# Foundations of
# ELECTRICAL
# ENGINEERING
## Second Edition

**J . R . C O G D E L L**

**Department of Electrical and Computer Engineering**
**University of Texas at Austin**

**P R E N T I C E   H A L L**
**Upper Saddle River, New Jersey 07458**

**Library of Congress Cataloging-in Publication Data**

Cogdell, J. R.
    Foundation of electrical engineerig / J. R. Cogdell. —2nd ed.
    p. cm.
    ISBN 0–13–092701–5
    1. Electric engineering I. Title.
621.3—dc20                 95—30313
1996                    CIP

Acquisitions Editors: Alan Apt, Linda Ratts-Engelman
Production Editors: Joe Scordato/Rose Kernan
Developmental Editor: Sondra Chavez
Copy Editor: Peter Zurita
Text Designer: Delgado Design, Inc.
Cover Designer: Bruce Kenselaar
Manufacturing Buyer: Donna Sullivan
Editorial Assistant: Kathryn Cassino
Art Director: Amy Rosen
Creative Director: Paula Maylahn

Printed in the United States of America
10  9  8  7  6

ISBN 0-13-092701-5

Prentice Hall International (UK) Limited, *London*
Prentice Hall of Australia Pty. Limited, *Sydney*
Prentice Hall Canada Inc., *Toronto*
Prentice Hall Hispanoamericana, S.A., *Mexico*
Prentice Hall of India Private, Limited, *New Delhi*
Prentice Hall of Japan Inc., *Tokyo*
Prentice Hall Asia Pte. Ltd, *Singapore*
Editora Prentice Hall do Brasil, Ltda., *Rio de Janeiro*

Dedicated to the Glory of God
to my wife Ann
and to my children
Amy, Thomas, and Christina

# Brief Contents

# Contents

# Preface

## THE NEED FOR THIS BOOK

About 10 years ago, I started teaching electrical engineering to nonmajors. We used a well-known text, but I found that my students had trouble with the book. The encyclopedic scope of this text of necessity forced it to be superficial. I wanted a text that presented the important ideas in depth and left many of the details for future learning in further study or professional practice. So I wrote *Foundations of Electrical Engineering*, choosing "Foundation" for the title to point to the few important principles that upheld the entire superstructure of electrical engineering.

This second edition has the same three principle goals as the first edition:

1. To explain well the foundational ideas of electrical engineering.
2. To emphasize the unity of the subject by frequent reminders of those basic ideas.
3. To bring understanding of circuits, electronics, systems, and electrical power engineering within the reach of all engineers.

My equal emphasis on electrical power engineering meets, I predict, an emerging need of our time. In the eyes of EE students, the technical challenge, professional opportunities, and personal enjoyment of electronics have totally eclipsed interest in electric power engineering. To most students, comparing power and electronics is like comparing a draft horse with a racing thoroughbred, with the result that many electrical engineering students avoid taking a single elective course in power. Thus, electric motors, like illumination engineering, must fall to the engineer who needs the information, such as the mechanical engineer who needs to select a motor to drive a pump. This book anticipates the need of all engineers to have more than superficial knowledge of electric power, motors, in particular.

## IMPROVEMENTS IN THE SECOND EDITION

While sharing in the goals of the first edition, this second edition differs in many ways. The entire text has been revised and refined, a new chapter has been added, and material has been rearranged to improve the logic and flow. The presentation has been improved by numerous graphical and pedagogical features. During the revision process, the entire book went through three drafts, two sets of reviews, and class testing at four universities.

## PREREQUISITES

We address this book to students who have completed 1 year of college calculus and physics. We work with linear differential equations and the algebra of complex numbers, but techniques of solution are explained in full. The part on motors begins with a chapter that summarizes the relevant material in electrical physics while introducing the notation and vocabulary of the developments to follow. A few simple ideas from mechanics are introduced in discussions of dynamic and steady-state operation of motors, primarily Newton's second law.

## PEDAGOGY OF THE BOOK

One way to view the structure of an engineering subject is shown in the following diagram:

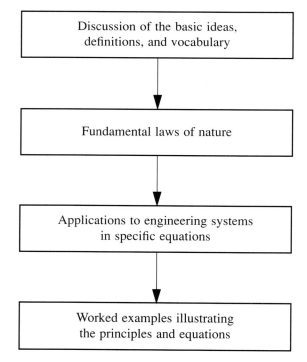

The instructor's emphasis goes from top to bottom. The structure in the instructor's (and author's) mind is, first, ideas and vocabulary, then laws, then equations, then examples—from the general to the specific. But most students seem to learn in the opposite order: first, examples, then equations, then laws, and finally ideas. One suspects some students never go beyond studying the examples, and certainly many believe the equations are what is important. When the instructor probes their understanding of the more general principles by giving a quiz problem that differs from previous examples, many students serve up memorized "solutions" or protest that "the quiz wasn't anything like the lectures and homework." The goals and needs of both instructors and students were paramount in the writing and design of this book.

## AIDS TO LEARNING

This text addresses the viewpoints of both students and instructors in a number of ways:

**Conservation of Energy**

- **Ideas.** We have identified eight basic ideas of electrical engineering and identified them with a light-bulb icon in the margin, as shown at left. These icons hopefully will convince students that electrical engineering is based upon a few foundational ideas that come up again and again.

**vocabulary**

- **Key terms** are italicized and emphasized by a note in the margin, as shown, when they are first introduced and defined. *Vocabulary* cannot be overemphasized because we communicate with others and, indeed, do our own thinking with words.

- **Major equations** are boxed in blue. This format, however, is used sparingly lest students think electrical engineering consists of a set of equations to be memorized.

- **Causality diagrams**[1] that show cause–effect relationships are given in complicated situations. One reason students have trouble solving problems is they look at equations and do not see what the important variables are. Understanding consists largely in knowing the causal connections between various factors in a problem so that equations are written with a purpose. Causality diagrams picture these cause–effect relationships.

**LEARNING OBJECTIVE**

**This alerts students to important material**

- **Objectives.** Chapters begin with stated objectives and end with summaries that review how those objectives have been met. In between, we place marginal pointers that alert the student where the material relates directly to one of the stated objectives. Our intention is to give road signs along the way to keep our travelers from losing their way.

---

| **EXAMPLE P.1** | **This is the title of an example** |
|---|---|

The 230 examples are boxed, titled, and numbered.

**SOLUTION:**
Solutions are differentiated from problem statement, as shown. Students are lured beyond passively studying the examples by a What if? challenge at the end.

| **WHAT IF?** | What if the student were asked to rework the example with a slight change?[2] The answer to the What If? challenge appears in a footnote for easy checking of results. |
|---|---|

---

[1] See page 341 for an example.
[2] That would get them involved, wouldn't it?

■ **Check your understanding** We have "Check Your Understanding" questions and problems, with answers, after major sections.

## PROBLEMS

Three types of problems have different levels of difficulty and appear at three places in the development:

1. What if? challenges follow most examples. These problems present a slight variation on the example and are intended to involve the student actively in the principles illustrated by the example. The answers are given in a footnote.

2. Check Your Understanding problems follow most sections. These are intended as occasions for review and quick self-testing of the material in the section. The answers follow the problems.

3. The 1035 end-of-chapter problems range from straightforward applications, similar to the examples to quite challenging problems requiring on insight and refined problem-solving skills. Answers are given to the odd-numbered problems. We are convinced that the only path to becoming a good problem solver passes through a forest of nontrivial problems.

## ACKNOWLEDGMENTS

I gratefully acknowledge the assistance of many colleagues at the University of Texas at Austin for helpful suggestions: Lee Baker, David Bourell, David Brown, John Davis, Mircea Driga, "Dusty" Duesterhoeft, Bill Hamilton, Om Mandhana, Charles Roth, Ben Streetman, Jon Valvano, Bill Weldon, Paul Wildi, Quanghan Xu, and no doubt others. My warmest thanks go to my friend, Jian-Dong Zhu, who worked side by side with me in checking the answers to the end-of-chapter problems. My heartfelt thanks for numerous corrections, improvements, and wise counsel go to my reviewers: William E. Bennett, U.S. Naval Academy; Richard S. Marleau, University of Wisconsin-Madison; Phil Noe, Texas A&M University; Ed O'Hair, Texas Tech University; and Terry Sculley and Carl Wells, Washington State University.

Special thanks go to my son, Thomas, who produced all the figures and made many significant suggestions. Thomas guided me through the maze of: producing the text in Microsoft WORD 5.0, drawing the figures with Claris CAD, generating the graphs with Mathematica, and editing the graphs in Adobe Illustrator.

I appreciate the suggestions and encouragement of my editors, Alan Apt and Linda Ratts-Engelman, and their associates, especially to Sondra Chavez for a lively E-mail dialog throughout the revision process.

I wish to thank my wife for her support and encouragement. Finally, I thank the Giver of all good gifts for the joy I have experienced throughout this labor of love.

*John R. Cogdell*

# PART 1

# Circuits

# 1

# Basic Circuit Theory

1. To understand what is a circuit and why circuits are important in electrical engineering
2. To understand the definition of current and use Kirchhoff's current law (KCL) to express conservation of charge
3. To understand the definition of voltage and use Kirchhoff's voltage law (KVL) to express conservation of electric energy
4. To understand how to use the voltage and current to calculate the power into or out of a circuit element
5. To understand the relationship between voltage and current in a resistor as described by Ohm's law
6. To understand how to combine resistances connected in series and how voltage divides between series resistances
7. To understand how to combine resistances connected in parallel and how current divides between parallel resistances
8. To understand how to analyze circuits containing one source and resistances in series and parallel

We begin our study of electrical engineering with the subject of circuits for three reasons. The most important is that almost every electrical device, from a radio to an electric motor, is a circuit, or at least contains circuits. The second reason is that the study of circuits is neither as abstract or as mathematically sophisticated as other electrical subjects such as electromagnetic fields. Finally, this subject has produced the language of electrical engineering. Learn the vocabulary of circuits and you can break into the conversation about electrical engineering.

## Place of Electrical Engineering in Modern Technology

**electrical
engineering**

**What is electrical engineering?**  Electrical engineering is, in one sense, the oppo-site of lightning.  Lightning unleashes electrical energy unpredictably and destructively.  *Electrical engineering* harnesses electrical energy for human good—for transporting en-ergy and information, for lifting the burdens of toil and tedium.  When electrical energy is important for its own sake, to turn motors or illuminate department stores, we think of the electrical power industry.  When energy is important for its symbolic (informa-tion) content, we think of the electronics industry.  Both use electrical energy for bene-ficial purposes.

This book explains the fundamental ideas and techniques of electrical engineering.  Our goal is to provide you with a strong foundation to solve basic and practical prob-lems and to furnish you with a vocabulary of words and ideas for clear thinking and clear communication.  All engineers need this background to contribute in a technology that is increasingly electrical.

**Foundational ideas in electrical engineering.**  Our focus will be on the ideas upon which electrical engineering is built.  These foundational ideas are as follows:

- **Conservation of charge** (Kirchhoff's current law) is one of the fundamental principles used in writing circuit equations.

- **Conservation of energy** (Kirchhoff's voltage law) applies in two forms: con-servation of *electric* energy is one of the fundamental principles used in writ-ing circuit equations; and conservation of energy generally is used in electrical/mechanical systems to develop equations and understanding.

- **The frequency domain** is a way of looking at the physical world in which frequency, not time, is the independent variable.

- **Equivalent circuits** model real devices by ideal electrical devices that have identical or similar characteristics.

- **Impedance level** determines how electrical devices interact.

- **Feedback** is a technique for bringing part of the output of an electronic de-vice back to the input to improve performance.

- **Analog information** uses an electrical signal proportional to the information content.

- **Digital information** uses a two-valued code to represent the information con-tent.

As we introduce, explain, and apply these ideas, we will remind you by the light bulb icon that a certain foundational idea is being used.  In this way, we hope to convince you that electrical engineering is based on relatively few ideas; the rest is detail.

**Why start with circuit theory?**  The first part of this book is about electric cir-cuit theory.  There are three reasons why we start with circuit theory.  It is an easy place to start, neither as abstract nor as mathematically sophisticated as other branches of electrical engineering.  More important, practically every electrical device is a circuit.

A radio is a circuit, as is the power distribution system that runs your lights and air conditioner. Hence, understanding of the methods of circuits opens the door to the study of all areas of electrical engineering.

Finally, the study of circuits provides a logical starting point because circuit theory has generated the language of electrical engineering. Even devices that are more sophisticated than an electrical circuit (an aircraft radar, for example) are described by electrical engineers in the language of circuits. Hence, our study of circuits introduces the ideas and language underlying much of electrical engineering.

## 1.2  PHYSICAL BASIS OF CIRCUIT THEORY

### Energy and Charge

**charge**

**Charge is a fundamental physical quantity.** *Charge*, like mass, is a property of matter; indeed, charge joins mass, length, and time as one of the fundamental units from which all scientific units are derived. The unit of electric charge is the coulomb (abbreviated C), named in honor of Charles de Coulomb (1736−1806). There are two types of charge, *positive* and *negative*. The names fit because the two types of charge produce opposite effects. Thus, equations describing the effects of charges encompass both types of charges if we associate a positive number with one type and a negative number with the other. Traditionally, the electron has been assigned a negative sign and the proton a positive. The magnitude of the charge of the electron is the smallest possible charge; in the MKS system of units, this is[1]

$$e = -1.602 \times 10^{-19} \text{ coulombs (C)} \tag{1.1}$$

Because the mass of the electron is $9.11 \times 10^{-31}$ kg, the charge-to-mass ratio of the electron is $1.76 \times 10^{11}$ in the MKS system. The charge on the proton is positive in sign and equal in magnitude to that of the electron, but the proton mass is 1846 times greater. Because the charge-to-mass ratio of the fundamental bits of matter is so great, electrical effects usually dominate mechanical inertia effects. Hence, we usually talk about charge as if it were not tied to mass—as if it were massless.

**electrostatic forces**

**Forces between charges.** We know about electric charges because charges exert forces on other charges. There are two types of forces between charges. Charges attract or repel each other due to *electrostatic forces*, which are described by Coulomb's law. Electrostatic forces are responsible for lightning, because charges are separated in clouds by droplet separation; and electrostatic forces are used in photocopy machines to form images on glass drums with charged bits of dry ink.

**magnetic forces**

*Magnetic forces* depend on moving charges (that is, on currents) and are described by Ampere's force law. Magnetic forces turn motors, deflect electron beams in TV tubes, and effect energy conversion in generators. Electrical engineers thus have both electrostatic and magnetic effects to use in manipulating electrical energy.

**energy**

**The importance of energy.** *Energy* is the medium of exchange in a physical system, like money in an economic system. Energy is exchanged whenever one physical

---

[1] Important physical constants are tabulated on the inside back cover of this book.

thing affects another. In mechanics, it takes force and movement to do work (exchange energy), and in electricity, it takes electrical force and movement of charges to do work (exchange energy). The electrical force is represented by the voltage and the movement of charge by the current in an electrical circuit.

## What Is Circuit Theory?

**OBJECTIVE 1**

**To understand what is a circuit and why circuits are important in electrical engineering**

**A circuit problem.** To see what circuit theory involves, consider the circuit consisting of the battery, light switch, two headlights, and connecting wire and chassis from a car, as shown in Fig. 1.1. When we pull the switch, we expect that the lights will glow and also get hot, which suggests that the battery is supplying energy to the headlights.[2] Figure 1.2 shows an electric circuit representing the physical situation depicted in Fig. 1.1, a 12.6-volt (V) battery symbol and two 5.25-ohm ($\Omega$) resistances, modeling the headlights, with lines representing the wire and chassis return. We may use circuit theory to calculate the current in the wires, the power out of the battery, and the energy into each headlight.

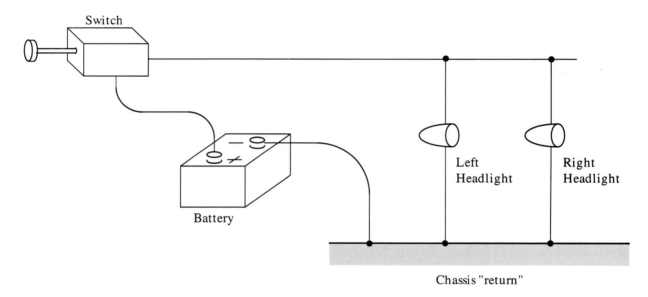

Switch

Battery

Left Headlight

Right Headlight

Chassis "return"

**Figure 1.1** Automotive lighting system.

**circuit theory**

**The nature of electrical circuit theory.** Soon we will present the definitions and laws that will allow us to make such calculations. Here we show what circuit theory encompasses. The solution of an engineering problem normally proceeds through four stages: first, a real-world problem is identified; second, the problem is modeled; third, the model is analyzed; and fourth, the results are applied to the original physical problem. In the case of the battery and headlights, we skipped the first and last steps,

---

[2] Most people assume that the energy flows through the wire, but it is more accurate to say that the wire guides the energy from the battery to the headlight.

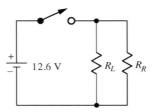

**Figure 1.2** Circuit representing automotive lighting system. The headlights are represented by resistances.

but we did model a physical situation (battery, switch, and headlight) with common circuit symbols and we plan to analyze the circuit model soon. *Circuit theory* consists only of the third step: taking a given circuit model and solving for certain results through the application of known circuit laws. This third step is what you will learn to do in the first part of this book. In the remainder, you use circuit theory in learning the principles of electronic and electromechanical systems. We begin with the definitions of current and voltage.

## 1.3 CURRENT AND KIRCHHOFF'S CURRENT LAW

**OBJECTIVE 2**

**To understand the definition of current and use Kirchhoff's current law (KCL) to express conservation of charge**

current

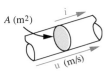

**Figure 1.3** Wire with current.

### Definition of Current

**Current is charge in motion.** In the experiment with the battery and headlights described before, we recognize that the headlights glow because of charges moving through the electrical conductors. An electrical conductor has mobile (conduction) electrons capable of moving in response to electric forces. A nonconductor has plenty of charges but its charges cannot move.

Consider a wire with a cross-section of $A$ m$^2$ with charges moving with a velocity $u$ from left to right, as pictured in Fig 1.3. If in a period of time $\Delta t$, $\Delta Q$ coulombs cross $A$ in the indicated direction, we define the *current* to be

$$i = \frac{\Delta Q}{\Delta t} \text{ C/s or ampere, A} \tag{1.2}$$

Note that the units of current are coulombs per second, but to honor André Ampère (1775—1836), we give this unit a special name, the ampere (A). A copper wire has a concentration of conduction electrons of $n_e = 1.13 \times 10^{29}$ electrons/m$^3$. If the electrons are moving with a velocity $u$, the number of electrons crossing $A$ in $\Delta t$ would be $\Delta n = n_e A u \, \Delta t$. Hence, the current would be[3]

$$i = \frac{\Delta Q}{\Delta t} = \frac{e \, \Delta n}{\Delta t} = e n_e A u \quad \text{A} \tag{1.3}$$

For example, consider electrons traveling downward in a No. 12 wire (0.081 in. in diameter) at a snail's pace of 0.1 mm/s. From Eq. (1.3), the charges constitute a current of $i = -5.8$ A downward, as shown in Fig. 1.4. We could also express this result by saying that the current is $i = +5.8$ A upward in Fig. 1.4(b).

---

[3] Note that $e$ is negative, so the direction of numerically positive (physical) current is opposite to the direction of electron motion.

**Reference directions.** That we can express the current two ways reveals the importance of reference directions. We write "downward," to indicate the direction to which we are referring current flow. To specify a current, we require a reference direction plus a numerical value, which may be positive or negative. In this book, the current reference directions are indicated by arrowheads drawn on the lines representing the conductors, as in Fig. 1.4, or with arrows beside the wires, or with subscripts. The relationship between the reference direction and the numerical sign of the current is shown in Fig. 1.4, which expresses the same current in all three ways. The direction of the *physical current* is opposite to the direction of electron motion and hence the physical current is by definition numerically positive.

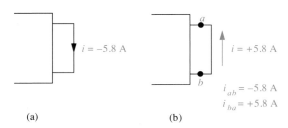

(a)     (b)     $i_{ab} = -5.8 \text{ A}$
        $i_{ba} = +5.8 \text{ A}$

**Figure 1.4**  Four notations for expressing the same current. The physical current is from $b$ to $a$.

**Assigning reference directions.** The engineer is responsible for assigning current reference directions as a beginning step in analyzing a circuit. These reference directions may be assigned without regard for the direction of the physical currents; they are assigned for bookkeeping purposes. This freedom in assigning reference directions will be clarified later when we state Kirchhoff's current law.

On the other hand, experienced engineers will usually define the current reference direction in the direction of the physical current if that direction is evident. They know that normally the physical current flows *out* of the + terminal on the battery, through the circuit, and returns into the − terminal. It is reasonable, therefore, to make your best guess as to which ways the physical currents go, but you must write and solve the equations to find out for sure.

**Summary.** Moving charges constitute a current. To specify the current in a conductor, we need both a reference direction and a numerical value, which can be positive or negative.

**A mechanical analogy.** For most students, an understanding of mechanics comes easier and earlier than an understanding of electrical phenomena. We have all experienced forces and motion, springs and inertia; and mechanics is taught early in most curricula. Because your intuition for mechanics is relatively well-developed, we present mechanical analogs for many electrical quantities and phenomena.

Velocity is the simplest analog for electric current, and displacement therefore would be analogous to charge accumulation. By these analogies, we mean that the equations relating these quantities are similar.

For example, if we know the velocity of an object, $u(t)$, the change in displacement, $x_2 - x_1$, during the period $t_1 < t < t_2$ would be

$$x_2 - x_1 = \int_{t_1}^{t_2} u(t)\, dt \tag{1.4}$$

as shown in Fig. 1.5(a). Similarly, if we know the current in a wire, $i(t)$, the charge $q$ passing a cross-section of the wire during the period $t_1 < t < t_2$ would be

$$q = \int_{t_1}^{t_2} i(t)\, dt \text{ coulombs} \tag{1.5}$$

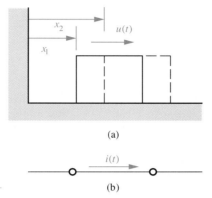

(a)

(b)

**Figure 1.5** The mechanical analog for current (b) is velocity (a).

as shown in Fig. 1.5(b). Velocity and displacement in general are vector quantities. Charge motion is also in general a vector quantity; but in circuits, the wires channel the current in established directions, and a plus or minus sign is all that remains of the "vectorness" of the current. Thus, charge flow in circuit theory corresponds to linear motion in mechanics.

---

**EXAMPLE 1.1** | **Electron Motion**

A steady current of $+10^{-6}$ A flows toward the right in a copper wire of 0.001 in. diameter. Find the speed and direction of the electron motion. How many electrons pass a cross-section of the wire in 1 μs?

**SOLUTION:**
Because the current to the right is positive, the electrons must be traveling to the left. From Eq. (1.3), their velocity would be

$$u = \frac{I}{A n_e |e|} = \frac{10^{-6}}{\pi (0.0005 \times 0.0254)^2 \times 1.13 \times 10^{29} \times 1.60 \times 10^{-19}} \tag{1.6}$$

$$= 1.09 \times 10^{-7} \text{ m/s}$$

The total charge passing a cross-section in $10^{-6}$ s would be

$$q = \int_0^{10^{-6}} i \, dt = 10^{-6} \text{ A} \times 10^{-6} \text{ s} = 10^{-12} \text{ C} \qquad (1.7)$$

The number of electrons would be

$$\frac{10^{-12} \text{ C}}{1.602 \times 10^{-19} \text{ C / electron}} = 6.24 \times 10^{6} \text{ electrons} \qquad (1.8)$$

**WHAT IF?** What if the speed is the same, but the diameter of the wire is doubled? What then would be the current?[4]

## Kirchhoff's Current Law

**Conservation of Charge**

**Conservation of charge and charge neutrality.** All the evidence suggests that the universe was created charge-neutral, that is, there exists somewhere a positive charge for every negative charge. As was implied in our discussion on electrostatic forces, positive and negative charges can be separated by natural causes (lightning) or man-made causes (TV tubes), but most matter does not contain surplus charge, that is, most matter is charge-neutral. Furthermore, charge is neither created nor destroyed in electrical circuits. This conservation principle leads directly to a constraint on the currents at a junction of wires.

**node**

**Kirchhoff's current law (KCL) at a junction of wires.** The junction of two or more wires is called a *node*. The constraint imposed by conservation of charge and charge neutrality is known as *Kirchhoff's current law* (KCL) and can be stated as follows: Because charge is conserved, the sum of the currents leaving a node is zero at all times. We could have written "currents entering a node" just as well. Another equivalent statement would be that the sum of the currents entering a node is equal to the sum of the currents leaving that node.

### Three forms of Kirchhoff's current law

1. The sum of the currents leaving a node is zero at all times.
2. The sum of the currents entering a node is zero at all times.
3. The sum of the currents referenced into a node is equal at all times to the sum of the currents referenced out of the node.

Figure 1.6 illustrates KCL at node *a*. Kirchhoff's current law (KCL) in the first form requires a + sign for currents referenced departing from the node and a − sign for currents referenced toward the node. In general form, KCL is

---

[4] The current would be 4 µA.

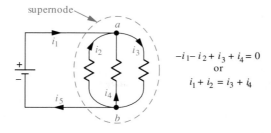

$$-i_1 - i_2 + i_3 + i_4 = 0$$
or
$$i_1 + i_2 = i_3 + i_4$$

**Figure 1.6** Conservation of charge at nodes $a$ and $b$ is expressed by Kirchhoff's current law (KCL). KCL also applies to the region encircled by the dashed line, a "supernode."

$$\sum_{node} \pm i_n = 0 \qquad (1.9)$$

The signs ($+$ or $-$) come from the reference directions; the $i$'s are counted $+$ if referenced departing from the node and $-$ if referenced entering the node.

**supernode**

**KCL applied to groups of nodes.** Kirchhoff's current law is one of the fundamental laws of electric circuits because it expresses the conservation of charge. Not only does it apply to a simple node, but it applies also to groups of nodes, which are often called *supernodes*. For example, if in Fig. 1.6 we add KCL for node $a$ to KCL for node $b$, the $i_2$ term must appear with opposite signs in the two equations; thus the two $i_2$ terms will cancel. For the same reason, the $i_3$ and $i_4$ terms will also cancel. Clearly, this cancellation will always occur for the internal currents in a group of nodes. Thus in Fig. 1.6, we can easily show that $i_1$ and $i_5$ are equal by applying KCL to the supernode enclosed with the dashed line.

| EXAMPLE 1.2 | KCL |

Two sources are connected to the same load, as shown in Fig. 1.7. The load current is 12 A, and the first source supplies 8 A. How much current is supplied by the second source ($i_2$)?

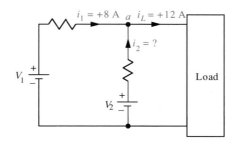

**Figure 1.7** The load is supplied by two sources. Two currents are known.

**SOLUTION:**
We may apply Kirchhoff's current law to node $a$. Summing currents leaving the node, we have

$$-i_1 - i_2 + i_L = 0 \Rightarrow -(+8) - i_2 + (+12) = 0 \qquad (1.10)$$

In Eq. (1.10), the $-(+8)$ term, for example, distinguishes between the $-$ due to the reference direction (outside the parentheses) and the $+$ associated with the numerical sign of the current (inside the parentheses). Thus,

$$i_2 = -8 + 12 = 4\,\text{A} \tag{1.11}$$

**WHAT IF?**

What if the reference direction for $i_2$ were down? What would $i_2$ be in that case?[5] Is the physical current different than before?[6]

### Check Your Understanding

1. The charge on the electron is $e = -1.60 \times 10^{-19}$. What is the current in a wire in which $10^8$ electrons pass a cross-section in 15 μs?

2. How many electrons pass a cross-section in 15 μs in a wire carrying 55 μA?

3. The physical current comes out of the plus or minus terminal of a battery. Which?

*Answers.* (**1**) 1.07 μA, sign not required; (**2**) $5.15 \times 10^9$ electrons; (**3**) plus, unless the battery is being charged.

## 1.4 VOLTAGE AND KIRCHHOFF'S VOLTAGE LAW

**OBJECTIVE 3**

To understand the definition of voltage and use Kirchhoff's voltage law (KVL) to express conservation of electric energy

voltage

### Definition of Voltage

**Voltage and energy exchanges.** Voltage expresses the potential of an electrical system for doing work. *Voltage* is defined to be the work done by the electrical system in moving a charge from one point to another in a circuit, divided by the charge. In Fig. 1.8, we show the circuit modeling the battery−headlight experiment described earlier. We have identified points in the circuit with the letters $a$, $b$, $c$, $d$, $e$, and $f$. After the switch is closed, the motion of charges around the circuit affects the transfer of energy from the battery to the headlights, which are represented by the resistances. The work done by the electrical system in moving a charge from $a$ to $b$ is indicated by the voltage: For high voltages, more work will be done. Specifically, the voltage from $a$ to $b$ is defined to be

$$v_{ab} = \frac{\text{work done by the electrical system in moving } q \text{ from } a \to b}{q} \tag{1.12}$$

The unit of voltage is energy/charge, joules per coulomb in the MKS system, but to honor Count Alessandro Volta (1745−1827), we use the special name volt (V) for this unit.

In our headlight circuit, the voltage between $e$ and $f$ is 12.6 because of the battery. With the switch open, the voltage does not get to the lights (resistances); with the

---

[5] The sign of $i_2$ would change to $-4$ A.

[6] No, the physical current is the same, 4 A upward.

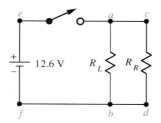

**Figure 1.8** Automotive headlight circuit.

switch closed, the voltage is applied to the lights. The lines in Fig. 1.8 represent ideal connections through the wires. After we explore the concept of voltage more thoroughly, we will present the laws that describe how the voltage distributes throughout the circuit when the switch is closed.

**Voltage as potential.** Although our example implies that charges must move for the voltage to exist, such motion is not required. If a bulb were burned out and no current existed, the voltage would still be present. The voltage expresses the *potential* for doing work, that is, it measures how much work would be done if a charge were moved from *a* to *b*. It is similar to a gravitational potential, which expresses the work that would be done in a gravitational field if a mass were moved from one point to another. For both a gravitational potential and an electric potential, the path of the charge does not matter. The charge can be moved from *a* to *b* through the bulb or it can be moved outside the bulb. In both cases, the work on the hypothetical charge, and hence the voltage, would be the same.

**Signs.** Both the work and the charge may be positive or negative; hence, voltage must also be a signed quantity. In the case where the battery turns on the headlight, energy is delivered by the electrical circuit to the thermodynamic system (heat and radiation), and in this case, the work done by the electrical system (via *q*) would be positive. On the other hand, chemical processes in the battery are delivering energy to the electrical circuit; in this case, the work done *by* the electrical system is negative in our definition of the voltage involving the battery. Voltage is thus the work done *by* the electrical system divided by the charge involved in doing that work, taking into account the signs of the work and the charge.

There is yet another way in which the sign of the voltage can be affected because the direction in which the charge is moved also must be considered. If we were to move a hypothetical positive charge from *a* to *b* in Fig. 1.8, positive work would be done and the voltage would be positive. If we were to move the hypothetical positive charge from *b* to *a*, negative work would be done and the voltage would be negative. To speak meaningfully of voltage as a signed quantity, we must have a clearly defined reference direction to indicate the assumed direction of travel.

---

**EXAMPLE 1.3** | **The Definition of Voltage**

For our battery in Fig. 1.8, $v_{ef} = +12.6$ V. Hence, if we move a charge of $+1$ C from *e* to *f* with our hand, the electrical system (the battery) would do $+12.6$ joules (J) of work (on us), which means that the charge would pull on us. But if we moved a charge of $-1$ C from *e* to

$f$, the work done by the electrical system would be $-12.6$ J, revealing that we would have to push on the charge to move it from $e$ to $f$.

> **WHAT IF?** What if an electron were moved from the negative ($f$) to the positive ($e$) terminal of the battery? How much work would be done by the electrical system?[7] Where does this energy come from (or go to)?[8]

**subscript notation**

**Voltage reference directions.** We will use two conventions for defining the reference direction of voltages. The more explicit convention uses subscripts, $v_{ab}$, as in Eq. (1.12), to define the beginning point ($a$), the ending point ($b$), and thus the direction traveled (from $a$ to $b$). By this convention, $v_{gh}$ would be the work done by the electrical system per charge in moving a charge from $g$ to $h$. Often in a circuit, however, we desire to express the voltage across a single element, as in the present case with the battery or the headlight. In this case, we can mark both ends of the circuit element with polarity symbols: a $+$ at one end and a $-$ at the other end. With this simpler notation, the convention is that the $+$ represents the first subscript and the $-$ the second subscript of the voltage. Figure 1.9 shows the battery/headlight circuit marked in this manner.

**physical voltage, physical polarity**

**Physical voltage.** The *physical polarity* of the voltage is the reference direction marking that gives a positive voltage. Thus, the physical voltage is always positive and has polarity markings assigned accordingly. That is, if the voltage with arbitrary $+/-$ reference direction assignment is numerically negative, the physical voltage is polarized in the opposite direction. Most voltmeters have red and black leads, with the black called "common." Such voltmeters will indicate a positive voltage when the common is connected to the minus polarity mark of the physical voltage and the red is connected to the plus polarity mark. On an auto battery, for example, the markings on the battery terminals are those of the physical voltage. Of course, we use the same convention on the battery symbol in circuit theory.

**A mechanical analog.** Force is a mechanical analog for voltage, in two senses. As external forces impart energy to mechanical systems and thus make things happen, so voltage sources (batteries, for example) impart energy to electrical circuits. Beyond this subjective analogy, however, we will show later in this chapter that equations involving voltage are similar in form to those involving force in mechanical systems.

## Kirchhoff's Voltage Law (KVL)

**IDEA Conservation of Energy**

**Conservation of energy.** Kirchhoff's voltage law (KVL) expresses conservation of electrical energy in electrical circuits. The charges traveling around a circuit transfer energy from one circuit element to another, but do not receive energy themselves on the average. This means that if you were to move a hypothetical test charge around a complete loop in a circuit, the total energy exchanged would add to zero. During part of

---

[7] Work $= -12.6 \times (-1.602) \times 10^{-19} = +2.02 \times 10^{-18}$ J.

[8] The energy comes from the battery and originates in the chemical system.

the loop, you would have to push on the charge to move it, but during other parts of the loop, it would pull on you.

**Forms of KVL.**   Because the energy sum is zero, it follows from the definition of voltage that the voltage sum around a closed loop is zero also.  This is *Kirchhoff's voltage law* (KVL):

$$\sum_{\text{loop}} \text{voltages} = 0 \qquad (1.13)$$

We can apply KVL to the circuit in Fig. 1.8 with these three results:

$$v_{ab} + v_{bf} + v_{fe} + v_{ea} = 0 \qquad (1.14)$$

$$v_{ab} + v_{bd} + v_{dc} + v_{ca} = 0 \qquad (1.15)$$

$$v_{ef} + v_{fd} + v_{dc} + v_{ce} = 0 \qquad (1.16)$$

We note the following:

■ Equation (1.14) was written around the loop containing the battery, the switch, and $R_L$, moving clockwise.

■ Equation (1.15) was written around the loop containing the two resistances, moving counterclockwise.

■ Equation (1.16) was written around the loop containing $R_R$, the switch, and the battery, moving counterclockwise.

■ In Eq. (1.16) we skipped some intermediate points; for example, we wrote $v_{fd}$ instead of $v_{fb} + v_{bd}$.

The direct connections between $a$ and $c$, $d$ and $b$, and $b$ and $f$ imply ideal connections, and hence no voltage, between these points.  Therefore,

$$v_{ac} = v_{bd} = v_{bf} = v_{df} = 0 \qquad (1.17)$$

and Eqs. (1.14) through (1.16) reduce to

$$v_{ab} + v_{fe} + v_{ea} = 0, \qquad v_{ab} + v_{dc} = 0, \qquad v_{ef} + v_{dc} + v_{ae} = 0 \qquad (1.18)$$

When we apply KVL to voltages whose reference directions are indicated with the + and − polarity convention, we find that we cannot guarantee, as in Eqs. (1.14) through (1.16), that all the signs in the resulting equation will be positive.  Thus, we must rewrite KVL in the form

$$\sum_{\text{loop}} \pm v\text{'s} = 0 \qquad (1.19)$$

In writing KVL equations with + and − polarity symbols, we write the voltage with a positive sign if the + is encountered before the − and with a negative sign if the − is encountered first as we move around the loop.  Applying this rule to Fig. 1.9,

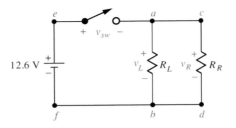

**Figure 1.9** Automotive circuit with voltages marked with the +/− convention.

we express KVL as

$$-(12.6) + v_{sw} + v_L = 0 \qquad (1.20)$$

Equation (1.20) results from starting at $f$ and proceeding clockwise around the loop including the switch and $R_L$. The minus sign results because we encounter the − first at the battery. The two plus signs occur because we encounter the + reference marks first for both $v_{sw}$ and $v_L$. All the signs in Eq. (1.20) result from the voltage reference directions marked in Fig. 1.9, not from the signs of the physical voltages.

---

**EXAMPLE 1.3** **Jump Starting a Car**

We have a weak battery with a voltage of 11.5 V and a strong battery with a voltage of 13.6 V. (This includes the benefits of the alternator charging the battery during the jump start.) What would happen in jump starting the car having the weak battery when the correct connections with the jumper cables are made, and what happens when the incorrect connections are made?

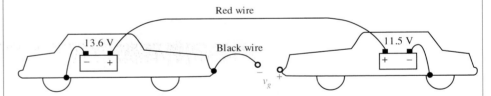

**Figure 1.10** Jump starting a car having a weak battery (correct connections).

**SOLUTION:**

Figure 1.10 shows the correct connections. According to the recommended procedure, we should first connect the positive terminals, as shown in Fig. 1.10, and then complete the circuit by connecting between points on the auto chassis away from the batteries, to reduce the danger of explosion. Thus, we are left with a voltage across the gap, $v_g$, before the final connection is made, due to the differing voltages of the two batteries. Using KVL, we determine the gap voltage to be

$$-v_g - 11.5 + 13.6 = 0 \Rightarrow v_g = -2.1 \text{ V} \qquad (1.21)$$

where $v_g$ is the voltage across the gap. The same voltage would exist between the jumper cable and the negative terminal of the battery.

Figure 1.11 shows the incorrect connections, where we connect the negative of one bat-

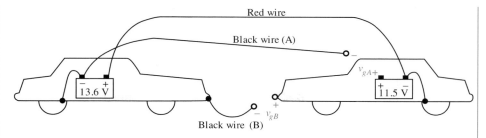

**Figure 1.11** Jump starting a car having a weak battery (incorrect connections).

tery to the positive of the other battery. From this bad start, we can continue in two ways. If we take the second jumper cable and proceed to connect between the two remaining battery terminals (A), we will have a gap voltage of

$$-v_{gA} + 11.5 + 13.6 = 0 \Rightarrow v_{gA} = +25.1 \qquad (1.22)$$

where $v_{gA}$ is the gap voltage with incorrect connection A. This large voltage presents a danger to both batteries and to the person making the connection.

**WHAT IF?**    What if we follow the recommended procedure and connect between the two chassis (B)? What then would be the gap voltage, $v_{gB}$?[9]

---

**EXAMPLE 1.4**    **KVL with Mixed Polarity Conventions**

Determine the unknown voltages, $v$ and $v_{cd}$ in Fig. 1.12.

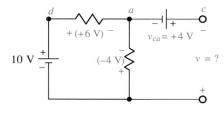

**Figure 1.12** The circuit has voltages marked with both the +/− and the subscript notations.

**SOLUTION:**

Here we have deliberately mixed the reference-direction conventions. We note that all the voltages around the leftmost loop are specified. Let us confirm that the given voltages satisfy KVL. We write a KVL loop equation going clockwise around the loop starting at the bottom of the battery:

$$- (10) + (+6) - (-4) = 0 \qquad (1.23)$$

In this equation, the signs outside the parentheses come from the reference directions and the signs inside come from the numerical values of the voltages. Thus, the minus sign is placed

---

[9] The gap voltage, $v_{gB}$, would be 13.6 V. This is still a dangerous situation.

before the first term because we encounter first the − polarity symbol on the battery, and the next sign is positive because we then encounter the first subscript of the voltage across a resistance. We note that KVL is satisfied.[10]

Let us proceed to determine the unknown $v$ by writing KVL around the rightmost loop. What loop? There is indeed a loop even though no path exists for current, for we could still move our hypothetical test charge around this closed path. Thus, KVL must be satisfied even when there is no path for current. Let us start at point $a$ and go counterclockwise:

$$-(-4) + (v) + v_{ca} = 0$$

$$v = -v_{ca} - 4 = -4 - 4 = -8 \text{ V} \qquad (1.24)$$

In the first form of Eq. (1.24), we have written the $v_{ca}$ term with a + sign because we are moving from the first subscript ($c$) to the second ($a$). Finally, we can determine $v_{cd}$ by writing KVL from $c$ to $d$ to $a$ to $c$:

$$v_{cd} + v_{da} + v_{ac} = 0$$

$$v_{cd} = -v_{da} - v_{ac} = -(+6) + (+4) = -2 \text{ V} \qquad (1.25)$$

Note that, in the second form of Eq. (1.25), we wrote $v_{da}$ as +6 because $d$ and the + symbol mark the same point in the circuit. That is, the convention for the + and − markings is that we move from the + to the −, which in this case is the same as moving from $d$ to $a$; hence, $v_{da}$ is +6 V. Note also that $v_{ac} = -v_{ca}$, as shown in what follows.

**WHAT IF?**    What if the 4-V battery were reversed? Find $v_{dc}$ for that condition.[11]

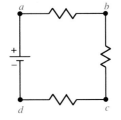

**Figure 1.13** Circuit for proving rules of subscript notation.

**Two rules for subscripts.** As a third application of KVL, we will demonstrate two properties of the subscript notation for voltages. For this purpose, we refer to Fig. 1.13. One application of KVL is to go from $a$ to $b$ and then return to $a$. The resulting equation is

$$v_{ab} + v_{ba} = 0 \Rightarrow v_{ab} = -v_{ba} \qquad (1.26)$$

Thus, we see that reversing the subscripts changes the sign of a voltage. This happens because the physical work done in moving a charge between two points is the negative of the work done in moving the same charge in the opposite direction.

Let us now determine $v_{ac}$ by moving from $a$ to $c$ to $b$ and back to $a$:

$$v_{ac} + v_{cb} + v_{ba} = 0 \Rightarrow v_{ac} = -v_{ba} - v_{cb} = v_{ab} + v_{bc} \qquad (1.27)$$

(We changed the signs in the next-to-last form by reversing the subscripts.) Note the pattern in the subscripts in the last form of Eq. (1.27): The second subscript ($b$) of the first voltage ($v_{ab}$) is identical to the first subscript of the second term ($v_{bc}$). The final form of $v_{ac}$ suggests that the middle point does not matter, that is, drops out. You can

---

[10] What would it mean if KVL were not satisfied around this loop? It would mean that the author, or the printer, had made an error, for a circuit in which KVL is not satisfied is not a circuit at all—it is nonsense, like $1 + 1 = 3$.

[11] The voltage would be 10 V.

verify this for yourself by writing $v_{ac}$ in terms of $v_{ad}$ and $v_{dc}$. You will get the equation

$$v_{ac} = v_{ad} + v_{dc} \tag{1.28}$$

Again the middle point drops out. This makes sense: It is like saying that the distance from New York to Los Angeles is the distance from New York to St. Louis plus the distance from St. Louis to Los Angeles. Clearly, "St. Louis" is a variable; we could have just as easily said Amarillo or Tucson. These two properties of the subscript notation will prove useful in later chapters.

### Check Your Understanding

1. If $v_{ab} = -5$ V, how much energy is required by an *external agent* to move $-2$ C of charge from $b$ to $a$?

2. If $v_{ab} = +2$ V and $v_{cb} = -1$ V, find $v_{ba}$ and $v_{ca}$.

3. A tape player requires three 1.5-V batteries. What voltage is developed if one battery is inserted backward?

4. Is it always true that $v_{ab} + v_{bc} + v_{ca} = 0$?

*Answers.* (1) $+10$ J; (2) $-2$ V, $-3$ V; (3) 1.5 V; (4) yes.

## 1.5  ENERGY FLOW IN ELECTRICAL CIRCUITS

### Voltage, Current, and Power

**OBJECTIVE 4**

**To understand how to use the voltage and current to calculate the power into or out of a circuit element**

**power**

**Power from voltage and current.** At the beginning of this chapter, we described electrical engineering as the useful control of electrical energy. Usually, energy is being exchanged between parts of a circuit, and the rate of energy flow, the power, must be calculated. We will now show that knowledge of voltage and current everywhere in an electrical circuit allows computation of energy flow (or power) throughout that circuit. Indeed, merely restating the definitions of voltage and current reveals their relationship to power flow. Voltage is the energy exchanged per charge and current is the rate of charge flow. *Power* is defined as the rate of energy exchange; hence, the power is by definition the product of voltage and current:

$$v \left( \frac{\text{work}}{\text{charge}} \right) \times i \left( \frac{\text{charge}}{\text{time}} \right) = \frac{\text{work}}{\text{time}} = \text{power} \tag{1.29}$$

Thus, if we know the voltage across a circuit component and the current through that element, we can determine the power into (or out of) that component by multiplying voltage and current (volts $\times$ amperes $=$ watts).

**source set, load set**  **Load sets and source sets.** We must consider reference directions when we write a power formula. The sign in the power formula depends on the *combination* of the voltage and current reference directions. We show both possibilities in Fig. 1.14. In a *source set*, Fig. 1.14(a), the current reference direction is directed *out of* the $+$ polarity marking (or the first subscript) of the voltage. This combination is normally used for a source of energy to the circuit such as a battery. In a *load set,* Fig. 1.14(b), the current reference direction is directed *into* the $+$ polarity marking (or the first subscript) of the voltage reference direction. This is the convention normally used with a resistance or

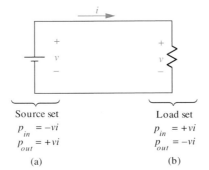

**Figure 1.14** Sign convention for power calculations. The source set (a) is normally used with sources such as batteries, and the load set (b) is normally used with passive circuit elements.

Source set
$p_{in} = -vi$
$p_{out} = +vi$
(a)

Load set
$p_{in} = +vi$
$p_{out} = -vi$
(b)

some other element that receives power from the circuit. For both cases in Fig. 1.14, we can speak of the power out of the component and the power into the component as meaningful quantities. For example, although a battery normally gives power to a circuit ($p_{out} = +$), it can be receiving power ($p_{out} = -$ or $p_{in} = +$) when the battery is being charged.

We must stress that the formulas given in Fig. 1.14 relate solely to reference directions. Any of the numerical values of the voltages, currents, or powers can be positive or negative. The direction of energy flow at a component will be established only after the sign depending on the reference directions is combined with the numerical signs of the voltage and current. The use of load and source sets will be clarified in the example of Fig. 1.15.

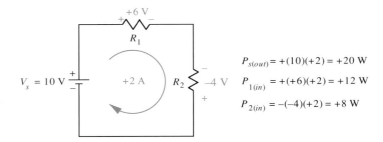

$P_{s(out)} = +(10)(+2) = +20$ W

$P_{1(in)} = +(+6)(+2) = +12$ W

$P_{2(in)} = -(-4)(+2) = +8$ W

**Figure 1.15** The battery and $R_2$ have source sets, but $R_1$ has a load set.

| EXAMPLE 1.5 | **Calculating the Power In and Out of Circuit Elements** |
|---|---|

Find the power out of the battery and the power into the two resistances. Show that energy is conserved.

**SOLUTION:**
With the battery, we have a source set because the current reference arrow is out of the + polarity marking. Hence, the battery supplies a power of $+vi$ or $+ (+10) (+2) = +20$ W. In the preceding sentence, the + of the "$+vi$" is from the source set of reference directions and the + of the "+20" comes from the combination of the reference directions and the numerical values of the voltage and current. The interpretation of the positive power out of the source is that the battery is delivering energy to the circuit. If the power out of the battery had been

negative, we would learn that the battery is being recharged by some other source in the circuit.

Resistance $R_1$ has a load set and proves to be receiving energy from the circuit. Resistance $R_2$ is also receiving energy from the circuit because a positive sign is produced by the combination of the minus sign from the reference directions and the minus sign of the voltage. Thus, in calculating power, we must continue to distinguish between signs arising from the reference directions and signs arising from the numerical values of the voltages and currents. Only the meaning of the power variable ("into" or "out of") and the numerical sign of the result allow the final conclusion as to which way energy is flowing at a given instant.

**Conservation of Energy**

The power out of the source in the previous example, $+20$ W, is equal to the sum of the powers into the resistances, $12$ W $+ 8$ W; hence, electric energy is conserved in the circuit. We call this conservation of *electric* energy because we have accounted for the energy entering and leaving the electrical system represented by the circuit. To be sure, total energy (electric plus other forms) would also be conserved; we simply have ignored the non electrical aspects of the system. For example, the battery might represent a chemical system, a solar cell, or a small electric generator powered by a windmill. To account for all energy, we would have to study these sources.

**Mechanical analogies.** We have presented mechanical force, velocity, and displacement as counterparts of voltage, current, and charge, respectively. Here we will review some of the relationships relating these mechanical variables to energy exchanged in a mechanical system. Then we will show the corresponding equations for the electrical variables.

The amount of energy exchanged, $dW$, by a force $f$ (newtons) operating through a distance, $dx$ (meters), would be

$$dW = f \, dx \text{ joules (J)} \tag{1.30}$$

When continuous motion is involved, the rate of energy exchanged, the power, $p$, would be

$$p = \frac{dW}{dt} = f \frac{dx}{dt} = fu \text{ watts (W)} \tag{1.31}$$

where $u$ is the velocity. Finally, the energy exchanged in a period of time $t_1 < t < t_2$ can be computed by integration:

$$W = \int_{t_1}^{t_2} p \, dt = \int_{t_1}^{t_2} fu \, dt \text{ J} \tag{1.32}$$

Equations (1.30) to (1.32) have electrical counterparts. When a charge $dq$ is moved from $a$ to $b$, the energy given by the electrical circuit would be

$$dW = v_{ab} \, dq \text{ J} \tag{1.33}$$

When continuous charge flow, a current, is involved, the rate of energy exchanged, the power, $p$, would be

$$p = \frac{dW}{dt} = v_{ab}\frac{dq}{dt} = v_{ab}i \ \text{W} \tag{1.34}$$

where $i$ is the current referenced from $a$ to $b$. Finally, the energy exchanged in a period of time $t_1 < t < t_2$ can be computed by integration:

$$W = \int_{t_1}^{t_2} p \ dt = \int_{t_1}^{t_2} v_{ab}i \ dt \ \text{J} \tag{1.35}$$

---

**EXAMPLE 1.6** | **Energy to Start Engine**

The starter motor of an automobile draws 60 A when turning over the engine. If the voltage is 12.6 V and the engine starts after 10 seconds, what is the power to the starter motor and the energy required to start the engine?

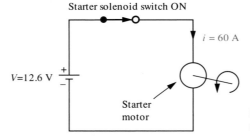

Starter solenoid switch ON

$i = 60$ A

$V = 12.6$ V

Starter motor

**Figure 1.16** Circuit model for the automotive starter circuit.

**SOLUTION:**
Figure 1.16 shows the circuit. The power out of the battery is

$$p_{\text{out}} = +Vi = + (+12.6)(+60) = 756 \ \text{W}$$

$$p_{\text{out of battery}} = p_{\text{into starter}} \tag{1.36}$$

The energy required to start the engine would be

$$W = \int_0^{10} p \ dt = 10p = 7560 \ \text{J} \tag{1.37}$$

---

**WHAT IF?** | What if it took 1 minute to start the car and the battery was recharged at a 20-A rate by the alternator? How long would it take to recharge the battery?[12]

---

[12] Three minutes.

**Summary.** Voltage and current allow us to monitor energy flow in an electrical circuit, are easily measured, and also obey simple laws, KVL and KCL. For these reasons, voltage and current are universally used by electrical engineers in describing the state of an electric network.

In the next section we define resistance and state Ohm's law. This addition allows us to develop basic techniques for analyzing electrical circuits.

### Check Your Understanding

1. A battery charger puts 5 A into a 12.6-V auto battery. What is the power into the battery?
2. Find the power *out of* $R_1$ and $R_2$ in Fig. 1.15.
3. A 1.5-V flashlight battery puts out 300 mA for 10 minutes. How much energy does this represent?

*Answers.* (1) 63.0 W; (2) $-12$ W, $-8$ W; (3) 270 J.

## 1.6 CIRCUIT ELEMENTS: RESISTANCES AND SOURCES

### Resistances and Switches

In the previous sections, we have defined current and voltage and shown how these describe energy exchanges in an electrical circuit. We have stated Kirchhoff's current law and Kirchhoff's voltage law, which express conservation of charge and electric energy in a circuit, respectively. For illustrative purposes, we have presented some *circuit elements*—sources, switches, and resistances—without careful definition or explanation. We now define and explain these circuit elements.

**Ohm's law.** Let us again think about the battery–switch–headlight circuit of Fig. 1.1. We know that chemical action produces charge separation within the battery. This charge separation appears at the battery terminals, and electrostatic forces are experienced by all the charges in the vicinity of the battery, significantly by charges in the wire and the headlights. Because of these forces, electrons move in the wire and headlight, a current exists in the circuit, and the lights glow.

It will not surprise you that the greater the voltage, the greater will be the resulting current. For a large class of conductors, the current increases in direct proportion to the voltage. Physical experimentation leads to the following equation, known as *Ohm's law*:

**OBJECTIVE 5**

**To understand the relationship between voltage and current in a resistor as described by Ohm's law**

$$i = \frac{v}{R} \qquad \text{or} \qquad v = Ri \tag{1.38}$$

In Eq. (1.38), $R$ is the *resistance* and has the unit volts per ampere, but to honor Georg Ohm (1787–1854), we use the unit ohm, abbreviated by the uppercase Greek letter omega, $\Omega$. Ohm's law relates voltage and currents for resistive elements. Later, we will discover other voltage–current relationships for capacitors and inductors. The resistance of a piece of wire is directly proportional to its length, to a property of the metal called resistivity, and inversely proportional to its cross-sectional area:

$$R = \frac{\ell \rho}{A} \qquad (1.39)$$

**resistance, resistor**

where $\ell$ is the length of the wire, $\rho$ is the metal resistivity, and $A$ is the area of the wire. The material from which the wire is drawn is an important factor: Copper is a good conductor; iron not so good. Table 1.1 gives the resistance of some common wires. The resistance of a wire also depends on its temperature, but the resistance often may be considered constant. In electronic circuits, we use resistors made out of a carbon-impregnated binder, high-resistance wire, or metals deposited on nonconducting surfaces. The physical behavior of such resistors leads directly to the circuit theory definition of an ideal resistance.[13]

**TABLE 1.1  Properties of Copper Wires**

| Wire Size (gage) | Diameter (in.) | Resistance ($\Omega$/1000 ft) | Nominal Current Limit (A) | Use |
|---|---|---|---|---|
| 12 | 0.08081 | 1.588 | 23 | Household wiring |
| 16 | 0.05082 | 4.016 | 13 | Extension cords |
| 24 | 0.0201 | 25.7 | 2 | Electronic wiring |
| 30 | 0.01003 | 103.2 | 0.52 | Computer circuits |

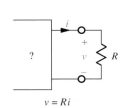

$$v = Ri$$

**Figure 1.17** The circuit symbol for a resistance. Note that the voltage and current reference directions form a load set.

**conductance**

**Circuit theory of resistance.** The circuit symbol for a resistance, $R$, is given in Fig. 1.17. Note that the reference directions of the voltage and current form a load set. We could also write Ohm's law for a source set, which would introduce a minus sign, but this is usually avoided.

Ohm's law is presented in graphical form in Fig. 1.18. We have shown voltage to be the independent variable (cause) and current to be the dependent variable (effect). The slope of the line is the reciprocal of resistance. Customarily, Ohm's law is also stated in terms of reciprocal resistance, which is called *conductance*:

$$i = Gv, \qquad \text{where} \qquad G = \frac{1}{R} \qquad (1.40)$$

The unit of conductance is amperes per volt, but we use siemens (the official unit) or mho (the unofficial but more common term). The symbol for siemens is S, and the common symbol for the mho[14] is the upside-down omega ($\mho$). Because we have a load set, the power into the resistance is $+vi$. We can express the power into a resistance in several ways, as follows:

---

[13] We should perhaps distinguish a *resistor* from a *resistance*. A resistor is a device, often cylindrical in shape, exhibiting the property of resistance, placed in an electrical circuit for the purpose of influencing some voltage or current. Wires, lightbulbs, heater elements, and resistors all exhibit resistance. However, in common parlance resistor and resistance are synonymous.

[14] "Ohm" spelled backward.

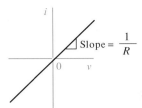

**Figure 1.18** Ohm's law in graphical form. We show the voltage as the independent variable (cause) and the current as the dependent variable (effect).

$$p = +vi = (Ri)\,i = i^2 R$$
$$= v\left(\frac{v}{R}\right) = \frac{v^2}{R} \text{ watts} \tag{1.41}$$

where $v$ is the voltage across the resistance and $i$ is the current through the resistance. Note that the power into a resistance is always positive. Resistance, therefore, always removes electrical energy from a circuit. Like the headlight circuit, the energy lost to the electrical circuit usually appears as heat (also some light in that case).

---

**EXAMPLE 1.7** | **Power in Resistances**

What is the maximum allowed voltage across a 1000-$\Omega$, $\frac{1}{2}$-watt resistance?

**SOLUTION:**
From Eq. (1.41), $v^2/1000 = 0.5$ W $\Rightarrow v = \sqrt{500} = 22.4$ V.

**WHAT IF?** What if it were a 500-$\Omega$, 2-W resistance and you wanted the maximum allowed current?[15]

---

**short circuit and open circuit**

**Open circuits and short circuits.** Figure 1.19 shows the characteristic of two special resistances. A short circuit ($R = 0$) permits current to flow ($i \neq 0$) without any resulting voltage ($v = 0$), and an open circuit ($R = \infty$) permits voltage ($v \neq 0$) with no current ($i = 0$). In both cases, Eq. (1.41) shows no power is required for the open or short circuit.

**Switches.** An ideal switch is a special resistance that can be changed from a short circuit to an open circuit to turn an electrical device ON or OFF. Ideal switches receive no electrical energy from the circuit.[16] Figure 1.20(a) shows a *single-pole, single-throw* switch in its open (OFF) state. Figure 1.20(b) shows a *single-pole, double-throw* switch, which switches one input line between two output lines. Figure 1.20(c) shows a *double-pole, single-throw* switch; the dashed line indicates mechanical coupling be-

---

[15] The maximum current would be 63.2 mA (milliamperes).
[16] Of course, some energy is required to "switch" the switch between states.

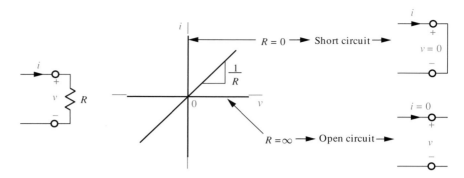

**Figure 1.19** Circuit symbol and graphical characteristic of a resistance. The characteristic of a short circuit ($R = 0$) is vertical and that of an open circuit ($R = \infty$) is horizontal.

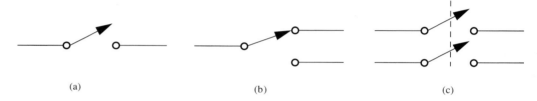

**Figure 1.20** Circuit symbols for switches: (a) A single-pole, single-throw switch in the OFF state; (b) a single-pole, double-throw switch; and (c) a double-pole, single-throw switch in the OFF state. The dashed line in (c) indicates mechanical coupling to ensure identical states for both poles.

tween the two components of the switch to cause simultaneous switching. Clearly, switches can have any number of *poles* and *throws*.

## Voltage and Current Sources

**ideal voltage source**

**Ideal voltage sources.** Figure 1.21 shows the circuit symbol, mathematical definition, and graphical characteristic of an ideal general and dc voltage source. The *ideal voltage source* maintains its prescribed voltage, independent of its output current. In general, an ideal voltage source may have positive or negative voltage, and it may be constant or time-varying. In this and the next chapter, we use the battery symbol for a constant (dc) voltage source and always consider the battery voltage to be positive. Note that we have used a source set for the voltage source. Normally, a voltage source would produce a positive current, the physical current, out of the + terminal and thus act as a source of energy for the circuit; but it is possible that some other, more powerful source might force the physical current *into* the + terminal of the voltage source to be positive, thus delivering energy to the source. When this happens for a battery, the current as defined is negative and we say that the battery is being charged.

The dc voltage source of circuit theory models an ideal battery. We recognize that a real battery does not maintain constant voltage under heavy load. Furthermore, real batteries store a finite amount of energy and need to be recharged or replaced fre-

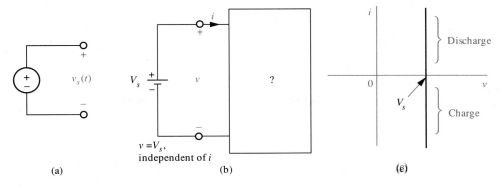

$v = V_s$,
independent of $i$

(a)     (b)     (c)

**Figure 1.21** (a) General symbol for a voltage source. (b) circuit symbol and mathematical definition for a dc voltage source, and (c) graphical characteristic for a dc voltage source. The source determines the voltage, but the current is determined by the load. Note that the voltage and current form a source set, so the power out of the source is positive for positive current.

quently. By contrast, the ideal voltage source can deliver energy without limit. A physical battery often can be represented as an ideal voltage source in a circuit problem.

**ideal current source**

**Ideal current sources.** Figure 1.22 shows the circuit symbol, mathematical definition, and graphical characteristic of ideal general and dc current sources. The *ideal current source* produces its prescribed current, independent of its output voltage. Like the ideal voltage source, an ideal current source will deliver any required amount of energy. Unlike the voltage source, there is no physical device at your local hardware store whose electrical properties resemble those of a current source; however, we can build electronic devices that act like current sources and the idea is useful in circuit analysis.

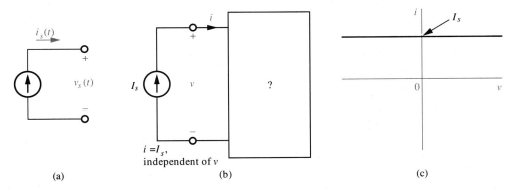

$i = I_s$,
independent of $v$

(a)     (b)     (c)

**Figure 1.22** (a) General symbol for a current source, (b) circuit symbol and mathematical definition for a dc current source, and (c) graphical characteristic for a dc current source. The source determines the current, but the voltage is determined by the load. Note that the voltage and current form a source set, so the power out of the source is positive for positive voltage.

**EXAMPLE 1.8**

**EXAMPLE 1.8**  **Voltage and Current Sources**

A constant voltage source is connected in series with a current source that produces a pulse of current. The pulse is 0.1 s in duration and triangular in shape, as shown in Fig. 1.23. Find the energy out of the current source.

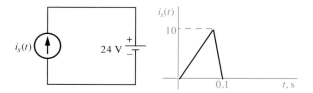

**Figure 1.23**  The current source provides a triangular pulse of current to the voltage source.

**SOLUTION:**
Kirchhoff's voltage law requires that the voltage across the current source be +24 V, with the + reference mark at the top. This voltage forms a source set with the current; hence,

$$p_{out} = +(+24)\,i_s(t) \Rightarrow W_{out} = \int p_{out}\,dt = 24 \int_0^{0.1} i_s(t)\,dt \tag{1.42}$$

But the integral is the area under the triangle in Fig. 1.23.

$$\text{Area} = \tfrac{1}{2}\,(0.1)\,(10) = 0.5 \text{ C} \Rightarrow W_{out} = 24 \times 0.5 = 12 \text{ J} \tag{1.43}$$

**WHAT IF?**   What would be the energy out of the current source if it was oriented with the arrow downward?[17]

## Analysis of DC Circuits

**Headlight circuit solved carefully.**   We now have defined sufficient concepts and conventions to analyze the headlight circuit in Fig. 1.9, which we repeat in Fig. 1.24. We have used the + and − polarity notation and assigned reference directions such that the current reference directions are the directions in which current would be numerically positive. The physical current will come out of the + on the battery, divide between the headlights, recombine, and then go into the − on the battery. Note that we have defined voltages $v_L$ and $v_R$ in load sets for the resistances and a source set for the voltage source. Going clockwise around the left loop, we find

$$-12.6 + v_{sw} + v_L = 0 \tag{1.44}$$

---

[17]$W_{out} = -12$ J.

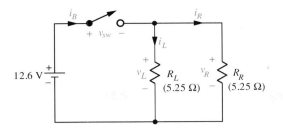

**Figure 1.24** Figure 1.8 repeated.

**Conservation of Energy**

and KVL clockwise around the loop created by the resistors is

$$-v_L + v_R = 0 \qquad (1.45)$$

We must solve these equations for two cases: the switch open (OFF) and the switch closed (ON).

With the switch OFF, the solution is trivial. The open switch blocks the voltage from being applied to the headlights; hence, the voltage across the headlights is zero and no current flows. Because $v_L = v_R = 0$, Eq. (1.44) reduces to

$$-12.6 + v_{sw} + 0 = 0 \Rightarrow v_{sw} = 12.6 \text{ V} \qquad (1.46)$$

Thus, all the voltage of the battery appears across the switch and no current flows in the resistances representing the headlights.[18] The power out of the battery is zero, and the power into each resistance is zero.

With the switch ON, $v_{sw} = 0$, and Eqs. (1.44) and (1.45) reduce to $v_L = v_R = 12.6$ V. The currents in the headlights follow from Ohm's law:

$$i_L = \frac{v_L}{R_L} = \frac{12.6 \text{ V}}{5.25 \text{ }\Omega} = 2.40 \text{ A} \qquad (1.47)$$

**Conservation of Charge**

and $i_R$ is the same. The current in the switch and battery may be determined from applying Kirchhoff's current law (KCL) to the node where the two resistances connect at the top:

$$-i_B + i_L + i_R = 0 \Rightarrow i_B = i_L + i_R = 2.40 + 2.40 = 4.80 \text{ A} \qquad (1.48)$$

Because $i_B$ and the battery voltage form a source set, the power *out of* the battery is

$$p_{out} = + (+12.6)(i_B) = +12.6 \times 4.80 = 60.5 \text{ W} \qquad (1.49)$$

The resistance voltages and current form a load set, so the power *into* each resistance is

$$p_{resistances} = + (+12.6)(+2.40) = 30.2 \text{ W} \qquad (1.50)$$

**Conservation of Energy**

We note that the power out of the battery equates to the sum of the powers into the resistances and, because the switch requires no power, conservation of electric energy is satisfied.[19]

---

[18] The reasoning is heuristic and intuitive. Reasoning from the definition of a switch given earlier is surprisingly complicated and lends no insight.

[19] We normally write numerical results to three-place accuracy, but in our calculations, we maintain full accuracy. This occasionally leads to apparent rounding errors, as here.

**Summary.** We applied Kirchhoff's laws directly to find the voltage, current, and power for each element in the headlight circuit with the switch OFF and ON. We found all currents positive because we took care to define our current variables according to the directions of the physical current in the circuit. We found all voltages positive because we used load sets for the resistances and switch. The power flow *out of* the battery and the power flow *into* each resistance is a physical reality, independent of the reference directions of the voltage and current variables, which are part of a man-made analysis scheme.

**Alternative solution based on series and parallel combinations.** We may find the voltages, currents, and powers in the circuit by an alternative method that employs equivalent circuits. Figure 1.25 shows the part of the circuit with the resistances. We note that both ends of the resistances are connected together; hence, both resistances have the same voltage, $v_p$, applied to them. This is called a *parallel connection*, referring not to the geometric positions of the resistances, but rather to the division of the current at the top and the recombining of the currents at the bottom. We have labeled the voltage and current of the parallel connection $v_p$ and $i_p$, respectively.

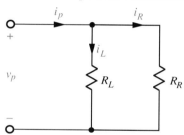

**Figure 1.25** The part of the headlight circuit with only the headlights. Our goal is to replace this with a simpler equivalent circuit.

**equivalent resistance**

We will now show that we may replace the two parallel resistances with a single *equivalent resistance*, that is, a single resistance that has the same external properties ($v_p$ and $i_p$) as the parallel resistances. Writing KCL in the form that the sum of the currents leaving a node equals the sum of the currents entering, we have

$$i_p = i_L + i_R \tag{1.51}$$

But from Ohm's law, we have

$$i_L = \frac{v_p}{R_L} \quad \text{and} \quad i_R = \frac{v_p}{R_R} \tag{1.52}$$

Substituting Eqs. (1.52) into Eq. (1.51), we obtain

$$i_p = \frac{v_p}{R_L} + \frac{v_p}{R_R} = v_p \left( \frac{1}{R_L} + \frac{1}{R_R} \right) \tag{1.53}$$

Equation (1.53) has the same form of Ohm's law, Eq. (1.38), if we introduce an equivalent resistance, $R_{eq}$, where

$$\frac{1}{R_{eq}} = \frac{1}{R_L} + \frac{1}{R_R} \Rightarrow R_{eq} = \frac{1}{1/R_L + 1/R_R} \qquad (1.54)$$

with the equivalent resistance, $R_{eq}$, defined in Eq. (1.54), Eq. (1.53) becomes

$$i_p = \frac{v_p}{R_{eq}} \qquad (1.55)$$

**Figure 1.26** The two parallel resistances in Fig. 1.25 are replaced by one equivalent resistance.

Thus we can replace the circuit in Fig. 1.25 by the equivalent circuit shown in Fig. 1.26, where $R_{eq}$ is given by Eq. (1.54). We note

- Equation (1.54) is awkward to write, so we introduce the parallel bars symbol, $R_{eq} = R_L \parallel R_R$, as a shorthand symbol for this operation. For example,

$$2 \parallel 5 = \frac{1}{1/2 + 1/5} = 1.43$$

- Equation (1.54) reduces to the product of the resistances over the sum of the resistances, and many students have memorized this formula for parallel resistances. We discourage the use of this formula for two reasons: (1) The formula is valid for two resistances, but not for three or more parallel resistances. Thus, this formula can get you in trouble because it is not general. (2) With a modern calculator, it is easier to calculate with Eq. (1.54) than with the product-over-sum formula. For example, on a reverse-Polish-entry calculator (H-P), we would calculate $2 \parallel 5$ in the following sequence of keystrokes: 2, 1/x, 5, 1/x, +, 1/x. It takes more keystrokes to execute the product-over-sum formula, because the resistance values need to be stored or entered twice. The product-over sum formula is useful, however, in mentally checking the magnitude of the combination of two parallel resistances.

- The concept of an equivalent resistance is very general and will be used throughout this book. Thus, the symbol $R_{eq}$ is used like "x" in algebra and is by no means reserved for parallel resistances. So when you read Eq. (1.54) read (or think) "the equivalent resistance *of two parallel resistances* is ..."

**Equivalent Circuits**

- The resistance in Fig. 1.26 is equivalent to the two resistances in Fig. 1.25 only in certain regards. Specifically, the two circuits are equivalent as far as the external voltage and current, $v_p$ and $i_p$, are concerned, but information about the internal currents, $i_L$ and $i_R$, is lost. Later in this section, we show how to recover this lost information.[20]

**Equivalent Circuits**

- The equivalent resistance defined earlier is one example of an equivalent circuit. An *equivalent circuit* is a circuit that represents in some important respects the properties of another, more complicated circuit. We shall encounter many types of equivalent circuits in our study of electrical engineering: The

---

[20] With the headlights, current $i_p$ divides equally between the two equal resistances.

equivalent resistance of two parallel resistors is simply the first use of an equivalent circuit.

■ In our circuit the two resistances represent two identical headlights, each having 5.25-$\Omega$ resistance. Thus for us, $R_L \parallel R_R = 5.25 \parallel 5.25 = 2.63\ \Omega$.

**Series resistances.** Because we will need the $R_{eq}$ symbol for another meaning in this section, let us use the symbol $R_p = R_L \parallel R_R$ to represent the parallel resistances. With this symbol, the circuit reduces to that shown in Fig. 1.27, where $R_{sw}$ represents the resistance of the switch ($R_{sw} = \infty$ for open and $R_{sw} = 0$ for closed). The voltage of the battery is represented by $v_B$.

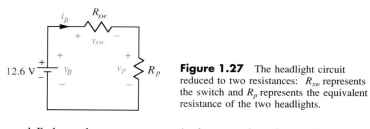

**Figure 1.27**  The headlight circuit reduced to two resistances: $R_{sw}$ represents the switch and $R_p$ represents the equivalent resistance of the two headlights.

We note that $R_{sw}$ and $R_p$ have the same current, $i_B$, because there is no place where the current divides. This is called a *series connection* when two circuit elements have the same current; so the battery, switch, and parallel resistances are connected in series. Two resistances in series can be replaced by an equivalent resistance, as we now show. We write KVL around the loop

$$-v_B + v_{sw} + v_p = 0 \Rightarrow v_B = v_{sw} + v_p \tag{1.56}$$

and introduce Ohm's law for both resistances:

$$v_{sw} = R_{sw}i_B \qquad \text{and} \qquad v_p = R_p i_B \tag{1.57}$$

**series connection**    Combining Eqs. (1.56) and (1.57), we find

$$v_B = (R_{sw} + R_p)\, i_B = R_{eq}i_B \tag{1.58}$$

where $R_{eq} = R_{sw} + R_p$ is the equivalent resistance of $R_{sw}$ and $R_p$ in series connection. Thus, we may determine the battery current as

$$i_B = \frac{v_B}{R_{eq}} \tag{1.59}$$

For an open switch, $R_{eq} = \infty + R_p$; hence, $i_B = 0$. For a closed switch, $R_{eq} = 0 + R_p$ and $i_B = 12.6/2.63 = 4.80\ \text{A}$. As before, this current divides equally between the two resistances (headlights) and the power is also as before.

**Summary.**  We have analyzed the automotive headlight circuit by two means. First we applied Kirchhoff's laws directly and treated the switch as a device that either blocked or allowed the voltage to reach the headlights. Then we treated the switch as a resistance that was either zero or infinity, and we used equivalent resistances to represent resistances in parallel and series. Electrical engineers often replace resistances in series or parallel with equivalent resistances. In the next section, we explore and generalize this technique of circuit analysis.

### Check Your Understanding

1. Ohm's law is written with a + sign when the reference directions of the voltage across and current through the resistance are related by a load set or source set?

2. A 1000-$\Omega$ resistance is rated at 5 W. What is the maximum current that should go through this resistance? The maximum voltage across the resistance?

3. A 5-A current source is connected in series with a 10-V battery, with the current source going into the minus terminal of the battery. What is the power into the battery?

*Answers.* **(1)** Load set; **(2)** 70.7 mA, 70.7 V; **(3)** −50 W.

## 1.7  SERIES AND PARALLEL RESISTANCES; VOLTAGE AND CURRENT DIVIDERS

### Series Resistances and Voltage Dividers

**OBJECTIVE 6**

**Understand how to combine resistances connected in series and how voltage divides between series resistances**

**Resistances in series.**  As stated before, two circuit elements are connected *in series* when the same current flows through them. Figure 1.28 shows a series connection of three resistances and a battery. It is important in our method to anticipate the direction of the physical current, so we have defined the current reference direction such that the current will be positive out of the + terminal of the voltage source; and we put the + and − polarity symbols on the resistance voltages according to load-set conventions. Because $i$ will be numerically positive, the $v$'s across the resistances will also be positive. We can write KVL around the loop, going clockwise.

$$-V_s + v_1 + v_2 + v_3 = 0 \Rightarrow V_s = v_1 + v_2 + v_3 \qquad (1.60)$$

Because the $v$'s are positive and their sum is $V_s$, the battery voltage divides between $v_1$, $v_2$, and $v_3$. To show how this division depends on the values of the resistances, we introduce Ohm's law:

$$\begin{aligned} V_s &= R_1 i + R_2 i + R_3 i \\ &= (R_1 + R_2 + R_3)\, i \\ &= R_{eq} i \end{aligned} \qquad (1.61)$$

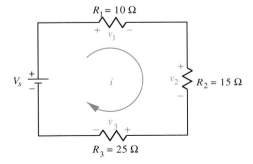

$R_1 = 10\ \Omega$
$v_1$
$V_s$
$i$
$v_2$  $R_2 = 15\ \Omega$
$v_3$
$R_3 = 25\ \Omega$

**Figure 1.28**  The three resistances have the same current and thus are in series. We may replace two or more resistances connected in series with a single equivalent resistance.

where $R_{eq}$ is an equivalent resistance. Thus, resistances connected in series add to an equivalent resistance as

$$R_{eq} = R_1 + R_2 + \cdots + R_n \text{ (all series resistances)} \tag{1.62}$$

Figure 1.29 shows a circuit that is equivalent to that in Fig. 1.28, except that the three resistances have been replaced by $R_{eq}$.

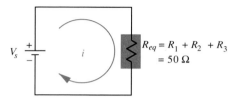

**Figure 1.29** The 10, 15, and 25-$\Omega$ resistances connected in series are represented by an equivalent resistance of 50 $\Omega$.

**Equivalent Circuits**

**Voltage dividers.** We set out to learn how the battery voltage, $V_s$, divides between the three resistances. We have determined the current:

$$i = \frac{V_s}{R_{eq}} = \frac{V_s}{50} \tag{1.63}$$

We can now obtain the voltage across the individual resistances from Ohm's law applied to the original circuit:

$$v_1 = R_1 i = R_1 \frac{V_s}{R_{eq}} = \frac{R_1}{R_{eq}} \times V_s = \frac{10}{50} V_s \tag{1.64}$$

Formulas for $v_2$ and $v_3$ can be written similarly. For example, if $V_s$ were 60 V, $v_1$ would be 12 V, $v_2$ would be 18 V, and $v_3$ would be 30 V. Our results are easily generalized to include an arbitrary number of series resistances; indeed, the voltage across the $i$th resistance would be

$$v_i = \frac{R_i}{R_{eq}} \times V_s \tag{1.65}$$

where

$$R_{eq} = R_1 + R_2 + \cdots + R_i + \cdots \text{ (all series resistors)}$$

As an intermediate result, we learned that series resistances can be replaced by a single resistance whose value is the sum of the values of the resistances in series.

---

**EXAMPLE 1.9** | **Voltage Dividers**

The circuit of Fig. 1.30 models a flashlight. The shaded boxes represent the batteries, but in this case, we have included the internal resistance of the battery in addition to its internal voltage source. We know that a battery has internal resistance because (1) it becomes hot when used heavily, (2) the battery voltage drops if current is flowing through the battery; and (3) the current it will produce is limited (actually to about 5 A). Calculate the voltage across the 2.5-$\Omega$ resistance representing the flashlight bulb when the switch is closed.

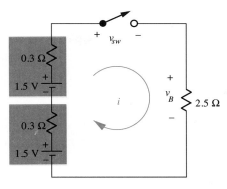

**Figure 1.30** Model of flashlight circuit. The shaded boxes represent the two dry-cell batteries, which not only produce voltage, but also have internal resistance. The 2.5-$\Omega$ resistance represents the bulb.

**SOLUTION:**
In the circuit of Fig. 1.30, all elements are in series because they have the same current. Kirchhoff's voltage law for the circuit, starting at the bottom and going clockwise, is

$$-(1.5) + 0.3\,i - (1.5) + 0.3\,i + v_{sw} + 2.5\,i = 0 \qquad (1.66)$$

We wrote the equation to show that the voltage from the batteries add to 3.0 V. With the switch closed, Eq. (1.65) gives the voltage across the bulb as

$$v_B = 3.0 \times \frac{2.5}{0.3 + 0.3 + 2.5} = 2.42 \text{ V} \qquad (1.67)$$

That the resistances are separated from each other by the voltage sources is irrelevant; the resistances share the same current and hence are connected in series.

**WHAT IF?**

What if the switch was corroded and had a resistance of 1.2 $\Omega$ when ON? What then would be the bulb voltage?[21]

## Parallel Resistances and Current Dividers

**OBJECTIVE 7**

**Understand how to combine resistances connected in parallel and how current divides between parallel resistances**

**Parallel resistances.** Resistances are said to be connected *in parallel* when they have the same voltage across them. Figure 1.31 shows a parallel combination of three resistances and a current source. We could have defined voltages for each resistance, but because the lines represent ideal connections (wires of zero resistance), the tops of the resistances are connected together and bottoms of the resistances are connected together, as pictured in Fig. 1.6. We were careful to define the currents through the resistances with reference directions such as the currents would be positive, assuming $I_s$ positive. We write KCL for node $a$:

---
[21] 1.74 V.

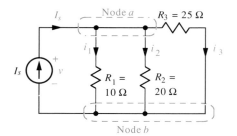

**Figure 1.31** Three resistors connected in parallel.

$$-I_s + i_1 + i_2 + i_3 = 0 \Rightarrow I_s = i_1 + i_2 + i_3 \tag{1.68}$$

Because the current reference symbols are directed into the + end of $v$ on the resistances, we have load sets; hence, we introduce Ohm's law, Eq. (1.38), into Eq. (1.68):

$$I_s = \frac{v}{R_1} + \frac{v}{R_2} + \frac{v}{R_3}$$

$$= v\left(\frac{1}{R_1} + \frac{1}{R_2} + \frac{1}{R_3}\right)$$

$$= v\,\frac{1}{R_{eq}} \tag{1.69}$$

**Equivalent Circuits**

where $R_{eq}$ is the equivalent resistance of $R_1$, $R_2$, and $R_3$ connected in parallel. The third form of Eq. (1.69) introduces a resistance, $R_{eq}$, that is equivalent to the three parallel resistances:

$$\frac{1}{R_{eq}} = \frac{1}{R_1} + \frac{1}{R_2} + \frac{1}{R_3} \Rightarrow R_{eq} = \frac{1}{1/R_1 + 1/R_2 + 1/R_3} \tag{1.70}$$

Many students have memorized the special case of Eq. (1.70) that applies to two resistances in parallel—the product over the sum. As stated earlier, we would encourage exclusive use of Eq. (1.70) for two reasons:

1. Equation (1.70) is the correct form regardless of the number of resistances.
2. Equation (1.70) is easier to implement on a calculator than the "product over the sum" for two parallel resistances.

Clearly, Eq. (1.70) represents an extension of Eq. (1.54) for three resistances, and we can use the notation: $R_{eq} = R_1 \| R_2 \| R_3$. In this case,

$$R_{eq} = 10 \| 20 \| 25 = \frac{1}{1/10 + 1/20 + 1/25} = 5.26\ \Omega \tag{1.71}$$

Thus, for the purpose of calculating the voltage across the three parallel resistances, we may replace the three resistances with an equivalent resistance of 5.26 Ω We now determine how the current $I_s$ divides between the three resistances.

**Current dividers.** We wish to use Eq. (1.69) in determining how the current $I_s$ divides between the three resistances. We can find the voltage from the last form of Eq. (1.69) and solve for the current in, say, $R_1$ from Ohm's law:

$$v = R_{eq} I_s \Rightarrow i_1 = \frac{v}{R_1} = \left(\frac{R_{eq}}{R_1}\right) \times I_s = \left(\frac{1/R_1}{1/R_1 + 1/R_2 + 1/R_3}\right) \times I_s \qquad (1.72)$$

The last form of Eq. (1.72) looks awkward but is the easiest form to implement on a calculator. Substituting the numbers, we learn that the current through $R_1$ is $0.526\, I_s$, or 52.6% of the total current. You can confirm for yourself that 26.3% passes through $R_2$ and 21.1% through $R_3$. These results are easy to generalize:  For any number of resistances that are connected in parallel, the current through the $i$th resistance, $R_i$, is

$$i_i = \frac{R_{eq}}{R_i} \times I_T = \frac{1/R_i}{1/R_1 + 1/R_2 + \cdots \text{(all parallel resistances)}} \times I_T \qquad (1.73)$$

where $I_T$ is the total current entering the parallel combination.

Equation (1.70) shows how to combine resistances in parallel. The addition of reciprocals is awkward to write but easy to accomplish on a calculator. Indeed, adding reciprocals with a calculator is just as simple as adding numbers except that you must hit the 1/x key on the calculator after entering the resistance values. After summing the reciprocals, you then hit the 1/x key to display the equivalent resistance of the parallel combination. If we desire a neat equation, we must use the conductances

$$G_{eq} = G_1 + G_2 + \cdots \text{(all parallel conductances)} \qquad (1.74)$$

In terms of conductances, the current divider relationship has the simpler form

$$i_i = \frac{G_i}{G_1 + G_2 + \cdots \text{(all parallel conductances)}} \times I_T \qquad (1.75)$$

---

**EXAMPLE 1.10** | **Parallel and Series Resistances**

Calculate the voltage across the four resistances in Fig. 1.32.

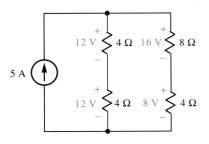

5 A

12 V    4 Ω    16 V    8 Ω

12 V    4 Ω    8 V    4 Ω

**Figure 1.32** The parallel paths each contain two resistances in series.

**SOLUTION:**

When we have two parallel connections of multiple resistances in a circuit, the voltage across the two parallel combinations divides independently in the two paths. In Fig. 1.32, the equivalent resistance seen by the current source is

$$R_{eq} = (4+4) \parallel (8+4) = 4.8 \ \Omega \tag{1.76}$$

and hence the total voltage across the parallel combination is $5 \times 4.8 = 24$ V with + at the top. This voltage divides independently in the two paths by a routine application of Eq. (1.65), with the results shown in Fig. 1.32.

**WHAT IF?**

What if the 8-$\Omega$ resistance were changed to 10 $\Omega$? What then would be the voltage across the 10-$\Omega$ resistance?[22] Across each of the two series 4-$\Omega$ resistances?[23]

**OBJECTIVE 8**

**To understand how to analyze circuits containing one source and resistances in series and parallel**

**The full voltage-divider/current-divider technique.** In the preceding sections, we learned about series and parallel combinations and how voltage and current divide in them, respectively. Let us now use these concepts to find the unknown voltages in the circuit shown in Fig. 1.33. We first will combine resistances to simplify the circuit. Notice that $R_2$ and $R_3$ are connected in parallel. We can replace them with an equivalent resistance of $4 \parallel 6$ or $2.4 \ \Omega$. This reduces the network to that shown in Fig. 1.34(a). The 2-$\Omega$ resistance is connected in series with the 2.4-$\Omega$ resistance and they can be combined into an equivalent resistance of 4.4 $\Omega$, Fig. 1.34(b). Clearly, the voltage across the current source, $V_s$, is 2A $\times$ 4.4 $\Omega$ = 8.8 V.

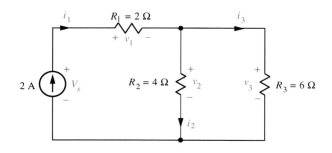

**Figure 1.33** Solve for the unknown voltages using the voltage-divider technique.

We will now restore the original circuit. Figure 1.34(c) is the same as Fig. 1.34(a), but because we are planning to divide the 8.8 V between the two resistances, we have defined voltages $v_1$ and $v_4$ with the proper polarity markings for that purpose. The original $v_1$ already has the desired polarity marking, and we introduced a $v_4$ for the voltage across the 2.4-$\Omega$ resistance. "Wait" (you might object), "that is a current source, not a voltage source you are dividing." True, but the voltage created by the current source divides in the series circuit. It does not matter whether we have a 2-A current source pro-

---

[22] 18.2 V.

[23] 12.7 V.

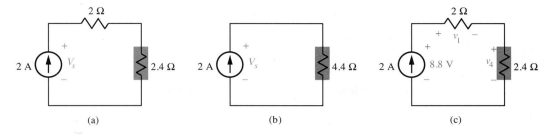

**Figure 1.34** Combining resistances in parallel and series simplifies the circuit to the point where the unknown voltage can be determined by a voltage divider.

ducing 8.8 V or an 8.8-V voltage source producing 2 A—the circuit will respond in the same way.[24] So we can divide the 8.8 V whether it is produced by a voltage or a current source. The results are

$$v_1 = 8.8 \times \frac{2}{4.4} = 4.00 \text{ V} \qquad \text{and} \qquad v_4 = 8.8 \times \frac{2.4}{4.4} = 4.80 \text{ V} \qquad (1.77)$$

Because $v_4$ is the voltage across the parallel combination of the 4- and 6-$\Omega$ resistances in the original circuit, $v_4$ is the same as $v_3$ and $v_2$ in the original problem, and $i_3$ follows from Ohm's law to be 0.80 A. The downward current through the 4-$\Omega$ resistance is 4.8 V/4 $\Omega = +1.2$ A.

**Reworking with current dividers.** We repeat using current dividers instead of voltage dividers. The 2 A passes through $R_1$, producing 4 V across it, and then divides between the $R_2$ and $R_3$. The current through $R_3$ can be determined directly by current division, as also can be the current through $R_2$. For example, Eq. (1.73) yields

$$i_3 = 2 \times \left( \frac{1/6}{1/6 + 1/4} \right) = 0.8 \text{ A} \qquad (1.78)$$

Note that $R_1$ has no influence on the division of the current between $R_2$ and $R_3$.

From the currents, we can calculate the voltages and complete the problem. For example, Eq. (1.38) yields

$$v_3 = R_3 i_3 = 6 \times 0.8 = 4.8 \text{ V} \qquad (1.79)$$

On more complicated circuits, both voltage and current dividers might be used to learn how voltage and current distribute throughout the circuit.

**Summary of this method.** In this method:

**1.** We use series and parallel combinations of resistances to simplify a circuit, beginning far away from and coming toward the source.

---

[24] The type of source would matter if we changed one of the resistances in the circuit, for in one case, the source current would remain constant, and in the other case, the source voltage would remain constant.

2. The entire circuit can be reduced to a single resistance across the source, although often the process does not have to be carried that far.

3. The circuit is then restored, voltages and currents being divided progressively to yield the individual currents and voltages throughout the circuit.

**Advantages of this method.** The genius of this method is that you are guided in the solution by the geometry of the circuit. This important information is neglected if you merely define variables and apply Kirchhoff's and Ohm's laws directly. This method avoids defining unnecessary variables; you merely introduce those needed to perform the voltage and current division. As a final advantage, we might suggest that this method, after you use it a while, will develop your intuition about what is happening in circuits.

**Weaknesses of this method.** Alongside these advantages, we must place certain limitations. As we presented it, the method works for circuits having only one source, although we will overcome this limitation in Chapter 2. More significantly, this method does not handle the sign for you; you are expected to bring to the problem sufficient insight to know which way the physical current goes. For only one source, this is frequently no problem; but you do have to remember to supply the sign and not look for the mathematics to produce it. Also, this method often requires that you analyze the entire circuit, solving for virtually every voltage and current, to determine any single unknown. Finally, there are circuits where this method fails.

Figure 1.35 shows such a circuit. Simple though this circuit is, no two resistances are in series or parallel. There is no place to start combining resistances. Chapter 2 explains several methods that can solve this circuit.

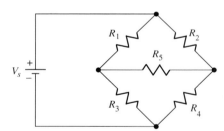

**Figure 1.35** This circuit cannot be solved by voltage and/or current dividers because no two resistances are in series or in parallel.

### Check Your Understanding

1. Two circuit elements are said to be in parallel if they share the same voltage or current?

2. In a current divider consisting of three resistances, the resistances are in the ratio $1:2:3$. What percent of the total current goes through the largest resistance?

3. What are $2 + 5 \| 7$ and $10 \| 12 + 7 \| (1 + 2)$?

4. Three resistances having the same value, $R$, are connected together to have an equivalent resistance of $1.5R$. How are they connected?

*Answers.* (**1**) Same voltage; (**2**) 18.2%; (**3**) 4.92, 7.55; (**4**) one in series with the other two in parallel.

# CHAPTER SUMMARY

We lay the foundation for the entire book in defining the electrical quantities used to describe most electrical systems, voltage and current, stressing that these track energy flow throughout a circuit. We present Kirchhoff's laws as expressions of conservation of charge and electric energy. Resistance is defined and Ohm's law is presented. With the definition of current and voltage sources, we begin to solve simple circuits. More complicated circuits are analyzed by combining series and parallel resistances, and voltage and current dividers are used to determine voltage and current throughout a circuit.

**Objective 1: To understand what is a circuit and why circuits are important in electrical engineering.** Circuits are the logical place to begin the study of electrical engineering because most electrical devices and applications involve circuits in one form or another. Circuits are relatively easy to understand and require simple mathematics.

**Objectives 2 and 3: To understand the definitions of current and voltage and how to use Kirchhoff's laws to express conservation of charge and energy.** Voltage and current are used to describe the state of an electric circuit for several reasons: they are easily measured, they describe the flow of energy in the circuit, and they obey simple constraints based on conservation of charge and energy. We stress the necessity of careful attention to signs in writing equations based on these laws because both voltage and current are described by both a magnitude and a sign with respect to a reference direction.

**Objective 4: To understand how to use the voltage and current to calculate the power into or out of a circuit element.** Power is the product of voltage and current, but again one must pay careful attention to signs, in this case the reference direction for the current relative to the reference direction for the voltage. We recommend using a load set for passive circuit elements such as resistors and using a source set for sources.

**Objective 5: To understand the relationship between voltage and current in a resistor as described by Ohm's law.** Ohm's law states that the current in a resistor is proportional to the voltage across the resistor. It follows that the power in a resistor is proportional to the square of the current through the resistor and the square of the voltage across the resistor.

**Objective 6: To understand how to combine resistances connected in series and how voltage divides between series resistances.** Resistors are in series when they have the same current through them. Resistors in series can be combined by adding their resistances. The voltage across resistors connected in series divides between the resistors in proportion to their resistance values.

**Objective 7: To understand how to combine resistances connected in parallel and how current divides between parallel resistances.** Resistors are in parallel when they have the same voltage across them. Resistors in parallel can be combined by adding the reciprocals of their resistances. The current into two or more resistors connected in parallel divides between the resistors in proportion to the reciprocals of their resistance values.

Objective 8: To understand how to analyze circuits containing one source and resistances in series and parallel. By combining resistors in series and parallel, simple circuits can be reduced to a form where the voltage and current throughout the circuit can be determined with voltage and current dividers.

Chapter 2 presents additional methods for circuit analysis, all based on the definitions and laws presented in this chapter.

## PROBLEMS

## Section 1.3: Current and Kirchhoff's Current Law

1.1. The allowed safe current for a No. 12 copper wire, 0.08081 inch in diameter, is 23 A.
   (a) How many coulombs of charge pass a cross-section of the wire in 1 minute?
   (b) At 23-A direct current, how fast are the electrons traveling in mm/s?

1.2. In a No. 10 copper wire 0.1019 inch in diameter, electrons are moving 1 ft every minute. What is the magnitude of the current in the wire?

1.3. The current in a wire is zero for $t < 0$ but begins increasing at a rate of 5 amperes/second at $t = 0$, as shown in Fig P1.3.
   (a) At what time is the current 7.2 A?
   (b) At what time have 12 C of charge passed a cross-section of the wire?

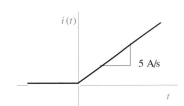

**Figure P1.3**

1.4. For the circuit in Fig. P1.4:
   (a) Write KCL for node $a$ using the first form of KCL on page 10.
   (b) Write KCL for node $b$ using the third form of KCL on page 10.
   (c) Add or subtract the equations resulting from KCL at nodes $a$ and $b$ to show that $i_1$ and $i_4$ are equal.

1.5. Use KCL to determine $i$ and $i_{ab}$ in the circuit shown in Fig. P1.5.

1.6. For the circuit in Fig. P1.6, compute the unknown currents using KCL.

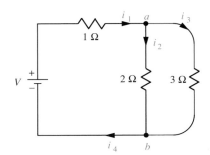

**Figure P1.4**

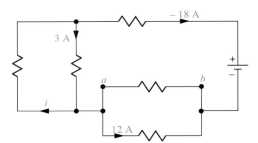

**Figure P1.5**

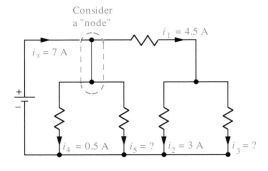

**Figure P1.6**

CHAPTER 1 BASIC CIRCUIT THEORY

**1.7.** In a simulated lightning bolt in a laboratory, the current increases linearly from 0 to 1500 A in 1 μs and then decreases linearly back to 0 in 4 μs, shown in Fig. P1.7, making a 5 μs total for the duration of the lightning. What is the total charge required?

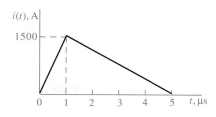

**Figure P1.7**

## Section 1.4: Voltage and Kirchhoff's Voltage Law

**1.8.** How much work is done by a 12.6-V battery if 1 microcoulomb of positive charge is pulled off the negative terminal and placed on the positive terminal?

**1.9.** If $v_{xy} = +120$ V and a $-4$-C charge is moved by an external agent from $y$ to $x$, how much work is done on the external agent by the electrical system?

**1.10.** In a cathode-ray tube (CRT), a beam of electrons is accelerated through a certain voltage ($V_{CRT}$), then allowed to drift through an evacuated space until it strikes the CRT surface, making a small spot of light. If $|V_{CRT}| = 9500$ V, what velocity do the electrons acquire from the voltage source? *Hint:* Equate the final kinetic energy of an individual electron with the electrical energy delivered by the source to one electron.

**1.11.** **(a)** Write KVL to determine $v_{ab}$ in the circuit Fig. P1.11.
   **(b)** If a battery (voltage source) were inserted between $c$ and $d$ to make $v_{ab} = 12.3$ V, draw the circuit showing the battery polarity and voltage magnitude.

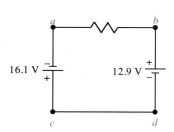

**Figure P1.11**

**1.12.** For a circuit, $v_{ab} = 9$ V, $v_{cb} = -5.2$ V, $v_{dc} = -11$ V, and $v_{de} = -4$ V. Using the rules for adding subscripts, determine $v_{ba}$, $v_{bd}$, and $v_{ae}$. *Hint:* Draw

a "circuit" showing the lettered points to aid in visualizing the patterns.

**1.13.** For the circuit shown in Fig. P1.13, find $V_1$, $v_{ad}$, $v_{bc}$, and $v_{ac} + v_{ce}$.

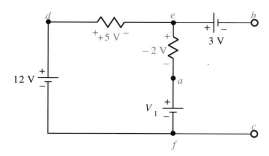

**Figure P1.13**

**1.14.** For the circuit shown in Fig. P1.14, use KCL and KVL to determine $i_1$, $i_2$, $v_{ad}$, and $v_x$.

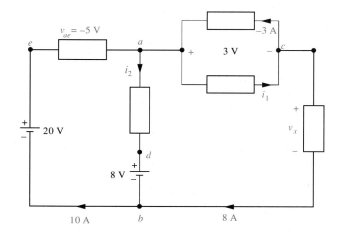

**Figure P1.14**

## Section 1.5: Energy Flow in Electrical Circuits

**1.15.** The MKS unit for energy is the joule, which is 1 watt-second, but the unit in common use by electrical utilities is the kilowatt-hour (kWh).
 (a) How many joules are there in 10 kWh?
 (b) At 9.35 cents/kWh, how many joules can one buy for a penny?

**1.16.** For the circuit shown in Fig. P1.16:
 (a) Use KCL and KVL to find $v_2$, $v_3$ and $i$.
 (b) Calculate the power *into* every resistance and the power *out of* every source. Show that energy is conserved, that is, that $p_{out} = p_{in}$.

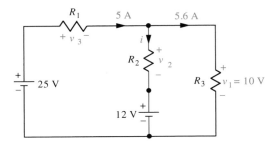

**Figure P1.16**

**1.17.** The circuit shown in Fig. P1.17 represents a battery charger charging a battery.
 (a) Find the power into the battery being charged.
 (b) What is the time it would take to impart 1 kilocoulomb ($10^3$ C) to the battery?
 (c) What energy is given to the battery in this period of time?

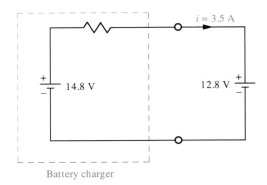

Battery charger

**Figure P1.17**

**1.18.** In Fig. P1.18, the power into the 5-V battery is $+10$ W. Determine the power into $R$ and the power out of the 9-V battery.

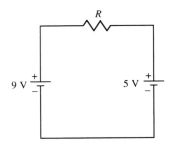

**Figure P1.18**

**1.19.** In the circuit in Fig. P1.19 determine the following:
 (a) $v_{ab}$.
 (b) $i$.
 (c) The sum of the powers into $R_1$, $R_2$, and the 2-V battery.

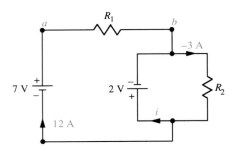

**Figure P1.19**

**1.20.** In the circuit shown in Fig. P1.20, give the values for the following:
 (a) $v_{ab}$.
 (b) $v_x$.
 (c) The power out of the 4-V battery.

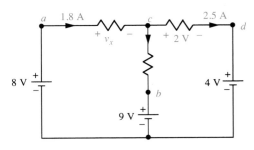

**Figure P1.20**

**1.21.** For the circuit shown in Fig. P1.21, compute the unknown voltages and currents. (You supply the voltage and current variables for the unknowns, including their reference directions.) Compute the power *into* the two resistances and the power *out of* both sources. Show conservation of power.

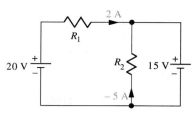

**Figure P1.21**

## Section 1.6: Circuit Elements: Resistors, Switches, and Sources

**1.22.** A resistor capable of handling safely 5 W is to be placed across the terminals of a 10-V voltage source. What range of resistances will not exceed the 5-W limit?

**1.23.** Find the value of $R_1$, $R_2$, and $R_3$ in Fig. P1.16.

**1.24.** A car radio designed to operate from a 6.3-V system uses 4.5 A of current, as shown in Fig. P1.24.
   **(a)** What resistance should be placed in series with this radio if it is to be used in a 12.6-V system?
   **(b)** What should be the power rating of this resistance?

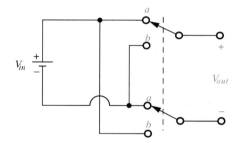

**Figure P1.25**

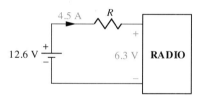

**Figure P1.24**

**1.25.** A voltage source, current source, and resistance are shown in series in Figure P1.25.
   **(a)** For $I_s > 0$, find the value of $V_s$ that makes the power into the voltage source equal to the power into the resistance. The required $V_s$ is a function of $I_s$ and $R$.
   **(b)** For $I_s < 0$, show that no positive value of $V_s$ will satisfy the conditions given in (a). Explain why this is true.

**1.26.** Figure P1.26 shows a voltage source and a switch.
   **(a)** Is the switch single- or double-pole?
   **(b)** Is the switch single- or double-throw?
   **(c)** What is the output voltage for the switch in position *a* and in position *b*?

**1.27.** Figure P1.27 shows a voltage source, light bulb, and two double-throw, single-pole switches.

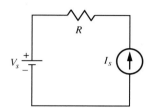

**Figure P1.26**

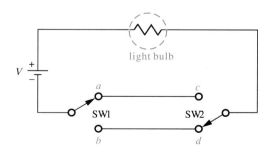

**Figure P1.27**

   **(a)** For the light bulb to be ON, what are the possible settings for the switches?

**(b)** Assuming that the light is ON, what happens to the light as a consequence of changing either switch?

**(c)** Assuming that the light is OFF, what happens to the light as a consequence of changing either switch?

*Note:* This is (for some reason) called a "three-way" switch and is often used in a long hall or stairway so that a light can be turned ON or OFF from either end of the hall.

1.28. Figures 1.28(a) and 1.28(b) show a resistance and a voltage source or current source, respectively. Plot of $V(R)$ and $I(R)$ vs. $R$ for the range $1 < R < 10\,\Omega$ in both cases. *Note:* Commonly, we consider $V(R)$ to mean that $V$ *depends* on $R$, so $V$ cannot be constant as $R$ is varied. But actually $V(R) =$ constant is a perfectly good mathematical function that happens to have a zero derivative everywhere.

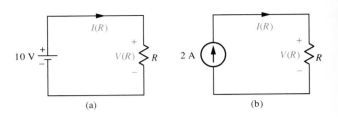

**Figure P1.28**

1.29. Figure 1.29 shows circuits containing voltage and current sources and resistances. Some circuits are valid (non contradictory) for all values of the variables, some are valid for no values, and some are valid for specific values of the variables. Classify each and tell what, if any, values of the $V$'s, $I$'s, and $R$'s lead to circuits compatible with the definitions of the sources and resistance.

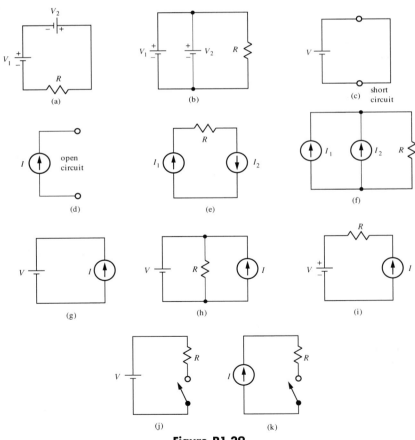

**Figure P1.29**

# Section 1.7: Series and Parallel Resistances; Voltage and Current Dividers

**1.30. (a)** Three resistors connected in series have resistance values in the ratio 1:1.5:3.3 and combine to an equivalent resistance of 150 Ω. What is the smallest resistor?

**(b)** The three resistors, still in series, are placed across a 300-V dc voltage source. What is the voltage that will appear across the largest resistor?

**1.31. (a)** Two series resistances are to work as a voltage divider, with the smaller receiving 30% of the total voltage. What are the resistors given that their equivalent resistance is 200 Ω?

**(b)** If both resistors are 2-watt resistors, what is the maximum total voltage the voltage divider can handle without exceeding this rating for either resistor?

**1.32.** For the circuit shown in Fig. P1.32, the arrow indicates that the resistor $R$ is variable; hence, the voltage across $R$, $v(R)$, will depend on the value of $R$, as the notation indicates. Determine the function and plot $v(R)$ for $0 < R < 40$ Ω, and find the value of $R$ to make the voltage 5.5 V.

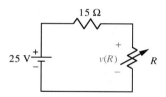

**Figure P1.32**

**1.33. (a)** Find the equivalent resistance of the parallel combination shown in Fig. P1.33.

**(b)** If 10 A enters the parallel combination, referenced in at $a$ and out at $b$, what is the current referenced downward in the 6-Ω resistance?

**(c)** What is the current referenced upward in the 2-Ω resistance?

**(d)** What is the voltage $v_{ab}$ for this current?

**1.34.** Consider three parallel resistances, $R_1$, $R_2$, and $R_3$, with a current of $I_T$ A passing through the parallel combination. Show that the power in the equivalent resistance, $R_{eq} = R_1 \| R_2 \| R_3$, is the correct value, that is, the sum of the powers in the resistances in the original circuit.

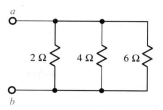

**Figure P1.33**

**1.35.** For the circuit shown in Fig. P1.35 determine the following:

**(a)** Find $R$ such that $i_R = 0.5$ A.

**(b)** What value of $R$ gives a power of 833 W in $R$?

**(c)** What is the maximum possible value of the power in $R$?

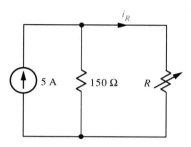

**Figure P1.35**

**1.36.** Design a current divider that has an equivalent resistance of 100 Ω and divides the current in the ratio of 5:2. This problem is summarized in Fig. P1.36.

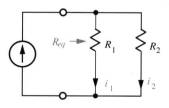

$$R_{eq} = R_1 \| R_2 = 100 \ \Omega$$

$$2i_1 = 5i_2$$

**Figure P1.36**

**1.37. (a)** Evaluate $R_{eq} = 8 + (3 + 4)\|6\ \Omega$.
  **(b)** Draw the circuit corresponding to this expression.

**1.38. (a)** What resistance in parallel with $105\ \Omega$ reduces the equivalent parallel resistance to $91.5\ \Omega$?
  **(b)** What is $1\|2\|4\|8\|16\|\cdots$?
  *Hint:* Write the expression for the total conductance. The result should be a familiar geometric series that is easily summed.

**1.39.** As the variable resistor in Fig. P1.39, $R$, varies from a short to an open circuit, the equivalent resistance should vary between 30 and 75 $\Omega$.
  **(a)** Design $R_1$ and $R_2$ to accomplish this result.
  **(b)** Find $R$ to give $R_{eq} = (30 + 75)/2\ \Omega$.

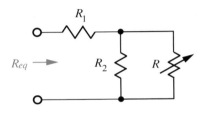

**Figure P1.39**

**1.40.** The resistance $R$ in Fig. P1.40 is variable from a short circuit to an open circuit.
  **(a)** Find the maximum and minimum equivalent resistance at the input.
  **(b)** What value of $R$ gives the average between $R_{max}$ and $R_{min}$?

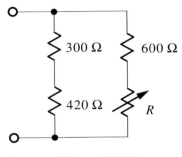

**Figure P1.40**

**1.41.** For the circuits shown in Fig. P1.41, find the indicated unknowns using voltage and current dividers.

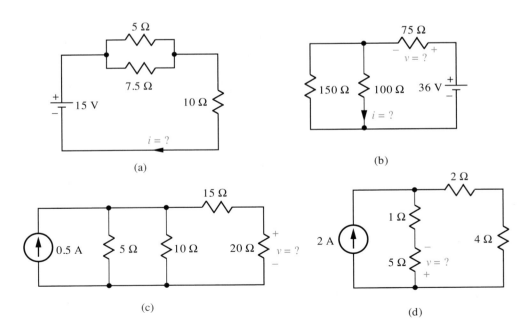

**Figure P1.41**

**1.42.** For the circuits in Fig. P1.42, find the indicated unknowns using voltage and current dividers.

**1.43.** For the circuit shown in Fig. P1.43, find the value of $R$ that makes the power into the 100-$\Omega$ resistor to be 10 W.

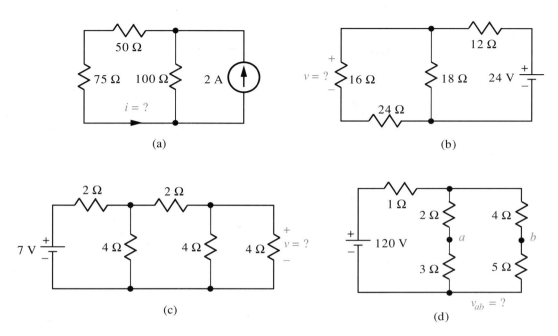

(a)

(b)

(c)

(d)

$v_{ab} = ?$

**Figure P1.42**

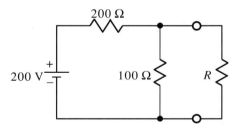

**Figure P1.43**

## General Problems

**1.44.** In the circuit shown in Fig. P1.44, all voltages are dc. The boxes represent unknown (and in some cases, weird) circuit elements. The current in No. 1 is also dc, as shown. The voltage across No. 1 is $v_{ab} = +40$ V. The current in No. 3 is the pulse of current shown in the figure and is described by the

equation $i_3(t) = 8(t - 2t^2)$, $0 < t < 0.5$, and $i_3 = 0$ at all other times.

(a) Find the work done by the electrical system in moving an electron from $c$ to $b$.

(b) What is the minimum power into No. 2 as time varies?

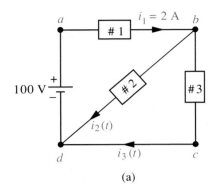

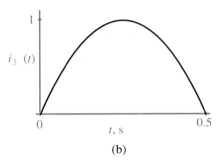

**Figure P1.44**

the initial charge separation neutralized by the lightning?

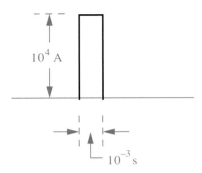

**Figure P1.46**

**(c)** How much charge is moved through No. 3 by current pulse $i_3(t)$?

**(d)** Find the electrical energy contributed to the circuit by No. 3 during the time period $0 < t < 0.5$ s.

**1.45.** In a semiconductor such as silicon, current is carried both by conduction electrons and by mobile "holes" that behave like positive charges having a charge equal in magnitude to that of the electron. Find the magnitude and direction of the current in a silicon diode of cross-sectional area $10^{-9}$ m² with electrons ($n_e$ of $10^{23}$ electrons/m³) traveling with 0.3 mm/s to the right and holes ($n_h$ of $1.5 \times 10^{22}$ holes/ m³) traveling to the left at 0.1 mm/s.

**1.46.** A lightning bolt might carry a current of $10^4$ A and last for about 1 ms, as shown in Fig. P1.46.

**(a)** How much charge is exchanged between ground and cloud in such a lightning bolt?

**(b)** How many raindrops had to fall, each having a deficiency of 10 electronic charges, to create

**1.47.** A battery can be rated in "A-h," ampere-hours. For example, a 60 A-h battery ought to put out 60 A for 1 h, or 1 A for 60 h, or some other combination multiplying to 60.

**(a)** How many coulombs of charge may one hope to get out of a fully charged 90 A-h battery?

**(b)** How many electrons would pass through the wire discharging such a fully charged battery?

**1.48.** A fully charged auto battery has a voltage of 12.6 V. As the battery discharges, the voltage drops. The voltage will drop to about 10.0 V as total discharge is approached, at which point the voltage drops to essentially zero if you try to draw current from the battery. Consider the case where we are discharging a 60-A-h battery over a 6-h period at a uniform 10-A rate. Assume battery voltage drops from 12.6 to 10.0 V at a linear rate.

**(a)** Describe the voltage as a function of time during discharge.

**(b)** Compute the total energy output of the battery for this discharge rate.

**(c)** Show that the energy output is independent of the discharge rate. *Hint:* Let $T$ be the time for discharge in hours and $60/T$ be the current.

**1.49.** Figure P1.49 shows the voltage and current for a semiconductor switch closure. Note the switch is not ideal in that voltage and current do not change instantaneously. This means that the

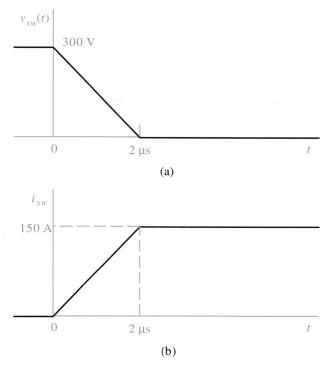

$v_{sw}(t)$

300 V

0    2 μs    t

(a)

$i_{sw}$

150 A

0    2 μs    t

(b)

**Figure P1.49**

switch will dissipate some energy during its operation.

**(a)** How much energy is used up in each switching operation? (Assume a source set of reference directions.)

**(b)** If the same energy were used in opening the switch, and the switch went through 5000 cycles each second, what is the average power lost in the switch? Each cycle involves opening and closing the switch.

1.50. Problems based upon circuit symmetry. The equivalent resistances in Fig. P1.50 may be solved readily using circuit symmetry. For example, in circuit (a), the circuit has even symmetry about the center line of the bridge; hence, any current that enters at the top divides equally. Consequently, the voltage across the middle resistance is zero, no current passes through it, and the left and right resistances are actually in series (have the same current). Using this approach, find the indicated equivalent resistance for all three circuits.

1.51. These problems are based upon infinite ladder circuits. The equivalent resistances of the circuits in Fig. P1.51 may be determined by considering the properties of infinity. In both cases, if you remove the first two resistances (the first rung of the ladder), the remaining circuit has an equivalent resistance that is closely related to that of the original problem. Find the equivalent resistance in parts (a) and (b).

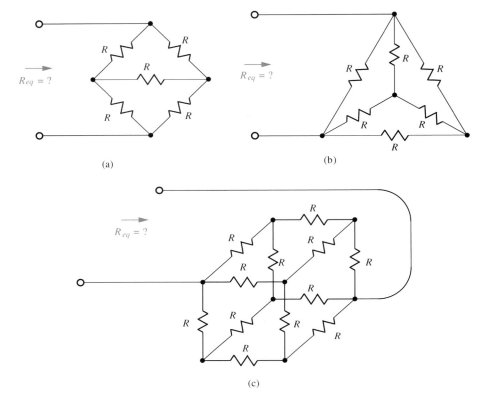

(a)

(b)

(c)

**Figure P1.50**

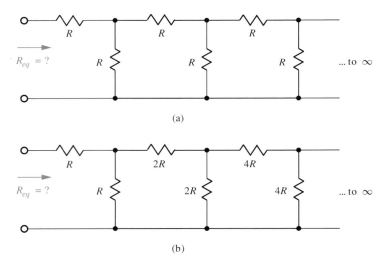

(a)

(b)

**Figure P1.51**

# Answers to Odd-Numbered Problems

1.1. **(a)** 1380 C; **(b)** 0.384 mm/s.

1.3. **(a)** 1.44 s; **(b)** 2.19 s.

1.5. $i = -15$A, $i_{ab} = 6$A

1.7. 3.75 mC.

1.9. $+480$ J.

1.11. **(a)** $-29$ V; **(b)** 41.3 V, $+$ at left.

1.13. 9 V, $-3$ V, $+4$ V, $+2$ V.

1.15. **(a)** $3.6 \times 10^7$ J; **(b)** $3.85 \times 10^5$ J/cent.

1.17. **(a)** 44.8 W; **(b)** 286 s; **(c)** 12,800 J.

1.19. **(a)** $+9$ V; **(b)** $-15$ A; **(c)** 84 W.

1.21. **(a)** $p_{sources} = 40 + 45$ W; **(b)** $p_{resistors} = 10 + 75$ W.

1.23. $R_1 = 3$ Ω, $R_2 = 3.33$ Ω, $R_3, = 1.79$ Ω

1.25. **(a)** $V_s = I_s R$; **(b)** same formula, but violates polarity convention for voltage sources.

1.27. **(a)** For ON,

| SW1 | SW2 |
|-----|-----|
| a | c |
| b | d |

**(b)** it goes OFF; **(c)** it comes ON.

1.29. **(a)** Valid for all $V_1$, $V_2$, and $R$; **(b)** valid for $V_1 = V_2$; **(c)** valid for $V = 0$, or not valid; **(d)** valid for $I = 0$, or not valid; **(e)** valid for $I_1 = I_2$; **(f)** valid for all $I_1$, $I_2$, and $R$; **(g)** valid for all $V$ and $I$; **(h)** Valid for all $V$, $I$, and $R$; **(i)** valid for all $V$, $I$, and $R$; **(j)** valid for all $V$, $R$, and switch positions; **(k)** valid for closed switch only.

1.31. **(a)** 60 Ω and 140 Ω; **(b)** 23.9 V.

1.33. **(a)** 1.09 Ω; **(b)** 1.82 A; **(c)** $-5.45$ A; **(d)** 10.9 V.

1.35. **(a)** 1350 Ω; **(b)** 74.9 Ω or 300 Ω; **(c)** 937.5 W.

1.37. 11.2 Ω.

1.39. **(a)** 30 Ω, 45 Ω; **(b)** 45 Ω.

1.41. **(a)** 1.15 A; **(b)** 0.160 A, $v = 20$ V; **(c)** 0.870 V; **(d)** $-5.00$ V.

1.43. 60.2 Ω.

1.45. $-5.05 \times 10^{-9}$ A to the right.

1.47. **(a)** 324,000 C; **(b)** $2.02 \times 10^{24}$ electrons.

1.49. **(a)** 0.0150 J; **(b)** 150 W.

1.51. **(a)** $1.62R$; **(b)** $1.78\ R$.

# 2

# The Analysis of DC Circuits

1. To understand the principle of superposition and use super-position to analyze circuits with multiple sources
2. To understand the origin of Thevénin's equivalent circuit and be able to derive the Thevénin equivalent circuit of a circuit with a load
3. To understand the significance of impedence level in interactions between circuits
4. To understand how to analyze a circuit using nodal analysis
5. To understand how to analyze a circuit using loop currents
6. To understand how to choose the most efficient manner for analyzing a circuit

Simple circuits can be analyzed by simple meth-ods, but not all circuits are simple. The methods of this chapter, although illustrated on relatively simple circuits, are general enough to han-dle complicated circuits.

The method of Thevénin equivalent circuits, further-more, yields an insight that figures explicitly or implicit-ly into virtually every electri-cal design.

Introduction. In Chapter 1, we defined voltage and current in terms of energy, charge, and time. We showed that knowing the voltage and current throughout a circuit allows the engineer to know how energy is entering, exiting, and moving throughout the circuit. We presented Kirchhoff's voltage and current laws as statements of conservation of energy and charge, expressed in terms of voltage and current. We gave special attention to voltage and current reference directions in the writing of circuit equations.

We then defined voltage sources, current sources, and resistances. We discussed Ohm's law, which relates the voltage across a resistance to the current through the resistance. We solved simple circuits involving sources, switches, and resistances. Finally, we showed that resistances in series (having the same current) and resistances in parallel (sharing the same voltage) can be combined into equivalent resistances that simplify circuit analysis. Voltage and current dividers were used to find how the voltage and current distribute in simple circuits.

The method of circuit analysis summarized on page 39 works well for simple circuits. In Chapter 2, we add methods of circuit analysis that are useful in more complicated circuits.

## 2.1 SUPERPOSITION

### Superposition Illustrated

Demonstration of the principle. The principle of superposition extends the method based upon resistance combinations taught in Chapter 1. Before giving a formal definition, we will illustrate the principle of superposition. We will solve for $v_2$ in the circuit in Fig. 2.1. Because the circuit has two sources, we cannot use voltage and current dividers. Thus, we will apply Kirchhoff's voltage and current laws, and Ohm's law. These are

$$\text{Ohm's law:} \quad v_1 = i_1 R_1 \quad \text{and} \quad v_2 = i_2 R_2 \tag{2.1}$$

$$\text{KVL:} \quad -v_1 + v_2 + V_s = 0 \tag{2.2}$$

$$\text{KCL:} \quad -I_s + i_1 + i_2 = 0 \tag{2.3}$$

First, we eliminate $i_1$ and $i_2$ with Ohm's law, so Eq. (2.3) becomes

$$\frac{v_1}{R_1} + \frac{v_2}{R_2} = I_s \tag{2.4}$$

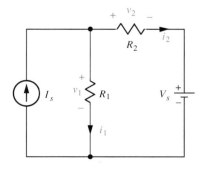

**Figure 2.1** Solve for $v_2$ using KVL and KCL.

When we eliminate $v_1$ between Eqs. (2.2) and (2.4), we obtain the following result:

$$v_2 = \frac{I_s - (V_s/R_1)}{(1/R_1) + (1/R_2)} = I_s(R_1 \parallel R_2) - V_s \times \frac{R_2}{R_1 + R_2} \qquad (2.5)$$

**Some observations based on the result.** The first form of Eq. (2.5) emerges from the algebra; the second form can be interpreted from the results of Chapter 1. Examination of Eq. (2.5) suggests the following:

1. There are two components of $v_2$, one for each source. This means that one part of $v_2$ is caused by the current source and the other part is caused by the voltage source.

2. The part of the voltage due to the current source is what would be caused by the current source acting alone, provided the voltage source is replaced by a short circuit. The current source sees two resistances in parallel if the voltage source is replaced by a short circuit. By *short circuit*, we mean an ideal connection having no voltage across it.

3. The part of the voltage due to the voltage source is what would be caused by the voltage source acting alone, provided the current source is replaced by an open circuit. By *open circuit*, we mean that no path exists for current flow. Note that if there is no current flow through the current source, the two resistances are connected in series and the voltage-divider form, the second term in Eq. (2.5), is easily identified.

4. The total voltage is the sum of the separate effects of the two sources, provided the polarity of the effects is considered. In this case, the current source produces a voltage with a polarity the same as the reference direction of $v_2$ and it appears with a positive sign. The voltage source produces a voltage with a polarity opposite to that of $v_2$, and this component appears in the summation with a negative sign.

These observations suggest the principle of superposition, which we now state.

## Principle of Superposition

**Principle stated.** The principle of superposition may be stated as follows: *The response of a circuit due to multiple sources can be calculated by summing the effects of each source considered separately, all others being turned OFF.* By OFF, we mean that current sources are replaced by open circuits and voltage sources are replaced by short circuits.

**Turned-OFF sources.** The concept of turning-OFF a source is important and bears elaboration. We start with the graphical presentation of the $i - v$ characteristics of a resistance in Fig. 2.2. Because the slope of the resistance characteristic is $1/R$, a zero-resistance line would have an infinite slope. Thus, any amount of current can pass without producing a voltage. On the other hand, the line for an infinite resistance would have zero slope, implying zero current no matter how large the voltage. In Fig. 2.2, we have called zero resistance a short circuit and infinite resistance an open circuit. The circuit symbol for a short circuit is merely a line, and the circuit symbol for an open circuit is a break in the line, indicating that there is no path for current.

**short circuit**

**open circuit**

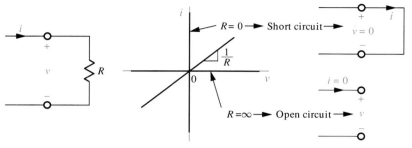

**Figure 2.2** The characteristic of a short circuit is vertical and the characteristic of an open circuit is horizontal.

From our earlier definition of a voltage source, we know that a voltage source establishes a certain voltage at its terminals, independent of the current. In Fig. 2.3, this is represented by a vertical line at $V_s$. It follows that a voltage source of zero volts would be represented by a vertical line of infinite slope through the origin, which is the same as the characteristic of a short circuit. Thus, a turned-OFF voltage source is a short circuit.

Figure 2.4 shows the definition of a current source. This is a horizontal line of constant current. A current source of zero value produces a horizontal line through the origin, the same characteristic as an open circuit. Thus, a turned-OFF current source is identical to an open circuit.

**Benchmark example.** We will use the principle of superposition to solve for the voltage across the 3-$\Omega$ resistance in the circuit shown in Fig. 2.5. We call this our "benchmark example" because we will solve this problem by every method presented in this chapter.

**Turn ON 4-A source.** There are three sources, so we will have to analyze three circuits, each having a single source. In Fig. 2.6, we calculate the voltage due to the 4-A current source, $v_4$. We have turned OFF the 5-A current source, replacing it with an open circuit; and we have turned OFF the 6-V source, replacing it with a short circuit. The re-

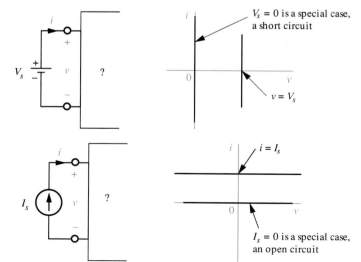

**Figure 2.3** The voltage source has a vertical characteristic. Zero voltage ($V_s = 0$) is equivalent to a short circuit.

**Figure 2.4** The current source has a horizontal characteristic. Zero source current ($I_s = 0$) is equivalent to an open circuit.

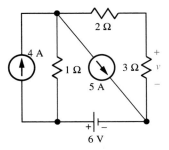

**Figure 2.5** We will calculate the contributions of each source to $v$ and add all results.

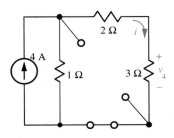

**Figure 2.6** The circuit with the 4-A source ON and the others OFF.

sulting circuit shows the 2- and 3-$\Omega$ resistances connected in series with each other and together in parallel with the 1-$\Omega$ resistance. We use a current divider, Eq. (1.73),

$$i = 4\,\text{A} \times \frac{1/(2+3)}{1/(2+3)+1/1} = 2/3\,\text{A} \tag{2.6}$$

and then calculate the voltage across the 3-$\Omega$ resistance from Ohm's law:

$$v_4 = 2/3\,\text{A} \times 3\,\Omega = 2.00\,\text{V} \tag{2.7}$$

The polarity resulting from the 4-A source is the same as the original polarity markings for $v$. Hence this contribution will appear with a $+$ sign in the final summation.

**Turn ON 5-A source.** Figure 2.7 shows the circuit with the 4-A and 6-V sources turned OFF. From the perspective of the 5-A source, the 2- and 3-$\Omega$ resistances are in series and together in parallel with the 1-$\Omega$ resistance. The voltage resulting from the 5-A source, $v_5$, can be calculated with the current-divider approach just used, but for practice, we will use voltage dividers. The voltage across the 3-$\Omega$ resistance is

$$v_5 = \underbrace{5 \times 1 \| (2+3)}_{\substack{\text{voltage across} \\ \text{parallel combination}}} \times \underbrace{\frac{3}{2+3}}_{\substack{\text{portion across} \\ \text{3-}\Omega\text{ resistor}}} \tag{2.8}$$

$$= 5 \times 0.833 \times 0.6 = 2.50\,\text{V}$$

Here the polarity is opposite to the reference direction of $v$, so we use a minus sign in the final summation.

**Turn ON 6-V source.** Finally, we calculate in Fig. 2.8 the contribution of the voltage source. With both current sources turned OFF, the three resistances are connected in series and the resulting voltage due to the 6-V source, $v_6$, is readily calculated by voltage division.

$$v_6 = 6 \times \frac{3}{1+2+3} = 3.00\,\text{V} \tag{2.9}$$

Note that the sign of $v_6$ will be positive in the final summation because the polarity of the voltage due to the voltage source is the same as that of $v$.

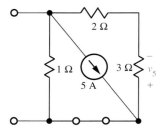

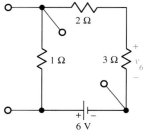

**Figure 2.7** The circuit with the 5-A source ON and the others OFF. Here the voltage produced is opposite to the reference direction in Fig. 2.5.

**Figure 2.8** The circuit with the 6-V source ON and the others OFF.

The principle of superposition states that we can now obtain the total voltage across the 3-$\Omega$ resistance by adding up the contributions of the three sources, supplying the signs from the polarity produced from each source:

$$v_3 = +v_4 - v_5 + v_6 = +2.00 - 2.50 + 3.00 = +2.50 \text{ V} \qquad (2.10)$$

---

**EXAMPLE 2.1**  **Reducing the Current to Zero**

Find the value of $I_s$ to reduce the voltage across the 4-$\Omega$ resistor to zero in Fig. 2.9.

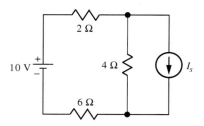

**Figure 2.9** The voltage and current sources cause voltages of opposite polarities across the 4-$\Omega$ resistor.

**SOLUTION:**

The voltage due to the 10-V source is

$$v_{10} = 10 \times \frac{4}{2 + 4 + 6} = 3.33 \text{ V} \qquad (2.11)$$

with the + at top. The voltage due to the current source is

$$v_{I_s} = I_s \times 4 \| (6 + 2) = I_s \times 2.67 \ \Omega \qquad (2.12)$$

with the + at the bottom. To add to zero, the two must be equal:

$$3.33 = I_s \times 2.67 \Rightarrow I_s = 1.25 \text{ A} \qquad (2.13)$$

**WHAT IF?**   What if the 2- and 6-$\Omega$ resistors were exchanged?[1]

---

[1] It would make no difference to the voltage across the 4-$\Omega$ resistor.

**Limitations of superposition.** Superposition works because Kirchhoff's laws and Ohm's law are linear equations. In all KVL and KCL equations, voltage and current appear in the first power; there are no squares or square roots or functions as $e^v$.

Superposition does not work for power calculations, however, because power calculations involve multiplication of voltage by current, or squaring a variable like $i^2R$. Thus, you will not get the correct total power by adding the power due to each source considered separately. Superposition can be used indirectly for power calculations, however, because the total current through a resistance can be computed using superposition and this total current can be then used to calculate correctly the power in that resistance. You can confirm for yourself the failure of superposition to compute power correctly by calculating the power in the 3-$\Omega$ resistance due to each source acting alone and testing to determine whether these powers add up to the true power calculated from the total voltage given in Eq. (2.10). Neither will superposition yield correct answers for circuits containing *nonlinear* electronic devices such as diodes or transistors.

**Summary.** Superposition is valid for computing the effects of individual sources on the voltages or currents throughout a circuit. As such, it allows us to extend the method of voltage and current dividers to circuits having multiple sources. Because this method develops intuition and thus aids in design, superposition is often used by circuit designers.

On the other hand, this method has weaknesses. One weakness is that you often have to analyze the circuit, perhaps several times, to calculate a single unknown current or voltage. With the simple examples we have given, this is fairly easy but in a large circuit this method becomes an ordeal. It would be much better to solve for the unknown without having to calculate every voltage and current along the way. Another weakness is the multiple solutions—much better to solve for the effects of all sources at once. Yet another weakness is that this method is somewhat unsystematic—many decisions have to be made along the way. The methods to be presented in the remainder of this chapter eliminate these weaknesses.

### Check Your Understanding

**1.** Is an infinite resistance equivalent to a turned-OFF voltage or current source?

**2.** A turned-OFF voltage source is equivalent to a resistance of what value?

**3.** Does superposition of powers give the correct value for computing the power out of a dc voltage source?

***Answers.*** **(1)** Current source; **(2)** zero ohms; **(3)** yes. Generally you *cannot* superpose powers but it works in this case because the voltage is the same in each calculation.

## 2.2   THÉVENIN'S AND NORTON'S EQUIVALENT CIRCUITS

### Example to Justify the Concept

**load**

We will analyze the circuit shown in Fig. 2.10 by a method that you will surely think strange. We are to determine the current in the variable load resistor $R_L$ as a function of that resistance. A *load* is an element in a circuit of particular importance; in one sense, the circuit exists to supply the load.[2]

Our method uses an equivalent circuit first proposed in the 1880s by a French telegrapher named M. L. Thévenin. Thévenin's equivalent circuit leads to one of the most useful ideas of electrical engineering, namely, the idea of the "output impedance"[3] of a circuit. This concept influences the thinking of electrical engineers in much of the work they do. We now justify the method as we analyze the circuit in Fig. 2.10 . Later we will distill the method into a simple procedure.

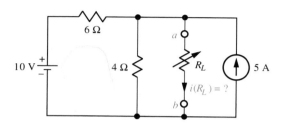

**Figure 2.10**  Solve for the current in $R_L$ as a function of $R_L$, $i(R_L)$

■ **Remove the load resistor.** Yes, the first step is to dismantle the circuit you are trying to analyze. In the lab, you could literally cut out the resistor; on paper, you merely erase it or redraw the circuit without it. Figure 2.11 gives the resulting circuit.

**open-circuit voltage**

■ **Measure** (in the lab) or calculate (on paper) the open-circuit voltage between $a$ and $b$, $v_{ab}$. We call $v_{ab}$ the *open-circuit voltage* because this voltage appears between $a$ and $b$ with the load removed, that is, with the circuit "open" between $a$ and $b$. This is a good opportunity for you to calculate $v_{ab}$ by superposition. You should get $v_{ab} = 4 + 12 = 16$ V.

■ **Connect** to $b$, but not to $a$, a voltage source equal to the open-circuit voltage (a 16-V battery in this case), as shown in Fig. 2.12. The voltage across the gap, $v_{aa'}$, is now zero. If you do not believe that, write KVL around $a$ to $b$ to $a'$ and back to $a$ and you ought to get zero for $v_{aa'}$.

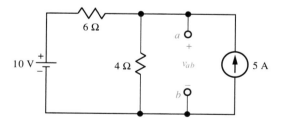

**Figure 2.11**  The open-circuit voltage is $v_{ab} = 16$ V.

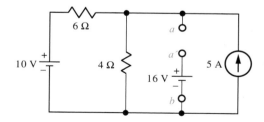

**Figure 2.12**  With the 16-V source inserted, $v_{aa'} = 0$ V.

---

[2] If you are making toast, the power system exists for the sake of the toaster.

[3] *Impedance* is a generalized form of resistance. The idea is defined precisely in Chapter 4. For now, we introduce the word as a synonym for resistance.

- **Reconnect** the load resistor between $a$ and $a'$. Because there is no voltage across the gap, replacing the resistor will disturb nothing and the voltage across the resistor will remain at zero. *Hence, no current will exist in the load resistor.* This is an important conclusion and deserves careful attention.

  By replacing the load, we have restored our original circuit, except that now we have inserted a voltage source in series with the load. That voltage source has a polarity *opposing* the flow of current through the load and has the exact magnitude to prevent any current from flowing. We might say that it "bucks out" the current in the load. In hydraulics, it would be like inserting a centrifugal pump to stop fluid flow.

- **Superposition.** Normally, we would calculate the total current in the modified circuit as the combined results of all three sources, but this time we will distinguish between the original sources and the inserted source, as indicated in the equation

$$i_{total} = i_{original} - i_{inserted} = 0 \qquad (2.14)$$

In Eq. (2.14), $i_{original}$ stands for the current through the load from the original sources in the circuit, the 10-V battery and the 5-A current source; and $i_{inserted}$ stands for the current due to the open-circuit voltage source that we inserted, a 16-V battery in this case. The minus sign comes from the polarity with which we inserted the battery, namely, so as to oppose the original current.

Conclusion. Equation (2.14) shows that the two components must be equal. The component due to the original sources is what we set out to calculate in the first place. Because this is equal to the current due to the inserted source, we can calculate the current due to one source instead of calculating the current due to the original sources (two in this case).

When we use superposition, we turn all the sources OFF except the source we are considering at the moment. Hence, we calculate the effect of the inserted source by turning OFF the original sources. This produces the circuit shown in Fig. 2.13. Now $R_L$ is seen to be connected in series with an output impedance of $R_{eq} = 4 \parallel 6 = 2.4 \, \Omega$ and the resulting current is thus

$$i(R) = \frac{v_{open \ circuit}}{R_L + R_{eq}} = \frac{16}{R_L + 2.4} \qquad (2.15)$$

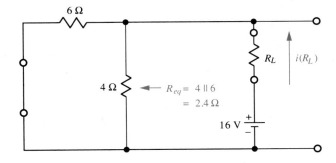

**Figure 2.13** With the original sources OFF, the circuit is reduced to an equivalent resistance.

Equation (2.15) gives the current in $R_L$ as a function of $R_L$, which was what we set out to find.

This was an easy problem to begin with, so you may wonder why we solved it by this roundabout method. The point is this: *We would have derived the same simple equation as Eq. (2.15) no matter how complicated the original circuit.* There could have been hundreds of sources and thousands of resistors in the original circuit and we still would have reduced the circuit to two parameters, an open-circuit voltage and an output impedance.

## Thévenin's Equivalent Circuit

**Equivalent Circuits**

**Basic concept.** Equation (2.15) suggests the simple equivalent circuit shown in Fig. 2.14. The Thévenin equivalent circuit consists of a voltage source, $V_T$, in series with an output impedance. The magnitude and polarity of $V_T$ are identical to the open-circuit voltage at $a–b$, the terminals of the load. The output impedance, $R_{eq}$, is computed at the load terminals with all sources in the circuit turned OFF.

Let us solve another problem using Thévenin's equivalent circuit, this time skipping the justifying steps. The circuit in Fig. 2.15 is drawn with everything in a box except the load. We wish to calculate the voltage across that load resistor. We replace the circuit in the box with the simpler circuit shown in Fig. 2.14.

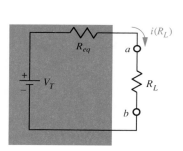

**Figure 2.14** Equivalent circuit suggested by Eq. (2.15).

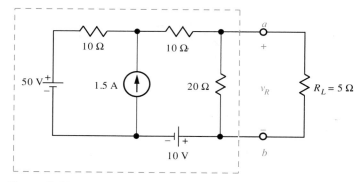

**Figure 2.15** Replace the circuit in the box by a Thévenin equivalent circuit.

**Thévenin voltage calculation.** First, we calculate the Thévenin voltage source, $V_T$, the open-circuit voltage between terminals $a$ and $b$ with $R_L$ removed. We use the method of superposition to find the current in the 20-Ω resistor and, from that, the open-circuit voltage. The current referenced downward with the 50- and 10-V voltage sources ON and the 1.5-A current source OFF would be

$$i_V = \frac{50 - 10}{10 + 10 + 20} = 1.00 \text{ A} \tag{2.16}$$

The downward current due to the 1.5-A current source acting alone would be

$$i_I = 1.5 \times \frac{1/(10 + 20)}{1/(10 + 20) + (1/10)} = 0.375 \text{ A} \tag{2.17}$$

Hence, the current referenced downward with all sources ON would be 1.375 A and the open-circuit voltage would be 1.375 A × 20 Ω = 27.5 V with the + at the top. The polarity is important because we require that the two circuits in the box in Figs. 2.15 and 2.16 be fully equivalent to the load. This requires that the polarity in the Thévenin equivalent circuit be identical to that in the original circuit.

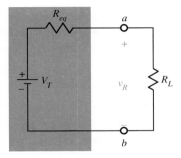

**Figure 2.16** The Thévenin equivalent circuit consists of the open-circuit voltage in series with the output impedance.

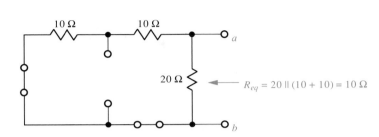

**Figure 2.17** Turning OFF the three sources leaves a series-parallel combination.

**Computing $R_{eq}$, the output impedance.** To make this computation, we turn OFF all three sources within the box, as shown in Fig. 2.17. Thus, with $R_{eq} = 10\ \Omega$, we now have the Thévenin equivalent circuit shown in Fig. 2.18.

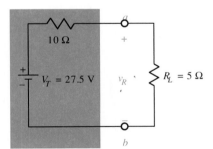

**Figure 2.18** The Thévenin equivalent circuit for the circuit of Figure 2.15.

The solution to our original problem is now easy:

$$v_R = 27.5 \times \frac{5}{5 + 10} = 9.17\ \text{V} \qquad (2.18)$$

**Benefits of the Thévenin equivalent circuit.** Of course, with modest effort, we could have computed this result directly from the original circuit in Fig. 2.15. With this method, however, we gain the freedom to ask many additional questions such as: What value of $R_L$ makes the voltage 30 V? What value of $R_L$ withdraws the most power from the circuit? These questions lead to mathematical complexities with the original circuit, but can be answered simply with the Thévenin equivalent circuit. The answer to the first question is that no value of $R_L$ will give 30 V. The investigation of the second question leads to an interesting and important result, to which we will soon turn.

**Equivalent Circuits**

**Equivalent circuits.** First, let us consider further what we mean by a Thévenin *equivalent* circuit. The equivalent circuit replaces the circuit within the box only for effects *external* to the box. We can no longer ask questions about the circuit in the box after we have replaced it by an equivalent circuit. For example, if we are interested in the current in the 20-Ω resistor or the total power consumed by the resistors in the box, the equivalent circuit is useless.

**Maximum power transfer.** Let us now investigate the question of maximizing the power in $R_L$ in Figure 2.15. We let load resistance $R_L$ be the independent variable, the power in the load be the dependent variable $P$, and find $P(R_L)$ using basic circuit techniques. The power in $R_L$ as a function of $R_L$, $P(R_L)$, is

$$P(R_L) = i^2 R_L = \frac{V_T^2 R_L}{(R_L + R_{eq})^2} = \frac{(27.5)^2 R_L}{(R_L + 10)^2} \tag{2.19}$$

**impedance match**   To maximize $P(R_L)$ as given in Eq. (2.19), we take the derivative with respect to $R$ and set it equal to zero. You can confirm that the maximum (or minimum) occurs at $R_L$ equals $R_{eq}$ (10 Ω). This is called an *impedance match*, when the load is equal to the output impedance of the circuit. To confirm that we have a maximum and not a minimum, a second derivative can be taken, but an easier way in this case is to make a simple sketch of $P(R_L)$ to show that we have found a maximum. Figure 2.19 shows a plot of Eq. (2.19).

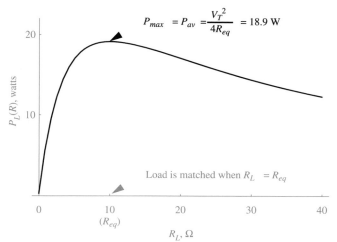

**Figure 2.19**  The power in $R_L$ is maximum when $R_L = R_{eq}$.

**Importance of maximum power transfer.** Obtaining the maximum power out of a circuit is important because often we deal in electronics with small amounts of power and wish to make full use of the power that is available. On a TV set, for example, we pull out the "rabbit ears" antenna to receive power from radio waves originating at a transmitter many miles away. The antenna does not collect much power, so the TV receiver is designed to make maximum use of the power provided by the antenna. Although our results were derived for a simple battery and resistor, they can be applied to a TV antenna. Figure 2.19 shows that we should design the receiver input circuit, represented here by a load resistor, to match the output impedance of the antenna for withdrawing the maximum power from the antenna.

optimum, optimize **Optimization.** When a design is the best possible under the constraints, the design is said to be *optimum*. Thus, the TV receiver input is *optimized* when its input impedance is matched to the output impedance of the antenna because this gives maximum power to the receiver.

---

**EXAMPLE 2.2** **Loudspeaker analysis**

Consider a stereo system that puts out 25 watts into each of two 8-$\Omega$ speakers. What would be the voltage provided by this amplifier to each speaker?

**SOLUTION:**

We assume that the speakers are adequately represented by 8-$\Omega$ resistances and that the speakers and amplifier output impedances are matched. Thus, the circuit we propose as a model for each channel is shown in Fig. 2.20.

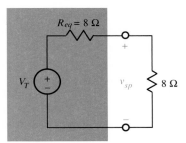

**Figure 2.20** Circuit model for one channel of the stereo output circuit.

We have used a general symbol for the voltage source because the audio voltage would certainly not be a constant voltage.[4] Because we have assumed that the load and output impedance of the amplifier are matched, this requires that $R_{eq}$ be also 8 $\Omega$. From the maximum in Fig. 2.19, we calculate the Thévenin voltage to be

$$\frac{V_T^2}{4 \times 8} = 25 \text{ watts/channel} \Rightarrow V_T = 28.3 \text{ V} \qquad (2.20)$$

The voltage across the speaker will be half this value because the Thévenin voltage divides equally between the output impedance and the 8-$\Omega$ speaker resistance. Hence, the answer is 14.1 V.

**WHAT IF?** What if 16-$\Omega$ speakers were used with this same stereo? What then would be the power in each speaker?[5]

---

[4] In Chapter 9, we study the appropriate model for such an audio signal. For now, we are merely interested in the voltage representing the output.

[5] The power would drop to 22.2 watts. This slight decrease shows the benefits of optimizing the amplifier/speaker power transfer. In general, when a system is optimized, performance is insensitive to changes such as using 16-$\Omega$ instead of 8-$\Omega$ speakers.

**Norton's equivalent circuit.** An American engineer named E. L. Norton (1889–1983) came up with a similar equivalent circuit. Norton's equivalent circuit consists of a current source connected in parallel with an output impedance, $R_{eq}$, as shown in Fig. 2.21. The derivation of the values for the impedance and the current source, $I_N$, is similar to that for Thévenin's circuit and will not be repeated here. Indeed, the output impedance is the same as before, namely, the resistance of the circuit presented to the load after all internal sources are turned OFF. The Norton current source has a magnitude identical to the current that would flow in a short circuit of the output terminals.

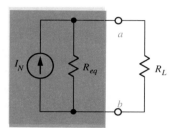

**Figure 2.21** The Norton equivalent circuit appears in the box.

To illustrate, we will find the Norton equivalent circuit for the circuit of Fig. 2.15. The value of the output impedance, $R_{eq}$, is the same as before, 10 Ω. The value of the Norton current source, $I_N$, can be determined by replacing the load with a short circuit. This gives the circuit in Fig. 2.22. The short circuit effectively removes the 20-Ω resistor from the circuit because it forces its voltage, and hence its current, to be zero. The current flowing through the short circuit is easily calculated. The result is 2.75 A from $a$ to $b$ in the short circuit; hence, the Norton equivalent circuit is that shown in Fig. 2.23. From this simple circuit, $v_R$ is seen to be $2.75 \times 10 \parallel 5 = 9.17$ V, as before. Notice that the polarity of the current source must produce the physical current from $a$ to $b$.

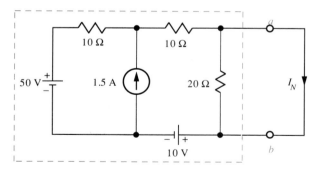

**Figure 2.22** Short the output to find $I_N$. The 20-Ω resistor is effectively removed for the calculation of $I_N$.

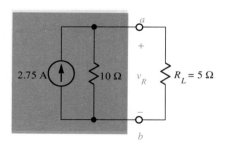

**Figure 2.23** Norton equivalent circuit.

**Relationship between Thévenin's and Norton's equivalent circuits.** If two circuits are equivalent to the same circuit, they must be equivalent to each other. Thus, if the Norton circuit in Fig. 2.21 is open-circuited, the voltage must be $V_T$, the same as the voltage source in the Thévenin circuit of Fig. 2.16. You can see that this proves true in the example, because $2.75\,\text{A} \times 10\,\Omega = 27.5\,\text{V}$. In general, it must be true that

$$V_T = I_N R_{eq} \tag{2.21}$$

Equation (2.21) is useful in theoretical work, but it also can be applied in the laboratory to find the output impedance of a source. In practice, we may be unable to get inside and turn OFF internal sources, for example, in a battery or an electronic circuit, but we can measure the open-circuit output voltage and the current that flows when the output terminals are shorted. From the measured voltage and current, we can compute the output impedance

$$R_{eq} = \frac{V_T}{I_N} \tag{2.22}$$

**Graphical Interpretation.** Figure 2.24(b) shows the output characteristic of any linear circuit, Fig. 2.24(a). The intercept on the voltage axis ($i_{out} = 0$) is the Thévenin, or open-circuit, voltage, and the intercept on the current axis ($v_{out} = 0$) is the Norton, or short-circuit current. The slope is the negative of the reciprocal of the output impedance, as required by Eq. (2.22).

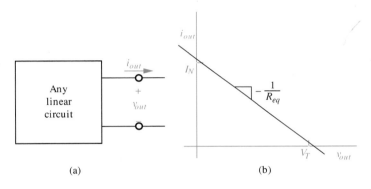

(a)                    (b)

**Figure 2.24:** (a) An arbitrary linear circuit, with the output voltage and current indicated. (b) The output characteristic of the circuit in graphical form. The intercepts are the Thévenin voltage and the Norton current, and the slope is the negative of the reciprocal of the output impedance.

**available power**

**Available power.** The maximum power that can be extracted from a circuit is called the *available power*, $P_{av}$, and is given by

$$P_{av} = P(R_{eq}) = \frac{V_T^2}{4R_{eq}} \tag{2.23}$$

as shown in Fig. 2.19. Note that sources with low output impedance can supply large amounts of power to an external load.

---

**EXAMPLE 2.3**    **Available Power from an Auto Battery**

The open-circuit voltage of a standard automotive battery is 12.6 V, and the short-circuit current is approximately 300 A. What is the available power from the battery?

**SOLUTION:**

From Eq. (2.22) we find the output impedance of the battery

$$R_{eq} = \frac{V_T}{I_N} = \frac{12.6}{300} = 0.042 \ \Omega \tag{2.24}$$

Therefore, the available power from Eq. (2.23) is

$$P_{av} = \frac{V_T^2}{4R_{eq}} = \frac{(12.6)^2}{4 \times 0.042} = 945 \ \text{W} \tag{2.25}$$

**WHAT IF?**

What if you compute the available power from one of the flashlight batteries in Fig. 1.30?[6]

---

**loading of a circuit, voltmeter**

**Loading of a circuit.** We also are concerned about the *loading* of circuits, which occurs when the output voltage is changed significantly by a load. Figure 2.25(a) shows a voltage divider creating a voltage $v$ and a *voltmeter* to measure the voltage. The voltmeter has an input resistance of 10 MΩ, and hence connecting it will change the voltage to be measured. We may determine the loaded voltage, $v'$, from the Thévenin equivalent circuit in Fig. 2.25(b).

$$v' = 3.85 \times \underbrace{\frac{10 \ \text{M}\Omega}{10 \ \text{M}\Omega + 308 \ \text{k}\Omega}}_{0.970} = 3.73 \ \text{V} \tag{2.26}$$

The loaded voltage, which is what the voltmeter will indicate, proves to be 3% lower

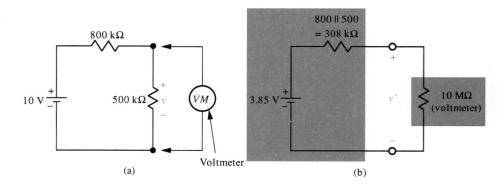

(a)

(b)

Voltmeter

**Figure 2.25:** (a) The amount of loading from the meter depends on the output impedance of the circuit at the point of measurement and the resistance of the meter; (b) Thévenin equivalent circuit showing the effect of meter loading.

---

[6] The available power is 1.875 W.

than the unloaded voltage of 3.85 V, which is what we are seeking to measure with the voltmeter. In practice, we can correct for loading error if we know the output impedance of the circuit and the input impedance of the meter.

## Impedance Level

**Impedance Level**

**impedance level**

**Definition of impedance level.** Impedance level is a broad concept that is better illustrated than defined. The resistance of a load is its impedance level, and the output impedance of a circuit to a load is the impedance level of the circuit seen by that load. Thus, the *impedance level* describes the approximate ratio of voltages to currents in a circuit or portion of circuit. The interaction of a circuit with a load depends on the relative values of their respective impedance levels.

**Circuit model.** Consider the Thévenin equivalent circuit shown in Figure 2.26, bearing in mind that this represents the most general circuit/load interaction possible. We now investigate the effect of the impedance level of circuit and load upon the transfer of power, voltage, and current.

**Power.** We have already shown that when the impedance level of the load is equal to the output impedance of the circuit, the power in the load is optimized, that is, is maximum. Hence, it would be fitting to say that this condition yields a transfer of power to the load. Figure 2.19 shows that the amount of power depends reciprocally on the output impedance level of the source and will be relatively insensitive to the load impedance, especially if the load impedance is greater than the source impedance.

**Voltage.** The voltage across the load in Fig. 2.26 is determined by voltage division to be

$$v_L = V_T \times \frac{R_L}{R_L + R_{eq}} = V_T \times \frac{1}{1 + R_{eq}/R_L} \tag{2.27}$$

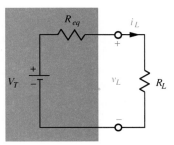

**Figure 2.26** This circuit models all circuit/load interactions.

When $R_L \gg R_{eq}$, we have $v_L \approx V_T$. Hence, when the impedance level of the load is large relative to that of the source, the voltage transferred to the load will be approximately equal to the open-circuit voltage and will be relatively insensitive to the load-impedance level. Hence, this condition transfers voltage to the load. This is the desired condition when we measure voltage, as before.

**Current.** When $R_L \ll R_{eq}$, the voltage to the load will be small, but the current will be

$$i_L = \frac{V_T}{R_L + R_{eq}} = \frac{V_T}{R_{eq}} \times \frac{1}{1 + R_L/R_{eq}} = I_N \times \frac{1}{1 + R_L/R_{eq}} \tag{2.28}$$

**ammeter**

Hence, when the load impedance is small compared with that of the source, the current will be approximately the Norton current, independent of $R_L$. Hence, current is transferred to the load in this condition. Thus, a meter to measure current, an *ammeter*, should have an impedance level that is low compared with the impedance level of the circuit to be measured.

**Importance of impedance level.** Consideration of impedance level has application for many circumstances. Consider the power system supplying energy for lighting, electric motors, etc. These appliances are designed to operate at a prescribed voltage; hence, the impedance level of the power system should be small compared with all the loads placed on it. Indeed, because all loads are placed in parallel, the output impedance of the power system should be small compared with the parallel combination of all loads on the system at any given time. If this were not the case, the voltage of the power system would fluctuate seriously according to the load on the system.

Everyone has had the experience of being shocked by sliding across a car seat in cold, dry weather. The spark can jump as much as 5 mm, which means that at least 15,000 V is developed. But the impedance level of the "circuit" is extremely high relative to the impedance of your body and therefore the voltage is not transferred to your body, just the current, which is extremely small. Hence, no harm is done. Of course, the opposite would be true if you were struck by lightning.

We showed before that in electronics, the impedance levels are controlled to optimize transfer of power between parts of the electronic circuit. Hence, in power, electronics, metering, and, indeed, many other contexts, the impedance levels of the various parts of the circuits are critical to performance.

## Source Transformations

**source transformations**

Transformations between Thévenin's and Norton's equivalent circuits can be used in connection with other methods of circuit analysis. For example, in Figure 2.15, we may transform the 50-V source in series with the 10-$\Omega$ resistance into a 5.0-A current source in parallel with 10 $\Omega$. Thus, the circuit becomes that shown in Fig. 2.27, and we may combine the two current sources to a single 6.5-A current source. Next, we may convert the 6.5-A source in parallel with 10 $\Omega$ to a 65-V voltage source in series with 10 $\Omega$ and then combine the 65-V source with the opposing 10-V source to yield Fig. 2.28. Clearly, $v_{ab} = V_T = 27.5$ V. When we switch back and forth between Thévenin and Norton equivalent circuits, these are *source transformations*.

**Benchmark example, solved with equivalent circuits.** Figure 2.29(a) gives the benchmark example of Fig. 2.5, with the 3-$\Omega$ resistor marked as the load. When we remove the load, KCL at the upper node shows a physical current of 1 A up in the 1-$\Omega$ resistor, and the open-circuit voltage therefore will be

$$V_T = +6\text{ V} - 1\text{ A} \times 1\ \Omega = +5\text{ V} \tag{2.29}$$

and the output impedance is clearly 2 $\Omega$ + 1 $\Omega$; thus, the problem reduces to that in Fig. 2.29(b). Clearly, the unknown voltage is +2.50 V. If you refer back to the previ-

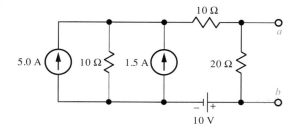

**Figure 2.27** Same circuit as Fig. 2.15, but with 50-V source transformed into a current source.

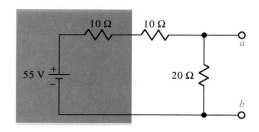

**Figure 2.28** After several source transformations, the Thévenin voltage can be determined by inspection.

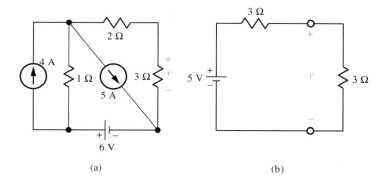

(a)

(b)

**Figure 2.29** (a) Benchmark example, Fig. 2.5, with the 3-Ω resistor marked as the load; (b) the reduced circuit.

ous solution of this problem using superposition, you will see the benefits of using the Thévenin equivalent circuit.

**Comparison of equivalent circuits with voltage and current divider techniques.** In closing this section, we wish to compare the method of equivalent circuits with our first method, voltage and current dividers. With voltage and current dividers, the strategy was to combine resistors until we have represented the entire circuit to the *source* as a single equivalent resistance. We then restore the original circuit, dividing voltage and current as we go. Eventually, we can calculate the current or voltage across a particular resistor of interest. If there are multiple sources, we must repeat this process for each source and use superposition. The methods of equivalent circuits and source transformations work in the opposite direction. Here we represent the entire circuit, including multiple sources, to the *load* of interest. We bring everything, as it were, to a particular point in the circuit that has special importance. For this reason, the method of equivalent circuits plays an important role in both design and analysis of electrical circuits.

## Check Your Understanding

1. A 1.5-V dry cell has a maximum (short-circuit) current of 300 mA. What is the internal resistance of the battery?

2. A circuit has an output voltage of 20 V and a short-circuit current of 0.5 A. What is the maximum power that can come out of this circuit?

3. Normally, we adjust a load for maximum power in a power circuit or an electronics circuit?

4. A circuit has a variable load, $R_L$. Power measurements show that the power into $R_L$ is maximum at 10 W with $R_L = 2\ \Omega$. What would be the open-circuit voltage, $V_T$?

***Answers.*** (**1**) 5 $\Omega$; (**2**) 2.5 W; (**3**) in electronics—power circuits want constant voltage; (**4**) 8.94 V.

## 2.3 NODE-VOLTAGE ANALYSIS

### Basic Idea

**A systematic method.** The methods presented thus far in Chapters 1 and 2 work well for simple circuits and are especially useful to designers. But the time comes when one must analyze a large circuit containing many circuit elements, and for this purpose, we will develop two systematic methods of circuit analysis. These methods develop sets of linear equations to be solved simultaneously for the unknown voltages or currents, a task for which computers are well suited. To keep the mathematics within bounds, however, we will limit our examples to relatively simple circuits.

**Node voltages.** Node-voltage analysis, or nodal analysis, is based on Kirchhoff's current law. We write KCL equations at all nodes except one, but we write these equations in such a way that current variables are never formally defined. We avoid defining current variables by expressing the currents in terms of the "node voltages" in a special way. Figure 2.30 shows a simple circuit with two voltage sources and a resistor. The point at the bottom we have denoted $r$ and the points at the ends of the resistor we have called $a$ and $b$. Using KVL and Ohm's law, we may express $i_{ab}$ thus:

$$-v_{ar} + v_{ab} + v_{br} = 0 \Rightarrow v_{ab} = v_{ar} - v_{br} \qquad (2.30)$$

$$i_{ab} = \frac{v_{ab}}{R_{ab}} = \frac{v_{ar} - v_{br}}{R_{ab}} \qquad (2.31)$$

**reference node, node voltage**

We will change the appearance of Eq. (2.31) by simplifying our notation: We drop the $r$ in the voltage subscript. The *reference node*, labeled $r$, is like an elevation datum in surveying: We measure all elevations (voltages) relative to it.[7] When we talk about the *node voltage* at $a$, $v_a$, we are to understand that we are talking about $v_{ar}$, the voltage be-

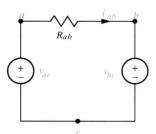

**Figure 2.30** The reference node is marked $r$.

---

[7] When we speak of the elevation of St. Louis as being 413 ft or at the Salton Sea as being −287 ft, we are talking about the elevation relative to mean sea level, to which we assign an elevation of zero.

tween node $a$ and the reference node, which is thus assigned a voltage of zero. Later, we will discuss how to choose the reference node; here we are interested in the pattern of subscripts in Eq. (2.31). With the change in notation, the form becomes

$$i_{ab} = \frac{v_a - v_b}{R_{ab}} \tag{2.32}$$

**Pattern of subscripts.** Equation (2.32) can be stated in words as follows: The current from $a$ to $b$ is the voltage at $a$, minus the voltage at $b$, divided by the resistance between $a$ and $b$.[8] The pattern established in Eq. (2.32) is so simple and intuitive that with it we can express currents without defining current variables. That is, we can keep the "current from $a$ to $b$" part in our heads and write on the paper the voltage at $a$, minus the voltage at $b$, divided by the resistance between $a$ and $b$, the right-hand side of Eq. (2.32).

---

**EXAMPLE 2.4** | **Constrained Nodes**

Determine the current through the 7-$\Omega$ resistor, referenced toward the left, in Fig. 2.31.

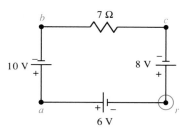

**Figure 2.31** Determine the current in the resistor, referenced toward the left, $c \rightarrow b$.

**constrained node**

**SOLUTION:**
This current would be the voltage at $c$, minus the voltage at $b$, divided by 7 $\Omega$. We may use KVL to determine $v_c$ and $v_b$. We begin at $b$, go to $r$, writing $v_{br}$, then to $a$ and back to $b$: $v_{br} - (6) + (10) = 0$; hence, $v_{br} = v_b = -4$ V. To find $v_c$, we go from $c$ to $r$, around the battery and then return through the 8-V battery: $v_{cr} + (8) = 0$; or $v_{cr} = v_c = -8$ V. So the current toward the left through the 7-$\Omega$ resistor would be:

$$\frac{v_c - v_b}{R_{cb}} = \frac{-8 - (-4)}{7} = -0.571 \text{ A} \tag{2.33}$$

In this circuit, the voltages at all nodes are constrained to the reference node by the voltage sources. In general, a *constrained node* is a node whose voltage is constrained to the voltage of another node by a voltage source. In this example, the nodes are constrained to the reference node and hence their node voltages are known absolutely.

---

[8] This applies only when there is a resistor between $a$ and $b$.

**WHAT IF?**

What if node $a$ were the reference node, zero volts? Find $v_c$, $v_b$, and $i_{cb}$.[9]

## Node-Voltage Technique

**OBJECTIVE 4**

**To understand how to analyze a circuit using nodal analysis**

We will find the voltage across the 3-Ω resistor in Fig. 2.32(a). We will analyze this circuit through the node-voltage method, which consists of the following steps:

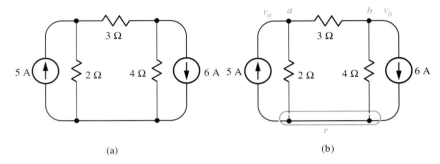

(a)

(b)

**Figure 2.32** (a) Find the voltage across the 3-Ω resistor. (b) Circuit with labeled nodes. The unknowns are $v_a$ and $v_b$.

1. **Define a reference node.** The circuit has three nodes. We may choose any of them as the reference node. Often, the node with the most wires is chosen as the reference node. In this case, the node at the bottom will be chosen. We mark the reference node with $r$, as shown in Fig. 2.32(b).

2. **Count the independent nodes.** Here we have three nodes, the reference node plus two independent nodes.[10] Thus, two equations will be written.

3. **Label the independent nodes.** We have already labeled the reference node; now we label the other nodes, as shown in Fig. 2.32(b). The node voltages, $v_a$ and $v_b$, are our secondary unknowns from which we will calculate the primary unknown, the voltage across the 3-Ω resistor. In nodal analysis, we calculate the node voltages; then we calculate from these the specified unknown in the problem, a current or voltage or power of interest.

**Conservation of Charge**

4. **Write KCL in a special form.** The special form is

$$\sum \text{Currents leaving the node in resistors}$$

$$= \sum \text{currents entering the node from current sources}$$

(2.34)

---

[9] $v_c = -14$ V, $v_b = -10$ V, $i_{cb} = -0.571$ A, the same as before.

[10] We define independent nodes on page 80.

But we avoid defining current variables by expressing currents with the node voltages:

$$\frac{v_a - (0)}{2} + \frac{v_a - v_b}{3} = + (5) \tag{2.35}$$

In Eq. (2.35), the left side represents the currents leaving node $a$ in the two resistors connected directly to node $a$, and the right side represents the current entering from the 5-A source. The current flowing through the 2-$\Omega$ resistor to the reference node is merely the node voltage, $v_a$, divided by the resistance between node $a$ and the reference node. We wrote the (0) for the voltage of the reference node as a reminder. The current from $a$ to $b$ through the 3-$\Omega$ resistance is derived from the pattern in Eq. (2.32). Similarly, we can write KCL for node $b$ with the node voltages:

$$\frac{v_b - v_a}{3} + \frac{v_b - (0)}{4} = - (+6) \tag{2.36}$$

where the first term on the left side represents the current flowing from node $b$ to node $a$. This is the negative of the second term in Eq. (2.35). This change in sign occurs because we are now expressing the current referenced in the opposite direction from before. Note also that the current source term on the right side has a negative sign because we are summing the currents *entering* the node from the sources. Equations (2.35) and (2.36) are rewritten:

$$(\tfrac{1}{2} + \tfrac{1}{3}) v_a - (\tfrac{1}{3}) v_b = 5$$
$$-(\tfrac{1}{3}) v_a + (\tfrac{1}{3} + \tfrac{1}{4}) v_b = -6 \tag{2.37}$$

We may solve these equations by any method, such as Cramer's rule for determinants, with the result

$$v_a = 2.44 \text{ V} \qquad \text{and} \qquad v_b = -8.89 \text{ V} \tag{2.38}$$

5. **Compute the primary unknown.** We can now calculate the original unknown from the resulting node voltages. The voltage across the 3-$\Omega$ resistor was specified, but we cannot calculate it without a polarity marking. If we wish the + polarity symbol at node $a$, we have the marking shown in Fig. 2.33. We can determine $v_3$ by writing KVL around the loop *rabr*:

$$v_{ra} + v_3 + v_{br} = 0$$
$$v_3 = - v_{ra} - v_{br} = v_{ar} - v_{br} = v_a - v_b \tag{2.39}$$

The second line of Eq. (2.39) was converted via Eq. (1.26) to a form where $r$ was the second subscript and then $r$ was dropped. Thus, $v_3$ with the polarity marking of Fig. 2.33 is $2.44 - (-8.89)$ or 11.3 V. Had we marked the + at node $b$, we would have followed a similar procedure. You can confirm for yourself that this would have reversed the right sides of Eq. (2.39) and resulted in $v_3'$ being $-11.3$ V, where the primed $v_3$ has the + at node $b$.

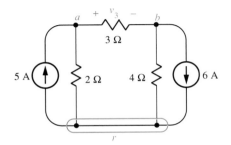

**Figure 2.33** Using $v_a$ and $v_b$ to determine $v_3$.

## Some Refinements

**How to handle voltage sources.** Nodal analysis deals routinely with current sources. The circuit of Fig. 2.34, however, is currently beyond the reach of the method. In Fig. 2.34, we have identified a reference node and labeled the other two nodes $a$ and $b$; we will find $v_a$ and $v_b$. To find the voltage at node $a$, we will write KVL from $r$ to $a$ and back to $r$ through the voltage source:

$$v_{ra} + 10 = 0 \Rightarrow v_{ar} = v_a = +10 \text{ V} \tag{2.40}$$

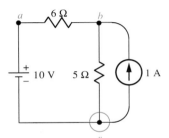

**Figure 2.34** Node voltage problem with a voltage source. The unknowns are $v_a$ and $v_b$.

The voltage source constrains $v_a$ to be $+10$ V. Thus, when we write KCL for node $b$, we treat $v_a$ as known rather than unknown:

$$\frac{v_b - (+10)}{6} + \frac{v_b - (0)}{5} = +(+1) \tag{2.41}$$

The solution for $v_b$ is 7.27 V.

We may also use a source transformation to convert the voltage source to a current source. The 10-V source in series with the 6-$\Omega$ resistance in Fig. 2.35(a) can be transformed to the Norton form in Fig. 2.35(b) using Eq. (2.21). In this form, the current sources can be added and the parallel resistances can be combined; so the voltage across the circuit is

$$v_{br} = v_b = \left(\frac{10}{6} + 1\right)(6 \parallel 5) = 7.27 \text{ V} \tag{2.42}$$

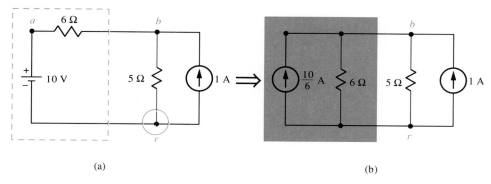

(a)                                                              (b)

**Figure 2.35** A source transformation allows solution without using constrained nodes. Note that the number of independent nodes does not change.

EXAMPLE 2.5 **Constrained Nodes**

Find the power in the 4-$\Omega$ resistor in Fig. 2.36.

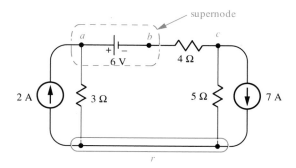

**Figure 2.36** Nodes $a$ and $b$ are constrained by the 6-V source.

**SOLUTION:**

Here we have one node constrained to another independent node rather than to the reference node. The voltages at nodes $a$ and $b$ are unknown, but they are not independent. If we knew the voltage at either of them, we could determine the voltage at the other; thus, it would be inappropriate to treat them as independent unknowns. We can determine the relationship between them by writing KVL from $r$ to $a$ to $b$ and back to $r$:

$$v_{ra} + 6 + v_{br} = 0 \Rightarrow -v_a + 6 + v_b = 0$$

$$v_b = v_a - 6 \tag{2.43}$$

In the second line of Eq. (2.43), we have written the equation with $v_a$ as our unknown and $v_b$ expressed from $v_a$. We can now write KCL for node $c$:

$$\frac{v_c - (0)}{5} + \frac{v_c - (v_a - 6)}{4} = -(+7) \tag{2.44}$$

In the second term on the left side, we write $(v_a - 6)$ for $v_b$ in expressing the current referenced out of node $c$ in the 4-Ω resistor.

The two constrained nodes are treated as a supernode, as shown in Fig. 2.36, and KCL is written as

$$\frac{v_a - (0)}{3} + \frac{(v_a - 6) - v_c}{4} = +(+2) \tag{2.45}$$

We now have two equations in two unknowns, $v_a$ and $v_c$, which yield $-2.75$ V and $-20.4$ V, respectively. From the second term in Eq. (2.45), we calculate the current in the 4-Ω resistor to be

$$\frac{(-2.75 - 6) - (-20.4)}{4} = 2.92 \text{ A} \tag{2.46}$$

The power in the 4-Ω resistor is

$$P_R = i_R^2 R = (2.92)^2 (4) = 34.0 \text{ W} \tag{2.47}$$

We could alternatively transform the 6-V source in series with the 4-Ω resistor to a 1.5-A current source in parallel with a 4-Ω resistance. The source transformation permits routine application of nodal analysis.

**Summary.** A voltage source will establish a constraint between two nodes. We can express the node voltage at one end of a voltage source in terms of the node voltage at the other end plus or minus the source value, depending on the polarity of the source. To determine the sign, we may have to write KVL around a loop containing the reference node and the two constrained nodes. Constrained nodes are treated as a supernode when KCL equations are written.

**independent node**

**Independent nodes.** The analysis of Fig. 2.36 shows that a first count of the nodes of a circuit could overestimate the number of unknown node voltages to be determined. If there are voltage sources, some nodes will be constrained and the number of unknowns, and equations to be solved, will be reduced. An *independent node* is a node whose voltage cannot be derived from the voltage of another node. When we analyze a circuit using the method of node voltages, we will have as many unknowns (and equations to solve) as we have independent nodes.[11]

Here is a rule for counting independent nodes: Turn OFF all sources and count the nodes that remain separated by resistors. The number of independent nodes is one less than the number of remaining nodes. Turning OFF all sources means that voltage sources are replaced by short circuits and current sources are replaced by open circuits. The second step in node-voltage analysis is to turn OFF all sources and determine the number of independent nodes. The third step is to label only the independent nodes, because these are the only secondary unknowns.

---

[11] The number of independent nodes may be reduced by combining resistances in series. If the primary unknown disappears, a voltage divider can find the voltage at the node that vanished.

EXAMPLE **2.6** **Counting the independent nodes on the benchmark example**

Count the independent nodes for the benchmark-example circuit in Fig. 2.37(a).

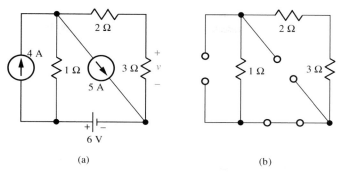

(a)                                    (b)

**Figure 2.37** (a) Benchmark example circuit. (b)The circuit with sources OFF. There are three nodes, of which two are independent, but one of these may be eliminated by combining the series resistances.

**SOLUTION:**
When we turn OFF the sources, we have the circuit in Fig 2.37(b). There are three nodes, two of which are independent. However, if we add the two series resistors to make a 5-$\Omega$ resistor and determine the unknown voltage with a voltage divider, we can get by with solving one nodal equation. Thus, we define the top node as node $a$ and write KCL in nodal form:

$$\frac{v_a - (+6)}{1} + \frac{v_a - (0)}{2+3} = +4 - 5 \Rightarrow v_a = \frac{6-1}{1.2} = 4.17 \text{ V} \qquad (2.48)$$

and hence from the voltage divider,

$$v = 4.17 \times \frac{3}{2+3} = 2.50 \text{ V} \qquad (2.49)$$

**WHAT IF?**     What if we had not combined resistors?[12]

## Critique

**A general method.** Nodal analysis is our first systematic method for analyzing circuits. It can be implemented somewhat routinely and always works. It is probably the favorite method of electrical engineers for analyzing electronic circuits because most

---

[12]Then we would have had to solve two equations in two unknowns, but the answer would have come out the same.

circuit components are connected to the electronic ground, which is used for a reference node.

The physical meaning of the node voltages is clarified by considering a voltmeter. The black voltmeter lead, often marked "common," should be attached to the reference node. If the red voltmeter lead is then touched to the nodes in the circuit, the voltmeter will indicate the node voltages.[13] Thus, node voltages are easily measured. Loop currents, the next method we present, also qualifies as a popular and powerful method, but measuring currents involves disconnecting the circuit and hence the loop currents are not easily measured. As you will see, the loop currents may not actually exist in the circuit either.

**What about KVL?**  We might pause to ask: How can we analyze a circuit without considering KVL? This is certainly what we appear to do when we use the method of node voltages. *Answer*: Kirchhoff's voltage law refers to individual voltages around a loop. Node voltages, on the other hand, are all referred to the same point. Hence, KVL does not apply directly.

**ground node**

**The reference node versus "ground."**  When the node voltage method is presented in books and used in practice, the reference node is often called the *ground node* and given the symbol ⏚ Strictly speaking, the ground in an electrical circuit identifies the point that is physically connected via a thick wire to the moist earth, usually for safety purposes. We discuss grounding in Chapter 5; here we only comment on the relationship between the reference node of nodal analysis and the physical ground of an electrical system.

The grounded portion of an electrical circuit usually has many wires connecting to it, and hence the electrical ground is often designated the reference node in a nodal analysis. But this is mere coincidence: The reference node and the ground are totally different concepts. We have avoided calling the reference node the "ground" to establish the concept of the reference node independent of the concept of electrical grounding. You should be aware, however, that many people use the terms interchangeably when discussing nodal analysis.

**potential difference, potential rise, potential drop**

**Node voltages and electrical potential.**  The analogy we made earlier between node voltages and elevations above mean sea level has a factual basis. Elevation is a measure of gravitational potential, and the node voltages are a measure of the electrical potential of the various nodes in an electrical circuit, relative to the reference node. What we have defined as the voltage between two points can also be called the *potential difference* between the points. Likewise, we can define *potential rises* and *potential drops* in a circuit; for example, the potential rises across a battery (going from − to +) and drops across a resistor (going from + to −). However, we will not speak of potential rises and drops in our development of circuit theory. Our definition of voltage is that of a potential drop.

## Check Your Understanding

**1.** What is the name of the point in a circuit defined to have zero volts?

---

[13] This assumes a modern electronic voltmeter that indicates the sign of the voltage. An old-fashioned analog meter might have to be reversed for negative node voltages.

**2.** If $v_{rb} = +5$ V, where $r$ is the reference node, what is the node voltage at node $b$?

**3.** If node $a$ is connected to the reference node by a 40-V voltage source with the $-$ at node $a$, what is $v_a$?

**4.** Two nodes are said to be constrained together when connected by a voltage source or a current source. Which?

*Answers.* (**1**) The reference node, not "ground"; (**2**) $-5$ V; (**3**) $-40$ V; (**4**) voltage source.

## 2.4 LOOP-CURRENT ANALYSIS

**OBJECTIVE 5**

**To understand how to analyze a circuit using loop currents**

## Simple Method of Loop-Current Analysis

**Introduction.** The method of loop currents is similar to nodal analysis, except that the variables are currents, not voltages, and the equations are based on KVL. The goal is to avoid defining unnecessary variables and to systematically write simultaneous equations for the unknown loop currents.

We will present the method by analyzing the circuit shown in Fig. 2.38(a); we are to solve for the voltage across the 2–$\Omega$ resistance using loop currents. We give step-by-step instructions:

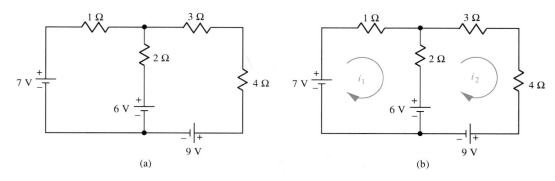

(a)                                     (b)

**Figure 2.38** (a) The voltage across the 2-$\Omega$ resistor is to be determined. (b) The same circuit with loop currents $i_1$ and $i_2$ defined.

**independent loop, loop current**

**1. Define and label loop currents.** Label the independent loops 1, 2, 3, ... and define loop currents $i_1$, $i_2$, $i_3$, ... going clockwise around the loops. An *independent loop* is a loop that does not pass through a current source. A *loop current* flows in a closed path, following a loop. In this circuit, both loops are independent loops and we get the picture of Fig. 2.38(b).

**Conservation of Energy**

**2. Write KVL** going with the currents around each loop in a special form:

$$\sum \text{Voltages across resistors in loop}$$

$$= \sum (+ \text{ or } -) \text{ voltage sources in loop}$$

(2.50)

On the right side of Eq. (2.50), we use $+$ if the voltage aids the loop current for that loop and $-$ if the voltage source opposes the loop current for that loop.

3. **Solve for the loop currents** and from them compute the currents, voltages, or powers required. Note that because we write one KVL equation for each loop and we have one loop current for each loop, we always get the same number of equations and unknowns. We will now follow this plan for the circuit in Fig. 2.38(a). The loop currents have already been defined in Fig. 2.38(b). The KVL equation for loop 1 is

$$i_1(1) + (i_1 - i_2)(2) = +(+7) - (+6) \tag{2.51}$$

The first term in Eq. (2.51) is the voltage across the 1–$\Omega$ resistance. We are going with the current and we are using a load set for the voltage across the resistance; thus we automatically get a + sign for that voltage. The second term is the voltage across the 2-$\Omega$ resistance. The downward current in that resistance is $i_1 - i_2$, the difference between the two loop currents. Because $i_1$ is referenced down and $i_2$ is referenced up, the current in the resistance is their difference. We are going with $i_1$, so we write the voltage across that resistance as $+i \times R$, where $i$ is the current referenced in the direction we are going, $i = i_1 - i_2$. Thus, the + sign in the second term is automatic, just like the + sign on the first term. The $+(+7)$ on the right side is due to the 7-V source. It has a + sign because that source tends to force the loop current in that loop ($i_1$) in its positive direction. The $-(+6)$ is due to the 6-V source. It has the minus sign outside the parentheses because it opposes $i_1$.

Of course, there are not two physical currents in the 2-$\Omega$ resistance, one going up and the other going down. The loop "currents" are mathematical variables that may or may not be identical to a current somewhere in the circuit. In this case, $i_1$ is the current in the 1-$\Omega$ resistance, $i_2$ is the current in the 3- and 4-$\Omega$ resistances, and $i_1 - i_2$ is the current referenced downward in the 2-$\Omega$ resistance.

The KVL equation for the second loop is

$$i_2(3) + i_2(4) + (i_2 - i_1)(2) = +(+6) - (+9) \tag{2.52}$$

We are now going with $i_2$ around loop 2. The first two terms in Eq. (2.52) are due to $i_2$ going through the 3- and 4-$\Omega$ resistances. We automatically get + signs because we are going in the same direction as the loop current. When we get to the 2-$\Omega$ resistance, we write the current as $i_2 - i_1$ because now we are going up, in the same direction as $i_2$. This term in Eq. (2.52) is the negative of the corresponding term in Eq. (2.51). The sign is changed because in both cases we are writing voltages across resistances going clockwise: in loop 1 this requires going downward through the 2-$\Omega$ resistance and in loop 2, this requires going upward.

We now have two equations in two unknowns:

$$(1 + 2)i_1 - (2)i_2 = +1 \tag{2.53}$$

$$(-2)i_1 + (3 + 4 + 2)i_2 = -3 \tag{2.54}$$

Therefore, $i_1$ is 0.130 A and $i_2$ is −0.304 A.

**4. Compute the primary unknown.** This result is not the end of the problem, however, for we set out to calculate the voltage across the 2-$\Omega$ resistance. We were silent about the reference direction of this voltage because we wanted to consider both possibilities. If we put the $+$ polarity symbol at the top of the 2-$\Omega$ resistance, the voltage would be $+(i_1 - i_2)\,(2\,\Omega)$ or $[0.130 - (-0.304)]\,(2) = +0.870$ V. If we put the $+$ polarity symbol at the bottom of the 2-$\Omega$ resistance, the voltage would be $(i_2 - i_1)(2\,\Omega)$ or $[(-0.304) - (+0.130)](2) = -0.870$ V.

---

**EXAMPLE 2.7**  **A Bridge Circuit**

Write the loop-current equations for the circuit in Fig. 1.35, redrawn in Fig. 2.39.

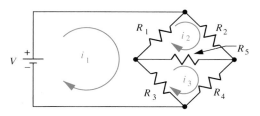

**Figure 2.39**  Bridge circuit from Chapter 1. No two resistors are in series or parallel, but loop current analysis works well.

**SOLUTION:**
This is often called a bridge circuit, and its analysis is beyond the method of series and parallel resistance combinations. The three loop currents are defined in Fig. 2.39. The KVL equation for loop 1 is

$$R_1\,(i_1 - i_2) + R_3\,(i_1 - i_3) = V \tag{2.55}$$

or

$$i_1\,(R_1 + R_3) - (R_1)\,i_2 - (R_3)\,i_3 = V \tag{2.56}$$

Inspection of Eq. (2.56) shows a simple pattern in the signs and coefficients of the three currents. The sign of the $i_1$ term is positive because we are going around loop 1 in the same direction as $i_1$. The other terms have minus signs because all the loop currents are referenced clockwise and thus go opposite directions in the resistances that are common to two loops. Similarly, the coefficient multiplying $i_1$ is the sum of the resistances in loop 1, and the coefficients multiplying the other currents are the negatives of the resistances in common between loop 1 and the loops of those currents. Note that Eqs. (2.53) and (2.54) follow these patterns. Thus, we may write the equation around the second loop as

$$-(R_1)\,i_1 + (R_1 + R_2 + R_5)\,i_2 - (R_5)\,i_3 = 0 \tag{2.57}$$

The zero is put on the right-hand side of the equation because there are no voltage sources in loop 2.

**WHAT IF?**
What if you had to produce the third equation for loop 3 on an exam. What would you write?[14]

---

[14] $-(R_3)i_1 - (R_5)i_2 + (R_3 + R_5 + R_4)i_3 = 0.$

## Some Extensions and Fine Points

How to handle current sources.  Perhaps you have noticed that, as it now stands, we cannot incorporate current sources into our loop-current method.  Current sources require a modest extension of the standard procedure.  Consider the circuit of Fig. 2.40.  The circuit has a current source; but, doing the obvious thing, we have defined and labeled our loop currents in the standard way.  The current source would constrain the two loop currents passing through it, for by definition of a current source, we must require that

$$i_2 - i_1 = 2\,\text{A} \tag{2.58}$$

Having two unknowns, we require another equation.  The second equation comes from KVL around the outer loop:

$$5i_1 + 8i_2 - 10 = 0 \tag{2.59}$$

In writing Eq. (2.59), we have departed from the standard procedure in two ways: We went around the outer loop, which does not follow any single loop current; and we wrote KVL with all terms on the left side of the equation, which is the way we originally learned to write KVL equations.  Equations (2.58) and (2.59) yield $i_1 = -0.462\,\text{A}$ and $i_2 = 1.538\,\text{A}$.  We note that $i_1$ is the current in the voltage source and the 5-$\Omega$ resistance, and $i_2$ is the current in the 8-$\Omega$ resistance.  Note that $i_2 - i_1$   2 A, as required by the current source.

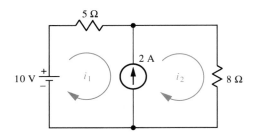

**Figure 2.40**  The current source constrains $i_1$ and $i_2$.

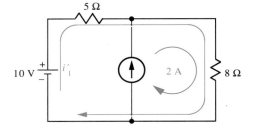

**Figure 2.41**  Loop current $i_1'$ is routed to avoid the current source.

**constrained loop current**

The solution just presented gives the correct answer but is not the recommended way to handle current sources.  We now present another solution that uses the concept of a *constrained loop current,* which is a loop current that is known because it passes through a current source.  Figure 2.41 shows the same circuit with one unknown loop current defined, $i_1'$, and one known loop current of 2 A defined to flow around the right loop.  "Wait," you should say, "that current will divide at the top and go both ways."  Yes, that is true, but bear with us until we finish and then you will understand this approach.  Because we now have only one unknown, we need only one equation, which comes from KVL around the loop of $i_1'$:

$$5i_1' + 8\,(i_1' + 2) - 10 = 0 \tag{2.60}$$

In Eq. (2.60) the term for the 8-$\Omega$ resistance includes the effect of both the unknown and the constrained loop currents. They add because both are referenced in the same direction through that resistance. The solution of Eq. (2.60) is routine: $i_1' = -0.462$ A. Using this and the constrained loop current, we calculate the current in the 8-$\Omega$ resistance to be $i_1' + 2 = 1.538$ A. Thus, by using the constrained loop concept to handle the current source, we get the same results for the physical currents as we obtained before with the first, more straightforward method.

---

**EXAMPLE 2.8**   **Redirecting the constrained current**

Constrain the 2-A loop current from the source to flow through the 5-$\Omega$ resistance and voltage source, as shown in Fig. 2.42, and solve for the physical currents again.

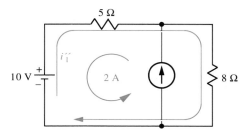

**Figure 2.42**   Again the loop current misses the current source. The constrained loop current is rerouted.

**SOLUTION:**
The KVL equation around the loop of $i''$ is

$$5\left(i_1'' - 2\right) + 8\,i_1'' - 10 = 0 \tag{2.61}$$

The solution of Eq. (2.61) is routine: $i_1'' = 1.538$ A, and the current referenced left to right in the 5-$\Omega$ resistance is $i_1'' - 2 = -0.462$ A. Again, we have the same answers for the physical currents.

**WHAT IF?**
What if you split the 2-A current and have two constrained loops of 1 A each?[15]

---

We have shown *how* the constrained loop current works, but *why* does it work? Who are we to make the current from the current source go wherever we wish? *Answer:* We are the ones defining variables in the problem. We are defining variables by numbering loops and by drawing currents going clockwise around these loops; and when there are current sources, we are defining variables by defining the paths in which those currents flow. Look at Figs. 2.41 and 2.42. The unknown loop current *appears* to be the same in both, but by changing the path of the 2-A current, we changed the *meaning*

---
[15] It works, but there is no advantage to doing it that way.

of the unknown loop current. Thus, we can handle current sources by defining their currents to flow in certain paths, modifying our interpretation of the unknown loop currents accordingly.

**Counting independent loops.** The first step in our standard procedure was to number the independent loops. We identify independent loops by turning OFF all sources, as we did when we wished to identify independent nodes in the method of node voltages. For example, when we turn OFF both sources in Fig. 2.40, the current source becomes an open circuit and the voltage source becomes a short circuit. We are left with one loop containing two resistances. Thus, we have one independent loop, requiring one unknown and one KVL equation.

**loop currents,**
**mesh currents**

**Loop currents and mesh currents.** What we have been using up to now are mesh currents, a special class of loop currents. In circuit terminology, a *loop* is any closed path. A *mesh* is a special loop, namely, the smallest loop one can have. A mesh is thus a loop that contains no other loops. In the fuller sense of the loop-current method, we can define the loop currents with great freedom, allowing them to go wherever we wish within certain guidelines. For our relatively simple circuits, the guidelines are that we must define the correct number of currents and that we must go through each resistance with at least one loop current.

We will rework the circuit in Fig. 2.38(a) as an example of this more general loop-current method. The circuit is redrawn in Fig. 2.43 with true loop[16] currents drawn as shown. We defined one current clockwise and the other counterclockwise to show the generality of the method. We write KVL around the loops of the unknown currents with the following results:

$$-7 + 1\,(i_1' - i_2') + 2i_1' + 6 = 0 \tag{2.62}$$

$$+7 - 9 + (3 + 4)i_2' + 1\,(i_2' - i_1') = 0 \tag{2.63}$$

Therefore, $i_1' = 0.435\,\text{A}$ and $i_2' = 0.304\,\text{A}$. Because $i_1'$ is the only current through the 2-$\Omega$ resistance, we must solve for it only to compute the voltage across that resistance, the original unknown. The result is $0.435\,\text{A} \times 2\,\Omega = 0.870\,\text{V}$, + at top, which agrees with our earlier result.

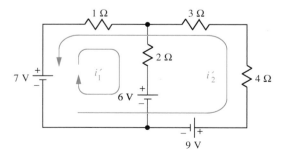

**Figure 2.43** These are true loop currents, not mesh currents.

---

[16]Actually $i_1'$ is also a mesh current, but is called a loop current here because it is used in the more general method.

The more general loop-current method is useful when we wish to determine only one current or voltage, because we can define all the unknown loop currents to avoid that path except one loop current. The resulting equations can then be solved for that one loop current, which will be the desired current. The trouble with the generalized loop-current method is that all the nice symmetries and automatic sign patterns of the mesh-current method vanish, and once again we are required to pay careful attention to signs.

**branch currents**

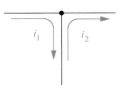

**Figure 2.44** Node with two loop currents.

**How we can ignore KCL?**   With the loop-current method, we solve for the currents of a circuit by writing only KVL equations. How can we ignore KCL? *Answer*: KCL applies to *branch currents*, currents that flow from one point to another through a direct path. We can ignore KCL because we defined the currents to flow in complete loops rather than from one point to another in the circuit. In Fig. 2.44, we show two loop currents passing through a node. If we wrote KCL for such a node, each loop current would contribute two equal and opposite terms: Each loop current must add to zero at every node. Thus, KCL is satisfied automatically when we use loop currents to describe the circuit; we have only to satisfy KVL to find the solution.

---

**EXAMPLE 2.9**   **Benchmark Example**

Solve the benchmark example by loop-current analysis.

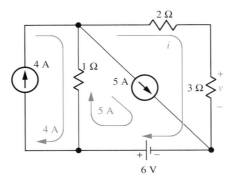

**Figure 2.45**   The benchmark example with loop currents defined. We have constrained currents such that only one current passes through the 3-Ω resistor.

**SOLUTION:**
Figure 2.45 shows the circuit marked for loop-current analysis. Note that we have one independent and two constrained loops. KVL around the loop is

$$2i + 3i - 6 + 1 \times (i + 5 - 4) = 0 \Rightarrow i = \frac{6 + 4 - 5}{2 + 3 + 1} = \frac{5}{6} \text{ A} \qquad (2.64)$$

and the unknown voltage is $3i = 2.50$ V, as before.

# Summary of Methods of Circuit Analysis

**OBJECTIVE 6**

**To understand how to choose the most efficient manner for analyzing a circuit**

**Which method to use?** We now have four methods for analyzing circuits: the method of current and voltage dividers augmented by superposition, Thévenin and Norton equivalent circuits, the method of node voltages, and the method of loop currents. How can we select the best one to use on a given circuit? Here are some of the factors to consider:

■ **Design or analysis?** Are we trying to design or analyze the circuit? If the circuit is completely specified and we are trying to determine some aspect of its response, say, the power out of a source or the voltage across some resistance, the nodal or loop methods are favored. These are general methods of analysis, which solve for the entire circuit response all at once. Special attention is not given toward the effect of a single resistance or source; rather, everything is incorporated into the equations at the beginning.

   On the other hand, if you are designing the circuit in some regard, the methods of voltage and current dividers or equivalent circuits are favored. These methods focus on the effects of individual resistances and sources at specific points in the circuit. Design must, of course, deal in such details and these methods are well suited for allowing the designer to control the way voltage and current distribute throughout a circuit.

■ **Number of equations?** How many equations must be solved? It is possible for a circuit to have more independent nodes than loops, or vice versa. The next example illustrates this point.

■ **Fine points.** Finally, there are numerous minor considerations that would suggest a method if those discussed fail to dictate a choice. If there are many current sources, nodal analysis is favored, but if many voltage sources, loop currents might be easier. If the unknown is a voltage, nodes might be best, but if the unknown is a current, loops might be more efficient. If there is only one source and the circuit is not too complicated, the method of voltage and current dividers is favored. These decisions come easily as a result of much experience in circuit analysis. As a beginner, you will have to practice the various methods on a number of circuits before you develop the ability to choose the most efficient method.

---

**EXAMPLE 2.10** **Loop Currents or Node Voltages?**

Find $i$ in the circuit shown in Fig. 2.46.

**SOLUTION:**

This circuit has two independent loops but only one independent node if we combine the series resistors. Thus, we favor nodal analysis for simpler mathematics.

   Choosing the node at the bottom for the reference node, we designate the voltage at the top node as $v$, the nodal equation is

$$\frac{v - (+10)}{2} + \frac{v - (0)}{1 + 3} + \frac{v - (+8)}{6} = 0 \qquad (2.65)$$

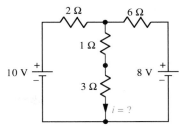

**Figure 2.46** The circuit has two independent loops but only one independent node.

The solution is $v = 6.91$ V, and the current downward is this voltage divided by 4 $\Omega$, or 1.73 A.

### Check Your Understanding

1. How many independent loops are there in the circuit in Fig. 2.15 with the load removed?

2. What is the name of a loop current passing through a current source?

3. If a circuit has five independent nodes and two independent loops, what method of analysis does this suggest?

4. In the standard method for mesh (loop) current analysis, what is the coefficient of the mesh current in the equation for that mesh?

*Answers.* **(1)** One independent loop; **(2)** a constrained loop current; **(3)** loop currents (two equations in two unknowns); **(4)** the sum of the resistances around its mesh.

## CHAPTER SUMMARY

Chapter 2 builds on Chapter 1 by giving a variety of methods for analyzing circuits. The various methods are compared for their advantages and disadvantages. The concept of impedance level was introduced to explain the interaction between parts of a circuit.

**Objective 1: To understand the principle of superposition and use superposition to analyze circuits with multiple sources.** Superposition is based on the linearity of Ohm's and Kirchhoff's laws. Using superposition, we can examine the effects of multiple voltage and current sources at a prescribed point in a circuit.

**Objective 2: To understand the origin of Thévenin's equivalent circuit and be able to derive the Thévenin equivalent circuit of a network with a load.** Thevenin's equivalent circuit is used to describe the interaction of a circuit with a load. The equivalent circuit consists of a voltage source, the open-circuit voltage, in series with a resistor, output impedance. A complicated problem can often be reduced to two simpler problems by using Thévenin's equivalent circuit.

**Objective 3: To understand the significance of impedance level in interactions between circuits.** The interaction between a circuit and a load depends on the output impedance level of the circuit relative to the input impedance level of the load. When the source impedance level is small relative to the load, voltage will be transferred to the load; when the source impedance level is large relative to the load, current will be transferred to the load; and when impedance levels are roughly the same, power will be transferred.

**Objective 4: To understand how to analyze a circuit using nodal analysis.** In nodal analysis, all voltages are defined relative to a reference node, which is assigned a voltage of zero. Equations are based on Kirchhoff's current law in a special form, resulting in simultaneous equations for the voltages at all nodes. This method of circuit analysis is systematic and efficient, especially when the circuit contains many loops but few nodes, as is common in electronic circuits.

**Objective 5: To understand how to analyze a circuit using loop currents.** Loop currents are mathematical variables defined to flow in closed loops. Equations for loop currents are based upon Kirchhoff's voltage law, although voltage variables are not defined. This method is systematic and efficient when the circuit contains voltage sources and few loops.

**Objective 6: To understand how to choose the most efficient manner for analyzing a circuit.** Our methods for circuit analysis now include voltage and current dividers plus superposition, Thévenin equivalent circuits, nodal analysis, and loop-current analysis. These methods are compared for ease of mathematics, for suitability in analysis or design, and for relative popularity and importance among practitioners.

The methods of this chapter are used throughout the remainder of the book to formulate circuit equations. In Chapter 3, we use them to formulate differential equations describing circuits containing resistors, inductors, and capacitors.

## PROBLEMS

## Section 2.1: Superposition

2.1. Find the current in the 20-$\Omega$ resistor in Fig. P2.1 using superposition.

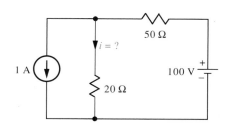

**Figure P2.1**

2.2. In Fig. P2.2, find $i$ using the principle of superposition.

2.3. For the circuit in Fig. P2.3, determine the current in the 10-$\Omega$ resistor with the reference direction shown using the principle of superposition.

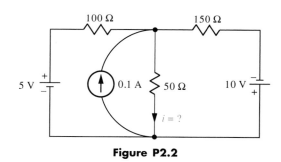

**Figure P2.2**

2.4. For the circuit shown in Fig. P2.4, determine the power into the 15-$\Omega$ resistor using superposition.

2.5. For the circuit shown in Fig. P2.5, determine the following:
   (a) Find $v$ using superposition
   (b) Determine the power out of the current source.

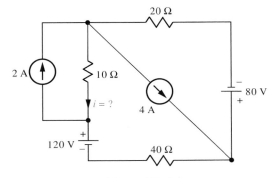

**Figure P2.3**

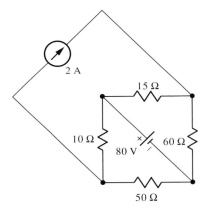

**Figure P2.4**

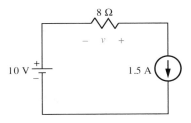

**Figure P2.5**

2.6. For the circuit shown in Fig. P2.6, determine the following:

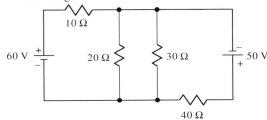

**Figure P2.6**

(a) Find the current in the 20–Ω resistance due to the 60-V source. (Do not consider the current due to the 50-V source.)

(b) With both sources operating, find the ratio of the current in the 30-Ω resistance to the current in the 20-Ω resistance.

## Section 2.2: Thévenin's and Norton's Equivalent Circuits

2.7. Place a connection (a short circuit, no resistor) between $a$ and $a'$ in Fig. 2.12. Solve for the current flowing down from $a$ to $a'$. The answer should be zero current, as argued in Section 2.2.

2.8. Develop a Thévenin equivalent circuit for the part of the circuit shown in the box in Fig. P2.8. Use this equivalent circuit to solve for $i$, as shown.

2.9. For the circuit in Fig. P2.9, determine the following:
(a) Replace the circuit in the box by a Thévenin equivalent circuit.
(b) Find $v_{ab}$ for $R_L = 3$ kΩ
(c) What value of $R_L$ receives maximum power from the circuit?
(d) What value of $R_L$ makes the current in the 6-kΩ resistor to be 0.1 mA?

2.10. A black box was connected to a variable resistor

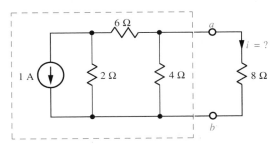

**Figure P2.8**

and the power in the resistor was measured as the resistance was varied. The results are shown in Fig. P2.10. From this graph, determine the Thévenin equivalent circuit for the circuit in the black box.

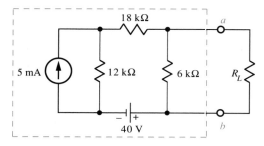

**Figure P2.9**

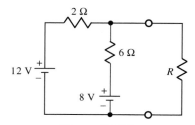

**Figure P2.13**

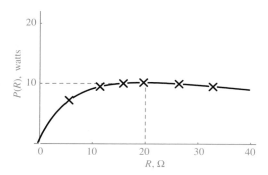

**Figure P2.10**

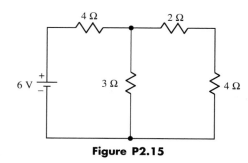

**Figure P2.15**

(a) Find the current in the 3-Ω resistor.
(b) What resistance, replacing the 3-Ω resistor, would draw one-half the current in part (a)?

2.16. For the circuit shown in Fig. P2.16, determine the following:

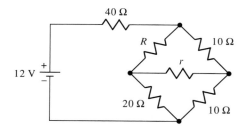

**Figure P2.16**

(a) What value of resistance, $R$ will reduce the current through $r$ to zero?
(b) For the value of $R$ in part (a), what is the current through the voltage source?

2.17 A circuit has a variable load, $R$. Power measurements show that the power into $R$ is maximum at 100 W with $R = 6\ \Omega$ What current would flow if $R$ were replaced by a 3-Ω resistor?

2.18. What value of $I_s$ reduces the circuit in Fig. P2.18 to a simple resistor as seen by the output terminals?

2.11. Rework Problem P2.8, this time using a Norton equivalent circuit for the portion of the circuit in the box.

2.12. A mysterious black box is found in the electrical engineering lab. A curious student measured the output voltage to be 6.3 V. Then he shorted the output through an ammeter (consider the ammeter to have zero resistance), which indicated a current of 126 A. Give the Norton equivalent circuit for the box. How much power can be gotten out of the box if a variable resistor is connected to its terminals and adjusted for maximum power?

2.13. For the circuit shown in Fig. P2.13, determine the following:
(a) Find the value of $R$ to receive maximum power.
(b) For the value of $R$ in part (a), find the power out of the 12-V source.

2.14. The starter motor on a car draws 75-A starting current, which lowers the battery voltage from 12.6 to 9.1 V. What would the battery voltage be if it were being charged at 30 A?

2.15. For the circuit shown in Fig. P2.15, determine the following:

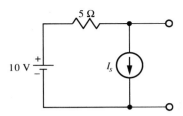

**Figure P2.18**

2.19. For the circuit shown in Fig. P2.19, find $I_s$ such that the current in the 120-Ω resistance is zero.

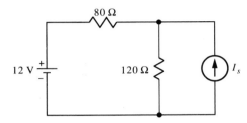

**Figure P2.19**

2.20. Using a Thévenin equivalent circuit, find $R$ in Fig. P2.20 such that $i = 0.5$ A.

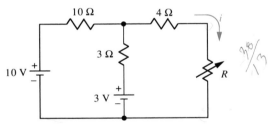

**Figure P2.20**

2.21. For the circuit in Fig. P2.21, find $V$ to make the current in the 5-Ω resistor to be zero.

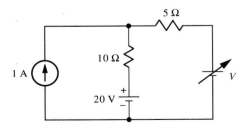

**Figure P2.21**

2.22. Show that the available power from a circuit is equal to the product of one-half the Thévenin voltage with one-half the Norton current. Express the output impedance in terms of the available power and the open-circuit voltage.

2.23. A student is testing a circuit containing batteries and resistors. The output voltage is 6.26 V when measured with a good (assume ideal) voltmeter, but 6.05 V when a 600-Ω resistor is connected across the output terminals. What current would result if the output were short-circuited?

2.24. The circuit in Fig. P2.24 shows the circuit for a voltage source and "potentiometer," which is a resistor with a sliding contact. The variable $x$ varies from 0 to 1, and the open-circuit voltage increases in proportion with $x$.
  (a) Determine a Thévenin equivalent circuit for the voltage source, with the voltage and output impedance functions of $x$.
  (b) What is the maximum output resistance if the total resistance of the potentiometer is $R$?
  (c) If the load resistor were equal to the resistance of the potentiometer, $R$, what would $x$ have to be to give an output voltage of $0.5\,V_s$?

2.25. A circuit, as shown in Fig. P2.25(a), has a variable load and ideal meters to monitor load voltage and current. The table in Fig. P2.25(b) shows partial results of a series of tests. Fill in the blank spaces in the table with the missing data.

2.26. A voltmeter has an impedance level (input resistance) that is 100 times the impedance level of the circuit it is measuring (the output resistance, with the meter as load). Find the % error in the meter reading, where

$$\% \text{ Error} = \frac{\text{true voltage} - \text{measured voltage}}{\text{measured voltage}}$$

2.27. A circuit is represented by a Thévenin equivalent circuit, as shown in Fig. P2.27. With no ammeter, the current would be $i = V/R_{eq}$. Find the impedance level of the meter in terms of $R_{eq}$ to cause a 1% error in the measurement. The definition of % error is given in the previous problem.

2.28. A voltmeter has a 1 MΩ (megohm = $10^6$ Ω) impedance level (input resistance). Find the voltage it would measure for the Thévenin voltage between $a$ and $b$ in Fig. P2.9 with no load other than the voltmeter.

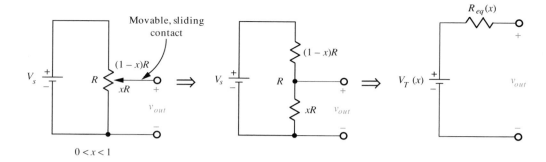

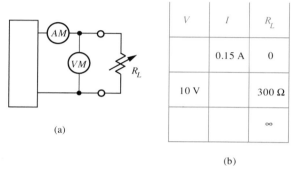

Figure P2.24

(a)

| V | I | $R_L$ |
|---|---|---|
|  | 0.15 A | 0 |
| 10 V |  | 300 Ω |
|  |  | ∞ |

(b)

Figure P2.25

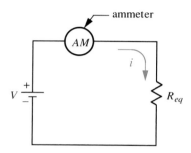

Figure P2.27

## Section 2.3: Node-Voltage Analysis

2.29. **(a)** For the circuit shown in Fig. P2.29, solve for $v_a$ and $v_b$ using node-voltage techniques.
   **(b)** Find the voltage across the three resistors (you supply reference directions), and show that KVL is satisfied.
   **(c)** Now double $v_a$ and repeat part (b). Note that KVL is still satisfied, even if *incorrect* node voltages are used. Of course, KCL would be violated.

2.30. For the circuit shown in Fig. P2.30, write the KCL equation for node $b$ using the node-voltage patterns and solve for $v_{br} = v_b$. Check your solution using the voltage-divider method.

2.31. For the circuit in Fig. P2.31, determine the following:
   **(a)** Write KVL to show $v_{ar} = v_a = +5$ V and $v_{cr} = v_c = -10$ V.
   **(b)** Find the current downward in the 50–Ω resistor by first solving for $v_b$ using nodal analysis.

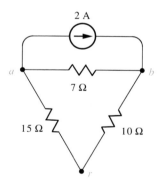

Figure P2.29

*Hint*: Nodes $a$ and $c$ are constrained to the reference node.

2.32. Using node-voltage analysis, solve for the indicated unknowns in Fig. P2.32. *Hints*: In parts (a) and (b), note that kV, mA, and volts make a consistent set of

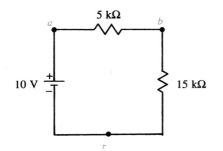

**Figure P2.30**

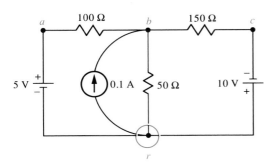

**Figure P2.31**

units; in part (c), find $v_a$, then $v_{10}$ from the voltage divider.

2.33. For Fig. P2.33, write the nodal equations, using the notation given. Do not solve the equations.

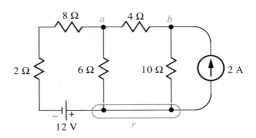

**Figure P2.33**

2.34. For Fig. P2.34, determine the current in the 100-$\Omega$ resistor with the reference direction given. Use nodal analysis.

2.35. For the circuit shown in Fig. P2.35, determine the following:
   (a) Using nodal analysis, find the current in the 10-$\Omega$ resistor for $R = 6\,\Omega$.

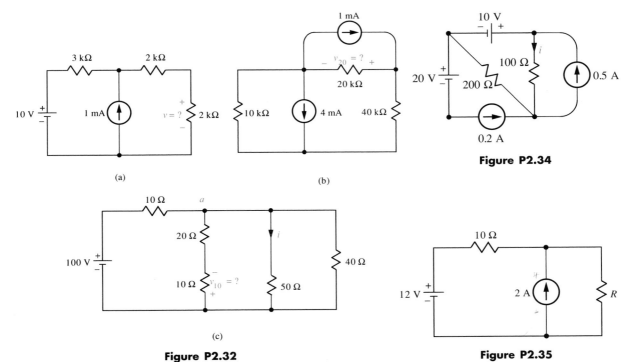

(a)

(b)

**Figure P2.34**

(c)

**Figure P2.32**

**Figure P2.35**

**(b)** Derive a Thévenin equivalent circuit with $R$ as the load.

**(c)** Find the value of $R$ that gives 10% of the current that would flow if the load were replaced by a short circuit.

2.36. Write the nodal equations for the circuit of Fig. P2.36 in the form

$$v_a(\quad) + v_b(\quad) = (\quad)$$
$$v_a(\quad) + v_b(\quad) = (\quad)$$

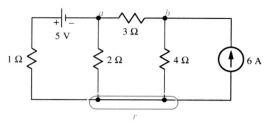

**Figure P2.36**

## Section 2.4: Loop-Current Analysis

2.37. Solve for all branch currents in the circuit of Fig. P2.37 using loop-current analysis.

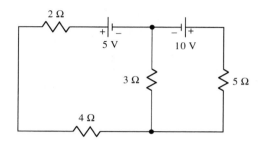

**Figure P2.37**

2.38. Find the power out of the 10-V source in Fig. P2.38 using loop currents to analyze the circuit.

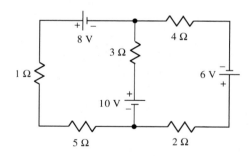

**Figure P2.38**

2.39. Solve for the current referenced downward in the 20-$\Omega$ resistor in the circuit of Fig. P2.39 using the constrained loop concept to handle the current source.

2.40. Solve for $i$ in Fig. P2.40 using the loop-current method.

2.41. For the circuit of Fig. P2.41, solve for $i_4$ using mesh-current variables to analyze the circuit. Note

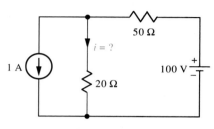

**Figure P2.39**

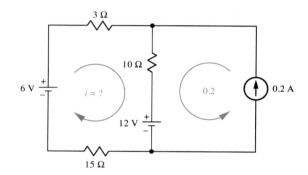

**Figure P2.40**

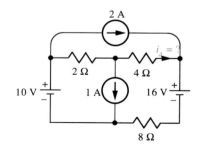

**Figure P2.41**

that you may direct the constrained loops to miss the 4-Ω resistor. Be sure to count independent loops before defining variables.

2.42. Solve for the power out of the 80-V source in the circuit of Fig. P2.42, using loop-current variables.

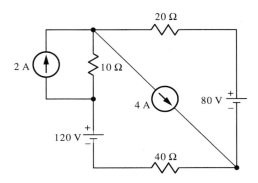

**Figure P2.42**

## General Problems

2.44. (a) Find the current in the 40-Ω resistor in Fig. P2.44 caused by the voltage sources. (Ignore the current caused by the current sources.)

(b) Find the current in the 40-Ω resistor in Fig. P2.44 caused by the current sources. (Ignore the current caused by the voltage sources.)

(c) Find the current in the 40-Ω resistor in Fig. P2.44 caused by all sources acting simultaneously.

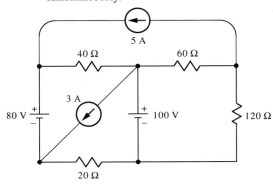

**Figure P2.44**

2.45. For Fig. P2.45, find R such that the power into the 200–Ω resistor is 12.5 W.

Remember to count independent loops first.

2.43. True loop (not mesh) currents are defined in Fig. P2.43 satisfying the rules given in Section 2.4. Write the KVL equations for the circuit using these loop variables. You are not required to solve the resulting equations.

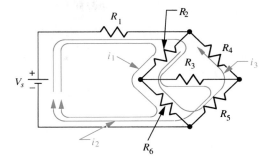

**Figure P2.43**

2.46. A 16-Ω loudspeaker draws maximum power from the output of its amplifier, which is capable of producing 25 W in the speaker. What would be the power produced in an 8-Ω speaker? Represent the loudspeakers as resistors of 16 and 8 Ω, respectively.

2.47. An electric stove (dc or ac, it does not matter, because the same power formulas apply) requires 230 V for the line voltage. The stove uses two heater elements that can be switched in one at time or placed in series or parallel, making four heating temperatures. If the highest setting requires 3000 W

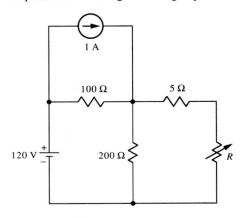

**Figure P2.45**

and the lowest 500 W, what are the powers for the two intermediate settings?

2.48. A voltmeter must draw some current from the circuit it is measuring in order to operate (see Fig. P2.48). The amount of current it draws depends on the meter scale and is specified in terms of the "ohms per volt" of the meter. For example, a 10-$k\Omega/V$ meter would have a resistance of 10 $k\Omega$ on the 1-V scale, 100 $k\Omega$ on the 10-V scale, and so on. For this problem, assume that we are measuring with a 10-$k\Omega/V$ meter.

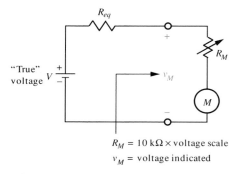

$$R_M = 10\ k\Omega \times \text{voltage scale}$$
$$v_M = \text{voltage indicated}$$

**Figure P2.48** Metering a voltage. The impedance of the meter, $R_M$, depends on what voltage scale is used.

(a) If we measure 5 V on the 10-V scale, what current does the meter draw from the circuit?

(b) If the output impedance of the circuit is 600 $\Omega$ and we measure 5 V on the 10-V scale, what is the true open-circuit voltage of the source, that is, what would be measured by an ideal meter that drew no current from the circuit?

(c) With our 10-$k\Omega/V$ meter, on an unknown circuit we measure 24 V on the 30-V scale but 30 V on the 100-V scale. Explain the reason for this apparent discrepancy and determine from these measurements the Thévenin equivalent circuit for the source we are measuring.

2.49. The ladder network shown in Fig. P2.49, if terminated with the proper value of $R_t$, has the property that the input current is divided by 2 at each node, as shown. What should be the value of $R_t$ for this property? What would be the input resistance to the ladder if the $R$, $2R$ pattern were continued infinitely?

2.50. After Norton died and went to heaven, he chanced to encounter Thévenin one day. They got into a discussion about whose equivalent circuit was

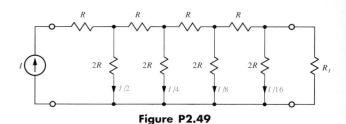

**Figure P2.49**

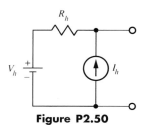

**Figure P2.50**

better. To maintain peace, they proposed the "Thevenort" circuit shown in Fig. P2.50.

(a) Give values of $V_h$, $I_h$, and $R_h$ that correspond to an open-circuit voltage ($V_{oc}$) of 5 V and a short-circuit current ($I_{sc}$) of 2 A. (The answer is not unique.)

(b) Give general relationships that relate $V_h$, $I_h$, and $R_h$ to the open-circuit voltage ($V_{oc}$) and the short-circuit current ($I_{sc}$).

2.51. Find the power in the 100-$\Omega$ resistor in Fig. P2.51 by a method of your own choosing.

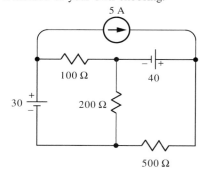

**Figure P2.51**

2.52. We have two batteries, A and B. Battery A has a voltage of 13.8-V and a short-circuit current of 350-A. Battery B has a voltage of 13.2-V and a short-circuit current of 220-A. The batteries may be connected in series or in parallel to give power to a single resistor. What connection, series or parallel, has the most power-producing capability, and what is the maximum power that can be obtained from that connection?

2.53. For the circuit in Fig. P2.53, find $v_{ab}$ by any method.

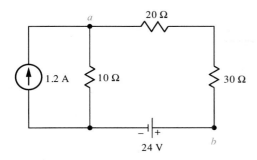

**Figure P2.53**

2.54. For the circuit in Fig. P2.54, find $v_{ab}$ by any method.

2.55. For the circuit in Fig. P2.55, find $v_{ab}$ by any method.

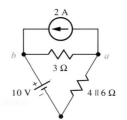

**Figure P2.54**

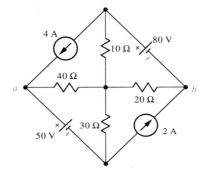

**Figure P2.55**

# Answers to Odd-Numbered Problems

2.1. 0.714 A.

2.3. −2.29 A.

2.5. **(a)** −12 V; **(b)** +3 W.

2.7. 0 A.

2.9. **(a)** 3.33 V, 5 kΩ; **(b)** 1.25 V; **(c)** 5 kΩ; **(d)** 1.10 kΩ.

2.11. **(a)** −0.250 A, 2.67 Ω; **(b)** −0.0625 A.

2.13. **(a)** 1.50 Ω; **(b)** 39.0 W.

2.15. **(a)** 3.60 V, 2.40 Ω, 0.667 A; **(b)** 8.40 Ω.

2.17. 5.44 A.

2.19. −0.150 A.

2.21. 30 V.

2.23. 0.301 A.

2.25.

| V | I | | $R_L$ |
|---|---|---|---|
| 0 | 0.15 | A | 0 |
| 10 V | 0.0333 A | | 300 Ω |
| 12.9 V | 0 | | ∞ |

2.27. $R/100$.

2.29. **(a)** $v_a(\frac{1}{7} + \frac{1}{15}) + v_b(-\frac{1}{7}) = -2$

$$v_a(-\frac{1}{7}) + v_b(\frac{1}{7} + \frac{1}{10}) = +2$$

**(b)** $v_{ar} = -6.56$ V, $v_{br} = +4.38$ V, $v_{ab} = -10.9$ V

**(c)** $v'_{ar} = -13.1$ V, $v'_{br} = 4.38$ V, $v'_{ab} = -17.5$ V.

2.31. **(a)** $v_a = +5$ V, $V_c = -10$ V; **(b)** 0.0455 A.

2.33. $v_a(\frac{1}{10} + \frac{1}{6} + \frac{1}{4}) + v_b(-\frac{1}{4}) = -\frac{12}{10}$

$v_a(-\frac{1}{4}) + v_b(\frac{1}{4} + \frac{1}{10}) = 2.$

2.35. **(a)** 0 A; **(b)** 32 V, 10 Ω; **(c)** 90 Ω.

2.37. 0.159 A downward on left, −1.35 A downward in middle, +1.19A downward on right.

2.39. 0.714 A.

2.41. −1.71 A.

2.43. $i_1(R_1 + R_2 + R_6) + i_2(R_1 + R_2) + i_3(R_6) = +V_s$
$i_1(R_1 + R_2) + i_2(R_1 + R_2 + R_3 + R_5) + i_3(R_2 - R_5) = +V_s$
$i_1(R_6 + R_2) + i_2(R_2 - R_5) + i_3(R_2 + R_6 + R_5 + R_4) = 0.$

2.45. 29.5 Ω.

2.47. 634 W, 2366 W.

2.49. **(a)** $2R$; **(b)** $R_{in} = 2R$ into series resistor, and $R$ into parallel resistor.

2.51. 768 W.

2.53. −10 V.

2.55. 129.5 V.

# 3

# The Dynamics of Circuits

Theory of Inductors and Capacitors

First-Order Transient Response of *RL* and *RC* Circuits

Advanced Techniques

Chapter Summary

Problems

**objectives**

1. To understand the properties of inductors and to be able to find the inductor voltage from the inductor current and vice versa

2. To understand the properties of capacitors and to be able to find the capacitor voltage from the capacitor current and vice versa

3. To understand how to analyze first-order transients by the initial-value/final-value method

In this chapter, we move from statics to dynamics. Inductors and capacitors are introduced, and we study energy transfer within circuits. Time enters as the independent variable by which circuit behavior is described.

## Time and Energy

**Statics and dynamics.** In mechanics, dynamics usually follows statics. Statics deals with the distribution of forces in a structure; time is not a factor. Dynamics deals with the exchange of energy between components in a system, and time is an important factor because energy cannot be exchanged except as a time process.

In our study of electrical circuits, we have not yet considered time as an important quantity. Our dc circuits involve only KVL, KCL, and Ohm's laws, and none of these equations has time as a factor. Indeed, even if we allowed one of our voltage or current sources to have an output that varied with time, the solution would not become more complicated. It would be like letting the force in a statics problem vary slowly with time: The method of solution would be valid provided rates of energy exchange between components of the system remain small. In a true dynamics problem, the rate of energy transfer between components must be considered.

With this chapter, we begin the study of electrical circuits in which rates of energy exchanged between circuit components are important. We begin by introducing the two circuit components that store energy in electrical circuits. The presence of inductors or capacitors in an electrical circuit suggests a true dynamics problem. We first identify the two types of energy that may be stored in a circuit.

**electric energy,
magnetic energy**

**Electric energy and magnetic energy storage.** To understand what we mean by magnetic energy and electric energy, let us recall from Chapter 1 that there are two types of forces between electric charges: electrostatic and magnetic. Here we wish to emphasize energy. From mechanics, you recall that when a displacement is made against a force, work is done (mechanical energy is exchanged). Similarly, if we displace a charge in the presence of a motional (magnetic) force, magnetic energy is exchanged. To store much magnetic energy, we must bring many moving charges close

**inductor, capacitor**

together, which is what an *inductor* does. On the other hand, when we move charges in the presence of positional (electrostatic) forces, electric energy is exchanged. To store electric energy, we must separate charges, yet keep them close together, which is what a *capacitor* does.

**Analogy between mechanical and electric energy.** Magnetic and electric energy are the two forms of electrical energy, arising from the two types of electrical force. In a mechanical system, we also have two types of force and two types of energy. Forces that depend on position, as in a spring or a gravitational field, store *potential energy*. Forces that depend on changes in velocity lead to *kinetic energy*. Potential energy and kinetic energy in a mechanical system are analogous to electric energy and magnetic energy in an electrical system. We must emphasize, however, that this is only an analogy. Magnetic energy is not kinetic energy; it is merely analogous to kinetic energy.

**OBJECTIVE 1**

**To understand the properties of inductors and to be able to find the inductor voltage from the inductor current and vice versa**

## Inductor Basics

**Physical inductor.** Figure 3.1(a) shows a coil of wire, which acts as an inductor. When current flows in the wire, moving charges are close together, magnetic forces are large, and magnetic energy is stored.

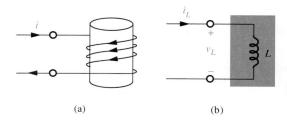

**Figure 3.1** (a) A coil of wire gets moving charges close together and acts as an inductor. (b) A circuit model for an inductor.

(a)                          (b)

**Circuit-theory definition of an inductor.** Figure 3.1(b) shows the circuit symbol for an inductor. The equation describing the voltage−current characteristics of an inductor is based on Faraday's law of induction and may be stated in differential or integral form:

$$v_L(t) = +\frac{d}{dt}Li_L(t) \qquad (3.1)$$

and

$$i_L(t) = i_L(0) + \frac{1}{L}\int_0^t v_L(t')\,dt' \qquad (3.2)$$

The circuit symbol and the accompanying equations together define a circuit-theory model for an ideal inductor. Normally, the inductance, $L$, is considered a constant and brought outside the derivative in Eq. (3.1). Chapter 13 discusses the calculation of the inductance of a coil. Note in Fig. 3.1(b) that $v_L$ and $i_L$ form a load set.

**Analogy with Newton's law.** Equation (3.1) is analogous to Newton's second law in Fig. 3.2. Just as changes in the velocity of a mass require a force, or vice versa, changes in the current through an inductor produce a voltage, or vice versa. If the current is increased (positive $di_L/dt$), the inductor physical voltage opposes the change. If the current is decreased (negative $di_L/dt$), the inductor acts momentarily as a source polarized to keep the current going. Thus, the physical polarity of the inductor voltage will tend to keep the current constant, just as a mass will tend to maintain constant velocity. Equation (3.2) is analogous to determining the velocity by integrating the acceleration, which is proportional to an exciting force. We note that only changes in current can be determined from the voltage across the inductor, just as only changes in velocity can be computed from the force acting on a mass. To determine the current fully, we need to know the inductance, the voltage as a function of time, and the initial current, $i_L(0)$.

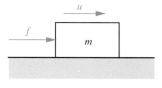

$$f = \frac{d}{dt}(mu)$$

**Figure 3.2** An inductor is analogous to mass.

EXAMPLE 3.1 **Battery-switch-inductor**

Find the current for $t > 0$ in the circuit shown in Fig. 3.3 if the switch closes at $t = 0$.

**SOLUTION:**
With the switch open, the current in the circuit must be zero. With the switch closed, $v_L = V$. We may find the current for $t > 0$ by integrating Eq. (3.2) with $v_L = V$:

$$i_L(t) = i_L(0) + \frac{1}{L} \int_0^t v_L(t')\, dt' = 0 + \frac{1}{L} \int_0^t V\, dt' = \frac{V}{L} \times t \tag{3.3}$$

Thus, the current increases linearly, as shown in Fig. 3.4. This circuit is analogous to a mass being accelerated by a constant force; theoretically the velocity will continue to increase so long as the force is applied.[1]

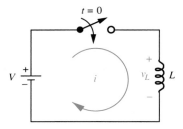

**Figure 3.3** The inductor will integrate the voltage to give the current.

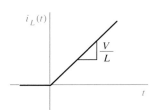

**Figure 3.4** The current increases linearly because the inductor voltage is constant.

**WHAT IF?** What if the switch is opened?[2]

---

 **Conservation of Energy**

**Stored magnetic energy in an inductor.** We pointed out that a load set of voltage and current is used to define the equation of an inductor. In Eq. (1.35), we compute the energy transferred by integrating the power. We thus can calculate the energy stored in the inductor by integrating its input power, $+v_L i_L$.

$$p_L = \frac{dW_m}{dt} = + v_L i_L = \left( L\,\frac{di_L}{dt} \right) i_L = \frac{d}{dt}\left( \frac{1}{2} L i_L^2 \right) \tag{3.4}$$

$$W_m = \int p_L\, dt = \int \frac{d}{dt}\left( \frac{1}{2} L i_L^2 \right) dt = \frac{1}{2} L i_L^2 \tag{3.5}$$

where $p_L$ is the power into the inductor and $W_m$ is the stored magnetic energy in the in-

---

[1] Until relativity effects must be considered.

[2] This is a tricky question and will be discussed later in the chapter. For now, suffice it to say that a spark would occur at the switch as it was opened.

ductor. The constant of integration is set to zero because there is no stored energy when the current is zero. The result in Eq. (3.5) is analogous to the kinetic energy in a moving mass, with inductance playing the role of mass and current playing the role of velocity.

**henry, millihenry, microhenry**

**Units of inductance.** The inductance, $L$, depends on coil dimensions and the number of turns of wire in the coil. The inductance also depends on the material (if any) located near the coil. In particular, the magnetic properties of iron increase greatly the inductance of a coil wound on an iron core. The units of inductance are volt-seconds per ampere, but to honor Joseph Henry (1797–1878), we use the name *henry* (H) for this unit; *millihenries* ($10^{-3}$ H or mH) and *microhenries* ($10^{-6}$ H or $\mu$H) are also in common use.

---

**EXAMPLE 3.2** | **Stored magnetic-energy calculation**

Use the definition of an inductor to compute the voltage across, the power into, and the energy stored in a 2-H inductor with current shown in Fig. 3.5.

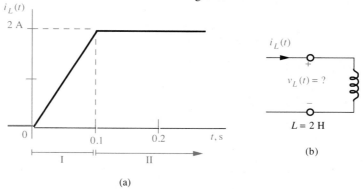

(a)

(b)

**Figure 3.5** A changing current will produce a voltage.

**SOLUTION:**

Because the current function is piecewise continuous, we cannot represent it by a single mathematical formula, but rather must represent it separately in its several regions. During interval I, $0 < t < 0.1$ s, the slope is constant at 20 A/s; thus, during this period, the inductor voltage will be 2 H $\times$ (+20 A/s), or +40 V. During interval II, $0.1$ s $< t < \infty$, the slope is zero and hence the voltage will be zero also.

When we compute the power into the inductor as the product of $v_L$ and $i_L$, we note that the power is positive during interval I and zero during II.

During interval I, $i_L = +20t$ and hence:

$$p_L(t) = +v_L i_L = \frac{d}{dt}(+2 \times 20t) \times 20t = +800t \text{ W} \tag{3.6}$$

where we have used Eq. (3.1) to calculate the inductor voltage. The magnetic energy stored in the inductor can be computed by integrating the input power, but the easier way uses Eq. (3.5), with the results shown in Fig. 3.6. During interval I, when the current is increasing in magnitude, we must supply power to the inductor to increase the stored magnetic energy.

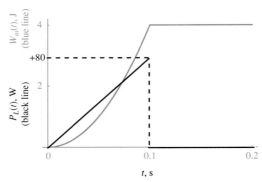

**Figure 3.6** The power curve (blue) is the slope of the stored energy.

$$W_m(t) = \frac{1}{2} L i_L^2 = \frac{1}{2} \times 2(20t)^2 = 400t^2 \text{ J} \tag{3.7}$$

During interval II, the current is constant and hence no energy is exchanged between inductor and source: The system "coasts forever" like a mass in constant motion.

**WHAT IF?** What if the times in Fig. 3.5 were doubled such that the current increased from 0 to 2 A in 0.2 second, etc.? Which of the following would not change in magnitude: inductor voltage, inductor power, final inductor stored energy?[3]

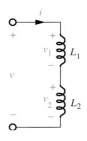

**Figure 3.7** The circuit model for a coil of wire must contain a resistance to account for loss.

**Conservation of Energy**

**Equivalent Circuits**

**Figure 3.8**
Inductors in series add like resistors in series.

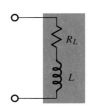

**Model for a real inductor.** The wire in a physical inductor would have resistance and would not store all the energy delivered to it. Some of the energy would heat the wire and be lost to the electrical circuit. This energy is not lost to the entire physical system because it appears as thermal energy. The equivalent circuit model for a real coil of wire, shown in Fig. 3.7, accounts for loss as well as the storage of magnetic energy.

An inductor that uses a ferromagnetic material such as iron to increase the magnetic energy storage will have losses and possibly some nonlinearities from the iron. For such inductors, the simple linear model in Fig. 3.7 may be inadequate. We will deal with such magnetic structures in Chapters 13 and 14.

**Inductors in series and parallel.** Figure 3.8 shows two inductors in series, which we may replace by a single equivalent inductor. KVL yields

$$v = v_1 + v_2 = \frac{dL_1 i}{dt} + \frac{dL_2 i}{dt} = \frac{d(L_1 + L_2)i}{dt} = \frac{dL_{eq} i}{dt} \tag{3.8}$$

where $L_{eq} = L_1 + L_2$ (series inductors). Thus, inductors in series add like resistors in series. Similarly, one can show that inductors in parallel add like resistors in parallel,

---

[3] The inductor voltage and power depend on rates of change, but the final stored energy depends only on the current and would not change in magnitude.

$$L_{eq} = L_1 \| L_2 = \frac{1}{1/L_1 + 1/L_2} \text{ (parallel inductors)} \tag{3.9}$$

## Capacitor Basics

**Physical capacitors.** Electric (electrostatic) forces arise from interactions between separated charges, and the associated energy is called electric energy. To store electric energy, we must separate charges, as in Fig. 3.9.

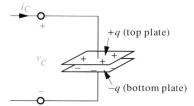

**Figure 3.9**  Structure having capacitance.

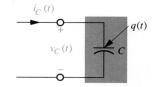

**Figure 3.10**  Circuit symbol for capacitance.

**Circuit-theory definition of a capacitor.** Figure 3.10 shows the circuit symbol for a capacitance. Capacitance is defined as the constant relating charge and voltage in a structure that supports a charge separation. If $q$ is the charge on the + side of the capacitor and the voltage is $v_C$, as shown in Fig. 3.9, the capacitance, $C$, is defined as

$$q = Cv_C \tag{3.10}$$

Chapter 13 discusses the physics of capacitance. For every charge arriving at the + side of the capacitor, a charge of like sign will depart from the − side and the structure as a whole will remain charge-neutral. Thus, KCL will be obeyed because charge flowing into the + terminal side is matched by charge flowing out of the − terminal, as for a resistor. If current is positive into the + terminal, positive charge will accumulate there and will be increasing in proportion to the current. From the definition of current, we can relate the charge in Eq. (3.10) and current as follows:

$$i_C = \frac{dq(t)}{dt} \tag{3.11}$$

where $q(t)$ is the charge in the + side of the capacitor. Thus, we may define the relationship between current and voltage for a capacitor as

$$i_C = \frac{d}{dt} \, Cv_C(t) = C\frac{dv_C(t)}{dt} \tag{3.12}$$

where the last form of Eq. (3.12) is valid if the capacitance is constant. Note that we have used a load set in Fig. 3.10 for the voltage and current variables.

**farad, microfarad, nanofarad, picofarad**

**Units of capacitance.** The unit of capacitance is the coulomb/volt, but to honor Michael Faraday (1791–1867), we use the name *farad* (F). Realistic capacitor values come small and usually are specified in microfarads ($10^{-6}$ F, or μF), nanofarads ($10^{-9}$ F, or nF), or picofarads ($10^{-12}$ F, or pF). When a capacitor is constructed from parallel

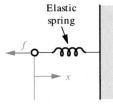

Elastic
spring

$f = Kx$ (reaction)

$u = \dfrac{dx}{dt} = \dfrac{1}{K}\dfrac{df}{dt}$

**Figure 3.11**
Mechanical analog for
capacitance.

plates, as in Fig. 3.9, the capacitance depends on the area, separation, and material (if any) between the plates.

**Mechanical analog of capacitance.** The mechanical analog of a capacitor is a spring, as shown in Fig. 3.11. The analog of velocity is current and thus displacement of the spring is analogous to charge. The voltage across a capacitor is analogous to the force produced by the spring. Comparison of the second equation in Fig. 3.11 with Eq. (3.12) shows that capacitance corresponds to the inverse of the stiffness constant, $K$, and thus capacitance is analogous to the compliance of a spring.

---

**EXAMPLE 3.3** | **Equation of RC circuit**

Derive the equation for the current in Fig. 3.12(a). Assume $v_C(0) = 0$.

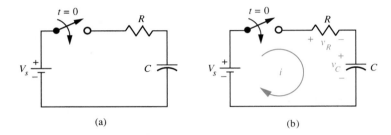

(a)                                    (b)

**Figure 3.12**   (a) Closing the switch will cause a momentary current. (b) The same circuit with variables defined.

**SOLUTION:**
Figure 3.12(b) defines the capacitor and resistor voltages in a load-set convention. With the switch closed, KVL is

$$-V_s + v_R(t) + v_C(t) = 0 \tag{3.13}$$

We may express both voltages in terms of the current if we differentiate Eq. (3.13):

$$0 + \frac{d}{dt}Ri(t) + \frac{dv_C(t)}{dt} = R\frac{di(t)}{dt} + \frac{i(t)}{C} = 0 \tag{3.14}$$

The last form in Eq. (3.14) is readily manipulated to the form

$$\frac{di}{i} = -\frac{1}{RC}\,dt \Rightarrow \ln i = -\frac{t}{RC} + \ln A \Rightarrow i(t) = Ae^{-t/RC} \tag{3.15}$$

where $A$ is a constant. The current will charge the capacitor until the capacitor voltage is equal to the battery voltage. Equation (3.16) equates the final charge on $C$ to the integral of the current.

$$q - q(0) = CV_s = \int_0^\infty i(t)\, dt = \left. \frac{Ae^{-t/RC}}{-1/RC} \right|_0^\infty = A(RC) \tag{3.16}$$

Because $v_C(0) = 0$, $q(0) = 0$, and the initial current is

$$i(o) = A = \frac{V_s}{R} \tag{3.17}$$

hence

$$i(t) = \frac{V_s}{R} e^{-t/RC} \tag{3.18}$$

**WHAT IF?**

What if the switch is opened after being closed a long time? What would happen to the capacitor voltage?[4]

**Integral _i–v_ equation.**  Equation (3.12) is useful in determining the current through a capacitor, given the voltage as a function of time. If we know the current and wish to determine the voltage, we must integrate. Let us consider that we know the capacitor voltage at some time, say, $t = 0$, and wish to determine the voltage at a later time, $t$. We can integrate Eq. (3.12) from 0 to $t$, with the result

$$v_C(t) = v_C(0) + \frac{1}{C} \int_0^t i_C(t')\, dt' \tag{3.19}$$

We have used $t'$ as the dummy variable of the integration process because $t$ is one limit of the integral.

| EXAMPLE 3.4 | Capacitor discharge and charge |

As an example of the use of Eq. (3.19), consider a capacitor with current, as shown in Fig. 3.13.

Here we know the voltage at the beginning time, $v_C(0) = -2$ V, and the current through the capacitor. We wish to compute the voltage for all $t > 0$. We will use Eq. (3.19), noting that we must divide the integration into several regions due to the piecewise nature of the current function. During interval I, $0 < t < 1$ ms, the current is zero; hence, the voltage does not change. During interval II, the slope of the current is 0.1 A/1 ms = 100 A/s; hence, the current is

---

[4] No current could flow after the switch opened, and according to Eq. (3.12), the voltage would remain constant. A real capacitor would discharge over time due to leakage current.

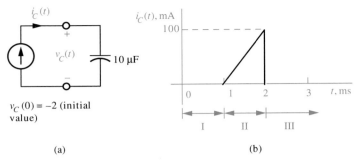

$v_C(0) = -2$ (initial value)

(a)

(b)

**Figure 3.13** (a) The capacitor has an initial voltage. (b) Current into the capacitor for positive time.

$$i_C(t) = 100(t - 1\text{ ms}) \text{ A}, \qquad 1\text{ ms} < t < 2\text{ ms} \tag{3.20}$$

Thus, during interval II, the voltage will be

$$v_C(t) = -2.0 + \frac{1}{10\mu\text{F}} \int_{1\text{ ms}}^{t} 100\,(t' - 1\text{ms})\,dt'\Big|_{\text{II: }1 < t < 2\text{ ms}}$$

$$= -2.0 + \frac{10^{+5} \times 100\,(t - 1\text{ms})^2}{2} \text{ V} \tag{3.21}$$

which indicates a parabolic increase, as shown in Fig. 3.14. The final value at $t = 2$ ms is $+3$ V, which is easily checked from the area under the current curve:

$$\Delta v_C = \frac{\Delta q}{C} = \frac{\text{area under current curve}}{C} = \frac{\frac{1}{2} \times 1\text{ms} \times 100\text{ mA}}{10\ \mu\text{F}} = +5 \text{ V} \tag{3.22}$$

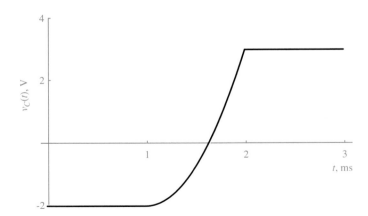

**Figure 3.14** Capacitor voltage for positive time.

After the current pulse, the capacitor voltage remains constant because the current is zero. This constant voltage would hold for an ideal capacitor; a physical capacitor would discharge eventually due to leakage current.

**WHAT IF?**

What if the current were constant at 100 mA for 1 ms $< t < 2$ ms? What then would be the final value?[5]

**Mechanical analogy.** The process of integrating current through a capacitor to determine voltage is analogous to integrating velocity to determine change in force in a spring problem. The only difference is that the value of the capacitance scales the integral of the current, whereas the scale factor depends on $K$, the spring constant, in the mechanical analog.

**Stored energy in a capacitor.** The charge separation in a capacitor stores electric energy. This energy is analogous to potential energy stored in a stressed spring. We may derive the stored electric energy in a capacitor by integrating the power into the capacitor,

$$W_e = \int p_C \, dt = \int v_C \times C \frac{dv_C}{dt} dt = \int d\left(\frac{1}{2} C v_C^2\right) = \frac{1}{2} C v_C^2 = \frac{1}{2}\frac{q^2}{C} \qquad (3.23)$$

where $p_C$ is the power into the capacitor and $W_e$ is the stored electric energy in the capacitor. The constant of integration must be zero because the uncharged capacitor stores no energy. We see from Eq. (3.23) that the stored energy depends uniquely on the voltage, or the charge, and the capacitance. For example, if we take a 10-μF capacitor and connect it briefly to a 12.6-V battery, the capacitor will receive $0.5 \times 10^{-5}(12.6)^2 = 7.94 \times 10^{-4}$ J from the battery. Although this is not much energy, it would take only about 1 μs to charge the capacitor. Hence, the rate of energy flow would be rather high, about 800 W.

**Capacitors in series and parallel.** Figure 3.15 shows two capacitors in series. KVL yields

$$v(t) = v_1 + v_2 = \frac{1}{C_1}\int_0^t i \, dt + \frac{1}{C_2}\int_0^t i \, dt = \frac{1}{C_{eq}}\int_0^t i \, dt \qquad (3.24)$$

where

$$C_{eq} = C_1 \| C_2 = \frac{1}{1/C_1 + 1/C_2} \quad \text{(series capacitors)}$$

Thus, capacitors connected in series combine numerically like resistors in parallel. Similarly, we can easily show that capacitors in parallel add like resistors in series, that is,

$$C_{eq} = C_1 + C_2 \quad \text{(parallel capacitors)} \qquad (3.25)$$

**Mechanical analog for resistance.** A mechanical analog for a resistance is frictional loss of a special type. Voltage is analogous to force, and current analogous to ve-

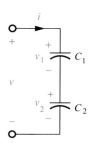

**Equivalent Circuits**

**Figure 3.15**
Capacitors in series add like resistors in parallel: $C_{eq} = C_1 \| C_2$.

[5] +8 V.

| TABLE 3.1 Summary of Mechanical and Electrical Analogs | |
| --- | --- |
| **Mechanical** | **Electrical** |
| Force | Voltage |
| Velocity | Current |
| Displacement | Charge |
| Mass | Inductance |
| Spring compliance | Capacitance |
| Shock absorber | Resistance |

locity. Voltage/current, or resistance, would thus imply a force that is proportional to velocity. We experience such a force when we try to move underwater. A common mechanical component having this property would be an automotive shock absorber. Table 3.1 summarizes the analogies between mechanical and electrical quantities.

### Check Your Understanding

1. An inductor has a stored energy of 5 J and an inductance of 0.1 H. What is the current through the inductor?

2. If an ideal 10-V battery were connected for 1 s to an ideal 1-H inductor, how much energy would be given to the inductor?

3. A capacitor has a stored energy of 500 μJ and a capacitance of 0.15 μF. What is the voltage across this capacitor?

4. What is the mechanical analog of an inductor?

*Answers.* **(1)** 10 A; **(2)** 50.0 J; **(3)** 81.6 V; **(4)** mass.

## 3.2 FIRST-ORDER TRANSIENT RESPONSE OF *RL* AND *RC* CIRCUITS

**transients, first-order transient**

**First-order transients.** In the major part of this chapter, we show how to analyze an important class of circuit problems. Typical situations are shown in Fig. 3.16. These circuits are characterized by having the following:

- ■ A single energy storage element, one capacitor or inductor
- ■ Loss, represented by one or more resistors
- ■ Constant sources
- ■ A switch[6] that either opens or closes at a known time, usually $t = 0$, causing a sudden change in the circuit
- ■ Only linear components.

In all cases, the circuit will have one dc state before the switch action and another dc state long after the switch action. Consequently, the state of the circuit goes through a transition. Because this transition lasts for a brief period of time, these problems are often called *transient* problems. We consider primarily circuits with one energy storage element, which lead to *first-order transients*.

---

[6] The pulse in Fig. 3.16(c) can be considered a voltage switched ON, then OFF.

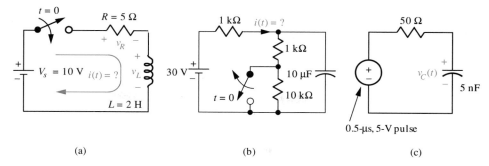

**Figure 3.16** Each circuit has one energy storage element, a constant source, and a sudden change.

These problems are important because they represent switching something on or off, which is often a critical period in the operation of a device. Also included in this class of problems are digital signals, such as a computer uses in processing information. Such digital signals can often be represented as a dc source being turned ON and OFF.

**system**

A *system* consists of several components that work together to accomplish some purpose. Thus, an electric circuit is a system. The type of circuits we will consider later are linear, so our results are typical of linear systems. Thus, in this section, we use some of the vocabulary associated with linear systems. Chapter 12 deals more fully with system theory.

## Classical Differential Equation Solution

**Deriving the differential equation.**  Our approach will be first to analyze a representative problem using the techniques of differential equations (DEs). Then we will develop a much simpler, more physical method that can also be applied to electrical, mechanical, thermal, or chemical problems that fall into the class described before. We now analyze the circuit of Fig. 3.16(a). With the switch open, the full 10 V appears across the switch because there is no current to cause a voltage across the resistor or the inductor. After the instant at which the switch is closed, KVL for the circuit is

$$-V_s + v_R(t) + v_L(t) = 0 \tag{3.26}$$

Equation (3.26) becomes a DE when we express $v_R$ and $v_L$ in terms of the unknown current, $i(t)$.

$$L\frac{di(t)}{dt} + Ri(t) = V_s, \qquad t > 0 \tag{3.27}$$

**steady-state or forced response**

**Form of the solution.**  Equation (3.27) is a linear DE with constant coefficients and a constant forcing term on the right side. The solution of a DE of this type usually proceeds by separating the unknown solution into two parts. In mathematics terminology, the parts are called the homogeneous part and the particular integral. In engineering terminology, the homogeneous part, the part of the solution identified with the voltage term on the right side of Eq. (3.27) is usually called the *forced response* or the *steady-state response*. In this problem, and all problems we solve in this chapter, this response must be constant because the forcing function is constant in time.

The *homogeneous solution* is determined by the left side of the equation, with the right side equal to zero. This part of the solution, also called in engineering terminology the *natural* or *transient response*, satisfies the equation with the forcing function set to zero. A linear DE with constant coefficients is always satisfied by a function of the form $e^{\alpha t}$, where $\alpha$ is an unknown constant with the dimensions of time$^{-1}$. The general solution to Eq. (3.27), therefore, must be of the form

$$i(t) = \underbrace{A}_{\substack{\text{forced} \\ \text{response}}} + \underbrace{Be^{\alpha t}}_{\substack{\text{natural} \\ \text{response}}} \tag{3.28}$$

where $A$, $B$, and $\alpha$ are unknown constants to be determined from Eq. (3.27) and the initial conditions of the circuit.

**Determining the unknown constants.** We can determine $A$ and $\alpha$ by substituting Eq. (3.28) back into Eq. (3.27).

$$LB(\alpha)e^{\alpha t} + R(A + Be^{\alpha t}) = V_s \tag{3.29}$$

The coefficient of the exponential term must vanish if the equation is valid for all times.

$$B(L\alpha + R)e^{\alpha t} + AR = V_s \Rightarrow \alpha = -\frac{R}{L} = -2.5 \text{ s}^{-1} \tag{3.30}$$

In engineering contexts, it is customary to express the exponential term in Eq. (3.28) in the form $e^{-t/\tau}$, where

$$\tau = -\frac{1}{\alpha} = \frac{L}{R} = \frac{2}{5} = 0.4 \text{ seconds} \tag{3.31}$$

for the circuit in Fig. 3.16(a). The *time constant*, $\tau$, is a characteristic time for the transient; we explore its significance shortly. Setting the coefficient of the exponential term to zero in Eq. (3.30) leads also to the value of $A$, the steady-state response.

$$AR = V_s \Rightarrow A = \frac{V_s}{R} = \frac{10}{5} = 2 \text{ A} \tag{3.32}$$

**Initial condition.** To determine $B$, we must consider the initial condition. The initial condition for this, and for all such systems, arises from consideration of energy. Time is required for energy to be exchanged and hence processes involving energy carry the system from one state to another, particularly when, as here, a sudden change occurs.

With the switch open, there is no current and no stored magnetic energy in the inductor. The closing of the switch will allow the inductor to store energy, but at the instant after the switch is closed, the stored energy must still be zero. Zero energy implies zero current because the stored energy in an inductor, Eq. (3.5), is $\frac{1}{2}Li^2$; hence, $i(0^+)$ is zero, where $0^+$ denotes the instant after the switch is closed. This condition leads to the value for $B$:

$$0 = A + Be^{-0/\tau} \Rightarrow B = -A = -2 \text{ amperes} \tag{3.33}$$

The final solution is given in Eq. (3.34) and plotted in Fig. 3.17.

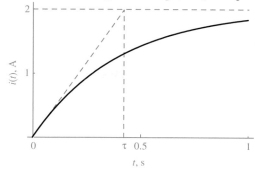

**Figure 3.17** Current for circuit in Fig. 3.16(a).

$$i\,(t) = \frac{V_s}{R} - \frac{V_s}{R}e^{-t/\tau} = 2 - 2e^{-t/0.4\ \text{s}}\ \text{A} \qquad (3.34)$$

**Physical interpretation of the solution.** The mathematical solution is complete, but we wish to examine carefully the physical interpretation of the response, for we will develop our simpler method from a physical understanding of this type of problem.

The current is zero before the switch is closed and approaches $V_s/R$ as a final value. This final value does not depend on the value of the inductor, but would be the current if no inductor were in the circuit. The inductor cannot matter in the end because we have a dc excitation in the circuit and eventually the current must reach a constant value. The constant current renders the inductor to act as a short circuit because an inductor will exert itself only when its current is changing.

Without the inductor, the current would change instantaneously from zero to $V_s/R$ when the switch is closed. The inductor effects a smooth transition between the initial and final values of the current. The smooth change moderated by the inductor takes place over a *characteristic time* of $\tau$, the *time constant*.

Note from Fig. 3.17 that the current initially increases with a rate as if to arrive at the final value in one time constant. This time constant for the *RL* circuit, $\tau = L/R$, can be understood from energy considerations. The inductor will require little energy if $L$ is small or $R$ is large; hence, the transition will be rapid for small $L/R$. But if the inductor is large or $R$ is small, much energy will eventually be stored in the inductor; hence, the transition period will be much longer for large $L/R$.

**Summary.** We see that the response consists of a transition between two constant states, an initial state and a final state. The energy storage element, the inductor, effects a smooth transition between these states. Because of the form of the DE for this class of problems, the transition between states is exponential and is characterized by a time constant. The stored energy in the inductor carries the state of the circuit across the instant of sudden change and leads directly or indirectly to the initial condition.

## A Simpler Method

We will now rework this problem using a more direct method. The goal is to write the circuit response directly based on physical understanding. There are four steps.

OBJECTIVE 3

To understand
how to analyze
first-order
transients by the
initial-value/final-
value method

1. **Find the time constant.** We already know the time constant for this type of problem, $\tau = L/R$, but in general, we can determine the time constant for a first-order system by putting the DE into the special form of Eq. (3.35). We divide by the coefficient of the linear term, so that $x$ appears in the equation without a multiplier.

$$\tau \frac{dx}{dt} + x = \text{constant} = x_\infty \tag{3.35}$$

In Eq. (3.35), $x$ refers to the physical quantity being determined. It would represent a voltage or current in a circuit problem, but in other physical systems, $x$ might represent a temperature, a velocity, or something else. When we put the DE in this form, $\tau$ will always be the characteristic time, the time constant. To put Eq. (3.27) into this form, we have to divide by $R$ to see that $\tau = L/R$ by this method.

Because the purpose of this method is to avoid DEs, we hesitate to suggest that you must write the DE to get started. Usually, you will know the equation of the time constant for the circuit or system from previous experience. For an *RL* circuit, for example, the time constant is always $L/R$. Because we solve circuits having only one energy storage element with this method, we have only one $L$. In Sec. 3.3, we show how to handle circuits with more than one resistor. Returning to the problem we are solving, we now know our time constant: $L/R = 0.4$ s for the circuit in Fig. 3.16(a).

2. **Find the initial condition.** The initial condition ($x_0$ in general, $i_0$ in this case) always follows from consideration of the energy condition of the system at the beginning of the transient. In this case, we argued earlier that because the inductor had no energy before the switch was closed, it must have no energy the instant after the switch is closed. Hence, the initial current is zero ($i_0 = 0$). Later, we discuss generally how to determine initial values in circuits.

3. **Find the final value.** The final value ($x_\infty$ in general, $i_\infty$ in this case) follows from the steady-state solution of the system. Earlier, we argued that the inductor approaches a short circuit. This is true because the final state of the circuit is a dc state, and the inductor has no voltage across it for a constant current. Thus, application of Ohm's law to the circuit in Fig. 3.16(a) shows that the final current must be $i_\infty = 2$ A.

If the DE has been written and put into the form of Eq. (3.35), then the final value is the constant on the right-hand side of the DE. In the final state, time derivatives must vanish and Eq. (3.35) reduces to $x = x_\infty$.

4. **Substitute the time constant and the initial and final values into a standard formula.**

$$x(t) = x_\infty + (x_0 - x_\infty)e^{-t/\tau} \tag{3.36}$$

Equation (3.36) is the solution for all first-order systems having dc (constant) excitation. In our case, the $x_0$ and $x_\infty$ are currents of known numerical value, so our solution is

$$i(t) = \frac{V_s}{R} + \left(0 - \frac{V_s}{R}\right)e^{-t/\tau}$$

$$= 2 + (0 - 2)e^{-t/0.4} \, \text{A} \tag{3.37}$$

As before, we see that as $t \rightarrow \infty$, $i(t) \rightarrow V/R = 2$ A, and initially $i(0) = 0$ because $e^0 = 1$. Equation (3.37) describes a *rising* exponential because the current begins at zero and increases to a final value.

Figure 3.18 shows a generalized plot of Eq. (3.36). The curve starts at $x_0$ and asymptotes to $x_\infty$. Its initial slope is such as to move from $x_0$ to $x_\infty$ in one time constant, but it only reaches $(1 - e^{-1})$ or 63% of the way during the first time constant. You might note that we have shown a discontinuity at the origin. This can happen in general, although it does not happen in our present example. We show a *falling* exponential in Fig. 3.18 because the curve decreases to a final value. The sign of the exponential determines whether the curve rises or falls.

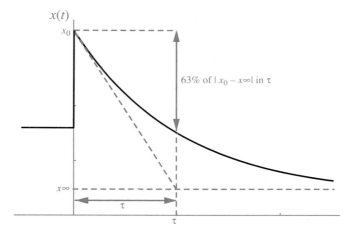

**Figure 3.18** Generalized response in Eq. (3.36).

**Summary.** Our direct method consists of determining three constants and substituting these into a standard formula. The time constant can be determined from the DE, but usually the formula for $\tau$ is known from prior experience. The other two constants are the initial value of the unknown, which is determined from energy considerations, and the final value, which is determined from the dc (static) solution. The energy storage element effects a smooth transition between the initial and final values and influences the initial value through energy considerations.

| EXAMPLE 3.5 | Same Circuit, Find the Voltage |
|---|---|

Determine the voltage across the inductor in Fig. 3.16(a).

**SOLUTION:**
We already know the time constant. The initial condition $v_L(0^+)$ follows indirectly from energy

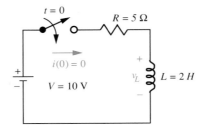

**Figure 3.19**    Because $i(0^+) = 0$, $v_L = V_S$.

considerations. The initial energy in the inductor is zero, which implies zero current. Consider the state of the circuit in Fig. 3.16(a) at the instant after the switch is closed, as shown in Fig. 3.19. Because of the inductor, there can be no current at this initial instant; hence there can be no voltage across the resistor. If there is no voltage across the resistor and no voltage across the switch, the full 10 V of the battery must appear across the inductor. Hence, the initial value of the inductor voltage is 10 V.

The final value of the inductor voltage must be zero because we have a dc source and eventually the current becomes constant. Consequently, $di/dt$ approaches zero, and the inductor voltage must also approach zero. We now know the time constant, the initial value, and the final value, and therefore we can write the full solution with our standard form,

$$v_L(t) = 0 + (10 - 0)\,e^{-t/0.4} = 10e^{-t/0.4} \text{ V} \tag{3.38}$$

The plot of Eq. (3.38) is shown in Fig. 3.20. Notice that we have shown a discontinuity in the inductor voltage at the origin. Before the switch closes, the inductor has no voltage. When the switch closes, the current begins to increase, but the inductor voltage instantly jumps to 10 V to oppose that increase. The initial rate of increase of the current is limited to

$$10 = 2\,\frac{di}{dt}\bigg|_{t=0^+} \quad \Rightarrow \quad \frac{di}{dt} = \frac{10}{2} = 5\,\frac{\text{A}}{\text{s}} \tag{3.39}$$

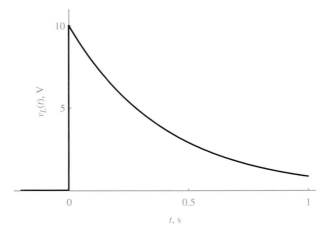

**Figure 3.20.**    Inductor voltage in Fig 3.16(a).

As the current increases, the voltage across the resistor increases accordingly, and the voltage across the inductor decreases. Finally, the current increases to a level where it is limited by the resistor. Thus, the inductor dominates the beginning and the resistor dominates the end of the transient.

**WHAT IF?**    What if we want the time when the stored energy in the inductor is one-half its final value?[7]

## RC **Circuits**

We have already written the DE for the *RC* circuit shown in Fig. 3.12(a) in Eq. (3.14). There we solved the problem by direct mathematical analysis. Here we will merely extract from that work the time constant for an *RC* circuit. We may put the last form of Eq. (3.14) into the required form for Eq. (3.35) by multiplying by *C*. The result is

$$RC \, \frac{di\,(t)}{dt} + i\,(t) = 0 \qquad\qquad (3.40)$$

and hence the time constant is

$$\tau = RC \qquad\qquad (3.41)$$

This will be the time constant for *all RC* circuits whether the resistor and capacitor are in series or parallel.

Armed with this result, we will now apply our direct method to the *RC* circuit shown in Fig. 3.12(a) with $R = 1000 \,\Omega$, $C = 1 \,\mu F$, and $V_s = 100$ V, which we repeat in Fig. 3.21. We will determine the voltage across the resistor, $v_R(t)$, assuming zero initial energy in the capacitor.

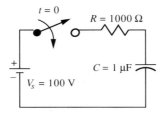

**Figure 3.21**   Figure 3.16(a) repeated with $C = 1 \,\mu F$ and $R = 1000 \,\Omega$.

**Time constant.**  From Eq. (3.41), the time constant for this circuit $\tau = RC = 1000 \times 10^{-6} = 1$ ms.

**Find the initial condition.**   The initial condition emerges from consideration of energy. The electric energy stored in a capacitor is given in Eq. (3.23) as $\frac{1}{2} C v_C^2$. The capacitor is unenergized at $t = 0^-$, the instant before the switch is closed. Hence it remains unenergized at $t = 0^+$, the instant after the switch is closed, because finite time

-------

[7]0.491 s.

is required for energy to be stored in the capacitor. At $t = 0^+$, therefore, KVL around the loop is

$$-100 + v_R(0^+) + \underbrace{v_C(0^+)}_{0} = 0 \Rightarrow v_R(0^+) = 100 \text{ V} \tag{3.42}$$

**Find the final value.** The final value of the resistor voltage follows from the requirement that the voltage and current eventually become constant. Because $dv_C/dt$ is zero, $i$ is zero, and $v_R$ must therefore be zero as $t \to \infty$.

**Substitute the time constant and the initial and final values into the standard form.** Now that we know the time constant, the initial value, and the final value for $v_R$, we substitute into the standard form of Eq. (3.36).

$$v_R(t) = 0 + (V_s - 0)e^{-t/\tau}$$

$$= 100\,e^{-t/1\text{ ms}} \text{ V} \tag{3.43}$$

Equation (3.43) is plotted in Fig. 3.22. As the current flows, charge accumulates and builds up voltage across the capacitor. The voltage across the resistor must diminish with time and eventually vanish. When the full voltage of the battery appears across the capacitor, the current stops.

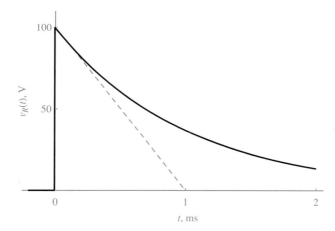

**Figure 3.22** Resistor voltage in Fig 3.21.

**Summary.** We have developed a direct method for analyzing first-order transient circuits involving one resistor and one inductor or capacitor. The method consists of determining the time constant, initial value, and final value of the unknown, and substituting into a standard formula. In the next section, we extend and generalize this method.

## 3.3 ADVANCED TECHNIQUES

**Equivalent Circuits**

### Circuits with Multiple Resistors

**Thévenin equivalent circuit.** Circuits with one inductor or capacitor but more than one resistor can be analyzed with the concept of equivalent circuits. The circuit in

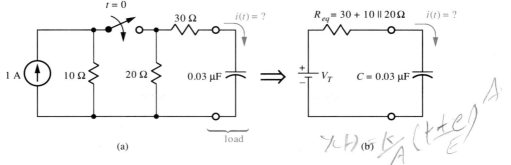

**Figure 3.23** (a) The three resistors can be combined using a Thévenin equivalent circuit; (b) the time constant is easily identified in this equivalent circuit.

Fig. 3.23(a), for example, can be reduced to the equivalent circuit in Fig. 3.23(b). From this equivalent circuit, clearly the time constant is $R_{eq}C$, where $R_{eq}$ is the output impedance of the circuit with all sources turned OFF and the switch closed. Thus, $R_{eq}$ is the output impedance of the circuit to the capacitor as a load. In this case, $R_{eq}$ is $30 + 20 \parallel 10 = 36.7 \, \Omega$, and thus $\tau$ is $36.7 \times 0.03 \times 10^{-6}$ or $1.1 \, \mu s$.

We may or may not be interested in the Thévenin equivalent circuit as a means for calculating the initial or final values of the unknown. That is a separate problem to be approached by the most efficient method. It is the *concept* of the Thévenin circuit, specifically the concept of the output impedance, or impedance level, that leads to the time constant for a transient circuit with multiple resistors. In general, the relevant resistance for the time constant is the output resistance presented to the energy storage element as a load.

---

**EXAMPLE 3.6** | **Three $R$'s and a $C$**

Find the time constant for the circuit of Fig. 3.16(b) for $t > 0$.

**SOLUTION:**
Here we clearly should not replace the circuit external to the capacitor with a Thévenin equivalent circuit, for then we would eliminate the unknown, $i(t)$. We invoke the concept of the equivalent circuit only to calculate the equivalent resistance seen by the capacitor with the switch open, $(1 \, k\Omega + 10 \, k\Omega) \parallel 1 \, k\Omega$ or $917 \, \Omega$. Thus, $\tau = 917 \times 10 \, \mu F = 9.17 \, ms$. We continue this example in what follows.

**WHAT IF?** What would be the time constant if the switch were closed at $t = 0$?[8]

---

initial and final values

## Initial and Final Values

**What we mean by "initial" and "final."** We now look generally at how to calculate the initial and final values. By *initial* we mean the instant after a change occurs

---

[8] $\tau = 5 \, ms$.

in the circuit, usually a switch closing or opening. This does not have to be the time origin, although often we define $t = 0$ as the time of switch action. By *final* we mean the steady-state condition of the circuit, its state after a large period of time. The final state may be hypothetical because the circuit may never reach that state due to subsequent switch action. We may first close a switch and then open it before the circuit reaches the final state. The circuit cannot anticipate the second switch action and hence reacts to the first switch action as if it *would* reach steady state. In this section, we develop guidelines for determining the final and initial states of the circuit.

### Determining final values.

Final values arise out of the eventual steady state of the circuit. All time derivatives must eventually vanish. Consequently, the current through capacitors and the voltage across inductors must approach zero, as suggested in

$$v_C \rightarrow \text{constant} \ \Rightarrow \ i_C = C\frac{dv_C}{dt} \rightarrow 0 \quad \text{as } t \rightarrow \infty$$

$$i_L \rightarrow \text{constant} \ \Rightarrow \ v_L = L\frac{di_L}{dt} \rightarrow 0 \quad \text{as } t \rightarrow \infty$$

(3.44)

Thus, capacitors act as open circuits and inductors act as short circuits in establishing final values, as shown in Figs. 3.24 and 3.25, respectively.

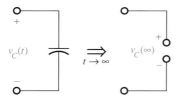

**Figure 3.24** The capacitor behaves as an open circuit as time becomes large.

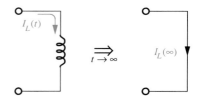

**Figure 3.25** The inductor behaves as a short circuit as time becomes large.

### Determining initial values.

Initial values always follow from energy considerations, The fundamental principle is that the stored electric energy in a capacitor and the stored magnetic energy in an inductor must be continuous. From continuity of energy, we conclude that the voltage across a capacitor and the current through an inductor must be continuous functions of time. Thus, we always calculate capacitor voltage or inductor current before the switch is thrown and then carry this value over to the moment after the switch is thrown. From these known values of the capacitor voltage or inductor current, required circuit unknowns can be calculated.

A model for an energized capacitor at the instant after the switch action is shown in Fig. 3.26. For that first instant, the charged capacitor acts like a voltage source because the voltage across the capacitor cannot change instantaneously. As current flows through the capacitor, its voltage will change, and hence the capacitor acts as a battery *only* at that first instant. Similarly, a current source models an energized inductor at the instant after switch action, as shown in Fig. 3.27. Although these models are valid only for the first instant of the new regime, they suffice for the calculation of the initial values of the circuit unknowns of interest.

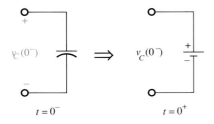

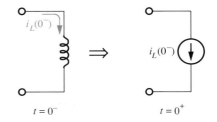

**Figure 3.26** A battery models the initial voltage of the capacitor.

**Figure 3.27** A current source models the initial current of the inductor.

**EXAMPLE 3.7** **Three *R*'s and an *L***

Find the voltage across the inductor in Fig. 3.28 after the switch is opened at $t = 0$.

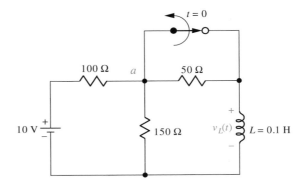

**Figure 3.28** After being closed a long time, the switch is opened.

**SOLUTION:**

The switch is opened after having been closed for a time long enough to establish steady state throughout the circuit. We determine the voltage across the inductor after the switch is opened. We first calculate the inductor current at the instant before the switch is opened. We note that with the switch closed and with the circuit in steady state, the 50-$\Omega$ resistor is short-circuited by the switch and the 150-$\Omega$ resistor is shorted by the switch and the dormant inductor. Thus, the current from the battery is 10 V/100 $\Omega$ or 0.1 A and this current flows through the switch and inductor.

This information does not give us the initial value of $v_L(t)$ directly, but it leads indirectly to the initial value through the analysis of the circuit in Fig. 3.29. We have replaced the inductor by a current source and eliminated the switch because it is now an open circuit. As you can see, we have labeled the circuit to suggest solution by nodal analysis. You may confirm that $v_a$ is zero at $t = 0^+$. From this information, we can calculate $v_L$ from KVL around the right-hand loop, with the result that $v_L(0^+) = -5$ V.

The time constant is $L/R_{eq}$, where $R_{eq}$ is the equivalent resistance seen by the inductor with the switch open. Thus, $R_{eq}$ is 50 + 150 ∥ 100 or 110 $\Omega$, and the time constant is 0.1/110 or 909 μs. Because the final value of the inductor voltage is zero, the full solution is

$$v_L(t) = 0 + (-5 - 0)\, e^{-t/909\ \mu s} = -5 e^{-t/909\ \mu s}\ \text{V} \tag{3.45}$$

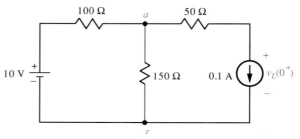

**Figure 3.29** Equivalent circuit at $t = 0^+$.

**WHAT IF?**

What if, after being open a long time, the switch is closed at $t = 0$? What is $v_L$ for that case?[9]

**Summary.** An energized capacitor acts as a voltage source in the calculation of initial values. A special case is an unenergized capacitor, which acts as a short circuit. In the calculation of final values, a capacitor acts as an open circuit.

An energized inductor acts as a current source in the calculation of initial values. A special case is an unenergized inductor, which acts as an open circuit. For final values, an inductor acts as a short circuit. We can solve for initial and final values by replacing capacitors and inductors by these models.

The initial and final values thus are derived from the analysis of a circuit containing only resistors and sources. These principles are valid for circuits containing multiple inductors and capacitors, which lead to higher-order DEs that cannot be solved by our four-step procedure. We introduce the transient analysis of such circuits in what follows, but deal fully with them in Chapter 12.

---

**EXAMPLE 3.8** | **Three *R*'s and a *C* (continued)**

Determine $i(t)$ for the circuit of Fig. 3.16(b).

**SOLUTION:**

We have already determined the time constant to be $\tau = RC = 9.17$ ms. To find the initial value, we must determine the voltage across the capacitor at $t = 0^+$. At the instant before the opening of the switch, the circuit will be in steady state; indeed, this is the final state from previous actions that established the circuit. Thus, the capacitor will act as an open circuit, as shown in Fig. 3.30.

The voltage across $C$ is 15 V because the 30 V of the source divides equally between the two 1-k$\Omega$ resistors, the 10-k$\Omega$ resistor being shorted by the switch. Consequently, the circuit that must be analyzed for the initial value of $i(t)$ is shown in Fig. 3.31. Notice that $i(0^+)$ can

---

[9] $v_L = 2.727 e^{-\tau/1.67 \text{ ms}}$.

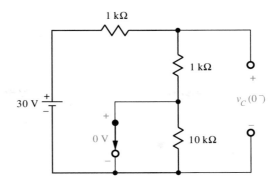

**Figure 3.30** The capacitor acts as an open circuit in the steady state before the switch is opened.

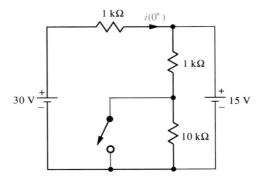

**Figure 3.31** The capacitor now acts as a battery in the initial-value calculation.

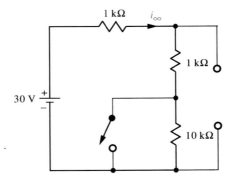

**Figure 3.32** Equivalent circuit for final-value calculation.

be determined by writing KVL around the outer loop containing the two sources, with the result $i(0^+) = 15$ mA.

The final value of $i(t)$ can be established from the equivalent circuit in Fig. 3.32, where the capacitor is again treated as an open circuit. The value of $i_\infty$ is easily derived from this series circuit: $i_\infty = 30$ V/12 k$\Omega$ = 2.5 mA. We now have determined the time constant, the initial value, and the final value; hence, the solution follows from Eq. (3.36).

$$i = 2.5 + (15 - 2.5)e^{-t/9.17\,\text{ms}}\ \text{mA} \tag{3.46}$$

**WHAT IF?**  What would be $i(t)$ if the switch were closed after being open a long time?[10]

## Pulse Problem

**Pulse circuits.**  We now consider the circuit in Fig. 3.16(c) as detailed in Fig. 3.33. Although this problem appears to differ significantly from the others, we can analyze it with the same techniques. The pulse is treated as a dc voltage that is turned ON, then OFF before steady state is reached.

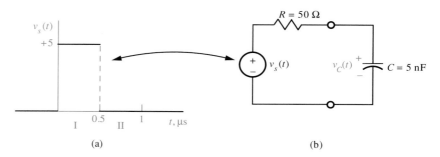

(a)                                    (b)

**Figure 3.33**  (a) Voltage pulse; (b) the capacitor is uncharged when the pulse begins.

**Charging transient.**  We assume that the capacitor is initially unenergized. When the source voltage jumps to +5 V, current will flow, and the capacitor will begin charging toward +5 V. Bear in mind that the circuit cannot anticipate the end of the pulse, but will respond as if a 5-V battery were attached. Thus, the transient proceeds toward a final value, even though that value will never be attained. During interval I, the time constant will be $RC = 0.25\ \mu$s, the initial value will be zero, and the final value would be +5 V. Thus, the capacitor voltage during interval I will be

$$v_C(t) = 5 + (0 - 5)e^{-t/0.25\,\mu\text{s}} = 5(1 - e^{-t/0.25\,\mu\text{s}})\ \text{V} \tag{3.47}$$

---

[10] $i(t) = 15 + (2.5 - 15)e^{-t/5\,\text{ms}}$ mA.

**Discharging transient.** When the end of the pulse comes along $0.5\,\mu s$ after the leading edge (the beginning), the capacitor now has a voltage across it. Because the pulse width is twice the time constant, the value of the capacitor voltage at the beginning of the second transient would be $5(1 - e^{-2}) = 4.32\,V$. This becomes the initial value for the transient during interval II. During this interval, the voltage source is OFF and thus is equivalent to a short circuit. The situation in interval II is therefore that shown in Fig. 3.34. We know the initial voltage, the final value is clearly zero, and the time constant is unchanged. Hence the capacitor voltage during interval II is

$$v_C(t) = 0 + (4.32 - 0)\,e^{-t'/0.25\,\mu s}, \qquad t' > 0$$

$$= 4.32\,\exp\left(-\frac{t - 0.5\mu s}{0.25\mu s}\right)V, \qquad t > 0.5\mu s \tag{3.48}$$

where $t'$ is time counted from the beginning of interval II. For example, at $t = 1\,\mu s$, we calculate the voltage to be

$$v_C(1\,\mu s) = 4.32\,e^{-(1.0-0.5)/0.25} = 0.585\,V \tag{3.49}$$

Putting the two parts of the transient together, we plot the results in Fig. 3.35.

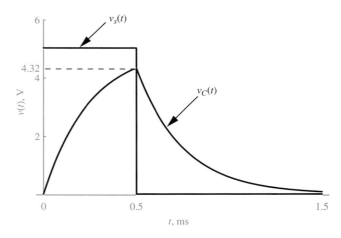

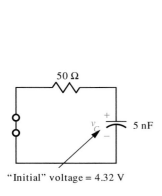

"Initial" voltage = 4.32 V

**Figure 3.34** During interval II, the "initial" voltage is 4.32 V.

**Figure 3.35** The capacitor voltage is a distorted version of the input pulse.

**Comparing a pulse with a battery–switch.** It is interesting to contrast the pulse problem with that shown in Fig. 3.36. Here we simulate the pulse with a battery and a switch that closes for $0.5\,\mu s$. The charging part of the transient will be the same as for the pulse problem, but when the switch is opened, there is no discharge path for the capacitor. Hence, the capacitor will charge up to 4.32 V in both cases, but with the battery–switch, no discharge will occur.[11]

---

[11] Except discharge that is due to leakage. This discharge will take place over a long period of time compared with the time constant if the physical circuit is well represented by the circuit model.

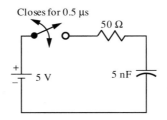

Figure 3.36 The battery–switch has the same Thévenin voltage but different output impedance from the pulse source.

**Impedance Level**

We can understand the difference between the pulse source and the battery–switch source by considering the Thévenin equivalent circuits for each. The Thévenin voltage source is the same for both, but the impedance level differs. With the switch closed, the output impedance is 50 Ω for both cases, but with the switch open, the output impedance becomes infinite (an open circuit) for the battery-switch source.

**A puzzle.** While we are considering battery-switch sources, let us consider what would happen in the circuit of Fig. 3.16(a) if we opened the switch after the current is established. Energy considerations require that the current in the inductor continue after the switch is opened. But no current can flow through an open switch. What will happen?

This question can be answered on two levels. At the theoretical level, we must outlaw this situation. We have created our dilemma by violating the definitions of the circuit elements we are using. Strictly speaking, we can no more open the switch on an energized inductor than we can short circuit an ideal voltage source—the definitions of these elements are contradictory. On the theoretical level, opening the switch on an inductor is like setting $1 = 0$ in mathematics—it is nonsense.

But this answer does not fully satisfy us, does it? There are, after all, real inductors and real switches. What happens when we perform the experiment? If you try it, you will witness a spark when you open a switch connected in series with an energized inductor. The voltage across the inductor, and hence the voltage across the switch, rises instantaneously to a high value, such that the air between the switch contacts becomes ionized. The ionized air provides a resistive path for deenergizing the inductor. Indeed, this is the principle behind the conventional automotive ignition system: the coil is the inductor, the points are the switch, and you know where the spark occurs.

## Higher-Order Transients

**Introduction.** This chapter, after introducing inductors and capacitors, has focused on first-order transients. We have analyzed circuits containing one energy-storage element by a method that built the solution out of the time constant, the initial and final values, and a standard formula.

Our method fails, however, when a circuit has two or more independent[12] energy-storage elements. In this concluding section, we give a brief introduction to such higher-order transients, and in Chapter 12 we develop a powerful method for analyzing this type of circuit.

---

[12]Two or more capacitors or inductors in series or parallel act as a single energy-storage element.

**Two capacitors.** Figure 3.37 shows a circuit with two capacitors, two resistors, two loops, and two nodes. We draw the circuit to indicate battery-switch input and an output voltage across $C_2$. The capacitors are initially uncharged (zero volts); we will find output voltage, $v_2$.

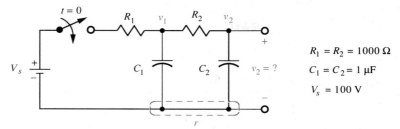

**Figure 3.37** Two independent capacitors will lead to a second-order DE.

**Deriving the DE.** We mentioned loops and nodes because we must choose how to analyze the circuit. We have chosen nodal analysis and labeled the circuit accordingly. Using the standard procedure, augmented by the definition of a capacitor, Eq. (3.12), we write KCL for node 1 as

$$\frac{v_1 - V_s}{R_1} + C_1\frac{dv_1}{dt} + \frac{v_1 - v_2}{R_2} = 0 \tag{3.50}$$

where the middle term is the current through $C_1$ to the reference node. Similarly, KCL for node 2 is

$$\frac{v_2 - v_1}{R_2} + C_2\frac{dv_2}{dt} = 0 \tag{3.51}$$

We develop the DE for $v_2$ by eliminating $v_1$ between Eqs. (3.50) and (3.51), which yields

$$C_1 C_2 \frac{d^2 v_2}{dt^2} + \left(\frac{C_2}{R_1} + \frac{C_1 + C_2}{R_2}\right)\frac{dv_2}{dt} + \frac{v_2}{R_1 R_2} = \frac{V_s}{R_1 R_2} \tag{3.52}$$

**Form of the solution.** We anticipate a solution of the form[13]

$$v_2(t) = A + Be^{\alpha t} \tag{3.53}$$

and generally we proceed as in the classical DE solution on page 116. However, the algebra gets out of hand quickly if we retain the symbolic notation, so we will use numbers from here on. We substitute $V_s = 100$ V, $R_1 = R_2 = 1000\ \Omega$, and $C_1 = C_2 = 1\ \mu$F, and calculate the coefficients as

---

[13] Because the circuit is second order, we will find two values of $\alpha$ that satisfy the circuit conditions and add a second exponential term.

$$10^{-12}\frac{d^2v_2}{dt^2} + 3 \times 10^{-9}\frac{dv_2}{dt} + 10^{-6}v_2 = 10^{-4} \tag{3.54}$$

Substitution of Eq. (3.53) into Eq. (3.54) yields

$$[(10^{-12})\,\alpha^2 + (3 \times 10^{-9})\,\alpha + 10^{-6}]\,Be^{\alpha t} + 10^{-6}A = 10^{-4} \tag{3.55}$$

which can be valid at all times only if

$$(10^{-12})\,\alpha^2 + (3 \times 10^{-9})\,\alpha + 10^{-6} = 0 \qquad \text{and} \qquad 10^{-6}A = 10^{-4} \tag{3.56}$$

The quadratic equation yields two roots, $\alpha_1 = -382$ and $\alpha_2 = -2618$, and the linear equation yields $A = 100$. Because we have two $\alpha$'s, we split the $B$ in Eq. (3.53) into two constants, and write the solution in the form

$$v_2(t) = 100 + B_1e^{-382t} + B_2e^{-2618t} \tag{3.57}$$

Before proceeding with the analysis, we need to relate Eq. (3.57) to our earlier results. We should not be surprised to learn that this second-order circuit has two time constants:

$$\tau_1 = \frac{1}{382} = 2.62 \text{ ms} \qquad \text{and} \qquad \tau_2 = \frac{1}{2618} = 382 \text{ }\mu s \tag{3.58}$$

Nor should we be surprised, after examining Fig. 3.37, to find the constant term is 100 V, because that would be the voltage across $C_2$ if we replace both capacitors with open circuits.

**Initial conditions.** To determine $B_1$ and $B_2$, we need to consider the initial conditions for the circuit. When the switch closes at $t = 0$, both capacitors will have zero volts and will act as short circuits. The voltage across $C_2$ cannot change instantaneously, so the initial condition on $v_2(t)$ is

$$\underbrace{v_2(0^+)}_{0} = 100 + B_1e^0 + B_2e^0 = 0 \;\Rightarrow\; B_1 + B_2 = -100 \tag{3.59}$$

Furthermore, the current through $R_1$ at $t = 0^+$ will all pass through $C_1$, because that path is a short circuit compared with the parallel path through $R_2$ and $C_2$. Thus, the initial current through $C_2$ will be zero, and the initial condition on $v_2(t)$ will be

$$\left.\frac{dv_2}{dt}\right|_{t=0^+} = 0 \;\Rightarrow\; B_1\,(+\alpha_1)\,e^{\alpha_1 t} + B_2\,(+\alpha_2)\,e^{\alpha_2 t} = 0 \tag{3.60}$$

Simultaneous solution of Eqs. (3.59) and (3.60) yields $B_1 = -117.1$ V and $B_2 = +17.1$ V; hence, the output voltage of the circuit in Fig. 3.37 is

$$v_2(t) = 100 - 117.1\,e^{-t/2.62\,\text{ms}} + 17.1\,e^{-t/382\,\mu s} \text{ V} \tag{3.61}$$

which is plotted in Fig. 3.38. The response is dominated by the longer time constant, with the shorter time constant showing its effect in keeping the slope zero at $t = 0^+$.

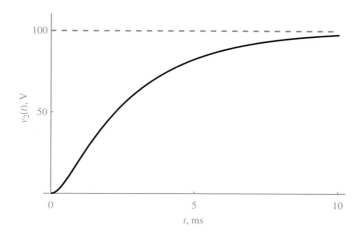

Figure 3.38 The second-order response looks like first-order except for the zero slope at the origin.

**Summary.** Although the analysis of the two-capacitor circuit in Fig. 3.37 was accomplished through a combination of classical DE and circuit-theory methods, nothing new emerged. We cannot use the initial-value/final-value method, but we still have time constants and the response looks similar to those we have seen in first-order circuits. As you will soon see, we must use capacitors *and* inductors to get something really different.

## An *RLC* Circuit

**Deriving the DE.** Figure 3.39 shows a series *RLC* circuit with a battery-switch input and an output of the voltage across the inductor. Because there is one loop, we will develop the DE through loop-current analysis. With the switch closed, the KVL equation following the loop current is

$$-V_s + Ri + v_C(0) + \frac{1}{C}\int_0^t i(t')\,dt' + \underbrace{L\frac{di}{dt}}_{v_L(t)\,=\,v_{out}(t)} = 0 \tag{3.62}$$

We have identified the last term as the output voltage because we wish to derive a DE for $v_L(t)$. We differentiate Eq. (3.62) once to get rid of the integral:

$$0 + R\frac{di}{dt} + \frac{i}{C} + \frac{dv_L}{dt} = 0 \tag{3.63}$$

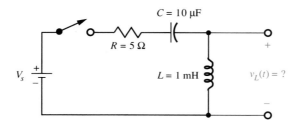

Figure 3.39 The series *RLC* circuit can exhibit oscillations.

This differentiation gets rid of the source voltage, but it will reappear when we consider initial conditions. The first term in Eq. (3.63) can easily be expressed in terms of $v_L$, but we must differentiate again to get rid of the current term:

$$\frac{R}{L}\frac{dv_L}{dt} + \frac{v_L}{LC} + \frac{d^2v_L}{dt^2} = 0 \tag{3.64}$$

where we have in Eqs. (3.63) and (3.64) used $di/dt = v_L/L$ repeatedly to convert variables from current to output voltage. We will consider solutions of Eq. (3.64) under two conditions: no loss ($R = 0$) and small loss ($R = $ small).

**No loss ($R = 0$) solution.** Setting $R = 0$ in Eq. (3.64) eliminates the first-derivative term and leaves

$$\frac{d^2v_L}{dt^2} + \frac{v_L}{LC} = 0 \tag{3.65}$$

Equation (3.65) is a homogenous second-order linear DE, and has two solutions, $\cos(\omega_0 t)$ and $\sin(\omega_0 t)$, where

$$\omega_0^2 = \frac{1}{LC} = 10^8 \tag{3.66}$$

Thus, the general solution of Eq. (3.65) is

$$v_L(t) = A\cos(\omega_0 t) + B\sin(\omega_0 t)$$
$$= A\cos(10^4 t) + B\sin(10^4 t) \tag{3.67}$$

**Initial conditions.** We assume that the capacitor is initially uncharged. Examination of Fig. 3.39 reveals that the full battery voltage must appear across the inductor at $t = 0^+$ because the current must be zero; hence, the voltage across both the resistor and the capacitor will be zero. This conclusion could be also deduced from Eq. (3.62) at $t = 0^+$. Thus, $v_L(0^+) = V_s$. Equation (3.67) thus requires that $A = V_s$. Similarly, we can reason from Eq. (3.63) at $t = 0^+$ that

$$\left.\frac{dv_L}{dt}\right|_{t=0^+} = -\frac{R}{L}v_L(0^+) = -\frac{R}{L}V_s = 0 \qquad \text{for } R = 0 \tag{3.68}$$

The requirement in Eq. (3.68) forces the sine term in Eq. (3.67) to be zero, and the output response to the switch closure is, therefore,

$$v_L(t) = V_s\cos(\omega_0 t) = 100\cos(10^4 t) \tag{3.69}$$

which is shown in Fig. 3.40.

**Interpretation.** We may understand this response physically in terms of the mechanical analog, which is shown in Fig. 3.41. The closing of the switch corresponds to the sudden application of a force to the spring–mass system, and the output voltage corresponds to the acceleration of the mass. The mass will respond immediately to the application of the force and will resonate with the spring in a lossless oscillation. Thus,

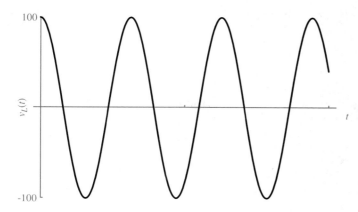

**Figure 3.40** Without loss, the response is a pure oscillation.

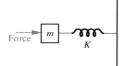

**Figure 3.41**
Mechanical analog to circuit in Fig. 3.39 with $R = 0$.

we expect the simple harmonic motion we see in Fig. 3.40. In the electric circuit, the "momentum" is associated with the current in the inductor, and the spring action associated with the capacitor.

**Low-loss response** ($R = 5\ \Omega$). We now discuss the response with small loss. The mathematics to derive the response is beyond our present ambition, especially since we deal with this problem thoroughly in Chapter 12. The response is

$$v_L(t) = e^{-2500t}[100\cos(9682t) - 25.8\sin(9682t)] \tag{3.70}$$

which is plotted in Fig. 3.42. You will note the similarity to the response for no loss, but of course the response dies out due to the loss in the resistor. With loss, the circuit will eventually reach steady state, which means zero voltage across the inductor.

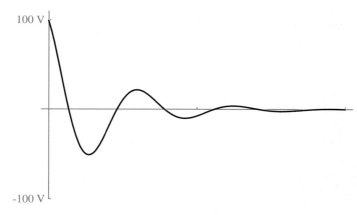

**Figure 3.42** With an inductor and a capacitor in the circuit, an oscillation is possible. This oscillation shows the effect of the losses in the resistor.

### Check Your Understanding

1. In the differential equation, $5\,dx/dt + 2x = 3$, what is the time constant? What is the final value for $x$?

2. In a first-order transient, if the initial current in a capacitor is 5 mA, what is the current one time constant later in time?

3. In using a Thévenin equivalent circuit to determine the equivalent resistance in an *RL* transient problem, what must be considered the load?

4. During a switch action, which is constant: voltage, current, stored energy, or power?

5. In a simple circuit containing a resistor and an energy-storage element (*L* or *C*), when the value of the resistor was doubled, the transient lasted twice as long. What was the other element?

6. As $t \to \infty$, what circuit element approaches a short circuit?

7. A capacitor will allow an instantaneous change in its current or voltage?

8. An *RC* circuit has a time constant of 10 ms. The capacitor is replaced by a 50-mH inductor and the time constant changes to 8 ms. What was *C*?

9. In a simple transient, the initial energy in an inductor is 10 mJ and the final energy is 0. What is the energy after two time constants?

*Answers.* (**1**) 2.5 s, 1.5; (**2**) 1.84 mA; (**3**) the inductor; (**4**) stored energy; (**5**) a capacitor; (**6**) an inductor; (**7**) its current; (**8**) 1600 µF; (**9**) 0.183 mJ.

## CHAPTER SUMMARY

Chapter 3 introduces inductors and capacitors as circuit elements that store magnetic and electric energy, respectively. Time processes enter into circuit analysis, and circuit behavior is described by differential equations. We focus on first-order systems: one inductor or capacitor in a circuit containing one or more resistors and switches.

**Objective 1. To understand the properties of inductors, and be able to find the inductor voltage from inductor current and vice versa.** Inductors store magnetic energy by getting currents close together. The inductor voltage is equal to the time derivative of the current times a constant, the inductance. An inductor tries to keep its current constant.

**Objective 2. To understand the properties of capacitors, and be able to find the capacitor voltage from capacitor current and vice versa.** Capacitors store electric energy by getting charges close together. The capacitor current is equal to the time derivative of its voltage times a constant, the capacitance. Capacitor voltage is temporarily constant when sudden changes occur on a circuit.

**Objective 3. To understand how to analyze first-order transients by the initial-value/final-value method.** When switches are opened or closed in a dc circuit containing a single energy-storage element, a first-order transient carries the circuit from one condition to another over a transient period of time. We develop a method for analyzing a first-order transient based upon the initial and final values of the electrical voltage or current of interest, plus the time constant of the circuit.

The chapter ends with a brief introduction to second-order circuits. First-, second-, and higher-order circuits are studied in detail in Chapter 12, where powerful methods of analysis are developed. In Chapter 4, first-order transients play a small role, but the chapter emphasizes steady-state response of circuits with alternating-current sources.

# PROBLEMS

## Section 3.1: Theory of Inductors and Capacitors

**3.1.** A 50-mH inductor has a current of $i_s(t) = 0$, $t < 0$, and $i_s(t) = 150t^3$ A, $t > 0$. Calculate the voltage across the inductor, $v_L(t)$, with the polarity shown in Fig. P3.1.

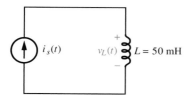

**Figure P3.1**

**3.2.** A 6.3-V battery is connected to an ideal 0.3-H inductor, as shown in Fig. P3.2.
 **(a)** Calculate the current as a function of time after the switch is closed.
 **(b)** At what time does the stored energy in the inductor reach 10 J? Verify the stored energy by integrating the input power (product of $v_L$ and $i_L$) from $t = 0$ to the time you calculate.

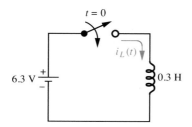

**Figure P3.2**

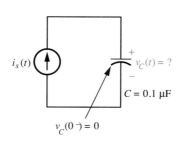

$v_C(0^-) = 0$

**Figure P3.6**

**3.3.** **(a)** Find the equivalent inductance of a 1-H inductor in parallel with a 2-H inductor.
 **(b)** Find the ratio of the stored energy in the inductors, $W_{m2}/W_{m1}$, if they initially have zero energy.
 **(c)** Repeat if the inductors are in series.

**3.4.** If an ideal 4.5-V battery were connected to an ideal 1-H inductor, how much energy would be given to the inductor in the first second?

**3.5.** Figure P3.5 shows a 20-μF capacitor that has a voltage

$$v_s(t) = 0, \qquad t < 0$$
$$v_s(t) = 10^4 t^2, \qquad 0 < t < 0.1 \text{ s}$$
$$v_s(t) = 100, \qquad t > 0.1 \text{ s}$$

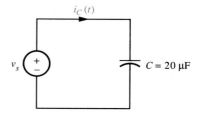

**Figure P3.5**

 **(a)** Find the current, $i_C(t)$.
 **(b)** At what time is the energy in the capacitor 50 mJ?
 **(c)** At what time is the power into the capacitor 1 watt?

**3.6.** A 0.1-μF capacitor is charged with a 1-μs pulse of current, as shown in Fig. P3.6. Find the voltage across the capacitor, with the polarity shown, as a function of time.

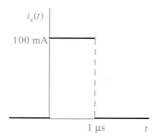

**3.7.** To move the spot of a CRT smoothly across the screen, the voltage across a pair of deflection plates must be increased in a linear fashion, as shown in Fig. P3.7. If the capacitance of the plates is 1 pF, find the resulting current through the capacitor.

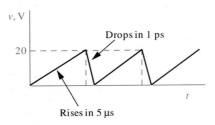

**Figure P3.7**

**3.8. (a)** Find the equivalent capacitance of a 1-μF capacitor in series with a 5-μF capacitor.
**(b)** Find the ratio of the stored energy in the capacitors, $W_{e2}/W_{e1}$, if they initially have zero energy.
**(c)** Repeat parts **(a)** and **(b)** if the capacitors are in parallel.

**3.9.** An inductor and a capacitor are placed in series with a current source whose current increases with time, as shown in Fig. P3.9 (b). The circuit is shown in Fig. P3.9 (a).
**(a)** Find the voltage across the inductor, $v_L(t)$.
**(b)** Assuming no initial charge on the capacitor, find its voltage, $v_C(t)$.
**(c)** Calculate the instant when the stored energy in the capacitor first exceeds that in the inductor.

**3.10.** For the circuit shown in Fig. P3.10, the voltage

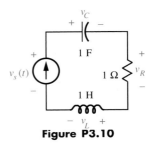

**Figure P3.10**

across the resistor is 0 V for negative time and $v_R = t$ V for positive time. The capacitor is initially unenergized.
**(a)** What is the stored energy in the inductor at $t = 2$ s?
**(b)** What is the voltage across the capacitor at the same time?
**(c)** What is the voltage across the source at the same time?

**3.11.** For the series $RLC$ circuit in Fig. P3.11, the voltage across the inductor is shown.
**(a)** Determine and sketch the voltages across the resistor and the capacitor. Assume $v_C = v_R = 0$ at $t = 0$.
**(b)** What is the value of $v_s$ at $t = 3$ ms?

**3.12.** In the circuit shown in Fig. P3.12, the initial voltage on the capacitor is 10 V, with the + at the bottom, and the initial current in the inductor is zero. The current into the capacitor is 5 A dc for $t > 0$, as shown.
**(a)** Find the source voltage.
**(b)** Determine the *two* times after $t = 0$ when the power out of the voltage source is zero.

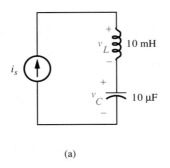

(a)

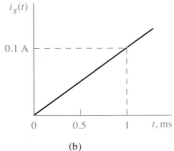

(b)

**Figure P3.9**

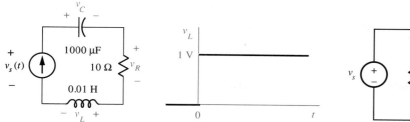

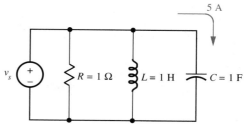

**Figure P3.11**

**Figure P3.12**

## Section 3.2: First-Order Transient Response of *RL* and *RC* Circuits

**3.13.** The solution of a first-order DE with constant coefficients and a constant term on the right side is $x(t) = 5 - 3e^{-t/1\text{ms}}$.
   **(a)** Plot this solution. What is the value at the origin and as time becomes large?
   **(b)** What is the DE that this solution satisfies? What initial condition? Verify by substitution that your DE is correct.

**3.14.** Verify that the standard solution, Eq. (3.36), satisfies Eq. (3.35) and has the required values at $t = 0$ and $t$ very large.

**3.15.** A system is described by the DE

$$\frac{1}{3}(dx/dt) + 5x = 10.$$

   **(a)** What is the time constant for this system?
   **(b)** What would be the final value, $x_\infty$?
   **(c)** If $x_0 = -2$, find and sketch $x(t)$ for $t > 0$.

**3.16.** The circuit shown in Fig. P3.16 has two capacitors, one of which is charged, and hence would appear to be second-order. Derive the DE for $i(t)$ and show that it has the form of Eq. (3.35). What is the time constant?

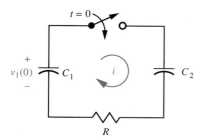

**Figure P3.16**

**3.17.** Figure P3.17 shows a switch that is changed from *a* to *b* at $t = 0$. Assume that the switch has been in position *a* for a long time before the switch action. Find $v_L(t)$, the voltage across the inductor with the polarity shown.

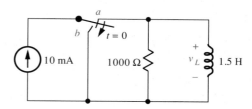

**Figure P3.17**

**3.18.** A current source is placed in series with a resistor and inductor, as shown in Fig. P3.18. During this period, the switch is open. Then the switch is closed, and the circuit is separated into two independent loops that share a common short circuit but do not interact.

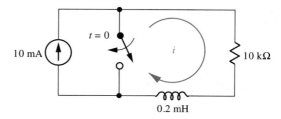

**Figure P3.18**

   **(a)** Calculate the current in the right-hand loop after the switch closes at $t = 0$.
   **(b)** Plot the current in the switch, referenced downward.

**3.19.** For the circuit shown in Fig. P3.19, assume that the switch has been in position *a* for a long time and then is changed to position *b*.

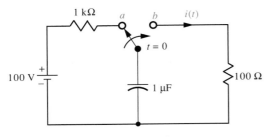

**Figure P3.19**

(a) Find and sketch $i(t)$.
(b) Calculate by integration the energy lost in the 100-$\Omega$ resistor during positive time. Confirm that all the energy stored initially in the capacitor is accounted for by the loss in the resistor.

**3.20.** The circuit shown in Fig. P3.20 has equilibrium established with the switch closed, then the switch is opened. Determine the voltage across the 5-k$\Omega$ resistor after the switch is opened.

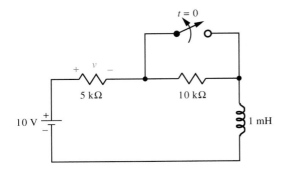

**Figure P3.20**

**3.21.** After being closed a long time, the switch in Fig. P3.21 is opened at $t = 0$.
(a) Find the voltage across the switch as a function of time for $t > 0$.
(b) In what period of time is half the initial stored energy in the capacitor lost to the resistor?

**3.22.** The switch in Fig. P3.22 is in position *a* for negative time, moved to *b* at $t = 0$, and to *c* at $t = 10$ ms. Sketch the voltage across the capacitor for $0 < t < 30$ ms. At what time should the switch be switched to *c* for no "transient"?

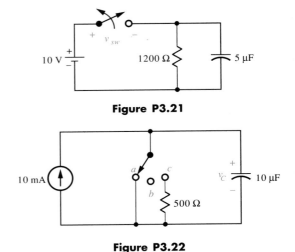

**Figure P3.21**

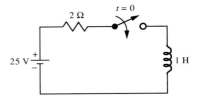

**Figure P3.22**

**3.23.** The switch in Fig. P3.23 is closed at $t = 0$. Find the time at which the power into the inductor is maximum.

**Figure P3.23**

**3.24.** A capacitor is charged to 100 V and disconnected. Leakage reduces its voltage to 35 V in 45 min. Estimate the additional time required for the voltage to drop to 8 V. *Hint:* The leakage is represented by a resistance in parallel with the capacitance.

**3.25.** For the circuit shown in Fig. P3.25, the switch is open a long time, closed for 1 second, and then opened again for a long time.
(a) Determine and sketch the current in the inductor.
(b) How much energy comes out of the battery in this process?

**3.26.** The switch in Fig. P3.26 is closed at $t = 0$. Find $di/dt$ at the instant of time when the stored energy in the inductor is 0.5 μJ.

**3.27.** For the circuit in Fig. P3.27, the original energy stored in the capacitor is 500 J and the switch is open. The switch is then closed for 1 second and

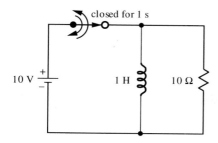

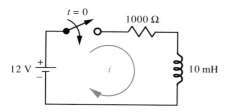

**Figure P3.25**

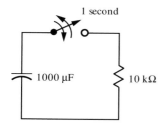

**Figure P3.26**

**Figure P3.27**

## Section 3.3: Advanced Techniques

**3.30.** For the circuit in Fig. P3.30 find the following:
(a) $\tau$.
(b) $i_0$.

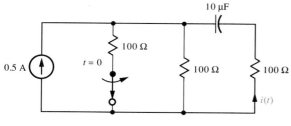

**Figure P3.30**

opened again after 1 second. Find the final energy stored in the capacitor.

**3.28.** The 1000-µF capacitor in Fig. P3.28 is charged to 10 V and the switch is closed at $t = 0$. The circuit must meet the requirement that the current exceeds 250 mA for at least 10 ms. Find $R$ to meet this requirement. (The answer is not unique.)

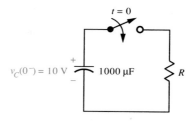

**Figure P3.28**

**3.29.** For the circuit shown in Fig. P3.29, the switch is open a long time, then closed at $t = 0$. It is required that the capacitor voltage equals or exceeds 0.75 V at $t = 10$ ms. Find $R$ to satisfy this criterion. (The answer is not unique.)

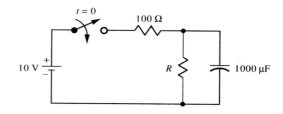

**Figure P3.29**

(c) $i_\infty$.
(d) $i(t)$.

**3.31.** After being closed a long time, the switch in Fig. P3.31 is opened at $t = 0$. Find the following:
(a) The time constant.
(b) The initial value of $i(t)$.
(c) The final value of $i(t)$.
(d) The time function, $i(t)$.

**3.32.** After being closed for a long time, the switch in Fig. P3.32 is opened at $t = 0$. Find the following:
(a) The voltage across the capacitor with + at top as a function of time.
(b) The integral of the current during the period $0 < t < \infty$.

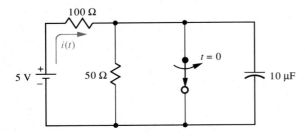

**Figure P3.31**

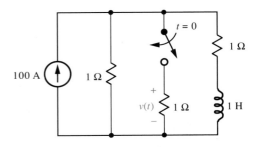

**Figure P3.34**

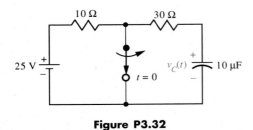

**Figure P3.32**

(c) The total energy given to the circuit by the battery during the period $0 < t < \infty$.

3.33. For the circuit shown in Fig. P3.33, the switch has been open a long time and is closed at $t = 0$.

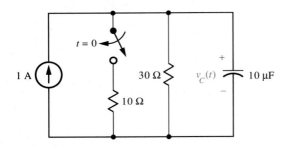

**Figure P3.33**

(a) What is the time constant of the circuit with the switch closed?
(b) Determine the capacitor voltage with the polarity shown and sketch.

3.34. For the circuit in Fig. P3.34, find $v(t)$ for $t > 0$ after the switch is closed.

3.35. For the circuit shown in Fig. P3.35, the switch is closed at $t = 0$ after being open a long time. Find the following:
(a) The voltage across the 10-$\Omega$ resistor for $t > 0$.
(b) The stored energy in the capacitor in the steady-state condition.

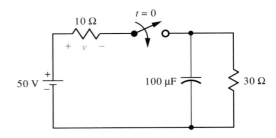

**Figure P3.35**

3.36. After being open a long time, the switch in Fig. P3.36 closes at $t = 0$. Find the power out of the 6-V source at $t = 10$ ms.

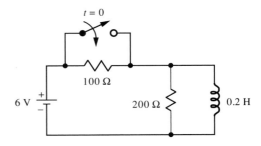

**Figure P3.36**

3.37. For the circuit shown in Fig. P3.37, the switch has been closed for a long time and then is opened at $t = 0$. Determine the voltage across the capacitor with the polarity shown.

3.38. For the circuit shown in Fig. P3.38, the switch is open a long time, closed for 5 ms, and then opened again. Find and sketch $i(t)$.

3.39. After being open a long time, the switch in Fig. P3.39 is closed at $t = 0$ for 1 ms, then opened again. Determine the voltage across the 125-$\Omega$ resistor for $t > 0$.

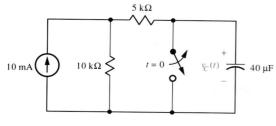

**Figure P3.37**

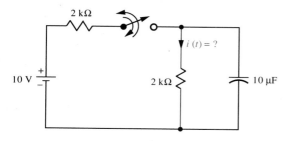

**Figure P3.38**

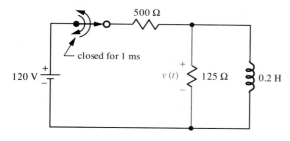

**Figure P3.39**

**3.40.** For the circuit shown in Fig. P3.40, the switch has been closed for a long time and then is opened at $t = 0$. Determine the current through the inductor with the reference direction shown.

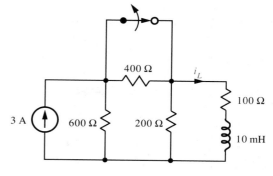

**Figure P3.40**

**3.41.** The parallel $RL$ circuit shown in Fig. P3.41 is excited by the current pulse as shown. Calculate and sketch the resulting voltage, $v_L$. Assume that the inductor is initially unenergized.

**3.42.** A pulse can be modeled as two sources, one switching the voltage on and the other switching it off, as shown in Fig. P3.42. Note that the two sources add to zero except during the period $0 < t < t_1$. The voltage across the capacitor can be calculated by superposition. Use this model to rework the problem in Fig. 3.33. Specifically, solve for the voltage across the capacitor at $t = 1.0$ μs and verify the result given on page 129, where $V = 5$ V, $R = 50$ Ω, and $C = 5$ nF.

**3.43.** The circuit in Fig. P3.43 is the same as in Fig. 3.37, except that the output is taken across $R_2$ instead of $C_2$.
(a) Derive the differential equation for $v_2$. [Should be very similar to Eq. (3.52).]
(b) Determine the initial conditions for the output voltage and its derivative, assuming the capacitors initially uncharged.
(c) Find $v_2(t)$.

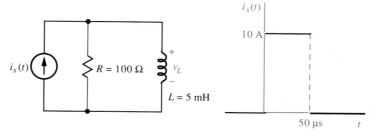

**Figure P3.41**

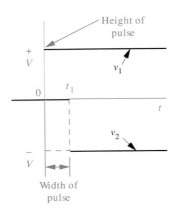

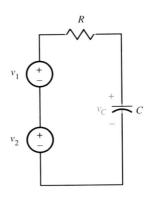

**Figure P3.42**

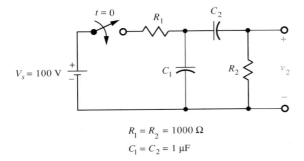

$R_1 = R_2 = 1000\ \Omega$

$C_1 = C_2 = 1\ \mu F$

**Figure P3.43**

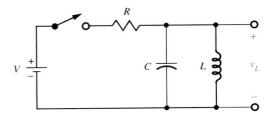

**Figure P3.44**

**3.44.** The *RLC* circuit in Fig. P3.44 is similar to that in Fig. 3.39, except the inductor and capacitor are in parallel rather than in series.
  (a) Derive the DE for $v_L(t)$.
  (b) Find the initial values for the $v_L(t)$ and its derivative.

**3.45.** The circuit in Fig. P3.45 has loop currents defined. Derive the DE for $i_2(t)$.

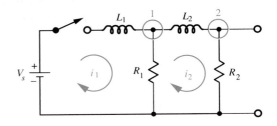

**Figure P3.45**

## General Problems

**3.46.** When the switch in the *RC* circuit of Fig. P3.46 is closed, for a period of time energy flows from the battery into the circuit. Once the current stops, the energy flow ceases.
  (a) Calculate by integration the total energy given to the circuit by the battery for $t > 0$. Show that this is $Vq$, where $q$ is the charge on the capacitor.
  (b) Show by direct calculation that one-half this total energy is stored in the capacitor and the

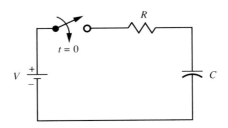

**Figure P3.46**

other half is lost to the circuit as losses in the resistor.

3.47. The switch in Fig. P3.47 is in position $a$ for a long time, then switched to $b$ for a period of time $\Delta t$, and then switched to position $c$. Find $\Delta t$ such that the voltage across the 50-$\Omega$ resistor is 60 V at 100 $\mu$s after the switch was switched to position $b$, that is, 100 $\mu$s $- \Delta t$ after the switch was put in position $c$. *Hint:* The equation is nonlinear and must be solved by numerical methods.

3.48. A microwave oven will boil water in 3 minutes, starting with water at 75°F. If the initial heating rate is 55°/minute, estimate the temperature to which the water would heat were it not for the phase change at 212°F. *Hint:* This fits the model for a first-order transient. The unknown is the final value of the temperature (which it never reaches).

3.49. The circuit in Fig. P3.49 will operate as a variable delay in operating the alarm. The alarm operates when its input current exceeds 100 $\mu$A. Find the range of $R$ such that the delay is between 0.1 and 1 second.

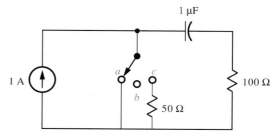

**Figure P3.47** The switch is in position $b$ for $\Delta t$ and then put in position $c$.

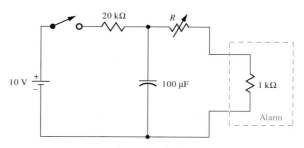

**Figure P3.49**

## Answers to Odd-Numbered Problems

3.1. $22.5t^2$, $t > 0$

3.3. **(a)** 2/3 H; **(b)** 1/2; **(c)** 2/1

3.5. **(a)** $0.4t$ for $0 < t < 0.1$ s, 0 elsewhere; **(b)** 0.0841 s; **(c)** 0.0630 s

3.7. 4 $\mu$A when increasing, $-20$ A when decreasing

3.9. **(a)** 1 V; **(b)** $10^7 t^2/2$, **(c)** 0.632 ms

3.11. **(a)** $i = 100t$, $v_R = 1000t$, $v_C = 10^5 t^2/2$, **(b)** $v_s = 4.45$ V at 3 ms

3.13. **(a)** Starts at 2 and approaches 5 for large time with 1 ms time constant; **(b)** $10^{-3} dx/dt + x = 5$ with $x(0) = 2$

3.15. **(a)** 1/15 s; **(b)** +2; **(c)** $x(t) = 2 - 4e^{-15t}$

3.17. $v_L(t) = -10e^{-t/1.5 \text{ ms}}$ V

3.19. **(a)** $i(t) = 1e^{-t/100 \mu s}$ A; **(b)** 5 mJ

3.21. **(a)** $10(1 - e^{-t/6 \text{ ms}})$ V; **(b)** 2.08 ms

3.23. 0.347 s

3.25. **(a)** $i_L(t) = 10$ A for $0 < t < 1$, $i_L(t) = 10e^{-(t-1)/0.1 \text{ s}}$ A, $t > 1$ s; **(b)** 60 J

3.27. 409 J

3.29. **(a)** $R > 19.5\ \Omega$ works

3.31. **(a)** 0.333 ms; **(b)** 50 mA; **(c)** 33.3 mA; **(d)** $i(t) = 33.3 + (50 - 33.3)e^{-t/0.333 \text{ ms}}$ mA.

3.33. **(a)** 75 $\mu$s; **(b)** $v_C(t) = 7.5 + (30 - 7.5)e^{-t/75 \mu s}$ V

3.35. **(a)** $v(t) = 12.5 + (50 - 12.5)e^{-t/0.75 \text{ ms}}$ V; **(b)** 70.3 mJ

3.37. $v_C(t) = 100(1 - e^{-t/0.6 \text{ s}})$ V

3.39. $v_L(t) = 24e^{-t/2 \text{ ms}}$ V for $t < 1$ ms and $-11.8e^{-(t-1 \text{ ms})/1.6 \text{ ms}}$ V for $t > 1$ ms

3.41. $v_L(t) = 1000e^{-t/50 \mu s}$ V for $t < 50$ $\mu$s and $-632e^{-(t-50 \mu s)/50 \mu s}$ V for $t > 50$ $\mu$s.

3.43. **(a)** Same as Eq. 3.52 except right-hand side $= 0$;

**(b)** $v_2(0^+) = 0$, $\left.\dfrac{dv_2}{dt}\right|_{t=0^+} = 10^5$ V/s;

**(c)** $v_2(t) = 44.7e^{-382t} - 44.7e^{-2620t}$ V

3.45. $L_1 L_2 \dfrac{d^2 i_2(t)}{dt^2} + [R_1 L_2 + (R_1 + R_2)L_1] \dfrac{di_2(t)}{dt}$
$+ R_1 R_2 i_2(t) = R_1 V_s$

3.47. 72.2 $\mu$s.

3.49. 3.36 k$\Omega < R_L < 33.6$ k$\Omega$.

# The Analysis of AC Circuits

objectives

1. To understand how to identify the amplitude, frequency, and phase of a sinusoidal function
2. To understand the phasor concept and be able to find the sinusoidal steady-state response of a circuit, given the differential equation
3. To understand how to use phasors and impedance to determine the sinusoidal steady-state response of a circuit
4. To understand the effect of varying frequency on series and parallel *RL*, *RC*, and *RLC* circuits
5. To understand admittance and its advantages in analyzing parallel impedances

Alternating-current circuits, except for automotive and other portable power systems, comprise the vast majority of all power distribution and power consumption circuits. This chapter introduces the methods by which ac circuits are analyzed.

## Importance of AC

**Historical perspective.** Thomas A. Edison was a clever, determined inventor whose activities excited the public imagination toward the practical uses of electricity. He pioneered in, among other things, the generation and distribution of electric power for lighting. But Edison was committed to direct current (dc). The power plants built by the Edison Electric Lighting Company produced dc.

Edison had many young inventors and scientists working for him. His was, in fact, the first industrial research laboratory. One of these underlings was Nikola Tesla, a young engineer from Croatia. Tesla appears to have been the first person to recognize the possibilities of ac and he is credited with inventing the ac induction motor. But his efforts to convince Boss Edison of the benefits of ac were in vain, and Tesla eventually quit.

Tesla went to a rival company and battle was pitched: Was it to be dc or ac? Nasty ads were placed in the newspapers by Edison's group, claiming that ac was unsafe. From our perspective, these warnings of the dangers of ac seem odd, but at the time they created a serious debate.

Edison was wrong and Tesla was right. Today, the vast majority of all electric power is generated, distributed, and consumed in the form of ac power. Before World War II, electrical engineering meant ac generators, motors, transformers, transmission lines, and the like. The ac power industry currently employs a mature technology and is a vital part of modern civilization.

In this chapter, you will learn how to analyze ac circuits and, more broadly, how electrical engineers think about ac waveforms. The techniques of ac analysis, once mastered, are powerful for solving problems and stimulating insight. We begin by acquainting you with the sinusoidal waveform.

## Sinusoids

**OBJECTIVE 1**

To understand how to identify the amplitude, frequency, and phase of a sinusoidal function

**Physical model for a sinusoid.** Most of us were introduced to sines and cosines through the study of triangles: sine equals opposite over hypotenuse, and that sort of thing. Later we learned that circular motion leads to sine and cosine functions. Figure 4.1 shows a crank. The horizontal projection of the crank is the length times the cosine of the angle $\phi$. If the rotation speed of the crank is uniform, the horizontal projection becomes a sinusoidal function of time. We may describe this waveform mathematically as a sine function or a cosine function, but we will simply call it a *sinusoid*, or sinusoidal waveform.

**sinusoid**

**Mathematical form for a sinusoid.** Electrical engineers have adopted the cosine function as the standard mathematical form for sinusoidal waveforms. Figure 4.2 shows the peak value, period, and phase of a sinusoidal waveform. The corresponding mathematical form is

$$v(t) = V_p \cos(\omega t + \theta) \tag{4.1}$$

**period,
event frequency**

The peak value of the voltage is $V_p$. The sinusoid repeats with a *period*, $T$, which determines the frequency of the sinusoid. The *event frequency*, namely, the number of cycles during a period of time, is the reciprocal of the period:

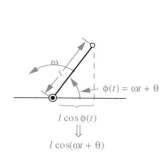

**Figure 4.1** The projection of the rotating crank is a sinusoid.

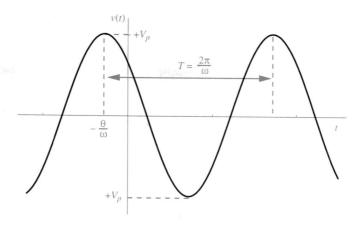

**Figure 4.2** The sinusoidal function is defined by its peak value, its phase, and its period (or frequency).

$$f = \frac{1}{T} \text{ hertz} \tag{4.2}$$

For example, if the period were 0.02 s, the event frequency would be 1/0.02, or 50 cycles per second. Because the unit "cycles per second" is awkward to say, most people tend to shorten it to "cycles," which is misleading to the novice and offensive to the purist. To honor Heinrich Hertz (1857–1894), the unit hertz, abbreviated Hz, has replaced cycles per second as the common unit for event frequency. So 50 hertz means 50 cycles/second.

**angular frequency**    When most people talk about a frequency, they mean the event frequency. When we write mathematical expressions for sinusoidal waveforms, however, we more often deal with the proper mathematical measure, the angular frequency, $\omega$ (Greek lowercase omega), in radians per second. Because there are $2\pi$ radians in a full circle (a cycle), the relationship between *angular frequency*, event frequency, $f$, and period, $T$, is

$$\omega = 2\pi f = \frac{2\pi \text{ radians}}{T \text{ second}} \tag{4.3}$$

The scientific dimensions of frequency are reciprocal seconds. The numerator of Eq. (4.3) represents an angle and is therefore dimensionless. Just as we retain radians or degrees to remind us which measure of an angle we are using, so we need to state the units for frequency to make explicit which frequency we mean, $f$ or $\omega$.

**Units of phase.** The phase of the sinusoid, $\theta$ (Greek lowercase theta), is what permits the waveform in Fig. 4.2 to represent a general sinusoid. We have drawn the curve for a phase of $\theta = +50°$, but we can shift the position of the sinusoid by varying the phase. The phase is related to the time origin when we use a mathematical description, but in an ac problem, what matters are the relative phases of the various sinusoidal voltages and currents.

Here you must tolerate one of the traditional inconsistencies of electrical engineers. The mathematical unit for $\omega t$ is radians and hence the correct unit for phase should also be radians. For example, we may wish to compute the time when the voltage reaches its positive peak. The cosine is maximum for zero angle, so the peak occurs when the total angle is zero:

$$\omega t_{peak} + \theta = 0 \Rightarrow t_{peak} = -\frac{\theta}{\omega} = -\frac{\theta}{2\pi}T \tag{4.4}$$

When we solve an equation like Eq. (4.4), we must use radian measure for the phase, as the last form of Eq. (4.4) suggests. But electrical engineers usually speak of phase in degrees, as we did before (+50°). Thus, for $\theta = 50°$,

$$t_{peak} = -\frac{50 \times (\pi/180)}{2\pi} \times T \tag{4.5}$$

where $\pi/180$ converts 50° to radians. This inconsistency is tolerable because only relative phase is what matters in most situations. Electrical engineers, like most people, still are more comfortable thinking about and sketching angles in degree measure. Probably you also think best in degree measure, so we will continue to express phase in degrees unless radians are required by the mathematics.

---

**EXAMPLE 4.1**  ## Sinusoids

A sinusoidal voltage is 20 V peak to peak, is 5 ms between peak and trough, and at $t = 0$ is $-3.6$V and decreasing. Find $v(t)$, and the value of the sinusoid at $t = 12$ ms.

**SOLUTION:**
Figure 4.3 shows the sinusoid. The amplitude is clearly 10 V. The period is the time between peaks, 10 ms; so the event frequency is

$$f = \frac{1}{T} = \frac{1}{10 \text{ ms}} = 100 \text{ Hz} \tag{4.6}$$

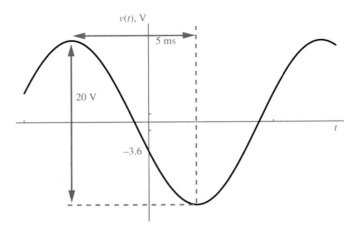

**Figure 4.3** Sinusoid described by peak-to-peak voltage, half-period, and value with trend at the origin.

and the radian frequency is

$$\omega = 2\pi f = 200\pi \text{ radians/second} \tag{4.7}$$

Therefore, the sinusoid is of the form

$$v(t) = 10 \cos(200\pi t + \theta) \text{ V} \tag{4.8}$$

For $v(0) = -3.6$V, we require $10 \cos(\theta) = -3.6$. The calculator gives $111.1°$ for $\cos^{-1}(-0.36)$, but we should realize that this is the principal value and $360° - 111.1° = 248.9°$ is also a possibility.

We decide between the two possible phases by choosing the one that gives a negative derivative. A simple way to determine the sign of the derivative is use the calculator to evaluate $\cos(\theta + 1°)$, which is equivalent to evaluating the function at a time slightly after the origin in time. The calculator gives $\cos(111.1° + 1°) = -0.376$, but $\cos(248.9° + 1°) = -0.344$. Hence, $111.1°$ is the correct phase because it gives a decreasing function at the origin. Therefore,

$$v(t) = 10 \cos(200\pi t + 111.1°) \text{ V} \tag{4.9}$$

The value at 12 ms would be

$$v(0.012) = 10 \cos(200\pi \times 0.012 + 111.1°) \text{ V} \tag{4.10}$$

where the first term is in radians: $200\pi \times 0.012 = 7.54$ radians ($= 432.0°$). Thus, the value at 12 ms would be

$$v(0.012) = 10 \cos(432.0° + 111.1°) = -9.985 \text{ V} \tag{4.11}$$

---

**WHAT IF?**

What if the voltage were $+3.6$V at $t = 0$ and increasing? What then would be the phase?[1]

---

**Some familiar frequencies.** Frequency is a familiar concept. When we speak of an engine speed as 4000 rpm, for example, we are indicating a frequency of 66.7 Hz, and each of the eight spark plugs would be firing with a frequency of 33.3 Hz. The power system frequency is 60 Hz in this country, although 50 Hz is used in much of the world, and 400 Hz is used in airborne and some naval applications.[2] When the radio announcer tells you that you are "tuned to 1200 on your radio dial," she is giving her station frequency, 1200 kHz (kilohertz) or $1.2 \times 10^6$ Hz. The FM stations broadcast at frequencies of about 100 MHz (megahertz) or about $10^8$ Hz. The UHF TV band extends to about 800 MHz, and communication satellites relay signals at about 5 GHz (gigahertz), or $5 \times 10^9$ Hz. The highest frequencies currently used for radio signals are about 300 GHz, $3 \times 10^{11}$ Hz. We find infrared, optical, and X-ray radiation at even higher frequencies.

Later in this book, we explore more fully the importance of frequency in electrical engineering, particularly in communication systems. In this section, we have introduced

---

[1] The phase would be $-68.9°$.

[2] Because motors and transformers are smaller and lighter at the higher frequency.

the concept of frequency, and in the next section, we show how ac waveforms are represented for ac circuit analysis.

## AC Circuit Problem

### The differential equation (DE).
Figure 4.4 shows the ac circuit we will analyze. The ac source has a frequency of 60 Hz, or $120\pi$ rad/s, and is connected by a switch that closes at $t = 0$. We wish to solve for the current, $i(t)$. After the switch is closed, we write KVL as

$$-v_s(t) + v_R(t) + v_L(t) = 0 \tag{4.12}$$

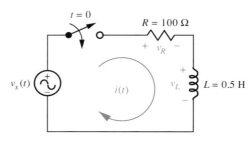

$v_s = V_p \cos(\omega t + \theta)$

$V_p = 100$ V, $f = 60$ Hz, $\theta = 30°$

**Figure 4.4** Solve for $i(t)$ for positive time. The switch closes at $t = 0$.

**Conservation of Energy**

We may introduce $i(t)$ through Ohm's law and the definition of inductance, with the result

$$L\frac{di}{dt} + Ri = V_p \cos(\omega t + \theta) \tag{4.13}$$

Equation (4.13) is a linear first-order DE, but the technique we used in Chapter 3 does not fit because we do not have a dc term on the right side.

### Form of the solution.
The character of the response, however, is similar to our earlier results. Here also there will be a transition from the state of the circuit before the switch was closed to the state with the closed switch. Here also the transition period is expressed in terms of the $L/R$ time constant of the circuit. In fact, the form of the solution is

$$i(t) = Ae^{-t/\tau} + i_{ss}(t), \qquad \text{with } \tau = \frac{L}{R} \tag{4.14}$$

where $A$ is an unknown constant, $\tau$ the time constant, and $i_{ss}(t)$ the particular integral, or steady-state current. The steady-state current, $i_{ss}(t)$, is no longer a constant, but results from a dynamic equilibrium between source, resistor, and inductor.

### Looking ahead.
Methods for determining the steady-state response are the focus of this chapter. Equation (4.13) can be integrated directly with the aid of an integrating factor. This approach fails, however, when we try it on more complicated circuits and,

besides, our goal is to learn how electrical engineers analyze ac problems. No electrical engineer would integrate this equation directly to find the steady-state solution. We will lead you down the traditional path—so please be patient. Once we arrive, you will be amazed how easily we can solve ac circuit problems.

### Check Your Understanding

1. What is the frequency in hertz of the ticking of a pendulum clock if it ticks twice every second?

2. If eight cycles of a sinusoidal waveform take 2 ms, find the angular frequency, $\omega$.

3. What is the value of $\cos(100t + 30°)$ at $t = 10$ ms?

4. What is the time between positive peaks for the sinusoidal waveform in the previous question?

*Answers.* (1) 2 Hz; (2) 25,100 rad/s; (3) 0.0472; (4) $6.28 \times 10^{-2}$ s.

## 4.2 REPRESENTING SINUSOIDS WITH PHASORS

### Sinusoids and Linear Systems

**Sinusoid in, sinusoid out.** An important idea is suggested in Fig. 4.5. Here we have represented the circuit as a linear system, linear because the equations of $R$ and $L$ are linear equations and a "system" because the circuit is an interconnection of such elements. (We could also have capacitors in our circuit, but that would complicate this first effort.) Think of the voltage source as an input to this system (the circuit in Fig. 4.4) and the current $i(t)$ as an output of the system.

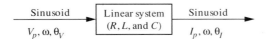

**Figure 4.5** A linear system responds at the frequency of excitation.

The important idea is the following: If the input is a sinusoid, the output is also a sinusoid at the same frequency. This assertion can be justified through examination of Eq. (4.13) and reflection on the properties of sinusoids. The sinusoidal steady-state solution of Eq. (4.13) must be a function that, when differentiated and added to itself, will result in a sinusoid of frequency $\omega$. The only mathematical function that qualifies is a sinusoid of the same frequency because the "shape" of the sinusoidal function is invariant to linear operations such as addition, differentiation, and integration.

**A mechanical analogy.** To get a feeling for this, think about a system of springs and masses. If you shake such a system with a certain frequency,[3] the entire system will shake at the same frequency. In other words, no new frequencies are generated in the system; the only frequency that exists is the one you applied externally. Therefore, if we apply a voltage at 60 Hz to the circuit in Fig. 4.4, the current will respond at 60 Hz.

**New unknowns.** The input voltage, being a sinusoid, is completely described by three numbers: the amplitude ($V_p = 100$ V), the frequency ($\omega = 120\pi$), and the phase

---

[3] The ac input is an electrical shaking.

($\theta_V = 30°$). The output current must also be a sinusoid, and hence can also be described by an amplitude ($I_p = ?$), frequency ($\omega = 120\pi$), and phase ($\theta_I = ?$). Because the output frequency is known, only the amplitude and phase need to be derived to determine the steady-state current. Our object, therefore, is to develop an efficient method for finding the amplitude and phase of the output; thus, $I_p$ and $\theta_I$ become our new unknowns. We now develop a mathematical model suited to finding the unknown amplitude and phase. The first step is to represent the amplitude and phase of a sinusoid by a complex number.

**A mathematical model.** We model a sinusoid as a rotating point in the complex plane. An initial difficulty at this stage is that many readers are not up to speed in the complex number system without review. So now we must follow a detour in this development to refresh your knowledge of the complex plane. If you do not need the detour, skip ahead to "Phasor Idea," page 161.

## Mathematics of the Complex Plane

Most of us were introduced to complex numbers through the study of quadratic equations. We discovered that the solution to certain equations like $x^2 + 4 = 0$ required the introduction of a new type of number:

$$x = \pm\sqrt{-4} = \pm i2 \tag{4.15}$$

**imaginary number, complex number**

The new numbers are called *imaginary* and the symbol $i$ is chosen (by mathematicians) to identify these new numbers, like "−" is used to identify negative numbers. The connotation of the word "imaginary" is unfortunate, because these new numbers are no less the product of mathematical imagination than "real" numbers. The solutions of other quadratic equations are combinations of the real and imaginary numbers, such as $2 \pm i\sqrt{2}$. These combinations are called *complex numbers*. Complex numbers are perhaps well named because the rules for manipulating them are more complicated than those for real numbers, but on the whole, the complex numbers represent a reasonable and useful extension of our number system.

We expect that you already have some skill in dealing with complex numbers. However, we will review the properties of complex numbers, because we will need many of these properties to understand fully why a rotating point in the complex plane is an ingenious tool for analyzing ac circuits. We now list and illustrate some of the important properties of complex numbers.

**Complex plane.** All numbers can be represented as points in a complex plane, such as we show in Fig. 4.6. The horizontal axis represents real numbers, and the vertical axis represents imaginary numbers. You will note that we have changed to $j$ instead of $i$ to indicate imaginary numbers. This is customary among electrical engineers to avoid confusion between imaginary numbers and currents, which have traditionally been symbolized by $i$. In Fig. 4.6, we show two complex numbers, $z_1$ and $z_2$, each having real and imaginary components. In general, we can state that a complex number has a real and imaginary part,

$$z = x + jy \tag{4.16}$$

In what follows, we give the principal algebraic and geometric properties of complex

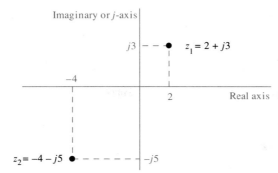

Imaginary or $j$-axis

$j3$ ---•  $z_1 = 2 + j3$

$-4$

$2$  Real axis

$z_2 = -4 - j5$ •------- $-j5$

**Figure 4.6** A complex number can be represented by a point in the complex plane.

numbers, for we need these properties to represent sinusoids as rotating points in the complex plane.

**Addition, subtraction, multiplication, and equality of complex numbers.** A good first approximation to the algebra of complex numbers is to use ordinary algebra plus two additions: (1) keep real and imaginary parts separate and (2) treat $j^2$ as $-1$. For example, when we add complex numbers, we add the real parts and the imaginary parts separately:

$$z_1 + z_2 = (2 + j3) + (-4 - j5) = (2 - 4) + j(3 - 5) = -2 - j2 \qquad (4.17)$$

and similarly for subtraction. Thus, complex numbers add and subtract like vectors in a plane. This is one of the few properties common between complex numbers and vectors.

Similarly, multiplication of $z_1$ and $z_2$ is

$$\begin{aligned}
z_1 z_2 &= (2 + j3)(-4 - j5) \\
&= 2(-4) + 2(-j5) + j3(-4) + j3(-j5) \\
&= -8 - j^2 15 - j10 - j12 \\
&= -8 + 15 + j(-10 - 12) \\
&= 7 - j22
\end{aligned} \qquad (4.18)$$

---

**EXAMPLE 4.2** **The square root of a complex number**

Find the square root of $-1 + j2$.

**SOLUTION:**
We have two unknowns, the real and the imaginary parts of the root, so we can proceed as follows:

$$\begin{aligned}
(x + jy)^2 &= -1 + j2 \\
x^2 + 2x(jy) + (jy)^2 &= -1 + j2 \\
x^2 - y^2 + j(2xy) &= -1 + j2 \\
x^2 - y^2 = -1 \quad \text{and} \quad 2xy &= 2
\end{aligned} \qquad (4.19)$$

Notice that we treated $j^2$ as $-1$, and we separated real and imaginary parts. Thus, an equation involving complex numbers is equivalent to two ordinary equations, one for the real part and one for the imaginary part. We can continue the problem by solving simultaneously for $x$ and $y$, but we will stop here. As we will soon see, there is a better way to find the roots of complex numbers.

**WHAT IF?**

What if you eliminate $y$ from Eq. (4.19) and got the equation $x^4 + x^2 - 1 = 0$? Because this equation has four solutions and we expect only two roots for the square root of $-1 + j2$, how to pick the right values of $x$?[4]

**Division, conjugation, and absolute values.** Division requires a trick to get the results into standard form:

$$\frac{z_2}{z_1} = \frac{-4 - j5}{2 + j3} = \frac{-4 - j5}{2 + j3} \times \frac{2 - j3}{2 - j3} \tag{4.20}$$

$$= \frac{(-4)(2) + (-j5)(-j3) + (-4)(-j3) + (-j5)(2)}{(2)^2 - (j3)^2}$$

$$= \frac{-8 - 15 + j(+12 - 10)}{4 + 9} = -\frac{23}{13} + j\frac{2}{13}$$

The first form we wrote to the right of the first equal sign is considered nonstandard because it contains a complex number in the denominator. To force the denominator to be real, we multiply top and bottom by the *complex conjugate* of z, which is the same complex number except that the sign of the imaginary part is changed. This causes the cross term in the product in the denominator to drop out and thus forces the denominator to be real and positive. Meanwhile, the numerator requires lots of careful work, but the rules are simple: Separate real and imaginary parts and let $j^2 = -1$. The final form is now considered standard because at a glance we can identify the real and imaginary parts of the quotient.

**complex conjugate**

If these tedious manipulations of complex numbers discourage you, take heart—there is a better way to multiply and divide complex numbers. Before we present this better way, however, we must look more closely at the complex conjugate. In Fig. 4.7, we show the complex conjugate of $z_1$, denoted by $z_1^*$, as the mirror image of $z_1$. We have already shown that the product of a complex number with its conjugate is a real and positive number:

$$zz^* = (x + jy)(x - jy) = x^2 - (jy)^2 = x^2 + y^2 \tag{4.21}$$

---

[4]The roots of the biquadratic are $x^2 = 0.618$ and $-1.618$. Because $x$ must be a real number in Eqs. (4.19), we have only $x = \pm\sqrt{0.618} = \pm 0.786$ .

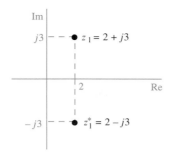

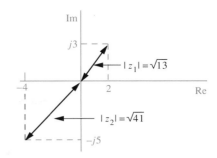

**Figure 4.7** The complex conjugate of $z_1$ is $z_1^*$.

**Figure 4.8** The magnitude of a complex number is its distance from the origin.

**absolute value**

This suggests the definition of the *absolute value* (or the magnitude) of a complex number:

$$|z| = \sqrt{zz^*} = \sqrt{x^2 + y^2} \tag{4.22}$$

The absolute value of a complex number thus is the Pythagorean sum of the real and imaginary parts. Geometrically, we identify this with the distance from the origin to the point representing the complex number, as shown in Fig. 4.8.

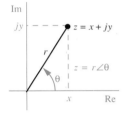

**Figure 4.9** Complex number in rectangular and polar forms.

**Polar form.** Figure 4.9 shows a general complex number. We have shown that $z$, a point in the complex plane, can be located either by its $x$, $y$ location or by a distance and an angle. We have used $r$ for the distance; clearly, $r$ is $|z|$, the absolute value of $z$. We call the $x$, $y$ form of $z$ the *rectangular* form and we call the $r$, $\theta$ form the *polar* form. We can symbolize the two forms as

$$z = x + jy = r \angle \theta = |z| \angle \theta \tag{4.23}$$

**rectangular form, polar form**

where the symbol $\angle$ is read "at an angle of." The right triangle yields simple transformations between *rectangular* and *polar* form:

$$x, y \iff r, \theta$$

$$x = r \cos \theta \qquad r = \sqrt{x^2 + y^2}$$

$$\iff$$

$$y = r \sin \theta \qquad \theta = \tan^{-1} \frac{y}{x} \tag{4.24}$$

Most engineering calculators have built-in functions for this transformation. Presumably, you have used this feature in working with vectors.[5]

At this stage of our review, the polar form represents only a notation. If we wanted to multiply or take the square root of a complex number, we would have to do it with the rectangular form. But the polar form is closely related to the exponential form, and because of this relationship, the polar form proves to be extremely useful, not merely as

---

[5] You will save yourself lots of time and grief by learning to use this feature.

a notation but also as a computational aid. All this arises out of Euler's theorem, an amazing relationship between the exponential function and angles in the complex plane.

**Euler's theorem.** The Swiss mathematician Euler (pronounced "oiler," as in Houston Oilers) discovered an important property of complex numbers. He began with the series expansion for the function $e^x$:

$$e^x = 1 + x + \frac{x^2}{2!} + \frac{x^3}{3!} + \cdots \tag{4.25}$$

and made a series expansion for $e^x$ when $x$ is imaginary, $x = j\theta$.

$$e^{j\theta} = 1 + (j\theta) + \frac{(j\theta)^2}{2!} + \frac{(j\theta)^3}{3!} + \cdots \tag{4.26}$$

Euler simplified with $(j\theta)^2 = -\theta^2$, $(j\theta)^3 = -j\theta^3$, ..., and followed the rule of grouping together real and imaginary parts. The results were

$$e^{j\theta} = \left(1 - \frac{\theta^2}{2!} + \frac{\theta^4}{4!} - \cdots\right) + j\left(\theta - \frac{\theta^3}{3!} + \frac{\theta^5}{5!} - \cdots\right) \tag{4.27}$$

The series in parentheses Euler identified as the expansions for cosine and sine. We would speculate that he wrote something like

$$e^{j\theta} = \cos\theta + j\sin\theta \quad (?) \tag{4.28}$$

The question mark is not there because of some suspicion about the mathematics—the algebra is correct—but it is there because Euler must have wondered what this could mean. Look, for example, at the strange combination of mathematical symbols on the left side of Eq. (4.28). A special number from differential calculus ($e$), the square root of $-1$, and the ratio of the arc to the radius of a circle ($\theta$)—what can these have to do with each other? And on the right side, we find the ratios of the legs to the hypotenuse of a right triangle. What can these have to do with $e$ and $j$?

**Interpretation.** The right side of Eq. (4.28) is interpreted in Fig. 4.10. Because the Pythagorean sum of cosine and sine is unity, the right side of Eq. (4.28) must be a point in the complex plane one unit from the origin located at an angle $\theta$ counterclockwise from the positive real axis, as shown. Euler's theorem requires that this point also be expressed by the function $e^{j\theta}$, as indicated by Eq. (4.28).

The best way to get acquainted with a new mathematical relationship often is to try it on some familiar specific cases to see how it works. Let us try Euler's formula on the

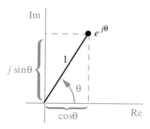

**Figure 4.10** Implication of Eq. (4.28).

identity $\sqrt{-1} = j1$. We will express the left side of this equation with Euler's formula and follow the rules of exponents:

$$\sqrt{-1} = \sqrt{e^{j\pi}} = (e^{j\pi})^{1/2} = e^{j\pi/2} \qquad (4.29)$$

$$= \cos\frac{\pi}{2} + j\,\sin\frac{\pi}{2}$$

$$= 0 + j1$$

The first substitution follows because $-1$ in the complex plane is one unit from the origin at an angle $\pi$ from the positive real axis. The second change replaces the square root symbol by the one-half power, and the third change follows an ordinary rule of exponents. The form on the second line is a direct application of Euler's formula, and the third line gives the cosine and sine of $\pi/2$ radians. We conclude that Euler's formula leads to the correct answer for this special case. If we tried it on other powers and roots, it would work there also.

**exponential form**

**Exponential form.** Comparison of Figs. 4.9 and 4.10 reveals that a complex number can be expressed as

$$z = re^{j\theta} \qquad (4.30)$$

where $r = |z|$. Clearly, this is closely related to the polar form, Eq. (4.23), and we have

$$z = r\angle\theta = re^{j\theta} = \underbrace{r\cos\theta}_{x} + j\underbrace{r\sin\theta}_{y} \qquad (4.31)$$

In Eq. (4.31), we normally express the angle of the polar form in degrees, whereas in the exponential form, the angle *must* be expressed in radians for the Euler formula to be valid. This inconsistency arises from our traditions but does not diminish the fact that both forms give the same information, namely, that the complex number falls in the complex plane at a radius $r$ and an angle $\theta$ counterclockwise from the positive real axis. We stress that the polar form is merely a compact notation, whereas the exponential form is a legitimate mathematical function.

**Multiplication, division, and conjugation revisited.** The laws of exponents reveal that the magnitude of the product of two complex numbers is the product of the magnitudes of the numbers and the angle of the product is the sum of their angles.

$$(z_1)(z_2) = (r_1 e^{j\theta_1})(r_2 e^{j\theta_2}) = r_1 r_2 e^{j(\theta_1 + \theta_2)} \qquad (4.32)$$

Although the proof rests on the exponential form, the results are more easily expressed in polar form:

$$(r_1 \angle \theta_1)(r_2 \angle \theta_2) = r_1 r_2 \angle (\theta_1 + \theta_2) \qquad (4.33)$$

Hence, to multiply two complex numbers, multiply their magnitudes and add their angles. In a similar way, we can show that dividing two complex numbers requires dividing the magnitudes and subtracting the angles:

$$\frac{r_2 \angle \theta_2}{r_1 \angle \theta_1} = \frac{r_2}{r_1} \angle (\theta_2 - \theta_1) \qquad (4.34)$$

| EXAMPLE 4.3 | Multiplication and division of complex numbers |
|---|---|

Use polar form to confirm Eqs. (4.18) and (4.20).

**SOLUTION:**
First, we convert $z_1$ and $z_2$ to polar form using Eq. (4.24):[6]

$$z_1 = 2 + j3 = 3.61 \angle 56.3°$$

$$z_2 = -4 - j5 = 6.40 \angle -128.7° \qquad (4.35)$$

We multiply using Eq. (4.33):

$$z_1 z_2 = (3.61)(6.40) \angle (53.6° - 128.7°) \qquad (4.36)$$
$$= 23.1 \angle -72.5° = 7 - j22$$

We divide using Eq. (4.34):

$$\frac{z_2}{z_1} = \frac{6.40}{3.61} \angle [-128.7° - (56.3°)] \qquad (4.37)$$

$$= 1.78 \angle (-185.0°) = -1.77 + j0.154$$

| WHAT IF? | What if you express the complex conjugate in polar form? You see how the polar form gets the same results directly.[7] |
|---|---|

**Summary of how to calculate with complex numbers.** When we add and subtract complex numbers, the rectangular form must be used. This is true because we add and subtract real and imaginary parts separately. When we multiply (or divide) complex numbers, the polar form should be used because the magnitudes multiply (or divide) and the angles add (or subtract).

For the analysis of ac circuits, we must master the manipulation of complex numbers. Our techniques require frequent changes between rectangular and polar form. In the days of slide rules, these conversions were a bother, but now they require a simple keystroke on the calculator. If you currently do not know about those keys, locate the manual on your calculator and look them up. This review of complex numbers is vital to your gaining skill in solving ac circuit problems. These operations, like the vector

---

[6] Actually, I used the button on my calculator marked $\rightarrow P$.

[7] If $z = r \angle \theta$, then $z^* = r \angle (-\theta) = r \cos \theta + jr \sin (-\theta) = r \cos \theta - jr \sin \theta$.

manipulations required in statics, are simple in principle, but care is required to produce correct answers consistently.

**Some examples.** Here are two additional examples of complex number manipulation, which give practice and show some new principles.

$$(2 - j6)(5\angle + 30°)^* = (6.32\angle - 71.6°)(5\angle - 30°) \tag{4.38}$$
$$= 31.6\angle - 101.6°$$
$$= -6.34 - j31.0$$

Note that complex conjugation merely changes the sign of the angle.

Find $z$, where $z^3 = -1 + j\,0.5$.

$$z^3 = -1 + j\,0.5 = 1.12 \angle 153.4° = 1.12\,e^{j(153.4)(\pi/180)}$$

$$z = (1.12e^{j2.68})^{1/3} = \sqrt[3]{1.12}\,e^{j2.68/3} \tag{4.39}$$
$$= \text{also } \sqrt[3]{1.12}\,e^{j(2.68+2\pi)/3} \text{ and } \sqrt[3]{1.12}\,e^{j(2.68+4\pi)/3}$$
$$= 1.04\angle 51.1°, 1.04\angle 171.1°, 1.04\angle 291.1°$$

To find all three cube roots, we must add $2\pi$ and $4\pi$ (one and two additional rotations) to the angle before dividing by 3.

## Phasor Idea

**Expressing a sinusoid with a complex number.** Now that we have reviewed the mathematics of the complex plane, we will return to the main quest, that of finding the steady-state solution of the ac circuit problem described in Fig. 4.4 and Eq. (4.13). Specifically, we wish to find a way to represent sinusoidal functions, such as that appearing in Eq. (4.1), repeated here

$$v_s(t) = V_p \cos(\omega t + \theta), \quad V_p = 100\text{ V}, \quad \omega = 2\pi \times 60, \quad \theta = 30° \tag{4.40}$$

Euler's formula, Eq. (4.28), allows us to express a sinusoidal waveform with the function

$$v_s(t) = V_p \cos(\omega t + \theta) = \text{Re}\{V_p e^{j(\omega t + \theta)}\} \tag{4.41}$$

where Re, the "real part of," is the complex-plane notation for the projection on the real axis. Equation (4.41) follows from Eq. (4.42), which expands Euler's formula:

$$V_p e^{j(\omega t + \theta)} = V_p[\cos(\omega t + \theta) + j\sin(\omega t + \theta)]$$
$$= \underbrace{V_p \cos(\omega t + \theta)}_{\text{real part}} + j\,\underbrace{V_p \sin(\omega t + \theta)}_{\text{imaginary part}} \tag{4.42}$$

**Rotating point in the complex plane.** The left side of Eq. (4.42) has great importance in this development and deserves more attention. We rearrange it

$$V_p e^{j(\omega t + \theta)} = V_p(e^{j\omega t})(e^{j\theta}) = (V_p e^{j\theta})e^{j\omega t} \tag{4.43}$$
$$= (V_p \angle \theta)e^{j\omega t} = (100\angle 30°)e^{j120\pi t}$$

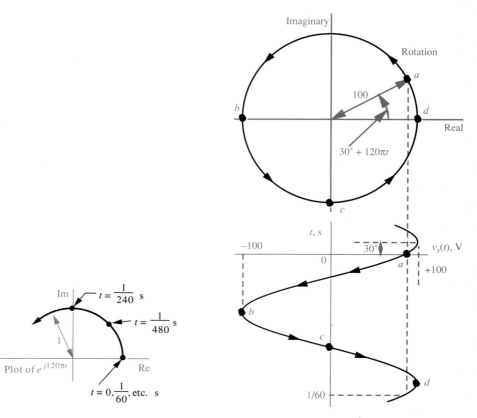

**Figure 4.11** Rotating point in the complex plane.

**Figure 4.12** The correspondence between the rotating point in the complex plane and the sinusoidal waveform.

The first line results from some juggling of terms and the rules for exponents. The second line emphasizes that this term consists of a complex constant, $V_p \angle \theta = 100 \angle 30°$, multiplied by a time function, $e^{j\omega t}$, which describes the rotation of a point in the complex plane. If we follow its progress as time increases, as shown in Fig. 4 11, we find it to be a point at unit distance from the origin rotating around the origin, starting at the real axis at $t = 0$ and passing through that point 60 times every second.

The time function $e^{j\omega t}$ describes a point rotating in the complex plane at an angular frequency of $\omega$ radians per second. When we multiply this rotation function by the complex number $V_p \angle \theta = 100 \angle 30°$, we move the point out to a magnitude of $V_p = 100$ and counterclockwise by an angle of $\theta = 30°$ at $t = 0$, as shown in Fig. 4.12 (point $a$). The rotation begins from that point and rotates around a circle of radius 100, 60 times a second. The projection on the real axis is shown below the complex plane. Clearly, we have the desired sinusoid—correct amplitude, phase, and frequency. Figure 4.12 is a graphical interpretation of Eq. (4.41), illustrated for the values appropriate for Eq. (4.40).

**Summary.** We have shown that a sinusoidal function can be represented by

$$v_s(t) = V_p \cos(\omega t + \theta) = \text{Re}\{\underline{\mathbf{V}}_s e^{j\omega t}\} \tag{4.44}$$

where $\underline{\mathbf{V}}_s = V_p \angle \theta = 100 \angle 30°$ is a complex number containing the amplitude and phase of the sinusoid. We use the uppercase bold, underlined symbols to indicate a complex number that does not vary with time. Thus, we can represent a sinusoid by a rotating point in the complex plane. To see why this is useful, we must return to the differential equation we are solving.

## Back to the Circuit Problem

**Using complex numbers to solve the DE.** Equation 4.45 is our DE,

$$L\frac{di}{dt} + Ri = V_p \cos(\omega t + \theta) = \text{Re}\{V_p \angle \theta e^{j\omega t}\} \tag{4.45}$$

$$= \text{Re}\{\underline{\mathbf{V}}_s e^{j\omega t}\}$$

We have introduced the complex number form for the sinusoidal voltage source.

**The new unknown.** Recall that we know something about the unknown current, $i(t)$. Earlier we argued that the current had to be a sinusoid of the same frequency as the input voltage. Only the amplitude and phase of the current must be determined. Using our scheme for representing sinusoids by complex numbers, we know that $i(t)$ may be represented in the form

$$i(t) = \text{Re}\{\underline{\mathbf{I}} e^{j\omega t}\}, \qquad \text{where } \underline{\mathbf{I}} = I_p \angle \theta_I \tag{4.46}$$

when $I_p$ is the peak amplitude and $\theta_I$ the phase of the current. We have thus introduced a complex number, $\underline{\mathbf{I}}$ as the unknown; everything else in the equation is known. We have numerical values for $L$, $R$, and $\underline{\mathbf{V}}_s$, and, of course, $\omega$ is known from the input. We can now substitute Eq. (4.46) into Eq. (4.45):

$$L\frac{d}{dt}\text{Re}\{\underline{\mathbf{I}} e^{j\omega t}\} + R \times \text{Re}\{\underline{\mathbf{I}} e^{j\omega t}\} = \text{Re}\{\underline{\mathbf{V}}_s e^{j\omega t}\} \tag{4.47}$$

We wish to avoid taking unnecessary excursions into mathematical proofs, so you will have to take our word for this assertion: The derivative can be taken inside the "real part" operation:

$$\frac{d}{dt}\text{Re}\{\underline{\mathbf{I}} e^{j\omega t}\} = \text{Re}\left\{\frac{d}{dt}\underline{\mathbf{I}} e^{j\omega t}\right\} = \text{Re}\left\{\underline{\mathbf{I}}\frac{d}{dt} e^{j\omega t}\right\} \tag{4.48}$$

$$= \text{Re}\{j\omega\underline{\mathbf{I}} e^{j\omega t}\}$$

We substitute the derivative back into Eq. (4.47). Because the "real part" operation distributes, we can collect terms:

$$\text{Re}\{L(j\omega\underline{\mathbf{I}} e^{j\omega t}) + R(\underline{\mathbf{I}} e^{j\omega t})\} = \text{Re}\{\underline{\mathbf{V}}_s e^{j\omega t}\} \tag{4.49}$$

$$\text{Re}\{(j\omega L\underline{\mathbf{I}} + R\underline{\mathbf{I}} - \underline{\mathbf{V}}_s) e^{j\omega t}\} = 0 \tag{4.50}$$

Equation (4.50) emerges from the algebra; but what does it mean? Look first at the term, $j\omega L\underline{I} + R\underline{I} - \underline{V}_s$. This represents a complex number that does not vary with time. Because it contains the complex number representing the unknown current amplitude and phase, $\underline{I}$, this term in Eq. (4.50) is an unknown constant, a point somewhere in the complex plane. Of course, the $e^{j\omega t}$ term rotates this unknown constant, and Re represents the projection of the rotating point on the real axis. The right side of Eq. (4.50) requires that this projection be zero at all times; hence, the complex constant must itself be zero. If the point were not rotating, many complex constants could have zero projection,[8] but the origin is the only point that continues to have zero projection when rotated about the origin.

**Conclusion.** Equation (4.50) requires

$$j\omega L\underline{I} + R\underline{I} - \underline{V}_s = 0 \qquad (4.51)$$

Equation (4.51) involves only complex constants; time is no longer a factor. We know all the constants except $\underline{I}$, so we can solve for the unknown $\underline{I}$:

$$\underline{I} = \frac{\underline{V}_s}{R + j\omega L} = \frac{100\angle 30°}{100 + j(120\pi \times 0.5)} \qquad (4.52)$$

$$= \frac{100\angle 30°}{213\angle 62.1°} = 0.469\angle - 32.1°$$

Recall that the magnitude of $\underline{I}$ represents the peak value of the sinusoidal steady-state current flowing in the $RL$ circuit and the angle of $\underline{I}$ represents the phase angle of the current. Hence, we may write

$$i_{ss}(t) = 0.469 \cos(120\pi t - 32.1°) \text{ A} \qquad (4.53)$$

This at last is the steady-state solution to the DE in Eq. (4.13) and hence this is the steady-state current that flows in the circuit shown in Fig. 4.4 after the transient period passes. Before finding the transient part of the solution, we will summarize the argument.

**Summary of the argument.** Because the development of Eq. (4.51) has taken many pages and extensive math review, you may feel that you have been led through a complicated argument. Actually, there are but a few steps:

1. We wrote the DE and focused on the steady-state solution.

$$L\frac{di}{dt} + Ri = V_p \cos(\omega t + \theta) \qquad (4.54)$$

2. We then represented the sinusoidal voltage and the unknown sinusoidal current by the real parts of rotating complex constants and took the derivative. The result was

$$\text{Re}\{j\omega L\,\underline{I}\,e^{j\omega t}\} + \text{Re}\{R\,\underline{I}\,e^{j\omega t}\} = \text{Re}\{\underline{V}_s\,e^{j\omega t}\} \qquad (4.55)$$

---

[8] All points on the imaginary axis have this property.

3. We then collected terms and reasoned that the resulting complex constant had to vanish when the equation is put into the form of Eq. (4.50). This amounts to the same thing as dropping Re and $e^{j\omega t}$ in Eq. (4.55). Note that we did not *cancel* these factors–that would be mathematically incorrect—but the result is the same as if we had canceled them.

4. The resulting equation is solved for $\underline{I}$, and the result is easily interpreted in terms of the amplitude and phase of the current in the circuit.

**Complete solution.** We may now determine the complete solution to Eq. (4.13) using principles developed in Chapter 3. The form of the solution is

$$i(t) = Ae^{-t/\tau} + 0.469 \cos(120\pi t - 32.1°) \qquad (4.56)$$

where $\tau = L/R = 1/200$ s and $A$ is an unknown constant to be determined from the initial condition. The initial current must be zero, $i(0^+) = 0$, due to the inductor; hence,

$$0 = Ae^{-0/\tau} + 0.469 \cos(-32.1°) \qquad (4.57)$$

Hence, $A = -0.397$. Thus, the total solution is

$$i(t) = -0.397e^{-200t} + 0.469 \cos(120\pi t - 32.1°)\,\text{A} \qquad (4.58)$$

This response is shown in Fig. 4.13. The current rapidly approaches the sinusoidal steady-state part of the solution after the switch is closed.

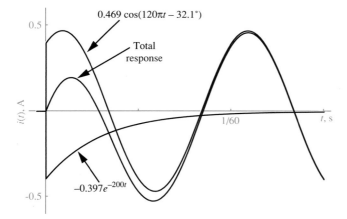

**Figure 4.13** The current is the sum of the transient and steady-state responses.

**phasor**

**Phasors.** Before giving further shortcuts and simplifications, let us summarize what we have learned and introduce some vocabulary. A *phasor* is a complex number containing the amplitude and phase of a sinusoid. The phasor produces the time-function sinusoid when rotated at the proper frequency and projected on the real axis. Because it is difficult to see a single point, phasors are usually drawn as an arrow from the origin, as in Fig. 4.14. Because phasors add like vectors, they are often incorrectly referred to as vectors.

The equation relating the sinusoid $v(t)$ and the phasor $\underline{V}$ is

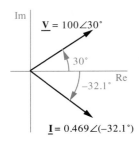

$$v(t) = \text{Re}\{\underline{\mathbf{V}}\, e^{j\omega t}\} \tag{4.59}$$

The phasor encodes the amplitude and phase of the sinusoid in the form $\underline{\mathbf{V}} = V_p \angle \theta$. Equation (4.59) can be differentiated to show that the phasor representing the derivative is

$$\frac{dv(t)}{dt} = \text{Re}\left\{\underline{\mathbf{V}}\,\frac{de^{j\omega t}}{dt}\right\} = \text{Re}\left\{\underbrace{j\omega\underline{\mathbf{V}}}_{\substack{\text{phasor} \\ \text{for derivative}}}\, e^{j\omega t}\right\} \tag{4.60}$$

**Figure 4.14** Voltage phasor and current phasor.

**The Frequency Domain**

**frequency domain, time domain**

Phasors can be added to represent the addition of two sinusoids of the same frequency, as is shown in the next example.

We use the expression *frequency domain* to refer to the form of the DE after it has been transformed into a complex equation. The DE is called the *time-domain* formulation of the problem, but the transformed equation belongs to the frequency domain—time is no longer a factor.

Equation (4.60) shows that the differentiation in the time domain corresponds to multiplication by $j\omega$ in the frequency domain. The phasor voltages and currents belong to the frequency domain. We move from the frequency domain to the time domain by rotating the phasors at the proper frequency and taking projections on the real axis.[9]

---

| EXAMPLE 4.4 | **Phasor addition** |

Add the two sinusoids $v_1(t) = 12\cos(100t)$ and $v_2(t) = 8\cos(100t - 48°)$.

**SOLUTION:**
First, we find the phasors

$$v_1(t) = 12\cos(100t) \Rightarrow \underline{\mathbf{V}}_1 = 12 \angle 0°$$

$$v_2(t) = 8\cos(100t - 48°) \Rightarrow \underline{\mathbf{V}}_2 = 8\angle - 48° = 5.35 - j5.94 \tag{4.61}$$

The sum, $v_1(t) + v_2(t)$, will be represented by the phasor sum, $\underline{\mathbf{V}}_1 + \underline{\mathbf{V}}_2$, which is

$$\underline{\mathbf{V}}_1 + \underline{\mathbf{V}}_2 = 12 + j0 + (5.35 - j5.94) \tag{4.62}$$

$$= 17.35 - j5.94 = 18.34\angle - 18.9°$$

Thus, the sum will be $v_1(t) + v_2(t) = 18.34\cos(100t - 18.9°)$.

**WHAT IF?**  What if it were the difference, $v_1(t) - v_2(t)$, you wanted?[10]

---

[9] That is the mathematical way. In practice, we take the magnitude and angle of the phasor and substitute into a standard cosine form, Eq. (4.1).

[10] $v_1(t) - v_2(t) = 8.92\cos(100t + 41.8°)$.

**OBJECTIVE 2**

**To understand the phasor concept and be able to find the sinusoidal steady-state response of a circuit, given the differential equation**

Shortening the procedure. This method for determining the sinusoidal steady state admits to additional shortcuts. If we compare Eq. (4.51) with the original DE, Eq. (4.13), we see a direct correlation between terms:

$$i(t) \Rightarrow \mathbf{I}, \qquad v_s(t) \Rightarrow \underline{\mathbf{V}}_s, \qquad \frac{d}{dt} \Rightarrow j\omega \qquad (4.63)$$

We have shown that these are legitimate transformations. These suggest a shorter method:

1. Write the DE.

2. Perform the transformations shown in Eq. (4.63) on the known sinusoidal source, the unknown voltage or current, and the d/dt.

3. Solve the resulting complex equation for the unknown.

4. Interpret the results by substituting the amplitude and phase back into the standard form for a sinusoid. This amounts to the transformation

$$\underline{\mathbf{V}} = V_p \angle \theta$$
$$\Downarrow \quad \Downarrow \quad \searrow$$
$$v(t) = V_p \cos(\omega t + \theta) \qquad (4.64)$$

---

**EXAMPLE 4.5** | **Short method**

Using the short method, determine the voltage in Figure 4.15.

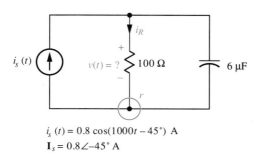

$i_s(t) = 0.8 \cos(1000t - 45°)$ A
$\mathbf{I}_s = 0.8 \angle -45°$ A

**Figure 4.15** Solve for the steady-state voltage across the parallel resistor and capacitor.

**SOLUTION:**
We use nodal analysis to derive the DE. At the top node, KCL is

$$\frac{v}{R} + C\frac{dv}{dt} = i_s(t) \qquad (4.65)$$

The second step is to transform this DE into a complex equation with the changes suggested by Eq. (4.63).

$$i_s \Rightarrow \mathbf{I}_s = 0.8\angle -45° \qquad v \Rightarrow \mathbf{V} = ? \qquad \frac{d}{dt} \Rightarrow j\omega \tag{4.66}$$

The resulting complex equation is

$$\frac{1}{R}\mathbf{V} + j\omega C\mathbf{V} = \mathbf{I}_s \tag{4.67}$$

We can solve the equation for $\mathbf{V}$, which represents the amplitude and phase of the unknown voltage. The results are

$$\mathbf{V} = \frac{\mathbf{I}_s}{1/R + j\omega C} = \frac{0.8\angle -45°}{1/100 + j1000 \times 6 \times 10^{-6}} \tag{4.68}$$

$$= \frac{0.8\angle -45°}{0.0117\angle 31.0°} = 68.6\angle -76.0° \text{ V}$$

The last step consists in writing the current in the standard form for sinusoids. From Eq. (4.64), we write

$$v(t) = 68.6\cos(1000t - 76.0°) \text{ V} \tag{4.69}$$

You must admit that apart from the complex arithmetic, which may still be unfamiliar to you, the derivation of the DE is now the most difficult part of the solution. We will soon introduce shortcuts for simplifying that part of the problem.

| EXAMPLE 4.6 | **Using sine form** |

In Fig. 4.16(a), we show a series $RC$ circuit, with the voltage across the capacitor given as $5\sin(500t)$ V. Determine the voltage across the source that produces this prescribed voltage.

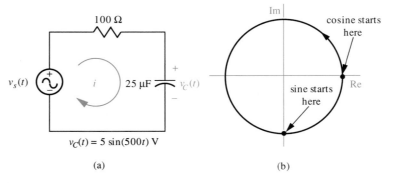

(a)

(b)

**Figure 4.16** (a) The voltage across $C$ is given; the source voltage is to be found. (b) The frequency domain equivalent of a sine function is $-j$ or $1\angle -90°$ because a rotating point starting at the bottom projects on the real axis as a sine function.

**SOLUTION:**

Considering that the current is $C(dv_C/dt)$, the voltage across the resistance is $RC(dv_C/dt)$; hence, the DE for the source voltage is

$$v_s(t) = 100 \times 25 \times 10^{-6} \frac{dv_C}{dt} + v_C \tag{4.70}$$

which transforms into the frequency domain as

$$\underline{\mathbf{V}}_s = 25 \times 10^{-4}(j500)\,\underline{\mathbf{V}}_C + \underline{\mathbf{V}}_C = (1 + j1.25)\,\underline{\mathbf{V}}_C \tag{4.71}$$

where $\underline{\mathbf{V}}_s$ and $\underline{\mathbf{V}}_C$ are phasors representing the voltages across the source and capacitor, respectively. Because $v_C(t)$ is a sine (instead of a cosine) function, we must represent it as

$$v_C(t) = 5\sin(500t) \Rightarrow \underline{\mathbf{V}}_C = -j5 \tag{4.72}$$

We may show that sine transforms into $-j$ by using the trigonometric identity $\sin x = \cos(x - 90°)$, but a graphical demonstration is shown in Fig. 4.16(b). We have identified $-j$ with sine because that point produces a sine function when rotated and projected onto the real axis: The projection is zero at $t = 0$, but increases to unity one-quarter of a period later. Finally, we substitute Eq. (4.72) into Eq. (4.71) and transform back into the time domain.

$$\underline{\mathbf{V}}_s = (1 + j1.25)(-j5) = 1.601\angle 51.3° \times 5\angle -90°$$

$$= 8.00\angle -38.7°$$

$$v_s(t) = 8.00\cos(500t - 38.7°)\ \text{V} \tag{4.73}$$

## Check Your Understanding

1. Convert $10 - j12$ and $-30 + j58$ to polar form.
2. What is the rectangular form for $4\angle 25°$ and $0.025\angle -140°$?
3. Convert $13.5\,e^{j0.86}$ to polar and rectangular forms.
4. What is the complex conjugate of $z = -2 + j6$?
5. Give both square roots of $1 + j1$.
6. What are the phasors representing $-6\cos(\omega t - 30°)$ and $5\sin(\omega t + 10°)$?
7. What is the time-domain sum of the two sinusoids in the previous question?
8. In transforming a DE into the frequency domain, what replaces $d/dt$?

*Answers.* **(1)** $15.6\angle -50.2°$, $65.3\angle 117.3°$;   **(2)** $3.63 + j1.69$, $(-1.92 - j1.61) \times 10^{-2}$; **(3)** $13.5\angle 49.3°$, $8.81 + j10.2$;   **(4)** $-2 - j6$;   **(5)** $1.19\angle 22.5°$, $1.19\angle 202.5°$; **(6)** $6\angle 150°$, $5\angle -80°$;   **(7)** $4.74\cos(\omega t - 156°)$;   **(8)** $j\omega$.

### The Final Shortcut

**Look at the answer.** Let us look again at the steady-state response of the *RL* circuit, shown again in Fig. 4.17. This is a simple circuit with *R* and *L* in series; we know the sinusoidal driving voltage and we have found the current. When expressed as phasor voltages and currents, our results were given in Eq. (4.52) as

$$\underline{I} = \frac{\underline{V}_s}{R + j\omega L} \tag{4.74}$$

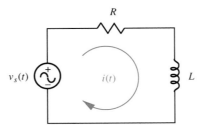

**Figure 4.17** The *RL* circuit again.

We interpret Eq. (4.74) to state that the phasor current is found by dividing the phasor voltage by the sum of the resistance and *jωL*. Because Eq. (4.74) closely resembles Ohm's law, every part of this expression has meaning to us except the *jωL* part. Clearly, this term represents the effect of the inductor in the circuit. What can it mean?

**The Frequency Domain**

**Impedance.** This question, or one similar to it, sparked long ago an idea that leads to the final shortcut in analyzing ac circuits—the idea of impedance. This idea is the following: Because we are dealing only with sinusoidal voltages and currents, and because these can be represented by complex numbers, why not represent *R*'s, *L*'s, and *C*'s by complex numbers also? This suggests transforming Ohm's law and the definitions of *L* and *C* into the frequency domain and representing them by complex equations.

**Impedance of an inductor.** Here is how it works for the inductor: The defining equation for an inductor is

$$v_L = L\frac{di_L}{dt} \tag{4.75}$$

Because we are dealing with sinusoids, we can transform this equation into a frequency-domain equivalent:

$$v_L(t) \Rightarrow \underline{V}_L, \qquad i_L(t) \Rightarrow \underline{I}_L, \qquad \frac{d}{dt} \Rightarrow j\omega \tag{4.76}$$

The result is

$$\underline{V}_L = L(j\omega\underline{I}_L) = j\omega L\underline{I}_L \tag{4.77}$$

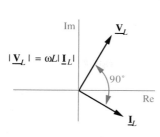

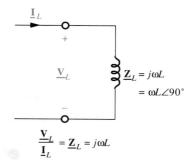

**Figure 4.18** For an inductor, current lags voltage by 90°.

**Figure 4.19** Representing an inductor by its impedance.

The phasor interpretation of Eq. (4.77) is shown in Fig. 4.18. Equation (4.77) gives both the magnitude and phase relationships between the phasor voltage and phasor current for an inductor. The magnitude of the phasor voltage is $\omega L$ times the magnitude of the phasor current. Because $j1 = 1 \angle 90°$, the phase of the phasor voltage leads the phase of the phasor current by 90°. We can verify this interpretation by taking the derivative in the time domain. If $i_L = I_p \cos(\omega t + \theta_I)$, then $v_L(t)$ is

$$v_L = L \frac{d}{dt} I_p \cos(\omega t + \theta_I) = -\omega L I_p \sin(\omega t + \theta_I) \qquad (4.78)$$

$$= \omega L I_p \cos(\omega t + \theta_I + 90°)$$

where we have used the identity that $-\sin\phi = \cos(\phi + 90°)$. We use the word "impedance" to refer to the complex number relating the phasor voltage and phasor current of an element in an ac circuit, as shown in Fig. 4 19.

We began using the word "impedance" back in Chapter 2 in connection with output impedance and impedance level, with the promise that a precise definition would follow. We define *impedance*, **Z**, as the phasor voltage divided by the phasor current,

**impedance**

$$\mathbf{Z} = \frac{\mathbf{V}}{\mathbf{I}} \qquad (4.79)$$

Applying this definition to Eq. (4.77), we obtain the result shown in Fig. 4 19:

$$\mathbf{Z}_L = j\omega L \qquad (4.80)$$

---

**EXAMPLE 4.6** **Impedance of an inductor**

Find the impedance of a 10-mH inductor at a frequency of 360 Hz.

**SOLUTION:**
The impedance is given by Eq. (4.80):

$$\mathbf{Z}_L = j\omega L = j2\pi \times 360 \times 0.01 = j22.6 \; \Omega \qquad (4.81)$$

$$= 22.6\angle +90° \; \Omega$$

**WHAT IF?** | What if the frequency is doubled?[11]

**Kirchhoff's laws in the frequency domain.** You will note that Fig. 4.19 also introduces the practice of putting the phasor voltage and current on the circuit diagram. This is legitimate and useful because, for sinusoidal voltages and currents, KVL and KCL can also be transformed directly into the frequency domain; for example,

$$-v_s(t) + v_R(t) + v_L(t) = 0 \;\Rightarrow\; -\mathbf{V}_s + \mathbf{V}_R + \mathbf{V}_L = 0 \qquad (4.82)$$

**Conservation of Energy**

Equation (4.82) gives the frequency-domain version of KVL as applied to the *RL* circuit. If there were nodes in the circuit, we could also write frequency-domain versions of KCL at these nodes.

**Summary.** We can represent all voltages and currents in an ac circuit as phasors. These phasors are complex numbers representing the amplitudes and phases of the waveforms in the sinusoidal steady state. Phasor voltages and currents obey KVL and KCL. We can also represent *R* and *L* (and *C*, when we get around to it) as complex numbers, which are called *impedances*. Figure 4.20 gives the impedance of *R*, which is Ohm's law for phasors. The impedance of a resistor is real because its voltage and current have the same phase.

**Representing the circuit in the frequency domain.** We can transform the entire circuit into the frequency domain, representing voltages and currents as phasors and representing the resistor and inductor as impedances. Because phasor voltages and currents obey KVL and KCL, we can use the techniques of dc circuit theory to solve

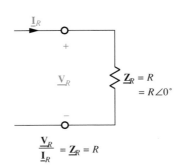

$$\frac{\mathbf{V}_R}{\mathbf{I}_R} = \mathbf{Z}_R = R$$

**Figure 4.20** The impedance of a resistor is real because no phase shift occurs.

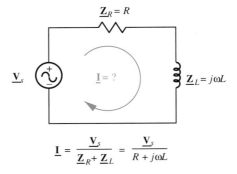

$$\mathbf{I} = \frac{\mathbf{V}_s}{\mathbf{Z}_R + \mathbf{Z}_L} = \frac{\mathbf{V}_s}{R + j\omega L}$$

**Figure 4.21** The frequency-domain version of the *RL* circuit.

[11] Then the impedance doubles in magnitude to 45.2 $\Omega$. The angle is unchanged.

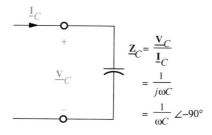

**Figure 4.22**   Impedance of a capacitor.

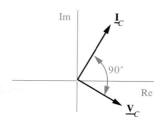

**Figure 4.23**   For a capacitor, the current leads the voltage by 90°.

the circuit, only we must now work with impedances as if they were "complex resistors."

**Benefits of the impedance concept.**   We can now solve our original problem in the frequency domain. Figure 4.21 shows the circuit transformed into the frequency domain. Because we have a simple series circuit, we can find $\mathbf{I}$ by the method of equivalent resistance (actually, equivalent impedance), combining the impedances of $R$ and $L$ in series. If we were faced with a more complicated circuit, we might analyze the circuit using node voltages, loop currents, or a Thévenin equivalent circuit. Through the concept of impedance, all the techniques of dc circuits can be applied to ac circuit problems. The DE does not have to be written.

**The impedance of a capacitor.**   We may use these techniques to derive the impedance of a capacitor, as symbolized in Fig. 4.22. We transform the definition of a capacitor into the frequency domain,

$$i_C = C\frac{dv_C}{dt} \ \Rightarrow \ \mathbf{I}_C = C(j\omega\mathbf{V}_C) = j\omega C\mathbf{V}_C \qquad (4.83)$$

Thus, the impedance of a capacitor is

$$\mathbf{Z}_C = \frac{\mathbf{V}_C}{\mathbf{I}_C} = \frac{1}{j\omega C} = \frac{j}{j^2\omega C} = -j\frac{1}{\omega C} = \frac{1}{\omega C}\angle -90° \qquad (4.84)$$

For a capacitor, the voltage lags the current by 90°, as shown in Fig. 4.23.

**Frequency–domain technique.**   We now illustrate the full use of the frequency domain in finding the sinusoidal steady-state response of a circuit.
We will find $v(t)$ in Fig. 4.24. The steps are as follows:

**1.** Transform the time domain variables to phasors.

$$v_s(t) = 10\cos(2000t + 20°) \ \Rightarrow \ \mathbf{V}_s = 10 \angle 20°$$

$$v(t) = ? \qquad\qquad\qquad \Rightarrow \mathbf{V} = ? \qquad (4.85)$$

**2.** Transform the circuit into the frequency domain as impedances.

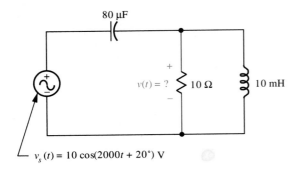

$v_s(t) = 10 \cos(2000t + 20°)$ V

**Figure 4.24** The circuit in the time domain.

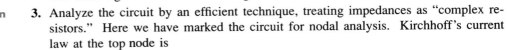

**Figure 4.25** The circuit in the frequency domain. Impedances replace $R$, $L$, and $C$.

$$R \Rightarrow \mathbf{Z}_R = R = 10 \ \Omega$$

$$L \Rightarrow \mathbf{Z}_L = j\omega L = j2000 \times 0.01 = j20 \ \Omega$$

$$C \Rightarrow \mathbf{Z}_C = \frac{1}{j\omega C} = -j\frac{1}{2000 \times 80 \times 10^{-6}} = -j6.25 \ \Omega \qquad (4.86)$$

The resulting circuit is shown in Fig. 4.25.

**IDEA** **Conservation of Charge**

3. Analyze the circuit by an efficient technique, treating impedances as "complex resistors." Here we have marked the circuit for nodal analysis. Kirchhoff's current law at the top node is

$$\frac{\mathbf{V}_a - 10 \angle 20°}{-j6.25} + \frac{\mathbf{V}_a - (0)}{10} + \frac{\mathbf{V}_a - (0)}{j20} = 0 \qquad (4.87)$$

which yields

$$\mathbf{V}_a = \frac{10 \angle 20°/(-j6.25)}{1/-j6.25 + 1/10 + 1/j20} = 10.8 \angle 62.3° \ \text{V} \qquad (4.88)$$

4. Transform the resulting phasor back into the time domain.

$$10.8 \angle 62.3° \Rightarrow v(t) = 10.8 \cos(2000t + 62.3°) \ \text{V} \qquad (4.89)$$

---

**EXAMPLE 4.7** **Voltage divider**

Figure 4.26(a) shows a circuit in the time domain in sinusoidal steady state. Determine the voltage across the resistor.

**SOLUTION:**
Figure 4 26(b) shows the circuit, source, and unknown transformed into the frequency domain. As discussed on page 169, we transform sine $\rightarrow 1 \angle -90°$ because the cosine function is standard. This changes the phase from $+20°$ for sine to $-70°$ for cosine. The phasor voltage

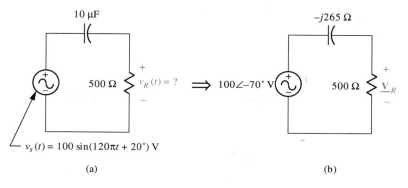

**Figure 4.26** (a) Time-domain circuit; (b) frequency-domain circuit.

across the resistor can be determined from a voltage divider:

$$\mathbf{Z}_C = \frac{1}{j120\pi \times 10 \times 10^{-6}} = -j265$$

$$\mathbf{V}_R = 100 \angle -70° \times \frac{500}{500 - j265} = 88.3 \angle -42.1° \text{ V} \tag{4.90}$$

The time-domain voltage across the resistor is thus

$$v_R(t) = 88.3 \cos(120\pi t - 42.1°) \text{ V} \tag{4.91}$$

**WHAT IF?**

What if the capacitor were replaced by a 1-H inductor?[12]

**Summary of the frequency-domain method.** We have developed an efficient method for finding the sinusoidal steady-state response of a circuit. The circuit is transformed into the frequency domain by replacing time-domain voltages and currents by phasors. The circuit elements $R$, $L$, and $C$ are replaced by their impedances $R$, $j\omega L$, and $1/j\omega C$, respectively. The circuit is analyzed by the most efficient means—voltage dividers, node voltages, Thévenin equivalent circuit, etc. The resulting phasor is then transformed back into the time domain.

## 4.4 PHASOR DIAGRAMS FOR *RL*, *RC*, AND *RLC* CIRCUITS

**OBJECTIVE 4**

To understand the effect of varying frequency on series and parallel *RL*, *RC*, and *RLC* circuits

**Varying the frequency.** You may wonder why we use the grandiose word "domain" for the techniques described before. You are correct in observing that we do not yet have much of a domain, only a technique for analyzing ac steady-state circuits at a single frequency. But there really is a domain; the exploration of this idea continues as an important theme for the remainder of this book. Extensive exploration of this concept is reserved for Chapters 9 and 12.

---

[12] $v_R(t) = 79.8 \cos(120\pi t - 107.0°)$.

The viewpoint in this section is that we have available a sinusoidal source, the frequency of which we vary. Here we explore the effects of frequency changes on the response of series and parallel circuits to gain insight into the properties of inductors and capacitors in ac circuits.

## *RL* Circuits

**Series *RL* circuit.** Figure 4.27 shows a series *RL* circuit excited by a current source. We will investigate the effect of the inductor as frequency varies. If there were no inductor in the circuit, it would exhibit the same behavior at all frequencies; all voltages and currents would be in phase with each other and in a fixed ratio. With an inductor in the circuit, however, the properties of the circuit change as frequency is varied.

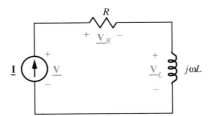

**Figure 4.27** Series *RL* circuit.

The impedance of the series circuit is

$$\mathbf{Z} = R + j\omega L \tag{4.92}$$

The relationship between the phasor voltage and current is thus

$$\mathbf{V} = \mathbf{Z}\mathbf{I} = (R + j\omega L)\,\mathbf{I} \tag{4.93}$$

$$= R\mathbf{I} + j\omega L\mathbf{I} = \mathbf{V}_R + \mathbf{V}_L$$

In Eq. (4.93), we have interpreted the two terms in the impedance as relating to the voltages across the resistor, $\mathbf{V}_R$, and the inductor, $\mathbf{V}_L$. Because the current is common to both *R* and *L*, we have drawn the phasor diagram in Fig. 4.28 with $\mathbf{I}$ as the phase reference, that is, $\mathbf{I} = I_p \angle 0°$. The phase of the voltage across the resistor, $\mathbf{V}_R$, is the same as the phase of $\mathbf{I}$, but the phase of the voltage across the inductor, $\mathbf{V}_L$, leads by 90°. The total voltage, $\mathbf{V}$, the phasor sum of $\mathbf{V}_R$ and $\mathbf{V}_L$, thus leads the current by a phase angle somewhere between 0° and 90°. The phase angle by which the voltage leads the current is the geometric angle of $\mathbf{Z}$ in the complex plane, $\theta$, as given in Eq. (4.94) and Fig. 4.29.

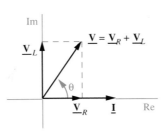

**Figure 4.28** The inductor causes current to lag.

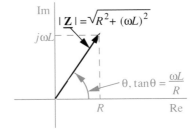

**Figure 4.29** The angle of the impedance represents the phase shift.

$$\underline{Z} = R + j\omega L = |\underline{Z}| \angle \theta \qquad (4.94)$$

where

$$|\underline{Z}| = \sqrt{R^2 + (\omega L)^2}, \qquad \theta = \tan^{-1} \frac{\omega L}{R}$$

**Frequency effects on the series *RL* circuit.**  Now let us examine what happens to the phasor diagram when frequency is varied, with $R$, $L$, and $\underline{I}$ held constant. Consider, first, very low frequencies. By "low," we mean those frequencies where the imaginary part of $\underline{Z}$ is small compared with the real part, that is, where $\omega L \ll R$. For low frequencies, the phase angle is small, meaning that $\underline{V}$ and $\underline{I}$ are almost in phase with each other, and the magnitude of the impedance is essentially equal to $R$. Thus, the inductor has little effect at low frequencies.

**Zero frequency = dc.**  We saw in Chapter 3 that inductors become invisible at dc once their initial energy requirements are met. The foregoing discussion shows inductors to be virtually invisible at low ac frequencies. Or we can put it the other way and treat dc behavior as a limiting case of ac as $\omega$ approaches zero. The mathematics supports this approach because $e^{j\omega t} \to 1$ as $\omega \to 0$. Whichever outlook we choose, the resistance dominates the behavior of the circuit at low frequencies.

As frequency increases, the presence of the inductor is shown by an increase in the impedance of the inductor and hence an increase in the voltage across the inductor. This increases the overall voltage and also the phase difference between the total voltage and the current. When $\omega L = R$, for example, the phase difference is 45° and the voltage is increased by $\sqrt{2}$ because the magnitude of the total impedance has increased by $\sqrt{2}$ from the dc value. As the frequency goes yet higher, the inductor comes to dominate the behavior of the circuit. The phase shift approaches 90° because the impedance approaches $j\omega L$.

**Mechanical analogy.**  To get a feeling for how the impedance of the inductor becomes large at high frequencies, imagine shaking a massive object in your hands. If you shake slowly (low frequencies), not much force is required, but as you attempt to shake faster, more force is required. Similarly, it takes more voltage to put the same current through an inductor as the frequency is increased.

**Motor application.**  The series *RL* circuit in Fig. 4.27 would be an appropriate circuit model for an electric motor under steady load. The resistance would represent heat and friction losses in the motor, plus the energy converted to mechanical form and applied to a mechanical load. The inductance would represent magnetic energy storage in the motor structure. If we were to draw the phasor diagram for the motor, it would look like Fig. 4.28 except that the voltage would normally be used as the phase reference, as in Fig. 4.30.

Voltage is customarily used as the phase reference in ac power circuits because lights, motors, heaters, and so on, are parallel loads requiring a standard voltage. Because voltage is the phase reference, current is said to *lag* for an inductive load and, as we will soon see, *lead* for a capacitive load.

**lagging and leading current**

**Resistive and reactive parts.**  The foregoing discussion suggests that an impedance can represent more than a physical resistor and a physical inductor in an ac circuit. The

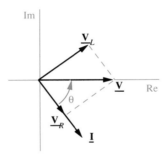

**Figure 4.30** Phasor diagram redrawn with voltage as the phase reference.

*real part* of the impedance represents losses to the circuit, that is, energy leaving electrical form and converted to heat or some other form of energy such as mechanical work. The *imaginary part* of the impedance represents energy storage, in this instance, magnetic energy storage in a motor. Because of these broader interpretations of impedance, which we will explore more fully in the next chapter, names are given to the real and imaginary parts of the impedance. The real part of $\mathbf{Z}$ is called the *resistive part* and the imaginary part is called the *reactive part*. The reactive part is given the symbol, $X$, as used in

**resistive, reactive, reactance**

$$\mathbf{Z} = R + jX = \text{(resistance)} + j\,\text{(reactance)} \tag{4.95}$$

Thus, the reactance of an inductor is $X_L = \omega L\ \Omega$, and the reactance of a capacitor is

$$X_C = -\frac{1}{\omega C} \tag{4.96}$$

Why do we need these new words? Why can't we speak in terms of inductance? One reason we have already given—that the impedance represents more than simple $R$ and $L$. The other reason becomes important when frequency is varied. The reactance of a true inductor varies linearly with frequency, but the reactance of more complicated circuits or devices does not vary linearly with frequency. Reactance is a more general concept than inductance.

---

**EXAMPLE 4.8**    **Reactance**

A load has a voltage of $10\cos(120\pi t + 12°)$ V and a current of $2.5\cos(120\pi t - 37°)$ A. What is the reactance of the load?

**SOLUTION:**
The load impedance is

$$\mathbf{Z} = \frac{\mathbf{V}}{\mathbf{I}} = \frac{10\angle 12°}{2.5\angle -37°} = 4\angle 49° = 2.62 + j3.02 \tag{4.97}$$

The reactance is thus $3.02\ \Omega$.

What if the voltage and current at twice the frequency are $10\cos(240\pi t + 12°)$ V and $1.5\cos(240\pi t - 54.5°)$ A? Can the load be a simple coil of wire?[13]

**Parallel *RL* load.** For the parallel *RL* load shown in Fig. 4.31, voltage is convenient as a phase reference from both practical and mathematical considerations. Since both *R* and *L* are connected in parallel with an ideal voltage source, we can determine their currents independently:

$$\mathbf{I}_R = \frac{\mathbf{V}}{\mathbf{Z}_R} = \frac{\mathbf{V}}{R}, \qquad \mathbf{I}_L = \frac{\mathbf{V}}{\mathbf{Z}_L} = \frac{\mathbf{V}}{j\omega L}, \qquad \mathbf{I} = \mathbf{I}_R + \mathbf{I}_L = \mathbf{V}\left(\frac{1}{R} + \frac{1}{j\omega L}\right) \tag{4.98}$$

The impedance of the parallel load is calculated according to the generalized concept of impedance:

$$\mathbf{Z} = \frac{\mathbf{V}}{\mathbf{I}} = \frac{1}{1/R + 1/j\omega L} = R \| j\omega L = |\mathbf{Z}| \angle \theta \tag{4.99}$$

where $\theta = \tan^{-1}(R/\omega L)$.

**Frequency effects on the *RL* parallel circuit.** Figure 4.32 shows the phasor diagram for the parallel *RL* circuit. The current lags the voltage because of the inductance. Let us now consider changes in the phasor diagram as frequency is varied. At low frequencies, $\omega L \ll R$, the current in the inductor is much larger than the current in the resistor because the reactance of the inductor approaches a short circuit at dc. This would cause the phase, $\theta$, to approach 90° (current lagging voltage).

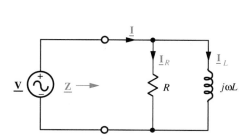

**Figure 4.31** Parallel *RL* circuit.

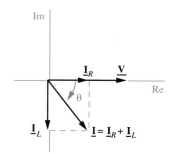

**Figure 4.32** Current still lags voltage due to the inductor.

---

[13] Yes, because the impedance is $2.66 + j6.11$, the load appears to have about 2.6 Ω resistance in series with about 8.1 mH of inductance.

As frequency increases, the reactance of the inductor will increase and the resistor gains importance. At $\omega L = R$, the current phase is $-45°$, current lagging voltage, and the magnitude of the total current will be $\sqrt{2}$ times the current in the resistor. As higher frequencies are reached, the reactance of the inductor exceeds that of the resistor, and the impedance of the parallel combination approaches that of the resistor.

| **EXAMPLE 4.9** | **Parallel to series conversion** |

Convert $100 \| j50$ into a series form $R + jX$.

**SOLUTION:**
Figure 4.33(a) shows the parallel circuit. We may derive the series form by evaluating $100 \| j50$ in rectangular form:

$$100 \| j50 = \frac{1}{1/100 + 1/j50} = 44.7 \angle 63.4 \qquad (4.100)$$

$$= 20 + j40 \ \Omega$$

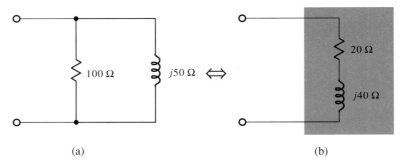

**Figure 4.33** (a) A parallel circuit and (b) a series circuit can be equivalent.

Figure 4.33(b) shows the series form. The two circuits are equivalent, however, at a single frequency only; they would exhibit different characteristics if the frequency changed.

| **WHAT IF?** | What if the frequency were doubled?[14] |

## RC Circuits

**Series *RC* circuit.** Figure 4.34 shows a series *RC* circuit. The impedance of the series combination is

---

[14] $\mathbf{Z} = 50 + j50 \ \Omega$.

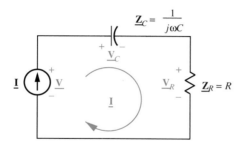

**Figure 4.34** Series *RC* circuit.

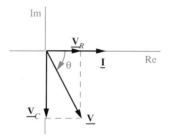

**Figure 4.35** Current leads voltage in the capacitive circuit.

$$\mathbf{Z} = R + \frac{1^{\cdot}}{j\omega C} = \sqrt{R^2 + \left(\frac{1}{\omega C}\right)^2} \angle \theta \qquad (4.101)$$

where $\theta = -\tan^{-1}(1/\omega RC)$.

Figure 4.35 shows the corresponding phasor diagram. We use the current as the phase reference, so the voltages are shown lagging. However, we would normally say the current leads voltage in a capacitive circuit because voltage would be considered the phase reference.

**Frequency effects on the *RC* series circuit.**  In this case, we will examine the frequency behavior by starting at high frequencies. At high frequencies, the reactance of the capacitor, $-1/\omega C$, is very small and the circuit appears resistive. The phase angle is nearly zero, with the current slightly leading the voltage. As frequency is decreased, however, the reactance of the capacitor increases. This increases $\mathbf{V}_C$, which increases the total voltage and the phase angle. At $1/\omega C = R$, the phase is 45°, leading current, and the voltage has increased by $\sqrt{2}$ from its high-frequency value. At low frequencies, the reactance of the capacitor becomes very large, approaching an open circuit at dc. Thus, at low frequencies, the capacitor dominates the behavior of the series combination, and the current phase approaches 90° leading the voltage.

---

**EXAMPLE 4.10** | **Series *RC***

At what frequency does a load consisting of 10 Ω in series with 0.01 μF produce a phase shift of 12.5° between voltage and current?

**SOLUTION:**
For a series *RC* circuit,  the phase of the impedance is given by the angle in Eq. (4.101); thus,

$$12.5° = \left| -\tan^{-1}\frac{1}{\omega RC} \right| \Rightarrow \frac{1}{\omega RC} = \tan 12.5°$$

$$\omega = \frac{1}{10 \times 10^{-8} \times \tan 12.5°} = 4.51 \times 10^7 \text{ rad/s} \qquad (4.102)$$

or about 7.2 MHz.

**WHAT IF?**    What if you want the frequency for $Z_{RC} = 13 \ \Omega$?[15]

**Parallel *RC* circuit.**    Figures 4.36 and 4.37 show a parallel *RC* circuit and the corresponding phasor diagram. The currents in the resistor and the capacitor are independent because they are connected in parallel with an ideal voltage source.

$$\mathbf{I}_R = \frac{\mathbf{V}}{R}, \qquad \mathbf{I}_C = \frac{\mathbf{V}}{1/j\omega C} = j\omega C \mathbf{V}$$

$$\mathbf{I} = \mathbf{I}_R + \mathbf{I}_C = \mathbf{V}\left(\frac{1}{R} + j\omega C\right), \qquad \theta = \tan^{-1}(\omega RC) \qquad (4.103)$$

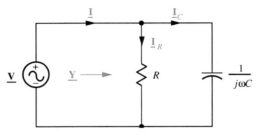

**Figure 4.36**    Parallel *RC* circuit.

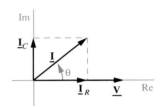

**Figure 4.37**    The capacitor causes the current to lead the voltage.

We can derive the impedance from Eq. (4.103), but Eq. (4.103) leads naturally to the definition of "admittance."

**OBJECTIVE 5**

**To understand admittance and show its advantages in analyzing parallel impedances**

**Admittance.**    Recall from Chapter 1 that we introduced the concept of conductance, $G = 1/R$, to simplify discussion of parallel resistors. There the concept of conductance brought few practical benefits, because modern calculators handle reciprocals without difficulty, but the corresponding concept in ac circuits has considerable theoretical and practical importance. *Admittance*, $\mathbf{Y}$, is defined as

$$\mathbf{Y} = \frac{\mathbf{I}}{\mathbf{V}} = \frac{1}{\mathbf{Z}} \qquad (4.104)$$

**admittance**

Clearly, the admittance of the parallel *RC* circuit in Fig. 4.36 is

---

[15] $\omega = 1.2 \times 10^7$ rad/s, or 1.92 MHz.

$$\mathbf{Y} = \frac{\mathbf{I}}{\mathbf{V}} = \frac{1}{R} + j\omega C = G + j\omega C \tag{4.105}$$

where we have introduced the conductance of the resistor, $G$. Admittance is useful for dealing with parallel circuits and has importance because parallel connections are common in practice. We have a specialized vocabulary associated with admittance. The real part of the admittance is called the *conductive part* or the *conductance*. The imaginary part of the admittance is called the *susceptive part* or the *susceptance*. Thus, we say that the conductive part of the admittance of a parallel $RC$ circuit is $G$ and the susceptive part is $\omega C$. The standard symbols for the conductance and susceptance are

**susceptance**

$$\mathbf{Y} = G + jB \tag{4.106}$$

where $B$ is a real number. For example, the conductive part of the parallel $RL$ circuit in Fig. 4.33(a) is 0.01 S (siemens) and the susceptive part is $B = -0.02$ S. Note that the susceptance of the inductive circuit is negative.

## *RLC* Circuits

Series *RLC*.   Figure 4.38 shows a series *RLC* circuit. The impedance of the circuit is

$$\mathbf{Z} = R + j\omega L + \frac{1}{j\omega C} = R + j\left(\omega L - \frac{1}{\omega C}\right) = |\mathbf{Z}|\angle\,\theta$$

where

$$|\mathbf{Z}| = \sqrt{R^2 + \left(\omega L - \frac{1}{\omega C}\right)^2} \quad \text{and} \quad \theta = \tan^{-1}\frac{\omega L - 1/\omega C}{R} \tag{4.107}$$

The reactive part of the impedance now combines the effects of the inductor and the capacitor. The frequency response of this reactive term gives this circuit interesting and useful characteristics. The phasor diagram is shown in Fig. 4.39. We have drawn the phasors showing the voltage across the inductor greater in magnitude than the voltage across the capacitor. This situation would be appropriate for high frequencies, where $\omega L > 1/\omega C$.

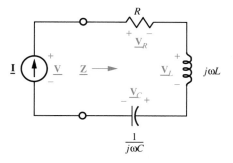

**Figure 4.38**   Series *RLC* circuit.

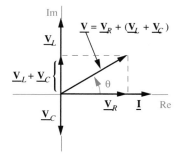

**Figure 4.39**   Above resonance, the inductor dominates, so current lags voltage.

The frequency characteristics of the series $RLC$ circuit combine those of the series $RC$ and $RL$ circuits. At dc, the circuit acts as an open circuit because of the capacitor. At low frequencies, the reactance of the capacitor dominates and the phase angle approaches 90°, with current leading voltage. As frequency increases, however, the inductive reactance becomes significant and at the resonant frequency grows to the point of canceling the negative reactance of the capacitor. This frequency occurs when

$$\omega_r L = \frac{1}{\omega_r C} \qquad \text{or} \qquad \omega_r = 1/\sqrt{LC} \qquad (4.108)$$

**series resonance**

and is called the frequency of *series resonance*. At resonance, the inductor and capacitor combination becomes invisible and $R$ is the total impedance of the circuit. As the frequency increases through resonance, the phase changes from leading to lagging (current lagging voltage), and at resonance, the phase is zero. At frequencies above resonance, the inductor dominates the circuit characteristics and the phasor diagram of Fig. 4.39 shows the trend. At very high frequencies the current phase approaches 90° lagging.

This circuit, with its series resonance, is used in electronics to select one group of frequencies from a broader group. For example, this circuit can be used as part of a radio filter that selects one station for reception, rejecting all others. We discuss this circuit more fully in Chapter 5, where we discuss energy in ac circuits. We will see that resonance occurs when magnetic and electric energy requirements are equal, just as a mechanical system resonates when kinetic and potential energy requirements are balanced.

**EXAMPLE 4.11**   **Series resonance**

Calculate the width of the resonance region for the circuit shown in Fig. 4.40.

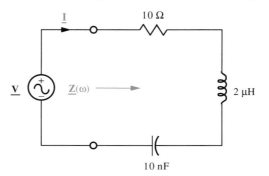

**Figure 4.40**   Series $RLC$ circuit. We will find the resonant frequency and the width of the resonance.

**SOLUTION:**
The impedance is

$$\mathbf{Z}(\omega) = 10 + j\left(2 \times 10^{-6}\omega - \frac{10^8}{\omega}\right)\Omega \qquad (4.109)$$

Resonance occurs when the total reactance is zero:

$$2 \times 10^{-6}\omega = \frac{10^8}{\omega} \Rightarrow \omega_r = 7.071 \times 10^6 (f_r = 1125 \text{ kHz}) \qquad (4.110)$$

where $\omega_r$ (or $f_r$) is the resonant frequency. At the resonant frequency of 1125 kHz, the impedance of the circuit is 10 $\Omega$ resistive. Frequencies will exist below and above resonance where the reactance is equal to the resistance, and the phase will be $\pm 45°$. We will consider these frequencies to define the width of the resonance. These frequencies occur at

$$\left| 2 \times 10^{-6}\omega - \frac{10^8}{\omega} \right| = 10 \qquad (4.111)$$

Equation (4.111) leads to the two quadratic equations:

$$2 \times 10^{-6}\omega - \frac{10^8}{\omega} = 10$$

and

$$2 \times 10^{-6}\omega - \frac{10^8}{\omega} = -10 \qquad (4.112)$$

which yield frequencies of 1592 and 796 kHz. At the lower frequency, the circuit would be capacitive, and the angle of the impedance would be negative (leading current). At the higher frequency, the circuit would be inductive, and the angle of the impedance would be positive (lagging current). Because these frequencies are in the AM radio band, this circuit might be used as a frequency filter in an AM radio.

**Parallel *RLC* circuit.** The parallel *RLC* circuit (Fig. 4.41) combines the properties of the parallel *RL* and *RC* circuits. The admittance of the circuit is

$$\mathbf{Y} = G + j\omega C + \frac{1}{j\omega L} = G + j\left( \omega C - \frac{1}{\omega L} \right) \qquad (4.113)$$

At low frequencies, the susceptance of the inductor $(-1/\omega L)$ is large and dominates the admittance expression. The admittance is large (infinite at dc) and the current phase approaches $-90°$. As frequency is increased, the inductive susceptance diminishes and the **parallel resonance** capacitive susceptance grows until they become equal. This is a *parallel resonance* and it occurs when $\omega_r C = 1/\omega_r L$, or $\omega_r = 1/\sqrt{LC}$, the same frequency as for series resonance. Thus, series and parallel resonance occur at the same frequency for the same ideal inductor and capacitor. At resonance, the admittance is pure conductance, $\mathbf{Y} = G = 1/R$. Thus, the impedance level at resonance is $R$.

As the frequency increases above resonance, the capacitive susceptance dominates, and as the frequency approaches very high frequencies, the admittance again becomes very large and the current phase approaches $+90°$. Thus, the admittance is minimum at resonance and becomes very large at low and high frequencies. Put differently, at low and high frequencies, the impedance is very small, approaching a short circuit, but the

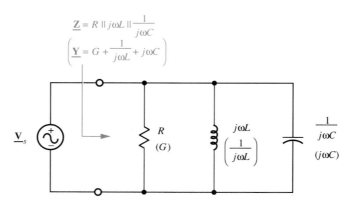

**Figure 4.41** Parallel *RLC* circuit. Admittance (in parentheses) is natural for parallel circuits.

impedance has a maximum at the frequency of parallel resonance. This contrasts with the series case, where the impedance is minimum at resonance.

### Check Your Understanding

1. What is the impedance, including units, of a 0.7-H inductor at 50 Hz?

2. What is the impedance of a 80-μF capacitor at 120 Hz?

3. A capacitor at 1 kHz has an impedance with a magnitude of 20 Ω. What is the magnitude of the impedance at 2 kHz?

4. What is the magnitude of the impedance of a 20-Ω resistor in series with a 20-mH inductor at 80 Hz?

5. What is the conductive part of $\mathbf{Y} = 0.012 \angle +12°$?

6. What is the reactive part of $\mathbf{Z} = 18 \angle -26°$?

7. If the current lags the voltage in an *RL* circuit, what type of circuit is it: series, parallel, or either?

8. At resonance, the input impedance to a series *RLC* circuit is a minimum or a maximum?

*Answers.* **(1)** $j220 \ \Omega$; **(2)** $-j16.6 \ \Omega$; **(3)** $10 \ \Omega$; **(4)** $22.4 \ \Omega$; **(5)** $11.7 \times 10^{-3}$ S; **(6)** $-7.89$; **(7)** either; **(8)** minimum.

## CHAPTER SUMMARY

Chapter 4 introduces methods for determining the steady-state response of circuits with sinusoidal sources. These methods are frequently required in electronics and electric power engineering. Complex numbers are used to describe voltage and current through phasors and resistors, inductors, and capacitors are described through their impedances. The frequency responses of simple circuits are considered.

**Time and frequency domain.** Table 4.1 summarizes the relationships between the time domain and the frequency domain that we have developed in this chapter.

### TABLE 4.1 Time-Domain and Frequency-Domain Transforms

| Time Domain | Frequency Domain |
| --- | --- |
| Sinusoid | Phasor |
| Phase angle | Angle in complex plane |
| $V_p \cos(\omega t + \theta)$ | $\underline{\mathbf{V}} = V_p \angle \theta$ |
| DEs | Arithmetic with complex numbers |
| $d/dt$ | $j\omega$ |
| Cosine function | $1 \angle 0°$ |
| Sine function | $-j = 1 \angle -90°$ |
| $R$, $L$, and $C$ | Impedances |
| $R$ | $\underline{\mathbf{Z}}_R = R$ |
| $L$ | $\underline{\mathbf{Z}}_L = j\omega L = \omega L \angle +90°$ |
| $C$ | $\underline{\mathbf{Z}}_C = \dfrac{1}{j\omega C} = \dfrac{1}{\omega C} \angle -90°$ |

**Objective 1: To understand how to identify the amplitude, frequency, and phase of a sinusoidal function.** We describe the parameters and mathematical properties of the generalized sinusoid, of which the sine and cosine functions are special cases.

**Objective 2: To understand the phasor concept and be able to find the sinusoidal steady-state response of a circuit, given the differential equation.** After a review of the algebra and arithmetic of complex numbers, a phasor is introduced as a complex number derived from the amplitude and phase of a sinusoidal time function. Using phasors, we can transform a linear differential equation into an algebraic equation that can be solved for the phasor representing the unknown voltage and current in the circuit.

**Objective 3: To understand how to use phasors and impedance to determine the sinusoidal steady-state response of a circuit.** When the phasor technique is applied to the definitions of resistors, inductors, and capacitors, the equations define the impedance of these circuit elements. Impedances can be combined in series and parallel like resistors at dc; indeed, using impedance all the techniques used to analyze dc circuits can be applied to ac circuits.

**Objective 4: To understand the effect of varying frequency on series and parallel *RL*, *RC*, and *RLC* circuits.** The magnitude of the impedances of inductors and capacitors depend on frequency. Thus, the phase and amplitude responses of circuits containing these elements depend on frequency. We study the frequency response of series and parallel first- and second-order circuits, especially noting the resonance response in *RLC* circuits.

**Objective 5: To understand how to define admittance and show its advantages in analyzing parallel impedances.** Admittance is the reciprocal of impedance and is frequently used in the analysis of parallel ac circuits.

Chapter 5 continues the study of ac circuits with an emphasis on energy processes.

## PROBLEMS

## Section 4.1: Introduction to Alternating Current

4.1. Find the frequencies in hertz and in radians per second for the following:
  (a) The rotation of the Earth on its axis relative to the Earth–Sun line.
  (b) The rotation of a bike tire (26-in. diameter) at 20 mph.
  (c) The second hand of a watch.
  (d) A dentist's drill rotating at 200,000 rpm.
  (e) A 33.3-rpm LP phonograph record.

4.2. The sidereal day measures the Earth's rotation relative to the fixed stars and is 3 minutes, 56 seconds shorter than the mean solar day. What is the Earth's angular velocity on its axis relative to absolute space in radians/hour? Give to five-place precision.

4.3. The maximum elevation angle of the sun in Ft. Collins, Colorado, is $E(t) = 48.4° + 23.5° \cos(\omega t - \theta)$.
  (a) If $t$ is in months, what is $\omega$?
  (b) Estimate $\theta$ in radians if $t = 0$ on January 1. *Hint:* The summer solstice, approximately June 23, is the day when the Sun should be at its maximum northerly position. Thus, $E(t)$ should be maximum on that day.
  (c) What is the maximum elevation angle of the Sun on July 4?

4.4. A sinusoidal function is shown in Fig. P4.4. Determine the frequency, phase, and amplitude for expressing this sinusoid in the standard form: $i(t) = I_p \cos(\omega t + \theta)$.

4.5. A sinusoidal function is shown in Fig. P4.5.
  (a) Determine the frequency, phase, and amplitude for expressing this sinusoid in the standard form: $v(t) = V_p \cos(\omega t + \theta)$.

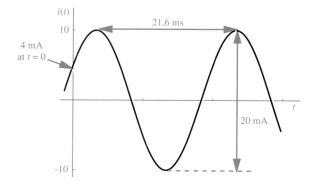

**Figure P4.4**

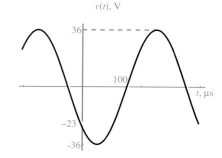

**Figure P4.5**

  (b) What is the first time after $t = 0$ that the voltage is at its maximum value?

4.6. Sketch the sinusoidal voltage $v(t) = 60 \cos(100\pi t - 120°)$ V.

4.7. (a) Sketch the sinusoidal voltage $v(t) = 420 \cos(1000t + 200°)$ mV.
  (b) What is the first time after $t = 0$ that this voltage is zero?

# Section 4.2: Representing Sinusoids with Phasors

**4.8.** Given three complex numbers:
$z = 6 - j2$, $w = 7 \angle 15°$, and $u = 10e^{j2.2}$.
 (a) Find $|z|$.
 (b) Find $u^*$ in rectangular form.
 (c) Evaluate $z/(w - u)$ and place the result in exponential form.
 (d) Solve for $s$ (a complex number) if $z(s - w) = u$ and express $s$ in polar form.

**4.9.** For the complex numbers $z_1 = -2 + j3$ and $z_2 = 1 - j6$, show the following:
 (a) $|z_1 \times z_2| = |z_1| \times |z_2|$.
 (b) $|z_1/z_2| = |z_1|/|z_2|$.
 (c) $|z_1| + |z_2| \neq |z_1 + z_2|$.

**4.10.** Given that $z = x + jy$ is a general complex number, show the following:
 (a) $\text{Re}\{z\} = (z + z^*)/2$.
 (b) $\dfrac{1}{z} = \dfrac{x}{x^2 + y^2} - \dfrac{jy}{x^2 + y^2}$ .
 (c) Solve for the first time when $\text{Re}\{ze^{j\omega t}\} = 0$ if $z$ is $2 - j6$ and $\omega = 100$.

**4.11.** Evaluate the following expressions:
 (a) $(1.4 + j6)\, 4 \angle 18° + 6 \angle +12°$.
 (b) $\dfrac{0.2 - j0.5}{13 + j7} \times \dfrac{1}{10 \angle +66°} - 10^{-3}$ .
 (c) $\dfrac{1}{\dfrac{1}{2 + j2} + \dfrac{1}{3 \angle + 40°}}$ .

**4.12.** (a) What is the phasor for $v(t) = 5.2 \cos(100t - 90°)$?
 (b) What time function is represented by the phasor $\mathbf{I} = 6 + j9\ \mu A$ if the frequency is 400 Hz?

**4.13.** Two 60-Hz sinusoidal voltages are described by the phasors $\mathbf{V}_1 = 20 \angle +10°$ V and $\mathbf{V}_2 = 9 - j\,17$ V.
 (a) Which has the larger amplitude?
 (b) Find $v_1(t) - v_2(t)$ at $t = 0$.
 (c) Find the first time after $t = 0$ when $v_1(t) = 0$.

**4.14.** (a) Sketch one cycle of the time function, $v(t)$, represented by the phasor
 $\mathbf{V} = e^{j\pi/3}$ mV, $f = 60$ Hz.
 (b) What is $\text{Re}\{(2 + j7)e^{j\omega t}\}$ V at $t = 0$?

**4.15.** Use phasor techniques in the following.
 (a) Find $2 \cos(100t - 45°) - 3 \cos(100t + 60°)$
 (b) Find $50 \sin(100t) + (d/dt) \cos(100t - 30°)$ .
 *Hint:* Do not take the derivative in the time domain; replace it by $j\omega$ in the frequency domain.

**(c)** Use phasor techniques to evaluate the derivative of $i(t) = 20 \sin(500t)$ at $t = 2$ ms.
 *Hint:* Write the formula in the time domain and transform into the frequency domain, using $j\omega$ for $d/dt$. Then put the specific $\omega$ and $t$ in the $e^{j\omega t}$ and take the real part.

**4.16.** On page 164, it was argued that, if $\text{Re}\{\underline{\mathbf{Z}}e^{j\omega t}\} = \text{Re}\{\underline{\mathbf{W}}e^{j\omega t}\}$ for all $t$, then $\underline{\mathbf{Z}} = \underline{\mathbf{W}}$. In effect, Re and $e^{j\omega t}$ can be dropped. Prove this by letting $\underline{\mathbf{Z}} = Z_r + jZ_i$ and $\underline{\mathbf{W}} = W_r + jW_i$ and evaluating the equation at the times when $\omega t = 0$ and $\omega t = \pi/2$.

**4.17.** Solve for $v(t)$ in the circuit shown in Fig. P4.17 using the phasor methods described in Section 4.2. You may use the short transformations in Eq. (4.63) if you wish.

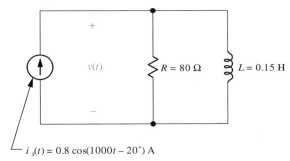

$i_s(t) = 0.8 \cos(1000t - 20°)$ A

**Figure P4.17**

**4.18.** Solve for $v_C(t)$ in the circuit shown in Fig. P4.18 using the phasor methods described in Section 4.2. You may use the short transformations in Eq. (4.63) if you wish.

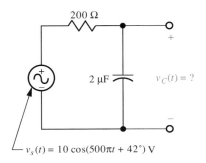

$v_s(t) = 10 \cos(500\pi t + 42°)$ V

**Figure P4.18**

**4.19.** Rework Problem P4.18 for the total response if the voltage is applied with a switch closure at $t = 0$. Assume the initial voltage on the capacitor is zero.

**4.20.** Find the steady-state value of the voltage across the inductor in the circuit of Fig. P4.20.

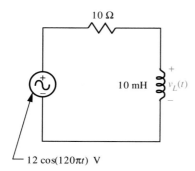

**Figure P4.20**

(a) Write the DE for $v_L(t)$.
(b) Transform into the frequency domain.
(c) Solve for the unknown phasor representing $v_L(t)$.
(d) Transform back into the time domain.

**4.21.** Find the steady-state value of the voltage across the resistance in the circuit of Fig. P4.21.
(a) Write the DE for $v_R(t)$.
(b) Transform into the frequency domain.
(c) Solve for the unknown phasor representing $v_R(t)$.
(d) Transform back into the time domain.

**4.22.** The mechanical system shown in Fig. P4.22 is excited by a rotating wheel that gives approximately a sinusoidal displacement for $x_1$. The differential

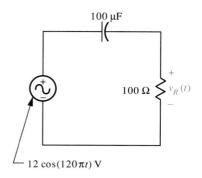

**Figure P4.21**

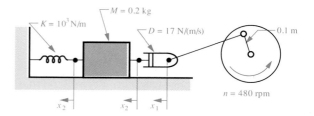

**Figure P4.22**

equation of the displacement $x_2$ is

$$M \frac{d^2 x_2}{dt^2} + D \frac{dx_2}{dt} + K x_2 = D \frac{dx_1}{dt}$$

(a) Find $\omega$
(b) Transform the DE to the frequency domain: $x_2(t) \Rightarrow \mathbf{X}_2$.
(c) Solve for $\mathbf{X}_2$.
(d) Write $x_2(t)$

## Section 4.3: Impedance: Representing the Circuit in the Frequency Domain

**4.23.** (a) What is the impedance of a 5-H inductor at 5 Hz in polar form?
(b) A resistor and capacitor, connected in series, have an impedance of $20 \angle -32°$ at a frequency of 2 kHz. Find $R$ and $C$.
(c) A resistor and capacitor, connected in parallel, have an impedance of $20 \angle -32°$ at 2 kHz. Find $R$ and $C$.

**4.24.** Make a chart for resistors, capacitors, and inductors with the following columns: name, symbol, time-domain equation, frequency-domain equation,

impedance in rectangular form, and impedance in polar form.

**4.25.** (a) What value of capacitance and what value of inductance have an impedance with a magnitude of 12 $\Omega$ at a frequency of 800 Hz?
(b) What would be the reactance of this $C$ and this $L$ at 1.6 kHz?
(c) What would be the impedance of this inductance and capacitor connected in series at a frequency of 1.2 kHz?

**4.26.** Using the frequency-domain versions of KVL and KCL, show that two impedances in series add like resistors in series, that is, $\mathbf{Z}_{eq} = \mathbf{Z}_1 + \mathbf{Z}_2$. Show also that two impedances in parallel add like resistors in parallel, that is,

$$\mathbf{Z}_{eq} = \mathbf{Z}_1 \| \mathbf{Z}_2 = \frac{1}{(1/\mathbf{Z}_1) + (1/\mathbf{Z}_2)}$$

4.27. Find the impedance in Fig. P4.27.

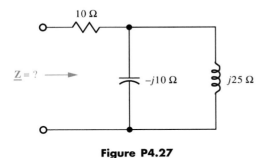

**Figure P4.27**

4.28. Determine the input impedance of the circuits shown in Fig. P4.28.

4.29. For the circuit shown in Fig. P4.29, determine $v(t)$ using phasor techniques. Sketch $v(t)$ in the time domain.

4.30. Use the techniques of the frequency domain to solve for $i(t)$ in the circuit shown in Fig. P4.30.
   (a) Find the frequency-domain version of the circuit, using phasors to represent sinusoidal functions, known and unknown, and impedances to represent circuit components.
   (b) Using parallel and series combinations, find $\mathbf{Z}_{eq}$ as seen by the voltage source.
   (c) Solve for $\mathbf{I}$.
   (d) Convert back to the time domain.

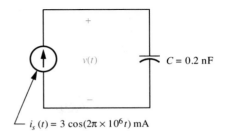

**Figure P4.29**

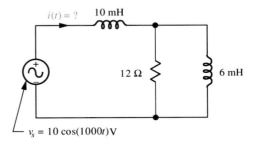

**Figure P4.30**

4.31. For the circuit in Fig. P4.31, find the first time after $t = 0$ when the instantaneous current is maximum, and give the maximum current.

4.32. The circuit shown in Fig. P4.32 is in sinusoidal steady state. The source voltage is shown in the graph. Sketch the capacitor voltage on the same graph.

4.33. Consider a 4-$\mu$F capacitor and a 10-$\Omega$ resistor.
   (a) They are connected in series. At what frequency in hertz is their series impedance 20 $\Omega$ in magnitude?

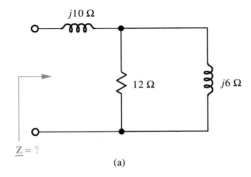

(a)

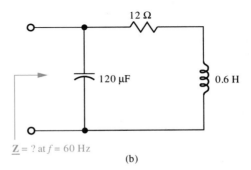

(b)

**Figure P4.28**

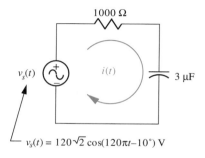

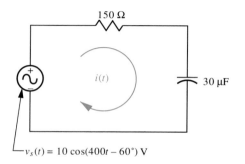

Figure P4.31

$v_s(t) = 120\sqrt{2}\cos(120\pi t - 10°)$ V

$v_s(t) = 10\cos(400t - 60°)$ V

Figure P4.34

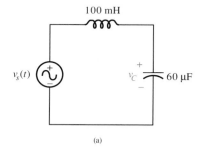

(a)

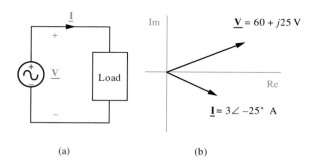

(a)          (b)

Figure P4.35

Assume the load consists of a resistor in series with a reactive component. The frequency is 60 Hz.
(a) What is the voltage at $t = 0$?
(b) What is the magnitude of the impedance?
(c) What is the resistance of the circuit?
(d) What is the reactive component (type and value)?

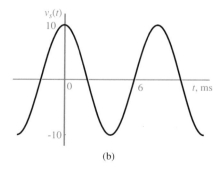

(b)

Figure P4.32

(b) If the resistor and capacitor are now placed in parallel, find the frequency at which their combined impedance is 7 Ω in magnitude.
(c) Still connected in parallel, at what frequency is the angle of the impedance $-45°$?

4.34. The circuit shown in Fig. P4.34 is in sinusoidal steady state. Determine the maximum value of the current and the first time after $t = 0$ at which the maximum current occurs.

4.35. Figure P4.35(a) shows a circuit in sinusoidal steady state, with the phasor diagram in Fig. P4.35(b).

4.36. A 60-Hz ac source and load are connected as indicated in Fig. P4.36. The phasor voltage is $\mathbf{V} = 120 + j0$ V and the phasor current is $\mathbf{I} = 7 - j5$ A.
(a) Find the instantaneous current at $t = 0$.

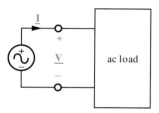

Figure P4.36

**(b)** What is the impedance of the ac load in rectangular form?

**(c)** Assuming that the load is a series resistor and inductor, find the value of the inductance.

**4.37.** For the circuit shown in Fig. P4.37, find the following:

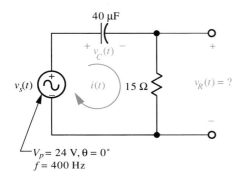

$V_p = 24$ V, $\theta = 0°$
$f = 400$ Hz

**Figure P4.37**

**(a)** Draw a phasor diagram showing $\underline{V}_s$, $\underline{I}$, $\underline{V}_R$, and $\underline{V}_C$. The voltages must be drawn to consistent scale and shown to add in accordance with the phasor KVL.

**(b)** Find $v_R(t)$ and sketch along with the source voltage.

**4.38.** Figure P4.38 shows an ac circuit in the frequency domain. The phasor voltage across the capacitor is given as a $10 \angle 45°$ V.

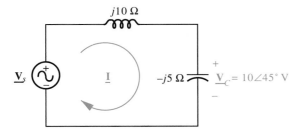

**Figure P4.38**

**(a)** Determine the phasor current in the circuit, $\underline{I}$.

**(b)** Determine the phasor source voltage, $\underline{V}_s$.

**4.39.** For the circuit shown in Fig. P4.39, find the following:

**(a)** At what frequency would the magnitude of the input impedance be 200 Ω?

**(b)** What is the angle of the impedance of this frequency?

**(c)** What value of $C$ should be added in series to make the circuit appear purely resistive at this frequency?

**(d)** What value of $C$ should be added in parallel to make the circuit appear purely resistive at this frequency? (This is not the same answer as the previous part.)

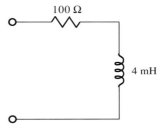

**Figure P4.39**

**4.40.** A resistor in series with a capacitor or inductor has a current of $i(t) = 1.2 \cos(1000t + 75°)$ mA and a voltage across the series combination of $v(t) = 0.8 \cos(1000t + 47°)$ V. What is the value of the resistance and the capacitor or inductor?

**4.41.** A resistor in series with a capacitor or inductor has a current of $i(t) = 12 \cos(1200t + 60°)$ mA and a voltage across the series combination of $v(t) = 0.8 \cos(1200t + 85°)$ V. What is the type and value of the resistor and the capacitor or inductor?

**4.42.** **(a)** Convert the circuit shown in Fig. P4.42 to the equivalent parallel circuit at $f = 1.2$ kHz.

**(b)** Find the impedances of the two circuits at a frequency of 1 kHz to show that the circuits are equivalent only at 1.2 kHz.

**4.43.** The circuit in Fig. P4.43 is to be represented by a Norton equivalent circuit. Determine $\underline{I}_N$ and $\underline{Z}_{eq}$.

**4.44.** **(a)** What is the total admittance of $\underline{Y}_1 = 1 + j6$ and $\underline{Y}_2 = 2.5 - j2.5$ connected in parallel?

**(b)** What is the magnitude of the input impedance of this parallel combination?

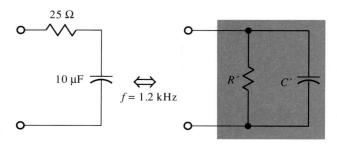

**Figure P4.42**

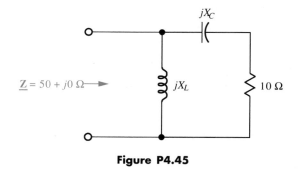

**Figure P4.43**

## General Problems

4.45. By proper choice of $X_C$ and $X_L$, the 10-$\Omega$ resistance in Fig. P4.45 can be transformed to "look" like a 50-$\Omega$ resistor at a specified frequency, as indicated in Fig. P4.45. Find $X_C$ and $X_L$ and, from them, $C$ and $L$ to accomplish this transformation at 1 kHz.

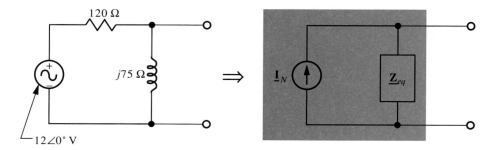

$v_1 = 100 \cos (120\pi t)$ V

$v_2 = 80 \sin (120\pi t)$ V

**Figure P4.46**

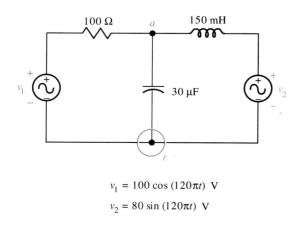

**Figure P4.45**

4.46. Find $v_a(t)$ in the circuit shown in Fig. P4.46 using nodal analysis.

4.47. The circuit shown in Fig. P4.47(a) is in sinusoidal steady state, with the output waveform, $v_{out}(t)$, shown in Fig. P4.47(b). On the same graph, sketch the input waveform, $v_{in}(t)$.

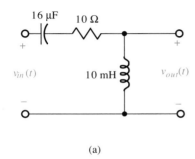

(a)

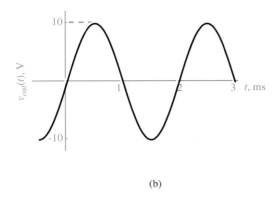

(b)

**Figure P4.47**

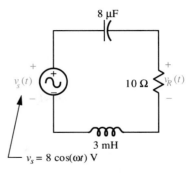

$v_s = 8 \cos(\omega t)$ V

**Figure P4.49**

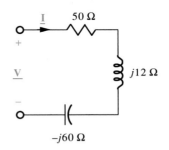

**Figure P4.50**

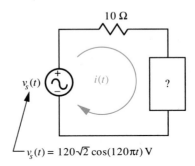

$v_s(t) = 120\sqrt{2} \cos(120\pi t)$ V

**Figure P4.51**

4.48. A voltage source with $v_s(t) = 120\sqrt{2} \cos(250t)$ V is connected in series with a 100-$\Omega$ resistance, a 0.2-H inductance, and a 25-$\mu$F capacitance.
   (a) Find the impedance of the circuit at the source frequency.
   (b) Determine the sinusoidal steady-state current, $i(t)$, in the series connection.
   (c) What is the first time after $t = 0$ when the voltage across the capacitance is zero?

4.49. For the circuit shown in Fig. P4.49, find the following:
   (a) $v_R(t)$ for $\omega = 0$, that is, for a dc voltage of 8 V.
   (b) $v_R(t)$ for $\omega = 4200$ rad/s.
   (c) The frequency in hertz for which the amplitude of $v_R(t)$ is maximum.

4.50. For the circuit in Fig. P4.50, $\underline{V} = 50 \angle 0°$ V.
   (a) Show $\underline{V}$ and $\underline{I}$ on a phasor diagram.
   (b) With $\underline{V}$ unchanged except that the frequency is doubled, show the phasor diagram. Use primed $\underline{V}$ and $\underline{I}$ for this case.

4.51. In Fig. P4.51, the design goal is to have $i(t)$ lead $v_s(t)$ by 55° of phase.

   (a) What is in the box: $R$, $L$, or $C$?
   (b) What is its numerical value?
   (c) What is the peak value of $i(t)$?
   (d) If the frequency were doubled, what would be the phase difference between $i(t)$ and $v_s(t)$? Consider phase positive if $i(t)$ leads $v_s(t)$. \

4.52. Figure P4.52(b) shows a circuit with an input and output voltage, and Fig. P4.52(a) shows the input voltage. Sketch the output voltage in the same graph.

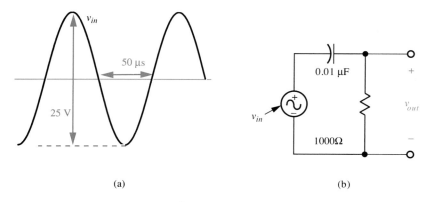

(a)                                        (b)

**Figure P4.52**

## Answers to Odd-Numbered Problems

4.1. **(a)** $7.27 \times 10^{-5}$ rad/s; **(b)** 4.31 Hz; **(c)** 0.105 rad/s; 3.02 radians, **(d)** 3,330 Hz; **(e)** 0.555 Hz.

4.3. **(a)** 0.524 rad/mo; **(b)** 3.02 radians, 173°; **(c)** 71.5°.

4.5. **(a)** $36 \cos(24500t + 130°)$; **(b)** 164 μs.

4.7. **(a)**

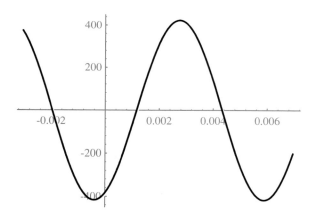

**(b)** 1.22 ms.

4.9. **(a)** 21.9 for both; **(b)** 0.593 for both; **(c)** 9.69 ≠ 3.61.

4.11. **(a)** $3.78 + j25.8$; **(b)** $(-4.48 - j1.10) \times 10^{-3}$; **(c)** $1.07 + j0.986$.

4.13. **(a)** $\underline{\mathbf{V}}_1$; **(b)** 10.7 V; **(c)** 3.70 ms.

4.15. **(a)** $4.01 \cos(100t - 91.2°)$; **(b)** $62.0 \cos(100t + 36.2°)$; **(c)** 5400 A/s.

4.17. $56.5 \cos(1000t + 8.07°)$ V.

4.19. $-8.34e^{-2500t} + 8.47 \cos(500\pi t + 9.86°)$ V.

4.21. **(d)** $11.6 \cos(120\pi t + 14.9°)$ V.

4.23. **(a)** 157 ∠90°; **(b)** 17.0 Ω, 7.51 μF; **(c)** 23.6 Ω 2.11 μF,

4.25. **(a)** 16.6 μF 2.39 mH.; **(b)** $X_C = -6$ Ω, $X_L = 24$ Ω; **(c)** $j10$ Ω.

4.27. 19.4 ∠ −59.0° Ω.

4.29. $2.39 \sin(2\pi \times 10^6 t)$ V.

4.31. 0.127 A, 15.2 ms.

4.33. **(a)** 2300 Hz; **(b)** 4060 Hz; **(c)** 3980 Hz.

4.35. **(a)** 60 V; **(b)** 21.7 Ω; **(c)** 14.6 Ω; **(d)** inductor, 42.5 mH.

4.37. **(a)** phasor diagram

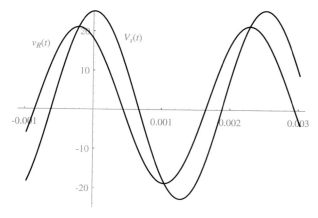

**(b)** 20.0 cos(800$\pi t$ + 33.6°) V.

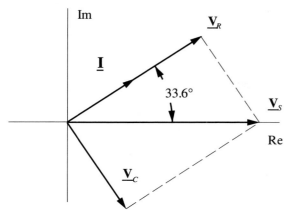

**4.39. (a)** 6890 Hz; **(b)** 60.0°; **(c)** 0.133 µF; **(d)** 0.100 µF for 400 Ω real.

**4.41.** 60.4-Ω resistor +23.5 mH inductor.

**4.43.** $\mathbf{I}_N = 0.1 \angle 0°$ A, $\mathbf{Z}_{eq} = 33.7 + j\,53.9$ Ω

**4.45.** $X_C = -20$ Ω, 7.96 µF, $X_L = 25$ Ω, 3.98 mH.

**4.47.** 4.86 cos(1000$\pi t$ − 131°) V.

**4.49. (a)** 0 V; **(b)** 4.03 cos(4200$t$ + 59.8°) V; **(c)** 1030 Hz.

**4.51. (a)** C; **(b)** 186 µF; **(c)** 9.73 A; **(d)** +35.5°.

# 5

# Power
# in AC Circuits

**objectives**

1. To understand how to calculate the time-average and effective values of periodic waveforms
2. To understand the energy and power requirements of resistors, inductors, and capacitors in the sinusoidal steady state
3. To understand how to calculate apparent, real, and reactive power flow in an electric network based on time-domain analysis
4. To understand how to calculate apparent, real, and reactive power in the frequency domain
5. To understand how to correct the power factor of a load
6. To understand how to use a Thévenin equivalent circuit to establish the load to withdraw maximum power from an ac source
7. To understand the voltage-, current-, and impedance-transforming properties of the transformer.
8. To understand the role of transformers in the transmission of electric power
9. To understand safe practice around electrical equipment

AC circuits are used universally for the generation, distribution, and consumption of electric power. This chapter examines energy processes in ac circuits. Additionally, we look into some matters of eminent practical importance, such as what meters indicate, what transformers do, and how to be safe around electrical equipment.

## Importance of Power and Energy

Power and energy are important in ac problems for several reasons. Energy concerns you as a user of electricity because the local electric utility makes you pay for the energy you use. More important, energy plays a vital role in describing the behavior of physical systems. The roller coaster problem of freshman physics—in which you compute the speed at some point on the track from a difference in height—exemplifies how energy considerations often sweep away many details of a problem and lead directly to a useful result. Indeed, the more experience you gain in analyzing physical systems, the more you should become impressed with the importance of energy in revealing the true workings of a system. Some feel, as does your author, that any analysis is incomplete until energy relationships are explored and understood. Finally, we should point out that modern civilization is characterized by the ready availability and varied uses of electric power. Lighting, electric motors, communication systems, and laptop computers, just to name a few useful applications, ultimately get their energy from the electric power system.

In this chapter, we investigate energy and power relationships in electric circuits. We begin by looking at averages because time-average power is frequently our focus. Then we examine energy and power relationships in the time domain. The frequency domain follows, and we succeed in expressing energy and power relationships with phasors. Finally, we introduce two topics of eminent practical value, transformers and electrical safety.

## Average Values of Electrical Signals

**What is an average?** Everybody knows how to calculate a numerical average. We compute the average of 12, 9, and 15 by adding the numbers (36), dividing by the number of values we are averaging (3), and getting the average (12). In general, the average of $n$ numbers, $x_i$, $i = 1, 2, \ldots, n$, is

$$X_{avg} = \frac{\sum_{i=1}^{n} x_i}{n} \quad \text{or} \quad nX_{avg} = \sum_{x=1}^{n} x_i \tag{5.1}$$

In the second form of Eq. (5.1), we see that the average value multiplied by the number of samples is equal to the sum of the numbers.

**average**    That is how to compute an arithmetic average, but what is the definition of an average? An *average* is a number[1] that characterizes in some aspect a body of information. The arithmetic average, for example, gives us some idea of the size of the numbers, such as the average price of gasoline in Kansas. There are many kinds of averages. The grade-point average provides an example near to the heart of most college students. This average characterizes the academic performance of a student even though many important factors, such as course load and difficulty, are ignored. Thus, an aver-

---

[1] More precisely, a *statistic*.

age is a number that characterizes a body of information in one particular way, omitting all the rest of the information.

### Computing time averages.

The time average of a periodic function can be generalized from the arithmetic average. The periodic voltage in Fig. 5.1 provides an example. Because the function is periodic, the average over all time will be the same as the average over one period; hence we can limit our attention to the time from $t = 0$ to $t = T$, as shown in Fig. 5.2. We can define the time average by analogy with the second form of Eq. (5.1): $n$ becomes $T$, the period; $X_{avg}$ becomes $V_{avg}$; and the summation of the numbers becomes the summation of all the heights of the voltage, which is the integral over the time period from 0 to $T$. Thus, we have the definition of *time-average* voltage:

$$TV_{avg} = \int_0^T v(t)\,dt \Rightarrow V_{avg} = \frac{1}{T}\int_0^T v(t)\,dt \tag{5.2}$$

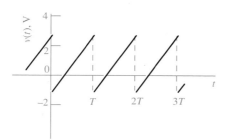

**Figure 5.1** Find the time-average value.

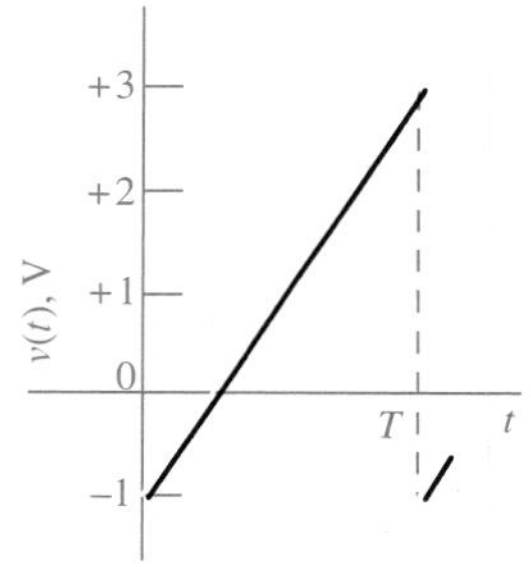

**Figure 5.2** One period of the waveform.

**time average**

The first form of Eq. (5.2) can be interpreted in terms of area, as shown in Fig. 5.3. Because $V_{avg}$ is a constant, the product on the left side represents the area on the $v(t)$ graph of a rectangle having base $T$ and height $V_{avg}$. The right side is the area under the $v(t)$ curve, counting the area above the $x$-axis as positive and the area below the $x$-axis as negative. This geometric interpretation is shown in Fig. 5.3. Equation (5.2) requires the two areas to be equal. The second form of Eq. (5.2) serves for computing averages.

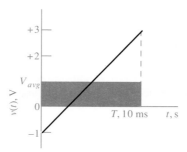

**Figure 5.3** The average multiplied by the period has the same area as the original waveform, counting the area below the $x$-axis as negative.

EXAMPLE 5.1

## Calculating the time average

Find the time-average value of the waveform in Fig. 5.1 for $T = 10$ ms.

**SOLUTION:**
We apply Eq. (5.2). The present example can be handled as the areas of triangles, but we will use calculus to illustrate the more general method. First, we derive the equation of $v(t)$ in the slope-intercept form: The intercept is $-1$; the slope is $3 - (-1)$ divided by 10 ms, or 400 V/s. Thus, the equation is

$$v(t) = -1 + 400t \qquad \text{(5.3)}$$

We now substitute into Eq. (5.2), with the resul

$$V_{avg} = \frac{1}{10 \text{ ms}} \int_0^{10 \text{ ms}} (-1 + 400t) \,$$

This is the value indicated on Fig. 5.3 and its

**WHAT IF?**  What if the time scale we change the averages?[2]

---

**dc value,
dc component**

**Some special averages.** Several resu
The time average of a dc (constant) volta
the time-average value of a signal, such a
*value* or *dc component* of the signal. An
soidal waveform is zero. The sinusoidal function has equal areas ab
time axis and thus has zero time-average (or dc) value.

   If we have the sum of two signals, say, two voltage sources connected in series, the average of the sum is the sum of the averages of the component signals. This follows from Eq. (5.2) because the integral distributes to the two functions.

$$(v_1 + v_2)_{avg} = \frac{1}{T} \int_0^T [v_1(t) + v_2(t)]\,dt$$

$$= \frac{1}{T}\left[\int_0^T v_1(t)\,dt + \int_0^T v_2(t)\,dt\right] = V_{1\,avg} + V_{2\,avg} \qquad \text{(5.5)}$$

One application of Eq. (5.5) would be the sum of a dc and a sinusoidal signal; the average would be the dc value because the sinusoidal part averages to zero.

---

[2] No. Both areas are scaled by the same amount.

## Effective or Root-Mean-Square (RMS) Value

**Time-average power.**    We will now consider the time-average power in a dc circuit, Fig. 5.4, where the resistor is hot because the electrical energy into the resistor appears as heat. From Chapter 2, we know that the power into the resistor is $V_{dc}^2/R$, but we will derive this result here from more general considerations, which we then apply to the heating of a resistor with an ac source. The instantaneous power (energy/time) into a circuit element is given by Eq. (1.29) as

$$p(t) = v(t) i(t) \tag{5.6}$$

For our dc circuit in Fig. 5.4, both voltage and current are constant, so the instantaneous power into the resistor is $v \times i = V_{dc} \times V_{dc}/R$, a constant. The time-average power, $P$, into $R$ is thus

$$P = \frac{1}{T} \int_0^T p(t)\,dt = \frac{1}{T} \int_0^T \frac{V_{dc}^2}{R}\,dt = \frac{V_{dc}^2}{R} \tag{5.7}$$

The time-average power determines how hot the resistor will become. The movement of charge through the resistor imparts thermal energy to the material. The input electrical power appears as a heat source internal to the resistor; the temperature of the resistor depends on this input and on its thermal coupling to the environment. The more power into the resistor, the hotter it will become. Physical resistors are rated for $\frac{1}{4}$, $\frac{1}{2}$, 1, 2 watts, and so on. The power rating indicates how much power the resistor can handle without burning out or changing its resistance value significantly.

**Power in AC circuits.**    Figure 5.5 shows the same circuit with an ac source. The instantaneous power is

$$p(t) = v(t) i(t) = V_p \cos(\omega t) \times \left[ \frac{V_p}{R} \cos(\omega t) \right] = \frac{V_p^2}{R} \cos^2(\omega t)$$

$$= \frac{V_p^2}{2R}[1 + \cos(2\omega t)], \qquad \omega = \frac{2\pi}{T} \tag{5.8}$$

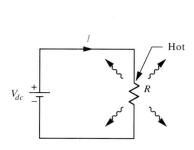

**Figure 5.4**   The heat is a measure of the average power.

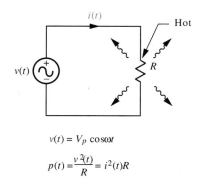

$$v(t) = V_p \cos \omega t$$

$$p(t) = \frac{v^2(t)}{R} = i^2(t) R$$

**Figure 5.5**   The heat is a measure of the time-average power.

where we have used the trigonometric identity

$$\cos^2 A = \tfrac{1}{2}[1 + \cos(2A)] \tag{5.9}$$

with $A = \omega t$.

Figure 5.6 shows a plot of the instantaneous power, Eq. (5.8). Although the charges move back and forth in the resistor, the power is always nonnegative, as shown mathematically from the squaring of the voltage in Eq. (5.8). The time-average power to the resistor, $P$, is the time average of the power curve:

$$P = \frac{1}{T} \int_0^T p(t)\,dt = \frac{V_p^2}{2R} = \frac{I_p^2 R}{2} \tag{5.10}$$

where $I_p = V_p/R$. The average value shown in Fig. 5.6 is half the peak, which is the average between the peak and valley.

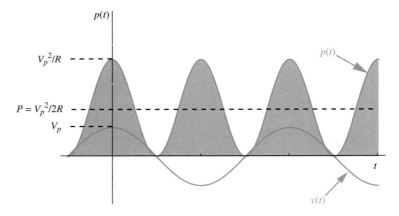

**Figure 5.6**  The energy flows into the resistor in spurts. The power is nonnegative at all times.

**Energy flow to the resistor.**  The nonnegative power results physically because the moving electrons heat the resistance material regardless of their direction of flow. The energy does not flow smoothly into the resistor, but flows in spurts, twice each cycle of the ac waveform, as shown in Fig. 5.6. Thus, the resistor is heated cyclically. In most resistors, this time variation is unimportant because thermal inertia smoothes out the heating variations and the temperature remains essentially constant. However, these variations can be a problem in incandescent lighting, where the thermal inertia of the filament is small. The power frequencies of 50 or 60 Hz were established high enough to make the flickering of the light (at 100 or 120 Hz) barely noticeable.

---

**EXAMPLE 5.2** | **Power rating of a resistor**

A 2-watt, 500-$\Omega$ resistor is operated at its maximum power with ac. Find the peak voltage across the resistor.

From Eq. (5.10), the requirement is

$$2 = \frac{V_p^2}{2 \times 500} \Rightarrow V_p = \sqrt{2000} = 44.7 \text{ V} \qquad (5.11)$$

**WHAT IF?**

What if you want the maximum ac current in a 5-W, 20-Ω resistor?[3]

**Effective or root-mean-square (rms) value of a sinusoid.** The analytic computation of Eq (5.10) appears in Eq. (5.12). The integral uses the trigonometric identity given in Eq. (5.9):

$$P = \frac{1}{T} \int_0^T \frac{V_p^2}{R} \cos^2(\omega t)\, dt = \frac{V_p^2}{RT} \int_0^T \left[ \frac{1}{2} + \frac{1}{2}\cos(2\omega t) \right] dt$$

$$= \frac{V_p^2}{RT} \left[ \frac{t}{2} + \frac{\sin(2\omega t)}{4\omega} \right]_0^T = \frac{V_p^2}{2R} \qquad (5.12)$$

**effective value**

Equation (5.12) leads to the effective value of the ac voltage. When we speak of effective, the "effect" to which we refer is the heating effect, or more generally the time-average energy conversion from electrical to nonelectrical form. The *effective value* of an ac waveform is the equivalent dc value that would heat the resistor as hot as the ac waveform heats it. For a sinusoid, this is

$$P = \frac{V_e^2}{R} = \frac{V_p^2}{2R} \Rightarrow V_e = \frac{V_p}{\sqrt{2}} \qquad (5.13)$$

where $V_e$ is the effective voltage. Equation (5.13) equates the time-average power from an equivalent dc source with magnitude $V_e$, the effective value, to the time average of power due to the ac source. Equation (5.13) defines the effective value of an ac source: The effective value of the sinusoidal voltage (or current, if we were dealing with current) is $1/\sqrt{2}$ or 0.707 times the peak value. For example, the ac voltage with a peak value of 44.7 V in the previous example would be equivalent in heating effect to a $44.7/\sqrt{2} = 31.6$-V battery, so this would be the effective value of the ac voltage. But we warn you that Eq. (5.13) applies only for the sinusoidal waveform, as we will illustrate shortly.

**root-mean-square (rms) value**

**Effective value in general.** The effective value is often referred to as the root-mean-square (rms) value. The general definition of effective or rms value of a periodic function is

---

[3] $I = 0.5$ A, rms.

$$P = \frac{V_e^2}{R} = \frac{1}{T} \int_0^T \frac{v^2(t)}{R}\,dt \Rightarrow V_e = \sqrt{\frac{1}{T} \int_0^T v^2(t)\,dt} \qquad (5.14)$$

where $T$ is the period. Here we have illustrated the definition of rms for voltage, $v(t)$, but a similar expression would apply for the effective value of a current. The effective, or rms, value is the square *root* of the *mean* (that is, the average, as in "mean sea level") of the *square* of the function.[4]   The practical importance of rms values is suggested by the fact that ac voltmeters and ammeters are calibrated to indicate rms for a sinusoid.

---

**EXAMPLE 5.3**   **Effective value of nonsinusoidal voltage**

Compute the rms value of the waveform in Fig. 5.1.

**SOLUTION:**
We derived the equation of the voltage during the first period to be

$$v(t) = -1 + 400t, \ \ 0 < t < 10 \text{ ms} \qquad (5.15)$$

Substituting into Eq. (5.14) and integrating, we obtain

$$V_e = \sqrt{\frac{1}{10 \text{ ms}} \int_0^{10 \text{ ms}} (-1 + 400t)^2\,dt} = 1.53 \text{ V} \qquad (5.16)$$

**WHAT IF?**   What if we added 1 to the voltage, making $v(t) = 400t$?[5]

---

**Measuring AC voltage.** Many ac voltmeters would not indicate the true rms (1.53 V) of the waveform in Fig. 5.1. A meter designed to square and average the instantaneous waveform could be complicated and expensive. Thus, for simple voltmeters, some other property of the waveform is measured and the rms is inferred from that, assuming a sinusoidal shape. For example, a common type of meter actually responds to the peak-to-peak value of the waveform, but the meter scale is marked to indicate the peak-to-peak value divided by $2\sqrt{2}$, which would be the rms for a sinusoid. Such a meter would indicate $4/2\sqrt{2} = 1.41$ V for the waveform in Fig. 5.1, not the true rms value of 1.53 V. Thus, meter readings require careful interpretation when measuring nonsinusoidals.

**Summary.** We can represent the power-producing capability of a waveform with an average value called the effective (or rms) value of the waveform. This is defined as the value that, when squared, is equal to the time average of the square of the waveform. For a dc waveform, the effective value is equal to the dc value. For a sinusoidal wave-

---
[4] The name *rms* gives the formula.
[5] $V_e = 2.31$ V.

form, the effective value is $1/\sqrt{2}$ times the peak value. For other waveforms, the effective value may be calculated by squaring and averaging. Electrical meters are designed to indicate the effective value of a sinusoidal waveform, but may not indicate the effective value for other wave shapes.

## Power and Energy Relations for R, L, and C

**Resistance.** We have discussed the power relationship for resistance in deriving the effective value of a sinusoid. As shown in Fig. 5.6, the energy flows unilaterally into the resistor, not smoothly, but in lumps.

$$p(t) = P_R[1 + \cos(2\omega t)] \tag{5.17}$$

where the time-average power into the resistor is

$$P_R = \frac{V_p^2}{2R} = \frac{V_e^2}{R} = I_e^2 R \tag{5.18}$$

where $V_e$ and $I_e$ are the effective voltage and current, respectively.

---

| **EXAMPLE 5.4** | **Resistance of a light bulb** |
|---|---|

Find the resistance of a 120-V, 100-watt light bulb.

**SOLUTION:**

The 120-V value represents the effective value of the standard voltage for lighting. According to Eq. (5.18), this indicates a resistance value of

$$R = \frac{V^2}{P_R} = \frac{(120)^2}{100} = 144 \ \Omega \tag{5.19}$$

The energy consumed by the bulb, operated for 24 hours, would be 24 hours × 0.100 kW, or 2.4 kWh (kilowatt-hours). This represents the total energy consumed, and at 6 cents/kWh, the bulb would operate for about 15 cents per day.

**WHAT IF?**  What if the lightbulb is a 130-V, 60-watt long-life bulb? Find its resistance.[6]

---

**Inductance.** We calculate the instantaneous and time-average magnetic energy stored by an inductor. The current and voltage for an inductor are

$$i_L(t) = I_p \sin(\omega t)$$

$$v_L(t) = L\frac{di}{dt} = +\omega L I_p \cos(\omega t) \tag{5.20}$$

---

[6] 282 Ω.

The instantaneous power into the inductor is the product of voltage and current:

$$p_L(t) = v_L(t)i_L(t) = +\omega L I_p \cos(\omega t) I_p \sin(\omega t)$$
$$= +\frac{\omega L I_p^2}{2} \sin(2\omega t) \tag{5.21}$$

where we have used the trigonometric identity $[\sin(\omega t)][\cos(\omega t)] = [\sin 2(\omega t)]/2$. The time-average power is zero, for the ideal inductor has no loss. Thus, an inductor gives back on the average as much energy as it receives.[7] For a 60-Hz source, the energy would pulsate in and out of the inductor 120 times per second. For this reason, heavy electrical equipment, such as transformers and motors, often hums audibly at 120 Hz.

**Stored energy in an inductor.** The magnetic energy stored in an inductor is given in Eq. (3.5) as

$$w_m(t) = \tfrac{1}{2} L i_L^2(t) \tag{5.22}$$

For the sinusoidal source, we find the instantaneous stored energy to be

$$w_m(t) = \frac{1}{2} L [I_p \sin(\omega t)]^2 = \frac{L I_p^2}{4} [1 - \cos(2\omega t)] \tag{5.23}$$

Figure 5.7 shows the power and stored energy in an inductor with a sinusoidal current. The stored energy is nonnegative and pulsates at twice the ac source frequency. While the stored energy is increasing, the power into the inductor is positive. During this period of time, the ac source supplies energy and the inductor acts as a load. While the stored energy is decreasing, the power into the inductor is negative, indicating that the inductor now acts as a source, returning energy to the ac source.

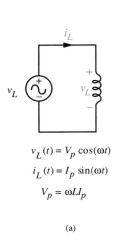

$$v_L(t) = V_p \cos(\omega t)$$
$$i_L(t) = I_p \sin(\omega t)$$
$$V_p = \omega L I_p$$

(a)

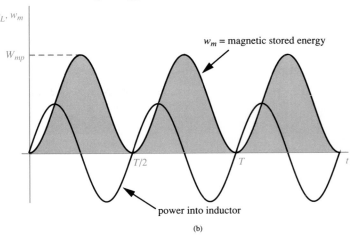

(b)

**Figure 5.7** Stored energy and power into an inductor.

---

[7] This is true only for an ideal inductor; a real inductor would have resistive losses.

The time-average stored energy is one-half of $\frac{1}{2} L i_p^2$, the peak stored energy shown by Eq. (5.23). This can be written

$$W_m = \tfrac{1}{2} L I_e^2 \tag{5.24}$$

where $W_m$ is the time-average stored magnetic energy, and $I_e$ is the effective value of the current. The time-average energy is important for two reasons. Although the time-average power into the inductor is zero, the time-average stored energy must be supplied to the inductor when the ac source is originally connected to the inductor. Additionally, the time-average stored energy indicates the magnitude of the energy pulsations in the inductor. Specifically, we know that the ac source must lend twice this amount of energy to the inductor twice each cycle.

---

**EXAMPLE 5.5** | **Stored energy in an inductor**

An ideal 0.1-H inductor has 30-Hz ac voltage applied to it, and the time-average stored energy is 5 J. What is the maximum power into the inductor?

**SOLUTION:**
From Eq. (5.24), we determine the effective value of the inductor current to be

$$I_e = \sqrt{\frac{2W_m}{L}} = \sqrt{\frac{2 \times 5}{0.1}} = 10 \text{ A} \tag{5.25}$$

Equation (5.21) gives the instantaneous power into the inductor, and the maximum power is simply

$$p_{max} = \frac{\omega L I_p^2}{2} = \omega L I_e^2 = 2\pi \times 30 \times 0.1 \times 10^2 = 1885 \text{ W} \tag{5.26}$$

**WHAT IF?** | What if the frequency is changed to 60 Hz but the inductance and stored energy remains the same?[8]

---

**Capacitance.** We will calculate the instantaneous and time-average electric energy stored by a capacitor. The voltage and current for a capacitor are

$$v_C(t) = V_p \cos(\omega t)$$
$$i_C(t) = C \frac{dv_C}{dt} = -\omega C V_p \sin(\omega t) \tag{5.27}$$

The instantaneous power into the capacitor is the product of voltage and current:

---
[8] 3770 W.

$$p_C(t) = v_C(t) i_C(t) = [V_p \cos(\omega t)][-\omega C V_p \sin(\omega t)]$$
$$= -\left(\frac{\omega C V_p^2}{2}\right) \sin(2\omega t) \tag{5.28}$$

where we have again used the trigonometric identity $[\sin(\omega t)][\cos(\omega t)] = [\sin 2(\omega t)]/2$. The average power is zero, which indicates that the capacitor is lossless.[9]

**Stored energy in a capacitor.** The pulsation of the power at twice the ac frequency corresponds to the shuttling of electric energy between source and capacitor. The stored electric energy in a capacitor is given in Eq. (3.23) as

$$w_e(t) = \tfrac{1}{2} C v_C^2(t) \tag{5.29}$$

For sinusoidal steady state, we find the instantaneous stored energy to be

$$w_e(t) = \tfrac{1}{2} C [V_p \cos(\omega t)]^2 = \frac{C V_p^2}{4}[1 + \cos(2\omega t)] \tag{5.30}$$

The stored energy is nonnegative and pulsates at twice the ac source frequency. While the stored energy is increasing, the power into the capacitor is positive. During this period, the ac source supplies energy and the capacitor acts as a load. While the stored energy is decreasing, the power into the capacitor goes negative, indicating that the capacitor is acting as a source, returning energy to the ac voltage source.

The time-average stored energy is one-half of $\tfrac{1}{2} C V_p^2$, the peak stored energy. This can be written

$$W_e = \tfrac{1}{2} C V_e^2 \tag{5.31}$$

where $W_e$ is the time-average stored electric energy, and $V_e$ is the effective value of the voltage.

---

**EXAMPLE 5.6** | **Stored energy in a capacitor**

Find the maximum current in a 120-μF capacitor that stores a time-average energy of 14 joules if the ac frequency is 60 Hz.

**SOLUTION:**
From Eq. (5.31), the effective value of the voltage is

$$\frac{1}{2} C V_e^2 = 14 \text{ J} \Rightarrow V_e = \sqrt{\frac{28}{120 \times 10^{-6}}} = 483 \text{ V} \tag{5.32}$$

So the effective current would be

$$I_e = \frac{V_e}{X_C} = \omega C V_e = 120\pi \times 120 \times 10^{-6} \times 483 = 21.9 \text{ A}. \tag{5.33}$$

---

[9] For an ideal capacitor; a real capacitor would have some loss, though not as much as a real inductor.

Hence, the maximum current would be $21.9\sqrt{2} = 30.9$ A.

What if the effective current were 20.0 A? Find the peak stored energy.[10]

## General Case for Power in an AC Circuit

We have dealt with resistance, inductance, and capacitance separately, and shown the role of each in power and energy relationships. We now consider the general case of circuits containing combinations of resistors, inductors, and capacitors. We think in terms of the circuit shown in Fig. 5.8, an *RLC* circuit, although our results and interpretations will apply to all ac circuits.

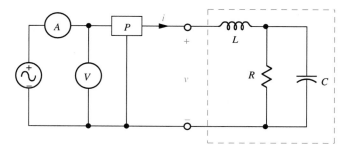

**Figure 5.8**  General *RLC* load with ammeter (*A*), voltmeter (*V*), and wattmeter (*P*).

This circuit will be analyzed in the frequency domain beginning on page 217. Here we assume it is described by an impedance, $\mathbf{Z} = |\mathbf{Z}| \angle \theta$. We are dealing here with power and energy in the time domain, so we express the relationship between voltage and current generally:

$$v(t) = V_p \cos(\omega t) \quad \text{and} \quad i(t) = I_p \cos(\omega t - \theta) \quad (5.34)$$

where $V_p = |\mathbf{Z}| I_p$. Note that $\theta$ is the angle of the impedance, which makes $\theta$ in this section have the opposite sign from Eq. (4.01). Although impedance is a frequency-domain concept and is computed in the frequency domain, the magnitude and angle of the impedance are real numbers that can be used in the time domain.

We investigate the time-average power into the *RLC* load through the use of two trigonometric identities. The instantaneous power is

$$p(t) = v(t)i(t) = V_p \cos(\omega t) I_p \cos(\omega t - \theta)$$

$$= \frac{V_p I_p}{2} [\cos\theta + \cos(2\omega t - \theta)] \quad (5.35)$$

The second form of Eq. (5.35) follows the application of the trigonometric identity:

---

[10]23.5 J.

$$(\cos A)(\cos B) = \frac{\cos(A - B) + \cos(A + B)}{2} \tag{5.36}$$

with $A$ identified with $\omega t$ and $B$ with $\omega t - \theta$. We may expand the second cosine in Eq. (5.36) further with the identity

$$\cos(C - D) = \cos C \cos D + \sin C \sin D \tag{5.37}$$

where $C = 2\omega t$ and $D = \theta$. Thus,

$$p(t) = \frac{V_p I_p}{2}[\cos\theta + \cos\theta\cos(2\omega t) + \sin\theta\sin(2\omega t)] \tag{5.38}$$

$$= \underbrace{P[1 + \cos(2\omega t)]}_{\text{one-way flow}} + \underbrace{Q\sin(2\omega t)}_{\text{two-way flow}}$$

where

$$P = \frac{V_p I_p}{2}\cos\theta = V_e I_e \cos\theta \tag{5.39}$$

and

$$Q = \frac{V_p I_p}{2}\sin\theta = V_e I_e \sin\theta \tag{5.40}$$

The second forms of Eqs. (5.39) and (5.40) are preferred because meters indicate effective values and because we usually speak in terms of effective values when discussing power relationships.

**real power, power factor**

**Interpretation of P.** The second form of Eq. (5.38) reveals the nature of power flow in sinusoidal steady state. The time average of the instantaneous power given by Eq. (5.38) is called the *real power, P,* given by Eq. (5.39). This power is the time-average rate of energy conversion from electrical to nonelectrical form, and this is the power that costs you money on your electric bill. Equation (5.39) reminds us of the power in the dc case, with effective instead of dc values for voltage and current, except that we now have the $\cos\theta$ factor. This added term is the *power factor, PF,* defined by

$$PF = \cos\theta = \frac{P}{V_e I_e} = \frac{P}{S} \tag{5.41}$$

where $S = V_e I_e$.

**apparent power**

In words, the power factor is the real power divided by the product of the effective voltage and the effective current, which is called the *apparent power, S.* The power factor is also the cosine of the phase angle between the voltage and current.

When voltage and current have the same phase, $\theta = 0$, the power factor is unity, and the power into the load is $V_e I_e$. When the voltage has a different phase from the current, the power factor is less than unity and the time-average power is decreased proportionally. This occurs symmetrically, whether the circuit is inductive (positive $\theta$) or capacitive (negative $\theta$). When the phase is $\pm 90°$, no time-average power is transferred to the load.

**Interpretation of** $P[1 + \cos(2\omega t)]$. Comparison of Eq. (5.38) with Eq. (5.8) suggests that the $P[(1 + \cos(2\omega t)]$ term represents the lumpy flow of energy from the source to the load, as shown in Fig. 5.6. This term in Eq. (5.38) represents a one-way flow of energy, from source to load, in contrast with the $Q$ term, which represents a two-way flow of energy.

**reactive power**    **Interpretation of** $Q \sin(2\omega t)$. The second term in Eq. (5.38) represents *reactive power*, energy loaned periodically to the reactive elements in the load. Equation (5.40) gives the magnitude of the reactive power, $Q$. This term averages zero and represents energy shuttled between source and load. The cases of pure resistance, inductance, and capacitance, the power and energy relationships are summarized in Table 5-1:

**TABLE 5-1**   **Power and energy relationships for pure resistance, inductance, and capacitance**

| Element | $\theta$ | P | Q | | Comment |
|---|---|---|---|---|---|
| resistance | $0°$ | $I_e^2 R$ | 0 | | real power only |
| inductance | $+90°$ | 0 | $V_e I_e \sin(+90°)$ $= +\omega L I_e^2$ $= +\omega W_{mp}$ | (5.42) | positive reactive power |
| capacitance | $-90°$ | 0 | $V_e I_e \sin(-90°)$ $= -\omega C V_e^2$ $= -\omega W_{ep}$ | (5.43) | negative reactive power |

In deriving the results in Table 5-1, we have used the following: $V_e = X_L I_e = \omega L I_e$, Eq. (4.95), and $W_{mp} = \frac{1}{2} L I_p^2 = L I_e^2$ as the peak magnetic stored energy in the inductance, Eq. (5.23); $I_e = V_e/|X_C| = \omega C V_e$, Eq. (4.96), and $W_{ep} = \frac{1}{2} C V_p^2 = C V_e^2$ as the peak electric stored energy, Eq. (5.30).

**Conservation of Energy**   **Reactive power.** From Eqs. (5.42) and (5.43), we see that the reactive power is a measure of the energy that the source has to lend to a reactive element in sinusoidal steady state. For an inductance, the reactive power is positive, and for a capacitance, the reactive power is negative.[11] The reactive power for a circuit containing several inductances and capacitances is the sum of reactive powers to each; hence, the reactive powers of inductances and capacitances tend to cancel. Adding Eqs. (5.42) and (5.43), we obtain

$$Q = Q_L + Q_C = \omega(W_{mp} - W_{ep}) \tag{5.44}$$

This subtraction is the basis of power-factor correction, which we will illustrate presently.

---

[11] The inductance is said to consume reactive power, and the capacitor is said to supply reactive power.

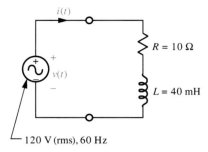

**Figure 5.9** Series *RL* circuit.

The analysis of the *RLC* load pictured in Fig. 5.8 will be resumed in the next section. Here, for simplicity, we work out power and energy calculations for the series *RL* circuit shown in Fig. 5.9.

---

**EXAMPLE 5.7**

## Power and energy of the series *RL* circuit

Find the power factor, the time-average power, the reactive power, and the peak stored energy for the series *RL* load shown in Fig. 5.9.

**SOLUTION:**

We are working in the time domain for our power calculations, but frequency-domain techniques are appropriate for finding the voltage and current that we need in the power calculations. We use the voltage source as our phase reference, so it would be represented by the phasor $\mathbf{V} = 120\sqrt{2} \angle 0°$. To calculate the current, we need the impedance,

$$\mathbf{Z} = 10 + j\,120\pi \times 0.04 = 10 + j\,15.1 = 18.1 \angle 56.4° \; \Omega \qquad (5.45)$$

so $|\mathbf{Z}| = 18.1 \; \Omega$ and $\theta = 56.4°$. The magnitude of the current is thus $120\sqrt{2}/18.1 = 6.63\sqrt{2}$ and the phase angle of the current is $-56.4°$. Thus, the time-domain voltage and current are

$$v(t) = 120\sqrt{2} \; \cos(120\,\pi t) \; \text{V}$$
$$i(t) = 6.63\sqrt{2} \; \cos(120\,\pi t - 56.4°) \; \text{A} \qquad (5.46)$$

The power factor is $PF = \cos 56.4° = 0.553$. From Eq. (5.39), we compute the time-average power delivered to the *RL* load by the ac voltage source to be

$$P = 120 \times 6.63 \times 0.553 = 440 \; \text{W} \qquad (5.47)$$

Because the inductor receives no time-average power, this power must represent electrical energy converted to thermal energy in the resistor. This interpretation is confirmed by direct calculation of the power into the resistor.

$$P_R = I_e^2 R = (6.63)^2 \, (10) = 440 \; \text{W} \qquad (5.48)$$

The reactive power from Eq. (5.40) is

$$Q = V_e I_e \sin\theta = 120 \times 6.63 \; \sin(+56.4°) = +663 \; \text{VAR} \qquad (5.49)$$

where VAR stands for "volt-ampere reactive," a unit intended to distinguish the reactive power from the real. The magnetic energy storage represented by the inductance has a peak value of

$$W_{mp} = LI_e^2 = 0.04 \times (6.63)^2 = 1.76 \text{ J} \tag{5.50}$$

You may confirm that Eq. (5.42) is satisfied. The instantaneous magnetic energy storage fluctuates between zero and the peak energy calculated in Eq. (5.50). This energy must be lent twice each cycle to the load by the source by means of reactive power flow.

---

**WHAT IF?** What if the inductor were replaced by a 200-μF capacitor? [12]

---

You may have noticed that we used rms values in every power and energy calculation in the foregoing example. However, we were careful to use peak values for time functions. This required inserting and taking out some $\sqrt{2}$ 's that never entered into the calculations. Many texts and most practitioners drop them and use rms values for everything, but we favor the more explicit approach and continue to use effective or peak values where each is more natural.

**Summary.** We have defined real and reactive power as

$$\underbrace{P = V_e I_e \cos\theta}_{\text{real power}} \quad \text{and} \quad \underbrace{Q = V_e I_e \sin\theta}_{\text{reactive power}} \tag{5.51}$$

where $V_e$ and $I_e$ are the effective values of the voltage and current, respectively. The definitions refer to circuits generally, but when applied directly to individual resistances, inductances, and capacitances, we have

$$P_R = I_e^2 R \quad \text{and} \quad Q_L = I_e^2 X_L \quad \text{and} \quad Q_C = I_e^2 X_C \tag{5.52}$$

where $X_C$ is numerically negative. Thus a resistance requires only real power; inductors and capacitors require reactive power of opposite signs.

We could push our investigation of power and energy in the time domain a little further, but we would rather move on to the frequency domain. The important question we ask is: Can such power calculations be made in the frequency domain without explicitly considering the time functions? The next section shows the answer to be yes; indeed, the frequency-domain viewpoint yields efficiency in calculation and suggests new insights.

### Check Your Understanding

1. What is the peak value of a sinusoidal current if a standard ac ammeter indicates 5 A?

2. A 120-V electric iron (for ironing clothes) converts approximately 1200 W of electrical power to heat. Estimate the rms current to the iron.

3. For a resistor, the time-average power is one-half the peak instantaneous power. (True/False?)

---

[12] $P = 522$ W, $Q = -692$ VAR, $W_{ep} = 1.84$ J.

**4.** In an ac circuit, the peak stored energy in a capacitor is $10\,\mu$J. What is the time-average stored energy?

**5.** What is the time-average value of $v(t) = 10 + 5\cos(100t)$ V?

**6.** If the power factor is 0.75, lagging, by what angle does the current lag the voltage?

**7.** Is the reactive power into a capacitor positive or negative?

**8.** For a dc voltage, a dc voltmeter measures 10 V. What is the time-average voltage? What is the rms value of the voltage? For an ac voltage, an ac voltmeter measures 10 V. What is the time-average value of the voltage? What is the rms value of the voltage?

*Answers.* **(1)** 7.07 A;  **(2)** 10 A;  **(3)** true;  **(4)** 5 µJ;  **(5)** 10 V;  **(6)** 41.4°;  **(7)** negative;  **(8)** 10 V, 10 V, 0 V, 10 V.

## 5.2 POWER AND ENERGY IN THE FREQUENCY DOMAIN

**Introduction.** The time-average (real) power in an ac circuit, given in Eq. (5.39), involves the peak (or rms) values of the voltage and current and the power factor, which is the cosine of the phase angle between the voltage and current. All these quantities can be expressed in the frequency domain; indeed, the frequency-domain concept of impedance provides the most efficient way to determine the magnitude and the phase angle of the current. Thus, we can calculate time-average power without transforming to the time domain. In this section, we show how to determine real, reactive, and apparent power in the frequency domain.

### Real and Reactive Power from Phasors

**Real power.** The time-average power into the load is given by Eq. (5.39) as

$$P = \frac{V_p I_p}{2}\cos\theta = \frac{1}{2}|\underline{\mathbf{V}}| \times \underbrace{|\underline{\mathbf{I}}|\cos\theta}_{\text{in-phase current}} \quad \text{watts} \tag{5.53}$$

Figure 5.10(b) and Eq. (5.39) suggest an interpretation of the power factor. If we associate the $\cos\theta$ with the magnitude of $\underline{\mathbf{I}}$, the term $|\underline{\mathbf{I}}|\cos\theta$ is the projection of the current phasor onto the voltage phasor. This part of the current is *in phase* with the voltage, and we conclude that the time-average power is given by the product of the voltage and the current in phase with the voltage. Thus, in the circuit of Fig. 5.9, repeated in Fig. 5.10(a),

$$P = \tfrac{1}{2}\,120\sqrt{2} \times 3.67\,\sqrt{2} = 440 \text{ W} \tag{5.54}$$

which agrees with Eq. (5.47).

**Reactive power.** Equation (5.40) for the reactive power can be interpreted as the product of the voltage with the *out-of-phase* component of the current, as shown in Fig. 5.10(b):

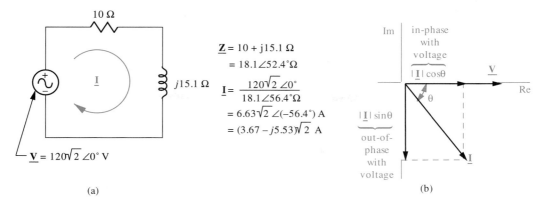

**Figure 5.10** (a) Solution in the frequency domain. (b) The phasor diagram shows the "in-phase" and "out-of-phase" components of the current.

$$Q = \tfrac{1}{2}|\underline{V}| \times \underbrace{|\underline{I}| \sin\theta}_{\text{out-of-phase current}} \quad \text{VAR} \tag{5.55}$$

where we consider lagging current to produce a positive out-of-phase component.[13] In the circuit in Fig. 5.10(a),

$$Q = \tfrac{1}{2} \ 120\sqrt{2} \times 5.53 \ \sqrt{2} = +663 \quad \text{VAR} \tag{5.56}$$

which agrees with Eq. (5.49). We showed in Eq. (5.42) the relation between reactive power and the stored-energy requirement of the inductor. We explore further the meaning of the reactive power in the following example.

---

**EXAMPLE 5.8**  **Real and reactive power in the *RLC* circuit**

Find the real and reactive power into the load in Fig. 5.11 with $R = 10 \ \Omega$, $L = 40$ mH, and $C = 120$ μF, and interpret these powers as lost or stored energy. The voltage is 120 V (rms) at 60 Hz.

**SOLUTION:**
Figure 5.11 shows the circuit in the frequency domain.
The impedance as seen by the voltage source is

$$\underline{Z} = j15.1 + 10 \ || \ (-j22.1) = 14.0 \ \angle \ 53.8° \ \Omega \tag{5.57}$$

so the current is

---

[13] Because $\theta$ is negative for lagging current, $Q$ would be negative for lagging current if strict mathematics were followed. In a power system, however, lagging current is "normal" and reactive power is defined to be positive for lagging, or inductive, current.

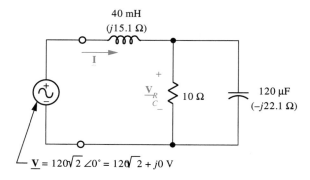

**Figure 5.11** General *RLC* load.

$$|\underline{I}| = \frac{120\sqrt{2} \angle 0°}{14.0 \angle 53.8°} = 8.55\sqrt{2} \angle -53.8° \qquad (5.58)$$

$$= (5.05 - j6.89)\sqrt{2} \ A$$

The real power to the load is the product of the rms voltage with the in-phase component of the rms current, $P = 120 \times 5.05 = 606$ watts, and the reactive power to the load is the product with the out-of-phase rms current, $Q = 120 \times 6.89 = 827$ VAR. Lagging current gives positive reactive power.

To interpret these powers in terms of lost or stored energy, we must complete the phasor analysis of the circuit. We find the voltage across the $R\|C$ by multiplying the current by the parallel impedance:

$$\underline{V}_{RC} = (8.55\sqrt{2} \angle -53.8°) \times 10\|(-j22.1) = 77.9\sqrt{2} \angle -78.1° \ V \qquad (5.59)$$

The energy lost to the circuit will be in the time-average power to the resistor, which is

$$P_R = \frac{V_R^2}{R} = \frac{(77.9)^2}{10} = 606 \text{ watts} \qquad (5.60)$$

where $V_R$ is the rms voltage across the resistor. The peak electric energy stored in the capacitor is

$$W_{ep} = \tfrac{1}{2} \ CV_C^2 = \tfrac{1}{2}(120 \times 10^{-6}) \times (77.9\sqrt{2})^2 = 0.728 \text{ J} \qquad (5.61)$$

where $V_C$ is the peak voltage across the capacitor. The peak magnetic energy stored in the inductor is

$$W_{mp} = \tfrac{1}{2} \ LI_L^2 = \tfrac{1}{2}(0.040) \times (8.55\sqrt{2})^2 = 2.92 \text{ J} \qquad (5.62)$$

where $I_L$ is the peak current through the inductor. These stored energies relate to the reactive power through Eq. (5.44):

$$Q = \omega(W_{mp} - W_{ep}) = 120\,\pi \times (2.92 - 0.728) = 827 \text{ VAR} \qquad (5.63)$$

which agrees with our earlier result.

**Summary.** The real (time-average) and reactive powers can be determined wholly in the frequency domain. The real power is the product of the voltage with the current in phase with the voltage, and the reactive power is the product of the voltage with the current out of phase with the voltage, with lagging current considered positive. The real power is the sum of the powers dissipated in the resistances of the load, and the reactive power is the product of the angular frequency with the difference between the magnetic and electric peak stored energies within the load.

## Complex Power

**complex power**

**Definition of complex power.** The complex sum of the real and reactive power in Eqs. (5.39) and (5.40) is called the *complex power* and can be written

$$\underline{S} = \tfrac{1}{2} \underline{V} \underline{I}^* = P + jQ \ \text{VA} \tag{5.64}$$

where $\underline{S}$ is the complex power in volt-amperes. The complex conjugate of the phasor current changes the sign of the imaginary part and thus introduces mathematically the customary change of sign in the out-of-phase current. The expression for the complex power in Eq. (5.64) also permits us to relax the requirement that the phasor voltage, $\underline{V}$, be a real quantity. Note that if

$$\underline{V} = |\underline{V}| \angle \theta_V \quad \text{and} \quad \underline{Z} = |\underline{Z}| \angle \theta \tag{5.65}$$

where $\theta_V$ is the phase of the voltage, no longer assumed zero, then

$$\underline{I} = \frac{\underline{V}}{\underline{Z}} = |\underline{I}| \angle (\theta_V - \theta) \Rightarrow \underline{I}^* = |\underline{I}| \angle (-\theta_V + \theta) \tag{5.66}$$

because the complex conjugate changes the sign of the current phase angle. The complex power, as defined in Eq. (5.64), would be

$$\underline{S} = \tfrac{1}{2} \underline{V} \underline{I}^* = \tfrac{1}{2} |\underline{V}| \angle\theta_V \times |\underline{I}| \angle(-\theta_V + \theta)$$
$$= \tfrac{1}{2} |\underline{V}||\underline{I}| \angle \theta = \tfrac{1}{2}|\underline{V}||\underline{I}| \ (\cos\theta + j\sin\theta) \tag{5.67}$$

Thus, the phase reference drops out for the complex power defined in Eq. (5.64) and only the phase difference between voltage and current remains.

---

[14] $P = 282$ watts and $Q = -711$ VARs.

**EXAMPLE 5.9** **Complex power**

Find the complex power into the circuit in Fig. 5.9 .

**SOLUTION:**
The phasor voltage is $\underline{V} = 120\sqrt{2} \angle 0°$ V and the current we found in Fig. 5.10 to be $\underline{I} = 6.63\sqrt{2} \angle -56.4°$ A in polar form or $\underline{I} = (3.67 - j5.53)\sqrt{2}$ A in rectangular form. The complex power is

$$\underline{S} = \tfrac{1}{2}\ \underline{V}\underline{I}^* = \tfrac{1}{2}\ (120\sqrt{2} + j0)\,(3.67\sqrt{2} + j5.53\sqrt{2})$$

(5.68)

$$= 120 \times 3.67 + j\,120 \times 5.53 = \underbrace{440}_{P} + \underbrace{j663}_{Q}\ \text{VA}$$

Thus, the real power is 440 W and the reactive power is +663 VAR. The positive sign indicates predominant magnetic energy storage. The $\sqrt{2}$'s all dropped out, as they always do in power calculations.

**WHAT IF?**

What if the resistor were increased to 12 $\Omega$? What would be the complex power in that case?[15]

**Apparent power.** The complex power is a complex number yielding information about the flow of time-average power and the shuttling of loaned energy between source and load in an ac circuit. The magnitude of the complex power, $S = |\underline{S}|$ is the *apparent power*. The apparent power results when you measure the voltage and current with meters and multiply the measured values without regard for phase.[16]

$$S = |\underline{S}| = \tfrac{1}{2}\ |\underline{V}||\underline{I}| = V_e I_e\ \text{VA}$$

(5.69)

Apparent power is important as a measure of the operating limits in electrical equipment such as transformers, motors, and generators. Losses in the wires are proportional to the square of the current in the machine regardless of the phase, whereas losses in the magnetic materials are roughly proportional to the square of the operating voltage. Machine limits are established by losses. Because electrical machinery is operated with the voltage more or less constant, apparent power limits imply current limits. In the previous example the apparent power is $120 \times 6.63 = 796$ VA.

**Summary.** The complex power gives concise information about power and energy flow in an ac circuit. The real part of the complex power is the time-average power in watts. The real power heats resistors, turns motors, and makes the electric meter revolve. The imaginary part of the complex power is the reactive power in VARs, which is proportional to the electrical energy lent to the load by the ac source twice each cycle. The reactive power is considered positive when the load is inductive and negative

---

[15] $\underline{S} = 465 + j584$ VA.

[16] In Eq. (5.69), we need not use $|\underline{I}^*|$ because the magnitude is the same for $\underline{I}$ and $\underline{I}^*$.

when the load is capacitive, although the latter is rare in power systems. The magnitude of the complex power is the apparent power in volt-amperes and indicates the operating level of a power system.

**power triangle**

**Power triangles.**   The apparent power, real power, and reactive power form a right triangle. Figure 5.12 shows this *power triangle* for the previous example. The angle at the origin is $\theta$, the angle of the impedance, $+\,56.4°$ in this case. When the current lags the voltage, the power triangle is drawn above the $x$-axis.

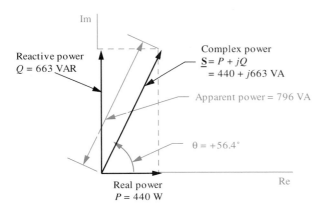

Reactive power
$Q = 663$ VAR

Complex power
$\underline{S} = P + jQ$
$= 440 + j663$ VA

Apparent power $= 796$ VA

$\theta = +56.4°$

Real power
$P = 440$ W

Re

**Figure 5.12**   The power triangle pictures complex, apparent, real, and reactive power.

Because the various kinds of powers form a triangle, and because the power factor is the cosine of an angle of that triangle, there follow a host of formulas relating power factor with the various types of powers. We now list several of these, which you can verify from the definitions and common trigonometric identities.

$$S = \sqrt{P^2 + Q^2} \tag{5.70}$$

$$PF = \frac{P}{S} = \frac{P}{\sqrt{P^2 + Q^2}} \tag{5.71}$$

$$Q = \pm\, S\sqrt{1 - (PF)^2} \quad (+ \text{ for lagging } PF) \tag{5.72}$$

Based on these formulas, and others that can easily be derived, a variety of problems in ac power systems can be analyzed, of which the following is typical.

**Determining apparent power, real power, and reactive power from measurements.**   Figure 5.8 shows an ammeter ($A$), voltmeter ($V$), and wattmeter ($P$) metering an $RLC$ load. We assume these meters are ideal and indicate measured values of $I_m$, $V_m$, and $P_m$. Because the meters indicate effective values, the measured apparent power would be the product of the meter indications:

$$S_m = V_m\, I_m \tag{5.73}$$

and Eq. (5.71) would give the measured power factor magnitude, $(PF)_m = P_m/S_m$.[17]   The measured reactive power follows from Eq. (5.70).

---

[17] Whether leading or lagging cannot be determined from these measurements.

$$Q_m = \pm \sqrt{S_m^2 - P_m^2} = \pm \sqrt{(V_m I_m)^2 - P_m^2} \tag{5.74}$$

## EXAMPLE 5.10 | Motors

A 230-V motor has a mechanical output power of 3 horsepower (hp). The input current, voltage, and power are measured to be 226 V, 15.6 A, and 2920 W, respectively. Calculate the efficiency, the power factor, and reactive power. Draw a phasor diagram, assuming lagging current.

### SOLUTION:
The measured apparent power is

$$S_m = V_m I_m = 226 \times 15.6 = 3530 \text{ VA} \tag{5.75}$$

The measured power factor is

$$PF_m = \frac{P_m}{S_m} = \frac{2920}{3530} = 0.828 \tag{5.76}$$

which corresponds to a phase angle of $\cos^{-1}(0.828) = 34.1°$, Eq. (5.41), assumed lagging current. The reactive power follows from Eq. (5.74):

$$Q = + \sqrt{S_m^2 - P_m^2} = \sqrt{(3530)^2 - (2920)^2} = +1980 \text{ VAR} \tag{5.77}$$

For the phasor diagram in Fig. 5.13, we have used the voltage for the phase reference, and shown the current lagging. The phase angle of the current follows from the power factor, $\theta = \cos^{-1}(0.828) = 34.1°$. The power triangle showing the real, reactive, and apparent powers would have the same angle but would be drawn above the real axis, similar to Fig. 5.12.

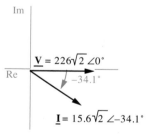

**Figure 5.13** Phasors representing motor voltage and current.

### WHAT IF?

What if the current were leading? What would change?[18]

---

[18]Only the signs of the phase angle and the reactive power.

The vocabulary and units of power in ac circuits. We now summarize the four types of power in ac circuits:

$P$ = real power = time-average power in watts
$Q$ = reactive power in VARs,[19] volt-amperes reactive
$S$ = apparent power in VAs, volt-amperes
$\underline{S}$ = complex power in VAs

The three units for ac power—watts, volt-amperes reactive, and volt-amperes—all have the scientific units for power, J/s. The related units of kW, kVAR , and kVA (k = $10^3$) and MW, MVAR, and MVA (M = $10^6$) are also common in the power industry. We use different units to clarify communication when speaking of the various kinds of "power" in ac circuits.

## Reactive Power in Power Systems

**Importance of reactive power.** Power companies have to be careful about the reactive power load on their systems. As stated before, the limits of larger power equipment such as generators and transformers are described by the apparent power, the Pythagorean sum of the real and reactive powers. Thus, if the reactive power becomes large, a piece of equipment may become overloaded even though the real power is moderate. Also, the reactive energy must be transported from generator to user, often over great distances. Reactive power increases line current, and hence increases line losses. The power company might surcharge industrial customers whose requirements for reactive power are great to pay for line losses.

**Power-factor correction.** Often, the industrial consumer can save money by placing a bank of capacitors in parallel with an inductive load to store energy locally. In effect, they receive the stored energy from the power company only once and then keep it "in house" with the capacitors. The customer thus *corrects* his power factor by creating a resonance between the electric energy stored by the added capacitance and the magnetic energy used by motors or other heavy equipment.

**Power-factor correction: current method.** The effect of adding parallel capacitance to correct the power factor can be understood from the phasor diagram of the currents. Figure 5.14 (b) shows the current phasors with the voltage as the phase reference. The load current, $I_{load}$, lags the voltage due to the magnetic equipment in the load. The in-phase current does useful work, and the out-of-phase current supplies the re-

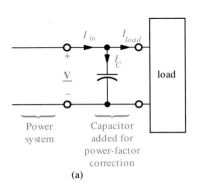

(a)

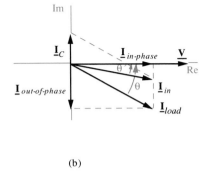

(b)

**Figure 5.14** (a) The capacitor corrects the lagging power factor of the load; (b) the leading current of the capacitor cancels part or all of the lagging out-of-phase current of the load. The input current is thus reduced.

[19] Rhymes with "jars."

quired magnetic energy. If the power factor is too low, capacitors are added in parallel with the load to draw leading current, which has the effect to improve the power factor from $PF = \cos \theta$ to $PF' = \cos \theta'$. The capacitive current is $I_C = \omega C V_e$ and the details amount to a simple problem in trigonometry, as shown by the following example.

## EXAMPLE 5.11 · Power factor correction (current method)

A 460-V, 60-Hz load uses 12 kW at a lagging power factor of 0.75. What capacitance should be placed in parallel with the load to correct the power factor to 0.9 lagging?

**SOLUTION:**
The rms load current is

$$I_{load} = \frac{P}{V \times PF} = \frac{12,000}{460 \times 0.75} = 34.8 \text{ A} \tag{5.78}$$

at a lagging phase angle of

$$\theta = \cos^{-1}(0.75) = 41.4° \tag{5.79}$$

With the voltage as the phase reference, the current is

$$\mathbf{I}_{load} = 34.8\sqrt{2} \ \angle -41.4° = (26.1 - j23.0)\sqrt{2} \text{ A} \tag{5.80}$$

The parallel capacitor will draw leading current but will not change the in-phase component. For a power factor of 0.9 lagging ($\theta = -25.8°$), the resultant out-of-phase component must be

$$23.0 - I_C = 26.1 \tan 25.8° = 12.6$$
$$I_C = 10.4 \text{ A} \tag{5.81}$$

where a lagging out-of-phase component is considered positive. The required capacitance is, therefore, 59.8 μF.

### WHAT IF?

What if the corrected power factor must be 0.95 lagging?[20]

**Power-factor correction: power method.** Power capacitors manufactured for power-factor correction are rated by voltage and reactive power.[21] Thus, the real and reactive power can be calculated directly, as shown by reworking the previous example on this basis.

---

[20] 83.2 μF.

[21] The frequency is assumed to be 60 Hz in the United States.

## EXAMPLE 5.12 Power factor correction (power method)

**ALTERNATE SOLUTION:**

A calculation of the complex power follows from the real power and power factor:

$$\underline{S} = \frac{P}{PF} \angle (\pm \cos^{-1} PF) = \frac{12,000}{0.75} \angle + \cos^{-1}(0.75) \tag{5.82}$$

$$= 16,000 \angle (+41.4°) = 12,000 + j10,600$$

where $+$ is used for lagging $PF$. The desired complex power is

$$\underline{S}' = \frac{12,000}{0.9} \angle \cos^{-1}(0.9) \tag{5.83}$$

$$= 12,000 + j5810$$

Because $\underline{S}' = \underline{S} + jQ_C$, the capacitor must contribute

$$Q_C = -4770 \text{ VAR} \tag{5.84}$$

as shown in Fig. 5.15. Thus we would use one 5-kVAR or five 1-kVAR, 460-V capacitors.

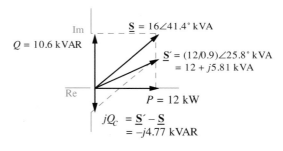

**Figure 5.15**   The power triangles before and after power-factor correction.

**WHAT IF?**   What if you wanted to correct to 0.95 $PF$ leading?[22]

---

## Reactive Power in Electronics

**OBJECTIVE 6**

To understand how to use an ac Thévenin equivalent circuit to establish the load to withdraw maximum power from an ac source

Reactive power also plays an important role in electronics. Here we normally deal with small amounts of power, and must make full use of the power that is available. To see the role of reactive power, let us examine the conditions for maximum power transfer in an ac circuit.

**Thévenin and Norton equivalent circuits for ac.**   In Chapter 2, we derived the Thévenin equivalent circuit using linearity and superposition. In Chapter 4, we re-

---

[22] $-14.5$ kVAR ($182 \ \mu$F).

duced ac problems to equivalent dc problems through the use of phasors, through which sources and circuits are represented by complex numbers. All the techniques we developed for dc circuits remain valid for solving ac circuits, including Thévenin and Norton equivalent circuits. In Fig. 5.16, we show a Thévenin equivalent circuit with a phasor voltage source, $\underline{\mathbf{V}}_T$, and an output impedance, $\underline{\mathbf{Z}}_{eq}$, which we have expressed as a resistive and reactive part for benefit of the derivation that follows. Recall that the circuit replaced by the Thévenin equivalent circuit can be arbitrarily complicated.

### Radio design.
Let us consider a typical situation that might arise in electronics, that of getting maximum power out of a radio antenna. Specifically, consider the telescoping AM radio antenna on an automobile, as suggested in Fig. 5.17. Radio waves are radiated by a commercial station, perhaps at considerable distance, and these waves interact with the antenna to give a small voltage, typically 10 mV, rms, between the fender and the base of the antenna.

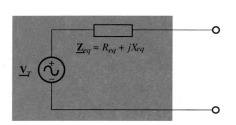

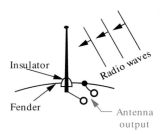

**Figure 5.16** For an ac circuit, the Thévenin voltage is a phasor and the output resistance becomes an impedance.

**Figure 5.17** The antenna and the radio waves can be represented by the Thévenin equivalent circuit shown in Fig. 5.16.

### Antenna impedance.
The derivation of the output impedance of such an antenna is complicated, but we can say a little based on our understanding of electric and magnetic energy. As a circuit element, the antenna represents a wire that leads nowhere, that is, an open circuit. The radio waves tend to make current flow on the wire, but a small current produces a buildup of charge on the wire and the current stops. Thus, we anticipate that an antenna of this type would build up charge but carry little current. This suggests that electric energy storage would dominate magnetic energy storage and that the output impedance would be capacitive. We have shown typical values in Fig. 5.18.

### Power transfer to the radio.
Our task is to specify the input impedance of the radio, $\underline{\mathbf{Z}}_L = R_L + jX_L$, to receive maximum power out of the antenna. The average power into the load would be $|\mathbf{I}|^2 R_L/2$, where $\mathbf{I}$ is the current in the load. This current is the antenna voltage divided by the total impedance in the circuit, the sum of $\underline{\mathbf{Z}}_{eq}$ and $\underline{\mathbf{Z}}_L$.

$$\mathbf{I} = \frac{\underline{\mathbf{V}}_T}{\underline{\mathbf{Z}}_{eq} + \underline{\mathbf{Z}}_L} = \frac{10\sqrt{2} \times 10^{-3} \angle 0°}{(10 + R_L) + j(X_L - 150)} \text{ A} \tag{5.85}$$

Because the phase does not matter in this power calculation, we will consider only the magnitude:

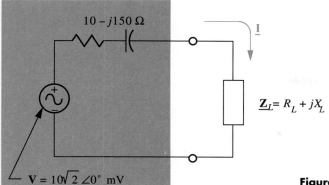

**Figure 5.18** Find $R_L$ and $X_L$ to maximize power in R

$$|\mathbf{I}| = \frac{10 \times 10^{-3}\sqrt{2}}{\sqrt{(10 + R_L)^2 + (X_L - 150)^2}} \; \text{A} \tag{5.86}$$

Consequently, the time-average power delivered to the radio by the antenna would be

$$P(R_L, X_L) = \frac{|\mathbf{I}|^2 R_L}{2} = \frac{2 \times (10^{-2})^2 R_L/2}{(10 + R_L)^2 + (X_L - 150)^2} \; \text{W} \tag{5.87}$$

**Maximizing the power.**  Equation (5.87) is the function to be maximized, so we might make an assault using the methods of differential calculus. Before taking derivatives, however, we should note the effect of the load reactance, $X_L$. Being in the denominator and being squared, the reactance term, $X_L - 150$, can only decrease the power. Clearly, the best we can do is set $X_L$ to $+150 \, \Omega$. Once we do that, the power is a function of $R_L$ only:

$$P(R_L + 150) = \frac{10^{-4} R_L}{(10 + R_L)^2} \Rightarrow R_L = 10 \, \Omega \;\; \text{for maximum power} \tag{5.88}$$

We have written by inspection the value of $R_L$ that gives maximum power because the problem has been reduced to that solved back in Chapter 2, Eq. (2.19). Once the load reactance ($X_L$) is adjusted to balance the reactance in the source, the maximum power follows from equating the resistance of the load to the resistive part of the output impedance of the source.  In summary,

$$\mathbf{Z}_L = \mathbf{Z}_{eq}^* = R_{eq} - jX_{eq} \tag{5.89}$$

**impedance matching**

gives maximum power to $R_L$. This is called *matching* the load impedance to the source.

Thus, the maximum power transfer will occur when the load has the same resistance as the source but the opposite reactance. We therefore create a local resonance from the viewpoint of the load, in effect balancing the equivalent stored energies. In the case solved before, you can confirm that the power delivered to the radio by the antenna is $2.5 \times 10^{-6}$ W. Not much power, but we know that it must be adequate because AM radios work. In Sec. 7.3, we will show how transistors are used to amplify these small signals to a level where loudspeakers produce audible sound.

---

**EXAMPLE 5.13** **Matching output cable**

A 1-MHz voltage source with an output impedance of 50 $\Omega$ must be attached to a load with a cable that has a capacitance of 300 pF. What should be the load to draw maximum power from the source?

**SOLUTION:**
Figure 5.19 shows the equivalent circuit. We have expressed the unknown load impedance also as admittance because we have a choice of two loads, depending upon whether we use a series or parallel form.

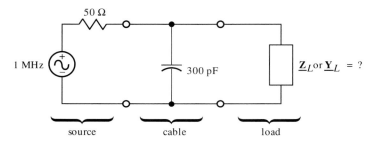

**Figure 5.19** The load impedance has to match the output impedance of the source, including the capacitance of the cable.

The output impedance to the load is

$$\mathbf{Z}_{out} = 50\Omega \| \, 300 \text{ pF @ } 1\text{MHz} = 50\| - j531 = 49.6 - j4.7\Omega \tag{5.90}$$

Maximum power transfer requires $\mathbf{Z}_L = \mathbf{Z}_{out}^*$, Eq. (5.89):

$$\mathbf{Z}_L = 49.6 + j4.7 = 49.6 \; \Omega \text{ in series with } 0.74 \; \mu\text{H} \tag{5.91}$$

The small value of inductance might cause a problem, so we should consider a parallel realization for the load. For a parallel load, the output admittance would be appropriate for

$$\mathbf{Y}_{out} = \frac{1}{R} + j\omega C = 0.02 + j\, 1.88 \times 10^{-3} \text{ mho} \tag{5.92}$$

The reciprocal of Eq. (5.89) is equally valid, so the load admittance for maximum power will be

$$\mathbf{Y}_L = 0.02 - j\, 1.88 \times 10^{-3} \text{ mho} \tag{5.93}$$

which is 50 $\Omega$ in parallel with 84.5 $\mu$H.

---

**WHAT IF?**
What if the frequency were 10 MHz?[23]

---

[23] The optimum load impedance would be 26.5 $\Omega$ in series with 0.4 $\mu$H or else 50 $\Omega$ in parallel with 1.7 $\mu$H.

A power system is designed to provide uniform voltage, independent of load. For this reason, the source impedance is always small relative to load impedance. Maximum power transfer is irrelevant to a power system.

## Check Your Understanding

1. If the current leads the voltage in an ac circuit, the reactive power is positive or negative?

2. If the real power is 600 W and the reactive power is −300 VAR, what is the apparent power?

3. The complex power depends on the relative phase between voltage and current, not the absolute phase. True/False?

4. An electronic circuit has an open-circuit voltage of 100 mV (rms) and an output impedance of $20 + j10\ \Omega$. What load will draw maximum power from this source? What will be the power in this load?

*Answers.*  (**1**) Negative;  (**2**) 671 VA;  (**3**) true;  (**4**) $20 - j\,10\ \Omega$, $1.25 \times 10^{-4}$ W.

## 5.3  TRANSFORMERS

### Transformer Principles

**Voltage transformation.**   A transformer is a highly efficient device for changing ac voltage from one value to another, for example, from 120 V to 6 V. Transformers come in all sizes, from the enormous transformers used in power substations to the small transformers used for doorbells.[24]

The transformer gives ac a feature lacking in dc power systems. Using a transformer, we can efficiently change ac voltage from small amplitudes to large amplitudes, or vice versa. Such changes are not simply accomplished with dc voltage.

**Current and impedance transformation.**   As we will soon prove, a transformer also transforms current, and, as a consequence of transforming voltage and current, also transforms impedance.   Indeed, the transformation of impedance is perhaps the most important property of the transformer.

**Common transformer applications.**   Transformers are indispensable to electrical systems; here are a few common applications:

Impedance level

■ **Power transformers.** Transformers are vital to high-voltage power distribution systems. This is an example of voltage transformation, but the main purpose is impedance transformation.  Power transformers are used to make the resistance and inductance of the transmission system look small relative to the load impedance; hence, the relative losses of the distribution system are reduced.

---

[24] Sometimes the word "transformer" is used for a device that employs a transformer but includes other controls or devices, such as the "transformers" used to power model railroad trains.

■ **Battery chargers.** Transformers reduce the power voltage from 120 V ac to some smaller value for charging of batteries through rectification.

■ **Arc welders.** Transformers are used to match the ac system to the impedance of the molten metal, which is close to a short circuit, so that power can be delivered to it.

■ **Doorbell and thermostat circuits.** Here, the transformer reduces the voltage to a small value for safety.

■ **Electronic power supplies.** This application is similar to a battery charger. The voltage is changed to the level required by the electronic circuits.

■ **Stereo output transformers.** Transformers are used to match the electronic output circuit to the impedance of the speakers, as well as to allow optimum use of different speaker systems with the same amplifier.

■ **Ignition coils.** The "coil" is a transformer that raises the voltage of the automotive electrical system to the high voltage required to create sparks in the cylinders.

■ **Etcetera.** We could multiply this list manyfold. The point is that transformers are used everywhere, not just in power circuits. In this section, we present ideal transformers and discuss some applications. In Chapter 6, we describe the use of transformers in power distribution systems. In Chapter 14, we analyze transformers from a physical basis and develop models for practical transformers.

**Transformer construction.** Figure 5.20 shows a simple transformer. Two coils are coupled by time-varying magnetic flux, which is channeled by an iron core. If we construct such a device, connect the primary coil to an ac voltage source, and connect the secondary coil to a resistive load, we would find that the resistive load becomes hot. This would demonstrate the flow of electrical energy from the ac source through the transformer and into the load. Furthermore, we would find that the transformer does not become very hot, suggesting that the transformer is an efficient device for coupling load and source.

**transformer primary and secondary**

**Transformer primary and secondary.** The coil connected to the ac source is called the *primary* and that connected to the load the *secondary*. There is nothing special about the two sides, for the transformer can convey power either way. In most applications, the power flows in only one direction and hence these names are useful.

**The ideal transformer.** In Chapter 14, we describe physical construction and circuit models of transformers. Here we define the ideal transformer as a circuit element and explore its properties in voltage, current, and impedance transformation. Primary and secondary voltage and current variables are defined in Fig. 5.21, which shows the circuit symbol for an ideal transformer. The primary variables form a load set and the secondary variables form a source set. These definitions are customary and indicate that the primary acts as a *load* to the power system supplying power to the transformer and the secondary acts as a *source* to the loads connected to it. We also define $n_p$ and $n_s$, the turns on the primary and secondary, respectively.

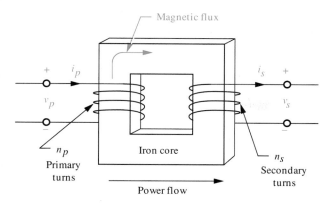

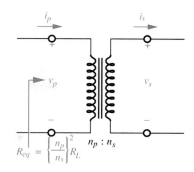

**Figure 5.20** A simple electrical transformer.

**Figure 5.21** Circuit symbol for an ideal transformer. The primary voltage and current form a load set, and the secondary voltage and current form a source set.

**ideal transformer**

**Voltage and current transformation in ideal transformers.** The primary and secondary voltages in the *ideal transformer* are related by

$$\frac{v_p}{n_p} = \frac{v_s}{n_s} \tag{5.94}$$

Thus, the side of the transformer with the larger number of turns has the larger voltage; indeed, the voltage per turn is constant for a given transformer. The primary and secondary currents in the *ideal transformer* are related by

$$n_p i_p = n_s i_s \tag{5.95}$$

Thus, the side of the transformer with the larger number of turns has the *smaller* current. For example, a transformer to increase the voltage would have a primary with few turns of large wire (small voltage, large current) and the secondary would have many turns of small wire (large voltage, small current).

---

**EXAMPLE 5.14** **Ideal transformers**

A transformer is required to produce 18 V (rms) and 650 mA from a 120-V rms line voltage. The primary uses 1000 turns of No. 30 wire. How many turns are required in the secondary and what would be the primary current?

**SOLUTION:**
Equation (5.94) is valid for instantaneous voltage in the time domain, so it transforms into the frequency domain as

$$\frac{\mathbf{V}_p}{n_p} = \frac{\mathbf{V}_s}{n_s} \Rightarrow \frac{120\sqrt{2}}{1000} = \frac{18\sqrt{2}}{n_s} \Rightarrow n_s = 150 \tag{5.96}$$

where $\underline{\mathbf{V}}_p$ and $\underline{\mathbf{V}}_s$ are the phasor primary and secondary voltages, respectively. The numerical version of Eq. (5.96) expresses only magnitudes because the phases must be the same. Using the same transformations in Eq. (5.95), we find the primary current to be

$$1000I_p = 150 \times 650 \text{ mA} \Rightarrow I_p = 97.5 \text{ mA} \tag{5.97}$$

**WHAT IF?**

What if the transformer primary uses only 500 turns?[25]

Equations (5.94) and (5.95) define the ideal transformer as a circuit element, with one restriction—no dc. The primary of the transformer is, like an inductor, a short circuit to dc and provides no coupling to the secondary unless voltage and current are changing.[26]

**Conservation of Energy**

**Conservation of power.** Multiplication of the left and right sides of Eqs. (5.94) and (5.95) shows that the instantaneous power into the primary, $p_{in}$, is equal to the instantaneous power out of the secondary, $p_{out}$

$$\frac{v_p}{n_p} \times n_p i_p = \frac{v_s}{n_s} \times n_s i_s \Rightarrow P_{in} = P_{out} \tag{5.98}$$

Thus, the *ideal* transformer has no losses and stores no energy.

Let us calculate the apparent power in the primary and secondary of the transformer in the previous example. The apparent power is the rms voltage times the rms current; hence,

$$S_p = 120 \times 97.5 \times 10^{-3} = 11.7 \text{ VA}$$

and

$$S_s = 18 \times 650 \times 10^{-3} = 11.7 \text{ VA} \tag{5.99}$$

Thus, apparent power is conserved by an ideal transformer. Because Eq. (5.98) shows that real power is conserved, it follows that reactive power is also conserved.

**Impedance Level**

**Impedance transformer.** Equations (5.94) and (5.95) reveal a very useful property of transformers—impedance transformation. Figure 5.22 shows an ideal transformer, a load resistor, $R_L$, connected to the secondary, and an equivalent resistance, $R_{eq}$, defined at the primary. The equations of the circuit are those of the ideal transformer in Eqs. (5.94) and (5.95) plus Ohm's law for $R_L$. If we divide Eq. (5.94) by Eq. (5.95), we obtain

$$\frac{1}{n_p^2} \frac{v_p}{i_p} = \frac{1}{n_s^2} \frac{v_s}{i_s} \tag{5.100}$$

---

[25] $n_s = 75$ turns, but $I_p = 97.5$ mA, the same.

[26] Practical transformers have a low frequency below which the coupling between primary and secondary begins to decrease, decreasing to zero at dc.

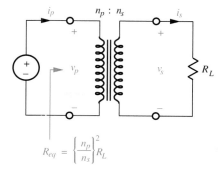

$$R_{eq} = \left\{ \frac{n_p}{n_s} \right\}^2 R_L$$

**Figure 5.22** The transformer will change $R_L$ to an equivalent resistance $R_{eq}$.

But $v_s/i_s$ is the load resistor, $R_L$, and $v_p/i_p$ defines the equivalent resistance, $R_{eq}$, into the primary, so Eq. (5.100) leads to the value of the equivalent resistance:

$$R_{eq} = \left( \frac{n_p}{n_s} \right)^2 R_L \tag{5.101}$$

**turns ratio**

Thus, the impedance level is transformed by the square of the *turns ratio*, $n_p/n_s$.[27] By using a transformer, we can make a large impedance appear small, or we can make a small impedance appear large.

---

**EXAMPLE 5.15** **Using a transformer to match impedances**

A source with an output resistance of 100 $\Omega$ must deliver power to a load of 500 $\Omega$. Find the turns ratio, $n_p/n_s$, to maximize load power.

**SOLUTION:**

As shown in Eq. (5.89), we must use an equivalent load impedance equal to the complex conjugate of the output impedance of the source. As shown in Fig. 5.23, this requires an impedance of 100 $\Omega$ looking into the primary of the transformer; thus, we need a transformer having $\sqrt{100/500}$ for a turns ratio. Because we wish to make the 500-$\Omega$ resistor look smaller, we must connect it to the high-voltage side of the transformer, the side with the more turns, and look into the low-voltage side to see the smaller impedance. A routine calculation shows an increase of 80% of the power in the load compared to a straight connection.

**WHAT IF?**  What if the required transformer were not available and a 1:2 transformer were used? What then would be the increase in load compared with a straight connection with no transformer?[28]

---

[27] The ratio of primary to secondary turns determines voltage, current, and impedance transformation properties. For this reason, the *turns ratio* is often stated as 1:$n$ (or $n$:1), where $n$ is not necessarily an integer and can be less than unity.

[28] Still 77.8%. Again this shows the importance of optimizing; small deviations do not matter.

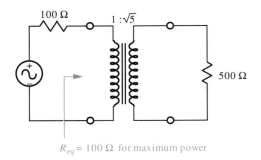

$R_{eq} = 100 \ \Omega$ for maximum power

**Figure 5.23**  The transformer turns ratio maximizes the power to the 500-$\Omega$ load.

**Impedance
Level**

**Analysis of circuits containing transformers.**  The equations relating transformer voltages and currents, Eqs. (5.94) and (5.95), may be used to analyze circuits
containing transformers.  However, transforming impedances usually works better.
Rather than writing equations for voltage and current, we deal with the ratio of voltage
to current, that is, the impedance level.

---

**EXAMPLE 5.16**  **Impedance transformation**

Solve for the load current, $\mathbf{I}_L$, in the ac circuit shown in Fig. 5.24(a).

**SOLUTION:**
We transform the load impedance into the primary and solve directly for the primary current.
Figure 5.24(b) shows the transformed impedance, and the primary current is easily determined:

$$\mathbf{I}_p = \frac{30\sqrt{2} \angle 0°}{20 + j20 + 2^2(2 - j10)} = 0.872\sqrt{2} \angle 35.5° \ \text{A} \qquad (5.102)$$

The secondary current, which is the load current, is greater by the turns ratio, Eq. (5.95), twice
as great in this case.  Thus the secondary current is $1.74 \ \sqrt{2} \angle 35.5°$ A.

---

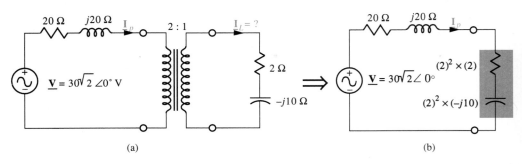

(a)  (b)

**Figure 5.24**  (a) Solve for $\mathbf{I}_L$; (b) equivalent circuit.

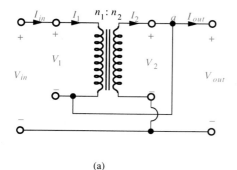

(a)

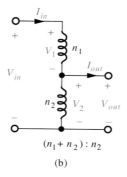

$(n_1 + n_2) : n_2$

(b)

**Figure 5.25** (a) The autotransformer connection; (b) the autotransformer connection drawn in the standard way.

**Autotransformers.** An autotransformer is a special transformer connection that is useful in power systems, motor starters, variable ac sources, and other applications. Figure 5.25(a) shows the autotransformer connection with the transformer primary and secondary drawn in the usual positions, and Fig. 5.25(b) shows the autotransformer drawn in a manner that clarifies the function of the transformer. In the step-down mode, which we have shown, the primary and secondary windings are connected in series for the new primary, and thus the input voltage is

$$V_{in} = V_1 + V_2 = \frac{n_1}{n_2} V_2 + V_2 = \frac{n_1 + n_2}{n_2} V_{out} \tag{5.103}$$

because $V_2 = V_{out}$. Hence, the voltage turns ratio is $(n_1 + n_2) : n_2$. The output current, from KCL at node $a$, is

$$I_{out} = I_1 + I_2 = I_1 + \frac{n_1}{n_2} I_1 = \frac{n_1 + n_2}{n_2} I_{in} \tag{5.104}$$

because $I_1 = I_{in}$. Equation (5.104) gives the same turns ratio as Eq. (5.103), which is consistent with conservation of apparent power.

The principal virtue of the autotransformer connection is that the apparent power rating increases. In effect, some of the power bypasses the transformer; only part of the power is transformed, as illustrated by the following example.

---

**EXAMPLE 5.17** **Autotransformers**

A 120/120-V, 12-kVA transformer is connected as an autotransformer to make a 240/120-V transformer. What is the apparent power rating of the autotransformer?

**SOLUTION:**

Figure 5.26 shows the transformer connection with rated voltage and current in the transformer. The current rating on both primary and secondary windings is 12 kVA/120 V = 100 A. In the autotransformer mode, the input apparent power is 240 × 100 = 24 kVA, and the output 120 × 200 = 24 kVA. Thus, the apparent power capacity of the 12-kVA transformer is doubled by the autotransformer connection. In effect, half the apparent power was transformed and half bypasses the transformer.

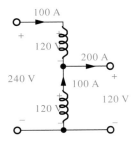

**Figure 5.26** The autotransformer connection increases the kVA limit.

## Transformer Applications in AC Power Systems

**Impedance transformation.** In this section, we explain why the impedance-transforming properties of transformers find their greatest application in electric power distribution. Figure 5.27 suggests the generation and delivery of electric power to a distant user over a distribution line. Although we have shown identical transformers at each end to simplify the analysis, in practice, the two transformers would not be identical because the power would be generated at a higher voltage than required by the consumer.

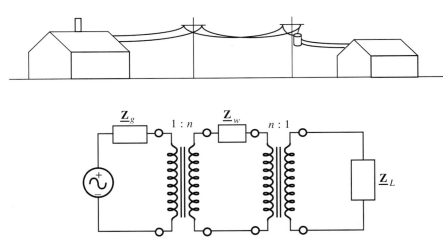

**Figure 5.27** Simple power distribution system and its equivalent circuit.

 **Impedance Level**

**System characteristics.** A power distribution system should offer constant voltage and high efficiency. The user wants constant voltage, independent of load, because her equipment is designed to operate at standard voltage. She requires, for example, that the voltage remain reasonably near 120 V whether she uses 1 kW or 10 kW of power. This requires, in turn, that the output impedance of the source, as seen from the user's point of view, be as low as possible. Of course, an ideal voltage source has zero output impedance, but the generator has an inherent output impedance, $\underline{\mathbf{Z}}_g$, and the distribution line has an impedance, $\underline{\mathbf{Z}}_w$, as shown in Fig. 5.27. The generator output impedance can be made quite small by good system design, but the resistance and reactance of the transmission line can only be reduced within limits due to the large distances.

The transmission system is required to be efficient to reduce costs and energy waste. The impedance-transforming properties of the transformers improve system characteristics, as shown in the following analysis.

**Transmission system analysis.** First, we transform $\mathbf{Z}_L$ with the transformer at the load. This raises the load impedance by a factor of $n^2$ and places it in series with $\mathbf{Z}_w$. We now can transform this series combination with the transformer at the generator, which lowers the impedances by $n^2$. The resulting equivalent circuit is shown in Fig. 5.28. Note that the load impedance appears with its true value in the final equivalent circuit, as does the generator impedance, but the impedance of the transmission line is reduced by the factor $n^2$. This will reduce its losses by the same factor.

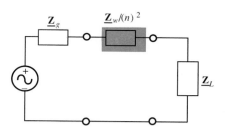

**Figure 5.28** Equivalent circuit for the power distribution system.

This reduction in transmission line losses can be understood by considering the current in the transmission line. The transformer at the generator increases the voltage and decreases the current by its turns ratio, the total power being unchanged. The transmission-line losses will be $I^2 R_w$, where $I$ is the rms current in the line and $R_w$ is the wire resistance. Reduction of the line current by $n$ therefore reduces these losses by $n^2$, and this reduction is reflected in the equivalent circuit in Fig. 5.28. For this reason, electrical power is distributed at extremely high voltages, up to 750 kV.

**Impedance Level**

Figure 5.28 also suggests that the voltage regulation at the load (voltage relatively independent of load current) is improved by the use of a high-voltage transmission line. The load impedance appears with its true value, which shows that the same equivalent circuit would have resulted had we transformed all impedances to the load end of the circuit. Thus, the output impedance of the generator-transmission-line system is $\mathbf{Z}_g + \mathbf{Z}_w/n^2$. The effect of the transmission-line impedance is therefore reduced by the square of the turns ratio, to the improvement of load-voltage regulation.

**EXAMPLE 5.18** | **Power distribution system**

Power is generated at 24 kV, 100 miles from a town that uses 50 MW at 12 kV, as shown in Fig. 5.29. The transmission line has an impedance of $0.1 + j0.8$ $\Omega$/mile. What should be the transmission voltage for an efficiency of 98.5% for the transmission system?

**SOLUTION:**
The load current is $(50 \times 10^6)/(12 \times 10^3) = 4167$ A, and hence the transmission line current is

$$I = 4167 \times \frac{12}{V} \tag{5.105}$$

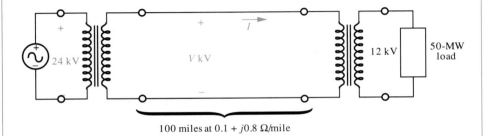

**Figure 5.29**  The transmission system is required to have 98.5% efficiency.

where $V$ (in kV) is the line voltage to be determined. The line resistance is 0.1 $\Omega$/mile $\times$ 100 miles $= 10\ \Omega$ and the allowed loss is 1.5% of the 50-MW load; hence,

$$\left(4167 \times \frac{12}{V}\right)^2 \times 10 = 0.015 \times 50 \times 10^6 \tag{5.106}$$

Thus, the required voltage is 183 kV, and the transformer turns ratios are chosen accordingly.

**WHAT IF?**    What if the line voltage is 138 kV?  What is the efficiency?[29]

**Multiple secondaries.**  Transformers may have multiple windings; for example, a transformer may have a 120-V primary and two secondaries, one with 12.6 V and one with 28 V.  Such transformers are used in both power and electronic applications. Figure 5.30 (a) shows a transformer with three windings, a primary with $n_1$ turns and secondaries with $n_2$ and $n_3$ turns, respectively, and appropriately defined voltage and current variables.  The voltage/turn is constant for the transformer, so the voltages are related by a simple extension of Eq. (5.94)

$$\frac{v_1}{n_1} = \frac{v_2}{n_2} = \frac{v_3}{n_3} \tag{5.107}$$

Thus, if we consider the primary voltage as given, we may calculate the secondary voltages based on the number of turns:

$$v_3 = \left(\frac{n_3}{n_1}\right) \times v_1 \qquad \text{and} \qquad v_2 = \left(\frac{n_2}{n_1}\right) \times v_1 \tag{5.108}$$

However,  Eq. (5.95) must be modified[30] to

$$n_1 i_1 = n_2 i_2 + n_3 i_3 \tag{5.109}$$

---

[29] 97.4%.

[30] This equation is derived in Chapter 14 as a form of Ampère's circuital law.

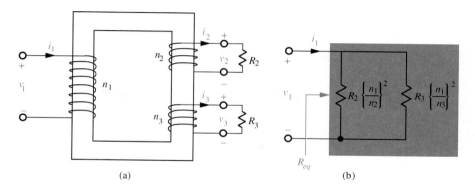

**Figure 5.30**    (a) The transformer has two secondaries.    (b) Although the secondaries appear to be in series, the equivalent circuit shows them to be in parallel.

One application of Eqs. (5.108) and (5.109) is to determine the equivalent impedance looking into the primary, given that the two secondaries are loaded with resistors $R_2$ and $R_3$, respectively.    If we divide Eq. (5.109) by the appropriate form of Eq. (5.108), we get the form

$$\frac{n_1 i_1}{v_1/n_1} = \frac{n_2 i_2}{v_2/n_2} + \frac{n_3 i_3}{v_3/n_3} \Rightarrow n_1^2 \times \frac{i_1}{v_1} = n_2^2 \times \frac{i_2}{v_2} + n_3^2 \times \frac{i_3}{v_3} \qquad (5.110)$$

and because

$$R_{eq} = \frac{v_1}{i_1}, \qquad R_2 = \frac{v_2}{i_2}, \qquad \text{and} \qquad R_3 = \frac{v_3}{i_3} \qquad (5.111)$$

Equation (5.110) becomes

$$\frac{1}{R_{eq}} = \left(\frac{n_2}{n_1}\right)^2 \times \frac{1}{R_2} + \left(\frac{n_3}{n_1}\right)^2 \times \frac{1}{R_3} \Rightarrow R_{eq} = \left(\frac{n_1}{n_2}\right)^2 \times R_2 \left\| \left(\frac{n_1}{n_3}\right)^2 \times R_3 \right. \quad (5.112)$$

In words, the primary sees the load impedances of both secondaries, transformed by the square of the turns ratios and connected in parallel. Figure 5.30(b) shows the equivalent circuit.

---

**EXAMPLE 5.19** **Two secondaries**

A 16-$\Omega$ speaker and an 8-$\Omega$ speaker are driven off the secondaries of a stereo output transformer.    Find the ratio $n_{16} : n_8$ such that equal power is given to both.    Find the ratio $n_p : n_{16}$ to make the primary see 100 $\Omega$.

**SOLUTION:**
To receive equal power,

$$\left(\frac{n_1}{n_{16}}\right)^2 \times 16 = \left(\frac{n_1}{n_8}\right)^2 \times 8 \Rightarrow \frac{n_{16}}{n_8} = \sqrt{\frac{16}{8}} = 1.414 \qquad (5.113)$$

For 100 Ω at the primary, each speaker must look like 200 Ω because they appear in parallel. Thus,

$$\left(\frac{n_1}{n_{16}}\right)^2 \times 16 = 200 \Rightarrow \frac{n_1}{n_{16}} = \sqrt{\frac{200}{16}} = 3.54 \qquad (5.114)$$

**WHAT IF?**   What if the 8-Ω speaker were 4 Ω instead?[31]

**Summary.** Transformers are used for voltage, current, and impedance transformation. Applications abound in both electronics and power systems engineering. Realistic power systems, however, would use three-phase voltages for generation and distribution of power, as we discuss in the next chapter.

### Residential AC Power

We do not recommend that you do it, but *if* you sought out the circuit breaker box[32] where you live, and *if* you removed the safety cover, you would discover three wires coming into the box from the transformer on the pole in the alley. One wire would be red, another black, and the third white.

**Circuit for 120/240-V circuits.** Figure 5.31(a) shows the usual arrangement at the transformer secondary. The white wire is the neutral and is grounded at the transformer by a wire that enters the moist earth and should also be grounded through the household

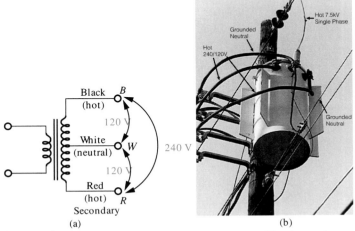

**Figure 5.31** (a) A 120/240-V household power system; (b) pole transformer.

---

[31] $n_{16}/n_4 = 2$, $n_1/n_{16} =$ same.

[32] Or the fuse box in older structures.

plumbing. The black and red wires are "hot," each carrying 120 V relative to the neutral. The neutral voltage is at the midpoint between the two lines that carry 240 V, and hence 120 V is developed between each hot line and the neutral, which is grounded.

The 240-V power is used for heavy equipment such as air conditioners, electric stoves, and certain power tools. Most appliances operate with 120 V, so the lighting and appliance circuits in the house are connected between a hot wire and neutral. The red color is not used in the household 120-V wiring: Black means hot and white neutral. Modern wiring codes require a third wire for a separate ground. The ground wires do not carry power like the neutral wire, but provide a separate ground connection independent of the power circuit.

---

**EXAMPLE 5.20** | **Center-tapped transformer**

A power transformer has a 7000-V primary and a center-tapped 240-V secondary. If the load on the 240-V circuit is 3000 W and the loads on each of the 120-V circuits are 1200 W, what is the current in the primary? Assume unity power factor for all loads, and consider the transformer ideal.

**SOLUTION:**

Figure 5.32 shows the circuit. The "center-tap" on the secondary is a connection in the middle of the secondary winding, and is equivalent to Fig. 5.30 with $n_2 = n_3$ and the bottom of the top winding connected to the top of the bottom winding. The problem is most easily worked by conservation of energy. Because the total load on the secondary is 5400 W and the power factor is unity, the input current must be

$$7000 \times I = 5400 \Rightarrow I = 0.771 \text{ A} \tag{5.115}$$

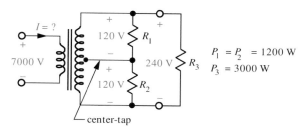

**Figure 5.32**   Center-tapped transformer circuit.

---

**WHAT IF?**

What if the power factor of the 240-V load were 0.9, lagging, with the same power? What then would be the primary current?[33]

---

[33] Including now the reactive power of $Q = 1453$ VARs, the current is 0.799 A.

**polarized**

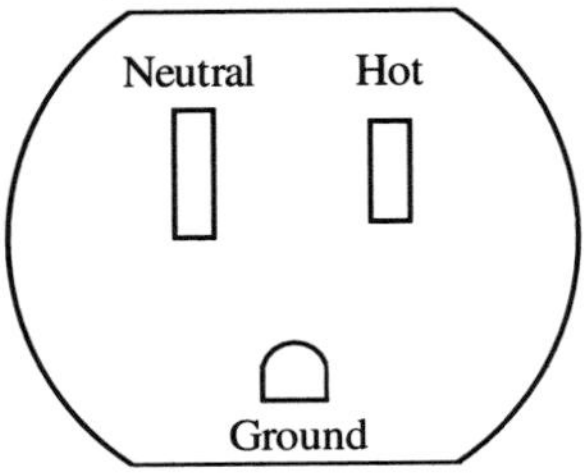

**Figure 5.33**
Grounded and polarized household outlet.

**Grounding of appliances.** Figure 5.33 shows a modern appliance outlet, which is both polarized and grounded with a three-wire system. The outlet and plug are said to be *polarized* because the hot and neutral connections differ in size. Some loads, such as table lamps, may work equally well, and be equally as safe, plugged in either way. Such a load would have an unpolarized plug, which would fit into the outlet either way. Other loads are equipped with polarized plugs that fit in only one way, thus controlling which wire connects to neutral. For safety, the neutral of the load (the male) cannot connect to the hot of the source because it is too large.

**Home wiring.** If you are wiring an appliance outlet (wall plug), pay close attention to polarity. Usually, the screw to which you should connect the hot (black) wire has a copper color and the screw to which you should connect the neutral (white) wire has a silver color. If you are installing a lighting fixture in a ceiling, the hot goes through the wall switch to the center of the receptacle and the neutral connects to the screw threads.

## Electrical Safety

**OBJECTIVE 9**

**To understand safe practice around electrical equipment**

Although use of electrical power is vital to our modern way of life, the average citizen is poorly informed of the dangers of electrical power. One person might fear to touch the terminals of a 12-V auto battery, whereas another might think nothing of sticking a finger into a light socket to see if there is any power.[34] This section presents some basic information about electrical safety to enable you to recognize a dangerous situation and hopefully stay out of trouble.

The circuit theory of this subject is simple enough: Ohm's law is the key,

$$I = \frac{V}{R} \tag{5.116}$$

where $R$ is you. Although we are accustomed to signs warning "DANGER, HIGH VOLTAGE," it is actually the current that affects our bodies. Many thousands of volts will do no more than startle, provided the current is small, as when we feel a small spark of static electricity after sliding across an auto seat. In the following, we speak first of the physiological effects of electric current on the human body. We then discuss body resistance and the resistance of typical surroundings. Finally, we offer some advice about electrical safety.

**Physiological effects of current.** Figure 5.34 shows the variety of effects that electrical current may have on the human body and the current levels at which they occur. Injury could be caused indirectly through being startled and losing muscular control or directly through burns. Death could result from suffocation, through loss of heart beat, or through severe burns. The large ranges in Fig. 5.34 represent variation between individuals in body size, condition, and tolerance to electrical shock. The region of the body through which the current passes is crucial; current passing through the lower part of the leg, for example, might be painful but would be unlikely to affect heart action.

---

[34] The battery is safe, but please keep your finger out of the light socket.

The surprising aspect of Fig. 5.34 is that small currents can have serious effects. This occurs because the communication system of the human body is electrical in nature and misbehaves under external electrical influence.

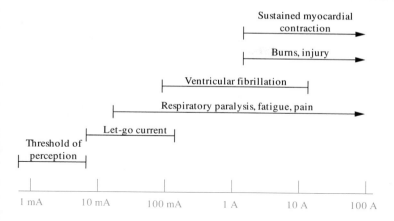

**Figure 5.34** Physiological effects of electricity. (Adapted from John G. Webster, *Medical Instrumentation, Application and Design*, Copyright © 1978 Houghton Mifflin Company. Adapted with permission.)

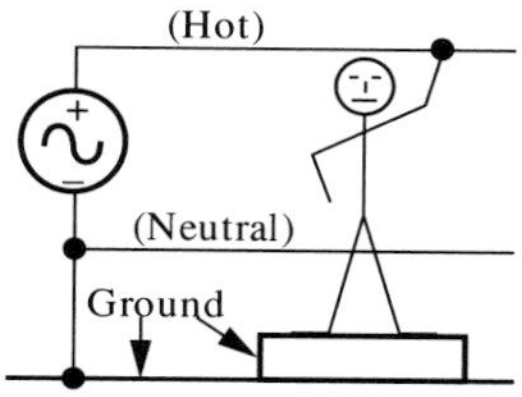

**Figure 5.35** Most shocks occur between the hot wire and ground.

**First aid for shock.** When a person is experiencing electrical shock, time becomes an important factor, for the damaging effects are progressive. Hence, it is important to remove the source of electrical energy from a shock victim before EMS is called.[35] Particularly serious is the condition of ventricular fibrillation, where the heart loses its synchronized pumping action and circulation ceases. This condition is very dangerous because the heart may not resume normal action when the source of electrical power is removed; sophisticated medical equipment is required to restore coherent heart action.

**Resistance.** Earlier, we stated that "the resistance is you." This would be true if you came into simultaneous contact with both wires of an electrical circuit, say, by grabbing a wire with each hand, but most serious electrical shocks occur through the situation portrayed in Fig. 5.35. Here we have shown the victim in simultaneous contact with the hot wire and with "ground." Ground may be the moist earth, the plumbing of a house, or even a concrete floor that is in contact with the plumbing. In this case, the resistance in Eq. (5.116) includes not only the resistance of the body, but also the resistance of the shoes and the resistance between the shoes and earth ground.

**Be aware of your surroundings.** To assess the danger of a given situation, we must estimate the resistance of the "circuit" of which our body might become an unhappy part. Table 5-2 shows some basic information to allow such an estimate of the total resistance to ground.

---

[35] Cardiopulmonary resuscitation (CPR) should be administered only by trained personnel.

## TABLE 5-2 Resistance for Safety Consideration

(a) For Various Skin-Contact Conditions

| Condition (area to situ) | Resistance | |
|---|---|---|
| | Dry | Wet |
| Finger touch | $40\,k\Omega$–1  M$\Omega$ | 4–15  k$\Omega$ |
| Hand holding wire | 15–50  k$\Omega$ | 3–6  k$\Omega$ |
| Finger–thumb grasp | 10–30  k$\Omega$ | 2–5  k$\Omega$ |
| Hand holding pliers | 5–10  k$\Omega$ | 1–3  k$\Omega$ |
| Palm touch | 3–8  k$\Omega$ | 1–2  k$\Omega$ |
| Hand around $1\frac{1}{2}$ in. pipe (or drill handle) | 1–3  k$\Omega$ | 0.1–1.5 k$\Omega$ |
| Two hands around $1\frac{1}{2}$ in. pipe | 0.5–1.5  k$\Omega$ | 250–750  $\Omega$ |
| Hand immersed | | 200–500  $\Omega$ |
| Foot immersed | | 100–300  $\Omega$ |
| Human body, internal, excluding skin $= 200 - 1000\,\Omega$ | | |

(b) For Equal Areas (130 square cm) of Various Materials

| Material | Resistance |
|---|---|
| Rubber gloves or soles | More than 20 M$\Omega$ |
| Dry concrete above grade | 1–5  M$\Omega$ |
| Dry concrete on grade | 0.2–1  M$\Omega$ |
| Leather sole, dry, including foot | 0.1–0.5 M$\Omega$ |
| Leather sole, damp, including foot | 5–20  k$\Omega$ |
| Wet concrete on grade | 1–5  k$\Omega$ |

*Source:* Adapted from Ralph Lee, "Electrical Safety in Industrial Plants," *IEEE Spectrum,* June 1971 © IEEE.

**EXAMPLE 5.20**

What would you experience if you were standing on moist ground with leather-soled shoes and you unwittingly grab hold of a 120-V wire?

**SOLUTION:**
Taking the lowest values in Table 5-2, we estimate the following resistances: 3 k$\Omega$ for the grasp, 200 $\Omega$ for the body, and 5 k$\Omega$ for the feet–shoes. Thus, the largest current you might carry would be (120 V)/(8.2 k$\Omega$), about 15 mA. From Fig. 5.34 we judge that there is a fair chance that you will be unable to release your grasp and that you might hence be unable to breathe. This is, therefore, a dangerous situation.

**WHAT IF?**

What if you had rubber-soled shoes?[36]

---

[36] No danger according to the chart.  Never willingly touch a live circuit.

**Skin resistance.**   One factor that Table 5-2 does not contain concerns the break-down voltage of skin resistance. At approximately 700 V (ac), the resistance of the skin drops to near zero: in effect, the current burns a hole in the skin. Thus, the resistance of the skin, which might save your life for a lower voltage, becomes ineffective at such high voltages. For this reason, high voltages are seldom used in industrial applications, and 240 V is the highest voltage used in residential wiring.

An interesting, and alarming, calculation the reader might wish to perform is the following: Making the most pessimistic assumptions about body resistance, resistance to ground, and loss of skin resistance (say, cuts or blisters on the hands and feet), calculate the least voltage that might prove fatal. Such a calculation would have you standing in water or on a metal floor without shoes. Although we are describing an unusual situation, we still urge you to make the calculation.[37]

**Precautions.**   Of more importance are the factors that increase your safety when working around electrical power. Make sure that the power is off before working on any electrical wiring or electrical equipment. Wear gloves and rubber-soled shoes. Avoid standing on a wet surface or on moist ground. Avoid working alone around exposed electric power.

**floating**

**Grounding.**   From our discussion of safety, you might notice that, from one point of view, the danger increases because the electrical power system is grounded. If the circuit were *floating*, that is, not grounded, the only way to get shocked would be to come into contact with both wires simultaneously, an unlikely event. How can we reconcile this viewpoint with the common idea that electrical circuits are grounded for safety? Actually, both ideas are valid, and there is no contradiction; there is more involved in the issue than we have discussed thus far.

**If the power system were floating.**   Suppose that the electrical power system in your building were floating. Everything would function correctly and safely until something went wrong with the equipment. But if, say, the wiring of the transformer on the pole became defective and a connection developed between primary and secondary, in this event, the 120-V circuits could float at 12,000 V or even 24,000 V. This would endanger virtually every piece of equipment on the line. Also, if the voltage suddenly were floated at 12,000 V, the danger to you becomes much greater. For this reason, the secondary of the transformer is grounded for protection of life and property. For if the secondary is grounded and a fault develops in the transformer, a large current flows immediately, a fuse or circuit breaker opens the circuit, and the source of power becomes disconnected from the offending part of the circuit.

**Why equipment is grounded.**   Given that the power system in the building should be grounded, the necessity for grounding the equipment with the three-wire system in Fig. 5.31 becomes apparent.   If a fault develops between the hot side of the power and the metal chassis of a piece of equipment, such as a washing machine, a fuse or circuit breaker will respond to the large current flowing through the ground connection and will remove power from the circuit containing the faulty connection. Hence,

---

[37] A 28-volt dc power supply can do it.

the safest way to install the power system involves grounding the power system and the equipment with which you might come into contact.

**Ground fault interrupters (GFIs).** The ground fault interrupter senses the current in the hot and neutral wires and opens the circuit when the current differs by about 5 mA. Thus, in Fig. 5.35, the most current that could pass a potential victim would be 5 mA, below the danger level. Modern building codes require GFIs be installed in bathrooms and increasingly GFIs are built into appliances such as hair dryers.

### Check Your Understanding

1. An ideal transformer has no losses. True/False?
2. In a transformer, a large number of turns on a winding goes with high or low voltage for that winding? What about current?
3. Transformers can be used to change voltage levels, current levels, impedance levels, or all three?
4. If we want to make a load impedance look smaller, which winding (primary or secondary) should have more turns?
5. To reduce losses in an electrical power transmission system, the voltage level should be raised or lowered?
6. If a larger voltage needs to be transformed to a smaller voltage, which side of the transformer should have the larger wire size?
7. What range of current through the human body is most likely to result in death, $i < 1$ mA, 100 mA $< i <$ 1 A, or 10 A $< i$?
8. In most electrocutions, current passes from the hot wire through the victim to the neutral wire or to earth ground?
9. When working on electrical devices, your body should be grounded for safety. True/False?

*Answers.* **(1)** true; **(2)** more turns go with the larger voltage and the smaller current; **(3)** all three; **(4)** secondary; **(5)** raised; **(6)** the low-voltage side; **(7)** 100 mA $< i <$ 1 A; **(8)** to earth ground; **(9)** false.

## CHAPTER SUMMARY

Understanding of energy processes requires insight and wise application in any physical system. This chapter focuses on both theoretical and practical aspects of energy processes in ac circuits, with an emphasis on electric power engineering.

**Objective 1: To understand how to calculate the time-average and effective values of periodic waveforms.** The process of time averaging is explained and applied to the calculation of the effective or root-mean-square value of a sinusoidal waveform. The effective value gives the power-producing ability of a waveform and is what is indicated by ac meters.

**Objective 2: To understand the energy and power requirements of resistors, inductors, and capacitors in the sinusoidal steady state.** The behavior of an interconnected system depends upon the behavior of its individual components. We show that energy shuttles in and out of inductors and capacitors, with energy needed in different times in the ac cycle. By contrast, energy flows one way into resistors, in which electrical energy is transformed into nonelectrical form, usually heat.

**Objective 3: To understand how to calculate apparent, real, and reactive power flow in an electric network based on time-domain analysis.** We show that the energy flow into a general ac circuit containing resistors, inductors, and capacitors consists of two terms, the real power carrying energy to the resistors, and the reactive power representing energy lent periodically to the inductors and capacitors of the circuit. However, the inductors and capacitors share energy and only the imbalance between electric and magnetic energy needs must be lent to the circuit periodically by the source.

**Objective 4: To understand how to calculate apparent, real, and reactive power in the frequency domain.** The energy processes described before appear in the frequency-domain description of the circuit. The various types of ac power are represented in a power triangle that pictures real, reactive, and apparent power, plus the angle of the power factor.

**Objective 5: To understand how to correct the power factor of a load.** This section presents a practical aspect of electric power utilization that falls to the user. Because power companies require that the customer's power factor be high, capacitors are often added locally to an installation to balance the energy needs of motors and other magnetic devices.

**Objective 6: To understand how to use a Thévenin equivalent circuit to establish the load to withdraw maximum power from an ac source.** This section describes a technique used in electronic systems to make optimal use of the small amounts of available energy. To effect maximum energy transfer, a local resonance is created between source and load, and resistive values of source and load are made equal.

**Objectives 7 and 8: To understand the voltage-, current-, and impedance-transforming properties of the transformer, especially their role in the transmission of electric power.** Transformers are used both in power and electronic circuits to change voltage, current, and impedance levels. This section introduces the ideal transformer as a circuit element and explores the use of transformers in effecting maximum energy transfer in electronic circuits and in improving efficiency in power distribution systems.

**Objective 9: To understand safe practice around electrical equipment.** Finally, we describe the type of circuit used in domestic power distribution. The dangers of electricity are discussed and safe practice is described. Electrical equipment should be grounded, but personnel should be isolated from electrical ground as much as possible.

Chapter 6 builds on these concepts to investigate the distribution of electric power in three-phase systems and its utilization in electric motors.

# PROBLEMS

## Section 5.1: AC Power and Energy Storage: The Time-Domain Picture

**5.1.** Compute the time average and the rms value for the waveforms shown in Fig. P5.1.

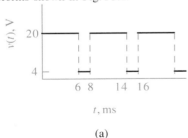

(a)

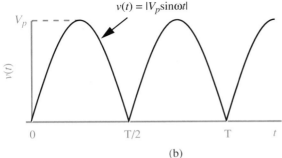

$$v(t) = |V_p \sin \omega t|$$

(b)

**Figure P5.1**

**5.2.** Show that ac and dc power are additive. That is, if $i(t) = I_{dc} + I_p \cos(\omega t)$, then the time average of $i^2(t)$ is $I_{dc}^2 + (I_p/\sqrt{2})^2$.

**5.3.** Figure P5.3 shows a periodic waveform.
   **(a)** Find the average value.
   **(b)** Find the effective value.

**5.4.** For the sawtooth waveform in Fig. P5.4, find the following:
   **(a)** The average value, $V_{dc}$.
   **(b)** The effective value, $V_e$.
   **(c)** What would be the average power if this were the voltage across a 10-$\Omega$ resistor?

**5.5.** **(a)** A current source having an rms value of 0.85 A is connected to a 12-$\Omega$ resistor. What is the power in the resistor?
   **(b)** If the current source in part (a) is sinusoidal with a period of 10 $\mu$s, what is the equation of the current as a function of time? (Assume the cosine form and phase $= +12°$.)

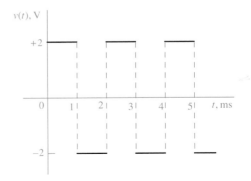

**Figure P5.3**

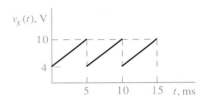

**Figure P5.4**

   **(c)** If the current in part (b) is put through an impedance of $12 \angle -60°$ $\Omega$ rather than a pure resistance, what now is the time-average power?

**5.6.** Figure P5.6 shows a periodic voltage waveform.
   **(a)** What is the time-average voltage?
   **(b)** If this voltage is applied to a 30-$\mu$F capacitor, what would be the effective value of the current in the capacitor?

**Figure P5.6**

**5.7.** For the circuit in Fig. P5.7, find the following:
  **(a)** Minimum instantaneous power into $R$.
  **(b)** Time-average power into $R$.
  **(c)** Maximum instantaneous power into $R$.
  **(d)** Time between maxima in the instantaneous power into $R$.

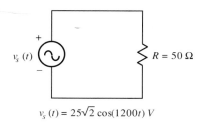

$$v_s(t) = 25\sqrt{2} \cos(1200t) \text{ V}$$

**Figure P5.7**

**5.8.** For the circuit shown in Fig. P5.8,
$v(t) = 240 \cos(\omega t)$ V and $i(t) = 5.5 \cos(\omega t)$ A. Find
the following:
  **(a)** Instantaneous power into the load at $t = 0$.
  **(b)** Time-average power into the load.
  **(c)** Effective value of the voltage.
  **(d)** Impedance of the load in polar form.

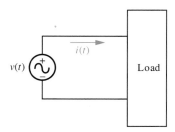

**Figure P5.8**

**5.9.** A circuit in sinusoidal steady state is shown in
Fig. P5.9.
  **(a)** Transform this circuit into the frequency
  domain.
  **(b)** What is the impedance, $\underline{\mathbf{Z}}_{eq}$, seen by the
  voltage source?
  **(c)** Find the time-domain current, $i(t)$.
  **(d)** Find the time-average power given to the
  circuit by the voltage source.
  **(e)** Find the peak electric energy stored in the
  capacitor.

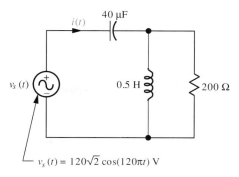

$$v_s(t) = 120\sqrt{2} \cos(120\pi t) \text{ V}$$

**Figure P5.9**

**5.10.** A voltage source with $v_s(t) = 120\sqrt{2} \cos(250t)$ V
is connected in series with a 100-$\Omega$ resistor, a 0.2-H
inductor, and a 25-$\mu$F capacitor.
  **(a)** Find the impedance of the circuit at the source
  frequency.
  **(b)** Determine the sinusoidal steady state current,
  $i(t)$, in the series connection.
  **(c)** Find the time-average power in the resistor.
  **(d)** Determine the reactive power in VARs given to
  the circuit by the source.

**5.11.** A 120-V(rms), variable-frequency source is
connected in series with a 100-$\Omega$ resistor and a
100-$\mu$F capacitor. Find the input power to the
circuit from the source at the frequency where the
power factor of the load is 0.75.

**5.12.** For the circuit shown in Fig. P5.12, $v(t) =$
$120\sqrt{2} \cos(120\pi t)$ V and $i(t) =$
$6.5 \cos(120\pi t + 30°)$ A. Find the following:
  **(a)** Effective current.
  **(b)** Time-average power out of the source.
  **(c)** Resistance, $R$.
  **(d)** Peak stored energy in the capacitor.

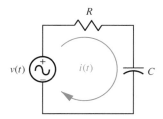

**Figure P5.12**

**5.13.** A 117-V rms, 60-Hz household circuit has two 75-W lights, $PF = 1$, and a fan using 500 VA at 0.78 $PF$ (lagging).
 (a) Draw the circuit, representing each load by its impedance. Include the switches for each load.
 (b) Determine the total current required for all loads operating simultaneously.
 (c) What capacitor in parallel with the loads will give unity power factor?

**5.14.** For the circuit shown in Fig. P5.14, find the following:
 (a) How much time-average power flows one way between the source and load?
 (b) How much energy is exchanged between the source and the load?
 (c) How much energy is exchanged between the capacitor and the inductor?

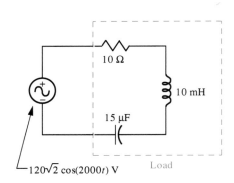

**Figure P5.14**

**5.15.** For the circuit shown in Fig. P5.15, find the following:
 (a) How much time-average power flows one way between the source and load?
 (b) How much energy is exchanged between the source and the load?
 (c) How much energy is exchanged between the capacitor and the inductor?

**5.16.** For the circuit in Fig. P5.16, find the following:
 (a) Find $i(t)$. Use time- or frequency-domain techniques.
 (b) What is the power factor for the load?
 (c) Compute the time-average power into the load.
 (d) Show that the time-average power into the load, $P$, is equal to the power dissipated in the resistor, $P_R$.
 (e) Calculate the peak and time-average magnetic energy stored in $L$.

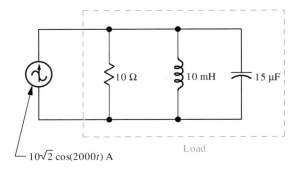

$10\sqrt{2}\cos(2000t)$ A

**Figure P5.15**

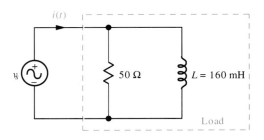

$v_s(t) = 100\sqrt{2}\cos(300\pi t)$ V

**Figure P5.16**

**5.17.** For the circuit shown in Fig. P5.17, find the following:
 (a) Solve for $v(t)$. Let the phase of $i(t)$ be zero.
 (b) Compute the time-average power into the circuit using the power factor.
 (c) Show that the time-average power into the entire circuit, $P$, is equal to the time-average power dissipated in the resistor, $P_R$.
 (d) Find the time-average electric stored energy.

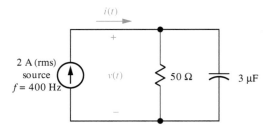

**Figure P5.17**

**5.18.** The circuit shown in Fig. P5.18 is in sinusoidal steady state.
   **(a)** Find $v_a(t)$ using nodal analysis.
   **(b)** What is the time-average power out of the left-hand source?

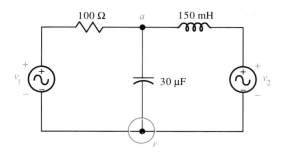

$$v_1 = 100 \ \cos(120\pi t) \ V$$
$$v_2 = 80 \ \sin(120\pi t) \ V$$

**Figure P5.18**

**5.19.** For the circuit shown in Fig. P5.19, find the time-average power out of the ac current source.

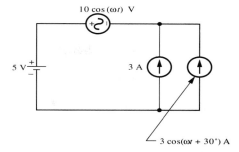

**Figure P5.19**

## Section 5.2: Power and Energy in the Frequency Domain

**5.20.** For the circuit shown in Fig. P5.20,
   $v(t) = 442\sqrt{2} \ \cos(120\pi t + 30°) \ V$ and
   $i(t) = 21\sqrt{2} \ \cos(120\pi t + 60°) \ A$.
   **(a)** What is the real power?
   **(b)** What is the reactive power?
   **(c)** What is the apparent power?
   **(d)** What is the impedance of the load in polar form?

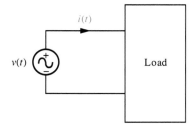

**Figure P5.20**

**5.21.** For the 60-Hz load shown in Fig. P5.21, the voltmeter measures 125 V, the ammeter measures 5.1 A, and the wattmeter measures 480 W. The load consists of a resistor and inductor. Find the following:
   **(a)** Power factor.

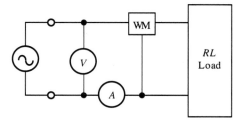

**Figure P5.21**

   **(b)** Leading or lagging?
   **(c)** Real power.
   **(d)** Apparent power.
   **(e)** Reactive power.
   **(f)** Average stored energy.
   **(g)** Draw a phasor diagram.

**5.22.** An impedance requires 80 V and 12 A as measured by standard ac meters. Figure P5.22 shows the phasor diagram. Find the following:
   **(a)** Apparent power (give units for all powers).
   **(b)** Power factor.
   **(c)** Real power.
   **(d)** Reactive power.
   **(e)** Impedance in rectangular form.

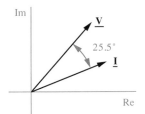

Figure P5.22

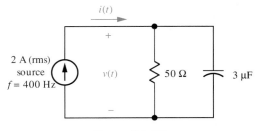

Figure P5.25

5.23. The complex power in a load is 1200 $\angle$ 25° volt-amperes. Determine the following:
(a) Apparent power (give units).
(b) Real power (give units).
(c) Reactive power (give units).
(d) Power factor, leading or lagging.

5.24. For the circuit shown in Fig. P5.24, the voltage and current are $\mathbf{V} = 120\sqrt{2} \angle 0°$ and $\mathbf{I} = 10\sqrt{2} \angle +25°$.
(a) Find the time-average power to the load.
(b) Find the peak instantaneous power to the load.
(c) Find the apparent power to the load.

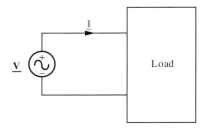

Figure P5.24

5.25. For the circuit shown in Fig. P5.25, find the following:
(a) The complex power.
(b) The real and reactive power, giving correct units.
(c) The apparent power, giving correct units.
(d) Draw a power triangle for this circuit.
(e) Verify Eq. (5.44) for this circuit.

5.26. An electric motor is monitored with an ammeter, voltmeter, and wattmeter, which indicate 5.2 A, 120 V, and 480 W, respectively. Assume 60 Hz.
(a) Draw a phasor diagram of the voltage and current, assuming the voltage at zero phase and lagging current.

(b) What is the reactive power to the motor, including the units?
(c) To improve the power factor of the motor, a capacitor is hung directly across the motor terminals. What value of capacitance will give unity power factor?

5.27. A 460-V load draws 18 kVA at 0.82 *PF*, lagging. Find the kVAR of capacitance required to correct the power factor to 0.93, lagging.

5.28. A 60-Hz single-phase, $\frac{1}{2}$-hp motor in a washing machine (120 V) has an efficiency of 78% at full load (rated output power) and a power factor of 0.72, lagging. Find the line current, the reactive power, and the apparent power to the motor. Draw a phasor diagram.

5.29. For the circuit shown in Fig. P5.29, the wattmeter reads 2400 W, the ammeter reads 14.0 A, and the voltmeter reads 45 V.
(a) What is $R$?
(b) What would be the peak value of the source voltage, $V_s$?

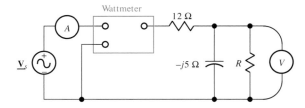

Figure P5.29

5.30. For the circuit shown in Fig. P5.30, the voltage and current are $v(t) = 110\sqrt{2} \cos(120\pi t + 32°)$ V and $i(t) = 4.8\sqrt{2} \cos(120\pi t - 21°)$ A.
(a) Find the complex power into the load, $\frac{1}{2}\mathbf{V}\mathbf{I}^*$.
(b) Draw a power triangle showing the numerical values of the real, apparent, and reactive powers.

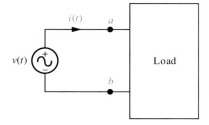

**Figure P5.30**

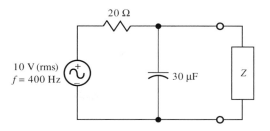

**Figure P5.31**

(c) Assuming that the load contains no electric energy storage, what is the peak value of the magnetic energy stored in the load?

(d) What value of capacitor connected between *a* and *b* will make the power factor as seen by the source to be 0.92, lagging?

5.31. For the circuit shown in Fig. P5.31, what should be the load impedance to draw maximum power from the circuit? Give component values, not just

impedance values. Assume a series circuit for the load.

5.32. The output impedance of a typical 120-V appliance wall outlet might be $0.2 + j0.4\ \Omega$.
   (a) What is the theoretical available power from the outlet?
   (b) Why would it be a bad idea to actually try to obtain that much power?

## Section 5.3: Transformers

5.33. An ideal transformer has 120 turns on the primary and 240 turns on the secondary. Find the primary and secondary currents for the circuit shown in Fig. P5.33.

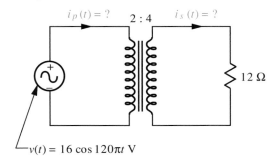

$v(t) = 16 \cos 120\pi t$ V

**Figure P5.33**

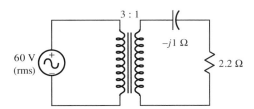

**Figure P5.34**

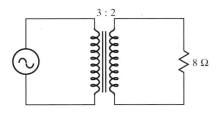

**Figure P5.35**

5.34. For the circuit in Fig. P5.34 containing an ideal transformer, find the following:
   (a) Secondary voltage.
   (b) Primary current.
   (c) Secondary current.
   (d) Power out of the source.

5.35. For the ideal transformer circuit shown in Fig. P5.35 a voltmeter measures 30 volts across the primary. What would the following measure?
   (a) A voltmeter across the secondary.

   (b) An ammeter in the primary.
   (c) An ammeter in the secondary.
   (d) A wattmeter in the primary.
   (e) A wattmeter in the secondary.

5.36. For the circuit in Fig. P5.36, containing the ideal transformer, find the following:
   (a) Primary current.

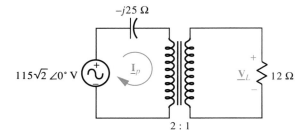

**Figure P5.36**

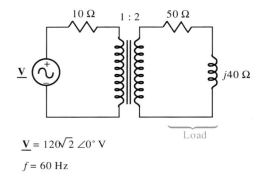

$\underline{V} = 120\sqrt{2} \angle 0° \text{ V}$

$f = 60 \text{ Hz}$

**Figure P5.38**

**(b)** Load voltage.

**(c)** Power out of the source.

5.37. The circuit shown in Fig. P5.37 is already in the frequency domain.

    **(a)** Find the rms value of the source voltage such that the power in the load is 1000 W.

    **(b)** For this value of source voltage, what is the apparent power to the load?

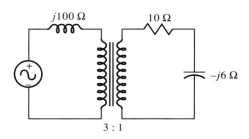

**Figure P5.39**

5.40. The circuit shown in Fig. P5.40 contains a step-up transformer, a transmission line with resistance of 0.5 Ω, a step-down transformer, and a load of 12 Ω. Find the value of $n$ to make the efficiency of the transmission circuit 99%.

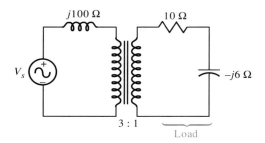

**Figure P5.37**

5.38. For the circuit shown in Fig. P5.38, find the following:

    **(a)** The real power into the load, with units.

    **(b)** The apparent power into the load, with units.

    **(c)** If a capacitor were placed in series with the 10-Ω resistor, what value of capacitance would maximize the power to the load?

5.39. The circuit shown in Fig. P5.39 is represented in the frequency domain. The source voltage is 120 V, rms.

    **(a)** Find the phasor current in the primary of the transformer, considering the voltage source the phase reference.

    **(b)** What is the effective voltage across the secondary of the transformer?

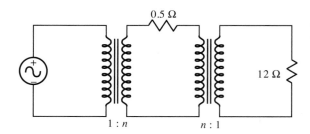

**Figure P5.40**

5.41. In the circuit in Fig. P5.41, the voltmeter measures 200 V. What would the following indicate?

    **(a)** A voltmeter in the primary?

    **(b)** An ammeter in the secondary?

    **(c)** An ammeter in the primary?

    **(d)** A wattmeter in the secondary?

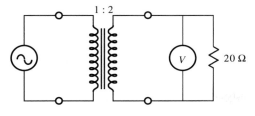

**Figure P5.41**

(e) A wattmeter in the primary?
(f) A dc ohmmeter connected between primary and secondary circuits?

5.42. For the circuit shown in Fig. P5.42, find the turns ratio $n_p/n_s$ such that the current in the secondary has a magnitude of 1 A (rms).

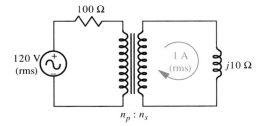

**Figure P5.42**

5.43. For the circuit shown in Fig. P5.43, find the turns ratio $n_p/n_s$ such that the current in the secondary has a magnitude of 2 A (rms).

5.44. Figure P5.44 shows a circuit in which an inductor is coupled with a transformer. Find the number of secondary turns such that the power factor seen by the generator is 0.85, lagging. There are 1000 turns on the primary.

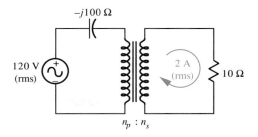

**Figure P5.43**

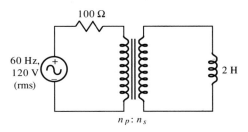

**Figure P5.44**

5.45. Power is generated at 480 V and utilized at 120 V. The generator is ideal, but the load is at some distance from the generator and hence line losses are appreciable, 1.2 Ω total for both wires. The equivalent load resistance would draw 15 kW at unity *PF* if 120 V were provided. Calculate the load voltage, the load power, and the efficiency of the transmission system under the following schemes:
(a) 4:1 transformer at the generator.
(b) 4:1 transformer at the load.
(c) 1:4 transformer at the generator and a 16:1 transformer at the load.

5.46. For the circuit shown in Fig. P5.46, the load impedance is fixed at 1000 Ω ‖ −j 3000 Ω,

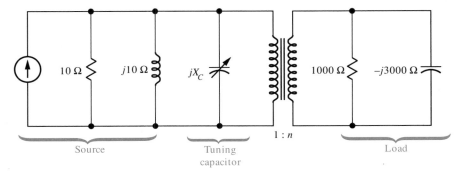

**Figure P5.46**

and the source output impedance is fixed at $10 \, \Omega \, \| \, j10 \, \Omega$. Maximum power transfer is to be achieved to the load with an ideal transformer with a turns ratio of $1{:}n$ and a "tuning capacitor" on the source side, represented by its reactance $+jX_C$ ($X_C < 0$). Find the values for $n$ and $X_C$ that achieve maximum power transfer.

## General Problems

**5.47.** With the circuit shown in Fig. P5.47, there is no value of the turns ratio, $n$, that will perfectly "match" the load to the source impedance, in the sense of eliminating all reactance and at the same time making the resistors match. However, there is still an optimum value of $n$ that maximizes the power in the load. Find that value of $n$.

**5.48.** The circuit shown in Fig. P5.48 is the Thévenin equivalent circuit of a loop antenna operating at a frequency of 570 kHz. Assuming that the input circuit of the radio consists of a capacitor in parallel with a resistor, what values of $R$ and $C$ will extract maximum power from the antenna.

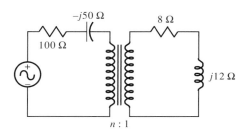

**Figure P5.47**

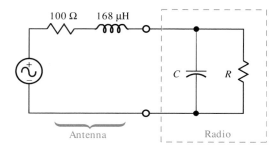

**Figure P5.48**

## Answers to Odd-Numbered Problems

**5.1.** (a) 16.0, 17.4 V; (b) $2V_p/\pi$, $V_p^2/2$.

**5.3.** (a) 0 V; (b) 2 V.

**5.5.** (a) 8.67 W; (b) $0.85\sqrt{2} \cos{(2\pi t/10^{-5} + 12°)}$ A; (c) 4.34 W.

**5.7.** (a) 0 W; (b) 12.5 W; (c) 25.0 W; (d) 2.62 ms.

**5.9.** (a,b) $99.9 \angle 19.6°$; (c) $1.20\sqrt{2} \cos{(120\pi t - 19.6°)}$ A; (d) 136 W; (e) 0.254 J.

**5.11.** 81.0 W.

**5.13.** (a)

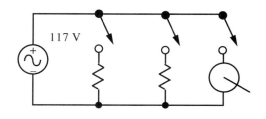

**(b)** $4.62 - j2.67$ A, rms; **(c)** 60.6 µF.

**5.15.** (a) 962 W; (b) 0.0962 J; (c) 0.144 J.

**5.17.** (a) $93.6\sqrt{2} \cos{(800\pi t - 20.7°)}$ V; (b) 175 W; (c) 175 W; (d) 0.0131 J.

**5.19.** $-13.0$ W.

**5.21.** (a) 0.753 ; (b) lagging; (c) 480 W; (d) 638 VA; (e) $+420$ VAR; (f) 0.557 J; (g) 41.2°.

**5.23.** (a) 1200 VA; (b) 1090 W; (c) $+507$ VAR; (d) 0.906, leading.

**5.25.** (a) $175 - j66.0$ VA; (b) 175 W, $-66.0$ VAR; (c) 187 VA; (e) 0.0263 J electric energy $\Rightarrow$ $-66.0$ VAR.

**5.27.** $-4.47$ kVAR $\Rightarrow$ 56 µF.

**5.29.** (a) 42.2 Ω; (b) 268 V.

**5.31.** 6.11 Ω in series with 3.67 mH.

**5.33.** secondary $= 2.67 \cos{(120\pi t)}$ A, primary $=$ $5.33 \cos{(120\pi t)}$ A.

5.35. **(a)** 20 V; **(b)** 1.67 A; **(c)** 2.50 A; **(d)** 50.0 W; **(e)** same.

5.37. **(a)** 337 V; **(b)** 1170 VA.

5.39. **(a)** $1.19\sqrt{2} \angle -27.1°$ A; **(b)** 41.5 V, rms.

5.41. **(a)** 100 V; **(b)** 10 A; **(c)** 20 A; **(d)** 2000 W; **(e)** 2000 W; **(f)** $\infty$ (no dc connection).

5.43. 5.74 and 1.74.

5.45. **(a)** 53.3 V, 2960 W, 44.4%; **(b)** 111 V, 12900 W, 92.8%; **(c)** 119.5 V, 14,900 W, 99.5%.

5.47. 2.78.

# 6

# Electric Power Systems

This chapter applies the concepts of Chapters 4 and 5 to power distribution systems and electric motors. Three-phase circuits are introduced, including three-phase transformers. The final section on electric motors examines motor/load interaction and shows how to analyze the nameplate information on the two most common types of electric motors.

## Importance of Electric Power Systems

In Chapters 4 and 5, we assumed that ac power is readily available as a sinusoidal voltage source with negligible output impedance. And this is what we assume in real life also. Our civilization is so dependent on reliable electric power that when the power fails, life seems to stop.

The generation and distribution of electric power is the business of large electric utility companies. Various fuels and sources are used, such as coal, natural gas, fuel oil, nuclear, and water power, not to mention some quaint and futuristic schemes such as wind power, tidal and wave power, solar power, and burning household garbage.

The normal way to generate[1] electrical power is to burn the primary fuel and produce high-pressure steam in a boiler. The steam drives a turbine that turns an electrical generator. The voltage from the generator is transformed to high voltage for transmission over long distances, as explained in Chapter 5. For reliability, all the generators in a geographic region are synchronized and are linked together with transmission lines to exchange real and reactive power.

Near the location of the industrial or residential customers, the voltage is lowered from transmission levels, typically, $120 - 500\,\text{kV}$, to distribution levels, typically $4.8 - 34\,\text{kV}$. For the residential consumer the voltage is lowered to $120/240\,\text{V}$, single-phase.

The power is generated, transmitted, and distributed in three-phase form. Only very near to the customer is the power changed from three-phase to single-phase power. This chapter begins with the introduction and study of three-phase electric systems. We then discuss three-phase transmission and distribution systems. Finally, we complete our study of electric power with an introduction to electric motors.

## Introduction to Three-phase Power Systems

Importance of three-phase systems. If you looked out your window at this moment, you would probably see some power lines. Count the wires and you will likely find there to be four. Go examine a pole closely and you will see that at each pole, one of the four wires is connected to a conductor that comes down the pole and enters the ground.

When you are driving cross country and see a large electrical transmission line, you will again see four wires. One of them, running along the top of the towers, will be noticeably smaller than the other three. If you look closely, you will again see that the small wire is grounded at every tower.

The three ungrounded wires in these transmission systems are driven by three ac generators. The grounded wire increases safety and protection from lightning. Power is conveyed by the three larger wires in the form of three-phase electric power. The overwhelming majority of the world's electric power is generated and distributed as three-phase power. For example, if you were to examine a catalog of industrial-grade motors, you will discover that all the larger electric motors, bigger than a few horsepower, would be three-phase motors.

---

[1] "Convert" would be a better word, because the energy is normally converted from chemical energy to heat, and finally to electrical energy.

**What is three-phase power?**  Physically, there are three wires that carry the power, and often a fourth wire, called the *neutral*, which is grounded. In enclosed cables, the active wires are normally colored red, black, and blue; and the neutral, if present, is white or gray. The phases are traditionally designated A, B, and C, and the time-domain voltages between them are as shown in Fig. 6.1. The voltages are expressed mathematically as

$$v_{AB}(t) = V_p\cos(\omega t)$$

$$v_{BC}(t) = V_p\cos(\omega t - 120°)$$

$$v_{CA}(t) = V_p\cos(\omega t - 240°)$$

(6.1)

**The Frequency Domain**

The frequency-domain picture for a three-phase system is shown in Fig. 6.2. We have used $\underline{\mathbf{V}}_{AB}$ as our phase angle[2] reference and shown $\underline{\mathbf{V}}_{BC}$ followed by 120°, then $\underline{\mathbf{V}}_{CA}$. This is known as an *ABC* phase sequence and corresponds to the time-domain representation in Fig. 6.1 and Eqs. (6.1).

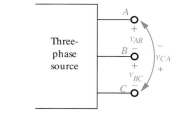

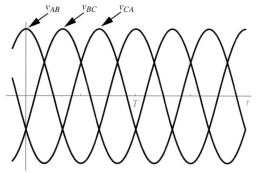

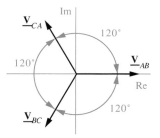

**Figure 6.1**  Voltages of a three-phase system in the time domain.

**Figure 6.2**  Voltages of a three-phase system in the frequency domain.

**Advantages of three-phase systems.**  We have shown in Fig. 5.6 that single-phase power produces a pulsating flow of energy. A *smooth* flow of energy from source to load is achieved by a balanced three-phase system. If we have identical resistive (R)

---

[2] We apologize for using "phase" to mean two separate concepts in this section, but this vocabulary is standard. The three voltages have different phases for their sources, and from this property, the sources themselves came to be called "phases." So "phase" means the phase angle of a sinusoidal quantity as well as the source of that sinusoid. In this section, we use "phase angle" to refer to the phase of a sinusoid.

loads connected between the three phases, the instantaneous flow of power would be given by Eq. (6.2). We use the trigonometric identity $\cos^2 \alpha = [1 + \cos(2\alpha)]/2$ to derive the second and third forms.

$$
\begin{aligned}
p(t) &= \frac{v_{AB}^2(t)}{R} + \frac{v_{BC}^2(t)}{R} + \frac{v_{CA}^2(t)}{R} \\
&= \frac{V_p^2}{2R}[1 + \cos 2(\omega t) + 1 + \cos 2(\omega t - 120°) + 1 + \cos 2(\omega t - 240°)] \\
&= \frac{3V_p^2}{2R} + \frac{V_p^2}{2R}\underbrace{[\cos(2\omega t) + \cos(2\omega t - 240°) + \cos(2\omega t - 480°)]}_{\text{add to zero at all times}}
\end{aligned} \tag{6.2}
$$

We see a constant term and a term that appears to be time-varying at twice the source frequency. Actually, *the second term adds to zero at all times*. This is easily shown by a phasor diagram; indeed, the phasors representing these terms give the same phasor diagram as Fig. 6.2.[3] Clearly, the phasor sum of the three symmetrical phasors is zero, and hence the fluctuating power term is also zero at all times. Thus, Eq. (6.2) reduces to

$$
p(t) = \frac{3V_p^2}{2R} \quad \text{(a constant)} \tag{6.3}
$$

This constant flow of energy effects general smoothness of operation in three-phase electrical equipment. A rough analogy is suggested by comparing an engine having one cylinder with an engine having many cylinders—clearly, the multicylinder engine runs smoother.

Compared with a single-phase system, distribution losses are proportionally less for a three-phase system. Additionally, three-phase motors offer advantages over single-phase motors in both startup and run characteristics. In short, three-phase systems are supremely important for the generation, distribution, and use of electrical power, particularly in industrial settings.

## Three-Phase Power Sources

**OBJECTIVE 2**

**To understand how to connect a generator in wye or delta**

**terminal**

**Three single-phase sources.** Three-phase generators produce three single-phase voltages with the required 120° phase-angle shifts, which are internally connected to produce a three-phase source. In this section, we pretend that the three single-phase voltages are brought out of the generator to a terminal board,[4] and our job is to connect the resulting six terminals together to produce a three-wire, three-phase source. The terminal board is shown in Fig. 6.3, and the phasor diagram of the available voltages is shown in Fig. 6.4.

**Delta (Δ) and wye (Y) connections.** The symmetry of the desired phasor voltages suggests that we require some sort of symmetrical connection for the three volt-

---

[3] A phase angle of −480° is the same as −120°.

[4] A *terminal* is the end of a wire from an electrical device. A *terminal board* is a place where terminals are made available for connection.

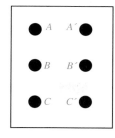

**Figure 6.3** External terminals for the three separate phases. These must be connected to produce a three-phase system.

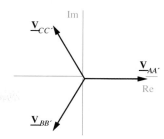

**Figure 6.4** Phasor voltages in the three coils. These must be connected externally to make a true three-phase system.

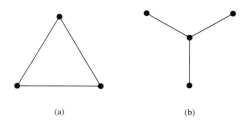

(a)  (b)

**Figure 6.5** The only two symmetrical configurations of three elements: (a) delta; (b) wye.

ages represented in Fig. 6.4. Only two symmetrical configurations exist for three elements connected end to end, and these are shown in Fig. 6.5. The closed ring is usually called a *delta* (for the Greek letter Δ), even when it is drawn upside down or on its side. The configuration with a common point is sometimes called a star configuration, but in three-phase terminology, it is more often called a *wye configuration* (a phonetic spelling of the letter Y), regardless of orientation.

These symmetric configurations suggest two solutions of the question posed earlier. We require three terminals for a source of three-phase power. The delta has three terminals, and hence the three-phase outputs connect these terminals. The wye, on the other hand, has four terminals, counting the common connection in the center. This gives us a place to connect the fourth wire mentioned earlier, the neutral wire that is grounded. We have to connect the terminals to have the geometric symmetry of the delta or wye configurations in Fig. 6.5, but we must also retain the electrical symmetry in Fig. 6.2.

**delta connection**

Delta connection. The delta ties the three generators in a closed ring. Figures 6.6(a) and 6.6(b) show one possible connection for the delta. We must be careful, however, when we close the ring, for the voltage must be small to avoid a large circulating current. Closing the delta is like jump starting a car having a weak battery, as shown in Fig. 6.6(c). The circuit can be closed if the polarities are correct. With the connection marked "Yes," there will be at most a small voltage across the gap and only small currents will flow through the batteries. But if the polarities are wrong, there will be approximately 24 V across the gap and a huge current will flow if the connection is made.

Similarly, if we are to close the ring of generators in Fig. 6.6(b), we require the voltage across the gap to be small. This requires that

$$\underline{\mathbf{V}}_{AC'} = \underline{\mathbf{V}}_{AA'} + \underline{\mathbf{V}}_{BB'} + \underline{\mathbf{V}}_{CC'} = 0 \qquad (6.4)$$

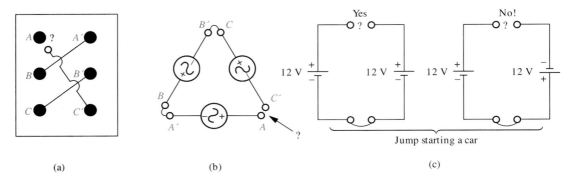

(a)  (b)  (c)

**Figure 6.6** (a) Potential delta connection; (b) The voltage across $A$ and $C'$ must be zero if the ring is to be closed; (c) The polarity must correct before closing the circuit.

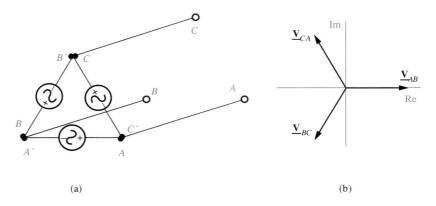

(a)  (b)

**Figure 6.7** Delta connection with phasor diagram.

Notice that Eq. (6.4) follows from the rule for adding subscripted voltages given on page 276 because $A'$ is connected to $B$ and $B'$ is connected to $C$. The general rule is

$$V_{AB} = V_{AX} + V_{XB} \tag{6.5}$$

We can extend this to $V_{AB} = V_{AX} + V_{YB}$ if $X$ and $Y$ are connected. The phasor diagram for the sum in Eq. (6.4) is easily derived from Fig. 6.4; clearly, the sum is small, ideally zero. Thus, it is safe to close the ring of generators and bring out the connected terminals as a three-phase source. Figure 6.7(b) shows the phasor diagram of the final connection in Fig. 6.7(a). Another possible delta connection would result with $A$ connected to $B'$, $B$ connected to $C'$, and $C$ connected to $A'$. We leave the investigation of this possibility to the reader.

**wye connection**

**Wye connection.** A wye connection results from connecting $A'$, $B'$, and $C'$, as shown in Fig. 6.8(a), with three wires for the three-phase power ($A$, $B$, $C$) and a common point ($A'B'C'$) for a neutral. With this connection, the magnitudes of $\underline{\mathbf{V}}_{AC}$, $\underline{\mathbf{V}}_{BA}$, and $\underline{\mathbf{V}}_{CB}$ are $\sqrt{3}$ greater than those of the component voltages, $\underline{\mathbf{V}}_{AA'}$, $\underline{\mathbf{V}}_{BB'}$, and $\underline{\mathbf{V}}_{CC'}$, and the phase angle of $\underline{\mathbf{V}}_{AC}$ lies at $-30°$ relative to $\underline{\mathbf{V}}_{AA'}$. These combinations are illus-

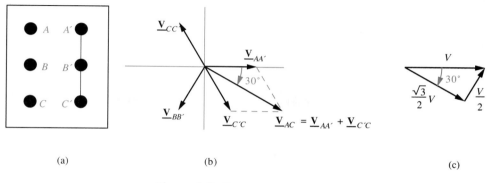

(a)              (b)              (c)

**Figure 6.8**   Possible wye connection.

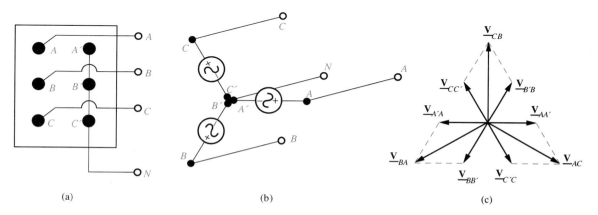

(a)              (b)              (c)

**Figure 6.9**   Wye connection.   The line voltages are $\sqrt{3}$ larger than the phase voltages.

trated in Fig. 6.8(b) by the forming of $\underline{\mathbf{V}}_{AC}$ through addition of $\underline{\mathbf{V}}_{AA'}$ and $\underline{\mathbf{V}}_{C'C}$, which is the negative of $\underline{\mathbf{V}}_{CC'}$. The $\sqrt{3}$ comes from the 30° right triangle, as shown in Fig. 6.8(c). In Figs. 6.9(a) and 6.9(b), we label the three lines $A$, $B$, and $C$, and the neutral $N$. Figure 6.9(c) shows the final phasor diagram of the wye connection. The wye connection leads to the four-wire system that we described at the beginning of this section.

**three-phase voltage, three-phase current, line voltage, line current**

**Three-phase voltage and current.**   The *three-phase voltage*, or *line voltage*, is the voltage between the lines carrying the power. The *three-phase currents*, or *line currents* are the currents in the three lines. For a balanced system, these quantities are simply the voltage and current measured by a voltmeter between any two lines and an ammeter in any of the lines. Hence, a 460-V three-phase system has 460 V (rms) between any two of the three lines carrying the power.

**Line and phase voltage and current for delta and wye connections.**   A three-phase generator consists of three interconnected single-phase generators,[5] as shown in Figs. 6.7 and 6.9. The *phase voltage*, $V_\phi$, and *current*, $I_\phi$, is the voltage across an individual generator and the current through that generator. For a delta connection,

**phase voltage phase current**

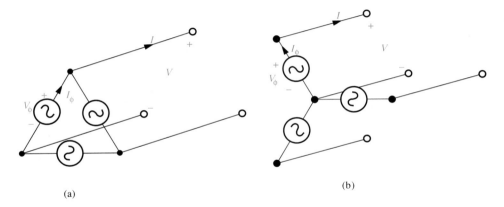

(a)

(b)

**Figure 6.10** Three-phase (line) and phase voltage and current for a (a) delta- and (b) wye-connected three-phase system.

the phase voltage is the three-phase, or line, voltage; but for a wye connection, the phase voltage is the three-phase voltage divided by $\sqrt{3}$, as shown in Fig. 6.9(c). The phase current is the same as the three-phase, or line, current for a wye connection, but for the delta connection, the phase current is the three-phase current divided by $\sqrt{3}$. The phase and line voltage and current are shown in Fig. 6.10 and summarized in Table 6.1.

| TABLE 6.1 | Relationships between Phase and Three-Phase Voltages for Wye and Delta Connections | |
|---|---|---|
| | **Three-Phase Voltage, $V$** | **Three-Phase Current, $I$** |
| **Wye** | $V_\phi = V/\sqrt{3}$ | $I_\phi = I$ |
| **Delta** | $V_\phi = V$ | $I_\phi = I/\sqrt{3}$ |

---

**EXAMPLE 6.1** | **Three-phase sources**

Three single-phase sources are wye-connected as a three-phase source that measures 208 V for the three-phase voltage. What would be the three-phase voltage if the generators were delta-connected?

**SOLUTION:**
The phase, or line-to-neutral, voltage of the wye-connected system is $208/\sqrt{3} = 120$ V. Thus, the delta connection would give a three-phase voltage of 120 V.

---

[5] Actually, there is only one generator, but it has three single-phase *windings* that are interconnected. Here we call these "generators" to indicate single-phase voltage sources.

What if one of the three phases in the delta is reversed, but the ring is not closed? What would be the voltages between the four sets of terminals?[6]

**Phase rotation.** The phase rotation came out *ABC* in both systems we developed, but *ACB* is also a possibility. The physical phase rotation is very important; for example, the rotational direction of a three-phase motor depends on the phase rotation of the input voltages. In practice, the three wires are arbitrarily labeled *A*, *B*, and *C*, and one of several techniques is used to determine whether the phase rotation is *ABC* or *ACB*.

**Other possible connections.** We have now shown the two ways for connecting the voltages in Fig. 6.3 to give a three-wire, symmetrical power system. Actually, we have shown one version of each way, for there is an alternative delta or wye. For example, we can make *A*, *B*, and *C* the neutral for a wye.

## Three-Phase Loads

**OBJECTIVE 3**

**To understand how to calculate voltage, current, and power in balanced wye- and delta-connected loads**

**Delta-connected resistors.** Like three-phase generators, three-phase loads can be connected in delta or wye. Figure 6.11 shows a balanced three-phase resistive load connected in delta. The source of the three-phase power is not shown; we assume *ABC* phase rotation and a three-phase voltage $V = |\underline{V}_{AB}| = |\underline{V}_{BC}| = |\underline{V}_{CA}|$. We show no neutral because the load offers no place for connecting a neutral. In practice, however, a delta-connected load, such as a three-phase motor, is housed in a physical structure that is normally grounded directly to earth ground and through a neutral. However, the motor circuit would be floating.

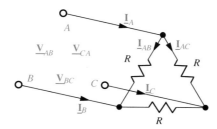

**Figure 6.11** Delta-connected load.

**Conservation of Charge**

With a load connected in delta, we must distinguish between the line currents and the phase currents flowing in the resistors. Figure 6.12 shows the phase currents, $\underline{I}_{AB}$, $\underline{I}_{BC}$, and $\underline{I}_{CA}$. These currents are in phase angle with the line voltages. Any line current, say, $\underline{I}_A$, can be determined by phasor addition of the phase currents. Kirchhoff's current law at the top node is

$$\underline{I}_A = \underline{I}_{AB} + \underline{I}_{AC} \tag{6.6}$$

---

[6] 120, 120, 120, and 240 V.

but

$$\mathbf{I}_{AC} = -\mathbf{I}_{CA} \tag{6.7}$$

and hence the currents add as in Fig. 6.12. The other line currents could be determined similarly; indeed, the picture develops like that of the wye generator connection in Fig. 6.9(c). We see that the line currents are $\sqrt{3}$ greater than the phase currents. Thus, the second row of Table 6.1 is valid for delta-connected loads as well as sources. For the resistive load, the phase angle of the line current in $A$ is in phase angle with the average of the phase angles of $\mathbf{V}_{AB}$ and $\mathbf{V}_{AC}$. The phase-angle relationships for a resistive load are shown in Fig. 6.13.

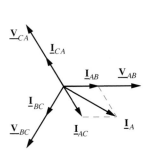

**Figure 6.12** Phase current addition to yield line current.

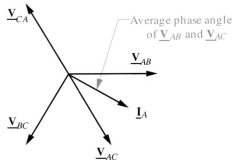

**Figure 6.13** For a resistive load, the line current is in phase angle with the average phase angle of the voltages to the other two lines.

---

| **EXAMPLE 6.2** | **Delta-connected load** |

A delta-connected resistive load has a line voltage of 460 V and a line current of 32 A. Find the resistance values.

**SOLUTION:**
The phase voltage is $V_\phi = 460$ V and the phase current is $I_\phi = 32/\sqrt{3} = 18.5$ A. Thus, the phase impedance is

$$|\mathbf{Z}_\phi| = \frac{V_\phi}{I_\phi} = \frac{460}{18.5} = 24.9 \ \Omega \tag{6.8}$$

| **WHAT IF?** | What if one of the resistors were missing? What would be the line currents?[7] |

---

[7] 32, 18.5, and 18.5 A.

**General loads in delta.** With balanced loads that are not resistive, the phasor diagram shown in Fig. 6.12 changes only slightly. The magnitude of the phase currents is computed by dividing the line voltages, which are also the phase voltages, by the magnitude of the phase impedance. The phase currents will lead or lag the line voltages according to the angle of the phase impedance. Hence, the line currents will also be shifted in phase angle by the angle of the impedance. We give an example later.

**Power in delta connections.** The total power to a load, $P_{3\phi}$, is the sum of the powers delivered to the three phase impedances; and this would be

$$P_{3\phi} = 3 P_\phi = 3 V_\phi I_\phi \times PF \qquad (6.9)$$

where $PF$ is the power factor of the phase impedance. In Eq. (6.9), $V_\phi$ and $I_\phi$ represent the rms values of the phase voltage and current. We desire, however, to express the total power in terms of line voltage and current. The phase currents are often inaccessible for measurements, but the line voltage and current always can be measured. Consequently, we introduce the line voltage and current:

$$P = 3V \frac{I}{\sqrt{3}} \times PF = \sqrt{3} VI \times PF \qquad (6.10)$$

where $V$ and $I$ are the rms line voltage and current, respectively. In the application of Eq. (6.10), the power factor is the cosine of the angle of the phase impedance and is *not* the phase angle between line current and line voltage. The power factor angle is, however, the angle between the phase angle of the line current and the average phase angle of the voltages to the two other lines, as illustrated in Fig. 6.13.

---

**EXAMPLE 6.3** | **Delta-connected _RL_ impedances**

A 230-V three-phase power system supplies 2000 W to a delta-connected balanced load with a power factor of 0.9, lagging. Determine the line currents, the phase currents, and the phase impedance. Draw a phasor diagram.

**SOLUTION:**
First, we calculate the magnitude of the line currents from Eq. (6.10).

$$P = \sqrt{3} VI \times PF \Rightarrow I = \frac{2000}{\sqrt{3}(230)(0.9)} = 5.58 \text{ A (rms)} \qquad (6.11)$$

The phase currents are smaller by $\sqrt{3}$, so

$$I_\phi = \frac{I}{\sqrt{3}} = \frac{5.58}{\sqrt{3}} = 3.22 \text{ A} \qquad (6.12)$$

This allows us to calculate the impedance in each phase of the delta. The angle of the impedance is implied by the power factor: $\theta = \cos^{-1}(0.9) = +25.8°$, + because the current is lagging (inductive).

$$Z_\phi = \frac{V_\phi}{I_\phi} \angle \cos^{-1}(PF) = \frac{230}{3.22} \angle \cos^{-1}(0.9) = 71.4 \angle +25.8° \, \Omega \qquad (6.13)$$

We can now draw the phasor diagram, Fig. 6.14. We use $\underline{V}_{AB}$ for the phase-angle reference, with the other line voltages placed symmetrically in $ABC$ sequence. The phase currents lag by 25.8°, as shown. The line currents can be computed by phasor addition of the phase currents, as we did in Fig. 6.12, but another approach is to use our earlier results to place the line currents behind the phase currents by 30° and greater by $\sqrt{3}$. Whichever way is chosen, only one line current need be determined, $\underline{I}_A$ for example, and the other two can be constructed by symmetry.

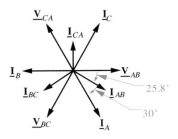

**Figure 6.14** Line voltages, phase currents, and line currents. The phase currents are $\sqrt{3}$ smaller than the line currents.

**WHAT IF?** What if the phase impedances are $\underline{Z}_\phi = 60 \angle -20°$? Find the new line current and power.[8]

**Wye-connected loads.** Figure 6.15 shows a load connected in wye.[9] We have shown no connection to the neutral, labeled $N$, but there would often be a connection between the load neutral and the source neutral, if such existed, and the neutral is often grounded. For a perfectly balanced load, no current would flow in the neutral connection because the three line currents add to zero. We now calculate the line-to-neutral voltages, $\underline{V}_{AN}$, $\underline{V}_{BN}$, and $\underline{V}_{CN}$, and the line currents, $\underline{I}_A$, $\underline{I}_B$, and $\underline{I}_C$.

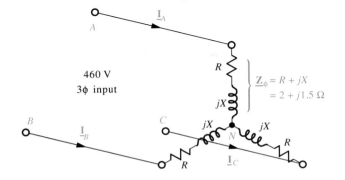

**Figure 6.15** Wye-connected load. To find the line currents, we must determine the line-to-neutral voltages.

---

[8] 6.64 A and 2485 W.

[9] On the input voltage, "$3\phi$" is a common abbreviation for "three phase."

**Line-to-neutral voltages.** The phase impedances are given, $\underline{\mathbf{Z}}_\phi$; hence, it is clear that the line currents can be determined once the line-to-neutral voltages are known; for example,

$$\underline{\mathbf{I}}_A = \frac{\underline{\mathbf{V}}_{AN}}{\underline{\mathbf{Z}}_\phi} \tag{6.14}$$

The line-to-neutral voltages can be determined from consideration of the symmetry of the circuit. It is convenient to pretend that we know the line-to-neutral voltages (which we do not) and determine from them the line-to-line voltages. The relationship between these two sets of three-phase voltages then becomes known and we henceforth can deduce either set of voltages from the other. We assume the *ABC* phase sequence; hence, the line-to-neutral voltages must appear as in Fig. 6.16, assuming that we make $\underline{\mathbf{V}}_{AN}$ the phase reference.

First, we determine $\underline{\mathbf{V}}_{AB}$. We can express $\underline{\mathbf{V}}_{AB}$ in terms of $\underline{\mathbf{V}}_{AN}$ and $\underline{\mathbf{V}}_{NB}$:

$$\underline{\mathbf{V}}_{AB} = \underline{\mathbf{V}}_{AN} + \underline{\mathbf{V}}_{NB} \tag{6.15}$$

Equation (6.15) becomes more useful when we reverse the subscripts on $\underline{\mathbf{V}}_{NB}$ and change the sign:

$$\underline{\mathbf{V}}_{BN} = -\underline{\mathbf{V}}_{NB} \;\Rightarrow\; \underline{\mathbf{V}}_{AB} = \underline{\mathbf{V}}_{AN} - \underline{\mathbf{V}}_{BN} \tag{6.16}$$

Equation (6.16) is represented in Fig. 6.16, with the negative of $\underline{\mathbf{V}}_{BN}$ drawn and added to $\underline{\mathbf{V}}_{AN}$. We note that $\underline{\mathbf{V}}_{AB}$ leads $\underline{\mathbf{V}}_{AN}$ by 30° and is somewhat greater in magnitude. The phasor addition is identical to that as shown in Fig. 6.8(b) and the magnitudes of phase and line voltages have the ratio $\sqrt{3}$, just as the currents in the delta-connected load. The remaining line voltages, $\underline{\mathbf{V}}_{BC}$ and $\underline{\mathbf{V}}_{CA}$, may be determined by similar reasoning, or more directly by arranging them in *ABC* sequence, each 120° from $\underline{\mathbf{V}}_{AB}$.

Figure 6.17 shows the results. The line-to-neutral voltages lag the corresponding line voltages by 30°, when we consider the two voltages with, say, *A* written first, like $\underline{\mathbf{V}}_{AB}$ and $\underline{\mathbf{V}}_{AN}$. But a better way to think about the phase angle is to realize that the phase angle of the corresponding line-to-neutral voltage lies between the phase angles of the two line-to-line voltages that connect to the same point. Thus, $\underline{\mathbf{V}}_{AN}$ will lie halfway between $\underline{\mathbf{V}}_{AB}$ and $\underline{\mathbf{V}}_{AC}$. This phase angle relation, together with the magnitude ra-

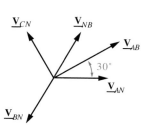

**Figure 6.16** Determining line-to-line voltages from line-to-neutral voltages.

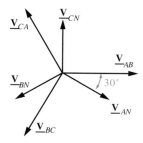

**Figure 6.17** The line-to-neutral voltages are smaller by $\sqrt{3}$ and lag line-to-line voltages by 30°.

tio of $1/\sqrt{3}$, allows us to determine easily the line-to-neutral voltages from the set of line-to-line voltages, or vice versa, as shown in Fig. 6.17.

---

**EXAMPLE 6.4** | **Wye-connected load**

Find the line and phase current, line and phase voltage for the wye-connected load shown in Fig. 6.15.

**SOLUTION:**
We make $\underline{\mathbf{V}}_{AB}$ the phase angle reference, that is, $\underline{\mathbf{V}}_{AB} = 460\sqrt{2} \angle 0°$V. Hence, the line voltage is 460 V (rms). From Fig. 6.17, we see that $\underline{\mathbf{V}}_{AN}$ will lie at $-30°$ and be smaller by $\sqrt{3}$, or $\underline{\mathbf{V}}_{AN} = 266\sqrt{2} \angle -30°$ V; so the phase voltage is 266 V (rms). Hence, the current in line $A$ is

$$\underline{\mathbf{I}}_A = \frac{\mathbf{V}_{AN}}{\mathbf{Z}_\phi} = \frac{266\sqrt{2} \angle -30°}{2 + j1.5} = \frac{266\sqrt{2} \angle -30°}{2.50 \angle 36.9°} = 106.2\sqrt{2} \angle -66.9° \text{ A} \qquad (6.17)$$

The other line currents can be determined similarly or by symmetry from $\underline{\mathbf{I}}_A$. Thus, the phase and line currents, which are the same for the wye-connected load, are 106.2 A.

---

**Power in wye-connected loads.**    The total power to the wye-connected load is three times the power to each phase of the load, $P_\phi$. Thus, we can compute the total power with

$$P_{3\phi} = 3P_\phi = 3V_\phi I_\phi \times PF \qquad (6.18)$$

where $P_{3\phi}$ is the power in the load, $V_\phi$ is the phase rms voltage, the line-to-neutral voltage in this instance, $I_\phi$ is the phase rms current, also the line current in this instance, and $PF$ is the power factor of the phase impedance.

---

**EXAMPLE 6.5** | **Power in wye-connected load**

Find the total power to the three-phase load in the previous example.

**SOLUTION:**
The phase voltage and current were determined to be 266 V and 106.2 A, respectively. The power factor is the angle of the phase impedance, $2 + j1.5 = 2.50 \angle 36.9°$; so the power factor is $\cos 36.9°$, lagging. Using Eq. (6.18), we find the power in the load to be

$$P_{3\phi} = 3(266)(106.2)(\cos 36.9°) = 67.7 \text{ kW} \qquad (6.19)$$

---

**WHAT IF?**    What if one phase impedance were missing?  What would be the power?[10]

---

[10] 33.9 kW.

**Using line voltage and current.** The neutral of the wye-connected load might not be accessible for voltage measurement; hence, it is desirable to express the total power in terms of the line voltage and current. Using the $\sqrt{3}$ ratio between phase voltage and line voltage, we may convert Eq. (6.18) to

$$P_{3\phi} = \left(\frac{V}{\sqrt{3}}\right)(I) \times PF = \sqrt{3}VI \times PF \qquad (6.20)$$

where $V$ is the line voltage, $I$ is the line current, and $PF$ is the power factor of the load. In Eq. (6.20), the power factor is the cosine of the angle of the phase impedance.

Equation (6.20) is identical to Eq. (6.10), which was developed for the delta-connected load. Thus, the formula is general and we mark it with a box due to its importance. Clearly, the two load configurations are indistinguishable to external measurement and only can be identified in practice by examining the internal connections in the three-phase load.

**Equivalent Circuits**

**Delta–wye conversions.** This does not mean, however, that the *same* set of phase impedances are equivalent when connected first in delta and then in wye. Indeed, the appearance of the circuits suggests that the delta gives parallel paths, whereas the wye gives series paths. This appearance suggests that the line current for the delta would be larger than for the wye if the same phase impedance were used for each connection. It can be shown that the ratio is 3:1; that is, three identical impedances will draw three times the current (and three times the power) when connected in delta, as compared to when they are connected in wye.

**Impedance Level**

Thus, the delta and wye are equivalent if the phase impedances differ by a factor of 3, with the delta connection having the higher impedance level. This equivalence, shown in Fig. 6.18, is often useful in solving three-phase problems. We leave proof of this equivalence for a problem at the end of this chapter.

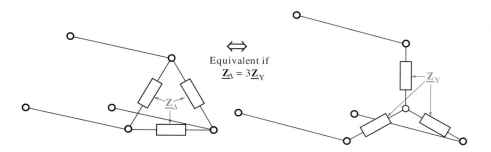

Equivalent if
$\underline{Z}_\Delta = 3\underline{Z}_Y$

**Figure 6.18** Delta and wye equivalence.

EXAMPLE 6.6 **Delta load with line losses**

Determine the power to the delta-connected load in Fig. 6.19.

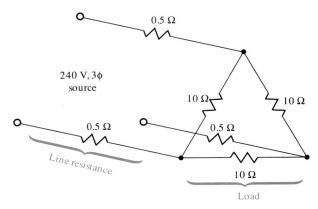

**Figure 6.19**  Find the power to the delta-connected load.

**SOLUTION:**

The 10-$\Omega$ resistors represent the load, but we must consider the resistance of the wires leading to the load, which is represented by the 0.5-$\Omega$ resistors. The presence of the wire resistance undermines our previous approach for solving delta-connected loads, but if we convert the delta to an equivalent wye load, we can solve the problem.

Figure 6.20 shows the circuit after conversion to wye. The wire resistance can now be combined with the load resistance to yield a phase resistance of 3.83 $\Omega$, and the rms line-to-neutral voltage is $240/\sqrt{3} = 139$ V. The line current thus is $139/3.83 = 36.1$ A, and the total power to the wires plus load is $\sqrt{3}\,(240)\,(36.1) = 15.0$ kW. The wire losses are $3(36.1)^2(0.5) = 1960$ W, the rest of the power going to the delta-connected load.

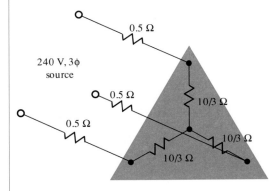

**Figure 6.20**  After converting the delta to a wye, we can determine the line currents.

**WHAT IF?**  What if you measured the voltage across a 10-$\Omega$ resistor in Fig. 6.19. What voltage would you measure?[11]

---

[11] 209 V.

# Per-Phase Equivalent Circuits

To understand
how to derive
and use the
per-phase
equivalent circuit
of a balanced
three-phase load

**Need for a simpler model.** Three-phase circuits are awkward to draw, and much of the drawing is unnecessary for a balanced circuit because each phase is identical. A single-phase model can represent the voltage, current, and power relationships in the three-phase circuit without this redundancy.

Equivalent
Circuits

The *per-phase equivalent circuit* is a single-phase circuit that represents a balanced three-phase circuit. The per-phase model can represent any three-phase system, whether source or load is connected in delta or wye; thus, the system is that shown in Fig. 6.21. The power source establishes the voltage, $V$, and the load determines the current and the power factor. The voltage, current, and power factor on the line indicate the power delivered to the load.

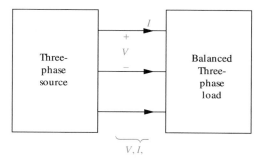

**Figure 6.21** The per-phase circuit is based on the line voltage, current, and power factor and not on the internal connections of source and load.

**Figure 6.22** The wye-wye circuit with neutral in place can be considered three single-phase circuits sharing a wire.

**Wye-wye basis.** The per-phase circuit is derived *as if* the three-phase source and load were wye-connected, as shown in Fig. 6.22. We have drawn the neutral connection dashed because it actually may be missing. Even if present, the current in the neutral will be zero for a balanced load, as indicated; thus, the neutrals of the source and the load are at the same voltage, as if connected by a short circuit. This equivalent short circuit connecting the neutrals divides the three-phase circuit into three, identical single-phase circuits sharing a common neutral. We may take the inner circuit, where we marked the voltage and current, as representing one-third of the three-phase system. The per-phase equivalent circuit, shown in Fig. 6.23, introduces the per-phase voltage, current, and impedance, $\mathbf{V}_{pp}$, $\mathbf{I}_{pp}$, and $\mathbf{Z}_{pp}$, respectively.

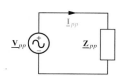

**Figure 6.23** Per-phase equivalent circuit.

**Relationship between three-phase and per-phase quantities.** The relationship between the three-phase quantities and the per-phase quantities are shown in Table 6.2. The per-phase voltage is $V/\sqrt{3}$ because, as shown in Fig. 6.22, the single-phase circuit consists of one line of the three-phase system plus the neutral. The currents and the power factor are the same. The per-phase impedance is the same as the load phase impedance if the load is wye-connected, but is one-third the load phase impedance if delta-connected. The power in the per-phase circuit is one-third the full power in the three-phase circuit, as the name "per phase" suggests. The same would be true for apparent, reactive, and complex power.

## TABLE 6-2 Relationships between Three-phase and Per-Phase Quantities

|  | Three-Phase Circuit | Per-Phase Circuit |
|---|---|---|
| Voltage | $V$ | $V_{pp} = V/\sqrt{3}$ |
| Current | $I$ | $I_{pp} = I$ |
| Impedance | $Z_\Delta$ or $Z_Y$ | $Z_{pp} = Z_Y$ or $Z_\Delta/3$ |
| Power factor | $PF$ | $PF = $ same |
| Power | $P_{3\phi} = \sqrt{3}\, VI \times PF$ | $V_{pp}I_{pp} \times PF = P_{3\phi}/3$ |

---

**EXAMPLE 6.7** | **Motor per-phase equivalent circuit**

A three-phase induction motor has the following specifications: 3 hp, 3515 rpm, 230 V, 8.8 A, efficiency $= 80.0\%$. Derive a per-phase equivalent circuit for the motor.

**SOLUTION:**

The per-phase voltage and current come directly from the three-phase voltage and current:

$$V_{pp} = \frac{230}{\sqrt{3}} = 133 \text{ V} \qquad \text{and} \qquad I_{pp} = 8.8 \text{ A} \tag{6.21}$$

and thus the magnitude of the per-phase impedance is established:

$$|Z_{pp}| = \frac{V_{pp}}{I_{pp}} = \frac{133}{8.8} = 15.1 \ \Omega \tag{6.22}$$

To determine the angle of the impedance, we need the phase angle of the current, which is not given, or the power factor, which is not given either but may be determined from the power quantities. The output power of the motor is 3 hp $\times$ 746 W/hp = 2240 W, and the input power follows from this and the efficiency:

$$\text{Efficiency} = \eta = \frac{P_{out}}{P_{in}} \Rightarrow P_{in} = \frac{P_{out}}{\eta} = \frac{2240}{0.800} = 2800 \text{ W} \tag{6.23}$$

Thus, the power factor of both the three-phase and the per-phase circuits is

$$PF = \frac{P_{pp}}{V_{pp}I_{pp}} = \frac{2800/3}{133 \times 8.8} = 0.798 \tag{6.24}$$

and hence the angle of the per-phase impedance is $\cos^{-1}(0.798) = 37.1°$ and the per-phase impedance is $\mathbf{Z}_{pp} = 15.1 \angle 37.1° = 12.0 + j9.09 \ \Omega$. Note: (1) we divided the total electrical input power by 3 to convert to power per phase, and (2) we assumed a positive angle for the impedance (inductive) because an induction motor draws lagging current. The per-phase equivalent circuit is that shown in Fig. 6.23 with $\underline{\mathbf{V}}_{pp} = 133\sqrt{2} \angle 0° \text{ V}$, $\mathbf{Z}_{pp} = 15.1 \angle 37.1° \ \Omega$, and $\underline{\mathbf{I}}_{pp} = 8.8\sqrt{2} \angle -37.1° \text{ A}$.

**unbalanced three-phase systems**

Unsymmetric loads. A per-phase equivalent circuit is possible only for a balanced system. A three-phase load becomes *unbalanced* when the phase impedances are not identical. This is an undesirable situation and is avoided in practice if possible. When unbalanced loads are connected in delta, calculation of the phase and line currents becomes tedious, though straightforward. All phase and line currents must be calculated individually because symmetry has been lost.

When unbalanced loads are connected in wye, the analysis is straightforward only when the neutral of the load is connected to the neutral of the three-phase source. With the neutral connected, the three loads operate in effect as single-phase loads that share the neutral connection. Current will flow in the neutral wire for an unbalanced load.

When there exists no neutral wire in the unbalanced wye connection, complications arise in the calculation of the line-to-neutral voltages and the line currents. Because the neutral of the load is no longer at the same voltage as the neutral of the source, the first step in solving the problem is to calculate the voltage of the neutral of the load. Then one can proceed to solve for the line currents. Such calculations are routinely performed with computers.

### Check Your Understanding

1. A three-phase circuit measures 762 V (rms) between earth ground and line $A$. What would be the voltage between lines $B$ and $C$?

2. For a delta-connected load, the phase and line currents are the same. True or false?

3. A three-phase load uses 50 kW at 480 V. The current is 64 A. Find the reactive power required by the inductive load.

4. Three 120-$\Omega$ resistors connected in wye are equivalent to what resistances connected in delta?

*Answers.* (1) 1320 V; (2) false; (3) +18.2 kVAR; (4) 360 $\Omega$.

## 6.2 POWER DISTRIBUTION SYSTEMS

Introduction. The power that is indispensable to our civilization is generated in large central power plants, transformed to high voltages for transmission over long distances, lowered to moderate voltages for distribution throughout a geographic region such as a small city, and finally reduced to the voltage levels required by industrial and

---

[12] $V_{pp} = 266$ V, $I_{pp} = 4.4$ A, and $\mathbf{Z}_{pp} = 60.4 \angle 37.1°\ \Omega$.

residential consumers. Only at the last stage is the power available in single-phase form; the generation, transmission, and distribution use three-phase.

In this section, we deal with the transmission and distribution aspects of the power system. In the next section, we deal with ac motors, which are a major consumer of electric power and have special importance to engineers. The operation of ac generators is described in Chapter 15.

**Voltage levels.** For reasons intrinsic to good design, large three-phase generators produce voltage in the range of 11–25 kV. As discussed in the previous chapter, the voltage is raised to much higher values, $120 - 500$ kV, for transmission. The voltage is lowered, perhaps by degrees, to smaller values, 7.2–23 kV, for distribution over a geographic area. As near to the customer as possible, within the building for a commercial customer or on a pole outside for a residential customer, the voltage is transformed finally to the standard utilization voltages, 120 and 240 V for residential, perhaps higher voltages for industrial customers. All these voltage transformations, with the exception of the last one, are performed by three-phase transformers.

## Three-Phase Transformers

Three-phase power may be transformed by three single-phase transformers or by a single three-phase transformer. Economics favors the latter for larger transmission transformers and the former for smaller distribution transformers. The principles are the same in both cases. We speak in the following as if we are using three single-phase transformers.

In three-phase transformation, primaries and secondaries can be connected in delta ($\Delta$) or wye (Y). This gives four possible combinations: Y–$\Delta$, $\Delta$–Y, $\Delta$–$\Delta$, and Y–Y. We now analyze the Y–$\Delta$ connection and summarize the other three connections in a table.

**The Y–$\Delta$ connection.** Figure 6.24 shows a Y–$\Delta$ connection in two circuit representations. We assume three single-phase transformers with voltages of $V_p:V_s$ and currents of $I_p:I_s$ with apparent power $S = V_p I_p = V_s I_s$. Operated at rated voltage and current, the primary line voltage and current are $V = \sqrt{3} V_p$ and $I = I_p$, for an apparent power of $\sqrt{3} VI = 3V_p I_p = 3S$. Thus, the apparent power rating of the three single-phase transformers connected for three-phase transformation is three times the apparent power rating of each component transformer. The secondary line voltage is $V_s$ and the rated current is $\sqrt{3} I_s$; hence, the apparent power rating again is $3S$. In both cases, the rating of the three-phase connection is three times the rating of the single-phase transformers. This is true for all four possible connections.

| **EXAMPLE 6.8** | **Y-$\Delta$ transformer connection** |
|---|---|

Three 2400/240-V, 24-kVA (each) single-phase transformers are connected with the 2400 side in wye and the 240 side in delta. Find the rated three-phase voltage, current, and apparent power on both sides of the transformer.

**SOLUTION:**
The allowed currents in the primary and secondary windings are 10 A and 100 A, respectively. Operated at rated voltage and current, the primary line voltage and current are $\sqrt{3} \times 2400 =$

4160 V and 10 A, respectively, for an apparent power of $\sqrt{3}\,VI = 72$ kVA. The secondary line voltage is 240 V and the rated current is $\sqrt{3} \times 100 = 173$ A. Hence, the apparent power in the secondary is also 72 kVA.

**WHAT IF?**  What if the transformers were connected Δ–Δ?[13]

The phasor diagram for the Y–Δ connection is shown in Figure 6.25. The secondary voltages are one-tenth the primary line-to-neutral voltage and 30° out of phase angle. This suggests that care should be used in designing and installing such systems because if multiple paths exist, and they do in most power systems, phase angles must be correct.

**Applications of transformer connections.** The four possible transformer connections are presented in Table 6.3. The winding (single-phase) voltage and current are $V_p$ and $I_p$ on the primary and $V_s$ and $I_s$ on the secondary, and the three-phase voltage and current are given in the table. Each of the connections find use:

■ **Wye–wye.** This connection is occasionally used in high-voltage transmission lines. In addition to providing a neutral, the wye connection has the virtue of having lower voltage across the windings and is desirable for high voltage

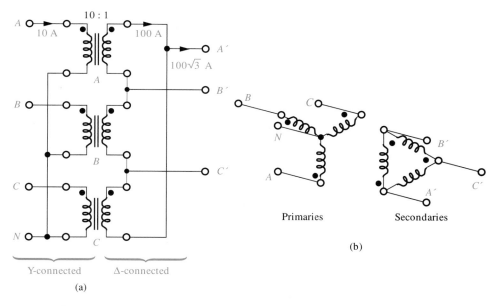

**Figure 6.24**  Three single-phase transformers in a Y-Δ connection:  (a) circuit diagram; (b) schematic diagram.

---

[13] Primary: 2400 V, 17.3 A, 72 kVA; secondary: 240 V, 173 A, 72 kVA.

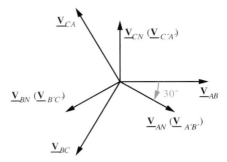

**Figure 6.25** Phasor diagram for a Y-Δ transformer connection.

**TABLE 6.3** **Voltage and Currents Resulting from Three-Phase Transformer Connections**[*]

| Connections | Primary $V$ | Primary $I$ | Secondary $V$ | Secondary $I$ |
|:-----------:|:-----------:|:-----------:|:-------------:|:-------------:|
| Y–Y | $\sqrt{3}V_p$ | $I_p$ | $\sqrt{3}V_s$ | $I_s$ |
| Y–Δ | $\sqrt{3}V_p$ | $I_p$ | $V_s$ | $\sqrt{3}I_s$ |
| Δ–Y | $V_p$ | $\sqrt{3}I_p$ | $\sqrt{3}V_s$ | $I_s$ |
| Δ–Δ | $V_p$ | $\sqrt{3}I_p$ | $V_s$ | $\sqrt{3}I_s$ |

[*]The winding (single-phase) voltage and current are $V_p$ and $I_p$ on the primary and $V_s$ and $I_s$ on the secondary. The three-phase voltage and current are $V$ and $I$, respectively.

connections. When used, Y–Y transformers often have a third set of windings, a *tertiary winding,* that is connected in delta to reduce harmonics[14] in the power system.

■ **Delta–wye.** This connection is used to step up the voltage from generation levels to the high voltages required for long-distance transmission. Also can be used to reduce from distribution levels to consumer voltage levels.

■ **Wye–Delta.** This connection is used to step down the voltage from transmission levels to distribution levels.

**open-delta connection**

■ **Delta–Delta.** This connection is used at distribution and consumer levels. This connection has the unique property that one leg of the delta can be omitted in the so-called $V$ or open-delta connection.[15] This configuration is useful because it can operate at 58% of the rating that the full delta would have and hence the open-delta connection is often installed in a growing system for later expansion.

**Per-phase equivalent circuits for transmission and distribution systems.** All the connections just listed, and indeed the entire transmission and distribu-

---

[14] Harmonics are discussed in Chapter 9.

[15] The open-delta connection is drawn in the figure for Problem P6.21.

tion system, can be represented by an equivalent per-phase (single-phase) circuit. After presenting per-unit calculations, we proceed to describe the properties of power transmission and distribution systems.

## Per-Unit Calculations

**per-unit calculations**

**Introduction.** The *per-unit* system of calculation is a method of *normalizing* electrical circuit calculations so that voltage transformations in transformers become inconsequential. Other benefits of the per-unit system are (1) many of the $\sqrt{3}$'s inherent in three-phase calculations are eliminated, and (2) on a per-unit basis all generators, transmission lines, transformers, motors, etc., look more or less alike.

**Base values.** In power system calculations, we are concerned with calculating voltages, currents, impedances, and the three types of power, apparent power ($S$), real power ($P$), and reactive power ($Q$). We need base values of these quantities to normalize actual circuit quantities; but voltage, current, impedance, and power are interrelated such that only two may be chosen as base values and the other two base values may be calculated. Normally, voltage (V or kV) and apparent power (VA, kVA, and MVA) are used as primary base values, and current and impedance base values are secondary.

**Converting to per unit (pu).** To convert a circuit quantity to per unit (pu), divide by the base value. Thus

$$V_{pu} = \frac{V}{V_{base}} \qquad \text{and} \qquad S_{pu} = \frac{S}{S_{base}} \qquad (6.25)$$

where the unsubscripted quantities are the circuit values. For example, we have a 240/120-V, 12-kVA transformer that is operated at 10 kVA with 220 V on the primary. If we use the rated values as base, the per-unit voltage and power are

$$V_{pu} = \frac{220\,\text{V}}{240\,\text{V}} = 0.917 \qquad \text{and} \qquad S_{pu} = \frac{10\,\text{kVA}}{12\,\text{kVA}} = 0.833 \qquad (6.26)$$

The per-unit quantities are unitless. We can normalize current and impedance also, but we must first establish consistent bases from the base voltage and apparent power.

**Base values for current and impedance.** Because the apparent power is voltage times current, we can derive the current base as

$$I_{base} = \frac{S_{base}}{V_{base}} = \frac{12\,\text{kVA}}{240\,\text{V}} = 50\,\text{A} \qquad (6.27)$$

and similarly for impedance

$$Z_{base} = \frac{V_{base}}{I_{base}} = \frac{V_{base}^2}{S_{base}} = \frac{(240\,\text{V})^2}{12\,\text{kVA}} = 4.8\,\Omega \qquad (6.28)$$

EXAMPLE 6.9 **Per-unit circuit calculations**

A 240/120-V, 12-kVA transformer that is operated at 220 on the primary has a 10-Ω load on the secondary. Derive a per-unit circuit and calculate the per-unit current in both primary and secondary and the per-unit power. Figure 6.26 shows the circuit.

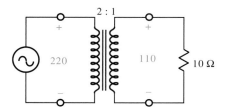

**Figure 6.26** The transformer will disappear in the per-unit circuit.

**SOLUTION:**

We have the base values for the primary in Eq. (6.26). We choose the rated voltage and the kVA for the secondary base values, which makes the transformer disappear, as we shall see. Thus, the base values for the secondary are, from Eqs. (6.27) and (6.28),

$$I_{base} = \frac{12\,\text{kVA}}{120\,\text{V}} = 100\ \text{A} \qquad \text{and} \qquad Z_{base} = \frac{(120\,\text{V})^2}{12\,\text{kVA}} = 1.2\ \Omega \qquad (6.29)$$

The per-unit voltage on both primary and secondary is 0.917, and the per-unit load impedance is

$$Z_{pu} = \frac{10\ \Omega}{1.2\ \Omega} = 8.33; \qquad \text{hence} \qquad I_{pu} = \frac{V_{pu}}{Z_{pu}} = \frac{0.917}{8.33} = 0.110 \qquad (6.30)$$

Thus, the current in the secondary is $0.110 \times 100\ \text{A} = 11\ \text{A}$. The per-unit current in the primary is the same, 0.110, because both actual and base currents are reduced by the turns ratio. Thus, the current in the primary is $0.110 \times 50\ \text{A} = 5.5\ \text{A}$. Note the per-unit voltage and current are the same on both sides of the transformer; it becomes in effect a 1:1 transformer, as shown in Fig. 6.27. Hence, the per-unit power is the same on both sides of the ideal transformer:

$$P_{pu} = V_{pu}I_{pu} = 0.917 \times 0.110 = 0.101 \qquad (6.31)$$

so the actual power is $0.101 \times S_{base} = 0.101 \times 12{,}000\ \text{VA} = 1210\ \text{W}$.

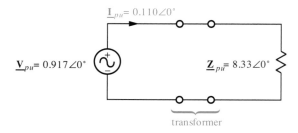

**Figure 6.27** The transformer is gone.

**WHAT IF?**

What if we used 10 kVA as the base apparent power? What would be the new bases? Would the per-unit quantities change? Would the actual quantities change?[16]

## Transmission Properties

**OBJECTIVE 6**

**To understand how the impedance of a transmission line affects power and voltage loss on the line**

**Introduction.** In this section, we investigate how the performance of a transmission system depends upon the real and reactive power passing through that system. Figure 6.28 shows a simple per-phase circuit model of a transmission system composed of a generator, a line represented by resistance and inductance, and a load. The transformers of the system are not shown because we can eliminate them either through reflecting all impedances to the transmission line part of the circuit or by using per-unit calculations. The resistance of the system will be ignored except when power loss calculations are made, and the reactance of the system consists of the inductive reactance of the transmission line and the transformers. The generator is represented by a voltage magnitude, $\underline{\mathbf{V}}_g = V_g \sqrt{2} \angle \delta$, at an angle, $\delta$, with respect to the load voltage.

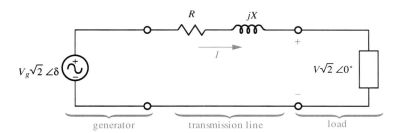

**Figure 6.28** Per-phase model of power transmission system.

generator    transmission line    load

**Analysis of the system.** In the following analysis, we assume that the load voltage, $\underline{\mathbf{V}} = V\sqrt{2} \angle 0°$, is fixed both in magnitude and angle. Thus, the current, and consequently the real and reactive power in the system, depend only on the load. We analyze the circuit to show how the rms voltage loss in the line, $\Delta V = V_g - V$, the phase angle shift, $\delta$, and the losses depend on the power flow in the system. Of course, we could perform an exact analysis, including the resistance, but we will gain adequate insight by ignoring the resistance.

Figure 6.29 shows the phasor diagram of the system. We have assumed the voltage across the impedance of the transmission system, $jX\underline{\mathbf{I}}$, to be small relative to the voltages of source and load because this is typical. If we ignore the small difference between $\underline{\mathbf{V}}_g$ and its projection on the real axis, we have

---

[16] On the primary, the new base current would be 41.7 A and base impedance 5.76 $\Omega$. On the secondary, the new base current would be 83.3 A and base impedance 1.44 $\Omega$. The per-unit quantities change to $I_{pu} = 0.132$ and $S_{pu} = 0.121$, but the actual currents and power are unchanged.

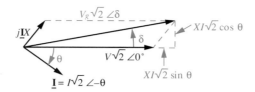

**Figure 6.29** Phasor diagram for the transmission system.

$$V_g = V + XI\sin\theta = V + \frac{XQ}{V} \tag{6.32}$$

because $Q = VI \sin\theta$. Thus, the voltage loss in the line, for fixed system reactance and load voltage, depends approximately on the reactive power flow:

$$\Delta V = \frac{X}{V} \times Q \tag{6.33}$$

**angle of transmission**

The *angle of transmission*, $\delta$, can be derived geometrically:

$$\delta = \sin^{-1}\left(\frac{XI\cos\theta}{V_g}\right) \approx \frac{XI\cos\theta}{V} = \frac{X}{V} \times P \tag{6.34}$$

because $P = VI \cos\theta$. Thus, the angle of transmission depends on the real power on the line. To find the line losses, we must include the line resistance, $R$:

$$P_{loss} = I^2R = \frac{S^2}{V^2} \times R = \frac{R}{V^2} \times P^2 + \frac{R}{V^2} \times Q^2 \tag{6.35}$$

Thus, both real and reactive power flow contribute to the loss in the transmission system.

---

| **EXAMPLE 6.10** | **Transmission line** |
|---|---|

A 345-kV (receiving end voltage) transmission line is 160 km long. The impedance/km is $0.034 + j0.32\ \Omega$/km per phase. The load requires 500 MW and 100 MVAR. At each end are 1000-MVA transformers with 0.1 per-unit reactance per phase based on the transformer voltage and apparent power rating. Find the voltage loss, $\Delta V$, the angle of transmission, and the line losses on a per-unit basis.

**SOLUTION:**
We use the line voltage and the transformer apparent power rating as bases. We need to calculate the base impedance to normalize the transmission line impedance.

$$Z_{base} = \frac{V_{base}^2}{S_{base}} = \frac{(345\,\text{kV})^2}{1000\,\text{MVA}} = 119\ \Omega \tag{6.36}$$

so the per-unit line impedance is

$$\mathbf{Z}_{pu} = \frac{\mathbf{Z}_{line}}{Z_{base}} = \frac{(0.034 + j0.32) \times 160}{119} = 0.0457 + j0.430 \qquad (6.37)$$

and hence $R_{pu} = 0.0457$ and $X_{pu} = 0.430 + 0.2$ after we add the reactance of the transformers. The per-unit powers are $P_{pu} = 500 \text{ MW}/1000 \text{ MVA} = 0.5$, and similarly $Q_{pu} = 0.1$. Thus, Eq. (6.33) gives the voltage drop to be

$$\Delta V_{pu} = \frac{X_{pu}}{V_{pu}} \times Q_{pu} = \frac{0.630}{1} \times 0.1 = 0.063 \qquad (6.38)$$

Hence, there is a 6.3% voltage drop over the transmission line. The angle of transmission is given by Eq. (6.34)

$$\delta \approx \frac{X_{pu}}{V_{pu}} \times P_{pu} = \frac{0.630}{1} \times 0.5 = 0.315 \text{ radians} = 18.1° \qquad (6.39)$$

Thus, there exists an 18.1° phase-angle shift between generator and load. Finally, the power loss is given by Eq. (6.35):

$$P_{loss(pu)} = \frac{R_{pu}}{V_{pu}^2} \times P_{pu}^2 + \frac{R_{pu}}{V_{pu}^2} \times Q_{pu}^2 \qquad (6.40)$$

$$= \frac{0.0457}{1^2} \times (0.5)^2 + \frac{0.0457}{1^2} \times (0.1)^2 = 0.0119$$

so the per-unit line loss is 1.19%, which on a base of 1000 MVA would be 11.9 MW. Thus the transmission efficiency is $(500 - 11.9)/500 = 97.6\%$.

**WHAT IF?**
What if the load were 800 MVA at a lagging power factor of 0.9? Find voltage and power loss in percent.[17]

**Power-factor correction in a transmission system.** Because the voltage and power loss in the transmission system depend on the reactive power flow, the power company has an interest in minimizing $Q$ in the system. This it does by forcing large consumers to control their power factor and by using capacitors in transmission and distribution systems. Figure 6.30(a) models a source, load, and distribution line, which includes resistance and inductance, and Fig. 6.30(b) shows capacitors added to the distribution system by the power company to improve performance. With leading current, the load voltage can be equal to or greater than the source voltage. Thus, adding capacitors to the system can reduce line power and voltage losses.

Figure 6.31(a) shows the phasor diagram for the system with 0.9 power factor, lagging current. The lagging current, combined with the inductive impedance of the line, results in a large voltage loss in the line. Figure 6.31(b) shows the phasor diagram with

---

[17] $\Delta V = 22.0\%$ and loss $= 4.06\%$.

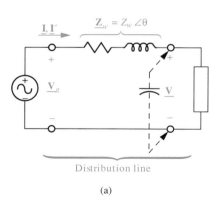

(a)                            (b)

**Figure 6.30** (a) Capacitors placed near the load improve efficiency and voltage regulation because the transmission system is inductive; (b) a 12.5-kV three-phase distribution power line with six capacitors between the lines and neutral.

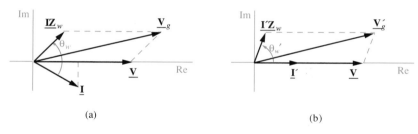

(a)                            (b)

**Figure 6.31** (a) Phasor diagram for the system with 0.9 power factor and no capacitors; (b) phasor diagram for the systems with the same load and unity power factor (with capacitors). Note that line current is smaller and $\underline{V}$ and $\underline{V}_g$ are more nearly equal in (b).

unity power factor and the same load. Here line current is smaller, and load and source voltages are more nearly equal.

### Check Your Understanding

1. If a line voltage is 0.9 per unit, what is the per-phase voltage (line-to-neutral) in per unit?

2. The base voltage is 13,200 V and the base power is 100 kVA. Find the base current and impedance.

3. If the $PF$ is 0.9 and the line loss is 1000 W, what would be the line loss if the $PF$ were corrected to unity?

*Answers.*    (1) 0.9, the $\sqrt{3}$'s go away;   (2) 7.58 A, 1742 Ω;   (3) 810 W.

**Introduction.** A large part of the load on an electric power system consists of electric motors. At home (air conditioners, hair dryer, blender), in the shop (tools, fans), in the office (printers, cooling fans for electronic devices), and of course in factories, electric motors are everywhere. Although there are many types of electric motors, at least 90% are induction motors: single-phase induction motors for small jobs and three-phase for big.

Chapters 15 to 17 present physical principles, electrical equivalent circuits, and applications of synchronous, induction, and dc motors. In this section, we give information relevant to all motors and discuss the steady-state and dynamic responses of motors. We give detailed analysis of nameplate information on three-phase and single-phase induction motors. Much practical information about a motor can be deduced from its nameplate by applying basic knowledge of ac circuits and simple mechanics.

## Terminology

**rotor, stator**

**Rotor and stator.** Figure 6.32 suggests an electrical motor. It has an electrical input of voltage and current, a mechanical output in the form of torque and rotation, and losses represented as heat. The motor consists mechanically of a *stator*, which does not rotate, a *rotor*, which can rotate, and an air gap to permit motion.

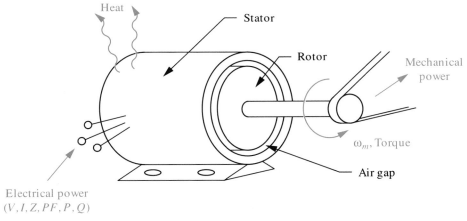

**Figure 6.32** A basic motor.

**armature, field**

**Armature and field.** Electrical force (torque) is produced by currents interacting with magnetic flux. We distinguish electrically between the *field* circuit, which produces a magnetic flux, and the *armature* circuit, which carries a current. The field usually has many turns of wire carrying relatively small currents, and the armature normally has few turns of larger wire carrying relatively large currents. Depending on the type of motor, the field might be on the rotor or stator, and the armature is always the opposite. For induction motors, the field is on the stator and the armature on the rotor.

**Types of electric motors.** Although there are many types of electric motors, we deal here with two types: the three-phase induction motor and the single-phase induction motor. After discussing certain general principles that relate to all motors, we discuss and analyze the nameplate information for both these types of motors.

## Motor Characterization in Steady-State Operation

**Electrical input.** We consider first steady-state operation, such as a fan motor turning at constant speed. The electrical quantities of interest in steady state are the input voltage, current, and the power factor. In many cases, analysis of the motor suggests an equivalent circuit that accounts for losses, energy storage, and the conversion of electrical power into mechanical power. The electrical operation depends on the mechanical load, as will be discussed presently.

**Mechanical output.** The output characteristic of a motor is the output torque, $T_M(\omega_m)$, as a function of rotation speed, $\omega_m$. The operating speed of the motor is jointly determined by the output torque characteristic of the motor and the torque requirement of the load.

**Basic equations for three-phase motor.** The input electrical power is

$$P_{in} = \sqrt{3}VI \times PF \qquad (6.41)$$

and the output mechanical power is

$$P_{out} = \omega_m \times T_M \qquad (6.42)$$

where $\omega_m$ is the mechanical speed in radians/second and $T_M$ is the output torque in newton-meters. Two other quantities of interest are the losses, $P_{loss}$, and the efficiency, $\eta$:

$$P_{loss} = P_{in} - P_{out} \text{ and } \eta = \frac{P_{out}}{P_{in}} \qquad (6.43)$$

**Basic equations for single-phase motors.** Equations (6.41) through (6.43) are also valid for single phase motors except that the input power equation lacks the $\sqrt{3}$ for single phase.

---

**EXAMPLE 6.11** | **Single-phase motor**

Consider a 60-Hz, single-phase induction motor with the following nameplate information: [18] 1 hp, 1725 rpm, 115 V, 14.4 A, efficiency = 68%. Find the output torque, the power factor, and the cost of operating the motor if electric power costs 9.6 cents/kWh.

**SOLUTION:**
The output power is 1 hp × 746 W/hp = 746 W, so the input power is, from Eq. (6.43),

$$P_{in} = \frac{P_{out}}{\eta} = \frac{746}{0.68} = 1097 \text{ watts} \qquad (6.44)$$

---

[18] We will discuss nameplate information presently. For now, assume that the actual operation of the motor is given by the nameplate information.

The power factor follows from Eq. (6.41) without the $\sqrt{3}$ :

$$PF = \frac{P_{in}}{VI} = \frac{1097}{115 \times 14.4} = 0.662 \qquad (6.45)$$

and the current is lagging for this type of motor. The output torque is

$$T_{out} = \frac{P_{out}}{\omega_m} = \frac{746}{1725\,(2\pi/60)} = 4.13 \text{ N-m} \qquad (6.46)$$

where the mechanical speed in rpm has been converted to radians/second. For continuous operation and nameplate conditions, the cost would be

$$\frac{1097 \text{ W}}{1000 \text{ W/kW}} \times \frac{24 \text{ hours}}{1 \text{ day}} \times \frac{9.6 \text{ cents}}{1 \text{ kWh}} \times \frac{1 \text{ dollar}}{100 \text{ cents}} = \$\ 2.53/\text{day} \qquad (6.47)$$

**WHAT IF?**    What if the motor is running without a load?[19]

## The Motor with a Load

OBJECTIVE 1

**To understand how motor and load interact to establish steady-state operation**

**Typical motor and load characteristics.** Figure 6.33 shows the diverse torque characteristics that can be achieved for several types of electrical motors. Even within a specific motor type, the designer can tailor the motor characteristics within broad limits. Figure 6.34 shows representative torque requirements for various mechanical loads.

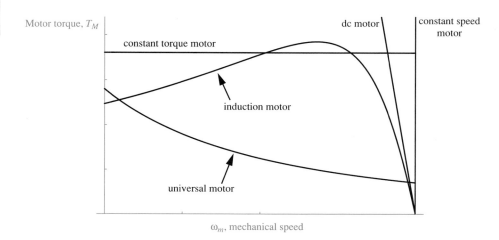

**Figure 6.33**    Motor torque characteristics.

---

[19] All we know in that case is that $P_{out} = 0$ and $T_M = 0$. But the cost would not be zero due to losses of the motor.

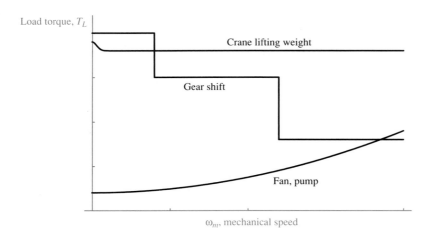

Load torque, $T_L$

Crane lifting weight

Gear shift

Fan, pump

$\omega_m$, mechanical speed

**Figure 6.34**   Load characteristics.

**blocked–rotor torque, breakover torque**

**Motor–load interaction.**    System operation is jointly determined by load require-ments, $T_L(\omega_m)$, and motor characteristics, $T_M(\omega_m)$. Consider, for example, connecting a three-phase induction motor to a fan starting from rest, as shown in Fig. 6.35. We have identified the motor-starting torque, often called the *blocked-*or *locked-rotor torque*, the maximum torque, often called the *breakover torque*, and the no-load speed. For rota-tion to occur, the starting torque of the motor must exceed the starting-torque require-ment of the load. The excess torque, $\Delta T(\omega_m) = T_M - T_L$, will accelerate the system to the speed where the two characteristics cross, which would be the steady-state speed of the motor–load system. This condition, $T_M = T_L$, determines the steady-state speed of the system. Thus, the speed, output torque, and output power of the motor depend in part on the load requirements. If, for example, the load required less torque, the motor would run slightly faster and supply less power.

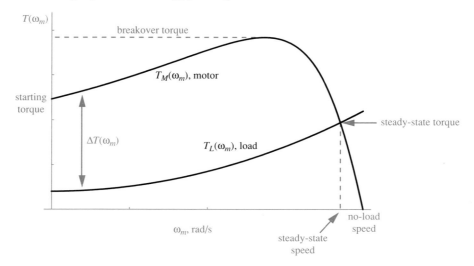

$T(\omega_m)$

breakover torque

$T_M(\omega_m)$, motor

starting torque

$\Delta T(\omega_m)$

$T_L(\omega_m)$, load

steady-state torque

$\omega_m$, rad/s

no-load speed

steady-state speed

**Figure 6.35**   Motor and load characteristics.  The load is accelerated by the excess torque, $\Delta T$.

## Dynamic Operation

**runup time**

In addition to steady-state operation, we are also interested in transient, or dynamic, operation. For example, we may need to predict the starting current and the time required to reach the steady-state speed, which is called the *runup time*. In dynamic operation, the rotor and load moments of inertia become factors, and energy processes are more complicated than for steady-state operation.

**Runup time.** We can calculate the time required to reach steady-state speed by integrating the equation of motion. In general, for a rotational system,

$$J\frac{d\omega_m}{dt} = T_M - T_L = \Delta T(\omega_m) \tag{6.48}$$

where $\omega_m$ represents mechanical rotation speed in radians/second, $J$ the combined moment of inertia of motor and load, $T_M$ the motor output torque, and $T_L$ the load torque requirement. We may integrate Eq. (6.48) from zero time, when the motor is stopped, to the runup time, $t_{ru}$, when the motor reaches the steady-state speed:

$$t_{ru} = \int_0^{\omega_{ss}} \frac{J\,d\omega_m}{\Delta T(\omega_m)} \approx \sum \frac{J\Delta\omega_m}{\Delta T(\omega_i)} \tag{6.49}$$

where $\omega_{ss}$ is the steady-state speed. We may approximate the runup time as indicated by the second form of Eq. (6.49) and illustrated in Fig. 6.36.

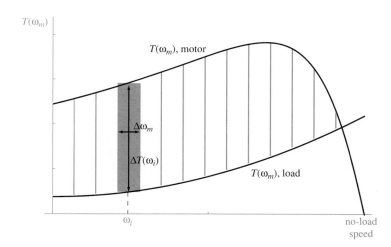

**Figure 6.36** Runup time calculation.

---

| EXAMPLE 6.12 | **Runup calculation** |
|---|---|

Consider a motor with a constant output torque of 5 N-m, driving a load requiring a torque proportional to speed. The steady-state speed is 800 rpm, and the combined moment of inertia of motor and load is 0.02 kg-m². Find the time required to reach equilibrium speed, starting from standstill.

**SOLUTION:**
The load requirement would be $T = C\omega_m$, where $C$ is a constant to be determined. The equilibrium speed would be $\omega_{ss} = 800 \times 2\pi/60 = 83.8$ rad/s; hence, the constant is

$$T_M - T_L = 0 \quad \Rightarrow \quad 5 = C \times 83.8 \quad \Rightarrow \quad C = 0.0597 \text{ N-m/(rad/s)} \tag{6.50}$$

By Eq. (6.49), the runup time is

$$t_{ru} = 0.02 \int_0^{83.8} \frac{d\omega_m}{5 - 0.0597\omega_m}$$

$$\tag{6.51}$$

$$= \frac{0.02}{-0.0597} \ln{(5 - 0.0597\omega_m)}\Big|_0^{83.8}$$

Equation (6.51) leads to an infinite result at the upper limit. The difficulty is that the system speed approaches steady state asymptotically, so theoretically it never reaches equilibrium.[20] One way to approximate the runup speed is to assume a "final" speed slightly below the steady-state speed. For Eq. (6.51), changing the upper limit to 98% of the steady-state speed gives a runup time of 1.311 s.

**WHAT IF?**

What if we define the final speed as 99.5% of final speed? What would be the runup time?[21]

**Summary.** In this section, we discussed some fundamentals that apply to all motors. We presented equations relating to the input electrical variables and the output mechanical variables. We discussed how the output-torque characteristic of the motor interacts with the torque requirement of the load to establish the steady-state speed, torque, and power in the motor–load system.

In the next sections, we present and interpret the nameplate information for a three-phase induction motor and a single-phase induction motor, with most of the emphasis on the former. These motors account for the vast majority of motor applications. Our purpose is to give sufficient information to analyze nameplate information. The details of motor models and operational characteristics for these and other electric motors are given in Chapters 15 to 17.

**OBJECTIVE 8**

To understand how to analyze and interpret nameplate information of induction motors

## Three-Phase Induction Motor Nameplate Interpretation

**Induction motor principle.** In an induction motor, the field windings are on the stator. The currents in the field windings set up a rotating magnetic flux, which in turn induces voltage in the rotor. The voltage in the rotor drives currents that interact with

---

[20] Of course, a real motor does reach equilibrium. Our linear *model* leads here to a mathematical problem.
[21] 1.78 seconds

the flux to produce torque. Because the relative motion between the rotating flux and the rotor conductors produce the voltage, the rotor will always turn slower than the flux rotates. The induction motor works like a fluid clutch or automatic transmission. Instead of fluid, the working medium is magnetic flux.

**Nameplate information.**  Three-phase induction motors are available from one-third horsepower to thousands of horsepower. The nameplate of a specific 60-Hz three-phase induction motor includes the following information:

- 50 horsepower
- Three phases
- 1765 rpm
- NEMA 326T frame
- 208-230/460 V
- 140-122/61 A
- Time rating: continuous

- Insulation class: F
- 1.15 service factor
- Maximum ambient temperature: 40°C
- NEMA code: G
- NEMA design: B
- NEMA nominal efficiency: 92.4%
- NEMA minimum efficiency: 91.0 %

The motor nameplate also might give the motor type: Dripproof, Totally Enclosed Fan Cooled (TEFC), explosion proof, etc.

**service factor**

**Power rating.**  The *power rating*[22] of this motor is 50 hp. This is a nominal rating and does not mean that the motor will put out 50 hp on all, or possibly on any, occasions. The actual power out of the motor depends on the load demands, as explained earlier. Nor is 50 hp the maximum power of the motor. The maximum power that the motor can put out on a continuous basis is the nameplate power times the service factor, 50 hp × 1.15 = 57.5 hp in this case. Thus, the *service factor* is something of a "safety factor," the 50-hp rating is, as we said before, the nominal power rating of the motor.

The nameplate power is significant in the following sense: *If* the motor is supplied with rated voltage, 460 V, and *if* the load demands exactly 50 hp, *then* the motor speed will be 1765 rpm *and* the input current will be 61.0 A.

**Motor speed.**  The nameplate *speed* is 1765 rpm, and the significance of this speed is given in the preceding paragraph. With a power frequency of 60 Hz, induction motors run slightly below the standard speeds of 3600, 1800, and 1200 rpm, for reasons that are discussed in Chapter 15. If this motor is unloaded, the motor speed will be approximately 1800 rpm.

**Motor output torque.**  The nameplate torque, $T_{NP}$, is not given but may be deduced from the output power and speed. Equation (6.42) yields

$$T_{NP} = \frac{P_{out}}{\omega_m} = \frac{50 \times 746}{1765 \times (2\pi/60)} = 202 \text{ N-m} \tag{6.52}$$

where we changed horsepower to watts and rpm to radians/second to make the units consistent. Again we stress that this is the nameplate torque; we do not know the actual torque unless we know what the load demands.

---

[22] The nameplate terms will be in bold italics in the following discussion, for easy reference.

**Torque vs. speed.** In the normal operating range, the output torque of a three-phase induction motor is approximately a straight line between zero torque at the no-load speed, $\omega_{NL}$, and nameplate torque at nameplate speed, as shown in Fig. 6.37. Thus, the torque equation is of the form

$$T(\omega_m) = \text{slope} \times (\omega_m - \omega_{NL}) \tag{6.53}$$

where the slope is $T_{NP}/(\omega_{NP} - \omega_{NL})$. Thus, the torque as a function of speed in the normal operating region is

$$T(\omega_m \text{ or } n) = T_{NP}\left(\frac{\omega_{NL} - \omega_m}{\omega_{NL} - \omega_{NP}}\right) = 202\left(\frac{1800 - n}{1800 - 1765}\right) \tag{6.54}$$

where we expressed speed in both rpm and rad/s.

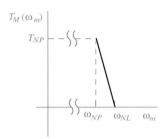

**Figure 6.37** The torque characteristic is a straight line between nameplate and no-load conditions.

---

**EXAMPLE 6.13** **Pump load**

The 50-hp motor with the torque given by Eq. (6.54) drives a pump with a torque requirement of

$$T_L = 1.2 + 100\left(\frac{n}{1800}\right)^2 \quad \text{N-m} \tag{6.55}$$

Find the speed at which the motor–pump operates and the power required by the pump.

**SOLUTION:**
The motor–pump will operate where the motor output matches the pump demand.

$$1.2 + 100\left(\frac{n}{1800}\right)^2 = 202\left(\frac{1800 - n}{1800 - 1765}\right) \tag{6.56}$$

which is a quadratic equation yielding $n = 1783$ rpm and $-188{,}598$ rpm. Clearly, the second answer represents the analytic extension of both motor and pump characteristics into regions where their models are invalid; the correct answer is 1783 rpm. The power is the speed in rad/s times the torque, which we can get from either motor or pump:

$$P_{out} = \omega_m T_M (\text{or } \omega_m T_L) \tag{6.57}$$

$$= 1783\,(2\pi/60)\left[1.2 + 100\left(\frac{1783}{1800}\right)^2\right] = 18{,}540 \text{ watts}$$

which is slightly less than 25 hp.

**WHAT IF?**

What if the pump torque required $T_L = 100 + n/18$ N-m?[23]

**NEMA frame 326T.** NEMA is an acronym for the National Electrical Manufacturers Association, an industry association that has standardized many aspects of electrical power equipment. In this case, the mechanical dimensions of motors are standardized; for example, the motor output shaft diameter is $2\frac{1}{8}$ inches and is centered 8 inches above the base of all motors built on a **NEMA 326T frame**.

**Voltage and current ratings.** The motor **voltage rating** is 208–230/460 V and the **current rating** is 140–122/61 A. We set aside the 208-V/140-A rating for a moment and concentrate on the 230/460-V rating. This reveals that each phase of the motor has multiple windings that can be connected in series or parallel. Figure 6.38(a) shows one phase of the high-voltage (460 V)/low-current (61 A) series connection, and Fig. 6.38(b) shows the low-voltage (230 V)/high-current (122 A) parallel connection. As you can see, the individual windings get the same voltage and current for both connections and the motor performance would be unchanged if indeed the voltage were exactly 230 or 460 volts. In practice, the series connection is preferred if 460-V three-phase power is available because the lower current requires smaller wire to supply the motor. Put another way, the impedance level of the motor is four times higher and the output impedance requirements of the power system are less demanding with the high-voltage/low-current connection.

**Impedance Level**

**The 208-V rating.** The 208-V rating tells us the lowest voltage the motor should be supplied, and the current for 50 hp would be 140 A. First of all, $208 = 120\sqrt{3}$, so 208-V systems exist as 120-V three-phase connected in wye. But more common is low

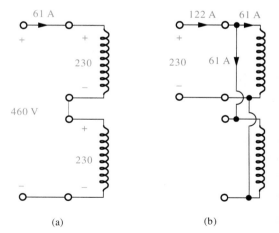

(a)

(b)

**Figure 6.38** (a) A series connection for high voltage and low current; (b) a parallel connection for low voltage and high current.

---

[23] $n = 1766$ rpm and power $= 49$ hp.

voltage due to older standards or long connecting wire, say, with pumps scattered around an oil field. Low voltage is dangerous to the motor because motors tend to overheat when the voltage is low, as explained in what follows, and heat shortens the motor lifetime.

**Constant impedance or constant power?** Up to this point, we have spoken of impedance as if it were constant, and this is true for many circuit elements. But a motor tends to take constant power from the electrical system and hence does not offer constant impedance. To see the difference, examine the contrast in Eq. (6.58):

$$Z = \frac{V}{I} = \frac{(\downarrow)}{(\downarrow)} \text{ but } P = \sqrt{3}VI \times PF = \sqrt{3}(\downarrow)(\uparrow) \times PF \tag{6.58}$$

For constant impedance, the current goes down when the voltage goes down. This is the characteristic of resistors, inductors, capacitors, and many other devices as well. But for constant power, the current goes *up* when the voltage goes down provided the power factor does not change. This is how a motor behaves because the power of the motor depends largely on load demands.

**Impedance Level**

Thus, low voltage forces a high current, even if the voltage source is ideal. In practice, the high current lowers the voltage further due to the output impedance of the power system. Thus, when you use a portable electric tool such as a chain saw or lawn mower, the manufacturer will warn you to use only 100 feet of extension cord: too long a cord produces low voltage, which produces higher current, which produces even lower voltage, etc. Because the resistive losses of the motor increase with the square of the current, the motor can rapidly overheat if the extension cord is too long.

---

**EXAMPLE 6.14** | **Long extension cord**

A saws-all electric saw is rated at 120 V, 8 A single phase. The saw is used with 100 ft of 16/3[24] extension cord. How much do the motor losses increase as a result of the extension cord?

**SOLUTION:**
The resistance for No. 16 wire is 4.02 Ω/1000 ft, and we have 200 feet of wire considering both conductors. Thus, the nominal 8 A of current causes a voltage drop of

$$\Delta V \approx \frac{4.02 \ \Omega}{1000 \ \text{ft}} \times 200 \ \text{ft} \times 8 \ \text{A} = 6.4 \ \text{V} \tag{6.59}$$

and hence the voltage at the saw is about 113.6 V, assuming 120 V for the supply. Because the saw requires constant power, this loss in voltage causes a further increase in current to

$$\Delta I \approx 8 \ \text{A} \times \frac{120}{113.6} = 8.45 \ \text{A} \tag{6.60}$$

which will cause a further decrease in voltage, but we will ignore further effects. The increase

---

[24] 16/3 = No. 16 power wires with a ground.

in motor loss will be

$$\Delta \text{loss} \approx \left(\frac{8.45}{8}\right)^2 = 1.116, \text{ or a } 11.6\% \text{ increase} \tag{6.61}$$

**WHAT IF?**   What if 150 ft of extension cord is used?[25]

**Thermal specifications.**   The *time rating* is continuous operation. The *insulation class* of F tells us that the maximum temperature of the insulation should not exceed 155°C. The importance of the *ambient temperature* of 40°C is self-evident. These specifications remind us again that the motor lifetime depends on the thermal environment affecting the temperature of its windings.

**NEMA code G.**   The *NEMA code* tells us the starting-current requirements of the motor. NEMA classifies motors according to locked rotor (starting) kVA, and code G means 5.60 to 6.29 kVA/hp. Hence, for this motor, the starting current lies between 609 and 684 A with the 460-V connection, and twice these values for the 230-V connection. Because of these large currents, large induction motors are frequently started with reduced voltage and the voltage is increased as the motor speed increases.

**NEMA design B.**   All three-phase induction motors have similar characteristics, but motors may be tailored somewhat for specific properties:

- Design A has high run efficiency, high breakover torque, with moderate starting torque and high starting current.
- Design B has moderate run efficiency, moderate starting torque with low starting current, and has moderate breakover torque.
- Design C is similar to design B but has higher starting torque and is more expensive.
- Design D has relatively low run efficiency, extremely high starting torque which is also the breakover torque, and low starting current.

Our motor is *design B*, which is the general-purpose motor.

**Efficiency.**   The nameplate gives a nominal (92.4%) and minimum (91.0%) *efficiency*. The nominal is what one would expect on an average, and we assume this value to calculate the nameplate input power from Eq. (6.43):

$$P_{in} = \frac{P_{out}}{\eta} = \frac{50 \times 746}{0.924} = 40,370 \text{ W} \tag{6.62}$$

and the input electrical power allows us to calculate the nameplate power factor from Eq. (6.41):

---

[25] The losses increase by 18.3%.

$$PF = \frac{P_{in}}{S} = \frac{40,370 \text{ W}}{48,600 \text{ VA}} = 0.831 \qquad (6.63)$$

where $S = \sqrt{3}\, VI = \sqrt{3} \times 460 \times 61 = 48,600$ VA is the nameplate VA rating of the machine. We also calculate the nameplate reactive power required by the motor:

$$Q_{in} = \pm \sqrt{S^2 - P_{in}^2} = + \sqrt{(48.6)^2 - (40.4)^2} = +27.0 \text{ kVAR} \qquad (6.64)$$

where the positive sign is used because an induction motor has lagging current.

The motor is designed to have maximum efficiency at nameplate conditions and hence the efficiency will be fairly constant in the vicinity of nameplate operation. However, the efficiency falls as the motor is lightly loaded.

**Summary.** We discussed the nameplate information for a three-phase induction motor. From the nameplate information, we deduced nameplate torque, the torque–speed characteristic, power factor, and reactive power. We stress again that the actual motor conditions depend on the load demands.

## Single-Phase Induction Motor

**Nameplate information.** Single-phase induction motors come in many varieties and sizes; we now discuss the type of single-phase motor used to power farm machinery, stationary shop tools, compressors, and the like.[26] Such induction motors are made in sizes from one-fourth horsepower to 10 horsepower and are used where three-phase power is unavailable. The nameplate information on one motor is as follows:

- Phase 1
- Frame L56
- Hz 60
- Volts 115
- 40°C
- SF 1.35
- Type CS
- HP 1/3
- RPM 1725
- Amps 5.8
- Insulation class A

We now discuss the nameplate information that is not self-evident.

**Type CS.** Single-phase induction motors come in three types, CS, SP, and CR:

- CS: A capacitor-start/induction-run motor has high starting torque and moderate run efficiency.
- SP: A split-phase motor has low starting torque and moderate run efficiency.
- CR: A capacitor-start/capacitor-run motor has high starting torque and high run efficiency, and is more expensive.

**RPM 1725.** This is self-evident. However, we should mention that the no-load speed of this motor would not be 1800, as for a three-phase motor, but would be somewhere around 1780–1790 rpm. Thus, we cannot derive the torque–speed characteristics

---

[26] Small fans, hand-held tools, and household appliances use other types of single-phase motors.

without measuring the no-load speed. Once we know the no-load speed, we can derive the torque-speed characteristic as for a three-phase motor.

**Other specifications.** The remainder of the specifications are similar to those for three-phase motors. Torque can be calculated from power and speed. Efficiency is not normally given, so losses and power factor cannot be calculated from the nameplate information.

### Check Your Understanding

1. In a motor the field current is usually larger than the armature current. True or false?

2. The output torque of a motor in operation depends in part on the load requirements. True or false?

3. The product of the power factor and the efficiency of an ac motor is always equal to the output mechanical power divided by the input electrical apparent power. True or false?

*Answers:* **(1)** False; **(2)** true; **(3)** true.

## CHAPTER SUMMARY

Chapter 6 introduces electric power distribution and utilization in electrical motors. Three-phase circuits investigated. The per-phase model is developed and per-unit normalization is defined and illustrated. System aspects of electric motors are discussed, and the analysis of the nameplate information for three- and single-phase electric motors is illustrated.

**Objective 1: To understand the nature and advantages of three-phase power.** The three-phase system is described in the time and frequency domains. The advantages include efficiency of distribution, smoothness of power flow, and characteristics in starting and operating induction motors.

**Objectives 2 and 3: To understand how to analyze a generator or load in wye or delta connection.** We derive the phase and amplitude relationships between line voltage, line current, and power and phase voltage, phase current, and power for both wye and delta connections. We show that three-phase power depends only on line voltage, current, and power factor and not on the load or source connections.

**Objective 4: To understand how to derive and use the per-phase equivalent circuit of a balanced three-phase load.** The per-phase equivalent circuit is a single-phase circuit that models the state of a balanced three-phase circuit. The per-phase current and power factor are the same as the three-phase line current and power factor, but the per-phase voltage is equal to the line-to-neutral voltage of the three-phase system. The per-phase power is one-third the three-phase power. The per-phase equivalent circuit is independent of the actual connection of the three-phase load or source.

**Objective 5: To understand how to connect single-phase transformers for three-phase transformation.** Three-phase power may be transformed either by one three-phase transformer or by three single-phase transformers. Connecting primaries and secondaries in wye or delta gives four possible connections, each having different voltage and current ratios and different advantages and disadvantages.

**Objective 6: To understand how transmission-line impedance affects power and voltage loss on the line.** Transmission of electrical power over large distances involves significant effects of line impedance. An approximate analysis shows the effect of line inductance on power angle and power magnitude. We introduce the definitions and advantages of the per-unit system of normalization.

**Objective 7: To understand how motor and load interact to establish steady-state operation.** We examine dynamic and steady-state interactions of motors with their loads. Motor power and speed depend on load demands.

**Objective 8: To understand how to analyze and interpret nameplate information of induction motors.** Nameplate information gives a benchmark for comparing motors. The nameplate directly or indirectly gives power, speed, torque, voltage, current, efficiency, and other information. The dangers of operating a motor at low voltage are illustrated.

Chapter 6 concludes the section on basic circuits with applications primarily in electric power engineering. Chapter 7 begins the section on electronics, in which electrical energy is used to symbolize information.

## PROBLEMS

## Section 6.1: Three-Phase Power

**6.1.** Pick two values of $\omega t$ in Eq. (6.2) and show by direct calculation that the time-varying terms cancel.

**6.2.** For Fig. 6.6(a), develop a delta connection by first connecting $A$ to $B'$. Draw a phasor diagram of the resulting system. Is the phase rotation $ABC$ or $ACB$?

**6.3.** Three 230-V (rms) generators are connected in a three-phase wye configuration to generate three-phase power. The load consists of three balanced impedances, $\mathbf{Z}_L = 2.6 + j1.8\ \Omega$, connected in delta.
  (a) Find the line current an ammeter would measure.
  (b) Find the apparent power.
  (c) Find the real power to the load.
  (d) What is the phase angle between $\mathbf{I}_A$ and $\mathbf{V}_{AB}$, assuming $ABC$ rotation?

**6.4.** For the three-phase power system shown in Fig. P6.4, a voltmeter measures 146 V between line $A$ and the neutral $N$. Find the following:
  (a) Line voltage.
  (b) Line current.
  (c) Load power factor.
  (d) Apparent power.
  (e) Real power.

**6.5.** In Fig. P6.5, the voltage between $A$ and $N$ is 120 V

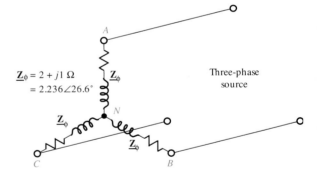

$\mathbf{Z}_\phi = 2 + j1\ \Omega$
$= 2.236\angle 26.6°$

Three-phase source

**Figure P6.4**

as measured by a standard meter. Let this voltage be the phase reference. The phase impedance is $\mathbf{Z}_\phi = 6.2 + j2.7 = 6.76\ \angle\ 23.5°\ \Omega$.
  (a) What is $\mathbf{V}_{AB}$ as a phasor?
  (b) What would an ammeter measure as the line current?
  (c) What is the apparent power?
  (d) What is the real power?

**6.6.** Figure P6.6 shows a three-phase source and load.
  (a) Draw appropriate connections.

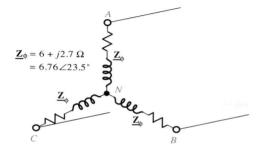

$$\underline{Z}_\phi = 6 + j2.7\ \Omega$$
$$= 6.76\angle 23.5°$$

**Figure P6.5**

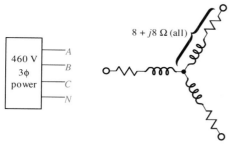

$8 + j8\ \Omega\ (\text{all})$

460 V
3ϕ
power

**Figure P6.6**

**(b)** Find the phase voltage.
**(c)** Find the line current.
**(d)** Determine the power factor.
**(e)** What is the power in the load?
**(f)** Assuming $\underline{V}_{AB} = 460\sqrt{2}\angle 0°$, find $\underline{I}_A$ as a phasor.

**6.7.** For the three-phase delta-connected load in Fig. P6.7, we have the line voltage and current to be $\underline{V}_{AB} = 480\sqrt{2}\angle 0°$ V and $\underline{I}_A = 10\sqrt{2}\angle -30$ A.
**(a)** What is $\underline{V}_{CA}$?
**(b)** What is the phase current in the load, rms value?
**(c)** What is the time-average power into the load?
**(d)** What is the phase impedance?

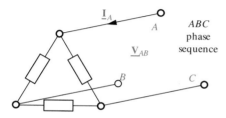

$\underline{I}_A$

$A$  ABC
phase
$\underline{V}_{AB}$  sequence

$B$  $C$

**Figure P6.7**

**6.8.** Three 230-V rms generators are connected in delta to form a three-phase source. A balanced wye-connected load has phase impedances of $12 + j7\ \Omega$. Find the rms values of the following:
**(a)** The phase voltage of the source.
**(b)** The line voltage of the system.
**(c)** The phase voltage of the load.
**(d)** The phase current of the load.
**(e)** The line current of the system.
**(f)** The phase current of the source.
**(g)** What is the power factor of the load?
**(h)** What is the real power to the load?

**6.9.** In the three-phase circuit shown in Fig. P6.9, find the following:
**(a)** The line current that would be measured by an ammeter.
**(b)** The power factor of the three-phase load.
**(c)** The voltage that would be measured between $B$ and $D$ by a voltmeter.

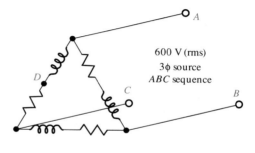

600 V (rms)
3ϕ source
$ABC$ sequence

All $\underline{Z}$'s = $20 + j11\ \Omega$

**Figure P6.9**

**6.10.** In the three-phase circuit shown in Fig. P6.10, find the following:
**(a)** The line current that would be measured by an ammeter.
**(b)** The power factor of the three-phase load.
**(c)** The voltage that would be measured between $B$ and $D$ by a voltmeter.

**6.11.** For the three-phase circuit connected in delta shown in Fig. P6.11, find the following:
**(a)** The load power factor. Assume lagging.
**(b)** The line current, rms.
**(c)** The magnitude of the phase impedance.
**(d)** The reactive power to each phase impedance.

**6.12.** For the three-phase circuit connected in delta shown in Fig. P6.12, find the following:

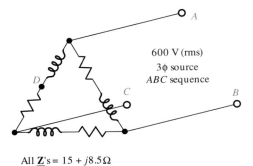

600 V (rms)
3φ source
$ABC$ sequence

All $\underline{Z}$'s = 15 + j8.5Ω

**Figure P6.10**

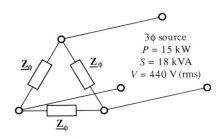

3φ source
P = 15 kW
S = 18 kVA
V = 440 V (rms)

**Figure P6.11**

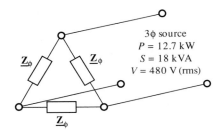

3φ source
P = 12.7 kW
S = 18 kVA
V = 480 V (rms)

**Figure P6.12**

(a) The load power factor. Assume lagging.
(b) The line current, rms.
(c) The magnitude of the phase impedance.
(d) The reactive power to each phase impedance.

6.13. For the three-phase system shown in Fig. P6.13, find the following:
(a) Phase voltage.
(b) Line voltage.
(c) Phase current.
(d) Line current.
(e) Phase impedance.
(f) Apparent power.
(g) Power factor.
(h) Real power to the load.

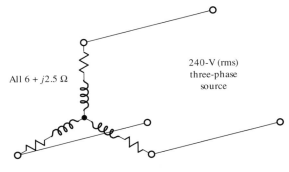

All 6 + j2.5 Ω

240-V (rms)
three-phase
source

**Figure P6.13**

6.14. A balanced, wye-connected three-phase load is shown in Fig. P6.14. The current in line $A$ is $\mathbf{I}_A = 8\sqrt{2} \angle 0°$ A. The voltage from $B$ to the neutral point is $\mathbf{V}_{BN} = 120\sqrt{2} \angle -90°$ V.
(a) Find the three-phase voltage that a voltmeter would read.
(b) Find the real and reactive power into the entire three-phase load.
(c) Determine $R$ and $L$, assuming 60-Hz operation.

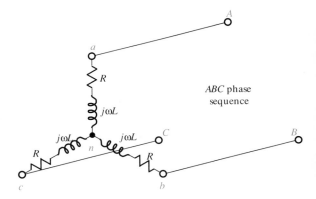

$ABC$ phase
sequence

**Figure P6.14**

6.15. Demonstrate the equivalence of the delta and wye circuits in Fig. 6.18. Assume an impedance $\mathbf{Z}_\Delta \angle \theta$ for the delta and an impedance $\mathbf{Z}_Y \angle \theta$ for the wye and compute the complex power for each. Equate these powers and confirm the 3:1 ratio shown in Fig. 6.18.

6.16. Three identical resistors are placed in a wye configuration and draw a total of 150 W from a three-phase source. What power would the same resistors draw if placed in delta?

**6.17.** For the three-phase circuit shown in Fig. P6.17, the 0.1-Ω resistors represent the resistance of the distribution system. Find the following:
  (a) Total power out of the source, including line and load.
  (b) Line losses.
  (c) Distribution system efficiency.

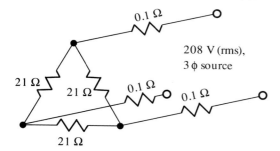

208 V (rms), 3 φ source

**Figure P6.17**

**6.18.** Using delta–wye transformations, determine the total power given to the delta and wye loads in Fig. P6.18, not counting the losses in the 0.1-Ω resistors that represent losses in the connecting wires. *Hint:* The neutrals of two balanced wye loads have the same voltage and hence may be considered as connected.

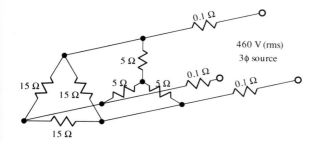

460 V (rms) 3φ source

**Figure P6.18**

**6.19.** The city of Austin, Texas, distributes power with a three-phase system with 12.5 kV between the power-carrying wires. But each group of houses is served from one phase and ground, and transformed to 240/120 V by a pole transformer, as shown in Fig. P6.19.
  (a) What is the turns ratio (primary/secondary turns), of the pole transformer to give 240 V, center-tapped?
  (b) When a 1500-W hair dryer is turned on, how

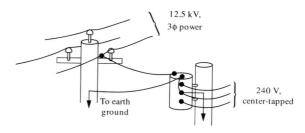

12.5 kV, 3φ power

To earth ground

240 V, center-tapped

**Figure P6.19**

much does the current increase in the high-voltage wire? Assume the power factor is unity and the transformer is 100% efficient.

**6.20.** A workman finds a three-phase cable with four wires. He labels the wires 1, 2, 3, and 4 and measures the following voltages: $V_{12} = 150$ V and $V_{23} = 260$ V. What are $V_{13}$ and $V_{34}$?

In the text, we showed how to transform three-phase power with the use of three single-phase transformers. There are two ways to transform three-phase power with *two* single-phase transformers. The next two problems investigate these methods. In them, we will transform 460 V three phase to 230 V three phase; hence, the transformers have a turns ratio of 2:1. *Hint:* In both figures, the geometric orientation hints of the phasor relationships.

**6.21.** The configuration shown in Fig. P6.21 is called the "open-delta" or V connection, for obvious reasons. Identical 2:1 transformers are used.
  (a) Show that if *ABC* is balanced 460-V three-phase, *abc* is 230-V balanced three phase. Consider the *ABC* voltages to be a three-phase set and prove the *abc* set is three-phase.
  (b) If the load is 30 kVA, find the required kVA rating of the transformers to avoid overload. [You can solve this independent of part (a).]

**6.22.** The circuit shown in Fig. P6.22 is called the T connection. For this connection, the 2:1 transformers are not identical but have different voltage and kVA ratings. The bottom transformer is center-tapped so as to have equal, in-phase voltages for each half.
  (a) Find the voltages $V_1$ and $V_2$ to make this transform 460-V to 230-V three-phase.
  (b) If the load is 30 kVA, find the required rating of each transformer to avoid overload.

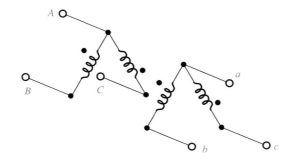

**Figure P6.21**   The *V* or open-delta transformer connection.

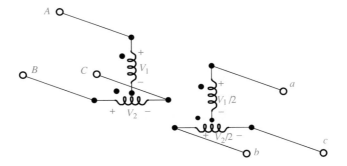

**Figure P6.22**   The *T*-transformer connection.

## Section 6.2: Power Distribution Systems

**6.23.** A wye-connected, balanced, three-phase load has a three-phase voltage of 480 V and requires a kVA of 20 kV at a *PF* of 0.94, lagging.

    **(a)** What is the per-phase, per-unit equivalent of the load, using the three-phase voltage and 42 kVA for bases?

    **(b)** What if the load is in delta?

**6.24.** A 500-MVA, 22-kV ac generator is represented on a per-phase equivalent circuit as an ideal ac voltage source in series with an inductive reactance. The internal reactance is Y-connected, 1.1 per unit. Find the actual reactances that are connected in Y.

**6.25.** A 12/138-kV, 50-MVA three-phase transformer has a per-phase inductive reactance of $j0.005\ \Omega$, referred to the primary side. Find the per-unit reactance for the transformer and give a per-unit, per-phase equivalent circuit for the transformer.

**6.26.** A transmission line has an impedance of $100 + j500\ \Omega$, including both wires. The $3\phi$

voltage at the generator output is 22 kV. The voltage is stepped up to 345 kV in a Δ–Y transformer connection, sent over a transmission line, and then stepped down to a nominal 23 kV with a Y–Δ transformer connection. The load is 30 MW at a lagging *PF* of 0.92.

    **(a)** Give a per-phase equivalent circuit showing the per-phase voltage and current on the line.

    **(b)** Find the approximate per-unit voltage loss. Ignore the transformer inductance.

    **(c)** Find the approximate per-unit power loss.

**6.27.** The circuit shown in Fig. P6.27 represents a 60-Hz power distribution system. The distribution voltage is 8 kV and the load is 20 houses, each requiring on the average 12 kW at 0.95 *PF*, lagging. The line impedance is shown. Assume an ideal transformer.

    **(a)** What would be the magnitude of the current in the primary of the transformer?

    **(b)** What are the line power losses?

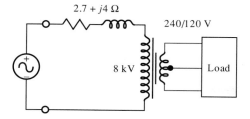

**Figure P6.27**

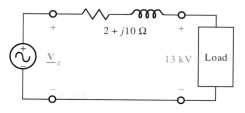

**Figure P6.28**

**(c)** What value of capacitor across the transformer primary minimizes line losses? Consider that the load voltage is constant.

**(d)** What are the line power losses with the corrected *PF*?

6.28. The circuit in Fig. P6.28 shows a load that requires 500 kVA at a lagging *PF* of 0.84, a voltage of 13 kV (maintained constant), and frequency of 60 Hz. The $2 + j10 \, \Omega$ represents the impedance of the distribution line. Making no approximations, you are to calculate the line losses and voltage difference between load and source voltage under two conditions:

**(a)** The circuit as shown.

**(b)** The circuit with a capacitor at the load to correct the power factor to unity with the same real power. Also determine the value of the required capacitor.

6.29. A 138-kV overhead line has a series resistance and inductive reactance of 0.16 and 0.41 $\Omega$/km, respectively. Find the magnitude of the voltage required at the sending end of the line for 138 kV at the receiving end if the line is 80 km long. The apparent power on the line is 12.5 MVA at 0.95 *PF*, lagging.

## Section 6.3: Introduction to Electric Motors

6.30. A motor has the output torque characteristic shown in Fig. P6.30. The load torque characteristic is

$$T_L(n) = 10 \left(\frac{n}{1200}\right)^2 \text{ N-m}$$

**(a)** Determine the operating speed.
**(b)** Determine the output power.
**(c)** What is the maximum possible output power from the motor?

characteristic is

$$T_L(n) = 3 + 4 \left(\frac{n}{1800}\right) \text{ N-m}$$

**(a)** Determine the operating speed.
**(b)** Determine the output power.
**(c)** What is the maximum possible output power from the motor?

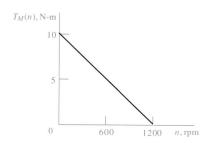

**Figure P6.30**

6.31. A motor has the parabolic output torque characteristic shown in Fig. P6.31. The load torque

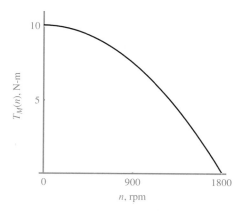

**Figure P6.31**

**6.32.** A motor has an output power given by the formula

$$P(\omega_m) = 12\omega_m - \frac{10\omega_m^2}{120\pi} \text{ watts}$$

(a) What is the starting torque of the motor?
(b) Find the no-load speed in rpm.
(c) Find the higher speed for 1-hp output power.
(d) Find the maximum output power.

**6.33.** A motor has an output torque characteristic given by the equation

$$T_M(\omega_m) = 50 - \frac{(\omega_m - 40)^2}{80} \text{ N-m}$$

where $\omega_m$ is the mechanical speed of the motor in radians/second.

(a) Find the no-load speed of the motor.
(b) What is the maximum torque of the motor?
(c) What is the maximum power of the motor?

**6.34.** The torque characteristics of two motors are shown in Fig. P6.34. The load requires a constant torque of 3 N-m.

(a) Which motor would have the longer runup time if starting the load from standstill?
(b) Determine the power required for the load in steady state if driven by motor #2.

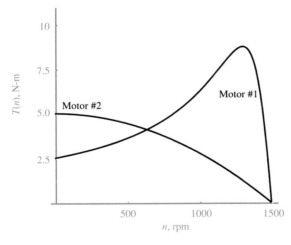

**Figure P6.34**

**6.35.** An electric motor has a torque-speed characteristic given by the equation

$$T_M(\omega_m) = \frac{100}{(5 + K\omega_m)^2} \text{ N-m}$$

where $K$ is a constant. The motor puts out 1 hp at 12,000 rpm.

(a) Find $K$.
(b) What is the starting torque?
(c) What is the maximum power out of the motor?

**6.36.** The output torque of a motor is given in Fig. P6.36.

(a) Find the blocked-rotor torque.
(b) Find the no-load speed in rpm.
(c) At what speed does the motor put out 12 hp?
(d) If a load requires 20 N-m, what speed would the motor-load run in rpm?

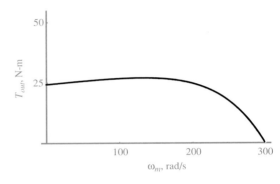

**Figure P6.36**

**6.37.** A motor has the torque given by the equation

$$T_M(\omega_m) = 50 + 0.1\omega_m - \frac{(\omega_m - 40)^2}{80} \text{ N-m}$$

(a) Find the starting torque.
(b) Find the no-load speed of the motor.
(c) Find the maximum torque of the motor.
(d) Find the maximum power of the motor.

**6.38.** A motor has an output torque characteristic that is well approximated by the function,

$$T(n) = 12 \cos\left(\frac{\pi}{2} \times \frac{n}{1200}\right) \text{ N-m},$$

where $0 < n < 1200$ is the speed in rpm.

(a) Find the starting torque.
(b) Find the no-load speed.
(c) Find the maximum power out of the motor in hp.

**6.39.** A motor with a moment of inertia $J = 0.5$ kg-m$^2$ is turning a load at a constant speed of 1160 rpm. When the load is suddenly disconnected, the instantaneous angular acceleration is $+12$ rad/s$^2$. Find the load torque at 1160 rpm.

**6.40.** Write the differential equation for a motor-load system where $T_M(\omega_m) = T_M$, a constant, and $T_L(\omega_m) = C\omega_m$, similar to the example on page 291. Use the notation $J$ = moment of inertia, $K$ = torque constant, and $\omega_{ss}$ = steady-state speed. This system fits the conditions of Chapter 3 transients; hence the initial value, final value, and time constant establish the response. Determine the time constant. Calculate the runup time for 98% of equilibrium speed based on the differential equation solution in terms of $T_M$, $J$, and $\omega_{ss}$.

**6.41.** A fan requires a driving torque of the form $T_L(\omega_m) = K\omega_m^2$. The fan requires $\frac{1}{2}$ hp of drive power on the shaft to turn 1800 rpm. The fan is driven by an electrical motor with the output characteristic given in Fig. P6.41.
  **(a)** Find the constant $K$, with torque and speed expressed in mks units, N-m and rad/s.
  **(b)** Find the speed in rpm at which the fan will operate.
  **(c)** Find the approximate time it takes the fan to reach its final speed. The moment of inertia of the motor/load is $J = 0.06$ kg-m$^2$.

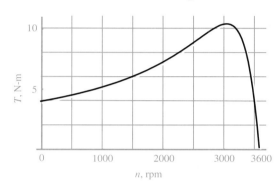

**Figure P6.41**

**6.42.** Calculate the steady-state speed and runup time for the motor and load used in the example on page 291 if the load torque requirement is changed to

$$T_L(\omega_m) = 0.001\,\omega_m^2 \text{ N-m.}$$

**6.43.** A motor–load system has a run–up characteristic given by

$$n(t) = 1180(1 - e^{-t/0.6s}) \text{ rpm.}$$

The motor–load moment is $J = 0.2$ kg-m$^2$, and the load torque requirement is constant at 8 N–m. Find the following:
  **(a)** Motor-starting torque.

**(b)** Motor torque at 1180 rpm.
**(c)** Time required to reach 96% of final speed.

**6.44.** A motor–load has a combined moment of inertia of 2 kg-m$^2$. The output torque of the motor is

$$T_M(n) = 10\left[1 - \left(\frac{n}{1800}\right)\right] \text{ N–m}$$

where $n$ is the speed in rpm. The required load torque is a constant 6 Nm.
  **(a)** What is the equilibrium speed in rpm?
  **(b)** How long would it take the system to reach 99% of the final speed starting from a standstill?

**6.45.** Figure P6.45 shows the input current, efficiency, and power factor of a 230-V three-phase motor from no load to full load.
  **(a)** What is the rated output power of the motor in hp?
  **(b)** What is the reactive power used by the motor at 50% load? The current is lagging.
  **(c)** What are the losses of the motor at no load?

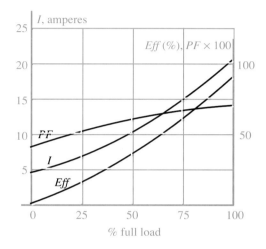

**Figure P6.45**

**6.46.** A 208-V three-phase motor runs 1720 rpm at a load requiring 9.0 N-m torque. The motor draws 5.5 A of current and the power factor is 0.92, lagging.
  **(a)** Find the input power.
  **(b)** Find the losses of the motor.
  **(c)** Find the efficiency of the motor.

**6.47.** A 60-Hz, three-phase induction motor has the following nameplate information: 25 hp, 1755 rpm, 91.7% eff., 230/460 V, 61.8/30.9 A, service factor 1.15.

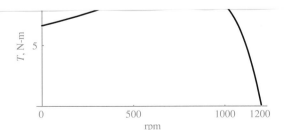

**Figure P6.58**

## General Problems for Chapter 6

**6.62.** Two pump jacks in the oil field require three-phase induction motors to drive the pumps. The wells are 325 yards apart and are connected by three No. 10

37 lb. **Motor B:** 1 hp, 1725 rpm, 115/230 V, 14.8/7.4 A, 1.0 SF, $182.99, 30 lb.
  **(a)** Assume that for each motor, the power factor and the efficiency are equal. Find the efficiencies of both motors.
  **(b)** If electric energy cost 3.6 ¢/kWh and the motors were run continuously at nameplate conditions, how soon (days) would Motor A justify its increased cost through saving of electric energy?

wires (1 Ω/1000 ft). One of the wells is shallow and requires a 10-hp motor; the other well is deep and requires a 50-hp motor. For the 10-hp motor the

(a) Find the torque output at nameplate conditions.
(b) What is the apparent power into the machine at nameplate conditions?
(c) Find the power factor at nameplate conditions.
(d) Determine the reactive power into the machine at nameplate conditions, assuming lagging current.

6.48. An induction motor has the following nameplate information: 60 Hz, three phase, 7.5 hp, 1750 rpm, 230/460 V, 22.0/11.0 A, 86.0% eff., NEMA frame 213T, 1.15 SF, $376 list, $250.79 wholesale, 129.0 lbs shipping weight. For this type of motor, the blocked rotor torque is 135 % and the breakover torque is 185% of the nameplate torque.
(a) Find the input power factor at nameplate conditions.
(b) Find the nameplate starting torque of the motor.
(c) Find the losses of the motor at nameplate conditions.

(a) Find the power factor at nameplate conditions.
(b) Find the output torque at nameplate conditions.
(c) Find the speed at which the motor and load will operate if the load requires a torque of

$$T_L(n) = 10 + 12.8(n/1800)^2 \text{ N-m.}$$

6.52. A three-phase, 60-Hz induction motor has the following nameplate information: 30 hp, 39 A, 1760 rpm, 460 V, 87.5 % eff, 1.15 SF. The no-load speed of the motor is 1799.4 rpm. The load torque is given by the equation

$$T_L(n) = 10 + 12\left(\frac{n}{1800}\right) + 15\left(\frac{n}{1800}\right)^2 \text{ N-m}$$

where $n$ is the speed in rpm. Find the operating speed of the motor/load system.

6.53. A three-phase, 60 Hz induction motor has the following nameplate information: 25 hp, 1755 rpm, 230/460 V, 64.0/32.0 A, 91.0 % efficiency, 1.15 SF.
(a) Find the reactive power requirement at

nameplate information is: 60 Hz, 1750 rpm, 230/460 V, 26.2/13.1 A, 88.5% eff., 1.35 SF. For the 50-hp motor, the nameplate information is: 60 Hz, 1775 rpm, 230/460 V, 90.2% eff., 121.4/60.7 A, 1.35 SF. The motor is connected for 460-V operation, and must be operated between 440 and 460 V for the warranties to be valid. Assume the motors are operated at their nameplate power. Power is brought to the motors from a 13-kV feeder line, and three single-phase transformers, connected in Y on the primaries and Δ on the secondaries, supply 460-V power to the line that serves the motors.
(a) Determine a suitable location for the transformers. That is, at what point between the motors should the transformers be located in order to minimize losses and to provide the acceptable voltages to the motors?
(b) Give the voltage and current in primary and

secondary windings of the single phase transformers.
(c) Find the overall efficiency of the system with both motors running at nameplate power.

6.63. A junior engineer needs 12 hp to drive a load, so he takes a 10-hp motor and a 2-hp motor, both three-phase, and puts them on the same shaft. The motor nameplates read: 10 hp, 1750 rpm, 60 Hz, 230/460 V, 26.2/13.1 A, 88.5% eff., 1.1 service factor; 2 hp, 1725 rpm, 60 Hz, 230/460 V, 6.6/3.3 A, 80.0% eff., 1.35 service factor. Assume operation in the small-slip region and negligible rotational loss.
(a) What speed does the system run, assuming exactly 12 hp for the load?
(b) Is either motor overloaded? To answer, you must calculate the motor power for both motors and explain your conclusion.

## Answers to odd-numbered problems

6.1. (a) $\cos(0°) + \cos(-240°) + \cos(-480°) = 0$ and $\cos(20°) + \cos(-220°) + \cos(-460°) = 0$.

6.3. (a) $218\sqrt{2} \angle -34.7°$ A; (b) 151 kVA; (c) 124 kW; (d) $-64.7°$.

6.5. (a) $120\sqrt{3}\sqrt{2} \angle +30°$; (b) 17.7 A;(c) 6390 W; (d) 5860 W.

6.7. (a) $480\sqrt{2} \angle -240°$ V; (b) 5.77 A rms; (c) 8.31 kW; (d) $83.1\sqrt{2} \angle 0°$ Ω.

6.9. (a) 45.5 A rms; (b) 0.876; (c) 311 V, rms .

6.11. (a) 0.833; (b) 23.6 A rms; (c) 32.3 Ω; (d) 3.32 kVAR .

6.13. (a) 139 V rms; (b) 240 V rms; (c) 21.3 A rms; (d) 21.3 A rms; (e) $6 + j2.5$ Ω; (f) 8860 W; (g) 0.923; (h) 8180 W.

6.15. (a) Proof .

6.17. (a) 6090 W; (b) 85.8 W; (c) 98.6 %.

6.19. (a) 30.1:1; (b) 0.208 A, rms .

6.21. (a) Calculate $V_{bc}$ from the other two and it comes out right; (b) 34.6 kVA for the two transformers.

6.23. (a) $2.10 \angle -19.9°$; (b) same .

6.25. (a) 0.00174 pu; (b) transformer is 1:1 with $j0.00174$ in primary or secondary .

6.27. (a) 31.6 A, rms; (b) 2690 W; (c) 3.27 μF; (d) 2430 W.

6.29. (a) $140,050 \sqrt{2} \angle 1.01°$ V.

6.31. (a) 1188 rpm; (b) 702 W; (c) 726 W at 1039 rpm .

6.33. (a) 103.2 rad/s; (b) 50 N-m; (c) 2740 W at 65.5 rad/s .

6.35. (a) $6.35 \times 10^{-3}$; (b) 4 N-m; (c) 787 W at 7520 rpm.

6.37. (a) 30 N-m; (b) 110 rad/s; (c) 54.2 N-m at 44.0 rad/s; (d) 3200 W at 70.1 rad/s.

6.39. (a) 6 N-m at 1160 rpm.

6.41. (a) $2.23 \times 10^{-4}$; (b) about 3500 rpm; (c) 3.6 s .

6.43. (a) 49.2 N-m; (b) 8 N-m; (c) 1.93 s .

6.45. (a) 7.1 hp; (b) 3030 VAR; (c) 771 W.

6.47. (a) 101 N-m; (b) 24.6 kVA; (c) 0.826; (d) $+13.9$ kVAR .

6.49. (a) $7.61/year .

6.51. (a) 0.818; (b) 30.4 N-m; (c) 1767 rpm.

6.53. (a) 15.2 kVAR; (b) 1845 W; (c) 101.5 N-m; (d) 1782 rpm .

6.55. (a) 4.09 N-m; (b) 65.3%; (c) 1070 VAR .

6.57. (a) 498 W and 18.4 N-m.

6.59. (a) 12.3 N-m; (b) 0.599; (c) 3.45 hp; (d) No way to determine.

6.61. (a) 84.0% for A and 66.2% for B; (b) 205 days .

6.63. (a) 183.0 rad/s; (b) 10.6 hp for 10 hp motor and 1.4 hp for 2 hp. Neither is overloaded.

# PART 2

# Electronics

# Semiconductor Devices and Circuits

1. To understand how to analyze half-, and full-wave rectifier circuits, with and without a filter capacitor
2. To understand the physical processes and the *i–v* characteristic of a *pn* junction
3. To understand the semiconductor processes in the *npn* bipolar junction transistor and the resulting input and output characteristics
4. To understand how to analyze a common-emitter amplifier-switch circuit
5. To understand how to analyze a common-emitter small-signal amplifier for operating point and gain
6. To understand FET operation and applications

In addition to resistors, capacitors, and inductors, electronic circuits use diodes, transistors, and other nonlinear devices. We analyze rectifier circuits that convert ac power to dc power and circuits that use transistors as switches or amplifiers.

## Introduction to Electronics

**power electronics**

Electronics and information. In Chapter 1, we distinguished between two branches of electrical engineering, power and electronics,[1] through their differing uses of electrical energy. In the power industry, electrical energy is generated from a primary source such as coal or water power and eventually converted into heat, illumination, mechanical work, or some other useful form. In electronics, electrical energy is used to symbolize, transport, and process information. Think of a telephone system, a radio, a computer, or a traffic control system—all use electrical energy to convey, process, and use information.

**signal**

In electronics, voltage and current become electrical *signals*; that is, they signify something else, as the root word "sign" suggests. The voltage generated when you speak into a telephone is a signal because it reproduces the acoustic vibrations in the air, these sounds have meaning, and information is exchanged in the conversation.

Chapters 7 through 12 discuss the main ideas used in electronics at the present time. As you will see from the historical survey to follow, electronics is a young enterprise. The current rate of progress in the field makes it difficult to anticipate what the future holds. But there are some major themes that, once understood, will give you a good grasp of the nature of electronics. Some of the important factors we address are (1) analog and digital representation and processing of information, (2) expanded use of the frequency domain, (3) application of the electrical properties of semiconductor materials, (4) feedback, and (5) utilization of nonlinear effects in circuits.

History of electronics. Before World War II, electronics had commercial importance primarily in radio broadcasting and in the telephone and telegraph industries. Most people who were active in these fields were educated through experience, including many physicists and electrical engineers. In those days, to study electrical engineering in college meant to study about power: motors, generators, lighting, transformers, and transmission lines.

World War II profoundly changed electronics. In addition to the obvious need to improve radio communication, one of the Allies' top-secret war projects focused on electronics. Everybody knows about the Manhattan Project and the atomic bomb. Through the work of the Radiation Laboratory in developing microwave radar, scientists and engineers made an equally important contribution toward ending the conflict. The best technical minds in the country were employed in these two projects and spectacular success crowned both efforts.

The postwar fruit of the Manhattan Project was more and bigger bombs, and even the peaceful application of nuclear technology continues to excite controversy. But widespread and, for the most part, benevolent have been the postwar fruits of the work of the Radiation Laboratory. The cathode-ray tubes (CRTs) that were developed as radar displays became TV picture tubes, and soon there were high-fidelity recordings to be enjoyed. Radar techniques developed to detect enemy aircraft allowed commercial avi-

---

[1] Chapter 18 deals with *power electronics*, which is the control of electrical power with electronic techniques.

ation to fly in all weather, and you could dial long distance directly and make yourself heard without shouting.

In the early 1950s, the development of the transistor inaugurated the first of several "solid-state revolutions." The integrated circuit followed and later the microcomputer on a "chip." The techniques of microelectronics seem limitless.

The idea of electronic computers was conceived before the war, but only modest applications were made, even during the war. An analog computer was developed to control naval gunnery, and some simple "logic" circuits emerged, but practical computers came after the war. The first digital computers were based on vacuum-tube technology and by present standards were gigantic, slow, and unfriendly to programmers. But when the idea of the digital computer merged with that of the transistor and later the integrated circuit, the development of computers became spectacular and continues so to this day.

**The nature of electronics.** Electronics is a big bag of tricks. Unlike circuit theory, which submits to an orderly and logical development, electronics employs a diversity of devices, techniques, and processes. It is difficult to apply a beginning knowledge of electronics, because electronic circuits are complicated. Did you ever, for example, examine the circuit diagram (the schematic) for a TV set? If one fell into your hands at this moment and you set about to apply your newly gained knowledge of Ohm's law, Kirchhoff's laws, and concepts such as impedance and Thévenin equivalent circuits, you would not make much progress in understanding such a circuit diagram.

Our goal in this second part of the book is to investigate the major themes currently driving electronics. We examine a few of the tricks in the electronics bag at the present time, but only enough to impart a beginning understanding of the nature of the subject. Do not expect to be able to fix your radio or interface a microcomputer after you master this part of the book. But you should understand how these systems work.

**Electronics in this book.** This chapter explains the physical operations of diodes and transistors, and then discusses some basic circuits that use these devices. Chapter 8, "Digital Electronics," shows how these basic circuits can be adapted to process information in digital form. Chapter 9, "Analog Electronics", details how these circuits are used to process information in analog form and expands our treatment of circuit theory into signal analysis. Chapters 10 to 12 show how analog and digital circuits are integrated into systems that monitor, control, or communicate. Finally Chapter 18, "Power Electronics Systems," deals with devices and circuits used to control electrical power.

## Ideal Diode

**Nonlinear devices.** The circuit theory developed in Chapters 1 through 6 applies to circuits that are linear. The defining equations for resistors, inductors, and capacitors describe linear relationships between voltage and current. Also linear are Kirchhoff's laws describing conservation of energy and charge in electric circuits. Many of the techniques that we developed are based on these linear properties—superposition and Thévenin equivalent circuits being obvious examples.

Electronics also uses resistors, inductors, and capacitors, and certainly Kirchhoff's laws are still valid. But electronic circuits employ many devices that are nonlinear in their characteristics. Diodes, transistors, and silicon-controlled rectifiers offer examples of such nonlinear electronic devices. The nonlinearities are not undesirable hindrances to the use of these and other devices; rather, they are useful because of their nonlinear properties.

### Graphical analysis.

Because of the importance of nonlinear devices, we employ more graphical analysis in electronics. Many of the circuit solution techniques we develop are based on graphical methods, and much of the information about device characteristics is given in graphical form. Figure 7.1 shows the graphical characteristics of a resistor, together with the extremes of an open circuit ($R = \infty$) and a short circuit ($R = 0$). Of course, the graphical form of Ohm's law is a straight line.

### Ideal diode characteristics.

Figure 7.2 shows the circuit symbol for an ideal diode, with the associated graphical characteristic, which is nonlinear. The ideal diode characteristic divides into two regions: the vertical region is called the forward-bias region and the horizontal region is called the reverse-bias region. Comparison with Fig. 7.1 suggests that the ideal diode acts as a short circuit in the forward-bias region and an open circuit in the reverse-bias region.

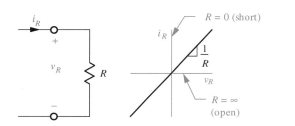

**Figure 7.1** Symbol and graphical definition of a resistor.

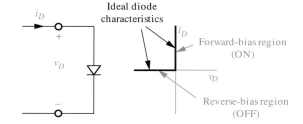

**Figure 7.2** Symbol and graphical definition of an ideal diode.

### ON and OFF.

The behavior of the device in terms of current flow is as follows: As long as the current is positive in the direction of the arrow of the circuit symbol, the diode acts as a short circuit and the current flows without hindrance. The diode is ON. When the voltage is positive in the direction opposite to the diode arrow, however, the diode acts as an open circuit and no current can flow. The diode is OFF. Thus, the current can flow in the direction of the arrow but cannot flow against the arrow.

### Mechanical analogs.

The diode can be considered as the electrical equivalent of the mechanical ratchet, such as is used to tighten the net on a tennis court. The mechanical ratchet allows motion or rotation in one direction only. Similarly, the diode allows charge motion in one direction only. Another analog would be a check valve that allows fluid flow in only one direction.

### Diode = switch.

The diode can also be considered a voltage-actuated switch. As long as the input voltage is positive (with the + at the top of the arrow), the switch is closed, current flows, and the diode is ON. But once the polarity of the voltage reverses, the switch opens, no current flows, and the diode is OFF.

The diode characteristic described is that of an ideal diode. Real diodes depart from this ideal characteristic, as is detailed in Section 7.2. But many of the common applications of the diode can be understood in terms of this ideal characteristic; hence, we present some applications before investigating the physical processes in semiconductor diodes.

## Rectifier Circuits

**power supply**

**DC and electronics.**  At the beginning of Chapter 4, we mentioned the struggle be-tween dc and ac to see which form of electrical power would dominate the fledgling electric power industry. Of course, ac came to be the common mode for the generation, distribution, and consumption of electric power.

With the ascendancy of electronics, however, dc has made a comeback, for almost all electronic circuits require dc power. You might suppose, therefore, that every elec-tronic device would contain a battery, but this is untrue. Batteries are expensive, heavy, short-lived, bulky, and filled with corrosive chemicals. Batteries are thus undesirable components and are avoided by designers except where portability is essential.

For this reason, most electronic equipment contains a power supply circuit. The function of the power supply is shown in Fig. 7.3. When you plug in and turn on your TV set, for example, the ac power enters the *power supply* section of the electronic cir-cuit, where it is converted to dc power. From there the dc power flows to other parts of the circuit. Such power supply circuits use the nonlinear properties of diodes in circuits called rectifiers.

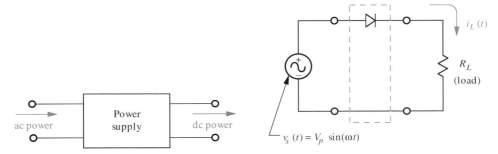

**Figure 7.3**  Most electronic circuits require a power supply.

**Figure 7.4**  Half-wave rectifier circuit.

**half-wave rectifier**

**Half-wave rectifier.**  Power supplies use diodes to convert ac to dc in rectifier cir-cuits; the diodes are said to "rectify" the ac. Figure 7.4 shows a basic rectifier circuit. This circuit is called a *half-wave rectifier* because it couples only the positive half of the input voltage to the load.  The ac voltage is represented as a sine function, the rectifier is an ideal diode, and the load is represented as a resistor, although in practice the load would be the electronic circuits that require dc power.

Figure 7.5 shows the rectifying effect of the diode. When the input voltage is posi-tive, the diode turns ON and current flows with a sinusoidal shape, but when the input voltage is negative, the diode turns OFF and no current flows. The resulting current flows in spurts, and the voltage across the load is that portion of the sinusoidal input that is positive. The diode blocks the negative part of the ac waveform.

**DC component.**  Admittedly, the output of the half-wave rectifier is not pure dc power. The output, however, does contain a dc component. Indeed, if we define the dc portion of the output as the time average defined in Sec. 5.1, we have a dc component of

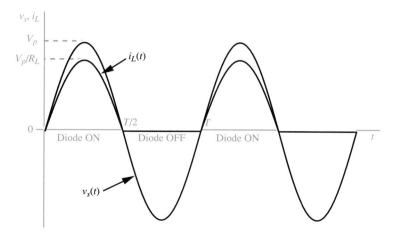

**Figure 7.5** Half-wave rectifier waveforms.

$$I_{dc} = \frac{1}{T} \int_0^T i_L(t)\,dt = \frac{1}{T}\left[\int_0^{T/2} \frac{V_p}{R_L}\sin(\omega t)\,dt + \int_{T/2}^T 0\,dt\right]$$

$$= \frac{V_p}{\pi R_L} \tag{7.1}$$

where $\omega = 2\pi/T$. This current would be indicated by a dc ammeter in series with the load. The dc component of the load voltage is

$$V_{dc} = I_{dc}R_L = \frac{V_p}{\pi} \tag{7.2}$$

---

**EXAMPLE 7.1**  **Half-wave rectifier**

A 24-V(rms) ac source is connected to a 20-Ω resistor with a diode in a half-wave rectifier circuit. Find the peak and the average current in the load.

**SOLUTION:**
Figure 7.4 shows the circuit. The peak current would be the peak positive voltage divided by the resistance, because the diode is ON for positive source voltage.

$$I_{peak} = \frac{V_p}{R_L} = \frac{24\sqrt{2}}{20} = 1.70 \text{ A} \tag{7.3}$$

The dc current is given by Eq. (7.1):

$$I_{dc} = \frac{V_p}{\pi R_L} = \frac{I_p}{\pi} = \frac{1.70}{\pi} = 0.540 \text{ A} \tag{7.4}$$

**full-wave bridge rectifier**

**Full-wave rectifiers.** The circuit in Fig. 7.6 (a) is called a *full-wave bridge rectifier* because it inverts or rectifies the negative half of the input voltage as well as the positive half.

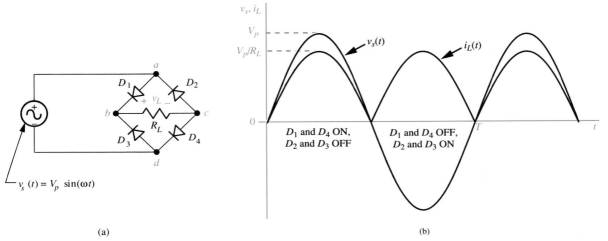

(a)                                           (b)

**Figure 7.6** (a) Bridge full-wave rectifier circuit; (b) waveforms for the bridge full-wave rectifier.

**Bridge-rectifier operation.** When the source voltage is positive, the current tends to flow through the rectifier from $a$ to $d$. Diode $D_1$ comes ON but $D_2$ cannot accommodate current from $a$ to $c$ and will turn OFF. From $b$, the current must flow through the resistor because $D_3$ will not permit current flowing directly from $b$ to $d$. Finally, $D_4$ will turn ON and the current will flow from $c$ to $d$. Thus, when the source voltage is positive, positive current flows out of the $+$ of the source through $D_1$, through the load resistor, and finally through $D_4$ and returns to the source. Diodes $D_2$ and $D_3$ are OFF during this part of the cycle. When the source voltage is negative, $D_2$ and $D_3$ turn ON while $D_1$ and $D_4$ turn OFF. Thus, during the second half of the cycle, positive current flows out of the minus terminal of the source, through $D_3$ from $d$ to $b$, through the load resistance, and back to the source through $D_2$. The two paths for the current are shown in Fig. 7.7. The current flows through the load from $b$ to $c$ during both parts of the cycle; thus, the current through the load is as shown in Fig. 7.6(b). The current again flows in spurts, but the full-wave rectifier leaves no idle time between spurts as does the half-wave rectifier.

As a power supply circuit, the full-wave rectifier does better than the half-wave rectifier. By inverting the negative portions on the input voltage, the circuit doubles the dc

---

[2] Then the negative part of the ac voltage would be coupled to the load. $I_{peak} = -1.70$ A and $I_{dc} = -0.540$ A.

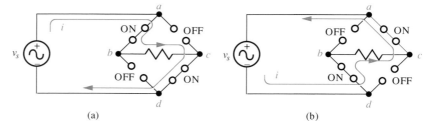

**Figure 7.7** Current paths for a bridge rectifier: (a) $v_s$ positive; (b) $v_s$ negative.

component in the output; hence, the dc component in the current is

$$
I_{dc} = \frac{1}{T} \int_0^T i_L(t)\ dt = \frac{2}{T} \int_0^{T/2} \frac{V_p}{R_L} \sin(\omega t)\ dt
$$

$$
= \frac{2V_p}{\pi R_L}
$$

(7.5)

and the dc load voltage is

$$
V_{dc} = I_{dc} R_L = \frac{2}{\pi} V_p
$$

(7.6)

---

**EXAMPLE 7.2**  **Full-wave rectifier**

A full-wave rectifier is required to provide 50 V dc and 2 A dc to a resistive load. Find the load resistance and the required rms ac voltage.

**SOLUTION:**
Figure 7.8 shows the bridge rectifier of Fig. 7.6(a), redrawn to put the load to the right. The load resistance is given by Ohm's law for the dc voltage and current:

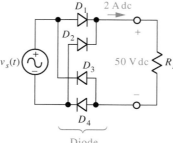

Diode
bridge

**Figure 7.8**  The diode bridge is drawn in the conventional manner.

$$R_L = \frac{V_{dc}}{I_{dc}} = \frac{50}{2} = 25 \ \Omega \tag{7.7}$$

The peak ac voltage is given by Eq. (7.6):

$$V_p = \frac{\pi(50)}{2} = 78.5 \ V \tag{7.8}$$

Hence, the rms voltage is $78.5/\sqrt{2} = 55.5$ V

> **WHAT IF?**    What if one of the diodes burned out and became an open circuit?[3]

**The diode bridge as a switch.**   The diodes act as switches that are activated by voltage. When the source voltage is positive, $D_1$ and $D_4$ are turned ON and thus $b$ and $c$ are connected to the $+$ and $-$ terminals of the source, respectively. When the source voltage becomes negative, $D_2$ and $D_3$ are turned ON and hence $b$ and $c$ are again connected to the source, this time with $b$ connected to the $-$ and $c$ to the $+$ terminal. Thus, $b$ is automatically connected to the physically positive terminal of the source while $c$ is connected to the physically negative terminal. This automatic switching action occurs regardless of the shape of the source voltage—the shape can be sinusoidal, triangular, or an unpredictable communication signal in a radio circuit. The effect of the diode bridge is thus to produce across the load an output voltage that is the absolute value of the input voltage: $v_L(t) = |v_s(t)|$.

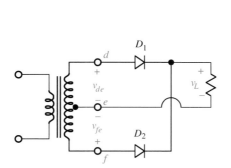

**Figure 7.9**  Full-wave rectifier using a center-tapped transformer.

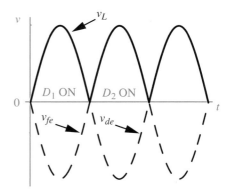

**Figure 7.10**    Waveform for the full-wave rectifier.

**Full-wave rectifier with center-tapped transformer.**   Figure 7.9   shows   a full-wave rectifier circuit that uses a transformer and two diodes. The transformer secondary is center-tapped to supply identical but opposite voltages to the two diodes.

---

[3] $I_{dc} = 1$ A, $V_{dc} = 25$ V.

Each diode acts as a half-wave rectifier: $D_1$ supplies the positive part of $v_{de}$ and $D_2$ supplies the positive part of $v_{fe}$, as shown in Fig. 7.10. The transformer gives this circuit the versatility to produce any desired dc voltage, depending on the turns ratio. It also allows both ac input and dc output to be grounded, which cannot be done with a bridge.

## Rectifier with Filter Capacitor

**filter, ripple**

**Filtering out the ripple.** The three rectifier circuits described produce a dc component in their outputs. We may describe their outputs as a desired dc component plus an undesired *ripple*, as shown in Fig. 7.11. A *filter*, as in Fig. 7.12, is a circuit used to remove an undesirable signal in a circuit. In this case, we need a filter to eliminate, or at least greatly reduce, the ripple component from the output of the rectifier. In Chapter 9, we consider filters generally; here we introduce the simplest of filters—we merely connect a capacitor across the load, as shown in Fig. 7.13. As we will see, the capacitor stabilizes the voltage across the load resistor.

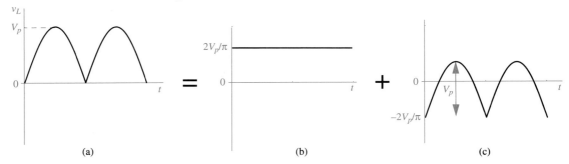

**Figure 7.11** The ripple is the undesirable portion of the output. (a) Rectifier output; (b) dc component; (c) ripple component.

**Charging the capacitor.** The source is $V_p \sin(\omega t)$, and thus passes through zero volts at $t = 0$, as shown in Fig. 7.14. As the voltage increases, diodes $D_1$ and $D_4$ turn ON and current flows through the load as before. Current also flows through the capacitor and charges it to the peak value of the input ac voltage. The first spurt of current is relatively large in Fig. 7.14 due to the initial charging of the capacitor.

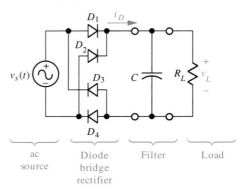

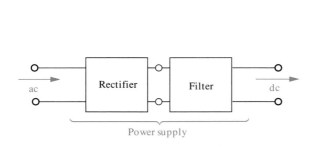

**Figure 7.12** A filter is used to reduce the ripple.

**Figure 7.13** Full-wave bridge rectifier with a capacitor filter.

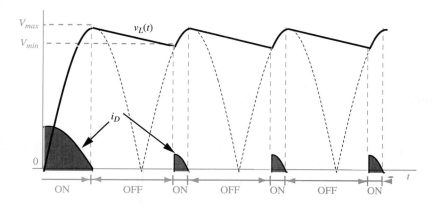

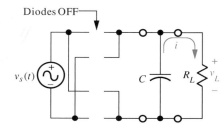

**Figure 7.14** Waveforms for the full-wave rectifier with a capacitor filter.

**Figure 7.15** When the diodes of the bridge are OFF, the capacitor discharges through the load.

**Holding the charge.** After its peak, the input voltage drops rapidly. If the voltage of the capacitor were to follow this voltage, a rapid discharge would have to occur. However, all diodes prevent discharge through the input source and are OFF when the input voltage drops below the voltage on the capacitor, because at that moment the diode becomes reverse biased. Hence, the filter capacitor and the load resistance become disconnected from the source, which continues with the negative part of its waveform.

**The discharge.** The capacitor discharges through the load resistor, as shown in Fig. 7.15. The discharge of a capacitor through a resistor is a problem we learned to solve in Chapter 3. To write the voltage as a function of time, we need to know the time constant, the initial value, and the final value. The time constant is $R_L C$, the initial value is $V_p$, and the final value would be zero if the discharge were allowed to go on forever. Thus, the voltage of the load and the capacitor during the discharge period, when the diodes are OFF, would be

$$v_L(t) = 0 + (V_p - 0)e^{-(t'/R_L C)} = V_p e^{-(t'/R_L C)} \qquad (7.9)$$

where $t'$ is measured from the peak.

**The recharge.** To function well as a filter, the circuit should have a time constant, $R_L C$, much longer than the period of the input ac voltage, usually $1/60$ s. The load voltage thus decreases only slightly between peaks. Figure 7.14 exaggerates the decrease from what it would be in practice. During this time the diode remains OFF until the input voltage becomes equal to the decreasing load voltage. As the input voltage again exceeds the load voltage, $D_2$ and $D_3$ turn ON and current again flows through the rectifier diodes. Most of the current goes to the capacitor, replenishing the charge lost during the discharge part of the cycle. After the pulse of current that initially charges the capacitor, current flows through the diode only during these brief recharging periods, as shown in Fig. 7.14.

**The dc load voltage.**  If the load voltage decreases only slightly during the period of the ac waveform, as shown in Fig. 7.14, the output voltage of the power supply remains approximately equal to the peak value of the input ac waveform. Thus, the first benefit of the filter capacitor is to increase the dc output from $(2/\pi)V_p$ to $V_p$. Second, the filter capacitor greatly reduces the ripple voltage. For the case we are considering, $R_L C \gg$ period, the exponential decrease of the load voltage is well approximated by a straight line, given by the two leading terms in a series expansion of the exponential:

$$v_L(t') = V_p\, e^{-(t'/R_L C)} = V_p\left(1 - \frac{t'}{R_L C} + \cdots\right) \tag{7.10}$$

where $t'$ is measured from the peak. Thus from its maximum value of $V_p$ the voltage decreases to a minimum value of approximately

$$V_{\min} \approx V_p\left(1 - \frac{T/2}{R_L C}\right) = V_p\left(1 - \frac{1}{2fR_L C}\right) \tag{7.11}$$

at the moment when the diode turns ON and permits recharging of the capacitor. In Eq. (7.11), $f$ represents the ac frequency, the reciprocal of the period. Consequently, the peak-to-peak ripple, $V_r$, is

$$V_r = V_{\max} - V_{\min} = \frac{V_p}{2fR_L C} \tag{7.12}$$

We note from Fig. 7.14 that a more accurate approximation to the dc component of the filtered output would be the average between the maximum and minimum voltages:

$$V_{dc} \approx \frac{V_{\max} + V_{\min}}{2} = V_p\left(1 - \frac{1}{4fR_L C}\right) \tag{7.13}$$

---

**EXAMPLE 7.3**  **Filtered full-wave rectifier**

Find the ripple and dc voltage out of the filtered full-wave rectifier in Fig. 7.16.

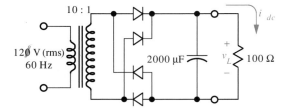

**Figure 7.16**  Full-wave rectifier circuit with a capacitor filter.

**SOLUTION:**

The input ac to the rectifier has an rms voltage of 12 V at 60 Hz. Thus, the peak value is $12\sqrt{2} = 17.0$ V. The time constant is

$$\tau = R_L C = 100 \times 2000 \times 10^{-6} = 200 \text{ ms} \tag{7.14}$$

which is long compared to the period of 16.7 ms. Thus the approximate analysis is valid. The maximum voltage across the load is $12\sqrt{2} = 17.0$ V. The minimum voltage is given by Eq. (7.11):

$$V_{min} \approx 17.0 \left[ 1 - \frac{1}{2 \times 60 \, (0.2)} \right] = 16.3 V \tag{7.15}$$

Thus, the ripple voltage is $17.0 - 16.3 = 0.71$ V peak-to-peak and the dc (time-average) voltage at the load is the average between the maximum and minimum, 16.3 V. The dc current in the load is 16.6 V divided by the load resistance, or 166 mA.

| **WHAT IF?** | What if the full-wave rectifier is replaced by a half-wave rectifier?[4] |

**Better filters.** We have investigated the benefits of the simplest possible filter. The performance of this filter is adequate for many applications, but high-quality power supplies employ more sophisticated filters. Some filters add inductors and additional capacitors to reduce the ripple; others employ electronic circuits to cancel the ripple.

## Check Your Understanding

1. An ideal diode uses no power because either its voltage or current is zero. (true or false?)

2. A half-wave rectifier circuit requires at least two diodes. (True or false?)

3. What is the average value of a full-wave rectified sinusoid having a peak value of 10 V before rectification?

4. A battery may be used as a filter in a power supply. (True or false?)

5. A rectifier circuit produces pure dc. (True or false?)

6. What is "filtered" by a filter circuit in a power supply?

7. An unfiltered full-wave rectifier puts out 12 V dc for a sinusoidal input. If a large capacitor is added across the load, what would be the new voltage, assuming ideal diodes?

8. In a good stereo, the sound does not go away immediately when you turn off the amplifier but fades out over a period of several seconds. Explain.

*Answers.* (1) true; (2) false; (3) 6.37 V; (4) true—the battery acts like an infinite capacitor; (5) false; (6) the ripple, everything but the dc; (7) 18.8 V; (8) the capacitor in the power supply has to discharge before the dc voltage is zero.

---

[4] The discharge time in that case is approximately $T$ so $V_{min} = 15.6$ V and $V_{dc} = 16.3$ V.

**Reasons for discussing the physical principles of diode operation.** The diode finds many uses as an electronic component. We have seen how diodes are used in power supplies to convert ac to dc, but this is only one of the many uses for diodes. Diodes are used extensively in analog electronic devices such as radios and audio systems, and are even more important in digital systems such as computers and digital watches.

The diode plays an important role in the study of electronics because it is a simple electronic device; hence, it presents a good starting place in exploring the bag of electronic tricks. The diode is also important in the teaching of electronics because it offers an opportunity to investigate the physical basis of semiconductor electronics, the processes that have produced essentially all the electronic equipment we require and enjoy in our lives and work. This section describes many of these semiconductor processes.

**Diode operation.** We have a genuine problem in helping you understand how a diode works. It is commonly asserted, and reasonably so, that we should explain the unknown in terms of the known. But your author must explain the unknown—how a diode works—in terms of other unknowns, namely, semiconductor processes such as holes, drift currents, uncovered charges, and depletion regions. Or, put another way, we are required to consider many physical processes before we can understand how a simple *pn*-junction diode operates. Understanding of the diode merits the effort, but our investment pays further dividends because modern electronics is founded on the manipulation of charges in semiconductor materials through such physical processes.

## Semiconductor Processes and the *pn* Junction

**OBJECTIVE 2**

**To understand the physical processes and the *i-v* characteristic of a *pn* junction**

**Crystalline nature of solids.** Matter exists in four states: gas, plasma, liquid, and solid. These may be understood in terms of the interaction between individual atoms or molecules comprising the matter. In a solid, the atoms remain in a fixed position relative to each other. Often the atoms exist in a regular crystalline order, held together by shared electrons in covalent bonds. Figure 7.17 shows a two-dimensional representation of such a lattice. The large circles with numbers represent the nuclei, the dots represent the valence electrons, and the curved lines represent the bonding effect of the electrons. The electrons are negatively charged and the nuclei are positively charged. Of course, there are many more electrons associated with each nucleus, but we have not represented these inner shells because these do not enter into the bonding process or the semiconductor processes we are investigating. We have represented the case where there are four electrons in the outer shell, which is typical of a semiconductor such as silicon. Because the individual atoms are electrically neutral, all the charge would be neutralized by the inner shells of electrons except for a positive charge of four times the electronic charge, which is thus the effective charge of the nucleus. This charge is indicated by the +4 in Fig. 7.17.

**insulator, conductor, conduction electrons**

**Insulators and conductors.** At zero absolute temperature, solids are either electrical conductors or insulators. The material represented by Fig. 7.17 would be an *insulator* because all the electrons are involved in the bonding. If such a material were placed in an electric circuit, no current would flow because no electrons are free to move. In a *conductor*, each atom has at least one excess electron that is not involved in the bond-

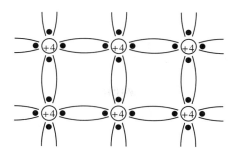

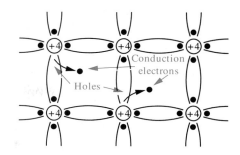

**Figure 7.17** Insulator.

**Figure 7.18** Semiconductor showing holes and electrons.

ing. Such excess electrons are known as *conduction electrons* and they move freely in response to electrical forces.

**Semiconductors.** Thermal energy has a strong effect on the conduction properties of solids. Thermal energy is distributed throughout the electrons and nuclei of the materials and this energy is stored, among other ways, in the physical movement, or vibration, of the electrons and nuclei. The vibrations may cause some of the bonding electrons to break loose from their bonding positions to become conduction electrons.

**semiconductor**

Materials that have no excess electrons and retain all their electrons in bonds at normal temperatures remain good insulators. Carbon in a diamond crystalline order and many plastics and ceramics furnish examples of good insulators at normal temperatures. In other materials that are good insulators at absolute zero, however, the electrons are not tightly held in the bonds, and in these materials, some of the electrons escape their bonds at normal temperatures to become conduction electrons. We have represented this condition in Fig. 7.18 with two electrons out of their bonding positions. Such a material is known as a *semiconductor* because it becomes a conductor at normal temperatures due to the electrons that have become conduction electrons.

**hole**

**Holes and hole movement.** When an electron leaves its bonding position, it leaves behind a vacant position, which is called a *hole*. We may think of the hole as having a positive charge because the nucleus adjacent to it now has charge not neutralized by the bonding electrons. Holes are also free to move under the influence of electrical forces because other bound electrons may move into the vacant location. If in Fig. 7.18 there were an electrical force tending to move electrons from left to right, the conduction electrons would move in response to such a force. But the electron next to the vacant position will also tend to move to the right and may leave one bonding position for a vacant position toward the right. Thus, we can envision the process represented in Fig. 7.19. First, the electron breaks its bond and becomes a conduction electron, creating a hole. Because there is an electric force tending to move electrons toward the right, there will also be a tendency for electrons remaining in bonds to move left to right; hence, the transitions labeled 2 through 5 are favored. The hole moves toward the left; in effect, a positive charge moves right to left because there is excess positive charge associated with the hole.

**carriers**

If a semiconductor were placed in a circuit where the voltage created a current, the current would be carried by both holes and electrons, which are said to be *carriers*. Note that the currents carried by the movement of holes and electrons are additive:

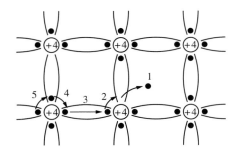

**Figure 7.19**  The movement of bound electrons produces hole movement.

holes moving toward the left carry a positive current toward the left; and electrons moving toward the right carry a negative current toward the right, which is a positive current toward the left. In a typical semiconductor, the holes move about one-third as fast as the electrons and hence carry about one-fourth the total current.

**Importance of thermal energy.**  We stated that hole–electron pairs are created because of thermal energy, and have shown how electrons changing bond positions due to thermal vibrations act like mobile positive charges. But we described these processes as if they were orderly and sedate, which they are not. For pure silicon at 300 K, there are approximately $1.5 \times 10^{16}$ conduction electrons/m³ and there are approximately $10^{22}$ hole-electron pairs/m³ created and eliminated through recombination per second through thermal action.

Hence emerges a picture of violent, random thermal motion of conduction electrons in a semiconductor. Many hole-electron pairs are created and many recombinations occur during short periods of time.

**n-type doping.**  We can increase the concentration of carriers by adding small amounts of impurities to the pure, *intrinsic*, semiconductor. Consider that we have intrinsic silicon, which has four bonding electrons per atom. If we add a small amount of an element that has five electrons in its valence shell, such as phosphorus, the impurity nuclei will bond into the lattice with one electron left over. This electron will be a conduction electron, as shown in Fig. 7.20, and there will also be one additional positive charge fixed into the lattice of nuclei because of the additional charge of the nucleus of the impurity atom. This process of adding impurities is called doping; Figure 7.20 shows *n-type doping,* so called because of the additional negative carriers. This would make an *n-type semiconductor* because it has an increased concentration of electrons. The impurity in this case would be called a *donor* atom because it donates an additional conduction electron to the semiconductor.

**p-type doping.**  Similarly, if we add an impurity with three electrons in its valence shell, we would create a hole for each impurity atom, as shown in Fig. 7.21. Here we have shown the hole and we have indicated that the nucleus is deficient one positive charge with a +3. If the hole were filled by a conduction electron, that region would in effect have a negative charge built into the lattice structure of the semiconductor. Such an impurity is called an *acceptor* atom because it accepts an electron from the conduction electrons in the semiconductor and an extra hole is created. A semiconductor that is doped with acceptor atoms is called a *p-type semiconductor* because it has an excess of holes, which act like mobile positive charges.

**intrinsic semiconductor n-type doping, n-type semiconductor, donor**

**acceptor, p-type semiconductor**

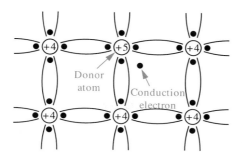

**Figure 7.20** An *n*-type semiconductor has extra conduction electrons.

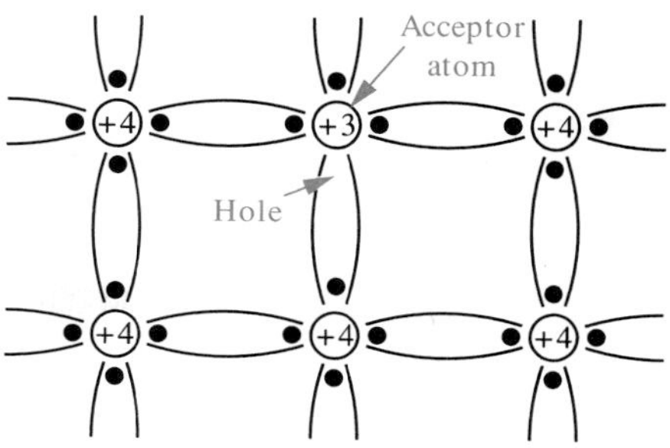

**Figure 7.21** A *p*-type semiconductor has extra holes.

The electrons donated by the donor atoms and the holes created by the acceptor atoms do not remain near their associated nuclei, but participate in the random thermal processes of all carriers. By doping the semiconductor, we have the ability to increase the carrier concentration and to control what type of carriers will dominate the conduction processes in the semiconductor.

**drift current**

**Drift currents**    We described what happens when a semiconductor is placed in an electric circuit. A current is formed by movement of both holes and electrons. If the semiconductor were *p*-type, most of the current would be carried by the holes. If the semiconductor were *n*-type, most of the current would be carried by the electrons. This type of current is called *drift current* because the carriers drift in a certain direction as dictated by an external voltage. Drift current is caused by an orderly process.

**diffusion, diffusion current**

**Diffusion currents**.   However, an excess of carriers in a certain region would tend to distribute uniformly throughout the material because of their random thermal movement. Such a flow is known as *diffusion*. A diffusion flow occurs when a bottle of a smelly chemical is opened in a room.  People near the open bottle would smell it first, and then those farther away. Eventually, everyone in the room would smell the chemical because the molecules would be distributed uniformly throughout the room by their thermal motion. In a similar way, carriers move away from regions of concentration due to their thermal motion. The resulting *diffusion current* is proportional to the rate of change of carrier concentration with respect to distance. Diffusion is a disorderly process because it is driven by thermal motion.

**Summary**.   An intrinsic semiconductor has many, but equal number of holes and electrons because thermal energy causes electrons to leave their bond positions, become conduction electrons, and leave behind a hole. We can create *p*-type or *n*-type semiconductors by doping the pure material with either acceptor or donor impurity atoms. The additional holes or electrons participate in the violent, random thermal motion of the carriers in the material. The carriers form currents either by the orderly process of a drift current or by the disorderly process of diffusion.

**Bound charges**.   There are also charges bound into the lattice structure associated with the acceptor or donor nuclei. The acceptor atoms act as stationary negative charges because their nuclei are deficient one positive charge relative to the other nuclei in the vicinity. The donor atoms act as stationary positive charges because their nuclei have one additional positive charge relative to the surrounding nuclei. Semiconductors are

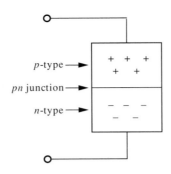

**Figure 7.22** The *pn* junction.

**Figure 7.23** Processes involved in the formation of a *pn* junction.

neutral in total charge because the excess mobile carriers neutralize the bound charges of the impurity atoms. All of these processes occur in a *pn* junction.

**pn junction**

**Structure.** A *pn* junction is formed at the boundary between regions of *p*-type semiconductor and *n*-type semiconductor, as shown by Fig. 7.22. When such a junction is formed, the sequence of events diagrammed in Fig. 7.23 occurs rapidly.

- **Diffusion currents.** Electrons in the *n*-type material diffuse toward the *p*-type material and holes in the *p*-type material diffuse toward the *n*-type material. These strong diffusion currents occur because the concentrations are unequal and the carriers are in violent thermal motion.

- **Recombination.** Recombinations occur immediately as the electrons that have diffused into the *p*-type material find holes to fill and holes that have diffused into the *n*-type material are filled by conduction electrons.

**depletion region, uncovered charge**

- **Depletion region.** There is a region on both sides of the junction that has a deficiency of carriers due to recombinations. This region is called a *depletion region*. We might anticipate a continual pouring of carriers into this depletion region were it not for another process that occurs.

- **Uncovered charge.** On the *p*-type material side of the junction in the depletion region, the acceptor atoms bound into the lattice structure are now uncovered. Because the electrons from the *n* side have recombined with many of the holes, the deficiency of charges in the nuclei of the acceptor atoms acts as an excess of negative charges fixed in this region. Similarly, the excess positive charges of the donor nuclei act as positive charges bound into the lattice structure, now uncovered because the electrons that formerly neutralized them have recombined with holes from the *p* side. Thus, we have *uncovered charges* bound into the lattice structure in the depletion region, as shown by Fig. 7.24.

- **The battery-capacitor effect.** This charge distribution acts similar to a capacitor, as shown in Fig. 7.25. Here we show a capacitor with a charge placed on it by a battery. The bottom plate of the capacitor has positive charges and the top has negative charges. If an electron were in the region between the plates, it would move downward, attracted by the positive charges below and

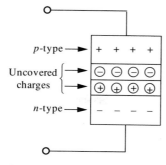

**Figure 7.24** Uncovered charge.

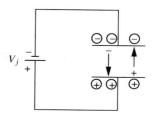

**Figure 7.25** The uncovered charges act like a charged capacitor.

repelled by the negative charges above. Similarly, a positive charge between the plates would move upward. This would be an orderly process and would create a drift current in this region if there were electrons or positive charges between the plates. Similarly, in Fig. 7.24 excess carriers in the depletion region experience forces from the uncovered, bound charges.

■ **Drift current.** These forces would tend to create a drift current upward as electrons are sent back toward the *n*-type material and holes are sent back toward the *p*-type material. Thus, we can envision the holes and electrons moving across the junction due to diffusion but moving the other way by the drift current caused by the uncovered charges.

■ **Dynamic equilibrium.** These two processes rapidly reach dynamic equilibrium. Another way to view this dynamic equilibrium is to consider that the uncovered charges constitute an internal battery–capacitor effect that automatically adjusts itself to stop the diffusion currents. Hence, we have a dynamic equilibrium between a disorderly process, the diffusion process, and an orderly process, the battery–capacitor effect.

**Bound charges.** Due to the uncovered charges, the *pn* junction diode has an internal voltage of approximately 0.7 V across its junction,[5] but no external voltage across the entire diode is produced. No current will flow unless the equilibrium is disturbed by an external voltage.

**Forward-bias characteristic.** If we add an external battery to the diode, as shown by Fig. 7.26, and if the polarity of the external battery is such as to oppose the internal battery–capacitor effect, the equilibrium will be disturbed and current will flow continually through the diode. In this case, the battery causes the holes in the *p*-type material and the electrons in the *n*-type material to move toward the junction. Because the drift process tending to prevent flow of carriers through the depletion region has been neutralized by the external battery, current is carried across the junction by the diffusion currents. The current increases dramatically with increases in the external voltage because it is driven by the energetic thermal motion of the carriers. If the external voltage exceeds the voltage of the internal battery–capacitor effect, large currents will flow:

---

[5] For a silicon-based *pn* junction. Other semiconductors give slightly different voltages.

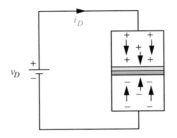

**Figure 7.26** Forward-biased *pn* junction.

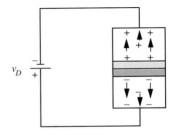

**Figure 7.27** Reverse-biased *pn* junction.

the diode is ON. Because this voltage is only about 0.7 V for a silicon diode, the forward-bias region of the diode approximates that of an ideal diode. A germanium diode requires about 0.2 V to cause substantial conduction and hence is more nearly ideal than a silicon diode.

**Reverse-bias characteristic.** If the polarity of the external voltage reinforces the influence of the internal battery–capacitor effect, the holes in the *p*-type semiconductor and the electrons in the *n*-type semiconductor will tend to move away from the junction, as shown in Fig. 7.27. The external voltage merely widens the depletion region and strengthens the restraining effect of the internal battery–capacitor effect. For this polarity of the external voltage, very little current will flow through the diode and an ideal diode is well approximated: the diode is OFF. The reverse-biased *pn* junction behaves as a capacitor due to the charge separation associated with the uncovered charges. In the next section we give the equation of a *pn*-junction diode and see how well an ideal diode approximates a semiconductor *pn* junction.

## Physical Properties of Real Diodes

**The *pn*-junction equation.** The voltage–current characteristic of the *pn*-junction diode is well described by

$$i_D = I_0\left[\exp\left(\frac{qv_D}{\eta kT}\right) - 1\right] \tag{7.16}$$

where

$\exp(x) = e^x$

$i_D =$ diode current, A

$v_D =$ diode voltage, V

$I_0 =$ a constant called the reverse saturation current, which depends on the semiconductor materials, manner of junction formation, and junction size

$q = |e|$, the magnitude of the electronic charge, $1.60 \times 10^{-19}$ C

$k =$ Boltzmann's constant, $1.38 \times 10^{-23}$ J/K

$T =$ absolute temperature, K

$\eta =$ a constant between 1 and 2, called the *ideality factor*, which depends on junction materials and method of formation

Figure 7.28 shows a plot of Eq. (7.16) for the parameters $\eta = 1.5$ and $I_0 = 10^{-9}$ A. These would be typical of a silicon diode at room temperature. If you wish to plot manually the $pn$-junction equation, it is useful to have $v_D$ as a function of $i_D$.

$$v_D = \eta V_T \ln\left(\frac{i_D}{I_0} + 1\right)$$ (7.17)

**voltage equivalent of temperature**

where $V_T = kT/q$ is called the *voltage equivalent of temperature* and has a magnitude of about 25.9 mV at $T = 300$ K.

If you compare the characteristics of a $pn$-junction diode, Fig. 7.28, with those of an ideal diode, Fig. 7.2, you might be disappointed, for the properties of a real diode appear quite nonideal. That impression is created by our plotting the $pn$-junction characteristic on an expanded voltage scale. Figure 7.29 shows the diode characteristics on the same scale as a 1-kΩ resistor.

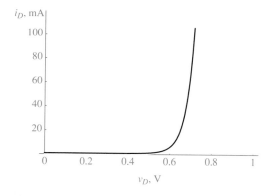

**Figure 7.28** Typical current–voltage characteristic for a silicon diode.

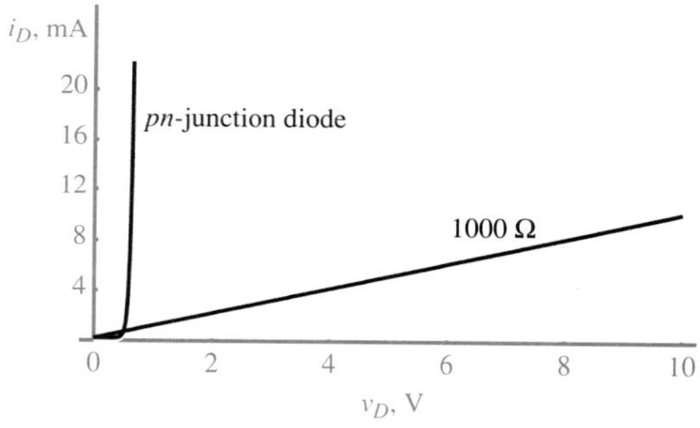

**Figure 7.29** A $pn$-junction diode characteristic compared with a 1-kΩ resistor.

**threshold voltage**

### Junction properties.
The properties of the $pn$-junction diode may be summarized in this fashion: Essentially, zero current flows in the reverse-bias region. Negligible current flows in the forward-bias region until a small *threshold voltage* is reached, after which the magnitude of the current rises rapidly. Once the current begins to rise, the voltage remains fairly constant. The threshold voltage is about 0.7 V for a silicon diode. The $pn$-junction equation, Eqs. (7.16) and (7.17), gives the precise characteristic, but the concept of a threshold voltage is used to simplify analysis for many diode applications. For the rectifier circuits presented earlier in this chapter, we may assume that the diodes will have a voltage of about 0.7 V when they are ON and thus the rectifier output voltages and currents will be reduced accordingly. When modeled by a threshold voltage, the voltage drop of the diode is easy to include in design and analysis of diode circuits.

### Power limits and heat transfer.
Temperature strongly affects the semiconductor processes upon which diode operation depends. In Eq. (7.16), temperature appears explicitly in the exponential term, but the reverse saturation current, $I_0$, is also strongly af-

fected by temperature. For this reason, the electronics designer must prevent the diode from getting too hot. Heat is produced by the electrical power given to the diode.

The power into a device is

$$p = vi \qquad (7.18)$$

The ideal diode requires no power because in the forward-bias region, the voltage is zero, and in the reverse-bias region, the current is zero; hence, the product of voltage and current is always zero. A real diode inherently receives little power because it also has small voltage when the current is high in the forward-bias region and low current when the voltage is high in the reverse-bias region. Even so, the small amount of power that is given to the diode is important because the heat is generated in the junction region, which is physically small. Thus, a small power can cause a significant rise in the junction temperature and affect diode performance. For this reason, diodes in power supplies are designed to have good heat conduction between the junction and the outer case of the diode, and the diode is mounted in such a way as to enhance heat transfer to the ambiance. Often, heat exchangers[6] and even fans are used to improve cooling of the diode. Occasionally, water cooling is used on large power supplies. Figure 7.30 shows a power semiconductor mounted on a heat sink.

**heat sinks**

**reverse-breakdown voltage**

**Breakdown.** A physical diode is also limited by the amount of voltage it can withstand in the reverse-bias region. Conduction is prevented in the reverse-bias region where an external voltage reinforces the effect of the uncovered charges in the depletion region, as suggested in Fig. 7.27. When too much voltage appears across the depletion region, however, the forces on the bound electrons in that region become so great that they can be stripped from their bonds. In this condition, a rapid buildup of current occurs, as shown in Fig. 7.31. The rapid buildup of current at the *reverse-breakdown voltage*, $-V_B$, increases the power into the junction region, and the diode fails.

**peak inverse voltage, PIV**

**Breakdown in power supplies.** Reverse breakdown must be avoided in power supply operation. Designers have available diode types with breakdown voltages[7] in excess of −1000 V. In the unfiltered half-wave rectifier shown in Fig. 7.4, the maximum diode voltage is $-V_p$, which occurs when the diode is OFF and the source at its maxi-

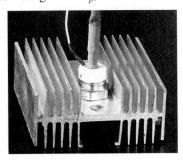

**Figure 7.30** Power semiconductor mounted on a heat sink.

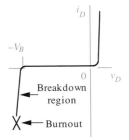

**Figure 7.31** When reverse-bias voltage exceeds the breakdown voltage, the current increases rapidly.

---

[6] Also called *heat sinks*.

[7] Also called *peak inverse voltage*, or *PIV*.

mum negative value. For successful operation in such a power supply, the *PIV* of the diode must exceed this voltage.

In the power supply in Fig. 7.9 with a capaciter, the maximum voltage across a diode is approximately $-2V_p$, as shown in Fig. 7.32. This maximum occurs because the capacitor holds the load voltage at approximately $+V_p$, whereas the voltage source swings negative to $-V_p$. To operate successfully in such a power supply, the diode must be able to withstand $-V_p$.

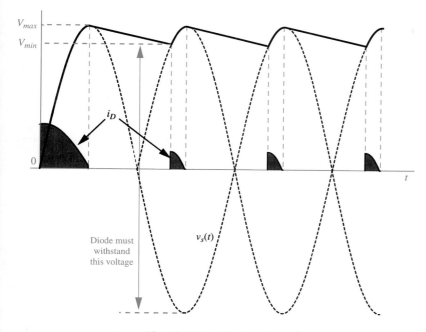

**Figure 7.32** To operate successfully in a rectifier, a diode must never have its breakdown voltage exceeded.

### Check Your Understanding

1. An intrinsic semiconductor has an excess of holes, conduction electrons, or nei her?
2. In a *pn* junction, the *p* stands for semiconductor material that has an excess of holes or electrons?
3. Which of the following are nonlinear devices: resistor, *pn*-junction diode, capacitor, short circuit, ideal diode?
4. In the ON state, current crosses a *pn* junction under the influence of a drift or diffusion process?

*Answers.* (1) Neither; (2) holes; (3) pn-junction diode and ideal diode; (4) diffusion.

## 7.3  BIPOLAR JUNCTION TRANSISTOR (BJT) OPERATION

### Importance of the Transistor

From your earlier experience with circuit theory, you will recall that one can do a fair amount of work solving a two- or three-loop ac circuit. That being true, do you wonder

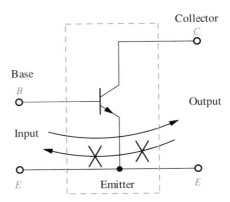

**Figure 7.33** Symbols for an *npn* transistor.

how electrical engineers can design circuits containing literally thousands of loops and nodes? For example, if you ever examine the circuit diagram for a relatively simple piece of electronics, say, a TV set or an FM radio, you would see hundreds of resistors and capacitors, not to mention diodes and transistors and other components.

**One-way property of the transistor.** The design of such complicated circuits is made possible by the unidirectional properties of transistors. The transistor is a three-terminal device connected normally as shown in Fig. 7.33. The transistor has an input and an output, suggesting that the cause–effect relationship goes from left to right. The input affects the output but the output has little effect on the input. This one-directional causality is indicated by marking an arrow from left to right and crossing out the arrow from right to left. We might say that the transistor is a "one-way street" to the electrical signal. This one-directional property of the transistor isolates the output from the input and allows electrical engineers to build complex circuits. This complexity can be mastered because circuits can be designed (or analyzed) one part at a time, unlike the two- or three-loop circuits that we studied in circuit theory, which must be analyzed all at once.

**Impedance Level**

**Other transistor properties.** Transistors can give signal gain, thus allowing small signals, such as a voltage induced in a radio antenna, to be amplified by stages until large enough to power a radio speaker. Transistors also can be used to couple circuits of greatly differing impedance levels, allowing more efficient transfer of signals between them. Transistors are used in digital circuits as electrically controlled switches. Finally, transistors offer a variety of nonlinear effects that are used in communication circuits for manipulating signals in the frequency domain. In this section, however, we limit our attention to the isolating, amplifying, and switching properties of the transistor.

**OBJECTIVE 3**

**To understand the semiconductor processes in the *npn* bipolar–junction transistor and the resulting input and output characteristics**

**Types of transistors.** All transistors accomplish the purposes stated before. There are *npn* and *pnp* bipolar junction transistors (BJTs) and there are *p*-channel and *n*-channel field-effect transistors (FETs). FETs can be either junction field-effect transistors (JFETs) or they can be metal-oxide semiconductor field-effect transistors (MOSFETs). In this section, we deal with the *npn* bipolar-junction transistor, which is symbolized in Fig. 7.33. In the next section, we deal with field-effect transistors.

## BJT Characteristics

As shown in Fig. 7.33, the transistor is a three-terminal device that is connected with one terminal in common between the input and output circuits. The parts of the transistor are the emitter $(E)$, the base $(B)$, and the collector $(C)$, each with appropriately labeled terminals. Our goal in this section is to describe the input and output characteristics of a typical *npn* transistor.

**Transistor input characteristic.** Figure 7.34 shows a simple diagram of the physical structure of an *npn* transistor in the common-emitter configuration. The structure is that of a sandwich, with the *p* material like a very thin piece of bologna between two thick pieces of *n*-material bread. The external connections are made through wires that are bonded to the three regions of the transistor. Depletion regions form at the two *pn* junctions, and, in the absence of external applied voltages, the orderly and disorderly processes rapidly come to equilibrium at both junctions. First we consider the effect of placing a voltage at the base–emitter $(B–E)$ junction, the input part of the transistor.

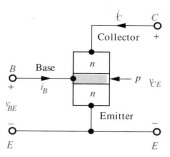

**Figure 7.34** Structure of an *npn* transistor structure.

Ignoring for the present the effect of the collector–base junction, we note that the base–emitter junction forms a *pn*-junction diode. We conclude that the input $i$–$v$ characteristic is like that of a diode, as shown in Fig. 7.35. The base current is very small until sufficient voltage exists across the junction to turn it ON, about 0.7 V for a silicon transistor. Once the junction is turned ON, the base current increases rapidly, with the base–emitter voltage remaining constant at about 0.7 V. Therefore, we can model the base–emitter characteristic as either an open circuit (for $v_{BE} < 0.7$) or else a constant voltage of 0.7 V once the input voltage tries to go above that value. This model is shown in Fig. 7.36. In justifying this model, we ignored the state of the output circuit ($v_{CE}$ and $i_C$); but as we stressed before, the output has negligible effect on the input.

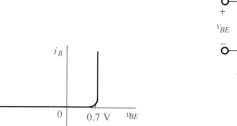

**Figure 7.35** Transistor input characteristic.

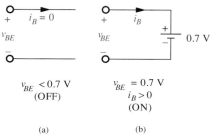

**Figure 7.36** Input circuit model of an *npn* transistor.

EXAMPLE 7.4 **Base current**

A 6-V battery in series with a 10-kΩ resistor is connected to the base circuit of an *npn* transistor, with the positive voltage connected to the base of the transistor. Find the base current.

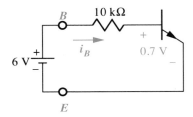

**Figure 7.37** The base-emitter circuit. We represent the base–emitter junction with a voltage of 0.7 V because it is ON for the input.

**SOLUTION:**
Figure 7.37 shows the base–emitter circuit. The *pn* junction between base and emitter will be ON, so the base–emitter voltage is approximately 0.7 V. Thus, KVL around the base emitter loop is

$$-6 + i_B \times 10 \text{ k}\Omega + 0.7 = 0 \quad \Rightarrow \quad i_B = \frac{6 - 0.7}{10 \text{ k}\Omega} = 0.530 \text{ mA} \quad (7.19)$$

**WHAT IF?** What if the required base current were 0.70 mA? Find the required base voltage if the 10-kΩ resistor is unchanged.[8]

## Output Characteristics

**Effect of doping.** Like the input characteristic, the output characteristics depend on whether the collector–base *pn* junction is forward-biased or reverse-biased. We assume that the input current to the base has been fixed at $i_B$, which requires approximately 0.7 V at the base region, considering the reference node to be the emitter. Now we increase the collector–emitter voltage, beginning at zero volts, and observe the collector current.

Consider, first, the holes and electrons in the base region. When we discussed the *pn* junction earlier in describing diode operation, we implied that the same density of holes exists in the *p* region as electrons in the *n* region. In this case, forward biasing the *pn* junction causes roughly as many holes to diffuse into the *n*-type material as electrons to diffuse into the *p*-type material. But if the *n*-type material were more heavily doped than the *p*-type material, the electron density would greatly exceed the hole density. For this case, a forward bias would produce many more electrons diffusing into the *p*-type material than holes diffusing into the *n*-type material. The diode would still work; however, the current would be carried across the junction largely by the electrons, and most of the recombinations would occur in the *p*-type material.

---

[8] 7.7 V.

**Emitter doping.** When a transistor is made, the emitter is doped more heavily than the base; hence, for an *npn* transistor, the conditions are those described earlier—excess electrons diffuse into the base region. For zero volts between collector and emitter, the base–collector junction is also forward-biased. Hence, electrons also tend to diffuse into the base from the collector region. Although there is a buildup of excess electrons in the base region, the only current that flows is that permitted by recombination of electrons in the base: This current is the $i_B$ assumed for the base–emitter bias circuit.

**saturation region**     **Saturation region.** If we now increase the collector–emitter voltage, we reinforce the orderly process forcing a drift current of electrons from the base to the collector. The result is a rapid buildup of collector current as excess electrons are permitted to pass into the collector region, where they flow through the collector–emitter circuit. This region of rapid increase in collector current is the *saturation region* labeled in Fig. 7.38.

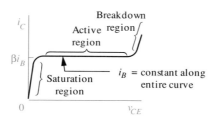

**Figure 7.38** Output current–voltage characteristic with base current held constant.

**active region**     **Active region.** By the time the collector–base voltage is about 0.2 to 0.4 V, all the excess electrons in the base region are being drawn into the collector region and the curve levels off, resulting in the active region in Fig. 7.38. In the *active region,* the collector current is controlled by the number of electrons injected into the base region by the emitter. This is controlled by the base–emitter voltage, which is controlled in turn by the amount of base current the base circuit allows. Thus, in the active region, the collector current is controlled by the base current.

Let us review the principal processes that occur in the active region. The external bias of about 0.7 V that is applied to the base–emitter junction diminishes the orderly process that might hold back the electrons in the heavily doped emitter region. These electrons diffuse into the base region, where a few, say, 1%, combine with holes and create the base current. The remaining 99% diffuse into the collector–base depletion region, where the orderly process of the uncovered bound charges forces them into the collector region. Thus, in the active region, the collector current is controlled by the base current.

**alpha,**
**beta,**
**current gain**     **Current gain of the transistor.** If we call $\alpha$ (alpha) the fraction of electrons that diffuse across the narrow base region, the fraction of electrons that recombine with holes in the base region to create the base current is $1 - \alpha$. The ratios of the base, collector, and emitter currents are thus

$$i_C = \alpha i_E \quad \text{and} \quad i_B = (1 - \alpha) i_E \quad (\alpha < 1) \qquad (7.20)$$

 **Conservation of Charge**

The value of $\alpha$ is fairly constant throughout the active region for a given transistor, and $\alpha$ characterizes the current gain of the device. Usually, the current gain is described in terms of the $\beta$ (beta) of the transistor, defined as

$$\beta = \frac{i_C}{i_B} = \frac{\alpha}{1 - \alpha} \tag{7.21}$$

In terms of $\beta$, the ratios of the currents become

$$i_C = \beta i_B, \qquad i_E = \frac{\beta + 1}{\beta} i_C = (\beta + 1) i_B \tag{7.22}$$

We stress that Eqs. (7.20) to (7.22) are valid only in the active region.

---

**EXAMPLE 7.5**  |  **Transistor currents**

A transistor has a $\beta$ of 150. Find the collector and emitter currents if $i_B = 10\ \mu\text{A}$.

**SOLUTION:**
Assuming the active region, we find from Eq. (7.22)

$$\begin{aligned} i_C &= 150 \times 10\ \mu\text{A} = 1.5\ \text{mA} \\ i_E &= (150 + 1) \times 10\ \mu\text{A} = 1.51\ \text{mA} \end{aligned} \tag{7.23}$$

**WHAT IF?**  |  What if the transistor is saturated?[9]

---

**Breakdown region.**  Figure 7.38 also shows a breakdown region, where the current increases rapidly with increasing collector–emitter voltage. In this region, the power into the transistor becomes excessive and thermal failure often occurs.

Normally, the output characteristics are shown for many values of base current, as in Fig. 7.39. Here we have given typical characteristics for a transistor with a $\beta$ of approximately 100 ($\alpha \approx 0.99$).

### Transistor Amplifier-Switch Circuit Analysis

**common-emitter connection**

**OBJECTIVE 4**

**To understand how to analyze a common-emitter amplifier-switch circuit**

**Problem statement.**  Figure 7.40 shows an important transistor circuit. This circuit uses an *npn* transistor in the *common—emitter connection*, meaning that the emitter of the transistor provides the common terminal between the input and output circuits. The circuit has an input voltage, $v_{in}$, and an output circuit with its output voltage, $v_{out}$. A dc voltage source, $V_{CC}$, in the output circuit supplies the energy required by the circuit, and two resistors, $R_C$ and $R_B$, control the currents and voltages applied to the transistor. The transistor input characteristics are those of a silicon *pn* junction, Fig. 7.35, and the output characteristics are shown in Fig. 7.39. Our goal is to determine how the output voltage depends on the input voltage.

---

[9] We then know that $i_C < 1.5$ mA and $i_E < 1.51$ mA.

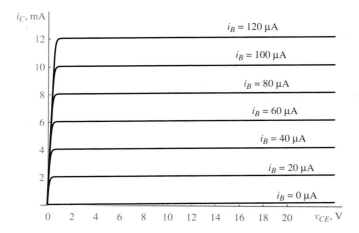

Figure 7.39 Typical *npn* transistor output characteristics.

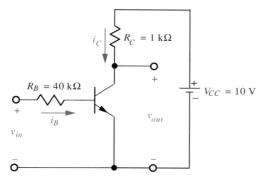

Figure 7.40 Transistor amplifier-switch circuit.

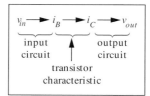

Figure 7.41 Causal relationships in the amplifier-switch circuit go from input to output.

**Causality.** Figure 7.41 shows the causal relationships for this circuit. The input voltage controls the base current through KVL in the input circuit. In the active region, the base current controls the collector current, as described by the transistor characteristics in Fig. 7.39. The collector current controls the output voltage, as determined by KVL in the output circuit. Our analysis proceeds therefore from input to output.

**Figure 7.42** Input circuit.

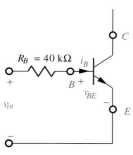

**Input-circuit analysis.** We begin at the input circuit, shown in Fig. 7.42. We first determine the base current, $i_B$, because this current controls the state of the transistor. Let us start with a negative value of $v_{in}$ and increase this voltage to positive values. Comparing the input circuit with the model of the input characteristics in Fig. 7.36, we note that no current flows until the input voltage becomes at least +0.7 V because the *pn* junction is OFF. This is known as *cutoff*, for no current flows in the base or in the collector. When the input voltage exceeds +0.7 V, the base–emitter junction turns ON and the second model circuit in Fig. 7.36 applies. Because in this case $v_{BE}$ is constant at 0.7 V, KVL requires the base current to be

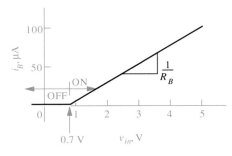

**Figure 7.43** Once the base-emitter junction is ON, the base current is limited by the base resistor, $R_B$.

$$-v_{in} + i_B R_B + 0.7 = 0 \Rightarrow i_B = \frac{v_{in} - 0.7}{R_B}, \qquad v_{in} > 0.7 \text{ V} \qquad (7.24)$$

**cutoff**

This current is graphed in Fig. 7.43. This completes our analysis of the input circuit.

---

**EXAMPLE 7.6** | **Ideal transistor**

Consider the base–emitter *pn* junction an ideal diode. What changes in Eq. (7.24) are required under this assumption?

**SOLUTION:**
The 0.7 represents the threshold voltage of the base–emitter *pn* junction. For an ideal diode, the threshold voltage is zero. Thus, the formula becomes

$$i_B = \frac{v_{in}}{R_B}, \quad v_{in} \geq 0 \text{ V} \qquad (7.25)$$

**WHAT IF ?** | What if the base voltage is negative and so large in magnitude as to cause reverse breakdown of the junction?[10]

---

**Output-circuit analysis.** The output characteristics of the transistor are controlled by the input circuit. In the active region the base current controls the collector current, which in turn determines $v_{out}$.

 **Conservation of Energy**

**Load-line analysis.** The concept of a load line offers an excellent way to understand the interaction of the transistor with the rest of the output circuit. In Fig. 7.44, we have shown the output circuit broken at the transistor collector and emitter connections. When we stand at that break and look to the left, we see the *i–v* output characteristics of the transistor, which are given in Fig. 7.39. If we look to the right, we see the *i–v* characteristics of the external circuit, $V_{CC}$ in series with $R_C$. Using KVL and Ohm's law,

---

[10] Good-bye transistor.

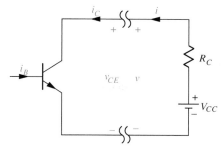

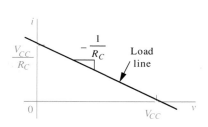

**Figure 7.44** The current–voltage character-istics of the left and right parts of the output circuit may be considered separately.

**Figure 7.45** The right half of the circuit is characterized by a load line.

we find the collector circuit $i$–$v$ characteristic to be

$$-V_{CC} + iR_C + v = 0 \implies i = \frac{V_{CC} - v}{R_C} \tag{7.26}$$

**load line**

When we plot current versus voltage for Eq. (7.26), Fig. 7.45, we observe a straight line with a voltage intercept of $V_{CC}$, a current intercept of $V_{CC}/R_C$, and a slope of $-1/R_C$. This line, known as the *load line*, represents the output circuit external to the transistor.

Figure 7.46 repeats Fig. 7.39 with the load line drawn for our specific values of $V_{CC} = 10$ V and $R_C = 1$ kΩ. The mental break in the output circuit was made for the purpose of examining independently the characteristics of the two parts of the circuit. When we mentally reconnect the circuit, the two voltages must be the same and the two currents must be the same. These requirements determine the current and voltage in the output circuit for a prescribed value of $i_B$.

**Input–output characteristic.** Consider now that the base current is 50 μA. Ac-cording to the transistor output characteristics, the transistor must operate on the line

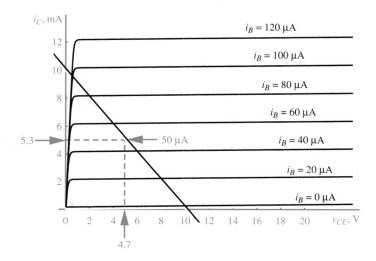

**Figure 7.46** Transistor output characteristic with load line.

corresponding to that base current. On the other hand, the collector circuit must operate on the load line. Both requirements are satisfied at the intersection of the two lines. For 50-μA base current, the intersection occurs at a collector current of 5.3 mA and a collector–emitter voltage of 4.7 V, as indicated in Fig. 7.46. This result demonstrates the method for finding the output voltage from the input voltage. For each input voltage, we can determine the base current, Eq. (7.24) and Fig. 7.43, and for each value of base current, we can determine the output voltage from the intersection with the load line. We can thus plot the input–output characteristic of the amplifier–switch. Such a plot is shown in Fig. 7.47.

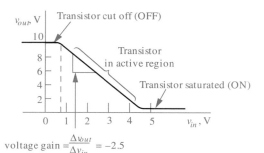

voltage gain $= \dfrac{\Delta v_{out}}{\Delta v_{in}} = -2.5$

**Figure 7.47**   Transistor amplifier-switch input-output characteristic.

---

**EXAMPLE 7.7**   **Different base current**

If the base current is 30 μA, find the input and output voltages.

**SOLUTION:**
The input voltage is given by Eq. (7.24):

$$v_{in} = i_B R_B + 0.7 = 0.03 \text{ mA} \times 40 \text{ k}\Omega + 0.7 = 1.9 \text{ V} \qquad (7.27)$$

The output voltage is given by the intersection of the $i_B = 30$ μA transistor characteristic with the load–line in Fig. 7.46, about $i_C = 3.1$ mA and $v_{CE} = v_{out} = 6.9$ V.

**WHAT IF?**   What if you want the input voltage corresponding to an output of 2 V?[11]

---

**Cutoff.**   Several features of Fig. 7.47 merit close attention. When the input voltage is less than $+0.7$ V, no base current flows and hence no collector current flows. The transistor is cut off. This cutoff condition fixes the output voltage at $V_{CC}$, 10 V in this case. Because no current flows in $R_C$, the full power supply voltage must appear across the transistor. This is like turning OFF a valve in a water pipe; the full pressure must be supported by the valve in the absence of flow.

---

[11] 3.74 V.

**Active region.** As the input voltage increases beyond $+0.7$ V, the base current begins to flow and the transistor moves out of cutoff into the active region. In the active region, the transistor amplifies small changes in the input voltage. The incremental *gain* of the amplifier is the slope of the input-output characteristic in the active region. The characteristic in Fig. 7.43 shows an incremental voltage gain of

$$A_v = \frac{\Delta v_{out}}{\Delta v_{in}} = \frac{-\Delta i_C\, R_C}{\Delta i_B\, R_B} = -\beta \frac{R_C}{R_B} = \frac{-100 \times 1\,\text{k}\Omega}{40\,\text{k}\Omega} = -2.5 \qquad (7.28)$$

The minus sign of the gain signifies the inversion of the incremental changes. That is, a small positive *change* in the input voltage produces a larger negative *change* in the output voltage.

**Saturation.** As the input voltage continues to increase, the base current eventually saturates the transistor. This is like opening fully a valve in a water pipe; the valve relinquishes control of the flow rate to the capacity of the supply. With the transistor saturated, the output voltage remains small, 0.2 to 0.4 V, and the collector current remains at approximately $V_{CC}/R_C = 10$ mA, even though the base current continues to increase as $v_{in}$ continues to increase. Thus in the saturation region the output voltage will remain small for increasing values of the input voltage.

---

**EXAMPLE 7.8** | **Saturation**

What is the base current required to saturate the transistor in Fig. 7.46?

**SOLUTION:**
The load line intersects the saturation region where the base current is approximately 95 μA.

**WHAT IF?** | What if the collector resistor, $R_C$, is changed from 1 to 2 kΩ? What is the base current required to saturate the transistor?[12]

---

## Transistor Applications

**Ideal and real switches.** An *ideal switch* is either an open circuit (OFF) or a short circuit (ON). A *real switch*, like the wall switch for the lights, has a large resistance when OFF and a small resistance when ON. To function properly as a switch, the device must have a large OFF resistance compared with the impedance level of the load such that almost all the voltage appears across the switch and very little voltage appears across the load. Likewise, in the ON state, the switch must have a small resistance compared with the impedance level of the load so that almost all the voltage appears across the load with very little voltage across the switch.

IDEA **Impedance Level**

---

[12] About 0.047 mA.

**The transistor as a switch.** Thus, the transistor can function as an electronic switch in the circuit shown in Fig. 7.40 if its OFF resistance is much larger than its load resistor, $R_C$, and its ON resistance is much smaller than its load resistor.

If the input voltage is less than 0.7 V, the transistor is cut off, that is, the electronic switch is OFF. If $R_C$ represented a light bulb, no current would flow through the bulb and it would not glow. If, for example, the input voltage exceeded about 4.0 V, the transistor would be saturated and our electronic switch would be ON. If $R_C$ were a light bulb, it would glow. Thus, we can use the transistor as a voltage-controlled switch to turn the bulb on and off.

**The importance of transistor switches.** The switching action of the transistor is one of its most valuable properties. This is true because digital circuits—computers, calculators, digital watches, and digital instrumentation—utilize transistors in switching operation. Some of the important applications of transistors in digital circuits are explored in Chapters 8 and 10.

**large signal amplifier**

**Large-signal amplifiers.** An amplifier is called a *large-signal amplifier* when the signal levels require the full transistor characteristics, from near cutoff to near saturation. Such amplifiers can furnish moderate amounts of power to transducers such as loudspeakers or control motors. The amplifier-switch circuit in Fig. 7.40 is limited to an output voltage of 10 V, peak to peak, but this limitation can be overcome by increasing the power supply voltage or the circuit complexity. As shown in Chapter 9, feedback techniques can be used to reduce distortion and generally improve the characteristics of large-signal amplifiers.

---

**EXAMPLE 7.9** | **Large-signal amplifiers**

What is the maximum peak-to-peak output voltage ($v_{CE}$) and the corresponding peak-to-peak input voltage?

**SOLUTION:**
Figures 7.46 and 7.47 show the maximum output voltage to be 10 V when the transistor is cut off and about 0.3 V when saturated; hence, the peak-to-peak is 9.7 V. The corresponding range at the input is shown by Fig. 7.47 to be 0.7 to 4.6 V.

**WHAT IF?** | What if you compute the large-signal gain from these peak-to-peak values?[13]

---

## Small-Signal Amplifiers

**stages of amplification**

**The importance of small-signal amplifiers.** Most amplifiers are small-signal amplifiers. Consider, for example, a radio that receives a signal of 10 mV and produces

---

[13] $A_V = -2.49$.

an output voltage of 10 V. Such a radio would require a voltage gain of 1000. This gain would be accomplished in *stages*, each transistor amplifier stage taking as its input the output of the previous stage. If each stage had a voltage gain of $\sqrt{10}$, six stages of amplification would provide the necessary gain. Of these, all but the last stage would be small-signal amplifiers.

**Equivalent Circuits**

**Converting the amplifier switch to a small-signal amplifier.** A small-signal amplifier must have a *dc bias* circuit for placing the transistor in its amplifying region, a means for introducing the input signal, and a means for supplying its output signal to the next stage. The circuit shown in Fig. 7.48 is the basic amplifier in Fig. 7.40 with a voltage divider added to provide bias at the input and with coupling at input and output. We symbolized the power supply connection with the terminal marked $+V_{CC}$, which appears as an open circuit but actually is connected through a dc power supply to ground. The two resistors $R_1$ and $R_2$ comprise a voltage divider to supply dc current to the transistor base to bias the transistor into its amplifying region. At the input, we have a Thévenin equivalent circuit of the signal source; this represents the previous stage of the amplifier or the origin of the signal such as a microphone or a radio antenna. The load, $R_L$, represents the input impedance of the next stage of the amplifier.

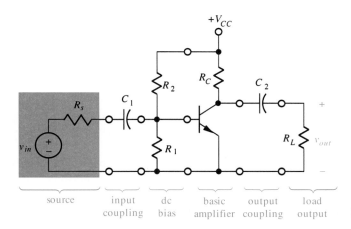

source    input coupling    dc bias    basic amplifier    output coupling    load output

**Figure 7.48**   Small-signal amplifier.

**coupling capacitors**

**Impedance Level**

**Coupling capacitors.** Capacitors $C_1$ and $C_2$ in Fig. 7.48 are coupling capacitors. Large capacitors block dc current but pass ac current. The infinite impedance of the capacitor at dc allows the dc state of each amplifier stage to be independent of the adjoining stages. If the impedance of the capacitors is small relative to the impedance level of the circuit, the time-varying signals will pass through the capacitors undiminished. Thus, the stages are isolated for dc but coupled for ac signals by the *coupling capacitors* at the input and output.

**OBJECTIVE 5**

**To understand how to analyze a common-emitter small-signal amplifier for operating point and gain**

**Bias voltage divider.** A dc current is supplied to the transistor base by the voltage divider, $R_1$ and $R_2$. Because the coupling capacitors act as blocks to the dc current, the equivalent circuit at dc is as shown in Fig. 7.49 (a). Although there is only one power supply, we have replaced the $+V_{CC}$ symbol with two voltages sources. We draw the circuit this way for two reasons: (1) to emphasize that the power supply acts independently on the bias and collector circuits, and (2) to help you recognize the voltage

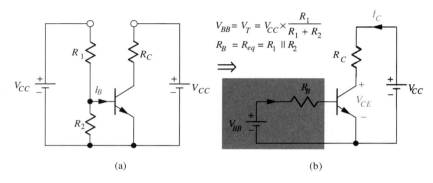

$$V_{BB} = V_T = V_{CC} \times \frac{R_1}{R_1 + R_2}$$

$$R_B = R_{eq} = R_1 \parallel R_2$$

$\Rightarrow$

(a)                                         (b)

**Figure 7.49** (a) DC bias circuit; (b) Thévenin equivalent circuit of the input portion of bias circuit.

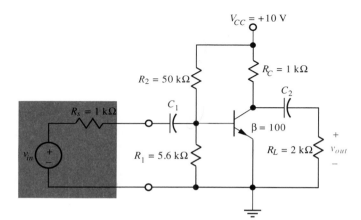

**Figure 7.50** Small-signal amplifier. The capacitors are assumed to have negligible impedance to the signal.

divider. The base circuit in Fig. 7.49 (a) can be reduced to the familiar circuit in Fig. 7.40 by converting the voltage divider to a Thévenin equivalent circuit, as shown in Fig. 7.49 (b). We used the symbol $V_{BB}$ for the open-circuit voltage at the base of the transistor. This plays the role of $v_{in}$ in Fig. 7.40 and Eq. (7.24).

**Bias analysis.** We continue this development for the specific circuit shown in Fig. 7.50. The open-circuit base dc bias voltage is

$$V_{BB} = 10 \times \frac{5.6 \text{ k}\Omega}{50 \text{ k}\Omega + 5.6 \text{ k}\Omega} = 1.0 \text{ V} \tag{7.29}$$

and the dc output impedance of the bias network, $R_B$, is

$$R_B = 5.6 \text{ k}\Omega \parallel 50 \text{ k}\Omega = 5.0 \text{ k}\Omega \tag{7.30}$$

Assuming a silicon transistor that requires a threshold voltage of $V_{BE} = 0.7$ V to turn ON the base–emitter junction, we can use the equivalent circuit in Fig. 7.36. Thus, the dc base current by Eq. (7.24) is

$$I_B = \frac{V_{BB} - 0.7}{R_B} = \frac{1.0 \text{ V} - 0.7 \text{ V}}{5.0 \text{ k}\Omega} = 60 \text{ } \mu\text{A} \tag{7.31}$$

Assuming the transistor to be in the active region, we calculate the collector dc current, $I_C$, to be

$$I_C = \beta I_B = 100 \times 60 \ \mu A = 6.0 \ mA \tag{7.32}$$

To confirm that the transistor is in the active region, not saturated, we must determine the dc collector–emitter voltage, $V_{CE}$. We could use a load line, but KVL around the collector–emitter loop in Fig. 7.49 (b) will do as well.

$$-V_{CC} + I_C R_C + V_{CE} = 0 \ \Rightarrow \ V_{CE} = 10 - (6.0 \ mA)(1 \ k\Omega) = 4.0 \ V \tag{7.33}$$

Thus, the transistor is operating near the middle of its active region. If there were no input signal, the transistor would have a steady voltage of +4.0 V across it, but the voltage across the 2-kΩ load resistor would remain zero because the dc voltage would be blocked by the output coupling capacitor, $C_2$.

---

**EXAMPLE 7.10** **Changing $R_B$**

What if $R_B$ were 2 kΩ but $V_{BB}$ were the same? What would be $V_{CE}$?

**SOLUTION:**
Equation (7.24) is still valid:

$$I_B = \frac{1.0 \ V - 0.7 \ V}{2 \ k\Omega} = 150 \ \mu A \tag{7.34}$$

But Eq. (7.32) is no longer valid because 150 μA of base current saturates the transistor, Fig. 7.46. Thus $V_{CE} \approx 0.3$ V and $I_C = I_{C \, (sat)} \approx 9.7$ mA.

**WHAT IF?** What if $V_{BB}$ and $R_B$ have their original values but $R_C$ is changed to 2 kΩ? Find $V_{CE}$.[14]

---

**small-signal component**

**DC and small signals.** We now consider the effect of an input signal. In general, all voltages and currents in the circuit will have two components, a dc component and a time-varying component, which we call the *small-signal* component. For example, the base current is

$$i_B(t) = I_B + i_b(t) \tag{7.35}$$

where $I_B = 60 \ \mu A$ and $i_b(t)$ is the small-signal component, with $i_b \ll I_B$.

**signal ground**

**Small-signal equivalent circuit.** What is the equivalent circuit that the signals "see," in the sense that Fig. 7.49 (a) is the circuit seen by the dc voltages and currents? Beginning at the input and moving toward the output, we now justify the circuit shown

---

[14]$V_{CE} = 0.3$ V, still saturated.

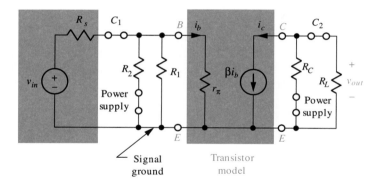

**Figure 7.51** Small-signal equivalent circuit.

**Equivalent Circuits**

in Fig. 7.51 as the appropriate small-signal equivalent circuit. The input source and its resistance, $R_s$, are now coupled to the amplifier with a short circuit representing the negligible impedance of $C_1$ to the signal. The base bias resistor $R_1$ appears as expected, but $R_2$ now connects to the *signal ground*[15] because of the low impedance of the power supply to the signal. The power supply circuit, not shown but represented by the $V_{CC}$ symbol, is connected to the circuit ground by a filter capacitor, as shown, for example, in Fig. 7.13. This filter capacitor not only filters the power supply output, but also provides a low-impedance path to ground for the signal.

**dependent current source**

**Transistor small-signal model.** The input impedance of the transistor is represented by a resistor, $r_\pi$, and the output by a dependent current source. Representing the base–emitter by a constant 0.7 V, as shown in Fig. 7.36 (b), is adequate for the dc solution but is not accurate for the signal: $r_\pi$ is a relatively low resistance in the range 300 to 1000 $\Omega$ that may be determined from theory,[16] from measured transistor input characteristics, or from published specifications of the transistor. The *dependent current source*,[17] $i_c = \beta i_b$, represents the current gain of the transistor.

In the output circuit, the collector bias resistor, $R_C$, is shown connected to the signal ground for the reason given before for $R_2$. Finally, the collector is connected to the load resistor, $R_L$, through the short circuit that represents the output coupling capacitor.

**Analyzing the small-signal circuit.** The small-signal equivalent circuit in Fig. 7.51 may be analyzed for the voltage gain, $A_v = v_{out}/v_{in}$, by the standard methods of circuit theory. Our analysis begins at the input with the calculation of $i_b$, the base signal current. From the base current, we can calculate the collector small-signal current, $i_c$, and then the small-signal output voltage.

The small-signal base current is easily calculated if the input source is converted to a Norton circuit, as shown in Fig. 7.52. We thus have a four-way current divider. The base current is the base voltage divided by $r_\pi$:

---

[15] The "signal ground" is the reference node for the signals in the circuit. Here it is identical to the power "ground." These "grounds" may not correspond to actual earth ground in the circuit. (See p. 82.)

[16] see Problem 7.31.

[17] A dependent current source is a current source whose value depends on a voltage or current elsewhere in the circuit. Here we have a current-controlled current source because the collector current depends on the base current in the active region.

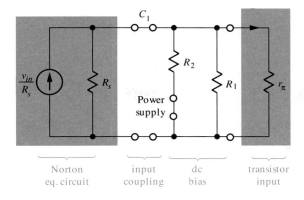

<br>

| | | | | |
|---|---|---|---|---|
| Norton eq. circuit | input coupling | dc bias | transistor input | |

**Figure 7.52** Analysis of the input circuit is simplified through use of a source transformation.

$$i_b = \frac{v_{in}}{R_s} \times \frac{R_s \| R_2 \| R_1 \| r_\pi}{r_\pi} \qquad (7.36)$$

For the values in Fig. 7.50 and $r_\pi = 450\ \Omega$, Eq. (7.36) leads to $i_b = v_{in}/1.54\ \text{k}\Omega$. The collector current is $\beta i_b$, and the output voltage is thus

$$v_{out} = -\beta i_b (R_C \| R_L) = -100 \frac{v_{in}}{1.54\ \text{k}\Omega}(1\ \text{k}\Omega \| 2\ \text{k}\Omega) = -43.3 v_{in} \qquad (7.37)$$

Thus, the voltage gain of the amplifier is $A_v = v_{out}/v_{in} = -43.3$. The minus sign represents inversion of the signal.

---

**EXAMPLE 7.11**  **Small signal amplifier**

What value of $R_L$ gives a gain of $-30$?

**SOLUTION:**
The only equation that changes is Eq.(7.37), which becomes

$$-30 v_{in} = -100 \frac{v_{in}}{1.54\ \text{k}\Omega}(1\ \text{k}\Omega \| R'_L) \qquad (7.38)$$

where $R'_L$ is the new load resistor. Equation (7.38) yields $R'_L = 858\ \Omega$.

**WHAT IF?**  What if $r_\pi$ was 740 $\Omega$, but $R_L$ was the original value of 2 k$\Omega$? Find the new voltage gain.[18]

---

[18] $A_v = -35.3$.

**Summary.** The calculation of the small-signal gain of the amplifier requires analysis of a dc equivalent circuit and a small-signal equivalent circuit. In the latter, the transistor is represented by its input resistance and a dependent current source, coupling capacitors by short circuits, and the power supply by a short circuit to signal ground. Because of the one-way property of the transistor, the analysis proceeds from input to output.

### Check Your Understanding

1. For a transistor, the conditions in the output (C–E) circuit have little influence on the input (B–E) circuit. (True or false?)

2. What type of semiconductor material is the base region for an *npn* transistor?

3. The input (B–E) current–voltage characteristic of a transistor is similar to that of a resistor, an ideal diode, a *pn*-junction diode, or an open circuit?

4. The load line intersects the current axis at the current that would flow if the transistor were replaced by a short circuit. (True or false?)

5. In the saturation region, the transistor acts as a switch that is ON or OFF?

6. To be used as an amplifier, the transistor must be biased into its cutoff, active, breakdown, or saturation region?

7. If the voltage gain of a transistor amplifier is negative, it means that the signal is diminished by the amplifier. (True or false?)

*Answers.* **(1)** True; **(2)** *p*-type; **(3)** a *pn*-junction diode; **(4)** true; **(5)** ON; **(6)** active; **(7)** false.

## 7.4  FIELD-EFFECT TRANSISTORS

**OBJECTIVE 6**

**To understand FET operation and applications**

The bipolar-junction transistor (BJT) was invented in 1947 and developed to usable form in the late 1950s. The field-effect transistor (FET) was also invented in the late 1940s but was made practical by manufacturing developments in the 1970s. Today, virtually all digital electronic systems such as watches and computers use integrated circuits of FETs operating as electronic switches.

Like the BJT, the FET comes in two polarity types: the *n*-channel corresponds to the *npn* and the *p*-channel corresponds to the *pnp*. We limit our study to *n*-channel devices. Unlike the BJT, FETs come in two varieties: the junction FET (JFET) and the metal-oxide semiconductor FET (MOSFET). We consider the JFET in detail and then deal briefly with the MOSFET because its properties are similar.

### Junction Field-Effect Transistors

The physical construction of an *n*-channel JFET is shown in Fig. 7.53 (a). The transistor has three terminals, gate (G), drain (D), and source (S). The input signal is the voltage applied between gate and source, $v_{GS}$, and the output signal is the current from drain to source, $i_D$. The gate is connected to the *p*-type semiconductor, and the drain and source are connected to the channel, which is *n*-type material. For proper operation, the *pn* junction between the gate and channel regions must be reverse-biased, $v_{GS} < 0$, so that a depletion region is formed, as shown. The depletion region acts as a nonconductor, but the remainder of the channel acts as a conductor and thus forms a "resistor" with

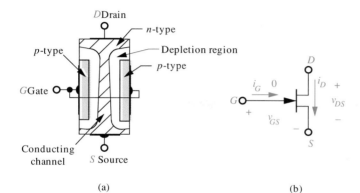

(a)

(b)

**Figure 7.53** (a) JFET construction; (b) JFET circuit symbol.

peculiar properties. The width of the depletion region and thus the width of the conducting channel depend on the gate voltage. The drain is operated at a positive voltage relative to the source, and hence the gate–drain end of the *pn* junction is more strongly reverse-biased than the gate–source end. For this reason, we show the conducting channel to be more narrow near the drain. The circuit symbol for the JFET is shown in Fig. 7.53(b). Notice that the arrow points from *p* to *n*, as for a diode.

**Impedance Level**

**Input characteristics.** Because the *pn* junction between gate and channel is reverse biased, very little current flows into the gate. Thus, we show $i_G \approx 0$ in Fig. 7.53(b), and the drain current flows through the channel and out the source connection. The gate controls the current in the channel through an electric field[19] that affects the depletion region. Because very little current flows into the gate, the input impedance level of the device is extremely high, up to $10^{12}\,\Omega$, and very little energy is required to control the device.

**ohmic region, pinchoff, saturation region**

**Output characteristics.** Like the BJT, the FET has several regions of operation, which we may examine by fixing the input voltage, $v_{GS}$, and observing the output current as we vary the output voltage, $v_{DS}$. Figure 7.54(a) shows the circuit for the experiment, and Fig. 7.54(b) shows the results. Consider first the top curve, where $v_{GS} = 0$ V. For small values of drain-source voltage, the current increases as for a resistor. This is the *ohmic region*. However, as $v_{DS}$ increases, the current begins to level off because the channel narrows at the drain end of the device. At the negative of the *pinchoff* voltage, $-V_P$, the conducting channel reaches a minimum size and the current becomes constant, independent of further increases in $v_{DS}$. This is the *saturation region*.[20] In the saturation region, the drain current is controlled totally by the input signal, and thus the saturation region for the FET corresponds to the active region for the BJT. Off the graph, to the right, is a breakdown region, where the current increases rapidly.

For smaller values of $v_{GS}$ (negative values), currents fall below the curve corresponding to $v_{GS} = 0$, and the device changes from the ohmic region to the saturation re-

---

[19] Electric fields are defined in Chapter 13. For now, think of an electric field as something to move the carriers.

[20] Warning: This "saturation region" is totally different from the saturation region for the BJT. Using the same term for both is unfortunate and confusing, but customary.

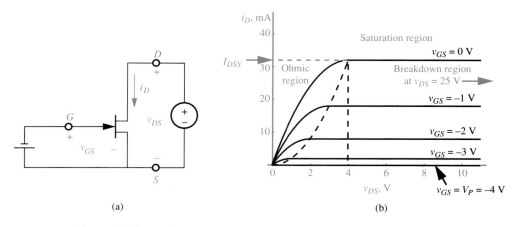

Figure 7.54 (a) Circuit for determining the output characteristic; (b) output characteristics for $V_P = -4$ V and $I_{DSS} = 32$ mA.

**Figure 7.54** (a) Circuit for determining the output characteristic; (b) output characteristics for $V_P = -4$ V and $I_{DSS} = 32$ mA.

gion at lower values of $v_{DS}$. For $v_{GS} < V_P$, the FET is cut off, meaning that no current flows, regardless of $v_{DS}$.

**Theoretical model.** In the ohmic region, the drain current is given by

$$i_D = \frac{2I_{DSS}}{V_P^2} \left[ (v_{GS} - V_P) v_{DS} - \frac{v_{DS}^2}{2} \right],$$

$$0 < v_{DS} < (v_{GS} - V_P), \ v_{GS} > V_P \tag{7.39}$$

where $I_{DDS}$ is the saturation current for $v_{GS} = 0$, as indicated in Fig. 7.54 (b). Equation (7.39) describes a parabola passing through the origin and tangent to the point of pinchoff. After pinchoff, the current is constant at the value

$$i_D = \frac{I_{DSS}}{V_P^2} (v_{GS} - V_P)^2, \qquad v_{GS} > V_P, \qquad v_{DS} > v_{GS} - V_P \tag{7.40}$$

---

**EXAMPLE 7.12** **FET characteristics**

What value of $v_{GS}$ corresponds to $i_D = 15$ mA and $v_{DS} = 6$ V?

**SOLUTION:**
This falls in the saturation region. Equation (7.40) yields

$$15 = \frac{32}{(-4)^2} [v_{GS} - (-4)]^2 \Rightarrow v_{GS} = -1.26 \text{ V} \tag{7.41}$$

**WHAT IF?** What if you are in the ohmic region with $i_D = 15$ mA and $v_{DS} = 1.5$ V?[21]

**Summary.** The JFET has four regions of operation. In the cutoff region, no current flows. In the ohmic region, the device behaves like a nonlinear resistor, with the resistance controlled mainly by the gate–source voltage. In the saturation region, the device behaves as a current source, with the current controlled by the gate–source voltage. Finally, in the breakdown region, the drain current increases rapidly. With the exception of the breakdown region, which is to be avoided, all the regions are useful.

**Determining the region of operation.** The region of operation for a JFET can be determined by the simple rules given in Table 7.1. We consider that the transistor has two ends: a gate–source end and a gate–drain end. The ends can be ON or OFF, depending on the voltage between the gate and the source or drain. For example, in the device shown in Fig. 7.54 (b), the pinchoff voltage is $-4$ V. Therefore, if the gate–source voltage is greater than $-4$ V, the gate–source end of the transistor will be ON, and if the gate–source voltage is less than (more negative than) $-4$ V, the gate–source end of the transistor will be OFF. Likewise, if the gate–drain voltage is greater than $-4$ V, the gate–drain end of the transistor will be ON; otherwise, it is OFF. With these definitions of ON and OFF, the transistor has the four states shown in Table 7.1.

**TABLE 7.1   Determination of Transistor Operating Region**

| Gate-Source End | Gate-Drain End | Condition |
| :---: | :---: | :--- |
| OFF | OFF | Cutoff region |
| OFF | ON | Reverse saturation |
| ON | OFF | Saturation region |
| ON | ON | Ohmic region |

We have already discussed rows 1, 3, and 4 in Table 7.1. Row 2 deals with a condition not previously discussed. For the gate–source end to be OFF and the gate–drain end to be ON, the drain voltage must be negative relative to the source voltage; and hence source and drain exchange roles. In this case, the current will flow from source to drain if we keep the same labels. This condition is useful also but will not be discussed further.

---

**EXAMPLE 7.13**   **Finding the region of operation**

An *n*-channel JFET has a pinchoff voltage of $-3$ V. The gate–source voltage is $-1$ V and the drain–source voltage is $+2$ V. What is the region of operation?

**SOLUTION:**
The gate–source voltage is greater than the pinchoff voltage, so the gate–source end is ON. The gate-drain voltage may be determined from KVL and the law of subscripts:

---

[21] $v_{GS} = -0.75$ V.

$$v_{GD} = v_{GS} + v_{SD} = v_{GS} - v_{DS} = -1 - (+2) = -3 \text{ V} \qquad (7.42)$$

This is equal to the pinchoff voltage, and hence the gate–drain end of the transistor is borderline between ON and OFF. Therefore the transistor is on the boundary between the ohmic region (row 4) and saturation (row 3).

**WHAT IF?**   What if $v_{GS} = -4$ V?[22]

## JFET Applications

**Variable resistance.** In the ohmic region, the JFET acts as a resistor between drain and source whose resistance is controlled by $v_{GS}$. For small signals of $v_{DS}$, the resistance, $r_{DS}$, can be determined from Eq. (7.39):

$$r_{DS} \approx \frac{1}{\partial i_D / \partial v_{DS}} = \frac{V_p^2}{2 I_{DSS}(v_{GS} - V_P)}, \qquad v_{DS} \ll v_{GS} - V_P \qquad (7.43)$$

Hence, the resistance is smallest for large $v_{GS}$.

**EXAMPLE 7.14**  **FET resistance**

Find the small-signal resistance of the transistor in Fig. 7.54(b) for $v_{GS} = 0$.

**SOLUTION:**
From Eq. (7.43),

$$r_{DS} \approx \frac{(-4)^2}{2(32 \times 10^{-3})(0 - (-4))} = 62.5\,\Omega \qquad (7.44)$$

**WHAT IF?**   What if you want $r_{DS} = 1000$ $\Omega$?[23]

**Small-signal amplifier.** Like the BJT, the JFET may be used as a small-signal amplifier. In this application, the JFET is biased into its saturation region, and small changes in $v_{GS}$ produce changes in the drain current that, passed through a resistor in the drain circuit, amplify the signal. To represent the JFET for this application, we require a small-signal model for the transistor, Fig. 7.55. The voltage and current variables are signal components and must remain much smaller than the dc bias voltages and current.

---

[22] Both ends are OFF. The transistor is cut off and $i_D = 0$.
[23] $v_{GS} = -3.75$ V.

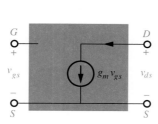

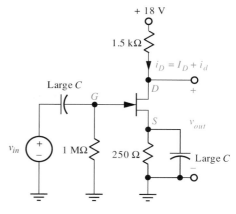

**Figure 7.55** Small-signal model for the JFET. The voltages and current are signal components of the total voltages and current. The gain-related parameter $g_m$ is the transconductance.

**Figure 7.56** A JFET amplifier. The capacitors block dc but act as short circuits for the signal.

**transconductance, voltage-controlled current source**

The gate circuit is shown as an open circuit because the gate draws no current. The drain–source circuit is shown as a voltage-controlled current source.[24] The *transconductance*, $g_m$, may be derived from Eq. (7.40):

$$g_m = \frac{\partial i_D}{\partial v_{GS}} = \frac{2I_{DSS}}{V_p^2} (v_{GS} - V_P)\Big|_{v_{GS} = V_{GS}} \tag{7.45}$$

where $V_{GS}$ is the dc bias voltage between gate and source. The use of Eq. (7.45) and the small-signal equivalent circuit are illustrated in the following analysis.

**JFET-amplifier bias analysis.** We will determine the small-signal gain of the amplifier shown in Fig. 7.56. The transistor has the output characteristics shown in Fig. 7.54 (b). Our first task is to determine the dc conditions in the circuit because the transconductance, $g_m$, depends on the dc conditions. To establish the bias condition, we must solve simultaneously for the dc gate–source voltage and the drain current. The source is not grounded but is biased to a positive voltage by the current passing through the 250-$\Omega$ resistor. The gate is grounded through the 1-M$\Omega$ resistor, but because no current flows in this resistor, the gate is at zero volts. Consequently, the gate–source voltage is

$$v_{GS} = v_G - v_S = 0 - 0.250i_D \tag{7.46}$$

where current is expressed in milliamperes and the reference node is the signal ground. We assume that the JFET is saturated and hence we obtain another equation relating the gate-source voltage and the drain current from Eq. (7.40).

---

[24] A *voltage-controlled current source* is a current source whose current depends on a voltage elsewhere in the circuit. The constant relating the signal current in the drain to the signal voltage between gate and source has units of siemens, or mhos (reciprocal ohms).

$$i_D = \frac{I_{DSS}}{V_P^2}(v_{GS} - V_P)^2 = \frac{32}{(-4)^2}[v_{GS} - (-4)]^2 \qquad (7.47)$$

When we eliminate $v_{GS}$ between Eqs. (7.46) and (7.47), we obtain a quadratic equation for the drain current. The two solutions are $i_D = 8.0$ and $32.0$ mA. The second value is unrealistic for several reasons.[25] The $I_D = 8.0$ mA can be accepted tentatively, but we must verify our assumption that the transistor is in the saturation region. With a drain current of 8 mA, the source voltage is $+2$ V and hence $v_{GS} = -2$ V. The gate–source end of the transistor is ON, as required for saturation. The drain voltage can be obtained from KVL as $+18$ V $-$ (8 mA $\times$ 1.5 k$\Omega$) $= +6$ V. Hence, the gate–drain voltage is $-6$ V and the gate–drain end of the transistor is OFF. Therefore, the transistor is operating in row 3 of Table 7.1, in the saturation region as assumed.

**Small-signal analysis.** Figure 7.57 shows the small-signal equivalent circuit for the amplifier in Fig. 7.56. Because the capacitors have a small impedance to the signal, we replaced them with short circuits. The power supply also has a small impedance to the signal, and hence we have connected one end of the 1.5-k$\Omega$ resistor to the signal ground. The transistor had been replaced by its equivalent circuit from Fig. 7.55. The transconductance of $8 \times 10^{-3}$ mhos has been determined from Eq. (7.45) for the dc operating conditions established before.

The analysis of the circuit proceeds from input to output. The gate–source signal voltage is equal to the input voltage because the source is connected to the signal ground. Thus, the signal current in the drain–source circuit is $(8 \times 10^{-3}) v_{in}$. This current flows upward through the 1.5-k$\Omega$ resistor, and hence the output voltage is

$$v_{out} = -(8 \times 10^{-3})v_{in} \times 1.5 \times 10^3 = -12.0\, v_{in} \qquad (7.48)$$

Thus, the voltage gain of the amplifier is $-12.0$. The minus sign indicates inversion of the signal.

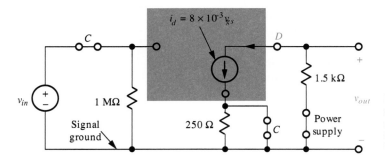

**Figure 7.57** Small-signal equivalent circuit. The transistor has been replaced by its small-signal model, and the capacitors and the power supply have been replaced by short circuits.

---

[25] See Problem 7.44.

EXAMPLE 7.15 **Grounding the source**

What is the drain current if the source is grounded in Fig. 7.56?

**SOLUTION:**

Because $v_G = 0$ and $v_S = 0$, then $v_{GS} = 0$. To find $i_D$, we must assume either the ohmic region, Eq. (7.39), or the saturation region, Eq. (7.40). Because the latter is simpler, we will see if it produces consistent results.

$$i_D = \frac{32}{(-4)^2}[0 - (-4)]^2 = 32 \text{ mA} \tag{7.49}$$

If this is the drain current, then the drain voltage is

$$v_D = 18\,\text{V} - (32 \text{ mA} \times 1.5 \text{ k}\Omega) = -30 \text{ V} \tag{7.50}$$

This would turn ON the gate–drain junction and thus the transistor cannot be in the saturation region; hence, Eq. (7.50) cannot be valid. This inconsistency shows that the transistor must be in the ohmic region.

**WHAT IF?**

What if you try it with Eq. (7.39)? What is $i_D$?[26]

---

**Impedance Level**

**JFET application as a switch.** Figure 7.58 (a) shows a circuit that uses a JFET as a voltage-controlled switch. Figure 7.58(b) shows the load line. With $v_{GS}$ less than $-4$ V, the transistor is cut off and the output voltage is $+10$ V. With $v_{GS} = 0$ V, the transistor is in the ohmic region and, as shown in Example 7.14 on FET resistance, has a resistance of about 63 $\Omega$. Thus, the FET switch must operate in circuits with high-impedance levels. In series with 2 k$\Omega$, this drops the output voltage to about 0.3 V. Thus, the JFET can act as a voltage-controlled switch.

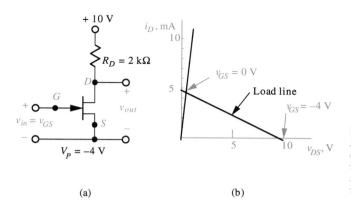

(a)

(b)

**Figure 7.58** (a) In this circuit, the JFET can operate as a switch; (b) by changing the input voltage from –4 to 0 V, the JFET can be changed from OFF to ON and the output voltage changed from 10 V to near zero.

[26] 6.98 mA.

**Summary.** In this section, we investigated the physical construction, input and output characteristics, and equivalent circuits appropriate to the various regions of operation of the *n*-channel JFET. We investigated its applications as a switch, a voltage-controlled resistor, and a small-signal amplifier. In the next section, we introduce briefly a class of devices very similar to the JFETs.

## Metal-Oxide Semiconductor Field-Effect Transistors (MOSFETs)

**Depletion-mode MOSFET.** Figure 7.59 (a) shows the physical structure of an *n*-channel depletion-mode MOSFET. The substrate of *p* material is maintained at a voltage equal to or less than any voltage anticipated at either source or drain so that a depletion region forms at the *pn* junction and isolates the channel from the substrate. Normally, the drain is operated positive relative to the source, and hence the substrate can be connected to the source to accomplish this purpose. On the circuit symbol, Fig. 7.59(b), the arrow in the substrate connection points from *p* to *n*.

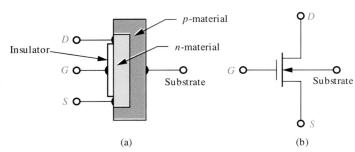

(a)                          (b)

**Figure 7.59** (a) Physical construction of an n-channel depletion-mode MOSFET. The substrate connection is kept at a dc voltage that is negative relative to all anticipated voltages at the source and drain. (b) The gate is shown insulated from the channel.

**threshold voltage (MOSFET)**

The gate is separated from the channel by an insulating layer and hence no current flows into the gate. If the gate has a large negative voltage relative to the channel, the carrier electrons are driven from the channel, which becomes a nonconductor and the channel is cut off. Like the JFET, there exists a critical voltage to cut off the channel. This is called the *threshold voltage*, $V_T$, and has the same effect as the pinchoff voltage for the JFET. Indeed, the depletion-mode MOSFET has similar characteristics to the JFET, except that the gate–source voltage can be positive. It has regions of cutoff, saturation, and ohmic operation, as described by Table 7.1. For example, if a depletion-mode MOSFET has a threshold voltage of –5 V, the gate–source voltage is $-2$ V, and the drain–source voltage is $+2$ V, then both ends of the device are ON (voltage is greater than the threshold) and hence operation falls in the ohmic region (row 4 of Table 7.1).

The depletion-mode MOSFET differs from the JFET in its physical construction and operating principles, but otherwise it functions similarly. Indeed, the equations describing operation are identical to Eqs. (7.39) and (7.40) except for a change in notation and the permitting of positive gate–source voltage. It can operate as a voltage-controlled resistor, small-signal amplifier, or switch.

**Enhancement-mode MOSFET.** Figure 7.60 (a) shows the physical structure of an enhancement-mode MOSFET, which differs from the depletion-mode device by having no *n*-type channel. For proper operation, the substrate must be connected to a voltage more negative than any voltage anticipated at either source or drain.

Both the drain-substrate and source–substrate *pn* junctions are reverse biased, and no channel exists until external voltage is applied to the gate. Thus, the device is cut off

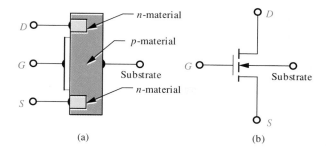

(a)                                    (b)

**Figure 7.60** (a) Physical structure of an enhancement-mode MOSFET. No channel exists until the gate-source voltage is large enough to create a channel out of the $p$-type substrate. (b) The circuit symbol for an enhancement-mode MOSFET. The broken line for the "channel" indicates that a channel does not exist naturally but must be created by the electric field between the gate and source.

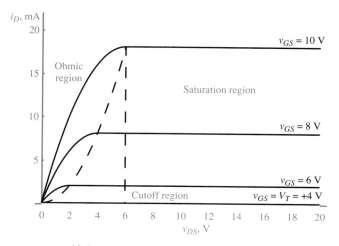

**Figure 7.61** Device characteristics for an enhancement-mode $n$-channel MOSFET for $K = 16$ mA and $V_T = +4$ V.

if the gate-source voltage is less than a positive threshold voltage. When the gate-source voltage exceeds the threshold voltage ($V_T$), the resulting electric field attracts electrons and repels holes in the $p$-type substrate, and a channel forms. The circuit symbol in Fig. 7.60 (b) shows a broken line for a "channel" to indicate that a channel does not exist naturally. As usual the arrow on the substrate connection points from $p$ to $n$, where $n$ refers to the $n$ channel formed by enhancement. The depletion- and enhancement-mode devices have identical characteristics except $V_T$ is negative for the former and positive for the latter. Equations describing operation in the ohmic and saturation regions of both types of MOSFETs are identical to those of the JFET except for a change in notation. In the ohmic region, the drain current is given by

$$i_D = \frac{K}{V_T^2} \left[ (v_{GS} - V_T)v_{DS} - \frac{v_{DS}^2}{2} \right], \qquad v_{GS} > V_T, \qquad v_{DS} < v_{GS} - V_T \qquad (7.51)$$

where $K$ is a constant, and in the saturation region, we have

$$i_D = \frac{K}{2V_T^2} (v_{GS} - V_T)^2 \qquad v_{DS} > v_{GS} - V_T \qquad (7.52)$$

For $K = 16$ mA and $V_T = +4$ V (enhancement mode), we have the characteristics shown in Fig. 7.61.

**Cutoff, ohmic, and saturation regions.** In the cutoff region, the drain–source circuit acts as an open circuit or a switch that is OFF. In the ohmic region, the enhancement-mode MOSFET acts as a voltage-controlled resistor, and in the saturation region it acts as a voltage-controlled current source. The region of operation may be determined from Table 7.1. For example, consider the top curve given in Fig. 7.61. With $v_{GS} = +10$ V, the source end of the transistor is ON because the gate–source voltage exceeds the threshold voltage of $+4$ V. If the gate-drain voltage is less than $+4$ V, then the gate–drain end of the transistor will be OFF and the transistor will be in the saturation region. This occurs for $v_{DS} > 10 - 4 = 6$ V. Hence, the transistor will be in the saturation region for drain–source voltages greater than 6 V and in the ohmic region for voltages less than 6 V.

**Circuit models for operation in the ohmic and saturation regions.** In the ohmic region, the transistor may be modeled as a voltage-controlled resistance. We may determine the transistor resistance in the ohmic region from Eq. (7.51) in the manner used to derive Eq. (7.43). For small-signal operation in the saturation region, the circuit model shown in Fig. 7.55 is valid. We may determine the transconductance for the model from Eq. (7.52) in the same manner as Eq. (7.45) was derived.

---

**EXAMPLE 7.16** | **MOSFET resistance**

Find the resistance of the MOSFET in Fig. 7.61 for small $v_{DS}$ and $v_{GS} = 10$ V.

**SOLUTION:**
From Eq. (7.51),

$$r_{DS} \approx \frac{1}{\partial i_D / \partial v_{DS}} = \frac{V_T^2}{K(v_{GS} - V_T)} = \frac{(+4)^2}{0.016(10-4)} = 167 \ \Omega \qquad (7.53)$$

**WHAT IF?** | What if a resistance of 100 $\Omega$ were required?[27]

---

**Summary.** The JFET and both types of MOSFETs have similar characteristics. The main difference between them is that the enhancement-mode MOSFET has a positive threshold voltage and the JFET and the depletion-mode MOSFETs have negative threshold voltages (called the pinchoff voltage for the JFET). Operation in the ohmic or saturation region may be determined in all cases from Table 7.1. These FETs can function as switches, voltage-controlled resistors, or small-signal amplifiers.

Circuit designers also have available $p$-channel JFETs and MOSFETs. These devices have identical characteristics except that all polarities of voltages and currents are reversed.

---

[27] $v_{GS} = 14$ V.

## Check Your Understanding

1. Why is the channel shown as a dashed line for the enhancement-mode MOSFET, yet shown as a solid line for the depletion-mode device?

2. For a JFET with $V_P = -5$ V and $v_{GS} = -3$ V, what range of drain–source voltage corresponds to operation in the ohmic region? Assume $v_{DS} > 0$ V.

3. For the device described in the previous problem and $I_{DS} = 20$ mA, determine the resistance of the device for small values of drain–source voltage.

4. An $n$-channel MOSFET has a threshold voltage of $-3$ V. Is this a depletion- or enhancement-mode MOSFET?

5. For the device described in the previous problem, assume the gate–source voltage is $-1.5$ V. What range of drain–source voltages corresponds to operation in the saturation region (positive voltages only)?

**Answers.** (1) Because the channel exists naturally for the depletion-mode device but must be created by the gate voltage for the enhancement-mode device; (2) $0 < v_{DS} < +2$ V; (3) 313 $\Omega$; (4) depletion mode; (5) $v_{DS} > 1.5$ V.

# CHAPTER SUMMARY

Electronics applies the circuit theory of nonlinear devices. We begin with the ideal diode and its applications in rectifier circuits. Semiconductor phenomena are introduced to describe the *pn* junction for understanding diodes, bipolar-junction transistors, and the various types of field-effect transistors. One-stage transistor circuits are analyzed to show the isolation, switching, and amplifying properties of transistors.

**Objective 1: To understand how to analyze half and full-wave rectifier circuits, with and without a filter capacitor.** After introducing the role of power supplies in electronic circuits, we study several rectifier configurations. The advantages of a filter capacitor are shown.

**Objective 2: To understand the physical processes and the *i–v* characteristic of a *pn* junction.** The variety of semiconductor processes at work in the *pn* junction are described, and the characteristic of the ideal *pn* junction is presented.

**Objective 3: To understand the semiconductor processes in the *npn* bipolar-junction transistor and the resulting input and output characteristics.** The roles of the two *pn* junctions of the BJT are discussed. The input characteristic is that of a *pn*-junction diode. The output characteristic depends on the state of the input circuit and includes cutoff, saturation, breakdown, and active regions.

**Objective 4: To understand how to analyze a common-emitter amplifier-switch circuit.** We derive the input–output characteristic of the common-emitter circuit. The effects of cutoff, saturation, and active regions are noted, and the amplifier gain in the active region is shown graphically and determined analytically.

**Objective 5: To understand how to analyze a common-emitter small-signal amplifier for operating points and gain.** The dc bias and output circuits are added to the basic common-emitter circuit to give a small-signal amplifier. The bias conditions are analyzed. The small-signal equivalent circuit is developed, including the equivalent circuit for the transistor, and analyzed for small-signal gain.

**Objective 6. To understand FET operation and applications.** Junction and MOS field effect transistors are described. Large- and small-signal circuits are analyzed.

Chapter 8 shows how transistor circuits in the switching mode are used to store and process information in digital form. Chapters 9, 10, and 11 show the roles of amplifier gain in analog and communication electronics.

## PROBLEMS

## Section 7.1: Rectifiers and Power Supplies

**7.1.** Figure P7.1 shows a sinusoidal voltage source, a diode, and a load resistor, $R$.
   **(a)** A dc voltmeter measures 12 V when connected between $A$ and $G$. What would an ac voltmeter measure between $B$ and $G$? Assume an ideal diode.
   **(b)** If a very large capacitor were connected between $A$ and $G$, what then would the dc meter read? Assume that $RC \gg T$, where $T$ is the period of the sinusoid.

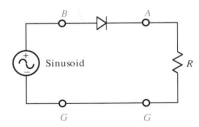

**Figure P7.1**

**7.2.** Using the unfiltered half-wave rectifier circuit shown in Fig. 7.4, design a power supply to produce 50 mA of dc current into a 600-$\Omega$ load. Give the circuit and the value that an ac voltmeter would indicate for the input voltage.

**7.3. (a)** Derive the equations for the dc voltage and ripple voltage for the half-wave rectifier shown in Fig. 7.4 with a capacitor across the load to reduce the ripple. Assume that the time constant of the $RC$ part of the circuit is large compared with the period of the input sinusoid. Have $f$ continue to represent the frequency of the input.
   **(b)** Using your results from part (a), design a 60-

Hz filtered power supply to provide 60 V dc, 40 mA dc to a load, with a ripple voltage of 0.3 V. You must specify the rms value of the input voltage and the value of the capacitor to be used. Assume ideal diodes. *Hint:* The dc voltage and current define an equivalent resistance for the load.

**7.4.** Draw the circuit of a 60-Hz filtered half-wave rectifier that will deliver 30 V dc and 270 mA dc to a resistive load. Specify the value of all components, including the equivalent load resistor. Assume an ideal diode. The peak-to-peak ripple voltage should not exceed 0.5 V. Also specify the rms input voltage.

**7.5. (a)** Draw the circuit of an unfiltered half-wave rectifier, with a generator, an ideal diode, and a 10-k$\Omega$ load.
   **(b)** Consider now that the generator puts out the square wave shown in Fig. P7.5. What would be the dc current in the load?

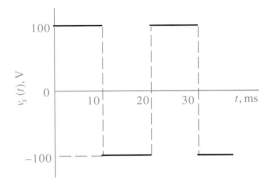

**Figure P7.5**

(c) Now add a 10-μF capacitor across the load. In this case, what would be the current in the load?

7.6. A simple rectifier circuit has the unsymmetric square waveform for an input as shown in Fig. P7.6. What is the average load voltage, with the polarity markings shown? Assume an ideal diode.

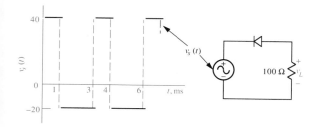

**Figure P7.6**

7.7. For the circuit shown in Fig. P7.7, the diode is an ideal diode.
(a) What fraction of the time does current flow in the load?
(b) Find the dc current through the load.
(c) If a 600-μF capacitor is added across the load to improve performance, find the dc current in that case.

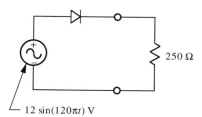

**Figure P7.7**

7.8. The load for the rectifier shown in Fig. P7.8 draws 10 mA dc regardless of the voltage.
(a) Name the type of rectifier (half-wave bridge, half-wave center-tapped transformer, full-wave bridge, full-wave center-tapped transformer)?
(b) Find the peak-to-peak ripple voltage across the load.
(c) Estimate the dc voltage across the load.

7.9. For the circuit shown in Fig. P7.9, assume ideal diodes.
(a) Is the circuit a half- or full-wave rectifier?
(b) Is the circuit a bridge or center-tapped rectifier?

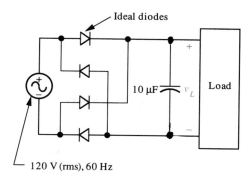

**Figure P7.8**

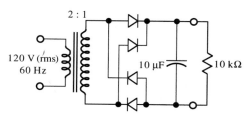

**Figure P7.9**

(c) What is the maximum load voltage?
(d) What is the minimum load voltage?
(e) What is the dc load voltage?

7.10. The rectifier circuit in Fig. P7.10(a) has a "sawtooth" input voltage as shown in Fig. P7.10(b). Assume an ideal diode.
(a) Determine the maximum and average current through the load.
(b) If a 5000 μF capacitor is placed across the load, determine the average and ripple voltage across the load.

7.11. In Fig. P7.11, the load requires 10 W of dc power. The capacitor has a value of 600 μF. Assuming an ideal diode, find the following:
(a) DC load voltage.
(b) DC load current.
(c) Ripple voltage at the load.
(d) Maximum reverse voltage across the diode.

7.12. The circuit for a power supply is shown in Fig. P7.12. Consider the diodes ideal except in (d).
(a) Is this a half-wave or full-wave rectifier?
(b) Is this a raw or filtered rectifier?
(c) Find the dc current in the load.
(d) Find the dc current in the load if one of the diodes burned out and became an open circuit.

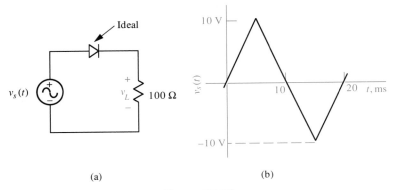

(a)

(b)

**Figure P7.10**

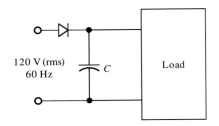

120 V (rms)
60 Hz

Load

$C$

**Figure P7.11**

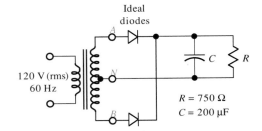

Ideal
diodes

120 V (rms)
60 Hz

$C$   $R$

$R = 750\ \Omega$
$C = 200\ \mu F$

**Figure P7.13**

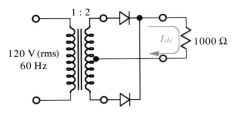

1 : 2

120 V (rms)
60 Hz

$I_{dc}$   $1000\ \Omega$

**Figure P7.12**

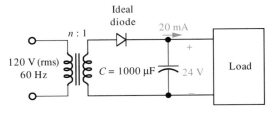

Ideal
diode

$n$ : 1

120 V (rms)
60 Hz

$C = 1000\ \mu F$   24 V   Load

20 mA

**Figure P7.14**

**7.13.** For the power-supply circuit shown in Fig. P7.13, an ac voltmeter measures 80 V between $A$ and $B$. Find the following:
  (a) Maximum load voltage.
  (b) Minimum load voltage.
  (c) DC load current.
  (d) DC voltage across the load if $C$ were removed.

**7.14.** The power-supply circuit shown in Fig. P7.14 converts 120-V (rms), 60-Hz voltage to 24 V dc, with 20 mA of dc current. Find the following:
  (a) Turns ratio of the transformer.
  (b) Equivalent load resistance.
  (c) Peak-to-peak ripple voltage.

## Section 7.2:  The *pn*-Junction Diode

**7.15.** (a) A *pn*-junction diode has a characteristic well described by Eqs. (7.16) and (7.17). Plot the $i$–$v$ characteristic in the region $0 < i_D < 100$ mA, assuming $I_0 = 10^{-10}$ A and $\eta = 1.4$. On a linear scale, plot both $i_D$ and $v_D$. Assume $T = 300$K.
  (b) If the diode in part (a) were placed in series with a 12-V source and a 500-$\Omega$ resistor, with the battery polarity such as to forward bias the

diode, what current would flow? You may use trial and error, an analytic, or graphical technique.

(c) What current would flow in part (b) if the battery were reversed so as to reverse bias the diode?

7.16. Figure P7.16 shows a piece of silicon that is doped with donor and acceptor atoms to form a *pn*-junction diode. Assume an ideality factor of 1.4.

(a) Where does there exist (1) more carrier electrons than holes; (2) more holes than carrier electrons; and (3) relatively few carriers?

(b) If you measured $i_D = 15$ mA of current for $v_D = 0.75$ V, what would you expect for $v_D = 0.80$ V? Assume a temperature of 300 K.

(c) What current would you expect for $v_D = -0.3$ V?

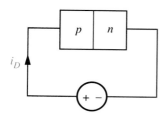

**Figure P7.16**

7.17. (a) The usual symbol for a *pn*-junction diode is shown in Fig. P7.17 together with a corresponding piece of silicon. Indicate which half is *p*-type material and which *n*-type

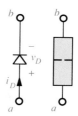

**Figure P7.17**

material. Which contains the donor and which the acceptor atoms?

(b) Indicate with an arrow the direction in which holes cross the junction due to diffusion (thermal motion) when the diode is ON.

(c) With the diode reverse-biased, the current is determined to be $10^{-11}$ A. How much voltage would it take to turn ON the diode to a current of 10 mA? Assume an ideality factor of 1.5 and $T = 300$K.

7.18. The circuit in Fig. P7.18 (a) shows a bridge rectifier with only one diode in place. The input voltage source is the "sawtooth" wave shown in Fig. P7.18 (b).

(a) Put the other three diodes in place such that the rectifier is functional.

(b) Find the time-average voltage across the load resistor with the polarity shown, assuming the diodes are ideal.

(c) Assuming real *pn*-junction diodes, what is the peak inverse voltage the diodes have to withstand to function satisfactorily in the circuit?

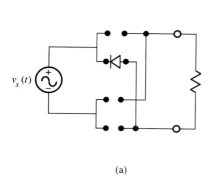

(a)

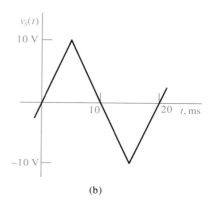

(b)

**Figure P7.18**

**7.19.** If the diodes in P7.12 were *pn*-junction diodes instead of ideal diodes, answer the following True or false questions.

   **(a)** The dc load voltage would decrease by approximately 0.7 V. (True or false?)

   **(b)** The reverse voltage might burn out one diode.(True or false?)

   **(c)** A large filter capacitor across the load would make little difference in the dc current. (True or false?)

   **(d)** Changing to a bridge rectifier would require the addition of two more diodes. (True or false?)

**7.20.** The circuit shown in Fig. P7.20 is a battery charger. The current flows when the instantaneous voltage out of the transformer exceeds the battery voltage plus the diode threshold voltage. As the battery is charged, its voltage increases until the current stops flowing. For this problem, however, consider the battery voltage constant at 12.6 V. Consider that it takes 0.7 V to turn ON the diode.

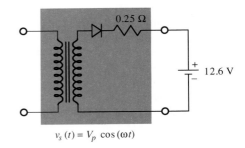

$$v_s(t) = V_p \cos(\omega t)$$

**Figure P7.20**

   **(a)** Find the peak value of the secondary voltage, $V_p$, such that the peak current in the battery is 10 A.

   **(b)** With this value for $V_p$, what percent of the time is the diode conducting?

   **(c)** What is the peak inverse voltage that the diode must withstand?

## Section 7.3: Bipolar-Junction-Transistor Operation

**7.21.** **(a)** For the transistor output characteristics shown in Fig. P7.21, determine the approximate value of $\beta$ in the active region.

   **(b)** What value of $\alpha$ does this imply?

   **(c)** If the collector current is saturated at a value of 28 mA, what is the collector–emitter voltage that results, and what is the base current required to saturate the transistor at this value of collector current?

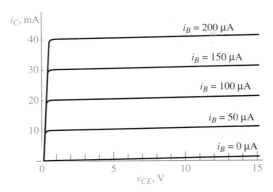

**Figure P7.21**

**7.22.** For the transistor amplifier shown in Fig. 7.40, change $V_{CC} = 12$ V and $R_B = 20$ kΩ.

   **(a)** Draw the new load line on the transistor characteristics in Fig. 7.46.

   **(b)** Find the input and output voltages for the following base currents: 0, 20, 40, 60, 80, 100, and 120 μA.

   **(c)** From part (b), plot $v_{out}$ vs $v_{in}$.

   **(d)** Find the incremental gain from the slope, $A_v = \Delta v_{out}/\Delta v_{in}$.

**7.23.** A transistor circuit is shown in Fig. P7.23(a), along with the transistor characteristics in Fig. P7.23(b). The base–emitter voltage is 0.7 V when ON.

   **(a)** What is the beta of the transistor?

   **(b)** Place a load line on the characteristics.

   **(c)** Find $R_B$ to give $v_{CE} = 10$ V.

   **(d)** What is the power out of the 12-V power supply with $v_{CE} = 10$ V?

   **(e)** Find $R_B$ to saturate the transistor.

   **(f)** Find $R_B$ to cut off the transistor.

**7.24.** A transistor circuit is shown in Fig. P7.24. The transistor output characteristics are shown in Fig. P7.21.

   **(a)** Draw the load line on the characteristics. Find the required current into the base to give a collector–emitter voltage of 6 V.

   **(b)** What value of the base voltage, $V_{BB}$, is required to give this amount of base current? Assume 0.7 V between base and emitter.

   **(c)** What value of $V_{BB}$ is required to saturate the transistor for this circuit? What is the collector current at saturation?

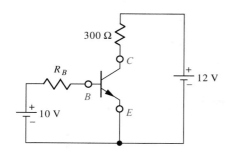

(a)

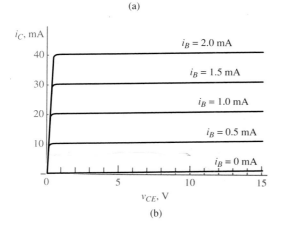

(b)

**Figure P7.23**

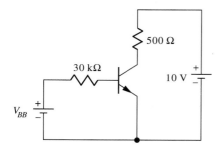

**Figure P7.24**

**7.25.** A transistor amplifier–switch circuit in Fig. P7.25(a) has a load line as shown on the transistor characteristics in Fig. P7.25(b). Assume that $v_{BE} = 0.7$ V when ON.

(a) What are $V_{CC}$, $R_C$, and $\beta$ for the transistor?

(b) What value of $v_{in}$ is required to saturate the transistor?

(c) What is the output voltage with the transistor $v_{in} =$ one-half the value in part (b)?

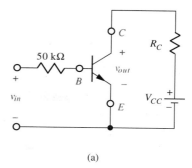

(a)

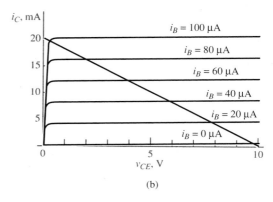

(b)

**Figure P7.25**

**7.26.** An amplifier-switch circuit is shown in Fig. P7.26. Assume that it takes 0.7 V to turn ON the base-emitter junction.

(a) The collector–emitter voltage $v_{CE} = 4.5$ V. Find the collector current, $i_C$.

(b) The current gain of the transistor is $\beta = 50$. Find the input voltage for the condition in (a).

(c) Find $v_{CE}$ if $v_{in} = 0$ V.

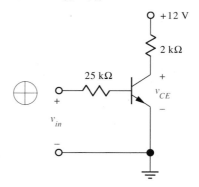

**Figure P7.26**

**7.27.** A transistor circuit is shown in Fig. P7.27. Transistor characteristics are those shown in Fig. P7.21. Assume 0.7 V for the base–emitter junction when ON.

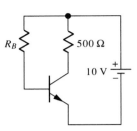

**Figure P7.27**

**(a)** Draw the load line. What value of $R_B$ will give a dc collector current of 15 mA?

**(b)** Find the voltage between collector and emitter for this value of $R_B$.

**7.28.** The BJT amplifier-switch circuit is shown in Fig. P7.28(a), with the transistor characteristics shown in Fig. P7.28(b). The input voltage is fixed at $v_{in} = +2.5$ V. The turn-ON voltage of the base–emitter junction is 0.7 V.
**(a)** Estimate $\beta$ for the transistor.
**(b)** Find the base current.
**(c)** Find $V_{CC}$ to give $v_{CE} = 3$ V for this value of $v_{in}$.
**(d)** With this value of $V_{CC}$ fixed, what value of $R_C$ ($\neq 5$ kΩ) will put the transistor barely in saturation?

**7.29.** The circuit shown in Fig. P7.29(a) is a standard amplifier-switch circuit. The transistor output

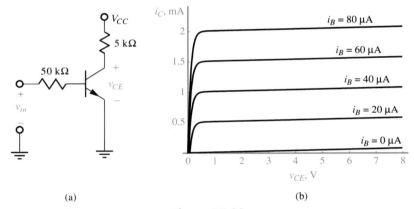

(a)                                              (b)

**Figure P7.28**

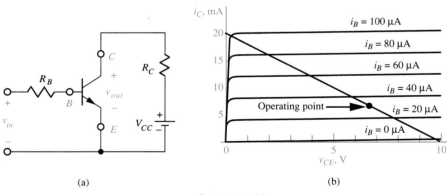

(a)                                              (b)

**Figure P7.29**

characteristics are shown, with the circuit load line in place. The operating point for $v_{in} = 2$ V is shown. Assume $V_{BE(ON)} = 0.7$ V.
(a) Find the power supply voltage, $V_{CC}$.
(b) Find the base resistor, $R_B$.
(c) Find the collector resistor, $R_C$.
(d) Estimate the $\beta$ of the transistor.

7.30. For the transistor amplifier shown in Fig. P7.30, find the following:
(a) What is the collector–emitter voltage, $v_{CE}$, if the transistor is cut off?
(b) What is the collector current, $i_C$, if $v_{CE} = 8$ V?
(c) What is the minimum base current required to saturate the transistor?
(d) What is the minimum value of $v_{in}$ to place the transistor in the active region?

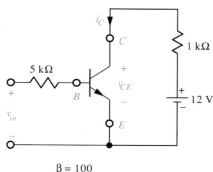

$\beta = 100$
$v_{BE} = 0.7$ V to turn ON
$v_{CE} = 0.3$ V at saturation

**Figure P7.30**

7.31. The input characteristic of a transistor is that of a *pn* junction, Eq. (7.17). For a transistor, we would associate the diode current with the base current, $i_B$, and the diode voltage with the base–emitter voltage, $v_{BE}$. The appropriate input resistance for the transistor in a small-signal equivalent circuit would be the slope of the input characteristic at the dc base current level: $r_\pi = dv_{BE}/di_B$ at $i_B = I_B$. Using Eq. (7.17) and ignoring the $+1$ term in the ln term, derive an expression for the input resistance to the transistor base. Also, evaluate with the result $r_\pi$ for the circuit of Fig. 7.50 and confirm that a value of 450 $\Omega$ is reasonable for $\eta \approx 1$.

7.32 Figure P7.32 (a) shows an amplifier-switch circuit and Fig. P7.32 (b) shows the output characteristics

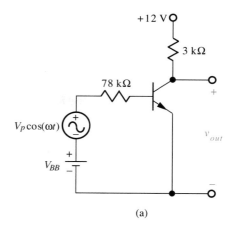

(a)

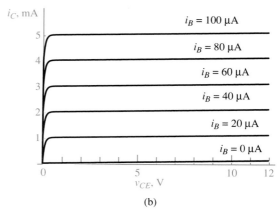

(b)

**Figure P7.32**

of the transistor. The input voltage consists of a dc and an ac source in series. Assume 0.7 V for the base-emitter junction when ON.
(a) Draw the load line.
(b) Find $V_{BB}$ to give an output voltage (with $V_p = 0$) of 8 V.
(c) With the value of $V_{BB}$ found in part (b), what is the largest value of $V_p$ that can be amplified without serious distortion?

7.33. For the transistor in Fig. P7.33, 0.7 V is required to turn ON the base–emitter junction, and $\beta$ is 100. Find $R_C$ and $R_B$ to make the collector current 5 mA and the collector–emitter voltage 4 V.

7.34. Figure P7.34 (a) shows a transistor amplifier–switch circuit and Fig. P7.34 (b) the transistor output characteristics.

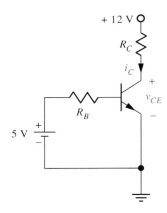

**Figure P7.33**

(a) What is $\beta$ for the transistor?
(b) Draw the load line.
(c) Estimate the base current required to saturate.
(d) Find the collector current for $v_{CE} = 12$ V.
(e) What is the voltage across $R_C$ if the transistor is cut off?

7.35. The transistor amplifier-switch in Fig. P7.35(a) has the input-output characteristic shown in Fig. P7.35(b). When the transistor is saturated, the power out of $V_{CC}$ is 110 mW. Find $V_{CC}$, $R_B$, and $R_C$.

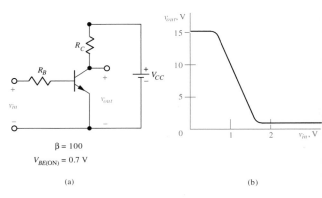

$\beta = 100$
$V_{BE(ON)} = 0.7$ V

(a)                                    (b)

**Figure P7.35**

7.36. For the transistor in Fig. P7.36, $\beta = 150$, $v_{CE(\text{sat})} = 0.3$ V, and $v_{BE(ON)} = 0.7$ V. Find the following:
(a) What are the values of $v_{CE}$ and $i_C$ at which the load line will cross the voltage and current axes on the transistor output characteristics.

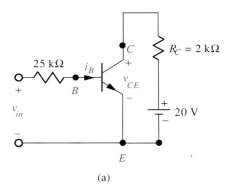

(a)

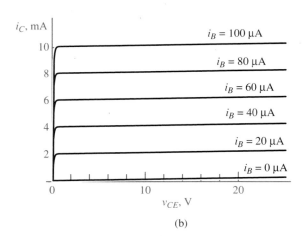

(b)

**Figure P7.34**

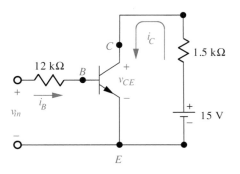

**Figure P7.36**

**(b)** What are the collector current and base current at saturation.

**(c)** What is the range (from ? to ?) of input voltages to have the transistor in the active region.

**7.37.** Figure P7.37 shows a transistor amplifier biased to operate as a small-signal amplifier.

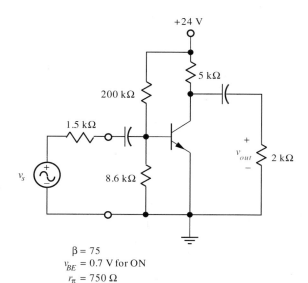

+24 V

5 kΩ

200 kΩ

1.5 kΩ

$v_{out}$

2 kΩ

$v_s$

8.6 kΩ

$\beta = 75$
$v_{BE} = 0.7$ V for ON
$r_\pi = 750\ \Omega$

**Figure P7.37**

**(a)** Draw the dc bias circuit and solve for the base and collector dc currents and the dc voltage from collector to emitter.

**(b)** Draw the small-signal equivalent circuit and solve for the voltage gain of the amplifier, $v_{out}/v_s$. Consider the capacitors as short circuits at the signal frequency. Let $r_\pi = 750\ \Omega$.

**(c)** Find the input impedance of the amplifier as seen by the input generator. This does not include the 1.5-kΩ source resistance.

**7.38.** In Fig. P7.38(a), we show a transistor amplifier-

switch circuit, with the output characteristics of the transistor in Fig. P7.38(b). The base–emitter voltage of the transistor is 0.7 V when ON.

**(a)** Draw the load line on the characteristics.

**(b)** What is the beta of the transistor?

**(c)** What would have to be the power rating of the 5-kΩ resistor to operate satisfactorily in all conditions of the input voltage.

**(d)** If the input voltage were 1.9 V, what would be the output voltage?

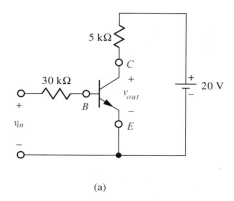

5 kΩ

C

30 kΩ

$v_{out}$

20 V

$v_{in}$

B

E

(a)

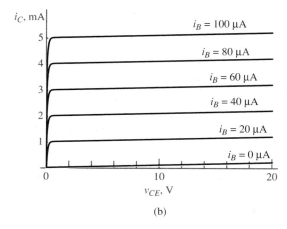

$i_C$, mA

$i_B = 100\ \mu A$

5

$i_B = 80\ \mu A$

4

$i_B = 60\ \mu A$

3

$i_B = 40\ \mu A$

2

$i_B = 20\ \mu A$

1

$i_B = 0\ \mu A$

0

10

20

$v_{CE}$, V

(b)

**Figure P7.38**

## Section 7.4: Field–Effect Transistors

**7.39.** For a JFET with $V_P = -2.5$ V and $v_{DS} = 2$ V, what range of gate–source voltage corresponds to operation in the ohmic region? Assume $v_{GS}$ and $v_{DS}$ both < 0 V.

**7.40.** For the JFET amplifier circuit in Fig. 7.56 with characteristics shown in Fig. 7.54, find the following:

**(a)** Redesign the circuit to have $i_D = 7$ mA by

changing the 250-$\Omega$ resistor to a different value. Find the corresponding value of $v_{DS}$.

**(b)** Determine the small-signal gain of the amplifier at the new operating point.

7.41. For the JFET amplifier circuit in Fig. 7.56, the designer wishes to increase the gain of the amplifier by changing the 1.5-k$\Omega$ resistor to a larger value.

**(a)** How large a resistor value can be used and still have the transistor in the saturation region?

**(b)** What is the small-signal gain with this limiting resistance?

7.42. The JFET in Fig. P7.42 has $I_{DSS} = 32$ mA and $V_P = -4$ V, and hence has the output characteristics shown in Fig. 7.54(b). Assume that the transistor is in the saturation region throughout this problem.

**(a)** Find $v_{GS}$ to give $i_D = 4$ mA.

**(b)** Find the required value of $R_S$ to give $i_D = 4$ mA.

**(c)** Find the drain voltage $v_D$ relative to ground, the reference node.

**(d)** Determine the voltage gain of the amplifier stage, $A_v = v_{out}/v_{in}$.

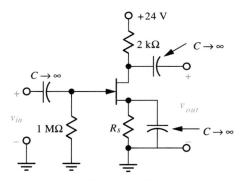

**Figure P7.42**

7.43. The JFET of Fig. P7.43 has $I_{DSS} = 32$ mA and $V_P = -4$ V, and hence has the output characteristics shown in Fig. 7.54. Assume that the transistor is in the saturation region throughout this problem.

**(a)** Find $i_D$ to give $v_{DS} = 12$ V.

**(b)** What value of $v_{in}$ gives $v_{DS} = 12$ V?

7.44. In solving for the dc conditions for the JFET amplifier circuit in Fig. 7.56 we referred to a quadratic equation derived from Eqs. (7.46) and (7.47).

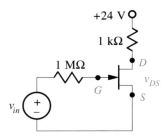

**Figure P7.43**

**(a)** Derive the quadratic equation and show that the solution is $I_D = 8.0$ and 32.0 mA.

**(b)** Show that 32.0 mA is not a realistic solution because it violates the assumed device characteristics.

7.45. An *n*-channel MOSFET has a threshold voltage of $-2$ V, and the drain–source voltage is $+3$ V. What range of gate–source voltages corresponds to operation in the ohmic region?

7.46. Show that Eqs. (7.51) and (7.52) match each other in both current and slope at the transition between the ohmic and saturation regions.

7.47. The MOSFET in Fig. P7.47 has the characteristics described by Eqs. (7.51) and (7.52), with $K = 16$ mA and $V_T = 4$ V, and displayed in Fig. 7.61. Determine the input–output characteristic, $v_{out}$ vs $v_{in}$ for the range $0 < v_{in} < 10$ V. *Hint:* A load line on the characteristics would be a good place to start.

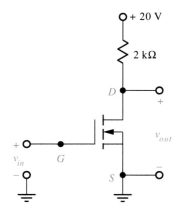

**Figure P7.47**

7.48. The MOSFET in the small-signal amplifier in Fig. P7.48 has the characteristics described by

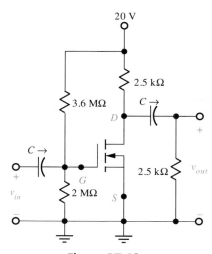

**Figure P7.48**

Eqs. (7.51) and (7.52), with $K = 16$ mA and $V_T = 4$ V, and displayed in Fig. 7.61. The capacitors may be treated as dc open circuits and signal short circuits.

**(a)** Determine the operating point for the dc drain current and drain–source voltage.

**(b)** Calculate the mutual conductance for the transistor, $g_m$, and draw the small-signal equivalent circuit for the amplifier, replacing the transistor with its small-signal equivalent circuit.

**(c)** Determine the small-signal gain of the amplifier, $v_{out}/v_{in}$.

## General Problems

**7.49.** Find the current in the diode in Fig. P7.49 by the following method: Plot the diode $i_D(v_D)$ characteristics; draw a load line; and find the intersection.

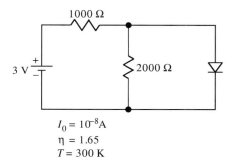

$I_0 = 10^{-8}$A

$\eta = 1.65$

$T = 300$ K

**Figure P7.49**

**7.50.** Repeat Problem 7.7 if the diode is a *pn*-junction diode that requires 0.7 V to turn ON.

**7.51.** The power supply circuit in the dashed-line-box in Fig. P7.51 can be represented by a Thévenin equivalent circuit for moderate values of $I_{dc}$. The diode requires 0.7 V to turn ON. Find $V_T$ and $R_{eq}$.

**7.52.** A three-phase system with a neutral is used in a rectifier configuration, as shown in Fig. P7.52. The time-domain line-to-neutral voltages are shown.

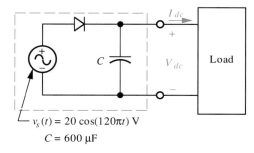

$v_s(t) = 20 \cos(120\pi t)$ V

$C = 600$ μF

**Figure P7.51**

**(a)** If a voltmeter measures 460 V between $A$ and $B$, what is the peak value of the voltage, $V_p$?

**(b)** Sketch the current in the load, $i_L(t)$.

**(c)** Find the dc current through the load.

**7.53.** A transistor circuit is shown in Fig. P7.53. The $\beta$ for the transistor is 125. The base–emitter voltage is 0.7 V when ON and the collector–emitter voltage is 0.2 V when the transistor is saturated.

**(a)** What range of input voltages corresponds to the transistor's being cut off? What is the collector current of the transistor when cut off?

**(b)** What range of input voltages corresponds to the transistor's being saturated? What is the collector current of the transistor when saturated?

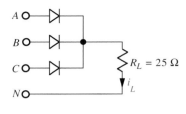

(a)

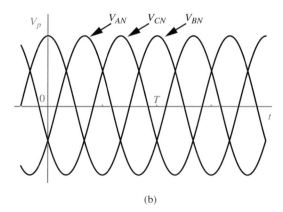

(b)

**Figure P7.52**

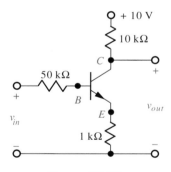

**Figure P7.53**

**7.54.** The circuit shown in Fig. P7.54 will operate as an ac/dc voltmeter, depending on the switch setting. The meter movement responds to dc, 0 to 100 μA full scale.

(a) Explain how the circuit works on dc. Mention what would happen if the input polarity were reversed.

(b) Explain how the circuit works on ac. What

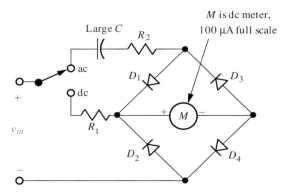

**Figure P7.54**

would happen in this case if the input leads were reversed?

(c) Determine $R_1$ so that the dc meter indicates full scale with 150 V dc input. Assume ideal diodes.

(d) Determine $R_2$ for the meter to read full scale with 150 V ac (rms) input. The meter movement registers full scale with 100 μA of dc current through it. Assume ideal diodes and that the capacitor is large.

**7.55.** A calculator "charger," shown in Fig. P7.55, is actually a simple transformer. The remainder of the power supply is located in the calculator, as shown. The battery pack has a voltage ranging from 3.0 V (discharged) to 3.6 V (charged). The current limit for the diode is 50 mA and its ON voltage is 0.7 V. No current should flow into the fully charged battery. Determine the turns ratio required for the "charger" and the minimum value of $R$.

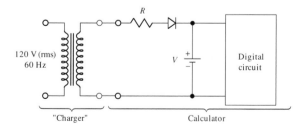

**Figure P7.55**

**7.56.** For Fig. P7.56, find the dc current from $a$ to $b$ for the following conditions:

(a) The load is a short circuit.

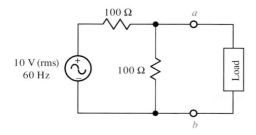

**Figure P7.56**

(b) The load is a 5-V battery, with + connected to *a*.

(c) The load is an ideal diode, with the allowed direction from *a* to *b* through the load.

**7.57.** A transistor circuit is shown in Fig. P7.57(a). The transistor characteristics are shown in Fig. P7.57(b). Determine $R_2$ to make the collector–emitter voltage +5 V, as shown on the circuit.

**7.58.** The transistor circuit shown in Fig. P7.58 has a constant voltage of +5 V at the base. The voltage at the emitter is 4.3 V because the ON voltage of the base-emitter junction is 0.7 V. The $\beta$ for the transistor is 100.

(a) Is the transistor in the active, cutoff, or saturation region?

(b) What is the base current if *a* and *b* have no load?

(c) If *a* is shorted to *b*, what is the current that would flow in the short circuit?

(d) Draw a Thévenin or Norton circuit with *a* and *b* as the output terminals. *Note:* Although the transistor is a nonlinear device, here it operates in a linear region of its characteristics. Hence, we may use an equivalent circuit to represent circuit output characteristics in that linear region.

**7.59.** The transistor in the circuit of Fig. P7.59 has a $\beta$ of 60, requires a base-emitter voltage of 0.7 V to turn ON, and saturates at a voltage of 0.3 V. The input voltage $v_{in}$, is zero for a long time, and then at *t* = 0, changes to a value $V_{in}$.

(a) Find the minimum value of $V_{in}$ to saturate the transistor for all positive times.

(b) Sketch the output voltage for positive time.

**7.60.** The circuit in Fig. P7.60 shows a standard switch-amplifier circuit, except that the collector and base currents (rather that collector-emitter voltage) are monitored with dc ammeters, *A*. An experiment is performed in which collector and base currents are

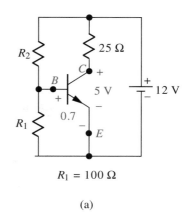

$R_1 = 100 \ \Omega$

(a)

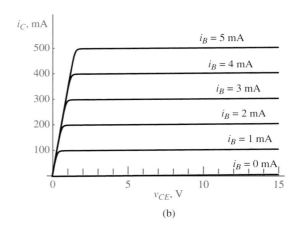

(b)

**Figure P7.57**

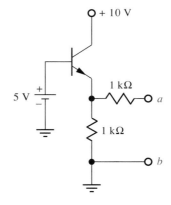

**Figure P7.58**

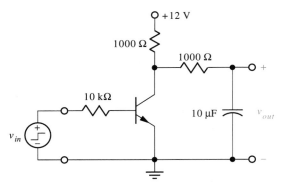

**Figure P7.59**

measured with dc ammeters as the input voltage is
changed, with the results shown in the table.

| $v_{in}$ (V) | $I_B$ (μA) | $I_C$ (mA) |
|---|---|---|
| 0 | 0 | 0 |
| 1 | 12 | 1.7 |
| 2 | 52 | 7.3 |
| 3 | 92 | 8.7 |
| 4 | 132 | 8.7 |

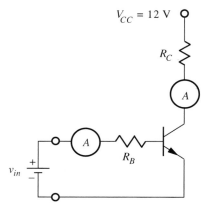

**Figure P7.60**

Assume that 0.7 V is required to turn ON the base–
emitter junction and that the collector–emitter
saturates at 0.3 V.
(a) Find $\beta$ for the transistor.
(b) Find the base resistor, $R_B$.
(c) Find the collector resistor, $R_C$.
(d) What is the input voltage that first saturates the
transistor?

# Answers to Odd-Numbered Problems

**7.1.** (a) 26.7 V; (b) 37.7 V
**7.3.** (a) $V_{dc} = V_p(1 - 1/(2fRC))$, $V_r = V_p/fRC$;
(b) 42.5 V, rms, 2230 μF
**7.5.** (a)

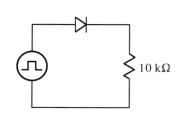

(b) 5.0 mA; (c) 9.76 mA
**7.7.** (a) 50%; (b) 15.3 mA; (c) 45.5 mA
**7.9.** (a) full wave; (b) bridge; (c) 84.9 V; (d) 77.8 V;
(e) 81.3 V
**7.11.** (a) 169 V; (b) 59.2 mA; (c) 1.65 V; (d) 339 V
**7.13.** (a) 56.6 V; (b) 53.4 V; (c) 73.3 mA; (d) 36.0 V

**7.15.** (a)

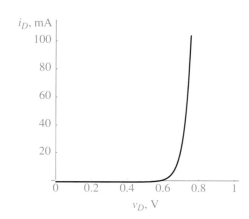

(b) 22.6 mA at 0.6975 V; (c) $-10^{-10}$ A
**7.17.** (a) $n$ top, $p$ bottom; (b) holes diffuse upward;
(c) 0.805 V
**7.19.** (a) True; (b) true; (c) false; (d) true

7.21. **(a)** 200; **(b)** 200/201; **(c)** $\approx$ 0.3 V, base current about 140 μA

7.23. **(a)** 20; **(b)** intercepts at 12 V and 40 mA; **(c)** $\approx$ 26.6 kΩ; **(d)** 80 mW; **(e)** 4.77 kΩ; **(f)** $\infty$ Ω to cut off

7.25. **(a)** 10 V, 500Ω, 200; **(b)** 5.7 V; **(c)** 5.3 V

7.27. **(a)** 124 kΩ; **(b)** $\approx$ 2.5 V

7.29. **(a)** 10 V; **(b)** 43.3 kΩ; **(c)** 500 Ω; **(d)** $\approx$ 200

7.31. exact is 432 Ω

7.33. $R_C = 1.6$ kΩ, $R_B = 86$ kΩ

7.35. **(a)** 15 V, 12.7 kΩ, 2.05 kΩ

7.37. **(a)** 35.1 μA, 2.63 mA, 10.8 V; **(b)** − 44.9; **(c)** 687 Ω

7.39. **(a)** −0.5 < $v_{GS}$ < 0 V

7.41. **(a)** 1.75 kΩ; **(b)** −14.0

7.43. **(a)** 12 mA; **(b)** −1.55 V

7.45. −2 < $v_{GS}$ <− 1 V

7.47. starts at 20 V, drops to about 3 V in the range from 6 to 10 V

7.49. $\approx$ 2.2 mA at voltage 0.51V

7.51. 19.3 V, 27.8 Ω

7.53. **(a)** $v_{in}$ < 0.7 V, 0 A; **(b)** $v_{in}$ > $\approx$ 1.95 V, 9.8 mA

7.55. **(a)** 39.5:1; **(b)** 12 Ω

7.57. 1.15 kΩ

7.59. **(a)** 4.60 V; **(b)** decays from 12 V to 0.3 V with a time constant of 10 ms.

# Digital Electronics

1. To understand how information is coded in digital form
2. To understand how to perform NOT, OR, NOR, AND, NAND, and XOR operations on binary variables
3. To understand how digital information is represented and manipulated with electronic circuits
4. To understand how to use Boolean algebra to simplify and manipulate logic expressions
5. To understand how to efficiently implement logic expressions using standard logic gates
6. To understand how flip flops are used to store and process digital information
7. To understand how a computer uses digital circuits to process information

The basic idea of digital electronics is simple enough: represent information by signals that are either ON or OFF, and then use electronic circuits to store or process the information. But this idea has affected not only technology, but most aspects of modern living—think "computer." Digital techniques increasingly dominate electronic systems and are replacing many mechanical systems such as clocks.

## What Is a Digital Signal?

**An historical example.** "Listen my children and you shall hear/Of the midnight ride of Paul Revere... ." According to Longfellow's poem, Paul Revere was sent riding through the New England countryside by a signal from the bell tower of the Old North Church in Boston. "One if by land and two if by sea." Thus, one light was to be displayed if the British forces were advancing toward Concord by the road from Boston, and two lights were to be displayed if they were crossing the Mystic River to take an indirect route. The message received by the patriot was coded in digital form. We would say today that two "bits" of information were conveyed by the code.[1]

Information can be communicated in digital form if a message is capable of being defined by a series of yes/no statements. There can be only two states of each variable used in conveying the information. Reducing information to a series of yes/no statements might appear to be a severe limitation, but the method is in fact quite powerful. Numbers can be represented in base 2, and the alphabet by a digital code. Indeed, any situation with a finite number of outcomes can be reduced to a digital code. Specifically, $n$ digital bits can represent $2^n$ states or possible outcomes.

**Digital Information**

**binary variables**

**Binary variables.** *Binary variables* are unusual mathematical variables because each can have only two values. We may call those two values by any names we wish: yes/no, true/false, ONE/ZERO, high/low, or black/white. When such variables were used primarily for analysis of philosophical arguments through symbolic logic, the values of the variables were called true or false. Recently, the names ONE/ZERO have come to be preferred by engineers and programmers dealing with digital codes. These names have the obvious advantage of fitting with the binary (base-2) number system for representation of numerical information.

**Numerical and nonnumerical codes.** Although other codes can be used, the most common digital code for numbers is in base 2. Table 8-1 shows the binary code for the numerals 0 to 9 and a few letters of a common code for the alphabet that is used in computers and communication.

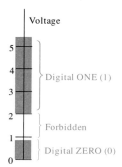

**Figure 8.1** Typical ranges of voltage represent digital ONEs and ZEROs.

**logic levels**

**Representing digital information electrically.** In digital electronics, digital variables are represented by *logic levels*. At any given time, a voltage is expected to have one value or another, or more precisely to lie within one region or another. In a typical system, a voltage between 0 and 0.8 V would be considered a digital ZERO, a voltage above 2 V would be considered a digital ONE, and anything between 0.8 and 2 V would be forbidden; that is, if the voltage fell within this range, you would know that the digital equipment needs repair. These definitions are shown in Fig. 8.1.

**Amplifier-switch logic levels.** As an illustration of a digital circuit, we analyze the BJT amplifier switch we studied in Sec. 7.3 as a NOT circuit. The output of a *NOT circuit* is the digital *complement*, or the opposite, of the input. First we represent the definition of the NOT circuit with the *truth table*[2] shown in Fig. 8.2: $A$ represents the

---

[1] Strictly speaking, two bits could indicate four possible messages and would require distinguishable lights, say, one red and one white.

| TABLE 8-1 | Some Common Digital Codes | |
|:---:|:---:|:---|
| **Symbol** | **Digital Code** | **Type of Code** |
| 0 | 0000 | Binary number |
| 1 | 0001 | Binary number |
| 2 | 0010 | Binary number |
| 3 | 0011 | Binary number |
| 4 | 0100 | Binary number |
| 5 | 0101 | Binary number |
| 6 | 0110 | Binary number |
| 7 | 0111 | Binary number |
| 8 | 1000 | Binary number |
| 9 | 1001 | Binary number |
| A | 1000001 | ASCII |
| B | 1000010 | ASCII |
| C | 1000011 | ASCII |

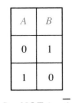

| $A$ | $B$ |
|:---:|:---:|
| 0 | 1 |
| 1 | 0 |

$B = \text{NOT}\, A = \overline{A}$

**Figure 8.2** NOT binary function.

**complement, NOT circuit, truth table**

**Figure 8.4** Digital definitions for the amplifier switch.

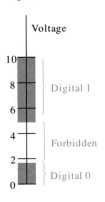

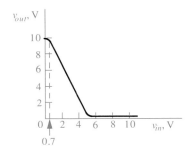

**Figure 8.3** Amplifier-switch input–output characteristic.

input, which may be either 1 or 0; $B$ represents the output, which may also be 1 or 0 but depends on the input. The NOT, or logical complement, operation is indicated algebraically by the equation under the truth table, $B = \overline{A}$.

We now define logic levels for the amplifier–switch we studied in Chapter 7 such that it performs the NOT function. The input–output characteristic of the circuit is repeated in Fig. 8.3. Clearly, we wish 10 V to be in the region for a 1 and 0.7 V to be in the region for a 0. That is, if the input were 10 V (digital 1), the output should be less than 0.7 V (digital 0), and vice versa. Hence, we might consider making the region for a digital 0 to be from 0 to 1 V, and the region for a digital 1 to be, say, from 8 to 10 V. This works but leaves insufficient range for a working digital system. We broaden the range of values in the regions for 1 and 0 to allow for variations in transistors or power supply voltage, noise that might get mixed with the signal, and other uncertainties. In the present case, we can determine by trial and error that the region 0 to 1.5 V as a digital 0 works well with 5 to 10 V as a digital 1; with these definitions, the circuit operates as a NOT circuit. These logic levels are shown in Fig. 8.4.

---

[2] A truth table systematically enumerates all possible states of the system. Here there are two states.

# Digital Representation of Information

### Elevator door controller.
Having explained the nature of digital signals, how digital information is represented electrically, and how transistor circuits have the possibility of performing digital operations, we turn to a more complete example showing how to represent a situation in digital form. Our purpose is to introduce the AND and OR digital functions and to illustrate further the language and mathematics of the digital approach.

The door on a typical elevator closes from two sources: (1) a passenger pushes a button or (2) a timer that closes the door automatically if empty. For safety, it also has an "electric eye" to prevent the door from closing on a passenger. Let us represent a command to close the door with the binary variable $D$ ($D = 1$ if the door is to close). The state of the door, $D$, will be controlled by three binary variables: $T$ represents the state of the timer ($T = 1$ means that the timer is running, time has not yet elapsed); $B$ represents someone's pushing a button for another floor ($B = 1$ means that a button has been pushed); and $S$ represents the state of the safety device ($S = 1$ means that someone is in the door). We see that $D$ is the dependent variable and is a function of three independent variables ($T$, $B$, and $S$). Keep in mind that these are all binary variables and hence can be only 1 or 0.

$$D = f(T, B, S) \qquad (8.1)$$

### Truth-table representation.
One useful method for describing a binary function is a truth table, as shown in Fig. 8.5. Here we have enumerated all possible combinations of the independent variables and shown the appropriate value of the dependent variable. In general, when there are $n$ independent variables, each having two possible states, there will be $2^n$ possible combinations, $2^3$ in this case, which may be enumerated to define the function. The truth table offers a systematic form for displaying such an enumeration. The name *truth table* originated historically from the application of this type of representation to the systematic investigation of logical arguments. Because of this association, digital circuits are often called *logic circuits*.

| $T$ | $B$ | $S$ | $D$ |
|-----|-----|-----|-----|
| 0 | 0 | 0 | 1 |
| 0 | 0 | 1 | 0 |
| 0 | 1 | 0 | 1 |
| 0 | 1 | 1 | 0 |
| 1 | 0 | 0 | 0 |
| 1 | 0 | 1 | 0 |
| 1 | 1 | 0 | 1 |
| 1 | 1 | 1 | 0 |

**Figure 8.5** Truth table for an elevator door controller.

### Truth table for elevator door.
Figure 8.5 presents the truth table for the elevator door function. The 1's and 0's in the first three columns result from a systematic counting of the eight combinations. We call it "counting" because the pattern counts in the base-2 number system. The pattern is clear: We alternated the 1's and 0's fastest for $S$, slower for $B$, and slowest for $T$, thus covering all possible combinations. These represent all values of our independent variables. For filling out the 1's and 0's in the last column, we looked first at the $S$ column, which represents the safety switch. We do not want the door to close when the safety switch indicates that someone stands in the door ($S = 1$), so we put 0 in the $D$ column ($D = 0$ means do not close the door) for every 1 in the $S$ column. This accounts for four of the eight states. The other four states depend on the button and the timer. If $S = 0$ (nothing blocking the door), the door should close if either the button is pushed ($B = 1$) or the timer expires ($T = 0$). We examine the remaining four states and put a 1 in column $D$ if there is a 1 in the $B$ column or a 0 in the $T$ column, or both.

### Interpretation of the truth table.
Three combinations close the door. The first, $TBS = 000$, represents the timer running out to close the door. The second, 010, repre-

sents a button being pushed and the timer running out simultaneously, and the third, 110, represents a button being pushed before the timer runs out. The other five combinations leave the door open.

**EXAMPLE 8.1**  **Electric fan**

An electric fan will cool ($C = 1$) if it is plugged in ($P = 1$) and the switch is ON ($S = 1$). Show the truth table for the operation of the fan.

**SOLUTION:**
There are two independent variables, $P$ and $S$, and one dependent variable, $C$. Thus, $n = 2$ and there are $2^n = 4$ states. The truth table, given in Fig. 8.6, shows that the fan must be plugged in and turned on to cool.

| $P$ | $S$ | $C$ |
|---|---|---|
| 0 | 0 | 0 |
| 0 | 1 | 0 |
| 1 | 0 | 0 |
| 1 | 1 | 1 |

**Figure 8.6** Truth table for the fan.

**WHAT IF?**
What if we consider the possibility of a faulty cord ($F = 1$ means bad cord). How many rows will there be now?[3]

**NOT function**

**OBJECTIVE 2**

**To understand how to perform NOT, OR, NOR, AND, NAND, and XOR operations on binary variables**

**OR function inclusive OR**

**AND fuction**

**NOT function.** The truth-table method is a brute-force way for describing a binary function. The same information can be represented algebraically through the AND, OR, and NOT binary functions. Consider first the NOT function, the logical complement, described in the truth table of Fig. 8.2. The NOT function is involved in this problem because NOT $S$ allows the door to close, and NOT $T$ prompts the closing of the door by the timer. The NOT function is represented algebraically by an overscore added to the variable or expression to be NOTed: $\overline{S}$ means NOT S. We need the NOT when a 0 is to trigger the OR or AND combinations because these trigger on a 1.

**OR function.** The OR binary function is defined in Fig. 8.7. The dependent variable $C = A$ OR $B$ is 1 when either $A$ or $B$ (or both) is (are) 1. This is thus the *inclusive* OR because it includes the case where both $A$ and $B$ are 1. The OR *function* is involved in our elevator problem in describing the combined effect of the timer and the button. We wish the door to close when the timer elapses ($T = 0$) OR the button is pushed ($B = 1$) or both. The way to express this algebraically is $\overline{T}$ OR $B$. The truth table for this function is shown in Fig. 8.8. In constructing the truth table in Fig. 8.8, we added a NOT $T$ column. Then we put a 1 in the last column wherever there is a 1 in either of the previous two columns because these are the variables we are ORing.

**AND function.** Next we need to account for the safety switch. The AND function is required because we must express the simultaneous occurrence of an impulse to close the door and the lack of an obstacle in the door. The truth table for the AND function appears in Fig. 8.9. Here we get a 1 only when $A$ AND $B$ is[4] 1. To complete the truth table for our door-closing variable, $D$, we must AND $\overline{S}$ with the last column in Fig. 8.8 to cover all the possibilities. Thus, we may state the door-closing function as

---

[3] Eight rows for the 8 states.
[4] This seems like bad grammar, but $A$ AND $B$ is a singular subject.

| A | B | C |
|---|---|---|
| 0 | 0 | 0 |
| 0 | 1 | 1 |
| 1 | 0 | 1 |
| 1 | 1 | 1 |

$C = A$ OR $B$

**Figure 8.7**  OR function.

| $T$ | $B$ | $\overline{T}$ | $B$ OR $\overline{T}$ |
|---|---|---|---|
| 0 | 0 | 1 | 1 |
| 0 | 1 | 1 | 1 |
| 1 | 0 | 0 | 0 |
| 1 | 1 | 0 | 1 |

**Figure 8.8**  Binary function $\overline{T}$ OR $B$.

| A | B | C |
|---|---|---|
| 0 | 0 | 0 |
| 0 | 1 | 0 |
| 1 | 0 | 0 |
| 1 | 1 | 1 |

$C = A$ AND $B$

**Figure 8.9**  AND function.

$$D = (\overline{T} \text{ OR } B) \text{ AND } \overline{S} \tag{8.2}$$

When interpreted as a binary or logical function, Eq. (8.2) states algebraically the same information as the truth table in Fig. 8.5, which we worked out by considering all possible combinations. We have now introduced a method of representing information in digital form and we have defined some basic logic relationships. We turn next to describing how electrical circuits can perform logical operations such as AND and OR.

---

**EXAMPLE 8.2**  **Fan motor again**

In Example 8.1, express $C$ in terms of $P$, $S$, and $F$ and the logical NOT, OR, and AND functions.

**SOLUTION:**
To operate, we must have power ($P = 1$) AND the switch must be ON ($S = 1$) AND the cord must NOT be faulty ($\overline{F} = 1$); hence the function is

$$C = P \text{ AND } S \text{ AND } \overline{F} \tag{8.3}$$

**WHAT IF?**  What if we include the possibility of a burned-out motor ($G = 1$ means good motor)?[5]

---

### Check Your Understanding

1. A truth table having five independent and three dependent binary variables would have how many rows?

2. How many bits of information (binary variables) are required to specify one of the 50 states in the United States?

3. If a signal in a digital system is between the regions for a 1 and a 0, you should assume 1, assume 0, or repair the circuit. Which?

*Answers.* (1) 32;  (2) 6 bits;  (3) repair the circuit.

---

[5]$C = P$ AND $S$ AND $\overline{F}$ AND $G$.

### NOT Circuit

**Circuit improvements.**   In Sec. 8.1, we showed that the transistor amplifier-switch circuit performs the digital NOT function, provided that we define a digital 1 as any voltage between 5 and 10 V and a digital 0 as any voltage between 0 and 1.5 V. We propose here three modifications of the circuit to improve its performance as a NOT circuit. Specifically, we add two diodes to the base circuit, lower the resistance in the base circuit to 10 kΩ, and lower the power-supply voltage to 5 V, all shown in Fig. 8.10.

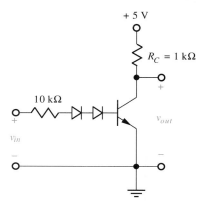

**Figure 8.10**   Improved NOT circuit.

**Analysis of the modified circuit.**   We assume the diodes and the base–emitter *pn* junction are OFF when the voltage across each is less than 0.7 V. After they are turned ON and current begins to flow, their voltage will remain at 0.7 V each. This is the simple model of the *pn* junction shown in Fig. 7.36.

**Base-circuit analysis.**   To derive the input–output characteristic of the circuit in Fig. 8.10, we increase the input voltage, beginning at zero volts. No current will flow into the base of the transistor until both diodes and the base–emitter junction turn ON, which requires about $3 \times 0.7$ or 2.1 V at the input. Once the voltage at the input rises to 2.1 V, therefore, the three *pn* junctions will turn ON, and the transistor will move out of cutoff. Once this occurs, Kirchhoff's voltage law in the base–emitter loop takes the form

$$i_B = \frac{v_{in} - 3 \times 0.7}{R_B} = \frac{v_{in} - 2.1}{10 \text{ k}\Omega} \; , \; v_{in} > 2.1 \tag{8.4}$$

**Collector-circuit analysis.**   The base current controls the current in the collector–emitter loop, the output part of the circuit. While the transistor is cut off, no collector current flows and the output voltage remains at +5 V. As the base current begins to flow, however, the transistor moves into the active region and the collector (output) voltage begins to fall. This moves the operating point from cutoff toward saturation, as shown on the load line in Fig. 8.11. Because we changed the power-supply voltage, the load line now goes from $V_{CC} = +5$ V on the voltage axis to 5 V/1 kΩ = 5 mA on the

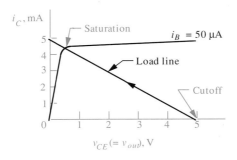

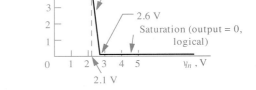

**Figure 8.11** Load line for improved circuit.

**Figure 8.12** Input-output characteristic of improved NOT circuit.

current axis. Because the transistor beta ($\beta$) is about 100, a base current of about 5 mA/100 = 50 $\mu$A is required for saturation; hence, we put the 50-$\mu$A characteristic on Fig. 8.11. Base currents between 0 and 50 $\mu$A put the transistor in the active region. Equation (8.4) requires, therefore, that input voltages between 2.1 and 2.6 V correspond to the active region. After the input voltage exceeds 2.6 V, the transistor is saturated; that is, the collector voltage ($v_{out}$) falls to about 0.4 V and further increases in base current cause little change in the output. Thus, the input–output characteristic of the modified amplifier–switch is shown in Fig. 8.12.

### Benefits of changing the circuit.
If you compare the characteristic in Fig. 8.12 with that in Fig. 8.3, you will note several differences. The slope is greater, higher gain, in the active region, a result of decreasing the resistance in the base circuit. We want higher gain, so that the transistor passes through the active region, the forbidden region in digital operation, with a smaller range of input voltage and hence passes through with greater speed. Next, the modified circuit remains in cutoff until the input exceeds 2.1 V, in contrast to 0.7 V for the unmodified circuit. Thus, two diodes in the base circuit increase the range for a digital 0 and enhance symmetry between the allowed ranges of the digital 0 and the digital 1. Finally, we note that the output voltage for a 1 is decreased from +10 to +5 V. We lowered the value of $V_{CC}$ for two reasons, to save diodes and to save power. We added two diodes to raise the threshold of the active region to roughly half of the +5 V. If we had to add enough diodes to raise the active region up to one-half of 10 V, we would have had to use five or six diodes; thus, we save diodes by lowering the power-supply voltage. We also save power by lowering the voltage because the saturation current is lowered correspondingly. The power used by the circuit when saturated is approximately $V_{CC}$ times the saturation current; hence, we use one-fourth the power with the smaller $V_{CC}$.

**Figure 8.13** Logic levels for improved NOT circuit.

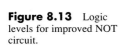

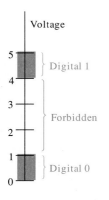

### Logic levels for the modified NOT circuit.
Appropriate digital levels for the modified amplifier–switch are shown in Fig. 8.13. The range 0 to 1.0 V defines a digital 0, 4.0 to 5.0 V defines a digital 1, and the range from 1.0 to 4.0 V is forbidden. We desire these broad, symmetrical regions for several reasons. Digital equipment is reliable and inexpensive because the exact voltages do not matter, as long as they lie in the ranges for a 0 or 1. Furthermore, broad well-separated regions for the logic levels immunize digital circuits to noise and false signals to some degree. We use these voltage ranges as our logic levels for the remainder of this section. Thus, a "1", meaning a dig-

ital 1, a symbol and not a number, means a voltage between 4.0 and 5.0 V, and a "0" means a voltage between 0 and 1.0 V.

---

<table>
<tr><td>**EXAMPLE 8.3**</td><td>**Other circuit changes**</td></tr>
</table>

If three diodes are used in the base circuit and the collector resistor is changed to 2 kΩ, do these logic levels still work?

**SOLUTION:**

The 2-kΩ collector resistor changes the base saturation current to 25 μA. Now the transition begins when $v_{in} = 2.8$ V and ends when $v_{in} = 2.8 + 25$ μA x 10 kΩ $= 3.05$V. Thus, we lose a bit of the symmetry but the logic levels still work.

**WHAT IF?**    How about three diodes and a 500-Ω collector resistor?[6]

---

## BJT Gates

**gates, NOR gate**

**NOR gate.**    Digital *gates* are circuits that pass or block signals moving through a logic circuit. We now examine the NOR *gate*, a circuit that combines the OR function with the NOT function. A simple NOR circuit is shown in Fig. 8.14(a). The inputs are *A* and *B*, and the output is *C*.

**OBJECTIVE 3**

**To understand how digital information is represented and manipulated in electronic circuits**

**NOR truth table.**    We will justify the truth table shown in Fig. 8.14(b). Because there are two inputs, there will be $2^n$ ($n = 2$) or 4 possible input combinations for *A* and *B*, which we have listed systematically in the truth table. The first of these (00) corresponds to having voltages below 1.0 V at both inputs. Although the three *pn* junctions (two diodes and the base–emitter junction) are slightly forward-biased, insufficient voltage is present to turn them ON and in particular the transistor base-emitter junction will not turn ON; hence, the transistor remains OFF. This cutoff condition causes the output to be +5 V, a digital 1; hence, we place 1 in the *C* column, first row. The next row has a digital 1 at *B* and a digital 0 at *A*. The voltage at *B* exceeds 4 V, which turns ON diodes $D_2$, $D_3$, and the base–emitter junction, leading to saturation and a digital 0 at the output. Notice that the voltage at *P* is at least $4 - 0.7 = 3.3$ V and the voltage at *A* is at most 1.0 V; hence, $D_1$ is OFF. This diode, acting as an open circuit in its OFF condition, prevents the signal at B from coupling back into the source of A. The last two rows in the truth table follow from similar considerations: clearly, if either (or both) of the inputs is (are) a 1, the transistor will turn ON, current will flow in the saturated transistor, and the output voltage will drop into the range for a digital 0. The diodes perform the OR operation and the transistor gives the NOT. Incidentally, we are not limited to two inputs; we can have three, four, or more inputs coming into the OR part of the circuit.

---

[6] Now the transition ends about 3.8 V; not enough margin.

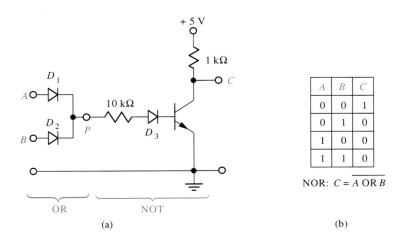

| A | B | C |
|---|---|---|
| 0 | 0 | 1 |
| 0 | 1 | 0 |
| 1 | 0 | 0 |
| 1 | 1 | 0 |

NOR: $C = \overline{A \text{ OR } B}$

(a)  (b)

**Figure 8.14** (a) NOR circuit; (b) truth table for the NOR function.

**Role of transistor.** The output $C$ is isolated by the transistor from affecting the inputs. The transistor firms up the output of the diode OR logic and isolates the input circuit from the output circuit. In the process of offering these benefits, the transistor inverts the digital signal and we thus pick up the NOT operation. If we require an OR circuit, we would put $C$ into a NOT circuit; this would NOT the NOR to give the OR operation.

**NAND gate**

**NAND gate.** The NAND circuit shown in Fig. 8.15(a) combines the AND and the NOT operations. Ignore for the moment the two inputs with their diodes and think of the circuit as a NOT circuit with the input (to the 10-k$\Omega$ resistor) connected to the +5-V power supply. Without action at the $A$ and $B$ inputs, the circuit would be a NOT circuit with the input locked at a digital 1 and the output locked at 0.

**NAND truth table.** Now let us consider the effect of the inputs. The first row of the truth table has both $A$ and $B$ at low voltage, below 1 V. This causes both $D_1$ and $D_2$ to turn ON and current flows through the 10-k$\Omega$ resistor, through the diodes, and to

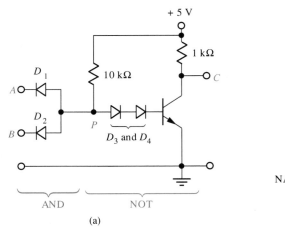

| A | B | C |
|---|---|---|
| 0 | 0 | 1 |
| 0 | 1 | 1 |
| 1 | 0 | 1 |
| 1 | 1 | 0 |

NAND: $C = \overline{A \text{ AND } B}$

(a)  (b)

**Figure 8.15** (a) NAND circuit; (b) truth table for the NAND function.

ground through whatever is controlling $A$ and $B$. The voltage at $P$ is at most $1 + 0.7 = 1.7$ V, not enough to turn ON diodes $D_3$ and $D_4$ and the base–emitter junction. Hence, the transistor is cut off and the output voltage is $+5$ V, a digital 1. The next state (01) leads to similar operation, the only difference being that the voltage at $B$ is now at least 4 V and hence $D_2$ is OFF. But the voltage at $P$ remains no higher than 1.7 V and the output remains at 1. Only if both $A$ and $B$ are a digital 1 does the current through the 10-k$\Omega$ resistor return to the transistor base, turn ON the base–emitter junction, saturate the transistor, and drop the output voltage to a digital 0. The input diodes perform the logical AND function and the transistor the NOT function, giving the entire circuit a NAND function. If we require the AND function, we can invert $C$ with a NOT circuit. If we add other inputs in parallel with $A$ and $B$, all would have to be at a digital 1 to give a digital 0 at the output.

## MOSFET Gates

A number of features make MOSFETs attractive as logic gates: They are small and easily fabricated in integrated circuits, they have a high input impedance, and they require very little power to hold and change logic states. In Sec. 7.4, we showed how a MOSFET can operate as a switch when used in series with a load resistor. The circuits used in practice replace the load resistor with another FET.

**driver transistor, load transistor**

**Using an *n*-channel depletion-mode MOSFET for a load.** Figure 8.16(a) shows a NOT gate that uses an enhancement-mode MOSFET as a switch, or *driver*, transistor, and a depletion-mode MOSFET as a *load* transistor. When the input voltage is less than the threshold voltage for the driver transistor, it will be OFF and no current will flow through the transistor. The load transistor will be in the ohmic region because the output voltage will be very near $V_{DD}$.

When the input voltage to the driver transistor is much greater than its threshold voltage, it allows current to flow, the output voltage drops, and the driver transistor enters the ohmic region. The load transistor moves into its saturation region and thus acts as a current source having a high output impedance. Because a large current would require high power, the load transistor is fabricated to have a relatively small current when in saturation with $v_{GS} = 0$.

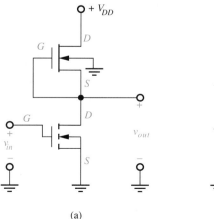

(a)

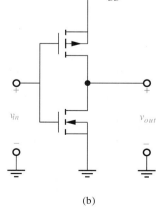

(b)

**Figure 8.16** (a) A NOT gate using an enhancement-mode *n*-channel FET for a driver transistor and a depletion-mode FET for a load transistor; (b) a NOT gate using two enhancement-mode MOSFETs, an *n*-channel driver and a *p*-channel load transistor.

**Using a _p_-channel enhancement-mode MOSFET for a load.** The NOT gate shown in Fig. 8.16(b) uses a _p_-channel enhancement-mode MOSFET for a load transistor. Here a low input voltage causes the driver transistor to be cut off and the load transistor to be in the ohmic region; hence, the output voltage is nearly $V_{DD}$. Likewise, an input voltage near $V_{DD}$ puts the driver transistor into the ohmic region and the load transistor into cutoff; hence, the output voltage is small. Note that in both states, one of the transistors is cut off and no dc current flows through the inverter. Current flows in the gate only during transitions, and hence this circuit uses very little power.

**NMOS, CMOS**

**NMOS and CMOS logic families.** The type of circuit shown in Figure 8.16(a) is called NMOS because the logic circuits are constructed entirely of _n_-channel MOS transistors. The type of circuit in Fig. 8.16b is called CMOS because it uses _p_-channel and _n_-channel, or complementary, transistors. Although we have shown only the NOT gate, families of logic elements including NAND and NOR gates are constructed of these transistors without use of resistors or capacitors.

The NOR, NAND, and NOT circuits are the basic building blocks from which digital systems are constructed. We will consider how large systems are formed after we have refined our mathematical language.

### Check Your Understanding

1. The BJTs in a digital watch spend the least time in the cutoff, saturation, or active region?
2. A transistor, among other things, produces the complement (or NOT) of a binary signal. True or false?
3. In the NAND circuit in Fig. 8.15, the "AND" part is done by the diodes or the transistor?
4. If the collector voltage is used to represent a digital signal, the output of a transistor in saturation would be 1 or 0?
5. The diodes in the base circuit of Fig. 8.10 are there to increase the gain. True or false?
6. In a three-input NAND gate, how many input states correspond to 1 at the output?
7. Which type of NOT gate would use less power, the BJT or the CMOS?

_Answers._ **(1)** Active; **(2)** true; **(3)** by the diodes; **(4)** 0; **(5)** false; **(6)** seven; **(7)** CMOS.

## 8.3 THE MATHEMATICS OF DIGITAL ELECTRONICS

### Need for a Mathematical Language

**realize a logic function**

We showed earlier how to express a digital function with a truth table. We termed this a brute-force method, for a truth table lists all possible states of the independent variables (the inputs) and lists the corresponding values of the dependent variables (the outputs). This way of expressing a digital function has several limitations. The truth table offers little guidance about how to _realize_ the logic function, how to assemble the required logical operations with digital circuits to produce the desired output. In our example about the elevator door, for example, we were able to translate the problem description into a logical function by common sense rather than through examination of the truth table. The techniques we develop in this section not only suggest a realization of the logic function but also permit manipulation of the function into different forms, thus offering alternative realizations. Also, we demonstrate ways to simplify logical expressions, thus permitting simpler realizations.

**Boolean algebra**

**Origins of Boolean algebra.** The algebra of two-valued variables is called *Boolean algebra* after George Boole, an English mathematician who first investigated this type of mathematics. Boole was interested in symbolic logic, the formal examination of logical arguments to establish their soundness or expose their fallacies. As we have already remarked, this early application of Boolean algebra has influenced the language of digital electronics.

**A warning.** Whereas the ideas, theorems, and applications of Boolean mathematics are relatively simple, the nomenclature and language can be confusing. One difficulty is that this mathematics uses some of the same symbols as ordinary algebra, but with different meanings. Thus, $A + B = C$ is a meaningful equation in both systems but has totally different meaning and is read differently as a binary expression.[7] Another difficulty is that common English words such as "and" are given technical meanings. Until you become accustomed to this new usage, many of the statements about Boolean variables sound like double talk.

## Common Boolean Theorems

**OBJECTIVE 4**

**To understand how to use Boolean algebra to simplify and manipulate logic expressions**

**Boolean variables.** A Boolean, or digital, or binary variable has two values, which we call 1 and 0. The values are *defined* to satisfy the definitions of OR, AND, and NOT in Fig. 8.17. The + sign is used for OR, the "•" symbol for AND, and the overscore for NOT or logical complement.

**One-variable theorems.** Theorems involving one variable, here $A$, are shown in Fig. 8.18. All of these may be verified by testing the validity of the expression for both states of $A$ and comparing with the definitions in Fig. 8.17.

| OR | AND | NOT |
|---|---|---|
| $1 + 1 = 1$ | $1 \bullet 1 = 1$ | $\overline{1} = 0$ |
| $1 + 0 = 1$ | $1 \bullet 0 = 0$ | $\overline{0} = 1$ |
| $0 + 1 = 1$ | $0 \bullet 1 = 0$ | |
| $0 + 0 = 0$ | $0 \bullet 0 = 0$ | |

**Figure 8.17** Basic definitions of OR, AND, and NOT functions.

| OR | AND | NOT |
|---|---|---|
| $1 + A = 1$ | $1 \bullet A = A$ | $\overline{\overline{A}} = A$ |
| $0 + A = A$ | $0 \bullet A = 0$ | |
| $A + A = A$ | $A \bullet A = A$ | |
| $A + \overline{A} = 1$ | $A \bullet \overline{A} = 0$ | |

**Figure 8.18** Boolean theorems for one variable.

**EXAMPLE 8.4** **Proof with truth table**

Verify $A \bullet \overline{A} = 0$ using a truth table.

**SOLUTION:**

Because $A$ has two states, the truth table has two rows, Fig. 8.19. The first column lists the

[7] For example, the equation $1 + 1 = 1$ is correct in Boolean mathematics but is incorrect in ordinary algebra.

two values of $A$. The second substitutes these into the expression to be proved. The third uses the definitions under NOT in Fig. 8.17, and the fourth uses definitions under AND in Fig. 8.17. The theorem is proved because the last column shows $A \cdot \overline{A} = 0$ for both states of $A$.

| $A$ | $A \cdot \overline{A}$ | Definition | Definition |
|-----|------------------------|------------|------------|
| 0 | $0 \cdot \overline{0}$ | $\overline{0} = 1$ | $0 \cdot 1 = 0$ |
| 1 | $1 \cdot \overline{1}$ | $\overline{1} = 0$ | $1 \cdot 0 = 0$ |

**Figure 8.19** Proof of the theorem $A \cdot \overline{A} = 0$ with a truth table.

**WHAT IF?**  What if you have to simplify $A + (A \cdot \overline{A})$?[8]

**Two or three variables.** Some useful theorems and properties involving two or three binary variables are shown in Fig. 8.20. Many of these are deceptively similar to the familiar properties of algebra. Note that we show the expressions involving AND operations both with and without the "•" symbol; thus, $AB$ means the same as $A \cdot B$. Writing the AND without any symbol is common, even though the confusion with ordinary multiplication is compounded.

Commutation:  $A + B = B + A; A \cdot B = B \cdot A; AB = BA$
Association:  $A + (B + C) = (A + B) + C; A \cdot (B \cdot C) = (A \cdot B) \cdot C; A(BC) = (AB)C$
Absorption:  $A + (A \cdot B) = A; A \cdot (A + B) = A; A(A + B) = A$
Distribution:  $A \cdot (B + C) = (A \cdot B + A \cdot C); A(B + C) = AB + AC$
$A + (B \cdot C) = (A + B) \cdot (A + C); A + BC = (A + B)(A + C)$
De Morgan's Theorems:  $\overline{A + B} = \overline{A} \cdot \overline{B}; \overline{A + B} = \overline{AB}; \overline{A \cdot B} = \overline{A} + \overline{B}; \overline{AB} = \overline{A} + \overline{B}$

**Figure 8.20** Some useful theorems and properties involving two or three binary variables.

**EXAMPLE 8.5**  **Absorption rule**

Verify the first absorption rule in Fig. 8.20.

**SOLUTION:**
Figure 8.21 shows the truth table. The last column is identical to the column for $A$, validating the theorem. Examination of the truth table shows how $B$ is "absorbed" by $A$: If $A = 1$, $B$ does not matter; and if $A = 0$, $B$ does not matter. Hence, $B$ is absorbed.

**Figure 8.21** Truth-table proof of the absorption theorem $A + (A \cdot B) = A$.

| $A$ | $B$ | $AB$ | $A + AB$ |
|-----|-----|------|----------|
| 0 | 0 | 0 | 0 |
| 0 | 1 | 0 | 0 |
| 1 | 0 | 0 | 1 |
| 1 | 1 | 1 | 1 |

**De Morgan's theorems.** *De Morgan's theorems* reveal how to distribute the NOT over variables that are ANDed or ORed. Figure 8.22 gives a proof for the first theorem.

[8] $= A + (A \cdot \overline{A}) = A$.

| $A$ | $B$ | $A+B$ | $\overline{A+B}$ | $\overline{A}$ | $\overline{B}$ | $\overline{A} \cdot \overline{B}$ |
|---|---|---|---|---|---|---|
| 0 | 0 | 0 | 1 | 1 | 1 | 1 |
| 0 | 1 | 1 | 0 | 1 | 0 | 0 |
| 1 | 0 | 1 | 0 | 0 | 1 | 0 |
| 1 | 1 | 1 | 0 | 0 | 0 | 0 |

**Figure 8.22** Truth-table proof of one of De Morgan's theorems, $\overline{A+B} = \overline{A} \cdot \overline{B}$.

**De Morgan's theorems**

The fourth and seventh columns are identical, thus proving the theorem. The form of De Morgan's theorems is that on the left side of the identities, the NOT covers two variables that are either ANDed or ORed, and on the right side, the NOT has been distributed to the individual variables. Both rules are summarized by the following statement: A NOT can be distributed in a logical expression involving two variables provided that ANDs are changed to ORs, and vice versa. This rule can be applied to expressions involving more than two variables, provided care is taken with the grouping of variables.

**Importance of De Morgan's theorems.** A transistor inverts the output signal relative to its input(s). We saw before in examining NOR and NAND gates that the diodes at the input perform the OR or AND logic and the transistor firms up the decision, isolates the input from the output, and inverts the signal in the process, thus adding the NOT unavoidably to the logical operation. This "NOT" makes De Morgan's theorem useful in digital electronics. We explore the usefulness of De Morgan's theorems in digital electronics after we have introduced symbols for the logic gates.

---

**EXAMPLE 8.6** | **Simplifying logic expressions**

Simplify the expression $\overline{(\overline{AB} + A)}$ using the theorems in Fig. 8.20.

**SOLUTION:**

$$\overline{(\overline{AB} + A)} = \overline{(\overline{A} + \overline{B} + A)} = \overline{1 + \overline{B}} = 0 \qquad (8.5)$$

Equation (8.5) shows that a logical expression that appears to depend on two input variables is in fact constant and remains in the 0 state, regardless of the values of $A$ and $B$.

**WHAT IF?** | What if you simplify $\overline{A \cdot B} + \overline{\overline{A} + B}$ ?[9]

---

**EXCLUSIVE OR, XOR**

**EXCLUSIVE OR (XOR) and the equality function.** The OR operation is an *inclusive* OR, meaning that it includes the case where both variables are 1. An EXCLUSIVE OR, or XOR, function is a logic function that takes the value 1, if either variable is 1 but takes the value 0 if both variables are either 1 or 0. The truth table for such a

---

[9] $\overline{A \cdot B}$.

| $A$ | $B$ | $A \oplus B$ | $\overline{A \oplus B}$ |
|-----|-----|--------------|-------------------------|
| 0   | 0   | 0            | 1                       |
| 0   | 1   | 1            | 0                       |
| 1   | 0   | 1            | 0                       |
| 1   | 1   | 0            | 1                       |

**Figure 8.23** EXCLUSIVE OR and EQUALITY functions.

function is given in Fig. 8.23. The third column contains the definition of the EXCLUSIVE OR, symbolized by a + inside a circle, $\oplus$. The bottom row of the table shows the exclusion of the state where both inputs are 1. The EXCLUSIVE OR indicates inequality between the variables, since the output 1 indicates that $A$ and $B$ are unequal. It follows that the complement of the EXCLUSIVE OR, $\overline{A \oplus B}$, indicates equality, as the last column of Fig. 8.23 shows.

### Check Your Understanding

1. Evaluate $D = \overline{B} + B(C + \overline{A})$ if $A = 1$, $B = 1$, and $C = 0$.
2. A digital system has three inputs, $A$, $B$, and $C$, and one output, $\overline{AB} + C$. How many of the possible input states correspond to a 1 at the output?
3. Under what condition is the Boolean expression $A + A = 1$ valid?
4. Simplify $\overline{A(1 + \overline{A}) + \overline{B}}$.
5. As a Boolean equation, $C + C = C$ is valid. True of false?

*Answers.* (1) 0; (2) 7 states; (3) if $A = 1$; (4) $AB$; (5) true.

## 8.4 COMBINATIONAL DIGITAL SYSTEMS

### Logic Symbols and Logic Families

**Logic symbols.** Digital systems consist of vast numbers of AND, NAND, OR, NOR, XOR, and NOT gates, plus memory and timing circuits that we discuss later, all interconnected to perform some useful task such as count and display time, measure a voltage, or perform arithmetic. If we were to draw a circuit diagram for such a system, including all the resistors, diodes, transistors, and interconnections, we would face an overwhelming task. And the task would be unnecessary because anyone who read the circuit diagram would group the components together into standard circuits and think in terms of the "system" functions of the individual gates. For this reason, we design and draw digital circuits with standard logic symbols, as shown in Fig. 8.24.[10]

The small circle at the output of the logic symbol indicates the inversion of the signal. Thus, without the small circles, the triangle of the NOT would represent an amplifier (or buffer) with *output = input*, and the second symbol would indicate an OR gate. As stated earlier, however, the common circuits are those that invert. These logic symbols show only the input and output connections. When wired into a digital circuit, the

---

[10]The + (OR) and • (AND) markings in the gates are optional. The shape of the gate symbol defines its function.

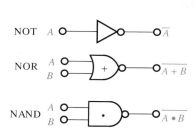

NOT $A$ — $\overline{A}$

NOR $A$, $B$ — $\overline{A + B}$

NAND $A$, $B$ — $\overline{A \cdot B}$

**Figure 8.24** Logic gate symbols for NOT, NOR, and NAND circuits.

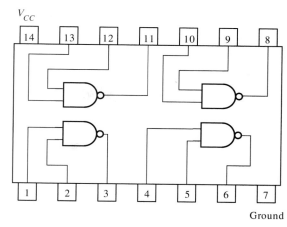

**Figure 8.25** Quad-NAND chip.

gates would have a power-supply voltage, $V_{CC}$, and grounding connections as well. Figure 8.25 shows the connections for a quadruple, two-input NAND gate. The supply voltage is applied between pins 14 and 7, with 7 grounded.

**Logic families.** If you wished to construct a digital circuit, you would not assemble a pile of diodes, resistors, and transistors and proceed to wire them together, first into standard gate circuits, and then into larger functions. You would purchase the gates already fabricated on an integrated circuit (IC), and packaged in a plastic capsule, as suggested by Fig. 8.26.[11] This commercial IC chip includes four NAND gates packaged together. An early and important step in the design would be to select a particular logic family, depending on the nature and working environment of your eventual product. The logic families are composed of a large selection of compatible circuits that can be connected together to make digital systems. The logic families differ in the details of the circuits used to perform the logical operations. Here are some of the logic families.

**Figure 8.26**
Physical appearance of a logic chip.

1. Diode–transistor logic (DTL) circuits are similar to the circuits in Figs. 8.14 and 8.15. These circuits are now obsolete. We used this simple type of logic only to illustrate the principles of logic gates.

2. High-threshold logic (HTL) circuits are similar to DTL gates but include a special diode in place of the two series diodes in Figs. 8.14 and 8.15, and use a larger power-supply voltage, $V_{CC}$. The special diode raises the threshold level for switching the transistor and hence separates the voltage regions for a 1 and 0 by a large margin, say, 10 V. This logic family is useful to prevent electrical noise, which might leak into the circuit, from affecting the operation. If, for example, your circuit must operate adjacent to a large dc motor or an arc welding machine, you would use HTL circuits.

3. Transistor–transistor logic (TTL) circuits use special-purpose transistors in place of the diodes. These circuits are widely used because they switch rapidly, require

---

[11] One reviewer suggested that these days you might order a special IC with the entire circuit on one chip.

modest power to operate, and are inexpensive. The circuits used in this logic family are considerably more complicated than the DTL circuits.

4. Complementary metal-oxide semiconductor (CMOS) logic circuits use field-effect transistors (FETs). These circuits require very little power to operate and are used where low power consumption is an important requirement, as in battery-operated calculators.

5. Emitter-coupled logic (ECL) gates switch very fast and are used in high-speed circuits such as high-frequency counters.

The design of logic circuits is highly sophisticated, and specialists in this area must become intimately familiar with all the possible products and logic families that are available at a given time.

## Realization of Logic Functions

**OBJECTIVE 6**

**To understand how to efficiently implement logic expressions using standard logic gates**

**NOT function.** Often when a NOT circuit is required, the designer will make one out of a NOR or a NAND circuit. Figure 8.27 shows the two ways to make a NOT (or inverter) out of a NAND circuit. These realizations are based on the first and third rows under AND in Fig. 8.18. The input to be fixed at a digital 1 in the lower realization would be attached to the $V_{CC}$ power supply through a resistor. Similarly, if we required an input to be fixed at 0, this input would be grounded. Grounding an input can be used to realize the NOT function with a NOR gate, which we leave as a problem at the end of the chapter.

**Realizing the elevator-door function.** In Sec. 8.1, we derived a logical expression for closing an elevator door. The logical expression, recast into the notation we developed, is given in Fig. 8.28. We first realize the function with NAND and/or NOR gates. The realization in Fig. 8.28 utilizes six gates: one NOR, one NAND, and four NOTs, which were accomplished with NANDs. This realization is based on direct translation of the logical expression into logic-gate symbols.

**Using De Morgan's theorem.** We may accomplish a simpler realization by manipulating the expression for $D$ into a more convenient form. Equation (8.6) shows such a manipulation.

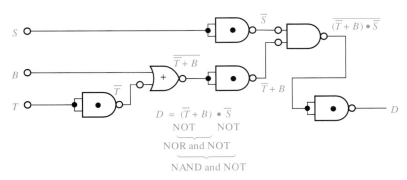

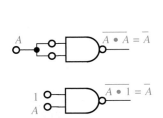

**Figure 8.27** NOT from a NAND.

**Figure 8.28** Straightforward realization of the elevator-door function using NAND and NOR gates.

$$\overline{\overline{(\overline{T} + B) \bullet \overline{S}}} = \overline{\overline{\overline{T} + B} + \overline{\overline{S}}} = \overline{\overline{\overline{T} + B} + S} \qquad (8.6)$$

In Eq. (8.6), the first form is the same expression for $D$ as in Fig. 8.28, except that we NOTed it twice. We do this because we want the final result for $D$ to be the NOT of something, to end with a NOR or NAND gate. The second form results from using De Morgan's theorem to distribute one of the NOTs to the individual terms. The third form is the same as the second, except that we have removed the double complement from $S$. This final form proves convenient for realization with NOR gates. Figure 8.29 shows the realization. We made a NOT out of NOR similar to the way we realized a NOT with a NAND earlier. De Morgan's theorem thus leads to a simpler realization.

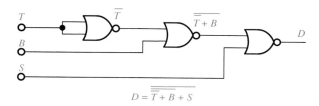

$$D = \overline{\overline{\overline{T} + B} + S}$$

**Figure 8.29**  Simple realization of the elevator-door function using NOR gates.

---

**EXAMPLE 8.7**

## Minimum gate realization

What are the fewest NAND or NOR gates to realize $A + BC$?

**SOLUTION:**

Apply the double NOT and use De Morgan's theorem on the inner NOT:

$$\overline{\overline{A + BC}} = \overline{\overline{A} \bullet \overline{BC}} \qquad (8.7)$$

The second expression requires two NANDs and a NOT, which can be made from a NAND. Thus, the answer is three NAND gates.

**WHAT IF?**   What if you try $A(B + C)$?[12]

---

## Binary Arithmetic

**binary numbers**

**Base-2 numbers.**   High-speed arithmetic is one of the spectacular achievements of digital electronics. Computers perform arithmetic with logic circuits through the representation of numbers as *binary numbers*, that is, in base-2 form. In this section, we investigate how binary arithmetic can be accomplished by digital circuits.

The development of efficient arithmetic methods was retarded for centuries by the lack of a convenient system and notation for the representation of numbers. The break-

---

[12] Two NORs and a NOT, or three NORs.

through came when the 10 Arabic[13] numerals were used to write numbers in base 10, that is, allowing the repetition of numerals, with the position representing powers of 10. For example, the number 806.1 means

$$806.1_{10} = 8 \times 10^2 + 0 \times 10^1 + 6 \times 10^0 + 1 \times 10^{-1} \qquad (8.8)$$

The advantage of such a system is that the addition and multiplication tables assume manageable size; and the rules for such operations follow simple patterns.

The triumph of the base-10 number system was so successful that, until recently, few could write and perform arithmetic in some other base. This is no longer true because "modern math" in the secondary school system includes arithmetic in nondecimal number bases. You presumably required little explanation of the binary counting already used in Fig. 8.5. In that table, the first row represents ZERO, the second ONE, and the seventh, for example, represents 6 in binary form:

$$6_{10} = 110_2 = 1 \times 2^2 + 1 \times 2^1 + 0 \times 2^0 \qquad (8.9)$$

**bit, word (binary)**

Thus, it takes three binary digits, or bits, to represent 6 in base 2, or binary, form. In general, $n$ bits can represent numbers 0 to $2^n - 1$ and, if we wish to consider plus or minus numbers, we require another bit to represent the sign. An ordered grouping of binary information, a group of bits, is called a *word*. Thus, a digital computer would represent a number as a word of, say, 32 bits, and hence be limited to numbers smaller than about 4 billion. We are speaking here of an integer format or straight binary for the numbers; we can, of course, use a floating or exponential form to represent a wider range of numbers.

---

**EXAMPLE 8.8** | **How many bits?**

How many bits of information are required to represent $10^6$ in binary form?

**SOLUTION:**
With $n$ bits, we can represent numbers up to $2^n - 1$. Thus, $2^n$ must exceed $10^6$. Take the log

$$n \log 2 > \log 10^6 = 6 \Rightarrow n > 19.9 \qquad (8.10)$$

Thus, 20 bits are required.

**WHAT IF?** | What if you want to represent the English alphabet, including capitals, and the 10 numerals. How many bits are required?[14]

---

**BCD, binary-coded decimal**

**Binary-coded decimal (BCD).** Thus far, we have presented pure decimal and pure binary representation of numbers. A hybrid system, binary-coded decimal (BCD), is frequently used in calculators and digital instrumentation. With BCD, the decimal format

---

[13] Actually, these symbols are thought to have been first used in ancient India and introduced into Western society through Islamic culture.

[14] Six bits.

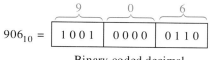

$$906_{10} = \boxed{1001 \quad 0000 \quad 0110}$$

Binary-coded decimal
(BCD)

**Figure 8.30** BCD representation of decimal 906.

of the numbers is preserved, but each digit is represented in binary form. Because we must represent 10 numerals (0, 1, 2, ..., 9), we require 4 bits of digital information for each numeral to be represented. Figure 8.30 offers an example, representing $906_{10}$ as a 12-bit BCD word. From Fig. 8.30, we deduce that $n$ bits, where $n$ is a multiple of 4, can represent numbers up to $10^{n/4} - 1$ in BCD form. This represents a reduction from what we can represent with pure binary, but facilitates input and output interactions between system and operator. Because we think in decimal, for example, we want 10 keys on our calculators for entering numbers and we also require outputs in decimal. The internal manipulation of the binary information is complicated somewhat by the BCD form, but this is a problem for calculator designers, who obviously are up to the challenge.

**hexadecimal number**

**Hexadecimal system.** With the emergence of microcomputers, which work with words of 8 and 16 bits, the hexadecimal system has gained importance. *Hexadecimal* is base 16 and requires 6 "new" number symbols in addition to the 10 Arabic numerals. For convenience in using standard printers, the letters A through F are used for 10 through 15, respectively. Thus, in hexadecimal the number A8F represents

$$A8F_{16} = 10 \times 16^2 + 8 \times 16^1 + 15 \times 16^0 = 2703_{10} \qquad (8.11)$$

The numbers 0 through 16 are represented in decimal, hexadecimal, and binary in Table 8.2.

| TABLE 8-2 Numbers in Decimal, Hexadecimal, and Binary | | |
|:---:|:---:|:---:|
| **Decimal** | **Hexadecimal** | **Binary** |
| 0 | 0 | 0000 |
| 1 | 1 | 0001 |
| 2 | 2 | 0010 |
| 3 | 3 | 0011 |
| 4 | 4 | 0100 |
| 5 | 5 | 0101 |
| 6 | 6 | 0110 |
| 7 | 7 | 0111 |
| 8 | 8 | 1000 |
| 9 | 9 | 1001 |
| 10 | A | 1010 |
| 11 | B | 1011 |
| 12 | C | 1100 |
| 13 | D | 1101 |
| 14 | E | 1110 |
| 15 | F | 1111 |
| 16 | 10 | 10000 |

# Digital Arithmetic Circuits

**BCD adder.** To illustrate digital computation, we design a logic circuit to add two decimal digits represented in BCD form. The problem is symbolized by

$$A + B = S \implies A_4 A_3 A_2 A_1 + B_4 B_3 B_2 B_1 = S_4 S_3 S_2 S_1 \qquad (8.12)$$

where in the second form the $A$'s and $B$'s with the subscripts are binary variables representing the 4 bits required for the BCD representation and the $+$ represents addition.

**First stage of the adder.** Addition in binary is illustrated in Eq. (8.13):

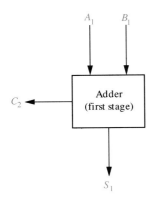

**Figure 8.31** The first stage of the adder has two inputs and two outputs.

$$
\begin{array}{r}
{}^{1}\phantom{0} \\
1001_2 \\
0101_2 \\
\hline
1110_2
\end{array}
\qquad (8.13)
$$

We have shown the carry for the binary addition in the traditional manner to emphasize that we must consider carries in the design of our circuit. That is, when we add in the lowest-order bits, 1 and 1, we obtain $10_2$, which is written as a 0 with a carry of 1. Thus, the binary circuit that adds the lowest-order bits must produce two binary outputs: the lowest-order bit of the sum and the carry to be added with the next-higher-order bits. Figure 8.31 indicates what the first stage of addition must accomplish. It must take two binary inputs, $A_1$ and $B_1$, and produce two outputs, the lowest-order bit of the sum, $S_1$, and the carry, $C_2$, to the next higher stage of addition. Examination of the truth table in Fig. 8.32 reveals that the carry bit is the AND of the inputs and the sum bit is the EXCLUSIVE OR of the two inputs:

$$C_2 = A_1 B_1 \qquad \text{and} \qquad S_1 = A_1 \oplus B_1 \qquad (8.14)$$

We thus need a realization for the XOR.

**Making an XOR.** We may express the EXCLUSIVE OR in terms of OR and AND functions through either of the following equivalent forms:

$$A_1 \oplus B_1 = A_1 \overline{B_1} + \overline{A_1} B_1 = (A_1 + B_1)\overline{A_1 B_1} \qquad (8.15)$$

The first form expresses the two ways the function can be 1: either ($A_1$ is 1 AND $B_1$ is 0) OR ($A_1$ is 0 AND $B_1$ is 1). The second form uses the ordinary OR and then removes the case where both $A_1$ and $B_1$ are 1 by ANDing with $\overline{A_1 B_1}$. We can manipulate either expression into a form suitable for realization with NAND and NOR gates, but in this case, the second expression should be chosen because it involves the AND of the two inputs, which we need for the carry bit. Using the double NOT and De Morgan's theorems, we express the EXCLUSIVE OR in the form

$$\overline{\overline{(A_1 + B_1)\overline{A_1 B_1}}} = \overline{\overline{(A_1 + B_1)} + \overline{A_1 B_1}} \qquad (8.16)$$

We use only NAND and NOR gates in our realization, so there is no benefit in canceling the double NOT on the $A_1 B_1$ term. Figure 8.33 shows the realization of the lowest bit adder and represents in detail what is indicated by Fig. 8.31.

**Higher stages of the adder.** The second and higher stages of the adder must

**Figure 8.32** Truth-table representation of the single-bit adder inputs and outputs.

| Inputs | | Outputs | |
|:---:|:---:|:---:|:---:|
| $A_1$ | $B_1$ | $C_2$ | $S_1$ |
| 0 | 0 | 0 | 0 |
| 0 | 1 | 0 | 1 |
| 1 | 0 | 0 | 1 |
| 1 | 1 | 1 | 0 |

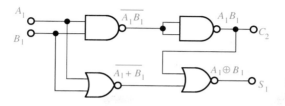

**Figure 8.33** Realization for the first stage of the adder.

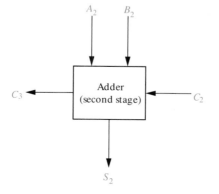

**Figure 8.34** The second stage of the adder has three inputs and two outputs.

| Inputs | | | Outputs | |
|---|---|---|---|---|
| $A_2$ | $B_2$ | $C_2$ | $C_3$ | $S_2$ |
| 0 | 0 | 0 | 0 | 0 |
| 0 | 0 | 1 | 0 | 1 |
| 0 | 1 | 0 | 0 | 1 |
| 0 | 1 | 1 | 1 | 0 |
| 1 | 0 | 0 | 0 | 1 |
| 1 | 0 | 1 | 1 | 0 |
| 1 | 1 | 0 | 1 | 0 |
| 1 | 1 | 1 | 1 | 1 |

**Figure 8.35** Truth-table representation of the second stage inputs and outputs.

consider the carry from the next-lower stage. Thus, these stages of addition must function with three inputs and two outputs, as indicated by Fig. 8.34 for the second stage. Figure 8.35 shows the truth table relating the two outputs to the three inputs. We will not complete the design of the higher-order stages of the BCD adder beyond developing Boolean expressions for the outputs.

**sum of products**

The truth table shows there to be four ways to achieve a 1 in the output bit, $S_2$, corresponding to the four 1's in the $S_2$ column. This last way is easiest to see because $A_2B_2C_2 = 1$ when all three variables are 1. The first way requires 1 when $A_2 = 0$, $B_2 = 0$, and $C_2 = 1$; hence, $\overline{A_2}\,\overline{B_2}C_2$ gives this 1. We then OR the group of ANDs. This form is called a *sum of products*. In this form, the second output bit of the sum would be

$$S_2 = \overline{A_2}\,\overline{B_2}C_2 + \overline{A_2}B_2\overline{C_2} + A_2\overline{B_2}\,\overline{C_2} + A_2B_2C_2 \tag{8.17}$$

Similarly, the carry bit from the second stage can be expressed

$$C_3 = \overline{A_2}B_2C_2 + A_2\overline{B_2}C_2 + A_2B_2\overline{C_2} + A_2B_2C_2 \tag{8.18}$$

The theorems of Boolean algebra permit simplification of Eq. (8.18). The last two terms can be combined as shown in Eq. (8.19). Thus, we can replace two terms by a simpler term.

$$A_2B_2\overline{C_2} + A_2B_2C_2 = A_2B_2(\overline{C_2} + C_2) = A_2B_2(1) = A_2B_2 \tag{8.19}$$

We could have used the same trick by combining the last term with either of the first two terms. Fortunately, the theorems of Boolean algebra allow us to insert[15] two additional $A_2B_2C_2$ terms in Eq. (8.18), and then combine them with each of the first two terms in the manner shown in Eq. (8.19). Thus, we reduce Eq. (8.18) to

$$C_3 = B_2C_2 + A_2C_2 + A_2B_2 \tag{8.20}$$

Given this success in simplifying Eq. (8.18), we might try to simplify Eq. (8.17) in a similar way, but our effort would be unsuccessful because Eq. (8.17) is already in its simplest form. Clearly, we could complete the realization of the BCD adder with NAND or NOR gates by manipulating these expressions for the sum and carry bits of the higher-order stages of the adder into suitable forms, as we did in Eq. (8.16).

**Karnaugh map**

## Karnaugh Maps

In the previous section, we used the theorems of Boolean algebra to reduce Eq. (8.18) to Eq. (8.20). It is unclear, however, when such simplifications can be achieved. The Karnaugh map furnishes a technique for simplifying a Boolean expression. By arranging the truth table into a geometric representation, one can identify algebraic relationships through the patterns of ONEs and ZEROs.

**Making a map.** The procedure for making a Karnaugh map is simple: Make a rectangular grid having 4, 8, 16, and so on, bins. Figure 8.36 shows such a map for $C_3$ as a function of $A_2$, $B_2$, and $C_2$. This map has eight bins because there are eight states to be represented. Each bin corresponds to one row of the truth table and is marked at top and side with its coordinates. For example, the bin in the lower-right corner of the map corresponds to $A_2 = 1$, $B_2 = 0$, and $C_2 = 1$, as marked at the top and side.

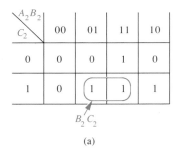

(a)

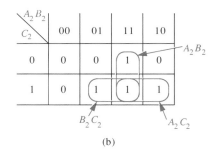

(b)

**Figure 8.36** (a) Karnaugh map showing $C_3$ as a function of $A_2$, $B_2$, and $C_2$; (b) the same Karnaugh map with all three patterns identified.

The ordering of the bins is arbitrary, provided (1) all combinations are represented only once and (2) each bin differs from adjoining bins by a change of only 1 bit. For this reason, we cannot count across the top in the usual way (00, 01, 10, 11) because 2 bits change between the second and third states. This second rule for arranging the coordinates ensures that spatial proximity is linked to algebraic closeness.

**Grouping the 1's for a sum-of-products expression.** The values of $C_3$ from the truth table go into the bins; hence, the four 1's under $C_3$ in Fig. 8.35 correspond to the four 1's in the eight bins in Fig. 8.36, each in the bin representing its row in the truth table. We now look for square and rectangular patterns of 1's. We have circled one

---

[15] Notice the third property of the OR in Fig. 8.18: $A = A + A + A + ...$, where we have expanded the expression to as many $A$'s as we require.

such pattern in Fig. 8.36(a) and marked it with $B_2C_2$ because $B_2 = 1$ AND $C_2 = 1$ uniquely identifies those adjacent bins. In other words, $A_2$ drops out because it is both 0 and 1 in that rectangle. The reason why we do not circle the three adjacent 1's is that this property of variables dropping out occurs only in rectangular patterns of two, four, eight, and so on, adjacent bins.

Figure 8.36(b) shows the same Karnaugh map with three patterns circled and identified. We now see that the 1's in the map may come from $B_2C_2$ OR $A_2B_2$ OR $A_2C_2$, which leads directly to Eq. (8.20).

**product of sums**

**Grouping the 0's for a product-of-sums expression.** We can derive an alternate expression for $C_3$ based on the zeros in the Karnaugh map. Figure 8.37(a) shows the Karnaugh map of Fig. 8.36 with a rectangle of zeros marked. We identify this group with $C_2 + A_2$ because both $C_2$ and $A_2$ must be ZERO to get ZERO in this rectangle. Figure 8.37(b) shows the Karnaugh map with all rectangles of ZEROs identified and marked with the variables that are ZERO in those rectangles. We build the function by ANDing these components, because the function is ZERO when one of these components is ZERO. This produces a *product-of-sums*[16] form for $C_3$:

$$C_3 = (C_2 + A_2)(C_2 + B_2)(A_2 + B_2)$$  (8.21)

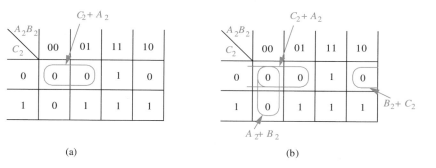

(a)                                   (b)

**Figure 8.37** (a) Karnaugh map of $C_3$ with a rectangle of ZEROs identified; (b) all rectangles identified. This leads to the product-of-sums form.

The product-of-sums form for $C_3$ is equivalent to the sum-of-products form, Eq. (8.20), as may be confirmed by expanding Eq. (8.21) and using the theorems in Fig. 8.20. However direct realization of Eq. (8.21) leads to a different circuit than Eq. (8.20) and may be simpler in some cases, though not in this case.

---

**EXAMPLE 8.9** | **Don't care**

**don't care**

A precision electronic oscillator uses a crystal that must be kept in an oven for stable operation. The oscillator has three states: OFF, STANDBY, and ON. The oven is kept operating in STANDBY and ON. We represent the states with a digital code: $S_1S_2 = 00$ (OFF), 01(STANDBY), and 10(ON), and design logic to operate the oven ($OV = 1$).

---

[16]"Sums" and "products" are not defined in Boolean algebra. The names are based on appearance.

**SOLUTION:**

Figure 8.38(a) shows the truth table and Fig. 8.38(b) the Karnaugh map. In both, the X represents a DON'T CARE state, meaning a state that cannot occur. In our design, we may assign a 1 or 0 to the DON'T CARE, whichever leads to the simplest realization, because that state can never occur.

| $S_1$ | $S_2$ | $OV$ |
|---|---|---|
| 0 | 0 | 0 |
| 0 | 1 | 1 |
| 1 | 0 | 1 |
| 1 | 1 | X |

(a)

| $S_1 \backslash S_2$ | 0 | 1 |
|---|---|---|
| 0 | 0 | 1 |
| 1 | 1 | X |

(b)

**Figure 8.38** (a) Truth table for the oven operation. The $X$ represents a DON'T CARE, which cannot happen in practice; (b) Karnaugh map for the oven function. The DON'T CARE can be considered a ZERO or ONE, whichever leads to the simpler expression.

Our realization function is based on the Karnaugh map. If we call the DON'T CARE a 0, we would have no simplifying rectangles formed, but if we call it a 1, we would have a simple product of sums form based on the one ZERO. Because $X = 1$, the one ZERO is described by $OV = S_1 + S_2$. Thus, our realization is an OR gate.

**WHAT IF?**  What if we insist on calling the $X$ a 0? What is the product-of-sums and sum-of-products functions in that case?[17]

**Further properties of Karnaugh maps.**  Other properties of the Karnaugh map are as follows:

■ There is no "edge" to the map. Bits on the far left are adjacent to bits on the far right. Figure 8.39(a) shows the same information as Fig. 8.36(b) rearranged in a different order. The pattern for $A_2C_2$ now rolls over to the left.

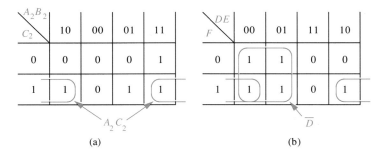

(a)

(b)

**Figure 8.39** (a) The same Karnaugh map as Fig. 8.36, with a different ordering of the columns. The $A_2C_2$ pattern now rolls over the edge of the map. (b) The identified pattern corresponds to $D = 1$.

---

[17] Sum of products: $OV = S_1\overline{S_2} + \overline{S_1}S_2 = S_1 \oplus S_2$ ; product of sums: $OV = (S_1 + S_2)(\overline{S_1} + \overline{S_2}) = S_1 \oplus S_2$.

- Patterns corresponding to independent variables that are 0 are identified as complements. For example, the four 1's in Fig. 8.39(b) correspond to $D = 0$; hence, we may identify them as $\overline{D} = 1$. The 1's in Fig. 8.39(b) thus may be identified as $\overline{D}$ OR $\overline{EF}$.

- DON'T CAREs are marked with $X$'s in the Karnaugh map and may be considered either as 0's or 1's, whichever gives the largest patterns. Because these states never occur in practice, we may safely assign them either value to give the simplest algebraic expression.

We leave for a homework problem the Karnaugh map for $S_2$, in Eq. (8.17), which has no rectangular groupings of 1's. Thus, no simplification of the expression for $S_2$ is possible.

### Check Your Understanding

1. What is $1011_2$ in hexadecimal (base 16)?
2. What is $C_{16}$ in decimal?
3. How many bits are required to represent a hexadecimal number?
4. Why would it be incorrect to label a Karnaugh map with 01, 11, 00, and 10 across the top?
5. If the state $A_2B_2C_2 = 010$ were impossible (a DON'T CARE) in the Karnaugh map in Fig. 8.36, what would be the simplest expression for $S_2$?

*Answers.* **(1)** $B_{16}$; **(2)** $12_{10}$; **(3)** 4 bits; **(4)** because more than 1 bit changes between 11 and 00 and also between 10 and 01; **(5)** $S_2 = B_2 + A_2C_2$.

---

## 8.5 SEQUENTIAL DIGITAL SYSTEMS

**combinational logic, sequential logic**

**OBJECTIVE 7**

**To understand how flip-flops are used to store and process digital information**

**stage of amplification**

The logic circuits in Section 8.4 are called *combinational* logic circuits because the output responds immediately to the inputs and there is no memory. A *sequential* logic circuit has memory; its output depends on the inputs *plus* its history. In this section, we show how memory is developed in logic circuits and how memory elements increase greatly the applications of logic circuits.

### Bistable Circuit

**Two-stage amplifier.** The basic memory circuit is the bistable circuit. Figure 8.40 shows two amplifier-switch circuits in cascade, the output of the first, $T_1$, providing the input to the second, $T_2$. This is a two-stage amplifier, for amplification takes place in two distinct *stages*.

**Input-output characteristic of the amplifier.** Each of these stages is identical to the original amplifier switch analyzed in Sec. 7.3, the input–output characteristic shown in Fig. 7.47. Cascading the two stages of amplification requires that we consider the output of the first stage as the input of the second stage. Figure 8.41 shows the overall input–output characteristic of the amplifier in Fig. 8.40. We derived this characteristic by increasing the input voltage starting with zero volts. With zero volts input, the first transistor, $T_1$, is cut off and $T_2$ is saturated. As the input voltage rises, $T_1$ leaves cutoff as the input voltage rises above 0.7 V, but $T_2$ remains saturated until the output of

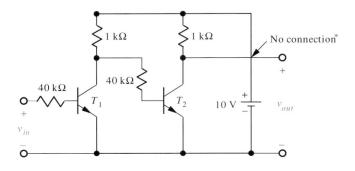

40 kΩ

1 kΩ   1 kΩ

40 kΩ

$T_1$   $T_2$   10 V   $v_{out}$

No connection*

$v_{in}$

* When wires cross in a circuit diagram, no electrical connection is implied unless a dot is placed at the intersection.

**Figure 8.40**   Two-stage amplifier.

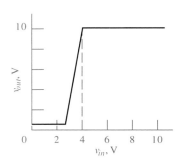

**Figure 8.41**   Input-output characteristic of two-stage amplifier.

the first stage drops to about 4 V. This output of 4 V requires an input of about 3 V (see Fig. 7.47); hence, the input to $T_1$ must increase to approximately 3 V before $T_2$ comes out of saturation and the output voltage of the entire two-stage amplifier begins to rise. In this region, both transistors are in the active region and the output rises rapidly. The second transistor reaches cutoff when the output of $T_1$ falls below 0.7 V, which occurs when its input exceeds 4 V. Thus, both transistors are in the active region for input voltages between 3 and 4 V as shown in Fig. 8.41.

**The latch circuit.**   What will happen if we connect the output of the two-stage amplifier to its input? Figure 8.42(a) shows the circuit redrawn with this connection and with $T_1$ turned around to emphasize the symmetry of the resulting circuit. We also have added inputs, which we discuss presently. This connection requires $v_{in} = v_{out}$, which defines a straight line passing through the origin and having a slope of unity. Figure 8.42(b) adds this line to the amplifier characteristic, which also has to be satisfied. This straight line is not a load line, but the same reasoning that we followed in thinking about load lines applies here: To satisfy both characteristics, the solution must lie at their intersection(s). The two intersections labeled $S_1$ and $S_2$ are stable solutions, but the intersection labeled $U$ is unstable or metastable.

**Mechanical analog.**   Figure 8.42(c) suggests a mechanical analog: The lever will have stable equilibria when resting against either wall but with a frictionless pivot the balanced position will be unstable and will not occur in practice.

**Latch action.**   The stable position marked $S_1$ occurs with transistor $T_2$ saturated and transistor $T_1$ cut off, and the stable position marked $S_2$ has transistor $T_2$ cut off and transistor $T_1$ saturated. The circuit will remain in one of these stable states forever unless an external signal forces it to the other stable state, just as the lever in Fig. 8.42(c) will lean against one wall unless an external force moves it to the other wall. By applying sufficient positive voltage to the input of the transistor that is cut off, we can switch the state of the circuit. The diodes are placed in the inputs to isolate the input drivers from the state of the circuit.

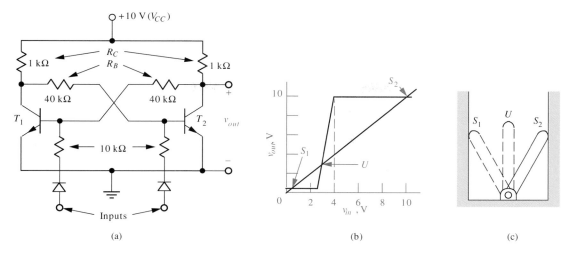

(a)                  (b)                  (c)

**Figure 8.42**   (a) Two-stage amplifier with output connected to input; (b) the circuit has two stable and one unstable operating point; (c) mechanical analog.

**latch**

### Latch function.

The circuit shown in Fig. 8.42(a) is called a *latch circuit* and it provides electronic memory. When you depress a button on your calculator, the signal sets latch circuits in the calculator to retain the keyed information after you release the button. The information thus retained is then available for processing after all numerical information is entered.

## Latches and Flip-Flops

### *S–R* latch.

We can realize the latch function with standard logic gates. Figure 8.43 shows a latch constructed from two NOR gates. The output of each NOR provides one of the inputs for the other NOR. The other inputs are labeled $S$ (for SET) and $R$ (for RESET). The outputs are labeled $Q$ and $\overline{Q}$ because the latch provides complementary outputs. This circuit, called an *S-R* latch, is similar in its operation to the circuit in Fig. 8.42(a).

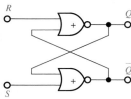

**Figure 8.43**   Latch from NOR gates.

### Latch states.

We can make a brute-force analysis of the circuit in Fig. 8.43 by pretending that the inputs are independent of the outputs, as shown in Fig. 8.44(a). Thus, the inputs to the NOR gates are $R$, $S$, $Q_{in}$, and $\overline{Q}_{in}$. With these "inputs," we can determine the outputs, $Q_{out}$ and $\overline{Q}_{out}$, from the characteristics of the NOR gates. Only the states that are self-consistent can actually exist in the flip flop in Fig. 8.43. The truth table in Fig. 8.44(b) gives the results. We require 16 rows for four input variables, with two output variables, $Q_{out}$ and $\overline{Q}_{out}$. We fill in the 0's and 1's in the first four columns to cover all possible input states by the usual method of binary counting. The columns under $Q_{out}$ and $\overline{Q}_{out}$ are filled in by using the outputs of the NOR gates, Fig. 8.14(b). For example, in the second row $R = 0$ and $\overline{Q}_{in} = 1$, so $Q_{out} = 0$; and $S = 0$ and $Q_{in} = 0$, so $\overline{Q}_{out} = 1$. After filling in all 0's and 1's, we compare the input $Q$'s with the output $Q$'s, and where they are different we know that this state is impossible. Impossible states are labeled "inconsistent."

(a)

| R | S | $Q_{in}$ | $\overline{Q_{in}}$ | $Q_{out}$ | $\overline{Q_{out}}$ | Interpretation |
|---|---|---|---|---|---|---|
| 0 | 0 | 0 | 0 | 1 | 1 | Inconsistent |
| 0 | 0 | 0 | 1 | 0 | 1 | Consistent, MEMORY with $Q_{out} = 0$ |
| 0 | 0 | 1 | 0 | 1 | 0 | Consistent, MEMORY with $Q_{out} = 1$ |
| 0 | 0 | 1 | 1 | 0 | 0 | Inconsistent |
| 0 | 1 | 0 | 0 | 1 | 0 | Inconsistent |
| 0 | 1 | 0 | 1 | 0 | 0 | Inconsistent |
| 0 | 1 | 1 | 0 | 1 | 0 | Consistent, SET |
| 0 | 1 | 1 | 1 | 0 | 0 | Inconsistent |
| 1 | 0 | 0 | 0 | 0 | 1 | Inconsistent |
| 1 | 0 | 0 | 1 | 0 | 1 | Consistent, RESET |
| 1 | 0 | 1 | 0 | 0 | 0 | Inconsistent |
| 1 | 0 | 1 | 1 | 0 | 0 | Inconsistent |
| 1 | 1 | 0 | 0 | 0 | 0 | Consistent, but forbidden |
| 1 | 1 | 0 | 1 | 0 | 0 | Inconsistent |
| 1 | 1 | 1 | 0 | 0 | 0 | Inconsistent |
| 1 | 1 | 1 | 1 | 0 | 0 | Inconsistent |

(b)

**Figure 8.44** (a) $S$–$R$ latch with inputs independent of outputs; (b) truth table for $S$–$R$ latch with identification and interpretation of the possible states.

**Interpretation of the stable states.**   We identify five consistent states, which therefore are stable states for the circuit. Two of these stable states we have identified as the MEMORY states; one state we have labeled SET, one RESET, and one FORBIDDEN. Thus, we reduce the truth table in Fig. 8.44(b) to that in Fig. 8.45(a).

The interpretations in Figs. 8.44(b) and 8.45(a) make sense in the following context: Information comes to the latch in pulses of 1's that come to $S$ or $R$. If we get a pulse at $S$, the latch output, $Q$, is set to 1. If we get a pulse at $R$, the output is reset to 0. If we get no pulse at either input, the output state remains in, or remembers, its present state. If it gets simultaneous pulses at $S$ and $R$, both outputs go to 0, which does not hurt anything, but then go to an indeterminate state when the inputs return to 0. This is undesirable because it leads to an unpredictable result; hence, this state is called FORBIDDEN.

The $S$–$R$ latch  made from NOT and NAND gates shown in Fig. 8.45(b) has the same properties as the $S$–$R$ latch we analyzed except that both its outputs go to 1's when 1's appear at both inputs. This type of $S$-$R$ latch forms the basis for the gated latch.

| R | S | Q | $\overline{Q}$ | Interpretation |
|---|---|---|---|---|
| 0 | 0 | 0 | 1 | MEMORY with $Q = 0$ |
| 0 | 0 | 1 | 0 | MEMORY with $Q = 1$ |
| 0 | 1 | 1 | 0 | SETS $Q \rightarrow 1$ |
| 1 | 0 | 0 | 1 | RESETS $Q \rightarrow 0$ |
| 1 | 1 | 0 | 0 | FORBIDDEN $Q = \overline{Q} = 0$ |

(a)

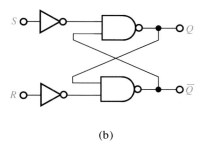

(b)

**Figure 8.45** (a) Truth table for an $S$–$R$ latch made from NOR gates; (b) an $S$–$R$ latch made with NAND gates. The properties of this latch are the same as shown in (a) except the outputs go to $Q = 0$ and $\overline{Q} = 1$ in the FORBIDDEN state.

## EXAMPLE 8.10  Stable states

Find the stable states of the logic circuit in Fig. 846(a).

**SOLUTION:**

Figure 8.46(b) treats $A$ and $B$ as independent inputs and then from them deduces the output from the NAND gate truth table in Fig. 8.46(b). We find the only stable state to be $A = 0$ with $B = 1$.

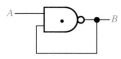

| $A$ | $B_{in}$ | $B_{out} = \overline{AB_{in}}$ | Result? |
|---|---|---|---|
| 0 | 0 | 1 | Inconsistent |
| 0 | 1 | 1 | Consistent |
| 1 | 0 | 1 | Inconsistent |
| 1 | 1 | 0 | Inconsistent |

(a)                      (b)

**Figure 8.46** (a) This circuit has stable states when input and NAND gate requirements are met, (b) The truth table with the inputs independent of the output.

**WHAT IF?**      What if the gate is a NOR?[18]

---

[18] One stable state with $A = 1$ and $B = 0$.

**glitch**

**Gated flip-flops.** The *S–R* latch requires a number of refinements to achieve its full potential for memory and digital signal processing. One problem is that the *S–R* latch responds to its input signals at *S* and *R* immediately and at all times. Timing problems can occur when logic signals that are supposed to arrive at the same time actually arrive at slightly different times due to separate delays. Such timing problems can create short, unwanted pulses called *glitches*.

The gated latch in Fig. 8.47(a) responds to the *R* or *S* inputs only when a gating signal arrives at the *G* (gate) input. Here we have built the latch out of NAND gates. In this form, the forbidden state at the inputs to the cross-coupled NANDs is 00, which corresponds to 11 at the *R* and *S* inputs, as before. This latch also has Preset (*Pr*) and Clear (*Cr*) inputs that set the latch independent of the input gates. These are active when in the 0 state, as indicated by the circle at their inputs on the logic symbol in Fig. 8.47(b). The truth table in Fig. 8.47(c) now lists the output state *after* the gating pulse, $Q_{n+1}$, as a function of the *R* and *S* inputs and the state, $Q_n$, *prior* to the gating pulse, $Q_n$. For example, with $RS = 00$, the gating signal produces no change in the output state, $Q_{n+1} = Q_n$. By using an inverter on the gate input, we could have the gating occur at $G = 0$. This would be indicated by a circle at the gating input (*G*) of the flip-flop symbol in Fig. 8.47(b).

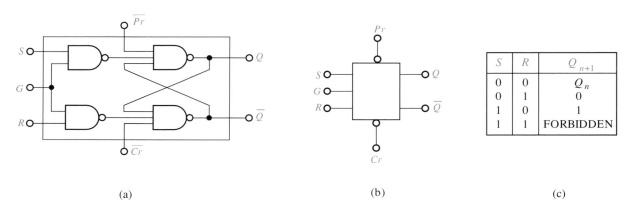

**Figure 8.47** (a) Gated latch; (b) logic symbol; (c) truth table.

The *R* and *S* inputs are thus active when the signal at the gate input is 1. Normally, such timing, or synchronizing, signals are distributed throughout a digital system by clock pulses, as shown in Fig. 8.48. The symmetrical clock signal provides two periods during each cycle when switching may be accomplished, that is, when $Ck \Rightarrow 1$ and when $\overline{Ck} \Rightarrow 1$.

**edge-triggering**

**Edge-triggered flip-flops.** The gating time of the inputs can be further reduced by making the clock input sensitive to transitions in the clock signal, which is known as *edge triggering*. The circuit can be designed to trigger at the leading or trailing edge of the clock. The symbol for an edge-triggered flip-flop is shown in Fig. 8.49 for both (a) leading and (b) trailing edge triggering. The distinguishing mark for edge triggering is a triangle at the clock input. Triggering at the edges of the waveform limits the time during which the inputs are active and thus serves to eliminate glitches. By using cir-

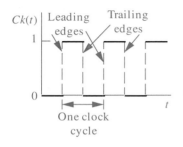

Figure 8.48 Clock signal.

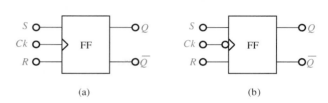

Figure 8.49 Logic symbols for edge-triggered flip flops: (a) leading edge triggering; (b) trailing edge triggering.

cuits that trigger at either the leading or trailing edges, the designer can pass signals in a circuit at two times in each clock cycle.

**toggle**

*J–K* **flip flops.** Another problem with the basic *S–R* latch is the forbidden state at the input. This can be eliminated by ANDing the inputs with the output of the flip flop, thus blocking one of the inputs, as shown in Fig. 8.50. The added gates here have the effect of inhibiting the 1 input to the gate whose output is 1. Therefore, with $J = 1$ and $K = 1$, the input that is passed will always change the state of the output. The truth table for the *J–K* flip-flop, Fig. 8.51, is the same as the truth table in Fig. 8.47(c), except that we indicate a change of output state, $Q_{n+1} = \overline{Q}_n$ for the hitherto forbidden input state. The *J–K* flip-flop thus gives us, in addition to a latched memory of the input, the capacity to *toggle*[19] at each clock pulse when both inputs are 1. This toggle feature reveals why we must use edge triggering for this flip-flop: If the clock pulse were extended in time, the state would oscillate back and forth and the eventual output would be indeterminate. The toggle mode of the *J–K* flip flop is useful in counters and frequency dividers.

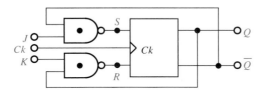

Figure 8.50 *J–K* flip flop.

| $J$ | $K$ | $Q_{n+1}$ | Meaning |
|---|---|---|---|
| 0 | 0 | $Q_n$ | MEMORY |
| 0 | 1 | 0 | RESET |
| 1 | 0 | 1 | SET |
| 1 | 1 | $\overline{Q}_n$ | TOGGLE |

Figure 8.51 Truth table for the *J–K* flip flop. $Q_n$ represents the state before the clock pulse and $Q_{n+1}$ the state after the clock pulse.

**D-type flip-flops.** The *J–K* flip flop can be converted to a *D*-type flip-flop[20] by connecting an inverter between the inputs, as shown by Fig. 8.52. This has the effect of shifting the input to the output at the active clock edge, as shown in Fig. 8.53.

---

[19] A lever-actuated switch, like the ordinary light on–off switch, is called a toggle switch. Thus, to toggle means to switch from one state to another.

[20] *D* for delay.

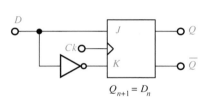

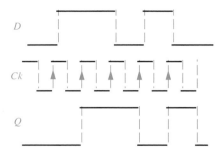

**Figure 8.52** $D$-type flip-flop.

**Figure 8.53** The output is delayed until the next active clock edge.

$T$-type flip flops. Tying the $J$ and $K$ inputs together produces a $T$-type flip-flop.[21] The $T$-type flip flop toggles with the clock pulse when $T = 1$ and does not toggle when $T = 0$. This is useful for counters and divide-by-2 applications. The logic symbol and truth table for the $T$-type flip-flop are shown in Fig. 8.54.

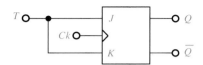

| $T$ | $Q_{n+1}$ |
|---|---|
| 0 | $Q_n$ |
| 1 | $\overline{Q}_n$ |

**Figure 8.54** $T$-type flip-flop with truth table.

Summary. In this section, we presented the $S$–$R$ latch as the basic memory element in logic circuits. A variety of refinements were given, leading to $J$–$K$, $D$, and $T$ flip-flops. In all cases, we have shown only one way to realize the characteristic of the different flip-flops. In the various logic families, these circuits could be realized through many variations, depending on the properties of the specific family. In the next section, we indicate how flip-flops can be used in digital systems.

## Flip-Flop Applications

Frequency dividers. The clock frequency can be halved with a $T$ flip-flop by setting the $T$ input to 1 and letting the clock toggle the output. This process can be continued to divide by 4, 8, etc.

Counters. Figure 8.55 illustrates the counting process. We begin with a cleared counter, that is, with all output $Q$'s at ZERO. As shown, every trailing edge of the clock pulse changes the state of FF0; hence, the output frequency of FF0 is half the clock frequency. Because this output is used as a clock for FF1, the frequency is again divided by 2, and so on down the counter. We have drawn two dashed lines to verify that the repeated divide-by-2 operation counts the input clock pulses. For example, after the end of the seventh input pulse, the state of the $Q$'s is 0111 $(= 7_{10})$, considering $Q_0$ as the lowest-order bit. The reader can verify the count after 12 pulses. Note that the chain counts input pulses in binary even if the clock pulses are unevenly spaced.

---

[21] $T$ for toggle.

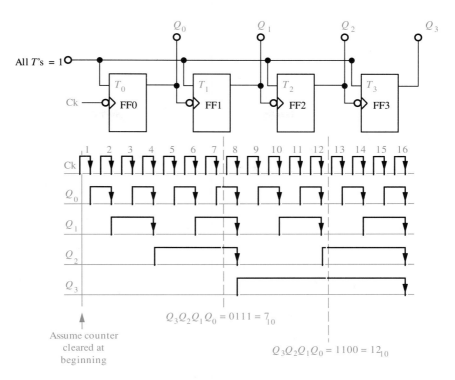

**Figure 8.55** Basic counter operation. The states count in binary, with $Q_0$ interpreted as the lowest-order bit.

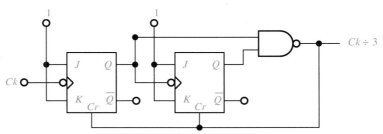

**Figure 8.56** Divide-by-3 circuit.

Division by a factor that is not an exact power of 2 can be accomplished by using an AND gate to detect the appropriate state. Figure 8.56 shows a divide-by-3 counter. If the two flip-flops start off cleared (both $Q$'s = 0), then at the end of the third clock cycle, both $Q$'s would be 1, which would produce a 1 at the AND output. This 1 clears the flip-flops and acts as output. Hence, we get one output pulse for every three input pulses.

**ripple counter, synchronous counter**

**A decade counter.** Figure 8.57 shows how to convert a binary counter to a decade counter. The AND gate detects a count of 10, $Q_3\overline{Q}_2Q_1\overline{Q}_0 = 1$, clears the counter, and provides an input to the next stage. The $Q_3Q_2Q_1Q_0$ output from the stage could be transferred to a BCD-to-decimal display while the counter is counting another sample of the input.

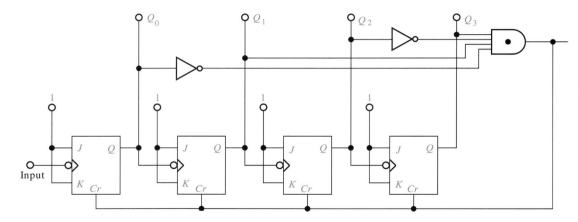

**Figure 8.57** One stage of a decade counter.

The types of counters that we have presented are called *ripple counters* because the flip-flop transitions move in sequence from left to right through the counter. By contrast, a *synchronous counter* uses a simultaneous clock pulse at all flip-flops, and controls the counting operation with external gates. Also possible are up–down counters that increase or decrease the count depending on an input command.

The digital designer has available frequency dividers, counters, and many other useful system functions on LSI (large-scale integration) chips. Such LSI circuits manage the internal connections and provide the external inputs and outputs.

**register, byte, word**

**Registers.** A *register* is a series of flip-flops arranged for organized storage or processing of binary information. Before describing several types of registers, we must introduce some concepts that relate to the use of registers in computers.

Information is represented in a computer by groups of 1's and 0's called *words*. Thus, a word in an 8-bit microprocessor might be 01101101, or 6D in hexadecimal. An 8-bit word is also called a *byte* and is a convenient unit for digital information. One byte can represent two BCD digits or an ASCII (American Standard Code for Information Interchange) alphanumeric symbol. Current microprocessors work with words of 4, 8, 16, or 32 bits, whereas larger computers work with words of 32 or more bits. A register in a computer with 8-bit words would require eight flip-flops to store or process simultaneously the 8 bits of information.

**bus**

Words of information are moved around in a computer or other digital system on a *bus*. As on a city bus line where passengers can enter or leave at a variety of points along the way, so on a computer bus the words can originate at any of the several registers or arrive at any of several destination registers. The bus itself consists of the required number of wires[22] connecting all potential source registers with all potential destination registers.

Figure 8.58 shows a bus of four wires connected to a destination register of four *D*-type flip-flops. At the leading edge of the LOAD signal, the information on the bus is

---

[22] Plus the common, which would be the signal ground. Actually, "conducting paths" is more appropriate, for no wires are used for internal information transfer on a microprocessor chip.

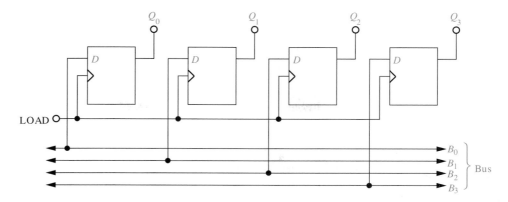

**Figure 8.58** Loading a register from a bus.

stored in the register. The information does not come down the bus and get off at the register; rather, the information appears simultaneously all along the bus and may be loaded simultaneously into several registers.

**Three-state gates.**    Whereas more than one register can be loaded simultaneously from the bus, only one register can put information on the bus at one time. We need a way to connect the outputs of all source registers to the bus such that only one register can transfer its output word to the bus at any time. An ordinary gate will not accomplish this, for its output must be either 1 or 0 and hence connecting the outputs of all source registers would result in a tug of war. A three-state gate, shown in Fig. 8.59, is required. In the absence of an ENABLE signal, the output of the gate approximates an open circuit and the gate is disconnected from the bus. When the ENABLE signal is present, the gate is connected to the bus and the output is 1 or 0 according to the input. Thus, we can connect all source registers to the bus with three-state gates and ENABLE one register at a time to transfer data to the bus.

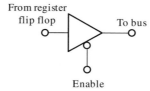

**Figure 8.59** Three-stage gate. When ENABLE is 1, the output is disconnected from the bus.

**parallel information, channel, serial information**

**Shift register.**    The data-storage register described in the preceding section transfers information with *parallel* input and parallel output. Sometimes digital information must be sent over one *channel*, as when a telephone circuit is used. In this case, bits are sent in time sequence, or *serial* form. When digital information must be received in serial form, a shift register may be used to accept the serial information and convert it to parallel form.

The $D$-type flip-flops in Fig. 8.60 will act as a shift register. Recall that the input to the $D$ flip-flop is shifted to the output by the clock pulse. Thus, the input to $D_3$ will appear at $Q_3$ after one clock pulse, at $Q_2$ after two, at $Q_1$ after three, and at $Q_0$ after four clock pulses. Hence, the 4-bit sequence (word) input at $D_3$ will fill the register

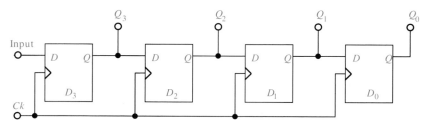

**Figure 8.60**  Shift register.

$Q_3Q_2Q_1Q_0$ after four clock pulses. The word can then be transferred to a parallel bus with three-state gates.

**EXAMPLE 8.11**  **Shift register**

The shift register in Fig. 8.60 receives a hexadecimal F (= 1111) in serial form at its input. Assuming that the register is initially cleared, what are the states after two clock pulses?

**SOLUTION:**

We assume the lowest-order bit arrives first, so after one clock pulse, this bit occupies $Q_3$ and $Q_2$, $Q_1$, and $Q_0$ are still cleared. Thus, the pattern is $Q_3Q_2Q_1Q_0 = 1000$. After two clock pulses, the state of the register is 1100.

**WHAT IF?**  What if you are loading a hexadecimal $9_{10}$ and you want the state after three clock pulses?[23]

The shift register takes a serial input and produces parallel output when operated in the manner of Fig. 8.60. The same register can accept a parallel word at the Preset inputs to the flip-flops. The word can then be driven out $Q_0$ by the clock to produce serial output.

**Binary multiplication.**  The shift register in Fig. 8.60 shifts its bit pattern one unit to the right with each clock pulse. A more versatile shift register results when the flip-flop inputs are connected with gates to their neighbors on left or right. Such a register can shift its bit pattern to the right or left, depending on which set of gates is ENABLED. This facility is useful in arithmetic operations. Multiplication by 10 in the decimal number system can be accomplished by shifting the decimal point one digit to the right. Similarly, multiplication by 2 in binary can be accomplished by moving the binary point one place to the right. This can be effected in hardware by shifting all bits one place to the left in a shift register, and clearly multiplication by $2^n$ requires $n$ left shifts. A combination of shifting and adding intermediate results is required for multi-

---

[23] $Q_3Q_2Q_1Q_0 = 0010$.

plication by numbers that are not exact powers of 2. In like manner, division can be accomplished by shifting bits to the right in a shift register.

**Summary.** In this section, we have shown how flip-flops are used to store digital information. Groups of flip-flops called registers can receive or deliver words of information in parallel with a bus, or information can be stored and delivered in serial form. The shift register is also useful in binary arithmetic operations. These are the principal components of computers, to which we now turn.

### Check Your Understanding

1. In the $S$–$R$ latch made with NOR gates in Fig. 8.43, the forbidden state is $R \bullet S = 1$ or 0?
2. Tying $J$ and $K$ together in a $J$–$K$ flip-flop makes what type of flip-flop?
3. If $Q = 1$ and $T = 0$ in the $T$-type flip-flop of Fig. 8.54, what will $\overline{Q}$ be after the clock pulse $(Ck)$?
4. How many latches are required to store a byte of information?
5. Which of the following have a forbidden state: $S$–$R$ latch, $J$–$K$ FF, $D$-type FF, $T$-type FF?

*Answers.* (1) $R \bullet S = 1$; (2) $T$, or toggle FF; (3) $\overline{Q} = 0$ after the clock pulse; (4) eight; (5) $S$–$R$ latch.

## 8.6 COMPUTERS

## Introduction

**OBJECTIVE 8**

**To understand how a computer uses digital circuits to process information**

Electrical engineers have produced some passing fads, but computers are here to stay. These versatile devices increasingly influence modern business and pleasure; seers predict an even broader place for computers in the future. The computer epitomizes many of the themes of this book. In Chapter 1, we stressed the speed with which electrical phenomena occur: computer magic arises, for the most part, out of the speed with which computers operate. We stressed in Chapters 1 and 7 that microscopic matter is electrical in nature: from manipulation of the electrical properties of matter come the tiny transistor switches and electrical connections that physically constitute computer circuits. The digital idea finds its fullest expression in computers.

Computers have changed drastically since their development four decades ago. The original computers were big and expensive; only large institutions could justify their purchase for demanding computational tasks. Costs were in hundreds of thousands, if not millions, of dollars. Large (mainframe) computers still command an important place in the computer market. Then came the minicomputer, about the size of a suitcase. The electronics of minicomputers utilize LSI digital circuits. These computers made possible the automation of process control and the processing of data in real time; costs were in tens of thousands of dollars.

Now we have microcomputers. The low cost of the basic computer chip is revealed by its use in toys that retail for less than $25. Small personal computers, including memory, keyboard, and elementary software, sell for hundreds of dollars; you provide a CRT for display. The computer on a chip finds more and more applications: smart typewriters, cash registers, appliances, and sewing machines; in the automobile, in electronic instruments, at the video arcade, in the nursery. Perhaps the desktop computer itself best demonstrates the potential of microprocessor technology.

Computers are complicated systems, not easily explained. Aside from the fundamental principles of the computer itself, a myriad of related topics could be discussed: interfacing the computer to peripheral devices such as keyboards, CRTs, and printers; software development, including programming languages, editors, assemblers, and compilers; information representation matters such as fixed- and floating-point representation of numbers, data structures, codes for representing text; and potential applications such as numerical calculation, word processing, accounting systems, real-time process control, and time sharing. To add to the complexity, the world of computers has developed its own esoteric and colorful language.

We have listed topics that, for the most part, we are *not* going to discuss in this section. Our brief introduction to this subject addresses two basic questions: What is a computer, and how does it work?

## Computer Architecture

The four basic elements of a computer are memory, an arithmetic-logic circuit, a control circuit, and input–output. These elements are present as well in a hand-held calculator. In that case, you supply the program by pushing the various buttons that sequence the calculations. When the calculator has the capability of storing a "program" of keystrokes, it is a computer, albeit a limited, slow, and highly specialized computer.

**Central processing unit (CPU).** Figure 8.61 shows the system configuration of a typical computer. The central processing unit (CPU) contains an arithmetic-logic unit (ALU), control circuits, and several registers for storage and general manipulation of words of data. The CPU is the brains of the computer and, at our level of understanding, the most complex and mysterious. Although we have touched on hardware implementation of binary arithmetic and data storage, the complexity of the CPU places it far beyond the level of this introduction.

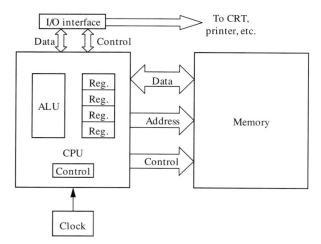

**Figure 8.61** Elements of a computer.

The CPU has an instruction register that is sequentially loaded with words from the program in memory. These instructions, mere strings of 1's and 0's, are decoded and executed by the CPU: words are brought from memory, placed in designated registers, processed according to the instruction, and then stored in memory at a specified location or perhaps transferred to an output device. Within the CPU are a number of registers to hold data and addresses of special places in memory relating to the program or to blocks of data. A program-counter register is incremented after each instruction is "fetched" from memory into the instruction register so that the CPU knows where to get the next instruction. The CPU communicates with memory by means of a two-way data bus, an address bus,[24] that controls the location in memory to furnish or receive data or program words, and a control bus that coordinates timing and order.

**random-access memory (RAM)**

**Memory.** Computer memory may be of several types. A *random-access memory* (RAM) is an array of memory registers with which data may be exchanged. The memory access is random because any memory location is equally accessible for reading or writing of data or program instructions. Normally, the program would not write into the portion of the memory containing program instructions, but the entire program must initially be loaded into memory. Most semiconductor memories are "volatile" because they lose the stored information when the computer is turned off. For this reason, and generally to store large amounts of information, magnetic disks or tapes are used for storage of digital information.

**read-only memory (ROM)**

Also important are *read-only memories* (ROMs), which contain information (usually programs) that can be read but not modified by the computer. Programmable ROMs (PROMs) allow the user to store information by burning microscopic fuses in the ROM. An erasable PROM (EPROM) can be reprogrammed after its information has been erased by ultraviolet light.

**Input/output (I/O).** Although self-contained for their internal calculations and data manipulations, computers must interact with the outside world. Often computer–person interaction is provided through terminals with keyboard and display and through printers and plotters. Such devices translate between people-oriented symbols, such as alphanumeric text or graphical representation of information, and computer-oriented representation, bits, 1's and 0's of information.

Computers interact with external systems such as robots, electronic instruments, and manufacturing processes. Such interactions often involve digital-to-analog (D/A) and analog-to-digital (A/D) conversion. The computer communicates with external devices over an external data bus, which is separate from the computer's internal data bus. Several protocols exist for announcing which component has information to transfer to the computer, for keeping two devices from "talking" at once, and for assuring that the target component "heard what was said."

**high-level language, assembly language, op code**

**Programming languages.** *Programming* is the art of translating a problem into words of 1's and 0's that the computer CPU executes to solve the problem. Figure 8.62 summarizes the communication problem: We think in terms of language, mathematical

---

[24] 16 bits for a 64K memory. In computer talk, K means $2^{10}$, or 1024. Thus, a 16-bit address can specify one location out of $2^{16}$, or 64 K, or 65,536 words.

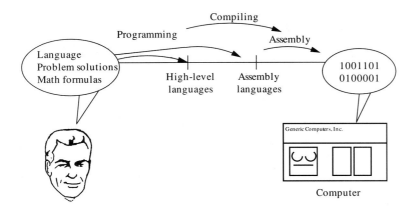

**Figure 8.62** Communicating with a computer.

notation, accounting conventions, and so on, and the computer "thinks" in 1's and 0's. Programming languages provide the bridge between human thought processes and the binary words that control computer operations. Computer languages that are deliberately close to human thought processes or notations are called *high-level languages*: FOR-TRAN, BASIC, LISP, ALGOL, C, FORTH, and PASCAL are examples of high-level languages. Low-level languages are called *assembly languages* and these are oriented toward the instructions that the specific computer can execute. The binary words are loaded into computer memory and executed as machine or object code. One line of code in a high-level language can produce many lines of machine code, whereas one line of assembly code, being close to the computer operations, will produce one or at most a few lines of machine code. For the microprocessor, the assembly language is also called the *op code* for the machine.

**compiler, assembler**

**Compilers, assemblers, loaders, and interpreters.** A *compiler* is a program that accepts as input a program in a high-level language, usually as a string of ASCII characters, and produces as an output either an assembly-language program or a machine-code program. The compiler is thus a computer program that performs language translation from one computer language to another language closer to what the computer uses. An *assembler* performs the same function, using the assembly (source) code as input and producing output in object code.

**loader, bootstrap**

Compilers and assemblers are large programs that function on a specific computer. Such programs thus would be developed and furnished by the computer manufacturer, often on a ROM chip, or perhaps by an institution providing computer services. The object code that is produced usually is stored on disk or magnetic tape or in memory at a different location from where it will eventually reside. After the compiler or assembler does its work, it often is erased from memory to make room for the program machine code and whatever data the program requires. A small program called a *loader* loads the machine code into memory for execution. When the program consists of several separate parts (main program, subroutines, functions), the loader puts these into consecutive memory and, in effect, tells each where all the others are so that they can communicate. When one begins with a completely empty memory, a small program called a *bootstrap* can be loaded into memory by means of a keyboard or front panel switches. The bootstrap program can load the loader, which loads the program and signals the beginning of execution.

Some high-level languages, such as BASIC, are interpreted instead of compiled. This means that the program is converted into machine language and executed line by line. This is inefficient in computer time but efficient for finding certain program errors because mistakes can be corrected as they occur without having to reexecute the program up to the point where the error has occurred. This is especially appropriate when the programmer is working on a small computer.

In the past, programs were usually punched on cards or perhaps paper tapes and read into the computer with a card (or paper-tape) reader. Modern systems use editors that allow typing of alphanumeric text directly into the computer and offer the programmer easy modification through a variety of editing commands. Indeed, the storage, editing, and manipulation of text have opened new computer applications for the production of printed matter.

## CHAPTER SUMMARY

Information may be represented in a variety of forms. The fundamental digital operations of AND, OR, and NOT are introduced. We show how electronic circuits can perform these operations once ONEs and ZEROs are represented as regions of voltage. Boolean algebra is introduced and logic expressions are placed in appropriate forms for realization by combinational logic circuits. Circuits with memory are developed based on the simple latch.

**Objective 1: To understand how information is coded in digital form.** Representing information in a series of "yes/no" questions might seem limiting, but the technique is quite powerful. Common alphanumeric and ad hoc codes are introduced.

**Objective 2: To understand how to perform NOT, OR, NOR, AND, NAND, and XOR operations on binary variables.** The basic operations between binary variables are defined and illustrated in the context of an example.

**Objective 3: To understand how digital information is represented and manipulated with electronic circuits.** A binary state is represented with an electrical signal that has one region for a ONE separated by a forbidden region from a region for a ZERO. By using such regions, simple circuits of diodes and transistors can perform the NOT, NAND, and NOR operations.

**Objective 4: To understand how to use Boolean algebra to simplify and manipulate logic expressions.** We use Boolean algebra to simplify and manipulate binary expressions into forms that permit minimal realization with logic circuits. De Morgan's theorems produce alternate forms of binary expressions for realization with NAND or NOR gates.

**Objective 5: To understand how to efficiently implement logic expressions using standard logic gates.** Logic expressions may be placed in a form that suggest direct realization with standard gates. Karnaugh maps allow the designer to reduce a truth table to a sum-of-products or product-of-sums form for realization with logic circuits.

**Objective 6: To understand how flip-flops are used to store and process digital information.** The basic latch has two stable states that can store of 1 bit of information. From this basis, a family of flip-flops is derived to store and process digital information.

**Objective 7: To understand how a computer uses digital circuits to process information.** The basic parts of a computer are described.

Chapter 9 presents the techniques of analog electronics, and Chapter 10 combines the techniques of digital and analog electronics for instrumentation systems.

## PROBLEMS

## Section 8.1 Digital Infomation

**8.1.** A room has a three-way switch system, meaning that changing either switch changes the state of the light. Let $S_A$ represent the switch at door $A$ and $S_B$ the switch at door $B$. Let $S_A = 0$ and $S_B = 0$ be a state with the light OFF ($L = 0$).
  **(a)** Develop a truth table relating the switch states to the digital variable $L$ representing the light.
  **(b)** Give a Boolean expression for $L$ as a function of $S_A$ and $S_B$.

**8.2.** An outside floodlight has an automatic device turning it ON at night ($D = 0$) and OFF during daylight hours ($D = 1$). It also has a switch ($S = 1$ for the switch ON, controlling power to the automatic device and bulb), and $B = 1$ means the floodlight bulb is functional (not burned out).
  **(a)** Let $F = 1$ indicate that there is light from the floodlight. Give a truth table for $F$ as a function of $D$, $S$, and $B$.
  **(b)** Write a Boolean expression for $F$.

**8.3.** A student is allowed to take a course ($C = 1$) if he or she pays the registration fee ($R = 1$) and either has the prerequisites ($P = 1$) or has the instructor's approval ($A = 1$).
  **(a)** Give a truth table for $C$ as a function of $R$, $P$, and $A$.
  **(b)** Write a Boolean expression for $C$.

**8.4.** A burglary alarm system sounds an alarm ($A = 1$) if the detectors detect activity ($D = 1$). The alarm system has a key to disable it during working hours ($K = 1$ disables the alarm) and also has a test button ($T = 1$ sounds the alarm if the system is not disabled).
  **(a)** Give a truth table relating the output $A$ to the inputs $D$, $K$, and $T$. Use $X$ for DON'T CARE states, that is, states that will never happen in practice.

  **(b)** Give a Boolean expression for $A$. Count DON'T CAREs as 1.
  *Comment:* In this situation, some states are impossible. We have excluded the case where $T = 1$ and $K = 1$. Such states are called DON'T CARE states and are indicated by an $X$ under $A$ in the truth table rather than a 1 or 0. The logical function is still valid; certain combinations of the independent variables never occur in practice. The designer therefore does not care about what the system does in these states. See page 405 for an example.

**8.5.** A student is sure to accept an invitation ($I = 1$) provided that the student likes the invitor ($L = 1$) and has no test the next day ($T = 0$). But if it's A Certain Friend ($F = 1$), the student will accept even if there is a test the next day.
  **(a)** Make a truth table relating the dependent variable, $I$, to the independent variables: $L$, $T$, and $F$.
  **(b)** Express the Invitation function, $I(L, T, F)$, in terms of ANDs and ORs. Count DON'T CAREs as 1. See the comment on DON'T CARE states in Problem 8.4 or the example on page 405.

**8.6.** In the 1980 NBA playoffs, the Philadelphia 76ers basketball team led the Boston Celtics three games to one; the 76ers could have won the best-of-seven series by winning any of the fifth, sixth, or seventh games. Let $G_5$, $G_6$, and $G_7$ be digital variables to describe the outcome of those games, with $G_5 = 1$ if the 76ers win the fifth game and $G_5 = 0$ if Boston wins, and so forth for $G_6$ and $G_7$. For the sake of completing the truth table, we will award the remaining games to the 76ers should they win the series before the seventh game. The dependent variable is $P = 1$ if the 76ers win the series and $P = 0$ if the Celtics win. Make a truth table showing the relationship between $G_5$, $G_6$, and $G_7$ as input

(independent) variables and $P$ as output (dependent) variable. This situation has some DON'T CARE states; see the comment in Problem P8.4.

## Problems on Section 8.2: The Electronics of Digital Signals

8.7. The circuit shown in Fig. P8.7 has digital input and output, connected by some switches. The input is a digital 1, but the output is 1 or 0, depending on the switches. Let $S_A = 1$ if switch A is closed and $S_A = 0$ if switch A is open, and the same for all switches. Write a Boolean expression for the output, $D$, as a function of $A$, $B$, and $C$.

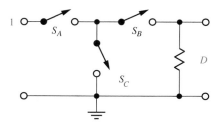

**Figure P8.7**

8.8. Figure P8.8 shows the input–output characteristic for a transistor circuit. The $\beta$ of the transistor is 125.
   (a) Draw a circuit with this characteristic. Let one of your resistors be 1 kΩ
   (b) Define logic levels for 0 and 1 such that the circuit exhibits the NOT function.
   (c) Modify the circuit such that it exhibits NOR behavior.

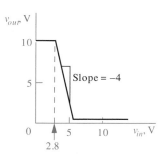

**Figure P8.8**

8.9. The circuit in Fig. P8.9 operates as a digital inverter. Assume a voltage of 0.7 V for a $pn$ junction that is ON, and a saturation voltage of 0.3 V for the transistor. The $\beta$ of the transistor is 50.
   (a) Find the minimum value of $v_{in}$ to saturate the

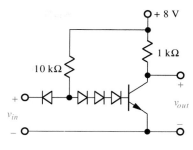

**Figure P8.9**

   transistor. What is the collector current in saturation? What current must the input draw to saturate?
   (b) Find the maximum of $v_{in}$ to leave the transistor in cutoff. What is the output (collector) voltage when the transistor is cut off? What current must the input draw to keep in cutoff?

8.10. The circuit in Fig. P8.10 uses switches to create logic inputs to a circuit. $S_A = 1$ indicates closure, and so on. Give the truth table for the circuit operation, using the usual convention for the output $C$. For the transistor, $\beta = 100$, $V_{CE(sat)} = 0.3$ V, and 0.7 V to turn ON a $pn$ junction.

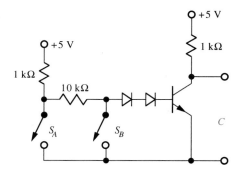

**Figure P8.10**

8.11. For the NOR gate in Fig. 8.14 to operate properly, the transistor must be saturated when the input is a digital 1. Assume that the transistor characteristics are those in Fig. 7.39 and that the minimum voltage input for a 1 is 4.0 V. Assume that the $pn$ junctions have a voltage of 0.7 V when ON.

(a) What is the largest value of $R_B$ (10 k$\Omega$ in Fig. 8.14 but now a variable) that allows the transistor to remain saturated for an input 1?

(b) Keeping $R_B$ at 10 k$\Omega$, what is the smallest value of the transistor $\beta$ that will keep the transistor saturated? (Now the transistor characteristics are different from those in Fig. 7.39.) Assume that $V_{CE(\text{sat})} = 0.5$ V.

## Problems on Section 8.3: The Mathematics of Digital Electronics

8.12. Make a truth table with two inputs, $A$ and $B$, and the outputs OR, NOR, AND, NAND, EXCLUSIVE OR, and the equality function.

8.13. With a truth table, verify the second of the absorption rules in Fig. 8.20.

8.14. Simplify the following Boolean expressions

(a) $\overline{\overline{A} + B(\overline{A} + B)}$ .

(b) $A(B + \overline{A}) + B(B + A)$ .

(c) $\overline{\overline{\overline{AB}}} + A + B$ .

8.15. Use the theorems of Section 8.3 to simplify the following digital functions:

(a) $\overline{\overline{A} + (B + A)\overline{B}}$ .

(b) $A + \overline{B(1 + \overline{A})AA}$ .

(c) $\overline{ABC} + \overline{A}B(C + A)$ .

(d) $A\overline{B}C + A + \overline{B}C$ .

8.16. Simplify each of the following Boolean expressions by applying the theorems in Sec. 8.3.

(a) $\overline{ABC} + \overline{AB\overline{C}}$ .

(b) $A + \overline{B}C + \overline{D}(A + \overline{B}C)$ .

(c) $A\overline{B}(C + D) + \overline{C + D}$ .

(d) $(A\overline{B} + \overline{C} + D\overline{E})(A\overline{B} + \overline{C})$ .

## Problems on Section 8.4: Combinational Digital Systems

8.17. Show two ways for realizing a NOT function with a NOR gate.

8.18. Give a realization of the Invitation function of Problem 8.5 with NOR and NAND functions.

(a) Do this directly with the function as you derived it.

(b) Use De Morgan's theorem to produce a simpler realization.

8.19. Show a way to make a three-input OR gate out of two-input OR gates.

8.20. The radio in a car should be ON ($R = 1$) if the ignition switch is either ON ($I = 1$) or in the accessory position ($A = 1$) and the radio on–off switch is also ON ($S = 1$). Watch for DON'T CAREs.

(a) Write a Boolean expression for $R$ as a function of $I$, $A$, and $S$.

(b) Give a realization with NOT, NOR, and NAND gates.

8.21. The safety system in Fig. P8.21 has three inputs. If two or more of these are 1 at the same time, an alarm should sound ($A = 1$).

(a) Give a truth table for $A$.

(b) Give a Boolean function for $A$.

(c) Simplify the results of part (b) if possible.

(d) Use De Morgan's theorem to put the Boolean expression in a form for NAND-gate synthesis.

(e) Give a logic circuit to perform the alarm function using only 2-input and 3-input NAND gates.

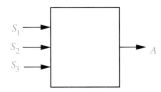

**Figure P8.21**

8.22. A student will pass ($P = 1$) if he has a good average ($A = 1$) and gets in all the required work ($W = 1$). But if he fails the final exam ($F = 1$), he will not pass.

(a) Make a truth table for $P$ as a function of $A$, $W$, and $F$.

(b) Give a Boolean expression for $P$.

(c) Give a realization using only two-input NOR gates.

8.23. A telephone-answering device has two incoming lines, $A$ and $B$. (Consider $A$ and $B$ as digital signals with $A = 1$ for a call on A, etc.) If a call comes in on either line, the "ring" signal is given ($R=1$) and stays on until the call is completed. If a second call comes in, the "second call" signal is given ($S = 1$) to a light.

**(a)** Give a truth table with $A$ and $B$ as inputs and $R$ and $S$ as outputs.

**(b)** Develop a combinational logic circuit using NAND and/or NOR gates that perform the necessary logic to activate the output signals.

**8.24.** Give a truth table for the logic circuit shown in Fig. P8.24. *Hint:* Consider the second input to the NOR gate to be independent of $B$, and then eliminate those states in which this input is not $\bar{B}$.

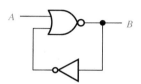

**Figure P8.24**

**8.25.** The digital circuit shown in Fig. P8.25 has three inputs and one output. Show the relationship between output and inputs with a truth table.

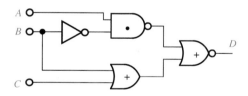

**Figure P8.25**

**8.26.** A Boolean expression is

$$D = A + (A + \bar{B})C.$$

**(a)** Give a truth table for $D$.

**(b)** Simplify $D$ if possible. You may use a Karnaugh map if you wish.

**(c)** Give a realization using only NAND gates. The inputs are $A$, $B$, and $C$, and the output is $D$.

**8.27.** Make a Karnaugh map for $S_2$ in Figure 8.35 and show that no rectangular patterns of 1's are present. This shows that no simplification of Eq. (8.17) is possible.

**8.28.** On the Karnaugh map in Fig. P8.28, mark the regions corresponding to the following:

**(a)** $A = 1$.

**Figure P8.28**

**(b)** $\bar{C} = 1$.

**(c)** $\overline{AB} = 1$.

**8.29.** The digital circuit shown in Fig. P8.29 has three binary inputs, $Q_2$, $Q_1$, and $Q_0$, and one output, $L$, which activates a light. The input is interpreted as a binary number between 0 and 7, and the output is supposed to activate the light ($L = 1$) if the input is divisible by either 2 or 3. Set $L = 1$ for $Q_0 + Q_1 + Q_2 = 0$ since zero is divisible by everything but itself.

**(a)** Give a truth table for $L(Q_2, Q_1, Q_0)$.

**(b)** Derive a sum-of-products expression for $L$ using a Karnaugh map.

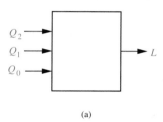

(a)

**Figure P8.29**

**8.30.** The digital circuit shown in Fig. P8.30 has three binary inputs, $Q_2$, $Q_1$, and $Q_0$, and one output, $L$, which activates a light. The input is interpreted as an English letter A through H with 000 representing A, 001 representing B, etc., through 111 representing H. The output is supposed to activate the light ($L = 1$) if the input letter appears in the expression "HARD TEST."

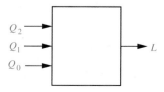

**Figure P8.30**

**(a)** Give a truth table for $L(Q_2, Q_1, Q_0)$.

**(b)** Derive a product of sums expression for $L$ using a Karnaugh map.

**8.31.** Make a Karnaugh map of the elevator-door function described in Fig. 8.5, and from the map, determine the logic function for $D$.

**8.32.** The seven-segment numerical display shown in Fig. P8.32 can display the integers 0 through 9, depending on which segments are illuminated. The driver accepts a BCD input and gives output 1's to the segments that should be lit and 0's to the segments that should not be lit.

**(a)** Construct the truth table for segments $a$ through $g$. Note that inputs corresponding to $10_{10}$ through $15_{10}$ do not occur and result in DON'T CAREs in the truth table.

**(b)** Develop a Karnaugh map for the $b$ segment.

**(c)** From the map, determine the logic function for $b$.

**(d)** Give a sum-of-products realization using 2- and 3-input NANDs.

**8.33.** Give the truth table for the logic circuit in Fig. P8.33.

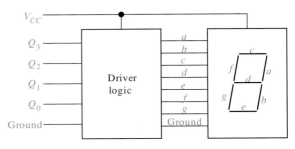

**Figure P8.32**

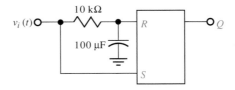

**Figure P8.33**

## Section 8.5: Sequential Digital Systems

**8.34.** For the bistable circuit in Fig. 8.42(a) to operate as described, sufficient current must flow into the base of the ON transistor to permit saturation (that is, $\beta i_B \geq i_{C(\text{sat})}$). For the resistor values shown, this imposes a minimum value of $\beta$.

**(a)** What is the minimum value of $\beta$ for the circuit in Fig. 8.42(a) to function as a bistable? Assume 0.7 V for the ON base–emitter voltage and 0.3 V for $V_{CE(\text{sat})}$.

**(b)** Find the formula for the minimum value of $\beta$ in terms of the power-supply voltage ($V_{CC}$), base resistor ($R_B$), and collector resistor ($R_C$).

**(c)** For the circuit in Fig. 8.42(a) and for a $\beta$ of 60, what voltage at the input to the OFF transistor is required to switch the circuit? Assume 0.7 V to turn ON the diode and transistor $pn$ junctions.

*Note:* The bistable will switch if the current into the ON transistor is dropped below the value required to saturate the transistor. This implies a certain voltage at the collector of the OFF (but coming ON) transistor. This implies in turn a certain collector current, and so on.

**8.35.** Design an $S$–$R$ latch circuit with NAND gates rather

than the NOR gates shown in Fig. 8.43. Determine the inputs (1 or 0) required to SET and RESET the flip-flop.

**8.36.** The $S$–$R$ latch in Fig. 8.43 has one input, $v_i(t)$, that goes from logical 0 to logical 1 at $t = 0$. The circuit has an external resistor and capacitor added, as shown in Fig. P8.36. Describe the output that occurs if $Q = 0$ for $t < 0$.

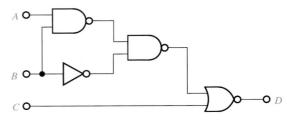

**Figure P8.36**

**8.37.** In a digital circuit, the edge-triggered flip-flops could use an input circuit similar to that shown in Fig. P8.37. Assume the gates treat a logical zero as any voltage in the range from 0 to 0.8 V and a logical one as any voltage in the range 2.3 and 5.0 V. In this case, the AND gates need to be open

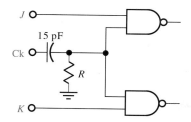

**Figure P8.37**

for at least 1 μs to pass the $J$ and $K$ signals. The capacitor is part of the integrated circuit and has a value of $15 \times 10^{-12}$ farad (15 pF). A 4- to 5-V pulse is used for the clock. Find the minimum value of $R$ to enable the edge-triggering feature to operate correctly.

**8.38.** Construct a truth table for the $J$–$K$ flip-flop in Fig. 8.50 with $J$, $K$, $Q_n$, and $\overline{Q}_n$ as inputs, $R$ and $S$ as intermediate outputs, and $Q_{n+1}$ and $\overline{Q_{n+1}}$ as outputs. Use the truth table to confirm the truth table in Fig. 8.51. You must eliminate all rows that contradict the requirement that the outputs be complements.

**8.39.** The logic circuit in Fig. P8.39 uses a $J$-$K$ flip-flop. There is one input, $J$, and the output is $Q$. Find the output, $Q_{n+1}$, after the clock pulse in terms of the input, $J$, and the output before the clock pulse, $Q_n$.

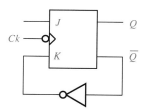

**Figure P8.39**

**8.40.** The circuit shown in Fig. P8.40 is not the usual latch because it uses one NAND and one NOR gate.
   **(a)** If $A$ and $B$ are both ZERO, determine which, if any, stable output states exist. That is, which combinations of $Q$ and $\overline{Q}$ can be present.
   **(b)** If $A$ and $B$ are both ONE, determine which, if any, stable output states exist.

**8.41.** Using $T$-type flip-flops and an AND gate, design a circuit to divide the clock frequency by 5.

**8.42.** The two $T$-type flip-flops in Fig. P8.42(a) are connected and clocked as shown in Fig. P8.42(b). Give the values of $Q_0$ and $Q_1$ at times $T_2$, $T_3$, $T_4$, and $T_5$ if the states are both zero at $T_1$.

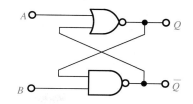

**Figure P8.40**

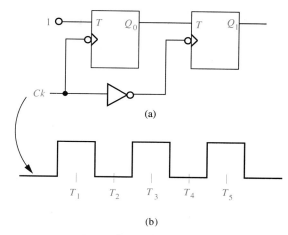

(a)

(b)

**Figure P8.42**

**8.43.** Repeat Problem 8.41, except use a NOR gate rather than an AND gate.

**8.44.** The $S$–$R$ latch shown in Fig. P8.44(a) is made with NOR gates, as in Fig. 8.43. The inputs are given in Fig. 8.44(b). At $t = 0$, $Q = 0$. Give $Q$ for $t > 0$. If $Q$ is indeterminate, mark ×'s on the time axis.

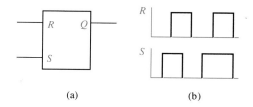

(a)                  (b)

**Figure P8.44**

**8.45.** Figure P8.45(a) shows the inputs and the clock of the $T$-type flip-flop in Fig. P8.45(b). Give the output function $Q(t)$ if $Q = 0$ at $t = 0$.

**8.46.** In the circuit shown in Fig. P8.46, $Q_0$ and $Q_1$ are both 1 at $t = 0$. Give $Q_0$ and $Q_1$ as functions of time along with a sketch of the clock pulses.

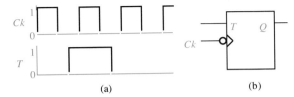

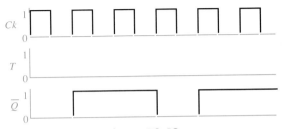

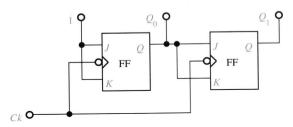

**Figure P8.45**

**Figure P8.49**

**(b)** Give a $T$ input signal that will produce this output.

8.50. The output of a $T$-type flip-flop can be expressed as $Q_{n+1} = T\overline{Q}_n + \overline{T}Q_n$, where $Q_{n+1}$ is the output after the clock pulse, $Q_n$ is the output before the clock pulse, and $T$ is the input.
   **(a)** Show by means of a truth table that this gives the same information as the truth table in Fig. 8.54.
   **(b)** Give the corresponding expression for the output of the $D$-type flip-flop.

8.51. Figure P8.51 shows a chain of $T$-type flip-flops. The initial state is $Q_0 = 1$, $Q_1 = 1$, and $Q_2 = 0$.
   **(a)** What will be the state of the outputs after one clock pulse?
   **(b)** What will the circuit do generally?

**Figure P8.46**

8.47. Two $J$–$K$ flip-flops are connected as shown in Fig. P8.47. Give $Q_0$ and $Q_1$ under a sketch of the clock pulses. $Q_0 = 0$ and $Q_1 = 0$ at $t = 0$.

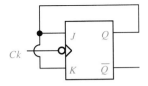

**Figure P8.47**

8.48. The $J$-$K$ flip-flop shown in Fig. P8.48 has its inputs tied together and tied to the output $Q$. Give the output as the clock pulses begin, assuming $Q = 1$ at $t = 0$.

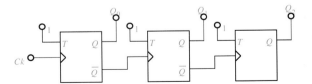

**Figure P8.51**

8.52. The $J$-$K$ flip-flop in Fig. P8.52 has its inputs tied together and tied to the output $\overline{Q}$. Give the output as the clock pulses begin, assuming $Q = 0$ at $t = 0$.

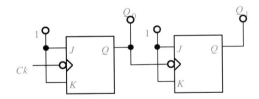

**Figure P8.48**

8.49 A $T$-type flip-flop has the clock and output shown in Fig. P8.49. The flip flop triggers on the lagging edge of the clock.
   **(a)** Draw the circuit showing flip-flop type, inputs, and output.

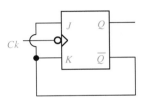

**Figure P8.52**

**8.53.** The *J-K* flip-flop in Fig. P8.53(a) has *K* set permanently at a digital 1, but *J* varies with time, as shown in Fig. P8.53(b). Show the output *Q* on the same time scale as the clock and *J* if $Q(0^-) = 0$.

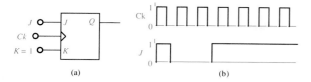

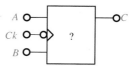

(a)          (b)

**Figure P8.53**

**8.54.** Figure P8.54 shows a *J–K* flip-flop with some external logic connected.
  **(a)** Is the flip flop leading- or lagging-edge triggered?
  **(b)** Make a truth table with *J* and $Q_n$ as inputs and $Q_{n+1}$ as output.
  **(c)** Give a Boolean expression for $Q_{n+1}(J, Q_n)$.

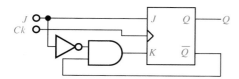

**Figure P8.54**

**8.55.** The *J-K* flip-flop is connected as shown in Fig. P8.55. Determine the output $Q_{n+1}$ as a function of the input *J* and the output from the previous state, $Q_n$.

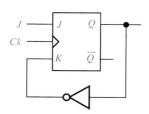

**Figure P8.55**

**8.56.** A chain of *T*-type flip-flops are connected as shown in Fig. P8.56, with the clock signal. Give the outputs at $Q_0$, $Q_1$, and $Q_2$ along with the clock signal. Assume $Q_0 = Q_1 = Q_2 = 0$ at $t = 0$.

**8.57.** Figure P8.57 shows a clocked circuit with two binary inputs and one binary output. What should go

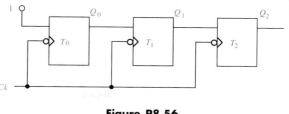

**Figure P8.56**

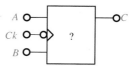

**Figure P8.57**

in the box such that the output after the clock pulse is equal to the product of the two inputs, with inputs and output considered base-2 numbers? That is, $C_{n+1} = A_n \times B_n$. You may use standard gates and flip-flops.

**8.58.** Figure P8.58 shows an ordinary *S–R* latch, except that an *RC* circuit is used in one of the connections. The time constant of the *RC* circuit is 0.5 second.
  **(a)** If $R = 0$ and $S = 0$ for a long time, what is *Q*?
  **(b)** Now *R* receives a 1-μs pulse. What happens?
  **(c)** Then 1 s later, *S* receives a 1-μs pulse. Explain what happens.

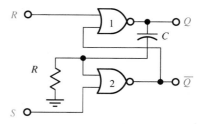

**Figure P8.58**

**8.59.** The circuits that perform multiplication in a calculator must handle the signs of the component numbers according to the usual rules of algebra. However, if the product is exactly zero, the sign should be set to positive so that a negative zero is not displayed. In Fig. P8.59, we display the portion of the circuit that determines the sign to be displayed. Consider the multiplication of $N_1$ and $N_2$. Let $S_1 = 1$ if the sign of $N_1$ is +, $S_2 = 1$ if the sign of $N_2$ is +, $Z = 1$ if the product is exactly zero, and

$S_R = 1$ if a + is to be displayed (including a positive zero).

(a) Make a truth table for the sign of the result, $S_R$, as a function of $S_1$, $S_2$, and Z.

(b) Give a Boolean expression for $S_R(S_1, S_2, Z)$. You may use $\oplus$ for the EXCLUSIVE OR if you wish. You may use a Karnaugh map.

(c) Give a realization using 2- and 3-input gates.

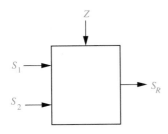

**Figure P8.59**

8.60. A calculator has a sign formed by two segments, as shown in Fig. P8.60. For plus, both a and b are lighted; for minus, only a is lighted. The calculator must compute the sign of the product of two signed

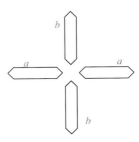

**Figure P8.60**

numbers. Let $S_1$ be the sign of one of the numbers ($S = 1$ means plus), and $S_2$ be the sign of the other number.

(a) Give a truth table for a and b as functions of $S_1$ and $S_2$.

(b) Design a logic circuit for b using NAND gates.

8.61. Figure P8.61 shows four $T$-type flip-flops clocked for synchronous counting. Using AND gates, design logic such that at the clock leading edge, $FF_1$ changes states when $Q_0 = 1$, $FF_2$ changes states when $Q_0 Q_1 = 1$, and $FF_3$ changes states when $Q_0 Q_1 Q_2 = 1$. What is the function of this circuit if $T_0 = 1$? What if $T_0 = 0$?

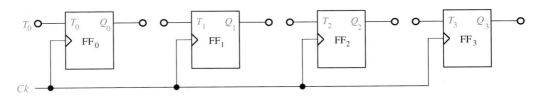

**Figure P8.61**

## General Problems

8.62. The *rise time* of a signal pulse is defined as the time it takes to go from 10 to 90% of the difference between its initial and final values. The circuit in Fig. P8.62 shows a digital inverter with a 15-pF ($15 \times 10^{-12}$F) capacitor representing the output capacitance of the transistor and the stray capacitance of the output circuit. Assume a voltage of 0.7 V for an ON $pn$ junction and a voltage of 0.2 V for the saturation value of the collector–emitter voltage. Calculate the rise time of the output of this circuit.

8.63 A remote door lock is operated by an electrical relay that requires 10 mA to operate, as shown in

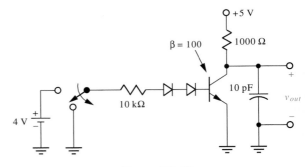

**Figure P8.62**

Fig. P8.63. The relay can be opened by either switch *A* or switch *B* or both. The information from the switches is combined in a logic circuit. The logic levels are 0 to 0.5 V for a ZERO and 4.5 to 5 V for a ONE. The logic circuit can put out only 0.5 mA into a short circuit and hence cannot operate the relay directly. Hence, a transistor is used to switch the relay, and the logic circuit controls the transistor.

(a) Design the required logic circuit using only NAND and/or NOR circuit.

(b) Determine the resistor *R*. The beta of the transistor is 200, and it requires 0.7 V to turn ON the base–emitter junction.

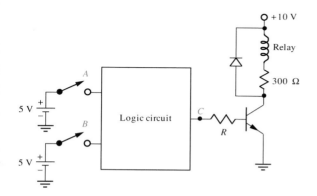

**Figure P8.63**

**8.64.** Design a digital circuit that will compare a digital signal with its value 1 second earlier and give an output of 1 if the values are the same but zero if different. You may use any kind of latch or flip-flop, NAND, NOR, AND, OR, or XOR gates.

**8.65.** A telephone-answering device has a switch on it that activates the response message ("After the tone, leave a message, etc.") after one, two, or four rings. The incoming ring signal is a burst of 24-volt, 20-hertz ac voltage, as shown in Fig. P8.65(b). The ring signal is ON for 2 seconds and OFF for 4 seconds.

(a) Design a clock-shaper circuit that will convert the ring signal to a digital signal with nominal +5-and 0-volt logic levels. That is, find suitable values of *R* and *C* in the rectifier circuit shown. Assume a high input-impedance level for the logic circuit.

(b) Design a logic circuit, Fig. P8.65(a), that will "count" the rings and furnish signals to the triple-pole, single-throw switch, as shown, for input to the message response. Assume the counter starts in the "clear" state, with 0 at all flip-flop *Q*s. [Assume you have suitable clock signals even if you draw a blank on part (a).]

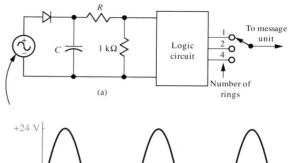

(a)

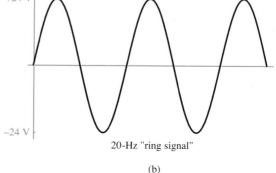

20-Hz "ring signal"

(b)

**Figure P8.65**

# Answers to Odd-Numbered Problems

**8.1. (a)**

| $S_A$ | $S_B$ | $L$ |
|-------|-------|-----|
| 0 | 0 | 0 |
| 0 | 1 | 1 |
| 1 | 0 | 1 |
| 1 | 1 | 0 |

**(b)** $L = (S_A$ AND NOT $S_B$) OR (NOT $S_A$ AND $S_B$).

**8.3. (a)**

| $R$ | $P$ | $A$ | $C$ |
|-----|-----|-----|-----|
| 0 | 0 | 0 | 0 |
| 0 | 0 | 1 | 0 |
| 0 | 1 | 0 | 0 |
| 0 | 1 | 1 | 0 |
| 1 | 0 | 0 | 0 |
| 1 | 0 | 1 | 1 |
| 1 | 1 | 0 | 1 |
| 1 | 1 | 1 | 1 |

**(b)** $C = R$ AND ($P$ OR $A$).

**8.5. (a)**

| $L$ | $T$ | $F$ | $I$ |
|-----|-----|-----|-----|
| 0 | 0 | 0 | 0 |
| 0 | 0 | 1 | 1 or $X$ |
| 0 | 1 | 0 | 0 |
| 0 | 1 | 1 | 1 or $X$ |
| 1 | 0 | 0 | 1 |
| 1 | 0 | 1 | 1 |
| 1 | 1 | 0 | 0 |
| 1 | 1 | 1 | 1 |

**(b)** $I = F$ OR ($L$ AND NOT $T$).

**8.7.** $D = S_A$ AND $S_B$ AND NOT $S_C$.

**8.9. (a)** 2.1$^+$ V, 7.7 mA, 154 µA; **(b)** 2.1$^-$ V, 8 V, 520 µA.

**8.11. (a)** 38 kΩ; **(b)** 24.

**8.13.**

| $A$ | $B$ | $A + B$ | $A(A + B)$ |
|-----|-----|---------|------------|
| 0 | 0 | 0 | 0 |
| 0 | 1 | 1 | 0 |
| 1 | 0 | 1 | 1 |
| 1 | 1 | 1 | 1 |

**8.15. (a)** $\overline{\overline{A} + (B + A)\overline{B}} = \overline{\overline{A} + A\overline{B}} =$
$\overline{\overline{AB} + \overline{A}\overline{B} + A\overline{B}} = \overline{\overline{A} + \overline{B}} = AB;$

**(b)** $A + \overline{B(1 + \overline{A})AA} = A + A\overline{B} = A;$

**(c)** $\overline{ABC} + \overline{AB}(C + A) = \overline{A} + \overline{B} + \overline{C} + \overline{A}\overline{B}C =$
$\overline{A} + \overline{B} + \overline{C} = \overline{ABC};$ **(d)** $A\overline{B}C + A + \overline{B}C =$
$A + \overline{B}C;$

**8.17.**

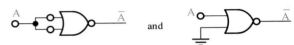 and

**8.19.**

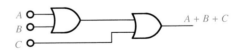

**8.21. (a)**

| $S_1$ | $S_2$ | $S_3$ | $A$ |
|-------|-------|-------|-----|
| 0 | 0 | 0 | 0 |
| 0 | 0 | 1 | 0 |
| 0 | 1 | 0 | 0 |
| 0 | 1 | 1 | 1 |
| 1 | 0 | 0 | 0 |
| 1 | 0 | 1 | 1 |
| 1 | 1 | 0 | 1 |
| 1 | 1 | 1 | 1 |

**(b, c, and d)**

$A = S_1 S_2 \overline{S_3} + \overline{S_1} S_2 S_3 + S_1 \overline{S_2} S_3$
$\quad + S_1 S_2 S_3 = S_1 S_2 + S_1 S_3 + S_2 S_3$
$\quad = \overline{(\overline{S_1 S_2})(\overline{S_1 S_3})(\overline{S_2 S_3})} \; ;$

**(e)**

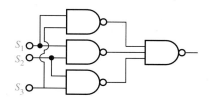

**8.23. (a)**

| A | B | R | S |
|---|---|---|---|
| 0 | 0 | 0 | 0 |
| 0 | 1 | 1 | 0 |
| 1 | 0 | 1 | 0 |
| 1 | 1 | 1 | 1 |

$R = A$ OR $B$, $S = A$ AND $B$

**(b)**

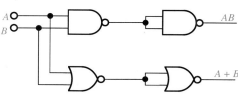

**8.25.** $D = \overline{\overline{A\overline{B}} + B + C} = \overline{\overline{A} + B + C}$

| A | B | C | $\overline{A} + B + C$ | D |
|---|---|---|---|---|
| 0 | 0 | 0 | 1 | 0 |
| 0 | 0 | 1 | 1 | 0 |
| 0 | 1 | 0 | 1 | 0 |
| 0 | 1 | 1 | 1 | 0 |
| 1 | 0 | 0 | 0 | 1 |
| 1 | 0 | 1 | 1 | 0 |
| 1 | 1 | 0 | 1 | 0 |
| 1 | 1 | 1 | 1 | 0 |

**8.27.**

| $A_2$ \ $B_2C_1$ | 00 | 01 | 11 | 10 |
|---|---|---|---|---|
| 0 | 0 | 1 | 0 | 1 |
| 1 | 1 | 0 | 1 | 0 |

**8.29. (a)**

|  | $Q_2$ | $Q_1$ | $Q_0$ | L |
|---|---|---|---|---|
| 0 | 0 | 0 | 0 | 1 |
| 1 | 0 | 0 | 1 | 0 |
| 2 | 0 | 1 | 0 | 1 |
| 3 | 0 | 1 | 1 | 1 |
| 4 | 1 | 0 | 0 | 1 |
| 5 | 1 | 0 | 1 | 0 |
| 6 | 1 | 1 | 0 | 0 |
| 7 | 1 | 1 | 1 | 0 |

**(b)**

| $Q_2$ \ $Q_1Q_0$ | 00 | 01 | 11 | 10 |
|---|---|---|---|---|
| 0 | 1 | 0 | 1 | 1 |
| 1 | 1 | 0 | 0 | 1 |

$L = \overline{Q_0} + \overline{Q_2}Q_1$

**8.31.**

| $T$ \ $BS$ | 00 | 01 | 11 | 10 |
|---|---|---|---|---|
| 0 | 1 | 0 | 0 | 1 |
| 1 | 0 | 0 | 0 | 1 |

$D = B\overline{S} + \overline{T}S$

**8.33.** $A$ drops out and $D = \overline{C + B}$, NOR

| B | C | D |
|---|---|---|
| 0 | 0 | 1 |
| 0 | 1 | 0 |
| 1 | 0 | 0 |
| 1 | 1 | 0 |

**8.35.**

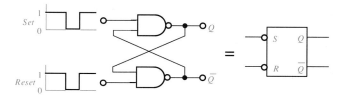

**8.37.** 120 kΩ.

**8.39.**

| $J$ | $K$ | $Q_n$ | $\overline{Q}_n$ | $Q_{n+1}$ |
|-----|-----|-------|------------------|-----------|
| 0 | 0 | 0 | 1 | 0 |
| 0 | 1 | 1 | 0 | 0 |
| 1 | 0 | 0 | 1 | 1 |
| 1 | 1 | 1 | 0 | 0 |

$$Q_{n+1} = J\overline{Q}_n$$

**8.41.**

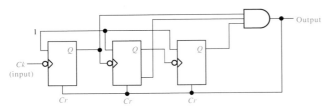

**8.43.**

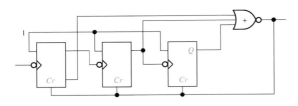

**8.45.**

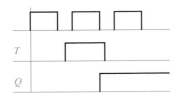

**8.47.**

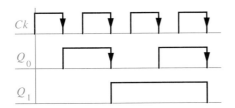

**8.49. (a)** $T$–flip flop, trailing-edge triggering. Input at $T$, output at $\overline{Q}$.

**(b)**

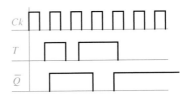

**8.51. (a)**

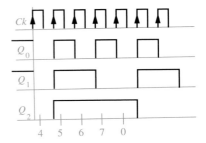

**(b)** This circuit counts up, modulo 8, starting with 3.

**8.53.**

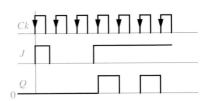

**8.55.**

| $J$ | $Q_n$ | $K$ | $Q_{n+1}$ |
|-----|-------|-----|-----------|
| 0 | 0 | 1 | 0 |
| 0 | 1 | 0 | 1 |
| 1 | 0 | 1 | 1 |
| 1 | 1 | 0 | 1 |

$$Q_{n+1} = J + Q_n$$

**8.57.** $C_{n+1} = A_n B_n$, the AND.

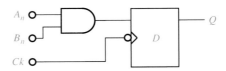

**8.59. (a)**

| $S_1$ | $S_2$ | $Z$ | $S_R$ |
|---|---|---|---|
| 0 | 0 | 0 | 1 |
| 0 | 0 | 1 | 1 |
| 0 | 1 | 0 | 0 |
| 0 | 1 | 1 | 1 |
| 1 | 0 | 0 | 0 |
| 1 | 0 | 1 | 1 |
| 1 | 1 | 0 | 1 |
| 1 | 1 | 1 | 1 |

**(b)** From the Karnaugh map,

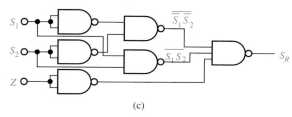

(c)

$$S_R = Z + S_1 S_2 + \bar{S}_1 \bar{S}_2 = Z + S_1 \oplus S_2$$

**8.61.** The circuit counts to 15 and resets to zero if $T_0 = 1$, and stops counting if $T_0 = 0$.

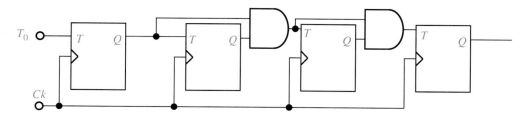

**8.63. (a)** A NOR gate; **(b)** 13.8 k$\Omega$ or less.

**8.65. (a)** 3800 $\Omega$, 93.2 $\mu$F; **(b)**

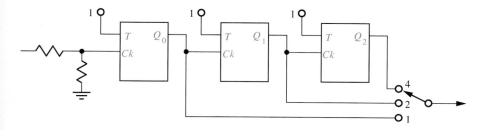

# 9

# Analog Electronics

1. To understand the concept of a spectrum as applied to periodic, non periodic, and random signals
2. To understand how to calculate the bandwidth required to pass pulses and other signals
3. To understand how filters modify spectra
4. To understand how to describe filters with Bode plots
5. To understand the nature and benefits of feedback
6. To understand the importance of loop gain in feedback systems
7. To understand the importance and applications of op amps in analog circuits

Analog techniques represent information by signals that mimic in some sense the quantity being symbolized, much as a mercury in a thermometer represents temperature. This chapter considers a variety of signal analysis and processing techniques. The operational amplifier is introduced and its basic applications in analog circuits are presented.

## Introduction

**Analog Information**

**analog**

**Contrast between analog and digital electronics.** We have already explored how transistors and diodes are used as switches to process information in digital form. In digital electronics, transistors are either conducting or not. The active region is used only in transition between states.

By contrast, analog electronics depends on the active region of transistors and other types of amplifying devices. In this context, *analog* means that information is encoded into an electrical signal that is proportional to the quantity being represented.

**Analog example.** In Fig. 9.1, our information originates physically in a musical instrument. The radiated sound is best understood as sound waves, which produce motion in the diaphragm of a microphone, which in turn produces an electrical signal. The variations in the electrical signal are a proportional representation of the sound waves. The electrical signal is amplified electronically, with an increase in signal power derived from the input ac power to the amplifier. The amplifier output drives a recording head that magnetizes a pattern on a moving magnetic tape. If the system is good, every acoustic variation of the air will be recorded on the tape and when the recording is played back through a similar system and the signal reradiated as sound energy by a loudspeaker, the resulting sound should faithfully reproduce the original music.

Systems based on analog principles form an important class of electronic devices. Radio and TV broadcasting are examples of analog systems, as are many electrical instruments used in monitoring deflection (strain gages, for example), motion (tachometers), and temperature (thermocouples). Many electrical instruments—voltmeters, ohmmeters, ammeters, and oscilloscopes—utilize analog techniques, at least in part.

**spectrum**

**Contents of this chapter.** Analog techniques employ the frequency-domain viewpoint extensively. We begin by expanding our concept of the frequency domain to include periodic, nonperiodic, and random signals. We will see that most analog signals and processes can be represented in the frequency domain. We introduce the concept of a *spectrum*, which is the representation of a signal as the simultaneous existence of many frequencies. Bandwidth in the frequency domain, the width of a spectrum, is related to information rate in the time domain.

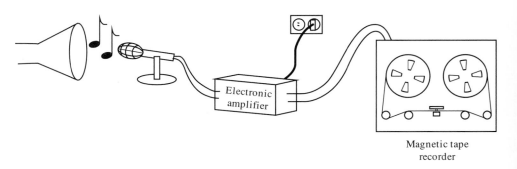

Electronic amplifier

Magnetic tape recorder

**Figure 9.1** Analog system.

This expanded concept of the frequency domain also helps us distinguish the effects of linear and nonlinear analog devices. In this chapter, linear circuits are shown to be capable of "filtering" out unwanted frequency components. Chapter 11 shows how new frequencies, created by nonlinear devices such as diodes and transistors, are used in radios and other communication systems.

Next we study feedback, a technique by which gain in analog systems is exchanged for other desirable qualities such as linearity or wider bandwidth. Without feedback, analog systems such as audio amplifiers would distort signals. Understanding the benefits of feedback provides the foundation for appreciating the many uses of operational amplifiers in analog electronics.

Operational amplifiers provide basic building blocks for analog circuits in the same way that NOR and NAND gates are basic building blocks for digital circuits. We conclude by describing some of the more common applications of op amps.

**Frequency-domain concepts.** We introduced the frequency domain in Chapter 4 for the analysis of ac circuits. There we showed that sinusoidal sources can be represented by complex numbers through

$$v(t) = V_p \cos(\omega t + \theta) = \text{Re}[\underline{\mathbf{V}} e^{j\omega t}] \tag{9.1}$$

where the phasor voltage, $\underline{\mathbf{V}} = V_p \angle \theta$, is a complex number representing the sinusoidal function in the frequency domain. The $e^{j\omega t}$ term produces sinusoidal behavior; however, when only one frequency is present, the frequency is not stated explicitly in the frequency domain. The time-domain and frequency-domain representations for a sinusoidal signal appear in Fig. 9.2.

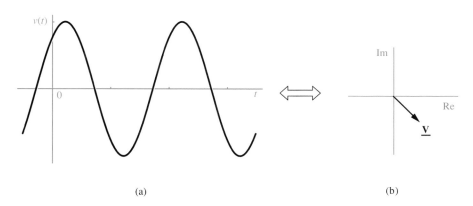

(a)

(b)

**Figure 9.2** Sinusoid in (a) the time domain and (b) the frequency domain.

## Frequency-Domain Representation of Periodic Functions

The Frequency Domain

**A periodic function.** Our representation of signals in the frequency domain is enriched when we consider periodic signals that are nonsinusoidal. As an example, we consider the function

$$v(t) = \frac{V}{2} + \frac{2V}{\pi}\left[\cos(\omega_1 t) - \frac{1}{3}\cos(3\omega_1 t)\right]$$

$$= \mathrm{Re}\left[\frac{V}{2} + \frac{2V}{\pi}e^{j\omega_1 t} + \frac{2V}{3\pi}\angle 180° e^{j3\omega_1 t}\right]$$

(9.2)

**harmonics**

Leaving aside for the moment the significance of this mathematical function, let us consider the time-domain representation in Fig. 9.3. In the time domain, we see nothing unusual except that we now have a more complicated function than a simple sinusoidal function. The dc component of the voltage is easily identified in Eq. (9.2) as $V/2$. The time-varying part of the function consists of two sinusoidal terms. Because the frequency of the second term is an integral multiple of the frequency of the first term, the frequencies are said to be *harmonically related*. The term *harmonic*[1] is used because in music the tones that share harmonics form pleasant-sounding chords. Because the two sinusoids are harmonically related, they form a stable pattern and thus repeat with the period of the lower frequency, $T = 2\pi/\omega_1$. This function in the time domain has three harmonic components: a dc component (zero frequency), a fundamental (or first harmonic), and a third harmonic. The dc component is described by its magnitude, and the two sinusoidal components are described by their amplitudes and phases.

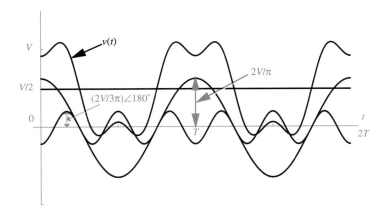

**Figure 9.3**  The time function.

**The spectrum.**  Because we now have three frequencies involved, we can no longer describe the signal in the frequency domain by a phasor in the complex plane. Frequency becomes important in a new way and cannot be relegated to the memory or the margin of the page. A common way to handle this new complexity is shown in Fig. 9.4. We make frequency, $\omega$, the independent variable and show the three harmonics at their frequencies. The magnitude (for the dc component) and phasors (for the ac components) are placed beside the various frequency components, drawn roughly to scale.

**voltage spectrum**

Figure 9.4 is a *voltage spectrum*; it shows how much voltage exists at the various frequencies.[2] The voltage spectrum in Fig. 9.4 is the frequency-domain representation of

---

[1] from the Greek, meaning "to fit together."

[2] Phase is expressed notationally but not pictured.

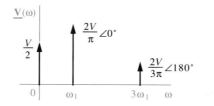

**Figure 9.4** Spectrum consists of three frequencies.

the time-domain voltage in Fig. 9.3. This concept of the frequency domain expands that presented in Chapter 4. Figures 9.3 and 9.4 portray the complementary nature of the two domains: time and frequency are shown as complementary variables.

---

**EXAMPLE 9.1** **What frequencies?**

What frequencies exist in the voltage output spectrum of a temperature sensor, with $t =$ hours after midnight?

$$i(t) = 10 + 2.6 \, \sin(0.262t) - 9.7 \, \cos(0.262t) + 2 \, \cos(0.524t + 60°) \text{ mV} \qquad (9.3)$$

**SOLUTION:**
The constant term is dc or zero frequency. The next two terms have the same frequency of 0.262 radian/hour, 0.0417 cycles/hour, or $T = 24$ h, and the last term has a frequency of 0.524 rad/hour, the second harmonic.

**WHAT IF?**
What if you want the voltage spectrum of the standard power voltage in the United States?[3]

---

**Fourier series.** In 1807, a French artillery officer immortalized his name among electrical engineers yet unborn by proposing that any periodic function can be expressed as a series of harmonically related sinusoids. Fourier's theorem expressed mathematically what musicians had long known by ear, that a steady tone consists of many harmonically related frequencies. The mathematical expression of Fourier's theorem, expressed for a periodic voltage, $v(t)$, is

$$v(t) = V_0 + V_1 \cos(\omega_1 t + \theta_1) + V_2 \cos(2\omega_1 t + \theta_2) + \cdots$$
$$+ V_n \cos(n\omega_1 t + \theta_n) + \cdots \qquad (9.4)$$

where $\omega_1 = 2\pi/T$, $T$ is the period of $v(t)$, $V_n$ is the amplitude of the $n^{th}$ harmonic, and $\theta_n$ its phase. Fourier's theorem shows that any periodic function can be expressed as a spectrum consisting of dc, a fundamental frequency, and all frequencies that are integral multiples of the fundamental.

---

[3] One frequency: $120\sqrt{2}$ V at 60 Hz.

**Spectra in music.** Fourier's theorem gives a mathematical explanation for many musical phenomena. Musicians know that the overtones of musical instruments are important. The piano sounds different from the harpsichord, for example, because the harpsichord strings are excited in a way that creates more sound energy at the higher harmonics than piano strings produce. In the language of the frequency domain, the various musical instruments sound different because they produce different acoustic spectra.

The musical scale is based on the harmonic relationship between the frequencies of the notes. The octave is a factor of 2 in frequency. Two tones are said to be consonant, to sound good together, when they are harmonically related. For example, in the pure scale the frequency of G would be 3/2 that of C. It follows that the third, sixth, ninth, ... harmonics of C coincide with the second, fourth, sixth, ... of G. This shared harmonic structure defines all major fifth intervals in the pure musical scale, and other consonant intervals share harmonics similarly.

Our digression on music was to show that frequency-domain concepts are commonplace in certain areas of experience. For our purposes, Fourier's theorem, as expressed by Eq. (9.4), shows that all periodic functions can be described by harmonic spectra. We bypass the mathematical procedures for computing the amplitudes and phases of the harmonics of a periodic function;[4] our primary purpose is the exploration of this expanded concept of the frequency domain.

**Two spectra.** We give two examples of Fourier series. The first is the Fourier series representation of the periodic series of pulses shown in Fig. 9.5 (a). The Fourier series for the square wave in Fig. 9.5(a) is

$$v(t) = \frac{V_s}{2} + \frac{2V_s}{\pi}\cos(\omega_1 t) - \frac{2V_s}{3\pi}\cos(3\omega_1 t) + \frac{2V_s}{5\pi}\cos(5\omega_1 t) - \cdots \qquad (9.5)$$

We showed only the first four components of the frequency-domain representation in Fig. 9.5(b). Comparison of Eqs. (9.2) and (9.5) shows that the first three frequency components of the square wave are those plotted in Fig. 9.3. Indeed, you should see some resemblance between the series of pulses and the sum of the dc, the fundamental, and

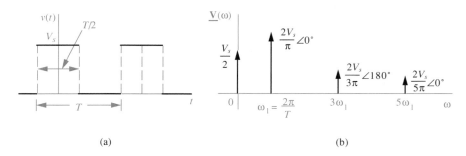

(a) (b)

**Figure 9.5** (a) Periodic time function; (b) voltage spectrum.

---

[4] These procedures are taught in courses in differential equations and signal analysis. Handbooks give the Fourier coefficients for many common periodical signals.

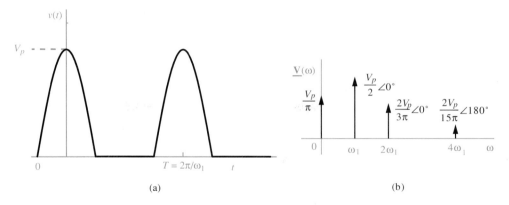

(a)

(b)

**Figure 9.6** (a) Half-wave rectified sinusoid; (b) voltage spectrum.

the third harmonic in Fig. 9.3. If the fifth harmonic were added, it would steepen the slope at the sides and flatten the top and bottom. With the addition of each higher harmonic, the series would better approximate the periodic pulses.

A second example of the Fourier series of a periodic function is shown in Fig. 9.6(a), the half-wave rectified sinusoid. The Fourier series is

$$v(t) = V_p \left[ \frac{1}{\pi} + \frac{1}{2} \cos(\omega_1 t) + \frac{2}{3\pi} \cos(2\omega_1 t) - \frac{2}{15\pi} \cos(4\omega_1 t) - \cdots \right] \qquad (9.6)$$

The spectrum, Fig. 9.6(b), consists of the fundamental plus all even harmonics, unlike that in Fig. 9.5(b), which contains odd harmonics only. We introduce these spectra for examples to be explored in this and later sections.

**Voltage spectra and power spectra.** The spectra shown in Figs. 9.5(b) and 9.6(b) are called *voltage spectra* because they correspond to the amplitudes and phases of the harmonics in their respective signals. In many applications, the power in a signal carries great importance; hence, we extend the concept of a spectrum to include power and energy concepts.

Power is defined as energy flow per unit time. Figure 9.7 shows a sinusoidal voltage source connected to a resistive load. The power into the resistor, as given in the figure, depends only on the amplitude and the resistance; frequency and phase do not matter. The factor of 2 in the denominator results from time averaging, Eq. (5.12), and can be absorbed into the voltage term if we use the rms instead of the peak value of the voltage.

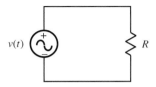

$v(t) = V_p \cos(\omega t + \theta)$ volts

$P_R = V_p^2 / 2R$ watts

**Figure 9.7** Average power in a resistor.

**power in volts²**

**Impedance Level**

**Conservation of Energy**

**Power in volts².**  The presence of the resistance in the power relationship in Fig. 9.7 poses a mild dilemma in developing the concept of the power spectrum of a signal. One possibility is to state explicitly the impedance level of an assumed load, say, 50 $\Omega$, and to compute the power that each harmonic would deliver to such a load. With this approach, watts would be the units of the power spectrum. The second possibility leaves the resistance term unstated. In this case, the "power" would be $V_p^2/2$, it being understood that to get actual power, one has to divide by an appropriate resistance. In this second approach, which is more general, the units of "power" are volts². Thus, the *power in volts²* is the power in $R$ multiplied by $R$.[5] One would be wise to state explicitly these units to stress that the power spectrum is of this second variety. Because of its generality, this second approach is frequently preferred and will be used here.

**Superposition of power.**  We stated before that the time-average power in a resistor does not depend on the frequency or phase of the sinusoidal source. It is easily shown, and is verified later, that the total power in a periodic signal is the sum of the power in its harmonics. Thus, the time-average power, $P$, in the periodic signal in Eq. (9.4) is

$$P = V_0^2 + \frac{V_1^2}{2} + \frac{V_2^2}{2} + \cdots + \frac{V_n^2}{2} + \cdots \tag{9.7}$$

The dc term is not divided by 2 because the effective value is the same as the peak value.

Thus, we can apply superposition to power provided the power contributions of the various sources are at different frequencies. In Chapter 2, we stressed that superposition applied only to voltage and current and not to power because there we were dealing only with sources at the same frequency. Thus, we may extend the principle of superposition to power provided (1) we are speaking of time-average power and (2) the sources have different frequencies.

**Effective value of a periodic signal.**  Equation (5.14) defines the effective value of a general signal. Substituting Eq. (9.7), leaving out R, and solving for the effective value, $V_e$, we find

$$V_e = \sqrt{V_0^2 + \frac{V_1^2}{2} + \frac{V_2^2}{2} + \cdots + \frac{V_n^2}{2} + \cdots} \tag{9.8}$$

Thus, the effective value of a periodic function is the Pythagorean sum of the effective values of all its component harmonics, including the dc component. In fact, the preceding equation and interpretation are valid for the spectra of non periodic functions, provided the time average is taken over a long period of time and provided no two component frequencies are the same.

---

[5] A good compromise is to call these units "watts in a 1-$\Omega$ resistor."

**EXAMPLE 9.2**

## Power in a periodic signal

Confirm the equivalence of power between the time and frequency domains for the series of pulses in Fig. 9.5(a).

**SOLUTION:**

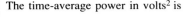

**Conservation of Energy**

The time-average power in volts$^2$ is

$$P_{avg} = \frac{2}{T} \int_0^{T/2} v^2(t) \, dt = \frac{2}{T} \int_0^{T/4} V_s^2 \, dt = \frac{2V_s^2}{T} \times \frac{T}{4} = \frac{V_s^2}{2} \text{ volts}^2 \qquad (9.9)$$

The power in the frequency domain would be the sum of the powers in the harmonics in Eq. (9.5)

$$P = \frac{V_s^2}{4} + \frac{2V_s^2}{\pi^2} + \frac{2V_s^2}{9\pi^2} + \frac{2V_s^2}{25\pi^2} + \cdots$$

$$= V_s^2 \left[ \frac{1}{4} + \frac{2}{\pi^2} \left( 1 + \frac{1}{9} + \frac{1}{25} + \cdots \right) \right] \text{ volts}^2 \qquad (9.10)$$

The infinite sum in Eq. (9.10) converges rapidly to the value $\pi^2/8$, as you can confirm from math tables or by summing terms with your calculator.

**WHAT IF?**

What if you confirm the power equivalence for the half-wave rectified signal in Fig. 9.06(a)?[6]

---

**Summary.**  We showed in this section that a periodic signal can be represented by an infinite series of sinusoidal components at frequencies harmonically related to the fundamental frequency of the signal. The voltage spectrum of a periodic signal consists, therefore, of a series of harmonics, each being described by an amplitude and phase. The power spectrum has no phase information and may be described in either watts or volts$^2$. The power spectrum accounts for the total power as the sum of the powers in the individual harmonics.

## Spectra of Nonperiodic Signals

**An important question.**  Granted this success in representing periodic signals in the frequency domain through Fourier series, we are emboldened to ask: How far can we carry this line of development? This is an important question, for in electronic systems, we must deal with both periodic and nonperiodic signals. Examples of periodic

---

[6] $P = \dfrac{V_p^2}{4}$ volts$^2$ (time domain);

$$P = V_p^2 \left\{ \frac{1}{\pi^2} + \frac{1}{2} \left[ \left( \frac{1}{2} \right)^2 + \left( \frac{2}{3\pi} \right)^2 + \left( \frac{2}{15\pi} \right)^2 \right] \right\} = 0.2497 V_p^2 \text{ volts}^2.$$

signals are, ac voltages, pulses sent out by radar transmitters, timing signals in a TV signal, clocking signals in a computer, and steady musical tones. Examples of nonperiodic signals are music, speech, information pulses in a computer, and radar pulse returns from a maneuvering target or a diffuse target, such as a thunderstorm. Thus, we must press for the extension of frequency-domain concepts to include a wider class of signals.

**A strategy.** How, then, might we explore the possibility of having a spectrum for a nonperiodic signal, such as a pulse that happens only once? One approach, which works in this case, begins with a periodic series of pulses and then increases the period, keeping the width of the individual pulses constant. As we let the period of the repeating pulses become larger and larger, in the limit we would have a single pulse. This limiting process in the time domain affects the spectrum, and the resulting spectrum corresponds to the spectrum of a single pulse.

**Spectrum of a series of narrow pulses.** Figure 9.8 suggests such a series of pulses by showing three pulses. The individual pulse widths are $\tau$, which is kept constant, and the period is $T$, which is allowed to increase so as to isolate a single pulse. The time origin is the center of one of the pulses; hence, the signal has even symmetry about the origin. This means that the Fourier series for these pulses contains harmonics in the form of Eq. (9.4), but every harmonic has a phase angle ($\theta$) of 0 or 180°, because these phases alone possess even symmetry. Because the phase of 180° is equivalent to a negative sign in front of the amplitude, the Fourier series for this signal must be of the form

$$v(t) = V_0 + V_1\cos(\omega_1 t) + V_2\cos(2\omega_1 t) + \cdots + V_n \cos(n\omega_1 t) + \cdots \tag{9.11}$$

where $\omega_1 = 2\pi/T$ and $V_n$ is the amplitude of the $n^{\text{th}}$ harmonic, which may be negative. The amplitudes can be computed by the standard methods of Fourier series, with the result

$$V_n = \frac{2V_s\tau}{T}\frac{\sin(n\omega_1\tau/2)}{n\omega_1\tau/2} = \frac{2V_s\tau}{T}\frac{\sin(n\pi\tau/T)}{n\pi\tau/T} \quad \text{V}, \qquad (n = 1, 2, 3, \cdots) \tag{9.12}$$

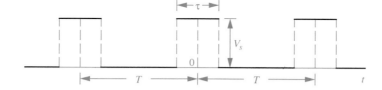

**Figure 9.8** Series of pulses.

Recall that the spectrum consists of components at $\omega = 0$, $\omega_1$, $2\omega_1$, ..., $n\omega_1$, ..., with harmonic amplitudes, except for $n = 0$, given by Eq. (9.12). We reserve as a problem the proof that Eq. (9.12) yields the results presented in Eq. (9.5) when $\tau = T/2$.

**The harmonics of the spectrum.** As an example, we plot in Fig. 9.9(b) the spectrum for the case where $T = 10\tau$. We see in Fig. 9.9(b) that there are now many

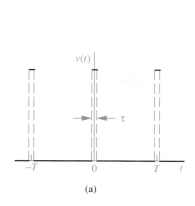

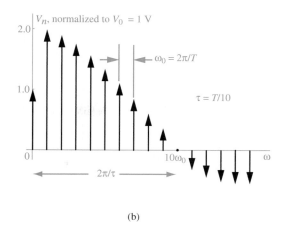

**Figure 9.9** (a) Time-domain and (b) frequency-domain representations for a series of pulses with period $T$ and width $\tau = T/10$.

harmonics that are significant, unlike the spectrum in Fig. 9.5(b), where the amplitudes fall off rapidly after the first few harmonics. The negative amplitudes indicate a phase of 180° from the tenth to the twentieth harmonics. The spectrum consists of a large number of harmonics spaced apart $\Delta f = 1/T$, where $T$ is the period of the time function.

### The amplitude of the spectrum.

Although for graphing purposes we have normalized the harmonic amplitudes to unity relative to the dc component, Eq. (9.12) reveals that the individual harmonics become small as $T$ is made large. There are two reasons for this decrease. As the period is increased, with $\tau$ kept constant, the pulses come less and less frequently and hence the power in the signal decreases accordingly. Specifically, the average power must decrease as $1/T$ due to the spreading of the pulses in time. Compounded with this effect, the power in any individual harmonic must decrease even faster because the power in the series of pulses distributes between an increasingly larger number of harmonics. As Eq. (9.12) shows, the power in, say, the first harmonic ($n = 1$) decreases as $(1/T)^2$ because power is proportional to the square of the amplitude.

### Isolating a single pulse.

With the aid of Fig. 9.9(b) and a measure of imagination, we can now anticipate what will happen to the spectrum as we allow the period, $T$, to approach infinity. As $T \rightarrow \infty$, the frequencies of the individual harmonics crowd closer and closer together and, in the limit, constitute a continuous spectrum. Individual harmonics must disappear because there is no longer any specific period; hence, frequency becomes a continuous variable. We conclude that a single pulse in the time domain contains all frequencies in the frequency domain.

### The voltage spectrum of a single pulse.

The shape of the spectrum will not change as $T$ becomes large. The period, $T$, affects the spacing of the harmonics, but the shape of the spectrum depends only on $\tau$. Thus, the shape of the spectrum retains the form in Eq. (9.12), which approaches

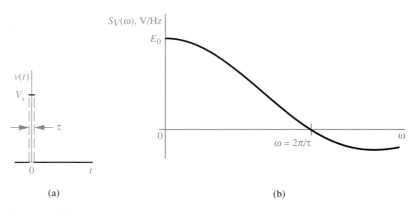

(a)                                              (b)

**Figure 9.10**   (a) Time-domain and (b) frequency-domain representations for a single pulse.

$$S_V(\omega) = E_0 \frac{\sin(\omega\tau/2)}{\omega\tau/2} \text{ V/Hz} \tag{9.13}$$

where the continuous variable $\omega$ replaces the discrete variable $n\omega_1$, $E_0$ is a constant, and $S_V(\omega)$ is the voltage spectrum of the pulse. This continuous spectrum is shown in Fig. 9.10(b).

**Power or energy spectrum?**   We wish also to investigate the power spectrum, but here we must be careful. As implied earlier, the single pulse carries no average power because the finite energy in the pulse is spread over all time, whereas power implies the continuous flow of energy as a time process. Consequently, we may meaningfully discuss the energy in the pulse but not the power. The voltage spectrum in Eq. (9.13), when squared, becomes an energy spectrum, not a power spectrum. The energy in the pulse distributes between the infinite number of frequencies making up the spectrum. Each individual frequency carries an infinitesimal quantity of energy, but taken together the spectrum accounts for the total energy of the pulse.

As in the case of periodic power spectra, we have the option of including resistance explicitly or omitting it to leave the definition of an energy spectrum more general. The units of the spectrum given in Eq. (9.13) are volts per hertz. The energy spectrum has the units joule-ohms per hertz, which requires division by a resistance and multiplication by a bandwidth in hertz to have the units for energy.

**Conservation of Energy**

**Spectrum amplitude.**   Let us apply this interpretation of the square of the voltage spectrum in computing the energy in the pulse in the frequency domain. We can equate this energy to the energy in the time domain to evaluate the constant $E_0$ in the spectrum in Eq. (9.13). To have a physical picture, and to get the units to work out to the proper units of energy, let us consider that the pulse has an amplitude of $V_s$ and is applied to a resistor of value $R$, as shown in Fig. 9.11. The total energy in the pulse is the integral of the power, Eq. (1.35). The required calculation is

$$W_R = \int_{-\infty}^{+\infty} vi \, dt = \int_{-\tau/2}^{+\tau/2} \frac{v^2}{R} \, dt = \frac{V_s^2}{R} \int_{-\tau/2}^{+\tau/2} dt = \frac{V_s^2 \tau}{R} \text{ J} \tag{9.14}$$

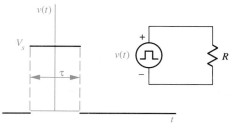

**Figure 9.11** Computation of the energy in a single pulse.

The frequency-domain calculation follows the same reasoning used in Eq. (9.10), except that here we replace the sum of the contributions of each individual harmonic with the integral of the continuous spectrum. We use the rms value of each contributing sinusoid; hence the amplitudes must be divided by $\sqrt{2}$. We no longer must treat the dc term separately because it carries an infinitesimal amount of energy. Equation (9.15) summarizes the required computation.

$$W_R = \frac{1}{R}\int_0^\infty \left[\frac{E_0}{\sqrt{2}}\frac{\sin(\omega\tau/2)}{\omega\tau/2}\right]^2 d\left(\frac{\omega}{2\pi}\right) = \frac{E_0^2}{2R}\left(\frac{1}{\pi\tau}\right)\int_0^\infty \frac{\sin^2 x}{x^2}dx$$

$$= \frac{E_0^2}{4R\tau} \quad \text{J} \tag{9.15}$$

You will note that we are integrating with respect to $\omega/2\pi$, which is the frequency in hertz. The second form of the integral results from a change in variables from $\omega$ to $x = \omega\tau/2$. The definite integral has the value $\pi/2$, leading to the final result. We now equate the two energy calculations in Eqs. (9.14) and (9.15), with the result

$$\frac{E_0^2}{4R\tau} = \frac{V_s^2\tau}{R} \quad \Rightarrow \quad E_0 = 2V_s\tau \quad \text{volt-second} \tag{9.16}$$

Thus the spectrum of the pulse in Fig. 9.10(a) is

$$S_V(\omega) = 2V_s\tau\frac{\sin(\omega\tau/2)}{(\omega\tau/2)} \quad \text{V/Hz} \tag{9.17}$$

---

**EXAMPLE 9.3**  **Pulse spectrum**

Find the total energy and spectrum amplitude of a 10-V, 0.2-μs pulse.

**SOLUTION:**
The total "energy" is given by Eq. (9.14), except that we remove the resistance, $R$, to make the equation more general. The energy is

$$W_V = V_s^2\tau = (10\text{ V})^2 \times 2 \times 10^{-7} = 2 \times 10^{-5}\text{ V}^2\text{-s} \tag{9.18}$$

The voltage spectrum of this pulse has the amplitude given by Eq. (9.16)

$$E_0 = 2V_s\tau = 2 \times 10 \times 2 \times 10^{-7} = 4 \times 10^{-6} \text{ V/Hz} \tag{9.19}$$

The rms value of this spectrum height is $4 \times 10^{-6}/\sqrt{2} = 2.83 \text{ μV/Hz}$.

**The Frequency Domain**

**Bandwidth.** The spectrum of the single pulse in Eq. (9.17) illustrates an important general relationship between the time and frequency domains. In Fig. 9.12, we show the energy spectrum of the pulse, $S_P(\omega)$,[7] which is the square of the voltage spectrum in Fig. 9.10. Clearly, most of the energy is contained in the frequency bandwidth below the first null at $2\pi/\tau$. Integration of the energy spectrum reveals that 90% of the total energy of the single pulse lies in the bandwidth between 0 and the first null in the spectrum. Thus, if we were to pass this spectrum through an ideal low-pass filter that eliminated all frequencies above the first null of the spectrum, most of the energy would go through and the pulse would appear in the time domain without serious change. Similarly, the representation of the periodic pulses, Fig. 9.5(a), by the dc and first two harmonics contains 90.5% of the energy in the entire series of pulses, as you can verify from Eq. (9.5). Figure 9.3 verifies that the shape of the pulses is relatively unchanged by the elimination of the higher harmonics. Later in this chapter, we investigate filtering in the frequency domain; here we merely wish to establish that there is an effective bandwidth in the frequency domain associated with a pulse.

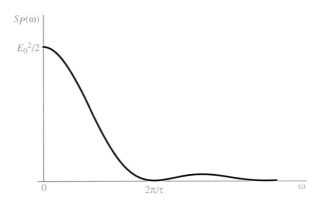

**Figure 9.12** Power spectrum of a single pulse. The bandwidth in Hz is approximately $1/\tau$.

We may determine this effective bandwidth by setting $\omega\tau/2$ equal to $\pi$, the angle in radians where the spectrum first goes to zero. Solving this equation and converting to frequency in hertz, we obtain

$$\frac{\omega\tau}{2\pi} = \pi \Rightarrow B = \frac{2\pi}{2\pi\tau} = \frac{1}{\tau} \text{ Hz} \tag{9.20}$$

where $B$ is the significant *bandwidth* in hertz.

---

[7] The subscript "$P$" indicates a power spectrum. In this context, this means that the voltage spectrum has been squared, not that the units are watts.

**Bandwidth and pulse width.** Important consequences follow from this approximate relationship between pulse duration in the time domain and bandwidth in the frequency domain. For one, we must provide adequate bandwidth if pulses are to pass through communication or computing systems without serious distortion. If, for example, we have a digital system that utilizes pulses of 1-μs duration, we must provide at least $1 \times 10^6$ Hz, or 1 MHz, of bandwidth to send those pulses to another location for recording or processing.

This reciprocal relationship between pulse length and bandwidth applies also to periodic pulses. The spectrum of the periodic pulses shown in Fig. 9.5(b) has the same general shape, and hence the same bandwidth, as that of the single pulse. Furthermore, this relationship between time duration and bandwidth does not depend on the exact shape of the pulses. The pulses may be rounded on top or triangular in shape: The same approximate bandwidth would be needed to preserve the identity of the pulses in passing through a communication system.

---

**EXAMPLE 9.4** | **Bandwidth of a pulse**

What is the bandwidth of the 10-V, 0.2-μs pulse in the previous example?

**SOLUTION:**
Using Eq. (9.20), we find

$$B = \frac{1}{\tau} = \frac{1}{2 \times 10^{-7}} = 5 \times 10^6 \,\text{Hz} \tag{9.21}$$

**WHAT IF?** What if you pass this pulse through an amplifier with a 1-MHz bandwidth? What would happen to the pulse?[8]

---

**Example from mechanics.** Let us imagine that we have a large bell and we strike this bell with a metal hammer. We know, of course, that the bell "rings", meaning that the mechanical resonances of the bell are excited to produce a ringing sound. The force between the hammer and the bell is of short duration, and this short pulse of force excites the bell structure. Because the energy spectrum of the short pulse is broad in bandwidth, the higher resonances of the bell are excited.

Pick up now a rubber hammer and again strike the bell. We would expect the bell to sound less harsh, more mellow. We can understand this change in sound in terms of the energy spectrum of the force from the rubber hammer. The rubber hammer remains in contact with the bell much longer because the rubber hammer is more compliant than the metal hammer. The result of this longer pulse of force is a smaller bandwidth of excitation; consequently, the higher-frequency resonances of the bell are not excited.

---

[8] The pulse would lose approximately 80% of its energy, and its shape would be smeared out to a width of 1 μs. Basically it wouldn't be a pulse anymore.

These higher resonances, which give the bell a harsh sound, are eliminated; hence, a mellow sound results with a rubber hammer.

## Spectra of Random Signals

**random signal**

### Importance of random signals.

A *random signal* is any signal that is unpredictable to us, either because it originates from chance events or because its complexity defies routine analysis. Examples of random signals are broadcast signals over radio and TV channels, digital signals passing from computer to computer, and the roar of a jet aircraft engine.

Information is carried by random signals. We say that a signal contains information when we know something new because we received the signal. This implies that a signal containing the information is unpredictable to us, that is, is random in the sense given earlier. The examples given before illustrate the information-carrying possibility for random signals.

### Characterization of random signals.

If we are to design electronic circuits to monitor, record, transmit, receive, and process random signals, we must develop appropriate concepts to characterize such signals. Probability and statistics deal with random phenomena. These types of mathematics do not allow us to predict random events, but they can describe the structure of the randomness. Consequently, the application of probability theory to communication systems has yielded many important results.

It is not our aim here to explore communication theory. We limit our characterization of random signals to that required for the discussion of simple communications systems, such as an AM radio. Our major goal is to show that random signals can be characterized by a power spectrum in the frequency domain. First, we discuss the power in a random signal; then we discuss the time structure and show, in consequence, how the power in the signal is distributed in the frequency domain.

### DC component of a random signal.

Figure 9.13 shows a random signal. This might represent an electrical signal monitoring the temperature at a certain point in a chemical plant. The average temperature would be indicated by the average value of the voltage, $v_{dc}$. We can denote this time average as

$$v_{dc} = \langle v(t) \rangle \qquad (9.22)$$

where the angle brackets indicate time average. This average could be approximated by

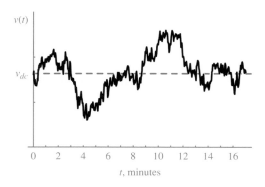

**Figure 9.13** Random signal.

averaging over a long period of time:

$$v_{dc} = \langle v(t) \rangle = \frac{1}{T}\int_0^T v(t)\ dt \tag{9.23}$$

Here $T$ would have to be large enough to include many random fluctuations, say, a period of hours for the function in Fig. 9.13. We acknowledge the possibility that at some future time, the plant might shut down and cool off, and hence the average temperature might change. But for normal operation, we assume there to be a meaningful average temperature as represented by the dc voltage in Eq. (9.23).

**AC component.** We may define the *ac component* of the random signal as the remainder after the average is subtracted:

$$v_{ac}(t) = v(t) - v_{dc} = v(t) - \langle v(t)\rangle \tag{9.24}$$

By "ac," we mean everything but the dc, the fluctuations in the signal. By definition, the time average of the ac component is zero:

$$\langle v_{ac}(t)\rangle = \langle v(t) - v_{dc}\rangle = \langle v(t)\rangle - v_{dc} = v_{dc} - v_{dc} = 0 \tag{9.25}$$

Because averaging is a linear process, we have distributed the averaging operation to the individual terms in Eq. (9.25).

**Power structure.** Leaving out the resistance for generality, we may define the power, $P$, to be

$$\begin{aligned} P &= \langle v^2(t)\rangle = \langle [v_{ac}(t) + v_{dc}]^2\rangle \\ &= \langle v_{ac}^2(t) + 2v_{ac}(t)v_{dc} + v_{dc}^2\rangle \text{ volts} \end{aligned} \tag{9.26}$$

Again we may distribute the time average.

$$\begin{aligned} P &= \langle v_{ac}^2(t)\rangle + 2\langle v_{ac}(t)\rangle v_{dc} + \langle v_{dc}^2\rangle \\ &= \langle v_{ac}^2(t)\rangle + v_{dc}^2 \text{ volts}^2 \end{aligned} \tag{9.27}$$

The middle term drops out because the time average of the ac component vanishes, as shown in Eq. (9.25). Equation (9.27) indicates that the total power of the random signal may be considered as the sum of the powers in the dc and ac components, acting independently.

$$P = P_{ac} + P_{dc} \tag{9.28}$$

These two types of power produce distinct components in the power spectrum of the random signal.

**Time structure of random signals.** The fluctuations of a random signal are characterized by a *correlation time*. This is the time, on the average, during which the fluctuations in the signal become independent of the past. In Fig. 9.13, for example, the correlation time is about 1 min. This correlation time suggests how far into the future

ac component

correlation time

**The Time Domain**

we might be able to predict the signal. If we know the voltage in Fig. 9.13 at some instant of time, we could predict its value 1 or 2 s later with confidence. But our uncertainty would grow as the prediction moves into the future, and we can say little if anything about the value of the fluctuations, say, some 3 minutes hence. Thus, correlation time characterizes the time structure of a random signal in a crude way.

Statistics gives a precise definition of the correlation time and furnishes numerical methods for estimating it for a random signal. Investigation of such mathematical techniques, however, would lead us far beyond our goal of developing the ideas we need to understand basic communication systems.

Given that we know the correlation time for a signal, we can approximate the signal with a train of pulses, as shown in Fig. 9.14. The approximation is poor for details of the fluctuation of the random signal, but does yield a crude representation of the time structure of the signal.

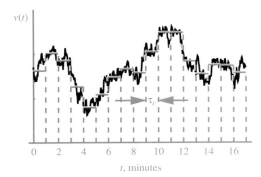

**Figure 9.14** Random signal approximated by pulses.

**The Frequency Domain**

**Spectra of random signals.** Let us now consider the spectrum of the random signal. A spectrum represents a time-domain signal as a sum of sinusoids. At first glance, it would appear to be impossible to represent an unpredictable random signal with stable, predictable sinusoids. This is true in part, for a random signal cannot be represented with a stable sum of sinusoids. The random signal contains sinusoids, but the phases of these sinusoids never stabilize, but rather vary randomly with time. An amplitude spectrum exists for random signals, but phase is meaningless. Thus, a power spectrum exists for a random signal but a voltage spectrum cannot be meaningfully defined.

**Bandwidth of a random signal.** The exact shape of the power spectrum of a random signal depends on the details of the nature of the fluctuations, but the meaningful bandwidth depends on the correlation time. If we were to consider the power spectrum of the pulses approximating the random signal in Fig. 9.14, all of them would have a significant bandwidth of

$$B \approx \frac{1}{\tau_c} \text{ Hz} \tag{9.29}$$

where $\tau_c$ denotes the correlation time. Thus, we would require approximately $1/60$ Hz of bandwidth to handle the random signal in Fig. 9.13, but if the correlation time were $1\ \mu s$, we would require about 1 MHz of bandwidth.

**Summary.** The power spectrum, $S_P(f)$, of a random signal will have one component due to the dc component and one component due to the ac component, as shown in Fig. 9.15. The dc component is represented by a discrete line at zero frequency, but the ac component is represented by a continuous spectrum. The units of this continuous spectrum are volts²/hertz or volts²-second. As shown, the area of the continuous power spectrum represents the total power in the random signal fluctuations and must give the same power as the time-domain representation,

$$P_{ac} = \langle v_{ac}^2(t) \rangle = \int_0^\infty S_{ac}(f)\,df \tag{9.30}$$

where $S_{ac}(f)$ represents the power spectrum of the fluctuations in the random signal. Figure 9.15 also shows the relationship between significant bandwidth and correlation time, as asserted in Eq. (9.29).

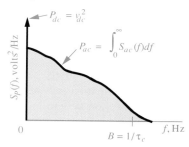

**Figure 9.15** Power spectrum of a random signal.

---

**EXAMPLE 9.5** | **Spectrum of the ac component**

An electrical signal has a total power of $100$ V². The time average of the signal is 5.5 V and the correlation time is 0.1 ms. Find the "power" and the bandwidth of the fluctuating component of the signal.

**SOLUTION:**

From Eq. (9.28), $P_{ac} = P - P_{dc} = 100 - (5.5)^2 = 69.8$ V². The bandwidth is approximately

$$B \approx \frac{1}{\tau_c} = \frac{1}{0.1 \times 10^{-3}} = 10^4 \text{ Hz} \tag{9.31}$$

The average power density in the spectrum of the fluctuations would be

$$S_{P(avg)} = \frac{P_{ac}}{B} = \frac{69.8}{10^4} = 6.98 \times 10^{-3} \text{ V}^2/\text{Hz} \tag{9.32}$$

**WHAT IF?** | What if the dc voltage were $-5.5$ V?[9]

---

[9] No difference in the ac spectrum.

# Bandwidth and Information Rate

Information.   Information has meaning in both technical and ordinary language. We might describe a book as containing information, and we might understand the gestures of a police officer directing traffic as offering information to motorists. In these instances, we think of information as offering knowledge—matters to be observed and acted upon.

The technical definition of information can cover these possibilities but deals primarily with the machine transmission or storage of symbols. With this theory, we may study the exchange of information between two computers or we may calculate the information stored in the genetic code. This mathematical theory of information is of recent origin, springing from the work of Claude Shannon (1916–). This theory deals with the probability of deciphering a known code that has been transmitted or stored in the presence of random disturbance. Information theory generally supports and enhances the commonsense understanding of information but also allows nonsense to be considered valid information. According to the mathematical theory, for example, the received message "3 = 5" is valid information if that is what the transmitter sent. In other words, the theory measures and describes objective information (messages sent and received), not subjective information (the meaning, validity, and importance of such messages).

**The Frequency Domain**

Information rate and bandwidth.   Our purpose here is to show an important relationship between the information rate of a communication system and the bandwidth required by that communication system in the frequency domain. For our purposes, it is unnecessary to distinguish between the common understanding of information and that of the mathematical theory because this relationship is valid in both senses. Our examples are based on the commonsense understanding of information. The conclusion we reach, however, can be supported with the mathematical theory. We consider one analog and one digital example.

**Analog Information**

Speech.   What is the band of audio frequencies necessary to communicate, say, over a telephone line? Experiments have established that the essential bandwidth of audio frequencies lies between about 800 and 2400 Hz. That is, if someone spoke to you via a telephone system that passed that band of frequencies, you could certainly understand what they said. Although this would be the minimum bandwidth for communication to occur, the phone company allocates the band of frequencies between about 400 and 3300 Hz. The additional bandwidth is not required for intelligibility but rather for recognition of the speaker. For satisfactory telephone service, we require not only to hear and understand the message, but also to recognize the speaker's voice. This recognition factor represents additional information content to the phone message.

An AM radio signal uses audio frequencies between 100 and 5000 Hz. This additional bandwidth is required for satisfactory transmission of music. Of course, FM radios sound better because their audio bandwidth is from 50 to 15,000 Hz. The large bandwidth enhances the quality of the music, a subjective measure of its information content.

A TV signal contains audio (voice) and video (picture). The audio bandwidth is similar to that of an FM radio, but the video requires much more bandwidth because the information rate is much higher. Of the 6-MHz bandwidth required for transmission of the entire TV signal, over 99% of the bandwidth is required for the video and synchronization signals, the remainder being used for the audio. Thus, we see a clear relationship between bandwidth and information rate in analog systems.

**Digital communications.** Early communication systems (signal fires, signal flags, Morse-code telegraph) were digital in their coding. The invention of the telephone in the 1870s inaugurated a century of analog communications, but in recent decades, digital methods have made a comeback. Indeed, except for local telephone service, modern communication systems use digital codes.

**baud**

The unit of digital information rate is the bit/second, or *baud*. The maximum baud rate of a communications system is determined by its bandwidth and its coding sophistication. Let us consider data rates for an ordinary phone line. Originally, data rates were deliberately slow, 110 baud, because the usual recipient of the information, a teletype, was essentially a mechanical typewriter that decoded and typed out the alphanumeric symbols as they arrived. Baud rates were increased for electronic "dumb" terminals to 1200 baud, which is about the limit for a phone line transmitting simple pulses, as shown by the next example. Modern modems utilize sophisticated codes to increase baud rates to about 20 kbaud. Such data rates are adequate for desktop computers, but the higher data rates required for business communications, for example, an airline reservation system, are achieved through increased bandwidth.

Increased bandwidths have been achieved by use of coaxial-cable and microwave systems at 100 Mbits/second, or megabaud, and a variety of optical communication technologies. Current optical systems use optical fibers to carry 3.4 gigabits/second,[10] or Gbaud, and experimental systems have achieved 34 Gbaud.

---

**EXAMPLE 9.6** | **Baud rate**

Determine the bandwidth required for a data rate of 1200 baud, using simple pulses to represent the bits of information.

**SOLUTION:**
Each bit (pulse) will require 1/1200 s to transmit, so the individual pulses will look as shown in Fig. 9.16. The pulse itself would occupy half the time space and hence the pulse width would be about 1/2400 s. Using the relation given in Eq. (9.20), we would expect that a bandwidth of about 2400 Hz would be required to send such a pulse without significant distortion; and therefore we would expect that an ordinary phone line would be adequate for connecting a computer with the remote terminal.

**WHAT IF?** | What if the baud rate were 100 Mbaud?[11]

---

**Summary.** We have expanded frequency domain concepts to periodic, non periodic, and random signals. We have investigated the relationship between time structure and

---

[10] "G" = giga = $10^9$.

[11] The required bandwidth would be 200 MHz.

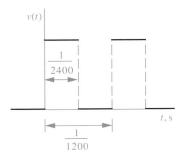

**Figure 9.16** Digital pulse train, 1200 pulses/second.

bandwidth. For random signals, bandwidth determines the maximum information rate for a system.

### Check Your Understanding

1. If the period of a periodic signal is 12 ms, what is the frequency in hertz of the third harmonic?

2. The most important harmonic output frequency of a power supply is the zeroth, first, second, or third harmonic of the input frequency. (Which?)

3. If a pulse has a width of 10 ms, what is the bandwidth in hertz required to carry the pulse without significant distortion?

4. If a computer terminal writes 30 characters/second, and each character requires 8 bits, what is the baud rate and the required bandwidth of the channel supplying data to the terminal?

5. The voltage spectrum or power spectrum gives amplitude and phase information? Which?

6. A random signal has a correlation time of 2 ms. What is the required bandwidth for a communication channel to carry this signal?

7. Which type(s) of signals has (have) a continuous spectrum: sinusoidal, periodic, a single pulse, a random signal?

*Answers.* (**1**) 250 Hz; (**2**) the dc, the zeroth harmonic, is the *only* desired output of a power supply; (**3**) 100 Hz; (**4**) 240 baud, 480 Hz; (**5**) voltage spectrum; (**6**) 500 Hz; (**7**) single pulse and random signal.

## 9.2 ELECTRICAL FILTERS

**OBJECTIVE 3**

**To understand how filters modify spectra**

**Introduction.** The frequency-domain representation of signals is important because we can use electrical filters to shape the spectrum of a signal. In this section, we analyze the properties of simple low-pass, high-pass, and band-pass filters. We develop the Bode plot as a convenient means for describing filter properties.

### Filter Concepts

**Filtering a rectified signal.** In Fig. 9.17, we show an *RC* low-pass filter. Consider the input voltage to be the half-wave rectified sinusoid in Fig. 9.6 (a); we wish to

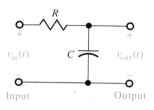

**Figure 9.17** Low-pass filter.

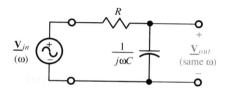

**Figure 9.18** Low-pass filter in the frequency domain. We derive the filter function.

determine the output voltage, $v_{out}$. This input waveform is chosen because we have studied its spectrum; it does not represent the simple rectifier circuits analyzed in Chapter 7 because the output of these rectifiers would be modified by the input impedance of the low-pass filter.

**Time-domain analysis.** We can write a DE for the output voltage but the solution is a bit tricky. Furthermore, the time-domain approach generates little insight into the behavior of the circuit. We approach the problem in the frequency domain.

💡 **The Frequency Domain**

💡 **The Time Domain**

**filter function**

**Filter function.** Figure 9.18 shows the $RC$ filter in the frequency domain, with $R$ and $C$ represented by their impedances. The input phasor, $\underline{\mathbf{V}}_{in}$, represents a single sinusoid at a frequency $\omega$. The output phasor, $\underline{\mathbf{V}}_{out}$, is readily determined with a voltage divider:

$$\underline{\mathbf{V}}_{out} = \underline{\mathbf{V}}_{in} \times \left( \frac{1/j\omega C}{R + 1/j\omega C} \right) = \underline{\mathbf{V}}_{in} \times \frac{1}{1 + j\omega RC} \tag{9.33}$$

The *filter function* is the ratio between output and input phasors

$$\underline{\mathbf{F}}(\omega) = \frac{\underline{\mathbf{V}}_{out}}{\underline{\mathbf{V}}_{in}} = \frac{1}{1 + j\omega RC} \tag{9.34}$$

**How the filter works.** The characteristics of the low-pass filter function, $\underline{\mathbf{F}}(\omega)$, can be understood from the effect of frequency on the impedance of the capacitor. Recall that the impedance of a capacitor has a magnitude of $1/\omega C$. At dc, the capacitor acts as an open circuit; hence, all the input voltage appears at the output, independent of $R$. At very low ac frequencies, the impedance of the capacitor is still very high compared to $R$. Specifically, as long as $1/\omega C \gg R$, the output voltage is approximately equal to the input voltage, and thus the filter gain is near unity. Thus, $\underline{\mathbf{F}}(\omega) \to 1$ as $\omega \to 0$, as shown mathematically by Eq. (9.34).

**low-pass filter**

At very high frequencies, the impedance of the capacitor approaches that of a short circuit and hence little voltage appears across the capacitor. As long as $R \gg 1/\omega C$, the current is approximately $\underline{\mathbf{V}}_{in}/R$ and the magnitude of the voltage across the capacitor, which is the output voltage, is $|\underline{\mathbf{V}}_{in}|/\omega RC$ and hence approaches very small values as $\omega$ increases. Thus, $\underline{\mathbf{F}}(\omega) \to 0$ as $\omega \to \infty$. Consequently, the gain of the low-pass filter becomes very small at high frequencies. This means that a high-frequency signal would be greatly reduced, whereas low-frequency components would not be reduced by the filter; that is, it will "pass" only components of the signal at low frequencies. The filter characteristic, $\underline{\mathbf{F}}(\omega)$, is shown in Fig. 9.19, plotted on a log scale to show a large range of frequencies.

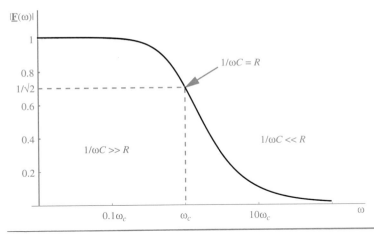

**Figure 9.19** Low pass-filter amplitude characteristic.

**Cutoff frequency.** The region of transition between these two types of behavior is centered on the frequency where the impedance of the capacitor is equal to that of the resistance:

$$R = \frac{1}{\omega_c C} \Rightarrow \omega_c = \frac{1}{RC} \qquad \text{and} \qquad f_c = \frac{1}{2\pi RC} \tag{9.35}$$

where $\omega_c$ is called the *cutoff frequency* and characterizes the region of frequency where filtering begins. The filter function can be expressed in terms of the cutoff frequency:

$$\mathbf{F}(\omega) = \frac{1}{1 + j\omega RC} = \frac{1}{1 + j(\omega/\omega_c)} = \frac{1}{1 + j(f/f_c)} \tag{9.36}$$

At $\omega = \omega_c$, or $f = f_c$, the filter function has the value $1/(1 + j1)$, which has a magnitude of $1/\sqrt{2} = 0.707.$[12] The significance of a voltage gain of 0.707 lies in the relationship between input and output power. Power is proportional to the square of the voltage; hence, at $\omega_c$, the output power is reduced by a factor of 2 from what it would have been in the absence of the filter. For this reason, the cutoff frequency, expressed in either rad/s or hertz, is often called the *half-power frequency*.

**Phase effects.** Figure 9.19 shows only the magnitude of the filter function, $|\mathbf{F}(\omega)|$ . The filter function is a complex function with real and imaginary parts. Thus, the filter affects both the magnitude and the phase of sinusoids passing through it. For example, at the cutoff frequency, the filter function has the value $1/(1 + j1) = 0.707 \angle -45°$. This phase shift is an unavoidable by-product of the filtering process that can cause problems in some applications. In audio systems, few problems occur due to phase shift because the ear is largely insensitive to phase, but in video systems, such phase shifts can degrade the performance.

---

[12] This has nothing to do with the rms value of a sinusoid.

**Frequency-domain analysis.**    We return to the problem of low-pass filtering a half-wave rectified sinusoid. We can express the input voltage as a spectrum, a sum of sinusoids. Each of these represents an ac source and by superposition leads to a straight forward ac circuit problem, which we can solve using phasors and impedance. Specifically, if we have an input sinusoid of frequency $\omega$ and phasor magnitude, $\underline{V}_{in}$, the output phasor can be determined from the filter function.

**Filtering a spectrum.**    Let us summarize the approach that we are following. The basic idea is indicated by Fig. 9.20. This is similar to Fig. 4.5, except that now we are willing to let the input phasor be a spectrum of frequencies. Specifically, we use superposition to determine the effect of the filter on each input frequency. We know that the circuit, being a linear circuit, creates no new frequencies; each harmonic in the input produces a harmonic in the output. The filter affects each of these frequencies differently because the impedance of the capacitor varies with frequency. This frequency dependence of the circuit is symbolized by the filter function, $\underline{F}(\omega)$ .

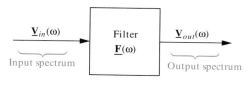

$$\underline{V}_{out}(\omega) = \underline{V}_{in}(\omega) \times \underline{F}(\omega)$$

**Figure 9.20**    Filtering a spectrum.

**Passing the signal through the filter.**    We now can determine the effect of the input voltage in Fig. 9.6(a) on the filter in Fig. 9.17 by treating separately each frequency component of the signal. This approach is suggested by Fig. 9.21, where we have indicated that the input can be represented as a series of voltage sources representing the dc component, the fundamental, the second harmonic, the fourth harmonic, and so on. Our analysis is based on superposition, adding up the effect of each input sinusoidal source, considered separately. This exchanges the solution of a DE in the time domain for a host of ac circuit solutions in the frequency domain.

**Input harmonics.**    Fourier analysis allows us to determine the amplitude and phase of the harmonics of the input signal. Equation (9.4) can be combined with Eq. (4.59) to become

$$v_{in}(t) = \text{Re}\{V_{in(dc)} + \underline{V}_{in(1)}e^{j\omega_1 t} + \underline{V}_{in(2)}e^{j2\omega_1 t}$$

$$+ \cdots + \underline{V}_{in(n)}e^{jn\omega_1 t} + \cdots \}$$

(9.37)

where $\underline{V}_{in(n)}$ represents the amplitude and phase of the $n^{\text{th}}$ harmonic of the input signal, as shown in the voltage spectrum in Fig. 9.6(b).

**Output harmonics.**    We must next evaluate the filter function at each harmonic frequency to see how each is affected in amplitude and phase by the filter. This is symbolized by

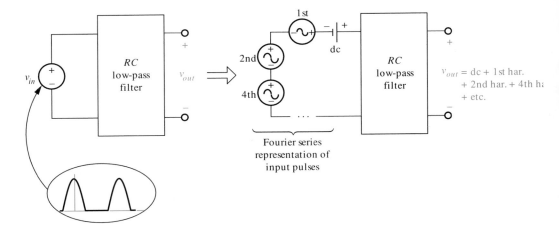

**Figure 9.21** Filtering a periodic signal in the frequency domain.

$$V_{out(dc)} = \mathbf{F}(0) \times V_{in(dc)}$$

$$\underline{\mathbf{V}}_{out(1)} = \mathbf{F}(\omega_1) \times V_{in(1)} \tag{9.38}$$

$$\underline{\mathbf{V}}_{out(n)} = \mathbf{F}(n\omega_1) \times V_{in(n)}$$

where $\underline{\mathbf{V}}_{out(n)}$ represents the amplitude and phase of the $n^{th}$ output harmonic and $\mathbf{F}(n\omega_0)$ is the filter function evaluated at the frequency of the $n^{th}$ harmonic. Finally, we sum the frequency components of the output and transform back to the time domain, as shown in

$$v_{out}(t) = \mathrm{Re}\{V_{out(dc)} + \underline{\mathbf{V}}_{out(1)}e^{j\omega_1 t} + \underline{\mathbf{V}}_{out(2)}e^{j2\omega_1 t}$$

$$+ \cdots + \underline{\mathbf{V}}_{out(n)}e^{jn\omega_1 t} + \cdots\} \tag{9.39}$$

**Filtering the half-wave rectified sinusoid.** So much for the general theory. We now work through the details for the problem presented in Fig. 9.21. Specifically, we assume a peak amplitude of 18 V and a fundamental frequency of 60 Hz for the half-wave rectified sinusoid. For the filter, we use $R = 500\ \Omega$ and $C = 20\ \mu\mathrm{F}$, for a cut-off frequency of

$$\omega_c = \frac{1}{RC} = \frac{1}{500 \times 20 \times 10^{-6}} = 100\ \mathrm{rad/s} \tag{9.40}$$

which is about one-fourth the fundamental frequency of $120\,\pi$ rad/s. The first few components in the output are as follows:

**DC term.** The dc input is $18/\pi = 5.730$ V. The filter function at dc is $\mathbf{F}(0) = 1$, so the output at dc is $\underline{\mathbf{V}}_{out}(0) = 5.73$ V.

**Fundamental.** The phasor for the fundamental is from Eq. (9.6):

$$\underline{V}_{in}(120\pi) = \frac{V_p}{2} \angle 0° = 9.0 \angle 0° \text{ V} \tag{9.41}$$

The filter function at the frequency of the fundamental is

$$\underline{F}(120\pi) = \frac{1}{1 + j(120\pi/100)} = 0.256 \angle -75.1° \tag{9.42}$$

Thus, the output phasor for the fundamental is

$$\underline{V}_{out}(120\pi) = 9.0 \angle 0° \times 0.256 \angle -75.1° = 2.31 \angle -75.1° \text{ V} \tag{9.43}$$

**Higher harmonics.**    Similarly, we can calculate the second and fourth harmonics of the output to be

$$\underline{V}_{out}(240\pi) = \frac{18 \times 2}{3\pi} \angle 0° \times \frac{1}{1 + j(240\pi/100)} = 0.502 \angle -82.4° \text{ V}$$

$$\underline{V}_{out}(480\pi) = \frac{18 \times 2}{15\pi} \angle 180° \times \frac{1}{1 + j(480\pi/100)} = 0.0505 \angle +93.8° \text{ V} \tag{9.44}$$

Similarly, the sixth harmonic is $\underline{V}_{out}(720\pi) = 0.0145 \angle -87.5° \text{ V}$.

**Time-domain output.**    Equation (9.45) gives the time-domain output voltage by converting each harmonic to a sinusoidal time function.

**The Time Domain**

$$v_{out}(t) = 5.73 + 2.31 \cos(120\pi t - 75.1°) + 0.502 \cos(240\pi t - 82.4°)$$

$$+ 0.0505 \cos(480\pi t + 93.8°) + 0.0145 \cos(720\pi t - 87.5°) + \cdots \text{ V} \tag{9.45}$$

From Eq. (9.45) and Fig. 9.22, the results of the filtering are apparent:[13]   no loss of dc but substantial reduction of the fundamental and higher harmonics.

## Bode Plots

**dB, Bode plot**

**Decibels of gain.**    The gain of amplifiers and the loss of filters are frequently specified in decibels, dB. This unit refers to a logarithmic measure of the ratio of output power to input power, as defined in

$$\text{Gain} = 10 \log\left(\frac{P_{out}}{P_{in}}\right) \text{ dB} \tag{9.46}$$

Because the power gain is proportional to the square of the voltage gain, the voltage gain in dB is defined to be

$$\text{Gain} = 10 \log\left|\frac{\underline{V}_{out}}{\underline{V}_{in}}\right|^2 = 20 \log\left|\frac{\underline{V}_{out}}{\underline{V}_{in}}\right| \text{ dB} \tag{9.47}$$

---

[13] Figure 9.22 includes only the five harmonics written in Eq. (9.45). If more harmonics were included, the curve would be smoother.

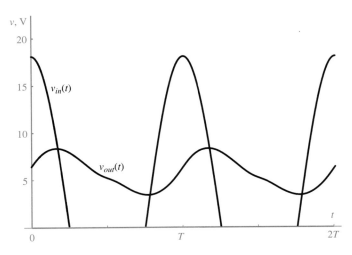

**Figure 9.22** The low-pass filter passes the dc but reduces the harmonics.

We note in comparing Eqs. (9.46) and (9.47) that power ratios require a factor of 10 in the dB calculation and voltage ratios a factor of 20.

---

**EXAMPLE 9.7** | **dB of gain**

An audio preamplifier gives an output voltage of 500 mV with an input of 10 mV. Find the dB gain of the amplifier.

**SOLUTION:**
Using Eq. (9.47), we find

$$G_{dB} = 20 \log \left( \frac{500}{10} \right) = 34.0 \, \text{dB} \tag{9.48}$$

**WHAT IF?** What if the input impedance level is 47 kΩ and the output impedance level is 1000 Ω?[14]

---

**Loss in dB.** A loss can also be described by Eq. (9.47), but the "dB gain" is negative for a loss: for example, the gain of a low-pass filter [Eq. (9.36)] at $\omega = \omega_c$ was shown to be $1/\sqrt{2}$; Eq. (9.47) yields

$$G_{dB} = 20 \log \left| \frac{\mathbf{V}_{out}}{\mathbf{V}_{in}} \right|_{\omega = \omega_c} = 20 \log |\mathbf{F}(\omega_c)| = 20 \log \frac{1}{\sqrt{2}} = -3.0 \, \text{dB} \tag{9.49}$$

---

[14] Then the dB of voltage gain is the same but the dB of power gain is 50.7 dB.

Thus, we could say that the gain of the filter at its half-power frequency is negative 3.0 dB or, equivalently, that its loss is 3.0 dB. For this reason, the critical frequency of a filter is often called its 3-*dB frequency* or *half-power frequency.*

The dB scale is also useful for expressing the power in a signal. In this context, the power is expressed as a logarithmic ratio between the signal power and an assumed power level, usually 1 W or 1 mW. Thus dBw, dB relative to 1 W, is defined as

$$\text{dBw} = 10 \log \frac{P}{1 \text{ watt}} \tag{9.50}$$

where $P$ is a power and dBw is that same power relative to 1 W, expressed in dB. Similarly, dBm normalizes signal power to a milliwatt, expressed in dB.

---

**EXAMPLE 9.8** | **Satellite transmitter**

A satellite transmitter has an output power of 1000 W. Express this power in dBw.

**SOLUTION:**
From Eq. (9.50), this power would be

$$\text{dBw} = 10 \log \frac{1000\text{W}}{1\text{W}} = 30 \text{ dBw} \tag{9.51}$$

**WHAT IF?** What if you want it in dBm?[15]

---

**Why dB is useful.** There are three reasons why electrical engineers use the dB scale for describing gains, losses, and signal levels. First, because of the compressive nature of the logarithmic function, the numbers involved in a dB calculation are quite moderate compared to a linear scale. This feature of dB measure is particularly useful when plotting quantities that vary greatly in magnitude.

**cascaded systems** **Cascaded systems.** The second virtue of dB measure is that the dB gains add when a signal is passed through cascaded systems. Figure 9.23 shows an amplifier *cascaded* with a filter, meaning that the output of the amplifier is the input to the filter. The combined voltage gain of the cascaded system is

$$\left| \frac{\mathbf{V}_3}{\mathbf{V}_1} \right| = \left| \frac{\mathbf{V}_2}{\mathbf{V}_1} \right| \times \left| \frac{\mathbf{V}_3}{\mathbf{V}_2} \right| = A \times |\mathbf{F}(\omega)| \tag{9.52}$$

where $A$ is the voltage gain of the amplifier. The dB gain of the cascaded system is

---

[15]60 dBm. In general, dBw = dBm −30 dB.

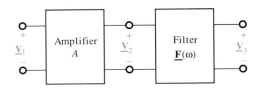

Figure **9.23** Cascaded systems. The output of the amplifier is the input to the filter.

$$G_{dB} = 20 \log \left| \frac{\mathbf{V}_3}{\mathbf{V}_1} \right| = 20 \log A + 20 \log |\mathbf{F}(\omega)|$$
$$= A_{dB} + F_{dB}$$

(9.53)

where $A_{dB}$ is the gain of the amplifier in dB and $F_{dB}$ is the gain of the filter in dB. Thus, dB gains add for cascaded systems. This feature results from the familiar technique for multiplying numbers by adding their logarithms. In these days of calculators, this adding of dB gains seems no great benefit, but the custom of using dB became universal among electrical engineers in an earlier day and will no doubt continue in the future.

**OBJECTIVE 4**

**To understand how to describe filters with Bode plots**

**Bode plots.** A third virtue of dB measure involves a special way of plotting the characteristic of a filter, amplifier, or spectrum. The Bode plot (named for H. W. Bode, 1905–1982) is a log power versus log frequency plot. For example, Fig. 9.24 shows the Bode plot of the function:

$$\mathbf{A}(f) = \frac{100}{1 + j(f/10)}$$

(9.54)

which combines an amplifier (voltage gain of $100 = 40$ dB) with a low-pass filter ($f_c = 10$ Hz). In Fig. 9.24, the vertical axis is proportional to log power expressed in dB. The horizontal axis expresses frequency on a log scale, although normally the frequency (not the logarithm of the frequency) is marked on the graph, as in Fig. 9.24. The log plot gives equal spacing on the graph to equal ratios of frequency—1:10, 10:100, etc.

**decade**

**Advantages of Bode plots.** The Bode plot is useful in two ways. As mentioned earlier, the log scales allow the representation of a wide range of both power and frequency. In this case, the vertical scale of 0 to 40 dB represents a range of power gain from 1 to $10^4$, or a voltage gain from 1 to 100. Similarly, the horizontal scale represents

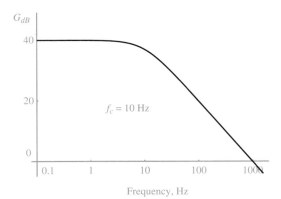

Figure **9.24** Bode plot.

four *decades*, factors of 10, in frequency. These wide ranges are possible because of the compressive nature of the logarithmic function.

**asymptotic Bode plot**
The other advantage of the Bode plot is that a filter characteristic can often be well represented by straight lines. The straight lines are evident in Fig. 9.24: The characteristic is quite flat for frequencies well below $f_c = 10$, and slopes downward with constant slope for frequencies well above this value. Only in the vicinity of $f_c$ does the exact Bode plot depart significantly from these straight lines. In the following section we examine in more detail the relationship between the exact Bode plot and the straight-line approximation, which is called the *asymptotic Bode plot*.

**Bode plot for a low-pass filter.** As shown in Eq. (9.36), the low-pass filter has the characteristic

$$\mathbf{F}(f) = \frac{1}{1 + j(f/f_c)} \tag{9.55}$$

The Bode plot represents the magnitude of the voltage gain and hence requires the absolute value

$$F_{dB}(f) = 20 \log \left| \frac{1}{1 + j(f/f_c)} \right| = 20 \log \frac{1}{\sqrt{1 + (f/f_c)^2}}$$

$$= -10 \log \left[ 1 + \left( \frac{f}{f_c} \right)^2 \right] \tag{9.56}$$

We may generate the exact Bode plot using normalized frequency $f/f_c$ for numerical calculation, Fig. 9.25(a), as shown in Fig. 9.25(b), where we show that the exact Bode plot approaches a straight line above and below the cutoff frequency, $f/f_c = 1$. At the cutoff frequency, the filter gain is −3.0 dB, as noted earlier.

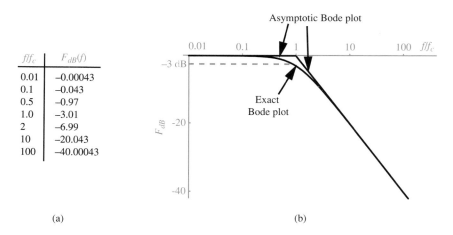

| $f/f_c$ | $F_{dB}(f)$ |
|---------|-------------|
| 0.01 | −0.00043 |
| 0.1 | −0.043 |
| 0.5 | −0.97 |
| 1.0 | −3.01 |
| 2 | −6.99 |
| 10 | −20.043 |
| 100 | −40.00043 |

(a)                                                                        (b)

**Figure 9.25** (a) Exact calculations; (b) Bode plot for the low-pass filter.

**Asymptotic Bode plots.** We may derive the asymptotic Bode plot by taking the limiting forms of Eq. (9.56). For frequencies well below the cutoff frequency, $f \ll f_c$, the gain is approximately

$$F_{dB} \approx -10 \log(1 + \text{small}) \approx -10 \log(1) = 0 \qquad (f \ll f_c) \qquad (9.57)$$

This accounts for the flat section. For frequencies well above the cutoff frequency, the gain approaches

$$F_{dB} \rightarrow -10 \log\left(\frac{f}{f_c}\right)^2 = -20 \log f + 20 \log f_c \qquad (f \gg f_c) \qquad (9.58)$$

Recalling that our horizontal variable is $\log f$, we see that Eq. (9.58) has the form of a straight line, $y = mx + b$, where $m = -20$, $x$ is $\log f$, and $b$ is $20 \log f_c$. Thus, the high-frequency asymptote will be a straight line when plotted against log frequency. When $\log f = \log f_c$, the $y$ of the straight line has zero value and hence the line passes through the horizontal axis at $f = f_c$. The slope is –20: Usually, we say that the slope is negative 20 dB/decade because dB of gain and decades of frequency are the units for a Bode plot.

The low- and high-frequency asymptotes of the exact Bode plot combine to form the asymptotic Bode plot. As shown in Fig. 9.25(b), the exact Bode plot is well represented by this approximation, the largest error being –3.0 dB at the cutoff frequency. For most applications, the asymptotic Bode plot gives an adequate picture of the filter characteristics.

---

| **EXAMPLE 9.9** | **Low-pass filter** |
|---|---|

An analog data acquisition system has a low-pass filter with a cutoff ($-3$ dB) frequency of 50 Hz. From the asymptotic Bode plot, find the frequency where the gain is $-6$ dB.

**SOLUTION:**
This is in the part of the characteristic described by Eq. (9.58)

$$-6 = 20 \log f + 20 \log 50$$
$$20 \log f = 39.98 \implies f = (10)^{1.999} = 99.76 \text{ Hz} \qquad (9.59)$$

**WHAT IF?**    What if you use the exact Bode plot?[16]

---

**high-pass filter**

**High-pass filter.** Figure 9.26 shows a high-pass filter, which blocks low frequencies and passes high frequencies. The filter characteristic can be determined by considering the circuit as a voltage divider in the frequency domain

---

[16] The exact $-6$ dB frequency is 86.33 Hz.

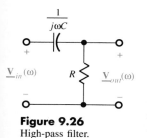

**Figure 9.26**
High-pass filter.

$$\mathbf{F}(\omega) = \frac{\mathbf{V}_{out}(\omega)}{\mathbf{V}_{in}(\omega)} = \frac{R}{R + 1/j\omega C} = \frac{j\omega RC}{1 + j\omega RC} = \frac{j(f/f_c)}{1 + j(f/f_c)} \qquad (9.60)$$

where $f_c = 1/2\pi RC$ is the cutoff frequency.

**How the filter works.** At low frequencies, $f \ll f_c$, the capacitor has a high impedance and allows little current; hence, little voltage develops across the resistor. Indeed, at zero frequency, dc, the capacitor acts as an open circuit and no voltage appears at the output. At high frequencies, $f \gg f_c$, the capacitor impedance is low, and essentially all the voltage appears across the resistor. Consequently, the filter passes high frequencies and blocks low frequencies. The transition between these two regimes occurs when the impedance of the capacitor is comparable to that of the resistor, and the cutoff frequency occurs where they are equal, as given again by Eq. (9.35).

**Asymptotic Bode plot for high-pass filter.** The asymptotic Bode plot for the filter function given in Eq. (9.60) may be derived by the same method used for the low-pass filter. The Bode plot is derived from the absolute value of the filter function,

$$F_{dB} = 20 \log \left| \frac{j(f/f_c)}{1 + j(f/f_c)} \right| = 20 \log \frac{f/f_c}{\sqrt{1 + (f/f_c)^2}} \qquad (9.61)$$

At frequencies well below the cutoff frequency, the frequency term in the denominator can be neglected and the asymptote becomes

$$F_{dB} = 20 \log \frac{f}{f_c} = 20 \log f - 20 \log f_c \qquad (9.62)$$

Plotted against $\log f$, this is a straight line with a slope of +20 dB/decade, passing through the horizontal axis at $f = f_c$, as shown in Fig. 9.27. For high frequencies, the filter function approaches unity, or 0 dB, also shown in Fig. 9.27. The exact Bode plot for the filter combines these two asymptotes and makes a smooth transition near the cutoff frequency. At the cutoff frequency, the exact Bode plot lies 3 dB below the intersection of the low- and high-frequency asymptotes.

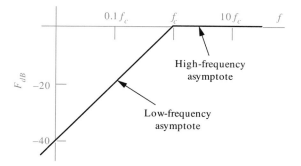

**Figure 9.27** Asymptotic Bode plot for a high-pass filter.

**Combining filter characteristics.** Figure 9.28 shows a combination of a low-pass filter, an amplifier, and a high-pass filter. As derived in Eq. (9.53) and shown in

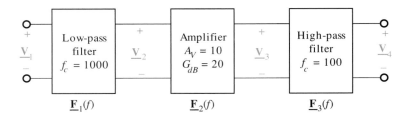

$$\underline{F}(f) = \underline{F}_1(f) \times \underline{F}_2(f) \times \underline{F}_3(f)$$

$$G_{dB} = F_{1(dB)} + G_{2(dB)} + F_{3(dB)}$$

**Figure 9.28**  Two filters and an amplifier in cascade.

Fig. 9.28, the dB gain of cascaded circuits is the sum of the dB gain of the components:

$$G_{dB} = F_{1(dB)}(f) + G_{2(dB)}(f) + F_{3(dB)}(f) \qquad (9.63)$$

**band-pass filter**

where $G_{dB}$ is the dB gain of the system. Thus, the Bode plots add to give the combined Bode plot of the cascaded system. Figure 9.29 shows the effect of adding up the individual Bode plots. The amplifier has a constant gain of 20 dB and raises the sum of the filter Bode plots by that amount. The high-pass filter blocks the low frequencies, and the low-pass filter blocks the high frequencies. The result is a *band-pass filter*; the "band" being passed in this case contains the frequencies between 100 and 1000 Hz. Thus, we combine filter effects by adding the Bode plots.

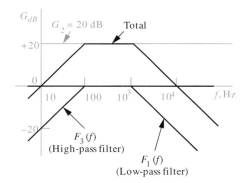

**Figure 9.29**  Adding Bode plots.

---

**EXAMPLE 9.10**  **Band-pass filter**

A band-pass filter for an audio equalizer is created by combining a low-pass filter with a cutoff frequency of 2 kHz with a high-pass filter with a cutoff of 1 kHz. What is the gain in dB at 1.5 kHz?

**SOLUTION:**
From the asymptotic Bode plots, we must say 0 dB. But the exact value from Eq. (9.60) and (9.36) is

$$G_{dB} = -20 \log \frac{1.5/1}{\sqrt{1 + (1.5/1)^2}} - 10 \log [1 + (1.5/2)^2]$$

$$= -1.60 - 1.94 = -3.54 \text{ dB}$$

(9.64)

Thus, this filter does not work well when the relative bandwidth is not large.

**A narrow-band RLC filter.** As shown before, we can produce a filter to pass the frequencies in a certain band by combining high-pass and low-pass *RC* filters. This approach works well only when the relative passband of frequencies is rather large. However, most communication systems, such as radios, require filters that pass a narrow band of frequencies. This is normally accomplished with *RLC* filters, such as appears in Fig. 9.30. This particular *RLC* filter produces a parallel resonance between the inductor and capacitor at about 1125 kHz, which is near the middle of the AM radio band. The resistance shown in parallel with the inductor is not present in the physical circuit but is placed in the circuit model to represent the losses of the inductor. For frequencies far away from the resonant frequency, the impedance of either the inductor or the capacitor becomes small and the filter response drops. At the resonant frequency, the inductance and capacitance resonate and the output is maximum.

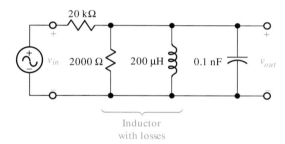

Inductor
with losses

**Figure 9.30** *RLC* band-pass filter.

Figure 9.31 shows the band-pass characteristics of this filter in linear and dB scales. It might be noted that this filter has an inherent loss, even at its maximum output, $-20.8$ dB in this case. Thus, such a filter must be used in conjunction with an amplifier to compensate for this loss. This is no disadvantage in most communication circuits, for the radio already must provide considerable amplification—this merely requires a bit more. We might mention in closing this section that the filter characteristic of the *RLC* filter in Fig. 4.41 is similar to that in Fig. 9.30. The parallel form of the filter is accomplished more easily in electronic circuits with realistic inductors and capacitors, and hence this is the form of narrow-band filter commonly used in radios. In Chapter 11, after we discuss the properties of nonlinear circuits, we discuss the role of such filters in typical radio circuits.

### Check Your Understanding

1. A filter normally changes the phase as well as the amplitude spectrum of the input signal. (True or False?)

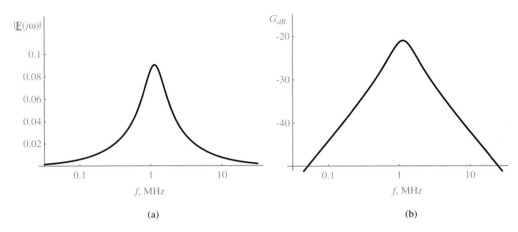

**Figure 9.31**   Narrow-band *RLC* filter characteristics:   (a) linear plot; (b) dB plot.

**2.** An *RC* high-pass filter passes a dc signal. (True or false?)

**3.** If one decade is a factor of 10, what ratio corresponds to one-fourth of a decade?

**4.** If the input to an amplifier is 5 mW and the output is 0.1 W, what is its gain in dB if input and output impedance levels are the same?

**5.** If an amplifier reduces the signal voltage by a factor of 4, what is its gain in dB?

*Answers.*  **(1)** True;   **(2)** false;   **(3)** 1.778;   **(4)** 13.0 dB;   **(5)** −12.0 dB.

## 9.3  FEEDBACK CONCEPTS

**feedback**

**Introduction to feedback.**   *Feedback* brings a sample of the output back to the input of an amplifier, device, or composite system.  The feedback signal is combined with the input signal to modify the input/output characteristics of the system.  This technique, first proposed by Harold S. Black in 1928, has profoundly affected the development of electronics, for reasons that are explained in this section.

We first examine feedback effects with an amplifier and then generalize to a system model.  The many benefits of feedback are discussed.  Section 9.4 shows how feedback is used with operational amplifiers to achieve a family of circuits useful for amplification and signal processing generally.

### A Feedback Amplifier

**OBJECTIVE 5**

**To understand the nature and benefits of feedback**

**Feedback**

**Amplifier with feedback.**   Figure 9.32 shows an amplifier that has been modified from straight amplification by having a sample of the output brought back to interact with the input as a feedback signal.  The main amplifier is represented by the top box: its input, $v_i$, and its output, $v_{out}$, are related by the main amplifier gain $A$, as indicated in the box. We assume an ideal amplifier with $A$ real and positive, infinite input impedance, and zero output impedance.  In the main amplifier, the signal goes from left to right.

A feedback circuit, represented by the bottom box, consists in this example of two resistors arranged as a voltage divider.  In the feedback circuit, the signal goes from

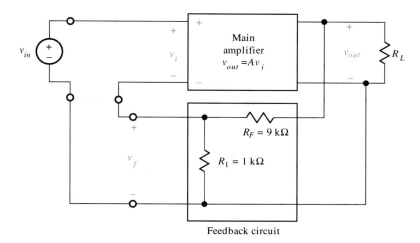

**Figure 9.32** Amplifier employing feedback.

right to left, from the output of the main amplifier back to its input. The input to the feedback circuit is $v_{out}$ and its output is $v_f$.

A voltage source, $v_{in}$, is located at the input to the entire "amplifier with feedback," that is, the entire system, feedback and all. The output of the feedback circuit, $v_f$, is part of the input loop, which also contains the voltage source and the input to the main amplifier.

**Analysis of amplifier gain.** We calculate the gain of the amplifier with feedback, $A_f$, which is the ratio of the output to the source voltage:

$$A_f = \frac{v_{out}}{v_{in}} \tag{9.65}$$

We can write three equations describing the system. They are as follows:

**1.** Definition of the main amplifier:

$$v_{out} = Av_i \tag{9.66}$$

**2.** Voltage divider for the feedback circuit:

$$v_f = \frac{R_1}{R_1 + R_F} v_{out} \tag{9.67}$$

**3.** KVL around the input loop:

$$-v_{in} + v_i + v_f = 0 \tag{9.68}$$

Equations (9.66) through (9.68) give us three equations relating four voltages. We can eliminate two voltages between the equations, reducing to one equation in two voltages. We require the ratio of $v_{out}$ to $v_{in}$ for computing the gain in Eq. (9.65), so we eliminate

$v_f$ and $v_i$. Some straightforward algebra produces

$$A_f = \frac{A(R_1 + R_F)}{R_1 + R_F + R_1 A} = \frac{A}{1 + [R_1/(R_1 + R_F)]A} \qquad (9.69)$$

Equation (9.69) exemplifies a more general relationship that we develop presently. We conclude from Eq. (9.69) that the gain with feedback, $A_f$, is smaller than the gain without feedback, $A$. Having lost gain, what have we achieved? Answer: We have improved the reliability, linearity, bandwidth, and impedance characteristics of the amplifier. We verify these benefits later in this section. First, we investigate how feedback works.

**Signal levels.**   We now examine the signal levels for the amplifier with feedback in Fig. 9.32 to get a picture of how feedback works. The gain of the main amplifier is $A = 200$ and the feedback circuit consists of $R_F = 9 \text{ k}\Omega$ in series with $R_1 = 1 \text{ k}\Omega$. According to Eq. (9.69), the gain of the amplifier with feedback is

$$A_f = \frac{200}{1 + [1 \text{ k}\Omega/(1 \text{ k}\Omega + 9 \text{ k}\Omega)](200)} = \frac{200}{1 + 20} = 9.52 \qquad (9.70)$$

We assume that the output voltage is 10 V and calculate the signal levels throughout the circuit. With 10 V at its output, the input voltage to the main amplifier, $v_i$, must be $10/200 = 0.050$ V. The input voltage to the entire amplifier is $v_{in} = 10/9.52 = 1.050$ V. The output of the feedback circuit, $v_f$, is

$$v_f = \frac{R_1}{R_1 + R_F} v_{out} = \frac{1 \text{ k}\Omega}{1 \text{ k}\Omega + 9 \text{ k}\Omega}(10) = 1.000 \text{ V} \qquad (9.71)$$

Hence, we confirm KVL around the input loop: $v_{in} = v_f + v_i$.

The calculation performed in the preceding paragraph moves from the output back to the input. The signal goes the other way, so let us think of the operation of the amplifier in time sequence. We apply 1.050 V at the input at some instant of time. Electronic circuits respond quickly but not instantaneously; hence the output signal at this initial instant is zero. Thus, the feedback voltage, $v_f$, is at first zero and the entire 1.050-V input appears at the main amplifier input, $v_i$. This signal is amplified by the main amplifier and the output voltage increases toward $200 \times 1.050$; but as the output increases, so does the feedback signal. Because the feedback signal subtracts from the 1.050-V input, the input voltage to the main amplifier diminishes as the output voltage rises. Thus, we have competing effects: The higher the output voltage rises, the more voltage feeds back and the more the input voltage to the main amplifier is reduced. In equilibrium, the feedback signal subtracts 1.000 V from the input voltage of 1.050 V and the remaining 0.050 V is amplified by the main amplifier to yield an output voltage of 10 V.

## System Model

sampling
connection

**System notation.**   A system representation of the feedback amplifier is shown in Fig. 9.33. This representation is characterized by the various blocks and circles connected with lines representing signal flow. Although our signals are voltages, customarily denoted with $v$'s, we have used a neutral symbol $x$ to denote the signals on the

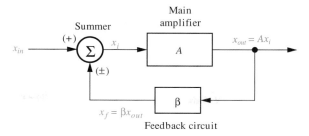

**Figure 9.33** System representation of feedback.

system diagram of Fig. 9.33. Use of a neutral symbol emphasizes that the *signal*, not the physical variable that represents the signal, is of primary importance from the system viewpoint. At some places in the system, the signal might be represented by a voltage, at others a current, at yet others a pressure or the physical displacement of a mechanical component. The system representation embraces such hybrid systems.

**System components.** We show four system components in Fig. 9.33. The main amplifier and the feedback circuit are obvious carryovers from the original formulation of the amplifier except that here we allow $A$ and $\beta$ to be negative. The direction of signal flow is indicated with arrowheads. At the output, we show a means for *sampling* the output; this represents the parallel connection to the output of the main amplifier. In other feedback arrangements, the feedback network might be placed in series with the load and main amplifier output; with this arrangement, the feedback network would sample the output current. Both possibilities are covered by the dot at the output.

**summer, comparator**

**Summer.** At the input, there is a circle containing a summation symbol to represent the *summer*, which represents the interaction of signals at the input of the system. In our previous example, this circle represents KVL in Eq. (9.68), which can be put into the form

$$v_i = + v_{in} - v_f \tag{9.72}$$

where the $+$ and $-$ signs on the summer in Fig. 9.33 are associated with the input and the feedback signals, respectively. We may think of the summer as having a gain of $+1$ for $v_{in}$ and a gain of $-1$ for $v_f$. The summer thus works as a differencer or subtractor in this case, but the symbol covers both possibilities, as indicated by the $+$ and $-$ signs. In other contexts, the summer at the input might be called a *comparator* because it compares the input with a sample of the output, furnishing the difference as input to the main amplifier.

**Analysis of the system.** The equations of the system are as follows:

**1.** Main amplifier:

$$x_{out} = Ax_i \tag{9.73}$$

**2.** Feedback circuit:

$$x_f = \beta x_{out} \tag{9.74}$$

**3.** Summer:

$$x_i = x_{in} \pm x_f \qquad (9.75)$$

In Eq. (9.75), we used a gain of $+1$ for the input signal but allowed for either $+1$ or $-1$ for the feedback signal. As before, we can eliminate two of the variables and solve for the ratio of the output and input signals to obtain the gain with feedback.

$$A_f = \frac{x_{out}}{x_{in}} = \frac{A}{1 - (\pm 1)(\beta)(A)} \qquad (9.76)$$

Equation (9.76) reduces to our earlier result, Eq. (9.69), when the minus sign is used for the summer and $R_1/(R_1 + R_F)$ is used for $\beta$.

**Loop gain.**   Another form for Eq. (9.76) is

$$A_f = \frac{A}{1 - L} \qquad (9.77)$$

**loop gain**

where $L = (\pm 1)(\beta)(A)$ is called the loop gain. The *loop gain* is the product of the gains of all the system components around the feedback loop, including signs. The basic idea of the loop gain is suggested in Fig. 9.34. To calculate or measure the loop gain, break the feedback loop at some convenient point, insert a test signal, $x_t$, and calculate or measure the return signal, $x_r$. The loop gain is the ratio $L = x_r/x_t$. The loop may be broken, both in analysis and in the laboratory, only at a point where the function of the various system components is unimpaired. Care must be taken to terminate the break with the same impedance as the circuit saw before the break. For example, it would be inconvenient in the circuit in Fig. 9.32 to open the loop between $R_F$ and $R_1$.

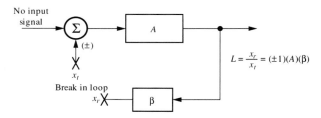

**Figure 9.34**   Determining the loop gain by breaking the loop at some point, inserting a test signal, and measuring the return signal.

**Loop gain**

What is the loop gain of the amplifier in Fig. 9.32?

**SOLUTION:**
The gain of the summer is $-1$, so the loop gain is

$$L = (-1)(A)(\beta) = -200 \times \frac{1}{10} = -20 \qquad (9.78)$$

Comparison of Eqs. (9.70) and (9.77) confirms this value.

**WHAT IF?** What if the voltage divider were eliminated and the output connected directly back to the input? Find the loop gain and the gain with feedback.[17]

**negative feedback, positive feedback**

**Sign of the loop gain.** The sign of the loop gain indicates the nature of the feedback. Negative loop gain indicates negative feedback. With *negative feedback*, the feedback signal subtracts from the input signal and the gain is reduced. Positive loop gain indicates *positive feedback* and is rarely used. Positive feedback increases the amplifier gain; indeed, for $L = +1$, the gain becomes infinite. This condition is used in the design of electronic oscillators, which can be considered amplifiers with output but no input.

**Magnitude of the loop gain.** The magnitude of the loop gain indicates the importance of feedback in influencing the system characteristics. When the magnitude of the loop gain is much larger than unity, the system properties are controlled largely by feedback considerations. We illustrate the importance of loop gain in the next section.

## Benefits of Negative Feedback

**static stability**

**Improved static stability.** By *static stability* we mean insensitivity[18] of performance to changes in the system parameters. For instance, in our earlier example, the gain of the main amplifier might decrease due to the deterioration of a circuit component or replacement of a transistor. Assume the gain of the main amplifier decreases from 200 to 100. Without feedback, this change might jeopardize the usefulness of the amplifier. With feedback, however, the new gain, $A_f'$, becomes

$$A_f' = \frac{100}{1 - (-1)(0.1)(100)} = 9.09 \qquad (9.79)$$

Thus, a 50% decrease in the gain of the main amplifier results in a 5% decrease in the overall gain of the system. We can see from Eq. (9.77) the cause of this robustness. When the magnitude of the loop gain is much greater that unity, the gain with feedback is approximately

$$A_f = \frac{A}{1 - L} \approx \frac{A}{-L} = \frac{A}{-(-1)(\beta)(A)} = \frac{1}{\beta} \qquad (9.80)$$

We see that, as loop gain increases, the gain with feedback approaches a value determined by $\beta$. Thus, the reduction of the main amplifier gain has little effect as long as the loop gain remains much larger than unity. The value of $\beta$ could depend on resistors only, as in Fig. 9.32, and thus be stable over long periods of time. In our example the reciprocal of $\beta$ is 10, and we see that the gain of the system, both before and after the gain decrease, falls close to this value. Often in a practical system, the main amplifier

---

[17]$L = -200, A_f = 0.995.$
[18]Could also be called robustness or immunity to change.

merely provides sufficient gain to keep the loop gain much larger than unity, for in this case, the $\beta$ of the feedback circuit determines the overall gain with feedback.

We used the word "static" to distinguish this type of stability from *dynamic stability*, the tendency of the system to vibrate or oscillate under the influence of external stimuli. With a bridge, for example, the static stability might be good, meaning that the bridge footings are sound and the bridge members are sufficiently stiff to hold the bridge solidly in place. But under the influence of traffic or wind, the bridge might shake and even collapse, as did the Tacoma Narrows bridge in 1940, and hence exhibit poor dynamic stability.

Although negative feedback improves static stability, feedback can cause dynamic instability in a system. Time delays, or the frequency-domain equivalent, phase shift, can convert negative feedback to positive feedback and hence cause dynamic instability or oscillations. This aspect of feedback theory is discussed in Chapter 12.

---

**EXAMPLE 9.12** **Static stability**

How large does the loop gain have to be such that a 10% change in main amplifier gain causes a 1% change in overall gain?

**SOLUTION:**

Let $A' = 0.9\,A$, which gives $L' = 0.9L$. Then

$$A'_f = 0.99 \times \frac{A}{1-L} = \frac{A'}{1-L'} = \frac{0.9A}{1-0.9L} \Rightarrow L = -10 \qquad (9.81)$$

**WHAT IF?** What if the loop gain is –50? What is the change in overall gain with feedback if $A$ changes by 10%?[19]

---

**Improved linearity.** Semiconductor devices such as transistors can be fairly linear in their active regions if signal variations are kept small, but large signals are often required. For example, the output amplifier in an audio system must produce a large signal to drive the speakers. Without feedback, such an amplifier would exhibit substantial distortion, but feedback techniques can be used to improve the linearity of the amplifier and thus reduce the distortion.

Equation (9.80) suggests how this is accomplished. The main amplifier introduces distortion into the system. If the loop gain is high, the system gain is determined by the $\beta$ of the feedback circuit, which depends on two resistors and not directly on the main amplifier gain. The resistors are linear components; hence, the amplifier with feedback produces minimal distortion if the loop gain is high. Thus, a large loop gain is always used when good linearity is required for large-signal amplification.

---

[19] The change is 2.17%.

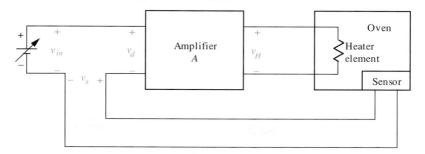

**Figure 9.35** Oven controller.

**Disturbance reduction.** Feedback can reduce unavoidable disturbances that enter a system. As an example, we consider the thermostatically controlled oven shown in Fig. 9.35. The input voltage to the system is compared with a voltage from a temperature sensor in the oven. The difference, $v_d$, is amplified and applied to a heater element, $v_H$. We analyze the static characteristics here and the dynamic characteristics in Chapter 12.

A simplified system diagram is shown in Fig. 9.36. The heater element has been represented as a box having a gain $A_H$, which is defined as the change in box temperature divided by the change in the heater voltage. Although the relationship between heat (power) and voltage is nonlinear for simplicity, we are treating small changes as linear effects. The oven temperature is influenced both by the internal heater and by the ambient temperature, whose changes represent a disturbance in the system. This effect is represented with a summer. The sensor is also represented by a gain factor, $A_S$, which would represent changes in sensor output voltage divided by changes in oven temperature.

The loop gain of the system is

$$L = -AA_H A_S \qquad (9.82)$$

Thus the relationship between oven temperature and input voltage is

$$T_{oven} = v_{in} \times \frac{AA_H}{1 - L} \qquad (9.83)$$

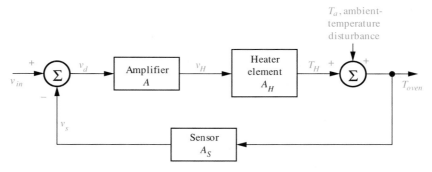

**Figure 9.36** System diagram for oven controller.

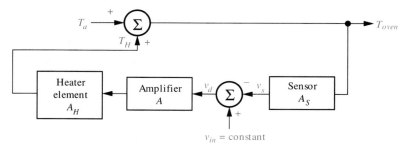

**Figure 9.37**  System diagram for controller with $T_a$ as input.

**Disturbance signal.**  Because we modeled the system as a linear system, we can use superposition to study the effect of the ambient temperature.  The disturbance signal, $T_a$, thus represents a second input to the system. We redraw the system diagram in Fig. 9.37 to clarify this role. Considering the gain of the summer to be +1, we can determine a relationship between ambient and oven temperature:

$$T_{oven} = T_a \frac{1}{1 - L} \tag{9.84}$$

where the loop gain, $L$, is the same as before.  We want a large loop gain to reduce the effect of changes in the ambient temperature.

---

**EXAMPLE 9.13** | **Loop gain**

Find the loop gain in the oven such that a $10°$ change in ambient temperature would cause a $0.1°$ change in oven temperature.

**SOLUTION:**
Interpreting Eq. (9.84) to apply to differences in temperature, we have

$$0.1° = 10° \times \frac{1}{1-L} \quad \Rightarrow \quad L = -99 \tag{9.85}$$

---

The effect of ambient temperature can be reduced to low levels, provided the system can be stabilized dynamically. This system is analyzed in greater detail in Chapter 12.

**Improved response time.**  Negative feedback can improve the response time of a system. Consider, for example, an electrical relay, as shown in Fig. 9.38. A relay is an electromagnet; when current passes through the coil, a magnetic force is produced at the gap and the lever closes against a spring. Such relays are used typically to activate switches and to operate locks and valves. We now analyze a relay having the following properties:

**relay**

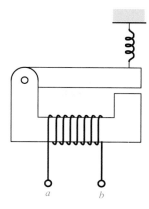

**Figure 9.38** Relay.

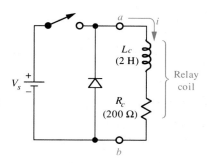

**Figure 9.39** Controlling circuit.

Current required to activate = 20 mA

Maximum current = 30 mA

Coil resistance, $R_c = 200\ \Omega$

Coil inductance, $L_c = 2$ H.

**Relay circuit.** A suitable circuit for energizing the relay is shown in Fig. 9.39. When the relay is to be activated, the switch is closed. Current, initially at $i_0 = 0$, increases exponentially toward a final value of $i_\infty = V_s/R_c$. As current builds up, the relay closes as the current exceeds 20 mA.

---

**EXAMPLE 9.14** | **Relay circuit design**

Find the shortest time for relay closure without exceeding relay limitations.

**SOLUTION:**

To close the relay as quickly as possible, the circuit requires a voltage source to be as large as possible. The voltage source is limited by the maximum current to be 30 mA × 200 $\Omega$ = 6 V. With that value of voltage, the time required for the relay to close is easily shown to be $\tau \ln 3$, where $\tau = L_c/R_c$ is the time constant, 2H / 200 $\Omega$ = 10 ms. Hence, in this case, the relay closes about 11.0 ms after the switch is closed.

**WHAT IF?** What if a resistor were placed in series with the relay?[20]

---

**free-wheeling diode**

**Why the diode?** Throughout the period when the relay current is increasing, the diode remains OFF; but when the switch is opened, the inductor reacts to keep the current going. This causes the diode to conduct and the current flows for a time through coil

---

[20] That would shorten the time of closure but increases the required voltage and circuit losses.

and diode, even with the switch open. The diode is thus placed across the relay coil to deenergize the inductance.[21] Without the diode, a spark would appear at the switch contacts, as discussed on page 130.

**Using feedback.** Let us suppose that the 11-ms response time is too slow. We can use a feedback technique to improve the relay speed. As shown in Fig. 9.40, we add an ideal amplifier, with high input impedance and low output impedance and a resistor to the relay circuit. The current-sampling resistor, $R_s$, produces a feedback signal that is proportional to the current in the relay coil. After the switch is closed, the equations of the system are, for the amplifier

$$v_{out} = A (V_s - v_f) = A (V_s - iR_s) \qquad (9.86)$$

and for the coil and feedback resistor,

$$v_{out} = L_c \frac{di}{dt} + (R_c + R_s)i \qquad (9.87)$$

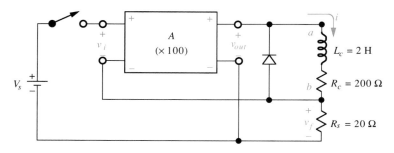

**Figure 9.40** Feedback circuit to improve response time. The 20-Ω resistor samples relay current and gives a feedback signal.

When we combine Eqs. (9.86) and (9.87), we obtain a differential equation describing the feedback system:

$$L_c \frac{di}{dt} + [R_c + (1 + A)R_s]i = AV_s \qquad (9.88)$$

which can be put into the standard form of Eq. (3.35):

$$\tau_f \frac{di}{dt} + i = \frac{AV_s}{R_c + (1 + A)R_s} \qquad (9.89)$$

where

$$\tau_f = \frac{L_c}{R_c + (1 + A)R_s} \qquad (9.90)$$

---

[21] This diode is called a *free-wheeling diode* because it allows the inductor current to continue after the source is removed.

This time constant with feedback is shorter than the original time constant. With the numerical values shown in Fig. 9.40, the time constant drops from 10 to 0.91 ms and the response time is reduced accordingly, from 11.0 to 1.0 ms.

---

**EXAMPLE 9.15** **Turn-off**

What is the turn-off time constant for the circuits shown in Figs. 9.39 and 9.40?

**SOLUTION:**
For the circuit of Fig. 9.39, the time constant with the switch is the same for turn on and turn off because the battery and ON diode are both low-impedance paths: $\tau = 10$ ms. When the input voltage is removed in the feedback circuit, both $v_{out}$ and $v_f$ drop instantly to zero and the inductor must deenergize through the free-wheeling diode as before. Thus, the turn-off time constant is 10 ms in both cases.

**WHAT IF?** What if you want to shorten the turn-off time constant by a factor of 10?[22]

---

**Improvement of frequency response.** As might be anticipated from the preceding example, and from the correspondence between the speed of response in the time domain and the bandwidth in the frequency domain, feedback can often improve the frequency response of a system. Let us reconsider the amplifier example in Fig. 9.32, except that we now introduce a bandwidth limitation to the main amplifier. We show the frequency-domain version of the circuit in Fig. 9.41, with the main amplifier now having a low-frequency gain of $A_0$ and a frequency cutoff of $\omega_c$.

$$A(\omega) = \frac{A_0}{1 + j(\omega/\omega_c)} \tag{9.91}$$

The main amplifier frequency response has the form of a low-pass filter, the loss of the high frequencies resulting from a limitation within the amplifier. This bandwidth limitation of the amplifier can be alleviated through negative feedback.

The equations of the system, Eqs. (9.66) to (9.68), transform into the frequency domain changed only in notation, and hence the amplifier characteristic with feedback becomes the frequency-domain version of Eq. (9.69):

$$\underline{A}_f(\omega) = \frac{A(\omega)}{1 + [R_1/(R_1 + R_F)]A(\omega)} = \frac{A_0/[1 + j(\omega/\omega_c)]}{1 + \beta A_0/[1 + j(\omega/\omega_c)]} \tag{9.92}$$

where $\beta = R_1/(R_1 + R_F)$. Equation (9.92) can be put into the form

$$\underline{A}_f(\omega) = \frac{A_0/(1 + \beta A_0)}{1 + j(\omega/\omega_{cf})} \tag{9.93}$$

---
[22] Then put an 1800-$\Omega$ resistor in series with the diode.

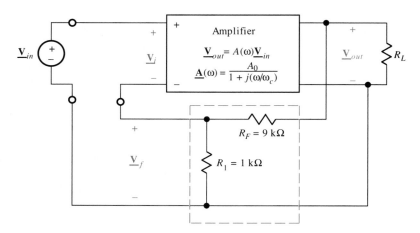

**Figure 9.41**   Improving bandwidth with feedback.

where $\omega_{cf} = (1 + \beta A_0)\omega_c$ is the cutoff frequency with feedback. Recognizing that the loop gain $L = -\beta A_0$, we see from Eq. (9.93) that the amplifier gain at low frequencies is reduced by the factor $1 - L$ and the cutoff frequency is increased by the same factor.

Bode plots for the amplifier with and without feedback are shown in Fig. 9.42. This application furnishes a good example of our claim that negative feedback trades gain for some other useful property. Here gain is exchanged for bandwidth. The inherent bandwidth limitation of the amplifier has been overcome through the use of negative feedback.

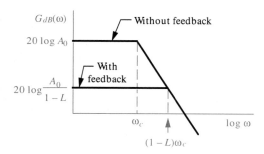

**Figure 9.42**   Feedback reduces gain but increases bandwidth.

We showed that negative feedback increases the bandwidth of a first-order system. Higher-order systems cannot always be improved by these means.

**Impedance Level**

**Impedance control.**   Feedback techniques can be used to change the impedance level of an electronic circuit. This is useful for reducing loading effects and for effecting maximum power transfer.

**common collector, emitter follower**

**Feedback analysis of emitter-follower circuit.**   The control of impedance levels through feedback is demonstrated by analyzing the *common collector*, or *emitter-follower*, circuit shown in Fig. 9.43. This amplifier is a variation on the amplifier-switch amplifier in Fig. 7.40 except that (1) the collector resistor is placed between the emitter

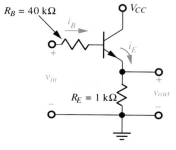

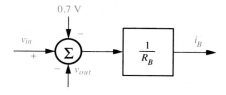

**Figure 9.43** For the common-collector or emitter-follower amplifier, the output is taken off the emitter.

**Figure 9.44** Ohm's law in the base-emitter circuit is represented by a summer and a scaler.

and ground and renamed $R_E$, and (2) the output is taken between the emitter and ground instead of the collector and ground.

**System analysis.** Our analysis considers only the active region, where the relationship between emitter and base currents from Eq. (7.22) is

$$i_E = (\beta + 1)i_B \qquad (9.94)$$

where $\beta$ is the current gain of the transistor. In the active region, $v_{BC} = 0.7$, so **KVL** around the base-emitter loop is

$$-v_{in} + R_B i_B + 0.7 + v_{out} = 0 \implies i_B = (v_{in} - 0.7 - v_{out}) \times \frac{1}{R_B} \qquad (9.95)$$

where we have written the equation for the base current to suggest a summer followed by a scaler box on a system diagram, Fig. 9.44. The remaining equations describing the circuit operation are Eq. (9.94) and Ohm's law for $R_E$: $v_{out} = R_E i_E$. All the emitter-follower equations are represented by the system diagram in Fig. 9.45.

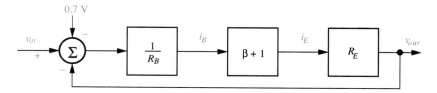

**Figure 9.45** System diagram for the emitter follower.

**Analysis of the system diagram.** We use Eq. (9.77):

$$A = \frac{1}{R_B} \times (\beta + 1) \times R_E$$

$$L = (-1)A \qquad (9.96)$$

$$A_f = \frac{A}{1 - L} = \frac{(\beta + 1)R_E/R_B}{1 + (\beta + 1)R_E/R_B}$$

Because our goal is to determine input and output impedance levels, we will ignore the effect of the 0.7-V term in Eq. (9.95), which merely describes a voltage offset in the output. For this goal, the gain with feedback is best expressed as a relationship between input and output voltages

$$v_{out} = v_{in} \times \frac{(\beta + 1)R_E/R_B}{1 + (\beta + 1)R_E/R_B} \tag{9.97}$$

**Input impedance.** The input impedance follows from Eq. (9.97) and the system diagram:

$$R_{in} = \frac{v_{in}}{i_B} = \frac{v_{out}/A_f}{v_{out}/(\beta + 1)R_E} = R_B(1 - L) = R_B + (\beta + 1)R_E \tag{9.98}$$

**Equivalent Circuits**

**Output impedance.** The output impedance can be derived from the open-circuit voltage and short-circuit current, as expressed in Eq. (2.22). The voltage calculated in Eq. (9.97) is the Thévenin voltage because no load is present at the output terminals. Thus, the open-circuit voltage is given by Eq. (9.97). The effect of shorting the output terminals can be seen from Fig. 9.43. Reducing $v_{out}$ to zero with the short kills the feedback and the Norton current flowing through the short will be the emitter current:

$$i_N = i_E\Big|_{v_{out} = 0} = v_{in} \times \frac{\beta + 1}{R_B} \tag{9.99}$$

Thus, the output impedance is

$$R_{eq} = \frac{v_T}{i_N} = \frac{v_{in} \times \dfrac{(\beta + 1)R_E/R_B}{1 - L}}{v_{in} \times (\beta + 1)/R_B} = \frac{R_E}{1 - L} \tag{9.100}$$

**Conclusions.** From the foregoing analysis, we conclude the following:

1. The feedback raises the input impedance from $R_B$ to $R_B \times (1 - L)$, Eq. (9.98). This change is desirable because a voltage amplifier with a large input impedance does not load its input source.

2. The final form of Eq. (9.98) shows that the transistor does not isolate the output circuit from the input circuit when the load is connected to the emitter. The input circuit looks through the emitter and sees the emitter resistor, increased by the current gain of the transistor, which is a feedback effect.

3. The output impedance is lowered from $R_E$ to $R_E/(1 - L)$. This is also a desirable change because a voltage amplifier should have low output impedance to avoid being loaded by its load and to have high available power.

4. The factor $1 - L$ appears in the gain, the input impedance, and the output impedance, underscoring the importance of this factor in all feedback calculations.

5. The feedback in this circuit is not introduced by bringing a connection from output to input, but occurs naturally in the circuit operation.

**6.** The analysis of the input and output impedances of an emitter-follower amplifier furnishes a good example of how circuit equations can be converted to system components such as summers and samplers. Once the conversion is made, the circuit can by analyzed by system techniques.

### Check Your Understanding

**1.** Sometimes the summer in a feedback system represents taking the difference, not the sum, of two signals. (True or false?)

**2.** For negative feedback, the loop gain must be positive or negative?

**3.** The loop gain is calculated or measured with the input source OFF. (True or false?)

**4.** If the loop gain in a feedback system is $-0.2$, feedback effects will not be very important in defining system characteristics. (True or false?)

**5.** Negative feedback, compounded with a phase shift in the loop, can cause dynamic instability. (True or false?)

*Answers.* **(1)** True; **(2)** negative; **(3)** true; **(4)** true; **(5)** true.

## 9.4 OPERATIONAL-AMPLIFIER CIRCUITS

### Introduction

**OBJECTIVE 6**

**To understand the importance and applications of op amps in analog circuits**

**operational amplifier, op amp**

**Importance of op amps.** An *operational amplifier*, *op amp* for short, is a high-gain electronic amplifier, normally controlled by negative feedback, that accomplishes many functions or "operations" in analog circuits. Such amplifiers were originally developed to accomplish operations such as integration and summation for solving differential equations with analog computers. Applications of op amps have increased until, at the present time, most analog electronic circuits are based on op-amp techniques. If, for example, you required an amplifier with a gain of $-10$, rarely would you design a circuit of the type in Fig. 7.48; convenience, reliability, and cost considerations dictate the use of an op amp. Thus, op amps form the basic building blocks of analog electronic circuits much as NOR and NAND gates provide the basic building blocks of digital circuits.

**Op-amp model and typical properties.** The typical op amp is a sophisticated transistor amplifier utilizing a dozen or more transistors, several diodes, many resistors, and perhaps a few capacitors. Such amplifiers are mass produced on semiconductor chips and sell for less than $1 each. These parts are reliable and rugged, approaching the ideal in their electronic properties.

Figure 9.46 (a) shows the symbol and the op-amp properties that interact with external signals. The two input signal voltages, $v_+$ and $v_-$, are subtracted and amplified with a large voltage gain, $A$, typically $10^5$ to $10^6$. The input resistance, $R_i$, is large, typically exceeding 10 MΩ; the output resistance, $R_{out}$, is small, 10 to 100 Ω. The amplifier is supplied with dc power from positive ($+V_{CC}$) and negative ($-V_{CC}$) power supplies. For this case, the output voltage lies between the power-supply voltages, as shown by Fig. 9.46 (b). Sometimes one power connection is grounded, for example, "$-V_{CC}$" = 0, in which case the output lies between 0 V and $+V_{CC}$. The power connections are seldom drawn on circuit diagrams.

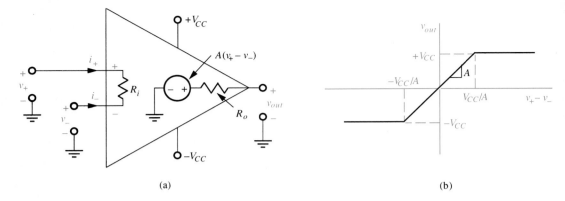

(a)

(b)

**Figure 9.46:** (a) Op-amp model. The amplifier circuit, whose details are omitted due to its complexity, has two dc power inputs, $V_{CC}$ and $-V_{CC}$, two signal inputs, $v_+$ and $v_-$, and one signal output, $v_{out}$; (b) input-output characteristic of an op amp. The sloped region is the amplifying region. The op amp saturates at the power-supply voltages.

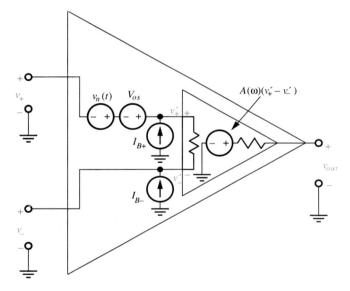

**Figure 9.47** An op amp has noise, offset voltage, bias currents, and limited bandwidth.

**Realistic op amps.** The model in Fig. 9.46 (a) approaches the ideal voltage amplifier: high input impedance, low output impedance, and high gain. Real op amps have these properties but also have undesirable features that limit their performance and influence circuit design. The circuit given in Fig. 9.47 models a number of the limitations of realistic op amps. These are as follows:

■ A dc offset voltage, $V_{os}$, is shown to indicate that the output of the op amp is nonzero with zero input voltage, that is, with $v_+ = v_-$.

■ Input dc bias currents, $I_{B+}$ and $I_{B-}$, are shown. Normally, these bias currents are expressed in terms of an offset bias current, $I_{os} = I_{B+} - I_{B-}$, and an average bias current $I_B = (I_{B+} + I_{B-})/2$.[23]

- A noise voltage, $v_n(t)$, represents broadband noise originating in the op amp. The magnitude of this noise is proportional to the square root of the bandwidth of the op amp in the circuit application, as discussed in Chapter 11.

- Gain–bandwidth limitation is indicated by making the op-amp gain $A(\omega)$, a function of frequency. The gain–bandwidth product is limited by inherent capacitance in the circuit and the semiconductor devices in the op amp, and often is deliberately limited by the chip designer to inhibit oscillations at high frequencies.

**Reducing the effects of op-amp imperfections.** The effect of dc offset voltage and current, $V_{os}$ and $I_{os}$, can be eliminated by introducing an external dc voltage to null the output voltage with $v_+ = v_-$. Application literature provided by the manufacturer gives information about canceling the effect of offset voltage and current.

The effect of the bias current, $I_B$, can be eliminated by providing equal dc impedance at the two inputs. In this way, the bias current produces equal voltages that cancel in the subtraction process.

The effect of input noise can be reduced by limiting the bandwidth of the system to that required by the signal. However, noise cannot be eliminated entirely and must be considered in the error analysis of the circuit employing the op amp.

The gain–bandwidth limitation of the op amp limits the product of the gain and bandwidth of the resulting amplifier employing the op amp. Generally, op amps with large gain–bandwidth products are more sophisticated and expensive than basic op amps.

**Summary.** The high gain of the op amp is converted to other useful features through the use of strong negative feedback. All the benefits of negative feedback are utilized by op-amp circuits. Furthermore, op amps are inexpensive and lead to easy designs that are easy to construct.

**Contents of this section.** We next analyze two common op-amp applications, inverting and noninverting amplifiers. We derive the gain of these amplifiers by a method that may be applied simply and effectively to any op-amp circuit operating in its linear amplifying region. We then discuss op-amp circuits for adding and subtracting signals, for converting a current signal to a voltage signal, and for integrating signals. We then consider nonlinear applications of op amps: comparators, log, and antilog amplifiers. In the next chapter, we consider additional applications of op amps.

## Basic Op-amp Amplifiers

**Inverting amplifier circuit.** The inverting amplifier, shown in Fig. 9.48, uses an op amp plus three resistors. The positive (+) input to the op amp is grounded through $R_2$; the negative (−) input is connected to the input signal via $R_1$ and to the feedback signal from the output via $R_F$. Note that $R_2 = R_1 \parallel R_F$ to reduce the effect of bias current. Throughout this section on linear op-amp circuits, we consider that the effect of offset voltage and current has been canceled to produce zero volts at the output for $v_+ = v_-$.

---

[23] These are the common-mode and difference-mode components in the bias currents, as defined in Chapter 10.

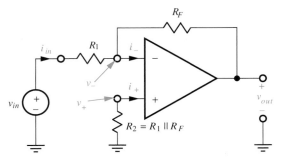

**Figure 9.48**  Inverting amplifier.

One potential source of confusion in the following discussion is that we must speak of two amplifiers simultaneously. The *op amp* is an amplifier that forms the amplifying element in a *feedback amplifier* that contains the op amp plus the associated resistors. To lessen confusion, we reserve the term "amplifier" to apply only to the overall, feedback amplifier. The op amp will never be called an "amplifier"; it will be called "the op amp." For example, if we refer to the input current to the amplifier, we are referring to the current through $R_1$, not the current into the op amp.

### Analysis of the inverting amplifier.

We could solve for the gain of the inverting amplifier in Fig. 9.48 either by solving the basic circuit laws, KVL and KCL, or by attempting to divide the circuit, in the style of Fig. 9.33, into the summer, main amplifier, and feedback system blocks. We, however, present a third approach that assumes that the op-amp gain is very high, effectively infinite. In the following, we give a general assumption, which may be applied to any op-amp circuit; then we apply this assumption specifically to the inverting amplifier. As a result, we establish the gain and input resistance of the inverting amplifier.

1. We assume that the amplifier operates in its linear amplifying region, the sloping region in Fig. 9.46(b). It follows that the output lies between the power-supply voltages. Thus, we assume that the negative feedback stabilizes the amplifier such that moderate input voltages produce moderate output voltages. If the power supplies are $+10$ V and $-10$ V, the output would have to lie between these limits. This assumption restricts our analysis to linear op-amp circuits.

2. Therefore, the difference between input voltages to the op amp is very small, essentially zero, because this difference is the output voltage divided by the large voltage gain of the op amp:

$$v_+ - v_- = \frac{v_{out}}{A} \approx 0 \quad \Rightarrow \quad v_+ \approx v_- \tag{9.101}$$

For example, if $|v_{out}| < 10$ V and $A = 10^5$, then $|v_+ - v_-| < 10/10^5 = 100$ μV. Thus, $v_+$ and $v_-$ will be equal within 100 μV or less. For the inverting amplifier in Fig. 9.48, $v_+$ is grounded through $R_2$; therefore, $v_+ \approx 0$ and $v_- \approx 0$. Consequently, the current at the input to the amplifier would be

$$i_{in} = \frac{v_{in} - v_-}{R_1} \approx \frac{v_{in}}{R_1} \tag{9.102}$$

**3.** Because $v_+ \approx v_-$ and the input impedance of the op amp, $R_i$, is large, the current into the + and − op-amp inputs is very small, essentially zero:

$$|i_+| = |i_-| = \frac{|v_- - v_+|}{R_i} \approx 0 \qquad (9.103)$$

For example, for $R_i = 10$ M$\Omega$, $|i_-| < 10^{-4}/10^7 = 10^{-11}$ A.

For the inverting amplifier, Eq. (9.103) implies that the current at the input, $i_{in}$, flows through $R_F$, as shown in Fig. 9.49. This allows us to compute the output voltage. The voltage across $R_F$ is $i_{in}R_F$ and, because one end of $R_F$ is connected to $v_- \approx 0$,

$$v_{out} = -i_{in}R_F = -\frac{v_{in}}{R_1} \times R_F \qquad (9.104)$$

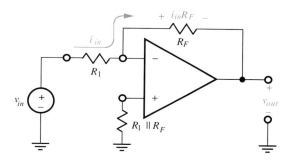

**Figure 9.49** The input current flows through the feedback circuit.

Thus, the voltage gain is

$$A_v = \frac{v_{out}}{v_{in}} = -\frac{R_F}{R_1} \qquad (9.105)$$

The minus sign in Eq. (9.105) means that the output is inverted relative to the input; a positive signal at the amplifier input produces a negative signal at the output = 180° phase shift.

**Impedance Level**

**Circuit impedance level.** Equation (9.105) shows the gain to depend on the ratio of $R_F$ to $R_1$, which implies that only the ratio matters, not the individual values of $R_1$ and $R_F$. This would be true if only the gain of the amplifier were important, but the input impedance to an amplifier is also important. The input resistance to the inverting amplifier follows from Eq. (9.102):

$$R_{in} = \frac{v_{in}}{i_{in}} \approx R_1 \qquad (9.106)$$

For a voltage amplifier, the input impedance level is an important factor, for if $R_{in}$ were too low, the signal source of $v_{in}$ could be loaded down by $R_{in}$. Thus, $R_1$ must be sufficiently high to avoid this loading problem. Once $R_1$ is fixed, $R_F$ may be selected to achieve the required gain. Therefore, the values of the individual resistors become important because they affect the input resistance to the amplifier.

EXAMPLE **9.16** **Amplifier design**

Design an inverting amplifier to have a gain of $-8$. The input signal comes from a pressure sensor having an output impedance of $100\,\Omega$.

**SOLUTION:**

To reduce loading, the input resistor, $R_1$, must be much larger than $100\,\Omega$. For a 5% loading effect, we set $R_1 = 20 \times 100\,\Omega = 2000\,\Omega$. To achieve a gain of $-8$ (actually 95% of $-8$, considering loading), we require that $R_F = 8 \times 2000 = 16\,k\Omega$.

**WHAT IF?**    What if you want a 1% loading effect and exactly $-8$ for the gain?[24]

**Circuit operation.** Feedback effects dominate the characteristics of the amplifier. When an input voltage is applied, $v_-$ increases, causing $v_{out}$ to increase rapidly in the negative direction. This negative voltage increases to the value where the effect of $v_{out}$ on the $-$ input via $R_F$ cancels the effect of $v_{in}$ through $R_1$. Put another way, the output will adjust itself to withdraw through $R_F$ any current that $v_{in}$ injects through $R_1$, because the input current to the op amp is extremely small. In this way, the output depends only on $R_F$ and $R_1$.

**Summary of the method.** The inverting-amplifier voltage gain and input impedance were determined from two principles:

**1.** The input voltages *at the op amp* are equal: $v_+ = v_-$.

**2.** The input currents *to the op amp* are negligible: $|i_+| = |i_-| \approx 0$.

These assumptions are valid for any good op amp operating with negative feedback in the linear region. We illustrate their application again in the next section.

**Noninverting amplifier.** For the noninverting amplifier shown in Fig. 9.50 the input is connected to the $+$ input through $R_2 = R_1 \parallel R_F$. The feedback from the output

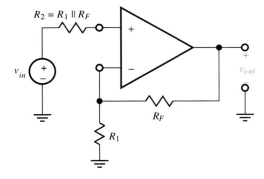

**Figure 9.50**   Non inverting amplifier.

---

[24]$R_{in} = 10\,k\Omega, R_F = 80.8\,k\Omega$.

connects through a voltage divider to the − op amp input, as required for negative feedback. We determine the gain with the analysis outlined earlier.

1. Because the input current to the op amp is very small, no signal voltage is lost across $R_2$ and hence $v_+ = v_{in}$.

2. Because $v_+ \approx v_-$, it follows that

$$v_- \approx v_{in} \qquad (9.107)$$

3. Because $i_- \approx 0$, $R_F$ and $R_1$ carry the same current. Hence, $v_{out}$ is related to $v_-$ through a voltage-divider relationship:

$$v_- \approx v_{out} \times \frac{R_1}{R_1 + R_F} \qquad (9.108)$$

Combining Eqs. (9.107) and (9.108), we establish the voltage gain to be

$$v_{in} = v_{out} \frac{R_1}{R_1 + R_F} \quad \Rightarrow \quad A_v = + \left( 1 + \frac{R_F}{R_1} \right) \qquad (9.109)$$

The + sign before the gain expression emphasizes that the output of the amplifier has the same polarity as the input: a positive input signal produces a positive output signal. Again, we see that the ratio of $R_F$ and $R_1$ determines the gain of the amplifier.

 **Impedance Level**

**Circuit operation.** When a voltage is applied to the amplifier, the output voltage increases rapidly until the voltage across $R_1$ reaches the input voltage. Thus, negligible input current flows into the amplifier, and the gain depends only on $R_1$ and $R_F$. The input impedance to the noninverting amplifier is very high because the input current to the amplifier is also the input current to the op amp, $i_+$, which is extremely small. Input impedance values exceeding 1000 MΩ are easily achieved with this circuit. This feature of high input impedance is an important virtue of the noninverting amplifier because loading of the input source is eliminated.

---

**EXAMPLE 9.17** | **Output impedance**

Find the output impedance of the noninverting amplifier.

**SOLUTION:**
Assume $v_{in} = 1$ V and calculate the Thévenin voltage and Norton current at the output. Assuming the loop gain is much greater than 1, the open-circuit output voltage is

$$V_T = 1\text{V} \times \left( 1 + \frac{R_F}{R_1} \right) \qquad (9.110)$$

Shorting the output to find the Norton current kills the feedback, $v_- = 0$, and $I_N = 1$ V × $A/R_o$, where $R_o$ is the output impedance of the op amp defined in Fig. 9.46 (a). Thus,

$$R_{out} = R_{eq} = \frac{V_T}{I_N} = \frac{1 + R_F/R_1}{A/R_o} = R_o \times \frac{R_1 + R_F}{AR_1} \qquad (9.111)$$

**WHAT IF?**    What if you apply the same analysis to the inverting amplifier?[25]

**Impedance levels.**   With the noninverting amplifier, the values of $R_1$ and $R_F$ may be chosen from a broad range as long as the ratio gives the desired gain. However, if the impedance level is too low, comparable to the output impedance of the op amp, the op amp might be loaded by its own feedback network, which would be undesirable. At the other extreme, very large resistors can act as sources of significant noise in the amplifier, increasing the output noise above that inherent to the op amp. Resistor noise is discussed in Chapter 11.

## Linear Op-Amp Circuits

**buffer**

**Impedance Level**

**Buffer or voltage follower.**   An amplifier with a gain of $+1$ results by eliminating $R_1 (= \infty)$ in the noninverting amplifier, as shown in Fig. 9.51. This *buffer* is used to control impedance levels in the circuit. The input impedance to the buffer is high and its output impedance is low. The output voltage from a source with high output impedance can  supply signal to one or more loads that have a low impedance via the buffer. The value of $R_F$ is arbitrary and can be chosen equal to the source impedance, $R_s$, to eliminate entirely the need for $R_2$.   Often $R_F = 0$ is used.

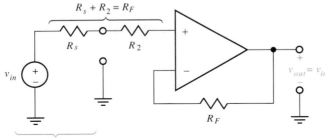

Source with high output impedance

**Figure 9.51**    The buffer or voltage-follower circuit.

**Current-to-voltage converter.**   Many devices produce current signals, whereas most electronic circuits require voltage signals. Figure 9.52 shows an op-amp circuit for converting a current signal to a voltage signal. This is the inverting amplifier with $R_1 = 0$. It has zero input impedance and hence does not load the input current source. The input current is converted to a voltage by flowing through the feedback resistor, as explained earlier.

---

[25] You must get the same answer because the circuits are identical with the input voltage OFF.  But seriously, see if you can derive it.

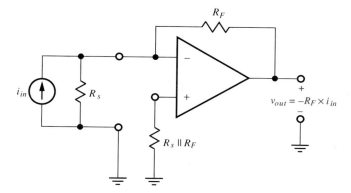

**Figure 9.52** A current-to-voltage converter.

## EXAMPLE 9.18 20-mA current-loop converter

Certain digital devices use a "20-mA current loop" to encode a digital signal. This means that a digital ONE is a current of 20 mA into a short circuit and a digital ZERO is 0 mA. Assuming the output impedance of the loop is 100 kΩ, design an op-amp interface to convert this current signal to a voltage signal with logic levels of 0 and +5 V.

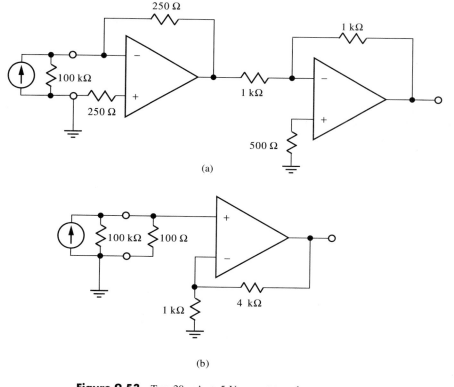

(a)

(b)

**Figure 9.53** Two 20-mA ⇒ 5-V current-to-voltage converters.

## SOLUTION:

One circuit is shown in Fig. 9.53(a). The feedback resistor must be $R_F = 5\,\text{V}/20\,\text{mA} = 250\,\Omega$. Because we require a positive output voltage, the current-to-voltage converter must be followed by an inverter, as shown in Fig. 9.53(a). Another approach is shown in Fig. 9.53(b). A 100-$\Omega$ resistor converts the 20 mA to a 2 V signal and the noninverting amplifier provides the gain to make 5 V. Here no inverter is required.

**Summing amplifier.** An inverting amplifier can accept two or more inputs and produce a weighted sum. Figure 9.54 shows a summer with two inputs. We may understand the operation of the circuit by applying the same reasoning we used earlier to understand the inverting amplifier. Because $v_- \approx 0$, the sum of the currents through $R_1$ and $R_2$ is

$$i_{in} = \frac{v_1}{R_1} + \frac{v_2}{R_2} \tag{9.112}$$

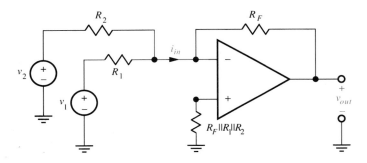

**Figure 9.54** Summer circuit.

The output voltage adjusts itself to draw this current through $R_F$, and hence the output voltage is

$$v_{out} = -i_{in}R_F = -\left(v_1 \times \frac{R_F}{R_1} + v_2 \times \frac{R_F}{R_2}\right) \tag{9.113}$$

The output is thus the sum of $v_1$ and $v_2$, weighted by the gain factors, $R_F/R_1$ and $R_F/R_2$, respectively. If the inversion produced by the summer is unwanted, the summer can be followed by an inverting amplifier with a gain of $-1$. Clearly, we could add other inputs in parallel with $R_1$ and $R_2$.

---

**EXAMPLE 9.19** | **A sinusoid with dc**

An op amp has power-supply voltages of $\pm 10$ V. The available input voltage is $v_{in} = 0.1 \cos(\omega t)$ V. Design a circuit to give an output of $v_{out} = 1 + \cos(\omega t)$ V.

## SOLUTION:

We use a summer and an inverter with unity gain. The summer has a gain of 10 for the sinusoid, but a gain of 0.1 for the power-supply voltage. Fig. 9.55 shows the circuit.

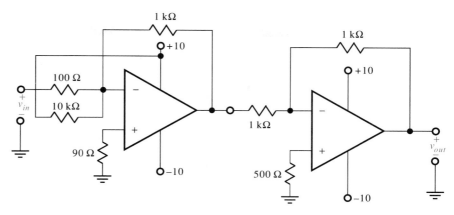

**Figure 9.55** The summer uses the power-supply voltage to produce a dc component in the output.

### WHAT IF?

What if the power supply is $\pm 8$ V? What changes?[26]

**Differencing amplifier.** The circuit in Fig. 9.56 produces an output proportional to the difference between the two inputs. The circuit is linear, so we may use superposition. The output due to $v_2$ is given by Eq. (9.105). The signal to the noninverting input is reduced by the voltage divider of $R_1$ in series with $R_F$. The output thus combines a voltage-divider relationship with the gain given by Eq. (9.109):

$$v_{out} = v_1 \times \frac{R_F}{R_1 + R_F} \times \left(1 + \frac{R_F}{R_1}\right) = v_1 \times \frac{R_F}{R_1} \tag{9.114}$$

Combining the effects from each input, we determine the output voltage to be

$$v_{out} = \frac{R_F}{R_1}(v_1 - v_2) \tag{9.115}$$

Thus, the amplifier subtracts the inputs and amplifies their difference.

**Impedance Level**

Two features of this subtractor circuit should be mentioned. Perfect subtraction requires a balance of the resistor values and thus may call for careful adjustment of the resulting circuit. Furthermore, the input impedances to the inputs are different, and therefore the balance could be affected if loading effects are significant. On the other

---

[26] The 10 k$\Omega$ changes to 8 k$\Omega$.

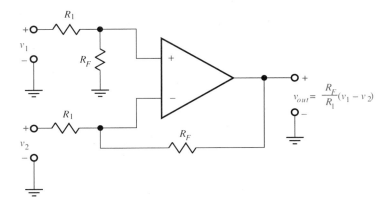

$$v_{out} = \frac{R_F}{R_1}(v_1 - v_2)$$

**Figure 9.56** This circuit subtracts and amplifies the inputs.

hand, the input impedances at the two inputs can be made equal by reducing the resistors in the voltage divider by the ratio $R_1/(R_1 + R_F)$, but this would forfeit the dc impedance balance seen at the op-amp inputs. In practice, a compromise might be required.

**Integrator.** Because a capacitor integrates current and an op amp can simulate a controlled current source, an op amp circuit can integrate its input voltage. The op-amp circuit of Fig. 9.57 uses a capacitor in the feedback path to integrate the input voltage and a voltage source $V_1$ that is disconnected at $t = 0$ to produce an initial voltage. Let us examine the initial state of the circuit before investigating what happens after the switch is opened. The input current to the amplifier, $v_{in}/R$, flows through the $V_1$ voltage source and into the output of the op amp. Because $v_+$ is approximately zero, so will be $v_-$, and hence the output voltage is fixed at $-V_1$ with the switch closed.

After the switch is opened at $t = 0$, the input current flows through the capacitor and hence $v_C$ is

$$v_C(t) = v_C(0) + \frac{1}{C} \int_0^t \frac{v_{in}(t')}{R} dt' \tag{9.116}$$

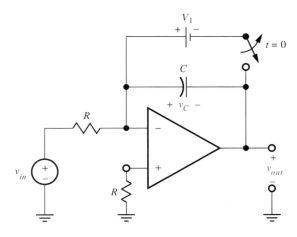

**Figure 9.57** Integrator circuit.

Thus, the output voltage of the circuit is

$$v_{out}(t) = -v_C(t) = -V_1 - \frac{1}{RC} \int_0^t v_{in}(t')\,dt' \qquad (t > 0) \qquad (9.117)$$

Except for the minus sign, the output is the integral of $v_{in}$ scaled by $1/RC$.

**EXAMPLE 9.20** **Integrator design**

Design a noninverting circuit that has an input impedance of 1 kΩ resistive, an initial voltage of +3 V, and an output that is 10 times the integral of the input voltage.

**SOLUTION:**

To have a noninverted output, we require an inverting amplifier and an integrator, which may be placed in either order. However, if the integrator were placed first, its drift due to unbalance would be amplified, so we use the circuit in Fig. 9.58.

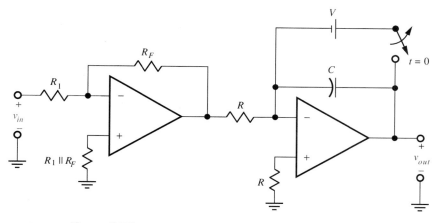

**Figure 9.58** An inverting amplifier followed by an integrator.

The input impedance requirement fixes $R_1$ as 1 kΩ, and the initial voltage requirement fixes $V$ as +3 V. Two of the three components ($C$, $R$, and $R_F$) may be chosen arbitrarily and the third adjusted to give the correct overall gain. We choose $C$ as a convenient value of 10 μF and choose $R_F$ as 20 kΩ to give the inverting amplifier a gain of −20. It follows from Eq. (9.117) that the integrator must have an $RC$ value of 2, and hence the value of $R$ must be 200 kΩ.

**WHAT IF?** What if you have only 1-kΩ resistors?[27]

---
[27] No problem. Use them with $C = 100$ μF.

## Nonlinear Op-Amp Circuits

Many circuits employing op amps are nonlinear, either because nonlinear elements such as diodes are used in the circuit or because the op amp operates outside its linear amplifying region. In this section, we discuss several nonlinear applications of op amps. Many more circuits are detailed in standard handbooks and application literature provided by manufacturers.

**Comparators.** Figure 9.59 (a) shows a basic comparator, and Fig. 9.59 (b) shows its input-output characteristic. No feedback is employed. When the input is less than $V_{th}$, the op amp is saturated at the value of the negative power supply, which is zero in this case. As the input voltage is increased past $V_{th}$, the op amp passes rapidly through its linear region and saturates at the voltage of the positive power supply. Because there is no feedback, transition between the two saturation voltages requires an input voltage range of a few millivolts at most. This circuit, therefore, gives a digital output for an analog input, depending on the region of the input voltage. Comparators have many applications, including alarm circuits, control circuits, and analog-to-digital converters.

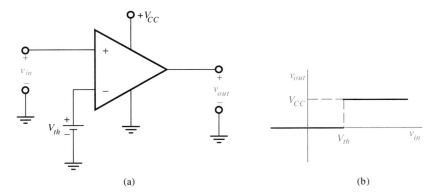

**Figure 9.59** (a) Basic comparator circuit; (b) the input–output characteristic.

A noisy signal, however, causes problems, as shown in Fig. 9.60 (a). The transition region is so narrow that an erratic output is likely to occur in the vicinity of the threshold, as shown in the bottom graph. The circuit shown in Fig. 9.60 (b) remedies this problem through the use of positive feedback. Figure 9.60 (c) shows the input–output characteristic of the modified circuit.

**Finding the thresholds.** As the input voltage increases, the output transition occurs when the input voltage reaches a threshold voltage, $V_{th(1)}$, which in this case is established from the power supply with a voltage divider. Because the input voltage to the op amp is reduced slightly by the feedback resistor, the transition occurs at the value given with the nodal analysis in Eq. (9.118). Because $v_{out} = 0$, KCL at the + input is

$$\frac{V_{th(1)} - V_B}{R_1} = \frac{V_B - 0}{R_F} \quad \Rightarrow \quad V_{th(1)} = V_B\left(1 + \frac{R_1}{R_F}\right) \tag{9.118}$$

As the op amp comes out of saturation in the lower state, the positive feedback produces a rapid transition to saturation in the upper state.

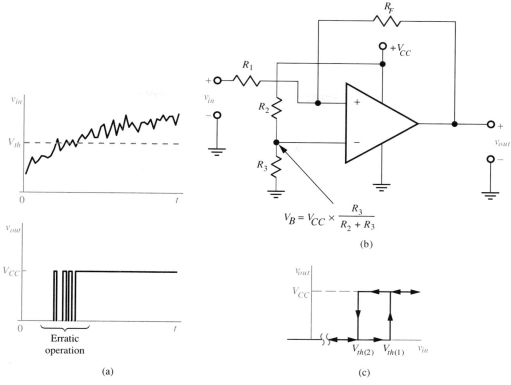

$$V_B = V_{CC} \times \frac{R_3}{R_2 + R_3}$$

(b)

(a)

(c)

**Figure 9.60** (a) A noisy signal can cause erratic operation if no hysteresis is provided; (b) a comparator with hysteresis created by positive feedback; (c) the input–output characteristic of the comparator with hysteresis.

As the input voltage is lowered and $v_{out} = V_{CC}$, the input voltage must be reduced to a value, $V_{th(2)}$, given by the nodal analysis in Eq. (9.119).

$$\frac{V_{th(2)} - V_B}{R_1} = \frac{V_B - V_{CC}}{R_F} \quad \Rightarrow \quad V_{th(2)} = V_B\left(1 + \frac{R_1}{R_F}\right) - V_{CC} \times \frac{R_1}{R_F}$$

$$= V_{th(1)} - V_{CC} \times \frac{R_1}{R_F}$$

(9.119)

Note that the width of the threshold region is $V_{CC} \times R_1/R_F$.

---

**EXAMPLE 9.21** | **Comparitor design**

Design a comparator with a hysteresis region 30 mV wide, centered on 5 V. The positive and negative power supplies are 15 and 0 V, respectively. The input impedance to the circuit should exceed 100 kΩ.

**SOLUTION:**

The specified threshold values are $V_{th(1)} = 5.015$ V and $V_{th(2)} = 4.985$ V. From the width of the threshold region, we find $R_1/R_F = 0.030/15 = 0.002$, and from Eq. (9.118) $V_{th} = 5.015/(1 + 0.002) = 5.005$ V. The input impedance is the sum of $R_1$ and $R_F$ because the op amp draws no current. We choose $R_F = 1$ M$\Omega$ and hence $R_1 = 2000$ $\Omega$. Here it is unnecessary to balance the input dc impedances at the op-amp inputs because the op amp is always saturated, and therefore bias currents have no effect. The voltage divider of $R_2$ and $R_3$ may be chosen at convenient values to give the required value of $V_{th}$.

**WHAT IF?**   What if $V_{th(1)} = 5.5$ V and $V_{th(2)} = 4.5$ V?[28]

**Logarithmic amplifier.** By placing a diode in the feedback path, as shown in Fig. 9.61, we create an amplifier whose output is proportional to the logarithm of the input. Applying the usual analysis, we see the input current to be $v_{in}/R$. The output voltage assumes a value to draw this current through the diode. The diode characteristic is well represented by the ideal $pn$-junction equation in Eq. (7.17); hence, the output voltage is

$$v_{out} = -\eta V_T \ln\left(\frac{v_{in}}{RI_0} + 1\right) \approx -\eta V_T \ln v_{in} + \eta V_T \ln RI_0 \qquad (9.120)$$

The output thus contains a factor proportional to the logarithm of the input voltage. The circuit in Fig. 9.61 can be followed by another op-amp circuit that subtracts the constant term and adjusts the gain of the log amplifier to a prescribed value. For example, the gain can be adjusted to produce an output in dB relative to 1 V. The circuit in Fig. 9.61 cannot deal with signals that go negative.

**Antilog amplifier.** With a diode in the input circuit, as shown in Fig. 9.62, the output voltage can be made proportional to the antilog, or exponential function.

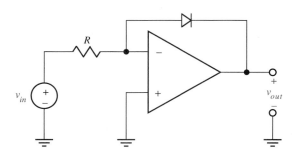

**Figure 9.61**   Logarithmic amplifier.

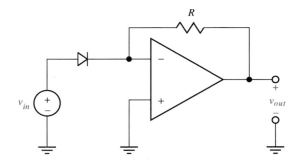

**Figure 9.62**   Antilog amplifier.

---

[28] $R_F = 1$ M$\Omega$, $R_1 = 66.7$ k$\Omega$, $V_{th} = 5.16$ V.

**Applications of log and antilog amplifiers.** The existence of log and antilog amplifiers makes possible analog circuits for multiplication and powers of analog signals. For example, if we wished a circuit to produce the product of two analog signals, we could take the log of each, add the logs, and take the antilog. If one or both of the inputs could go both positive and negative, they would have to be put through circuits that produce the absolute value, with the signs handled by a separate logic circuit.

Excellent analog multipliers and other nonlinear circuits are commercially available. Such circuits operate according to the principles outlined earlier but contain more complicated circuits to compensate for temperature effects and generally improve performance. Our purpose here is to show some representative nonlinear applications of op amps.

**Summary.** In this section we introduced the op amp as an inexpensive and versatile circuit component for processing analog signals. We described a method for determining circuit operation when the op amp is operating in its linear region. We dealt with representative circuits for amplification, addition, subtraction, and integration of signals. We also described several nonlinear applications of op amps, including comparators, log, and antilog converters. In Chapter 10, we show additional applications of op amps.

### Check Your Understanding

1. An ideal op amp has infinite gain, infinite input impedance, and infinite output impedance. (True or false?)

2. In a noninverting op-amp amplifier the feedback resistor is five times the value of the resistor between the inverting input and ground. If the output is $-6$ V, what is the voltage at the input?

3. For a voltage gain of $+5$ in an op-amp amplifier, the feedback comes from the output to which input terminal? Which input gets the input signal?

4. What operation is performed in an inverting amplifier if the feedback resistor is replaced by a capacitor? By a diode?

5. If an op amp has $\pm 8$ V for plus-and-minus power-supply values and a gain of 80 dB, at what value of $v_+ - v_-$ does the op amp saturate?

6. The voltage-follower amplifier inverts the signal. (True or false?)

*Answers.* **(1)** False; the output impedance should be zero; **(2)** $-1.0$ V; **(3)** feedback to inverting $(-)$, input to noninverting $(+)$; **(4)** becomes an integrator; becomes a log amplifier; **(5)** $\pm 0.8$ mV; **(6)** false.

# CHAPTER SUMMARY

Information may be represented in analog form. Signal spectra for periodic, nonperiodic, and random signals are described. Spectra may be modified with filters to improve signal characteristics. Feedback concepts are introduced generally and illustrated with linear and nonlinear operational-amplifier circuits.

**Objective 1: To understand the concept of a spectrum as applied to periodic, nonperiodic, and random signals.** Spectra consist of the simultaneous occurrence of sinusoids of different frequencies. Periodic signals have harmonic spectra of discrete frequencies. Nonperiodic and random signals have continuous spectra.

**Objective 2: To understand how to calculate the bandwidth required to pass pulses and other signals.** The bandwidth of the spectrum of a signal is related to the scale of time structure of the signal. For a random signal, the bandwidth determines the information rate.

**Objective 3: To understand how filters modify spectra.** The frequency dependence of the impedances of capacitors and inductors permits the design of filter circuits to modify spectra. We discuss low- and high-pass $RC$ filters and two types of band-pass filters.

**Objective 4: To understand how to describe filters with Bode plots.** A Bode plot is a log-log plot of filter response or signal spectrum. Bode plots accommodate a wide range in frequency and response level, and the Bode plots of simple filters are easily approximated by straight lines.

**Objective 5: To understand the nature and benefits of feedback.** Feedback combines the input with the output of a system. Negative feedback can improve the robustness, linearity, noise immunity, bandwidth, time-response, and impedance characteristics of a system. Positive feedback is used in oscillator circuits.

**Objective 6: To understand the importance of loop gain in feedback systems.** The sign of the loop gain determines if the feedback is negative or positive. The magnitude of the loop gain determines if feedback effects in the system are strong or weak.

**Objective 7: To understand the importance and applications of op amps in analog circuits.** An op amp amplifies the difference between two input signals with high gain. Op amps are the basic building blocks of analog circuits. Using op amps with negative feedback, we can build inverting and noninverting amplifiers, adders and subtracters, and current-to-voltage converters. Using op amps with positive feedback, we can build comparators and multipliers of analog signals.

Chapter 10 combines the techniques of digital and analog electronics in instrumentation systems.

## PROBLEMS

## Section 9.1: Frequency-Domain Representation of Signals

9.1. In Austin, Texas, the maximum average daily temperature occurs in mid-July and is 84.5°F. The minimum daily average temperature is 49.1°F and occurs in mid-January.
   (a) Based on this information, and assuming that the daily average temperature $T(t)$ is well represented by the dc and first harmonic terms of a Fourier series such as Eq. (9.4), find $T_0$, $T_1$, $\theta_1$, and $\omega_1$. Let $t$ be the time in months, with $t = 0$ on January 1, 1 on February 1, and so on.

   (b) From your result, estimate the expected average temperature for Christmas Day.

9.2. Consider a square wave similar to the one in Fig. 9.5(a), except that it goes from +3 to –1 V and has a pulse width of 2 ms, and has a spectrum similar to that shown in Fig. 9.5 (b).
   (a) What is $V_0$?
   (b) Find the frequency (in hertz), the amplitude, and the phase (in degrees) of the eleventh harmonic.

**9.3.** What would be the first three terms of the Fourier series for the half-wave rectified sinusoid in Fig. 9.6(a) if the origin were drawn at the beginning of the pulse? *Hint:* Change variables from $t \Rightarrow t' - T/4$, where $t'$ is the origin in the new time system.

**9.4.** Show that the Fourier harmonic spectrum of a full-wave rectifier sinusoid is

$$v_{FW}(t) = V_p\left[\frac{2}{\pi} + \frac{4}{3\pi}\cos(2\omega_1 t) - \frac{4}{15\pi}\cos(4\omega_1 t) + \cdots\right]$$

Note that $v_{FW}(t) = v_{HW}(t) + v_{HW}(t + T/2)$.

**9.5.** A Fourier series is

$$v(t) = -10 + 5\cos(300\pi t) + 3\cos(600\pi t - 90°) + \cdots \text{ V}$$

**(a)** Would this signal have a continuous or a discrete spectrum?
**(b)** What is the total "power" in volt² in the three harmonics given?
**(c)** If the voltage were increased by 5 V dc, how would the Fourier series change?
**(d)** What is the frequency of the third harmonic in hertz?

**9.6.** A periodic waveform has the form

$$v(t) = 2 + 3\sin(150\pi t) + 0.5\cos(450\pi t) \text{ V}$$

**(a)** What is the time average of $v(t)$?
**(b)** Find the period of $v(t)$.
**(c)** Find the rms value of $v(t)$.

**9.7.** Figure P9.7 shows a series of pulses in the time domain. Find the following:
**(a)** Frequency of the third harmonic in Hz.
**(b)** Power in volt² in the dc component.
**(c)** Amplitude of the third harmonic.
**(d)** Total power in volt² in all ac harmonics.

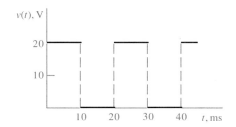

**Figure P9.7**

**9.8.** In Washington, DC, the maximum elevation ang of the sun at summer solstice, June 23, is about 73 and at winter solstice, December 23, about 27°. The maximum elevation can be described by a Fourier series of only two terms. What is the minimum length of the shadow of the Washington Monument, 555 feet in height, on the Fourth of July?

**9.9.** An unfiltered half-wave power supply produces 18.2 V dc from a 60-Hz sinusoid. What is its output power in volt² in the range of frequencies between 100 and 320 Hz?

**9.10.** A periodic waveform is shown in Fig. P9.10. This voltage can be represented by the following Fourier series:

$$v(t) = V_0 + V_1\cos(\omega_1 t + \theta_1) + V_2\cos(2\omega_1 t + \theta_2) + V_3\cos(3\omega_1 t + \theta_3) + \cdots$$

Find the following:
**(a)** $V_0$.
**(b)** $\omega_1$.
**(c)** $V_1$.
**(d)** $\theta_2$.
**(e)** $V_3$.

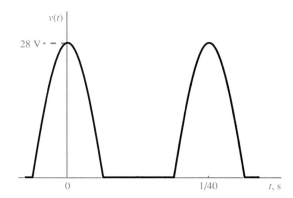

**Figure P9.10**

**9.11.** Show that Eq. (9.12) for $\tau = T/2$ gives the same harmonic amplitudes and phases as those in Eq. (9.5).

**9.12.** The nominal bandwidth of a standard telephone line is 4 kHz. What is the approximate duration of the shortest pulse that can be sent over such a telephone line? Given that the width between pulses should be equal to the pulse width, how many pulses per second can be sent over a phone line using simple pulses?

half-wave rectified sinusoid in Fig. 9.6(a), ~~ction of the total power is carried by the dc ~~'t?

~~er" spectrum of a random signal is shown ~~ig. P9.14.

(a) What is the dc value of the signal, assuming that it is negative?
(b) What power does this signal give to a 5-Ω resistor?
(c) What is the approximate correlation time for this signal?

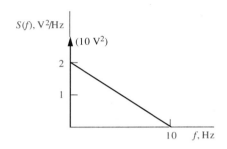

**Figure P9.14**

**9.15.** The effective bandwidth of standard AM radio is 5000 Hz. If such a radio were tuned off a station, receiving only static, what would be the approximate correlation time for the static?

## Section 9.2: Filters

**9.19.** A 60-Hz half-wave rectified sinusoid with a peak value of 10 V is filtered by a low-pass filter, as shown in Fig. P9.19. Calculate the dc and the peak value of the fundamental at the output.

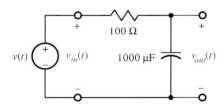

$v(t)$ = half-wave rectified sinusoid
$V_p$ = 10 V
$f$ = 60 Hz

**Figure P9.19**

**9.20.** Make asymptotic Bode plots of the magnitude of the following filter functions:

**9.16.** The effective bandwidth of standard FM radio is 15,000 Hz. If such a radio were tuned off a station, receiving only static, what would be the approximate correlation time for the static?

**9.17.** Figure P9.17 shows the power spectrum of a random signal.
(a) What is the average value of the signal?
(b) What is the approximate correlation time of the signal?
(c) What is the total power from this signal into a 50-Ω resistor?

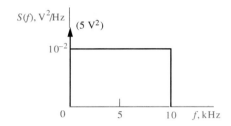

**Figure P9.17**

**9.18.** A computer-based communication system has an information rate of 3000 characters/second, where each character is represented by a byte of digital information. What is the approximate bandwidth required by this system? State assumptions.

(a) $\mathbf{F}(\omega) = \dfrac{25}{1 + j(\omega/250)}$

(b) $\mathbf{F}(\omega) = 50 \times \dfrac{j\omega}{100 + j4\omega}$

(c) $\mathbf{F}(f) = 10^{-2} \times \dfrac{1 + j(f/10)}{1 + j(f/1000)}$

**9.21.** Show that the loss of the low-pass filter in Fig. 9.17 is approximately 1 dB at a frequency one octave (factor of 2) below the cutoff.

**9.22.** The gain in dB of a filter is shown in the Bode plot of Fig. P9.22.
(a) Is this a high-pass, low-pass, or band-pass filter?
(b) What is the gain in dB at 500 Hz?
(c) Estimate the cutoff frequency of the filter.
(d) If the input voltage to the filter were $v_{in}(t) = 5 \cos(2000\,t)$ V, what would be the

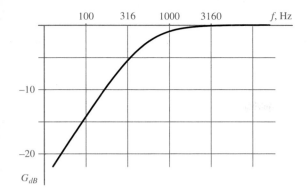

**Figure P9.22**

output in the form $v_{out}(t) = A \cos(2000t + \theta)$? In other words, find $A$ and $\theta$.

**9.23.** The input to a filter is the time function $v_{in}(t) = 10 + 5 \sin(8000t)$. The asymptotic Bode plot of the filter characteristic is shown in Fig. P9.23.

(a) Is the filter high-pass or low-pass?

(b) What is the frequency in hertz of the fundamental of the input?

(c) What is the input "power" in volt²?

(d) What is the output "power" in volt²?

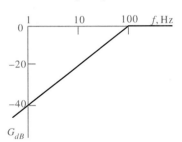

**Figure P9.23**

**9.24.** For the square wave shown in Fig. P9.24, determine the following:

(a) dc component.

(b) Frequency of the fifth harmonic.

(c) rms amplitude of the fifth harmonic.

(d) After passing through a low-pass filter with a cutoff frequency of 100 Hz, what is the output peak amplitude of the fundamental?

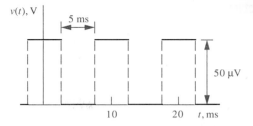

**Figure P9.24**

**9.25.** The input signal to an *RC* low-pass filter is $v(t) = 5 + 5 \sin(1000t)$. Draw the circuit diagram of a filter such that the power in the output is 90% dc power. The filter uses a 10-µF capacitor.

The half-wave rectified sinusoid in Fig. P9.26(a) is passed through an *RL* filter, as shown in Fig. P9.26(b). What percent of the output "power" in volt² is in its second harmonic?

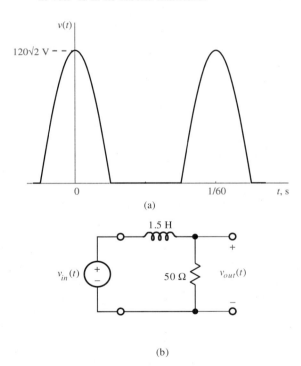

**Figure P9.26**

the signal levels with $v_{out} = 10$ V for the
Fig. 9.32 with reduced gain, $A = 120$.

large does the amplifier gain, $A$, have to be in
the feedback amplifier in Fig. 9.32 before the gain
with feedback is within 1% of $1/\beta$ with negative
feedback? What is the loop gain for this value of $A$?

9.29. A voltage amplifier has a gain of −500. Fifteen
percent of the output voltage is added to an input
voltage to provide the input voltage to the amplifier.
The feedback is negative.
(a) What is the gain of the feedback system?
(b) If you wished to double this gain, how could
this be accomplished?

9.30. A feedback system employs negative voltage
feedback. Assume that for a test, the feedback path
is opened at the point shown in Fig. 9.34, and 5 mV
is fed into the input to the amplifier. Under these
conditions, the output voltage is observed to be 5 V
and the return from the feedback loop is 0.5 V.
(a) What is the loop gain?
(b) What is the gain of the feedback amplifier with
the loop closed?

9.31. The system diagram in Fig. P9.31 shows a feedback
path.
(a) Find the loop gain.
(b) Find the gain of the system with feedback.

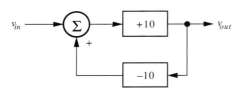

**Figure P9.31**

9.32. The amplifier in Fig. P9.32 employs feedback
derived from a voltage divider. The voltage
amplifier has infinite input impedance, zero output
impedance, and a gain given as $v_{out} = -50v_i$.
(a) Draw a system diagram of the amplifier, being
sure to put the correct sign on the summer.
(b) Determine the loop gain.
(c) Find the gain with feedback.

9.33. The feedback amplifier shown in Fig. P9.33 uses a
current amplifier and has a single resistor, $R_F$,
providing feedback. In your analysis, assume that
$R_F \gg R_L$, such that the output voltage is

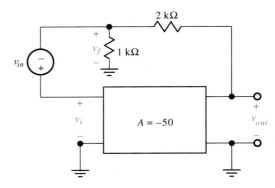

**Figure P9.32**

$v_{out} \approx i_{out} R_L$. Assume that the input impedance of
the current amplifier is very low and $A_i$ is a positive
number.
(a) Derive the gain with feedback, $A_f = v_{out}/i_{in}$, by
using KCL, Ohm's law, and the gain equation
for the current amplifier.
(b) For $A_i = 500$ and $R_L = 10 \, \Omega$, find $R_F$ for an
overall gain of −500 $\Omega$.
(c) Put the results from part (a) in the form of
Eqs. (9.73) to (9.75) and draw the system
diagram corresponding to this amplifier.
(d) What is the loop gain of the amplifier?
(e) If $A_i \Rightarrow \infty$, what is the limiting form for $A_f$?

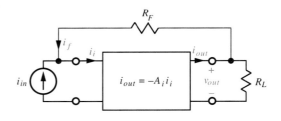

$$A_f = \frac{v_{out}}{i_{in}} \text{ volt /ampere}$$

**Figure P9.33**

9.34. Assume that the amplifier in Fig. 9.32 has a severe
nonlinearity, as shown by the input-output
characteristic in Fig. P9.34. Without feedback, this
would cause much distortion in the amplifier output.
Derive and sketch the overall (with feedback)
characteristics of $v_{out}$ vs. $v_{in}$ with feedback to
demonstrate the benefits of feedback in reducing the

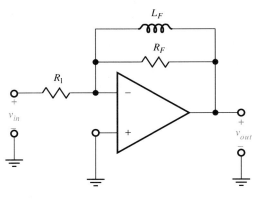

**Figure P9.48**

closed at $t = 0$. Assume that the op amp behaves in a linear manner.

**9.49.** For the op-amp circuit shown in Fig. P9.49, what are the voltages at points $a$ and $b$ relative to ground?

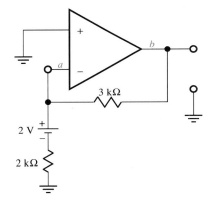

**Figure P9.49**

**9.50.** The op-amp circuit shown in Fig. P9.50 has plus-and-minus power supplies at $\pm 10$ V. The switch is closed at $t = 0$.
   **(a)** Find the value that the output would reach if the output transistors in the op amp did not saturate.
   **(b)** Find the time when the output saturates, assuming that this occurs at 10 V of output voltage.

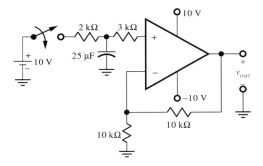

**Figure P9.50**

**9.51.** For the op-amp circuit shown in Fig. P9.51, find the following:
   **(a)** Input resistance seen by $v_{in}$.
   **(b)** Voltage gain $v_2/v_{in}$.
   **(c)** Voltage gain $v_3/v_{in}$.
   **(d)** If $v_{in} = 1$ V and the switch opened at $t = 0$, as shown, how long would it be until the magnitude of the output voltage is 1 V?

**9.52.** Design a comparator circuit that has output levels of 0 and $+5$ V (these are the power-supply values) and makes its transition at an input voltage of $+3$ V for increasing inputs and $+2$ V for decreasing inputs.

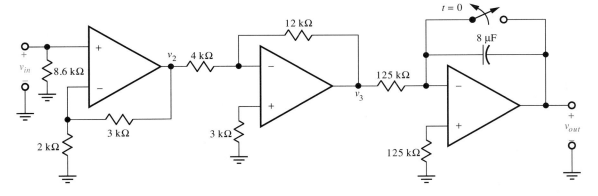

**Figure P9.51**

# General Problems

**9.53.** The circuit in Fig. P9.53 is a comparator with hysteresis. The op amp has a voltage gain of $10^5$ and its output saturates at $\pm 9$ V.

**(a)** Is the feedback positive or negative?

**(b)** Determine the voltage that will cause the output to change from $-9$ V to $+9$ V for increasing inputs.

**(c)** Determine the voltage that will cause the output to change from $+9$ V to $-9$ V for decreasing inputs.

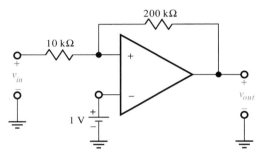

**Figure P9.53**

**9.54.** The filter shown in Fig. P9.54 uses a resistor, a capacitor, and an ideal transformer with a turns ratio of 4:1. Make a Bode plot of the gain of this filter. There is no load on the output.

**9.55.** The frequency characteristic of an $RC$ filter circuit is described by the Bode plot shown in Fig. P9.55(a). Find the output voltage of the circuit, $v_{out}(t)$, if a 10-

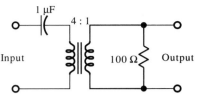

**Figure P9.54**

V battery is connected for 10 ms, as indicated by Fig. P9.55(b).

**9.56.** The circuit shown in Fig. P9.56(b) can be considered a filter followed by an amplifier or it can be considered as a filter combining resistors, a capacitor, and an op amp. The input to the filter is the square wave shown in Fig. P9.56(a).

**(a)** Taking the second approach, determine the filter function relating the output and input voltages in the frequency domain.

**(b)** Determine the frequency in hertz at which the gain of the filter is −5 dB.

**(c)** What would be the average value of the output?

**(d)** What would be the power in volts$^2$ in the first harmonic, or fundamental, of the output voltage?

**9.57.** The filter shown in Fig. P9.57(b) has no input initially; then, at $t = 0$, a series of pulses begins, as shown in Fig. P9.57(a) and continues for a long time.

**(a)** What is the output voltage at the end of the first pulse, at $t = 5$ ms?

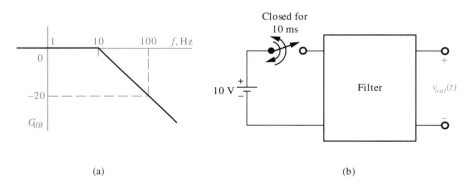

**Figure P9.55**

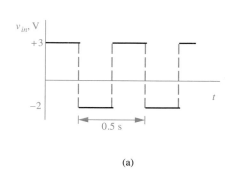

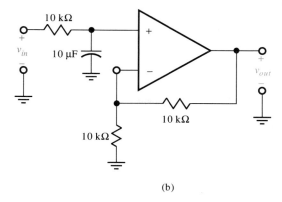

(a)    (b)

**Figure P9.56**

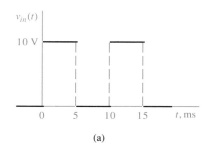

(a)

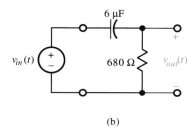

(b)

**Figure P9.57**

**(b)** After a long period of time with the pulses continuing, what are the amplitude of the dc and first-harmonic components in the output spectrum?

9.58. Figure P9.58 shows a standard noninverting op-amp amplifier circuit.

**(a)** Represent the entire amplifier in a system diagram with main amplifier, summer, $\beta$ network, and sampler. What are $A$, $\beta$, and the sign of the summer in this amplifier?

**(b)** Find the loop gain for this amplifier.

**(c)** Find the exact gain of the amplifier (no approximation) and compare with the gain derived in the text, Eq. (9.109).

9.59. A voltage is given by the expression

$$v(t) = 12 + 6\sin(200\pi t) - 3\cos(300\pi t)\,\text{V}$$

**(a)** What is the fundamental frequency in hertz?

**(b)** Find the total power in volts$^2$.

**(c)** Find the rms value of this voltage.

**(d)** If passed through a low-pass filter that reduces the 100-Hz component by 3 dB, how much in dB would the 150-Hz component be reduced?

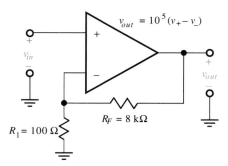

**Figure P9.58**

9.60. Using the circuit in Fig. P9.60, design an amplifier that produces an output of $20\log(v_{in}/1\,\text{V})$, that is, the output is the input voltage in dB compared with 1 V. Assume that the diode characteristic is described by Eq. (7.17) (ignore the $+1$ term) for $\eta = 1.4$, $I_0 = 2 \times 10^{-10}$ A, and $V_T = 0.0259$ V. Specify $R_F$ for the required gain and $V_B$ to remove the constant term in Eq. (9.120). (*Note:* $V_B$ could be obtained with a voltage divider connected to the negative power supply.)

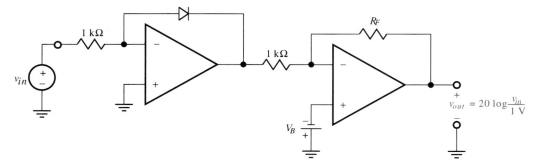

**Figure P9.60**

**9.61.** For the circuit shown in Fig. P9.61 find the following:
  **(a)** Find the sign of $A$ for the feedback to be negative.
  **(b)** We want a gain magnitude of 10 for the system. Find $R_F$.

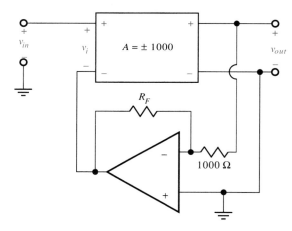

**Figure P9.61**

**9.62.** For the circuit shown in Fig. P9.62, find the following:
  **(a)** The loop gain
  **(b)** The gain with feedback.

**9.63.** The analysis of the passive low-pass filter in Sec. 9.2 ignores the loading at input and output. Consider now the circuit in Fig. P9.63, which contains a source resistance $R_s$ and a load resistor $R_L$. The filter function $\mathbf{F}(\omega) = \mathbf{V}_{out}/\mathbf{V}_{in}$ will be identical in form to that in Eq. (9.36), except (1) the gain will no longer be unity in the region below the critical frequency, $\omega_c$, and (2) the equation for $\omega_c$ is

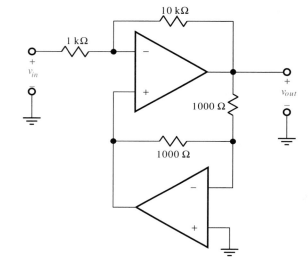

**Figure P9.62**

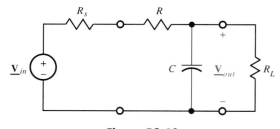

**Figure P9.63**

changed because it depends on the source and load resistances. Determine the revised expressions for $\omega_c$ and $\mathbf{F}(\omega)$.

**9.64.** The small-signal amplifier in Fig. 7.50 has an input impedance $Z_{in} = R_B \parallel r_x$ where $R_B = R_1 \parallel R_2$, which often is unacceptably low for a voltage

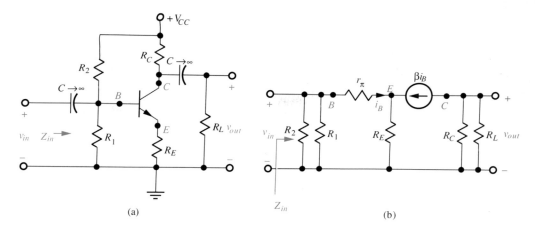

Figure P9.64

amplifier because $r_\pi$ is relatively small. A circuit in which feedback improves the input impedance is shown in Fig. P9.64(a). The small-signal equivalent circuit for the amplifier is shown in Fig. P9.64 (b). This circuit uses feedback to control impedance. The feedback is proportional to the emitter current and is subtracted from the input voltage at the base of the base–emitter $pn$ junction.

(a) Show that the input impedance to the transistor base is raised from $r_\pi$ to $r_\pi + (1 + \beta) R_E$, where $\beta$ is the current gain of the transistor. *Hint:* This circuit is similar to the emitter-follower circuit, especially in feedback effects.

(b) For the transistor ($r_\pi = 450 \ \Omega$) and component values in Fig. 7.50, but with an $R_E = 10 \ \Omega$ added to the base, calculate the input impedance and gain of the amplifier.

**9.65.** The power supply shown in Fig. P9.65 consists of a full-wave rectifier, an $LC$ filter, and a resistive load. If the filter is designed correctly, the current in the inductor will be continuous, two diodes will always be conducting, and the rectifier output, $v_{FW}(t)$, will be a full-wave rectified waveform having a spectrum:

$$v_{FW}(t) = V_p \left[ \frac{2}{\pi} + \frac{4}{3\pi} \cos(2\omega_1 t) \right.$$
$$\left. - \frac{4}{15\pi} \cos(4\omega_1 t) + \cdots \right]$$

where $\omega_1$ is the input frequency, 60 Hz in this case. Because the current in the inductor is mostly dc and second harmonic, the condition for continuous

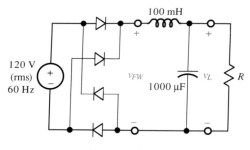

Figure P9.65

current is that the peak value of the second harmonic current be less than the dc current.

(a) Determine the maximum value of $R$ for continuous current in the inductor. Consider only dc and second harmonic. *Hint:* Treat the capacitor as a short circuit for ac.

(b) With the value determined in part (a), approximate the percent ripple in the load voltage, $V_{p-p}/V_{dc} \times 100\%$, where $V_{p-p}$ is the peak-to-peak in the load voltage. Make reasonable approximations.

**9.66.** Figure P9.66 shows a standard op-amp circuit, except for the capacitor in the feedback circuit. The switch is closed at $t = 0$. Determine the output voltage as a function of time after the switch closure at the input. *Hint:* You may use the methods of Chapter 3, but you may have to use the methods of this chapter to write the DE to determine the time constant. Assume linear operation of the op amp.

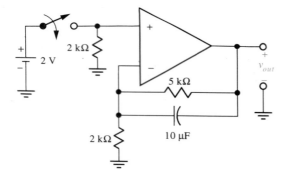

**Figure P9.66**

9.67. The op-amp circuit shown in Fig. P9.67 is assembled with the switch closed and then the switch is opened at $t = 0$. Determine the output voltage to show the voltage before the switch is

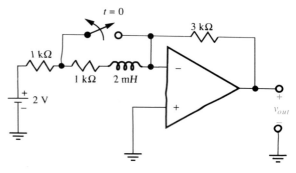

**Figure P9.67**

opened and the transient as a result of opening the switch. Make a sketch of $v_{out}$. *Hint:* You may use the methods of Chapter 3. You may have to use the methods of this chapter to write the DE to determine the time constant.

## Answers to Odd-Numbered Problems

9.1. (a) $T_0 = 66.8°$, $T_1 = 17.7°$, $\theta_1 = -195°$, and $\omega_1 = 2\pi/12$ rad/mo; (b) 50.3°

9.3. $v_{HW}(t) = V_p [1/\pi + (1/2) \sin(\omega_1 t) - (2/3\pi) \cos(2\omega_1 t)]$, $n = 4, 8, 12, \ldots$, the same as before, but if $n = 2, 6, 10, \ldots$, change the signs to $-$.

9.5. (a) Discrete (b) 117 V²; (c) the dc would change to $-5$ V; (d) 450 Hz.

9.7. (a) 150 Hz; (b) 100 V²; (c) 4.24 V; (d) 100 V².

9.09. 76.6 V².

9.11. Proof depends on $\sin(n\pi) = 0$ for $n$ even, $-1$ for $n = 1,5,9, \ldots$, and $+1$ for $n = 3, 7, 11, \ldots$

9.13. 40.5%.

9.15. 0.2 ms.

9.17. (a) $\pm 2.236$ V; (b) 100 μs; (c) 2.10 W.

9.19. 3.18 V dc, 0.133 V peak.

9.21. $-0.969$ dB.

9.23. (a) High Pass; (b) 1270 Hz; (c) 112.5 V²; (d) 12.5 V².

9.25. Standard low-pass filter with resistance of 187 Ω.

9.27. $v_{out} = 10$ V, $v_i = 0.083$ V, $v_f = 1.000$ V, $v_{in} = 1.083$ V.

9.29. (a) $-6.58$; (b) 0.075 approximate, 0.074 exact.

9.31. (a) $-100$; (b) 0.0990.

9.33. (a) $Gain = -\dfrac{A_i R_L}{1 + (R_L/R_F)A_i}$ ; (b) 556 Ω;

(c)

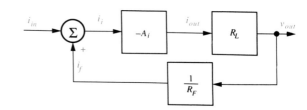

(d) $L = -\dfrac{R_L}{R_F}A_i = -8.99$ ; (e) $A_f \Rightarrow R_F$.

9.35. (a) 0.660 V; (b) 9.16 ms.

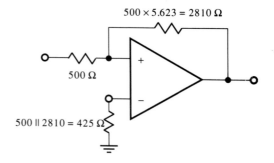

**9.37.** $15 \text{dB} = 10^{15/20} = 5.263$, $R_1 = 500 \ \Omega$.
$R_F = 2.81 \ \text{K}\Omega$, inverting amplifier.

**9.39.** (a) 6.02 dB; (b) $3R$.

**9.41.** $v_{out} = - v_{in} (R_F/R_1) + V$.

**9.43.** (a) $v_{out} = v_{in} \dfrac{-A}{1 + R_1/R_F + AR_1/R_F}$ ;

(b) the same answer; (c) $A \gg 1$ and $AR_1/R_F \gg 1$
such that $A_f \Rightarrow -R_F/R_1$.

**9.45.** The gain is between $-12.3$ and $-8.18$.

**9.47.**

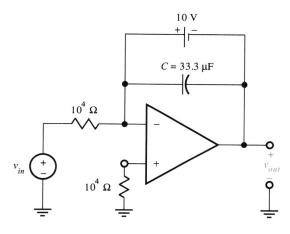

**9.49.** $v_a = 0$, $v_b = -3$ V.

**9.51.** (a) 8.6 k$\Omega$; (b) 2.5; (c) $-7.5$; (d) 0.133 s .

**9.53.** (a) positive; (b) 1.5 V; (c) 0.6 V.

**9.55.** $v_{out} = 10\,(1 - e^{-t/15.9 \text{ ms}})$ for $0 < t < 10$ ms and $v_{out}$
$= 4.67$ V for $t > 10$ ms .

**9.57.** (a) 7.06 V; (b) dc $= 0$, fundamental $= 5.93$ V peak.

**9.59.** (a) 100 Hz; (b) 166.5 V²; (c) 12.9 Vrms;
(d) $-5.12$ dB.

**9.61.** (a) $-1000$; (b) 99 $\Omega$ .

**9.63.** $\omega'_c = 1/[C \times R_L \| (R + R_s)]$ and
$$\mathbf{F}(j\omega) = \left( \frac{R_L}{R_L + R + R_s} \right) \times \frac{1}{1 + j(\omega/\omega'_c)} \ .$$

**9.65.** (a) 113 $\Omega$; (b) 7.4%.

**9.67.** $v_{out} = -3 + 3e^{-t/1\mu s}$ V.

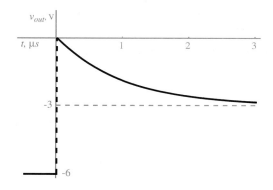

# PART
# 3
# Systems

# 10

# Instrumentation Systems

1. To understand how to perform worst-case and statistical error analysis
2. To understand how to recognize floating signals and be able to amplify difference-mode signals
3. To understand analog signal and noise spectra and how active filters can improve system performance
4. To understand the principles of cabling, grounding, and shielding to reduce interference
5. To understand digital signal sampling, conversion, and processing

Instrumentation systems combine analog and digital techniques to acquire, condition, store, and process data. Issues such as error analysis and noise reduction are considered, and new applications for op amps are presented.

## General Considerations

Data gathering and reduction were once simple but tedious tasks. Meters were read by eye and results were recorded by hand. At best, a continuously recording strip chart left a wiggly line of data to be examined for trends, interpolated by eye, and analyzed by hand calculations.

Computers have made data gathering and reduction quick, automatic, and sophisticated. The computer can monitor many inputs, adjust the gain of analog channels to keep data within a prescribed range, filter incoming signals to improve data quality, process and record data, furnish displays, and produce control outputs.

**Analog Information**

**An instrumentation system.**   Figure 10.1 shows an instrumentation system that employs analog and digital processing. We now discuss the various subsystems as a an introduction to the structure of this chapter.

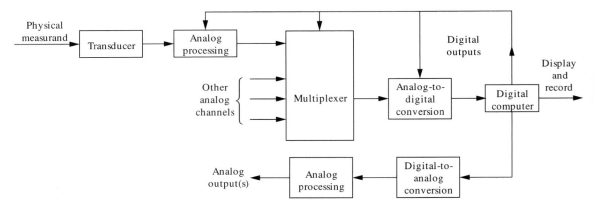

**Figure 10.1**   Instrumentation system.

**The Frequency Domain**

**Transducer.**   The transducer produces an electrical output indicative of some physical *measurand* such as pressure, temperature, or angular position. Transducers are discussed in this introductory section.

**measurand**

**Analog processing.**   Amplification and filtering are normally required to prepare the signal for conversion to digital form. Figure 10.1 shows a control signal coming from the computer into this subsystem because often the gain of an analog channel is controlled to keep the signal within a prescribed range. Analog processing is discussed in Sec. 10.2.

**Multiplexer.**   Typically, several analog channels are processed sequentially through a multiplexer, which is a digitally controlled switch. The multiplexer accepts parallel inputs from several analog channels and provides one analog output at a time for conversion to digital form. Multiplexers are discussed in Sec. 10.3.

**Digital Information**

**Analog-to-digital (A/D) conversion.**   The A/D converts the information from analog to digital form. Often, the time variations of the analog signal must be arrested with a sample-and-hold circuit while A/D conversion is taking place. We discuss two types of A/D converters in Sec. 10.3.

**Digital computer.** The brains of the entire operation, and the immediate recipient of the information, is a digital computer. This might be a microprocessor dedicated to the instrumentation system or it might be a general-purpose computer that is structured to perform the required data-acquisition function simultaneously with other activities. For example, a desktop personal computer can be adapted to accept analog and digital data inputs, and standard programs are available to supervise the data-gathering activity. We do not investigate the processing and storage functions of the computer in this chapter except for a brief discussion of digital filtering.

**Digital-to-analog (D/A) conversion.** Often, the computer must provide outputs in analog form. If, for example, the data monitor were part of a control system, the computer might furnish analog output signals as feedback to the controller of the process affecting the physical measurand. We discuss D/A converters in Sec. 10.3.

**Processing of analog outputs.** Analog outputs often require filtering and amplification for controlling process functions. However, no new topics are introduced, so we have no further discussion of analog outputs.

## Transducers

**transducer, sensor**

A *transducer*, also called a *sensor*, converts a physical quantity to an electrical signal. Most transducers produce analog signals, but some have digital outputs. Many types of transducers exist for most types of physical measurands; they differ in physical processes, noise, accuracy, linearity, ruggedness, output impedance, frequency response, and need for frequent calibration. After discussing bridge circuits and strain gages, we describe some common transducers used to measure position and angle, pressure, flow rate, and temperature.

### Bridge circuits.

Many transducers employ a resistor whose resistance changes as a function of the measurand. The most common circuit used to convert a resistance change to a voltage change is the Wheatstone-bridge circuit, shown in Fig. 10.2. The bridge consists of two voltage dividers, and the output voltage is the difference in the voltages created by the voltage dividers. Application of the voltage-divider relationship, Eq. (1.65), gives the output voltage:

$$v_{out} = V \times \left( \frac{R_0}{R_1 + R_0} - \frac{R_2}{R_3 + R_2} \right) \tag{10.1}$$

**balanced bridge**

The bridge is *balanced* when the output voltage is zero, which requires

$$\frac{R_0}{R_1} = \frac{R_2}{R_3} \tag{10.2}$$

If the bridge is approximately balanced, small changes in $R_0$ from balance, $\Delta R_0$, produce corresponding small changes in output voltage, given by

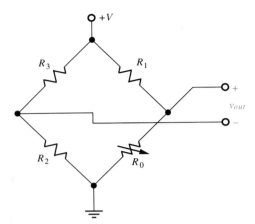

**Figure 10.2** The Wheatstone-bridge circuit converts a resistance change in $R_0$ to a change in output voltage.

$$\Delta v_{out} = V \times \frac{R_1 \, \Delta R_0}{(R_0 + R_1)^2} \tag{10.3}$$

**look-up table**

but large changes in $R_0$ are related to the changes in output voltage by the nonlinear relationship given by Eq. (10.1). Furthermore, the change in the resistance of the transducer is often nonlinear. Thus, the measurement system may have to process this nonlinear information to determine the measurand. With a computer-based system, this conversion is often performed by means of a *look-up table* that stores the nonlinear function in the computer.

---

**EXAMPLE 10.1** | **Balanced bridge**

Temperature is measured by a temperature-sensitive resistor called a thermistor. The nominal 10-k$\Omega$ thermistor is placed in a balanced bridge that has all resistors of 10 k$\Omega$ How much does $R_0$ have to increase to give a $v_{out} = 1/50 \times V$?

**SOLUTION:**
Using Eq. (10.3) with $R_1 = R_0$, we find

$$\frac{1}{50} \times V = V \times \frac{\Delta R_0}{4R_0} \quad \Rightarrow \quad \Delta R_0 = \frac{R_0}{12.5} = 800 \; \Omega \tag{10.4}$$

**WHAT IF?** What if you use the exact relationship in Eq. (10.1)?[1]

---

[1] $\Delta R_0 = +833$ or $-769 \; \Omega$.

**Strain gages.** Another common measurement component is the strain gage, which can be used to indicate strain, force, pressure, or acceleration. A *strain gage* is a resistor that is attached to a mechanical member to share the elongation of the member. A bonded strain gage, shown in Fig. 10.3 (a), is a resistance that is bonded to the member with an adhesive. Elongation changes the resistance of the gage by stretching the wire. The bonded strain gage is placed in a bridge circuit to produce an output voltage. Bonded strain gages are temperature-sensitive, and normally a second strain gage that shares the thermal environment, but not the strain, is used in the same bridge to minimize thermal effects.

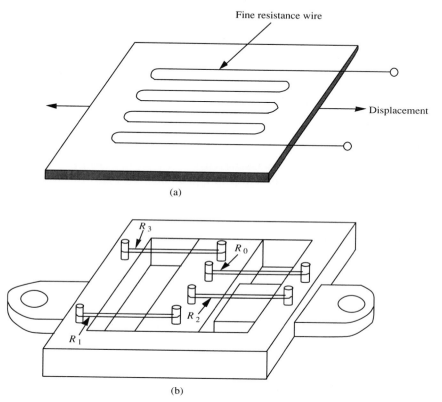

**Figure 10.3** (a) Bonded strain gage; (b) unbonded strain gage.

An unbonded strain gage is more sensitive than the bonded variety. As shown in Fig. 10.3(b), the entire bridge circuit is placed in a fixture that strains all four resistors, and temperature effects tend to cancel. More sensitive yet is the semiconductor strain gage, in which a special semiconductor material is bonded to the mechanical member. However, the semiconductor strain gage must be used in a temperature-controlled environment because its resistance is influenced strongly by temperature.

**Position transducers: potentiometers.** Figure 10.4 shows (a) translational and (b) rotational potentiometers. The potentiometer consists of a fixed resistor with a movable contact that responds to physical movement, thus changing the resistance ratio and

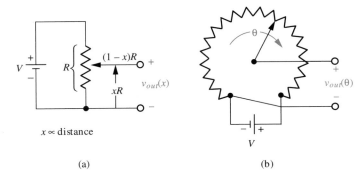

(a)

(b)

**Figure 10.4** (a) Translational potentiometer; (b) rotational potentiometer.

hence the output voltage of the voltage divider. The resulting change in resistance could be used in a bridge circuit or could produce a voltage directly, as shown in Fig. 10.4. The unloaded output voltage in Fig. 10.4(a) is

$$V_{out}(x) = V \times \frac{xR}{xR + (1-x)R} = xV \qquad (0 < x < 1) \qquad (10.5)$$

Potentiometers are available in which the output voltage relates to the physical movement through linear or logarithmic functions. Rotational potentiometers are available in single- or multiturn versions.

**Position transducers: linear variable differential transformers.**    The linear-variable differential transformer uses variable coupling between the primary and two secondaries of a transformer to create ac voltages that depend on the position of a magnetic slug. The diodes and resistors shown in Fig. 10.5 rectify the ac voltages and produce a dc output voltage that, after suitable filtering, gives an indication of the position of the magnetic slug. With the slug in the center, equal voltages are created across the two resistors and the output voltage is zero. With the slug off center, the voltages become unequal and produce an output voltage whose polarity indicates the direction of movement.

**Pressure transducers: diaphragm type.**    Pressure can be converted to force or displacement through the use of a diaphragm, bellows, or spiral tube. Therefore, pressure can be measured with a strain gage or some other means for monitoring force or displacement.

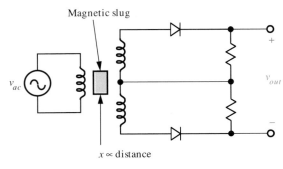

**Figure 10.5** The linear-variable differential transformer.

**Pressure transducers: integrated-circuit pressure cells.** Pressure cells based on semiconductor sensors are manufactured complete with bridge circuit and amplifiers. In effect, the input to the cell is a pressure, and the output is an electrical signal.

**Fluid-flow transducers.** Fluid flow in a pipe can be monitored through the differential pressure across an orifice or screen mesh. Fluid flow can also be measured through a turbine placed in the stream. The rotation rate of the turbine can be measured digitally to determine flow rate.

**Temperature transducers.** Many types of temperature sensors are available because almost all physical processes are affected by temperature. Sensors differ according to range and precision; a different transducer would be used to measure temperatures in the range of 5000°F than to monitor the temperature for an air-conditioning system. In the following, we describe two common types of temperature transducers that produce electrical outputs.

**thermistor**

**Temperature transducers: thermistors.** A *thermistor* is a resistor, made of a semiconductor, whose resistance depends on temperature. The change of intrinsic-carrier concentration with temperature produces a resistance that decreases strongly with increasing temperature. A typical temperature range for a thermistor is −100° to +300°C, and the resistance change is nonlinear. For monitoring of small temperature changes, the thermistor may be placed in a bridge circuit, but for large temperature changes, other circuit arrangements may be required.

---

**EXAMPLE 10.2** | **Thermistor**

A thermistor has a resistance given by

$$\ln\left(\frac{R(T)}{R_0}\right) = \alpha\left(\frac{1}{T} - \frac{1}{T_0}\right) \tag{10.6}$$

where $R(T)$ is the resistance at $T$ in Kelvin, $R_0 = 500\ \Omega$ at $T_0 = 20°C$ (293 Kelvin), and $\alpha = 4000$ is a parameter of the semiconductor. Find the temperature for $R(T) = 1000\ \Omega$

**SOLUTION:**
From Eq. (10.6),

$$\ln\left(\frac{1000}{500}\right) = 4000\left(\frac{1}{T} - \frac{1}{293}\right) \Rightarrow T = 278.8\ K\ (5.8°\ C) \tag{10.7}$$

**WHAT IF?** What if you solve for $R(T)$ for these parameters?[2]

---

[2] $R(T) = 5.89 \times 10^{-4}\ e^{4000/T}\ \Omega$.

**Temperature transducers: thermocouples.** A *thermocouple* is a junction between two dissimilar metals that produces a voltage that depends on the junction temperature. Thermocouples utilize this effect to monitor temperatures in a wide range, up to 2500°C. As shown in Fig. 10.6, two junctions are required, with a reference junction kept at constant temperature, often 0°C in an ice slush. Many types of metals are used, depending on the temperature range required, and typical temperature coefficients are $+50\ \mu V/°C$.

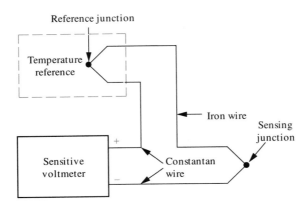

**Figure 10.6** A thermocouple-based temperature measurement requires two junctions, one at a known temperature.

**Summary.** In this section, we discussed the more common transducers used to measure displacement, force, pressure, fluid flow, and temperature. Sensors are available for measurement of virtually any physical variable. The technology of measurement is advanced and diverse; the best source of information is application literature from manufacturers.

## Error Analysis

**Need for error analysis.** Errors are introduced into a measurement system by the transducer, by the noise and nonlinearities of the analog electronics, by A/D conversion, and by digital signal processing. Error analysis combines the errors from the various components and processes to estimate the total error in the measurement. Some of the contributing errors are random errors describable by statistical methods, and some of the errors are estimates of uncertainty in calibration and system properties. Such errors may be combined only by making assumptions; and error analysis, even when undertaken with total objectivity, can be controversial. This section presents basic methods of error analysis.

**Exact and linearized error analysis.** The output of a measurement system depends on many factors, and in principle all can introduce errors. For a simple example, let us say we require a current source of magnitude, $I$, which we establish from a voltage source $V$, a resistance $R$, and the op-amp circuit shown in Fig. 10.7.

**Sources of error.** We assume the magnitude of the error in $V$ to be $\delta V$, the magnitude of the error in $R$ to be $\delta R$, and we ignore other sources of error such as finite loop gain, op-amp power-supply fluctuations, and thermal noise. The interpretation of the errors in $V$ and $R$ depends on the method of analysis employed, as is discussed in what

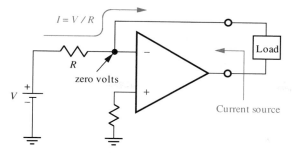

**Figure 10.7** A current source simulated with an op amp.

follows. These errors are not known quantities but rather uncertainties that we are willing to estimate. For example, $\delta V$ would depend on output ripple, noise introduced into the wiring, the influence of variations in line voltage and temperature on the voltage source, and whatever else might conceivably influence the input voltage. Likewise, $\delta R$ might be estimated from temperature change and calibration uncertainty. Usually, the magnitude of each error is estimated, the sign assumed randomly plus or minus. Our purpose in this section is to show how such "known" errors may be combined to estimate an overall error.

In this context, Ohm's law takes the form

$$I \pm \delta I = \frac{V \pm \delta V}{R \pm \delta R} \tag{10.8}$$

where $\delta I$ is the magnitude of the uncertainty in the output current. For purposes of illustration, we assume $V = 10$ V, $\delta V = 200$ mV, $R = 500\ \Omega$, and $\delta R = 1\%$. Equation (10.8) may be used to determine $\delta I$ by either the *worst-case* or the *statistical* error analysis shown in what follows.

**worst-case error analysis**

**Exact worst-case analysis.**   *Worst-case error analysis*, as the name implies, assumes that the errors are at their maximum and add in the worst possible way. The errors in this case, $\delta V$ and $\delta R$, are interpreted to be the maximum errors in the various factors, and the signs are chosen such that the effects of all errors are cumulative.

---

**EXAMPLE 10.3** | **Worst-case errors**

Calculate the worst-case error in the current-source output using the uncertainties given before.

**SOLUTION:**

Equation (10.8) gives a maximum current with maximum voltage and minimum resistance:

$$I + \delta I = \frac{V + \delta V}{R - \delta R} = \frac{10 + 0.2}{0.99 \times 500} = 20.606 \text{ mA} \tag{10.9}$$

and similarly a minimum output current of

$$I + \delta I = \frac{V - \delta V}{R + \delta R} = \frac{10 - 0.2}{1.01 \times 500} = 19.4059 \text{ mA} \tag{10.10}$$

Equations (10.9) and (10.10) may be solved for $I$ and $\delta I$ to yield

$$I = 20.006 \text{ mA} \quad \text{and} \quad \delta I = 0.600 \text{ mA} \qquad (10.11)$$

which may be expressed as

$$I = 20.006 \pm 0.600 \text{ mA (worst case)} \qquad (10.12)$$

In the example, the average value given by Eq. (10.12) is very near to the nominal value of 20 mA calculated before, because the relative errors are small. We put "worst-case" by our stated error to make explicit the method of error calculation and interpretation.

**Linearization.** Equation (10.8) is a simple expression, but usually many factors are involved in an error analysis, and the large number of variables and the nonlinear character of the expressions can lead to mathematical difficulties. For this reason, a linearized analysis is often performed. A linearized approximation to Eq. (10.8) is legitimate if the errors are small on a percent basis. We may linearize Eq. (10.8) by power-series expansion to the form

$$I(1 \pm \varepsilon_I) = \frac{V(1 \pm \varepsilon_V)}{R(1 \pm \varepsilon_R)} \approx \frac{V}{R} \times (1 \pm \varepsilon_V \pm \varepsilon_R \pm \text{higher order terms in } \varepsilon\text{'s}) \qquad (10.13)$$

where $\varepsilon_I = \delta I/I$, $\varepsilon_V = \delta V/V$, and $\varepsilon_R = \delta R/R$ are the normalized errors. The first term on the right side does not involve the errors and is the nominal output current. We may drop the higher-order terms and cancel the zeroth-order term on both sides of Eq. (10.13) to obtain a form involving only the errors:

$$\pm \varepsilon_I = \pm \varepsilon_V \pm \varepsilon_R \qquad (10.14)$$

Equation (10.14) is valid with the $\varepsilon$'s as normalized errors or as percent errors. In this simple case, both sources of error receive equal weight in establishing the resultant error, but in more complicated systems, the weights can differ.

---

**EXAMPLE 10.4** **Percent errors**

If the power supply voltage has a value of 10 V with an uncertainty of $\pm 200$ mV and a 1% tolerance 500-$\Omega$ resistor is used, what is the worst-case error in the current using a linearized analysis?

**SOLUTION:**
The nominal current is 20 mA. We interpret the $\varepsilon$'s in Eq. (10.14) as describing percent errors; hence we have

$$\varepsilon_V = \pm 2\% \pm 1\% = \pm 3\% \qquad (10.15)$$

where we have assumed that errors add. Thus, the worst case error is 3% of 20 mA, or 0.6 mA worst case.

**Summary.** In our examples, the difference between exact and linearized analysis is small because the errors are small. Worst-case analysis is pessimistic because it assumes that all errors are at their maximum values and that all the effects of errors accumulate. For this reason, worst-case error analysis is used primarily when life, property, or product acceptability is dependent on the results.

**Statistical error analysis.** A *statistical* analysis of system errors considers that errors are independent random variables described by probability density functions. The underlying mathematical models are beyond the scope of our treatment. Use of statistical techniques with the full nonlinear expressions is difficult at best, and usually a linearized analysis is performed.

With this model, the quoted errors of the $\varepsilon$'s are standard deviations and they combine in a Pythagorean addition. If we assume a standard deviation of 2% in $V$ and 1% in $R$.

$$\varepsilon_I = \sqrt{(2)^2 + (1)^2} = 2.24\% \text{ (1 s.d.)} \tag{10.16}$$

Note the following:

- With Pythagorean addition, the total errors are strongly dominated by the larger contributors. Small errors do not matter unless there are many of them.

- The "(1 s.d.)" means one standard deviation and implies the statistical method for combining errors. For our example, the statistical method yields a current of $20.00 \pm 0.45$ mA (1 s.d.). Normally, Gaussian statistics are assumed, and the results imply that the true current lies within the stated error bounds with a probability of 68% and within twice the error bounds with a probability of 95%.

Statistical error analysis is optimistic because it assumes that the errors can be small and that error cancelations occur to some extent. Experience shows that this method is usually valid, and its simplicity makes it popular.

## Check Your Understanding

1. The voltage applied to a Wheatstone bridge influences the output voltage unless the bridge is balanced. True or false?

2. Reversing both diodes in the linear-variable differential transformer does not change the output voltage. True or false?

3. A measurement system has three sources of error, which produce maximum errors of 1%, 1.8%, and 2.7%. What is the worst-case error possible in the output?

4. Repeat the previous problem if the errors are standard deviations. What is the standard deviation due to the combined errors?

*Answers.* (**1**) True; (**2**) false: the output changes sign; (**3**) 5.5% (worst case); (**4**) 3.40% (1 standard deviation).

The purpose of the analog section of the instrumentation system is to provide the A/D converter with analog information as free from noise as possible and in the acceptable voltage range. This involves amplification, gain control, removal of unwanted dc voltage, filtering, and cabling the system to minimize interference. In this section, we first treat matters relating to amplification and gain control, then deal with analog filtering techniques, and end with a brief section on grounding and shielding of instrumentation cables.

## Instrumentation Amplifiers

**Power ground, signal ground, single-ended signal, floating signal**

**Single-ended and floating signals.** In Chapter 5 we discussed grounding for safety; the *power ground* is the point of a circuit connected to earth by a large wire. By contrast, the *signal ground* of an electronic circuit is a connected set of conductors distributed to many points of the circuit to give a common reference voltage. Signal ground may or may not correspond to power ground. When the signal voltage appears between a wire carrying the signal and the signal ground, as shown in Fig. 10.8(a), the signal is *single-ended*. When the signal voltage appears between two wires independent of signal ground, as shown in Fig. 10.8(b), the signal is *floating*. The voltage source $v_{cm}$ in Fig. 10.8(b) might be voltage introduced by the circuit of the transducer or might represent noise induced in both wires carrying the signal. The floating signal can be considered two single-ended signals, with the real signal being their difference.

**OBJECTIVE 2**

**To understand how to recognize floating signals and be able to amplify difference-mode signals**

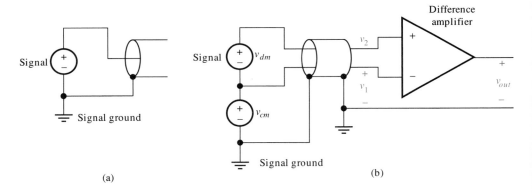

**Figure 10.8** (a) Single-ended signal; (b) floating signal.

**difference amplifier**

**Impedance Level**

**Amplifying floating signals.** With a single-ended signal, the standard op-amp amplifiers presented in Chapter 9 could be used. The noninverting amplifier would be favored because its high input impedance minimizes loading effects. A floating signal requires a *difference amplifier*, that is, an amplifier that subtracts the signals between the two input conductors and amplifies their difference. We presented a circuit that accomplishes this in Fig. 9.56, but that circuit suffers from a low input impedance. After discussing difference- and common-mode signals, we present an amplifier for floating input with high input impedance.

**Difference- and common-mode signals.** Signals of the type shown in Fig. 10.8(b) are described by a difference-mode signal and a common-mode signal. As shown in Fig. 10.9, the *difference-mode* signal, $v_{dm}$, is the difference between the two input voltages, as shown in Fig. 10.8(b). The *common-mode* signal is the average between $v_1$ and $v_2$ and is the voltage that the difference amplifier is required to reject, or at least minimize. The common- and difference-mode voltages relate to the single-ended voltages as

$$v_{dm} = v_2 - v_1 \qquad\qquad v_2 = v_{cm} + \frac{v_{dm}}{2}$$
$$\Leftrightarrow$$
$$v_{cm} = \frac{v_2 + v_1}{2} \qquad\qquad v_1 = v_{cm} + \frac{v_{dm}}{2} \qquad (10.17)$$

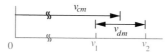

**Figure 10.9** The difference-mode signal is the difference between two voltages, and the common-mode signal is their average.

**Common-mode rejection.** An amplifier with a floating input, as shown in Fig. 10.8(b), ideally should have equal but opposite gains for both inputs, but in practice has slightly unequal gains. Let the gain for the noninverting input be $+A_2$ and the gain for the inverting input be $-A_1$, where both $A$s are positive. The output, therefore, is

$$v_{out} = +A_2 v_2 - A_1 v_1 = \underbrace{\left(\frac{A_1 + A_2}{2}\right)}_{\substack{\text{difference-mode} \\ \text{gain, } A_{dm}}} \times v_{dm} + \underbrace{(A_2 - A_1)}_{\substack{\text{common-mode} \\ \text{gain, } A_{cm}}} \times v_{cm} \qquad (10.18)$$

where the difference-mode gain, $A_{dm}$, is the average of $A_2$ and $A_1$ and the common-mode gain, $A_{cm}$, is the difference between $A_2$ and $A_1$. The *common-mode rejection ratio*, CMRR, is the ratio

$$\text{CMRR} = \left|\frac{A_{dm}}{A_{cm}}\right| \qquad (10.19)$$

A difference amplifier should have a large common-mode rejection ratio. A typical op amp would have a CMRR of 70 dB, which means that the gain for the difference-mode signal is $10^{+70/20} = 3162$ times the gain for the common-mode signal. In a given circuit application, the amplifier utilizing the op amp would have effects from the external circuit that would degrade the CMRR from that of the op amp alone. The magnitude of the common-mode voltage also has to lie within acceptable bounds for the op amp to operate satisfactorily.

---

**EXAMPLE 10.5** | **Bridge outputs**

The Wheatstone bridge in Fig. 10.2 operates with $V = 12$ V, $R_1 = R_2 = R_3 = 10$ kΩ, and $R_0 = 12$ kΩ. With these values, the voltage across $R_0$ is $v_2 = 6.545$ V and the voltage across

$R_2$ is $v_1 = 6.000$ V. We assume that this signal is amplified by a difference amplifier with a CMRR of 70 dB. What is the normalized error in the output due to the common-mode component?

**SOLUTION:**
The common-mode and difference-mode voltages can be determined from Eqs. (10.17), with the result $v_{dm} = 0.545$ V and $v_{cm} = 6.273$ V. Assuming a difference-mode gain of $A_{dm}$, the common-mode gain would be smaller by 70 dB: $A_{cm} = A_{dm}/3162$. The normalized error in the output due to the common-mode signal is, therefore,

$$\frac{6.273 \, A_{dm}/10^{70/20}}{0.545 \, A_{dm}} = 3.64 \times 10^{-3} = 0.364\% \tag{10.20}$$

**WHAT IF?**    What if $R_0 = 11$ k$\Omega$ and the CMRR $= 72$ dB?[3]

**Impedance Level**

**Instrumentation amplifier.**    The instrumentation amplifier shown in Fig. 10.10 has high and equal input impedances at both inputs and an output voltage that amplifies the difference between the input voltages. We recognize that the output op amp provides subtraction and amplification with a gain of $R_F/R_1$, as shown in Eq. (9.115). We may analyze the input stage by the methods of Sec. 9.4, p. 490. Because $v_+ \approx v_-$ for both amplifiers, the voltages at the top and bottom of $R_2$ are $v_2$ and $v_1$, respectively. The current in $R_2$ is thus

$$i = \frac{v_2 - v_1}{R_2} \tag{10.21}$$

Because the op-amp inputs have negligible input current, the current through $R_2$ must also go through both $R_3$'s, so the difference in output voltages is

$$v_2' - v_1' = iR_2 + 2iR_3 = (v_2 - v_1)\left(1 + \frac{2R_3}{R_2}\right) \tag{10.22}$$

Hence, the input stage gives a gain of $(1 + 2R_3/R_2)$, in addition to providing high and equal input impedances to the sources of $v_2$ and $v_1$. The difference-mode gain of the instrumentation amplifier shown in Fig. 10.10 is thus

$$A_{dm} = \frac{R_F}{R_1}\left(1 + \frac{2R_3}{R_2}\right) \tag{10.23}$$

The common-mode gain of the circuit depends on the CMRR for the output amplifier and the degree to which the $R_F/R_1$ ratios are matched for the two inputs to the subtractor circuit.

---

[3] The error would be 0.540%.

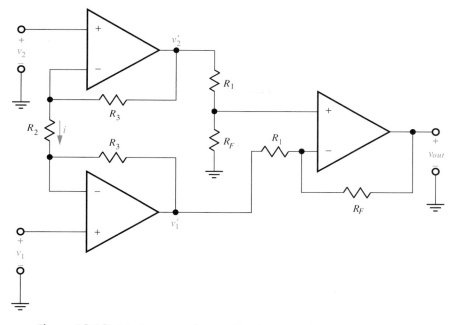

**Figure 10.10** The instrumentation amplifier has coupled noninverting amplifiers for high-input impedance, followed by a difference amplifier.

<table>
<tr><td>**EXAMPLE 10.6**</td><td>**Instrumentation-amplifier design**</td></tr>
</table>

A strain gage has a maximum output signal of 10 mV and a maximum of 1 V is allowed by the A/D converter. Design an instrumentation amplifier with the required gain using $R_2 = 10 \text{ k}\Omega$ and $R_1 = 10 \text{ k}\Omega$.

**SOLUTION:**

The required gain is $20 \log (1 \text{ V}/10 \text{ mV}) = 40$ dB. We choose 20 dB/stage of amplification. This requires

$$10^{20/20} = 10.0 = 1 + \frac{2R_3}{R_2} \Rightarrow R_3 = 4.5R_2 = 45 \text{ k}\Omega$$

(10.24)

$$10^{20/20} = 10.0 = \frac{R_F}{R_1} \Rightarrow R_F = 10R_1 = 100 \text{ k}\Omega$$

**WHAT IF?**      What if the top $R_3 = 46 \text{ k}\Omega$ and the bottom $R_3 = 44 \text{ k}\Omega$?[4]

---

[4] No problem: "$2R_3$" $= R_{3(\text{top})} + R_{3(\text{bottom})} =$ same.

**Amplifier with bias removal.** If the information appears as small changes in a dc voltage, we can use the amplifier shown in Fig. 10.11 to remove all or part of the dc voltage from the signal.[5] This circuit consists of a voltage-follower input stage, for high input impedance, followed by a subtractor. The dc input to the subtractor is derived from a potentiometer. The resistance of the potentiometer, $R_p$, should be somewhat less than $R$ to avoid loading effects and maintain constant gain for the signal.

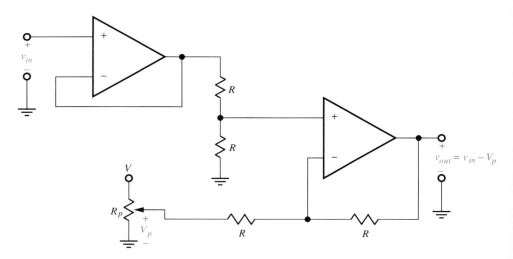

**Figure 10.11** This amplifier can be used to remove a dc bias from a signal.

**attenuator**

**Programmable attenuator.** An *attenuator* reduces the signal level by a prescribed amount. Attenuation is required when the signal level is too large for the A/D converter or some other component in the system. The inverting amplifier shown in Fig. 10.12 (a) has voltage gains of $-1$, $-0.5$, $-0.1$, $-0.05$, or $-0.01$, depending on the switch settings. The table in Fig. 10.12 (b) shows the standard settings, with a "1" indicating that the switch is closed. The attenuation in dB is the negative of the gain in dB. The switches might be relay switches or FET switches, controlled by an overrange indication from the A/D converter.

**Summary.** In this section we discussed a number of op-amp circuits that are useful in analog conditioning of signals. We defined difference-mode and common-mode signals and introduced the common-mode rejection ratio for an amplifier. We now discuss active filtering of analog signals.

## Analog Active Filters

**active filter**

**The Frequency Domain**

The analog section of an instrumentation system normally involves filtering. The filters typically are *active filters* employing op amps with frequency-dependent feedback networks. In this section, we first discuss sources of analog noise and then present representative active filter circuits for low-pass and high-pass filters.

---

[5] If the signal spectrum is not too low, a blocking capacitor can remove the dc and pass the signal. The circuit of Fig. 10.11 works for all signal frequencies.

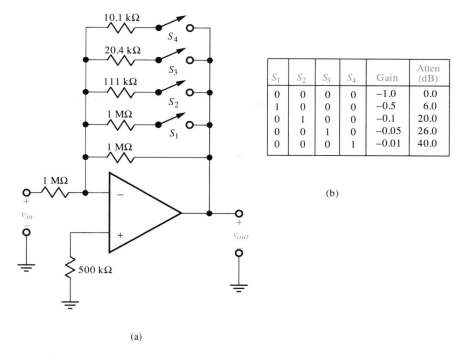

(a)

| $S_1$ | $S_2$ | $S_3$ | $S_4$ | Gain | Atten (dB) |
|---|---|---|---|---|---|
| 0 | 0 | 0 | 0 | −1.0 | 0.0 |
| 1 | 0 | 0 | 0 | −0.5 | 6.0 |
| 0 | 1 | 0 | 0 | −0.1 | 20.0 |
| 0 | 0 | 1 | 0 | −0.05 | 26.0 |
| 0 | 0 | 0 | 1 | −0.01 | 40.0 |

(b)

**Figure 10.12** This programmable attenuator reduces the signal level by factors up to 100, depending on the switch settings.

**OBJECTIVE 3**

**To understand analog signal and noise spectra and how active filters can improve system performance**

**Signal and noise spectra.** The transducer output signal has a time structure that may be described in the frequency domain by a spectrum. The transducer spectrum must be estimated as a basis for designing the filters of the analog section of the system. Noise from several sources is also present in the system. The purpose of the analog filter is to pass the transducer signal and to eliminate as much of the noise as possible. Because the signal and noise spectra typically overlap, the filter cannot fully eliminate the noise.

The spectrum of the signal is determined by the time variations in the measurand and the construction of the transducer. The specifications of the manufacturer of the transducer should give some indication of the time response.

**EXAMPLE 10.7** **Transducer bandwidth**

A temperature transducer is specified as having a 0.5-s time constant. What signal bandwidth might be expected from this transducer?

**SOLUTION:**
The specification of a time constant implies a first-order system like an $RC$ low-pass filter, presumably due to the thermal inertia of the material. Because the 3-dB frequency for such a filter is $f_c = 1/(2\pi RC)$, with $RC = \tau$, the time constant, a good estimate of the transducer signal bandwidth, $B$, is

$$B \approx \frac{1}{2\pi\tau} = \frac{1}{2\pi \times 0.5} = 0.318 \text{ Hz} \tag{10.25}$$

Variations of the temperature at higher frequencies would have little effect on transducer output.

**Types of noise.**   The principal components of the noise in the system are wide-band noise, $1/f$ noise, and interference. Figure 10.13 represents the spectra of wideband and $1/f$ noise. The wide-band noise consists of thermal noise, shot noise, and partition noise. Thermal noise arises in all resistors and is thermodynamic in origin; Chapter 11 gives more details. Shot and partition noise components arise in transistors due to the discrete character of electrical carriers and become a problem at small current levels. Interference is man-made noise that can be reduced by proper circuit layout, shielding, and grounding techniques, as discussed in the next section.

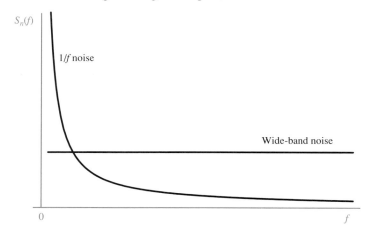

**Figure 10.13**   Two unavoidable noise components are $1/f$ and wide-band noise.

**1/f noise, drift, chopped signal**

**1/f noise.**   The $1/f$ noise component, which exists in all natural processes, shows the accumulated effects of small changes. For example, resistors and transistors are constantly changing in their microstructure due to heat, cosmic-ray damage, vibration, and a myriad of other effects. These combine to produce *drift*, that is, a slow meandering of signal values. Because the signal normally has a $1/f$ component of its own, which is part of its information content, the $1/f$ noise component cannot be eliminated by straightforward filtering.

**synchronous detection, chopping**

**Reducing 1/f noise.**   An important technique to minimize this noise component is the synchronous modulation/detection system shown in Fig. 10.14(a). The signal from the transducer is *chopped* or modulated by switching between the transducer output and a reference signal, as shown in Fig. 10.14(b). After amplification and analog filtering, the output component at the chopping frequency is detected by a phase-selective detector. The benefit of this scheme is that $1/f$ noise contributed by the electronic system is reduced because only these signal components near the modulation frequency are de-

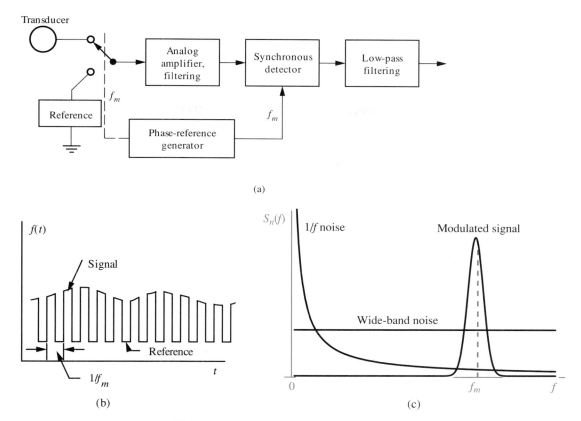

(a)

(b)

(c)

**Figure 10.14** (a) The lock-in detection system chops the signal at a frequency $f_m$ and detects the information at that frequency; (b) the slow variations in the signal are modulated by the chopping; (c) the effect of the modulation is to move the information to a higher frequency so that $1/f$ noise can be eliminated by the filtering and detection process.

tected. In effect, the modulation moves the information to a high frequency so that the $1/f$ noise can be filtered, as shown in Fig. 10.14(c). In Chapter 11, we again encounter modulation and detection in communication systems.

**active filter, passive filter**

**Active filters.** An *active filter* combines amplification with filtering. The *RC* filters investigated in Chapter 9 are *passive filters* because they provide only filtering. An active filter uses an op amp to furnish gain but has capacitors added to the input and feedback circuits to shape the filter characteristics.

We derived the gain of an inverting amplifier in the time domain. In Fig. 10.15, we show the frequency-domain version. We may easily translate the earlier derivation into the frequency domain:

$$v_{in} \Rightarrow \underline{\mathbf{V}}_{in}(\omega), \qquad v_{out} \Rightarrow \underline{\mathbf{V}}_{out}(\omega)$$

$$A_V = -\frac{R_F}{R_1} \Rightarrow \underline{\mathbf{F}}(\omega) = \frac{-\underline{\mathbf{Z}}_F(\omega)}{\underline{\mathbf{Z}}_1(\omega)} \tag{10.26}$$

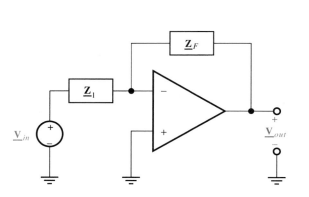

**Figure 10.15** Active filter circuit. $\underline{Z}_F$ and $\underline{Z}_1$ shape the filter characteristic.

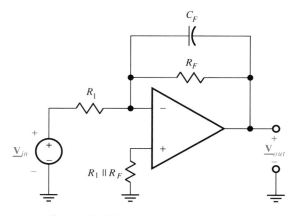

**Figure 10.16** Low-pass active filter circuit.

The filter function, $\underline{F}_V(\omega)$, is thus the ratio of the two impedances with an inversion, and in general gives gain as well as filtering.

**Low-pass active filter.** Placing a capacitor in parallel with $R_F$, Fig. 10.16, will at high frequencies tend to lower the magnitude of $\underline{Z}_F$ and hence reduce the gain of the amplifier; consequently, this capacitor converts an inverting amplifier into a low-pass filter with gain. We may write

$$\underline{Z}_F(\omega) = R_F \| \frac{1}{j\omega C_F} = \frac{1}{1/R_F + j\omega C_F} = \frac{R_F}{1 + j\omega R_F C_F} \qquad (10.27)$$

Because $\underline{Z}_1 = R_1$, the filter function from Eq. (10.26) is

$$\underline{F}_V(\omega) = -\frac{R_F}{R_1} \frac{1}{1 + j\omega R_F C_F} = A_V \frac{1}{1 + j(\omega/\omega_c)} \qquad (10.28)$$

where $A_V = -R_F/R_1$ is the gain without the capacitor, and $\omega_c = 1/R_F C_F$ is the cutoff frequency. The gain of the amplifier is approximately constant until the frequency exceeds $\omega_c$, after which the gain decreases with increasing $\omega$.

---

**EXAMPLE 10.8** **Low-pass active filter**

A pressure transducer requires a low-pass filter with a gain of 20 dB and an input impedance of 1 kΩ. The time constant of the transducer is 100 ms. Design a suitable filter for this application.

**SOLUTION:**
The low-frequency gain is $A_v = -10^{20/20} = -10$, so $R_F = 10R_1 = 10$ kΩ. From Eq. (10.25), we estimate the required cutoff frequency to be $1/(2\pi \times 0.1) = 1.59$ Hz. This is the critical frequency; thus, from the discussion of Eq. (10.28), we calculate

$$C_F = \frac{1}{\omega_c R_F} = \frac{1}{2\pi \times 1.59 \times 10^4} = 10\mu F \qquad (10.29)$$

The Bode plot of this filter function is shown in Fig. 10.17. The shape is identical to that of the low-pass filter in Fig. 9.25, but there is an increase in gain due to the op amp.

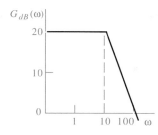

**Figure 10.17** Bode plot for an active low-pass filter.

**WHAT IF?**

What if the gain is to be 27 dB and the critical frequency 3 Hz?[6]

**High-pass active filter.** The high-pass filter shown in Fig. 10.18 uses a capacitor in series with $R_1$ to reduce the gain at low frequencies. For this filter, $\mathbf{Z}_F = R_F$ and $\mathbf{Z}_1 = R_1 + 1/j\omega C_1$; hence, the filter function is

$$\mathbf{F}_V(\omega) = -\frac{R_F}{R_1 + 1/j\omega C_1} = A_V \times \frac{j\omega/\omega_c}{1 \times j(\omega/\omega_c)} \qquad (10.30)$$

where $A_V = -R_F/R_1$ is the gain without the capacitor, and $\omega_c = 1/R_1 C_1$ is the cutoff frequency, below which the amplifier gain is reduced. The Bode plot of this filter characteristic is shown in Fig. 10.19. This Bode plot is identical to that of the high-pass filter given in Fig. 9.27 except for the increase in gain due to the op amp.

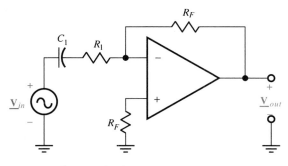

**Figure 10.18** High-pass filter circuit.

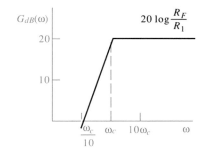

**Figure 10.19** Bode plot for active high-pass filter for $R_F = 10R_1$.

---

[6] $R_F = 22.4$ k$\Omega$ and $C_F = 2.37$ $\mu$F.

**Butterworth-filter characteristics.** The general low-pass Butterworth-filter characteristic is

$$|\mathbf{F}(f)| = \frac{1}{\sqrt{1 + (f/f_c)^{2n}}} \tag{10.31}$$

where $n$ is the order of the filter and $f_c$ is the critical frequency. For $n = 1$, we have the characteristic of the low-pass filter discussed in Chapter 9. The filter characteristics for $n = 1$ and $n = 2$ are shown in the asymptotic Bode plots of Fig. 10.20. The second-order filter characteristic drops at $-40$ dB/decade after the critical frequency is passed.

**Low-pass, two-pole Butterworth filter.** The circuit shown in Fig. 10.21 gives a second-order Butterworth-filter characteristic. This circuit combines positive and negative feedback, and its principles of operation are complex. We will confirm the characteristic by using the op-amp analysis techniques developed in Chapter 9.

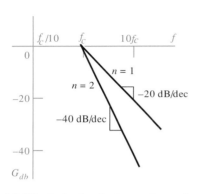

**Figure 10.20**  Bode plots for first- and second-order Butterworth low-pass circuits.

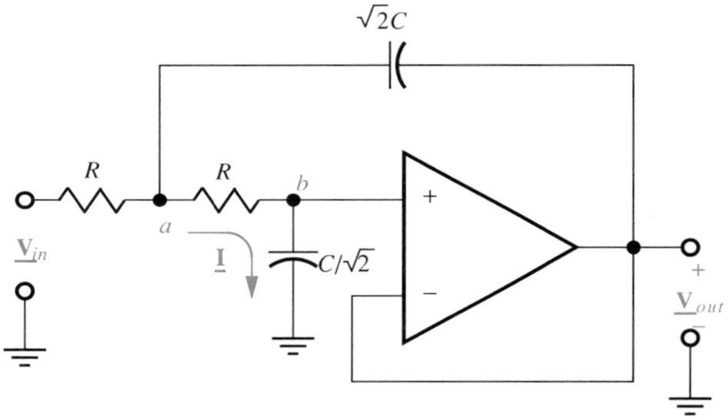

**Figure 10.21**  Second-order Butterworth low-pass-filter circuit.

**Analysis of Butterworth-filter circuit.** Applying the op-amp principles of Sec. 9.4, p. 490, we require that the input voltage to both op-amp inputs be essentially $\mathbf{V}_{out}$. Thus, the current $\mathbf{I}$ shown in Fig. 10.21 is

$$\mathbf{I} = j \frac{\omega C}{\sqrt{2}} \mathbf{V}_{out} \tag{10.32}$$

Hence, the voltage at point $a$ is

$$\mathbf{V}_a = \mathbf{V}_{out} + R\mathbf{I} = \mathbf{V}_{out}\left(1 + \frac{j\omega RC}{\sqrt{2}}\right) \tag{10.33}$$

We can now write KCL for node $a$, which is a standard nodal equation:

$$\frac{\left(1 + j\dfrac{\omega RC}{\sqrt{2}}\right)\mathbf{V}_{out} - \mathbf{V}_{in}}{R} + \frac{\left(1 + j\dfrac{\omega RC}{\sqrt{2}}\right)\mathbf{V}_{out} - \mathbf{V}_{out}}{1/j\sqrt{2}\,\omega C} + j\frac{\omega C}{\sqrt{2}}\mathbf{V}_{out} = 0 \tag{10.34}$$

Equation (10.34) has the solution

$$\underline{\mathbf{V}}_{out} = \frac{\underline{\mathbf{V}}_{in}}{1 - (\omega RC)^2 + j\sqrt{2}\,\omega RC} \qquad (10.35)$$

For the Bode plot, we require the square of the magnitude of the filter gain:

$$|\underline{\mathbf{F}}(\omega)|^2 = \left|\frac{\underline{\mathbf{V}}_{out}}{\underline{\mathbf{V}}_{in}}\right|^2 = \frac{1}{[1 - (\omega RC)^2]^2 + (\sqrt{2}\,\omega RC)^2} = \frac{1}{1 + (\omega RC)^4} \qquad (10.36)$$

which is the required Butterworth characteristic, Eq. (10.31) for $n = 2$ and

$$f_c = \frac{1}{2\pi RC} \qquad (10.37)$$

---

**EXAMPLE 10.9** **Butterworth filters**

Design a second-order low-pass Butterworth filter with a 3-dB frequency of 8 Hz. The output impedance of the input transducer is less than $100\ \Omega$.

**SOLUTION:**
The critical frequency given by Eq. (10.37) is the 3-dB frequency. The design requires one choice. We may ensure that the filter has insignificant loading of the signal source by making $R$ much greater than $100\ \Omega$. Accordingly, we choose $R = 10\ \text{k}\Omega$ and Eq. (10.37) determines the value of $C$ to be

$$C = \frac{1}{2\pi R f_c} = \frac{1}{2\pi(10^4)8} = 1.99\ \mu F \qquad (10.38)$$

This is not the value of either capacitor in the circuit in Fig. 10.21 but is rather the geometric mean between the two capacitors. The capacitors are thus approximately $2.8\ \mu F$ and $1.4\ \mu F$, and the required circuit is shown in Fig. 10.22.

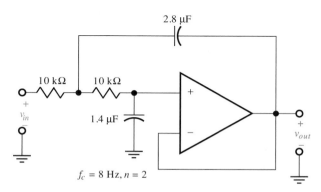

**Figure 10.22** Second-order low-pass Butterworth filter circuit.

**Other filters.**   Standard designs exist for high-pass Butterworth filters and wide- and narrow-band band-pass Butterworth filters, as well as several other filters having superior characteristics to the Butterworth in some aspects. Handbooks and application literature give practical circuits for many active filter circuits. Filter manufacturers produce filters of prescribed characteristics for high-frequency, extremely narrow-band band-pass, and narrow-band band-reject filters.

## Cabling, Grounding, and Shielding Techniques

**Interference, EMI**

**Impedance Level**

**Sources of interference.**   Unwanted, man-made electrical signals constitute a class of noise called *interference*.[8] Interference may couple into a transducer circuit via an electric field, a magnetic field, or a common ground wire. Electric-field interference arises from high-voltage or high-frequency signals and couples into high-impedance portions of electronic circuits. Magnetic fields induce signals by coupling to loops of wire in a low-impedance electronic circuit. Both types of interference may be reduced by proper circuit layout, shielding, and grounding techniques.

**OBJECTIVE 4**

**To understand the principles of cabling, grounding, and shielding to reduce interference**

**Reducing interference.**   Sensitive electronic equipment picks up interference in the vicinity of high-power electrical equipment such as motors, welders, and transformers, near radio and TV stations, or near power-electronic equipment such as motor controllers and large power supplies. Interference may be reduced by avoiding such locations if possible and shielding electronic circuits with grounded metallic cabinets and power lines with metal conduit. Circuits susceptible to magnetic interference may be shielded by magnetic foil. Low-level signals should be protected by twisted-pair conductors within a braided outer conductor.

**signal ground**

**Grounding.**   The signal ground is a network of wires, all tied together, to provide a reference potential of zero volts to all parts of the circuits. Grounding problems arise because currents flow in ground wires, and because the ground wires have resistance and inductance, voltage differences are created between different portions of the grounding system. Such differences can create false signals at low-level inputs. One precaution is to connect all grounds within a system to a common point through separate wires so that ground currents do not share wires, but this is usually unnecessary. A more practical technique is to provide a separate grounding system for high-level signals and signals that have rapid transitions that is isolated from the grounding system for low-level instrumentation signals.

Long cable runs between instruments or between a transducer and its analog electronics can cause special problems in grounding. When connected through the cable in an attempt to provide a common ground between two separate systems, as shown in Fig. 10.23, as much as 100 mV of voltage can exist between "ground" *a* and "ground" *b*

---

[7]The gain is $-5.37$ dB at 10 Hz.

[8]Or *EMI* for electromagnetic interference.

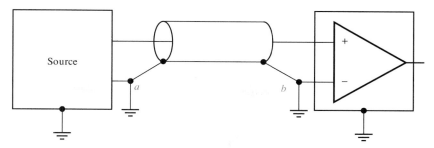

**Figure 10.23** Electronic circuits with grounds connected through the connecting cable. This approach can cause interference problems if the two "ground"s are not at the same potential.

due to interference signals. This connection is unacceptable unless signals are much larger than that level of interference.

The cabling connection shown in Fig. 10.24(a) allows separate grounds. The input to the receiving chassis is floating, with the cable shield as one input. The connection in Fig. 10.24(b) uses a common ground, but the signal is carried by a twisted-pair shielded cable and thus floats. The signal-carrying wires are twisted to reduce magnetic coupling.

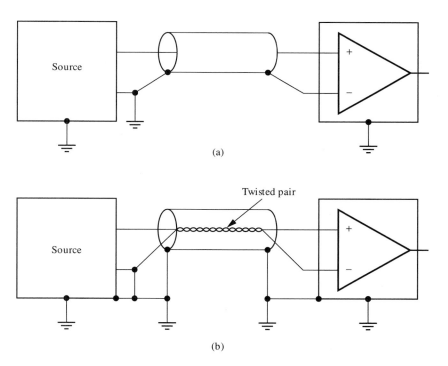

**Figure 10.24** (a) No common ground is provided in this connection; (b) here a common ground is provided, but the signal is separate from the ground connection.

## Check Your Understanding

1. Grounding one part of a floating input produces a single-ended input. True or false?

2. The voltages of a floating input are $+1.5$ V and $-0.8$ V. Find the common-mode and difference-mode components.

3. A difference amplifier has a voltage gain of 15,000 and a common-mode rejection ratio of 65 dB. What is the gain for the common-mode component of the input?

4. What would be the gain of the programmable attenuator in Fig. 10.12 if all switches were closed?

5. Show that the product of the voltage gain and the bandwidth of the low-pass filter in Fig. 10.16 is independent of the resistor in the feedback path.

6. The grounding system used in Fig. 10;23 would be acceptable for logic signals with a 5-V amplitude. True or false?

7. Twisted-pair cables are used to reduce electric-field or magnetic-field interference. Which?

*Answers.* (1) True; (2) $V_{cm} = 0.35$ V, $V_{dm} = 2.3$ V; (3) 8.44; (4) $0.00629 = -44.0$ dB; (5) gain $\times B = 2\pi/R_1 C_F$; (6) true; (7) magnetic-field interference.

---

## 10.3 DIGITAL SIGNAL PROCESSING

**OBJECTIVE 5**

To understand digital signal sampling, conversion, and filtering

A/D, ADC, ADC precision

### Analog-to-Digital Conversion

**Introduction.** An *analog-to-digital converter* (ADC or A/D) changes an analog signal to a digital signal for processing in digital form. Figure 10.25(a) shows an ADC with analog input, a *GO* input to initiate conversion, outputs to indicate the status of the conversion, and three output bits. If the ADC is linear, the digital output will be related to the analog input as indicated in Fig. 10.25 (b). The *precision* of the ADC is the number of output bits, in this case 3. The *range* of the ADC is given by the maximum and minimum input voltages that can be converted with at most a one-half least-significant-bit (LSB) error.

---

**EXAMPLE 10.10** **Errors in an ADC**

The full-scale (FS) input voltage of a 3-bit ADC is 10 V. As shown in Fig. 10.25(b), the range of the ADC is from 625 mV (1/16 FS) to 8.125 V (13/16 FS).[9] Find the worst-case error and rms error from digitizing the analog signal.

**SOLUTION:**
The worst-case error is 1/16 FS, or 0.625 V, as shown in Fig. 10.25(b). The rms error requires computing the rms value of a sawtooth waveform with a peak value of 0.625 V. We integrate over one-half the error cycle:

---

[9] If we use 111 for an overrange indication.

$$V_e^2 = \frac{1}{\text{FS}/16} \int_{-\text{FS}/32}^{+\text{FS}/32} (0.625)^2 \left(\frac{v_e}{\text{FS}/32}\right)^2 dv_e = \left(\frac{0.625}{3}\right)^2 \qquad (10.39)$$

where $V_e$ is the rms error and $v_e$ is the error voltage, the difference between the sloping and stair-step functions in Fig. 10.25(b). Thus, the rms error is $0.625/\sqrt{3} = 0.361$ V.

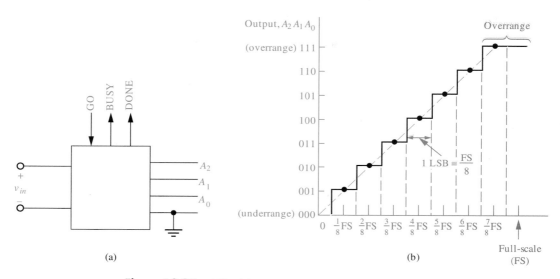

**Figure 10.25**  a) The A/D converter takes an analog input and converts to a parallel digital output; (b) the output binary word depends on the analog input.

**Underflow and overflow.**  Voltages below 625 mV would give an output of 000, indicating underrange, or *underflow*, and voltages above 9.375 V would give an output of 111 plus an overrange, or *overflow,* indication. The underrange and overrange indications can be used to control the gain of the analog channel to keep the analog voltage within the range of the ADC. The *resolution* of the ADC is the FS voltage divided by the number of output states, in this case, $10 \text{ V}/2^3 = 1.25$ V, and corresponds to 1 bit. Typical commercial ADCs have 8- and 12-bit precision, indicating 256 and 4096 states, respectively.

**underflow, overflow, ADC range, ADC resolution**

**Two-bit flash A/D converter.**  Figure 10.26(a) shows a 2-bit flash ADC; "flash" because it yields instantaneous output. The resistors in series set up three reference voltages, and the analog input voltage is compared simultaneously with all references, with the results shown in the truth table of Fig. 10.26(c). The lowest comparator indicates underflow and the highest indicates overflow. The middle three comparators indicate which of the four possible ranges contains the input, and the logic circuit in the dash-line box converts this information to a binary output code. The A/D conversion takes place almost instantaneously. This type of ADC, also called a *parallel encoder*, is available commercially in 4- and 8-bit versions. Figure 10.26(b) shows that the ranges for this converter are set up with an offset from a linear function passing through the origin, unlike the ideal in Fig. 10.25(b).

**flash converter, underflow, overflow, parallel encoder**

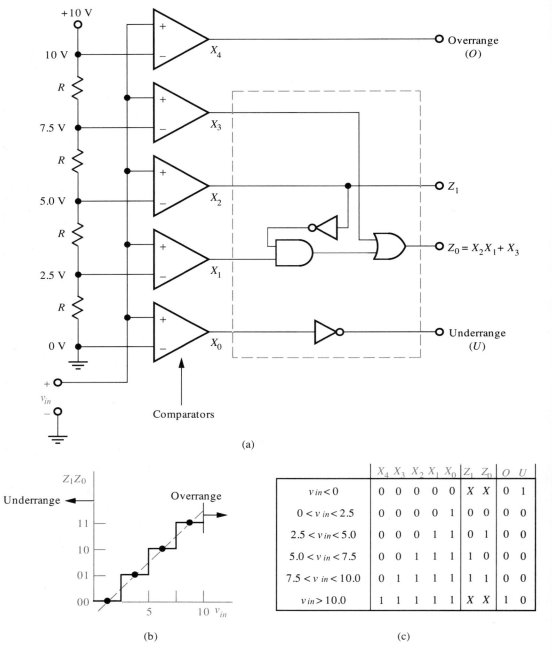

**Figure 10.26** (a) The 2 bit flash ADC converter compares the input with ranges of voltage; (b) the output–input characteristic of the ADC; (c) the truth table of the ADC, including overrange and underrange indications.

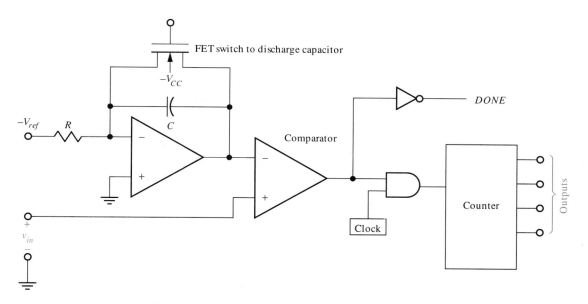

**Figure 10.27** The single-slope converter counts clock pulses until an increasing ramp voltage exceeds the input voltage.

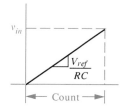

**Figure 10.28** The count is proportional to the input voltage.

**Single-slope ramp analog-to-digital conversion.** A single slope ramp converter uses an integrator to generate a linearly increasing voltage to compare with the unknown voltage. The circuit is shown in Fig. 10.27 uses an op amp to integrate an input reference voltage. This gives an output ramp function shown in Fig. 10.28. While the ramp is increasing, the AND gate allows the counter to count clock pulses, but when the comparator indicates that the ramp voltage has exceeded the analog input, the count stops, $DONE = 1$, and the counter output is displayed as indicated in Fig. 10.27. The capacitor is then discharged electronically, and the ADC is ready to begin its conversion cycle again.

---

**EXAMPLE 10.11** | **ADC**

An 8-bit ADC has a range from 0-10 V and a 100-kHz clock frequency. Find the time it takes to make the conversion and the required ramp slope.

**SOLUTION:**
Eight bits corresponds to a count of $2^8 = 256$ from the clock, which requires $256 \times T = 256 \times 10^{-5} = 2.56$ ms. The slope in Fig. 10.28 is $(10\text{ V})/(2.56\text{ ms}) = 3906$ V/s. For $V_{ref} = 8$ V, $RC = 2.05$ ms.

**WHAT IF?** What if a 1-MHz clock is used on a 12-bit converter?[10]

---

[10] Converts in 4.10 ms; $RC = 3.28$ ms.

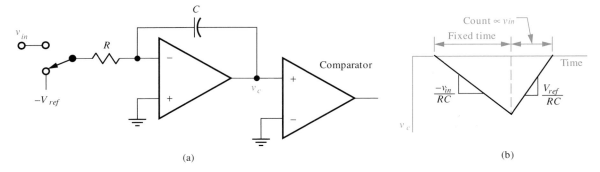

**Figure 10.29** (a) Dual-slope ramp conversion input stage; (b) the number of counts while the voltage is coming to zero indicates the analog input voltage.

**Dual-slope A/D ramp conversion.** Dual-slope conversion has several advantages over single-slope conversion. Figure 10.29 (a) shows the input to the integrator connected first to the unknown analog input voltage, and the output voltage increases in the negative direction a fixed amount of time, normally a multiple of the power-line period to reject this form of interference. The input then is switched to a known reference voltage of opposite polarity, and clock pulses are counted until the integrator voltage passes through zero, Fig. 10.29(b). The advantage of this scheme is that the unknown is compared to the voltage reference, independent of variations in the clock frequency. This is the method employed in most digital voltmeters.

## Sampling

**multiplexer**

Typically, transducers monitoring physical processes produce data rates well below the capability of a computer. Thus, many inputs can be monitored simultaneously. Numerous analog inputs may be sampled at discrete times sequentially through a *multiplexer*, which is essentially an electronic multipole switch. A sample-and-hold circuit may be required to arrest change in an input while A/D conversion is being performed. Finally, the discrete samples of the time-varying inputs may be processed as a time sequence by the computer by techniques known as digital filtering. Processes associated with the sampling of the analog inputs are discussed in this section.

**Analog multiplexers.** The analog multiplexer, AMUX, shown in Fig. 10.30(a) accepts eight analog inputs. A 3-bit address $B_2 B_1 B_0$ selects the input to connect to the output. By cycling through all inputs, the ADC can sequentially convert all inputs to digital form for processing by a computer.

**FET switch.** Figure 10.30(b) shows how the AMUX uses an FET switch to connect and disconnect an input from the output. The FET is used as a voltage-controlled switch. With zero voltage on the gate, the drain–source resistance is many megohms and the input voltage is blocked. With sufficient voltage applied to the gate, the FET is placed in the ohmic region, and the drain–source resistance is 25 to 100 $\Omega$, allowing the analog input to appear across the 47-k$\Omega$ resistor and the output. The internal logic in the AMUX decodes the channel address and connects one channel at a time with a "break-before-make" connection to ensure that no two input channels are shorted together through the switches.

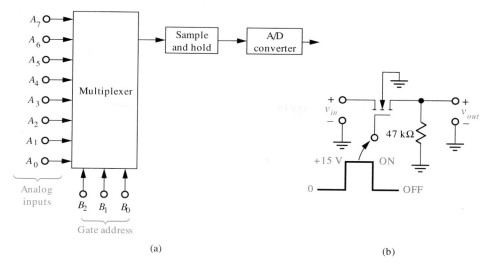

(a)

(b)

**Figure 10.30** (a) This multiplexer has eight analog inputs. The input selected by the incoming address is connected to the sample-and-hold circuit for analog-to-digital conversion. (b) The FET switch is an open circuit except when its gate is at +15 volts, connecting input to output.

---

**EXAMPLE 10.12** **AMUX loss and cross coupling**

The output impedances of the analog inputs to a 8-input AMUX is 100 $\Omega$. The FET OFF resistance is 10 M$\Omega$ and its ON resistance is 60 $\Omega$. Find the loss of the AMUX when the FET is ON.

**SOLUTION:**
One channel is ON and seven channels are OFF. The equivalent circuit is shown in Fig. 10.31. The output voltage compared with the open-circuit voltage at the analog input is given by a voltage divider:

$$\frac{v_{out}}{v_{in}} = \frac{47\text{k}\Omega \| (10\text{M}\Omega/7)}{47\text{k}\Omega \| (10\text{M}\Omega/7) + 100 + 60} = 0.996(-0.03\text{dB}) \qquad (10.40)$$

**WHAT IF?**
What if the FET is OFF? Find the isolation assuming another switch ON. [11]

---

**sample and hold**  **Sample-and-hold circuit.** Figure 10.32 shows a *sample-and-hold* circuit, which is used to arrest time variations in the input signal during ADC processing. The circuit uses two voltage-follower amplifiers to buffer input and output. An FET switch is acti-

---

[11] The isolation is 100 dB.

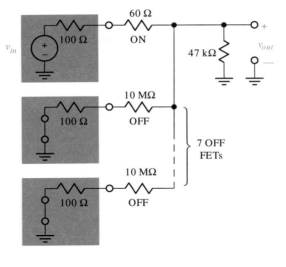

**Figure 10.31** Circuit with one FET ON and the other seven OFF.

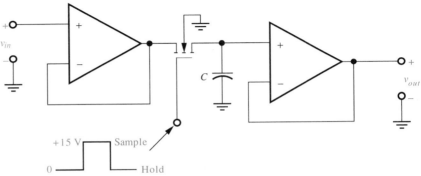

**Figure 10.32** The sample-and-hold circuit uses a capacitor to remember the voltage after the FET switch is gated ON briefly.

vated long enough for the capacitor to charge to the input voltage, and then the capacitor holds the voltage while A/D conversion is taking place. The capacitance is a compromise between the requirements for rapid charging and long voltage-retention time: The small capacitor required for rapid charging places a limit on how long the capacitor can hold the voltage to a prescribed tolerance, considering the leakage current through the FET and into the op amp.

---

**EXAMPLE 10.13** **Capacitance design**

In the sample-and-hold circuit of Fig. 10.32, the FET ON resistance is 25 Ω and the requirement is for charging to 99% of the input value in 1 μs. Find the required capacitance.

**SOLUTION:**
Assuming $v_C(0) = 0$ V, the transient is of the form

$$v_C(t) = V_\infty(1 - e^{-t/\tau}) \tag{10.41}$$

where $V_\infty$ is the output of the buffer and $\tau = RC = 25C$, assuming negligible output impedance from the buffer. Thus,

$$e^{-1\,\mu s/\tau} = 0.01 \quad \Rightarrow \quad \tau = 0.217\,\mu s \quad \Rightarrow \quad C = 8.7\,nF \tag{10.42}$$

**WHAT IF?**

What if the output impedance of the buffer is $5\,\Omega$ and a $10\,nF$ capacitor is used? What is the error in capacitor voltage for $1\,\mu s$ ON time?[12]

**Discrete samples.** Let us consider that we have a data-acquisition system with several inputs. We use an AMUX to sample the inputs with the sample-and-hold circuit holding the sampled voltages long enough for A/D conversion. The end result of this operation is a sequence of samples representing the time structure of each input, as shown by Fig. 10.33 (a). The discrete sampling of the time structure of the input raises two questions: "What is an appropriate sampling rate?" and "How should we process the samples to improve the information content of the data?"

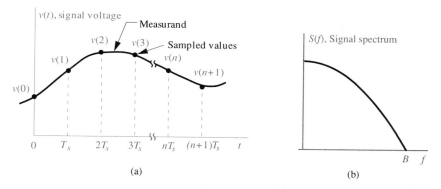

(a)

(b)

**Figure 10.33** (a) The continuous waveform is sampled at a frequency $f_s = 1/T_s$ producing a sequence of discrete values, $v(0)$, $v(1)$, ...; (b) the spectrum of the signal waveform before sampling. The Nyquist criterion states that the sampling frequency must be at least twice the signal bandwidth to avoid loss of information and prevent confusion.

**Nyquist sampling criterion.** The question of how often to sample is answered by the *Nyquist criterion*, which states that no information is lost through the sampling process if the sampling frequency $f_s$ satisfies the following criterion:

$$f_s > 2\,B \tag{10.43}$$

**aliasing**

where $B$ is the bandwidth of the waveform being sampled, as shown in Fig. 10.33(b). Thus, you must sample twice during each period of the highest frequency in the signal.

---

[12] 3.6%.

If the Nyquist criterion is violated by sampling too slowly, information is lost and the information content of the sampled values becomes confused through *aliasing*, the mixing of high frequencies into the signal band. For a wideband signal, the bandwidth prior to sampling should be limited to prevent aliasing.

<table>
<tr><td>**EXAMPLE 10.14**</td><td>**Nyquist Sampling**</td></tr>
</table>

A temperature transducer has a 0.5-s time constant. The signal bandwidth of this transducer was determined on p. 537 to be 0.318 Hz. What is an appropriate time between samples to monitor the temperature information out of the transducer?

**SOLUTION:**
The calculated bandwidth is not an exact guide because some signal spectrum lies above this critical frequency. To prepare this signal for sampling, we might use a second-order Butterworth low-pass filter with a critical frequency of 0.4 Hz, and then sample at 0.9 Hz to be safe. Thus, a sample every 1.11 seconds would get all the information that passes the filter.

**Digital filtering.** Digital filtering concerns the processing of the samples. Of course, the samples may be used directly, but often signal characteristics are improved by processing the samples. To illustrate this technique, we consider two sample-processing schemes for the filter indicated by Fig. 10.34.

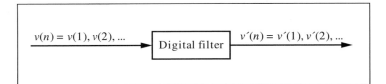

$v(n) = v(1), v(2), \ldots$   Digital filter   $v'(n) = v'(1), v'(2), \ldots$

**Figure 10.34** The digital filter accepts discrete input samples and uses a numerical procedure to produce output discrete data. The "filter" is a software algorithm in the computer.

**FIR, nonrecursive**

**FIR and IIR filtering.** The first is called a *finite impulse response* (*FIR*, or *nonrecursive*) filter, because it calculates the output, $x'(n)$, from previous values of the input, $x(n)$, $x(n-1)$, .... Consider, for example, the FIR filter represented by the calculation

$$x'(n) = \frac{x(n) + x(n-1)}{2} \tag{10.44}$$

**IIF, recursive**

The output is the running unweighted average of the current and previous sample of the input. By contrast, an infinite impulse (*IIF*, or *recursive*) filter calculates $x'(n)$ from previous inputs, $x(n)$, $x(n-1)$, ..., and previous outputs, $x'(n-1)$, $x'(n-2)$, ... An example is

$$x'(n) = \frac{x'(n-1) + x(n)}{2} \tag{10.45}$$

which averages the input with the previous output to give the new output.

We may compare the response of the FIR and the IIR filters described by Eqs. (10.44) and (10.45) by examining their responses to a sudden increase of the input. Figure 10.35(b) shows the responses calculated in the table in Fig. 10.35(a) for the filter algorithms given in Eqs. (10.44) and (10.45). We filled in between the samples with lines to aid in identification of the responses. The IIF algorithm has a greater smoothing effect because it has a longer memory of the past history of the input.

|  |  | 0 | 1 | 2 | 3 | 4 |
|---|---|---|---|---|---|---|
| Input | $x(n)$ | 0 | 1 | 1 | 1 | 1 |
| FIR | $x_1'(n)$ | 0 | 0.5 | 1 | 1 | 1 |
| IIR | $x_2'(n)$ | 0 | 0.5 | 0.75 | 0.88 | 0.94 |

(a)

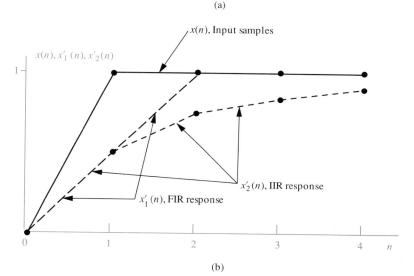

(b)

**Figure 10.35** (a) Table showing input and output of a digital filter with the filter algorithms given in Eqs. (10.44) and (10.45). The input is a sudden increase in the input value. (b) Plots of input and output samples.

Digital filters and their effects are an established technique of digital-signal processing. Digital filters exist to simulate analog filters such as the Butterworth filters and to eliminate discrete frequencies, 60-Hz hum, for example.

## Digital-to-Analog Conversion

The instrumentation system shown in Fig. 10.1 includes the possibility of an analog output from the computer because often the purpose of the data-gathering function is to control the processes being monitored. For example, the temperature of chemical reagents might be monitored to maintain a prescribed temperature through heaters. In this section we discuss digital-to-analog converters (D/A converters or DACs).

**DAC, D/A**

**Function.** The *digital-to-analog converter* (DAC or D/A) accepts a digital input and produces an analog output. The input–output characteristics are the same as those shown in Fig. 10.25(b) for the ADC, except that the vertical axis represents the input and the horizontal axis represents the output. Depending on details of the construction and specifications, the output might be offset from zero in the manner of Fig. 10.26(b). We will show circuits for two representative 3-bit DACs.

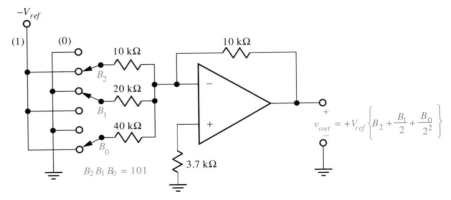

**Figure 10.36** This 3-bit digital-to-analog converter circuit sums voltages.

**Voltage-summing DAC.** The circuit shown in Fig. 10.36 uses a binary-weighted sum of inputs controlled by three single-pole, double-throw switches representing the digital word. The principle of operation of a summing amplifier circuit is discussed on page 498. Here each input is either $-V_{ref}$ or 0 V, depending on the switch setting. The switch positions shown correspond to the binary word $B_2B_1B_0 = 101$, and the output is $1.25V_{ref}$. Clearly, 000 produces zero output and 111 produces $1.75V_{ref}$. The least significant bit is thus $0.25V_{ref}$ for this DAC.

**Ladder DAC.** The circuit shown in Fig. 10.37(a) is based on the properties of the $R$-$2R$ ladder network, which are indicated in Fig. 10.37(b). We use the principle of superposition to examine the effect of the LSB input ($B_0$). Note that the equivalent resistance of the ladder is $2R$ into the series resistors and $R$ into the parallel resistors going to the inputs. Thus, the equivalent resistance values are the same, regardless of the length of the ladder. At each input, the input resistance is $3R$, so the input current from the source at $B_0$ is $I_0 = -V_{ref}/3R$. The $R-2R$ ladder network halves the current at each node. By the time the input current at $B_0$ reaches the op-amp input, it is halved three times, a factor of 8, such that the current into the op amp is $-V_{ref}/24R$. As explained on page 493, this current goes through the feedback resistor of $6R$ and produces an output voltage of $+V_{ref}/4$. The input of each higher-order bit produces a larger voltage by a factor of 2 because the current is halved one less time. Thus, the input at $B_2$ produces an output voltage of $+V_{ref}$, and generally the ladder can be extended to a larger number of bits for an 8- or 12-bit DAC.

---

**EXAMPLE 10.15** | **R-2R ladder DAC**

Find the input current to the inverting amplifier in Fig. 10.37(a) for $V_{ref} = 10$ V and $R = 2$ kΩ.

**SOLUTION:**
The properties of the $R$–$2R$ ladder are such that the impedance is $2R$ to ground each direction from the node above the $2R$ resistor connected to $-V_{ref}$. Thus, the source current at $B_0$ is

$$I_0 = \frac{-V_{ref}}{2R + 2R \| 2R} = \frac{-V_{ref}}{3R} = \frac{-10}{6 \text{ k}\Omega} = -1.67 \text{ mA} \qquad (10.46)$$

The input current at $B_2$ is the same. The input to the inverting amplifier is $I_0/2 + I_0/8 = -1.04$ mA, and $v_{out} = +1.04$ mA $\times 6 \times 2$ k$\Omega = 12.5$ V.

**WHAT IF?**

What if you calculate the most current that the $R$-$2R$ ladder can draw from the $V_{ref}$ power supply in Fig. 10.37(a)?[13]

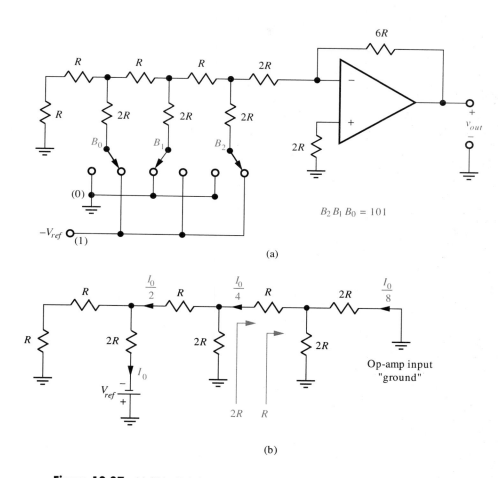

$B_2 B_1 B_0 = 101$

(a)

Op-amp input "ground"

(b)

**Figure 10.37** (a) This digital-to-analog converter is based on the current-division properties of the $R$-$2R$ ladder circuit; (b) the $R$-$2R$ ladder network divides the current by a factor of 2 at each node.

---

[13] Each input sees $3R$, so $I_{ref} = -5$ mA for $B_2 B_1 B_0 = 111$.

### Check Your Understanding

1. The increment of voltage corresponding to the least significant bit for an 8-bit ADC would be one-half the increment of voltage for a 4-bit ADC. True or false?

2. The underrange signal on the ADC in Fig. 10.26(a) would be a digital one for a negative input signal. True or false?

3. The dual-slope ramp conversion ADC is immune to minor variations in the clock frequency. True or false?

4. A sample-and-hold circuit may not be required if the ADC is fast enough in its conversion speed. True or false?

5. If the output signal from a temperature-indicating device contains no significant information beyond 1 Hz in its output spectrum, what is the maximum sampling period that can be used for this device without losing information?

6. A digital filter filters digital signals. True or false?

7. What is the increment in output voltage corresponding to a 1-bit change in the least significant bit for a 8-V full-scale ADC with a precision of 8 bits?

8. Show that the op-amp bias current sees the same impedance at the $+$ and $-$ input terminals in Fig. 10.37(a).

*Answers.*   **(1)** False;   **(2)** true;   **(3)** true;   **(4)** true;   **(5)** 0.5 s;   **(6)** false;   **(7)** 31.25 mV;   **(8)** $6R \parallel (2R + R) = 2R$.

## CHAPTER SUMMARY

This chapter builds on the material in Chapter 8, "Digital Electronics", and Chapter 9, "Analog Electronics". We introduce transducer technology and error analysis, but focus on the processing of analog and digital signals. Active filters improve the-signal-to noise ratio by eliminating noise out of the signal bandwidth. Filters must limit signal bandwidth to eliminate confusion and loss of information due to sampling. The sampling process involves analog multiplexing and a sample-and-hold circuit to enable analog-to-digital conversion. Finally, we show how digital signals are converted to analog form for control and display purposes.

**Objective 1: To understand how to perform worst-case and statistical error analysis.**   Measurements should have stated errors that combine the various error contributions of components of the instrumentation system. Errors may be combined on a worst-case or statistical basis. The meaning of stated errors should be explicit.

**Objective 2: To understand how to recognize floating signals and be able to amplify difference-mode signals.**   A signal is floating when the information voltage is present between two wires, neither of which is grounded. Practical systems can within limits reject the average voltage and amplify the difference voltage.

**Objective 3: To understand analog signals and noise spectra and how active filters can improve system performance.**   Several types of noise spectra are present in a system. Filtering can be effective when the signal and noise have different spectra. Active filters use negative feedback in an op-amp circuit to give gain and filtering.

**Objective 4: To understand the principles of cabling, grounding, and shielding to reduce interference.** Construction of instrumentation systems requires attention to the nature of the noise environment and the nonideal nature of connections between system components. Sensitive electronic equipment must be shielded from electric- and magnetic-field interference, and may require separate grounding systems for low-level signals.

**Objective 5: To understand digital-signal sampling, conversion, and processing.** The Nyquist sampling theorem gives the minimum sampling rate for an analog signal based upon the signal bandwidth. Sampled analog signals can be stored in sample-and-hold circuits for conversion to digital form. Once in digital form, the signals may be filtered by numerical algorithms.

Chapter 11 deals with another application of electronics, communication systems. Nonlinear effects, which constitute noise in instrumentation systems, are the key to the frequency-shifting operations common to all communication systems.

## PROBLEMS

## Section 10.1: Introduction to Data-acquisition Systems

**10.1** Find the resistor values for a Wheatstone bridge that uses a voltage of 8 V and a 10-$\Omega$ change from balance in one resistor produces a 10-$\mu$V change in the output voltage. Assume all resistors the same at balance.

**10.2.** A thermistor is used in the bridge circuit shown in Fig. P10.2. The characteristic of the thermistor is

$$\ln\left[\frac{R(T)}{R_0}\right] = 4000\left(\frac{1}{T} - \frac{1}{T_0}\right)$$

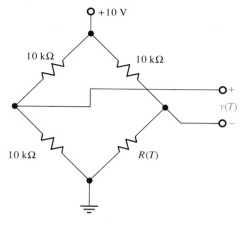

**Figure P10.2**

where $R(T)$ is the resistance at temperature $T$ in kelvin, and $R_0$ is the resistance at temperature $T_0$, in this case 10 k$\Omega$ at 20°C. Find and plot the output voltage of the bridge as a function of temperature in the range $0 < T < 100°$C Note: °C + 273 = kelvin.

**10.3.** The circuit in Fig. P10.3 represents an unbonded strain gage. All four resistors are affected by changes in the length of the device, $\Delta d$, with opposite resistors charged in opposite directions. Determine the output voltage as a function of $\Delta d$.

**10.4.** The potentiometer transducer in Fig. P10.4 gives an output voltage proportional to the displacement $x$ only if there is no load ($R_L = \infty$); otherwise, loading effects make the output nonlinear. Determine the ratio of the load resistance, $R_L$, to the potentiometer resistance, $R_p$, such that the maximum error is 1% of full scale. *Hint:* Find the maximum value of the output resistance and make this 1% of the load resistance.

**10.5.** A voltage in a first-order transient circuit decays from 10 to 0 V with an $RC$ time constant. If the resistance can vary by 5% and the capacitor by 10%; find the following:

  **(a)** The percent of variation in the time constant using an exact and a linearized analysis.

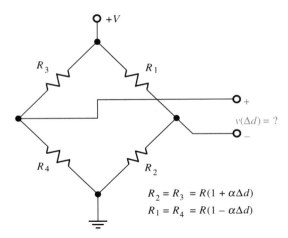

$$R_2 = R_3 = R(1 + \alpha\Delta d)$$
$$R_1 = R_4 = R(1 - \alpha\Delta d)$$

**Figure P10.3**

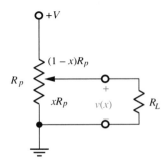

**Figure P10.4**

**(b)** The percent of variation in the voltage at $t = RC$, where $RC$ is the nominal time constant. Use the exact analysis.

**10.6.** A measurement of $y$ is derived from two measurements, $y = x_1 + x_2$, where $x_1 = 6\,(1 \pm 3\%)$ and $x_2 = 3\,(1 \pm 5\%)$.
- **(a)** Find $y$, assuming errors in the components are maximum errors. Use worst-case conditions.
- **(b)** Find $y$, assuming errors in the components are 1 standard-deviation errors. Use statistical error analysis.

**10.7.** The resistive voltage divider in Fig. P10.7 is built with 10% tolerance resistors.
- **(a)** Determine the exact limits of the output voltage if $R_2 = 2R_1$ (nominal values).
- **(b)** Explain why the limits do not give a 20% error due to each 10% error.

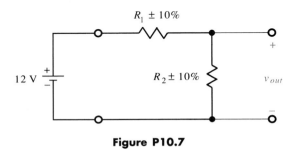

**Figure P10.7**

**10.8.** Assume that you have a number of measurements of the same physical quantity, all of comparable accuracy. Show that the standard deviation of the average is reduced by $1/\sqrt{n}$ from the standard deviation of a single measurement, where $n$ is the number of samples that are averaged. To improve the accuracy by a factor of 10, how many independent measurements must be made?

## Section 10.2: Analog Signal Processing

**10.9.** For the instrumentation amplifier in Fig. 10.10, assume that the two $R_3$'s are not identical but differ by a normalized error of $\varepsilon_R$. That is, assume $R_{3(\text{bottom})} = R_{3(\text{top})}(1 \pm \varepsilon_R)$.
- **(a)** Using the op amp analysis technique from Chapter 9, determine the error in the output due to this asymmetry.
- **(b)** Does this affect the common-mode rejection ratio or just the difference-mode gain of the amplifier?

**10.10.** Determine the output of the noninverting amplifier in Fig. 9.50 if the amplifier has finite gain ($A_d$) and a finite common-mode rejection ratio ($A_c = A_d/$CMRR). Express your answer is terms of $A_d$, CMRR, $R_1$, and $R_F$.

**10.11.** An amplifier has a gain of 50 dB for the difference input and a common-mode rejection ratio of 72 dB. The input signals are 1.012 and 1.006 V. What is the percent of error in the output signals due to the common-mode component?

**10.12.** Find the gain in dB of the attenuator in Fig. 10.12 when the input digital signal to the switches is $S_1 S_2 S_3 S_4 = 1010$.

**10.13.** What is the most attenuation in dB that can be produced by the attenuator in Fig. 10.12 and what is the switch configuration to achieve this attenuation? *Hint*: More than one switch can be closed.

**10.14.** Design an attenuator similar to the one in Fig. 10.12 that gives 0, 2, 4, or 6 dB of attenuation. The input impedance should be 1 MΩ.

**10.15.** The circuit in Fig. 10.11 has a gain of unity for the signal only if the loading due to the potentiometer is ignored. Find the ratio $R_p/R$ such that the gain of the signal channel is always between 0.97 and 1.00.

**10.16.** Design an op-amp-based amplifier with the following characteristics:
- ■ Amplifies the difference between two signals
- ■ Filters the signal with the filter function shown in Fig. P10.16
- ■ Has an input impedance of 1 kΩ at both inputs
- ■ Uses one 0.1-μF capacitor
- ■ Uses no more than two op amps

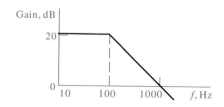

**Figure P10.16**

**10.17.** The sound energy in the voice has a power spectrum with most of the energy between 500 and 3000 Hz. Design an active filter to pass only this band of frequencies and also give a gain of 15 dB. Use no capacitor larger than 1 μF. Combine the first-order high-pass and low-pass characteristics.

**10.18.** For the active filter circuit shown in Fig. P10.18, find the following:
- **(a)** Find the filter function $\mathbf{F}(j\omega)$.
- **(b)** If the input voltage is 2 V dc, what is the output voltage?

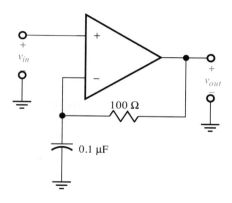

**Figure P10.18**

- **(c)** Is there a critical frequency? If so, what is it in hertz, and does the gain begin to decrease or increase at the critical frequency?

**10.19.** The Bode plot of the gain of a single-ended active filter is shown in Fig. P10.19.
- **(a)** Draw an active filter circuit to give this characteristic.
- **(b)** If the circuit capacitor is 12 μF, find the resistors.
- **(c)** At what frequency is the amplitude of the output voltage equal to the input voltage if the signal is a sinusoid?
- **(d)** If $v_{in}(t) = 5\sqrt{2}\cos(2400\pi t)$ is the input signal, which is the output signal in the time domain?

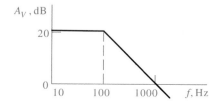

**Figure P10.19**

**10.20.** For the op-amp circuit shown in Fig. P10.20 find the following:
- **(a)** If a 1-V battery is connected from ground to the input, with the + of the battery connected to ground, what is the voltage of points $a$ and $b$ relative to the ground?
- **(b)** Now instead of a battery, the input is a 1-V pulse. What is the duration of the shortest pulse that the amplifier can pass without serious distortion?

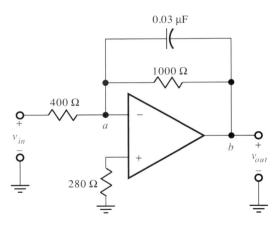

**0.03 μF**

**1000 Ω**

**400 Ω**

$a$

$v_{in}$

**280 Ω**

$b$

$v_{out}$

**Figure P10.20**

**10.21.** Design an active filter having a gain of +22 dB, a phase shift of 180°, an input resistance of 860 Ω in the passband, and a high-pass characteristic with a cutoff frequency of 1250 Hz.

**10.22.** Derive the filter function, $\mathbf{F}(\omega) = \mathbf{V}_{out}/\mathbf{V}_{in}$, for the high-pass filter shown in Fig. 10.18. Confirm the formula for the cutoff frequency, $\omega_c$. What is the input impedance in the band of frequencies above the cutoff frequency, $\omega_c$?

**10.23.** Design an active high-pass filter with a cutoff

frequency of 5000 Hz, an input impedance of 1000 Ω in the high-frequency region, and a gain of +20 in the passband. *Hint*: Use a passive high-pass filter at the input of a noninverting amplifier.

**10.24.** An op-amp amplifier is required to pass pulses of 1-ms width but to eliminate unwanted frequencies higher than those required for the pulse. The gain must be −3. Assume that you have a 0.0033-μF capacitor available. Give the circuit and component values.

**10.25.** In an audio system, an amplifier is required that will give a gain of 10 (+ or − , it does not matter) and have upper and lower cutoff frequencies to exclude signals outside the normal audio region, 30 to 20,000 Hz. Combine high-pass and low-pass active filters and design a circuit that will accomplish this. Assume that the largest capacitor you have available is 200 μF.

**10.26.** A second-order Butterworth low-pass filter with gain has a cutoff frequency of 100 Hz. The gain at 10 Hz is 20 dB. What would be the gain in dB at 10 kHz?

**10.27.** **(a)** Design a second-order low-pass Butterworth filter with a cutoff frequency of 1000 Hz. The largest capacitor may be no more than 0.1 μF.
**(b)** Determine the gain (amplitude and phase shift) at 500, 1000, and 5000 Hz.

## Section 10.3: Digital Signal Processing

**10.28.** An 8-bit ADC has a range from 0 to a full-scale value of 8 V.
**(a)** What nominal increment in input voltage causes a 1-bit change at the output?
**(b)** What range of input voltages corresponds to the output of 00001101? Use the no-offset characteristic similar to that shown in Fig. 10.25(b).

**10.29.** Verify the logic for $Z_0$ and $Z_1$ in the 2-bit flash ADC in Fig. 10.26(a) by making Karnaugh maps for $Z_0$ and $Z_1$ with $X_1$, $X_2$, and $X_3$ as inputs.

**10.30.** Redesign the flash ADC in Fig. 10.26(a) to have a characteristic passing through the origin. In other words, what would be the voltage-reference levels (and the resistors in the voltage-divider circuit) such that the transition to 01 is at $v_{in} = 0.125V_{ref}$, to 10 at $v_{in} = 0.375V_{ref}$, and so on.

**10.31.** An 8-bit ADC of the type shown in Fig. 10.27 takes 10 ms to make its conversion.
**(a)** What is the clock frequency?
**(b)** If the input range is 0 to 8 V and the reference voltage is 10 V, what is the $RC$ product for the integrator?

**10.32.** The sample-and-hold circuit in Fig. 10.32 was designed in the text to have an 8.7-nF capacitor. If the combined leakage current due to the FET, op-amp input bias current, and capacitor leakage were 1 nA, how long does the capacitor hold the voltage to 99% of a 10-V capacitor voltage when the FET is turned OFF?

**10.33.** The FET switches used in the multiplexer in Fig. 10.30(a), one of which is shown in Fig. 10.30(b), have a resistance of 25 Ω when ON and a resistance of 10 MΩ when OFF. Assume that inputs $A_0$ through $A_7$ come from sources with a 100-$\Omega$ output impedance. Determine the coupling in decibels from the channel that is ON to the other seven channels that are OFF. *Note:* The eight channels are switched by eight FETs, all of which connect to the same 47-k$\Omega$ resistor for an output.

**10.34.** The sample-and-hold circuit in Fig. 10.32 uses an input voltage-follower amplifier with an output impedance of 2 $\Omega$ and an output voltage-follower amplifier with an input impedance of 20 M$\Omega$. The FET resistance is 25 $\Omega$ when ON and 10 M$\Omega$ when OFF. The FET is ON for 1 $\mu$s and OFF for 1 $\mu$s for the ADC to make its conversion. Under these conditions, what is the optimum capacitor to maximize the voltage at the end of the 2-$\mu$s cycle, and what is the final voltage as a percent of the input voltage to the sample-and-hold circuit?

**10.35.** Determine the response of the two digital filters shown in Fig. 10.35 (a) to the sudden increase at the input if the filters use three terms: for the FIR filter, $x'(n) = [x(n) + x(n-1) + x(n-2)]/3$, and for the IIR filter, $x'(n) = [x(n) + x'(n-1) + x'(n-2)]/3$.

**10.36.** Show that the FIR digital filter in Eq. 10.44 will remove a 60-Hz component in the data if the sampling period is 1/120 s.

**10.37.** A transducer signal is sampled every 5 s. The output spectrum is sufficiently broad to cause confusion if the transducer bandwidth is not limited prior to sampling. Determine the cutoff frequency of a simple low-pass filter to ensure that 99% of the power to the sampler lies within the Nyquist limit. Assume a worst-case transducer spectrum that is white noise.

## General Problems

**10.38.** The highway department wishes to study the roughness of certain highways. For this purpose, a vehicle is instrumented with a downlooking sonar ranging unit and the associated electronics and data-recording equipment, as suggested by Fig. P10.38. The truck moves at 50 mph and road height variations are thereby converted to a continous time signal. The sonar spot size is 3 inches in diameter, so roughness at smaller scales is lost. Of course, the vehicle shock-absorber/spring system acts as a high-pass filter, so the really low frequencies are lost. The output voltage of the sonar unit is analog with voltages in the range of 0 to 100 mV. The sonar unit is followed by a low-pass filter, an amplifier, a sample-and-hold circuit, and an 8-bit ADC that requires a positive input voltage in the range of 0 to 5 V. The output of the ADC goes into a computer, which actively controls the sample-and-hold circuit and the ADC.

(a) What would be an appropriate cutoff

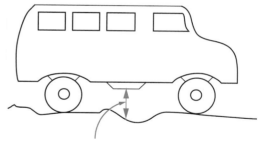

Sonar measures this distance

**Figure P10.38**

frequency for the filter such that noise outside the data spectrum is eliminated?

(b) Design the amplifier. Assume an input impedance of 1 k$\Omega$ and an ideal op amp.

(c) What is the minimum sampling rate for the system to record all the data?

(d) What voltage difference does 1 bit represent at the output of the ADC?

# Answers to Odd-Numbered Problems

**10.1.** All 2 MΩ.

**10.3.** $v(\Delta d) = -\alpha\Delta d \times V$.

**10.5.** **(a)** Exact: $+15.5\%$, $-14.5\%$; linearized: $\pm15\%$; **(b)** $V = 3.656 \pm 15.1\%$.

**10.7.** **(a)** $v_{max} = 8.516$ V and $v_{min} = 7.448$ V, $v = 7.982 \pm 6.69\%$; **(b)** $R_2s$ in the numerator and denominator are correlated; also $R_1 = R_2$ should not preserve percent accuracy.

**10.9.** **(a)** $v'_1 - v'_1 = (v_1 - v_2) \times [1 + R_{3(top)}/R_2 \times (2 \pm \varepsilon_R)]$; **(b)** does not affect the common-mode gain, just the difference-mode gain.

**10.11.** 4.22%.

**10.13.** $-44.0$ dB.

**10.15.** $R_p/R = 0.255$.

**10.17.**

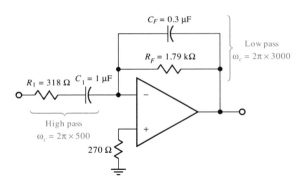

**10.19.** **(a)** Standard low-pass filter; **(b)** $R_F = 5.3$ kΩ, $R_1 = 530$ Ω; **(c)** 1000 by inspection; **(d)** $0.587 \cos(2400\pi t - 85.2°)$ V.

**10.21.**

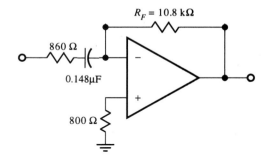

**10.23.**

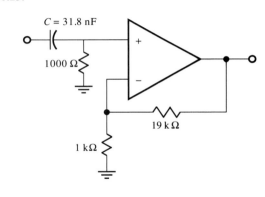

**10.25.**

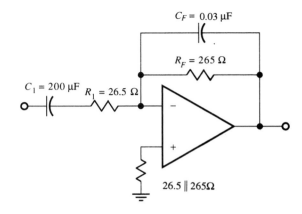

**10.27.** **(a)** "$C$" = 70.7 nF and $R$ = 2250 $\Omega$;
**(b)** 0.970 $\angle$ −43.3°, 0.707 $\angle$ −90°,
0.03997 $\angle$ −163.6°.

**10.29.**

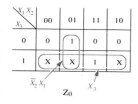

$Z_0$

$Z_1$

**10.31.** **(a)** 25,600 Hz; **(b)** 0.0125 s.

**10.33.** −100 dB.

**10.35.** FIR is 0, 0.333, 0.667, 1, 1, 1, …; IIR is 0, 0.333, 0.444, 0.592, 0.679, 0.757, 0.812, 0.856, etc.

**10.37.** 1.57 mHz.

# Communication Systems

1. To understand the effects of nonlinear circuits on the spectra of signals
2. To understand the superheterodyne radio circuit and be able to relate RF, LO, and IF frequencies
3. To understand the properties of free and guided electromagnetic waves as they relate to communication systems
4. To understand the properties of antennas and their role in communication systems

# objectives

Modern communication systems continue to proliferate: cellular phones, computer networks, TV satellites and optical links for telephone service. Differing in details, these and other communication systems all use the same basic techniques of modulation, transmission, reception, and demodulation in a superheterodyne radio circuit. We also consider antennas and radio-wave propagation.

**communication systems**

### Introduction to communication systems.

As a pipeline moves liquid from one location to another, so a *communication system* moves information from one location to another. A communication system consists of a source of information with some sort of encoder, a recipient of information with the appropriate decoder, and a medium connecting the two. Some examples are obvious: the telephone system, commercial TV broadcasting, and computer networks for stock-market transactions. Some are not so obvious: an internal bus in a computer, a police radar for measuring speed, and a system for collecting tolls from moving trucks on a toll road.

Electric signals have replaced smoke signals, Pony Express, and carrier pigeons in communication systems for several reasons. Electric signals travel with speeds approaching the speed of light. Electric signals in the form of radio waves go almost anywhere. At certain broadcast frequencies, the radio waves follow the Earth's curvature and also reach distant points by bouncing off the ionosphere. Electric signals lend themselves to a variety of ingenious coding schemes such as amplitude modulation, frequency modulation, and various digital codes.

### Contents of this chapter.

In this section, we focus on the system used in commercial amplitude-modulation (AM) radio. First, we look at how information is encoded onto and decoded from AM radio signals. The explanation requires expansion of our understanding of the frequency domain to include nonlinear effects. Then we consider the various forms of electromagnetic waves used in radio systems. We examine several common types of antennas, both in transmitting and receiving. Finally, we consider the details of two communication systems.

## General Principles of Nonlinear Devices in the Frequency Domain

**OBJECTIVE 1**

**To understand the effects of nonlinear circuits on the spectra of signals**

### Linear circuits.

Linear circuits create no new frequencies. In Chapter 4, we showed that if you excite a circuit at a certain frequency, it will respond only at that frequency. Our analysis of ac circuits using phasors and impedance is founded entirely on this principle.

### Nonlinear circuits with one input frequency.

Nonlinear circuits create new frequencies. We discovered in Chapter 7 that a diode, a nonlinear device, can rectify a signal, thus producing, in addition to the frequency of the input sinusoid, frequency components at dc and all the even harmonics of the input frequency. These new frequencies are created by the nonlinear action of the diode.

**frequency multipliers**

The spectrum of a rectified sinusoid is one instance of the general principle suggested in Fig. 11.1. For a nonlinear circuit with a sinusoidal input, the output of the circuit in general contains all the harmonics of the input. The amplitudes of the various output harmonics depend on the details of the circuit, but in principle, all harmonics are produced.

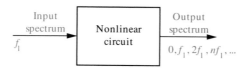

**Figure 11.1** Nonlinear circuits create new frequencies.

**Using these new frequencies.** This property of nonlinear circuits finds direct application in many practical devices. One familiar example is a power supply, where the dc output is the zeroth harmonic of the input. Another application occurs in the generation of stable high-frequency sinusoids for precision communication systems or spectroscopic measurement systems. Often high-frequency signals of the required stability are generated by taking the output of a highly stable oscillator with a low frequency, say, 5 MHz, and putting this signal through a chain of *frequency multipliers* until it reaches the required high frequency, say, 3240 MHz. In such a scheme, the output of the multiplier chain is harmonically related to the low-frequency source and hence exhibits the same relative stability.

**harmonic distortion, intermodulation distortion**

On the other hand, the creation of new frequencies may be undesirable. A good audio amplifier should have low *harmonic distortion*, meaning that it should not generate harmonics of the audio signal. The amplifier should also have low *intermodulation distortion*. This term refers to the creation of new frequencies through the interaction of separate frequencies in the audio spectrum. Nonlinearities in the amplifier can cause both of these undesirable effects on the signal spectrum.

**Nonlinear circuits with two input frequencies.** The creation of harmonics in a nonlinear circuit, suggested in Fig. 11.1, is a special case of a more general property of nonlinear circuits suggested by Fig. 11.2. Here is a nonlinear circuit with two input frequencies, and the output in general contains all the harmonics of both input frequencies *plus* all the sum and difference frequencies of those harmonics. For example, if we had inputs of 30 and 100 Hz, the output would contain not only the harmonics of 30 (60, 90, 120, ...) and the harmonics of 100 (200, 300, ...), but the output would also contain the various sum and difference frequencies, such as $100 - 30$, $100 + 30$, $200 - 30$, $200 + 30$, $100 - 2 \times 30$, $100 + 2 \times 30$, $200 - 2 \times 30$, .... Radio systems use such new frequencies to encode communication signals.

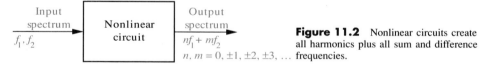

**Figure 11.2** Nonlinear circuits create all harmonics plus all sum and difference frequencies.

---

**EXAMPLE 11.1** | **Output spectrum**

If two frequencies, $f_1 = 5$ MHz and $f_2 = 7$ MHz, are the inputs to a nonlinear circuit, what harmonics ($n$ and $m$) give rise to an output frequency of 3 MHz?

**SOLUTION:**
The potential output frequencies are

$$f = nf_1 + mf_2, \text{ where } n, m = 0, \pm 1, \pm 2, ..., \tag{11.1}$$

where $f$ represents all possible output frequencies and $f_1$ and $f_2$ are the input frequencies. By trial and error, we find that $n = 2$ and $m = -1$ works, and also $n = -12$ and $m = 9$.

**WHAT IF?** | What if it is 2 MHz you want?[1]

**Importance of filtering.** Although a multitude of frequencies can appear in the output of a nonlinear circuit, not all these frequencies are useful. The circuit designer must ensure that only the desired frequencies are strong in the output and that undesired components are minimized. Filters are used to remove unwanted frequency components in the output spectra of nonlinear devices. Only through careful control of the filtering properties of such circuits can the benefits of nonlinear action be achieved.

The design and operation of nonlinear circuits are complicated by the creation of new frequencies and the filtering of these frequencies to enhance desired and diminish unwanted components. In the following, we examine the applications of a few nonlinear circuits, emphasizing especially their role in communication systems. Our goal is to develop a sufficient basis for discussing the operation of AM and FM radio and the telephone system.

## Modulation and Demodulation

**OBJECTIVE 2**

**To understand the superheterodyne radio circuit and be able to relate RF, LO, and IF frequencies**

**modulation, carrier**

**Analog Information**

**The Time Domain**

**modulation index**

**Amplitude modulation.** In communication engineering, *modulation* is the process by which information at a low frequency is coded as part of a high-frequency signal. The higher frequency is called the *carrier* because it carries the information signal. In this section, we examine the amplitude-modulation (AM) scheme that is widely used in commercial broadcasting of radio and TV signals. Initially, we explain the nature of amplitude modulation, emphasizing the frequency-domain viewpoint throughout. Then we discuss why modulation is required in communication systems. Finally, we present a circuit that accomplishes amplitude modulation.

**AM signals in the time domain.** Let us first consider the nature of amplitude modulation and how modulation affects the spectrum of the carrier. Equation (11.2) gives the equation of a modulated carrier in the time domain,

$$\underbrace{v_{AM}(t)}_{\text{AM signal}} = V_c \underbrace{[1 + m_a \cos(\omega_m t)]}_{v_e(t),\text{ the envelope}} \underbrace{\cos(\omega_c t)}_{\text{carrier}} \tag{11.2}$$

were $\omega_m$ is the angular frequency of the modulating sinusoid, $\omega_c$ is the frequency of the modulated carrier, and $V_c$ is its amplitude. The parameter $m_a$, the *modulation index*, indicates the degree of modulation. The modulation index is proportional to the amplitude of the modulating signal, which is indicated by $V_m$ in Fig. 11.3, subject to the restriction that $m_a$ never exceeds unity; that is, $m_a \leqslant 1$.

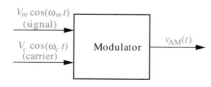

$$v_{AM}(t) = V_c [1 + m_a \cos(\omega_m t)] \cos(\omega_c t)$$

**Figure 11.3** A modulator circuit has two inputs and one output.

---

[1] $n = -1$ and $m = +1$ or $n = +6$ and $m = -4$ give 2 MHz.

The character of the modulated carrier and the role of the modulation index are shown in Fig. 11.4, which has modulated carriers for $m_a = 0.5$ and $m_a = 1.0$. Let us examine the role of the various factors characterizing the AM signal. The carrier is the sinusoid whose amplitude is being modulated. The carrier frequency controls the spacing of the zero crossings and individual peaks of the composite waveform. If we were to keep everything else the same yet double the carrier frequency, everything would look the same except there would be twice as many peaks and zero crossings. In other words, the hills and valleys of the amplitude would look the same, but the underlying sinusoid would have a higher frequency.

The amplitude of the carrier, $V_c$, characterizes the overall strength of the signal. With a broadcast signal, the amplitude of the carrier depends on the power of the station transmitter, the distance to the receiver, and the gains of the transmitting and receiving antennas.

The frequency of the modulating signals, $\omega_m$, determines the time between the hills and valleys of the envelope, $v_e(t)$, as defined in Eq. (11.2). If, for example, the modulat-

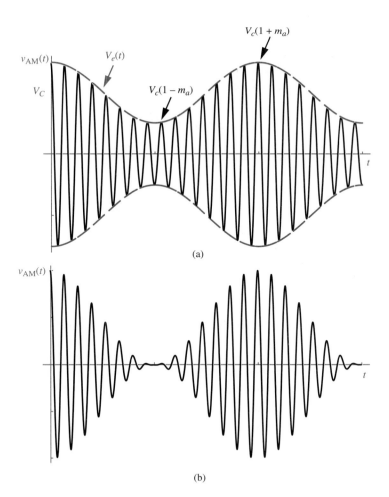

(a)

(b)

**Figure 11.4**  Two AM waveforms: (a) $m_a = 0.5$; (b) $m_a = 1.0$.

ing frequency were doubled, the envelope of the carrier would vary up and down twice as fast.

Finally, the modulation index controls the degree of modulation, the ratio of hills to valleys in the envelope. This parameter is limited to values less than unity, so the envelope factor in Eq. (11.2), $v_e(t)$, never goes negative. The modulation index is proportional to the amplitude of the modulating signal. The design of the modulator must ensure that the maximum amplitude of the modulating signal can be accommodated without exceeding the allowed value of unity.

$$m_a = KV_m, \quad \text{but} \quad m_a \leqslant 1 \tag{11.3}$$

where $K$ is a constant.

---

**EXAMPLE 11.2** | **AM signal**

An AM signal has zero crossings every 0.1 μs, a maximum amplitude of 12 V, and a minimum amplitude of 8 V, separated by 50 μs. Find the carrier frequency, the modulation index, and the modulation frequency.

**SOLUTION:**
The carrier period is $10^{-7}$ s; so the carrier frequency is $10^7$ Hz, or 10 MHz. The carrier modulation index can be derived from the ratio of maximum and minimum voltages:

$$\frac{1 + m_a}{1 - m_a} = \frac{12}{8} \quad \Rightarrow \quad m_a = 0.2 \tag{11.4}$$

Finally, the modulation period must be twice the time between maximum and minimum amplitude; hence,

$$T_m = 2 \times 50 \text{ μs} \quad \Rightarrow \quad f_m = \frac{1}{100 \text{ μs}} = 10 \text{kHz} \tag{11.5}$$

**WHAT IF?**

What if you want the carrier voltage?[2]

---

**AM modulator circuit.** The circuit of Fig. 11.5 acts as a simple modulator circuit. Ignore for the moment the $RC$ filter between $a$–$b$ and $c$–$d$, and consider the part of the circuit that consists of two generators, a diode, and a resistor. The generator marked $v_c(t)$ is the carrier and has a high frequency. The generator marked $v_m(t)$ is the modulating signal, and it has a lower frequency and a smaller amplitude than the carrier.

**Unfiltered output.** Consider now the action of the diode on the signal at $a$–$b$. When the instantaneous carrier voltage, $v_c(t)$, exceeds the instantaneous modulating voltage, $v_m(t)$, the diode turns ON and current flows clockwise around the circuit. The

---

[2] 10 V peak.

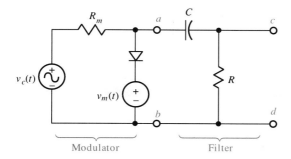

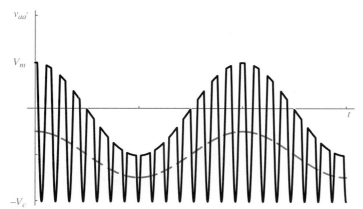

**Figure 11.5** AM modulator circuit.

**Figure 11.6** Unfiltered output of a AM modulator.

output voltage in this case is equal to the instantaneous modulating voltage plus a small voltage required to turn ON the diode. On the other hand, when the instantaneous carrier voltage is smaller than the instantaneous modulating voltage, the diode is OFF and no current flows. During this time, there is no voltage drop across the resistor; hence, the voltage at $a$–$b$ is equal to the carrier voltage. The result is shown in Fig. 11.6.

**Filtered output.** The signal at $a$–$b$, shown in Fig. 11.6, differs from a pure AM signal in two respects:

1. only the top is modulated, the bottom being flat, and
2. the carrier waveform is not round on top and is thus not a pure sinusoid with varying amplitude.

We can solve the first problem by filtering out the dc and the component at $\omega_m$, the dashed line in Fig. 11.6. These components we can eliminate with a high-pass filter that passes the carrier while rejecting the modulating frequency. This is the function of the high-pass filter between $a$–$b$ and $c$–$d$.

The other problem, that the tops of the modulated carrier are distorted, implies that some higher harmonics of the carrier are also created in the modulator circuit. These also can be eliminated with a filter. With proper filtering, the output of the modulator in Fig. 11.6 looks like the ideal AM waveform in Fig. 11.4.

**Spectrum of an AM signal.** The spectrum of an AM signal can be determined through expansion of Eq. (11.2) with the trigonometric identity

$$\cos a \cos b = \tfrac{1}{2}[\cos(b+a) + \cos(b-a)] \tag{11.6}$$

When we expand Eq. (11.2) and apply Eq. (11.6), letting $a = \omega_m t$ and $b = \omega_c t$, we obtain

$$v_{AM}(t) = V_c \cos(\omega_c t) + m_a V_c \cos(\omega_m t)\cos(\omega_c t)$$

$$= V_c \cos(\omega_c t) + \frac{m_a V_c}{2}\left[\cos \underbrace{(\omega_c + \omega_m)}_{\substack{\text{sum}\\\text{frequency}}} t + \cos \underbrace{(\omega_c - \omega_m)}_{\substack{\text{difference}\\\text{frequency}}} t\right] \tag{11.7}$$

**sidebands**

This reveals a spectrum with three frequency components: the carrier at $\omega_c$, an *upper sideband* at $\omega_c + \omega_m$, and a *lower sideband* at $\omega_c - \omega_m$. The spectra before and after modulation are shown in Fig. 11.7. We broke the frequency scale in Fig. 11.7 because the carrier frequency is normally much higher than the modulating frequency.

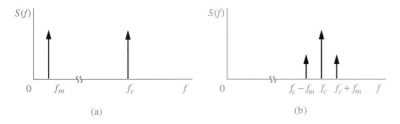

**Figure 11.7**  Modulation in the frequency domain:  (a) before modulation; (b) after modulation.

---

**EXAMPLE 11.3** | **AM spectrum**

The emergency warning broadcast tone is 853 Hz.  Broadcast on a carrier of 1200 kHz, what would be the upper and lower sidebands?

**SOLUTION:**
Simply add and subtract the modulation frequency from the carrier frequency:  1,200,853 Hz and 1,199,147 Hz, respectively.

**WHAT IF?**  What if the tone of A, 440 Hz, is broadcast on a carrier of 820 kHz? Where are the sidebands?[3]

---

**Modulation with a broadband signal.**    If your AM radio received the AM signals in Fig. 11.4, and if the modulating frequency were in the audio band, you would hear a steady tone from the radio speaker, and you might suppose some sort of test was underway. In normal broadcasting, the program material would be music and voice sig-

---

[3] The sidebands are 819,560 and 820,440 Hz.

nals, not steady tones. The modulated signal would thus be of the form

$$v_{AM}(t) = V_c[1 + m_a s(t)] \cos(\omega_c t) \tag{11.8}$$

where $s(t)$ represents the program material and hence would generally be a broadband function. In Eq. (11.8), $s(t)$ must remain smaller than unity so that the product $m_a s(t)$ never exceeds unity at any time.

**RF**

**Spectrum of broadband signals.** When the program information consists of a broadband signal such as music or voice, the individual frequencies comprising the spectrum of the audio signal are shifted to the sidebands. By law, the spectrum of the audio signal of standard AM broadcasting is limited to frequencies between 100 and 5000 Hz. The effect of modulating with such a signal is indicated by Fig. 11.8. The sidebands now become continuous spectra. The upper sideband is identical in shape with the audio signal, whereas the lower sideband is the mirror image. The bandwidth of the radio-frequency (RF) spectrum is twice the audio bandwidth; thus, 10 kHz of RF bandwidth is required for each AM station.

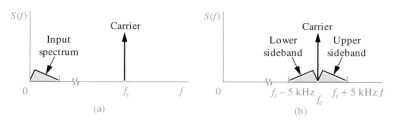

**Figure 11.8** Modulation with a broadband spectrum: (a) before modulation; (b) after modulation.

If you could examine the spectrum of radio waves received by an AM radio antenna, you would see carriers for each station in your area, each bracketed by its upper and lower sidebands. Because the AM broadcast band covers frequencies from 535 to 1605 kHz, and because carriers can be spaced at 10-kHz intervals, there are channels for 106 AM stations, although obviously most channels are unoccupied in a given geographic area.

**single sideband**

**Standard AM and single-sideband modulation.** Because AM detectors are simple, standard AM modulation with both sidebands is used for commercial broadcasting. However, this AM system is inefficient in its use of the available bandwidth and the transmitter power. Bandwidth is wasted because, although both sidebands and carrier are broadcast, all the information is contained in one sideband. Power is wasted because the carrier and one of the sidebands carry no information not already contained in the other sideband. For these reasons, sophisticated radio communication systems, such as a telephone company uses for long-distance messages, employ *single–sideband* modulation for economy in both power and bandwidth. Single–sideband modulation, as the name suggests, transmits only one of the sidebands over the communication path, and the receiver must generate the carrier and missing sideband to detect the information.

| EXAMPLE 11.4 | **Telephone supergroup** |
|---|---|

A telephone company uses frequencies between 312 and 552 kHz for a supergroup. The frequency band carries phone channels that have a 4-kHz bandwidth, single-sideband modulation. How many simultaneous phone conversations can be carried by a supergroup.

**SOLUTION:**

With single-sideband modulation, the RF bandwidth is equal to the information bandwidth, which is 4 kHz for a phone channel. The number of channels is, therefore, $(552 - 312)/4 = 60$ channels.

| **WHAT IF?** | What if double-sideband modulation were used?[4] |
|---|---|

**Benefits of modulation.** Modulation shifts the information from the audio band to the RF radio band. We modulate to solve antenna problems, filtering problems, and confusion problems. The last problem is the easiest to understand: Clearly, we cannot allow all radio stations to broadcast their signals in the same frequency band because then our radios would receive all stations simultaneously. Hence, modulation allows different portions of the RF spectrum to be assigned to different radio stations, who place their signals into their allotted frequency bands. We choose stations by tuning our radio receivers to these bands.

The antenna problems solved by modulation are addressed in the section on antennas later in the chapter. We will consider how modulation solves filtering problems later in this section, after we have discussed AM detectors and mixers. Having shown how the information in the audio band is shifted to higher frequencies for broadcast, we now turn to the inverse operation, how your radio shifts the signal back to the audio band so that you can hear it.

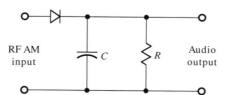

**Figure 11.9** AM detector circuit.

## Radio Receivers

**Introduction.** The radio receiver is also based on the principle of spectrum shifting with nonlinear devices. We begin by discussing an AM detector or demodulator, but the heart of the radio is the mixer, another nonlinear device. The AM radio circuit exemplifies the importance of the frequency-domain viewpoint in communication engineering.

---

[4] Then the bandwidth of the supergroup could handle 30 channels.

**AM detector.** Figure 11.9 shows a simple circuit that will extract the audio information from the AM signal envelope. This is the half-wave rectifier circuit of page 317, with a filter capacitor. The diode allows the capacitor to charge to the peak voltage of the input, and the resistor represents the load.

To function as an AM detector, this circuit requires an $RC$ time constant intermediate between the period of the carrier and that of the audio information, that is,

$$\frac{2\pi}{\omega_c} < RC < \frac{2\pi}{\omega_m} \tag{11.9}$$

With this provision, the detection of the envelope of the carrier takes place as suggested by Fig. 11.10. The output of the detector follows the peaks of the input and hence approximates the envelope of the AM signal. The period of the carrier is drawn relatively large, resulting in a jagged appearance for the output; but in practice, the period of the carrier is so short that the output is smooth. The small amount of jaggedness, which is inevitable, constitutes a high-frequency noise component in the output, easily removed with a low–pass filter. Disregarding this noise component, we see that the effect of the detector in the frequency domain is to shift the information in the sidebands back to the audio band, as shown in Fig. 11.11.

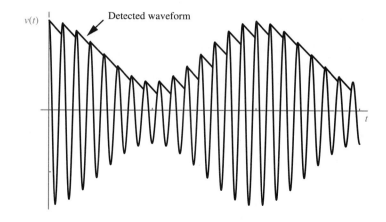

**Figure 11.10** Output of AM detector.

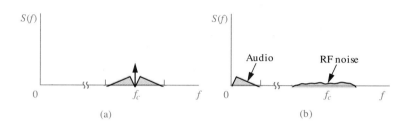

**Figure 11.11** Effect of a AM detector in the frequency domain: (a) detector input spectrum; (b) detector output spectrum.

EXAMPLE 11.5 **AM detector**

An AM radio receives a minimum carrier frequency of 540 kHz and a maximum modulation frequency of 5 kHz. Find a suitable $RC$ time constant for the AM detector.

**SOLUTION:**
From Eq. (11.9),

$$\frac{1}{540 \times 10^3} < RC < \frac{1}{5 \times 10^3} \tag{11.10}$$

One approach is to use the geometric mean between the two limits:

$$RC = \sqrt{1.85 \ \mu s \times 200 \ \mu s} = 19.2 \ \mu s \tag{11.11}$$

**WHAT IF?** What if the simple average is used?[5]

---

**demodulation, mixing**

**Demodulation.** Figures 11.8 and 11.11 reveal that the detector inverts the modulation process. For this reason, the word *demodulation* is often used to describe this process. We now have all the makings of a radio: We can shift the audio information to the sidebands of a carrier for broadcast and we can shift the information spectrum back to the audio region for conversion to acoustic waves with loudspeakers. However, standard radios use *mixing*, another nonlinear process, to shift the spectrum of the received signal to an intermediate frequency between the RF and the audio. A *mixer*, like a modulator, is a nonlinear circuit with two inputs and one output, as suggested by Fig. 11.12 (a). Indeed, modulators and mixers operate on similar principles yet differ in their function in communication systems.

**Mixer.** Figure 11.12 (b) shows a circuit that acts as a mixer. The input called $\underline{\mathbf{V}}_2$ at $\omega_2$ is the RF carrier and sidebands. The input $\underline{\mathbf{V}}_1$ at $\omega_1$ is the local-oscillator (LO) signal, to be explained in what follows. The frequency of the mixer output is placed intermediate between the RF and the audio, and hence is called the intermediate frequency (IF). We resonate the inductor and capacitor at the intermediate frequency; hence, the capacitor's impedance at RF will be so small that the RF current will be controlled by the diode characteristic [Eq. (7.16), assume $\eta = 1$].

$$i_D = I_0(e^{v_D/V_T} - 1) = I_0\left[1 + \frac{v_D}{V_T} + \frac{1}{2}\left(\frac{v_D}{V_T}\right)^2 + \cdots - 1\right]$$

$$= a_1 v_D + a_2 v_D^2 + \cdots \tag{11.12}$$

 **Impedance Level**

where $a_1$ and $a_2$ are constants. Because the impedance level of the $LC$ filter at RF is small, the voltage across the diode is approximately the sum of the two voltage sources:

---

[5] The answer is $RC = 101 \ \mu s$, but this is not a good method.

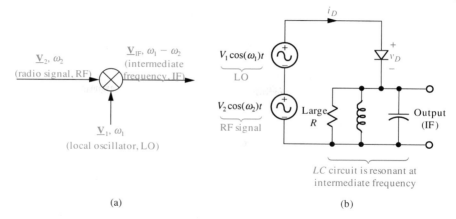

(a)                                    (b)

**Figure 11.12** (a) Mixer input and output frequencies; (b) mixer circuit. The *LC* filter presents a small impedance at the radio frequency but a large impedance at the intermediate frequency.

$$v_D \approx V_1 \cos \omega_1 t + V_2 \cos \omega_2 t \tag{11.13}$$

and therefore the power-series form of Eq. (11.12) has many terms involving the two input frequencies.

**Mixer output frequencies.** Table 11-1 shows some of the terms that will appear in the mixer output, and we have entered in the last column the frequency components that will be produced. The output provides an example of the principle suggested in Fig. 11.2, that a nonlinear circuit with two input frequencies will in general create all the harmonics of those input frequencies, plus the sums and differences of those harmonics. Had we extended our power series in Eq. (11.12) to higher-order terms and used trigonometric identities to expand these terms, we would have verified the presence of all higher harmonics, with their sums and differences.

**TABLE 11.1  Some of the Frequencies Created in the Mixer**

| Time-Domain Expansion | Frequency Component |
|---|---|
| $i_D = a_1[(V_1 \cos(\omega_1 t) + V_2 \cos(\omega_2 t)] + a_2[V_1 \cos(\omega_1 t) + V_2 \cos(\omega_2 t)]^2 + \ldots$ | |
| $= a_1 V_1 \cos(\omega_1 t)$ | $\omega_1$ |
| $+ a_1 V_2 \cos(\omega_2 t)$ | $\omega_2$ |
| $+ a_2 V_1^2 \cos^2(\omega_1 t) \{= a_2(V_1^2/2)[1 + \cos(2\omega_1 t)]\}$ | dc, $2\omega_1$ |
| $+ 2a_2 V_1 V_2 \cos(\omega_1 t) \cos(\omega_2 t) [= a_2 V_1 V_2 \cos(\omega_1 t + \omega_2 t)$ | $\omega_1 + \omega_2$ |
| $+ a_2 V_1 V_2 \cos(\omega_1 t - \omega_2 t)]$ | $\omega_1 - \omega_2$ |
| $+ a_2 V_2^2 \cos^2(\omega_2 t) \{= a_2(V_2^2/2)[1 + \cos(2\omega_2 t)]\}$ | dc, $2\omega_2$ |

**The intermediate frequency.**  Only one frequency is desired; all others are noise to be eliminated by filters. We require the difference frequency, $\omega_1 - \omega_2$, listed in the second column in Table 11.1. This component represents a shift of the information in the carrier and sidebands to the intermediate frequency. Figure 11.13 shows the effects of mixing and demodulation. The higher frequency, $f_1$, is called the *local-oscillator* (LO) frequency, because this frequency is generated within the radio by an oscillator circuit. The mixer combines this frequency with the carrier and sidebands and shifts the entire RF spectrum to the *intermediate frequency* (IF). The IF signal is amplified and filtered and then detected by a normal AM detector; the audio signal is thus recovered. This audio signal is further amplified, low-pass filtered, and furnished to a loudspeaker.

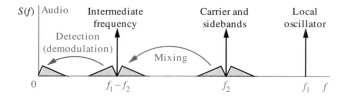

**Figure 11.13**  Mixing and demodulation in the frequency domain.

---

**EXAMPLE 11.6**  **AM system**

Consider a standard AM radio receiving a signal broadcast on a carrier of 1200 kHz. The standard IF for the AM radio is 455 kHz; find the LO frequency.

**SOLUTION:**
If the LO is placed above the RF, the LO frequency would be the sum of the RF and IF frequencies; hence, the local oscillator frequency must be $1200 + 455 = 1655$ kHz.  The resulting AM radio system is shown in Fig. 11.14.

**WHAT IF?**    What it the LO is below the RF?[6]

---

**The Frequency Domain**

**Filtering.**  We now give the reasons for shifting the information to an IF rather than using direct demodulation of the RF signal. As a preliminary, we review the filtering that we have already encountered in the circuit. We require low-pass filtering at the output of the AM detector to separate the audio signal from the detector noise. This filtering is usually incorporated into the audio amplifier circuit and is relatively easy to accomplish because of the wide difference in frequency between the audio spectrum and the noise spectrum.

Similarly, we need filtering at the mixer output to eliminate all but one of the frequencies created by the nonlinear action of the mixer diode. This filtering is likewise easily accomplished because again there is a large difference between the desired and

---

[6]This is a bad idea, but if you insist, 745 kHz.

the undesired frequency components in the mixer output. As we will see, this filtering is accomplished by the IF amplifier.

**Reasons for using an intermediate frequency.** The principal filtering task of the radio, and the most demanding, is the filtering of the RF spectrum to eliminate all the other radio stations that are broadcasting simultaneously with the station of interest. If Figure 11.13 portrayed the true effect of mixing, it would show the signals from many AM radio stations side by side in the RF spectrum, and the radio has to select one and eliminate the rest. How is this filtering accomplished?

The obvious solution is to put a narrow-band filter in the RF amplifier to select the desired station and reject the rest. The two reasons why this is impractical are: (1) the requirements on such a filter would strain the limits for practical inductors and capacitors; and (2) the requirement for a *tunable* filter would further complicate the design of a narrow-band RF filter.

Let us consider the second difficulty first. To construct a radio, we need to filter out all the radio stations except one; but we also need to be able to tune the radio to any of the available stations. We have not discussed tunable filters hitherto, nor will we here except to assert that they are difficult to design. The other problem is that, even without the requirement that the filter be tunable, it would be challenging to design an RF filter selective enough to reject all but one of the available radio stations. The combination of these two difficulties has driven radio designers to use intermediate frequencies, because mixing to an IF lessens both difficulties.

**IF amplifier.** In Fig. 11.14, we have followed the mixer with an IF amplifier/filter. In the AM radio, this amplifier would have high gain only for frequencies within $\pm 5$ kHz of the IF frequency of 455 kHz and hence would act as a filter eliminating all frequencies out of this band of frequencies. The IF amplifier is "fixed-tuned," that is, its passband remains the same as you tune the radio; and because its operating frequency is relatively low, it can provide effective filtering and high gain. Consequently, not only does the IF amplifier/filter eliminate the undesired frequencies created by the mixer, it eliminates the radio stations adjacent to the desired station. Thus, it performs the same function as an RF filter, but it filters at a lower frequency and does not need to be tunable.

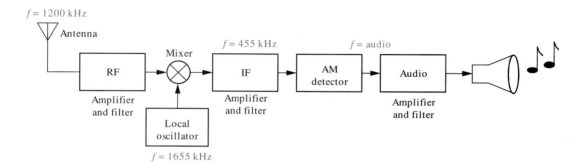

**Figure 11.14**   Standard AM radio system tuned to 1200 kHz.

**Selecting stations.** The radio is tuned by varying the local-oscillator (LO) frequency. When you turn the tuning knob on a radio, the principal effect inside the radio is to vary the frequency of the LO. We saw before that to receive a radio station broadcasting at 1200 kHz, we had to set the LO frequency to 1655 kHz. Clearly, if we increase the LO to 1665 kHz, the station broadcasting at 1210 kHz would now be mixed into the bandpass of the IF amplifier/filter, and the station at 1200 kHz would be eliminated. By this technique, one radio station is selected and all others are rejected.

**Image band.** To the previous filtering actions of the radio circuit, we must add yet one more. In Fig. 11.14, you will note that the box representing the RF amplifier is also called a filter. This does not contradict our earlier assertion that practical problems prevent us from designing a narrow-band RF filter. Some filtering of the RF spectrum is necessary to eliminate the image band of the mixer. To explain the image of the mixer and why we need one more filter to get rid of it, we must refer back to our explanation of mixer operation. You will note in Table 11.1 that the term relating to the mixer action was of the form $\cos[(\omega_1 - \omega_2)t]$. This is the logical way to write this term if $\omega_1$, the LO frequency, is higher than the RF frequency and if only one RF frequency comes into the mixer. But if the RF frequency were higher than the LO frequency, we would write the mixer term as $\cos[(\omega_1 - \omega_2)t]$. So if, for example, our LO were tuned to 1655 kHz and there were an RF input at $1655 + 455 = 2110$ kHz, then this frequency would also be mixed into the IF passband.

**image band**

**Image rejection.** We conclude that the mixer would not distinguish between RF frequencies above and below the LO frequency and hence would mix both into the IF amplifier/filter passband. Without additional filtering, the radio would receive two stations simultaneously, one above and one below the LO frequency. This second, undesirable frequency is called the *image band* of the mixer, and hence a broad-band RF amplifier/filter is required to eliminate any station broadcasting in the image band before it reaches the mixer.

---

**EXAMPLE 11.7** | **Image band**

A microwave receiver is tuned to a carrier of 4226 MHz, has an IF of 60 MHz with a 4-MHz IF bandwidth, and an LO frequency below the carrier. What is the image frequency band for this receiver?

**SOLUTION:**
The LO would be at $f_{RF} - f_{IF} = 4166$ MHz. The center of the image band would be below the LO by the IF, so $f_{image} = f_{LO} - f_{IF} = 4166 - 60 = 4106$ MHz. Hence, the image band would be $4106 \pm 2$ MHz = 4104 to 4108 MHz.

**WHAT IF?** What if the LO is above the RF?[7]

---

[7]4344 to 4348 MHz.

### The superheterodyne receiver.
The mixer and IF amplifier characterize the *superheterodyne receiver*, which combines amplification, filtering, and spectrum shifting. Obviously, much amplification is required because of the small signals picked up by the antenna, and we indicated amplification in Fig. 11.14 at RF, IF, and audio-frequencies. Spectrum shifting is performed by the mixer, to lower the spectrum of the information from the RF band to the IF band; and spectrum shifting is also accomplished by the AM detector to move the information back into the audio frequency band. Filtering is done at RF to eliminate signals in the mixer image band; filtering is done by the IF amplifier to eliminate unwanted mixer products and adjacent radio signals; and filtering is done at the audio frequencies to eliminate noise created by the detector.

**The Frequency Domain**

The radio provides an excellent example of the importance of the frequency-domain viewpoint in electrical engineering. Of the three essential processes involved in radio circuits, two (filtering and spectrum shifting) are accomplished in the frequency domain. We now present two additional examples using superheterodyne techniques

### Frequency-Modulation (FM) radio.
The frequency of a radio wave is less vulnerable to noise than the amplitude, so frequency modulation (FM) is used when high quality sound or other information is required. Commercial monaural FM broadcasting uses an RF bandwidth of 150 kHz, and stereo uses 200 kHz for sum (Left – Right) and difference (Left – Right) channels. The FM band is from 88 to 108 MHz with stations given 200 kHz in which to broadcast 15 kHz of audio bandwidth. The noise-suppression properties of FM therefore come at a cost of greater bandwidth.

**Feedback**

### FM receivers.
Figure 11.15 shows the basic FM receiver. This is a superheterodyne receiver with an IF of 10.7 MHz and an IF bandwidth of 200 kHz. The detection scheme puts the FM signal, shifted to the IF, through a frequency-sensitive circuit that converts the FM to AM for demodulation with rectifier diodes similar to AM radio. A limiter circuit prior to detection eliminates AM noise in the signal. A signal proportional to the IF frequency is fed back to the LO to lock the LO frequency to the station frequency, thus eliminating drift.

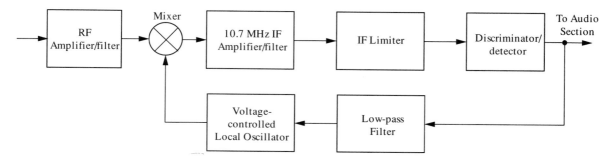

**Figure 11.15** Basic FM system receiver. The LO is part of a feedback loop to lock onto the station frequency.

**Analog Information**

### Telephone systems.
The traditional telephone circuit is a loop of wire from the central exchange to each subscriber. The voice spectrum of approximately 250–3300 Hz is sent over the wire in the base band, that is, without frequency shifting. Switching signals were obtained by opening and closing the loop at a rate of approxi-

mately 10–12 pulses/second and relays counted the pulses at the exchange to route the call. The ring signal was about 90 to 100 V ac at approximately 20 Hz.

The modern system used a tone system to transmit switching information and semiconductor switching computers have replaced the relays. The "ring" signal is commonly a tone that activates an audible device in the telephone receiver.

**Digital Information**

The local exchange switches up to $10^4$ lines with the signal at the base band with a 4-kHz bandwidth. Between exchanges, the voice information is modulated with signal sideband plus carrier into groups of 12 adjacent channels between 60 and 108 kHz. These groups, 12 channels, are then placed into a supergroup of 60 channels between 312 and 552 kHz, and finally 10 supergroups, 600 channels, are placed into a mastergroup between 564 and 3084 kHz. For long distance, the voice channels are modulated to yet higher frequency for transmission by coaxial cable, line-of-sight microwave, or satellite link. Currently digital systems using optical fibers are replacing traditional analog systems.

## Noise in Receivers

**noise, interference**

**Importance of noise.** When we spoke of op amps in Chapter 9, we asserted that gain is cheap. With radio receivers, gain is not as cheap as with op amps, but we can still achieve as high a gain as we wish by adding more stages of amplification. We might suppose, therefore, that we can successfully detect any input RF signal, no matter how weak, simply by having adequate gain in the receiver. This is not true, however, because the sensitivity of a radio receiver is limited by random noise. *Noise*, by definition, is any undesired signal in the system, whether natural or man-made. Man-made noise is called *interference*; Chapter 10 showed techniques to reduce its effects.

**blackbody radiation, shot noise, flicker noise**

**Sources of natural noise.** Natural noise in communication systems comes from two sources. Some noise comes into the receiver from the antenna; for example, in an AM receiver, we can hear a sporadic crackling noise from lightning during storms. Other sources of noise that enter the system through the antenna are atmospheric gases (thermal noise) and extraterrestrial objects such as the sun and our galaxy (cosmic noise).

The second source of noise is the receiver itself. Just as any body radiates *blackbody radiation* due to the thermal motion of its atomic constituents, so also resistors radiate their own type of thermal noise into the circuits of which they are a part. We investigate resistor noise in what follows. Transistors add, in addition to thermal noise, *shot noise* due to the discrete charges that carry the current across the *pn* junctions, and *flicker* or 1/f noise, due to slow changes in device properties from aging, temperature, and other physical changes.

**Equivalent Circuits**

**The Frequency Domain**

**Thermal noise.** The thermal radiation of resistors plays an important role in the description of noise because resistors provide a simple calibration for noise signals. Figure 11.16(a) shows a resistor, $R$, and indicates the noise voltage generated by the thermal motion of the carriers in the resistor. The Thévenin equivalent circuit in Fig. 11.16(b) separates the noise voltage from the resistance, which here is noise-free. The power spectrum of the noise voltage in volts²/hertz is shown in Fig. 11.16(c),

$$S_n(f) = 4kTR \ \text{V}^2/\text{Hz} \tag{11.14}$$

**white noise**

with $k$ = Boltzmann's constant of $1.38 \times 10^{-23}$ J/K. We note the following:

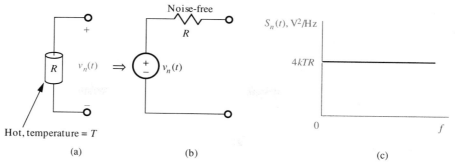

**Figure 11.16**  (a) A noisy resistor; (b) Thévenin equivalent circuit of a noisy resistor; (c) power spectrum of thermal noise.

- The noise spectrum is *white noise*, meaning that all frequencies are present equally, at least throughout the radio spectrum. Thus, a resistor produces a noise power that is proportional to the bandwidth of the circuit.

- The intensity of the power spectrum is proportional to the temperature of the resistor. For sensitive amplifiers, we may measure the noise of the system by comparing system noise to the noise from a resistor of known temperature.

- The intensity of the power spectrum is proportional to the resistance. For this reason, large values of resistance are avoided in sensitive electronic amplifiers. The *available power* out of a circuit is the maximum power that the circuit is capable of delivering into a matched load (see Chapter 2, page 69). The available power spectrum from the circuit in Fig. 11.16(b) is.

**available power**

$$S_{av}(f) = \frac{S_n(f)}{4R} = kT \text{ W/Hz} \qquad (10.15)$$

where $S_{av}(f)$ is the available power spectrum in watts/hertz. Thus, the total power a noisy resistor will contribute to a matched circuit is

$$P = kTB \quad \text{W} \qquad (11.16)$$

where $B$ is the bandwidth in hertz. Equation (11.16) is useful in determining the signal-to-noise ratio in a communication circuit, once we have defined the noise figure and system temperature of an amplifier.

**system temperature**

**System temperature.**   The noise originating in the resistors and semiconductors in a radio amplifier is generally broadband or white noise, at least over the bandwidth of the radio. Thus, we may represent the noise *as if* it originated in a resistor at the input of the radio. Figure 11.17(a) shows the true situation: An amplifier with a power gain of $G$ and a bandwidth of $B$ has internal noise sources that produce $N_s$ watts of noise at its output. In Fig. 11.17(b) we show an equivalent amplifier, assumed to be noise-free, with the same noise at its output *attributed* to a noisy resistor at the input. The *system temperature* is defined as the temperature the resistor required in Fig. 11.17(b) to produce the same amount of output noise as in Fig. 11.17(a). Using Eq. (11.16), we can express

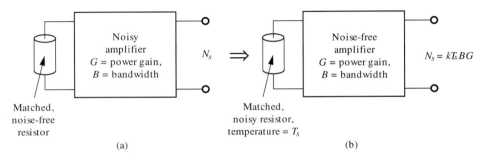

**Figure 11.17** (a) Amplifier with output noise; (b) the system temperature is the temperature of the input resistor to give the same output noise.

the output noise as

$$N_s = kT_s GB \quad \Rightarrow \quad T_s = \frac{N_s}{kGB} \ \text{K} \tag{11.17}$$

where $T_s$ is the system temperature and $N_s$ is the output noise produced by the amplifier. All the internally generated noise is *referred to the input* of the receiver and then expressed as a temperature. The system temperature describes the sensitivity of the amplifier; the lower the system temperature, the more sensitive the amplifier.

**operating noise figure**

**Noise figure.** The *operating noise figure* is defined as the input signal-to-noise ratio divided by the output signal-to-noise ratio. Figure 11.18 shows an amplifier with input signal and noise, $S_{in}$ and $N_{in}$, and output signal and noise, $S_{out}$ and $N_{out}$. The *operating noise figure* is defined to be

$$F = \frac{S_{in}/N_{in}}{S_{out}/N_{out}} = \frac{N_{out}}{N_{in}G} = \frac{N_{in}G + N_s}{N_{in}G} = 1 + \frac{N_s/G}{N_{in}} = 1 + \frac{T_s}{T_{in}} \tag{11.18}$$

where $F$ is the operating noise figure of the amplifier and is often expressed in decibels: $F_{dB} = 10 \log F$ and $T_{in}$ is the input noise expressed as a temperature. The first form on the right side of Eq. (11.18) is the definition of operating noise figure. The second form introduces the gain, $G = S_{out}/S_{in}$, and the third form breaks the output noise into two components, the amplified input noise and the internally generated noise. The last form shows that the noise figure depends on the internally generated noise, referred to the input of the amplifier, compared with the input noise. Thus, the operating noise figure depends in part on the input noise and not on the amplifier only. The operating noise figure is useful in performing signal-to-noise calculations in a communication system.

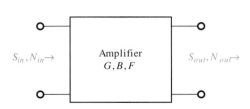

$S_{in}, N_{in} \rightarrow$    Amplifier $G, B, F$    $S_{out}, N_{out} \rightarrow$

**Figure 11.18** Amplifier with signal and noise at input and output.

EXAMPLE 11.8 **Operating noise figure**

The signal-to-noise ratio for a TV signal from a satellite antenna is +50 dB, and the operating noise figure of the amplifier in the radio receiver is 20 dB. Find the output signal-to-noise ratio of the receiver.

**SOLUTION:**

When we convert the definition of the noise figure in Eq. (11.18) to dB by taking 10 times the log of each side of the equation, we have

$$\left.\frac{S}{N}\right|_{out,\,db} = \left.\frac{S}{N}\right|_{in,\,dB} - F_{dB} \quad \Rightarrow \quad \left.\frac{S}{N}\right|_{out,\,dB} = 50\ dB - 20\ dB = 30\ dB \qquad (11.19)$$

**standard noise figure**

**Standard noise figure.** For purposes of comparing amplifiers, we use the *standard noise figure*, in which the input noise is assumed to be the thermal noise of a matched resistor at a temperature of 290 K. For this case, $N_{in} = k(290)\,GB$; and from Eq. (11.18), we can express the standard noise figure as

$$F = 1 + \frac{T_s}{290} \qquad (11.20)$$

EXAMPLE 11.9 **Amplifier comparison**

One amplifier has a standard noise figure of 1.25 and another has a system temperature of 75 K. Which is the more sensitive amplifier?

**SOLUTION:**

To compare the amplifiers, we must express their noise contributions in the same terms. The first amplifier has a system temperature of

$$T_s = 290(F - 1) = 72.5\ K \qquad (11.21)$$

and thus produces slightly less noise than the second amplifier.

**WHAT IF?**

What if you use the 75-K amplifier in a satellite receiver that is looking at the cold sky, assuming an noise input of 20K? What is the operating noise figure?[8]

---

[8] 6.77 dB.

**EXAMPLE 11.10** | **Output noise**

We assume the 72.5-K amplifier is used in a receiver with a gain of 120 dB, a bandwidth of 4 MHz, and an output impedance of 50 $\Omega$. What would be the output noise power due the amplifier and what would be the peak-to-peak noise voltage into a 50-$\Omega$ load?

**SOLUTION:**
The output available power can be determined from Eq. (11.17) as

$$N_s = kT_sGB = 1.38 \times 10^{-23} \times 72.5 \times 10^{120 \text{ dB}/10} \times 4 \times 10^6 \qquad (11.22)$$
$$= 4.00 \times 10^{-3} \text{ W}$$

This would be the power into a matched load of 50 $\Omega$, and thus the rms voltage would be

$$\frac{V_{rms}^2}{50} = 4.00 \text{ mW} \Rightarrow V_{rms} = 0.447 \text{ V} \qquad (11.23)$$

The output voltage would be a random signal with a correlation time of $\tau = 1/B = 0.25$ µs. A good rule of thumb for such random voltages is that the peak-to-peak voltage is five to six times the rms value; thus, we would expect a peak-to-peak output voltage of about 3 V.

### Check Your Understanding

1. If the input spectrum to a circuit contains a fundamental and third harmonic and the output contains in addition a second harmonic, is the circuit linear or nonlinear?
2. The input of a nonlinear system contains frequencies of 30 and 100 Hz. Which of the following can be in the output: 0, 70, 95, 100, 115, 210, 270 Hz?
3. The most critical filtering in a superheterodyne radio is done by the RF amplifier, mixer, IF amplifier, or audio amplifier. Which?
4. In a communication system, a carrier of 500 kHz is amplitude-modulated with a 5-kHz tone. What is the required radio-frequency bandwidth to pass the signal?
5. In a radio, the RF amplifier is required to remove the LO, IF, or image band of the mixer. Which?
6. If in a radio, the RF frequency is 22 MHz, the IF frequency is 5 MHz, and the LO frequency is 27 MHz, what is the image frequency?
7. An amplifier has a standard noise figure of 6 dB. What is its system temperature?
8. Calculate the available noise power from a 300-K, 5-k$\Omega$ resistor in the bandwidth from 0 to 10 MHz.

*Answers.* (1) Nonlinear; (2) 0, 70, 100, 210, and 270 Hz; (3) IF amplifier; (4) 10 kHz; (5) image band of the mixer; (6) 32 MHz; (7) 865 K; (8) $4.14 \times 10^{-14}$ W.

**Introduction.** Modern communication systems use electromagnetic (EM) waves as the medium for transmitting information. Guided EM waves are used in telephone and cable-TV systems, and radiated EM waves are broadcast by radio and TV stations and narrowcast by radar and space communication systems. In this section, we survey the physical properties of EM waves as they relate to communication systems, emphasizing the transmission of EM power from one antenna to another.

**History.** In early experiments in electricity, a connection between light, electric phenomena, and magnetic phenomena was unanticipated. It was known that moving charges produce a magnetic field (Ampère's circuital law) and that a changing magnetic flux produces an electric field (or a voltage, which is Faraday's law).[9] But no one related these phenomena to light. One of the major triumphs of mathematical physics occurred when James Clerk Maxwell (1831–1879) realized that mathematical consistency required that a changing electric field produce a magnetic field. When Maxwell added the needed term to the then-known equations, thus formulating Maxwell's equations, he showed that coupled electric and magnetic fields exist in the form of waves. Moreover, his predicted velocity of these waves corresponded to the known velocity of light. Thus, Maxwell unified electrical science, and showed that light consists of electromagnetic waves. Maxwell's predictions were soon confirmed experimentally by Heinrich Hertz.

**The electromagnetic spectrum.** Maxwell discovered what we call the electromagnetic spectrum, summarized in Fig. 11.19. The figure incorporates the relationship between frequency and wavelength:

$$\lambda = \frac{c}{f} = \frac{3 \times 10^8}{f} = \frac{300}{f_{\mathrm{MHz}}} \qquad (11.24)$$

where $\lambda$ is the wavelength in meters, $c$ is the velocity of light in meters/second, $f$ is the frequency in hertz, and $f_{\mathrm{MHz}}$ is the frequency in megahertz. Figure 11.19 shows the way that electromagnetic waves are guided from point to point. We discuss wave guiding structures in what follows. Also shown are the ways in which free waves are affected by earth and ionosphere for long-distance communication, which we also discuss. The last column shows some of the applications of electromagnetic waves in the various frequency-wavelength ranges.

**Free and guided electromagnetic waves.** Figure 11.19 distinguishes between free waves and guided waves. Guided waves are one-dimensional waves guided by wires, coaxial cables, and the like. Free waves are launched by antennas and spread out in two- or three-dimensional space. We must investigate both types of waves to understand communication systems. We begin with guided waves.

---

[9] These fields and laws are discussed in Chapter 13.

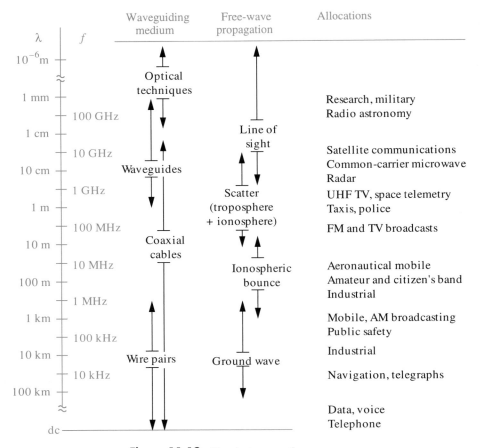

**Figure 11.19** The electromagnetic spectrum.

## Guided Electromagnetic Waves

**transmission lines**

**Introduction.** Along many rural roads, you see wires strung on high poles. The power line is usually on top, with the telephone cable below. These two examples of transmission lines exemplify two major applications, communication and distribution of electric power. The basic principles are the same for both types of lines, but in this section, we survey the major concepts of transmission lines used in communication systems.

A *transmission line* guides waves of EM energy from source to load. Such lines may be parallel wires, as described before, coaxial cables such as distribute TV and other communication services in urban areas, or an internal bus in a computer. Any "circuit" in which the distributed capacitance and inductance of the conductors becomes a factor in circuit performance is a transmission line. Put another way, any circuit whose physical dimensions are not greatly smaller than a wavelength at the highest significant frequency must be considered a transmission line. The analysis of waves on transmission lines fits nicely on the foundation of circuit theory that we have laid, but space limitations prohibit development here.

The following are properties of transmission lines:

- Wave *velocity* on an overhead transmission line is the velocity of light, $3 \times 10^8$ m/s in air. In coaxial cables, the waves are slowed down by the plastic that separates inner and outer conductors. The formula for the wave velocity is

$$v = \frac{1}{\sqrt{LC}} \text{ m/s} \tag{11.25}$$

where $L$ is the distributed inductance of the line in henrys/meter and $C$ is the distributed capacitance of the line in farads/meter. For example, a common coaxial cable, RG-58 in Fig. 11.20, has $L = 0.253$ µH/m and $C = 101$ pF/m, so the wave velocity is $1.98 \times 10^8$ m/s. The wavelength at any frequency can be calculated from Eq. (11.24) if instead of $c$ we substitute the velocity on the transmission line.

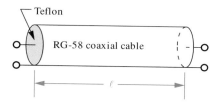

Inductance = 0.253 H/meter × $\ell$
Capacitance = 101 pF/meter × $\ell$

**Figure 11.20** RG-58 coaxial cable. The cable also has a small resistance, which causes loss.

- Power loss on the line is caused by distributed resistance and dielectric losses. For example, the loss of RG-58 is 5 dB/100 ft at 100 MHz.

- *Dispersion* describes the tendency of waves at different frequencies to travel at different velocities on the line. Dispersion causes distortion in the spectra of communication signals sent over transmission lines, but filters at the receiving end can compensate partially.

- The *characteristic impedance* gives the ratio of the voltage to the current waves that move along the line. The characteristic impedance, $Z_0$, of the transmission line is given by

$$Z_0 = \sqrt{\frac{L}{C}} \ \Omega \tag{11.26}$$

For example, the characteristic impedance corresponding to the values of $L$ and $C$ given above is $50.0 \ \Omega$.

- *Reflection* occurs when the impedance of the load at the receiving end of the line differs from the characteristic impedance of the line. Reflections are avoided if possible because power is lost to the load, and often the reflected waves interfere with the source of the signal. When the load has the same impedance as the characteristic impedance of the line, the load is matched to the line, and hence no reflection occurs, as indicated in Fig. 11.21.

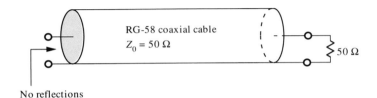

RG-58 coaxial cable
$Z_0 = 50 \ \Omega$

$50 \ \Omega$

No reflections

**Figure 11.21** A matched transmission line with load. No reflection occurs at the load.

---

**EXAMPLE 11.11** | **Transmission-line parameters**

A 10-meter piece of transmission line has a measured capacitance of 705 pF. A pulse traverses the length of the line in 50 ps. Find the inductance/meter for the line.

**SOLUTION:**
The capacitance must be 70.5 pF/m, and the velocity of the pulse on the line must be

$$v = \frac{10 \text{ m}}{50 \times 10^{-9}\text{s}} = 2.00 \times 10^8 \text{ m/s} \qquad (11.27)$$

From Eq. (11.25), we find

$$L = \frac{1}{v^2 C} = \frac{1}{(2.00 \times 10^8)^2 \times 70.5 \times 10^{-12}} = 0.355 \text{ μH/m} \qquad (11.28)$$

**WHAT IF?**
What if you need to match this transmission line with a resistor? What value should you use?[10]

## Free Electromagnetic Waves

**What we mean by "free."** In this section, we deal with electromagnetic waves that are free of man-made guiding structures. Such unconfined waves spread out in space. They may spread out in three dimensions, like waves radiated from a satellite antenna, or they may spread out in two dimensions, like waves radiated by a broadcast antenna and guided by the surface of the Earth. The distribution of energy flow in such waves is affected by the source of the energy, usually an antenna, and by the matter that the waves encounter, for example, by reflection from the ionosphere.

Free electromagnetic waves are used in almost all communication systems except local telephone and cable TV systems. For this reason, we need to understand the character of such waves, how they are launched, how they interact with Earth, obstacles, and the ionosphere, and how they are received. In this section, we focus on the character of the waves; in the next section, we look at how the waves are launched and received by antennas.

---

[10]71 Ω.

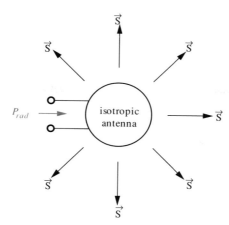

**Figure 11.22** An isotropic antenna radiates energy in all direction equally. The antenna does not focus the energy.

isotropic antenna

**Conservation of Energy**

**Spherical waves.** The simplest case is that of waves that travel away in all directions from a source. Such waves consist of coupled electric and magnetic fields traveling near the speed of light. We may describe the waves by their polarization and power density, the power per unit area in the wave in watts per square meter. We begin with the isotropic (all-directional) antenna. Such an antenna is defined[11] to radiate equally in all directions, as suggested in Fig. 11.22. Because the energy travels outward in straight lines, and because energy is conserved, the power passing a spherical surface of radius $R$ must account for all the power radiated by the antenna.[12] Thus, the power density is

$$S_{iso}(R) \times 4\pi R^2 = P_{rad} \Rightarrow S_{iso}(R) = \frac{P_{rad}}{4\pi R^2} \text{ W/m}^2 \quad (11.29)$$

**polarization**

**Figure 11.23**
Geometry of a wave traveling away from a source. The wave direction and power density are indicated by $\vec{S}$. The electric and magnetic fields are indicated by $\vec{E}$ and $\vec{H}$, respectively.

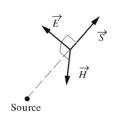

where $P_{rad}$ is the total power radiated, $4\pi R^2$ is the area of a sphere of radius $R$, and $S_{iso}(R)$ is the power density at a distance $R$ from the source of the radiation. The power density is a vector quantity, having a direction in space away from the source. Equation (11.29) indicates that spherical waves weaken due to spreading as they travel away from their source.

**Polarization.** Electromagnetic waves consist of electric and magnetic fields that, at any point, also have directions in space. Figure 11.23 shows the situation: the wave direction and power density are indicated by $\vec{S}$. The electric field, $\vec{E}$, and the magnetic field, $\vec{H}$, are directed at right angles to the direction of $\vec{S}$ and at right angles to each other. Thus, at a location we can describe a radio wave in terms of its direction of travel and its polarization, for example, $E$-field vertical relative to the Earth's surface.

Polarization is important because most antennas produce and receive only one polarization. Thus, if a satellite transmits vertical polarization and your local antenna re-

---

[11] It has been proved that an isotropic antenna is incompatible with Maxwell's equations and thus can never be constructed. It is a useful concept, however.

[12] There is a delay, of course, between the time of radiation and the time of passing the sphere. Equation (11.29) assumes steady power levels.

ceives only horizontal polarization, the radio waves arriving at your location will not be collected by the antenna. Commercial AM broadcast signals are vertically polarized, but FM and TV signals are required to use horizontal polarization. Circular polarization uses both vertical and horizontal polarizations, with a 90° phase shift between the two. Due to multiple reflection, however, transmitted signals can become in part depolarized, so the orientation of the receiving antenna is often not critical. At microwave[13] frequencies, aligning antenna and wave polarization is very important.

**Surface waves.**    At lower frequencies such as are used for AM broadcasting, radio waves can be guided by the surface of the Earth. These surface waves follow the curvature of the Earth and do not depend upon line-of-sight between transmitting and receiving antennas. In addition to the loss due to the spreading of the wave, a surface wave also diminishes due to resistive losses in soil.

**Plane waves.**    Radio waves originate from finite sources and hence have curvature as they spread out in space. However, for practical purposes, the radius of curvature is usually large enough to treat them as plane waves. In determining the intensity of such waves, we must consider the distance to the source, but in considering the local nature of the waves, we usually consider them as plane waves.

**Radio-wave phenomena.**    Earlier, we mentioned two effects that can happen to radio waves: they can be reflected and they can become depolarized. Among the more important effects on radio waves due to their interaction with matter are the following:

**reflection, depolarization, refraction, diffraction, scattering, Doppler shift, attenuation**

■ *Reflection* can occur from the Earth's surface, bodies of water, buildings, and, at low frequencies, the ionosphere. Reflection is used in radar to locate the range and direction of a target. Sometimes reflectors are elevated on towers in microwave relay stations, as shown in Fig. 11.24. At low frequencies, the reflection of radio waves from the ionosphere allows long-distance communication.

■ *Depolarization* occurs when a wave loses its pure polarization in the horizontal or vertical direction and becomes a partial mix of the two.

■ *Refraction* refers to the bending of a wave toward the direction of denser matter. For example, radio waves in the lower atmosphere are refracted toward the Earth's surface because the atmosphere is more dense at the Earth's surface. This has the effect of extending the "radio horizon" slightly and is beneficial in line-of-sight microwave transmission systems.

■ *Diffraction* occurs when waves spread into a shadow region behind an obstacle. Diffraction allows radio waves to be received beyond the radio horizon and behind buildings.

■ *Scattering* occurs when radio waves bounce off a multitude of small objects and "scatter" in all directions. For example, a wave that was reflected from the surface of the ocean would be in part scattered by the irregular surface.

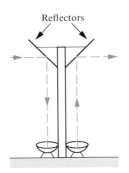

**Figure 11.24**  A microwave relay station using reflectors.

---

[13] Generally, above about 1000 MHz, but "microwave" refers more to the type of structures used to control the energy than to the absolute frequency.

- *Doppler shift* occurs when a wave reflecting from a moving target is shifted in frequency. This effect allows a radar to measure the speed of a target.

- *Attenuation* refers to the absorption of electromagnetic energy by matter. Rain and atmospheric gases cause attenuation at high microwave frequencies.

**Summary.** We investigated the behavior of free electromagnetic waves. We showed how waves diminish through spreading as they travel away from sources, and we described the various effects that can influence their travel through the atmosphere. We now describe the means for launching and receiving the waves.

## Antennas

**antenna**

**What is an antenna?** An *antenna* is a structure that couples between a guided and a free electromagnetic wave. Most antennas can be used for both transmitting and receiving waves. The transmitting and receiving properties of an antenna are closely related, but are described in different terms. Figure 11.25 represents an antenna as a transmitting device. It receives power, $P_{in}$, from a circuit and radiates power in the form of radio waves, which we describe by their polarization and their power density as a function of distance from the antenna, $S(R)$. As a circuit element, the antenna is described by its input impedance, $\mathbf{Z}_{in}$. The radiation efficiency, $\eta$, is the ratio of the radiated power to the input power:

$$\eta = \frac{P_{rad}}{P_{in}} \tag{11.30}$$

**Antenna gain.** Parabolic reflectors, such as shown in Fig. 11.26(a), are used in radar and satellite communication systems because they focus the radiated power into a narrow region of space. Simple wire antennas, such as shown in Fig. 11.26(b), focus the power only slightly and are used for broadcast applications. The focusing ability of an antenna is described by the antenna gain, which is defined as

$$G = \eta \frac{S(R)}{S_{iso}(R)} \tag{11.31}$$

**antenna gain**

where $G$ is the antenna gain. The antenna gain involves an efficiency factor and a focusing factor. The efficiency factor, $\eta$, describes how much of the power delivered to the antenna is radiated; $1 - \eta$ is the fraction lost in resistance and other losses. The focusing factor is the ratio of the power density radiated by the antenna divided by the

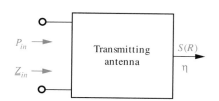

**Figure 11.25** A transmitting antenna receives power from a circuit and radiates an electromagnetic wave.

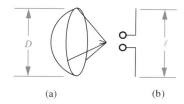

**Figure 11.26** (a) A parabolic reflector-type antenna; (b) a wire-type antenna.

power density of an isotropic antenna. The *antenna gain* thus is the power density of the antenna compared to that of a lossless antenna that does not focus at all. A simple wire antenna has a maximum gain in the range 1.5 to 2.0. A large parabolic reflector may have a gain exceeding 1000. The antenna is normally positioned to focus the energy in a preferred direction, and thus we deal usually with the maximum gain of the antenna.

We may combine Eqs. (11.29), (11.30), and (11.31) to obtain an important equation relating power density to distance from the antenna:

$$S(R) = \frac{P_{in}G}{4\pi R^2} \tag{11.32}$$

Equation (11.32) assumes spherical-wave spreading of the waves and also the absence of reflection, attenuation, and the like.

---

**EXAMPLE 11.12** **Transmitting antenna**

A parabolic antenna has a maximum gain of 22 dB. How much power do we have to deliver to the antenna to produce a power density of $2\ \mu W/m^2$ at a distance of 10 miles?

**SOLUTION:**

Because 10 miles $= 1.61 \times 10^4$ meters, and $G = 10^{22/10} = 158$, we find from Eq. (11.32)

$$P_{in} = \frac{4\pi(1.61 \times 10^4)^2 \times 2 \times 10^{-6}}{158} = 41.1 \text{ W} \tag{11.33}$$

**WHAT IF?** What if the distance were doubled?[14]

---

**Equivalent Circuit**

**Receiving antennas.** Figure 11.27 represents a receiving antenna. The input to the antenna is a plane wave of a given polarization and power density. As a circuit element, the antenna is characterized by its Thévenin equivalent circuit. Although in practice the equivalent circuit is not easy to determine, we may work directly with the available power from the antenna.

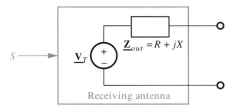

**Figure 11.27** A receiving antenna. The input is a plane wave and the output is power furnished to a circuit.

---

[14] Then we need four times the power, 164.3 W.

As mentioned before, the available power of a circuit is the maximum power that the circuit is capable of delivering into a matched load. The load on the antenna is the input impedance of the radio receiver attached to the antenna, which must be $\underline{Z}_{out}^* = R - jX$ to receive the available power from the antenna. The ability of the antenna to collect power from a radio wave and deliver it to a circuit is characterized by the *effective area* of the antenna:

$$A_{eff} = \frac{P_{av}}{S} \tag{11.34}$$

where $P_{av}$ is the available power in watts, $S$ is the incident power density in W/m$^2$, $A_{eff}$ is the effective area of the antenna in square meters, and we have assumed that the antenna is correctly oriented to receive the polarization of the incident radio wave. It can be shown[15] that the effective area of any antenna is related to its gain by

$$A_{eff} = \frac{\lambda^2}{4\pi} G \tag{11.35}$$

where $\lambda$ is the wavelength in meters. Equations (11.32), (11.34), and (11.35) permit us to calculate the coupling of transmitter and receiver through a radio link.

---

**EXAMPLE 11.13** **Receiving antenna**

The power radiated in the previous example is received by an identical antenna at a frequency of 5020 MHz. Find the available power from the receiving antenna.

**SOLUTION:**

The wavelength from Eq. (11.24) is $300/5020 = 5.97 \times 10^{-2}$ meters, so the effective area by Eq. (11.35) is

$$A_{eff} = \frac{(5.97 \times 10^{-4})}{4\pi} \times 10^{22/10} = 4.50 \times 10^{-2} \ \text{m}^2 \tag{11.36}$$

From Eq. (11.34), we can calculate the available power as

$$P_{av} = S \times A_{eff} = 2 \times 10^{-6} \times 4.50 \times 10^{-2} = 9.01 \times 10^{-8} \ \text{W}$$

---

**Communication equation.** In the communication link pictured in Fig. 11.28, a transmitter delivers $P_{in}$ of power to a transmitting antenna. A receiving antenna at a distance $R$ accepts a portion of the radio wave and delivers an available power $P_{rec}$ to a receiver with a matched input impedance. We consider only the line-of-sight wave and

---

[15] The proof of Eq. (11.35) from Maxwell's equations is difficult. A relatively simple proof can be obtained from thermodynamic equilibrium by considering resistors attached to each antenna. For the resistors to reach thermodynamic equilibrium through radiative heat transfer, Eq. (11.35) must be true. In other words, if Eq. (11.35) were not true, a perpetual motion machine theoretically could be constructed out of resistors and antennas.

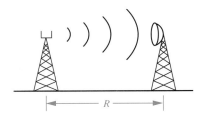

**Figure 11.28** A radio transmission link with transmitting and receiving antennas.

thus neglect reflection, scattering, and the like. Combining Eqs. (11.32) and (11.34), we determine the received power, $P_{rec}$, to be

$$P_{rec} = \frac{P_{in}G_t}{4\pi R^2} \times A_{eff} \qquad (11.37)$$

where $G_t$ is the gain of the transmitting antenna and $A_{eff}$ is the effective area of the receiving antenna. We may change the form of Eq. (11.37) by use of Eq. (11.35), with the result

$$P_{rec} = \frac{P_{in}G_tG_r}{(4\pi R/\lambda)^2} \qquad (11.38)$$

**space loss**

where $G_r$ is the gain of the receiving antenna. The coupling between transmitter and receiver depends, therefore, on the gains of the transmitting and receiving antennas and on the distance between antennas measured in wavelengths. The denominator in Eq. (11.38) is often called the *space loss* in the link and is often given in decibels. We illustrate its use in what follows; then we discuss two common types of antennas.

---

**EXAMPLE 11.14** **Space loss**

What is the space loss in dB for the communication link described in the previous two examples?

**SOLUTION:**
The distance normalized to wavelengths is

$$\frac{R}{\lambda} = \frac{16,100}{5.97 \times 10^{-2}} = 2.69 \times 10^5 \qquad (11.39)$$

The space loss in dB is

$$dB = 10 \log\left(4\pi \frac{R}{\lambda}\right)^2 = 10 \log\left(4\pi \times 2.69 \times 10^5\right)^2 = 130.6 \text{ dB} \qquad (11.40)$$

**WHAT IF?** What if the distance were doubled?[16]

---

**Reflector-type antennas.** Figure 11.26(a) shows a reflector-type antenna commonly used in microwave communication systems. The metallic reflector is parabolic in shape, and a "feed" at the focus of the parabola radiates or receives the radio waves. Power is coupled between the transmitter (or receiver) and the feed through a transmission line. In the transmit mode, a spherical wave is radiated by the feed in the direction of the reflector, and the reflector redirects the spherical wave into one direction, as shown in Fig. 11.29. In the receive mode, the incoming plane wave is reflected from the parabolic reflector and converted into a spherical wave that converges on the feed. The feed collects power from the incoming spherical wave.

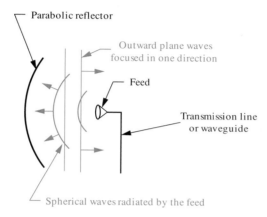

**Figure 11.29** The parabolic reflector transforms the spherical waves radiated by the feed into plane waves focused in one direction. The plane waves eventually spread through diffraction into a beam.

A reflector antenna is most naturally described in terms of its effective area. A good rule of thumb is that about 50% of the incident energy that strikes the reflector is collected by the feed; the effective area is about

$$A_{eff} \approx \frac{1}{2} A_{geo} = \frac{1}{2}\left(\frac{\pi}{4}\right)D^2 = \frac{\pi D^2}{8} \tag{11.41}$$

where $A_{geo}$ is the geometric area of the reflector and $D$ is its diameter. Equation (11.35) gives the approximate gain of a reflector-type antenna as

$$G \approx \frac{4\pi}{\lambda^2} A_{eff} = \frac{\pi^2}{2}\left(\frac{D}{\lambda}\right)^2 \tag{11.42}$$

Thus, the gain of the antenna depends on the diameter measured in wavelengths. Equation (11.42) allows estimation of the gain of a microwave antenna based on its size and operating frequency.

---

[16] 136.6 dB.

EXAMPLE 11.15 **Antenna size**

Find the diameter of the antennas used in the examples on transmitting and receiving antennas. The antennas are parabolic reflectors with a 22-dB gain at a frequency of 5020 MHz.

**SOLUTION:**
The wavelength was calculated as 5.97 cm. Using Eq. (11.42), we find the diameter to be

$$10^{22/10} = \frac{\pi^2}{2}\left(\frac{D}{5.97 \text{ cm}}\right)^2 \Rightarrow D = 33.8 \text{ cm} \tag{11.43}$$

**WHAT IF?**   What if the frequency were doubled?   What would be the gain at the higher frequency?[17]

**Wire-type antennas.**   Figure 11.26 (b) shows a common wire-type antenna called a *dipole*. This antenna is used on TV receivers and is closely related to the telescoping antenna used on automobiles. For good antenna properties, the length of the antenna, $\ell$, should be either one-half or a full wavelength of the electromagnetic wave.[18] Because the half-wave dipole is the smallest efficient antenna, this explains why audio signals must be modulated to higher frequencies for effective radiation. The half-wave dipole has a gain of about 1.5, and an input resistance of about 50 Ω. Thus, the effective area of this antenna is

$$A_{eff} = 1.5 \frac{\lambda^2}{4\pi} \tag{11.44}$$

**Other antenna types.**   Multiple dipole antennas are often used in tandem arrangements called *arrays*. A common housetop TV antenna is an array antenna of several dipole antennas with slightly different lengths to increase the gain and bandwidth of the antenna. Often an AM station uses an array of two or more dipoles on separate towers to direct their signals toward populated areas.

**array**

An external antenna is avoided in an AM radio by using a small, multiturn coil wound on a ferrite rod. A horn antenna may be used for a microwave antenna, much as a megaphone is used by a cheerleader to focus his or her voice. The cornucopia antennas used in microwave relay systems combine a horn with a parabolic reflector, as indicated in Fig. 11.30 (b).

**Summary.**   We discussed the components of a communication system. Transmitting antennas radiate waves that are received by an antenna, which furnishes power to a radio receiver. The receiver amplifies and filters the signal, plus the inevitable noise, and

---

[17] 28 dB.

[18] For practical reasons, the length of an auto antenna is much less than the wavelength, which is about 300 m for AM signals. For this reason, auto antennas are inefficient.

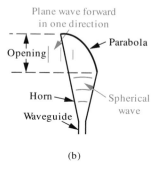

Plane wave forward
in one direction

Opening

Parabola

Horn

Spherical
wave

Waveguide

(b)

(a)

**Figure 11.30** (a) A cornucopia horn; (b) antenna cross-section.

delivers the signal to the ultimate user of the information. We next consider two representative communication systems.

## Check Your Understanding

1. A 0.5-μs pulse is transmitted down a RG-58 coaxial cable. How much space on the line does the pulse occupy at any given time?

2. One way that radio waves are bent is through refraction. True or false?

3. What is the wavelength of a radio wave with a frequency of 15 MHz?

4. An isotropic source radiates 10 W. What is the power density at a distance of 1 mile?

5. A wave with a power density of $2 \times 10^{-9}$ W/m² falls on an antenna with an effective area of 10 m². How much power is available from the antenna to its receiver?

6. What is the space loss in decibels between two antennas that are $10^4$ wavelengths apart?

7. What is the gain at 3000 MHz of a reflector-type antenna that has a diameter of 3 ft?

*Answers.* (1) 99.0 m; (2) true; (3) 20.0 m; (4) 0.307 μW/m²; (5) $2 \times 10^{-8}$ W; (6) $63.3 \times 10^{-12}$ or $-102.0$ dB; (7) 412.6, or 26.2 dB.

## FM Broadcast Station

**General description.** Frequency modulation uses a wide bandwidth to achieve its remarkable noise-repression characteristics; specifically, a stereo FM station uses 200 kHz of RF bandwidth for an audio bandwidth of 50 to 15,000 Hz. The University of Texas at Austin operates an FM radio station, KUT, on a carrier frequency of 90.5 MHz. The station radiates approximately 15 kW of RF power.

**Antenna system.** The station employs an array of 12 helical antennas, radiating circular polarization. The Federal Communication Commission requires horizontal polarization for FM, as stated before, but permits circular polarization. Circular polarization is desirable because orientation of the receiver antenna becomes unimportant.

Frequencies exceeding about 20 MHz do not normally bounce off the ionosphere; hence, reception is limited to line-of-sight, extended somewhat by refraction and by diffraction over the radio horizon. The array of transmitting antennas directs power out toward the horizon. The gain of the array, considered as a single antenna, is about 6.4 (8.1 dB). The transmitter output is about 17 kW, of which 80% is radiated by the antenna; thus, the radiated power is 13.6 kW. The station announcers claim "100,000 watts," which presumably takes account of the antenna gain and normal media exaggeration.

**Coverage.** The antenna is located west of Austin on a tower that is 528 ft high. Assuming a perfect sphere, we calculate through simple geometry the distance, $D$, to the line-of-sight horizon to be

$$D = \sqrt{2R_{eq}h} \qquad (11.45)$$

where $h$ is the antenna height and $R_{eq}$ is the equivalent radius[19] of the Earth, $1.3 \times 3956$ miles. Substitution into Eq. (11.45) yields a distance of about 32 miles to the radio horizon. The antenna tower is about 8 miles west of Austin on a high hill, which extends the radio horizon somewhat.

With Eq. (11.38), we may calculate the received power at the radio horizon. The wavelength is 300/90.5 m, and we assume a gain of 1.5 for the receiving antenna. Under these assumptions, the received power is $3.4 \times 10^{-6}$ watts. Some noise would be broadcast with the signal; the FCC requires a 60-dB or better signal-to-noise ratio. Some noise would also be added to the signal due to thermal radiation of the Earth and atmosphere, but the main source of noise would be the receiver. We assume a standard noise figure of $F = 5$; hence, the noise power in the 200-kHz bandwidth of the receiver would be

$$N = k(F - 1)T_0B = 1.38 \times 10^{-23}(5 - 1) \times 290 \times 200 \times 10^3 \qquad (11.46)$$
$$= 3.2 \times 10^{-15} \text{ W}$$

---

[19] The Earth's radius is increased by 30% to account for refraction.

where $T_0$ is the standard temperature (290 K) and the noise is referred to the input of the receiver. Thus, the signal-to-noise ratio is about 90.3 dB for a receiver at the radio horizon. This signal is much stronger than required for line-of-sight operation. The station is therefore extending coverage beyond the horizon.

## Speed-Measuring Radar

**Radar concepts.** Radar is an acronym for *RA*dio *D*irection *A*nd *R*ange. A conventional radar sends out a pulse of power that reflects from a target such as an airplane and returns to the radar site. The direction to the target is determined from the directionality of the antenna, and the range to the target is determined from the time delay between transmission and reception of the pulse. Such radars are used for airplane traffic control, weather detection, and a variety of military and space applications.

A police radar measures neither direction nor range but speed. A continuous microwave signal is radiated from a directional antenna, bounces off a vehicle, and returns to the point of origin. The return signal is received with the same antenna and diverted to a receiver. The motion of the vehicle Doppler shifts the frequency of the return signal, allowing accurate determination of speed. In this section, we perform some representative calculations for such a radar.

**Radar equation.** Figure 11.31 pictures the situation. The power density at the vehicle would be given by Eq. (11.32), repeated here:

$$S = \frac{PG}{4\pi R^2} \text{ W/m}^2 \tag{11.47}$$

**radar cross section** where $G$ is the gain of the antenna, $P$ is the power to the antenna, and $R$ is the distance. The reflection from the target back toward the transmitter is described by the *radar cross section*, $\sigma$, which has the units of square meters. The radar cross-section includes two factors: the total power reflected and the directionality of that reflection toward the transmitter. Hence, the equivalent power reflected back toward the transmitter, $P_{ref}$, is

$$P_{ref} = \frac{PG\sigma}{(4\pi R)^2} \text{ W} \tag{11.48}$$

**Figure 11.31** A speed-measuring radar.

This power weakens due to spreading and produces a power density at the transmitter/receiver of

$$S_{rec} = \frac{PG\sigma}{(4\pi R^2)} \text{ W/m}^2 \tag{11.49}$$

where $S_{rec}$ is the power density at the transmitter/receiver. The power available from the antenna is

$$P_{av} = \frac{PG\sigma A_{eff}}{(4\pi R^2)^2} = \frac{\lambda^2 PG^2\sigma}{(4\pi)^3 R^4} \quad \text{W} \tag{11.50}$$

**radar equation** where $A_{eff}$ is the effective area of the transmitter/receiver antenna. The second form of Eq. (11.50) uses the relationship between effective area and gain from Eq. (11.35). Equation (11.50) is called the *radar equation* and relates the available power to the transmitted power, the radar cross-section of the target, and the gain of the radar antenna.

### Received power calculation.
Modern police radars use a frequency of 24,150 MHz, which corresponds to a wavelength of 1.242 cm. The antenna is a horn with a 4-in. diameter. The gain of the antenna from Eq. (11.42) is about 330. The power source in the radar is a solid-state device, and the radiated power is a minimum of 10 mW. The radar cross-section of an automobile, being an irregularly shaped object, is a statistical quantity because the incident energy reflects from many points on the surface and combines in a random fashion in various directions. We use a nominal value of 0.01 m². We assume a range of 100 yards (91.4 m). Substitution of these numbers into the radar equation, Eq. (11.50), yields an available power of

$$P_{av} = \frac{\lambda^2 PG^2\sigma}{(4\pi)^3 R^4} = \frac{(0.0124)^2(10 \times 10^{-3})(330.1)^2(0.01)}{(4\pi)^3(91.4)^4} \tag{11.51}$$

$$= 1.212 \times 10^{-14} \quad \text{W}$$

Assuming the receiver is matched to the antenna system, this is the received power, which we must compare with the noise in the system to determine the signal-to-noise ratio.

### Signal-to-noise estimation.
To determine the noise level in the receiver, we must know the noise figure and the bandwidth. Because the noise power out of the receiver is proportional to bandwidth, the minimum bandwidth is used. The minimum bandwidth depends in turn on the maximum speed that the system would expect to encounter in practice. We assume 150 mph (67.0 m/s) and use the Doppler equation:

$$\Delta f = f \times \frac{2v}{c} = 24.15 \times 10^9 \times \frac{2(67.0)}{3 \times 10^8} = 10.8 \text{ kHz} \tag{11.52}$$

This would be the bandwidth of our receiver. The noise in the receiver depends on the input noise from the antenna and the receiver noise figure, with the major contribution coming from the receiver. A worst-case standard noise figure for a receiver of this type is $F = 10$. Using Eqs. (11.20) and (11.17), we estimate the noise, referred to the receiver input, to be

$$N = k(F-1)T_0 B = 1.38 \times 10^{-23}(10-1) \times 290 \times 10.8 \times 10^3 \tag{11.53}$$

$$= 3.89 \times 10^{-16} \quad \text{W}$$

The signal-to-noise ratio is thus about 31.2. This is not very impressive, and speeding tickets would be easy to discredit if this were the end of the story.

Equation (11.53) gives the signal-to-noise ratio if only one sample of the speed were obtained, but the radar would be able to collect many samples in a short time. Let us assume that the radar collects samples over 0.5 s before displaying the speed. This means that a counter determines the frequency of the return for 0.5 s, and then the results are displayed, scaled to indicate miles per hour. The correlation time of the receiver noise is approximately $1/B = 0.1$ ms, and hence the number of independent samples is approximately 5000. A well-known rule of statistics is that accuracy improves as the square root of the number of independent samples, which would be about 70 in this case. Thus, the signal-to-noise ratio of the speed measurement is about 2200, or 33.4 dB. This gives an accurate measurement of target speed.

## CHAPTER SUMMARY

Telecommunications is at present a dynamic area of technical and economic growth. A world-wide communication network for computers has emerged, and cellular pager and telephone coverage is spreading rapidly. Optical systems based on digital codes are replacing microwave systems based on analog techniques in all long-distance communication.

In this chapter, we considered the components of communication systems. We showed how nonlinear devices called modulators are used to shift communication signals to high frequencies for transmission, and we showed how similar principles are used in radio receivers to recover the information. These techniques have been adapted to optical systems and continue to be the basis of communication systems.

We described the properties of the free and guided EM waves used in communication systems. We defined the concepts used to describe the properties of transmitting and receiving antennas, and we used these to derive a communication equation for the power delivered to a radio receiver. Finally, we examined the details of two communication systems, emphasizing signal-to-noise calculations.

**Objective 1: To understand the effects of nonlinear circuits on the spectra of signals.** When two sinusoids are combined in a nonlinear circuit, all the harmonics of both and all sums and differences of the harmonics of both are created. This effect can be used to shift information in one band of frequencies to another. Modulation shifts information at low frequencies to high frequency for broadcasting or some other form of transmission. Mixing and demodulation shift the information back to lower frequency for application.

**Objective 2: To understand the superheterodyne radio circuit and be able to relate RF, LO, and IF frequencies.** The superheterodyne radio circuit combines several types of filtering with frequency shifting and amplification. The genius of the technique is the local oscillator–mixer–intermediate-frequency circuit.

**Objective 3: To undestand the properties of free and guided electromagnetic waves as they relate to communication systems.** Free and guided electromagnetic waves are used to transport communication signals. Wave effects such as dispersion, diffraction, and scattering limit communication systems in various ways.

Objective 4: To understand the properties of antennas and their role in communication systems. Antennas couple between free and guided electromagnetic waves. In transmission, antennas are described by their gain and receiving antennas are described by their effective area. We derive a communication equation relating received power to transmitted power, antenna properties, and distance between transmitting and receiving antennas. Two practical systems are analyzed.

This chapter concludes the section dealing with electronic techniques. The next chapter introduces mathematical methods for system analysis that are used in all types of systems, especially control systems.

## PROBLEMS

## Section 11.1: Radio Principles

11.1. A nonlinear circuit has input frequencies at 300 and 200 Hz. How many output frequencies are there below 1000 Hz, and what are these frequencies?

11.2. The input of a *linear* system contains frequencies of 40 and 100 Hz. Which of the following can be in the output: 0, 70, 100, 120, 210, and 270 Hz? Which of these can be in the output for a *nonlinear* system of the same input frequencies?

11.3. In a superheterodyne radio receiver, the receiver bandwidth is 100 to 101 MHz and the image bandwidth is 120 to 121 MHz. What is the LO frequency? What is the IF?

11.4. The AM radio band of carrier frequencies is 540 to 1600 kHz and the standard IF is 455 kHz. Calculate the image frequency when the radio is tuned to the bottom of the band to receive a station broadcasting with a carrier of 540 kHz. Is this image in the AM band?

11.5. An AM receiver has 10 channels, each 100 kHz wide, covering the bandwidth from 16 to 17 MHz. The IF is 2.6 MHz, with a 100-kHz bandwidth. Assume the LO frequency is below the RF. The LO is not continuously tuned, but each LO frequency is generated from a harmonic of a lower frequency, so the LO frequency is changed by selecting and amplifying the appropriate harmonic of a low-frequency oscillator
(a) What is the minimum LO frequency?
(b) What is the maximum frequency of the low-

frequency oscillator from which the LO frequencies are derived?
(c) What are the harmonic numbers that must be selected to tune the receiver to all 10 channels?
(d) If the receiver receives digital pulses, what is the approximate baud rate it can receive?

11.6. For the simplest design of the local oscillator (LO) in a radio, the ratio of the maximum to minimum LO frequencies should be as low as possible (that is, the percent tuning range of the LO should be minimum). To show why the LO is placed above the RF band, calculate the ratio $f_{max}/f_{min}$ for the LO both above and below the RF in the standard AM radio.

11.7. For a standard AM superheterodyne radio receiver tuned to the station with a carrier of 1600 kHz find the following:
(a) What is the IF frequency?
(b) What is the LO frequency?
(c) What is the IF bandwidth?
(d) What is the maximum RF bandwidth?
(e) Where does most of the gain occur?
(f) Where does most of the filtering occur?
(g) How is the receiver tuned to another station?

11.8. A superheterodyne radio receiver has the following characteristics: the antenna receives an RF spectrum of 10.160 MHz $\pm$ 32 kHz, with a voltage level of 4 $\mu$V; the RF amplifier has a gain of +15 dB; the mixer has a gain of $-12$ dB; the

IF amplifier has a center frequency of 1.5 MHz and a gain of +120 dB; the second detector has a gain of −16 dB (based on audio voltage vs. IF voltage); and the audio amplifier has a gain of +20 dB. Find the following:

(a) LO frequency, assuming that the LO is above the RF frequency.

(b) IF bandwidth required.

(c) Audio outuput voltage.

(d) Maximum bandwidth of the RF amplifier.

**11.9.** The FCC has allocated the band from 88 to 108 MHz for FM broadcasting, with 200 kHz for each station. The intermediate-frequency amplifier in an FM receiver has a center frequency of 10.7 MHz and a bandwidth of 200 kHz.

(a) What is the number of FM stations that can be assigned different carrier frequencies in the total FM band?

(b) What range is required for the frequency of the local oscillator in an FM receiver, assuming that the LO is located above the RF frequency?

(c) What is the maximum frequency that might be mixed into the IF passband from the image band of the mixer?

**11.10.** An FM radio receiver receives carriers at frequencies of 88.1, 88.3, . . . , 107.7, and 107.9 MHz. The RF bandwidth required by each station for the FM information is 200 kHz, the IF

is 10.7 MHz, and the audio bandwidth is 50 to 15,000 Hz.

(a) Find the lowest and highest LO frequency. State assumptions.

(b) Find the image frequency of the first detector when the LO is tuned to its lowest frequency.

(c) What would be an appropriate bandwidth for the IF amplifier?

(d) What would be highest frequency amplified by the audio amplifier?

**11.11.** An amplifier with a 290-K matched resistor at its input produces a certain amount of noise at its output. When the resistor is cooled to 77 K, the output noise power is observed to diminish by 15%. What is the system temperature of the amplifier?

**11.12.** A communication system has a bandwidth of 5 kHz and an output power spectrum of $2 \times 10^{-4}$ $(V)^2/Hz$ into a matched 100-$\Omega$ resistor. What is the rms current in the resistor?

**11.13.** A satellite receiver has a standard noise figure of 1.2. Its antenna looks at the cold sky and provides an input temperature, $T_{in}$, of 30 K.

(a) Find the operating noise figure of the receiver.

(b) If the satellite transmits with a signal-to-noise ratio of 70 dB, find the output signal-to-noise ratio of the receiver. The received power from the satellite is $6 \times 10^{-8}$ watts in the 4-MHz bandwidth.

## Section 11.2: Electromagnetic Waves

**11.14.** The distributed inductance and capacitance of a lossless vacuum-filled coaxial transmission line are

$$L = \frac{\mu_0}{2\pi} \ln\left(\frac{b}{a}\right) \text{ H/m} \quad \text{and} \quad C = \frac{2\pi\varepsilon_0}{\ln(b/a)} \text{ F/m}$$

where $b$ = inner radius of outer conductor and $a$ = outer radius of the inner conductor; $\mu_0 = 4\pi \times 10^{-7}$ H/m, and $\varepsilon_0 = 8.854 \times 10^{-12}$ F/m.

(a) Find the wave velocity in the cable.

(b) Determine the characteristic impedance if $b = 4a$.

**11.15.** A certain 60-Hz power transmission line has an

inductive reactance of 1.4 $\Omega$/mile and a capacitive susceptance of 3.0 $\mu\mho$/mile.

(a) Convert these to H/m and F/m, as required for the calculation of the wave velocity and characteristic impedance.

(b) Determine the wave velocity and characteristic impedance of this transmission line.

**11.16.** Consider the Sun as an isotropic radiator of energy. The power density at the surface of the Earth is about 1000 W/m². Determine the total power radiated by the Sun, assuming 92.8 million miles distance between Sun and Earth.

**11.17.** An antenna with a gain of 12 dB radiates 10 W

of power. What is the power density at 1-km distance?

**11.18.** The effective area of an antenna at 3000 MHz is 5 m². What is its gain in dB at that frequency?

**11.19.** Two half-wave dipoles, each having a gain of 1.3, are separated by 100 m. A 10-W signal at 100 MHz is transmitted by one antenna.
   **(a)** What is the available power at the receiving antenna?
   **(b)** What is the open-circuit rms voltage at the receiving antenna, assuming a 50-$\Omega$ output impedance?

**11.20.** A 10-ft-diameter satellite TV receiving antenna operates over a frequency range of 3700 to 4200 MHz. What is the maximum and minimum gain in decibels over this range of frequency?

**11.21.** An antenna produces at a certain point a wave intensity of $10^{-7}$ W/m², whereas an isotropic antenna gives a wave intensity of $10^{-8}$ W/m². What is the gain of the antenna?

**11.22.** The beam width of a reflector-type antenna describes the angular width of the region in space into which it focuses its radiated energy. Using Eqs. (11.32) and (11.42) and conservation of energy, show that the conical beam width ($\theta$) of a reflector-type antenna is approximately

$$\theta = \frac{4}{\pi}\sqrt{2}\left(\frac{\lambda}{D}\right) \text{ radians}$$

where $D$ is the antenna diameter and $\lambda$ is the wavelength.

**11.23.** Using Eq. (11.42), find the gain of a 6-ft-diameter reflector antenna at 500 MHz in dB.

**11.24.** A communication satellite transmitter radiates 10 watts of power. The satellite antenna focuses the power to cover the entire USA, exclusive of Alaska and Hawaii, more or less uniformly. (Assume a size 1000 miles × 3000 miles, and a satellite height of 22,000 miles.)
   **(a)** Estimate the average power density on the surface.
   **(b)** The frequency is 6 GHz. Estimate the size of the satellite antenna.

## Section 11.3: Examples of Communication Systems

**11.25.** For the FM station example, calculate the received power at the radio horizon (32 miles) and confirm the S/N of 90.3 dB, as stated in the text, page 605.

**11.26.** If a ship-borne radar must detect any target out to 10 miles, how high does the radar antenna have to be relative to the level of the sea?

**11.27.** It is desired to increase the range of an air-control radar by a factor of 50%.
   **(a)** If only the transmitted power is increased,

what is the required percent of increase in power?
   **(b)** If, rather than increasing the power, the reflector-type antenna is replaced by a larger antenna, what is the percent of increase in antenna diameter?

**11.28.** What would be the signal-to-noise ratio for the police radar if the device measured the speed for 0.3 s instead of 0.5 s?

**11.29.** Confirm that the gain of the police radar antenna described on page 606 is about 330.

## Answers to Odd-Numbered Problems

**11.01.** $0 = \text{dc}$, $100 = 300 - 200$, $200$, $300$, $400 = 2 \times 200$, $500 = 200 + 300$, $600 = 2 \times 300$, $700 = 300 + 2 \times 200$, $800 = 4 \times 200$, $900 = 3 \times 300$.

**11.03.** LO = 110.5 MHz, IF = 10 MHz.

**11.05.** **(a)** 13.45 MHz; **(b)** 50 kHz; **(c)** All odd harmonics between 269th and 287th; **(d)** 50 kbaud.

**11.07.** **(a)** 455 kHz; **(b)** 2055 kHz; **(c)** 10 kHz; **(d)** 910 kHz; **(e)** in the IF amplifier; **(f)** in the IF amplifier; **(g)** by changing the LO frequency

**11.09.** **(a)** 100; **(b)** 98.8 MHz < LO < 118.8 MHz; **(c)** 129.4 MHz.

**11.11.** 1130 K.

**11.13.** **(a)** 2.93 (4.67 dB); **(b)** 1.38 (1.40 dB).

**11.15.** **(a)** 2.31 μH/m and 4.95 pF/m; **(b)** 296,000 km/s and 683 Ω.

**11.17.** 12.6 μW/m$^2$.

**11.19.** **(a)** 9.63 × 10$^{-5}$ W; **(b)** 0.139 V, rms.

**11.21.** 10 (10 dB).

**11.23.** 45.8 (16.6 dB).

**11.25.** 90.3 dB.

**11.27.** **(a)** 406%; **(b)** 50%.

**11.29.** 330.

# 12

# Linear Systems

objectives

1. To understand the class of functions that can be described by complex frequencies
2. To understand how to use generalized impedance to find the forced and natural response of a system
3. To understand how to recognize conditions for undamped, underdamped, critically damped, and overdamped responses in second-order systems
4. To understand how to use system notation to describe the properties of composite systems
5. To understand the role of loop gain in the dynamic response of a feedback system

This chapter on linear systems expands in several directions the tools for analysis of circuits presented in Chapters 1 to 4. The concept of frequency is generalized, and we expand frequency-domain techniques to a wide class of behavior. The results are then generalized to include systems with nonelectrical components and systems with feedback.

# Introduction to Linear Systems

**What is a system?** A *system* consists of several components that together accomplish some purpose. For example, an automobile has a motor, steering mechanism, lights, padded seats, entertainment system, and more, operating together to give safe and pleasant transportation. Likewise, a stand-alone ac generator requires a control system to regulate the frequency and voltage of its output. Often, systems are modeled with linear equations. The analysis of such linear systems has furnished a powerful language for system description that builds on our earlier study of the frequency domain. This chapter introduces system models and explores basic techniques of linear system description and analysis.

**Contents of this chapter.** We begin by generalizing the concept of frequency. We then introduce the language of system notation by defining the generalized impedance of electrical circuits. From this impedance, we determine the natural frequencies and natural response of electrical circuits, and we then investigate the transient response of first- and second-order circuits. Next, this viewpoint is applied to a composite system involving electrical and thermal components, an oven. Finally, we regulate the oven with a feedback system and investigate the transient response and dynamic stability of the feedback system.

## 12.1 COMPLEX FREQUENCY

**Definition of complex frequency.** We resume our exploration of the frequency domain through the following definition of complex frequency. A time-domain variable, say, a voltage, is said to have a *complex frequency* $\underline{s}$ when it can be expressed in the form given in Eq. (12.1)

$$v(t) = \text{Re}\,\{\underline{V}e^{\underline{s}t}\} \tag{12.1}$$

where $\underline{V}$ is a complex number, a phasor, and

$$\underline{s} = \sigma + j\omega \quad \text{s}^{-1} \tag{12.2}$$

where $\underline{s}$, $\sigma$, and $\omega$ all have units of inverse seconds, $\text{s}^{-1}$. Equation (12.1) is a slightly modified version of, say, Eq. (4.44), except that frequency is now a complex number.

**Functions that can be represented by complex frequencies.** Before we explore the implications of complex frequency, we wish to relate Eq. (12.1) to familiar results. We have in previous chapters introduced several important functions that can be represented by complex frequencies.

**When $\underline{s}$ is zero.** When the complex frequency in Eq. (12.1) is zero, $\underline{s} = 0$, the voltage is a constant, or a dc voltage:

$$v(t) = \text{Re}\,\{\underline{V}e^{0t}\} = V_{dc} \quad \text{for } \underline{s} = 0 \tag{12.3}$$

**When $\underline{s}$ is real and negative.** When the complex frequency $\underline{s}$ is real, $\underline{s} = \sigma$, the time-domain voltage is

$$v(t) = \text{Re}\,\{\underline{V}e^{\sigma t}\} = Ae^{\sigma t} \quad \text{for } \underline{s} = \sigma \tag{12.4}$$

where $A$ is a constant. For negative $\sigma$, the voltage is a decreasing exponential function, such as we encountered in first-order transient problems in Chapter 3. Specifically, the time constant is the negative of the reciprocal of $\sigma$:

$$\sigma = -\frac{1}{\tau} \qquad \text{where} \quad \tau = R_{eq}C \quad \text{or} \quad \frac{L}{R_{eq}} \quad \text{s} \qquad (12.5)$$

---

**EXAMPLE 12.1** **Transient problem**

Find the complex frequency representing the response of the circuit in Fig. 12.1.

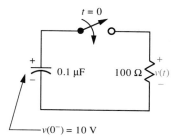

**Figure 12.1** The circuit response can be described by a complex frequency.

**SOLUTION:**

Using the techniques from Chapter 3, we find the response to be

$$v(t) = v(0^-)e^{-t/RC} = 10e^{-10^5 t} \quad \text{V} \qquad (12.6)$$

Comparison with Eq. (12.4) shows $\underline{s} = \sigma = -10^5 \text{ s}^{-1}$.

**WHAT IF?** What if the switch is open?[1]

---

**When $\underline{s}$ is real and positive.** If $\sigma$ is positive in Eq. (12.4), the voltage is an increasing exponential, which we have not encountered before. Figure 12.2 shows the time functions that result from zero and real complex frequencies. Thus, a complex frequency that is real includes the response that we studied as a transient solution in Chapter 3, except that we now include growing as well as decaying exponentials. Later we show that a growing exponential represents a possible response of an unstable system.

**When $\underline{s}$ is pure imaginary.** When the complex frequency is pure imaginary, Eq. (12.1) takes the form of a sinusoidal function, such as we studied in Chapter 4. In this case,

---

[1] Then the only possible response is $\underline{s} = 0$. In effect the resistance becomes infinite, but a constant voltage and a constant current (zero current) are still possible.

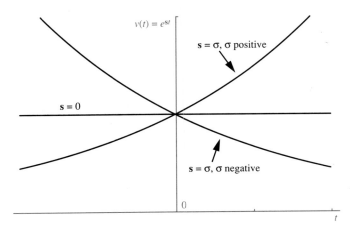

**Figure 12.2** Time-domain responses for complex frequencies that are real.

$$v(t) = \text{Re}\{\underline{V}e^{j\omega t}\} = V_p \cos(\omega t + \theta) \tag{12.7}$$

where $\underline{V} = V_p e^{j\theta}$, with $V_p$ the peak value and $\theta$ the phase of the sinusoidal function. Imaginary complex frequencies are used in the analysis of ac circuits.

**Sinusoid = two complex frequencies.** From another point of view, we may represent a sinusoidal function by two complex frequencies. This is implied by the "real part" operation in Eq. (12.1), because an alternate way to express the real part is through the identity in Eq. (12.8)

$$\text{Re}\{\underline{z}\} = \tfrac{1}{2}(\underline{z} + \underline{z}^*) \tag{12.8}$$

where $\underline{z}^*$ is the complex conjugate of $\underline{z}$. Thus, Eq. (12.7) can be expressed in the form

$$V_p \cos(\omega t + \theta) = \text{Re}\{\underline{V}e^{j\omega t}\} = \frac{\underline{V}}{2}e^{j\omega t} + \frac{\underline{V}^*}{2}e^{-j\omega t} \tag{12.9}$$

When we compare Eq. (12.9) with Eq. (12.1), we see that two complex frequencies, $\underline{s} = j\omega$ and $\underline{s} = -j\omega$, express a sinusoidal function. In our consideration of complex frequency, we often find this second point of view to be useful.

**Frequency and complex frequency.** We have a slight semantic problem in speaking of complex frequency. When the complex frequency $\underline{s}$ is imaginary, the frequency, $\omega$, is said to be real. Thus, a sinusoidal function has a real frequency, but is described by a complex frequency that is imaginary. As shown before, a complex frequency that is real corresponds to a growing or decaying exponential function.

**General interpretation of complex frequency.** We now consider the meaning of $e^{\underline{s}t}$, with $\underline{s} = \sigma + j\omega$. In general

$$v(t) = \text{Re}\{\underline{V}e^{\underline{s}t}\} = \text{Re}\{\underline{V}e^{(\sigma+j\omega)t}\} \tag{12.10}$$
$$= e^{\sigma t}\text{Re}\{\underline{V}e^{j\omega t}\} = V_p e^{\sigma t}\cos(\omega t + \theta)$$

Equation (12.10) expresses a time function that combines sinusoidal behavior with the

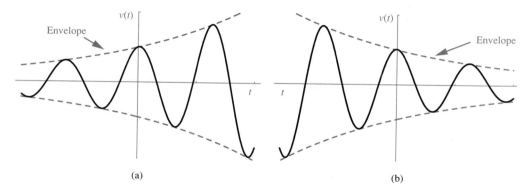

**Figure 12.3** The function $\mathrm{Re}\{e^{(\sigma+j\omega)t}\}$ for (a) $\sigma$ positive and (b) $\sigma$ negative.

exponential behavior that we hitherto have associated with transients. Equation (12.10) also can be considered a sinusoidal function in which the peak value of the sinusoid changes exponentially with time. Figure 12.3 shows the character of the time function in Eq. (12.10).

**The s-plane.** A complex number, $\underline{s}$, can be represented by a point in the complex plane. In Fig. 12.4, we show such an $\underline{s}$-plane and identify the regions of complex frequency corresponding to possible time responses.

- ■ The origin corresponds to a constant or dc function.
- ■ Complex frequencies on the real axis correspond to growing and decaying exponential functions.
- ■ Complex frequencies on the imaginary axis correspond to sinusoidal functions.
- ■ The region to the right of the vertical axis, the right-half plane, corresponds to sinusoids that are growing exponentially.
- ■ The left-half plane corresponds to sinusoids that are decreasing exponentially.

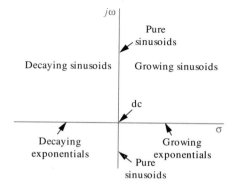

**Figure 12.4** The $\underline{s}$-plane and associated time functions.

EXAMPLE 12.2 **Complex frequency**

What complex frequency corresponds to the function

$$v(t) = 100e^{1000t} \sin(400\pi t + 75°) \text{ V} \qquad (12.11)$$

**SOLUTION:**
There are two frequencies: $\sigma = 1000$ comes from the exponential part and $j\omega = \pm j400\pi$ comes from the sinusoidal part. Thus,

$$\underline{s}_1 = 1000 + j400\pi \qquad \text{and} \qquad \underline{s}_2 = 1000 - j400\pi \qquad (12.12)$$

**WHAT IF?** What if the function were cosine instead of sine?[2]

**The Time Domain**

**The Frequency Domain**

**eigenfunction**

**Time domain and frequency domain.** The introduction of complex frequency expands our concept of the frequency domain to cover a wider class of time-domain behavior. We now have a frequency-domain representation of exponentially growing or decreasing time functions that may oscillate. As hinted before, this expansion will allow frequency-domain techniques to be applied to transient problems as well as sinusoidal steady-state problems such as we studied in Chapter 4. Furthermore, these new functions allow the study of a wider class of transient problems.

**Importance of $e^{st}$.** The function $e^{st}$ is a mathematical probe[3] we use to investigate the properties of linear systems. At this point, we wish to look ahead and anticipate later results. We find that all linear systems are characterized by certain complex frequencies. Once we determine these frequencies for a given system, say, a feedback amplifier, we can determine from them the system response in the time domain or the frequency domain. We may thereby examine transient and steady-state responses, and we can determine if the system is stable or unstable. In the following section we show how to determine these characteristic frequencies and how to derive from them the time-domain response of the system.

**Summary.** In this section, we have generalized frequency to include growing or decreasing exponentials and exponentially growing or decreasing sinusoids. Such complex frequencies allow frequency-domain techniques to be applied to a wide class of systems. The characteristics of linear systems are often described in terms of complex frequency.

**Check Your Understanding**

**1.** What complex frequency or frequencies describe(s) an $RC$ transient with a dc source if $R = 100 \ \Omega$ and $C = 10 \ \mu\text{F}$.

---

[2] The "sin/cos" and "75°" affect the phase but not the complex frequency.
[3] The mathematical term for $e^{st}$ is the *eigenfunction* for a linear DE.

**2.** What is the time between zero crossings for a function described by the complex frequency $\underline{s} = -2 + j10$?

**3.** A pure sinusoid may be described by a complex frequency that is pure imaginary, two complex frequencies that are pure imaginary, either, or neither. Which?

**4.** Complex frequencies near the origin in the $\underline{s}$-plane describe functions that vary slowly with time. (True or False?)

**Answers.** (1) 0 (for the source) and $-1000$ s$^{-1}$ (for the circuit); (2) 0.314 s; (3) either, depending on context; (4) true.

## 12.2 IMPEDANCE AND THE TRANSIENT BEHAVIOR OF LINEAR SYSTEMS

### Generalized Impedance

**generalized impedance**

**Impedance of R, L, and C.** We may use complex frequency to generalize the concept of impedance. We use the technique presented in Chapter 4, where only real frequency was considered. As before, we argue that $e^{\underline{s}t}$ is a function that is indestructible to linear operations such as addition, differentiation, and integration. To determine the impedance, therefore, we excite a circuit with a voltage $\mathrm{Re}\{\underline{V}e^{\underline{s}t}\}$ and calculate a response, $\mathrm{Re}\{\underline{I}(\underline{s})e^{\underline{s}t}\}$.

The *generalized impedance* is defined as

$$\underline{Z}(\underline{s}) = \frac{\underline{V}(\underline{s})e^{\underline{s}t}}{\underline{I}(\underline{s})e^{\underline{s}t}} \ \Omega \tag{12.13}$$

We illustrate with an inductor, as shown in Fig. 12.5. The equations are

$$v(t) = L\frac{d}{dt}i(t) \Rightarrow \underline{V}(\underline{s})e^{\underline{s}t} = L\frac{d}{dt}\underline{I}(\underline{s})e^{\underline{s}t} = \underline{s}L\underline{I}(\underline{s})e^{\underline{s}t} \tag{12.14}$$

where we have omitted the "real part of" for simplicity. The differentiation is performed only on the $e^{\underline{s}t}$ function because this is the only function of time. Thus the generalized impedance of an inductor is

$$\underline{Z}_L(\underline{s}) = \frac{\underline{V}(\underline{s})e^{\underline{s}t}}{\underline{I}(\underline{s})e^{\underline{s}t}} = \underline{s}L \ \Omega \tag{12.15}$$

In like manner, we can establish the generalized impedances of resistors and capacitors:

$$\underline{Z}_R(\underline{s}) = R \ \Omega, \quad \text{and} \quad \underline{Z}_C(\underline{s}) = \frac{1}{\underline{s}C} \ \Omega \tag{12.16}$$

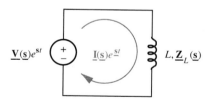

**Figure 12.5** An inductor excited by $\underline{V}e^{\underline{s}t}$.

**OBJECTIVE 2**

To understand
how to use
generalized
impedance to
find the forced
and natural
response of a
system

**Application of generalized impedance.** We now analyze the *RL* circuit shown in Fig. 12.6(a). In the frequency domain, Fig. 12.6(b), the impedances combine like resistors at dc:

$$\mathbf{Z}(\mathbf{s}) = 2\|(1 + \mathbf{s}/2) = \cfrac{1}{\cfrac{1}{2} + \cfrac{1}{1 + \mathbf{s}/2}} = \frac{2(\mathbf{s} + 2)}{(\mathbf{s} + 6)} \ \ \Omega \tag{12.17}$$

We use the complex impedance function in Eq. (12.17) to explore the transient response of the circuit.

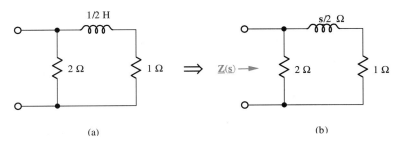

**Figure 12.6** An *RL* circuit in (a) the time domain; (b) the frequency domain.

(a)

(b)

## Transient Analysis

**Forced and natural response.** When we excite a circuit with a voltage or current source, we force a certain response from the circuit. For example, if we apply a dc source, we expect a dc response. But, as we saw in Chapter 3, part of the transient response of the circuit takes a form that is natural to, and determined by, the circuit itself. Thus, the response is always of the form, say, for a current:

$$i(t) = i_f(t) + i_n(t) \tag{12.18}$$

where $i_f(t)$ is the forced response and $i_n(t)$ is the natural response. We now explore the role of complex frequency and the impedance function in determining the forced and natural responses of a linear circuit.

**Forced response from impedance.** The forced response of the circuit may be determined directly from the impedance function when the forcing function, input current or voltage, is of the form $e^{\mathbf{s}t}$. We evaluate the impedance function at the value of $\mathbf{s}$ of the forcing function. For example, if the voltage is a known function with a complex frequency $\mathbf{s} = \mathbf{s}_f$, the current must be of the same form and can be determined from Eq. (12.19)

$$\frac{\mathbf{V}_f e^{\mathbf{s}_f t}}{\mathbf{I}_f e^{\mathbf{s}_f t}} = \mathbf{Z}(\mathbf{s}_f) \ \ \Rightarrow \ \ \mathbf{I}_f e^{\mathbf{s}_f t} = \frac{\mathbf{V}_f}{\mathbf{Z}(\mathbf{s}_f)} \times e^{\mathbf{s}_f t} \tag{12.19}$$

where $\mathbf{V}_f$ and $\mathbf{I}_f$ are phasors describing the source and response, respectively. The response in the time domain is thus

$$i_f(t) = \text{Re}\{\mathbf{I}_f e^{\mathbf{s}_f t}\} = \text{Re}\left\{\frac{\mathbf{V}_f}{\mathbf{Z}(\mathbf{s}_f)} e^{\mathbf{s}_f t}\right\} \tag{12.20}$$

When the exciting function is not of the form $e^{st}$, the forced response must be determined by other methods, such as Laplace transform theory.

---

**EXAMPLE 12.3**   **Forced response with voltage source**

For the circuit in Fig. 12.6, a voltage source is connected to the input, $v_f(t) = 2e^{-t}$ for all time. Find the forced current response at the input.

**SOLUTION:**
The complex frequency of the input is $\mathbf{s}_f = -1 \ \text{s}^{-1}$. The current must be of the form $I_f e^{-t}$, where $I_f$ is a constant. From Eqs. (12.19) and (12.17),

$$\frac{2e^{-t}}{I_f e^{-t}} = \mathbf{Z}(-1) = \frac{2(-1+2)}{-1+6} = 0.4 \ \Rightarrow \ I_f = \frac{2}{0.4} = 5 \ \text{A} \tag{12.21}$$

Thus, $i_f(t) = 5e^{-t}$ A. This is the forced response of the circuit to the exponential voltage source.

**WHAT IF?**   What if $v(t) = 2e^{-2t}$ ?[4]

---

**EXAMPLE 12.4**   **Forced response with a current source**

Find the forced response of the circuit in Fig. 12.6 if excited by a current source with $i_f(t) = 1.5 \cos(2t + 42°)$.

**SOLUTION:**
The input can be represented by a phasor $i_f(t) = \text{Re}\{1.5 \angle 42° \, e^{j2t}\}$, so $\mathbf{s}_f = j2$. Thus, the phasor representing the forced voltage response is

$$\mathbf{V}_f = \mathbf{I}_f \times \mathbf{Z}(j2) = 1.5 \angle 42° \times \frac{2(j2+2)}{j2+6} = 1.34 \angle 68.6° \tag{12.22}$$

Thus, the voltage produced in steady state is $v_f(t) = 1.34 \cos(2t + 68.6°)$ V. All this should look familiar to you because this is merely ac circuit analysis such as we studied in Chapter 4.

---

**Finding the natural response.**   The impedance function can also assist us in finding the natural response of the circuit. Consider the case of a circuit excited by a volt-

---

[4] Then $If = \infty$ by our method. More advanced methods must be used in that case.

age source and we wish to determine the current. The natural response of a linear circuit or system must be of the form

$$i_n(t) = \mathrm{Re}\{\underline{\mathbf{I}}_n e^{\underline{\mathbf{s}}_n t}\} \tag{12.23}$$

where $\underline{\mathbf{I}}_n$ is an unknown phasor and $\underline{\mathbf{s}}_n$ is the natural frequency of the system. We can determine the natural frequency from the impedance function. The natural frequency corresponds to the case where the exciting voltage is zero but the current is nonzero, being established solely by the circuit. The impedance function thus becomes

$$\underline{\mathbf{Z}}(\underline{\mathbf{s}}) = \frac{\mathbf{V}(\underline{\mathbf{s}}) e^{\underline{\mathbf{s}}t}}{\mathbf{I}(\underline{\mathbf{s}}) e^{\underline{\mathbf{s}}t}} = \frac{0}{\neq 0} \tag{12.24}$$

Equation (12.24) can be valid only if the natural frequency makes the impedance zero:

$$\underline{\mathbf{Z}}(\underline{\mathbf{s}}_n) = 0 \tag{12.25}$$

We illustrate with the circuit in Fig. 12.6 with the impedance function derived in Eq. (12.17). The circuit has only one natural frequency, which may be determined by setting the impedance to zero:

$$\frac{2(\underline{\mathbf{s}}_n + 2)}{(\underline{\mathbf{s}}_n + 6)} = 0 \;\Rightarrow\; \underline{\mathbf{s}}_n = -2 \tag{12.26}$$

The natural frequency in this first-order circuit corresponds to the negative of the reciprocal of the time constant. Because we are exciting the circuit with a voltage source, the time constant must be determined with the input shorted.

---

**EXAMPLE 12.5** **Transient with voltage source**

Find the current input to the circuit in Fig. 12.6 if the voltage source input of Fig. 12.7 is applied as an input.

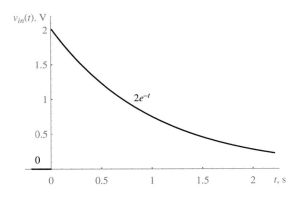

**Figure 12.7** The input voltage is zero for negative time and a decreasing exponential for positive time.

### Solution:

The current consists of a forced and a natural component, as in Eq. (12.18). The forced component is derived in Eq. (12.21) and the natural response is of the form of Eq. (12.23) with $\underline{s}_n = -2$, as shown in Eq. (12.26). Thus, the current produced by the voltage in Fig. 12.7 must be of the form

$$i(t) = 5e^{-t} + Ae^{-2t} \tag{12.27}$$

where $A$ is to be determined from the initial conditions. In this case, the initial current must be 1 A because the initial voltage is 2 V and the inductor acts as an open circuit.[5] Thus, $A$ comes from Eq. (12.27) at $t = 0$:

$$1 = 5e^0 + Ae^0 \Rightarrow A = -4 \tag{12.28}$$

The input current is, therefore,

$$i(t) = 5e^{-t} - 4e^{-2t} \text{ A} \tag{12.29}$$

which is shown in Fig. 12.8.

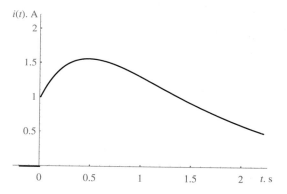

**Figure 12.8**  Response of the circuit of Fig. 12.6 to the voltage source of Fig. 12.7.

**Open-circuit and short-circuit natural frequencies.** We showed that the value of $\underline{s}$ that makes the impedance function go to zero corresponds to the natural frequency with a turned-OFF voltage source at the input.[6] In Fig. 12.9, for example, the inductor sees an equivalent resistance of 1 $\Omega$ if the 2-$\Omega$ resistor is shorted; thus, the short-circuit time constant of the circuit is $L/R = 0.5$ s. This time corresponds to a natural frequency of $\underline{s}_n = -2$, Eq. (12.5).

Additional information can be derived from the value of $\underline{s}$ that makes the impedance function go to infinity. Infinite impedance corresponds to input current, $\underline{I}(\underline{s})$, going to zero, an open circuit, with input voltage, $\underline{V}(\underline{s})$, nonzero.

---

[5] See the discussion on p. 124.

[6] A turned-OFF voltage source is equivalent to a short circuit; see p. 58.

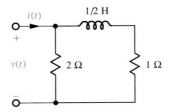

**Figure 12.9** Circuit of Fig. 12.6(a) repeated.

$$\mathbf{Z}(\mathbf{s}) = \frac{\mathbf{V}(\mathbf{s})\,e^{\mathbf{s}t}}{\mathbf{I}(\mathbf{s})\,e^{\mathbf{s}t}} = \frac{\neq 0}{0} \qquad (12.30)$$

For Eq. (12.17), this requires

$$\frac{2(\mathbf{s}+2)}{(\mathbf{s}+6)} = \frac{\neq 0}{0} \;\Rightarrow\; \mathbf{s}_n = -6 \qquad (12.31)$$

This natural frequency corresponds to the negative of the reciprocal of the time constant of the circuit with the input open-circuited. The open circuit corresponds to exciting the circuit with a current source, that is turned OFF for the natural frequency.

---

**EXAMPLE 12.6** **Transient with a current source**

Find the voltage produced in the circuit of Fig. 12.6 if the current in Fig. 12.10 were applied.

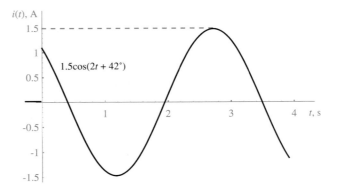

**Figure 12.10** The current source is zero for negative time and a sinusoid for positive time.

**SOLUTION:**
The resulting voltage has a forced and a natural component. The forced response was calculated in Eq. (12.22). The natural response is of the form of Eq (12.23) with $\mathbf{s}_n = -6$, as derived in Eq. (12.31). Combining the forced and natural responses, we find the input voltage to be

$$v(t) = 1.34\cos(2t + 68.6°) + Be^{-6t} \quad \text{V} \qquad (12.32)$$

where $B$ is a constant to be determined from the initial conditions. As argued before, the inductor acts initially as an open circuit, so the initial value of the voltage must be $1.5 \cos 42°\text{A} \times 2\,\Omega = 2.23$ V. From Eq. (12.32) at $t = 0$,

$$2.23 = 1.34 \cos(0 + 68.6°) + Be^0 \Rightarrow B = 1.74\text{ V} \tag{12.33}$$

Hence, the voltage produced by the current in Fig. 12.10 in the circuit in Fig. 12.9 is

$$v(t) = 1.34 \cos(2t + 68.6°) + 1.74e^{-6t}\quad\text{V} \tag{12.34}$$

which is shown in Fig. 12.11.

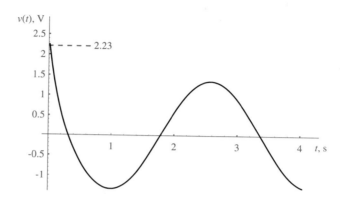

**Figure 12.11**    Voltage response of the circuit of Fig. 12.9 to the current source in Fig. 12.10.

**zero,
pole**

## Summary.
The value of $\underline{s}_n$ that sets the impedance function to zero is called a *zero* of the impedance function and corresponds to the short-circuit natural frequency. The value of $\underline{s}_n$ that makes the impedance function go to infinity is a *pole* of the impedance function and corresponds to the open-circuit natural frequency of the circuit. These natural frequencies are normally called the zeros and poles of the impedance function.

## Poles and zeros.
The impedance function of a complicated circuit generally takes the form of Eq. (12.17), except that the numerator and denominator are polynomials in $\underline{s}$. Thus, the function can always be factored into the form

$$\frac{\mathbf{V}(\underline{s})\,e^{\underline{s}t}}{\mathbf{I}(\underline{s})\,e^{\underline{s}t}} = \mathbf{Z}(\underline{s}) = K\frac{(\underline{s} - \underline{z}_1)(\underline{s} - \underline{z}_2)}{(\underline{s} - \underline{p}_1)(\underline{s} - \underline{p}_2)(\underline{s} - \underline{p}_3)} \tag{12.35}$$

where $K$ is a constant, and we assumed a second-order polynomial in the numerator and a third-order polynomial in the denominator.[7] In Eq. (12.35), $\underline{z}_1$ and $\underline{z}_2$ are called the zeros of the function because these are the values of $\underline{s}$ at which the function goes to zero. Likewise, $\underline{p}_1$, $\underline{p}_2$, and $\underline{p}_3$ are called the poles of the function because these are the values of $\underline{s}$ at which the function goes to infinity.

---

[7] This indicates a circuit with three independent energy-storage elements.

**Natural frequencies.** As we have shown, the zeros correspond to the short-circuit natural frequencies and the poles correspond to the open-circuit natural frequencies of the circuit. Except for a multiplicative constant, the poles and zeros of the impedance function fully establish the behavior of the circuit. They give the natural frequencies, as we have illustrated before, and they also give directly the forced response to excitations of the form $e^{\underline{s}t}$, such as dc ($\underline{s} = 0$) or ac ($\underline{s} = j\omega$).

**transfer function**

**Second-order circuit.** The circuit of Fig. 12.12 is identical to that in Fig. 12.6 except that a 2-H inductor is added at the input and the voltage across the 1-$\Omega$ resistor is taken as an output.[8] The ratio of the output and the input is the *transfer function*, $\mathbf{T}(\underline{s})$

$$\frac{\mathbf{V}_{out}(\underline{s})\,e^{\underline{s}t}}{\mathbf{V}_{in}(\underline{s})\,e^{\underline{s}t}} = \mathbf{T}(\underline{s}) \tag{12.36}$$

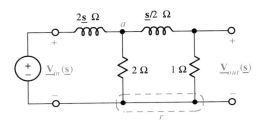

**Figure 12.12** The same circuit as that in Fig. 12.6 with an added inductor. An output voltage is indicated because we will derive the transfer function.

The transfer function is like an impedance function except it relates circuit variables at different places in a system. The transfer function is a generalization of the filter functions presented in Chapters 9 and 10.

**Transfer-function derivation.** We now derive the filter function with a nodal analysis. Because the output is open-circuited, we first determine the voltage at $a$, and then find $\mathbf{V}_{out}(\underline{s})$ with a voltage divider. Kirchhoff's current law for node $a$ in the frequency domain becomes

$$\frac{\mathbf{V}_a - \mathbf{V}_{in}}{2\underline{s}} + \frac{\mathbf{V}_a - (0)}{2} + \frac{\mathbf{V}_a - (0)}{\underline{s}/2 + 1} = 0 \tag{12.37}$$

**Conservation of Charge**

which, after a bit of algebra, becomes

$$\mathbf{V}_a = \frac{\underline{s} + 2}{\underline{s}^2 + 7\underline{s} + 2} \times \mathbf{V}_{in} \tag{12.38}$$

Using a voltage divider relationship, we find the transfer function to be

$$\mathbf{T}(\underline{s}) = \frac{\mathbf{V}_a}{\mathbf{V}_{in}} \times \frac{\mathbf{V}_{out}}{\mathbf{V}_a} = \frac{\underline{s} + 2}{\underline{s}^2 + 7\underline{s} + 2} \times \frac{1}{\underline{s}/2 + 1} = \frac{2}{\underline{s}^2 + 7\underline{s} + 2} \tag{12.39}$$

---

[8] And we have labeled the circuit for nodal analysis.

The methods we developed for transient analysis work equally well for transfer functions, as shown by the following example.

---

**EXAMPLE 12.7** | **Transient analysis of transfer function**

The circuit of Fig. 12.12 has a switched-battery input, as shown in Fig. 12.13. Find the output voltage.

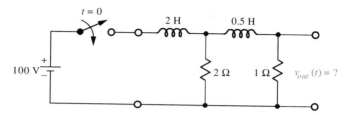

**Figure 12.13** The circuit of Fig. 12.12 with a switched-battery input. We determine the output voltage.

**SOLUTION:**

The output voltage consists of a forced and natural component. The forced component has a frequency of $\underline{s}_f = 0$, because the input is dc. The output voltage in the frequency domain will therefore, be from Eq. (12.36) at $\underline{s} = 0$

$$\frac{\mathbf{V}_f e^{0t}}{100e^{0t}} = \mathbf{T}(0) = 1 \qquad (12.40)$$

Thus, the forced component of the output voltage is 100 V. This occurs because the inductors become short circuits at dc.

The natural response corresponds to having nonzero output with zero input:

$$\frac{\mathbf{V}_{out}}{\mathbf{V}_{in}} = \mathbf{T}(\underline{s}) = \frac{\neq 0}{0} \qquad (12.41)$$

which can be valid only if the denominator of Eq. (12.39) is set to zero:

$$\underline{s}^2 + 7\underline{s} + 2 = 0 \implies \underline{s}_n = -0.298, -6.70 \quad \text{s}^{-1} \qquad (12.42)$$

Thus, we have two natural frequencies that are real and negative. The output is, therefore, of the form

$$v_{out}(t) = 100 + Ae^{-0.298t} + Be^{-6.70t} \quad \text{V} \qquad (12.43)$$

Where $A$ and $B$ are constants. The two inductors block the initial voltage from the output; hence, hence, the initial conditions on $v_{out}(t)$ are

$$v_{out}(0^+) = 0 \qquad \text{and} \qquad \left.\frac{dv_{out}(t)}{dt}\right|_{t=0^+} = 0 \qquad (12.44)$$

We may substitute Eq. (12.43) into Eqs. (12.44) and solve simultaneously for $A$ and $B$, with the result

$$v_{out}(t) = 100 - 104.66e^{-0.298t} + 4.66e^{-6.70t} \text{ V} \qquad (12.45)$$

which is plotted in Fig. 12.14

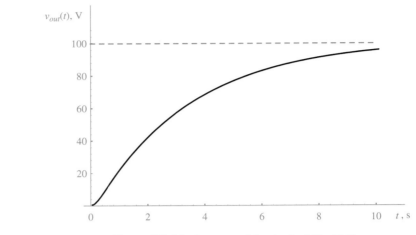

**Figure 12.14**   Response of the circuit of Fig. 12.13.

   The time constants derived from Eq. (12.45) do not correspond to any $L/R$ combination in the circuit, but are influenced by the interactions of all components. When the energy-storage elements in a circuit are all inductors or all capacitors, the natural frequencies are always real and negative.

## Frequency Response

**Poles, zeros, and frequency response.**   The poles and zeros of a transfer function define the frequency response of the circuit in sinusoidal steady state. In this context, the system acts as a filter with $\underline{s} = j\omega$ and the poles and zeros correspond to the critical frequencies defining the Bode plot.

---

**EXAMPLE 12.8**  **Bode plot of filter function**

Give the filter function and Bode plot of the network in Fig. 12.12.

**SOLUTION:**

The filter function $\mathbf{F}(j\omega)$ is the transfer function given in Eq. 12.39 with $\underline{s} = j\omega$

$$\mathbf{F}(j\omega) = \frac{2}{(j\omega)^2 + 7(j\omega) + 2} = \frac{2}{(j\omega + 0.298)(j\omega + 6.70)} \qquad (12.46)$$

where we have factored the denominator using the results of the previous example. Equation (12.46) can be placed in the form

$$\mathbf{F}(j\omega) = \frac{1}{(1 + j\omega/0.298)(1 + j\omega/6.70)} \tag{12.47}$$

This is the response of a low-pass filter with critical frequencies at $\omega_{c1} = 0.298$ and $\omega_{c2} = 6.70$ rad/s. The asymptotic Bode plot of this filter function is shown in Fig. 12.15. Thus, we see that the poles of the transfer function correspond to the critical frequencies of the filter response; indeed, these critical frequencies are often called the "poles" of the filter.

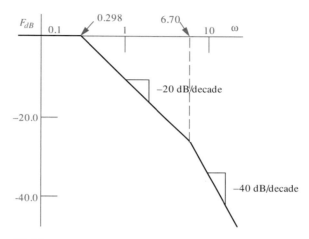

**Figure 12.15**   Bode plot of the circuit of Fig. 12.12. The poles of the transfer function correspond to the critical frequencies of the filter, as indicated in the Bode plot.

## Check Your Understanding

1. What is the impedance of a 100-µF capacitor at a complex frequency of $\underline{s} = -100 \text{ s}^{-1}$?

2. An impedance consists of $R = 100 \ \Omega$ and $C = 10 \ \mu\text{F}$ in series. What impedance does this present to an input voltage $v(t) = 10e^{-500t}$.

3. A 10-$\Omega$ resistor is connected in series with a 100-µF capacitor. At what complex frequency does this combination look like a short circuit?

4. An impedance with a zero at $\underline{s} = 0$ passes a dc current. True or false?

5. The open-circuit natural frequencies of a circuit correspond to the zeros of the impedance function. True or false?

6. A circuit with two inductors must have natural frequencies that are real. True or false?

*Answers.*  (1) $-100 \ \Omega$; (2) $-100 \ \Omega$; (3) $-1000 \text{ s}^{-1}$; (4) true; (5) false; (6) true.

## Types of Natural Responses in *RLC* Circuits

**Transfer function of an *RLC* circuit.** The circuit of Fig. 12.16 can exhibit an oscillatory response because the circuit contains an inductor and capacitor. This circuit can be analyzed as a voltage divider:

$$\underline{T}(\underline{s}) = \frac{\underline{V}_{out}(\underline{s})\,e^{\underline{s}t}}{\underline{V}_{in}(\underline{s})\,e^{\underline{s}t}} = \frac{R\|1/\underline{s}C}{\underline{s}L + R\|1/\underline{s}C} = \frac{1}{LC}\ \frac{1}{\underline{s}^2\ +\ (\underline{s}\,/\,RC)\ +\ 1\,/\,(LC)} \tag{12.48}$$

where $\underline{T}(\underline{s})$ is the transfer function.

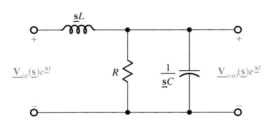

**Figure 12.16** An *RLC* circuit in the frequency domain. The transfer function is the ratio of output to input voltage.

**OBJECTIVE 3**

**To understand how to recognize conditions for undamped, underdamped, critically damped, and overdamped responses in second-order systems**

**Natural frequencies of the circuit.** The poles of the transfer function correspond to an output voltage with no input voltage, and hence are the natural frequencies of the circuit with the input short-circuited. These poles are investigated in detail because they reveal the various types of behavior that can result with an *RLC* circuit. We may determine the poles with the quadratic formula

$$\underline{s}^2 + \frac{\underline{s}}{RC} + \frac{1}{LC} = 0 \ \Rightarrow \ \underline{s}_n = -\frac{1}{2RC} \pm \sqrt{\left(\frac{1}{2RC}\right)^2 - \frac{1}{LC}}\ \ \text{s}^{-1} \tag{12.49}$$

There are four possibilities, depending on the relative values of $R$, $L$, and $C$. The possibilities are undamped, underdamped, critically damped, and overdamped responses.

**undamped response**

**Undamped behavior.** First, we consider the case where the resistance is infinite, which is equivalent to removing the resistor from the circuit. Equation (12.49) gives imaginary roots:

$$\underline{s}_1 = +j\omega_0 \qquad \text{and} \qquad \underline{s}_2 = -j\omega_0 \ \text{s}^{-1} \tag{12.50}$$

where $\omega_0 = 1/\sqrt{LC}$ rad/s. Thus, with no resistance, the short-circuit natural frequencies are imaginary, meaning that the natural response of the circuit is a sinusoid of constant amplitude. This may be understood as a lossless resonance, with $\omega_0$ the resonant frequency. With no resistor, any energy imparted to the circuit alternates between the inductor and capacitor and produces a sinusoidal output. This is called an *undamped response* because the oscillations do not diminish with time.

**damped oscillation, damping constant**

**Underdamped behavior.** For large but finite resistance, the square root remains imaginary, and the roots of the quadratic are complex:

$$\underline{s}_{1,2} = -\alpha \pm \sqrt{\alpha^2 - \omega_0^2} \quad \text{or} \quad \underline{s}_{1,2} = -\alpha \pm j\omega \quad s^{-1} \qquad (12.51)$$

where $\alpha = 1/2RC \ s^{-1}$ and $\omega = \sqrt{\omega_0^2 - \alpha^2} \ s^{-1}$. The two roots are complex conjugates and correspond to an exponentially decreasing sinusoid, a *damped oscillation*. Thus, the natural response of the circuit is of the form

$$v_{out}(t) = Ae^{-\alpha t}\cos(\omega t + \theta) \qquad (12.52)$$

where $A$ and $\theta$ are constants. The constant $\alpha$ is called the *damping constant* and is the reciprocal of the time constant of the dying oscillation. The frequency of the oscillation, $\omega$, is less than the resonant frequency, $\omega_0$, because the exchanges of energy between inductor and capacitor are slowed down by loss in the resistor.

**underdamped response**

**Condition for underdamped response.** The exponentially decreasing oscillation is called an *underdamped response*. The condition for an underdamped response is

$$\alpha < \omega_0 \quad \text{or} \quad R > \frac{1}{2}\sqrt{\frac{L}{C}} \qquad (12.53)$$

Thus, for large values of resistance, the response of the circuit is dominated by the resonance of the inductor and capacitor, but the oscillations die out in time due to the loss in the resistor.

**critical damping**

**Critical damping.** *Critical damping* occurs when $\alpha = \omega_0$, and the roots of Eq. (12.49) become real and equal. This is interesting mathematically but unimportant in practice because it exists only for one exact value of resistance, given by Eq. (12.53) with an equality sign. Even if we wished to produce this type of response in a physical circuit, we would be able to achieve the required resistance only with great care or good fortune. For us, critical damping is important as the boundary between underdamped oscillations and overdamped behavior.

**overdamped response**

**Overdamped behavior.** When $\alpha > \omega_0$, the roots of Eq. (12.49) are real, negative, and unequal.

$$\underline{s}_1 = -\alpha + \sqrt{\alpha^2 - \omega_0^2} \quad \text{and} \quad \underline{s}_2 = -\alpha - \sqrt{\alpha^2 - \omega_0^2} \qquad (12.54)$$

Thus, the *overdamped response* has the form

$$v_{out}(t) = Ae^{\underline{s}_1 t} + Be^{\underline{s}_2 t} \qquad (12.55)$$

where $\underline{s}_1$ and $\underline{s}_2$ are real, negative numbers. This response consists of two time constants, which are the negatives of the reciprocals of $\underline{s}_1$ and $\underline{s}_2$. Thus, for small resistance, the increased loss eliminates the resonance between the inductor and capacitor.

**Summary.** The natural frequencies of the *RLC* circuit are derived from the roots of a quadratic equation. The roots may be imaginary, complex, real and equal, or real and unequal. Imaginary roots indicate an undamped oscillation. Complex roots indicate a damped oscillation. Real, unequal roots indicate two time constants and no oscillation. Real, equal roots represent the mathematical boundary between oscillatory and non oscillatory behavior. These time-domain responses are derived through the application of frequency-domain techniques.

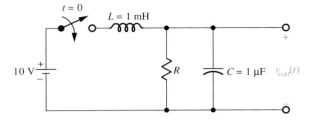

**Figure 12.17** An *RLC* circuit with a source in the time domain.

### *RLC* Circuit Transient Behavior

**Forced response.** We now investigate the time-domain response of the circuit shown in Fig. 12.17, in which a dc voltage is applied to the *RLC* circuit of the previous section. The output voltage consists of two components, a natural response and a forced response due to the dc input. We may determine the forced response by the methods presented in Chapter 3, by treating the capacitor as an open circuit and the inductor as a short circuit. Alternately, we may consider the input as $10e^{\mathbf{s}_f t}$, with $\mathbf{s}_f = 0$, and derive the forced response from the transfer function given in Eq. (12.48) with $\mathbf{s} = 0$. Using the latter method, we find the forced component of the output voltage to be

$$\frac{V_{out}e^{0t}}{V_{in}e^{0t}} = \mathbf{T}(0) \Rightarrow V_{out} = T(0) \times 10e^{0t} = 10 \text{ V} \tag{12.56}$$

This indicates a dc output of 10 V due to the battery. The total response is therefore,

$$v_{out}(t) = 10 + v_n(t) \text{ V} \tag{12.57}$$

where $v_n(t)$ is the natural response. Several forms are possible for the natural response, depending on the resistance.

**Natural response: undamped case.** We consider first the response for $R = \infty$:

$$v_{out}(t) = 10 + A \cos(\omega_0 t + \theta) \tag{12.58}$$

where $A$ and $\theta$ must be determined from the initial conditions.

**Initial conditions.** We may establish the initial conditions of the output voltage through the techniques presented in Chapter 3. The capacitor acts initially as a short circuit; hence, the output voltage must be zero at $t = 0^+$:

$$0 = 10 + A \cos \theta \tag{12.59}$$

The inductor acts initially like an open circuit. Consequently, the initial current through the capacitor is also zero, and the derivative of the output voltage must also be zero at $t = 0^+$:

$$\left.\frac{dv_{out}(t)}{dt}\right|_{t=0^+} = 0 \Rightarrow (0) = -\omega_0 A \sin\theta \tag{12.60}$$

so $\theta = 0$ and Eq. (12.59) yields $A = -10$ V.[9] Hence, the response is

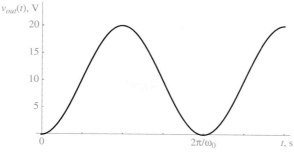

**Figure 12.18** Response of the circuit of Fig. 12.17 with $R = \infty$. The peak voltage is twice the input voltage, a property of the circuit that finds many applications.

$$v_{out}(t) = 10 - 10\cos(\omega_0 t) \tag{12.61}$$

This response is shown in Fig. 12.18.

**resonant charging**

**Resonant charging.** The voltage on the capacitor reaches twice that of the input because the inductor gives a momentum to the current to continue charging past the equilibrium point. If a diode is placed in series with the inductor to prevent the discharge of the capacitor, the addition of the diode and inductor results in a fourfold increase in stored energy in the capacitor, compared to charging through a resistor. This technique is known as *resonant charging* of the capacitor, and applications are found in radar and power electronics.

**Underdamped response.** For the inductance and capacitance values given in Fig. 12.17, the value of the resistance for critical damping is given by Eq. (12.53) with an equality sign:

$$R_c = \frac{1}{2}\sqrt{\frac{L}{C}} = \frac{1}{2}\sqrt{\frac{10^{-3}}{10^{-6}}} = 15.8 \ \Omega \tag{12.62}$$

where $R_c$ is the resistance for critical damping. We consider first the underdamped response, which implies a resistance larger than the critical value. We assume $R = 5R_c = 79.1 \ \Omega$. The resonant frequency and damping coefficient derived from Eq. (12.51):

$$\omega_0 = \frac{1}{\sqrt{LC}} = 31{,}600 \ \text{s}^{-1} \quad \text{and} \quad \alpha = \frac{1}{2RC} = 6320 \ \text{s}^{-1} \tag{12.63}$$

and thus the natural frequencies, determined from Eq. (12.51), are

$$\underline{s}_1 = -6320 + j31{,}000 \quad \text{and} \quad \underline{s}_2 = -6320 - j31{,}000 \tag{12.64}$$

The total response is

$$v_{out}(t) = 10 + Ae^{-6320t}\cos(31{,}000t + \theta) \tag{12.65}$$

The initial conditions are the same as for the undamped response. Hence, at $t = 0^+$,

---

[9] An identical answer results from $\theta = \pi$ and $A = +10$.

$$0 = 10 + A\cos\theta \tag{12.66}$$

and

$$\left.\frac{dv_{out}(t)}{dt}\right|_{t=0^+} = 0 \Rightarrow 0 = A(-6320\cos\theta - 31{,}000\sin\theta) \tag{12.67}$$

Equations (12.66) and (12.67) yield $\theta = -11.5°$ and $A = -10.21$ V. The solution is, therefore,

$$v_{out}(t) = 10 - 10.21e^{-6320t}\cos(31{,}000t - 11.5°)\ \text{V} \tag{12.68}$$

which is shown in Fig. 12.19.

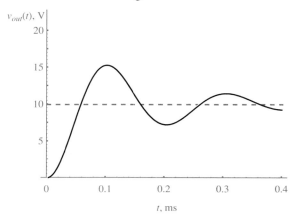

**Figure 12.19** Underdamped response for the circuit in Fig. 12.17 with $R = 79.1\ \Omega$.

**Overdamped response.** To obtain an overdamped response, we use a resistance one-fifth the critical value given by Eq. (12.62): $R = R_c/5 = 3.16\ \Omega$. With this resistance, $\alpha = 158{,}000$, and Eq. (12.54) gives the natural frequencies:

$$\underline{s}_1 = -3190\ \text{s}^{-1} \qquad \text{and} \qquad \underline{s}_2 = -313{,}000\ \text{s}^{-1} \tag{12.69}$$

Thus, the output voltage is

$$v_{out}(t) = 10 + Ae^{-3190t} + Be^{-313{,}000t}\ \text{V} \tag{12.70}$$

where $A$ and $B$ are constants. The first term is the forced response, which is the same as before. The second term has a time constant of 0.313 ms and the third term a time constant of 3.19 μs. The initial conditions are the same as before; hence, we may solve for $A$ and $B$ from the equations

$$0 = 10 + A + B \qquad \text{and} \qquad 0 = -3190A - 313{,}000B \tag{12.71}$$

which yield $A = -10.10$ V and $B = 0.10$ V. Thus, the overdamped response is

$$v_{out}(t) = 10 - 10.10e^{-3190t} + 0.10e^{-313{,}000t}\ \text{V} \tag{12.72}$$

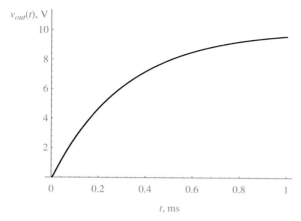

**Figure 12.20** Overdamped response for the circuit of Fig. 12.17.

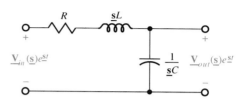

**Figure 12.21** This is a series *RLC* circuit when driven by a voltage source.

This response is shown in Fig. 12.20. The third term in Eq. (12.72) has a brief influence to give the zero derivative at the origin, but otherwise the response is that of a first-order transient of the *RL* part of the circuit.

### Parallel and series *RLC* circuits.

The circuit of Fig. 12.17, when excited by a voltage source, is a parallel *RLC* circuit. With the source turned OFF, the resistor, inductor, and capacitor are connected in parallel. In the circuit shown in Fig. 12.21, the resistor, inductor, and capacitor are connected in series. The analysis of the series *RLC* circuit for the transfer function, natural frequencies, and transient response follows the same lines as for the parallel circuit, but the results differ in detail. We leave the analysis of the series *RLC* circuit for the reader.

### Relationship with Laplace transform theory.

The Laplace transform gives a strong mathematical foundation to the techniques used in this chapter and is closely associated with linear system theory. Although the Laplace transform yields the total response of a circuit or system, including initial conditions, its primary importance lies in furnishing the tools for describing linear systems that we have developed in this chapter.

**The Frequency Domain**

### Frequency domain.

The functions such as $\mathbf{V}(\mathbf{s})$ and $\mathbf{I}(\mathbf{s})$, which we have been treating as constants, can be considered *transforms* of the time-domain voltage and current. These transforms can be interpreted as generalized spectra of the time-domain functions. Similarly, generalized impedances and transfer functions are frequency-domain transforms of the linear differential equations that describe the circuit or system component in the time domain.

### Summary.

In this section, we used complex frequency to investigate transient behavior of first- and second-order circuits. Natural responses have been decreasing exponentials or exponentially decreasing sinusoids. The natural frequencies and the character of the natural response may be determined from the poles and zeros of the impedance or transfer functions. In the next section, we illustrate how the transfer function describes the properties of a linear-system component.

## Check Your Understanding

1. Describe the largest number and the character of the natural frequencies of the following circuits: (a) two resistors and a capacitor; (b) one resistor and two capacitors; (c) three resistors and two inductors; (d) and two resistors, a capacitor, and an inductor.

2. Determine the natural frequencies of the circuit in Fig. 12.17 if the resistor has the value for critical damping.

*Answers.* (1) (a) One natural frequency, real and negative; (b) one natural frequency, real and negative; (c) two natural frequencies, real and negative; and (d) two natural frequencies, either complex with negative real part or both real and negative; (2) $\underline{s} = -31,623 \text{ s}^{-1}$ (repeated).

## 12.4 SYSTEM ANALYSIS

**OBJECTIVE 4**

**To understand how to use system notation to describe the properties of composite systems**

**Introduction.** In this section, we explore the notation and techniques commonly used to describe linear systems. Our example is a thermostatically controlled oven. We determine its response when controlled by a feedback control system. Although heating of the oven is inherently nonlinear, we linearize the problem to use the techniques of the frequency domain. We show that a second-order system, two independent modes of energy storage, is unconditionally stable, although the system response may be unacceptable. We then show that a third-order system can become unstable for large loop gain.

**Problem description.** In Chapter 9, p. 479, we discussed a system for controlling an oven with a feedback control system. We described the system in general terms and mentioned briefly the dynamic stability of the system. We now possess the tools to investigate the system stability. Figure 12.22 shows the oven control system. The oven is heated by a resistive element driven by an amplifier. The oven temperature is monitored by a sensor, which produces a voltage proportional to its temperature. The op amp is driven by the difference between an input set voltage and a feedback signal from the sensor.

### System Functions

**system function**

We now express the properties of the sensor in the frequency domain through a system function. A *system function*, $\underline{F}(\underline{s})$, relates the transforms of input and output in the equation

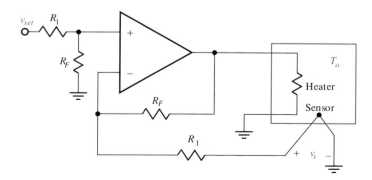

**Figure 12.22** Oven control system.

$$\frac{\mathbf{X}_{out}(\mathbf{s})}{\mathbf{X}_{in}(\mathbf{s})} = \mathbf{F}(\mathbf{s}) \tag{12.73}$$

where the $\mathbf{X}$'s are frequency-domain transforms of the time-domain input and output variables. The system function is similar to the transfer function except that the input and output variables may be any of a wide class of variables. In this case, the input is the oven temperature and the output is the sensor voltage.

**Sensor-system function.** We assume the sensor produces a voltage proportional to the oven temperature, $v_s = K_s T_o$, and responds to changes in oven temperature with a time constant $\tau_s$. The specification of a time constant implies a first-order system. To satisfy both properties, the output voltage of the sensor must satisfy the DE

$$\tau_s \frac{dv_s}{dt} + v_s = K_s T_o(t) \tag{12.74}$$

where $v_s(t)$ is the sensor voltage, $\tau_s$ is the time constant of the sensor, and $T_o(t)$ is the oven temperature. We may transform Eq. (12.74) into the frequency domain by assuming input temperature and output voltage to be of the form $e^{st}$, with the results

$$(\tau_s \mathbf{s} + 1)\mathbf{V}_s(\mathbf{s}) = K_s \mathbf{T}_o(\mathbf{s}) \quad \Rightarrow \quad \mathbf{V}_s(\mathbf{s}) = \underbrace{\frac{K_s / \tau_s}{\mathbf{s} + (1/\tau_s)}}_{\substack{\text{system function} \\ \text{for sensor}}} \times \mathbf{T}_o(\mathbf{s}) \tag{12.75}$$

where $\mathbf{V}_s(\mathbf{s})$ is the transform of the sensor voltage and $\mathbf{T}_o(\mathbf{s})$ is the transform of the oven temperature. Thus, we may represent the sensor in the frequency domain by the system component shown in Fig. 12.23.

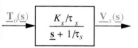

**Oven-system function.** The oven temperature will be controlled by the temperature of the heater element. We will assume a time constant of $\tau_o$ for this process. Thus the heater temperature and oven temperature are related by a system function similar to the sensor

$$\mathbf{T}_o(\mathbf{s}) = \underbrace{\frac{1/\tau_o}{\mathbf{s} + (1/\tau_o)}}_{\substack{\text{system function} \\ \text{for over}}} \times \mathbf{T}_H(\mathbf{s}) \tag{12.76}$$

where $\tau_o$ represents the oven time constant and $\mathrm{T}_H(\mathbf{s})$ is the transform of the heater temperature.

**Heater voltage.** Although the heater is nonlinear, we consider only small changes in the signal levels and assume that a linear increment in voltage produces a linear increment in power in the heater, and hence a linear increment in the heater temperature. There is a time constant associated with the thermal mass of the heater element, but we ignore this effect in the present analysis. Thus, we assume for now that changes in heater voltage produce proportional and instantaneous changes in the temperature of the

**Figure 12.23**
System component representing the sensor. The input and output are frequency-domain transforms of the oven temperature and sensor voltage, respectively.

heater element. These changes are represented in the time domain and frequency domain by

$$T_H(t) = K_H v_H(t) \implies \underline{\mathbf{T}}_H(\underline{s}) = K_H \underline{\mathbf{V}}(\underline{s}) \tag{12.77}$$

where $\underline{\mathbf{V}}_H(\underline{s})$ is the transform of the heater voltage and $K_H$ deg/V is a constant relating heater temperature to changes in heater voltage.

**System diagram.**  We may represent the interaction of the various system variables by the system diagram shown in Fig. 12.24. The amplifier is represented by a summer (differencer) and a gain of $R_F/R_1$.

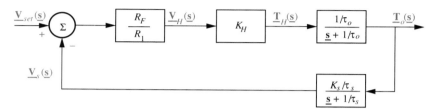

**Figure 12.24**  System diagram for the oven control system.

**Summary.**  In this section, we introduced the system functions of the various components of a feedback control system. Each variable is represented by its frequency-domain transform. Each component is represented by its system function. We may now use feedback theory to determine the overall system function of the controller. We determine the natural frequencies of the system and, from these, the transient response of the system in the time domain.

## Dynamic Stability of Feedback Systems

**Feedback analysis.**  The gain with feedback of an amplifier with feedback is given in Eq. (9.77) as

$$A_f = \frac{A}{1 - L} \tag{12.78}$$

where $A_f$ is the gain with feedback, $A$ is the gain without feedback, and $L$ is the loop gain. Here we are expressing the system properties in the frequency domain, so our signals and gains are complex functions of $\underline{s}$. The gain without feedback in Fig. 12.24 is the product of the system functions between input and output:

$$\underline{\mathbf{A}}(\underline{s}) = \frac{R_F}{R_1} \times K_H \times \frac{1/\tau_o}{\underline{s} + 1/\tau_o} \tag{12.79}$$

and the loop gain is the product of the system functions around the loop:

$$\underline{\mathbf{L}}(\underline{s}) = (-1)\frac{R_F}{R_1} \times K_H \times \frac{1/\tau_o}{\underline{s} + 1/\tau_o} \times \frac{K_s/\tau_s}{\underline{s} + 1/\tau_s} = +\frac{L_0/\tau_o \tau_s}{(\underline{s} + 1/\tau_o)(\underline{s} + 1/\tau_s)} \tag{12.80}$$

where $L_0 = -(R_F/R_1)K_H K_s$ is the dc loop gain at $\underline{s} = 0$, a dimensionless quantity.

**System natural frequencies.** Our investigation of the dynamic behavior of the system does not require that we substitute Eqs. (12.79) and (12.80) into Eq. (12.78). We are interested in the natural response of the system, when the input voltage is zero but the output is nonzero. This can occur only at the poles of the overall system function with feedback, which requires $1 - \mathbf{L}(\mathbf{s}) = 0$. Thus we may determine the natural frequencies from the quadratic equation

$$1 - \frac{L_0/\tau_s \tau_o}{(\mathbf{s} + 1/\tau_s)(\mathbf{s} + 1/\tau_o)} = 0 \;\Rightarrow\; \mathbf{s}^2 + \left(\frac{1}{\tau_o} + \frac{1}{\tau_s}\right)\mathbf{s} + \frac{1 - L_0}{\tau_o \tau_s} = 0 \qquad (12.81)$$

We continue our analysis assuming a time constant of 300 s for the oven and a time constant of 30 s for the sensor. The roots of Eq. (12.81) for dc loop gains of $L_0 = -1$, $-10$, and $-50$ are given in Fig. 12.25(a). The associated dynamic responses shown in Fig. 12.25(b) are derived in the next section.

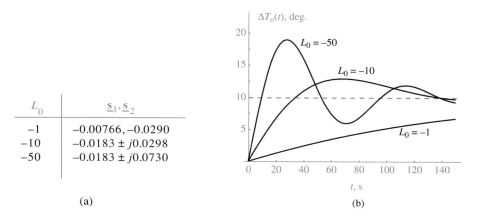

| $L_0$ | $\mathbf{s}_1, \mathbf{s}_2$ |
|---|---|
| $-1$ | $-0.00766, -0.0290$ |
| $-10$ | $-0.0183 \pm j0.0298$ |
| $-50$ | $-0.0183 \pm j0.0730$ |

(a)  (b)

**Figure 12.25** (a) Natural frequencies for dc loop gains of $-1$, $-10$, and $-50$; (b) the output temperature response to a sudden increase in input voltage for the various dc loop gains.

**Dynamic response: overdamped case.** We may determine the dynamic response of the circuit from the natural frequencies, which are the poles of the overall system function with feedback, and from the initial and final conditions of the output. We assume in this section that the input voltage is increased suddenly to produce an eventual 10°F increase in the oven temperature. For $L_0 = -1$, the natural frequencies of the system are given in Fig. 12.25(a) as $\mathbf{s}_1 = -0.00766$ and $\mathbf{s}_2 = -0.0290$. The response is overdamped, and the total response is of the form

$$\Delta T_o(t) = A + Be^{-0.00766t} + Ce^{-0.0290t} \qquad (12.82)$$

where $\Delta T_o(t)$ is the change in the oven temperature and $A$, $B$, and $C$ are constants to be determined from the initial and final conditions. The final condition is that $\Delta T_o(t)$ should approach $+10°F$ as $t \rightarrow \infty$; hence, $A = +10$.

**Initial conditions.** The initial conditions can be deduced from the time delays in the system. Because it takes time for the oven to heat up, the initial value of $\Delta T_o(t)$ is zero,

$\Delta T_o(0^+) = 0$. The initial value of the derivative is not affected by the feedback effects because of the time delay in the sensor. Because the feedback reduces the final value by the factor $1 - L_0$, the initial derivative is that of the function

$$T_o(t) = \underbrace{\Delta T_o(\infty)(1 - L_0)}_{\substack{\text{final temperature} \\ \text{with no feedback}}} (1 - e^{-t/\tau_o}) \tag{12.83}$$

Therefore, the initial value of the derivative of $\Delta T_o(t)$ is

$$\frac{d\Delta T_o(t)}{dt}\bigg|_{t=0^+} = \frac{\Delta T_o(\infty)(1 - L_o)}{\tau_o} \tag{12.84}$$

With these two initial conditions, we can readily determine the constants $B$ and $C$ in Eq. (12.82). The initial condition on the temperature increment is

$$0 = 10 + B + C \tag{12.85}$$

and the initial condition on the derivative of $\Delta T_o(t)$ for $L_0 = -1$ follows from Eqs. (12.82) and (12.84):

$$\frac{10}{300} \times [1 - (-1)] = -0.00766B - 0.0290C \tag{12.86}$$

Simultaneous solution of Eqs. (12.85) and (12.86) yields $B = -10.466$ and $C = +0.466$. Hence, the response of the system with a loop gain of $-1$ to a sudden increase in input voltage is

$$\Delta T_o(t) = 10 - 10.466e^{-0.00766t} + 0.466e^{-0.0290t} \tag{12.87}$$

which is shown in Fig. 12.25(b). We note that the transient is dominated by the longer time constant of $1/0.00766 = 130.5$ s. This is the time constant of the oven, sped up by a factor of approximately 2 by the feedback.

**Dynamic response: underdamped case.**   For dc loop gains greater than 2.025, the roots of Eq. (12.81) are complex, indicating underdamped response. For $L_0 = -10$, the roots are given in Fig. 12.25(a) as $\underline{s}_{1,2} = -0.0183 \pm j0.0298$. The form of the response can be written in several ways, but the form given in Eq. (12.88) is most convenient for our analysis.

$$\Delta T_o(t) = A + e^{-0.0183t}[B \cos(0.0298t) + C \sin(0.0298t)] \tag{12.88}$$

where, again, $A$, $B$, and $C$ are constants to be determined from the initial and final conditions. The final value, as before, is $A = +10$. The initial condition is $\Delta T_o(t) = 0$, as before, which allows $B$ to be determined by inspection as $-10$ because the sine term in Eq. (12.88) vanishes at $t = 0$. The initial value of the derivative is given by Eq. (12.84):

$$\frac{d\Delta T_o(t)}{dt} = \frac{10}{300} \times [1 - (-10)] = 0 - 0.0183B + 0.0298C \tag{12.89}$$

which yields $C = +6.159$. Hence, the response for a dc loop gain of $-10$ is

$$\Delta T_o(t) = 10 + e^{-0.0183t}[-10\cos(0.0298t) + 6.159\sin(0.0298t)] \qquad (12.89)$$

This response is shown in Fig. 12.25(b), where we have also shown the response for a dc loop gain of −50.

stable

**Summary of feedback effects for second-order systems.**    Figure 12.25(b) reveals the effects of feedback on the second-order system, which has delays due to thermal energy storage in both oven and sensor. As the magnitude of the dc loop gain is increased, the response goes from overdamped to underdamped. The character of the various responses is shown in Fig. 12.25(b), which indicates that the system speeds up with increasing loop gain. However, the use of excessive feedback causes a severe overshoot problem.

In a feedback system, instability is caused by excessive phase shift around the feedback loop. If at some frequency the phase shift approaches −180°, negative feedback becomes positive feedback and oscillations can occur. A second-order system is unconditionally *stable*, meaning that oscillations always die out, regardless of the amount of feedback, because the −180° phase shift is never reached. As we see in the next section, a third-order system can have growing oscillations if the loop gain is high. Such unstable behavior renders the system useless and can make it dangerous to life and property.

**Control theory.**    Figure 12.25(b) shows that large loop gain degrades the dynamic response of the system by causing a "hunting" type of response. But with low loop gain, we lose the benefits of feedback. One goal of control theory is to achieve an acceptable compromise between these two effects by modifying the system properties with electrical filters.

**Dynamic analysis of third-order system.**    We now repeat the analysis of the oven-control system considering the delay in the heater element. When the power is applied to the heater element, its temperature increases with a time constant $\tau_H$. This changes the system function of the heater element in Fig. 12.24 to that shown in Fig. 12.26. The analysis of the feedback system proceeds as before, and the natural frequencies are the roots of $1 - \mathbf{L}(\mathbf{s}) = 0$. This results in the cubic equation

$$\left(\mathbf{s} + \frac{1}{\tau_H}\right)\left(\mathbf{s} + \frac{1}{\tau_o}\right)\left(\mathbf{s} + \frac{1}{\tau_s}\right) + \frac{L_0}{\tau_H \tau_o \tau_s} = 0 \qquad (12.91)$$

We determined the roots of Eq. (12.91) assuming time constants of 15 s, 300 s, and 30 s

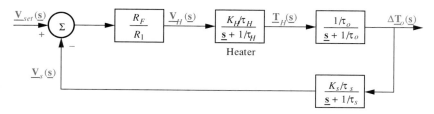

**Figure 12.26**    System diagram for the oven-control system with an additional time constant due to the heater element.

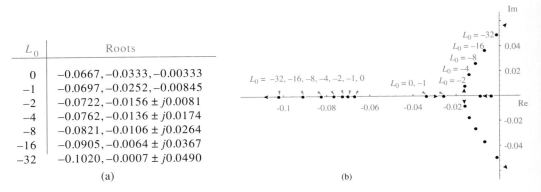

| $L_0$ | Roots |
|---|---|
| 0 | $-0.0667, -0.0333, -0.00333$ |
| $-1$ | $-0.0697, -0.0252, -0.00845$ |
| $-2$ | $-0.0722, -0.0156 \pm j0.0081$ |
| $-4$ | $-0.0762, -0.0136 \pm j0.0174$ |
| $-8$ | $-0.0821, -0.0106 \pm j0.0264$ |
| $-16$ | $-0.0905, -0.0064 \pm j0.0367$ |
| $-32$ | $-0.1020, -0.0007 \pm j0.0490$ |

(a)

(b)

**Figure 12.27**   (a) Natural frequencies for the system in Fig. 12.26; (b) root plot for third-order system with increasing loop gain.

for the heater, oven, and sensor, respectively. Figure 12.27(a) tabulates the roots for various values of dc loop gain.

**Root-locus plot.**   Figure 12.27(b) shows the motion of the natural frequencies in the complex plane as the magnitude of the dc loop gain is increased. For a loop gain of $-1$, all three roots are real, indicating exponential behavior in the time domain. For loop-gain magnitudes greater than about 1.3, two roots become complex and begin to move toward the real axis as the oscillation frequency increases. For loop-gain magnitudes greater than about 25, the roots move into the right half of the complex plane, indicating oscillations that increase with time, similar to the response shown in Fig. 12.3(a). This type of response indicates dynamically unstable behavior. The three poles cause excessive phase shift at high frequency, the feedback becomes positive, and oscillations grow until limited by nonlinear effects.

**Summary.**   In this section, we explored the dynamic response of second- and third-order feedback systems. We modeled system components and derived the system function with feedback. The dynamic response of the second-order system was found to be unconditionally stable but can exhibit an unacceptable hunting response if the loop gain is too high. The third-order system has similar behavior but can go unstable as loop gain is increased.

# CHAPTER SUMMARY

This chapter introduces the tools and concerns of linear system analysis. We generalize the concept of frequency to include exponential growth and decay, plus damped or growing oscillations. We demonstrate the significance of the poles and zeros of the impedance and system functions in establishing the transient and steady-state response of a system. We explore the various transient responses of which second-order systems are capable. Finally, we investigate the effect of loop gain on the response and dynamic stability of a feedback system.

**Objective 1. To understand the class of functions that can be described by complex frequencies.** Complex frequencies can represent constant signals, growing and decaying exponentials, sinusoidal functions, and growing and decaying sinusoidal functions. These functions have a broad practical significance, but also are useful as a mathematical probe to explore the behavior of linear systems.

**Objective 2. To understand how to use generalized impedance to find the forced and natural response of a system.** We generalize the impedance expressions from Chapter 4 using complex frequency to include a broader class of behavior than simple sinusoids. The poles and zeros of an impedance or transfer function determine both the natural and forced responses when the circuit is excited at a complex frequency.

**Objective 3. To understand how to recognize conditions for undamped, underdamped, critically damped, and overdamped responses in second-order systems.** We study *RLC* circuits as an example of a second-order system. The four types of response are named and described.

**Objective 4. To understand how to use system notation to describe the properties of composite systems.** Hybrid and nonelectrical linear systems can be described by complex-frequency techniques. The idea of system analysis is to focus on the dynamic interaction of system components without excessive attention to physical details.

**Objective 5. To understand the role of loop gain in the dynamic response of a feedback system.** We analyze second- and third-order systems with feedback. We show that second-order systems are unconditionally stable, but response may be unacceptable for high loop gain. Third- and higher-order systems can become unstable, with growing oscillations driving the system beyond linear operation, if loop gain is sufficiently high. We use the root-locus description in the stability analysis.

Throughout this chapter, frequency-domain concepts are emphasized. Input and output signals have been the frequency-domain transforms of time-domain signals and system functions replace differential equations representing dynamic behavior. The techniques introduced in this chapter will prove helpful in the remainder of the book, which deals with the transient and steady-state performance of electrical motors.

# PROBLEMS

## Section 12.1: Complex Frequency

**12.1.** The half-life of the exponential decay of carbon 14 is 3730 years. What complex frequency in $s^{-1}$ describes this process?

**12.2.** A decaying sinusoid has a complex frequency $\underline{s} = -2 + j1$ and has its maximum value at $t = 0$. What is the angle of the phasor representing this signal in the frequency domain?

**12.3.** A decaying sinusoid crosses zero every 10 ms and each positive peak is 90% of the previous positive peak. What complex frequency describes this function?

**12.4.** A time-domain function is shown in Fig. P12.4. The function is of the form
$$v(t) = A + Be^{\sigma t}\cos(\omega t)$$

**(a)** From the graph, determine $A$, $B$, $\sigma$, and $\omega$.

**(b)** Estimate the complex frequencies that can be used to describe this function?

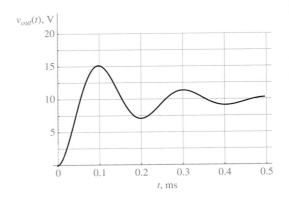

**Figure P12.4**

# Section 12.2: Impedance and the Transient Behavior of Linear Systems

**12.5.** Consider a resistor, $R$, in series with a capacitor, $C$.

**(a)** Determine the generalized input impedance as a function of complex frequency and, from that, the pole and zero of the circuit.

**(b)** What is the interpretation of the pole?

**(c)** What is the interpretation of the zero?

**12.6.** The circuit shown in Fig. P12.6 is excited by a voltage source that is zero for negative time and exponential for positive time, as indicated.

**(a)** Determine the impedance of the circuit, $\mathbf{Z}(\mathbf{s})$.

**(b)** What is the complex frequency of the source for $t > 0$?

**(c)** What is the natural frequency of the circuit?

**(d)** Determine the forced response of the current.

**(e)** Determine the total response of the current for $t > 0$, including the initial condition.

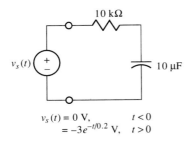

$$v_s(t) = 0 \text{ V}, \qquad t < 0$$
$$= -3e^{-t/0.2} \text{ V}, \quad t > 0$$

**Figure P12.6**

**12.7.** A circuit has the impedance function

$$\mathbf{Z}(\mathbf{s}) = 10^4 \frac{\mathbf{s}^2 + 4\mathbf{s} + 1}{\mathbf{s}(\mathbf{s} + 2)} \ \Omega$$

**(a)** What is the impedance at dc?

**(b)** What are the natural frequencies of the circuit if the input is shorted?

**(c)** What are the natural frequencies if the input is open-circuited?

**(d)** In addition to resistors, this circuit has one inductor, or one capacitor, or two inductors, or two capacitors, or one capacitor and one inductor? Which combinations are possible (may be more than one)? Explain your answer.

**(e)** If the circuit is excited with a current source of value $-2e^{-t}$ A that is suddenly turned on at $t = 0$, what is the forced response of the voltage at the input to the circuit?

**(f)** What is the total response for $t > 0$ for this input voltage if the initial value of the voltage and its rate of change are zero?

**12.8.** A system has a transfer function

$$\mathbf{T}(\mathbf{s}) = \frac{K}{(\mathbf{s} - \mathbf{s}_1)(\mathbf{s} - \mathbf{s}_2)} .$$

The input voltage is zero for negative time and $+10$ for positive time. With this input the output is

$$v_{out}(t) = 5 + 10e^{-t} - 5e^{-2t} \text{ V}.$$

**(a)** Find $K$, $\mathbf{s}_1$, and $\mathbf{s}_2$.

**(b)** If the input voltage is $3e^{-t/2}$ for $t > 0$, find the output voltage for $t > 0$, assuming the same initial conditions.

**12.9.** Determine the open-circuit and short-circuit natural frequencies for the circuits shown in Fig. P12.9 and interpret these in terms of the time constants of the circuits.

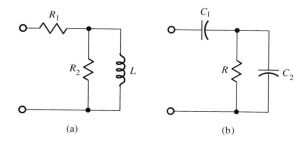

(a)                    (b)

**Figure P12.9**

**12.10.** Figure P12.10 (a) shows the input function to the low-pass filter shown in Fig. P12.10 (b). Determine the equation of the output voltage in the time domain.

**12.11.** The circuit shown in Fig. P12.11 is excited by a voltage source that is zero for negative time, but $v(t) = 100e^{-10,000t}$ V for positive time. Determine the current for positive time, assuming zero current at $t = 0$.

**12.12.** The impedance of the circuit in Fig. P12.12 has one zero at $\underline{s} = 0$ and one pole at $\underline{s} = -1 \text{ s}^{-1}$. At $\underline{s} = +1 \text{ s}^{-1}$, the impedance into the circuit has a value of 15 Ω. The circuit is excited by a current source that is zero for negative time and has a value of $i(t) = 0.5e^{-2t}$ A for positive time. Determine the input voltage, as shown, assuming $v(0+) = +2$ V.

**12.13.** An $RC$ network has the impedance function

$$\underline{Z}(\underline{s}) = 100 \frac{\underline{s}^2 + 25\underline{s} + 100}{\underline{s}(\underline{s} + 8)} \ \Omega$$

**(a)** Does the circuit allow a dc current?

**(b)** Find the impedance of the circuit at a frequency of 5 Hz.

**(c)** If the circuit is excited with a current source, what is (are) the natural frequency (frequencies) of the circuit?

**(d)** If the circuit source is $3e^{-10t}$ A, what input voltage results?

**(e)** What are the short-circuit natural frequencies of the network?

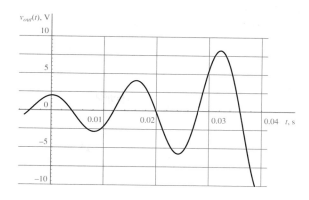

(a)

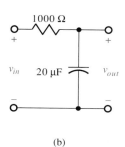

(b)

**Figure P12.10**

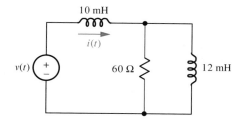

**Figure P12.11**

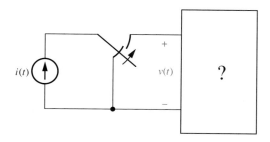

**Figure P12.12**

**12.14.** The system diagram shown in Fig. P12.14 gives the relationship between input and output voltage in the frequency domain. No voltage is applied prior to $t = 0$.

**(a)** Does this system pass a dc signal? How do you know?

**(b)** If the input is $v_{in}(t) = 2e^{-10t}$ for $t > 0$, and $v_{out}(0^+) = 0$, find the output for $t > 0$.

**(c)** If the input is $v_{in}(t) = 2\cos(2t)$ for $t > 0$, and $v_{out}(0^+) = 0$, find the output for $t > 0$.

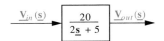

**Figure P12.14**

## Section 12.3: Transient Response of *RLC* Circuits

**12.15.** For the *RLC* circuit of Fig. 12.16, what would be the natural frequencies of the network if $R$ and $L$ were exchanged? What would be the initial value and initial derivative of the output response to the sudden application of an input voltage?

**12.16.** For the series *RLC* circuit of Fig. 12.21, with $L = 1$ mH and $C = 1$ μF, find the following:

**(a)** Determine the transfer function, $\mathbf{T(s)}$.

**(b)** From the transfer function, determine the natural frequencies of the circuit if excited by a voltage source.

**(c)** What is the value of resistance for critical damping of the circuit? Is this different from the critical value given in Eq. (12.62) for the parallel *RLC* circuit?

**(d)** For resistances one-half and twice the critical value established in part (c), determine the natural frequencies of the circuit and write the corresponding time responses with unknown constants.

**(e)** Consider that a 10-V source is suddenly applied to the input in the manner shown in Fig. 12.17. What are the initial value and initial derivative of the output voltage? Work out the complete response for the overdamped case calculated in part (d).

**12.17.** For the circuit shown in Fig. P12.17, find the following:

**(a)** Find the input impedance, $\mathbf{Z(s)}$.

**(b)** Determine the open-circuit natural frequencies.

**(c)** What value (range) of resistance corresponds to behavior that is (1) undamped, (2) underdamped, (3) critically damped, and (4) overdamped?

**12.18.** A circuit impedance has the pole–zero pattern shown in Fig. P12.18 and has an impedance magnitude of 30 Ω at $\mathbf{s} = +1$ s$^{-1}$. The circuit is excited by a voltage source that is zero for

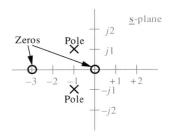

**Figure P12.17**

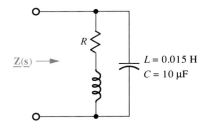

**Figure P12.18**

negative time and has a value of $v(t) = 5\cos(2t)$ for positive time. Determine the current into the circuit for positive time, assuming zero for the initial value and initial derivative of the current.

**12.19.** Figure P12.19 shows a circuit with a disconnected source.

**(a)** Find the generalized impedance of the circuit, $\mathbf{Z(s)}$.

**(b)** What is the impedance at $\mathbf{s} = 0$?

**(c)** What is the impedance at $\mathbf{s} = \infty$?

**(d)** If the switch is closed, what are the natural frequencies of the circuit?

**(e)** What is the character of the response (undamped, underdamped, critically damped, overdamped)?

**(f)** What is the initial value of the current in the resistor?

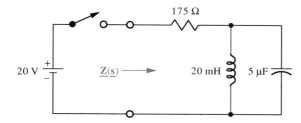

**Figure P12.19**

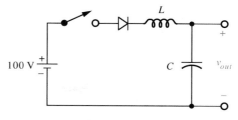

**Figure P12.20**

**(g)** What is the final value of the current in the resistor?

**12.20.** Figure P12.20 shows an undamped *LC* circuit that resonant charges the capacitor to twice the power-supply voltage, and the diode holds the voltage until the capacitor is discharged. Determine the inductance and capacitance to store 2 J of energy in the capacitor in 1 ms from the time of switch closure. Assume an ideal diode.

**12.21.** A circuit has the impedance function

$$\underline{\mathbf{Z}}(\underline{\mathbf{s}}) = 12 \, \frac{\underline{\mathbf{s}}}{\underline{\mathbf{s}}^2 + 9\underline{\mathbf{s}} + 6} \, \Omega$$

**(a)** What is the impedance at dc?

## Section 12.4: System Analysis

**12.22.** A simplified analysis of an electric-oven control system includes the following effects:
- When the heater element in turned on, it heats with a time constant of 15 s.
- If the heater element were fully hot, the air in the oven would heat with a time constant of 3 min.
- The time constant of the thermostat is negligible.
- If the heater element were left on a long time,

**(b)** What are the natural frequencies of the circuit if the input is shorted?

**(c)** What are the natural frequencies if the input is open-circuited?

**(d)** In addition to resistors, this circuit has one inductor, or one capacitor, or two inductors, or two capacitors, or one capacitor and one inductor? Which combinations are possible (may be more than one)? Explain your answer.

**(e)** If the circuit is excited with a current source of value $-2e^{-2t}$ A that is suddenly turned on at $t = 0$, what is forced response of the voltage at the input to the circuit?

**(f)** What is the total response for the input voltage if the initial value of the voltage and its rate of change are zero?

the oven would heat to 600°F relative to ambient temperature.

Figure P12.22 shows a block diagram of the system. The output of the thermostat is compared to the oven-temperature setting, and the output of the comparator is represented as a dashed line to the switch.

**(a)** Determine the form of the transfer functions for the heater and oven-temperature blocks.

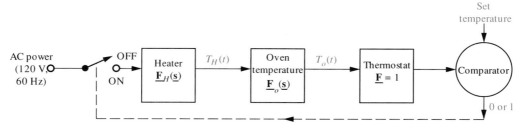

**Figure P12.22**

**(b)** Derive the system function from the input of the heater to the output of the thermostat.

**(c)** What is the form of the output signal in the time domain, given that the oven is excited with a constant voltage at the heater element?

**(d)** Determine the time required to heat the oven to 350°F and compare that time with the time required if there were no heat-up delay in the heater element. Assume an ambient temperature of 75°F.

**12.23.** A feedback system is shown in Fig. P12.23.

**(a)** What is the system function with feedback?

**(b)** Find $A$ for critical damping, that is, to put the system on the boundary between under- and overdamped behavior.

**(c)** For a value of $A$ 10 times that computed in part (b), what is the form of the natural response of the system?

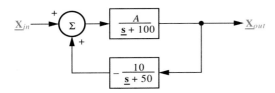

**Figure P12.23**

**12.24.** Show that in the absence of feedback, the final oven temperature used as an example in Sec. 12.4 reaches $10(1 - L_0)$, where $L_0$ is the dc loop gain and the final change in the oven temperature is 10°F. *Hint:* Determine the increment in input temperature to produce a 10°F change in the oven temperature with feedback operating.

**12.25.** Determine from Eq. (12.81) the value of dc loop gain to give critical damping. Show that this is $-2.025$ for $\tau_o = 300$ s and $\tau_s = 30$ s, as stated in the text.

**12.26.** Show from Eq. (12.81) that the second-order

system cannot become dynamically unstable, regardless of the dc loop gain.

**12.27.** A linear system is described by the differential equation

$$\frac{d^2 x_{out}}{dt^2} + 5\frac{dx_{out}}{dt} + 16x_{out} = 5\frac{dx_{in}}{dt},$$

where $x_{out}$ is the output signal and $x_{in}$ is the input signal. A fraction of the output, call it $\beta$, is fed back to the input and subtracted from the input in a negative feedback system.

**(a)** Draw a block diagram of the system in the frequency domain.

**(b)** What range of $\beta$ gives transient behavior that is overdamped?

**12.28.** The block diagram for a linear process is shown in Fig. P12.28.

**(a)** Determine the maximum value of $B$ for an overdamped response.

**(b)** Find the transfer function for $B = 0.1$.

**(c)** What value(s) of $\underline{s}$ allow output with no input?

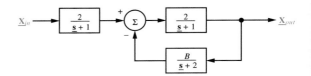

**Figure P12.28**

**12.29.** The circuit shown in Fig. P12.29 has a main amplifier and a feedback network. The main amplifier has a gain of 500, infinite input impedance, zero output impedance, and a $-3$-dB point at 5 kHz (one pole only). Find $C$ such that the poles are real and negative and differ by a factor of 2.

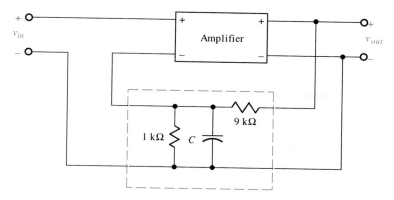

**Figure P12.29**

# Answers to Odd-Numbered Problems

**12.1.** $5.89 \times 10^{-12}$ s$^{-1}$.

**12.3.** $-5.27 + j314$.

**12.5.** (a) $\underline{\mathbf{Z}}_{eq} = (\underline{s}RC + 1)/\underline{s}C$; (b) at dc, we can have voltage, but no current, open-circuit natural frequency; (c) at $\underline{s} = -1/RC$, we can have current but no voltage, short-circuit natural frequency.

**12.7.** (a) $\infty$; (b) $-0.268$, $-3.73$ s$^{-1}$; (c) $0$, $-2$ s$^{-1}$; (d) must have two energy-storage elements and block dc: 2 $Cs$ or $LC$ is possible; (e) $-4 \times 10^4 e^{-t}$ V; (f) $v(t) = 2 \times 10^4(1 + e^{-2t} - 2e^{-t})$.

**12.9.** (a) short circuit: $-(R_1 \| R_2)/L$, open circuit: $-R_2/L$; (b) $-1/R(C_1 + C_2)$, open circuit: $0$, $-1/RC_2$.

**12.11.** $i(t) = 5\,(e^{-10^4 t} + e^{-1.1 \times 10^4 t})$ A.

**12.13.** (a) No dc current; (b) $116\angle -27.2°$; (c) $0$, $-8$ s$^{-1}$; (d) $-750 e^{-10t}$ V; (e) $-5$, $-20$ s$^{-1}$.

**12.15.** Same as before, $0$ initial value but $V/RC$ for initial derivative.

**12.17.** (a) $\dfrac{R + \underline{s}L}{\underline{s}^2 LC + \underline{s}RC + 1}$;

(b) $\underline{s} = -\dfrac{R}{2L} \pm \sqrt{\left(\dfrac{R}{2L}\right)^2 - \dfrac{1}{LC}}$;

(c) 77.5 $\Omega$ is critical damped, undamped is 0, underdamped up to 77.5 $\Omega$, overdamped over 77.5 $\Omega$.

**12.19.** (a) $\dfrac{175(\underline{s}^2 + 10^7) + 2 \times 10^5\,\underline{s}}{\underline{s}^2 + 10^7}$ $\Omega$;

(b) 175 $\Omega$, by inspection of the circuit; (c) 175 $\Omega$, by inspection of the circuit; (d) $\underline{s} = -571 \pm j3110$ s$^{-1}$; (e) underdamped; (f) 20/175 A; (g) 20/175 A.

**12.21.** (a) 0 $\Omega$; (b) 0 s$^{-1}$; (c) $-0.725$, $-8.27$ s$^{-1}$; (d) two inductors because it is second-order and it approaches a short at dc, or could be $LC$. (e) $-6e^{-2t}$ V; (f) $v(t) = -6e^{-2t} + 4.99e^{-0.725t} + 1.01e^{-8.27t}$ V.

**12.23.** (a) $\dfrac{A(\underline{s} + 50)}{(\underline{s} + 100)(\underline{s} + 50) + 10A}$; (b) 62.5;

(c) $-75.0 \pm j75.0$ s$^{-1}$.

**12.25.** For critical damping, $\dfrac{1}{4}\left(\dfrac{1}{\tau_o} + \dfrac{1}{\tau_s}\right)^2 = \dfrac{1 - L_0}{\tau_o \tau_s}$

**12.27.** (a)

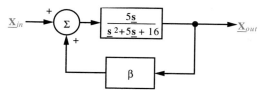

(b) $\beta < -2.60$.

**12.29.** 8.05 µF.

# PART

# 4

# Motors

# 13

# The Physical Basis of Electromechanics

1. To understand the definition of the electric field and its relationship to voltage
2. To understand the definition and nature of magnetic fields and their relationship to current and magnetic materials
3. To understand how to calculate voltage in stationary and moving wires with Faraday's law
4. To understand how to calculate stored energy in linear and nonlinear magnetic systems
5. To understand how to analyze and model energy conversion in a linear transducer

Electrical physics underlies all the material in this book, but this review is useful because principles of electromechanical devices are based on electric and magnetic fields. This review will help you understand the basic laws that govern important electric power devices such as motors and transformers.

# Introduction to Electromechanics

**Importance of electrical energy conversion.**   Electric motors are such an important part of modern civilization that we hardly notice them. But if you look, you see them everywhere: in your car (windshield wipers, starter motor, window lifts); in the office (floor buffers, hard disk drives on computers); in the home (hair dryers, clocks, large appliances); and of course in the factory. Electromechanical devices are also required in the generation of electric power from basic energy sources and in the distribution of such power to customers. Also important are the electrical transformer, which operates on principles similar to those of electromechanical devices, and other magnetic devices such as electrical relays, bells (doorbells, alarm bells), solenoids (electric locks, starter solenoids on cars), magnets, and inductors used in electronics and fluorescent lights.

**Purpose and scope of Part IV on motors.**   In Chapters 5 and 6, we surveyed the field of electric power, including an introduction to electric motors.  Our primary purpose in Part IV is to explain the principles of the common types of electric motors and generators, and to describe their characteristics and typical applications. We also give some details on electric transformers and some of the miscellaneous electromechanical devices just named. We end with a study of the electronic control of electric power.

**Motor principles and applications.**   Few engineers outside the major manufacturers design a new electrical motor. Thus, we do not emphasize the design of electromechanical equipment; rather, we aim at imparting a physical understanding of electromechanics and the practical knowledge that would guide one to choose the right device for a specific need.

**Contents of this chapter.**   Here we review the electrical physics underlying electromechanics. We define electric and magnetic fields, and we state the basic laws that operate in electromechanical devices. Magnetic field and force concepts are emphasized because virtually all electromechanical devices utilize magnetic phenomena.

## 13.1  ELECTRIC FORCES AND ELECTRIC FIELDS

### Forces between Charges

**electrostatic force, electric energy**

**Two experimental results.**   Figure 13.1(a) shows an experiment that one can perform with a battery and two sheets of metal. The battery forces opposite charges to the sheets, and the sheets exhibit an small attractive force tending to pull them together. This force can be explained as an attraction between the excess positive and negative charges on the sheets. We call the force an *electrostatic force* because it is associated with the relative location of the charges; and energy associated with this type of force is called electrostatic energy, or more simply, *electric energy*. Electrostatic forces are responsible for lightning, because charges become separated through the breakup of water droplets in clouds, and electrostatic forces are used in photocopy machines to form images on a selenium surface with charged bits of dry ink. Electrostatic forces indicate the presence of an electric field.

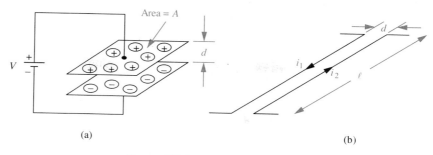

(a)                                                    (b)

**Figure 13.1**  Two simple experiments.

**magnetic force,**
**magnetic energy**

Figure 13.1(b) shows another simple experiment with currents in long, parallel wires, which for the current directions indicated exhibit a small force of repulsion. This type of force requires moving charges; thus, such a force exists between currents. This we call *magnetic force*, and energy associated with this type of force is *magnetic energy*. Such magnetic forces operate in electric motors and magnets and also can be used to deflect beams of electrons in TV tubes. Magnetic forces indicate the presence of a magnetic field.

**Forces and fields.**  It is convenient to describe these forces in terms of electric and magnetic fields. Rather than thinking of the forces as produced directly between stationary and moving charges, we assert that one set of charges, due to its presence and motion, sets up electric and magnetic fields, and that other charges experience force through interacting with, or responding to, these fields.

## Electric Fields

**electric field**

**Definition of an electric field.**  An *electric field* is defined as the vector force on a stationary charge divided by that charge; thus,

$$\vec{E} = \frac{\vec{f}}{q} \ \text{N/C}$$

(13.1)

where $\vec{E}$ is the vector electric field in newtons/coulomb and $\vec{f}$ is the vector force in newtons on the charge $q$ in coulombs. The direction of the electric field is the direction of force on a positive charge.  A single positive charge produces an electric field directed outward from the charge. Although the electric field is a vector field, we deal only with cases where the direction of the electric field is evident so as to eliminate the need for vector mathematics.

**dipole**

**Electric-field patterns.**  Figure 13.2(a) shows the electric field pattern from an isolated positive charge; Fig. 13.2(b) shows the electric field pattern of a *dipole*, an associated pair of equal but opposite charges; and Fig. 13.2(c) shows the electric field for a capacitor.  In all cases, the electric-field lines start on positive charges and end on negative charges.

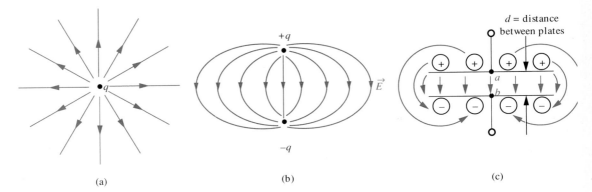

**Figure 13.2** Electric-field distributions for (a) single charge, (b) an electric dipole, and (c) a capacitor.

---

**EXAMPLE 13.1**  **Force on a water droplet**

A water droplet having an excess charge of $5e$ is located in a vertical electric field of $+10,000$ V/m. What is the force on the droplet?

**SOLUTION:**
Using Eq. (13.1) and $e = -1.60 \times 10^{-19}$ C, we find the force to be

$$f = 5 \times (-1.60 \times 10^{-19}) \times 10^4 = -8.01 \times 10^{-15}\,\text{N} \qquad (13.2)$$

**WHAT IF?**    What if you want the direction?[1]

---

**Dimensions of an electric field.**  The units of an electric field are newton/coulombs, but this is equivalent to volt/meter, as shown by the following:

$$\frac{\text{N}}{\text{C}} = \frac{\text{N} \times \text{meter}}{\text{C} \times \text{meter}} = \frac{\text{joule}}{\text{C}} \times \frac{1}{\text{meter}} = \frac{\text{volt}}{\text{meter}} \qquad (13.3)$$

because a joule/coulomb is a volt. Thus, we can interpret an electric field as a voltage per unit distance, or alternately, we can interpret a voltage as the integral of an electric field. We now investigate this second interpretation.

**voltage, fringing**

**Voltage and electric fields.**  Recall that the *voltage* from point $a$ to point $b$ is defined as the work done by the electrical system in moving a charge from $a$ to $b$, $W_{ab}$, divided by the magnitude of the charge:

$$V_{ab} = W_{ab}/q \qquad (13.4)$$

---
[1] Downward, opposite the field direction.

Let us consider the charged capacitor of Fig. 13.1(a), shown in cross-section in Fig. 13.2(c). Opposite excess charges spread over the top and bottom plates of the capacitor. The electric field is directed from the positive to the negative charges because that is the direction a positive charge would tend to move. Between the plates of the capacitor, the electric-field is essentially constant in magnitude and direction, but the electric field lines outside the plates spread out, which is called *fringing*.

**Voltage calculation.** The work done by the electrical system in moving a test charge $q$ from $a$ to $b$ is defined in Eq. (13.4) as $W_{ab} = qV_{ab}$. We can express this work mechanically in terms of force and displacement, with the integral of the vector dot product of the force and displacement:

$$W_{ab} = \int_a^b \vec{f} \cdot \vec{d\ell} = q \int_a^b \vec{E} \cdot \vec{d\ell} \ \text{J} \tag{13.5}$$

where $\vec{f} = q\vec{E}$ is the force on the test charge and $\vec{d\ell}$ is the vector increment of distance along the path of the line integral. Two comments are required before we continue to investigate the relationship between voltage and the electric field.

1. The relationship between the electric field and voltage that follows from Eq. (13.5) results from defining voltage as the voltage (or potential) *drop* from point $a$ to point $b$.

2. We use the notation of vector calculus in writing the equations describing electric (and magnetic) fields because these are required to express the relationships mathematically. We apply the equations only in situations where, due to symmetry, we do not require application of vector calculus. In the present instance, for example, we perform the line integral only in the region where the electric field is important, and we follow a path aligned with the electric field. On this path, the vector line integral becomes an ordinary integral.

The integral in Eq. (13.5) describes the summation of the electric-field component times the increment in distance in the direction of the path followed. For the capacitor, we perform the integral near the middle of the capacitor, where the electric field goes directly from the top to the bottom plate, and we move the charge in a straight line from top to bottom. Thus, the line integral reduces to the ordinary integral:

$$W_{ab} = \int_a^b f \ dx = \int_a^b qE \ dx \ \Rightarrow \ V_{ab} = \frac{W_{ab}}{q} = \int_a^b E \ dx \ \text{V} \tag{13.6}$$

where $E$ is the magnitude of the electric field and $dx$ is the incremental displacement of $q$ in moving from $a$ to $b$. Electric fields associated with charge distributions, like gravitational fields, are conservative fields, which means that the work done, and hence the voltage, is independent of the path taken from $a$ to $b$. Equation (13.6) shows that the voltage between two points can be expressed as the integral of the electric field or, alternatively, that a voltage indicates the presence of an electric field.

**Electric field in the capacitor.** We may apply Eq. (13.6) to the capacitor shown in Fig. 13.2(c) to determine the electric field between the plates of the capacitor, given the voltage. In this region, $E$ is constant:

$$V_{ab} = \int_a^b E \ dx = E \int_a^b dx = Ed \Rightarrow E = \frac{V_{ab}}{d} \ \text{V/m} \tag{13.7}$$

where $d$ is the distance between the plates. Equation (13.7) suggests the interpretation mentioned earlier, that the electric field is a voltage per unit distance in space.

**Summary.**  Electric fields are produced by charges and exert force on other charges. An electric field can be considered a voltage stretched over space.

---

**EXAMPLE 13.2** | **Electric field in a capacitor**

A cylindrical capacitor is constructed by rolling a 0.0005-inch-thick plastic material between metal conductors. The maximum electric field the plastic material can tolerate is $50 \times 10^6$ V/m. What should be the voltage rating of the resulting capacitor?

**SOLUTION:**
From Eq. (13.7) we calculate the maximum voltage to be

$$V_{max} = E_{max} \times d = 50 \times 10^6 \ \text{V/m} \times 0.0005 \ \text{in.} \times 0.0254 \ \text{m/in.} = 635 \ \text{V} \tag{13.8}$$

---

### Check Your Understanding

**1.** Give the units for an electric field.

**2.** An electron accelerates downward under the influence of an electric field. What is the direction of the field?

**3.** Estimate the electric field at an appliance outlet.

***Answers.*** (**1**) Newtons/coulomb or volts/meter; (**2**) upward; (**3**) $\approx$ 12 kV/m.

## 13.2 MAGNETIC FORCES AND MAGNETIC FIELDS

### Currents and Magnetic Forces

**Force equation.**  Magnetic force is produced when one set of moving charges interacts with another set of moving charges; or more simply, magnetic forces exist between currents. In Fig. 13.1(b), we show two long parallel wires of length $\ell$ separated by a distance $d$. The total force of repulsion, $F$, acting on the wires is described by Ampère's force law:

$$F = \mu_0 \frac{i_1 i_2 \ell}{2\pi d} \ \text{N} \tag{13.9}$$

where $\mu_0$ is the permeability of free space and has a numerical value of $4\pi \times 10^{-7}$ henry/meter in the mks system. In Eq. (13.9), $i_1$ and $i_2$ are referenced in opposite directions.

---

**EXAMPLE 13.3** | **Force in a lamp cord**

Estimate the force/meter between the two wires carrying current to a 60-W, 120-V lamp.

**SOLUTION:**
The current is 60 W/120 V = 0.5 A (rms). Thus, from Eq. (13.9)

$$\frac{F}{\ell} = 4\pi \times 10^{-7}\frac{(0.5)(0.5)}{2\pi(2 \times 10^{-3})} = 2.50 \times 10^{-5} \ \text{N/m} \qquad (13.10)$$

where we have used 2 mm as the distance between the two conductors.

**WHAT IF?** | What if you want the force between two conductors in a power plant with 8 kA separated by 6 inches?[2]

---

Our approach here, as for electrostatics, is to assert that one current produces a magnetic field in its vicinity, and the other current interacts with that field to experience a force. Here we consider the force on the wire carrying $i_2$ due to the magnetic field produced by $i_1$. Thus, we divide the problem into two parts: first, the relationship between $i_1$ and its magnetic field, $H_1$; and, second, the interaction of $i_2$ with $H_1$ to produce a force on the wire carrying $i_2$.

**Currents and their magnetic fields.**   Currents produce magnetic fields just as stationary charges produce electric fields. Magnetic fields are vector fields, but we can gain a sufficient understanding of the nature of magnetic fields and of many important devices using magnetic fields without vector mathematics. Because the current produces a magnetic field, we anticipate a theory for determining the field, given the current. Such a theory exists, but is mathematically difficult to apply. There is a relatively simple relationship, Ampère's circuital law, that allows us to determine the magnetic field in several important geometries.

**Ampere's circuital law.**   Unlike electric fields, which start on positive charges and end on negative charges, magnetic field lines encircle their source currents. Figures 13.3(a) and 13.3(b) show magnetic field configurations from a long straight wire and a coil of wire, respectively. Ampère's circuital law is a conservation principle that relates the integral of the magnetic field around a closed contour to the current passing through the area enclosed by the contour.

---

[2] 84.0 newtons/meter.

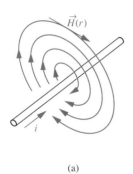

(a)

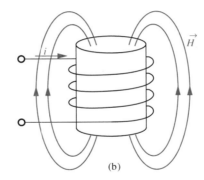

(b)

**Figure 13.3** The magnetic field encircles the current.

$$\oint_C \vec{H} \cdot \vec{d\ell} = i \tag{13.11}$$

where $\vec{H}$ is the magnetic field in amperes/meter, $\vec{d\ell}$ is a vector element of distance, $C$ is the contour of integration, and $i$ is the current passing through the area bounded by $C$. This gives the picture of magnetic-field lines circling currents, but always in such a way that, if you follow a magnetic-field line, the spatial integral of the magnetic-field strength around the path equals the current encircled. If the path is farther away from the current, the field will be weaker because the integration path length is longer.

**Magnetic field of a long straight wire.** We use Ampere's circuital law to calculate the magnetic field due to an infinitely long wire, suggested in Fig. 13.3(a). Here the magnetic-field lines must by symmetry encompass the current in circular paths, as shown, and hence the magnitude of the magnetic field $\left|\vec{H}(r)\right|$ at a radius $r$ from the wire must be constant in magnitude. Thus, the magnetic field is given by

$$\oint \vec{H} \cdot \vec{d\ell} = \left|\vec{H}(r)\right| \oint \left|\vec{d\ell}\right| = \left|\vec{H}(r)\right| \times 2\pi r = i \tag{13.12}$$

or

$$H(r) = \left|\vec{H}(r)\right| = \frac{i}{2\pi r} \frac{\text{A}}{\text{m}} \tag{13.13}$$

where $H(r)$ is the magnitude of the magnetic field at radius $r$. Thus, the magnetic field is proportional to the current and, in this case, inversely proportional to the distance from the wire.

**Magnetic forces.** We return to Fig. 13.1(b) and the force equation in Eq. (13.9), which we rearrange into the form

$$f_2 = \frac{F}{\ell} = \mu_0 \left(\frac{i_1}{2\pi d}\right) i_2 = \mu_0 H_1 i_2 \ \text{N/m} \tag{13.14}$$

**magnetic field**

where $f_2$ is the force in newtons/meter on $i_2$, and $H_1$ is the magnetic field due to $i_1$ at the location of $i_2$.[3]  Although derived for a specific geometry, Eq. (13.14) is valid generally and, indeed, can serve as a definition of *magnetic field*. The force per meter on the wire carrying $i_2$ depends on the magnetic field due to $i_1$ at the wire and the current in the wire. Later, we reformulate Eq. (13.14) in vector form and elaborate on the importance of the quantity $\mu_0 H_1$. For now, we accomplished our goal of separating the force into two terms: the magnetic field produced by $i_1$ and the force between that field and the wire carrying $i_2$.

---

| **EXAMPLE 13.4** | **Wire force** |
| --- | --- |

A wire carrying 1000 A experiences a force of 2 N/m.  What is the magnetic field at the wire?

**SOLUTION:**
From Eq. (13.14),

$$H = \frac{F/\ell}{\mu_0 i} = \frac{2}{4\pi \times 10^{-7} \times 1000} = 1590 \text{ A/m} \tag{13.15}$$

Actually, this is the component of $\vec{H}$ perpendicular to $i$; thus, 1590 A/m is the minimum field at the wire.

## Direction of the Magnetic Field

**Right-hand rule.** Ampère's circuital law, as stated, gives only the magnitude of the magnetic field. To determine the direction of the field, we use the right-hand rule. Actually, there are several forms of the right-hand rule that relate the directions of current and magnetic field. In Fig. 13.3(a), the convenient form is: Take the *wire* in your right hand with your thumb in the direction of the current; your fingers then encircle the wire in the direction of the magnetic field.

For a coil, as in Fig. 13.3(b), the following is convenient: Take the *coil* in your right hand with the fingers pointing in the direction of the conventional current. Then your thumb points in the direction of the magnetic field *inside* the coil.

**magnetic-field direction, north and south magnetic poles**

**Magnetic poles.** The direction of the magnetic field as given by the right-hand rule is consistent with the definition based on the magnetic-pole concept, which came first historically. The early theory of magnetism was developed along the same lines as electrostatics through the concept of magnetic poles. A compass was thought to consist of a north and a south magnetic pole, with the north pole of the compass indicating the direction of north. The *direction of the magnetic field* is defined as the direction a compass would indicate as northerly. Because opposites attract, it follows that the north *geographic* pole contains a south *magnetic* pole, as indicated in Fig. 13.4(a). A *north magnetic pole* is defined to be a region where the magnetic-field lines emerges from an object, the Earth in this case, and a *south magnetic pole* is a region where the magnetic-field lines enter an object.  Thus, Fig. 13.4(a) shows the magnetic field lines emerging

---

[3] Equation (13.14) is valid if $\vec{H}_1$ is perpendicular to the direction of $i_2$.

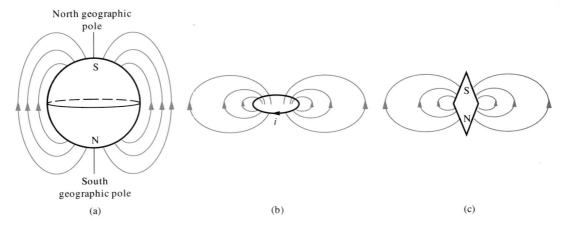

**Figure 13.4** (a) Terrestrial magnetic field; (b) field from a current loop; (c) magnetic dipole.

from the north *magnetic* pole at the south *geographic* pole and disappearing into the south *magnetic* pole located at the north *geographic* pole.

**magnetic dipole, magnetic moment**

A compass is analogous to an electric dipole and is called a *magnetic dipole* or *magnetic moment*. A small loop of current also has a dipole field as shown in Fig. 13.4(b), and Fig. 13.4(c) shows a dipole created by a pair of magnetic poles. Although isolated magnetic poles, magnetic charges, have not been detected by physicists, some basic atomic particles possess a magnetic moment.

## Magnetic Effects in Matter

**ferromagnetism, magnetic domain**

**Ferromagnetism.** Magnetic fields interact with matter through several effects. The important effect from an engineering viewpoint is ferromagnetism, which arises out of the inherent magnetic moment associated with the spin of the orbiting electrons, Fig. 13.5(a). In certain materials, notably iron, the magnetic moments of the orbital electrons interact with each other to produce a region of magnetic coherence over an extended region of the material, a *magnetic domain*. A magnetic domain can be thought of as a microscopic magnet and is capable of interacting significantly with an external field. Under normal conditions, the magnetic domains are randomly oriented, as suggested by Fig. 13.5(b), and produce no net effect. However, under the influence of an external magnetic field, the boundaries of the domains move such that the magnetic domains in the direction of the applied field grow in size at the expense of those in other directions, and the net effect is a considerable enhancement of the magnetic flux. This effect, called *ferromagnetism*, can establish large magnetic fluxes as required for electromechanical devices.

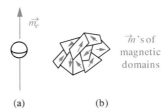

**Figure 13.5** (a) Electron spin; (b) magnetic domains in iron. Microscopic magnetic moments are denoted by $\vec{m}$.

**magnetic flux density**

**Magnetic flux density.** Consider the state of matter that is magnetized by an external field, such that the magnetic domains produce a net magnetic moment. We define the magnetic dipole density, $\vec{M}$, as the vector sum of all the magnetic moments over a volume of space, divided by that volume. The magnetic dipole density characterizes the effect of the magnetic field on the magnetic state of the matter. The *magnetic flux density*, $\vec{B}$, combines the applied and the induced magnetism, as defined in Eq. (13.16):

$$\vec{B} = \mu_0(\vec{H} + \vec{M})$$

$$(13.16)$$

The units of magnetic flux density are webers/meters$^2$, which has been given the honorary unit tesla (T) after Nikola Tesla (1856–1943).

**Causal relationships.** The causal relationships in producing magnetic flux are summarized in Fig. 13.6. The magnetic field, $\vec{H}$, can be thought of as a magnetic stress on space, and the magnetic flux density, $\vec{B}$, a magnetic strain. In other words, the magnetic field, $\vec{H}$, tends to magnetize space, and the magnetic flux density, $\vec{B}$, is the total magnetic effect that results.

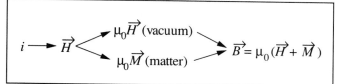

**Figure 13.6** Causality diagram for the magnetization of space. The current creates the magnetic field that magnetizes space and any matter in space. The net magnetization combines both effects.

**Magnetic properties of iron.** Because iron is important to electromechanics, we concentrate on the ferromagnetic properties of iron. For moderate applied fields, the induced magnetic dipole density is proportional to the applied field, and the magnetic flux density is proportional to the magnetic field. Equation (13.17) expresses this proportionality

$$\vec{M} \propto \vec{H} \Rightarrow \vec{B} = \mu_i\vec{H} = \mu_0\mu_r\vec{H}$$

$$(13.17)$$

**permeability, relative permeability**

where $\mu_i$ is called the *permeability* of the iron. If we think of $\vec{H}$ as the cause of the magnetization and $\vec{B}$ as the effect, then the constant $\mu$ in Eq. (13.17) indicates the magnitude of the induced effect. The constant $\mu_r$ is called the *relative permeability* of the material and is essentially unity for all materials except ferromagnetic materials, notably iron, for which the value of the relative permeability lies typically in the range 1000 to 10,000. Thus for iron, a small magnetic cause, $\vec{H}$, creates a large magnetic effect, $\vec{B}$.

**hysteresis curve**

**Magnetic saturation and hysteresis.** A more complete picture of magnetic effects in iron must show the effects of magnetic saturation and hysteresis, as indicated in Fig. 13.7. Here we show the effect of applying an external magnetic field to unmagnetized iron. The magnetism curve starts at the origin (*a*) and increases linearly as the magnetic field magnetizes the iron. The slope of the curve in this region is $\mu = \mu_0\mu_r$, Eq. (13.17). Eventually, however, all the magnetic domains align with the applied magnetic field, and the curve flattens out as the iron becomes magnetically saturated (*b*). If the applied field is then reduced to zero, the flux density follows a different curve because the iron tends to retain its previous magnetized state. The thermodynamic forces

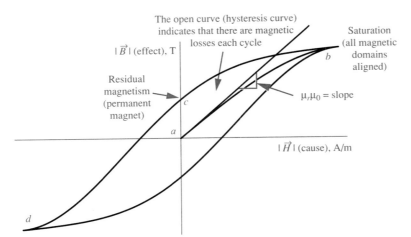

The open curve (hysteresis curve) indicates that there are magnetic losses each cycle

Saturation (all magnetic domains aligned)

$|\vec{B}|$ (effect), T

$b$

$\mu_r\mu_0$ = slope

Residual magnetism (permanent magnet)

$c$

$a$

$|\vec{H}|$ (cause), A/m

$d$

**Figure 13.7** A magnetic hysteresis curve for iron.

that disorient the magnetic domains in the iron do not fully overcome the order imposed by the external field, and the iron retains a residual magnetism ($c$). We thus have produced a permanent magnet. As we reverse the applied magnetic field, the iron eventually becomes magnetized in the reverse direction until it again saturates ($d$). If we continue to cycle the magnetic state of the iron by applying ac current to the coil creating the applied magnetic field, the curve continues to follow an S-shaped curve, which is called a *hysteresis curve*. The area enclosed by the hysteresis curve is the energy loss per unit volume per cycle. This loss heats the iron and is one reason why electric motors and transformers become hot.

### Air and iron paths for magnetic flux.

An iron path has a strong effect on the magnetic flux density, as illustrated by the hypothetical experiment shown in Fig. 13.8. Figure 13.8(a) shows a coil energized by a current. The resulting magnetic field, $\vec{H}$, has the shape shown and conforms to Ampère's circuital law, Eq. (13.11). Because $\vec{M}$ is zero for air, the magnetic flux density is given by $\vec{B} = \mu_0\vec{H}$ and is relatively small. An identical coil wound around an iron core, Fig. 13.8(b), produces a rather different flux pattern. The magnetic field, $\vec{H}$, is distorted by the presence of the iron. The magnetic fields in the region around the coil have roughly the same magnitude as before, because Ampère's circuital law must still be satisfied for the same coil and current. Within the iron, however, the magnetic flux density, $\vec{B}$, is much larger than before by the magnitude of $\mu_r$, say, 5000, resulting in a large magnetic flux that follows the iron path.

### Interaction with current.

The force given in Eq. (13.14) has a direction in space. A general form of Ampère's force law that gives the direction is the vector cross product of current and flux density,

$$\vec{f}_2 = \vec{i}_2 \times \vec{B}_1 \, \text{N/m} \tag{13.18}$$

where $\vec{f}_2$ is the vector force per unit length on the wire carrying $\vec{i}_2$ and $\vec{B}_1$ is the vector flux density due to $\vec{i}_1$. Equation (13.18) is a form of Ampère's force law.

### Right-hand rule.

We also have a right-hand rule relating current, magnetic flux density, and force from Eq. (13.18). In this case, point the fingers of your right hand in the direction of the current; then bend them in the direction of the magnetic flux. Your

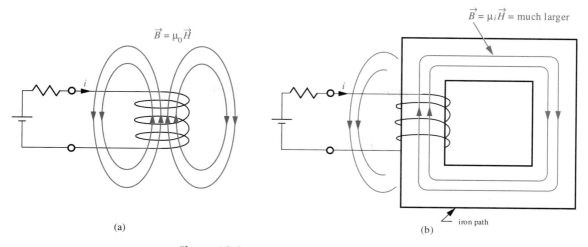

(a)                      (b)

**Figure 13.8**   (a) A coil in air; (b) the iron path for flux of the same coil,

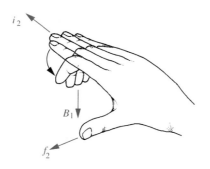

**Figure 13.9**   For the direction of $\vec{i_2} \times \vec{B_1}$, put the fingers of the right hand in the direction of $\vec{i_2}$, and then swing to the direction of $\vec{B_1}$. The thumb points in the direction of the force.

thumb indicates the direction of the force, as shown in Fig. 13.9, consistent with the definition of a vector product in a right-hand system, as Eq. (13.18) requires.

---

**EXAMPLE 13.5**    **Right-hand rule**

Work out the magnitude and directions of the flux and force for the case shown in Fig. 13.1(b) using the appropriate right-hand rules.

**SOLUTION:**

Putting the thumb of the right hand in the direction of $i_1$, we determine from the right-hand rule that $B_1$ is upward at the position of the wire carrying $i_2$ and has a magnitude, from Eq. (13.13), of $\mu_0 i_1 / 2\pi d$. Crossing $\vec{i_2}$ into $\vec{B_1}$, we see that the force on the wire carrying $i_2$ is directed away from the wire carrying $i_1$.

**WHAT IF?**      What if the currents are in the same direction?[4]

---

[4] The wires are attracted.

**Summary.** Iron enhances greatly the magnetic flux and controls its distribution in space. Large magnetic flux densities produce correspondingly large forces on conductors carrying currents. Thus, electromechanical devices normally use magnetic structures made of iron.

## Magnetic Flux ($\Phi$) and Magnetic Flux Linkage ($\lambda$)

Magnetic flux density is an important quantity because magnetic flux, of which $\vec{B}$ gives the spatial distribution, plays an important role in electromechanical energy conversion. In this section, we discuss the properties of magnetic flux and then begin our examination of the role played by magnetic flux in electromechanical energy conversion.

**Properties of magnetic flux.** Magnetic flux lines encircle the currents that generate them. Thus, magnetic flux lines exist only in closed loops. This means that magnetic flux is conserved in any closed spatial region: What goes in must come out. This is expressed by

$$\oiint_S B_\perp \, da = 0 \tag{13.19}$$

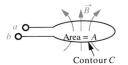

**Figure 13.10** A one-turn coil.

where $S$ is a closed surface, $da$ is a differential element of area on the surface, and $B_\perp$ is the component of magnetic flux density perpendicular to $da$. Magnetic flux lines, therefore, behave like the flow lines of an incompressible fluid. It follows that the amount of magnetic flux passing through a loop of wire having an area $A$ enclosed by the contour of the wire $C$, as shown in Figure 13.10, is a uniquely defined quantity,

$$\Phi = \int_A B_\perp \, da \tag{13.20}$$

**magnetic flux**

Equation (13.20) gives a mathematical expression for calculating the *magnetic flux*, $\Phi$, passing through such an area. The magnetic flux is a scalar quantity with units of webers (Wb), after Wilhelm Weber (1804–1891).

---

**EXAMPLE 13.6** | **Flux in a coil**

A circular coil has a diameter of 2 cm and a flux of $5 \times 10^{-8}$ Wb passing through it. Find the average flux density in the coil.

**SOLUTION:**
The average flux density would be the flux divided by the area

$$B_{avg} = \frac{\Phi}{A} = \frac{5 \times 10^{-8}}{\pi(0.01)^2} = 1.59 \times 10^{-4} \text{ tesla} \tag{13.21}$$

**WHAT IF?** What if the coil is in air and you want the average magnetic field?[5]

---

$$i \longrightarrow \vec{H} \longrightarrow \vec{B} = \mu\,\vec{H} \longrightarrow B_\perp\,da \longrightarrow \lambda = n\Phi$$

**Figure 13.11** Extension of causal diagram in Fig. 13.6 to include magnetic flux and flux linkage.

**magnetic flux linkage**

**Flux linkage.** For a coil of wire, the number of turns in the coil becomes important. The flux passing through the coil is the product of the number of turns, $n$, and the flux passing through a single turn, $\Phi$. This product is called the *magnetic flux linkage* of the coil, $\lambda$:

$$\lambda = n\Phi \text{ weber-turns} \tag{13.22}$$

Fig. 13.11 shows the causality relationships between $i$, $\vec{H}$, $\vec{B}$, $\Phi$ and $\lambda$.

The definition of flux linkage in Eq. (13.22) assumes that every turn of the coil has the same flux passing through it. Faraday's law, discussed in the next section, shows that the concept of flux linkage, broadly construed, is not founded on this assumption.

### Check Your Understanding

1. A wire is stretched around the equator, closed into a loop, and excited by a current traveling westward. Does the magnetic field from the current aid or oppose the Earth's magnetic field above the surface of the Earth?

2. At the south geographic pole, which direction (N, E, S, W, up, or down) does a magnetic compass indicate as "north"?

3. What is the value of the integral of the magnetic field around the electric cord of a lighted 120-V, 60-W electric light?

4. A cosmic ray with a positive charge is deflected in what direction by the Earth's magnetic field?

*Answers.* (1) aid; (2) up; (3) zero because the currents in the two wires add to zero; (4) eastward.

## 13.3 DYNAMIC MAGNETIC SYSTEMS

### Induced Voltage

**OBJECTIVE 3**

**To understand how to calculate voltage in stationary and moving wires with Faraday's law**

**Faraday's law.** In 1831, Michael Faraday published his law of electromagnetic induction relating voltage to time-varying magnetic flux:

$$v_t = \frac{d\Phi}{dt} \text{ V} \tag{13.23}$$

where $v_t$ is the voltage per turn induced by a time-varying magnetic flux, $\Phi$, through a coil. A coil having $n$ turns constitutes a series connection of the $n$ turns; hence, the total induced voltage is

$$v = nv_t = n\frac{d\Phi}{dt} = \frac{d\lambda}{dt} \text{ V} \tag{13.24}$$

---

[5] For air, $\mu = \mu_0$, so the average magnetic field is $1.59 \times 10^{-4}/\mu_0 = 127$ A/m.

| | |
|---|---|
| **EXAMPLE 13.7** | **Induced voltage** |

An inductor has 120-V, 60-Hz voltage applied. Calculate the flux linkage.

**SOLUTION:**
Letting the ac line voltage have a phase of zero, we have $v(t) = 120\sqrt{2}\cos(120\pi t)$. We may integrate Eq. (13.24) to give

$$\lambda = \int 120\sqrt{2}\cos(120\pi t)\, dt = \frac{\sqrt{2}}{\pi}\sin(120\pi t) + C \qquad (13.25)$$

where the constant of integration, $C$, represents a possible dc flux. The magnitude of the ac flux linkage is thus $\sqrt{2}/\pi = 0.450$ weber-turn.

**The importance of flux linkage.** Equation (13.24) shows that the induced voltage is the time derivative of the flux linkage of a coil. The last form of the equation is valid, and indeed serves as a definition of the flux linkage when all the magnetic flux does not pass through every turn of a coil. For example, if we crumpled a length of wire into a random tangle, we would not have a coil with well-defined turns, but the flux linkage would still be a meaningful quantity and would still be related through Eq. (13.24) to the induced voltage. In other words, the tangle of wire would still have an inductance. We investigate the relationship between flux linkage and inductance after we consider the sign of the induced voltage.

**Figure 13.12** Lenz's law expresses an action-reaction principle determining the polarity of the induced voltage.

**Lenz's law.** The polarity of the induced voltage may be determined through Lenz's law. Consider the situation shown in Fig. 13.12 and assume that the magnetic flux, $\Phi$, is changing with time. According to Faraday's law, a voltage $v_{ab}$ is induced. Lenz's law states that if the loop were closed, $a$ connected to $b$, the current would flow in the direction to produce a flux *inside the coil* opposing the original flux change. For example, let us say that the flux is increasing in the coil in Fig. 13.12. If we connected a resistor between $a$ and $b$, then current would flow to generate a *reaction* magnetic flux opposing the increase; in this case, the reaction flux would be downward. Using the right-hand rule, we point our right-hand thumb downward and determine that the current flows clockwise as seen from the top. The current flows through the external connection from $a$ to $b$; hence, the induced voltage $v_{ab}$ must be positive. The external circuit will see $a$ as $+$ and $b$ as $-$ because current flows out of the $+$ and into the $-$ *from the viewpoint of the external connection*. Thus, if $\Phi$ were increasing, $v_{ab}$ would be numerically positive.

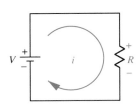

**Figure 13.13** The physical current flows *out of* the $+$ on the source (battery) and *into* the $+$ on the load.

This reasoning is based on the fact that *for a source*, the physical current flows out of the $+$ terminal, as shown in Fig. 13.13. The voltage described by Faraday's law acts as a source for the external circuit; thus, the $+$ polarity marking should be put at the terminal where the current flows out. Of course, if the coil is open-circuited, no current will flow, but the $+$ voltage is produced nevertheless.

**Inductance.** The circuit-theory concept of inductance is related to the flux linkage through Faraday's law. We have but to compare Faraday's law in Eq. (13.24) with the circuit-theory definition of inductance in Eq. (3.1):

$$v = \frac{d}{dt}\lambda \quad \text{and} \quad v = \frac{d}{dt}Li \qquad (13.26)$$

**inductance**

to define *inductance* as

$$\lambda = Li \implies L = \frac{\lambda}{i} \qquad (13.27)$$

Four comments:

1. Equation (13.27) defines inductance. To calculate the inductance of a coil, assume a current, determine the flux linkage, and use Eq. (13.27).

2. Although we normally write the definition of inductance with the inductance treated as a constant, and hence bring $L$ outside the derivative in Eq. (13.26), the form shown is required when the inductance can change with time, as would be the case, for example, if a coil were part of a moving system.

3. The polarity of the voltage in Eq. (13.24), which may be resolved through application of Lenz's law, is established in the circuit-theory case through a standard sign convention. We use a load-set convention for inductors, Fig. 13.14, which fixes the relationship between the voltage polarity and the current reference direction (and hence the direction of the magnetic flux).

4. In a *linear* magnetic system, the flux linkage is proportional to the current, and hence the inductance defined in Eq. (13.27) is constant and depends only on the geometry of the coil and the magnetic properties of the surroundings. However, if iron is involved in the inductor, then the inductance can be a function of the current because the *B–H* curve, Fig. 13.7, is not linear.

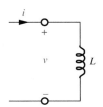

**Figure 13.14** The load set of voltage and current variables expresses Lenz's law for the circuit variables.

---

| **EXAMPLE 13.8** | **Inductance calculation** |
|---|---|

In Example 13.7, the current in the inductor is 200 mA(rms). Calculate the inductance.

**SOLUTION:**
The peak current is $200\sqrt{2}$ mA and the peak flux linkage is $\sqrt{2}/\pi$; hence, from Eq. (13.27),

$$L = \frac{\lambda_{peak}}{i_{peak}} = \frac{\sqrt{2}/\pi}{0.2\sqrt{2}} = 1.59 \text{ H} \qquad (13.28)$$

**WHAT IF?**   What if you use impedance instead of flux linkage to calculate the inductance?[6]

---

[6] The impedance magnitude is 600 $\Omega$; $L = 600/(2\pi \times 60) = 1.59$ H, as before.

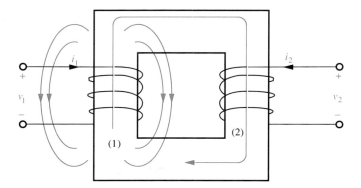

**Figure 13.15** Magnetic system with two coupled coils. The flux in coil (2) has contributions from $i_1$ and $i_2$.

**Coupled coils.** When a magnetic system has multiple coils, the flux linkage in a coil can have contributions from all other coils. Consider, for example the two-coil system shown in Fig. 13.15. The flux linkage in coil (1) has contributions from coils (1) and (2):

$$\lambda_1 = n_1(\Phi_{11} \pm \Phi_{12}) = \lambda_{11} \pm \lambda_{12} \tag{13.29}$$

where $\Phi_{11}$ is the flux in coil (1) due to $i_1$ and $\Phi_{12}$ is the flux in coil (1) due to $i_2$. The sign depends on the relative polarity of the coils. Faraday's law for the voltage in coil (1) is

$$v_1 = \pm\left(\frac{d\lambda_{11}}{dt} \pm \frac{d\lambda_{12}}{dt}\right) \tag{13.30}$$

where the signs are established by Lenz's law.

**Mutual inductance.** The circuit model for the coils involves circuit elements such as the self-inductance of coil (1), $L_{11}$, and the mutual inductance, $M_{12}$, between coils (1) and (2), where

$$L_{11} = \frac{\lambda_{11}}{i_1} = \frac{n_1\Phi_{11}}{i_1} \qquad \text{and} \qquad M_{12} = \frac{\lambda_{12}}{i_2} = \frac{n_1\Phi_{12}}{i_2} \tag{13.31}$$

In these terms Eq. (13.30) becomes

$$v_1 = L_{11}\frac{di_1}{dt} + M_{12}\frac{di_2}{dt} \tag{13.32}$$

**Figure 13.16** The standard dot convention with polarities defined in the customary manner. When physical currents are both into the dots, the fluxes from the coils add. This convention leads to the positive signs in Eqs. (13.33).

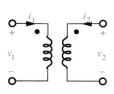

The signs in Eq. (13.32) are all positive because we adopted the standard dot convention for polarities shown in Fig. 13.16. According to this convention, positive currents into the dots produce fluxes that add. That convention, and the load sets relating voltage and currents, yields positive signs in the coupled equations of the system:

$$v_1 = L_{11}\frac{di_1}{dt} + M_{12}\frac{di_2}{dt}$$
$$\tag{13.33}$$
$$v_2 = M_{21}\frac{di_1}{dt} + L_{22}\frac{di_2}{dt}$$

**About self- and mutual inductance.** What we have hitherto called "inductance" is simply the self-inductance of an isolated coil. The mutual inductance has two important properties:

■ **Reciprocity.** It can be shown from Kirchhoff's laws that, for linear media, $M_{12} = M_{21}$. Thus it is customary to drop the double subscripts and use $L_1$, $L_2$, and $M$ for the self-inductances and mutual inductance for two coupled coils. With more than two coils, the double subscripts must be retained for the mutual inductances.

■ **Coefficient of coupling.** From conservation of energy and the nonnegative property of energy, it can be shown that the mutual inductance is equal to or smaller than the geometric mean of the self-inductances:

$$M = k\sqrt{L_1 L_2}, \qquad \text{where } 0 < k < 1 \tag{13.34}$$

where $k$ is the coefficient of coupling between the coils. When all of the flux in coil (1) also passes through coil (2), $k = 1$, but for weakly coupled coils, $k$ is near zero.

---

**EXAMPLE 13.9** | **Coupled coils**

Two coils have self-inductances of $L_1 = 100$ mH and $L_2 = 1$ mH, and a coupling coefficient of $k = 0.5$. Find $v_1(t)$ and $v_2(t)$ if $i_1 = 10 \cos(4000\pi t)$ mA and $i_2 = 0$, open circuit.

**SOLUTION:**
From Eq. (13.34),

$$M = 0.5 \times \sqrt{100 \times 1} = 5 \text{ mH} \tag{13.35}$$

Thus, from Eqs. (13.33):

$$v_1(t) = 0.100 \times \frac{d}{dt}[0.01 \cos(4000\pi t)] = -12.6 \sin(4000\pi t) \text{ V}$$
$$v_2(t) = 0.005 \times \frac{d}{dt}[0.01 \cos(4000\pi t)] = -0.628 \sin(4000\pi t) \text{ V} \tag{13.36}$$

**WHAT IF?** What if $i_1 = 0$ and $i_2 = 10 \cos(4000\pi t)$ mA?[7]

---

## Stored Energy in a Magnetic System

**IDEA Conservation of Energy**

We apply conservation of energy to a lossless magnetic system represented by the inductor in Fig. 13.14. We may compute the energy stored in the system by integrating the input power, $p = vi$. The incremental energy input is then

---

[7] $v_1(t) = -0.628 \sin(4000\pi t)$ V  and  $v_2(t) = -0.126 \sin(4000\pi t)$ V.

$$dW_m = p\,dt = vi\,dt = \frac{d\lambda}{dt}\,i\,dt = i\,d\lambda \tag{13.37}$$

**OBJECTIVE 4**

**To understand how to calculate stored energy in linear and nonlinear magnetic systems**

where $dW_m$ is the incremental increase in the stored magnetic energy in time $dt$. The total stored energy is thus

$$W_m = \int_0^\lambda i(\lambda')\,d\lambda' \tag{13.38}$$

where $\lambda'$ is a dummy variable of integration. The integral in Eq. (13.38) corresponds to the shaded area in Fig. 13.17.

---

**EXAMPLE 13.10** | **Maximum energy**

Find the maximum energy that can be stored in a magnetic system in which $\lambda = 10(1 - e^{-2i})$ Wb-turns.

**SOLUTION:**

The maximum energy is stored when the current goes to infinity and the flux linkage goes to 10 webers. From Eq. (13.38),

$$i(\lambda) = -\frac{1}{2}\ln\left(1 - \frac{\lambda}{10}\right) \Rightarrow W_m = \int_0^{10} -\frac{1}{2}\ln\left(1 - \frac{\lambda}{10}\right)d\lambda = 5\text{ J} \tag{13.39}$$

**WHAT IF?** What if $\lambda = 5\sqrt{i}$? What is the maximum energy for this system?[8]

---

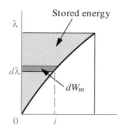

**Figure 13.17** The stored energy corresponds to the shaded area.

**Linear magnetic systems.** When a magnetic system is linear, the inductance is constant and Eq. (13.38) can be evaluated as shown in Eq. (13.40):

$$W_m = \int_0^\lambda \frac{\lambda'}{L}\,d\lambda' = \frac{\lambda^2}{2L} = \frac{1}{2}Li^2 \tag{13.40}$$

where $i$ is the final value of the current. Thus, for a linear inductor, the stored energy depends on the final state of the current, or flux linkage, and the inductance, which characterizes the geometry of the system. Of course, this is the relationship derived in Chapter 3 for linear inductors, Eq. (3.5).

**Relating $\lambda$ and $i$ to $\vec{B}$ and $\vec{H}$** Because the flux linkage, $\lambda$, is proportional to the magnetic flux density, $\vec{B}$, and the magnetic field, $\vec{H}$, is proportional to the current, it

---

[8] No limit exists.

follows that the $\lambda$–$i$ graph, as shown in Fig. 13.17, and the $B$–$H$ plot, as exemplified by Fig. 13.7, would be identical except for scaling factors. This proportionality has several implications:

- Because the shaded area in Fig. 13.17 represents the stored energy, the corresponding area in the $B$–$H$ curve must relate to energy. Indeed, the area in the $B$–$H$ diagram corresponding to the shaded area in Fig. 13.17 represents the stored energy per unit volume in the magnetic system.

$$w_m = \int_0^B H \, dB' = \frac{B^2}{2\mu_0} = \frac{\mu_0 H^2}{2} \quad \text{J/m}^3 \tag{13.41}$$

  where $w_m$ is the energy density, and $H$ and $B$ are the magnitudes of the magnetic field and flux density, respectively. The second and third forms in Eq. (13.41) assume a linear medium. The total energy in the system may be computed from the integral of the energy density over the entire volume of the magnetic system.

$$W_m = \int_V w_m \, dv \quad \text{joules} \tag{13.42}$$

  when $dv$ is a differential volume element of the volume, $V$.

- If the magnetic system contains iron, the $\lambda$–$i$ curve will possibly be nonlinear and exhibit hysteresis, as shown in Fig. 13.7. When there is hysteresis, the magnetic system returns less energy to the external system than it received when energized. Thus, there is magnetic loss resulting physically from the reorientation of the magnetic domains by the external source. The loss per unit volume is the area inside the hysteresis curve in the $B$–$H$ diagram. The energy lost to the electrical system through hysteresis loss appears as thermal energy in the iron.

## Conductors Moving in Magnetic Flux

**Faraday's law.**  Faraday's law in Eq. (13.24) is valid also for coils in which the wire is moving through the magnetic flux, provided the rate of flux change includes the effect of the motion. An alternate approach is to separate the voltage induced by a time-varying flux from the voltage induced in a moving conductor.

**OBJECTIVE 3**

To understand how to calculate voltage in stationary and moving wires with Faraday's law

**Faraday's law for moving conductors.**  The calculation of the voltage induced in a moving conductor can be complicated, but the case of a straight wire moving through a uniform magnetic flux field is

$$v = \vec{\ell} \cdot \vec{u} \times \vec{B} = \ell u \, B_\perp \, \sin\theta \tag{13.43}$$

where $\vec{\ell}$ is the vector length of the wire with the arrowhead at the $+$ end for $v$, $\vec{u}$ is its velocity, $\vec{B}_\perp$ is the flux density perpendicular to the wire, and $\theta$ is the angle between the motion and the perpendicular flux direction, as shown in Fig. 13.18.  If the two ends

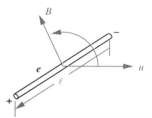

**Figure 13.18** A conductor moving through magnetic flux generates a voltage called an electromotive force (emf).

of the bar were connected through a resistor, current would flow in the direction of $\vec{u} \times \vec{B}$, out of the end marked $+$ and into the end marked $-$ in Fig. 13.18. Thus, the force on a positive carrier is positive in the direction indicated by the vector product $\vec{u} \times \vec{B}$. This force can be combined with the electrostatic force in the Lorentz force law for the force on a moving charge:

$$\vec{f} = q(\vec{E} + \vec{u} \times \vec{B}) \tag{13.44}$$

**Electromotive force (emf).**    The generation of a voltage by a magnetic flux, whether through flux change or through motion, indicates the presence of an electric field in the wire. This electric field integrated with Eq. (13.6) through the conductor path produces the voltage. The voltage described by Faraday's law is called an *electromotive force,* or *emf,* because such voltages can deliver energy to an electric circuit. The electric field due to a charge distribution is always conservative; KVL expresses conservation of energy for the resulting voltages. But the voltages induced by magnetic

**electromotive force, emf**

flux are nonconservative and, like a dc battery, can keep a current going indefinitely. Thus, an emf indicates an energy–conversion process.

---

**EXAMPLE 13.11**  **Rotating loop**

Find the voltage induced in the rectangular loop of wire shown in Fig. 13.19. The loop has a length of $\ell$, a width $W$, and is turning with an angular velocity $\omega$, as shown.

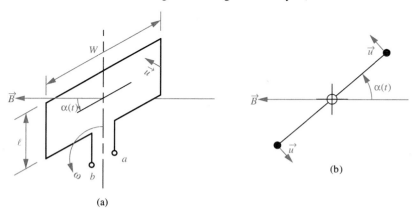

**Figure 13.19** A rectangular loop of wire turning in a magnetic flux density generates an ac voltage: (a) perspective view, (b) axial view.

The plane of the coil makes an angle $\alpha(t)$ relative to the direction of the magnetic flux density, as shown in Fig. 13.19(b). The emf is produced in the parts of the coil that are parallel to the axis of rotation; the linear velocity of this wire is $u = \omega W/2$. The angle between $\vec{u}$ and $\vec{B}$ is $90° - \alpha(t)$; hence, the emf from one wire is

$$v = \ell u \, B_\perp \sin[90° - \alpha(t)] = \ell \omega \frac{W}{2} B_\perp \sin[90° - \alpha(t)] \qquad (13.45)$$

$$= \frac{\omega \Phi_m}{2} \cos[\alpha(t)]$$

where $\Phi_m = B_\perp W \ell$ is the maximum flux in the coil, when $\alpha(t) = 90°$. An equal voltage is induced in the other wire. The voltages add in series, so the total motion-induced voltage is

$$v_{ab} = \omega \Phi_m \cos[\alpha(t)] = \omega \Phi_m \cos(\omega t) \qquad (13.46)$$

because $\alpha(t) = \omega t$. Note that $\vec{u} \times \vec{B}$ would force current out of terminal $a$, which gives the polarity.

**WHAT IF?**

What if you use Eq. (13.23)?[9]

## Electromechanical Energy Conversion

In this section, we show how Faraday's law and Ampere's force law describe the transformation of energy from electrical form, voltage and current, to mechanical form, force and velocity, and vice versa.

**OBJECTIVE 4**

**To understand how to analyze and model energy conversion in a linear transducer**

**Electromechanical transducer.** We will investigate the energy conversion process for the transducer shown in Fig. 13.20(a). The magnetic flux is furnished by an external magnet. The electrical circuit consists physically of a battery ($V$), a resistor ($R$), two stationary rails, and a movable bar that can roll or slide along the rails with electrical contact. We assume that the bar has an active length $\ell$ between the rails and is initially stationary. We close the switch and observe the sequence of effects that follow:

1. Current does not start immediately due to the inductance of the circuit.[10] The time constant of $L/R$ is very small, however.

2. The current quickly reaches the value $V/R$.

3. A force is exerted on the bar due to the interaction between the current and magnetic flux. The magnitude of this force, by Eq. (13.18), is $F = iB\ell$ to the right, and the bar begins to move with a velocity $u$. The instantaneous mechanical power *out of* the bar, $p_m$, is

$$p_m = Fu = iB\ell u \quad \text{W} \qquad (13.47)$$

---

[9] The flux through the coil is $\Phi(t) = \Phi_m \sin[\alpha(t)] = \Phi_m \sin(wt)$, and the emf by Faraday's law is $v_{ab} = d\Phi(t)/dt = \omega \Phi_m \cos(\omega t)$. The sign determined from Lenz's law is the same for both methods.
[10] It is a one-turn coil.

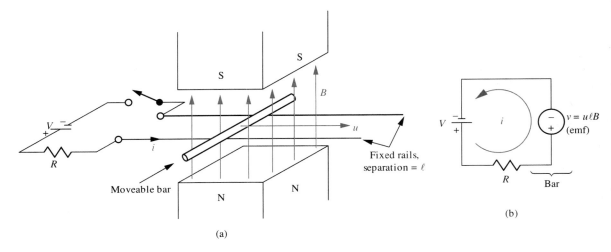

(a)

(b)

**Figure 13.20** (a) A simple transducer; (b) the moving bar presents a back emf to the circuit.

This power comes from the electrical circuit, ultimately from the battery, and accelerates the bar, does work against an external force, or both.

**Equivalent Circuits**

4. The motion of the bar produces an electromotive force. This is the condition shown in Fig. 13.18 with $\theta = 90°$; thus, by Eq. (13.43), $v = uB\ell$. The polarity of the emf is positive where the current enters the moving bar. The equivalent circuit, shown in Fig. 13.20(b), models the electrical aspects of the system. The moving bar generates a "back" emf that opposes the current.

**Conservation of Energy**

5. The instantaneous electrical power *into* the bar, $p_e$, is

$$p_e = vi = uB\ell i \tag{13.48}$$

Comparison of Eqs. (13.48) and (13.47) shows that the electrical input and the mechanical output powers are equal.

6. The dynamics of the electromechanical system involve the electrical system

$$i = \frac{V - v}{R} = \frac{V - B\ell u}{R} \tag{13.49}$$

and the mechanical system

$$F = B\ell i = B\ell \left( \frac{V - B\ell u}{R} \right) = \text{mechanical force balance} \tag{13.50}$$

7. The bar has an equilibrium speed of $u = V/\ell B$ at which the current, and hence the generated force, is zero. If moved faster by an external mechanical force, the bar becomes a generator, reverses the current direction, and supplies electrical power to the resistor and battery. In this circumstance, we could easily show that the input mechanical power is equal to the electrical output power supplied by the bar to the resistor and battery.

**Causality diagram.** Fig. 13.21 shows causality for the electromechanical transducer. The mechanical system is unspecified except that the bar is free to move.

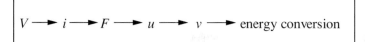

**Figure 13.21** Causality diagram for the electromechanical transducer. The mechanical system is unspecified, but it is assumed that the electrical force causes motion.

We draw four conclusions:

1. The electrical input power to the bar (ignoring resistive losses) is transformed to mechanical output power with 100% efficiency.

2. The energy lost to the electrical circuit via the emf appears as mechanical energy. The emf voltage source represents electrically the coupling between electrical and mechanical systems.

3. This structure is a two-way transducer between the electrical and mechanical systems. The bar may represent an electrical load or source, depending on its velocity.

4. The magnetic flux, though an agent in the electromechanical coupling, does not participate directly in the energy exchange.

Whether motor or generator, the moving bar couples energy between electrical and mechanical systems with 100% efficiency. We have ignored mechanical losses such as friction and electrical losses associated with the resistance of the bar, but these are modeled easily in their respective systems.

---

**EXAMPLE 13.12** **Accelerating bar**

Assume the bar has a mass $M$ but no friction. Determine its motion.

**SOLUTION:**
From Eq. (13.50),

$$M \frac{du}{dt} = \frac{B\ell}{R}(V - B\ell u) \quad \Rightarrow \quad \frac{MR}{(B\ell)^2} \frac{du}{dt} + u = \frac{V}{B\ell} \tag{13.51}$$

Comparison with Eq.(3.35) shows that the bar accelerates to a final velocity $u_\infty = V/B\ell$ with a time constant $\tau = MR/(B\ell)^2$.

**WHAT IF?**    What if there is a frictional force $Du$?[11]

---

[11] Then $u_\infty = VB\ell/[RD + (B\ell)^2]$   and   $\tau = MR/[RD + (B\ell)^2]$.

**Summary.** Through an analysis of a linear transducer, we established several important concepts. We showed that currents in wires moving through a magnetic flux effect electromechanical energy conversion. The moving conductor generates an electromotive force. When the current flows against the electromotive force, electrical energy is converted to mechanical energy; hence, the system acts as an electric motor. When the current is driven by the electromotive force, mechanical energy is converted to electrical energy, and the system acts as an electric generator. In both cases, an emf voltage source in the equivalent circuit represents the exchange of energy between the electrical and mechanical systems.

### Check Your Understanding

1. Figure 13.22(a) shows a one-turn coil. The magnetic flux is decreasing. Mark the physical polarity (+ and −) on the coil terminals according to Lenz's law.

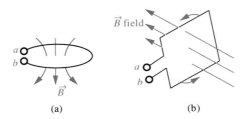

$\vec{B}$ field

(a)

(b)

**Figure 13.22** (a) A one-turn coil; (b) a rotating coil.

2. For the rotating coil shown in Fig. 13.22 (b), determine the numerical sign of $v_{ab}$ at the moment and angle shown.

3. What are the units of $\vec{u} \times \vec{B}$ in terms of volts, amperes, meters, and/or seconds? All are not required.

4. The deflection of the electron beam in a TV tube is accomplished with magnetic flux. If the TV set is facing south and the beam is deflected west, what is the direction of the magnetic flux established by the deflection coils?

*Answers.* (**1**) $b$ is +; (**2**) $v_{ab}$ is negative; (**3**) volts/meter, same as for electric fields; (**4**) down.

## CHAPTER SUMMARY

This chapter reviews the basic laws underlying electromechanical devices:

1. Ampère's circuital law, Eq. (13.11), which relates a current to the magnetic field it creates.

2. Ampère's force law, Eq. (13.18), which describes the force/meter on a current-carrying conductor in magnetic flux.

3. Faraday's law, Eq. (13.24), which describes the emf produced by changing flux and/or moving conductors.

The presentation and exploration of these laws require definition of a number of quantities and explanation of practical matters such as the magnetic properties of iron.

The section on dynamic magnetic systems is important because Faraday's law, stored magnetic energy, and electromotive forces generated by moving conductors are the heart of electromechanics. The analysis of the linear transducer, which can act as either motor or generator, introduces the main ideas that are explored in the next four chapters.

**Objective 1: To understand the definition of electric field and its relationship to voltage.**    An electric field is voltage stretched over space.    The electric field is important to our purpose because electric fields are present in energy conversion.

**Objective 2: To understand the definition and nature of magnetic fields and their relationship to current and magnetic materials.**    Magnetic fields support the efficient transformation of energy between electrical and mechanical forms. Ampere's circuital law relates a current to its magnetic field.    Ferromagnetic materials, notably iron, increase the magnitude of the magnetic field and direct its path through space.

**Objective 3: To understand how to calculate voltage in stationary and moving wires with Faraday's law.**    A voltage is generated by a changing magnetic flux or by motion of a conductor through a magnetic flux.    In a generator such voltage represents energy entering the electrical circuit, and in a motor such voltage represents energy leaving the electrical circuit as mechanical work.

**Objective 4: To understand how to calculate stored energy in linear and nonlinear magnetic systems.**    We derive the equation for stored magnetic energy from the principle of conservation of energy.    Stored energy provides the basis for calculating magnetic force in a magnetic system.

**Objective 5: To understand how to analyze and model energy conversion in a linear transducer.**    To introduce energy conversion, we analyze the coupling between a dc circuit and a mechanical system represented by a moveable bar carrying current.    We see that the magnetic field supports the energy transformation, but does not exchange energy.    The energy-conversion efficiency is 100% between electrical and mechanical forms, although electrical and mechanical losses lower conversion efficiency in a real transducer.

In adopting a modest mathematical level, we presented the physics in a piecemeal manner that obscures the unity and elegance of the subject. In some cases, we have given only a special case of a physical law or treated a vector equation as if it were a scalar equation. Many details and subtleties were ignored. Our goal was to introduce the important concepts and equations that are used in the following chapters, not to give a full exposition of electrical physics.

Chapter 14 builds on the physical principles and laws reviewed in this chapter in the analysis of magnetic structures, specifically inductors, transformers, and transducers.

# PROBLEMS

## Section 13.2: Magnetic Forces and Magnetic Fields

**13.1.** Two infinite wires carry currents of $I$ in opposite directions, as shown in Fig. P13.1. At what value(s) of $x$ outside the wires does the magnetic field have the same magnitude as it has at $x = 0$?

**Figure P13.1**

**13.2.** An infinite straight wire carries 10 A dc, as shown in Fig. P13.2. A nearby rectangular loop carries 5 A dc.
  (a) Find the flux passing through the rectangular loop due to the 10-A current. Count downward as positive.
  (b) Find the total force on the rectangular loop. Give the direction of the force relative to the infinite wire. *Hint:* The forces on the radial sides of the loop cancel by symmetry.

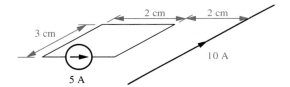

**Figure P13.2**

**13.3.** An auto battery is being charged with a current of 20 A.
  (a) Estimate the magnetic flux density at the top of the battery, neglecting any effect due to the iron in the vicinity.
  (b) Draw a picture showing the battery and the direction of the flux.

**13.4.** Two parallel infinite wires, $a$ and $b$, are 4 meters apart, as shown in Fig. P13.4. In the plane of the wires, the flux is upward for $x < 0$ and for $1 < x < 4$, the cross-hatched regions shown. The current in $a$ is 2 A, into the paper, as shown. Determine the current in $b$ in magnitude and direction.

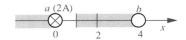

**Figure P13.4**

**13.5.** Two wires, infinite in the $y$-direction, are located at $x = 0$ and $x = 1$ cm, as shown in Fig. P13.5. The wires carry dc currents of 6 A and 3 A, as shown.
  (a) Find the magnetic field at $z = 0$, $x = 0.3$ cm. Give direction and magnitude.
  (b) What is the force per meter on the wire labeled $b$?
  (c) If the magnetic field were integrated in a circular path at radius $r = 10$ meters from the $y$-axis, what would be the magnitude of the result?

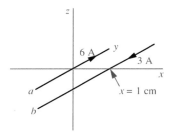

**Figure P13.5**

**13.6.** An infinite wire with 0.1-inch diameter carries 2 A in the $-z$-direction, as shown in Fig. P13.6. The wire is on the axis of an iron pipe with an ID of 0.75 inch and an OD of 1.0 inch. The permeability of the iron is 1200 $\mu_0$; assume $\mu_0$ elsewhere.
  (a) Find the magnitude of the magnetic field and the magnetic flux density at the surface of the wire.
  (b) Find the approximate magnitude of the magnetic field and the magnetic flux density in the iron.
  (c) Find the magnetic flux/meter between the wire and the iron.

**13.7.** In a power plant, a large current is divided between three symmetrically placed conductors, as

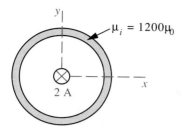

**Figure P13.6**

shown in Fig. P13.7. The centers of the conductors are a distance 20 cm apart, and all conductors carry the same current $i(t) = 1000 \cos(\omega t)$ A.

**(a)** Find the peak force/meter exerted on any of the conductors by the other two conductors.

**(b)** Find the peak value of the magnetic flux density at a point $b$ halfway between two of the conductors.

**(c)** Approximate the peak magnetic field at a distance of 10 meters from the wires, assuming no iron in the vicinity.

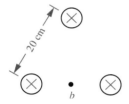

**Figure P13.7**

**13.8.** Three infinite, parallel wires of infinitesimal cross-section carry currents of $+1$ A, $-3$ A, and $+2$ A (all dc currents), respectively, as shown in Fig. P13.8. Note that $d_1$ and $d_2$ are positive numbers that sum to 1 meter. Assume that $d_1$ and $d_2$ are adjusted such that the net force on the center conductor is zero.

**(a)** Find the force/meter on the 1-A conductor counting force to the right as positive.

**(b)** Find the force/meter on the 2-A conductor also.

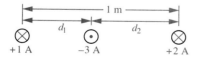

**Figure P13.8**

**13.9.** For the two wires shown in Fig. P13.5; Find the following:

**(a)** At what point on the $x$-axis between the wires is the flux density a minimum?

**(b)** At what finite point on the $x$-axis is the flux density zero?

**13.10.** An infinite wire along the $y$-axis has 10 A in the $+y$ direction, as shown in Fig. P13.10. Locate a second wire on the $x$–$y$ plane such that there is zero magnetic field at $x = 1$ cm and also the force between the wires is 0.002 newton/meter. Give the direction of the force (attraction or repulsion?).

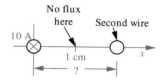

**Figure P13.10**

**13.11.** Figure P13.11 shows two infinite wires aligned with the $x$- and $y$-axes. The wires carry 1 A dc in the $+y$ and 1.5 A dc in the $-x$ directions, as shown.

**(a)** Where in the $x$–$y$ plane is the magnetic field zero?

**(b)** In what regions of the $x$–$y$ plane is the magnetic flux density out of the paper (in the positive $z$-direction)?

**(c)** Calculate the torque on the conductor carrying 1 A due to the field from the conductor

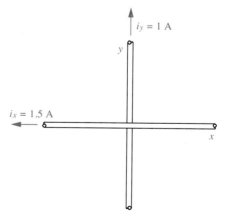

**Figure P13.11**

carrying 1.5 A. Calculate either total torque or torque per meter, whichever is appropriate.

13.12. Two infinite wires are 2 cm apart and have diameters of 3 mm each, as shown in Fig. P13.12. Each carries a current of 10 A, in opposite directions. Find the flux/meter passing between the wires, counting upward as positive.

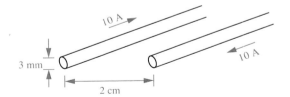

**Figure P13.12**

13.13. Figure P13.13 shows a strip conductor carrying a current $I$ in the $+y$-direction (into the paper.) The conductor is very thin and has a width $w$. The current is evenly distributed along the width of the conductor. The strip conductor can be analyzed as many wires, side by side, each having a current $di = (I/w)\,dx$ A.
   (a) What is the direction of the magnetic field at $x = a$?
   (b) What is the magnitude of the magnetic field at $x = a$?

(c) What is the direction of the magnetic field at $y = b$?
(d) What is the magnitude of the magnetic field at $y = b$?

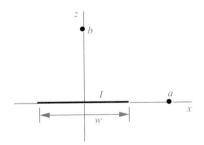

**Figure P13.13**

13.14. Assuming that lightning consists of electrons moving from earth to cloud, what direction (north, east, south, or west?) would a lightning bolt tend to move due to magnetic forces? Explain your answer.

13.15. The Lone Ranger is pursuing an outlaw who is fleeing toward the setting sun. He fires a silver bullet, which had a slight positive charge on it, toward the fugitive. Which way is the bullet deflected by the Earth's magnetic field (up, down, north, south, east, or west)?

## Section 13.3: Dynamic Magnetic Systems

13.16. For the circuit and coil in Fig. P13.16, find the following:
   (a) Draw the magnetic flux pattern, including flux direction.
   (b) Would a compass needle inside the coil indicate north to be up or down?
   (c) If the inductance of the coil were $L = 0.05$ H, find its magnetic flux linkage. Note that the wire in the coil and the rest of the circuit has a resistance of 1 $\Omega$, in addition to the 2 $\Omega$ in the lumped resistance.
   (d) As the battery weakens and the current decreases, an induced voltage appears across the coil. Would the $+$ of the induced voltage be at the top or bottom of the coil?

13.17. The Earth's magnetic field at the equator has a strength of about 30 μT. Consider an aircraft flying east over the equator at 600 mph. The wing span is

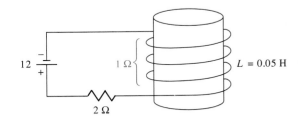

**Figure P13.16**

100 ft and the fuselage 15 ft in diameter.
   (a) To what part of the aircraft do the conduction electrons tend to move?
   (b) What is the maximum emf created by the aircraft's motion?

13.18. Figure P13.18 shows a lossless, nonlinear inductor that is energized with a battery. After the switch is

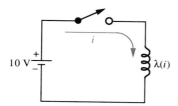

**Figure P13.18**

closed, the current is observed to increase as $i(t) = 0.05t^{1.2}$ A. Determine the flux linkage as a function of the current, $\lambda(i)$.

13.19. An inductor with a nonlinear magnetization curve described by $i = 0.2\lambda^2$ is connected to a 12-V battery by a switch that closes at $t = 0$, as shown in Fig. P13.19. Determine the stored energy as a function of time after the switch closure.

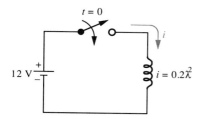

**Figure P13.19**

13.20. Figure P13.20 shows a nonlinear, lossless inductor with a flux linkage relationship $\lambda(i) = 3\sqrt{i}$ weber with $i$ in amperes. The inductor is energized by a battery through a switch that is closed at $t = 0$.
(a) Determine the time after switch closure when the power into the inductor is 12 W.
(b) At what time is the stored energy 100 J?

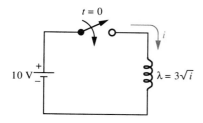

**Figure P13.20**

13.21. Two parallel infinite wires, each carrying a current $i$ in the same direction, set up a magnetic field. The wires are a distance $d$ apart, as shown in cross-section in Fig. P13.21. A conducting bar of length $\ell$ moves upward midway between the wires at a velocity $\vec{u}$. Derive a formula for the emf generated in the bar as a function of time, counting $t = 0$ when the bar passes the plane of the wires.

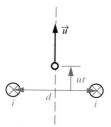

**Figure P13.21**

13.22. Figure P13.22 shows a permanent magnet that has a loop of wire around one of its poles.
(a) Draw the magnetic flux pattern, including the direction of the flux.
(b) As the loop of wire is lifted vertically, is voltage $v_{ab}$ positive or negative?

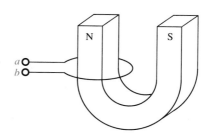

**Figure P13.22**

13.23. An infinite wire carrying a current $i$ puts flux through a rectangular loop, as shown in Fig. P13.23. Note that the differential area of integration is $w\,dr$, where $w$ is the width of the loop and $r$ is the distance from the wire.
(a) Determine the flux in the loop, with direction, for $w = 10$ cm and $i = 1$ A. This flux should be independent of $R_1$.
(b) Determine the voltage $v_{ab}$ if $di/dt = 100$ A/s.

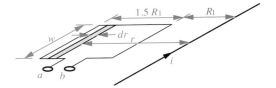

**Figure P13.23**

13.24. Figure P13.24 shows a homopolar generator, which consists of a conductor rotated in the presence of a magnetic flux. In this case, sliding contacts are made at the outer radius, $r_o$, and the radius of the axis, $r_i$. Determine the emf $v_{ab}$ as a function of the magnetic flux density, $B$, the angular velocity, $\omega$, $r_i$, and $r_o$.

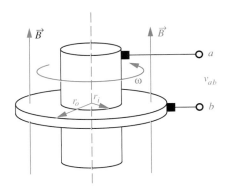

**Figure P13.24**

13.25. A wire is bent in a 90° angle and rotated in a uniform magnetic field with a flux density $B$, as shown in Fig. P13.25. Determine the emf produced, including the polarity.

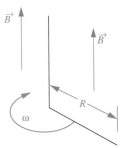

**Figure P13.25**

13.26. A circuit is shown is Fig. P13.26 that has a nonlinear inductor with a flux linkage-current relation $\lambda(i) = 5(1 - e^{-i})$ webers with $i$ in amperes. The current source is OFF for a long time and then suddenly becomes a constant value of 2 amperes.
   (a) Write a differential equation for the current in the inductor. You do not have to solve the equation.
   (b) Determine the final stored energy in the inductor.

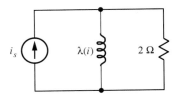

**Figure P13.26**

13.27. The relationship between the flux linkage and current for a magnetic system is plotted in Fig. P13.27 and is approximated by the equation $\lambda = 2 \ln (i + 1)$. Calculate the stored energy for $i = 0.4$ A.

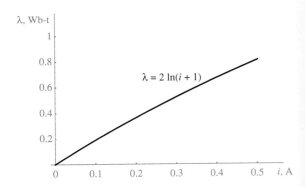

**Figure P13.27**

13.28. A nonlinear inductor is described by the equation $\lambda(i) = 1 - e^{-3i}$ webers, with $i$ in amperes. This inductor has an initial current of 1 A, as shown in Fig. P13.28, and then is connected to a 3-$\Omega$ resistor.
   (a) Derive a DE for the current, $i(t)$.
   (b) During the course of the transient, find the

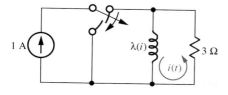

**Figure P13.28**

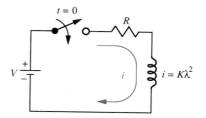

**Figure P13.30**

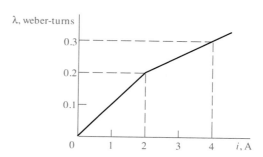

**Figure P13.31**

total energy given to the resistor. *Hint*: This would be the energy stored initially in the magnetic system.

**13.29.** A lossless, nonlinear inductor has a characteristic $\lambda(i) = K\sqrt{i}$, where $K$ is a constant and we consider only positive values of $i$. The inductor is energized by means of a battery and resistor, as shown in Fig. P13.29, with a final current of $V/R_1$. After a steady-state current is reached, at $t = 0$ the switch connects the inductor to a second resistor, giving its stored energy to the second resistor.
   **(a)** What is the stored magnetic energy in the inductor at the instance the switch is thrown?
   **(b)** Determine the flux linkage as a function of time, $\lambda(t)$, in the deenergization process.

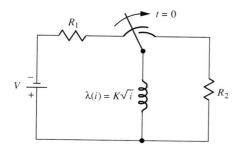

**Figure P13.29**

**13.30.** The circuit in Fig. P13.30 has a nonlinear inductor described by the equation $i = K\lambda^2$. The switch is closed at $t = 0$.
   **(a)** Write the DE for the current in terms of $V$, $R$, $K$, and time.
   **(b)** Find the current as time becomes very large.
   **(c)** Find the stored energy as time becomes very large in terms of $V$, $R$, $K$, and time.

**13.31.** Figure P13.31 shows the magnetic flux linkage of a coil as a function of the current. The curve is nonlinear due to saturation of the iron in the

system. The model uses straight-line approximations.
   **(a)** What is the inductance of the coil for currents below 2 A?
   **(b)** If the current starts at zero and increases at a rate of 100 A/s, determine the resulting voltage as a function of time during the first 40 ms. Plot the voltage during this time period.
   **(c)** Determine the stored energy of the system for a current of 4 A. *Hint*: You don't need to do any integrals; Just determine the areas geometrically.

**13.32.** Standard No. 12 wire has a diameter of 80.8 mils (thousandths of an inch), a weight of 19.77 pounds/1000 ft, and a capacity of 30 A under ideal conditions. In Fig. P13.32, we show two No. 12 wires of infinite length, each carrying the same unknown current $I$. The bottom wire is fixed, and the upper wire is free to float vertically.
   **(a)** Mark the direction of current in the upper wire such that it will tend to float, and indicate the pattern of magnetic flux in the vicinity of the wires.
   **(b)** Determine the minimum current $I$ at which the

**Figure P13.32**

top wire just begins to float. (1 lb of force = 4.448 newton.)

13.33. A circuit consists of two parallel rails, shorted together at one end, and a movable bar, as shown in Fig. P13.33. A magnetic flux is perpendicular to the plane of the circuit and has a direction out of the paper, as shown. The magnetic flux density is uniform in space but

increasing with time.

(a) Which way does induced current flow in the circuit?

(b) Which way does the bar tend to move?

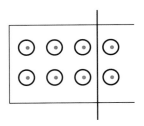

**Figure P13.33**

## Answers to Odd-Numbered Problems

13.1. $\pm 0.707d$.

13.3. (a) Approximately $2.5 \times 10^{-5}$, depending on the size of the assumed path around the battery for Ampère's circuit law;
(b)

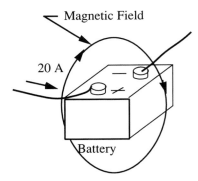

13.5. (a) 387 A/m $-z$ direction; (b) $3.60 \times 10^{-4}$ N, repulsion; (c) $4.77 \times 10^{-2}$ A/m.

13.7. (a) 1.73 N/m; (b) $1.15 \times 10^{-3}$ T;
(c) 47.7 A/m.

13.9. (a) 0.586; (b) 2 cm.

13.11. (a) along the line $y = -1.5x$;

(b)

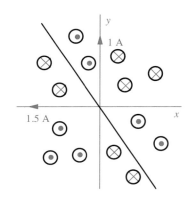

(c) a constant $1.5\mu_0/2\pi$ N-m/meter of torque.

13.13. (a) $-z$-direction; (b) $\dfrac{I}{2\pi w}\ln\!\left(\dfrac{a + w/2}{a - w/2}\right)$;
(c) $+x$-direction; (d) $\dfrac{I}{2\pi w}\tan^{-1}\!\left(\dfrac{b^2 + (w/2)^2}{b^2 - (w/2)^2}\right)$.

13.15. Down.

13.17. (a) Electrons to the bottom; (b) $3.68 \times 10^{-2}$ V.

13.19. (a) $115t^3$ J.

13.21. $2\mu_0\ell i u^2 t/\pi\,[(ut)^2 + (d/2)^2]$ .

13.23. **(a)** $1.83 \times 10^{-8}$ Wb, upward;
**(b)** $1.83 \times 10^{-6}$ V, $b$ positive.

13.25. $V = \omega B R^2/2$, plus at the axis of the wire.

13.27. 0.127 J.

13.29. **(a)** $\dfrac{K}{3}\left(\dfrac{V}{R_1}\right)^{1.5}$;

**(b)** $\lambda = \dfrac{1}{R_2 t/K^2 + (1/K)\sqrt{R_1/V}}$.

13.31. **(a)** 0.1 H;

**(b)**

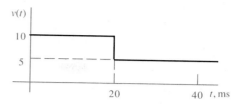

**(c)** 0.50 J.

13.33. **(a)** The current is clockwise, force to the left, opposing the flux increase inside the loop;
**(b)** Left, to decrease area.

# 14

# Magnetic Structures and Electrical Transformers

1. To understand the function and analysis of magnetic structures
2. To understand the physical basis for transformer models.
3. To understand how to derive a transformer equivalent circuit from opencircuit/shortcircuit measurements and use it to calculate the efficiency and percent regulation
4. To understand how to calculate the magnetic force in a magnetic structure

Electric motors and transformers are heavy because they contain iron structures to increase and control magnetic flux. This chapter uses the basic laws of magnetism to model inductors, transformers, and electromechanical transducers designed to produce force or torque.

## Introduction to Magnetic Structures

**magnetic structure,**
**magnetic circuit**

**Magnetic structures** A *magnetic structure*[1] is an iron structure that increases the amount of magnetic flux and controls its distribution in space. Figure 14.1 shows several types of magnetic structures. The transformer in Fig. 14.1(a) changes electrical voltage, current, and impedance levels. Relays, Fig. 14.1(b), are electrical actuators used in switches, locks, and the like. In electric motors and generators, Fig. 14.1(c), magnetic structures control the magnetic flux that produces torque. Transducers, such as the loudspeaker in Fig. 14.1(d), form yet another class of magnetic structures that includes phonograph pickups, tape heads, and tachometers. Finally, we should mention the ordinary inductors used as circuit elements, many of which require magnetic structures.

Although we stated before that magnetic structures are made out of iron, some use other magnetic materials. Materials research has produced ferrite ceramic materials with

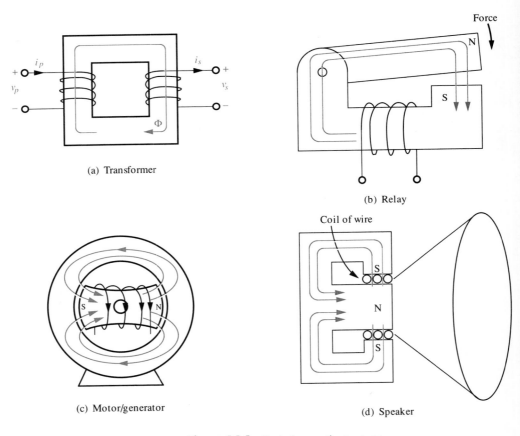

(a) Transformer

(b) Relay

(c) Motor/generator

(d) Speaker

**Figure 14.1** Typical magnetic structures.

---

[1] More commonly called a "magnetic circuit."

excellent magnetic properties, and a special class of electric motors, not to mention other devices, employ such materials in their magnetic structures. However, most magnetic structures are made of iron because of its low cost and excellent magnetic properties.

**Chapter Contents.** First, we demonstrate methods of analysis for magnetic structures, continuing the themes of Chapter 13. We then analyze a transformer, beginning from the definition of an ideal transformer and then developing models to describe real transformers. Finally, we study forces generated by magnetic structures, using conservation of energy as a basis for calculating force and torque in electromechanical systems.

## Toroidal Ring

Figure 14.2 shows a toroidal iron ring with a gap. We analyze this magnetic structure as an extended example. A coil of wire carrying current drives the magnetic system. We determine the magnetic field, flux density, and flux in the toroid and air gap.

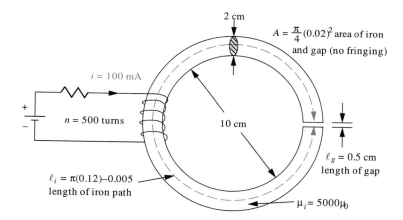

**Figure 14.2** A toroidal magnetic structure with a gap.

**Gaps in magnetic structures.** You may wonder why we have included a gap in the iron ring, because it reduces the flux. We include the gap because many electromechanical devices require such a gap. In Fig. 14.1, for example, the relay, motor, and loudspeaker must have gaps. The magnetic flux in such devices couples the electrical and mechanical systems, and the gap is required to permit motion.

**Assumptions.** Our analysis of the iron ring is based on several assumptions.

- We assume that the relative permeability of the iron is large and constant. Hence, we neglect magnetic saturation and hysteresis.

- We assume that the significant magnetic flux remains in the iron except at the gap, where the flux must pass through air. This reduces Ampère's circuit law to a scalar integral because the flux direction is assumed to be circumferential.

- We assume that the flux density is constant in magnitude, meaning that the flux density does not vary significantly across the cross-section of the toroid and does not vary around the ring.

■   We assume that fringing in the gap is negligible. This means that the flux density of the gap does not vary over its cross-section and is circumferential, as in the iron.

These assumptions are reasonable in view of the discussion of the effect of the iron structure, as discussed on page 664.

**Magnetomotive force (mmf).**   The analysis begins with Ampère's circuital law Eq. (13.11), around the axis of the toroid:

$$\oint H \, d\ell = \text{current enclosed} = ni \text{ ampere-turns} \tag{14.1}$$

The current enclosed by this path is the product of the current and the number of turns in the coil, which is called the *magnetomotive force*, or *mmf*. The name recognizes that the current-carrying coil energizes the magnetic system in the same way an electromotive force energizes an electric circuit.

**Iron and gap.**   We separate the integral of the magnetic field into two terms:

$$\oint H \, d\ell = \int_{\text{iron}} H_i \, d\ell + \int_{\text{gap}} H_g \, d\ell$$
$$= H_i \ell_i + H_g \ell_g = ni \quad \text{A-t} \tag{14.2}$$

where and $H_i$ and $H_g$ are the magnetic fields within the iron and gap, respectively, and $\ell_i$ and $\ell_g$ are the nominal distances within the iron and gap, respectively. The integral in Ampère's circuital law has contributions from both iron and gap. Because the field is constant along the path, $H$ can be brought outside the integrals, leading to the last form of Eq. (14.2).

**Magnetic flux.**   The magnetic fluxes in the iron and gap are also easily derived:

$$\Phi_i = \int B_i \, da = B_i A_i \qquad \text{and} \qquad \Phi_g = \int B_g \, da = B_g A_g \tag{14.3}$$

where $da$ is a differential area in the cross-section, $B_i$ and $B_g$ are the magnetic flux densities, $A_i$ and $A_g$ the cross-section areas, and $\Phi_i$ and $\Phi_g$ the fluxes in the iron and gap, respectively. Conservation of magnetic flux, Eq. (13.19), requires equal fluxes by integrating over the cross-section.

$$\Phi_i = \Phi_g = \Phi \tag{14.4}$$

where $\Phi$ is the magnetic flux in the magnetic structure.

**Iron and gap permeabilities.**   The magnetic fields and flux densities are related by the permeabilities of the iron, $\mu_i$, and gap, $\mu_0$:

$$H_i = \frac{B_i}{\mu_i} \qquad \text{and} \qquad H_g = \frac{B_g}{\mu_0} \tag{14.5}$$

Because the direction of these vector fields is constrained by the magnetic structure, we can treat them as scalar quantities.

**Analytical result.** Combining Eqs. (14.2) through (14.5), we can eliminate all unknown quantities except the flux, with the result

$$\Phi = \frac{ni}{(\ell_i/\mu_i A_i) + (\ell_g/\mu_0 A_g)} \quad \text{Wb} \tag{14.6}$$

**Numerical results.** When we substitute the current of 0.1 A and the dimensions of the structure in Fig. 14.2 and assume that the relative permeability of the iron is 5000,[2] we obtain the numerical result

$$\Phi = \frac{500(0.1)}{1.88 \times 10^5 + 1.27 \times 10^7} = 3.89 \times 10^{-6} \text{ Wb} \tag{14.7}$$

We can now determine the values of the various field quantities:

$$B_i = B_g = \frac{\Phi}{A} = \frac{3.89 \times 10^{-6}}{3.14 \times 10^{-4}} = 1.24 \times 10^{-2} \text{ T}$$

$$H_i = \frac{B_i}{\mu_i} = \frac{1.24 \times 10^{-2}}{5000(4\pi \times 10^{-7})} = 1.97 \text{ A/m} \tag{14.8}$$

$$H_g = \frac{B_g}{\mu_0} = 9850 \text{ A/m}$$

We also can determine the flux linkage and the inductance of the structure,

$$\lambda = n\Phi = 1.95 \times 10^{-3} \quad \text{and} \quad L = \lambda/i = 19.5 \text{ mH} \tag{14.9}$$

In the next section, we discuss and generalize this analysis, using the calculated magnitudes to justify several approximations.

## Principles of Analysis of Magnetic Structures

**Magnetomotive force.** Examination of the results of the previous section indicates that the magnetic flux depends on several factors. Notice first the role of the magnetomotive force, mmf $= ni$. The formal units of mmf are amperes, but ampere-turns, A-t, is commonly used to distinguish mmf from current. Magnetic systems are energized by current-carrying coils, and the mmf acts as the magnetic drive for the system. The "polarity" of the mmf is given by the right-hand rule. If there were more coils contributing to the flux, the mmfs would add or subtract according to this polarity.

**Gain and loss of mmf.** Equation (14.2) can be written in the form

$$ni - H_i\ell_i - H_g\ell_g = 0 \tag{14.10}$$

which suggests that mmf is gained in the coil and lost to the path around the toroid. For example, the mmf lost to, or required to magnetize, the gap is $H_g\ell_g$. In fact, the magnetic field can be considered as the loss in mmf per unit length along the field lines.

---

[2] That is, $\mu_i = 5000\mu_0$.

| EXAMPLE 14.1 | **mmf in toroid** |
|---|---|

Find the fraction of the mmf required to magnetize the iron in the toroid.

**SOLUTION:**
The total mmf of the coil is 500 turns $\times$ 0.1 A = 50 A–t. The mmf lost to iron and the gap, respectively, is

$$H_i \ell_i = 1.97 \times (\pi \times 0.12 - 0.005) = 0.73 \text{ A-t}$$

$$H_g \ell_g = 9850 \times 0.005 = 49.27 \text{ A-t}$$

(14.11)

Thus, 1.47% of the coil mmf is used to magnetize the iron and 98.5% to magnetize the air in the gap.

**Conservation of magnetic flux.** Another important principle, although it applied trivially in our example, is conservation of magnetic flux. Had our magnetic structure contained branches and parallel paths, such as suggested in Figs. 14.3 and 14.15, we would have required conservation of magnetic flux at each such junction.

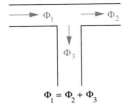

$$\Phi_1 = \Phi_2 + \Phi_3$$

**Figure 14.3**
Conservation of magnetic flux at a junction.

**Reluctance.** Equation (14.6) can be cast into the form

$$\Phi = \frac{ni}{\mathfrak{R}_i + \mathfrak{R}_g} = \frac{\text{mmf}}{\text{reluctance}}$$

(14.12)

where

$$\mathfrak{R}_i = \frac{\ell_i}{\mu_i A_i} = 1.88 \times 10^5 \frac{\text{A-t}}{\text{Wb}} \quad \text{and} \quad \mathfrak{R}_g = \frac{\ell_g}{\mu_0 A_g} = 1.27 \times 10^7 \frac{\text{A-t}}{\text{Wb}}$$

(14.13)

**reluctance**

are the reluctances of the iron and gap, respectively. *Reluctance* indicates the mmf required to magnetize a portion of a magnetic structure. Because the iron and gap are in series, have the same flux, their reluctances add to give the total reluctance of the path. The coil mmf is divided by this combined reluctance to give the flux in the system.

**Role of iron.** In Eq. (14.7), the reluctance of the iron path is small relative to the reluctance of the gap because of the large permeability of the iron. The total reluctance is approximately that of the air gap, and hence the magnetic flux of the system is in effect determined by the dimensions of the air gap. This is typical: The iron does such an effective job in guiding the magnetic flux that the magnetic system is limited by the air gap. As shown in the previous example, the mmf of the coil is used largely to magnetize the gap, and very little mmf is required to magnetize the iron.

**Combining reluctances.** Reluctances in series or parallel may be combined like resistances in series or parallel. Equation (14.12) illustrates a series addition. Parallel magnetic paths are sometimes used in transformers.[3]

---

[3] See Fig. 14.15.

**Nonlinear effects.** When saturation of the iron becomes a factor, several changes occur in the analysis. The equations become nonlinear and hence require numerical or graphical solution. Also, when the iron becomes saturated, the reluctance of the iron part of the path increases and becomes more of a factor in limiting the magnetic flux. This is frequently the case in practice, for practical devices often are operated partially saturated. However, our study of magnetic structures excludes the effects of saturation except for models of loss in inductors or transformers.

**Inductance.** The inductance is closely related to the reluctance of the system. The definition of inductance, Eq. (13.27), becomes

$$L = \frac{\lambda}{i} = \frac{n\Phi}{i} = \frac{n}{i} \times \frac{ni}{\Re} = \frac{n^2}{\Re} \text{ H} \qquad (14.14)$$

Note that small reluctance corresponds to large inductance. The last two forms of Eq. (14.14) are valid only when the magnetic system is linear.

---

**EXAMPLE 14.2** | **Winding an inductor**

An inductor has 125 turns and an inductance of 150 mH. A 100-mH inductor is required. How many turns should be removed?

**SOLUTION:**
We may use scaling principles because $L \propto n^2$. Thus,

$$\frac{100 \text{ mH}}{150 \text{ mH}} = \left(\frac{n'}{125}\right)^2 \Rightarrow n' = 102 \text{ turns} \qquad (14.15)$$

Thus, 23 turns should be removed.

**WHAT IF?** What if, instead of removing turns, more turns are added, but wound in the opposite direction. How many reverse turns should be added?[4]

---

**Summary.** In this section, we introduced the concept and function of a magnetic structure. We showed the role of magnetomotive force and reluctance in the analysis of magnetic structures. We now apply these concepts in the study of electrical transformers. In the next chapter, we introduce the cylindrical magnetic structures used in motors.

**Check Your Understanding**

1. A magnetic system is shown in Fig. 14.4.
   (a) For $i > 0$, mark the direction of the magnetic flux in the iron.
   (b) If $i$ were decreasing at a rate of 20 A/s, find $v_{ab}$.

---

[4] Twenty-three turns again.

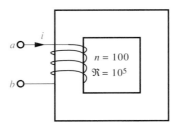

**Figure 14.4**

2. A magnetic structure has 1000 turns and an inductance of 12 H. Find the reluctance.

3. A magnetic structure has 1000 turns and an inductance of 12 H. It is scaled down by a factor of 2 in every physical dimension, but the number of turns is unchanged. Find the new inductance using scaling principles.

4. The flux is 0.1 Wb in a one-loop magnetic structure. It has an air gap with an area of 0.1 m$^2$ and a length of 1 mm.
   (a) What is the flux density in the air gap?
   (b) What is the reluctance of the air gap?
   (c) What mmf is required to force this flux across the air gap?

*Answers.* (1) (a) Up in the coil side, down in the other side; (b) –2 V; (2) 83,300 A-t/Wb; (3) 6 H; (4) (a) 1 T, (b) 7.96 × 10$^3$ A-t/Wb, (c) 796 A-t.

## 14.2 ELECTRICAL TRANSFORMERS

### Introduction to Transformers

**transformer**

An electrical *transformer* consists of two or more coils, or windings, tightly coupled by magnetic flux that is guided by a magnetic structure. Chapter 5 showed how transformers are used for voltage transformation, current transformation, and impedance transformation. Chapter 6 presented three-phase transformer connections and introduced applications in power distribution systems. In this chapter, we develop a physical understanding of transformers, leading to realistic models for transformers. Our treatment of transformers in this chapter is oriented toward power transformers.

**Section Contents.** We begin with a brief review of ideal transformer relationships, and then analyze the transformer as a magnetic structure. From this analysis, supplemented by physical considerations, we develop equivalent circuit models for single- and three-phase transformers.

**Ideal Transformers.** In Chapter 5, we introduced the ideal transformer with the symbol shown in Fig. 14.5(a) and Eqs. (14.16) and (14.17) relating the sinusoidal steady-state voltages and currents in the primary and secondary:

$$\frac{\mathbf{V}_p}{n_p} = \frac{\mathbf{V}_s}{n_s} \tag{14.16}$$

$$n_p \mathbf{I}_p = n_s \mathbf{I}_s \tag{14.17}$$

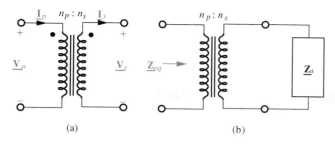

**Figure 14.5** (a) Circuit symbol for an ideal transformer; (b) impedance transformation.

**Impedance Level**

Division of Eq. (14.16) by Eq. (14.17) shows that the transformer changes impedances by the square of the turns ratio, Fig. 14.5(b),

$$\underline{Z}_{eq} = \frac{\underline{V}_p}{\underline{I}_p} = \left(\frac{n_p}{n_s}\right)^2 \frac{\underline{V}_s}{\underline{I}_s} = \left(\frac{n_p}{n_s}\right)^2 \underline{Z}_s \tag{14.18}$$

where $\underline{Z}_{eq}$ is the equivalent impedance into the primary. Our purpose in the following section is to show the physical basis for these relationships and to investigate the extent to which they describe real transformers. The analysis is based on the physical laws from Chapter 13 and the concepts of magnetic structures from the previous section.

## Analysis of a Transformer as a Magnetic Structure

**OBJECTIVE 2**

**To understand the physical basis for transformer models**

We now analyze the structure shown in Fig. 14.6, where turns, area, path length, permeability, and circuit variables are defined. We assume a sinusoidal steady state, and hence use phasors to represent voltage, current, field, and flux quantities. The voltage relationship in Eq. (14.16) follows from Faraday's law Eq. (13.24), if we assume the same flux in the primary and secondary windings.

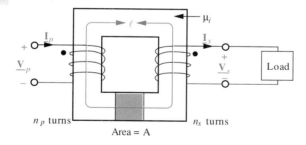

**Figure 14.6** Transformer conventions and dimensions.

**stray or leakage flux**

**Leakage flux.** In a real transformer, not all flux follows the iron path, and hence the ideal voltage relationship of Eq. (14.16) does not apply strictly to a real transformer. However, in a well-designed magnetic structure, only a small amount of flux escapes from the iron to become *stray* or *leakage flux*; hence, the ideal voltage relationship is very nearly obeyed in a real transformer. In the following, we assume that all flux couples primary and secondary coils, and later we insert small series inductors into our equivalent circuit to account for leakage flux.

**Faraday's law.** From Faraday's law, Eq. (13.24), we gain an important relationship between voltages and flux values. Applied to the primary, Faraday's law is

$$v_p(t) = n_p \frac{d\Phi(t)}{dt} \quad \Rightarrow \quad \underline{V}_p = n_p(j\omega)\underline{\Phi} \qquad (14.19)$$

where the first form is in the time domain and the second a phasor relationship in the frequency domain. We discuss Eq. (14.19) after we discuss notation.

**Important change in phasor notation.** In Eq. (14.19) and *henceforth*, the magnitude of a phasor quantity is the *rms* or *effective* value of the corresponding sinusoid. This is the custom in the study of electromechanics and power systems. Formulas for power and energy quantities lose the factor of $\frac{1}{2}$ as in Eq. (5.12), and phasor diagrams portray relationships between phase and rms amplitude. Time-domain quantities continue to use peak values.

**Voltage and flux.** The quantity $\underline{\Phi}$ in Eq. (14.19) is the phasor representation of the flux, phase and rms amplitude. The $j$ factor on the right side indicates that the flux lags the voltage by 90° in phase. Because the maximum value of the flux is frequently critical, the magnitude of Eq. (14.19) is often written

$$V_p = \frac{\omega n_p}{\sqrt{2}}\Phi_{max} \qquad (14.20)$$

where $\Phi_{max}$ is the maximum flux and $V_p$ is the rms magnitude of the primary voltage.[5] Clearly, Eqs. (14.19) and (14.20) also could have been written for secondary voltages. Equation (14.16) results when the common factors are eliminated between Eq. (14.19) and the corresponding equation involving the secondary voltage.

---

**EXAMPLE 14.3** | **Doorbell ringer**

A doorbell ringer has 200 turns and operates on 6-V, 60-Hz voltage. Find the maximum flux in the magnetic structure.

**SOLUTION:**
From Eq. (14.20),

$$6 = \frac{120\pi \times 200}{\sqrt{2}}\Phi_{max} \Rightarrow \Phi_{max} = 1.13 \times 10^{-4} \text{ Wb} \qquad (14.21)$$

---

**WHAT IF?** | What if the circular cross-section has a diameter of 1 cm? What is the maximum flux density?[6]

---

[5] We used $V_p$ for peak voltage earlier, but here it means rms voltage in the *primary.*
[6] 1.43 tesla.

**Polarities and the dot convention.** The voltage polarity between transformer windings is indicated by the dots in Figs. 14.5(a) and 14.6. Once the voltage polarity is established, the current reference directions are automatic. The reference direction of the *primary* current is *into* the dot, but the reference direction of the *secondary* current is *out of* the dot. Thus, the primary is represented as a load set, and the secondary is represented as a source set. This is the convention we used since Chapter 5.

**Lenz's law.** The dot on the primary is assigned arbitrarily, and a load set of voltage and current reference directions is assigned with the + on the voltage corresponding to the dot. The + of the secondary voltage reference direction is then determined by the right-hand rule and Lenz's law in the following manner. Assume current flows into the dot on the primary and use the right-hand rule to establish the flux direction. Then take the secondary coil in your right hand with the thumb *opposite* to the flux from the primary. Your fingers then indicate the direction that secondary current would flow if allowed. The dot is placed on the end of the secondary coil where current would exit.[7] The dot corresponds to the + on the reference direction of the secondary voltage.

**Ampère's circuital law.** The currents in primary and secondary are related through Ampère's circuital law:

$$\oint \underline{\mathbf{H}} \, d\ell = n_p \underline{\mathbf{I}}_p - n_s \underline{\mathbf{I}}_s \tag{14.22}$$

where $\underline{\mathbf{H}}$ is the phasor magnetic field in the magnetic structure. The minus sign of the $n_s \underline{\mathbf{I}}_s$ term in Eq. (14.22) follows from Lenz's law. We placed the dots in Fig. 14.6 such that the flux from $\underline{\mathbf{I}}_s$ would *oppose* the flux created by $\underline{\mathbf{I}}_p$; hence, the mmfs of the two coils subtract. We can change the left-hand side of Eq. (14.22) by introducing the concepts of magnetic structures:

$$\oint \underline{\mathbf{H}} \, d\ell = \underline{\mathbf{H}}\ell = \frac{\mathbf{B}_i}{\mu_i} \times \ell = \frac{\Phi}{A} \times \frac{\ell}{\mu_i} = \Phi \times \Re_i \tag{14.23}$$

where $\Re_i$ is the reluctance of the iron, and $\Phi$ is the phaser coupling flux. Thus, Eq. (14.22) can be rearranged to the form

$$\underline{\mathbf{I}}_p = \frac{n_s}{n_p} \underline{\mathbf{I}}_s + \frac{\Phi \Re_i}{n_p} \tag{14.24}$$

We can introduce the primary voltage into Eq. (14.24) by introducing Eq. (14.19), with the result

$$\underline{\mathbf{I}}_p = \frac{n_s}{n_p} \underline{\mathbf{I}}_s + \frac{\underline{\mathbf{V}}_p}{j\omega L_i} \tag{14.25}$$

where $L_i = n_p^2 / \Re_i$ from Eq. (14.14).

---

[7] A consequence of these conventions is that currents into the dots give flux in the same direction.

### Equivalent circuit.

Equation (14.25), interpreted as KCL, suggests the equivalent circuit shown in Fig. 14.7. Subject to the assumptions we have made, a real transformer is represented by an ideal transformer and an inductor. The inductor accounts for the magnetic energy of the flux; thus in this circuit model of the transformer, derived from Ampère's circuital law, real power is conserved, but reactive power is not because the transformer requires inductive current to magnetize the iron.

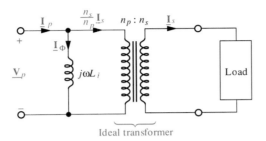

**Figure 14.7** The inductor represents the energy stored in the magnetic flux.

### Causality in a transformer.

Normally, the transformer primary is connected to an ac voltage source of constant voltage and the secondary to a load. The causal relationships for the transformer are shown in Fig. 14.8. By Faraday's law, the primary voltage must be matched by time-varying flux linkage in the primary winding, which in turn requires fields and the magnetizing current, $\mathbf{I}_\Phi$, represented by the inductor in Fig. 14.7. The changing flux in the secondary coil causes the secondary voltage, which causes load current in the secondary that is reflected back to the primary. If the secondary is open circuited, the lower path in Fig. 14.8 is eliminated and the only primary current is the magnetizing current.

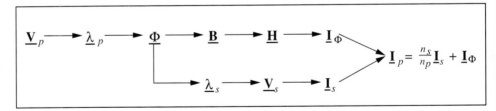

**Figure 14.8** Causality diagram for a transformer.

OBJECTIVE 3

To understand how to derive a transformer equivalent circuit from open-circuit/short-circuit measurements and use it to calculate efficiency and percent regulation

## Transformer Equivalent Circuits

To model a real transformer with an equivalent circuit, we need to account for the power loss and energy storage of the transformer, as well as the transformation properties represented by an ideal transformer. We showed that Ampère's circuital law introduces an inductor in the equivalent circuit of the transformer. Similarly, the other significant effects in the transformer are represented by circuit elements in the equivalent circuit.

### Iron losses.

Iron loss comes from two effects. *Eddy currents* are induced by the changing flux in the iron and generate heat in the resistance of the iron. Eddy-current loss may be reduced but not eliminated by fabricating the magnetic structure out of thin, insulated laminations. As discussed in Chapter 13, page 664, *hysteresis loss* represents the work done in the iron to cyclically reorient the magnetic domains. Iron and eddy-current losses vary approximately as $\Phi_{max}^2$ and hence are proportional to $V_p^2$, Eq. (14.20). These *iron losses*, therefore, may be modeled by a resistance in parallel with the primary voltage.

**Copper losses.** The losses in the resistance of primary and secondary windings are called *copper losses*.[8] These losses are modeled in the equivalent circuit by resistances, $R_p$ and $R_s$, in series with the primary and secondary of the ideal transformer.

**iron loss, eddy-current loss, hysteresis loss**

**Leakage flux.** Some flux escapes the iron path and thus fails to couple primary and secondary, as shown in Fig. 14.9. The energy associated with this flux is modeled by inductors, $L_p$ and $L_s$, in series with the primary and secondary resistances. In the ac equivalent circuit, these inductances become primary and secondary leakage reactances, $X_p$ and $X_s$.

**copper loss**

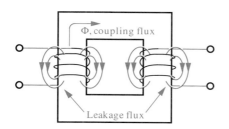

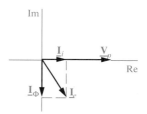

**Figure 14.9** Some leakage flux escapes the iron path.

**Figure 14.10** The exciting current consists of an in-phase component to supply iron losses and an out-of-phase component to supply energy stored in the magnetic structure.

**exciting current**

**Exciting current.** Figure 14.11 shows the *exciting current*, $\mathbf{I}_e$, required to magnetize the iron, which is detailed in Fig. 14.10. The in-phase component, $I_i$, supplies the iron losses, and the out-of-phase magnetizing current, $I_\Phi$, supplies the magnetic energy in the iron. If the secondary were an open circuit, the current in the primary would be the exciting current and the power into the primary would be the iron loss.

**Equivalent circuits.** We have now considered the significant loss and energy-storage effects in a real transformer. An equivalent circuit that accounts for these various effects in a real transformer is given in Fig. 14.11. Figure 14.12 transforms the secondary series impedance to the primary, where it is combined with the primary series impedance to give the *series winding impedance*, $R_w + jX_w$. In normal operation, the exciting current is small compared with the total input current, so we may move $R_i$ and $X_i$ to either position shown in Fig. 14.11 without significant change.

**Equivalent Circuits**

**series winding impedance**

---

[8] Although occasionally aluminum and other metals are now used for wires in transformers and other electrical apparatus, originally only copper was used. For this reason, resistive losses are called "copper losses," regardless of the metal.

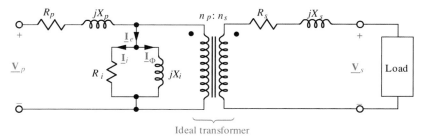

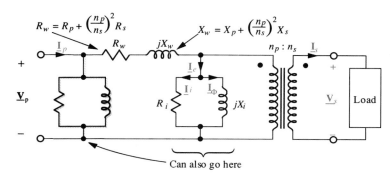

**Figure 14.11** The resistors account for losses. The inductors account for stored magnetic energy. The series elements model losses and energy storage proportional to current squared, and the parallel components model losses and energy storage proportional to voltage squared.

**Figure 14.12** Combining the series elements causes insignificant error. The parallel elements can be put on either side of the series elements with negligible change.

**Use of the equivalent circuit.** Circuit models of transformers are used to predict power and voltage loss in the transformer under various operating conditions. Such models are used in analysis of power systems to determine load flows, fault conditions and system performance generally. We give examples after showing how to determine the series and parallel elements in the equivalent circuit.

## Transformer Open-Circuit (OC)/Short-Circuit (SC) Test

**Transformer nameplate.** A transformer nameplate normally gives the nominal primary and secondary voltages, apparent power rating for output, and the series impedance, $|R_w + jX_w|$ in Fig. 14.12 in per-unit. The ratio of primary and secondary voltage gives the transformer turns ratio, but the other parameters in the equivalent circuit model must be measured.

---

| **EXAMPLE 14.4** | **Transformer ratings** |
|---|---|

A 10-kVA, 60-Hz, single-phase transformer is rated 2400/240 V. This transformer is used with the high-voltage side as the primary. Find the turns ratio and the nominal current ratings on the primary and secondary.

**SOLUTION:**
The turns ratio is derived from the nameplate voltages:

$$\frac{2400}{n_p} = \frac{240}{n_s} \Rightarrow \frac{n_p}{n_s} = \frac{10}{1} \tag{14.26}$$

The nominal current ratings follow from the voltage and apparent power rating:

$$I_s = \frac{\text{apparent power}}{V_s} = \frac{10,000 \text{ VA}}{240 \text{ V}} = 41.7 \text{ A} \tag{14.27}$$

and similarly for the primary, $I_p = 4.17$ A.

---

**WHAT IF?**

What if the transformer is excited at 2400 V on the primary, but the actual load is 2000 VA with $PF = 0.87$, lagging. Find the nominal primary current.[9]

---

**Open-circuit (OC) test.** The exciting current and its associated parameters, $R_i$ and $X_i$, are determined by an open-circuit measurement. For safety, the transformer is excited at rated voltage on the low-voltage side with the high-voltage side open.[10] The voltage, $V_s$, exciting-current magnitude, $I'_e$, and power, $P'_i$, into the low-voltage winding allows determination of $R'_i$ and $X'_i$, where the primed quantities are referred to the low-voltage side of the transformer, or secondary. The power indicated in the open-circuit measurement is iron loss only because currents and thus copper losses are very small. The voltage must be at rated value so that the flux levels are normal and the iron loss is that associated with normal usage.

**Determination of circuit parameters.** The in-phase, $I'_i$, and out-of-phase $I'_\Phi$, components of the exciting current can be determined as follows:

$$I' = \frac{P'_i}{V_s} \quad \text{and} \quad I'_\Phi = \sqrt{(I'_e)^2 - (I'_i)^2} \tag{14.28}$$

These lead directly to the circuit parameters

$$R'_i = \frac{V_s}{I'_i} \quad \text{and} \quad X'_i = \frac{V_s}{I'_\Phi} \tag{14.29}$$

---

**EXAMPLE 14.5** | **OC test**

The 10-kVA, 2400/240-V, 60-Hz, single-phase transformer in the previous example has an OC test excited on the 240-V side. The measured exciting current is 1.2 A and the measured power is 170 W. Find $R'_i$ and $X'_i$.

---

[9] 0.833 A. The power factor does not matter since apparent power is given.

[10] The primary may be the low- or high-voltage side of the transformer, depending on the application. In this analysis, the primary is the high-voltage side.

**SOLUTION:**

From Eqs. (14.28),

$$I_i' = \frac{170}{240} = 0.708 \text{ A} \qquad \text{and} \qquad I_\Phi' = \sqrt{(1.2)^2 - (0.708)^2} = 0.969 \text{ A} \qquad (14.30)$$

Thus, from Eqs. (14.29),

$$R_i' = \frac{240}{0.708} = 339 \text{ } \Omega \qquad \text{and} \qquad X_i' = \frac{240}{0.969} = 248 \text{ } \Omega \qquad (14.31)$$

**WHAT IF?**      What if you transform the parameters to the primary?[11]

**Short-circuit (SC) test.**      The combined winding resistance, $R_w$, and leakage reactance, $X_w$, in Fig. 14.12 are determined by shorting the low-voltage winding and exciting the high-voltage side at reduced voltage to produce the rated primary current, $I_p$. The primary voltage, $V_{sc}$, current, $I_{sc}$, and power, $P_c$, are measured; and $R_w$ and $X_w$ are determined as follows:

$$I_{sc}^2 R_w = P_c \implies R_w = \frac{P_c}{I_{sc}^2} \qquad (14.32)$$

and

$$\frac{V_{sc}}{I_{sc}} = \sqrt{R_w^2 + X_w^2} \implies X_w = \sqrt{(V_{sc}/I_{sc})^2 - R_w^2} \qquad (14.33)$$

Performing the SC test at rated current ensures that the measured power is the copper loss of the transformer under nameplate conditions because the flux levels and hence iron losses are extremely low at the reduced voltage.

---

**EXAMPLE 14.6**   **SC test**

The 10-kVA, 2400/240-V, 60-Hz, single-phase transformer in the previous example has the 240-V winding shorted. It is found that 72.0 V on the 2400-V winding produces the rated current of 4.17 A with an input power of 162 W. Find $R_w$ and $X_w$.

**SOLUTION:**
Using Eq. (14.32),

$$R_w = \frac{162}{(4.17)^2} = 9.32 \text{ } \Omega \qquad (14.34)$$

and using Eq. (14.33),

$$X_w = \sqrt{(72.0/4.17)^2 - (9.32)^2} = 14.5 \text{ } \Omega \qquad (14.35)$$

---

[11] The (turns ratio)$^2$ is $(10)^2$, so 33.9 kΩ and 24.8 kΩ.

**Equivalent Circuits**

**Summary.** The OC/SC test determines the series and parallel components in the transformer model. Voltage, current, and power measurements are made. Figure 14.13 shows the equivalent circuit derived in the previous three examples.

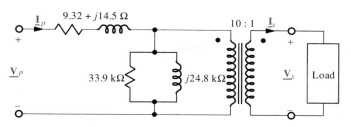

**Figure 14.13** Model for 10-kVA, 2400/240-V transformer derived from the OC/SC tests.

**Transformer calculations.** The equivalent-circuit model of a transformer permits the calculation of transformer efficiency and voltage regulation. Exact calculations may be made based upon load power and power factor, PF, requirements, but approximate calculations are usually adequate.

**Efficiency.** The efficiency of the transformer is based on the power passing through the transformer and its losses.

$$\eta = \frac{P_{out}}{P_{in}} = \frac{P_{out}}{P_{out} + P_c + P_i} \tag{14.36}$$

where $\eta$ is the efficiency, usually given in percent. The output power is determined by the load requirements, and the transformer copper loss, $P_c$, and iron loss, $P_i$, can be derived from the equivalent circuit.

---

**EXAMPLE 14.7** | **Efficiency calculation**

The 10-kVA, 2400/240-V, 60-Hz, single-phase transformer in the previous examples, which is modeled by the equivalent circuit in Fig. 14.13 provides 8 kVA at 0.94 PF (lagging) and 230 V to a load. Find the transformer efficiency under these conditions.

**SOLUTION:**

The output power is $P_{out} = 8000 \times 0.94 = 7520$ W. The iron losses may be estimated from the nominal primary voltage and the parallel resistor in the equivalent circuit, $R_i = 33.9$ kΩ. The nominal primary voltage is derived from the secondary voltage and the turns ratio.

$$V_p = \frac{10}{1} \times 230 = 2300 \text{ V} \tag{14.37}$$

Hence, the iron loss is

$$P_i = \frac{(2300)^2}{33,900} = 156 \text{ W} \tag{14.38}$$

To estimate the copper losses, we need the nominal primary current:

$$I_s = \frac{8{,}000 \text{ VA}}{230 \text{ V}} = 34.8 \text{ A} \Rightarrow I_p = \frac{n_s}{n_p} \times I_s = \frac{1}{10} \times 34.8 = 3.48 \text{ A} \qquad (14.39)$$

to find the power in the series resistance, $R_w = 9.32 \ \Omega$:

$$P_c = (3.48)^2 \times 9.32 = 113 \text{ W} \qquad (14.40)$$

We use nominal and not exact primary voltage and current in these approximate calculations. From Eq. (14.36), we determine the approximate transformer efficiency to be

$$\eta = \frac{P_{out}}{P_{out} + P_c + P_i} = \frac{7520}{7520 + 113 + 156} = 0.965 \, (96.5\%) \qquad (14.41)$$

**WHAT IF?**     What if you calculate the exact efficiency based on a full analysis of the equivalent circuit in Fig. 14.13?[12]

**Voltage regulation.**     The percent regulation is defined as:

$$\% \text{ Reg} = \frac{V_s \,(\text{no load}) - V_s \,(\text{loaded})}{V_s \,(\text{loaded})} \times 100\% \qquad (14.42)$$

where $V_s$ (no load) is the magnitude of the secondary voltage with no load and $V_s$ (loaded) is the magnitude of the secondary voltage under given load conditions. If the primary voltage is constant, the no-load secondary voltage will be approximately

$$V_s \,(\text{no load}) \approx \frac{n_s}{n_p} \times V_p \qquad (14.43)$$

Thus, we need to use the equivalent circuit in Fig. 14.12 to calculate the primary voltage required to supply the specified secondary voltage and power.

Let $\underline{\mathbf{V}}_s$ and $\underline{\mathbf{I}}_s$ be the required phasor secondary voltage and current. Then KVL in the primary in Fig. 14.12 is

$$\underline{\mathbf{V}}_p = \frac{n_p}{n_s} \times \underline{\mathbf{V}}_s + \left( \frac{n_s}{n_p} \times \underline{\mathbf{I}}_s \right) \times (R_w + jX_w) \qquad (14.44)$$

where $\underline{\mathbf{V}}_p$ is the actual (not nominal) primary voltage and we have again ignored the exciting current, $\underline{\mathbf{I}}_e$.

---

[12] Then you are in for a lot of unnecessary work. The answer is still 96.5% to three-place precision.

**Percent regulation**

The 10-kVA, 2400/240-V, 60-Hz, single-phase transformer in the previous example, which is modeled by the equivalent circuit in Fig. 14.13, provides 8 kVA at 0.94 *PF* (lagging) and 230 V to a load. Find the percent regulation under these conditions.

**SOLUTION:**
For 8000 VA at 230 V with 0.94 *PF* lagging, the current is

$$\mathbf{I}_s = \frac{8,000}{230} \angle - \cos^{-1}(0.94) = 34.8 \angle - 20.0° \text{ A} \tag{14.45}$$

Using Eq. (14.44), we find the primary voltage to be

$$\mathbf{V}_p = \frac{10}{1} \times 230 \angle 0° + \left(\frac{34.8}{10} \angle - 20.0°\right) \times (9.32 + j14.5) = 2348 \angle 0.887° \text{ V} \tag{14.46}$$

The no-load secondary voltage is thus 2348/10 = 234.8 V. Thus, Eq. (14.42) gives the percent regulation:

$$\%\text{Reg} = \frac{234.8 - 230}{230} \times 100 = 2.09\% \tag{14.47}$$

## Why Voltage and Apparent Power (kVA) Rating Are on the Nameplate

**Voltage rating.**   Transformers are rated for a specific voltage and apparent power, kVA. The magnetic structure is designed for a specific maximum flux, which by Faraday's law implies a specific voltage rating because the frequency and number of turns are constant. To operate the transformer at a voltage considerably higher than the design value would give excessive losses and invite eventual failure. To operate at a lower voltage would underutilize the transformer.

**Apparent power rating.**   Transformers are rated for a specific apparent power because operating voltage and current determine transformer losses, which heat the transformer winding.   Excessive operating temperature of the transformer windings deteriorates wire insulation and hence reduces reliability and transformer lifetime. Thermal design, environment, and transformer loss combine to establish the apparent power limits of the transformer.

In addition to iron loss, we have copper losses in the primary and secondary windings; hence, the maximum current is limited likewise by the amount of heat the transformer can dissipate. Thus, the transformer is rated according to the product of rated voltage and rated current, or apparent power.

We may distinguish two apparent power limits:

1. The rated apparent power is the operating level that may be sustained under a worst-case thermal environment. For example, a small pole-hung transformer would be rated for a hot summer day, in full Sun and with no wind. These would be the

most severe conditions expected, and the transformer would be expected to perform satisfactorily under such conditions.

2. The actual limit for the transformer would depend on the operating conditions. For example, a transformer rated for conditions in Texas could be operated at higher levels of apparent power in Alaska. In a given application, the operating level of the transformer depends on the load and may be safely below the rated or actual limits of the transformer.

When transformers have multiple primary and/or secondary windings, the kVA rating is independent of the way in which the transformer is connected, as shown by the following example.

---

**EXAMPLE 14.9**  |  **Transformer connections**

Consider a 480:240/240:120 transformer with a 8.8-kVA rating. The voltage rating reveals that both primary and secondary have two identical windings, which may be connected in series or parallel. Find the individual winding voltages and currents for both connections at nameplate conditions.

**SOLUTION:**

Figure 14.14(a) shows the windings in series. The primary voltage is 480 V, the series connection of two 240-V windings, and the secondary voltage is 240 V. From the kVA rating, we calculate the primary current as 18.3 A and the secondary current as 36.7 A as shown.

Figure 14.14(b) shows the parallel connection of both windings. From the kVA calculation, we now have twice the current in primary and secondary, but with parallel connections, this current is divided between two windings to give the rated current in each winding, as shown.

---

**WHAT IF?**  |  What if primary is connected in series and secondary in parallel? What is the voltage and kVA rating in this configuration?[13]

---

**Summary.**  The magnetic structure in the previous example operates at the same flux level in both connections, and the currents in the individual windings are unchanged; hence, the losses for the two cases are identical. Similar results are obtained for three-phase transformer connections. Consequently, the transformer is rated according to its apparent power; the power factor and hence the real power flowing through the transformer are not directly a limiting factor.

## Models of Three-phase Transformers

**Three-phase transformers.**  Three-phase systems constitute the overwhelming majority of all power generation and distribution systems. Chapter 6 discussed the use of transformers in such systems. Transformation of three-phase power from one voltage

---

[13] The voltage ratio is 480/120 V and the kVA rating is unchanged.

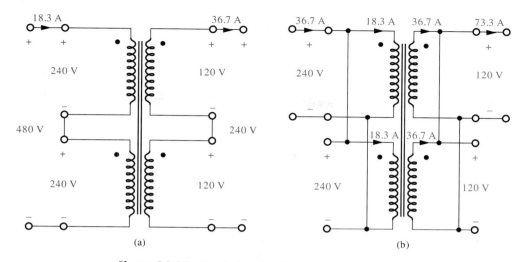

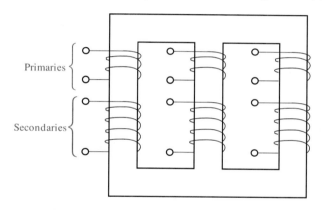

**Figure 14.14** (a) Windings in series; (b) windings in parallel.

**Figure 14.15** A three-phase transformer wound on a common magnetic structure.

level to another may be accomplished by three single-phase transformers or by one three-phase transformer. Figure 14.15 shows one possible configuration for a three-phase transformer.

A three-phase transformer is cheaper, smaller, and more efficient than three single-phase transformers, but the latter configuration is more versatile. For example, should a single transformer fail, only one transformer would have to be replaced, and in certain cases, the system could continue operation at reduced load until the replacement arrived.

**Per-phase equivalent circuit model for three-phase transformers.** Three-phase transformers, whether realized in a single unit or with three single-phase transformers, may be modeled by a per-phase equivalent circuit[14] identical to that shown in Fig. 14.12. In this case, all power quantities represent one-third the actual quantities, and voltages are reduced by $\sqrt{3}$ from three-phase values. The per-phase cir-

---

[14] Per-phase equivalent circuits are explained on page 275.

cuit represents transformer loss and energy storage and does not depend on whether windings are connected in wye or delta.

---

EXAMPLE 14.10 **Per-phase calculations**

A 2400/480-V, 60-kVA, 60-Hz, three-phase transformer is modeled by the equivalent circuit shown in Fig. 14.16. Find the efficiency of the transformer at nameplate kVA with 0.9 *PF*, lagging.

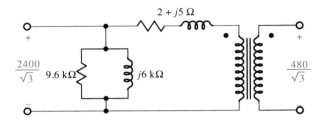

**Figure 14.16**   Per-phase model for a three-phase transformer.

**SOLUTION:**

Efficiency is given by Eq. (14.36), which may be applied to the entire transformer or to its per-phase representation. Choosing the former, we find the output power to be

$$P_{out} = S \times PF = 60,000 \times 0.9 = 54,000 \text{ W} \tag{14.48}$$

The iron loss per phase are represented by the parallel resistance in Fig. 14.16. Thus, the iron loss in the transformer is

$$P_i = 3 \times \frac{(2400/\sqrt{3})^2}{9600} = 600 \text{ W} \tag{14.49}$$

To find the copper loss, we must find the nominal current in the transformer primary. Equation (6.20) gives

$$I_p = \frac{S}{\sqrt{3}V} = \frac{60,000 \text{ VA}}{\sqrt{3} \times 2400 \text{ V}} = 14.4 \text{ A} \tag{14.50}$$

Because per-phase current levels are the same as the actual transformer, the nominal current in the 2-Ω series resistor in Fig. 14.16 is 14.4 A; hence, the copper loss in the three-phase transformer is

$$P_c = 3 \times (14.4)^2 \times 2 \text{ } \Omega = 1250 \text{ V} \tag{14.51}$$

As before, we multiply by 3 because the 2 Ω resistor is a per-phase resistance. Using Eq. (14.36), we find the efficiency to be

$$\eta = \frac{P_{out}}{P_{out} + P_c + P_i} = \frac{54,000}{54,000 + 1250 + 600} = 96.7\% \tag{14.52}$$

---

## Check Your Understanding

1. The basic laws describing the transformer are Coulomb's law, Ampère's circuital law, Faraday's law, and/or Ohm's law. Which two?

2. Many turns on a winding go with high or low voltage on a transformer? Which?

3. A transformer has 500 turns on the side connected to the power source and 25 turns on the side connected to the load. If the load requires 120 V, what should be the voltage of the power source?

4. A single-phase transformer has 300 turns on the side connected to the source of power and 27 turns on the side connected to the load. If the load requires 100 A, what would be the current capacity on the other side?

5. In the transformer circuit shown in Fig. 14.17, what do the following measure?
   (a) An ammeter in the secondary?
   (b) A voltmeter in the primary?
   (c) A voltmeter in the secondary?
   (d) A wattmeter in the primary?
   (e) A wattmeter in the secondary?

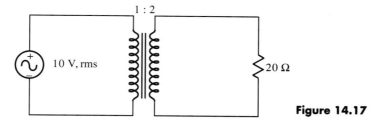

**Figure 14.17**

6. A 560-V rms, 20-kVA, three-phase transformer operates fully loaded with a power factor of 0.85, lagging.
   (a) What is the per-phase voltage?
   (b) What is the per-phase current?

*Answers.* (1) Ampère's circuital law and Faraday's law; (2) high voltage; (3) 2400 V; (4) 9.0 A; (5) (a) 1 A, (b) 10 V, (c) 20 V, (d) and (e) 20 W; (6) (a) 323 V, (b) 20.6 A.

## 14.3 FORCES IN MAGNETIC SYSTEMS

Figure 14.18 shows a magnetically driven mechanical actuator, which might operate a lock or ring a bell. The magnetic structure is iron, with a hinged member. The electrical input is produced by a coil with $n$ turns. Our goal in this section is to develop means for determining the magnitude and direction of the force produced by this electromechanical system.

### Magnetic-Pole Approach

Everyone has handled permanent magnets and knows about the magnetic compass. The properties of such can be described in terms of magnetic poles. We can use the concept of magnetic poles to build an intuitive understanding of the force in our actuator and to determine the direction of the force.

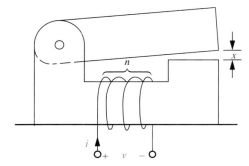

**Figure 14.18** A magnetic actuator.

**Relationship between magnetic poles and flux.** We already discussed magnetic poles and terrestrial magnetism on page 661 in defining the direction of a magnetic field. In speaking of a magnetic pole, we assume that there is a physical body, a piece of iron or perhaps the Earth, as shown in Fig. 14.19(a) with magnetic flux leaving or entering its surface. If magnetic flux is leaving the surface, as at the south *geographic* pole, we attribute this flux to the presence of a north *magnetic* pole within the surface, which is acting as a source for the flux. Alternatively, if flux lines are entering the surface, as at the north *geographic* pole, we attribute this flux to the presence of a south *magnetic* pole within the surface.

Because opposite poles attract and like poles repel, we can use the pole concept to determine the direction of forces and torques. Consider again the device in Fig. 14.18. If *i* is positive, then by the right-hand rule the direction of the magnetic flux is as shown in Fig. 14.19(b). The top member thus contains a north magnetic pole because *from the viewpoint of the gap* it produces the magnetic flux. Likewise, the bottom of the gap contains a south magnetic pole because the flux enters the bottom surface. We conclude that a force of attraction exists between the north and south magnetic poles, tending to close the gap. It is easily shown that the force is independent of the direction of the current.

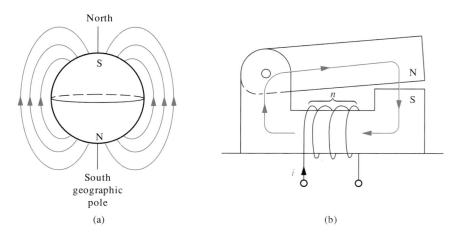

**Figure 14.19** (a) The Earth's magnetic poles and flux; (b) the actuator with magnetic poles shown.

**Conclusion.** This viewpoint gives us a qualitative understanding of the magnetic forces in the system but no quantitative information. Soon we will develop a method, based on conservation of energy, that gives both qualitative and quantitative information, albeit at the cost of some abstraction.

## Analysis from Current–Flux Interaction

In Eq. (13.18), we presented Ampère's force law for the force per meter on a current-carrying conductor in a magnetic flux:

$$\vec{f} = \vec{i} \times \vec{B} \text{ N/m} \tag{14.53}$$

This expression may be used to determine the force on a system of current-carrying conductors, as in a motor, if the magnetic flux density and currents are known. However, magnetic structures such as shown in Fig. 14.19(b) do not permit force calculation by Eq. (14.53) because the force is produced by magnetic dipoles in the magnetic material.

**Conservation of Energy**

## Analysis from Energy Considerations

**Modeling an electromechanical transducer.** The basic approach of this section is suggested in Fig. 14.20. Here we model the actuator with an electrical input, and we include resistive losses as part of the electrical part of the system. The electrical circuit terminates into a box labeled "ideal transducer." The ideal transducer is assumed to be lossless. Thus, it stores magnetic energy, which can be returned to the electrical circuit, and converts the remainder of the input electrical energy to mechanical energy. The output of the transducer is a developed force and a mechanical displacement. We show the developed mechanical energy going into another box representing mechanical losses, and output energy; but this box does not concern us here. We consider only the conversion of electrical into mechanical energy in the middle box and, from the conservation of energy, determine the developed mechanical force.

**OBJECTIVE 4**

**To understand how to calculate the magnetic force in a magnetic structure**

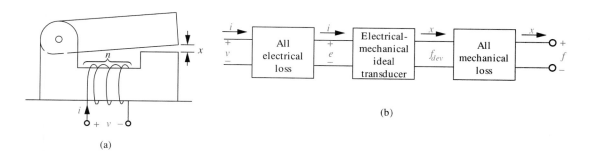

(a)

(b)

**Figure 14.20**   (a) A magnetic transducer; (b) a model for energy analysis.

**Equivalent Circuits**

**Electrical model.** Figure 14.21 models the actuator electrically. We separate the copper loss from the magnetic energy storage in the inductance. The emf, $e$, produced by the changing inductance flux linkages, $\lambda$, represents electrical energy entering the magnetic system.

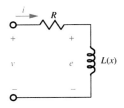

**Analysis.** Our assumptions and the conservation of energy require that the input electrical energy into the ideal transducer is either stored or converted to mechanical energy. Equation (14.54) expresses conservation of energy on an incremental scale:

$$\underbrace{ei\,dt}_{\substack{\text{electrical}\\\text{energy}\\\text{in}}} = \underbrace{dW_m(\lambda, x)}_{\substack{\text{increase}\\\text{in stored}\\\text{energy}}} + \underbrace{f_{dev}(\lambda, x)\,dx}_{\substack{\text{mechanical}\\\text{energy out}}} \tag{14.54}$$

**Figure 14.21** Electrical model for the actuator.

where $e$ is the emf, $dW_m(\lambda, x)$ is the stored magnetic energy as a function of flux linkage and mechanical displacement, and $f_{dev}$ is the magnetic force developed on the mechanical system. Faraday's law requires

**Conservation of Energy**

$$e\,dt = \frac{d\lambda}{dt}dt = d\lambda \tag{14.55}$$

Hence Eqs. (14.54) and (14.55) combine to

$$i\,d\lambda = dW_m(\lambda, x) + f_{dev}(\lambda, x)dx \tag{14.56}$$

Subject to certain mathematical assumptions to be discussed in what follows, the incremental stored energy change must satisfy the chain rule of calculus:

$$dW_m(\lambda, x) = \underbrace{\frac{\partial W_m(\lambda, x)}{\partial \lambda}}_{x = \text{constant}} d\lambda + \underbrace{\frac{\partial W_m(\lambda, x)}{\partial x}}_{\lambda = \text{constant}} dx \tag{14.57}$$

But Eq. (14.56) can be rearranged to the form

$$dW_m(\lambda, x) = i(\lambda, x)d\lambda - f_{dev}(\lambda, x)dx \tag{14.58}$$

Because Eqs. (14.57) and (14.58) are valid for arbitrary $d\lambda$ and $dx$, the coefficients of $d\lambda$ and $dx$ must be equal:

$$i(\lambda, x) = \underbrace{\frac{\partial W_m(\lambda, x)}{\partial \lambda}}_{x = \text{constant}} \quad \text{and} \quad f_{dev}(\lambda, x) = -\underbrace{\frac{\partial W_m(\lambda, x)}{\partial x}}_{\lambda = \text{constant}} \tag{14.59}$$

The second equation in Eq. (14.59) gives the developed magnetic force as a function of the stored energy.

**Stored-energy-state function.** We can determine the stored magnetic-energy-state function, $W_m(\lambda, x)$, by integrating Eq. (14.56), provided we keep $x$ constant ($dx = 0$). Thus, our strategy is to start with a system with no energy storage, move $x$ to the position at which we want to know the force (say, $x = 1$ mm), and then integrate the electrical energy input as we energize the system electrically. This determines the magnetic stored energy as

$$W_m(\lambda, x) = \int_0^\lambda \underbrace{i(\lambda', x)}_{x = \text{fixed}} d\lambda' \tag{14.60}$$

where $\lambda'$ is a dummy variable for integration.

---

**EXAMPLE 14.11** | **Stored energy**

Determine the state function for the stored magnetic energy of the system shown in Fig. 14.20(a).

**SOLUTION:**

Consider $x$ as a constant throughout the following development. The total flux is given by Eq. (14.12):

$$\Phi = \frac{ni}{\mathfrak{R}_i + \mathfrak{R}_g(x)} \text{ Wb} \tag{14.61}$$

where the reluctances of iron and gap are

$$\mathfrak{R}_i = \frac{\ell_i}{\mu_i A_i} \qquad \text{and} \qquad \mathfrak{R}_g(x) = \frac{x}{\mu_0 A_g} \tag{14.62}$$

Note that the mechanical displacement enters the analysis through its effect on the reluctance of the gap. The flux linkage is derived from Eq. (14.9)

$$\lambda = n\Phi = \frac{n^2 i}{\mathfrak{R}_i + \mathfrak{R}_g(x)} \text{ Wb-t} \tag{14.63}$$

Because Eq. (14.60) requires the current as a function of flux linkage, we rearrange Eq. (14.63) to the form

$$i(\lambda, x) = \frac{1}{n^2}[\mathfrak{R}_i + \mathfrak{R}_g(x)]\lambda \tag{14.64}$$

and integrate:

$$W_m(\lambda, x) = \int_0^\lambda i(\lambda', x)\, d\lambda' = \frac{1}{n^2}[\mathfrak{R}_i + \mathfrak{R}_g(x)]\int_0^\lambda \lambda'\, d\lambda'$$

$$= \frac{1}{2n^2}[\mathfrak{R}_i + \mathfrak{R}_g(x)]\lambda^2 \tag{14.65}$$

---

**Force determination.** Equation (14.60) gives the energy-state function required for calculating the force. To compute the developed force, Eq. (14.59) requires that we take the partial derivative of $W_m(\lambda, x)$ with respect to $x$, with $\lambda$ held constant.

$$f_{dev}(\lambda, x) = -\frac{\partial W_m(\lambda, x)}{\partial x}\Bigg|_{\lambda = \text{constant}} \tag{14.66}$$

Equation (14.66) gives the force on the mechanical system as a function of the flux linkage.

---

**EXAMPLE 14.12** **Force calculation**

Compute the force on the actuator in Fig. 14.20(a).

**SOLUTION:**
Equation (14.66) requires that we take the partial derivative of $W_m(\lambda, x)$ with respect to $x$, with $\lambda$ held constant. Using the results from the previous example, Eq. (14.65), we find

$$f_{dev} = -\frac{\partial}{\partial x}\frac{1}{2n^2}\left[\mathfrak{R}_i + \frac{x}{\mu_0 A g}\right]\lambda^2 = -\frac{\lambda^2}{2n^2\mu_0 A_g} \tag{14.67}$$

Equation (14.67) gives the force on the mechanical system as a function of the flux linkage.

**WHAT IF?** What if we wish to have the force as a function of the current? [15]

---

**Torque in rotational systems.** Clearly, this theory can be adapted to a rotational system, such as shown in Fig. 14.22. Specifically, $W_m(\lambda, x)$ becomes $W_m(\lambda, \theta)$, and the torque is

$$T_{dev}(\lambda, \theta) = -\frac{\partial W_m(\lambda, \theta)}{\partial \theta}\Bigg|_{\lambda = \text{constant}} \tag{14.68}$$

where $T_{dev}(\lambda, \theta)$ represents the developed torque. In this case, the dependence of the reluctance on $\theta$ becomes the important factor.

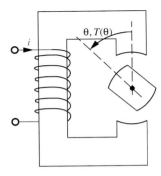

**Figure 14.22** A magnetic structure involving rotation.

---

[15] We may reintroduce Eq. (14.63) to yield $f_{dev} = -(ni)^2/[\mathfrak{R}_i + \mathfrak{R}_g(x)]^2 \times (1/2\mu_0 A_g)$.

**Discussion of examples.**   The minus sign means that the force is directed opposite to the direction of increasing $x$ and tends therefore to decrease $x$ to close the gap. This we anticipated from the argument based on magnetic poles. If the flux linkage is prescribed,[16] the force is independent of the gap width.

**Constant-current excitation.**   The form of the force with constant-current excitation is given in footnote 15. The force depends on the square of the mmf. To see how the force depends on the width of the gap, we assume that the reluctance of the iron is negligible compared with the reluctance of the gap. Under this assumption, the developed force, $f_{dev}$, reduces to

$$f_{dev} = -\frac{1}{2}\frac{(ni)^2}{(x/\mu_0 A_g)^2}\frac{1}{\mu_0 A_g} = -\frac{(ni)^2\mu_0 A_g}{2x^2} \tag{14.69}$$

and hence the force varies as the inverse square of the gap width.

**Zero gap?**   Although Eq. (14.69) leads to infinite forces as $x$ approaches zero, this is unrealistic for two reasons. For one, the gap cannot have zero width because of surface roughness; hence, a minimum effective value of $x$ exists. Also the finite permeability of the iron limits the force. If we were to determine the maximum force, we would have to consider carefully the properties of the iron, both the finite value of permeability and also the saturation effects.

**Mathematical and physical assumptions.**   The assumptions underlying the derivation of Eqs. (14.60) and (14.66) are as follows:

- The magnetic system must be lossless. Because most magnetic systems do have some loss, this assumption weakens the analysis slightly, meaning that the accuracy of the results is compromised by magnetic losses.

- The stored energy must be zero if the current or flux linkage is zero. This assumption rules out forces due to permanent magnets.[17]

- Only magnetic energy is stored in the system. This means no capacitors or springs can be hidden in the system, and velocities have to be small. This is no problem, because we are dealing with known systems and virtual displacements.

- The stored-energy function must be a single-valued state function. This requires that the stored energy depends only on the final value of $\lambda$ and $x$, and not on how the system is energized. Because most magnetic systems exhibit some hysteresis, this assumption also weakens the analysis.

- The requirements that flux linkage be constant corresponds, by Eq. (13.24), to $e = 0$, but this is a requirement of the mathematical form, not the physical excitation. The force depends only upon the state of the excitation; the $dx$'s and $d\lambda$'s are mental, not physical, changes.

---

[16] As in Example 14.3.

[17] For an analysis that includes permanent magnets,   see *Electrical Machines, 5th ed.*, A. E. Fitzgerald, Charles Kingsley, Jr., and Stephen D. Umans, New York: Mc-Graw Hill, pp. 32f.

**Summary.** We derived and applied an expression for the force developed in a magnetic system. The formula is based upon the conservation of energy and the mathematical properties of the energy-state function.

## Coenergy and Magnetic Force

**Changing** $\lambda \to i$. The requirement that energy and force be expressed in terms of flux linkage is inconvenient because flux linkage is difficult to measure and control in a circuit. For this reason, we now develop a modification of the analysis based upon a change of electrical variables and the concept of magnetic coenergy. We change variables beginning with a basic rule of calculus:

$$d(i\lambda) = id\lambda + \lambda di \implies id\lambda = d(i\lambda) - \lambda di \tag{14.70}$$

In the transformation, $W_m(\lambda, x)$ is merely changed to $W_m(i, x)$ symbolically. After some rearrangement, Eq. (14.56), which expresses conservation of energy, becomes

$$d[i\lambda - W_m(i, x)] = \lambda(i, x) di + f_{dev}(i, x) dx \tag{14.71}$$

**coenergy**

We now define a new type of energy function called the *coenergy*, $W'_m(i, x)$, as

$$W'_m(i, x) = i\lambda(i, x) - W_m(i, x) \tag{14.72}$$

and thus Eq. (14.71) becomes

$$dW'_m(i,x) = \lambda(i, x) di + f_{dev}(i, x) dx \tag{14.73}$$

The chain rule of calculus requires

$$dW'_m(i, x) = \underbrace{\frac{\partial W'_m(i, x)}{\partial i}}_{x\, =\, \text{constant}} di + \underbrace{\frac{\partial W'_m(i, x)}{\partial x}}_{i\, =\, \text{constant}} dx \tag{14.74}$$

Equations (14.73) and (14.74), which must be valid for arbitrary $di$ and $dx$, require

$$\lambda(i, x) = \underbrace{\frac{\partial W'_m(i, x)}{\partial i}}_{x\, =\, \text{constant}} \quad \text{and} \quad f_{dev}(i, x) = + \underbrace{\frac{\partial W'_m(i, x)}{\partial x}}_{i\, =\, \text{constant}} \tag{14.75}$$

**Force determination.** We determine the force by the same procedure as before. First, hold $x$ constant and calculate the coenergy by integrating Eq. (14.73):

$$W'_m(i, x) = \int_0^i \lambda(i', x) di' \tag{14.76}$$

and then calculate the developed force from Eq.(14.75):

$$f_{dev}(i, x) = + \frac{\partial W'_m(i, x)}{\partial x}\bigg|_{i\, =\, \text{constant}} \tag{14.77}$$

| EXAMPLE 14.13 | Force calculation using coenergy |
|---|---|

Find the force in the magnetic structure in Fig. 14.20(a) using coenergy.

**SOLUTION:**

The flux linkage is given by Eq. (14.63). Thus, the coenergy function is

$$W'_m(i,x) = \int_0^i \lambda(i',x)\,di' = \frac{n^2 i^2}{2[\Re_i + \Re_g(x)]} \tag{14.78}$$

Equation (14.77) gives the force as

$$
\begin{aligned}
f_{dev} &= +\frac{\partial W'_m(i,x)}{\partial x} = -\frac{(ni)^2}{2[\Re_i + \Re_g(x)]^2}\frac{\partial \Re_g(x)}{\partial x} \\
&= -\frac{(ni)^2}{2\mu_0 A_g[\Re_i + \Re_g(x)]^2}
\end{aligned} \tag{14.79}
$$

This is the same answer as in footnote 15.

**Conservation of Energy**

**What is coenergy?** Mathematically, coenergy is the function calculated by Eq. (14.76). Graphically, coenergy is the area under the $\lambda$–$i$ curve, as shown in Fig. 14.23(a). But these answers do not explain coenergy. Let us begin with the question, "What is energy?" The answer is not obvious; certainly, many brilliant minds pondered the physical creation before coming on the concept of energy and postulating its conservation. Our frequent use of the concept of energy has perhaps dulled us to its abstract quality.

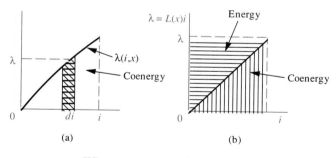

(a)     (b)

**Figure 14.23**  (a) Coenergy is the area under the curve; (b) for a linear magnetic system, energy and coenergy are equal.

**energy**    Whatever we say about energy from a physical point of view, *energy* is a descriptor of a system that has useful conceptual and mathematical properties. Conservation of energy leads to important relationships between variables, sometimes allows shortcuts in an analysis, and usually gives insight into the operation of a physical system. In the present context, for example, conservation of energy allows us to calculate the magnetically generated force on a mechanical system.

Similarly, coenergy is a mathematical function with useful properties. Here coenergy gives us an alternative means to compute the magnetically generated force. But as a basic principle of science, coenergy has minor importance compared with energy.

Energy is the area above the $\lambda$–$i$ curve, Fig. 13.17, and coenergy is the area below the curve in Fig. 14.23(a). Energy and coenergy are equal when we have a linear relationship between $\lambda$ and $i$, as in Fig. 14.23(b). This is the case that follows, where we apply these ideas to circuit theory.

## Circuit Approach

From an electrical point of view, the mechanical actuator pictured in Fig. 14.20(a) is simply an inductor, as shown in Fig. 14.21. The inductance depends on the reluctance of the magnetic structure,[18] which depends on $x$, the width of the gap. Thus, we may write the flux linkage, $\lambda = L(x)i$, where $L(x)$ is the inductance as a function of the mechanical variable, and the coenergy is thus

$$W'_m(i,x) = \int_0^i L(x)i'\,di' = \tfrac{1}{2}L(x)i^2 \tag{14.80}$$

The force is

$$f_{dev} = \partial W'_m(i,x) = \frac{1}{2}i^2\frac{dL(x)}{dx} \tag{14.81}$$

For an ac current, the time-average force is determined from the time average of the square of the ac current, which is by definition the square of the rms current:

$$\langle f_{dev}\rangle = \frac{1}{2}\langle i(t)^2\rangle\frac{dL(x)}{dt} = \frac{1}{2}I_e^2\frac{dL(x)}{dx} \tag{14.82}$$

where $<\,>$ denotes the time average and $I_e$ is the effective value of the current.

---

**EXAMPLE 14.14** **Rotational transducer**

The rotational magnetic structure in Fig. 14.22 has $n$ turns and a reluctance that depends on angle as

$$\Re(\theta_m) = \frac{\Re_o}{|\theta_m| + 0.01} \tag{14.83}$$

where $0 < |\theta_m| < 0.2$ radians. The structure is excited by an ac current $i(t) = I_p\cos(\omega t)$. Find the time-average torque at $\theta_m = 0.1$ radian.

**SOLUTION:**
The inductance for $\theta_m > 0$ is

---

[18] See Eq. (14.14).

$$L(\theta_m) = \frac{n^2}{\mathfrak{R}(\theta_m)} = \frac{n^2}{\mathfrak{R}_o}(\theta_m + 0.01) \qquad (14.84)$$

Adapting Eq. (14.82) for rotational motion,

$$\langle T_{dev} \rangle = \frac{1}{2}\left(\frac{I_p}{\sqrt{2}}\right)^2 \frac{d}{d\theta_m}\left[\frac{n^2}{\mathfrak{R}_o}(\theta_m + 0.01)\right] = \frac{n^2 I_p^2}{4\mathfrak{R}_o} \qquad (14.85)$$

Thus, the torque is independent of angle for $0 < |\theta_m| < 0.2$ radian.

> **WHAT IF?**
>
> What if $\theta_m = -0.1$ radian?[19]

**Where is the magnetic energy?**   As Eq. (14.65) implies, the total magnetic energy divides between iron and the gap in proportion to the reluctances. Because the relative permeability for iron is so large, most of the magnetic energy is stored in the air gap, even though the volume of the gap is relatively small.

### Check Your Understanding

1. In a magnetic system in which the reluctance of the magnetic structure decreases with increasing $x$, does the magnetic force tend to increase or decrease $x$?

2. The sum of the energy and coenergy of a magnetic system is constant if the current into the system is constant, even if a mechanical part of the magnetic structure is moved. True or false?

*Answers.* (**1**) Increase; (**2**) false.

## CHAPTER SUMMARY

In this chapter, we apply the physical laws from Chapter 13 to magnetic structures. We analyze the electrical transformer and present equivalent circuit models based on these laws, supplemented with reasoning based on energy considerations. We derive expressions for magnetically generated forces and torques in magnetic structures that have movable members.

The energy in a magnetic system is stored in the space comprising that system, primarily in the gaps. We visualize the magnetic fields as exerting a stress on the material and the space, and hence being the vehicle for force and energy storage. This analysis is applied in the next chapter, where we determine the torque developed in a cylindrical magnetic structure.

**Objective 1: To understand the function and analysis of magnetic structures.**   The function of a magnetic structure is to increase the amount of magnetic flux and to direct its path through space. The analysis of a magnetic structure is based on Ampère's circuital law and leads to the definition of reluctance as the ratio between

---

[19] $\langle T_{dev} \rangle = -n^2 I_p^2 / 4\mathfrak{R}_o$.

magnetomotive force and the flux in the system. The inductance is determined by the reluctance and the number of turns in the coil driving the system.

**Objective 2: To understand the physical basis for transformer models.** A transformer consists of two or more coils tightly coupled by a magnetic structure. The voltage ratio of an ideal transformer is derived from Faraday's law, and the current ratio is derived from Ampère's circuital law. Real transformers have stray and magnetizing flux, iron losses, and winding resistance.

**Objective 3: To understand how to derive a transformer equivalent circuit from open-circuit/short-circuit measurements and use it to calculate the efficiency and percent regulation.** A transformer equivalent circuit model includes, in addition to an ideal transformer, resistors to represent iron and copper loss and inductors to represent stray and magnetizing flux. The circuit elements in the equivalent circuit can be determined by voltage, current, and power measurements on the transformer with the output open and, with reduced voltage, with the output shorted.

**Objective 4: To understand how to calculate the magnetic force in a magnetic structure.** Among the various methods for calculating forces in magnetic structures, a method based on virtual displacement is the most general. In this method, the energy of the system is calculated as a function of the flux linkage and the mechanical variable, and then the force or torque is determined as the partial derivative with respect to the mechanical variable with flux linkage constant. An alternative method uses the coenergy function in a similar procedure.

In Chapter 15, we apply the principles of Chapter 14 to cylindrical structures to determine flux and torque related to motor operation.

## PROBLEMS

## Section 14.1: Analysis of Magnetic Structures

14.1. A toroidal inductor has a circular cross-section and the dimensions shown in Fig. P14.1, and no gap. Assume $\mu_r = 6000$ and $H$ is constant in the iron.

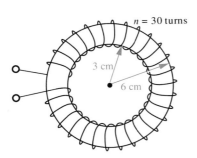

**Figure P14.1**

Use the average radius for computing the path length. Find the inductance.

14.2. The iron structure shown in Fig. P14.2 has a relative permeability of 2500. The structure has a winding (not shown) of 1500 turns.
   (a) Find the reluctance of the iron structure.
   (b) Find the stored energy in the system if excited at a steady value of $B = 1.1$ T.

14.3. A lossless toroidal inductor with a gap is represented in Fig. P14.3. The reluctances of the iron and air gap are 10,000 and 100,000 A-t/Wb, respectively.
   (a) If $i = 1$ A dc, what is the flux in the system?
   (b) Under these conditions, an electron passes through the gap traveling outward from the center. What would be the effect on its

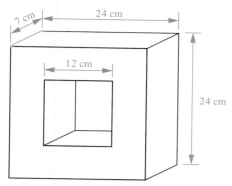

**Figure P14.2**

motion?

(c) If $i = 1$ A (rms) ac at 60 Hz, what would be the rms voltage per turn in the coil?

(d) What is the impedance of the inductor at 60 Hz?

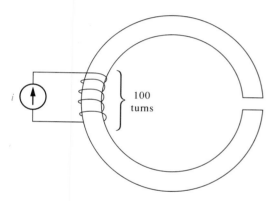

**Figure P14.3**

14.4. A 12-V (rms), 60-Hz electrical relay has 1000 turns and draws 12 mA (rms) of current. Assume that the relay magnetic system acts as a linear inductor, and neglect resistance.

(a) What is the mmf operating in the magnetic structure?

(b) What is the peak flux in the relay?

(c) What is the reluctance in the magnetic structure?

14.5. An iron ring weighing 3.65 kg and having a relative permeability of 5000 has some wire wrapped around it and is excited by an ideal ac voltage source. The current is measured. A small gap is then cut in the ring, and the current is

observed to increase by a factor of 10. How much do the filings weigh? The density of iron is 7.65 g/cm$^3$.

14.6. An inductor is shown in Fig. P14.6.

(a) What is the reluctance of the iron path?

(b) A 60-Hz ac voltage of 120 V rms is applied to the coil input. What is the maximum of the magnetic flux in the iron?

(c) What is the rms current required to supply this flux?

(d) The iron hysteresis and eddy-current losses are found to be 15 W. Give a parallel equivalent circuit for the inductor that accounts for the loss and energy storage.

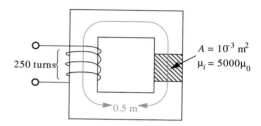

**Figure P14.6**

14.7. The ferrite toroid shown in Fig. P14.7 has a circular cross-section, an ID of 6 mm, an OD of 8 mm, and $\mu_i = 1600\mu_0$. The inductance is maximized by winding No. 32 wire (diameter = 8 mils = $8 \times 10^{-3}$ inches) in the hole until the inner hole of the toroid is completely filled.

(a) Estimate the inductance.

(b) The inductor is constructed according to the procedure given and the inductance is measured. The measured value is found to be only 60% of the required value. The inductor is redesigned by physically scaling up the toroid by a factor $x$ ($x =$ scaling factor > 1) but keeping the wire diameter the same, as in Fig. P14.7(b). Estimate $x$ to give the correct inductance.

14.8. A toroidal inductor is wound for maximum inductance by filling the "hole of the donut" totally with wire. The inductance is found to be 200% of the required value, so it is decided to make a smaller inductor. If the same wire is used and again the hole is filled, determine the scaling factor to make the new scaled-down version have the required inductance.

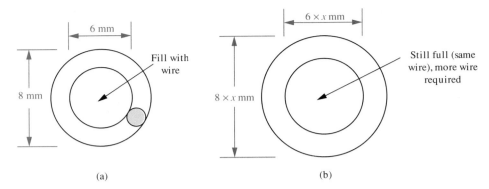

(a)                                                  (b)

**Figure P14.7**

14.9. An iron ring with a relative permeability of 2000 has a coil with $n$ turns wound on it. The inductance of the structure is measured at 60 mH. Give the new inductance as the following changes are made one at a time (and then restored before the next change).
(a) The number of turns is changed to $n/2$.
(b) The relative permeability increases to 4000.
(c) The entire structure is scaled up in every dimension by 25%, but the number of turns is constant.
(d) The windings are replaced by wires with half the original diameter, but the number of turns remains at $n$.

(e) We cut a gap in the iron such that 0.5% of the path length is now an air gap.

14.10. An iron-core inductor has a length of 0.5 m, a cross-sectional area of 0.01 m², and is wound with 100 turns of No. 23 wire, which has 20.4 $\Omega$/1000 ft. The density of the iron is 7.65 g/cm³. The loss in the iron is 1 watt/kilogram at a maximum flux density of 1.4 tesla and is proportional to flux squared. The inductor is excited at 250 V rms, 60 Hz. Find the iron and copper losses and, from these, a circuit model that is valid at 60 Hz. Ignore flux that escapes the iron, and assume the ac resistance is 10% higher than the dc. Let $\mu_i = 6000\mu_0$.

## Section 14.2: Electrical Transformers

14.11. Figure P14.11 shows an ideal magnetic structure ($\mu_i = \infty$), which thus becomes an ideal transformer, except that it has two secondaries, each with a resistor attached.
(a) Mark polarity dots on the two secondaries.
(b) Determine the equivalent resistance into the primary. *Hint:* Use fundamental laws.

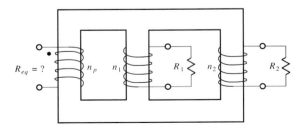

**Figure P14.11**

14.12. Figure P14.12 shows an ideal magnetic structure ($\mu_i = \infty$), which thus becomes an ideal transformer, except that it has two secondaries, each with a resistor attached.
(a) Mark polarity dots on the two secondaries.
(b) Determine the equivalent resistance into the primary. *Hint:* Use fundamental laws.

14.13. A transformer has 1000 primary turns and 100 secondary turns. The reluctance of the magnetic structure is $\Re = 10^5$ A-t/Wb. Assume no leakage flux, no iron losses, and ignore wire resistance.
(a) If the primary voltage is 120 V, 60 Hz, and the secondary is open-circuited, how much current will flow in the primary?
(b) If the secondary has a resistance of 30 $\Omega$ connected to it, what will be the current in the resistor?

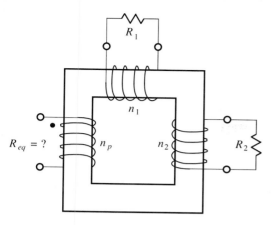

**Figure P14.12**

**(c)** For the circuit in part (b), what would be the magnitude of the current in the primary?

**14.14.** Figure P14.14 shows the approximate model for a nominal 880/220-V, 60-Hz, single-phase transformer with all internal impedances referred to the primary.

**(a)** What term(s) in the model account for the following:
  **i.** Secondary copper losses?
  **ii.** Magnetic energy stored in the iron?
  **iii.** Faraday's law?
  **iv.** Magnetic energy stored in the primary leakage fields?
  **v.** Core losses due to eddy currents and hysteresis losses?

**(b)** If the transformer heat exchanger is capable of dissipating 300 W without undue temperature rise, estimate the rated kVA of the transformer.

**(c)** What would be the approximate efficiency at rated kVA if the output power factor were 0.92?

**14.15.** A 2400/120-V, 30-kVA, 60-Hz single-phase transformer draws 2 kVA at a 0.2 power factor

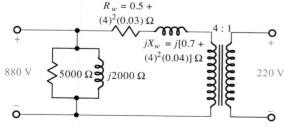

**Figure P14.14**

(lagging) at a no load. The series winding resistance and reactance due to stray inductance are $3.5 + j5.0\ \Omega$, referred to the primary.

**(a)** Determine the equivalent circuit for the transformer.

**(b)** Estimate the efficiency of the transformer if it serves a 30-kVA load at a 0.9 power factor (lagging) with rated secondary voltage.

**(c)** Estimate the voltage regulation under these load conditions.

**14.16.** Consider a 60-Hz, single-phase transformer with the following specifications: Core: area $= 0.1\ m^2$, length 2 m, $\mu_r = 5000$; windings: 150 primary and 15 secondary turns; coil impedances: primary $= 0.5 + j0.8\ \Omega$; secondary $= 0.005 + j0.008\ \Omega$; Allowable losses: 4000 W, divided equally between iron and windings. Also, we know that for 2000-W loss in the iron, the maximum magnetic flux density is $B_m = 1.4$ T.

**(a)** Find the allowable kVA for the transformer.

**(b)** Determine the equivalent circuit for the transformer.

**14.17.** Two coils are wound on a piece of iron, as shown in Fig. P14.17. A 120-V, 60-Hz source is connected to one of the coils and a 10-$\Omega$ resistor to the other.

**(a)** Put polarity marks on the resistor such that the voltages on both coils are in phase.

**(b)** Draw an equivalent circuit without using an ideal transformer that permits calculation of in-phase and out-of-phase components of the input current. Ignore iron and copper losses and leakage inductance.

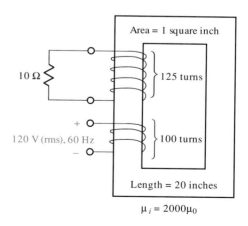

**Figure P14.17**

**(c)** In this situation, are the coils attracted or repelled by the currents in the wires? Explain.

**14.18.** A 72-VA, 60-Hz, single-phase transformer has an equivalent circuit shown in Fig. P14.18.

**(a)** What is the no-load current if excited on the 120-V side?

**(b)** Estimate the losses in the transformer at full load, resistive load.

**(c)** Estimate the input voltage required for full load if the output voltage is 36 V and the output current lags the voltage by 25°.

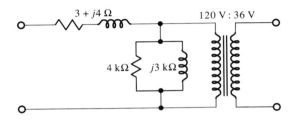

**Figure P14.18**

**14.19.** A 60-Hz, single-phase, iron-core transformer with $\mu_i = 4200\mu_0$, area $= 0.05$ m², and nominal length of 2 m has 1000 turns on the high-voltage (HV) and 200 turns on the low-voltage (LV) side. At the rated voltage, the peak flux density in the iron is 1.2 tesla.

**(a)** Find the rated voltage (rms value) at both the HV and LV sides.

**(b)** What rms magnetizing current is required on the HV side?

**(c)** The rated current in the transformer is 50 A on the HV side. The losses at rated current are 3000 watts. Give an equivalent circuit for the transformer, neglecting iron losses and leakage inductance.

**14.20.** Figure P14.20 shows a 20-kVA, single-phase, 8600/240-V (center-tapped), 60-Hz, pole transformer.

**(a)** What is in the cylinder physically and what is the electrical model for it? No values are required.

**(b)** At rated load and unity power factor, the iron losses are 4% and the copper losses 6% of the output power. What does that tell you about the equivalent circuit? Refer to the high-voltage side.

**(c)** Find the input real power if we have 5 kVA at $PF = 1$, lagging, between $A$ and $N$, 3 kVA at

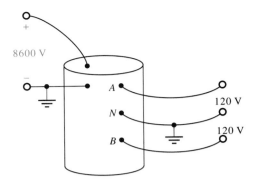

**Figure P14.20**

$PF = 0.75$, lagging, between $B$ and $N$, and 6 kVA at $PF = 0.95$, lagging, between $A$ and $B$.

**(d)** Discuss the kVA limits of the transformer for New Year's Day in Detroit.

**14.21.** A 50-kVA, 2300/230-V, 60-Hz, single-phase transformer has an iron structure 0.03 m² in area, 1 m in length, and $\mu_i = 3000\mu_0$. The peak flux density in the iron is 0.6 T. With no load and rated voltage, the input current on the high-voltage side is 0.3 A, rms.

**(a)** Estimate the turns on the high-voltage and low-voltage windings.

**(b)** Find the dc current required on the high-voltage side to magnetize the iron to 1.2 T, assuming no saturation occurs.

**(c)** Estimate the iron loss at rated voltage.

**(d)** Estimate the current magnitude, rms, on the high-voltage side with full output kVA and rated voltage at $PF = 1$.

**14.22.** An open-circuit (OC)/short-circuit (SC) test is performed on a single-phase transformer in the standard manner, with the results in Table P14.22 Quantities not measured are noted "NM."

**TABLE P14.22**

| Quantity | OC Side 1 | OC Side 2 | SC Side 1 | SC Side 2 |
|---|---|---|---|---|
| Voltage, V | 7500 | 240 | 372 | 0, NM |
| Current, A | 0, NM | 3.62 | 2 | NM |
| Power, W | NM | 290 | 245 | NM |

**(a)** What is the transformer apparent power rating?

**(b)** Give an equivalent circuit for the transformer, referred to the HV side.

**(c)** Find the magnetizing current, $I_\phi$, if excited on the high-voltage side

**(d)** Estimate the transformer efficiency if supplying 12 kVA at $PF = 1$ and rated voltage.

**14.23.** (Requires material in Chapter 12.) A transformer is modeled by the simplified equivalent circuit shown in Fig. P14.23. The ac source is connected at $t = 0$.

**(a)** Derive the transfer function of the transformer, $\mathbf{T}(\mathbf{s}) = \mathbf{V}_{out}(\mathbf{s})/\mathbf{V}_{in}(\mathbf{s})$.

**(b)** Find the steady-state response. You may use the transfer function or ordinary ac circuit analysis.

**(c)** Find the natural frequencies and the form of the natural response.

**(d)** Apply the initial conditions and determine the total response.

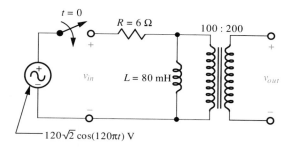

**Figure P14.23**

**14.24.** (Requires material in Chapter 12.) The equivalent circuit for a single-phase transformer is shown in Fig. P14.24. Although normally such equivalent circuits are valid in a narrow range of frequencies, we consider this model valid at all frequencies, including dc and complex frequencies.

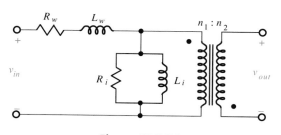

**Figure P14.24**

**(a)** Find the transfer function, $\mathbf{T}(\mathbf{s}) = \mathbf{V}_{out}(\mathbf{s})/\mathbf{V}_{in}(\mathbf{s})$.

**(b)** If an ideal 10-V dc battery were connected to the input at $t = 0$, find the output voltage as a function of time for positive $t$. For this part, consider $n_1 = 100$, $n_2 = 200$, $R_w = 2\ \Omega$, $L_w = 0.2$ H, $R_i = 1000\ \Omega$, and $L_i = 10$ H. The initial condition on the derivative of the output voltage is $10^5$ V/s.

**14.25.** An iron-core inductor with 1000 turns draws 12 mA rms, if excited by 120-V rms, 60-Hz source.

**(a)** Find the peak flux in the inductor.

**(b)** Find the reluctance of the iron magnetic structure.

**(c)** Find the equivalent circuit if the copper loss due to the resistance of the wire is 0.1 W under these conditions. Use a series model.

**(d)** Find the current if 1000 more turns are added to the inductor.

**14.26.** A 60-Hz, 240/120-V single-phase, transformer with $\mu_i = 4500\mu_0$ is shown in Fig. P14.26. The primary resistance is 0.3 $\Omega$ and the primary leakage reactance is 0.8 $\Omega$. The secondary resistance is 0.075 $\Omega$ and the secondary leakage reactance is 0.15 $\Omega$.

**(a)** Find the reluctance of the magnetic structure.

**(b)** Determine the magnetizing current, $I_\phi$, required on the high-voltage side to magnetize the iron for the voltages shown.

**(c)** If the hysteresis and eddy-current losses are 60 W, what is the in-phase current in the primary required to supply these losses? There is no load on the secondary.

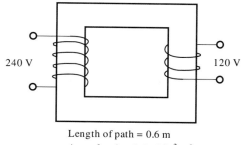

Length of path = 0.6 m
Area of path = $1.6 \times 10^{-3}$ m$^2$
Primary turns = 300
Secondary turns = 150
$\mu_i = 4500\mu_0$

**Figure P14.26**

**(d)** What is the no-load current?

**(e)** Give the equivalent circuit for the transformer with all circuit elements referred to the primary.

**(f)** If the total losses of the transformer must be kept below 135 W, what should be the kVA rating of the device?

**14.27.** A single-phase, 60-Hz transformer is 20 kVA, 1320/440, 85% efficient at full load, unity power factor. At no-load, the transformer current on the HV side is 1.5 A and the power is 1000 W.

**(a)** There are 120 turns on the 440 V side. Find the turns on the 1320 V winding.

**(b)** What would be the no-load current if the transformer were excited from the LV side?

**(c)** Estimate the copper losses of the transformer at the operating level of 15 kVA.

**(d)** Find the reluctance, $\mathfrak{R}$, of the iron core of the transformer.

**14.28.** A 60-Hz, single-phase transformer has 100 turns and 240 V rms on the primary. The graph of primary current as a function of secondary current for a resistive load is shown in Fig. P14.28.

**(a)** What is the primary/secondary turns ratio?

**(b)** What is the exciting current?

**(c)** Estimate the reluctance of the magnetic structure.

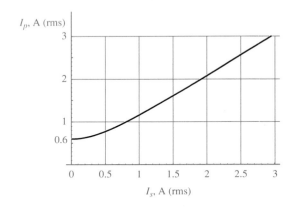

**Figure P14.28**

**14.29.** Figure P14.29 shows the equivalent circuit for a 2400/240-V, 60-Hz, 75-kVA, single-phase transformer. Assume that the transformer is operating at rated secondary voltage and apparent power, with a 0.9 power factor (lagging).

**(a)** What is the turns ratio?

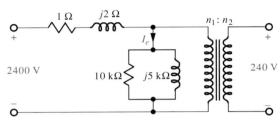

**Figure P14.29**

**(b)** Estimate the iron losses.

**(c)** Estimate the copper losses.

**(d)** What is the efficiency?

**(e)** What would be the exciting current, $I_e$?

**(f)** Estimate the input power factor. *Hint:* Determine the reactive powers since you know the real powers.

**14.30.** Figure P14.30 shows the equivalent circuit for a 1-MVA, 60-Hz, single-phase transformer. The voltages given are nameplate values.

**(a)** What current would flow on the high-voltage side if the low-voltage side were open-circuited?

**(b)** Estimate the copper losses at full load.

**(c)** Estimate the iron losses at full load.

**(d)** Estimate the efficiency at full load and unity power factor.

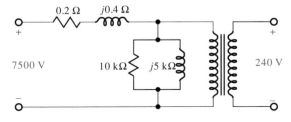

**Figure P14.30**

**14.31.** A single-phase, 60-Hz transformer has an iron structure length of 1 m and a cross-sectional area of $4 \times 10^{-3}$ m². The iron has a permeability of $5000\mu_0$ and is at rated voltage when operated to a maximum flux density of 1.4 tesla. Side 1 has 500 turns and side 2 has 1000 turns. We ignore iron and copper losses.

**(a)** Find the rms magnetizing current if excited on the low-voltage side at rated voltage.

**(b)** Find the rms magnetizing current if excited on the high voltage side at rated voltage.

**(c)** Find the rated rms voltage on the high-voltage side.

**(d)** Find the rated rms voltage on the low-voltage side.

**(e)** Find the volt-amperes required to excite the transformer.

**14.32.** The equivalent circuit in Fig. P14.32 represents a 240/120-V, 60-Hz, 10-kVA, single-phase transformer.

    **(a)** What is the exciting current for the transformer referred to the high-voltage side?

    **(b)** Estimate the transformer losses if the transformer is operating at 80% capacity.

    **(c)** If operating at 80% rated capacity and a power factor of 0.9 lagging, estimate the input voltage and power to the transformer.

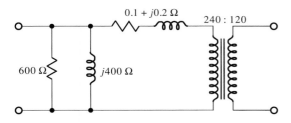

**Figure P14.32**

**14.33.** The equivalent circuit for a 460/230-V, 9.2-kVA, 60-Hz, single-phase, transformer is shown in Fig. P14.33(a).

    **(a)** Figure P14.33(b) shows a table to record the results of a standard open-circuit/short-circuit test. Fill in every slot, even if the quantity normally would not be measured. Assume that the wattmeters are connected to measure the input power on the side supplying the power.

    **(b)** If the secondary voltage is 230 V and the current 10 A with unity power factor, find the primary voltage and the efficiency.

**14.34.** A 60-Hz, single-phase, transformer is tested with a standard open-circuit/short-circuit test at nameplate voltage and current values, with the results shown in Table P14.34.

**TABLE P14.34**

| Test | Primary | | | Secondary | | |
|------|---------|---|---|-----------|---|---|
| | $V$ | $I$ | $P$ | $V$ | $I$ | $P$ |
| SC | 28 | 20 | 350 | 0 | N/A | N/A |
| OC | 480 | 0 | N/A | 240 | 1.93 | 290 |

    **(a)** Find the exciting current, as seen from the primary.

    **(b)** Find the apparent power rating of the transformer.

    **(c)** Estimate the efficiency if operated at 80% full-load capacity and 0.95 *PF*.

    **(d)** Estimate the voltage regulation at this load.

**14.35.** A single-phase transformer operated at unity power factor has a maximum efficiency of 94%, which occurs at a load of 30 kVA. What is its efficiency at a load of 20 kVA, unity power factor? *Hint*: It can be shown that the maximum transformer efficiency, if power factor is constant, occurs when iron and copper losses are equal.

**14.36.** A 480/120-V, 20-kVA, 60-Hz, single-phase transformer has 400-W iron losses and 500-W copper losses when operating at rated voltage and current. Because the transformer is used in a tropical country, the total losses must be kept less than 90% of the rated losses. What is the derated kVA of the transformer for operating in that location, assuming nameplate voltage?

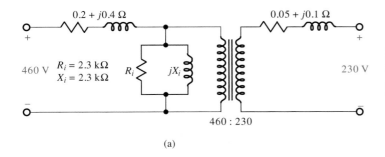

| Condition | $V_H$ | $I_H$ | $P_H$ | $V_L$ | $I_L$ | $P_L$ |
|-----------|-------|-------|-------|-------|-------|-------|
| Open circuit | | | | | | |
| Short circuit | | | | | | |

(b)

**Figure P14.33**

**14.37.** A 240/120-V, 720-VA, 60-Hz, single-phase transformer has a standard OC/SC test. The power into the transformer is 25 W in the open-circuit test and 30 W on the short-circuit test.
  **(a)** Find the current in the low-voltage winding during the short-circuit test, assuming that the voltage is applied to the high-voltage side.
  **(b)** Find the voltage across the high-voltage winding during the open-circuit test, assuming that the voltage is applied to the low-voltage side.
  **(c)** Estimate the efficiency if operated with a 0.95 power factor and full load.

**14.38.** A 50-kVA, 2400/240-V, 60-Hz, single-phase, transformer is tested in an open-circuit/short-circuit test, with the results shown in Table P14.38.
  **(a)** Derive an equivalent circuit for the transformer with all components referred to the primary.
  **(b)** The load on the transformer is 50 kVA with a power factor of 0.9, lagging. The output voltage is 240 V. Find the efficiency.
  **(c)** Estimate the input voltage required for the condition described in part (b).

**TABLE P14.38**

| Test | Primary | | | Secondary | | |
|------|---|---|---|---|---|---|
|      | V | I | P | V | I | P |
| OC | — | — | — | 240 | 4.22 | 650 |
| SC | 72 | 20.8 | 800 | — | — | — |

**14.39.** A 60-Hz transformer has an area of 0.01 m² and is made of iron with $\mu_i = 2400\mu_0$ and mass density 7.65 g/cm³. The transformer is shown in

Fig. P14.39(a) and the equivalent circuit is shown in Fig. P14.39(b). The primary has 300 turns and the secondary 75 turns. At the rated kVA, the maximum flux density is 1.1 T and the total losses are 2000 W.
  **(a)** Show the winding direction for the secondary side in accordance with the dots shown.
  **(b)** Find the nominal voltages at primary and secondary sides, effective values.
  **(c)** Estimate the transformer efficiency if operated at rated kVA and $PF = 1$.
  **(d)** Estimate the mass of the transformer if 70% of the weight is in the iron core.

**14.40.** Figure P14.40 shows (a) the circuit symbol, (b) the wiring connection, and (c) the equivalent circuit for the same transformer connected as a normal transformer and (d) as an *autotransformer*. (See pages 235, for more information about autotransformers.) This transformer is a 720-VA, 120/120-V, 60-Hz transformer when connected in the normal way. Assume the same flux levels in both connections.
  **(a)** What are the primary and secondary voltages of the autotransformer?
  **(b)** What are the parameters in the equivalent circuit of the autotransformer shown in Fig. P14.40(d)?
  **(c)** What is the apparent power rating of the autotransformer, assuming the same losses in both cases?

**14.41.** A single-phase, 60-Hz, 20-kVA transformer has two 460-V primary windings and two 230-V secondary windings, as shown in Fig. P14.41.
  **(a)** Find the nominal primary and secondary voltage and rated current for each of the four possible connections shown in Table P14.41

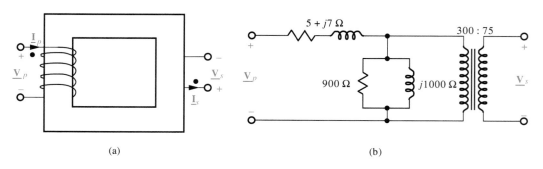

(a)                    (b)

**Figure P14.39**

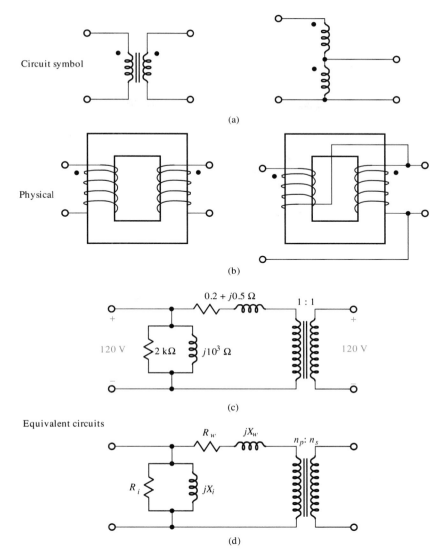

Circuit symbol

(a)

Physical

(b)

$0.2 + j0.5\ \Omega$

1 : 1

120 V

$2\ \mathrm{k}\Omega$   $j10^3\ \Omega$

120 V

(c)

Equivalent circuits

$R_w$   $jX_w$   $n_p : n_s$

$R_i$   $jX_i$

(d)

**Figure P14.40**

| TABLE P14.41 | | | | |
| --- | --- | --- | --- | --- |
| **Primary/Secondary Connection** | $V_p$ | $I_p$ | $V_s$ | $I_s$ |
| Series/series | | | | |
| Series/parallel | | | | |
| Parallel/series | | | | |
| Parallel/parallel | | | | |

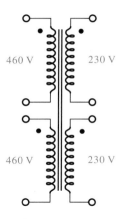

**Figure P14.41**

**(b)** Show the connections of the windings for the parallel/series connection and show the rated current in each winding.

**14.42.** A transformer, Fig. P14.42(a), has the following nameplate information: 10 kVA, 60 Hz, and 1380/440 V. Tests show the transformer efficiency at 92.0% at nameplate operation with unity power factor, and 89.3% at half-load (5 kVA) and unity power factor.

**(a)** What resistive load on the 440-V output gives the rated load?

**(b)** Find the no-load losses of the transformer.

**(c)** The transformer is connected as an autotransformer as shown in Fig P14.42(b). Under these conditions, what is the output voltage?

**(d)** Still connected as an autotransformer, what is the kVA rating of the transformer in this connection. (The answer is *not* 10 kVA.)

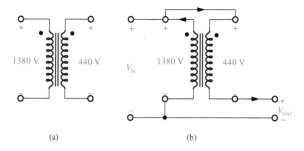

**Figure P14.42**

**14.43.** A three-phase 60-Hz transformer is used to reduce 4160 V to 240 V. The rating of the transformer are

30 kVA. When operated at rated kVA, the transformer losses are 1150 W, which are 30% iron losses and 35% each primary and secondary copper losses. At a load of 20 kW, 0.85 power factor, lagging, estimate the efficiency of the transformer.

**14.44.** A 30-kVA, 60-Hz, three-phase transformer has an efficiency of 94% at full load and 93% at half load, unity *PF*, and the same primary voltage in both cases. Find the iron loss of the transformer.

**14.45.** Three 25-kVA, 8600/1200-V, 60-Hz, single-phase transformers are connected in a delta-wye connection for three-phase operation, with the high-voltage side in wye and the low-voltage in delta. With the transformers operating at rated kVA, the iron loss/transformer is 550 W and the copper loss/transformer is 600 W.

**(a)** Draw a circuit diagram showing the single-phase transformer connections. No voltages are required.

**(b)** Find the low-voltage and high-voltage three-phase line voltages if the single-phase transformers are operated at their rated voltages.

**(c)** If 50 kVA is the load on the three-phase system, find the nominal line current on the high-voltage side. Ignore the exciting current for the transformers.

**(d)** Estimate the efficiency under the condition in part (c) and a *PF* of 0.7.

**(e)** In a per-phase equivalent circuit, what would be the value of the resistance representing the copper losses if placed on the low-voltage side?

**14.46.** The model shown in Fig. P14.46 is the per-phase model for a three-phase, 60-Hz transformer. The transformer is operating at an output load of 30 kW at 0.8 *PF*, lagging, with 240-V output voltage.

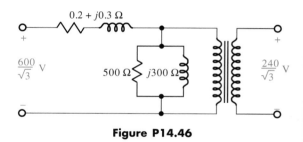

**Figure P14.46**

(a) Estimate the copper losses of the transformer.

(b) Estimate the iron losses of the transformer.

(c) Find the exciting current on the low-voltage side if power is applied to that side.

(d) Estimate the transformer efficiency.

(e) If the transformer has been designed for maximum efficiency at the nameplate apparent power and unity power factor, what is the nameplate kVA rating. *Hint:* For fixed *PF*, transformer efficiency is maximum when iron and copper losses are equal.

14.47. A three-phase, 60-Hz transformer is connected Y–Δ and rated 13 kV/480 V, 25 kVA. The efficiency is 95% at full-load, unity power factor, and losses are divided 60% iron, 40% copper. Determine the per-phase equivalent circuit for the transformer with numerical values for the turns ratio, the resistors in the circuit, and the voltage levels. No reactance values are required. Refer impedance values to the HV side of the transformer.

14.48. Three single-phase transformers are connected as a three-phase transformer. The high-voltage side is in wye and the low-voltage side is in delta. The per-phase equivalent circuit is shown in Fig. P14.48; also it is known that at full load (rated kVA), the iron and copper losses are equal.

(a) Find the turns ratio of the single-phase transformers.

(b) Find the ratio (full load current)/(exciting current), magnitudes only.

(c) Estimate the transformer efficiency at 80% full load and 0.75 power factor, lagging.

(d) What voltage in Fig. P14.48 corresponds to a physical voltage in the real system?

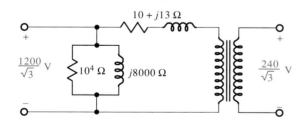

**Figure P14.48**

14.49. The per-phase equivalent circuit for a three-phase, 60-Hz transformer is shown in Fig. P14.49, along with rated voltage and current.

(a) Find the nameplate kVA.

(b) Find the nameplate primary voltage.

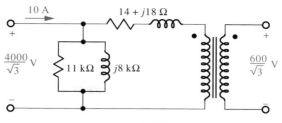

**Figure P14.49**

(c) Find the exciting current on the high-voltage primary.

(d) Estimate the transformer losses at 80% nameplate kVA.

14.50. A three-phase transformer has the following information: 60 Hz, 50 kVA, 4160/600 V, 95% efficiency at full load, and *PF* = 1, no-load current is 4% of full-load current, and at full load, losses divide equally between iron and copper losses.

(a) Determine a per-phase equivalent circuit for the transformer, evaluating numerically all the components you can, plus rated voltages and currents.

(b) Estimate the efficiency of the transformer at a load of 30 kVA, 0.95 *PF*, lagging.

14.51. Figure P14.51 shows the per-phase equivalent circuit for a 20-kVA, three-phase transformer. The rated voltages for the transformer are 4000/2300 V.

(a) Find the magnitude of the exciting current for the three-phase transformer if excited on the high-voltage side.

(b) Estimate the efficiency of the transformer at rated kVA and a *PF* of 0.82 lagging.

(c) Estimate the voltage regulation of the transformer under the conditions in part (b).

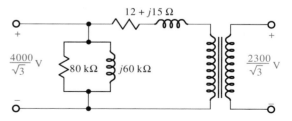

**Figure P14.51**

14.52. A three-phase transformer has the following parameters: 2400/480 V, 60 Hz, 60 kVA, primary resistance of 1 Ω per phase, primary leakage reactance of 1.3 Ω per phase, secondary resistance of 0.04 Ω per phase, secondary leakage reactance of 0.06 Ω per phase, iron losses of 600 W, and no-load current of 0.240 A on high-voltage side, which is the primary.

(a) Give the per-phase equivalent circuit for the transformer with all circuit quantities referred to the primary.

(b) For rated output voltage and kVA with 0.9 power factor, lagging, determine the input line voltage.

(c) Estimate the efficiency for the conditions in part (b).

(d) Estimate the voltage regulation for the conditions in part (b).

14.53. A three-phase, 60-Hz transformer is required to connect a 1320-V distribution line to a 460-V motor. We require a Y on the low-voltage side to provide a grounded neutral. The input is to be Δ-connected. The motor requires 10 kW at a power factor of 0.82, lagging.

(a) What are the phase voltages and currents on both sides of the transformer? Ignore losses.

(b) Give the per-phase circuit of the transformer and load, assuming an ideal transformer.

14.54. In Chapter 6, we showed how to transform three-phase power with the use of three single-phase transformers. There are two ways to transform three-phase power with *two* single-phase transformers. This problem investigates these methods. In this problem, we transform 460 V three-phase to 230 V three-phase; hence, the transformers have a turns ratio of 2:1. *Hint:* In both figures, the geometric orientation hints of the phasor relationships.

(a) The configuration shown in Fig. P14.54(a) is called the "open-delta" or V connection, for obvious reasons. Identical transformers are used.

  (1) Show that if *ABC* is three-phase, *abc* is also three-phase. Consider the *ABC* voltages to be a three-phase set and prove the *abc* set is three-phase.

  (2) If the load is 30 kVA, find the required rating of the transformers to avoid overload.

(b) The configuration shown in Fig. P14.54(b) is called the T connection. For this connection, the transformers are not identical but have different voltage and kVA ratings. The bottom transformer is center-tapped so as to have equal, in-phase voltages for each half.

  (1) Find the voltage, $V_{AX}$, to make this transform three-phase.

  (2) If the load is 30 kVA, find the required kVA rating of each transformer to avoid overload.

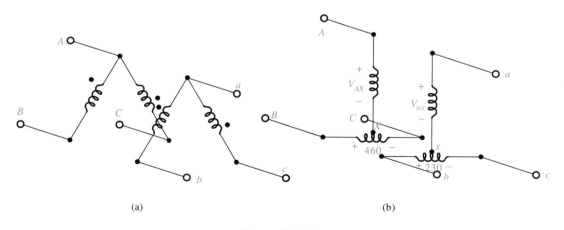

(a)                                (b)

**Figure P14.54**

# Section 14.3: Forces in Magnetic Systems

**14.55.** The reluctance of a magnetic system is given by the formula

$$\mathfrak{R}(x) = \frac{10^6}{x + 0.001}$$

with $x$ in meters. Find the force generated by the system at 1000 A-t of mmf as a function of $x$.

**14.56.** The current and flux linkage of a magnetic system are related by the formula

$i = \lambda[(1 + \sin(2|\theta|)], \qquad |\theta| < \pi/2$

with $\theta$ in radians. If $i = 1.2$ A, find the angle at which the torque is $-0.3$ N-m.

**14.57.** A magnetic structure with ideal iron properties is used to magnetize an air gap with an area of 2 cm$^2$ and a gap width of 2 mm. The mmf of the coil wound on the iron is 1000 ampere-turns.
(a) Find $H$ in the air gap.
(b) What is the force between pole faces?

**14.58.** A magnetic structure has a reluctance given by the expression. $\mathfrak{R}(x) = 10^5 + 10^4 x$ henries$^{-1}$, where $x$ is a mechanical displacement in cm. The structure has 100 turns of wire.
(a) If the coil has a current
$i(t) = 0.01 \cos(120\pi t)$ A and $x = 0$, find the rms voltage across the coil.
(b) Find the time-average force at $x = 0$ for the current in part (a).
(c) If $i = 10$ A dc and $x = 1 + 0.1 \sin(120\pi t)$ cm, estimate the resulting voltage.

**14.59.** An ac relay has a cross-sectional area of 1 cm$^2$ and a path length of 10 cm in iron with $\mu_i = 5000\mu_0$. With the relay open, the gap is 2 mm, and with the relay energized, the minimum average gap is 0.1 mm due to roughness and misalignment. The relay coil has 3000 turns and operates from 24 V (rms), 60 Hz ac.
(a) Find the current into the relay with the gap closed.
(b) Find the time-average force on the movable member at maximum gap width.
(c) Find the time-average force on the movable member at minimum gap width.

**14.60.** The device shown in Fig. P14.60 is a doorbell ringer, where a magnetic force operates against a spring (not shown). The ringer is excited by 12 V rms, 60-Hz ac. The inductance of the structure is $L(x) = 2e^{-x/2}$ H, with $x$ in inches.
(a) At $x = 0$, what is the rms current in the coil?

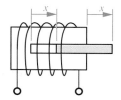

**Figure P14.60**

(b) At $x = 0$, what is the time-average force on the plunger? Consider the force positive if it is in the direction to increase $x$. *Hint:* Distance must be expressed in meters.

**14.61.** The magnetic structure shown in Fig. P14.61(a) has an inductance given by the graph in Fig. P14.61(b). Find the force at $d = 0.5$ cm and $i = 1.0$ A.

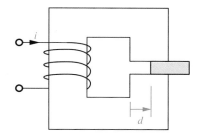

(a)

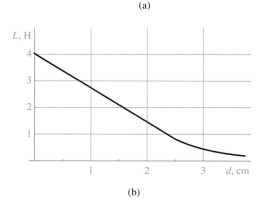

(b)

**Figure P14.61**

**14.62.** An electromechanical transducer is shown in Fig. P14.62(a). The coil has 1000 turns, and you may neglect stray flux and losses. An experiment

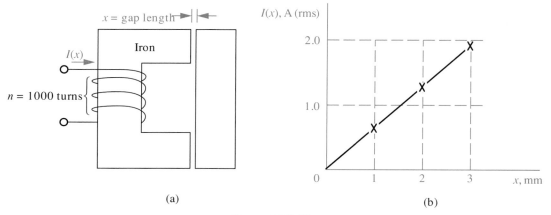

(a)

(b)

**Figure P14.62**

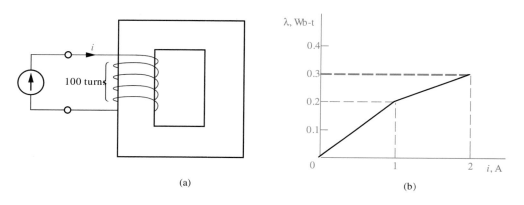

(a)

(b)

**Figure P14.64**

is performed in which the coil is excited with 120-V (rms) ac and the current is measured as the gap length is changed. The results are given in Fig. P14.62(b). From these data, you are to determine the time-average force developed across the gap at $x = 2$ mm. The frequency is 60 Hz.

14.63. The flux linkage created by a current $i$ is given by the equation $\lambda = (1 + x/10)i$, where $x$ is a mechanical displacement in the system in centimeters.

(a) Find the energy required to increase the current from 0 to 2 A for $x = 0$.

(b) What magnetically generated force operates on the mechanical system in the direction of increasing $x$ for $i = 2$ A?

14.64. A magnetic structure, with its flux-linkage-current curve, is shown in Fig. P14.64.

(a) Find the inductance for $i < 1$ A.

(b) Determine the energy required to increase the current from 0 to 1 A.

(c) Determine the energy required to increase the current from 1 to 2 A.

(d) The current is kept at 2 A and a 1-mm gap is sawed in the iron path. The filings are found to weigh 10 g and the density of the iron is 7.65 g/cm$^3$.

(1) What is the final flux linkage after the gap is opened?

(2) As the sawing is going on, does the source maintaining the current receive or give energy to the magnetic system?

**14.65.** Consider a magnetic structure with a moving mechanical member. Figure P14.65 shows the flux linkage–current characteristic for the structure for two values of mechanical displacement. The areas of several parts of the diagram are given.

(a) Estimate the mechanical force generated by the structure at $\lambda = 1.8$ Wb−t, $i = 1.0$ A, and $x = 1.0$ cm.

(b) Estimate the stored energy at the same point.

(c) Estimate the inductance at $x = 1.0$ cm for small currents.

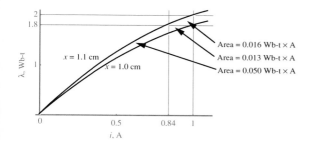

**Figure P14.65**

**14.66.** A 100-turn linear inductor has an inductance $L = 5\sqrt{x} + 0.001$ H, where $x$ is a mechanical displacement in meters. The inductor is excited by a 24-V, 60-Hz voltage source.

(a) Find the peak flux in the inductor.

(b) Find the time-average force tending to increase $x$ at 1 mm.

**14.67.** For the rotational device in Fig. P14.67, the reluctance of the air gap is $\mathcal{R}(\theta) = 10^5(1 + |\theta|)$, where $\theta$ is expressed in radians and $\theta < \pi/2$. Neglect mmf losses in the iron.

(a) Find the torque at $\theta = +\pi/4$ for a current of 10 A and 100 turns.

(b) Find the inductance of the system at the same angle.

(c) How much coenergy is stored at this angle and current?

**14.68.** A doorbell circuit uses 12 V rms for safety, a simple switch on the front porch, and a magnet to vibrate a clapper for a small bell, as shown in Fig. P14.68. The magnet is wound with 2500 turns of fine enamel-insulated wire. The iron in the magnet and clapper has $6000\mu_0$, but the system reluctance is limited mainly by the two 0.1-inch gaps, each of which with an area of 1 cm².

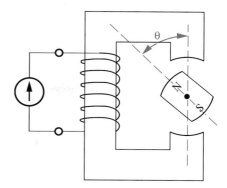

**Figure P14.67**

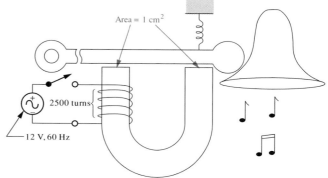

**Figure P14.68**

(a) Find the maximum flux density in the iron.

(b) Find the rms current through the switch when closed.

**14.69.** A 120-V/6-V, 60-Hz transformer is to be wound on a square iron core with a 5-cm outer size and a 3-cm inner hole. The area is 1 cm², and the nominal length of the path is 16 cm. To make it easy to wind, the top or the core is bonded after winding, and the bonding substance has a thickness of 0.05 mm. Assume these gaps have a permeability of $\mu_0$. The permeability of the iron is $6000\mu_0$, and the maximum flux density is to be 1.0 tesla at rated voltage.

(a) Find the number of turns on the primary and secondary windings.

(b) Calculate the magnetizing current on the 120-V side, rms value.

(c) Estimate the time-average force developed on the bonding substance at rated voltage.

**14.70.** A magnetic transducer has a 2 cm × 2 cm member that slides out, as shown in Fig. P14.70. The effective gap on the member is 0.1 mm on each side. The mmf is 1000 A-t. Find the force exerted on the moving member at $x = 1$ cm if the reluctance of the iron is ignored.

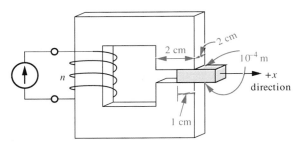

**Figure P14.70**

**14.71.** A 120-V, 60-Hz hair clipper Fig. P14.71(a) has a vibration motor dimensioned in Fig. P14.71(b). The spring is adjusted to resonate with the mass of the vibrator for maximum motion. The coil has 5000 turns, the average gap size is about 0.08 in., and the areas are as shown. Ignore mmf losses in the iron. Assume lateral motion.
  **(a)** At what frequency should the spring–mass system resonate?

**(b)** Estimate the input current required, assuming the real power into the motor is 25 W. Assume that the in-phase and magentizing current add in parallel.
**(c)** Give a parallel equivalent circuit for the vibrator motor.

**14.72.** Figure P14.72 shows a magnetic structure with a rotational permanent magnet in the gap. A steady current is applied to the coil. Experimentally, it is determined that the torque that must be applied to keep the magnet in equilibrium at $\theta_m$ is
$T(\theta_m) = 5 \sin \theta_m + 1.5 \sin(2\theta_m)$ N-m.
  **(a)** Identify which term in the torque expression comes from the permanent magnetism and

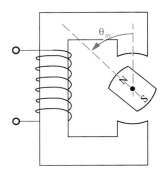

**Figure P14.72**

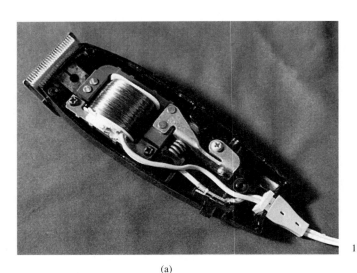

(a)

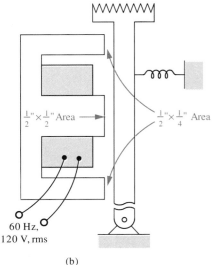

(b)

**Figure P14.71**

which from the induced magnetism.

**(b)** Determine the polarity of the electromagnet and show the corresponding current direction on the coil.

**(c)** If the permanent magnet is moved from $\theta_m = 0°$ to $\theta_m = 180°$ in the positive $\theta_m$ direction, how much work is done on the electrical system? Assume lossless and linear magnetic properties.

**(d)** Mark the polarity of the induced voltage on the coil for the rotation in part (c).

**14.73.** A magnetic structure has a rotating member that is permanently magnetized. With 1-A dc current in the direction shown, the torque in the positive $\theta_m$ direction is found to be

$$T(\theta_m) = -5\sin\theta_m - 0.3\sin(2\theta_m)\,\text{N-m}.$$

**(a)** What would be the torque equation if the dc current were doubled?

**(b)** What would be the torque equation if the dc current were reversed?

**(c)** What would be the equation for the time-average torque if the current were $i(t) = 1\cos(120\pi t)\,\text{A}$?

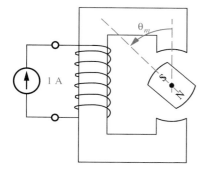

**Figure P14.73**

**14.74.** The $\lambda$–$i$ curve shown in Fig. P14.74 describes the magnetic characteristics of a magnetic structure that has a moveable member. The curves for two positions of that member are shown. The moveable member is set at $x = 0$ and the current is increased from zero to 10 A.

**(a)** How much energy was put into the system by increasing the current from zero to 10 A?

**(b)** With the current maintained at 10 A, the moveable member moves from $x = 0$ to $x = 1$ mm. How much work was done by the electrical system in this change?

**(c)** What was the average force exerted by the

electrical system on the moveable member as the value of $x$ was changed?

**(d)** Is the force at $x = 0.5$ mm greater than, less that, equal to, or cannot tell relative to the average force? Choose one answer and explain.

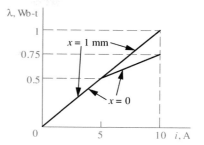

**Figure P14.74**

**14.75.** An electrical weighing device is constructed by using a magnetic structure with a gap, as shown in Fig. P14.75. The force puts a strain on the iron, which changes the gap width, which affects inductance. The circuit uses an ac constant voltage source and uses the current as an indication of the force acting on the system. Consider the iron ideal ($\mu_i = \infty$) and neglect any losses in the wire.

**(a)** Define the variables you need and derive a formula for the current in terms of the gap width and whatever variables you introduce.

**(b)** Discuss the effect of the magnetic forces on the accuracy of the system.

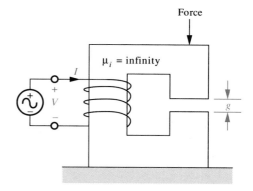

**Figure P14.75**

**14.76.** Figure P14.76 shows an electromechanical

transducer. When the coil is excited, the moveable member rotates, as measured by an angle $\theta_m$. The reluctance of the iron structure is given by $\mathfrak{R}(\theta_m^\circ) = 9000/(\theta_m^\circ + 3^\circ)$, where $\theta_m^\circ$ is the angle in degrees and must be in the range from $5^\circ$ to $20^\circ$. Find the torque generated at $\theta_m^\circ = 12^\circ$ and a current of 1.5 A dc.

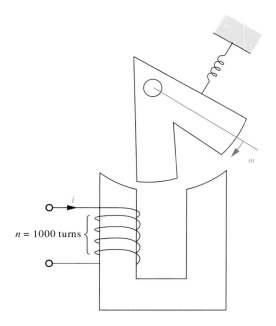

**Figure P14.76**

14.77. The toroidal ring in Fig. P14.77 has two gaps, which remain equal. The nominal radius is $R$, there are $n$ turns on the coil, and the cross-sectional area is $A$. The permeability of the iron is $\mu_i$. Determine the force required to hold the top in equilibrium as a function of current and gap distance $x$.

14.78. A magnetic structure is shown in Fig. P14.78. The

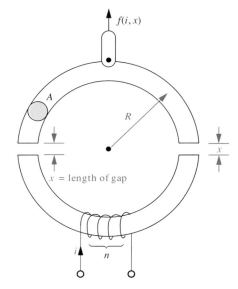

**Figure P14.77**

iron cross-section is square, $a \times a$. The iron is ideal. The coil has $n$ turns and a dc current of $I$. Due to fringing, the effective area of the gap depends on $g$, such that the gap area is approximately $(a + g)^2$. Find the force on the top pole face.

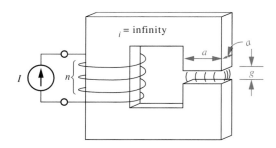

**Figure P14.78**

# Answers to Odd-Numbered Problems

14.1. 17.0 mH.

14.3. **(a)** $9.09 \times 10^{-4}$ Wb; **(b)** deflected out of the paper; **(c)** 0.343 V, rms; **(d)** 34.3 Ω.

14.5. 6.57 g.

14.7. **(a)** 54.6 mH; **(b)** 1.19.

14.9. **(a)** 15 mH; **(b)** 120 mH; **(c)** 75 mH; **(d)** no change; **(e)** 5.46 mH.

14.11. **(a)** Dots are at the bottom **(b)** $R_{eq} = (n_p/n_1)^2 R_1 + (n_p/n_2)^2 R_2$.

14.13. **(a)** 31.8 mA; **(b)** 400 mA; **(c)** 51.1 mA.

**14.15. (a)**

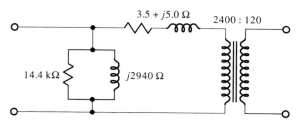

**(b)** 96.6%. **(c)** 2.55%.

**14.17. (a)** Both dots at the top or both at the bottom;
**(b)**

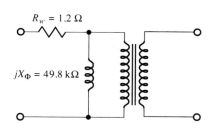

**(c)** repelled.

**14.19. (a)** 16,000 V and 3200 V; **(b)** 0.322 A;
**(c)**

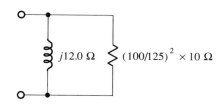

**14.21. (a)** 479 and 48; **(b)** 0.655 A; **(c)** 430 W;
**(d)** 21.9 A.

**14.23. (a)** $\mathbf{T}(\mathbf{s})$ , $= 2\mathbf{s}/(\mathbf{s} + 75.0)$ ; **(b)** $v(t) =$
$235\sqrt{2}\ \cos(120\pi t + 11.3°)$ V; **(c)** –75.0 s$^{-1}$; **(d)**
$12.9e^{-75t} + 235\sqrt{2}\cos(120\pi t + 11.3°)$ V.

**14.25. (a)** $4.50 \times 10^{-4}$ Wb; **(b)** $3.77 \times 10^{4}$ H$^{-1}$;
**(c)** 694 Ω in series with 26.5H; **(d)** 3.00 mA.

**14.27. (a)** 360 turns; **(b)** 4.5 A; **(c)** 1420 W; **(d)**
$47.9 \times 10^{4}$ H$^{-1}$.

**14.29. (a)** 10:1; **(b)** 576 W; **(c)** 977 W; **(d)** 97.8%;
**(e)** 0.537 A; **(f)** 0.888 lagging.

**14.31. (a)** 0.315 A; **(b)** 0.158 A; **(c)** 1490 V; **(d)** 746 V;
**(e)** 235 VA.

**14.33. (a)**

| Condition | $V_H$ | $I_H$ | $P_H$ | $V_L$ | $I_L$ | $P_L$ |
|-----------|-------|-------|-------|-------|-------|-------|
| OC | 460 V | 0 | 0 | 230 V | 0.566 A | 92 W |
| SC | 17.9 V | 20 A | 160W | 0 | 40 A | 0 |

**(b)** 461 V and 95.8%.

**14.35.** 93.5%.

**14.37. (a)** 6 A; **(b)** 240 V; **(c)** 92.6%.

**14.39. (a)**

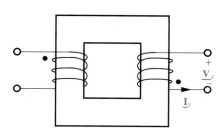

**(b)** 880 V and 220 V; **(c)** 86.9% at 13.3 kVA; **(d)**
111.8 kg.

**14.41. (a)**

| Primary/secondary connection | $V_p$ | $I_p$ | $V_s$ | $I_s$ |
|------------------------------|-------|-------|-------|-------|
| series/series | 920 V | 21.7 A | 460 V | 43.5 A |
| series/parallel | 920 V | 21.7 A | 230 V | 87.0 A |
| parallel/series | 460 V | 43.5 A | 460 V | 43.5 A |
| parallel/parallel | 460 V | 43.5 A | 230 V | 87.0 A |

(b)

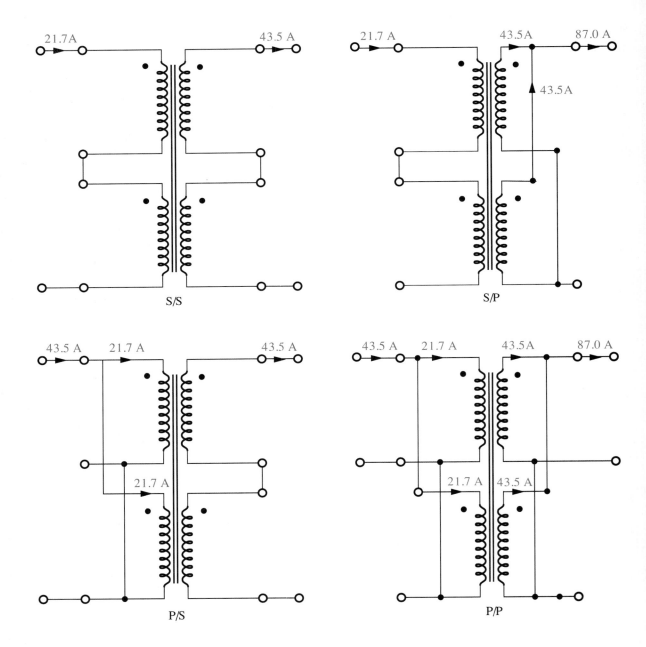

S/S

S/P

P/S

P/P

**14.43.** 96.0%.

**14.45.** (a)

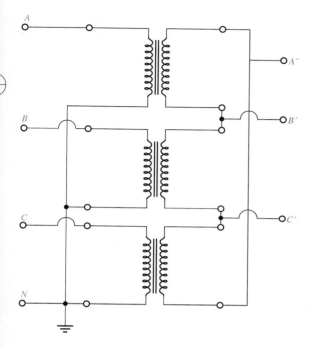

(b) 14,900 V, 1200 V; (c) 1.94 A; (d) 93.5%;
(e) 0.461 Ω/phase.

**14.47.**

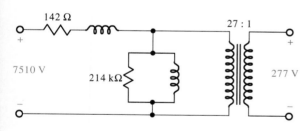

**14.49.** (a) 69.3 kVA; (b) 4000 V; (c) 0.357 A, rms; (d) 4140 W.

**14.51.** (a) 0.0481 A, rms; (b) 97.0%; (c) 2.31%.

**14.53.** (a) 1320 V on the primary, 266 V on the secondary, 5.33 A on primary, 15.3 A on secondary;
(b)

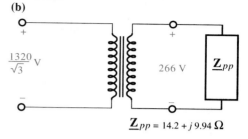

$\mathbf{Z}_{pp} = 14.2 + j\,9.94\ \Omega$

**14.55.** 0.5 N independent of $x$.

**14.57.** (a) $5 \times 10^5$ A-t/m; (b) $-31.4$ N.

**14.59.** (a) 6.75 mA; (b) 1.79 N; (c) 1.79 N.

**14.61.** $-66.7$ N.

**14.63.** (a) 2 J; (b) +20 N.

**14.65.** (a) $+63.0$ N on the basis of energy, 79.0 N on the basis of coenergy, average $= 71.0$ N; (b) 0.8 J approx; (c) 34 approximate.

**14.67.** (a) $-1.57$ N-m; (b) 56.0 mH; (c) 2.80 J.

**14.69.** (a) 4500 and 225 turns; (b) 15.8 mA;
(c) $3.98 \times 10^{-2}$ N.

**14.71.** (a) 120 Hz; (b) 0.330 A; (c) 576 Ω in parallel with $j471\ \Omega$.

**14.73.** (a) $T(\theta_m) = -1.0 \sin \theta_m - 1.2 \sin(2\theta_m)$ N-m;
(b) $T(\theta_m) = +0.5 \sin \theta_m - 0.3 \sin(2\theta_m)$ N-m;
(c) $T(\theta_m) = -0.15 \sin(\theta_m)$ N-m.

**14.75.** (a) $A =$ area, $g =$ gap, $n =$ turns, $V =$ rms voltage, and $\omega =$ electrical radian frequency

$$I = \frac{V}{\omega n^2 \mu_0 A}\, g\ ;\ \text{(b)}\ f = -V^2/2\,\omega^2 n^2 \mu_0 A,$$

independent of $g$, so magnetic force does not affect the scheme.

**14.77.** $f_{dev} = -\dfrac{1}{2}(ni)^2 \left(\dfrac{1}{\Re_i + 2x/\mu_0 A}\right)^2 \times \dfrac{2}{\mu_0 A}$ .

The external force is "+".

# CHAPTER

# 15

# The Synchronous Machine

Flux and Torque in Cylindrical
Magnetic Structures

Rotating Magnetic Flux for AC
Motors

Synchronous Generator
Principles and Characteristics

Characteristics of the
Synchronous Motor

Chapter Summary

Problems

1. To understand how magnetic flux is created and distributed in the air gap of a cylindrical magnetic structure
2. To understand how magnetic flux is made to rotate in cylindrical magnetic structures
3. To understand the role of the rotor and stator flux in the operation of synchronous generators
4. To understand the characteristics of the synchronous generator when operated into a large power system
5. To understand the characteristics of the synchronous motor, particularly the effect of field current on the power factor

The synchronous machine produces the ac power that we use in home, office, and factory. To understand and develop circuit models for this important machine, we must analyze the means by which suitable magnetic flux is established in cylindrical structures, and by which this flux is made to rotate. Rotating flux is required for steady torque in both synchronous and induction machines.

## Introduction to Motor/Generators

**Importance of the synchronous machine.**    The three-phase synchronous machine can be used as a generator or motor. As a motor, it has highly specialized properties and serves a narrow range of applications. The synchronous generator is the workhorse of the electric power industry for generating ac electric power. On a smaller scale, the automotive alternator is a small three-phase synchronous generator with six or eight diodes to rectify the ac to dc for charging the battery and supplying the electrical system.

**General characteristics of the synchronous machine.**    Figure 15.1 shows the external connections of a synchronous machine. Energy can be converted from mechanical to electrical form, generator action, or from electrical to mechanical form, motor action. The machine has two electrical connections: a dc field connection and a three-phase ac armature connection. The mechanical connection is a rotating shaft. As we will establish later, the machine has the following characteristics:

**Conservation of Energy**

- The dc field circuit, placed on the rotor, is essentially a rotating electromagnet whose flux is controlled by the dc field current.

- The armature circuit is placed on the stator and carries three-phase currents.

- The flow of real power through the system is determined by the mechanical input because the mechanical system exchanges real power only.[1] The power supplied to the dc field circuit supplies ohmic losses in the field winding but does not enter directly into the energy-conversion process. For generator action, the mechanical input power, minus the losses, becomes three-phase electrical output power. For motor action, the real power from the electrical input, minus the losses, becomes mechanical output power.

- When the load on a generator is a large power system, the reactive power flow is controlled by the dc field current. When the synchronous machine is operated as a motor, the reactive power required, and thus the power factor, is con-

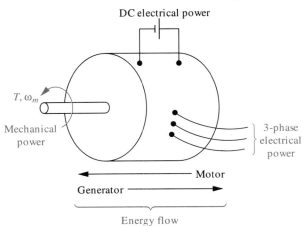

**Figure 15.1**  A synchronous machine can act as generator or motor.

---

[1] Mechanical energy flows smoothly because the inertia and general stiffness of the system eliminate fluctuations in mechanical stored energy.

trolled by the field current. This direct control of reactive power flow is a surprising, and extremely useful, property of the synchronous machine.

## Conditions for Motor/Generator Action

**Torque generation.** The steady transformation of electrical into rotational mechanical power or vice versa requires both torque and rotation.

$$P_{dev} = T_{dev} \times \omega_m \tag{15.1}$$

**stable equilibrium, unstable equilibrium**

where $P_{dev}$ is the developed power, $T_{dev}$ is the developed torque, and $\omega_m$ is the mechanical angular speed of the rotor. Let us consider first the means for producing torque. Figure 15.2(a) shows a compass at an angle $\theta_m$ relative to a magnetic flux. At $\theta_m = 0°$, the compass is in *stable equilibrium*: no torque is produced. For $\theta_m$ in the first quadrant, as shown in Fig. 15.2(a), a torque in the negative $\theta_m$ direction tends to restore equilibrium. This torque increases up to $\theta_m = 90°$ and then decreases to zero at $\theta_m = 180°$, where the compass has an *unstable equilibrium*. The equilibrium is unstable because a small displacement, either way, produces torque tending to increase the displacement. The $T_{dev}(\theta_m)$ curve shown in Fig. 15.2(b) is sinusoidal because the lever arm for the torque varies as $\sin \theta_m$.

We consider now the torque generated by the stator and rotor magnetic poles in Fig. 15.3. Because opposite poles attract, we also have a stable equilibrium at $\theta_m = 0$, an unstable equilibrium at $\theta_m = 180°$, and a maximum restoring torque around $\theta_m = +90°$. Although it is not obvious, the torque characteristic for this structure is that shown in Fig. 15.2(b), as is demonstrated later in this chapter. Thus, torque can be generated magnetically through a displacement between stator and rotor poles.

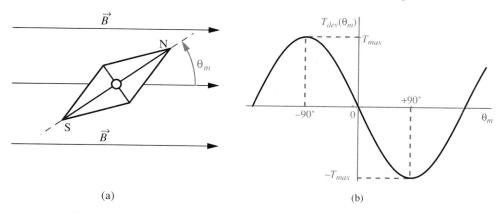

(a)     (b)

**Figure 15.2** (a) Compass in magnetic flux; (b) torque as a function of displacement angle.

**Ways to achieve motor action.** As indicated by Eq. (15.1), sustained torque and rotation are required to convert electrical energy to mechanical energy and vice versa. Electrical motors operate from this principle but differ in (1) how the rotor and stator poles are produced and (2) whether the rotor or stator poles cause rotation. For a synchronous machine, the stator flux (poles) rotates due to the three-phase currents and torque is developed when the electromagnet on the rotor is rotating at the same speed.

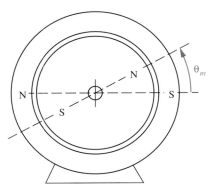

**Figure 15.3** Stator and rotor poles.

**Chapter Contents.** We begin by showing how stator magnetic flux is established by coils in the stator of cylindrical magnetic structures. We then introduce rotor flux and investigate the torque between stator and rotor. Then we show how the stator flux is made to rotate in two- and three-phase stators. A model for a synchronous machine is then presented. Performance characteristics for synchronous generators and motors are then explored.

## 15.1 FLUX AND TORQUE IN CYLINDRICAL MAGNETIC STRUCTURES

### Analysis of Cylindrical Magnetic Structures

**Role of iron and the air gap.** In this section, we show how currents on the inner surface of the stator produce magnetic flux in the air gap. We begin by reviewing magnetic-structure concepts from the previous chapter. Figure 15.4 shows a simple magnetic structure with a gap. The mmf of the coil produces a magnetic flux that is limited by the reluctances of the iron and the air gap. As derived in Sec. 14.1, the total flux is

$$\Phi = BA = \frac{\text{mmf}}{\text{reluctance}} = \frac{ni}{\mathfrak{R}_i + \mathfrak{R}_g} \tag{15.2}$$

where $\Phi$ is the flux, $B$ the flux density, $A$ the area, $ni$ the mmf, and the $\mathfrak{R}$'s the reluctances of the iron and the gap. Because the relative permeability of iron is large, the flux is limited mainly by the air gap.

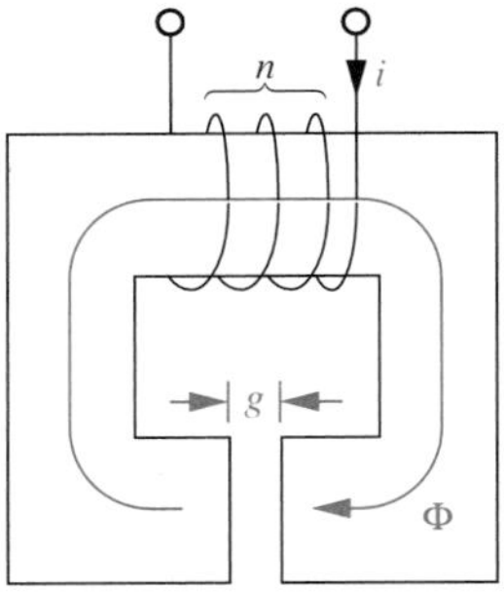

**Figure 15.4** Magnetic structure with a gap.

**Description of structure.** Most alternating-current motors have an iron structure with cylindrical symmetry. Figure 15.5(a) shows an axial view of such a cylindrical magnetic structure with the current-carrying wires on the stator side of the air gap. The currents in the coil go from front to back on the bottom, cross over to the top at the back, and return on top, as shown in Fig. 15.5(b). The wires lie in slots that have been milled in the inner circumference of the stator. The stator structure for a small motor is shown in Fig. 15.6. The rotor is assumed to be a coaxial iron cylinder in our analysis. We will determine the air-gap flux density established by the stator currents.

> **OBJECTIVE 1**
>
> **To understand how magnetic flux is created and distributed in the air gap of a cylindrical magnetic structure**

**Right-hand rule.** We may apply the right-hand rule to the currents in Fig. 15.5(a) by putting the fingers of the right hand around the rotor in the direction of the stator currents and noting that the thumb is horizontal and pointing to the right. Hence, the mag-

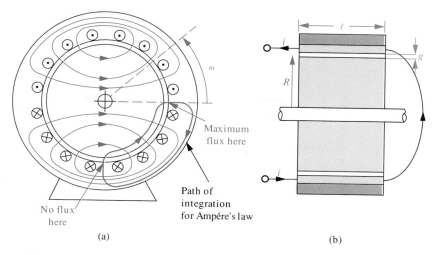

**Figure 15.5** Cylindrical magnetic structure: (a) axial view; (b) side view. The mechanical angle is $\theta_m$, and the width, radius, and length of the air gap are $g$, $R$, and $\ell$, respectively.

**Figure 15.6** Four-pole stator structure for a single-phase induction motor. The main windings for the motor are horizontal and vertical. The smaller starter windings are on the diagonals. The windings may be connected in parallel for 120-V operation or in series for 240-V operation.

netic flux in the rotor and air gap is directed to the right, as shown. The magnetic flux density is maximum at $\theta_m = 0°$ and $180°$ and zero at $\theta_m = -90°$ and $+90°$, as indicated.

**Flux distribution.** Although Fig. 15.5 suggests one conductor in each slot, in practice there are many, as shown in Fig. 15.6. The mmf of the coil, which is distributed around the circumference, is tapered sinusoidally. This sinusoidal distribution is accomplished by having heavy concentrations in the center of the coil, tapered to few wires[2] at the edge of the windings. The resulting flux distribution, shown in Fig. 15.5(a), has no

---

[2] Do not worry about those partially filled slots; we fill them later with more coils.

flux crossing the air gap at the top and bottom, maximum flux density in the air gap in the positive radial direction at $\theta_m = 0°$, and maximum flux density in the air gap in the negative radial direction at $\theta_m = 180°$. This pattern may be interpreted as a distributed south magnetic pole in the stator centered at $\theta_m = 0°$ and a distributed north magnetic pole in the stator centered at $\theta_m = 180°$. Thus, we are describing a two-pole structure. Because of the sinusoidal taper of the mmf, the flux density is sinusoidal in form:

$$B(\theta_m) = B_c \cos \theta_m \tag{15.3}$$

where $B_c$ is the maximum flux density at $\theta_m = 0°$. The flux crosses the air gap radially.

**Maximum flux density.** We may determine the maximum flux density, $B_c$, by applying Ampère's circuital law around the indicated path of integration in Fig. 15.5(a). The path encloses half the wires in the coil, so the result is

$$\oint \vec{H} \cdot \vec{dl} = \text{enclosed current} = \frac{n}{2} i \tag{15.4}$$

where $n$ is the number of turns in the coil and $i$ is the current in each turn. The line integral has four contributions, two from crossing the air gap twice and two from the paths within the rotor and stator iron. We assume that the magnetic field in the iron makes a negligible contribution to the line integral because the iron has a large $\mu_i$. Because of symmetry, the flux density at the bottom is zero and hence no contribution is made by crossing the air gap at $\theta_m = -90°$. This leaves the contribution from crossing the air gap at $\theta_m = 0°$. Because we are crossing in the same direction as the flux, Eq. (15.4) reduces to

$$H_{gap} g = \frac{B_c}{\mu_0} g = \frac{n}{2} i \tag{15.5}$$

and thus the maximum flux density due to a single coil is

$$B_c = \frac{\mu_0 n i}{2g} \tag{15.6}$$

Thus, the maximum flux density depends on the mmf of the coil and the gap width if we neglect the mmf required to magnetize the iron.

---

**EXAMPLE 15.1** **Maximum flux density**

A small motor has an air-gap radius of 5 cm and a gap width of 1.0 mm. We wish to establish a maximum flux density of 1.4 T in the machine. Find the required rms mmf.

**SOLUTION:**
We can determine the peak mmf directly from Eq. (15.6):

$$1.4 = \frac{4\pi \times 10^{-7} n I_p}{2 \times 1.0 \times 10^{-3}} \Rightarrow n I_p = 2230 \text{ A-t, peak} \tag{15.7}$$

Thus, the rms mmf would be $2230/\sqrt{2} = 1580$ A-t.

---

**WHAT IF?** What if there are 36 slots and the rms current is 5 A? How many wires/slot on the average are required?[3]

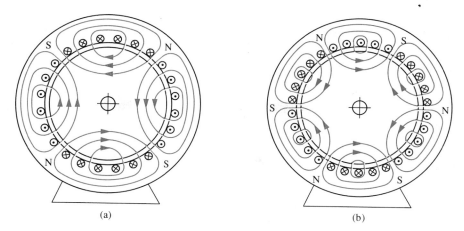

**Figure 15.7** (a) Four-pole, two-coil stator; (b) six-pole, three-coil stator.

**winding**

**For *P* poles.** We now consider magnetic structures with more than two poles. Figures 15.7(a) and 15.7(b) show stators wound for four and six poles, respectively. As more coils are added to the winding, two additional poles are added for each additional coil. The general form of Eq. (15.3) is

$$B(\theta_m) = B_c \cos\left(\frac{P}{2}\,\theta_m\right) \tag{15.8}$$

where $P$ is the number of poles and $P/2$ is the number of coils in the *winding*.[4] Note that $B_c$ is still given by Eq. (15.6), with $n$ still being the number of turns in one coil.

## Torque Development between Rotor and Stator Fluxes

**Introduction.** We showed before that we need rotor and stator poles to have torque between the rotor and stator. In this section, we assume that we have both rotor and stator fluxes, that each varies sinusoidally in space, and that they combine to produce the total flux in the air gap. In the next section, we show the means by which the rotor flux is established. Here we investigate the developed torque and introduce the various power angles that play a role in synchronous motor characteristics.

**Stop the rotation.** During motor or generator operation, the rotor and stator fluxes rotate in synchronism around the cylindrical structure. However, the developed torque depends on the flux magnitudes, the angles between the fluxes, and the geometry of the machine. In the following, we assume for simplicity that the fluxes are stationary.

**rotor–stator power angle**

**Combining fluxes.** We assume the stator flux, $B_S(\theta_m)$, is horizontal and has two poles:

$$B_S(\theta_m) = B_S \cos\theta_m \tag{15.9}$$

---

[3] 18 wires/slot.

[4] A winding is a series connection of coils.

where $B_S$ is the maximum stator–flux density. As shown in Figure 15.8, the rotor flux density, $B_R(\theta_m)$, is displaced from it by a physical angle $\delta_{RS}$, which is called the *rotor–stator power angle*, measured positive from the stator magnetic axis to the rotor magnetic axis.

$$B_R(\theta_m) = B_R \cos(\theta_m - \delta_{RS}) \tag{15.10}$$

where $B_R$ is the maximum rotor-flux density. The total air–gap flux density is the sum of the two, which may be combined like phasors[5] to produce

$$\underline{\mathbf{B}}_{RS} = \underline{\mathbf{B}}_R \angle -\delta_{RS} + \underline{\mathbf{B}}_S \angle 0° = \underbrace{\sqrt{B_R^2 + B_S^2 + 2B_R B_S \cos\delta_{RS}}}_{B_{RS}} \angle -\delta_S \tag{15.11}$$

**rotor power angle**      where $\theta_m = \delta_S$ is the angle of the maximum of the combined flux density, $B_{RS}$. The phasorlike addition of the rotor and stator fluxes is shown in Fig. 15.9,[6] where we also define the *rotor power angle*, $\delta_R$, as the angle between the rotor pole and the maximum of the total flux density. Because the sum of two spatial sinusoids is still sinusoidal, the total flux density is

$$B_{RS}(\theta_m) = B_{RS} \cos(\theta_m - \delta_S) \tag{15.12}$$

This flux density is used to calculate the coenergy of the system, from which the developed torque is derived.

**Coenergy determination.**   As shown in Sec. 14.3, we may determine the developed torque on the rotor by taking the partial derivative with respect to the angle of ei-

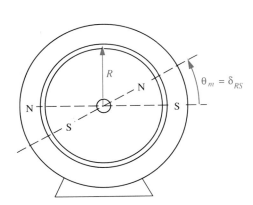

**Figure 15.8**  Rotor and stator poles are displaced by the rotor-stator power angle, $\delta_{RS}$.

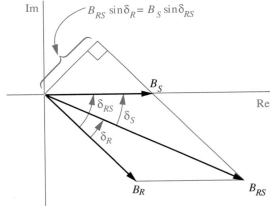

**Figure 15.9**  The rotor and stator fluxes combine by the law of cosines to produce the total (rotor–stator) flux density. The rotor–stator power angle, $\delta_{RS}$, is the angle between the rotor and stator poles. The rotor power angle, $\delta_R$, is the angle between the rotor poles and the total flux density maximum.

---

[5] These are stationary fluxes distributed sinusoidally in space. We are merely using the phasor technique to add two sinusoids.

[6] The angles appear reversed because of the way we define phasors. We marked them to correspond to spatial angles.

ther the energy or the coenergy functions. In the present case, we are assuming that the rotor and stator poles (fluxes) are constant in magnitude and vary only in relative position (angle). This requires constant current excitation, which suggests using the coenergy function. However, in this linear magnetic system, the coenergy and the energy are equal and are both proportional to the square of the total flux density. As shown in Sec. 14.3, almost all the energy is stored in the air gap, so we must substitute Eq. (15.11) into Eq. (13.41) and (13.42) and integrate over the air-gap volume. The result is

$$W'_m(\delta_{RS}) = \frac{\pi R \ell g}{2\mu_0}(B_R^2 + B_S^2 + 2B_R B_S \cos \delta_{RS}) \tag{15.13}$$

where $W'_m$ is the coenergy of the system and $R$, $\ell$, and $g$ are the air-gap radius, length, and width, respectively, as defined in Fig. 15.5(b).

**Torque.**    We consider the stator poles stationary and determine the torque on the rotor poles.  Equation (14.77) gives the developed torque as the partial derivative of the coenergy function with respect to the rotor–stator power angle, with the rotor and stator flux-density magnitudes kept constant.

$$T_{dev}(\delta_{RS}) = +\frac{\partial W'_m}{\partial \delta_{RS}} = -\frac{\pi R \ell g}{\mu_0}B_R B_S \sin \delta_{RS} \tag{15.14}$$

Figure 15.9 shows

$$B_S \sin \delta_{RS} = B_{RS} \sin \delta_R \tag{15.15}$$

which allows an alternative form of Eq. (15.14):

$$T_{dev}(\delta_{RS}) = -\frac{\pi R \ell g}{\mu_0}B_R B_{RS} \sin \delta_R \tag{15.16}$$

Equation (15.14) confirms that the torque is zero for $\delta_{RS} = 0$ and negative if $\delta_{RS}$ is positive, meaning the magnetic interaction tends to align the rotor with the stator poles.

**Summary.**    Equation (15.14) gives the magnetically generated torque between two sets of poles with an angle $\delta_{RS}$ between them. The maximum torque depends on the product of the individually contributing fluxes and the geometric factors. The torque characteristic given in Eq. (15.14) is shown in Fig. 15.2(b).  In the next section, we show how the stator poles are made to rotate in space so that torque between the stator and the rotating rotor can be sustained.

**For P poles.**    For more than two poles, Eq. (15.8) requires that we place a $P/2$ in front of all mechanical angles relating to magnetic fluxes.  In particular, the torque derived in Eq. (15.14) increases by $P/2$ because

$$\frac{\partial}{\partial \delta_{RS}}\cos\left(\frac{P}{2}\delta_{RS}\right) = \frac{P}{-2}\sin\left(\frac{P}{2}\delta_{RS}\right) \tag{15.17}$$

Thus, the general torque is

$$T_{dev}(\delta_{RS}) = -\frac{\pi R \ell g P}{2\mu_0} B_R B_S \sin\left(\frac{P}{2}\delta_{RS}\right) = -\frac{\pi R \ell g P}{2\mu_0} B_R B_{RS} \sin\left(\frac{P}{2}\delta_R\right) \qquad (15.18)$$

where $\delta_{RS}$ is the mechanical angle between the rotor and stator poles, measured positive from stator poles to rotor poles, and $\delta_R$ is the mechanical angle between the total flux and the rotor poles.

**electrical units, electrical degrees**

**Mechanical angles expressed in electrical units.** Often mechanical angles are expressed in *electrical units,*[7] which is mechanical angle $\times$ $P/2$. In electrical angle units, the $(P/2)$'s go away in the various flux equations, and after the $P/2$ is placed in the torque equation, all machines are equivalent to a two-pole machine. Converting mechanical angle to electrical angle has the added advantage that physical angles in electrical units correspond directly to electrical phase angles.

### Check Your Understanding

**1.** A cylindrical magnetic structure cannot have an odd number of magnetic poles. True or false?

**2.** In Fig. 15.6, the wires that can be seen are not the wires that produce the motor flux, but are the crossover wires between poles. True or false?

**3.** For large flux, the air gap in a machine should be as large or as small as possible. Which?

**4.** If the maximum torque in Fig. 15.2(b) is 5 N-m, determine the work required to move the rotor from its position of stable equilibrium to the position of unstable equilibrium.

**5.** For maximum torque, the rotor and stator fluxes should be aligned. True or false?

**6.** The rotor–stator power angle is $10°$ in a six-pole machine. How many electrical degrees is that?

*Answers.* (**1**) True; (**2**) true; (**3**) small; (**4**) 10 J; (**5**) false; (**6**) $30°$.

## 15.2 ROTATING MAGNETIC FLUX FOR AC MOTORS

**OBJECTIVE 2**

**To understand how magnetic flux is made to rotate in cylindrical magnetic structures**

### Two-Phase Rotating Flux

The previous section showed how magnetic flux is produced in a cylindrical magnetic structure and how torque is developed between rotor and stator flux. This section shows how the stator flux, or the stator magnetic poles, is made to rotate. Although the three-phase motor is more common than the two-phase, the latter offers a convenient place to start. We therefore consider a two-pole stator, like that in Fig. 15.5, with two coils: an $h$ coil that creates a magnetic flux pattern with its maximum in the horizontal plane (shown), and a $v$ coil that creates a magnetic flux pattern with its maximum in the vertical plane (not shown).

**Sinusoidal mmfs.** The wires/slot distributions for both coils are tapered to produce flux patterns that are sinusoidal in space. Hitherto, we have been considering only the $h$

---

[7] As *electrical degrees.*

coil, for which the wires are most dense on the top and bottom of the stator; the wires for the $v$ coil are most dense on the sides of the stator and share intermediate slots with the $h$ coil. The two coils are identical except for their orientation in space. If $i_h(t)$ is the current in the $h$ coil and $i_v(t)$ the current in the $v$ coil, then the magnetic flux densities in the air gap by Eqs. (15.6) and (15.3) would be

$$B_h(t, \theta_m) = \frac{\mu_0 n}{2g} i_h(t) \cos \theta_m \quad \text{and} \quad B_v(t, \theta_m) = \frac{\mu_0 n}{2g} i_v(t) \sin \theta_m \quad (15.19)$$

Both fluxes are radial across the air gap and have their maximum densities at $\theta_m = 0°$ and $\theta_m = +90°$, respectively.

The two-phase currents are

$$i_h(t) = I_p \cos (\omega t), \text{ excites } B_c \text{ in the } h\text{-direction}$$

$$i_v(t) = I_p \sin (\omega t), \text{ excites } B_c \text{ in the } v\text{-direction}$$

$$(15.20)$$

where $I_p$ is the peak current in each coil, $\omega$ is the electrical angular frequency, and a $90°$ phase shift between the two phases is indicated by the sine and cosine functions shown in Fig. 15.10. The two flux-density components are

$$B_h(t, \theta_m) = B_c \cos(\omega t) \cos \theta_m$$

$$B_v(t, \theta_m) = B_c \sin(\omega t) \sin \theta_m$$

$$(15.21)$$

where $B_c$ is the peak flux density created by each coil separately, Eq. (15.6).

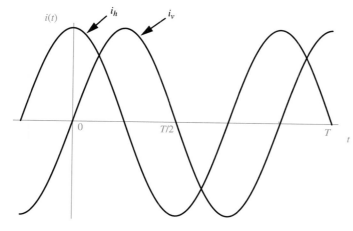

**Figure 15.10** The two-phase system has a $90°$ phase shift between the two phases.

**Rotating flux.** When both coils are excited simultaneously, the fluxes add as scalars because both are radial, and the flux pattern moves in the counterclockwise direction, as demonstrated mathematically in Eq. (15.22):[8]

---

[8] Using the trigonometric identify in Eq. (5.37).

$$B(t, \theta_m) = B_h(t, \theta_m) + B_v(t, \theta_m)$$
$$= B_c[\cos(\omega t) \cos \theta_m + \sin(\omega t) \sin \theta_m] \qquad (15.22)$$
$$= B_r \cos(\omega t - \theta_m)$$

where $B_r = B_c$ is the magnitude of the rotating flux density. The flux density retains a stable pattern that rotates in space with the following properties:

- The magnitude is equal to the peak flux density from each contributing coil.
- If time is fixed, the flux is sinusoidal in space with the maximum flux density at $\theta_{max} = \omega t$ if $t = 0$ when the maximum flux is at $\theta_m = 0°$.
- At a fixed $\theta_m$, the flux-density magnitude is sinusoidal in time. The time of peak flux density is $t_p = \theta_m/\omega$.
- The flux, therefore, exhibits angular wave motion, a rotating wave of flux.

**synchronous speed**

**For P poles.**    For more than two poles, the pattern of the magnetic flux advances one pole pair for each electrical cycle; hence, the mechanical speed of the flux pattern is slower than for two poles.  If there are $P$ poles, the flux density pattern will be

$$B(t, \theta_m) = B_r \cos\left(\omega t - \frac{P}{2}\theta_m\right) \qquad (15.23)$$

and the *synchronous speed*, $\omega_s$, therefore, will be

$$\omega_s = \frac{\omega}{P/2} \text{ spatial rad/s} \qquad (15.24)$$

where $\omega$ is the electrical angular frequency in radians/second, and $P$ the number of stator poles. Table 15.1 gives common synchronous speeds for 60 Hz.

| TABLE 15-1 | Synchronous Speeds for 60 Hz | |
|---|---|---|
| $P$ | $\omega_s$ | rpm |
| 2 | $2\pi \times 60$ | 3600 |
| 4 | $2\pi \times 30$ | 1800 |
| 6 | $2\pi \times 20$ | 1200 |

**EXAMPLE 15.2** | **50-Hz motor**

A two-phase, four-pole motor is operated at 50 Hz.  The motor windings create counterclockwise rotation with a maximum flux density of 1.3 tesla.  Find the synchronous speed and give the equation of the flux density, assuming the maximum flux density is at $\theta_m = 0°$ at $t = 0$.

**WHAT IF?** What if you want the speed in rpm?[9]

**Phase reversal.** If either the horizontal or vertical coil is reversed in polarity, the direction of flux rotation will change to clockwise; thus, the general expression for the flux density is

$$B(t, \theta_m) = B_r \cos\left(\omega t \mp \frac{P}{2}\theta_m\right) \qquad (15.26)$$

where the minus sign goes with rotation in the positive $\theta_m$ direction and the plus with rotation in the negative $\theta_m$ direction.

## Three-Phase Rotating Flux

**Three-phase windings.** Figure 15.11 shows a two-pole magnetic structure wound with three coils separated, by 120° in space. Note that coil $a$ corresponds to our $h$ coil from before, with the currents entering on the bottom and returning on the top, but coil $b$ currents enter in the first quadrant and those of coil $c$ enter in the second quadrant.[10] As before, the coil mmfs are tapered sinusoidally and share slots between their most

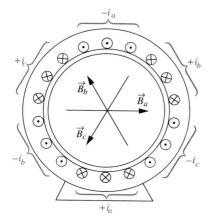

$$B_a = Ki_a(t)\cos\theta_m$$
$$B_b = Ki_b(t)(\cos\theta_m - 120°)$$
$$B_c = Ki_c(t)(\cos\theta_m - 240°)$$

**Figure 15.11** A three-phase cylindrical structure.

---

[9] $50 \pi \times 60/2\pi = 1500$ rpm.

[10] In practice, the three coils are internally connected in wye or delta, and only three wires are connected externally to the three-phase system.

dense regions. The equations of the flux patterns from the coils, given in Fig. 15.11, show that the maximum from coil $a$ lies in the horizontal plane, and the maxima from coils $b$ and $c$ are displaced 120° and 240° in space, respectively.

### Analysis of three-phase system.

The three-phase currents are shown in Fig. 6.1:

$$i_a(t) = I_p \cos(\omega t)$$

$$i_b(t) = I_p \cos(\omega t - 120°)$$  (15.27)

$$i_c(t) = I_p \cos(\omega t - 240°)$$

so, for example, the flux density from coil $a$ is

$$B_a(t, \theta_m) = B_c \cos(\omega t) \cos \theta_m \qquad (15.28)$$

where $B_c$ is the peak flux density from one coil alone, Eq. (15.6). The combined flux density is

$$B(t, \theta_m) = \underbrace{B_c[\cos(\omega t) \cos \theta_m}_{\text{phase } a} + \underbrace{\cos(\omega t - 120°) \cos(\theta_m - 120°)}_{\text{phase } b} \qquad (15.29)$$

$$+ \underbrace{\cos(\omega t - 240°) \cos(\theta_m - 240°)]}_{\text{phase } c}$$

We use the trigonometric identity in Eq. (5.36) to obtain the results

$$B(t, \theta_m) = B_c\{\tfrac{3}{2}\cos(\omega t - \theta_m) + \tfrac{1}{2}[\cos(\omega t + \theta_m) + \cos(\omega t + \theta_m - 240°)$$

$$+ \cos(\omega t + \theta_m - 480°)]\} \qquad (15.30)$$

The three bracketed terms add to zero at all times because they form a balanced three-phase set.[11] Hence, Eq. (15.30) reduces to

$$B(t, \theta_m) = \tfrac{3}{2}B_c \cos(\omega t - \theta_m) = B_r \cos(\omega t - \theta_m) \qquad (15.31)$$

where $B_r = \tfrac{3}{2}B_c$ is the magnitude of the rotating flux density with all coils operating together, a 50% increase in the flux density above what each gives individually. Equation (15.31) has the same form as Eq. (15.22) and represents a rotating flux pattern. It is easily shown that changing the three-phase sequence from $abc$ to $acb$ reverses the direction of rotation to give Eq.(15.31) with $-\theta_m$ for $abc$ rotation and $+\theta_m$ for $acb$.

## Single-Phase Expressed as Rotating Flux

Figure 15.12 shows a cylindrical magnetic structure with one winding excited by a single-phase current. The magnetic flux density in the air gap is given by

$$B(t, \theta_m) = B_c \cos \theta_m \cos(\omega t) \qquad (15.32)$$

---

[11] Considering that $-480°$ is the same as $-120°$.

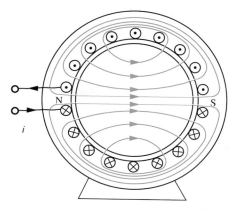

**Figure 15.12** Magnetic flux due to a single coil.

Using the identity in Eq. (5.36) with $a = \omega t$ and $b = \theta_m$, we may expand this into two terms:

$$B(t, \theta_m) = \underbrace{B_r \cos(\omega t - \theta_m)}_{\text{positive rotation}} + \underbrace{B_r \cos(\omega t + \theta_m)}_{\text{reverse rotation}} \tag{15.33}$$

where $B_r = B_c/2$ is the rotating flux density in each direction. Therefore, we may consider a single-phase oscillating flux as composed of two counter rotating fluxes. This viewpoint is useful in understanding the characteristics of single-phase induction motors in the next chapter.

**Coils, windings, phases, and poles.** We have now discussed cylindrical magnetic structures for one-, two-, and three-phase systems. Two- and three-phase synchronous machines exist,[12] although two-phase is rare. Equation (15.6) gives the maximum flux density produced in the air gap by a single coil, where $n$ is the number of turns in the coil. Table 15.2 shows the magnitude of the rotating flux density and the number of windings and coils required in such machines. The number of poles is $P$.

**TABLE 15-2 Rotating Flux Magnitude, Windings, and Coils for Single-, Two-, and Three-phase Machines**

| Phases | $B_r$ | Windings | Coils |
|--------|-------|----------|-------|
| 1 | $B_c/2$ | 1 | $P/2$ |
| 2 | $B_c$ | 2 | $P$ |
| 3 | $1.5B_c$ | 3 | $3P/2$ |

---

[12]Of course, some ac electric clocks and timers are single-phase synchronous machines. But these operate on different principles than those discussed in this section.

**General results.** The results of the previous sections are summarized by the general equation for a rotating flux wave:

$$B(t, \theta_m) = B_r \cos\left[\omega t \mp \frac{P}{2}(\theta_m - \theta_{m0})\right] \tag{15.34}$$

where all the quantities have been defined previously except $\theta_{m0}$, which is the position of the flux maximum at $t = 0$.

---

**EXAMPLE 15.3** | **Rotating flux**

A six-pole magnetic structure produces a clockwise rotating flux that has a north pole at $\theta_m = -90°$ at $t = 0$. The synchronous speed is 800 rpm. Give the equation of the flux density, counting flux positive in the outward radial direction. The maximum flux density is 0.92 T.

**SOLUTION:**
The synchronous speed is $\omega_s = 800 \times (2\pi/60) = 83.8$ rad/s, so for $P = 6$, Eq. (15.24) gives the electrical frequency as $\omega = (6/2) \times 83.8 = 251$ rad/s. For clockwise rotation, we use the bottom sign in Eq. (15.34). Because the north pole on the stator represents flux in the negative direction, across the air gap, we have

$$B(t, \theta_m) = -0.92 \cos\{251t + (6/2)[\theta_m - (-90°)]\}$$
$$= -0.92 \cos(251t + \theta_m + 270°) \text{ T} \tag{15.35}$$

---

**WHAT IF?**  What if you want to eliminate the minus sign?[13]

---

**Check Your Understanding**

1. The vector magnetic flux density in the gap of a machine changes only in magnitude, not in direction. True or false?

2. If we reverse the connections to both windings of a two-phase cylindrical structure, the direction of rotation of the magnetic flux density will reverse. True or false?

3. If we change the phase sequence of a three-phase cylindrical structure, the direction of rotation of the magnetic flux will reverse. True or false?

4. Three-phase rotating fluxes go faster than two-phase. True or false?

**Answers.** (1) True; it is always radial across the air gap; (2) false; (3) true; (4) false.

---

[13] $B(t, \theta_m) = +0.92 \cos(251t + \theta_m + 90°)$ T.

## Synchronous Generator Construction and Equivalent Circuit

**Stator construction.**    The stator of the synchronous machine was described and analyzed in the previous section. Three-phase stator currents produce magnetic flux that rotates at synchronous speed, which depends on the electrical frequency and the number of poles.

**cylindrical rotor, salient-pole rotor**

**Rotor construction.**    The rotor of a synchronous machine is a dc electromagnet. The dc current may be supplied to the rotor through a brush–slip ring assembly[14] or may be supplied by rectification of an ac voltage that is induced in a separate winding on the rotor. Figure 15.13 shows *cylindrical* and *salient-pole*[15] rotor construction. The magnetic structure of the cylindrical rotor is symmetric, and a sinusoidally tapered rotor flux is produced by tapered distribution of the rotor mmf. The magnetic structure of the salient–pole rotor is unsymmetrical: The dc coil mmf is concentrated by coils wound around the pole pieces, and a sinusoidal flux distribution is accomplished by tapering the width of the air gap. To develop torque, the same number of poles must be used on stator and rotor. Electrically, the rotor carries the field circuit, in the sense that it holds many turns of small wire carrying relatively small current.

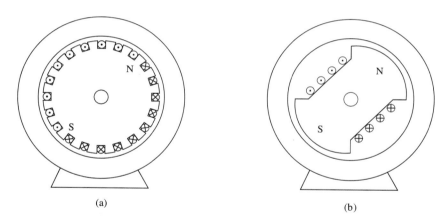

(a)                                                (b)

**Figure 15.13**   (a) Cylindrical rotor; (b) salient-pole rotor.

**OBJECTIVE 3**

**To understand the role of the rotor and stator flux in the operation of synchronous generators**

**The field-generated emf.**    Assume the rotor is rotating in the positive $\theta_m$ direction at synchronous speed. Because the rotor flux density is sinusoidal in space, the flux density at $\theta_m = 0°$ is a sinusoidal time function representable by a phasor. We count time from the moment when the rotor N magnetic axis passes $\theta_m = 0°$, so the rotor flux density phasor, $\mathbf{B}_R$, is

$$\mathbf{B}_R = B_R \angle 0°$$   (15.36)

---

[14] The brush on the stator makes sliding contact with a cylindrical surface that rotates on the rotor.
[15] Salient means, among other things, outstanding or jutting out.

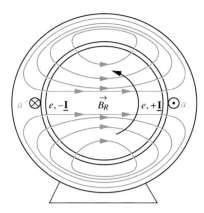

**Figure 15.14** The loop a–a' has voltage induced by the rotating flux.

where $B_R$ is the maximum rotor flux density and the electrical frequency is $(P/2)\omega_s$. The flux waves generate voltage in the stator coils, which in turn produce current in the stator and load. To fix ideas, we concentrate on the loop of wire a–a' in Fig. 15.14. From Eq. (13.43), we determine the emf in this loop to be

$$e = 2\vec{\ell} \cdot \vec{u} \times \vec{B} = 2\ell\omega R B_R \text{ V} \qquad (15.37)$$

where $\ell$ is the axial length of the machine, and $R$ is the nominal radius of the air gap, as shown in Fig. 15.8. The polarity of $e$ is $+$ at $a$ and $-$ at $a'$.[16] The phasor emf, $\underline{\mathbf{E}}_f$, of the entire coil is approximately

$$\underline{\mathbf{E}}_f = 2n\ell\omega R B_R \angle 0° \qquad (15.38)$$

where $n$ is the number of turns in the coil centered on a–a'. If there were no stator currents, $\underline{\mathbf{E}}_f$ would be the voltage in the coil[17] due to the rotation of the rotor field.

**Effect of stator currents.** The phase of the current in a–a', $\mathbf{I}$, depends on the load impedance, but the flux caused by the stator current, $\underline{\mathbf{B}}_s$, lags by 90° $(= -j)$ due to the right-hand rule.[18] Equations (15.6) and (15.31) give this flux density as

$$\underline{\mathbf{B}}_s = -j\,\frac{3}{2}\,\frac{\mu_0 n\mathbf{I}}{2g} \qquad (15.39)$$

where $g$ is the width of the air gap and the $\frac{3}{2}$ comes from the increase of rotating flux due to the other two phases. Thus, if stator current exists, the flux density in the air gap, $\underline{\mathbf{B}}_{RS}$, will be the sum of the rotor and stator fluxes:

---

[16] Recall that $\vec{u}$ is the velocity of the wire *relative to the flux*, which is downward at the right and upward at the left.

[17] Later we use $\underline{\mathbf{E}}_f$ as the per-phase excitation voltage, which might differ from the definition in Eq. (15.38) by $\sqrt{3}$.

[18] Put your right-hand fingers around the rotor in the direction of the current in a–a', and your thumb points downward. This 90° spatial angle is transformed into a phase shift by the rotation.

$$\mathbf{B}_{RS} = \mathbf{B}_R + \mathbf{B}_S \qquad (15.40)$$

We may convert Eq. (15.40) to a voltage equation by multiplying by $2\ell\omega Rn$:

$$\underbrace{2\ell\omega Rn\mathbf{B}_{RS}}_{\mathbf{V}} = \underbrace{2\ell\omega Rn\mathbf{B}_R}_{\mathbf{E}_f} - j\omega \underbrace{\frac{n^2}{2g/3\mu_0\ell R}}_{L_s} \mathbf{I} \qquad (15.41)$$

### Circuit interpretation of Eq. (15.41).

If $\mathbf{I}$ were zero, the voltage produced by the rotation of the rotor flux would be $\mathbf{E}_f$; think of it as the Thévenin voltage of the generator.[19] The $\mathbf{V}$ term is the output voltage of the generator with stator current flowing because $\mathbf{B}_{RS}$ is the flux density[20] in the air gap. The last term in Eq. (15.41) suggests an inductive reactance:

$$X_s = \omega \frac{n^2}{\Re_g} = \omega L_s, \text{ where } \Re_g = \frac{2g}{3\mu_0\ell R} \qquad (15.42)$$

**Equivalent Circuits**

where $L_s$ is the effective inductance of the stator winding and $X_s$ is its effective reactance at the ac frequency.

**excitation voltage, synchronous reactance**

### Per-phase equivalent circuit.

The derivation of Eq. (15.41) has been approximate in part, but the form and interpretation are correct and lead to a valid per-phase equivalent circuit, as shown in Fig. 15.15(a). The effect of the rotor flux is represented by the *excitation voltage*, $\mathbf{E}_f$, which is controlled by the dc field current, $I_f$, as shown in Fig. 15.15(b). However, we should not consider the excitation voltage as physically

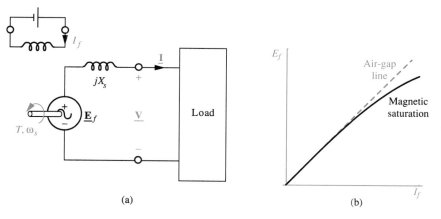

**Figure 15.15** (a) Per-phase equivalent circuit for a synchronous motor; (b) the field determines the magnitude of the excitation voltage, $\mathbf{E}_f$.

[19] In practice, large synchronous generators are operated with some magnetic saturation. The attendant nonlinear behavior weakens the strict applicability of Thévenin's theorem. Our brief theory assumes linearity.

[20] There is only one flux pattern in the machine. We conceptually divide it into rotor and stator components for analysis.

present in the machine because the rotor flux occupies the same space as the flux due to the stator currents represented by the per-phase *synchronous reactance*, $X_s$. The flux that exists physically in the machine is the rotor–stator flux. By Faraday's law, the per-phase voltage induced in the stator coils by the motion of the total flux around the structure must be the per-phase terminal voltage, $\underline{\mathbf{V}}$.

**Summary.** Figure 15.16 shows the causal factors at work in the synchronous generator. The circuit aspects are shown in the per-phase equivalent circuit in Fig. 15.15(a), which represents the rotating rotor flux by the excitation voltage and represents the rotating stator flux by the synchronous reactance times the stator current. The sum of the rotor and stator fluxes, which is the actual physical flux in the machine, is represented in the equivalent circuit by the sum of the excitation voltage and the voltage drop across the synchronous reactance. Faraday's law becomes

$$\underline{\mathbf{V}} = \underline{\mathbf{E}}_f - jX_s\underline{\mathbf{I}} \tag{15.43}$$

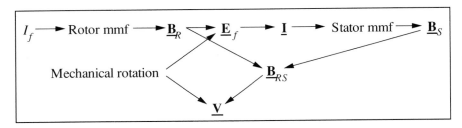

**Figure 15.16** Causal relationships in the synchronous generator. The real voltage in the generator, $\underline{\mathbf{V}}$, is generated by the real flux density, $\underline{\mathbf{B}}_{RS}$.

Losses and leakage flux in the stator circuit have been ignored. The magnitude of the excitation voltage is controlled by a dc field current. The equivalent circuit in Fig. 15.15(a) applies only to cylindrical-rotor machine because it ignores the asymmetry in the magnetic structure of a salient-pole rotor.

## Generator Operation in Stand-alone Power Systems

**System characteristics.** Most synchronous generators are used in large power systems and hence are used in tandem with many other generators. However, a synchronous generator may serve as the sole generator in an isolated power system. In this section, we examine the characteristics of the synchronous generator in such stand-alone applications.

Figure 15.17 suggests a stand-alone system. We note two generator inputs: the throttle on the mechanical drive and the dc field current. This power system has the following characteristics:

- The frequency is determined by the speed of the mechanical drive. The electrical frequency is $(P/2)\omega_m$, where $\omega_m$ is the mechanical speed of the rotor. Thus, tight control of the speed is required if the system frequency needs to be constant, say, for time keeping. Otherwise, the system frequency could vary somewhat without degrading the performance of most loads.

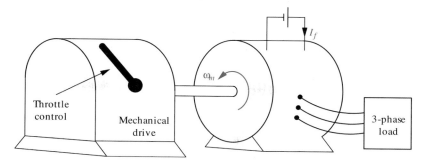

**Figure 15.17** A stand-alone power system.

- The voltage of the system is controlled in part by the field current. Increasing the field current produces an increase in the generated voltage. However, the following example shows that the voltage of the system also depends on the load impedance.

---

**EXAMPLE 15.4** | **Stand-alone generator**

A 230-V, four-pole, 60-Hz, three-phase generator is required to supply 10 kW to a load at a *PF* of 0.9, lagging. The synchronous reactance of the generator is 3.0 $\Omega$ and we neglect all losses and leakage reactance.[21] What would be the output voltage of the generator if the load were disconnected?

**SOLUTION:**

The output voltage with no load would be the magnitude of $\underline{E}_f$, which we can determine from the equivalent circuit in Fig. 15.15(a). The per-phase voltage and current are

$$\underline{V} = \frac{230}{\sqrt{3}} \angle 0°$$

and

$$\underline{I} = \frac{10,000}{\sqrt{3} \times 230 \times 0.9} \angle -\cos^{-1}(0.9) = 27.9 \angle -25.8° \text{ A} \tag{15.44}$$

The excitation voltage is determined by solving Eq. (15.43):

$$\underline{E}_f = \underline{V} + jX_s\underline{I} = \frac{230}{\sqrt{3}} + j3.0 \times 27.9 \angle -25.8° = 185.3 \angle 24.0° \tag{15.45}$$

This per-phase voltage is equivalent to a three-phase voltage of 321 V.

**WHAT IF?** | What if you want to know the torque requirement on the engine driving the generator?[22]

---

[21] Here, as in transformers, not all flux couples rotor and stator.

**Summary.** A stand-alone synchronous generator requires control systems to regulate both generator speed, which determines electrical frequency, and output voltage, which is strongly dependent on the load.

## Power Angles

**Definitions of power angles.** In Sec. 15.1, we investigated the combination of rotor and stator fluxes to produce a rotor–stator flux. In the course of that development, we introduced the angles $\delta_R$ and $\delta_S$ as the physical angles of the rotor and stator fluxes relative to the total flux. Here we investigate more fully these power angles, which correspond to physical angles between the various contributors to the total flux and correspond also to the phase angles between these sinusoidal quantities considered as phasors.

**Power angles and phasor diagrams.** Figure 15.18(a) shows the various power angles as physical angles and Fig. 15.18(b) shows the phasor fluxes at $\theta_m = 0°$. The rotor flux-density phasor is aligned with the N rotor pole because this puts flux across the air gap in the positive (outward) direction. The stator flux-density phasor, however, is aligned with the S stator pole, because this draws flux across the air gap in the positive (outward) direction. The rotor and stator fluxes combine to produce the rotor–stator flux. The rotor power angle, $\delta_R$, is positive when the rotor poles lead the air-gap flux maximum.

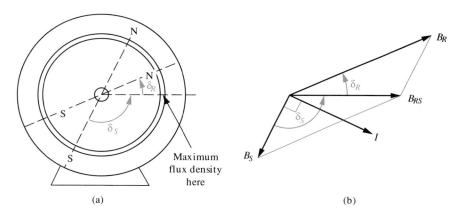

**Figure 15.18** The rotor and stator fluxes combine to give the total flux. This is the pole arrangement in the previous example. (a) Pole arrangement; (b) phasor representation of current and flux density at $\theta_m = 0°$.

**Torque and power angles.** Equation (15.18), repeated here,

$$T_{dev}(\delta_{RS}) = -\frac{\pi R\ell g P}{2\mu_0} B_R B_S \sin\left(\frac{P}{2}\delta_{RS}\right) = -\frac{\pi R\ell g P}{2\mu_0} B_R B_{RS} \sin\left(\frac{P}{2}\delta_R\right) \quad (15.46)$$

gives the output torque of the machine in terms of the rotor power angle. The second

---

[22] 53.1 N-m.

form is useful because its two flux quantities are tied to controlled quantities: The rotor flux is controlled by the dc field current, and the rotor–stator flux is linked to the output voltage. For fixed field excitation and output voltage, the torque depends on the rotor power angle, $\delta_R$.

We show the correspondence between the fluxes and the phasor diagram of the stand-alone operation in the previous example. The circuit and its phasor diagram are shown in Fig. 15.19. The voltage generated in the stator windings, $\underline{V}$, is the phase reference. The current and excitation voltage are shown. The excitation voltage is in phase with the rotor flux density, and the generated voltage in the stator is in phase with the rotor–stator flux density; thus, the phase angle between $\underline{E}_f$ and $\underline{V}$ is the rotor power angle, $\delta_R$. The rotor power angle is particularly important in understanding the operation of a synchronous generator in a large power system. The negative of $jX_s\underline{I}$ represents the stator flux density.

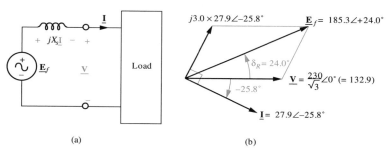

(a)                                          (b)

**Figure 15.19** (a) Circuit and (b) phase relationships, for example, of a stand-alone generator. The pole arrangement and flux-density phasors are shown in Fig. 15.18.

## Synchronous Generator Operation in a Large Power System

OBJECTIVE 4

To understand the characteristics of the synchronous generator when operated into a large power system

In this section, we examine the characteristics of synchronous generators when operated in large power systems where many loads and many generators are interconnected over a geographic region. Such interconnections are used to enhance reliability, to permit maintenance on individual generators, and to permit exchange of electric power between participating power companies, as discussed in Sec. 6.2.

**Power grids.** In such power grids, many generators are operated in tandem. All generators are synchronized and interconnected by long-distance transmission lines. From the viewpoint of an individual generator, the power system is the load into which the generator delivers real and reactive power. The characteristics of such a load, however, are quite different from those of a passive load.

**infinite bus**

**The infinite bus.** The power system is modeled as *infinite bus* in that it maintains constant frequency and constant voltage, both amplitude and phase, independent of the operation of the generator under consideration. The frequency of the system may be considered constant, being established by the controlled rotation of many generators. Thus, if we increase the mechanical drive to an individual generator, we do not increase frequency as in stand-alone operation; rather, we contribute more real power to the grid. Likewise, if we increase the dc field current on an individual generator, we do not increase the output voltage as in stand-alone operation; rather, we change the reactive power contributed to the system. Such independent control over real and reactive output power is demonstrated in the following analysis.

**Operation into an infinite bus.** Figure 15.20 shows the per-phase circuit of a synchronous generator operating into an infinite bus. The real power out of the generator is

$$P_{out} = 3VI \cos \theta \qquad (15.47)$$

where $\theta$ is the angle between the per-phase output voltage and current, and $V$ and $I$ are rms per-phase values. The phasor diagram for such a system is shown in Fig. 15.21.

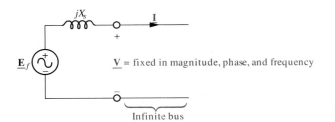

$\underline{V}$ = fixed in magnitude, phase, and frequency

Infinite bus

**Figure 15.20**  Per-phase model of synchronous generator operating into an infinite bus.

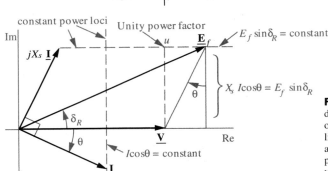

**Figure 15.21**  Per-phase phasor diagram for a synchronous generator operating into an infinite bus. The dashed lines show the loci of the excitation voltage and current phasors for constant output power as the magnitude of the excitation voltage is varied.

We now consider the changes in the phasor diagram as the dc field current is varied, thus changing the *magnitude* of the excitation voltage. We assume that the mechanical drive torque and speed are kept constant, and hence the input and output real powers of the generator remain constant. The line voltage of the infinite bus is fixed; and, hence, from Eq. (15.47), we see that $I \cos \theta$ must remain constant. Thus, the tip of the current phasor follows the dashed vertical line passing through the real axis at the in-phase current required to deliver the real power. As the dc field current is changed, the magnitude and phase of the output current vary, but the component of the current *in phase* with the bus voltage remains constant.

Figure 15.21 shows the rotor power angle, $\delta_R$, as the phase angle by which the excitation voltage, $\underline{E}_f$, leads the bus voltage, $\underline{V}$. By KVL, the excitation voltage is the phasor sum of $\underline{V}$ and $jX_s\underline{I}$; hence, from the geometry shown in Fig. 15.21, it follows that

$$X_s I \cos \theta = E_f \sin \delta_R \qquad (15.48)$$

where $E_f$ is the magnitude of the per-phase excitation voltage. We may therefore modify Eq.(15.47) to the form

$$P_{out} = \frac{3VE_f}{X_s} \sin \delta_R \qquad (15.49)$$

Thus, for constant power (drive throttle) and constant line voltage, $E_f \sin \delta_R$ remains constant. The tip of the excitation voltage phasor, therefore, follows the dashed horizontal line shown in Fig. 15.21.

**The Effect of dc field current on power factor.** With these two loci in mind, we can estimate the effects of changing the dc field current for a synchronous generator operating into an infinite bus. Consider, for example, the effect of decreasing the dc field current on the phasor diagram in Fig. 15.21. Decreasing the field current reduces the magnitude of $E_f$, which moves the tip of $\mathbf{E}_f$ back along the horizontal dashed line toward point $u$. At the same time, the output voltage, $\mathbf{V}$, is fixed; and, hence, the phasor $jX_s\mathbf{I}$, which is parallel to the line connecting $\mathbf{V}$ and $\mathbf{E}_f$, must swing toward a vertical position. Hence, current $\mathbf{I}$ must swing toward a horizontal position, with its tip remaining on the vertical dashed line. Consequently, as the dc field current is decreased, the current becomes more in phase with the output voltage, the power factor moves toward unity, and the magnitude of the current decreases. At point $u$, $\mathbf{E}_f$ lies directly above $\mathbf{V}$, and the current is in phase with the per-phase output voltage. At this point, we have a right triangle, and the excitation voltage is

$$E_{fu}^2 = V^2 + (X_s I)^2 \qquad (15.50)$$

where $E_{fu}$ is the magnitude of the excitation voltage required for unity power factor. As the magnitude of $\mathbf{E}_f$ is further decreased, the current swings ahead of the output voltage and begins to lead. The angle of the current relative to the output voltage is controlled, therefore, by the magnitude of the excitation voltage, which is controlled in turn by the dc field current. The in-phase component of the current is constant but the out-of-phase component varies in magnitude and sign. Hence, the reactive power exchanged between the generator and power system is controlled by the dc field current.

Figure 15.22 shows the effect of the dc field current on the current magnitude and power factor of a synchronous generator with constant output power. The output current leads the output voltage for small field current, an *underexcited* generator, and decreases in magnitude as field current increases. A minimum is reached for unity power factor at $u$, and then the current increases and begins to lag the output voltage, an *over excited* generator.

**underexcited, overexcited generator**

**Summary.** The real power output is controlled by the throttle on the mechanical drive to the generator. The sign and magnitude of the reactive power are controlled by the dc field current. With an overexcited generator, with $\mathbf{E}_f$ beyond point $u$ in Fig. 15.21, the generator supplies positive reactive power. With an underexcited generator, with $\mathbf{E}_f$ to the left of point $u$ in Fig. 15.21, the generator supplies negative reactive power. Equation (15.50) defines the boundary between overexcited and underexcited behavior and corresponds to unity power factor.

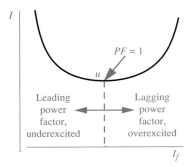

**Figure 15.22**  Effect of field current on output current of a synchronous generator with output power kept constant.

---

**EXAMPLE 15.5** | **Supplying reactive power**

A 600-V (line voltage), three-phase synchronous generator supplies 25 kW. The synchronous reactance is 10.0 Ω. Calculate the per-phase excitation voltage to give unity power factor and determine what excitation voltage causes the generator to supply +10 kVAR of reactive power in addition to the real power.

**SOLUTION:**
The required line current for unity power factor is

$$I = \frac{P}{3V} = \frac{25 \times 10^3}{3(600/\sqrt{3})} = 24.1 \text{ A} \tag{15.51}$$

and, hence, from Eq. (15.50), the required excitation voltage

$$E_{fu} = \sqrt{V^2 + (X_s I)^2} = \sqrt{(600/\sqrt{3})^2 + (10.0 \times 24.1)^2} = 422 \text{ V} \tag{15.52}$$

Note that we use the per-phase voltage in the calculations. For the second part of the problem, we find the apparent power:

$$S = \sqrt{P^2 + Q^2} = \sqrt{(25)^2 + (10)^2} = 26.9 \text{ kVA} \tag{15.53}$$

The power factor is $PF = 25/26.9 = 0.928$ and the phase angle of the current is $\theta = \tan^{-1}(10/25) = 21.8°$, lagging, and the magnitude of the new current, $I'$, is

$$I' = \frac{I}{PF} = \frac{24.1}{0.928} = 25.9 \text{ A} \tag{15.54}$$

From Eq. (15.43), the new phasor excitation voltage $\underline{E}'_f$ is

$$\underline{E}'_f = \underline{V} + jX_s\underline{I}' = \frac{600}{\sqrt{3}} + j10.0 \times 25.9 \angle -21.8° \tag{15.55}$$

$$= 504 \angle 28.5° \text{ V}$$

Thus, a 19% increase in the excitation voltage over the value required for unity power factor adds +10 kVAR of reactive power.

**Output power and power angle.**    Figure 15.23 shows Eq. (15.49) and the effect of rotor power angle on generated power with output voltage and field excitation constant. The rotor power angle, $\delta_R$, is the angle in space, measured in electrical units, by which the physical axis of the rotor leads the total flux in the air gap. As the drive torque is increased, the rotor pulls more on the flux, and more energy is converted from mechanical to electrical form. The output power can be increased up to a limit, as seen in Fig. 15.23, beyond which the motor-generator loses synchronism and runs away. In practice, generators are operated with power angles around 15–25° and thus stay well away from runaway.

Figure 15.23 indicates that negative power angles correspond to negative output power, to motor action. In this case, the air-gap flux leads the axis of the rotor, the electrical system pulls on the mechanical system, and electrical energy is converted to mechanical energy. The characteristics of the synchronous motor are investigated in the next section.

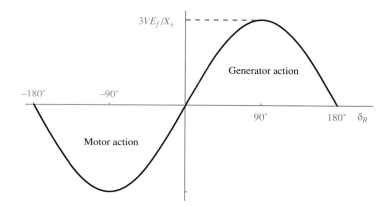

**Figure 15.23**  Output power vs. rotor power angle for a synchronous generator with constant excitation and output voltage.

## Check Your Understanding

**1.** The stator current in a loaded synchronous generator will be minimum with the excitation voltage smaller than, equal to, or greater than the per-phase output voltage. Which?

**2.** A permanent magnet could be used as the rotor of a synchronous generator. True or false?

**3.** In a cylindrical-rotor synchronous generator, increasing the dc field current increases the magnitude of the output current. Is the current leading or lagging?

**4.** It is impossible for a cylindrical-rotor synchronous generator to operate with a rotor power angle beyond +90°. True or false?

*Answers.*  (**1**) Greater than; (**2**) true; (**3**) lagging; (**4**) true.

## Generator and Motor Comparison

**Equivalent Circuits**

**Changed conventions.** Figure 15.24 shows reference directions appropriate for (a) generator and (b) motor operation. We note that a load set of voltage–current reference directions are used for the motor, with appropriate changes in the circuit equation and power formula.

In the formula for power in Fig. 15.24(b), we changed the *meaning* of the current variable (from output to input current) and we accordingly changed the *meaning* of the power from output electrical power to output mechanical power. However, the meaning of the power angle is unchanged, and hence the power angle must be negative for positive output power as a motor. Put another way, we fixed the power equation in Fig. 15.24(b) by negating power and current variables in the power equation in Fig. 15.24(a). In the parts involving the power factor, we absorb the minus sign by changing the *meaning* of the power and current variables. But no meanings were changed in the form involving the power angle, and the minus sign therefore remains. Thus, the power angle must be negative for motor action.

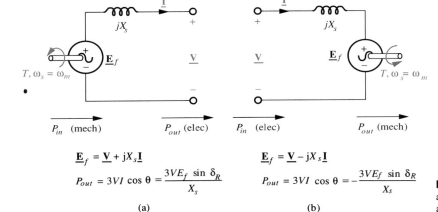

$$\mathbf{E}_f = \mathbf{V} + jX_s\mathbf{I}$$

$$P_{out} = 3VI \cos\theta = \frac{3VE_f \sin\delta_R}{X_s}$$

(a)

$$\mathbf{E}_f = \mathbf{V} - jX_s\mathbf{I}$$

$$P_{out} = 3VI \cos\theta = -\frac{3VE_f \sin\delta_R}{X_s}$$

(b)

**Figure 15.24** Reference conventions and resulting equations for (a) generator and (b) motor operation.

**Phasor diagrams for generator and motor.** Figure 15.25 compares phasor diagrams for generator and motor operation. The $jX_s\mathbf{I}$ phaser leads the stator current for a generator but lags for a motor, a consequence of the change of the current reference direction for the motor in Fig. 15.24(b).

**OBJECTIVE 5**

To understand the characteristics of the synchronous motor, particularly the effect of field current on the power factor

**Analysis of the equivalent circuit.** Kirchhoff's voltage law for the stator circuit of the motor, Fig. 15.24(b), is

$$\mathbf{V} = \mathbf{E}_f + jX_s\mathbf{I} \quad \Rightarrow \quad \mathbf{E}_f = \mathbf{V} - jX_s\mathbf{I} \tag{15.56}$$

The phasor diagram reflecting Eq. (15.56) is shown in Fig. 15.26, where $\theta$ is the phase angle between per-phase voltage and current and is shown negative in Fig. 15.26 (lagging current). The angle $\delta_R$ is the rotor power angle defined in Fig. 15.18 and is the

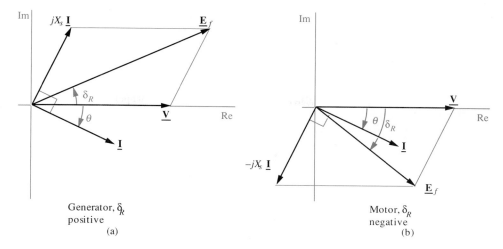

Generator, $\delta_R$
positive
(a)

Motor, $\delta_R$
negative
(b)

**Figure 15.25** Per-phase diagrams for: (a) synchronous generator and (b) synchronous motor.

physical angle, multiplied by $P/2$ for machines with more than two poles, between the rotor–stator flux and the rotor flux. This power angle appears between the per-phase voltage and the excitation voltage because the former represents the total flux and the latter the rotor flux.

The input electrical power to the machine is

$$P = 3VI \cos \theta = -\frac{3VE_f}{X_s} \sin \delta_R \qquad (15.57)$$

Using geometric reasoning on Fig. 15.26, we may determine the reactive power into the machine to be

$$Q = 3VI \sin (-\theta) = \frac{3V^2}{X_s} - \frac{3VE_f}{X_s} \cos \delta_R \qquad (15.58)$$

The excitation voltage may be eliminated between Eqs. (15.57) and (15.58) to give the rotor power angle in terms of the real and reactive power into the machine.

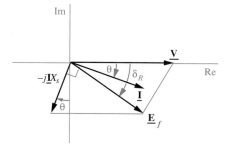

**Figure 15.26** Phasor diagram for the synchronous motor. The applied per-phase voltage is the phase reference, and the current is shown lagging by a phase angle $\theta$. The voltage across the synchronous reactance is shown lagging the current by 90°.

$$\tan \delta_R = \frac{P}{Q - (3V^2/X_s)} = \frac{P}{Q - (V_L^2/X_s)} \tag{15.59}$$

where $V_L$ is the three-phase voltage $(= \sqrt{3}V)$.

---

**EXAMPLE 15.6** | **Synchronous motor**

A 480-V three-phase, six-pole synchronous motor has 50-hp output power at unity power factor with a field current of 5 A dc. The field current is increased to 6 A dc. Find the new power factor and the new input current. Ignore losses, assume that the synchronous reactance is 3.2 Ω, and assume that the excitation voltage is proportional to field current.

**SOLUTION:**
First, we find the excitation voltage for unity power factor. For 50 hp out, no losses, and unity power factor, the current is

$$I = \frac{P}{3V} = \frac{50 \times 746}{3(480/\sqrt{3})} = 44.9 \text{ A} \tag{15.60}$$

and is in phase with the input voltage. By KVL in Eq. (15.56), the phasor excitation voltage is

$$\mathbf{E}_{fu} = \frac{480}{\sqrt{3}} - j3.2 \times 44.9 \angle 0° = 312.1 \angle -27.4° \tag{15.61}$$

where $\mathbf{E}_{fu}$ is the excitation voltage for unity power factor. Hence, for unity power factor, the magnitude of the per-phase excitation voltage is 312.1 V and the rotor power angle is $-27.4°$. When we increase the dc field current from 5 to 6 A dc, the magnitude of the excitation voltage increases proportionally:

$$E'_f = \frac{6}{5} \times 312.1 = 374.5 \text{ V} \tag{15.62}$$

where the prime refers to conditions after the field current is changed. Changing the field current does not change the real power output of the motor because that is established by the speed, which is constant, and the torque requirement of the load at that speed. Thus, we may determine the new rotor power angle from Eq. (15.57):

$$312.1 \sin(-27.4°) = 374.5 \sin(\delta'_R) \implies \delta'_R = -22.5° \tag{15.63}$$

And the new reactive power can be determined from Eq. (15.58):

$$Q' = \frac{3(480/\sqrt{3})^2}{3.2} - \frac{3(480/\sqrt{3})(374.5)\cos(-22.5°)}{3.2}$$
$$= -17,900 \text{ VAR} \tag{15.64}$$

The reactive power is negative, meaning that the new current leads the per-phase voltage. The new power factor may be determined from the real and reactive powers:

$$PF = \frac{P}{\sqrt{P^2 + Q^2}} = \frac{50 \times 746}{\sqrt{(50 \times 746)^2 + (-17,900)^2}} = 0.902 \qquad (15.65)$$

Hence, the new current magnitude is $44.9/0.902 = 49.7\,A$, and the new phase angle is $\cos^{-1} 0.902 = 25.6°$ with current leading voltage.

---

**WHAT IF?**

What if you use Eq. (15.56) instead of Eq. (15.64)?[23]

---

**overexcited motor**

### Effect of varying the field current with constant output power.

Figure 15.27 shows a phasor diagram for a synchronous motor that is *overexcited* because the excitation voltage is greater than that required to give unity power factor. Let us consider the effect of reducing the excitation voltage, reducing field current, while the output power and per-phase voltage are kept constant. By Eq. (15.57), $E_f \sin \delta_R$ must remain constant, so the tip of $\mathbf{E}_f$ must move along a horizontal line. Likewise, for constant power, the in-phase component of the current, $I \cos \theta$ must remain constant; hence, the tip of the current phasor moves along a vertical line. At point $u$, the tip of $\mathbf{E}_f$ ($E_{fu}$) lies below $\mathbf{V}$ and the current is in phase with the per-phase voltage. If the excitation voltage is larger than $E_{fu}$, the current phase must swing ahead of the per-phase voltage and a leading power factor is produced. If the excitation voltage is less than $E_{fu}$, the current phase must lag the per-phase voltage and a lagging power factor is produced. The out-of-phase component of the current of the synchronous motor thus can be controlled by the field current, as with a synchronous generator.

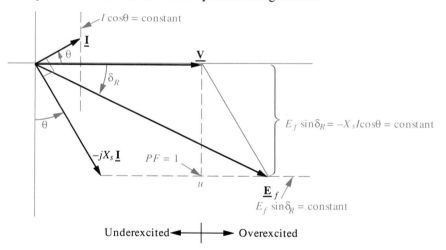

**Figure 15.27** Phasor diagram for the synchronous motor. The motor draws leading or lagging current, depending on the magnitude of the excitation voltage.

---

[23] $I' = (374.5 \angle -22.5° - 480/\sqrt{3}\,)/(-j3.2) = 49.7 \angle +25.7°$. This current leads to the same $P$, $Q$, and $PF$.

so we may determine $E_f$ from Eq. (15.69) with $\delta_R = -15.8°$.

$$250 \times 746 = -\frac{3(2300/\sqrt{3})E_f \sin(-15.6°)}{15}$$

$$-\frac{3}{2}\left(\frac{2300}{\sqrt{3}}\right)^2 \left(\frac{1}{8} - \frac{1}{15}\right)\sin(-2 \times 15.8°) \tag{15.72}$$

Thus, $E_f = 1470$ V. We may determine the reactive power from Eq. (15.70) with $\delta_R = 0°$:

$$Q = -\frac{3(2300/\sqrt{3})(1470)}{15} + 3\left(\frac{2300}{\sqrt{3}}\right)^2 \left(\frac{1}{15} + 0\right) \tag{15.73}$$

$$= -37,400 \text{ VAR}$$

The machine is overexcited and draws negative reactive power.

**Reluctance torque.** We may determine the developed torque from Eq. (15.69):

$$T_{dev} = \frac{P_{dev}}{\omega_s} = -\frac{3VE_f}{\omega_s X_d}\sin \delta_R - \frac{3}{2}\frac{V^2}{\omega_s}\left(\frac{1}{X_q} - \frac{1}{X_d}\right)\sin(2\delta_R)$$

$$= -T_f \sin \delta_R - T_\Re \sin(2\delta_R) \tag{15.74}$$

**reluctance torque**

The $\sin(2\delta_R)$ term in Eq. (15.74) reveals the presence of reluctance torque due to the salient poles. In Eq. (15.74), $T_f$ is the maximum torque[27] due to the rotor field and $T_\Re$ is the maximum reluctance torque due to the asymmetry of the rotor magnetic structure. This *reluctance torque* arises because the rotor magnetic structure tries to come into alignment with the stator poles. Reluctance torque is due to induced magnetic poles on the rotor protrusions and would be present if the rotor had no field coils.

| **EXAMPLE 15.9** | **Reluctance torque** |

The 60-Hz motor in the previous example has 12 poles. Find the equation of the torque and identify the terms due to rotor field and reluctance.

**SOLUTION:**
For 12 poles and 60 Hz, the synchronous speed is $20\pi$ rad/s. Substitution of the excitation voltage into the first term in Eq. (15.74) fields a maximum torque of 6210 N-m due to the rotor dc current. The second term yields 2460 N-m for the maximum reluctance torque. For the rotor power angle calculated, the output torques due to the two components are 1690 N-m and 1280 N-m, respectively, and hence about 43% of the output torque is due to reluctance torque. The reluctance torque improves the characteristics of the motor because it increases the maximum possible torque and causes the motor to run with a smaller rotor power angle. Figure 15.28 shows the torque characteristic of this machine.

---

[27] Recall that $\delta_R$ is negative.

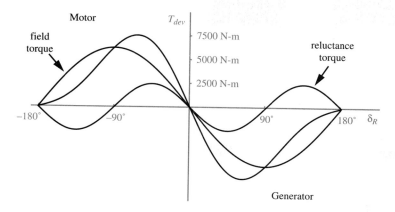

**Figure 15.28** Developed torque in a salient-pole motor. The reluctance torque improves the motor characteristic by giving a higher slope in the operating region and a larger maximum torque.

## Check Your Understanding

1. For a cylindrical-rotor synchronous motor, the torque is 500 N-m with a rotor power angle of $-30°$. What is the maximum torque available from this machine without changing the excitation voltage?

2. The effect of the reluctance torque is to degrade the performance of a salient-pole synchronous motor. True or false?

3. An important virtue of a synchronous motor is (a) easy speed control, (b) high efficiency, or (c) adjustable power factor. Which?

4. A 25-hp synchronous motor with eight poles has a rated output torque twice that of a 25-hp synchronous motor with four poles. True or false?

5. Explain why a factory uses a combination of synchronous and induction motors.

*Answers.* (**1**) 1000 N-m; (**2**) false; (**3**) adjustable power factor; (**4**) true; (**5**) induction motors have lagging current and synchronous motors can draw leading current.

## CHAPTER SUMMARY

Chapter 15 begins by showing that steady energy transformation requires both torque and rotation. Torque is produced between misaligned rotor and stator magnetic poles. Rotating flux is produced in cylindrical structures by ac excitation. The synchronous machine is studied as a generator, with emphasis on operating into a large power grid. We show that real and reactive output powers can be controlled independently. Similarly, the real power to the synchronous motor is determined by load demand but the reactive power is controlled by field current.

**Objective 1: To understand how magnetic flux is created and distributed in the air gap of a cylindrical magnetic structure.** Magnetic flux is created in a cylindrical structure by distributed coils placed in slots on the inner surface of the stator. The magnitude of the maximum flux density can be determined through Ampère's circuital law. The number of poles is twice the coils/phase. The wire density is tapered to produce a sinusoidally tapered flux pattern.

**Objective 2. To understand how magnetic flux is made to rotate in cylindrical magnetic structures.** The flux pattern is rotated by exciting spatially separated coils with two- or three-phase currents. The direction of rotation depends on the phase relationships between the exciting currents. The speed of flux rotation equals the ac frequency divided by the number of pole pairs.

**Objective 3: To understand the role of the rotor and stator flux in the operation of synchronous generators.** The rotor of the synchronous machine is an electromagnet whose poles match the stator poles. When rotating in synchronism with the stator, a steady torque is produced on the rotor structure. The torque requirement of the load determines the power angle by which motor poles follow stator poles in the rotation.

**Objective 4: To understand the characteristics of the synchronous generator when operated into a large power system.** When operated into an infinite bus, the real power output of the synchronous generator is determined by the input mechanical drive to the rotor. The reactive power is controlled in sign and magnitude by the strength of the rotor flux, which is established by the dc field current to the rotor. Normally, the field is overexcited to produce the lagging current required by magnetic loads.

**Objective 5. To understand the characteristics of the synchronous motor, particularly the effect of field current on the power factor.** The real power into the synchronous motor is determined by the torque requirement of the load. The reactive power, sign and magnitude, is controlled by the dc field current. Normally, the field is overexcited to draw leading current to balance the lagging current required by induction motors.

Synchronous motors are specialized devices with limited applications. Chapter 16 takes up three-and single phase induction motors, which constitute the vast majority of ac motors.

## PROBLEMS

## Section 15.1: Flux and Torque in Cylindrical Magnetic Structures

**15.1.** If you wanted the magnetic flux density to be 0.4 T at $\theta_m = 42°$ in Fig. 15.5(a), what would the mmf of the coil have to be? The gap is 0.5 mm wide.

**15.2.** The cylindrical magnetic structure shown in Fig. P15.2(a) has 24 slots with tapered windings, as shown in the table in Fig. 15.2(b). The gap width is 1 mm and the mmf loss in the iron may be neglected. The current is 20 A into the paper on the bottom half and out on the top half. Determine the maximum magnetic flux density in the air gap and determine the location of the maximum.

**15.3.** Two magnetic structures with cylindrical geometry are shown in Fig. P15.3. A dc current $i$ flows in at the cross and out at the dot, with one wire in each slot. The rotor is a permanent magnet with poles and orientation shown.

(a) How many stator poles are there in each case?
(b) In each case, determine the direction of the torque on the rotor, if there is any torque.

**15.4.** We wish to design a cylindrical magnetic structure to produce a four-pole flux pattern. We require N poles at $\theta_m = -45°$ and $+135°$. The peak value of the flux density is 1.0 T, the gap width is 0.9 mm.

(a) Draw the magnetic structure required and show the locations of the coils and currents on the stator. Mark $\times + i$ for where $i$ enters the paper, etc.

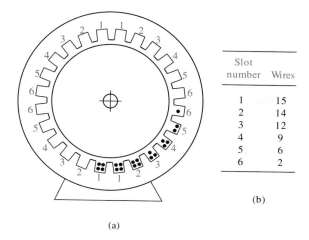

| Slot number | Wires |
|:-----------:|:-----:|
| 1 | 15 |
| 2 | 14 |
| 3 | 12 |
| 4 | 9 |
| 5 | 6 |
| 6 | 2 |

(b)

(a)

**Figure P15.2**

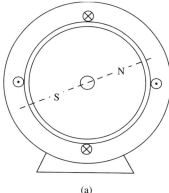

(a)　　　　　　　　(b)

**Figure P15.3**

**(b)** How many turns/coil are required if the peak current is 10 A?

**(c)** If there are 24 slots in the stator, give the number of wires in each slot to approximate a sinusoidal mmf.

## Section 15.2: Rotating Magnetic Flux for AC Motors

**15.5.** A cylindrical rotor and a three-phase, two-pole stator are excited by dc and 60-Hz ac currents, respectively. The rotor is locked and stationary in the position shown in Fig. P15.5. The rotor-flux density is constant with 1.0 T maximum, sinusoidally distributed in space. The stator produces a flux density with 0.5 T maximum, sinusoidally distributed in space and rotating

counterclockwise, as shown in Fig. P15.5. The maximum of the flux density due to the stator currents is at $\theta_m = 0°$ in space at $t = 0$.

**(a)** At $t = 1/360$ s, what is the magnitude and direction (in space) of the air-gap vector flux density at $\theta_m = 0°$?

**(b)** At $t = 1/360$ s, at what angle in space ($\theta_m$) is the magnetic-flux density a maximum?

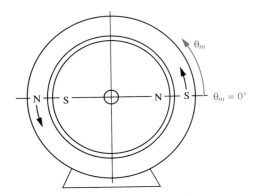

**Figure P15.5**

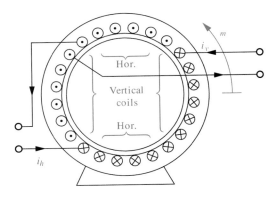

**Figure P15.6**

**(c)** At $t = 1/360$ s, what direction would the rotor tend to move if freed?

**15.6.** A cylindrical magnetic structure is wound with two coils, as shown in Fig. P15.6. One, excited by $i_h$, produces a horizontal flux, and the other, excited by $i_v$, produces a vertical flux. The horizontal flux density is

$$B_h(t, \theta_m) = \frac{\mu_0 n i_h(t)}{2g} \cos \theta_m$$

and the vertical flux density is

$$B_v(t, \theta_m) = \frac{\mu_0 n i_v(t)}{2g} \sin \theta_m$$

where $n$ is the number of turns in each coil and $g$ is the gap width. Find the magnetic flux density at a mechanical angle of $30°$, that is, find $B(t, \theta_m = 30°)$ for the following conditions. In each case, explain the nature of the flux (rotating?, which way?, oscillating?, direction?, etc.).
**(a)** $i_h = 2I_p$ dc and $i_v = -I_p$ dc.
**(b)** $i_v = 0$ and $i_h = I_p \cos(\omega t)$.
**(c)** $i_v = I_p \sin(\omega t)$ and $i_h = 0$.
**(d)** The currents in parts (b) and (c) at the same time.

**15.7.** Table P15.7 has columns for time-domain expressions for magnetic flux densities in an air gap, as a function of angle in space, and a description of the field or the source of the field. Fill in the missing information.

**15.8.** Write mathematical expressions for the following air-gap flux densities. Assume 60 Hz.
**(a)** A two-pole, single-phase oscillating flux with peaks in the vertical direction and nulls in the horizontal direction. Assume that the flux density has a maximum of 0.5 T at $t = 0$.
**(b)** A two-pole rotating flux that moves counterclockwise and has its positive peak of 0.5 T at $\theta_m = 180°$ at $t = 0$.
**(c)** A four-pole rotating flux that rotates clockwise and has its negative peak of 0.6 T at $\theta_m = -90°$ at $t = 0$.

**15.9.** A cylindrical magnetic structure has a flux pattern in its air gap given by the expression

$$B(t, \theta_m) = 1.5 \cos(800 \pi t + \theta_m - 60°)$$

**(a)** How many magnetic poles are indicated?
**(b)** Where is the maximum flux density at $t = 0$?
**(c)** What is the rotation direction and speed in rpm?

| TABLE P15.7 | | | |
| --- | --- | --- | --- |
| **Flux density** | **Poles** | **Synchronous speed** | **Description** |
| $1.5 \cos(200\pi t + \theta_m)$ $1.2 \cos(30t - 3\theta_m)$ $1.0 \cos(100\pi t) \sin(2\theta_m)$ | | | |

**(d)** Sketch a pattern of currents on the stator that produces this flux at $t = 0$.

**15.10.** Give the mathematical expressions in the time domain for the following fluxes. The frequency is 60 Hz. The radially outward direction is considered positive in the air gap.

**(a)** A four-pole oscillating flux. One maximum flux density of 1.2 T occurs at $\theta_m = -45°$ at $t = 0$.

**(b)** A two-pole rotating flux, clockwise rotation, North magnetic pole in the stator crosses $\theta_m = 0°$ at $t = 0$. The maximum flux density is 0.6 T.

**15.11.** A rotating flux is created with 16 coils, spaced evenly around a cylindrical stator. The coils are connected to two-phase current so as to create a rotating flux in the CCW direction. The flux rotates at 600 rpm and has a maximum of 1.0 T in the vertical direction, $\theta_m = 90°$ at $t = 0$. Find the magnitude and sign of the outward-directed flux density at $\theta_m = 234°$ and $t = 10$ ms.

**15.12.** A three-phase stator produces a rotating flux that is described by the equation

$$B(t,\theta_m) = 1.5 \cos(\omega t + 3\theta_m + 60°) \text{ T}$$

**(a)** How many poles does the stator have?

**(b)** Where ($\theta_m = ?$) is the flux density maximum at $t = 0$?

**(c)** If two wires of the three-phase system were reversed, what would change in the flux-density expression?

**(d)** If the electrical frequency of the stator currents were 30 Hz, what would be the speed in rpm of the stator flux rotation?

**(e)** If the stator windings were reconnected into Y instead of Δ, what would be the resulting rotating flux? Assume constant voltage. Consider the phase rotation as original.

**15.13.** Figure P15.13(b) shows a two-phase, two-pole stator with current directions. Figure P15.13(a) shows a two-phase current with the period given.

**(a)** Where ($\theta_m = ?$), is the flux density maximum at $t = 0$? Count the positive as maximum where the flux is outward across the air gap.

**(b)** Which way does the flux rotate?

**(c)** Give the equation of the flux density as a function of time and mechanical angle, assuming that the maximum flux density is 0.72 T.

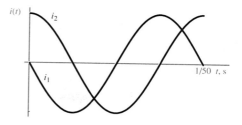

(a)

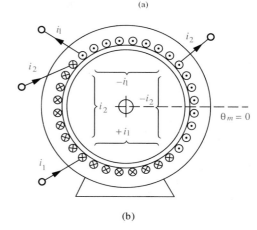

(b)

**Figure P15.13**

**(d)** Find the synchronous speed of the flux pattern in rpm.

**15.14.** Figure P15.14(b) shows a three-phase, two-pole stator with current directions. Figure P15.14(a) shows a three-phase current with the period given.

**(a)** Where ($\theta_m = ?$), is the flux density maximum at $t = 0$? Count the positive as maximum where the flux is outward across the air gap.

**(b)** Which way does the flux rotate?

**(c)** Give the equation of the flux density as a function of time and mechanical angle, assuming that the maximum flux density is 0.72 T.

**(d)** Find the synchronous speed of the flux pattern in radians/second.

**15.15.** A cylindrical magnetic structure has four coils on it, excited by 60-Hz, two-phase currents such that four counterclockwise rotating magnetic poles are produced. At $t = 0$, the N pole is at $\theta_m = 0°$. The maximum value of the magnetic flux density in the air gap is 0.85 T.

**(a)** Draw a cylindrical magnetic structure and

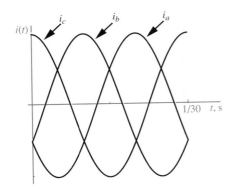

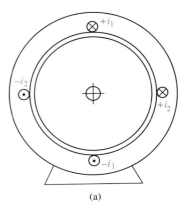

(a)

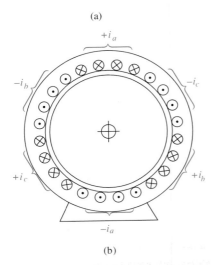

(a)

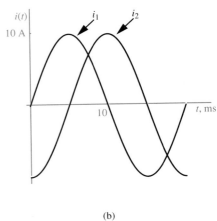

(b)

**Figure P15.16**

**Figure P15.14**

indicate the magnetic poles and sketch the magnetic flux patterns at $t = 0$.

**(b)** Write an expression for $B(t, \theta_m)$.

**(c)** Find a time when the flux density at $\theta_m = 45°$ is $+ 0.6$ T.

**15.16.** A cylindrical magnetic structure is wound with two coils, which we have symbolized with a single wire and labeled "1" and "2" in Fig. P15.16(a). The coils have 90 turns each and the air gap is 1 mm. Currents $i_1$ and $i_2$ are shown in Fig. P15.16(b). The coils overlap and are sinusoidally tapered.

**(a)** Is this a single-phase, two-phase, or three-phase system?

**(b)** Determine the location of the magnetic flux density maximum at $t = 0$.

**(c)** Determine the direction of rotation of the flux.

**(d)** Determine the synchronous speed in rpm.

**(e)** Determine the maximum value of the magnetic flux density.

**(f)** Write an expression for $B(t, \theta_m)$.

**15.17.** Write the equation for the magnetic flux density in the air gap of a cylindrical magnetic structure having the following properties:

- The machine has 18 coils, excited by three-phase ac currents to produce a rotating flux.
- The synchronous speed of the flux pattern is 1500 rpm in the CCW direction.
- The maximum flux-density is 0.8 T.
- The stator coils are tapered to produce a sinusoidal spatial flux pattern.
- The flux-density maximum is horizontal at $t = 0$.

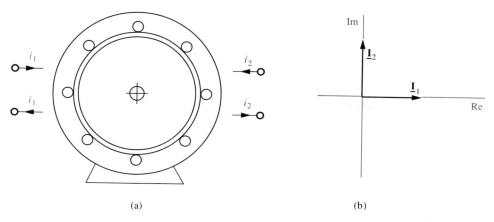

(a)                                          (b)

**Figure P15.18**

**15.18.** A cylindrical magnetic structure is shown in Fig. P15.18(a) with the windings simplified, showing a single wire for each distributed winding. You are to show the external connections so that two-phase currents produce a four-pole flux rotating in the clockwise direction. The phasors for $i_1$ and $i_2$ are shown in Fig. P15.18(b).

  (a) On the diagram place by the wires $+ i_1$ where the current enters the paper and $- i_1$ where the current comes out of the paper, and similarly for $i_2$. Connect the wires at the side.

  (b) Draw the flux pattern at $t = 0$.

**15.19.** A three-phase cylindrical magnetic structure has $P = 2$ poles.

  (a) The windings are excited with balanced three-phase 50-Hz currents. Describe in words the character and behavior of the flux in the machine.

  (b) Give a mathematical expression for the flux density in the time domain as a function of mechanical angle, using the standard notation. Assume the maximum air-gap flux density at $\theta_m = 0°$ at $t = 0$. Let $B_r$ be the maximum flux density in the air gap, and assume clockwise rotation.

  (c) Give a phasor representing the flux density at $\theta_m = 30°$.

  (d) If each coil has 100 turns and carries a current of 2 A and the gap width is 0.5 mm, what is the maximum flux density for the machine?

**15.20.** A counterclockwise rotating wave of flux density is represented at $\theta_m = 0°$ by the expression

$B(t, 0°) = 0.5 \cos(120\pi t - 45°)$ T. What is $B(t, \theta_m)$ generally, assuming a four-pole machine?

**15.21.** A rotating flux density is
$B(t, \theta_m) = 1.2 \cos[100\pi t + 4 (\theta_m - 30°)]$ T
The machine is three-phase, excited by 50-Hz currents.

  (a) How many magnetic poles does the machine have?

  (b) In which direction does the field rotate?

  (c) Find the first time after $t = 0$ when a positive flux maximum passes the angle $\theta_m = 0°$.

**15.22.** A cylindrical magnetic structure is shown in Fig. P15.22(a). The slots are numbered, and Table P15.22 gives the number of wires and

**TABLE P15.22**

| Slot | Coil for $i_a$<br>Wires, direction | Coil for $i_b$<br>Wires, direction |
|---|---|---|
| 1 | 19, + | 5, + |
| 2 | 14, + | 14, + |
| 3 | 5, + | 19, + |
| 4 | 5, − | 19, + |
| 5 | 14, − | 14, + |
| 6 | 19, − | 5, + |
| 7 | 19, − | 5, − |
| 8 | 14, − | 14, − |
| 9 | 5, − | 19, − |
| 10 | 5, + | 19, − |
| 11 | 14, + | 14, − |
| 12 | 19, + | 5, − |

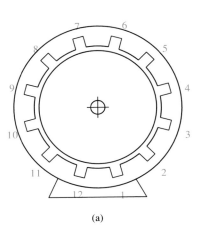

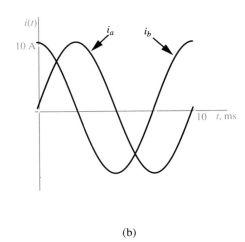

(a)

(b)

**Figure P15.22**

current direction (+ into the paper) for the two coils that are wound on the stator. The currents are shown in Fig. P15.22(b).
- **(a)** What is the maximum magnetic flux density if the gap is 1 mm wide?
- **(b)** How many poles in this structure?
- **(c)** What is the direction of rotation?
- **(d)** What is the synchronous speed of rotation?
- **(e)** Write the equation for $B(t, \theta_m)$.

15.23. A magnetic structure has a grand total of 600 turns. These are organized into two windings for two-phase operation, for four rotating poles. The OD of the rotor is $3.110 \pm 0.001$ inches and the ID of the stator is $3.136 \pm 0.001$ inches. The two-

phase currents are 60 Hz with the same peak current in both phases. The windings are sinusoidally tapered. There are 40 slots on the stator.
- **(a)** What is the rotational speed of the flux in radians/second?
- **(b)** To reverse the direction of flux rotation, would one or both of the two-phase currents have to be reversed?
- **(c)** If the least acceptable value of the peak magnetic flux density required were 1.1 T, what would be the rms current required in each winding?
- **(d)** Find the maximum number of wires in any slot.

## Section 15.3: Synchronous Generator Principles and Characteristics

15.24. A three-phase, four-pole, 60-Hz synchronous generator is operated in a stand-alone system. The load impedance is 2 Ω real per phase and requires 208 V (line voltage). The synchronous reactance of the generator is 2 Ω per phase. Stator resistance may be ignored.
- **(a)** What value of open-circuit line voltage is produced to yield the required value with the load in place? Assume a linear magnetic structure.
- **(b)** What is the load current and power?
- **(c)** What is the required input torque, ignoring losses?

15.25. A six-pole, three-phase, 60-Hz, Y-connected synchronous generator produces a line voltage of

8600 V. The stator windings are capable of carrying a current of 12 A. The synchronous reactance is 60 Ω. At a given moment, the field current is 10 A dc, and the generator is producing nameplate output at 0.8 *PF*, lagging, into a passive load. Neglect losses.
- **(a)** Find the input torque and speed in rpm.
- **(b)** Draw a phasor diagram showing $\mathbf{I}$, $jX_s\mathbf{I}$, $\mathbf{V}$, $\delta_R$, and $\mathbf{E}_f$.
- **(c)** If the load were suddenly removed, to what would the line voltage jump? Assume the magnetic structure is linear.

15.26. A three-phase 12-pole, 60-Hz, synchronous generator operates into a 600-V infinite bus and delivers 20 kW at unity power factor. The synchronous reactance is 10 Ω. Ignore resistive losses.

(a) What is the per-phase current?

(b) What is the excitation voltage, $E_f$, magnitude only?

(c) What is the rotor power angle?

(d) Determine the input torque.

**15.27.** An open-circuit/short-circuit test is performed on a three-phase synchronous generator, with the results shown in Fig. P15.27. The nameplate voltage is 240 V, and the nameplate current is 12 A, as shown.

(a) Explain why the voltage curve is curved but the current curve is straight.

(b) Estimate the per-phase synchronous reactance of the machine.

(c) Is the field current for nameplate operation, $PF = 1$, less than, equal, or greater than 4 A?

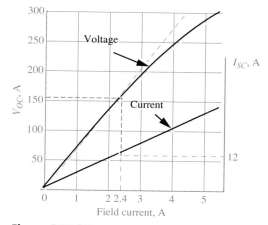

**Figure P15.27** Open-circuit/short-circuit test data.

**15.28.** A three-phase synchronous generator has a no-load output voltage of 2400 V at a field current of 12 A dc. Connected to a 2300-V infinite bus, the mechanical drive is adjusted such that the generator puts out 48 kW and + 12 kVAR with this same field current. Assume a linear magnetic structure.

(a) Calculate the synchronous reactance per phase.

(b) To increase the reactive power output to 24 kVAR, what should be the field current? The real power output stays the same.

**15.29.** A three-phase synchronous generator produces a real power of 100 kW and a reactive power of

+ 50 kVAR into an infinite bus at 1200 V. The synchronous reactance of the generator is 10 Ω, and the losses may be ignored.

(a) Draw a per-phase phasor diagram showing the bus voltage, $\mathbf{V}$, the line current, $\mathbf{I}$, the power factor angle, $\theta$, the rotor power angle, $\delta_R$, and the excitation voltage, $\mathbf{E}_f$,

(b) The drive torque is increased 10%. Indicate which of the quantities in part(a) increase in magnitude, which remain the same, and which decrease.

**15.30.** The phasor diagram for a 60-Hz, three-phase synchronous generator is shown in Fig. P15.30. Note that all sides and two angles of the triangle are shown. The current is 21 A, and the generator has four poles. The diagram shows per-phase values.

(a) Is the generator overexcited or underexcited?

(b) What is the rotor power angle?

(c) What is the power factor and is it leading or lagging?

(d) Determine the synchronous reactance.

(e) Determine the input power and torque, ignoring losses.

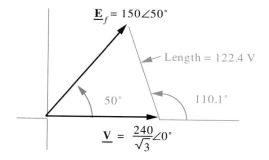

**Figure P15.30**

**15.31.** A 60-Hz, six-pole, three-phase synchronous generator is operated at nameplate kVA with the per-phase phasor diagram shown in Fig. P15.31. Ignore losses.

(a) Find the kVA of the machine.

(b) Find the input torque to the generator.

(c) Find the synchronous reactance per phase of the machine.

**15.32.** A three-phase, two-pole, 60-Hz, 10-MVA, 13-kV synchronous generator has a synchronous reactance of 10.0 Ω. Neglect losses.

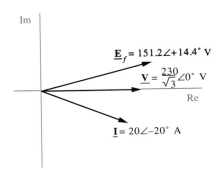

$\underline{E}_f = 151.2\angle +14.4° \text{ V}$

$\underline{V} = \dfrac{230}{\sqrt{3}}\angle 0° \text{ V}$

Re

$\underline{I} = 20\angle -20° \text{ A}$

**Figure P15.31**

**(a)** At nameplate kVA and 0.9 *PF*, lagging, what is the torque required to drive the machine?

**(b)** If the condition described in part (a) requires a field current of 50 A, what field current would correspond to unity power factor and the same real power out?

**(c)** Estimate how low the field current could be reduced without the generator losing synchronism under the same real power load.

## Section 15.4: Characteristics of the Synchronous Motor

**15.33.** Upper Slobovia runs on 60 Hz and Lower Slobovia runs on 50 Hz. Your assignment as an engineer in the Slobovia Light and Power Company is to design an interconnection between the two three-phase systems.

**(a)** Show how you would accomplish this.

**(b)** Specify the type of machine or machines, how many poles, rotational speeds, how to connect electrically and mechanically, and whatever else you wish to add.

**15.34.** A three-phase synchronous motor is rated at 6 kVA. The per-phase voltage is $240\sqrt{3}$ V. Tests were performed with no load, with the following results: Minimum (essentially zero) input current was observed at a field current of 8 A, and nameplate kVA was drawn at 10 A. Neglect magnetic saturation and losses throughout this problem.

**(a)** What is the nameplate per-phase current and what was the phase of this current during the second test? Draw a phasor diagram of this situation. Assume $\underline{V}$ at an angle of $0°$.

**(b)** A motor is now loaded. If the field current is then adjusted for nameplate kVA at unity power factor, what current is required in the field? Draw a phasor diagram for this situation.

**15.35.** A three-phase, 20-hp, four-pole, 60-Hz, 600-V synchronous motor has 60 N-m of output torque with a leading power factor of 0.92 and an efficiency of 89.5%. Find the input current.

**15.36.** A 460-V, three-phase, six-pole, 60-Hz synchronous motor has a nameplate output power of 10 hp. The per-phase synchronous reactance is 15 $\Omega$. At nameplate output power, the motor requires a dc current of 3 A in the rotor field for unity power factor. Ignore losses.

**(a)** Find the input current per phase for unity power-factor operation at $P_{out} = 10$ hp

**(b)** It is desirable to have the motor draw leading current from the bus. Find the field current for a leading angle of 30° at $P_{out} = 10$ hp. Assume that the magnetic structure is linear, that is, assume that the excitation voltage is proportional to the field current.

**(c)** For the condition in part(a), the load is suddenly dropped (say, the output shaft breaks!). Find the resulting per-phase current and the power factor.

**15.37.** Two identical synchronous machines are operated as a motor–generator set, as shown in Fig. P15.37. The rotor fields are connected in series so that they have the same field currents. The synchronous reactance of both machines is 2 $\Omega$, and ignore all losses. The machine that is operated as a motor is connected to a 240-V infinite bus. The field current is adjusted to give minimum motor current (ideally zero) when the generator has no load.

**(a)** What is the output line voltage with no electrical load?

**(b)** Without a change in the field currents, the generator is now loaded with real 5 $\Omega$/phase. Find the output line voltage and current.

**(c)** Assuming that the output voltage with no load is in phase with the input voltage to the motor, what is the phase of the output voltage in part (b) relative to the voltage on the infinite bus?

**15.38.** Two 50-kVA[28] three-phase synchronous machines (with 12 and 10 poles, respectively) are used to tie together a 60-Hz system and a 50-Hz system, as shown in Fig. P15.38. The 60-Hz system is

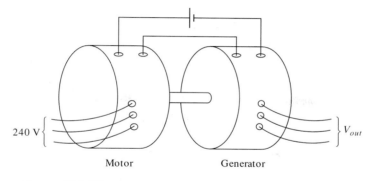

**Figure P15.37** A motor–generator set. The dc field currents are equal.

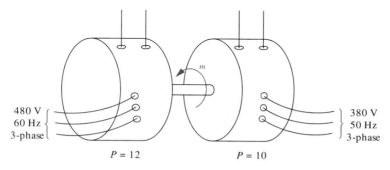

**Figure P15.38** A 60-to-50-Hz converter.

considered an infinite bus, and the 50-Hz machine is the sole generator in its system. The synchronous reactances are 1.7 and 1.2 $\Omega$, respectively, at the appropriate frequencies. The field currents are set to give the nameplate voltages with unity power factor and nameplate kVA on both machines. Neglect losses.

**(a)** What is the mechanical speed of the machines in rpm?

**(b)** For nameplate operation at unity power factor, what is the per-phase resistance of the load on the 50-Hz system?

**(c)** For the situation described in part (b), draw a per-phase phasor diagram showing $\mathbf{E}_f, \mathbf{I}, \mathbf{V}$, and the rotor power angle, $\delta_R$, for the motor.

**(d)** What would be the no-load line voltage on the 50-Hz system, assuming linear magnetic structures?

**15.39.** Figure P15.39 shows a per-phase phasor diagram for a 12-pole, three-phase synchronous machine.

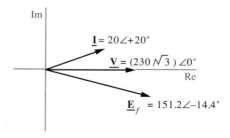

**Figure P15.39**

**(a)** Is the machine operating as a motor or a generator?

**(b)** What is the voltage and apparent power into/out of the machine?

**(c)** Determine the synchronous reactance of the machine.

**(d)** For the same real power, what magnitude of excitation voltage yields unity power factor?

**(e)** If the motor were stopped and used as a brake,

---

find the maximum torque it could hold. Assume both rotor and stator currents must be derated by 50% from those implied in the phasor diagram due to loss of cooling by convection.

**15.40.** A 50-hp, 480-V, 8-pole, 60-Hz, three-phase synchronous motor has a power factor of 0.8, leading, at full-load output. When the mechanical load is removed, the current into the motor is 40 A. Neglect losses. Find the synchronous reactance.

**15.41.** A cylindrical-rotor, 60-Hz, three-phase, 12-pole synchronous motor operates from 2300 V and produces 500 hp. The motor operates with unity power factor with an excitation voltage of $E_f = 1620$ V per phase. Neglect losses. Determine the following:
(a) The current.
(b) The synchronous reactance.
(c) The torque.
(d) The rotor power angle.

**15.42.** A 100-hp, 480-V, 8-pole, 60-Hz, three-phase synchronous motor has nameplate power at unity power factor with a field current of 5 A dc. What field current corresponds to 80 hp out and a 0.9 *PF*, leading? The synchronous reactance is 1 Ω. Neglect losses. Assume that the excitation voltage is proportional to the field current.

**15.43.** The per-phase phasor diagram for a three-phase, 60-Hz, 8-pole synchronous motor is shown in Fig. P15.43. Note that all sides and two angles of the triangle are shown. The current/phase is 21 A (rms).
(a) Is the motor overexcited or underexcited?
(b) What is the rotor power angle?
(c) What is the power factor and is it leading or lagging?
(d) Determine the synchronous reactance per phase.

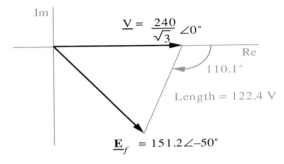

**Figure P15.43**

(e) Determine the output power and torque, neglecting mechanical losses.

**15.44.** A 10-kVA, 600-V, three-phase synchronous motor operates at nameplate kVA with 10-hp output power. The field current is 5 A and the synchronous reactance is 30 Ω/phase. Find the field current for unity power factor, assuming that 5 A overexcites the machine. Ignore losses and assume excitation voltage proportional to field current.

**15.45.** A three-phase, 30-hp, 12-pole, cylindrical rotor, 600-V synchronous motor has a synchronous reactance of 8 Ω. At full load, the field current is adjusted for minimum motor current and unity power factor. Ignore losses.
(a) Find the rotor power angle under these conditions.
(b) With the same field current, what is the greatest torque surge the motor can handle without losing synchronism?
(c) If the field current is increased 10% (assume a linear increase in excitation voltage) and the load torque is held constant, what is the reactive power drawn by the motor?

**15.46.** The diagram in Fig. P15.46 shows the per-phase phasor diagram for an 8-pole, 460-V, 60-Hz, three-phase synchronous motor. With the per-phase voltage as the phase reference, the excitation voltage is $286\angle-21.8°$ V. The synchronous reactance is 6 Ω. Ignore losses.
(a) Find the per-phase current.
(b) Find the power factor.
(c) Determine the developed torque.

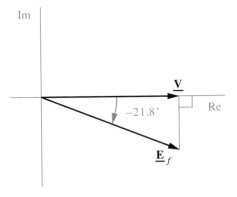

**Figure P15.46**

**15.47.** A three-phase synchronous motor operates under the following conditions: 208 V, 20 A, 0.866 *PF*, leading, and 3.8-A dc field current. The synchronous reactance is 8.5 Ω. For the same mechanical load, find the field current for a power factor of unity and the corresponding output power in hp.

15.48. A three-phase, 60-Hz, 460-V, 6-pole, 10-hp synchronous motor has a synchronous reactance of 30 Ω. Ignore losses.
   (a) The motor output power is 8 hp and the field current 2 A for a power factor of unity. Find the input current under these conditions.
   (b) If the output power increases to 10 hp and the field current is not changed:
      (1) Does the current increase, decrease, or stay the same?
      (2) Does the current lag, lead, or remain in phase?
   (c) Find the new field current to give unity power again if the magnetic flux is proportional to the field current.

15.49. A test is performed on a three-phase, 460-V synchronous motor. The load is kept constant at rated load, and input current is measured while the field current is varied. The results are shown in the Fig. P15.49. The nameplate current is marked on the graph at 24 A. Ignore losses and assume that the excitation voltage is proportional to field current.
   (a) What is the apparent power rating of the motor?
   (b) What is the nameplate output power in hp?
   (c) What range of field currents corresponds to overexcited operation.
   (d) Determine the synchronous reactance of the motor.

15.50. A 240-V, three-phase, 60-Hz synchronous machine has an open-circuit voltage described by the equation $V_{OC} = 100I_f$, where $I_f$ is the field dc current. The short-circuit current is $I_{SC} = 34I_f$, where $I_{SC}$ is the short-circuit line current.
   (a) What is the per-phase synchronous reactance, $X_s$? Ignore any resistance in the stator windings.
   (b) What field current is required to generate 20 kW at unity power factor with nameplate voltage?
   (c) What is the power angle for part(b)?
   (d) The machine is run as a motor. The field current is adjusted to give a leading power factor of 0.707, with an output power of 25 hp at 240 V. Sketch the per-phase phasor

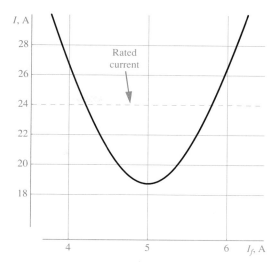

**Figure P15.49**

diagram, showing $\underline{V}, \underline{I}$, and $\underline{E}_f$. What field current is required?

15.51. A 60-Hz, three-phase synchronous motor has four poles and a 5-hp rating. Ignore losses. The motor operates at 440 V with the power factor adjustable, according to the field current.
   (a) If the field current is adjusted for minimum input current with the nameplate output power, what would be that current?
   (b) If the field current is increased to change the current 10% above the minimum value, what then would be the reactive power into the motor? The output real power is unchanged.
   (c) Give the output torque at full load in metric units.
   (d) If it took a 21% increase in field current to produce the 10% increase in input current, what would be the synchronous reactance? Assume that the excitation voltage is proportional to the field current.

15.52. An eight-pole, 480-V, 68-kVA, 60-Hz, 75-hp synchronous motor is connected to a load. The field current is varied, and the line current is measured to follow the curve shown in Fig. P15.52. The minimum current is 57 A, and at 14 A of field current, the current is 93 A. (*Note:* The kVA rating is higher than the real power rating because the motor is required to handle a reactive power load in addition to the real power load.) Assume linear magnetic structure and neglect losses.

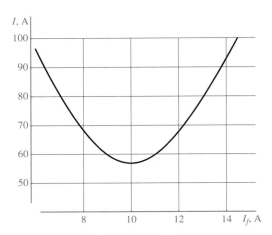

**Figure P15.52**

(a) What is the load on the motor?
(b) Which part of the graph corresponds to leading current and which to lagging?
(c) Find the output torque of the motor.
(d) At full load, what is the limiting power factor of the motor?
(e) At the load represented by the graph, what is the reactive power the motor can handle?
(f) Find the synchronous reactance of the machine.
(h) What field current corresponds to a reactive power of −30 kVAR with the load on the graph?

15.53. (Requires material in Chapter 12.) A three-phase,

12-pole, 460-V, 60-Hz synchronous motor has a synchronous reactance of 4 Ω, an output power of 25 hp, and a leading power factor of 0.866. Ignore losses

(a) Draw a per-phase phasor diagram showing per-phase voltage, current, and excitation voltage.
(b) Find the torque the motor can develop before losing synchronism.

15.54. A three-phase, 60-Hz, 460-V, 12-pole, 15-hp synchronous motor operates at nameplate power and the field current is adjusted for unity power factor. Ignore electrical and mechanical losses in this problem.

(a) Find the motor speed in rpm.
(b) Find the motor output torque.
(c) Find the input current/phase.
(d) If the mechanical load is removed, the current changes to 8 A. Find the phase of the current relative to the per-phase voltage and the synchronous reactance of the motor.

15.55. Adapt Eqs. (15.69) and (15.70) for cylindrical rotor generators by substituting $X_s$ for $X_d$ and $X_q$. Determine the power factor in Example 15.5 using only these adapted formulas based on complex power and Eq. (15.59), which is derived from them.

15.56. Calculate the maximum torque available from the motor in Example 15.9 on reluctance torque.

## Answers to Odd-Numbered Problems

15.1. 428 A-t.

15.3. Left: (a) 4 poles on the stator; (b) no torque; right: (a) 2 poles on the stator; (b) CCW (+ direction) torque.

15.5. (a) 1.25 T; (b) 19.1°; (c) CCW.

15.7. (a)

| Flux density | Poles | Synchronous speed | Description |
|---|---|---|---|
| $1.5 \cos(200\pi t + \theta_m)$ | 2 | 6000 rpm | Rotating CW wave |
| $1.2 \cos(30t - 3\theta_m)$ | 6 | $300/\pi$ rpm | Rotating in CCW direction |
| $1.0 \cos(100\pi t) \sin(2\theta_m)$ | 4 | — | No rotation, oscillation at 50 Hz |

15.9. (a) 2; (b) 60°; (c) 24,000 rpm in CW direction; (d)

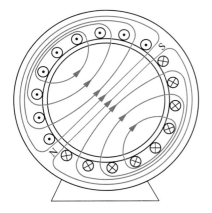

**15.11.** −0.809 T.

**15.13.** **(a)** −90°; **(b)** CW (− direction); **(c)** 0.72 cos[$100\pi t + (\theta_m + 90°)$]; **(d)** 3000 rpm.

**15.15.** **(a)**

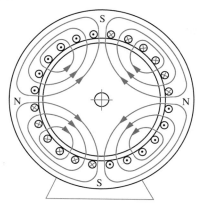

**(b)** 0.85 cos[$120\pi t − 2(\theta_m − 90°)$] T; **(c)** −0.006255 s, and can add multiples of 1/120 s.

**15.17.** $B(t,\theta_m) = 0.8 \cos(942t − 6\theta_m)$ T.

**15.19.** **(a)** Rotating wave of flux; **(b)** $B_r \cos(\omega t + \theta_m)$; **(c)** $B_r \angle 30°$; **(d)** 0.377 T.

**15.21.** **(a)** 8; **(b)** CW (−direction); **(c)** 1/600 s.

**15.23.** **(a)** $60\pi$ rad/s; **(b)** just one; **(c)** 7.12 A; **(d)** 23 wires.

**15.25.** **(a)** 1140 N-m at 1200 rpm;
**(b)**

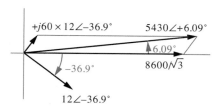

**(c)** 9400 V.

**15.27.** **(a)** Flux levels are high for the voltage measurement but low for the current measurement; **(b)** 7.46 Ω; **(c)** greater.

**15.29.** **(a)**

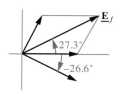

**(b)** **V** is the same, **I** increases, $\theta$ decreases, $\delta_R$ increases, **E**$_f$ same.

**15.31.** **(a)** 7.97 kVA; **(b)** 59.6 N-m; (c) 2.00 Ω.

**15.33.** **(a)**

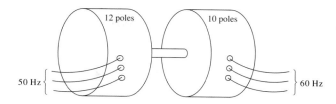

**(b)** rotational speed = 720 rpm; field currents are adjusted to make reactive powers balance.

**15.35.** 13.2 A.

**15.37.** **(a)** 240 V; **(b)** 25.7 A, 223 V; **(c)** −42.0°.

**15.39.** **(a)** Motor; **(b)** 230 V, 7970 VA; **(c)** 2.00 Ω; **(d)** 138 V; **(e)** 120 N-m.

**15.41.** **(a)** 93.6 A; **(b)** 9.91 Ω; **(c)** 5940 N-m; **(d)** −34.9°.

**15.43.** **(a)** Underexcited; **(b)** −50.0°; **(c)** 0.937, lagging; **(d)** 5.83 Ω; **(e)** 87.0 N-m.

**15.45.** **(a)** −26.4°; **(b)** 800 N-m; **(c)** 426 V.

**15.47.** 2.86 V, 8.35 hp.

**15.49.** **(a)** 19.1 kVA; **(b)** 14.8 kW; **(c)** > 5 A; **(d)** 3.72 Ω.

**15.51.** **(a)** 4.89 A; **(b)** −1710 VAR; **(c)** 19.8 N-m; **(d)** 31.6 Ω.

**15.53.** **(a)**

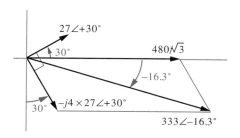

**(b)** 1060 N-m.

**15.55.** The same answers.

# 16

# Induction Motors

The induction motor is the workhorse of electric motors. The induction effect drives motors from a small fan circulating air in a refrigerator to a 1000-hp motor driving a compressor in an airport refrigeration system. This chapter explains this induction effect and its utilization in both three-phase and single-phase motors.

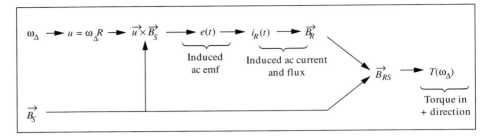

**Figure 16.3** Cause and effect in an induction motor.

induced in each conductor. From the viewpoint of the rotor, an ac voltage is induced in the conductor to drive these currents. For this reason, we show in Fig. 16.3 that the steady motion produces a time-varying emf, $e(t)$.

**Induced rotor flux.** The induced rotor currents produce a magnetic flux, $\vec{B}_R$. Applying the right-hand rule, you determine that this magnetic flux is directed downward, as shown in Fig. 16.1(a). If we associate magnetic poles with $\vec{B}_R$, we require a north pole at the bottom to act as source for the induced flux in the gap, and a south at top, as shown in Fig. 16.1(a). The stator flux and induced rotor flux combine to a rotor–stator flux in the gap, $\vec{B}_{RS}$, and a torque is produced, as described in Sec. 15.1. The torque is counterclockwise, in the positive $\theta_m$ direction, because the rotor magnetic poles seek to align with their opposites on the stator. From the viewpoint of Eq. (15.14), the power angle $\delta_{RS}$ is $-90°$ and the developed torque is thus in the positive $\theta_m$ direction, opposing the torque we apply to cause the rotation. Here are some observations and consequences based on these effects:

- The induced currents and the resulting flux are caused by the stator flux, $\vec{B}_S$. The stator flux is created by dc currents and is not rotating. Although the rotor turns physically, the pattern of currents and induced magnetic flux does not rotate. Thus, the rotor–stator flux pattern, $\vec{B}_{RS}$, is constant in time and space for a given rotation speed ($\omega_\Delta$).

- The power angle $\delta_{RS}$ is $-90°$ for small slip speed.

- The developed torque, $T_{dev}$, is proportional to the induced currents and the sine of the power angle and hence varies with slip speed:

$$T_{dev}(\omega_\Delta) \propto -i_R(\omega_\Delta)\sin\delta_{RS} = -i_R(\omega_\Delta)\sin(\theta_R) \qquad (16.1)$$

where $i_R(\omega_\Delta)$ represents the rotor current, $\theta_R$ the position of the rotor north pole, because $\delta_{RS} = \theta_R - \theta_S$ and $\theta_S = 0°$.

- The mechanical input power that we must supply to turn the rotor against the developed torque is

$$P_{in} = P_R = \omega_\Delta T_{dev}(\omega_\Delta) \qquad (16.2)$$

**Conservation of Energy**

where $P_R$ is the rotor copper loss. This power is converted into rotor-copper losses because resistive loss in the rotor conductors is the only energy-conversion mechanism at work if we ignore mechanical losses.

- For the two-pole structure shown in Fig. 16.1(a), the currents induced in each rotor conductor are sinusoidal at an electrical radian frequency of $\omega_e = \omega_\Delta$. If there were more than $P = 2$ poles, the rotor electrical frequency would be $\omega_e = (P/2)\omega_\Delta$.

<table>
<tr><td>EXAMPLE 16.1</td><td>Rotor current</td></tr>
</table>

The rotor in Fig. 16.1(a) has a resistance of 0.0005 $\Omega$/conductor and is turning 15 rad/s relative to a maximum flux density of 1T. The length is 3.4 cm and radius 3.8 cm. Find the current in the conductor directly under a stator pole, assuming perfect short circuits at the end.

**SOLUTION:**
The emf is given by Eq. (13.43):

$$\text{emf} = \ell \omega_m R B_S = 0.034 \times 15 \times 0.038 \times 1 = 0.0194 \text{ V} \tag{16.3}$$

and hence the current is the emf divided by the resistance, or 38.8 A.

**WHAT IF?**

What if there are 24 slots on a side, and the currents are tapered sinusoidally? What is the total rotor current?[1]

## Developed Torque, $T_{dev}(\omega_\Delta)$

**Factors influencing torque characteristics.** The developed torque, which counters the applied torque causing the rotation, depends on the slip speed, $\omega_\Delta$, through three factors:

- The induced voltage increases in proportion to the slip speed because the speed of the conducting bars relative to the magnetic flux increases. This increase in ac voltage causes the induced current to increase as slip speed increases.

- The impedance of the rotor circuit increases with slip speed because of the increase in the frequency of the induced voltage. At very small slip speeds, the impedance is largely resistive, but at larger slip speeds, the inductance of the rotor dominates. Thus, the current tends to approach a maximum value, where the increase in ac voltage is offset by the corresponding increase in impedance.

- The rotor–stator power angle between rotor and stator poles (fluxes) increases beyond the optimum value of $-90°$ because of the phase delay of the rotor currents associated with the inductance. This increase in power angle causes a lessening of the torque at high slip speeds, as shown by Eq. (16.1).

---

[1] Approximately 590 A.

**Combined effect.**    If we examine the dependence of torque given in Eq. (16.1) and then consider the dependence of induced current and power angle on slip speed, we predict the torque versus mechanical speed, $\omega_m = -\omega_\Delta$, characteristic shown in Fig. 16.4. The developed torque, being a counter-torque, has a sign opposite to that of the mechanical speed. For small slip speeds, the torque magnitude increases with slip speed, reflecting the linear increase of emf and current. However, the curve levels off and eventually decreases as slip speed increases because the induced current levels off and because the power angle increases beyond $-90°$. Hence, the torque reaches a maximum and then decreases due to the increasing power angle.

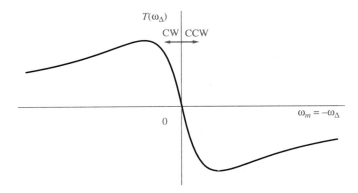

**Figure 16.4**   Developed torque versus speed with a stationary stator flux created by dc stator currents.

**Summary.**    This completes our mental experiment with dc stator currents. We examined the physical principles at work in the induction motor. We looked at the emf and the resulting current and magnetic flux of the rotor. We examined the frequency of the emf and currents in the rotor. We showed how torque is developed. We developed a formula for the rotor-copper losses, Eq. (16.2). Finally, we anticipated how the developed torque depends on slip speed. In the next section, we excite the stator with three-phase ac currents and the rotating flux creates motor action.

## Three-Phase Induction-Motor Characteristics

**Effect of rotation.**    We now apply three-phase currents to the stator field windings. As shown in Chapter 15, the stator flux rotates at synchronous speed. In comparison with our mental experiment, the stator currents change from dc to ac, and the synchronous speed changes from $\omega_s = 0$ to $\omega_s = (2/P)\omega$, where $\omega$ is the electrical angular frequency of the three-phase status currents.

**Slip.**    We assume now that the rotor is turning slower in the positive direction than synchronous speed, such that it is slipping backward by $\omega_\Delta$ relative to the synchronous speed; thus, the rotor speed changes from $\omega_m = -\omega_\Delta$ to

$$\omega_m = \omega_s - \omega_\Delta = \omega_s - s\omega_s = (1 - s)\omega_s \quad \text{rad/s} \tag{16.4}$$

**slip**

where s is the normalized slip speed, or more simply the *slip*:

$$s = \frac{\omega_\Delta}{\omega_s} = \frac{\omega_s - \omega_m}{\omega_s} \tag{16.5}$$

Although the rotor is now turning at a high speed, the electrical voltage and currents in the rotor are still generated by the *relative* motion between the rotor conductors and the stator flux; hence, the rotor voltage and current have an electrical frequency of

$$\omega_e = \omega_\Delta \times \frac{P}{2} = s\omega \qquad (16.6)$$

where $\omega$ is the stator electrical frequency, normally $2\pi \times 60$ rad/s. Even though the rotor is not turning at synchronous speed, the rotor flux is still locked to the stator flux, as in our mental experiment, and hence the rotor *flux* rotates at synchronous speed.

**Torque generation.**   From the viewpoint of the rotor, there is electrically no difference between stationary stator flux and rotating stator flux, provided the slip speed is the same. For the same slip speed, the emf, currents, and rotor magnetic flux are the same in both cases, and hence the developed torque is also the same. The torque characteristic of the motor with ac current, therefore, is identical to Fig. 16.4, except that it now is shifted to the right by the synchronous speed, as shown in Fig. 16.5. Figure 16.5 gives the speed in units of mechanical speed, $\omega_m$, and also in slip, $s$. Zero slip corresponds to rotation at synchronous speed and a slip of unity corresponds to a stationary rotor, $\omega_m = 0.$[2]

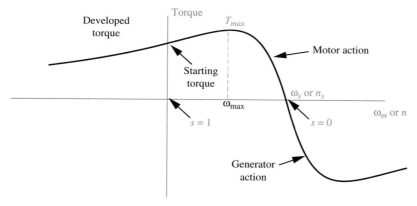

**Figure 16.5**   Developed torque versus rotational speed and slip with rotating stator flux.

**blocked rotor**

**Torque characteristic.**   From Fig. 16.5, we note the following motor characteristics:

**induction generator**

- Positive mechanical speeds below synchronous speed, $0 < \omega_m < \omega_s$, produce motor action because torque is developed in the same direction as the rotation.

- Mechanical speeds exceeding synchronous speed, $\omega_m > \omega_s$, produce generator action because the developed torque is opposite the direction of rotation. External mechanical torque is required to drive the rotor against this counter-torque. The electrical power generated has the same frequency as the currents in the stator field windings. This generator produces power when connected to a three-phase power source, but has poor characteristics when connected only

---

[2] Also called "blocked or locked rotor."

to a load. Such *induction generators* find application in wind-power generators and small power plants.

- When the mechanical speed is equal to the synchronous speed, $\omega_m = \omega_s$, neither motor nor generator action results; the system is merely idling. In this condition, an external mechanical drive is required to supply the mechanical losses.

- For $\omega_m \approx \omega_s$, the torque is proportional to slip. This is the region where the motor is normally operated.

- A point of maximum torque, $T_{max}$ exists at a speed of $\omega_{max}$. This speed is slightly below the speed for maximum output power.

- The starting condition corresponds to $s = 1$. The starting torque is positive and hence this motor is self-starting.

**developed torque and power, output torque and power, windage**

**Power relationships.** We can derive several useful power relationships from basic principles and from the results of our mental experiment, which gave an expression for the rotor-copper losses in Eq. (16.2). At this point, we must distinguish between the *developed* torque and power and the *output* torque and power. The *developed torque* is the magnetically generated torque and is the torque we have been discussing. The *output torque* is smaller due to the torque required to overcome bearing and *windage* losses, the loss due to air movement. Similarly, the *developed power* is $P_{dev} = \omega_m T_{dev}$, and represents the power converted from electrical to mechanical form. The *output power* is $P_{out} = \omega_m T_{out}$ and is smaller than the developed power because of the mechanical losses.

The developed power is

$$P_{dev} = \omega_m \times T_{dev} = (1 - s)\omega_s T_{dev} \qquad (16.7)$$

where $T_{dev}$ is the developed torque and we introduced the synchronous speed through the relationship $\omega_m = (1 - s)\omega_s$. As shown in Eq. (16.2), the power lost in the rotor-copper losses is

$$P_R = \omega_\Delta \times T_{dev} = s\omega_s T_{dev} \qquad (16.8)$$

**air-gap power**

The power crossing the air gap from the stator to the rotor, the *air-gap power*, $P_{ag}$, by conservation of energy must be the sum of the developed power and the rotor copper losses:

$$P_{ag} = P_{dev} + P_R = (1 - s)\omega_s T_{dev} + s\omega_s T_{dev} = \omega_s T_{dev} \qquad (16.9)$$

**Conservation of Energy**

Equation (16.9) shows how air-gap power divides between the rotor-copper losses and the developed power, and it also shows that developed torque is proportional to air-gap power because the synchronous speed is constant.

**Conservation of Energy**

**Power flow.** The meaning of the air-gap power is illustrated by Fig. 16.6, which shows the flow of real power in the motor. A portion of the input power becomes copper and iron loss in the stator windings. We have yet to focus on this loss, but it will be represented in the equivalent circuit developed in the next section. The remainder of the input power crosses the air gap into the rotor, similar to power moving from primary to secondary in a transformer. The air-gap power splits into two terms: the rotor-copper loss, which heats the rotor, and the developed power, which turns the rotor and load.

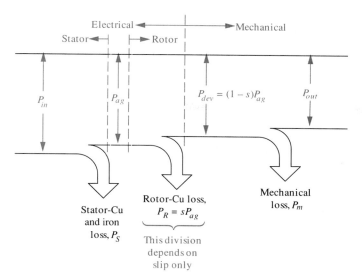

**Figure 16.6** Power flow in the induction motor.

From Eqs. (16.7)–(16.9), it follows that the air-gap power divides between rotor-copper loss and developed power in a ratio that depends only on the slip speed.

$$P_{ag} = \underbrace{(1-s)P_{ag}}_{=P_{dev}} + \underbrace{sP_{ag}}_{=P_R} \Rightarrow \frac{P_{dev}}{P_R} = \frac{1-s}{s} \qquad (16.10)$$

---

**EXAMPLE 16.2** | **Accounting for the power**

A three-phase, four-pole, 60-Hz induction motor has a full-load output power of 5 hp at 1740 rpm. The motor efficiency is 87.5% at full load. The mechanical losses account for 5% of the total losses. Determine all the power quantities in Fig. 16.6.

**SOLUTION:**
The input power is $5 \times 746/0.875 = 4263$ W, and hence the total losses are $4263 - 5 \times 746 = 533$ W. Of these losses, 5% are mechanical, so the mechanical losses are 26.6 W and electrical losses are 506 W. The developed power is

$$P_{dev} = P_{out} + P_m = 5 \times 746 + 26.6 = 3760 \text{ W} \qquad (16.11)$$

where $P_m$ is the mechanical loss. To determine the air-gap power from the developed power, we need the slip. The synchronous speed, from Table 15.1, is 1800 rpm; hence, the slip is

$$s = \frac{n_s - n}{n_s} = \frac{1800 - 1740}{1800} = 0.0333 \qquad (16.12)$$

From Eq. (16.10), the air-gap power is

$$P_{ag} = \frac{P_{dev}}{1-s} = \frac{3760}{1 - 0.0333} = 3890 \text{ V} \qquad (16.13)$$

Again, from Eq. (16.10), the rotor-copper loss is

$$P_R = sP_{ag} = 0.0333 \times 3890 = 130 \text{ W} \qquad (16.14)$$

and hence the stator loss is $506 - 130 = 376$ W.

---

**WHAT IF?**    What if there were no load? What would be the developed power?[3]

---

**Summary.**   Table 16.1 compares the mental experiment with motor action. All torques are developed torques.

**TABLE 16.1  Comparison of Mental Experiment, DC Stator Currents, with Motor Action, Three-Phase AC Stator Currents**

| Aspect | Mental Experiment (DC Stator Currents) | Motor Action (AC Stator Currents) |
|---|---|---|
| Synchronous speed | 0 | $\omega_s = \omega/(P/2)$ |
| Slip speed | $\omega_\Delta$ | $\omega_\Delta = s\omega_s$ |
| Mechanical speed | $-\omega_\Delta$ | $\omega_s - \omega_\Delta = (1-s)\omega_s$ |
| Developed torque | $T(\omega_\Delta)$ | $T(\omega_\Delta) = T(s) = \text{same}$ |
| Rotor-copper loss | $\omega_\Delta T(\omega_\Delta)$ | $\omega_\Delta T(\omega_\Delta) = s\omega_s T(s) = \text{same}$ |
| Air-gap power | 0 | $\omega_s T(s)$ |
| Developed power | $-\omega_\Delta T(\omega_\Delta)$ | $\omega_m T(\omega_\Delta) = (1-s)\omega_s T(s)$ |

### Check Your Understanding

1. For maximum torque, rotor and stator poles should be aligned, 0°, or spatially orthogonal, 90°. Which?

2. In the mental experiment, all input mechanical power goes into stator loss, rotor-copper loss, or the dc source supplying the stator flux. Which?

3. The slip speed is defined as positive in the negative angular direction. True or false?

4. The effect of rotor inductance is to increase or decrease developed torque as slip speed increases. Which?

5. What is the slip if the rotor is turning at synchronous speed for a six-pole machine?

6. Determine the output speed in rpm of a four-pole, three-phase induction motor operating at 60 Hz and having a slip of 3%.

7. The more poles an induction motor has, the faster it turns. True or false?

---

[3] 26.6 W, assuming the mechanical losses are constant. The slip is extremely small and hence the rotor copper loss is negligible.

8. In a two-pole, three-phase induction motor, the frequency is 60 Hz and the slip is 5%. Find the following:
   (a) Rotational speed of the rotor (rpm).
   (b) Rotational speed of the rotor flux (rpm).
   (c) Frequency of the stator currents (Hz).
   (d) Frequency of the rotor currents (Hz).

9. If the developed power in a three-phase induction motor is 15 times the rotor-copper loss, what is the slip?

*Answers.* (1) 90°; (2) rotor-copper loss; (3) true; (4) decrease; (5) zero; (6) 1746 rpm; (7) false; (8) (a) 3420 rpm, (b) 3600 rpm, (c) 60 Hz, (d) 3 Hz; (9) 6.25%.

## 16.2 EQUIVALENT CIRCUITS FOR THREE-PHASE INDUCTION MOTORS

### Physical Basis for Equivalent Circuit

**Energy processes.** In this section, we develop an equivalent circuit to account for every major energy process in the motor. As for a transformer, we need resistors to represent rotor-copper, stator-copper, and iron losses; and we need inductors to represent magnetic energy stored in the stray rotor and stator fields and in the flux coupling rotor and stator across the air gap. We also use a resistor to account for the energy leaving the electric circuit as developed mechanical power.

**Stator circuit.** The per-phase stator circuit in Fig. 16.7 accounts for stator-copper losses, $R_S$, stray magnetic fields, $X_S$, and the electromotive force, $\underline{V}_S$, induced in the stator coils by the rotating air-gap flux. The electrical frequency of stator voltage and currents is that of the ac power connecting to the stator, normally 60 Hz. Three times the complex power $\underline{V}_S \underline{I}_S^*$ into the stator emf represents the power and magnetic energy leaving the stator and passing into the air gap. The real power accounts for rotor-copper losses and developed mechanical power. The reactive power accounts for stored energy in the air gap and stray fields in the rotor.

**blocked rotor reactance**

**Rotor circuit.** The per-phase rotor circuit shown in Fig. 16.7 shows an emf, $\underline{V}_R$, an inductor, $jsX_R$, a resistor, $R_R$, and a short circuit. The electrical frequency of the rotor

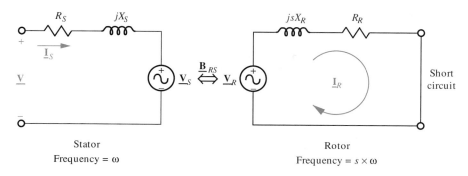

**Figure 16.7** Per-phase equivalent circuit for rotor and stator. The region between the circuits represents the air gap, which stores magnetic energy and provides coupling between the stator and rotor.

emf and current is $s$ times the stator frequency, Eq. (16.6), and hence the reactance of the rotor is shown to be proportional to slip. The reactance $X_R$ is the *blocked rotor reactance* because the slip is unity with the rotor stationary. The rotor-copper loss is

$$P_R = 3 \, |\mathbf{I}_R|^2 \, R_R \qquad (16.15)$$

where the factor of 3 accounts for the three phases. Rotor iron losses will be discussed later.

**Mechanical output?** The equivalent circuit shown in Fig. 16.7 is at present unable to account for the stored energy in the air gap or for the developed mechanical power. Application of Ampère's circuital law introduces a term to account for stored magnetic energy in the air gap. Application of Faraday's law *plus* the conservation of energy introduces a resistor into the rotor circuit to account for the developed mechanical power.

**Ampère's circuital law.** Ampère's circuital law may be applied to the induction motor in the same way it was applied to electrical transformers, Eq. (14.22). We introduce $n_S$ and $n_R$ as the equivalent turns for the stator and rotor, respectively, and integrate the magnetic field around a suitable path. The results can be put into the form of Eq. (14.25)

$$\mathbf{I}_S = \frac{n_R}{n_S}\mathbf{I}_R + \frac{\mathbf{V}_S}{jX_{ag}} \qquad (16.16)$$

where $X_{ag}$ is a reactance accounting for the stored energy in the air gap. Thus, *for the currents only*, the coupling between rotor and stator are represented by the ideal transformer shown in Fig. 16.8(a).

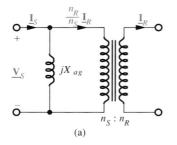

(a)

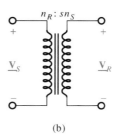

(b)

**Figure 16.8** (a) Per-phase equivalent circuit showing currents in the stator and rotor. The reactance represents stored energy in the air gap. (b) Per-phase equivalent circuit showing voltage induced in the stator and rotor windings by the rotating flux. The rotor voltage is reduced by the factor $s$ because the rotor is moving in the same direction as the flux.

**Faraday's law.** Again in analogy with the transformer, Eq. (14.19), the emfs in stator and rotor are related by Faraday's law. However, we must reduce the emf in the rotor by the slip because the electrical frequency in the rotor is $s\omega$. Hence, by Eq. (15.41)

$$\mathbf{V}_S = n_S \omega R \ell \, \mathbf{B}_{RS} \qquad (16.17)$$

where $R$ and $\ell$ are the radius and length of the air gap, respectively, but

$$\mathbf{V}_R = n_R s \omega R \ell \, \mathbf{B}_{RS} \qquad (16.18)$$

where $\underline{\mathbf{B}}_{RS}$ is the air-gap flux density. We may eliminate the flux density to obtain

$$\frac{\underline{\mathbf{V}}_S}{n_S} = \frac{\underline{\mathbf{V}}_R}{sn_R} \tag{16.19}$$

which suggests the ideal transformer in Fig. 16.8(b). However, the equivalent turns ratio of the voltage transformation is lower than that shown in Fig. 16.8(a) by the factor $s$.

**Rotor impedance.**  The rotor voltage and current are related through

$$\underline{\mathbf{I}}_R = \frac{\underline{\mathbf{V}}_R}{R_R + jsX_R} \tag{16.20}$$

where $R_R$ is the equivalent rotor resistance per phase and $X_R$ is the per-phase reactance of the blocked rotor, at the frequency of the stator voltage.

**Nonconservation of electric energy.**  We now have satisfied all circuit requirements except conservation of electric energy. Equations (16.16) and (16.19) require an ideal transformer with a voltage turns ratio $n_S{:}sn_R$ and a current turns ratio of $n_S{:}n_R$. Such a transformer would not obey conservation of energy, and of course it *should* not because *electrical* energy is not conserved in this device due to the mechanical output.

**Conservation of Energy**

**The Steinmetz transformation.**  We can eliminate this strange transformer by scaling up the rotor voltage to "impose" conservation of *electrical* energy on the circuit. We divide the numerator and denominator of the right side of Eq. (16.20) by $s$:

$$\underline{\mathbf{I}}_R = \frac{\underline{\mathbf{V}}_R/s}{(R_R/s) + jX_R} \tag{16.21}$$

where $\underline{\mathbf{V}}_R/s$ is a scaled-up rotor voltage. The transformation in Eq. (16.21) was first proposed by Carl Steinmetz (1865–1923). We now may use a normal ideal transformer to express voltage and current relationships between the stator and scaled rotor circuits. The secondary circuit in Fig. 16.9 now accounts for all the power passing from stator to rotor, *including that transformed to mechanical power*. We make the following observations:

- In transforming Eq. (16.20) into Eq. (16.21), rotor voltages and impedance values were scaled upward by $1/s$, but rotor current was unchanged. Thus, the rotor current in Fig. 16.9 is the true rotor current.

- The rotor reactance, $X_R$, is the per-phase reactance of the blocked rotor, as if the frequency in the rotor circuit were the same as the frequency in the stator circuit. Of course, the frequencies differ in stator and rotor circuits, but the impedance scaling compensates for the different frequencies.

**Conservation of Energy**

- The rotor part of Fig. 16.9 now accounts for all the power crossing the air gap into the rotor. This air-gap power divides between rotor-copper loss and developed mechanical power. The scaled-up resistor $R_R/s$ must therefore account for both powers. Because the rotor current appears at its true value, we may calculate and subtract the rotor-copper loss from the air-gap power to find the

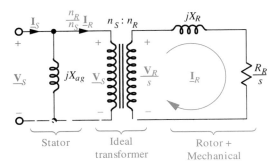

**Figure 16.9** Equivalent circuit with rotor voltage and impedance scaled by a factor of $1/s$. This circuit accounts for electrical energy and energy converted to mechanical form.

developed mechanical power:

$$P_{dev} = 3\left[|\mathbf{I}_R|^2\frac{R_R}{s} - |\mathbf{I}_R|^2 R_R\right] = 3|\mathbf{I}_R|^2 R_R \times \frac{1-s}{s} \tag{16.22}$$

**Equivalent Circuits**

Hence, $[(1-s)/s] \times R_R$ is an equivalent resistance accounting for the developed mechanical power per phase. We have thus modeled the developed mechanical power in our equivalent electrical circuit, as identified in Fig. 16.10. The first resistor represents power leaving the electrical circuit and entering the mechanical world as *disordered* mechanical energy, as heat. The second resistor in the rotor circuit represents power leaving the electrical circuit and entering the mechanical world as *ordered* mechanical energy as work. Figure 16.10 also shows resistors and reactances in the stator circuit to account for stator-copper, $R_S$, and iron loss, $R_i$, and magnetic energy as storage due to leakage flux and air-gap flux, $X_S$.

■ The kinship between the equivalent circuit in Fig. 16.10 and that of a transformer, Fig. 14.11, is evident. The only difference is that the load representing the mechanical work is always resistive and is derived from the electrical, $R_R$, and mechanical, $s$, conditions in this electromechanical device.

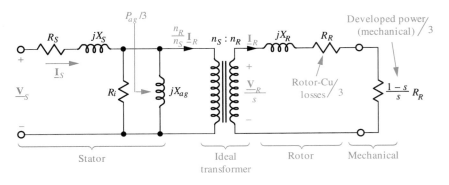

**Figure 16.10** Equivalent circuit with the $R_R/s$ term divided into two resistors, one accounting for rotor electrical loss and the other accounting for developed mechanical power.

- The air-gap power in the rotor circuit divides into developed mechanical power and rotor-copper losses in the ratio $(1 - s) : s$, as we established earlier, Eq. (16.10), from our mental experiment and conservation of energy.

**Impedance Level**

- We may simplify Fig. 16.10 through the impedance-transforming properties of an ideal transformer. Specifically, we multiply secondary (rotor) impedances by $(n_S/n_R)^2$ to obtain the primed values in Fig. 16.11, which represent rotor impedances referred to the stator circuit and frequency. Because energy-related quantities are unchanged by this transformation, the equivalent circuit in Fig. 16.11 can be used to determine many quantities of interest, such as input current, motor efficiency, and output torque as a function of speed.

- The development of the per-phase equivalent circuit in Fig. 16.11 has been inexact in a number of ways. We have been vague in defining rotor and stator turns and in specifying means for determining rotor resistance and reactance. With a more refined analysis, these factors could be defined and calculated, but we do not require such detail. We are interested in the performance and overall characteristics of the motor. Our purposes are served by knowing the nature of the equivalent circuit and identifying the critical parameters. These machine parameters, such as the rotor resistance transformed into the stator, can be measured or deduced from the external characteristics of the machine. From the equivalent circuit, we will be able to predict how motor characteristics depend on the various circuit model parameters, and thus we can gain an understanding of some of the design decisions that must be made in developing an induction motor.

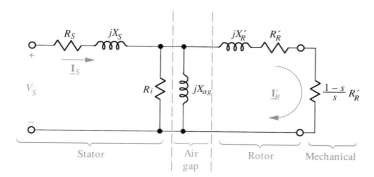

**Figure 16.11** In this equivalent circuit, rotor impedance elements are transformed to the stator.

## Applications of Equivalent Circuit

**Motor analysis.** We begin by analyzing a motor in steady state.

---

**EXAMPLE 16.3** | **Induction-motor analysis**

A 60-Hz, 230-V, three-phase, 5-hp, 1740-rpm induction motor is described by the per-phase equivalent circuit in Fig. 16.12. Analyze the circuit at nameplate speed to determine the input current, developed power, and efficiency.

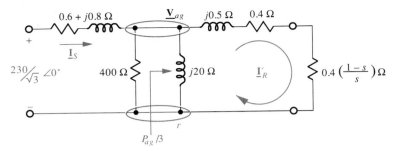

**Figure 16.12** Per-phase equivalent circuit for the motor.

**SOLUTION:**

From the nameplate speed, we learn that this is a four-pole motor; hence the synchronous speed is 1800 rpm and the slip is

$$s = \frac{n_s - n}{n_s} = \frac{1800 - 1740}{1800} = \frac{1}{30} = 0.0333 \qquad (16.23)$$

The resistor representing the developed power is

$$R'_R \times \frac{1 - s}{s} = 0.4 \times 29 = 11.6 \ \Omega \qquad (16.24)$$

and the rotor impedance is $12 + j0.5 \ \Omega$.

The analysis of the equivalent circuit is a straightforward but nontrivial task. We performed a nodal analysis, as indicated in Fig. 16.12, with $\underline{V}_{ag}$ the unknown. We skip the details; the results are

$$\underline{V}_{ag} = 121.3 \ \angle -1.91° \ \text{V}; \ \underline{I}_S = 12.3 \ \angle -33.9° \ \text{A}; \ \underline{I}'_R = 10.1 \ \angle -4.3° \ \text{A} \qquad (16.25)$$

From the results of Eq. (16.25), we can determine the motor performance. The air-gap power is

$$P_{ag} = 3 \times (I'_R)^2 \times \left(\frac{R'_R}{s}\right) = 3 \times (10.1)^2 (12 \ \Omega) = 3670 \ \text{W} \qquad (16.26)$$

and the developed power is

$$P_{dev} = (1 - s)P_{ag} = (1 - 0.0333) \times 3670 = 3550 \ \text{W} \qquad (16.27)$$

The mechanical losses are very small, so this is approximately the output power: $P_{out} = 3550/746 = 4.76$ hp. The developed torque, which is approximately the output torque, is

$$T_{dev} = \frac{P_{dev}}{\omega_m} = \frac{P_{ag}}{\omega_s} = \frac{3670}{60\pi} = 19.5 \ \text{N-m} \qquad (16.28)$$

The power factor is derived from the angle of the stator current: $PF = \cos 33.9° = 0.830$, lagging. The input power is

$$P_{in} = 3VI \times PF = 3 \times \frac{230}{\sqrt{3}} \times 12.3 \times 0.830 = 4050 \qquad (16.29)$$

Thus, the efficiency and total losses are approximately

$$\eta = \frac{P_{out}}{P_{in}} = \frac{3550}{4050} = 87.6\% \qquad \text{and} \qquad P_{loss} = P_{in} - P_{out} = 403 \text{ V} \qquad (16.30)$$

> **WHAT IF?** What if you want the rotor-Cu, stator-Cu, and iron losses?[4]

**Starting current and torque.** To calculate the starting torque, we set $s = 1$ and calculate the developed torque. A stationary rotor has no mechanical losses; hence, the developed torque is the starting torque. We can determine the developed torque from the air-gap power and the synchronous speed, Eq. (16.9), and specifically the starting torque,[5] $T_{st}$, is

$$T_{st} = \frac{P_{ag}(s = 1)}{\omega_s} \qquad (16.31)$$

---

**EXAMPLE 16.4** | **Starting torque**

Calculate the starting torque for the motor described in Example 16.3.

**SOLUTION:**
We show the equivalent circuit for $s = 1$ in Fig. 16.13. The starting current is

$$\mathbf{I}_{st} = \frac{230/\sqrt{3} \angle 0°}{0.6 + j0.8 + 400 \| j20 \| (0.4 + j0.5)} = 81.8 \angle -52.8° \text{ A} \qquad (16.32)$$

The input power is

$$P_{in} = 3 \times \frac{230}{\sqrt{3}} \times 81.8 \times \cos 52.8° = 19,700 \text{ W} \qquad (16.33)$$

After we subtract stator-copper losses, we have an air-gap power of 7630 W; hence, the torque is $7630/60\pi = 40.5$ N-m, approximately twice the run torque of 19.5 N-m.

> **WHAT IF?** What if we ignore the $400 \| j20 \ \Omega$ parallel impedance?[6]

---

[4] $P_R = 3 \times (10.1)^2(0.4) = 122$ W; $P_{S(Cu)} = 3 \times (12.3)^2(0.6) = 271$ W; and $P_i = 3 \times (121.3)^2/400 = 110$ W.
[5] Also called "blocked rotor torque."
[6] $I_{st} = 81.0$ A, $T_{st} = 41.7$ N-m.

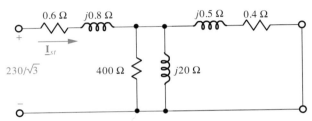

**Figure 16.13** Per-phase equivalent circuit for $s = 1$.

**Improving starting characteristics.** We should not, however, take too seriously the details of these calculations of conditions at starting. Soon we show that the rotor conductors are shaped to lower starting current and increase starting torque; hence, our model is not accurate for starting performance calculations.

**The rotor is the load.** We demonstrated that the motor performance can be calculated from the equivalent circuit in Fig. 16.11. However, we may simplify the equivalent circuit for purposes of deriving the output-torque characteristics. Figure 16.14 shows the results of representing the power system, stator, and air gap by a Thévenin equivalent circuit, considering the rotor equivalent circuit to be the load.

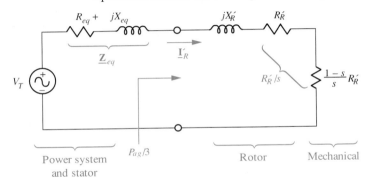

**Figure 16.14** The per-phase Thévenin equivalent circuit presented to the rotor.

---

| **EXAMPLE 16.5** | **Thévenin equivalent circuit** |
|---|---|

Derive the per-phase Thévenin equivalent circuit for the 5-hp motor described by the equivalent circuit in Fig. 16.12.

**SOLUTION:**
The open-circuit voltage with the load (rotor) removed is

$$\mathbf{V}_T = \frac{R_i \| j X_{ag}}{R_S + j X_S + R_i \| j X_{ag}} \times \mathbf{V} \tag{16.34}$$

$$= \frac{400 \| j20}{0.6 + j0.8 + 400 \| j20} \times \frac{230}{\sqrt{3}} \angle 0° = 127.5 \angle 1.54° \text{ V}$$

The output impedance seen by the rotor looking back into the air gap is

$$Z_{eq} = R_{eq} + j X_{eq} = R_i \| j X_{ag} \| (R_S + j X_S) \tag{16.35}$$

$$= 400 \| j20 \| (0.6 + j0.8) = 0.555 + j0.783 \ \Omega$$

**Torque characteristic.** Equation (16.9) shows that the developed torque may be derived from the synchronous speed and the air-gap power, which we may derive from the equivalent circuit in Fig. 16.14.

$$P_{ag} = 3 \times (I_R')^2 \times \frac{R_R'}{s} = \frac{3V_T^2 R_R'}{s\left[(R_{eq} + R_R'/s)^2 + X_T^2\right]} \qquad (16.36)$$

where $V_T$ is the rms magnitude of the Thevénin voltage and $X_T = X_{eq} + X_R'$ is the total reactance. Thus, the developed torque is

$$T_{dev} = \frac{P_{ag}}{\omega_s} = \frac{3V_T^2 R_R'}{s\omega_s\left[(R_{eq} + R_R'/s)^2 + X_T^2\right]} \qquad (16.37)$$

**Features of the torque characteristic.** Figure 16.15 shows the developed torque characteristic of an induction motor for several values of $R_R'$. We note the following features:

**small-slip region**

- ■ The maximum torque[7] is independent of rotor resistance, but the speed at which the maximum torque occurs decreases with increasing rotor resistance.

- ■ Near synchronous speed, the torque is a linear function of slip. This *small-slip region*, to be discussed presently, is the normal operating region of the motor.[8]

- ■ The slope of the torque characteristic in the small-slip region decreases as the rotor resistance increases. For a given load-torque requirement, the motor runs slower and has more rotor losses, Eq. (16.8), for larger rotor resistance. Thus, small values of $R_R'$ are desirable to increase efficiency.

- ■ The starting torque is larger for large rotor resistance. Thus, larger values of $R_R'$ are desirable and a compromise is indicated.

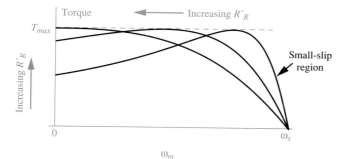

**Figure 16.15** Torque characteristics for several values of rotor resistance.

---
[7] Also called "breakover torque."
[8] See page 294 for a previous discussion of this region.

**Small-slip region.** In the normal operating region near synchronous speed, the denominator of Eq. (16.37) is dominated by the $R'_R/s$ term; hence, we may approximate Eq. (16.37) in the small-slip region by

$$T_{dev}(s) \approx s \times \frac{3V_T^2}{\omega_s R'_R} \tag{16.38}$$

Thus, the torque in the small-slip region is proportional to slip and inverse to rotor resistance, as suggested in Fig. 16.15. The developed mechanical power in the small-slip region is

$$P_{dev}(s) = \omega_m T_{dev}(s) = (1-s)\omega_s T_{dev}(s) = 3(1-s)s\frac{V_T^2}{R'_R} \tag{16.39}$$

The dependence of developed torque on slip allows the prediction of output power and speed throughout the small-slip region.

---

**EXAMPLE 16.6** | **Speed for 2 hp**

Find the speed at which the 5-hp motor used in the previous examples has an output power of 2 hp, assuming mechanical losses of 15 W.

**SOLUTION:**
The developed power for 2 hp would be $2 \times 746 + 15 = 1507$ W. Using Eq. (16.39) and the results of the previous example, we find the required slip:

$$1507 = 3(1-s)s\frac{(127.5)^2}{0.4} \Rightarrow s^2 - s - 0.0124 = 0 \tag{16.40}$$

Thus, $s = 0.0125$ (1.25%) and $\omega_m = (1 - 0.0125)60\pi = 186.1$ rad/s (1777 rpm).

**WHAT IF?** | What if you remove the load? Find the no-load speed in rpm.[9]

---

**wound rotor**

**Effect of rotor resistance.** High efficiency and relatively constant operating speed require small values of the rotor resistance, but high starting torque and moderate starting currents require relatively high values of rotor resistance. This dilemma for the designer can be resolved in two ways. The first requires a different type of rotor from the squirrel-cage type. For a *wound rotor*, slots are milled in the rotor and three-phase coils are wound in the slots. These coils are connected to external resistors through a brush slip-ring assembly. With a wound rotor, we can maximize starting torque with external resistors and then remove all resistance for running. We can also achieve limited

---

[9] 1799.8 rpm, assuming the 15-W mechanical loss is the developed power.

control of motor speed with a wound-rotor induction motor. However, the wound-rotor machine is more expensive and requires more maintenance than the squirrel-cage motor.

**Shaped-rotor conductors.** The alternative to the wound rotor is a squirrel-cage rotor with shaped conductors. Figure 16.16 shows two extremes. With small conductors near the surface of the rotor, we have relatively large resistance and small leakage inductance because the nearby air gap limits the leakage flux that encircles the currents in the rotor conductors. Thus, the conductors in Fig. 16.16(a) give good starting characteristics but poor run characteristics. On the other hand, the larger, deeper conductors in Fig. 16.16(b) have relatively small resistance and large leakage inductance. Such a rotor gives excellent run characteristics but produces a low starting torque because the high inductance dominates during starting.

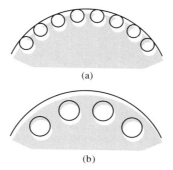

(a)

(b)

**Figure 16.16** (a) Small, shallow rotor conductors give good starting but poor running characteristics; (b) large, deep rotor conductors give poor starting but good running characteristics.

However, we can have both types at once; or rather we can shape the conductors to have a high-resistance, low-inductance portion near the surface and a low-resistance, high-inductance portion deeper in the rotor. At starting, the rotor currents have a high frequency, and the large inductance therefore shields the deeper conductors. The starting currents flow mostly in the surface conductors, which have relatively large resistance. As the motor comes up to speed, however, the rotor frequency decreases, and most of the rotor current shifts to the deeper, low-resistance conductors. Thus, for starting, we have relatively high resistance and for running relatively low resistance in the rotor.

**NEMA[10] design classes.** Figure 16.17(a) shows some of the common classes of shaped conductors, with typical torque characteristics resulting from each shown in Fig. 16.17(b). Clearly, the designer can, within limits, control the characteristics of the squirrel-cage motor by shaping the rotor conductors. The design classes in Fig. 16.17 refer to standard designations of squirrel-cage, three-phase induction motors to meet typical run and starting requirements:

- Designs A, not shown in Fig. 16.17(b), and B have normal starting torque, but design B has lower starting current. Both have low slip, less than 5%, at rated output power. Typical applications are fans, blowers, rotary pumps, unloaded compressors, some conveyors, metal-cutting machine tools, and miscellaneous machinery.

---

[10] See pages 295 and 297 for information about NEMA.

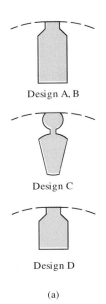

Design A, B

Design C

Design D

(a)

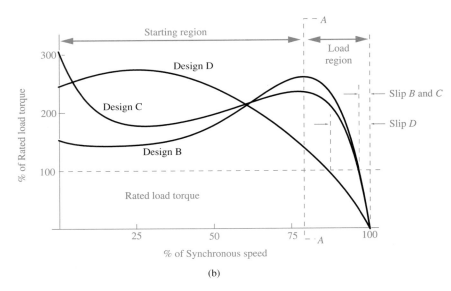

(b)

**Figure 16.17** (a) Typical slots shaped to compromise starting and running characteristics; (b) typical torque characteristics corresponding to the shaped slots in part (a). (Figure courtesy of the Lincoln Electric Company.)

- Design C has high starting torque and relatively low starting current, and runs with low slip at rated output power. Typical applications are starting of high-inertia loads such as large centrifugal blowers, flywheels, and crusher drums. Loaded starting of piston pumps, compressors and conveyors also require this design class.

- Design D has high starting torque and low starting current, but runs with relatively high slip, up to 11%, at rated output power. This design is required for very high inertia and loaded starts and also for loads having considerable variation in load torque throughout a load cycle. Typical applications are punch presses, shears and forming machine tools, cranes, hoists, elevators, and oil-well pumping jacks.

- Design E, not shown, is a new NEMA design for high-efficient motors. The motor has a large starting current.

## Dynamic Response of Induction Motors

**run-up time**

**Introduction.** Up to this point, we have considered motor performance in steady state. In Chapter 6, we had a brief introduction to dynamic characteristics of motors in general and considered the *run-up time*, the time required for the motor to reach steady state.

In this section, we analyze the dynamics of loaded induction motors in two cases: where the motor drive is constant but the load torque changes; and where the motor drive frequency and voltage are changed but the load torque characteristic is constant.

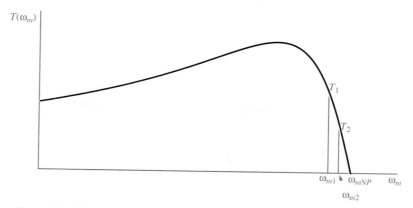

**Figure 16.18** The motor characteristic does not change, but the load-torque requirement changes suddenly from $T_1$ to $T_2$.

## Response to torque changes.

Figure 16.18 shows the first response we will analyze. The motor is supplying torque $T_1$ and running at $\omega_{m1}$, and the torque suddenly changes to $T_2$. The speed of the motor/load eventually changes to $\omega_{m2}$; we now analyze the dynamics of the change, assuming that the motor operates in its small-slip region and that mechanical losses are negligible. The motor torque curve is

$$T_M(\omega_m) = \frac{\omega_s - \omega_m}{\omega_s - \omega_{mNP}} \times T_{NP} \tag{16.41}$$

where $T_M$ is the motor developed torque and $NP$ signifies a nameplate quantity. The dynamics of the motor/load system is governed by

$$J\frac{d\omega_m}{dt} = T_M - T_L \tag{16.42}$$

where $T_L$ is the load torque and $J$ is the total moment of the system. When we substitute Eq. (16.41) into Eq. (16.42), we have

$$J\frac{d\omega_m}{dt} + \frac{T_{NP}}{\omega_s - \omega_{mNP}} \times \omega_m = \frac{\omega_s}{\omega_s - \omega_{mNP}}T_{NP} - T_L \tag{16.43}$$

## Sudden change in torque.

Equation (16.43) is valid for arbitrary changes in the load torque, but here we consider only a sudden change. In this case, the right-hand side of Eq. (16.43) changes from one constant to another; thus, we have a simple first-order transient of the type we studied in Chapter 3. Therefore, we may determine the motor response from the initial and final values plus the time constant. The initial and final values are shown in Fig. 16.18 and may be determined from the required load torques and Eq. (16.41). When we put Eq. (16.43) into the form of Eq. (3.35), we find the time constant:

$$\tau = \frac{J}{T_{NP}} \times (\omega_s - \omega_{mNP}) \tag{16.44}$$

Thus, the response of the motor to the sudden change in torque shown in Fig. 16.18 is

$$\omega_m(t) = \omega_{m2} + (\omega_{m1} - \omega_{m2})e^{-t/\tau} \qquad (16.45)$$

**EXAMPLE 16.7** | **Change in load**

Find the change in speed of the 50-hp motor analyzed in Chapter 6 if the load torque changes from half the nameplate torque to full nameplate torque. Assume the moment of inertia of motor and load is 1.1 kg-m², and that the no-load speed is the synchronous speed.

**SOLUTION:**
The analysis of the motor nameplate information is given on pages 292–298. The nameplate torque is found in Eq. (6.52) as 202 N-m and the nameplate speed is 1765 rpm for the 60-Hz motor. The final speed in this example is the nameplate speed, and the initial speed for the half-nameplate torque is 1782.5 rpm, halfway between the nameplate speed and the no-load speed of 1800 rpm. The time constant given by Eq.(16.44) is

$$\tau = \frac{1.1}{202} \times (1800 - 1765) \times \frac{2\pi}{60} = 0.0200 \text{ s} \qquad (16.46)$$

Expressing Eq. (16.45) in rpm, we find the motor response to the change in load torque:

$$n(t) = 1765 - 17.5e^{-t/20 \text{ ms}} \text{ rpm} \qquad (16.47)$$

which is shown in Fig. 16.19.

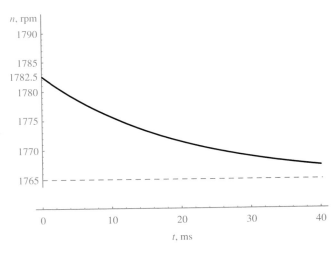

**Figure 16.19** Response of motor speed to sudden change in load torque requirement.

**WHAT IF?** | What if the torque suddenly changed back to half the nameplate value?[11]

**System function.** The preceding analysis can be translated into the system notation of Chapter 12. If we divide Eq. (16.43) by the moment of inertia and use Eq. (16.44), we have

$$\frac{d\omega_m(t)}{dt} + \frac{\omega_m(t)}{\tau} = \frac{\omega_s}{\tau} - \frac{T_L(t)}{J} \tag{16.48}$$

If we now, in the manner introduced in Chapter 12, consider all time variation of the form $e^{st}$, Eq.(16.48) takes the form

$$\left(\mathbf{s} + \frac{1}{\tau}\right)\mathbf{\Omega}_m(\mathbf{s}) = \frac{\omega_s}{\tau} - \frac{\mathbf{T}_L(\mathbf{s})}{J} \quad \Rightarrow \quad \mathbf{\Omega}_m(\mathbf{s}) = \frac{\omega_s/\tau - \mathbf{T}_L(\mathbf{s})/J}{\mathbf{s} + 1/\tau} \tag{16.49}$$

where in the last form we solved for the transform of the output speed, $_m(\mathbf{s})$, in terms of the transform of the input torque variations, $\mathbf{T}_L(\mathbf{s})$, and the constants of the system.

**System diagram.** Equation (16.49) is represented by the system diagram in Fig. 16.20, which shows a simple first-order system.

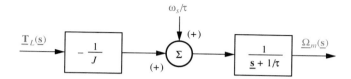

**Figure 16.20** System diagram for an induction motor with constant input voltage and frequency but changing load torque requirement.

**Changing motor-drive frequency.** In contrast to the passive system just analyzed, active control of the system speed can be accomplished through changing the drive frequency.[12] Such motor drives normally vary the applied voltage in proportion to the frequency to keep the motor flux, controlled by Faraday's law, Eq.(14.19), roughly constant.[13] Thus, the per-phase voltage to the motor varies as

$$V(\omega) = \frac{\omega}{\omega_{NP}} \times V_{NP} \tag{16.50}$$

where $\omega_{NP}$ and $V_{NP}$ are nameplate frequency and per-phase voltage, respectively. In the small-slip region, the torque of the motor is given by Eq. (16.38):

$$T_M(\omega) = s \times \frac{3V^2}{\omega_s R'_R} = \frac{\omega_s - \omega_m}{\omega_s^2} \frac{3(\omega/\omega_{NP})^2 V_{NP}^2}{R'_R} \tag{16.51}$$

But the synchronous speed, $\omega_s$, also depends on the electrical frequency, $\omega$, Eq. (15.24):

---

[11] $n(t) = 1782.5 - 17.5e^{-t/20 \text{ ms}}$ rpm.

[12] Variable-frequency motor drives are discussed in Chapter 18.

[13] This is called a "constant volts/hertz" drive.

$$\omega_s = \frac{2}{P}\omega \qquad (16.52)$$

There is, therefore, a cancellation of the square of the electrical frequency in the numerator and denominator of Eq. (16.51), and the result takes the form

$$T_M(\omega) = \left(\frac{2}{P}\omega - \omega_m\right) \times K_T \qquad (16.53)$$

where $K_T$ is a torque constant that can be evaluated from either Eq. (16.51) or, better, from the nameplate torque:

$$T_{NP} = \left(\frac{2}{P}\omega_{NP} - \omega_{mNP}\right)K_T \qquad (16.54)$$

---

**EXAMPLE 16.8** | **Torque constant**

Find the torque constant, $K_T$, in Eq. (16.53) for the 50-hp motor used in Example 16.7.

**SOLUTION:**
The motor torque constant comes from Eq. (16.54) and the motor nameplate torque, 202 N-m, and speed, 1765 rpm:

$$K_T = \frac{202}{(1800 - 1765) \times 2\pi/60} = 55.1 \qquad (16.55)$$

---

**System diagram.** Equation (16.53) suggests the system diagram shown in Fig. 16.21, in which $\underline{\Omega}(\underline{s})$ and $\underline{\Omega}_m(\underline{s})$ represent the transforms of electrical frequency and mechanical speed, respectively.

**Torque model.** To proceed with the analysis, we must assume a model for the torque. We assume the linear model shown in Fig. 16.22

$$T_L(\omega_m) = K_0 + K_1\omega_m \qquad (16.56)$$

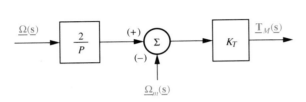

**Figure 16.21** System diagram for induction motor with constant volts/hertz drive. The two inputs are the frequency-domain transform of electrical frequency and mechanical speed.

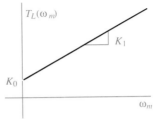

**Figure 16.22** Linear torque model.

where $K_0$ and $K_1$ are constants. If the load-torque requirements were not linear, Eq. (16.56) could represent a linearization of the exact characteristic in the vicinity of the operating point.

**Dynamic analysis.** Newton's law for motion, Eq. (16.42), becomes

$$J\frac{d\omega_m}{dt} = T_M(t) - (K_0 + K_1\omega_m) \tag{16.57}$$

When we place the term containing the output speed on the left-hand side, we have

$$J\frac{d\omega_m}{dt} + K_1\omega_m = T_M(t) - K_0 \tag{16.58}$$

Transforming Eq. (16.58) to the frequency domain, we have

$$(J\underline{s} + K_1)\underline{\Omega}_m(\underline{s}) = \underline{T}_M(\underline{s}) - K_0 \tag{16.59}$$

When we solve for the output speed and combine with the motor function in Fig. 16.21, we get the system diagram for the motor/load shown in Fig. 16.23.

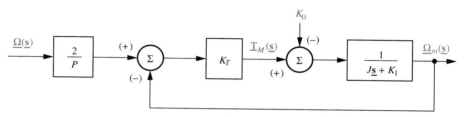

**Figure 16.23** System diagram for an induction motor with constant volts/hertz drive with a linear model for load torque.

**System time constant.** Figure 16.23 shows the motor/load system to be first-order with a feedback loop. We may determine the time constant of the system by finding the pole of the system, as discussed on page 639. This requires

$$1 - \underline{L}(\underline{s}) = 0 \Rightarrow 1 - (-1)\frac{K_T}{J\underline{s} + K_1} = 0 \tag{16.60}$$

Where $\underline{L}(\underline{s})$ is the loop gain. Equation (16.60) yields

$$\underline{s} = -\frac{K_T + K_1}{J} \Rightarrow \tau = \frac{J}{K_T + K_1} \tag{16.61}$$

Thus, the time constant depends on the moment of inertia and the combined torque constants from the motor and load.

**EXAMPLE 16.9**

## System time constant

Calculate the time constant for the 50-hp motor driving a load at nameplate torque. Assume that the load torque is proportional to speed and that the combined moment of the system is 1.1 kg-m$^2$.

**SOLUTION:**

For the time constant, we must calculate the two torque constants. The motor-torque constant was determined in Example 16.8. Because the load-torque is proportional to speed, $K_0$ is zero in Eq. (16.56) and the load torque constant is

$$K_1 = \frac{202}{1765 \times 2\pi/60} = 1.09 \tag{16.62}$$

Using Eq. (16.61), we find the time constant of the motor/load system:

$$\tau = \frac{1.1}{55.1 + 1.09} = 0.0196 \text{ s} \tag{16.63}$$

Thus, if the motor input frequency were suddenly changed from 60 to 45 Hz, the system would slow down approximately 25% with a time constant of 19.6 ms.

**WHAT IF?** What would be the time constant if the load torque were constant at nameplate value?[14]

**Summary.** We analyzed an induction motor with a load in two cases: where the motor drive is constant but the load changes, and where the motor-drive frequency changes while the load-torque model is constant. System models were developed describing both cases, and time constants were determined. In the next section, we consider how to select a motor to drive a load that is varying.

## Motor-Size Choice for Fluctuating Load Torque

**Load requirements.** We wish to select a motor to drive the periodic torque shown in Fig. 16.24. The required speed is about 1800 rpm, so we will select a four-pole, 60-Hz, three-phase induction motor. Table 16.2 shows information for a wide selection of four-pole motors from a single manufacturer; our job is to select the appropriate motor for this load.

**Power requirements.** Because motor powers are listed, we may convert the torques in Fig. 16.24 to power by multiplying by a nominal speed, say, 1750 rpm:

$$P_1 = 1750 \times \frac{2\pi}{60} \times 90 = 16,490 \text{ W} \ (= 22.1 \text{ hp}) \tag{16.64}$$

and similarly we get 9.83 hp for the low-torque level. These are the powers that the

---

[14] 20.0 ms.

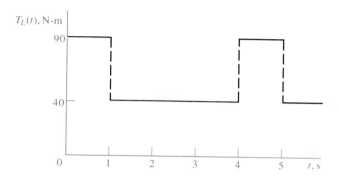

**Figure 16.24** Time-varying torque.
We must select a motor to drive this load.

| TABLE 16.2 | Induction-Motor Nameplate Information | | | | | |
|---|---|---|---|---|---|---|
| **hp** | **rpm** | **Volts**[*] | **Amps** | **Eff.** | **SF** | **Weight, lb.** |
| 1/3 | 1725 | 230 | 1.5 | 66.0 | 1.15 | 16 |
| 1/2 | 1725 | 230 | 2.2 | 69.0 | 1.15 | 18 |
| 3/4 | 1725 | 230 | 2.8 | 76.0 | 1.15 | 23 |
| 1 | 1725 | 230 | 3.8 | 72.0 | 1.15 | 27 |
| 1.5 | 1725 | 230 | 5.2 | 80.0 | 1.15 | 41 |
| 2 | 1715 | 230 | 5.8 | 80.0 | 1.0 | 50 |
| 3 | 1735 | 230 | 8.9 | 84.0 | 1.0 | 75 |
| 5 | 1725 | 230 | 13.2 | 85.5 | 1.0 | 97 |
| 7.5 | 1750 | 230 | 19.6 | 87.5 | 1.0 | 133 |
| 10 | 1750 | 230 | 25.0 | 88.5 | 1.0 | 172 |
| 15 | 1760 | 230 | 38.4 | 88.5 | 1.0 | 271 |
| 20 | 1755 | 230 | 49.2 | 89.5 | 1.0 | 317 |
| 25 | 1760 | 230 | 60.6 | 91.0 | 1.0 | 415 |
| 30 | 1750 | 230 | 73.8 | 91.0 | 1.0 | 477 |
| 40 | 1775 | 230 | 103.8 | 90.2 | 1.0 | 351 |
| 50 | 1775 | 230 | 119.6 | 91.7 | 1.0 | 420 |
| 60 | 1780 | 230 | 148.4 | 91.7 | 1.0 | 528 |
| 75 | 1780 | 230 | 176.6 | 91.7 | 1.0 | 627 |
| 100 | 1775 | 230 | 232.0 | 92.4 | 1.0 | 759 |

[*]*These motors also operate at 460 V with half the listed current.*

load requires on a cyclical basis. We require that the motor operate with an adequate torque reserve and that the motor not overheat.

**Torque reserve.** Because motors in this power range are required by **NEMA** to have a breakover torque that is 200% of the nameplate torque, we conservatively require that the motor selected have a 60% reserve. Any motor rated 22.1 hp/1.6 = 13.8 hp or higher possesses adequate torque reserve by this criterion.

**Maximum-horsepower choice.** Clearly, we may choose a 25-hp motor and be assured that the motor will not overheat, because a 25-hp motor can produce 22.1 hp continuously. However, this is almost certainly an overdesign, and will increase costs and motor size and weight. Furthermore, motors are designed to have maximum efficiency near their rated values; hence operating costs might also increase.

**Average-horsepower choice.** The average power required by the load is

$$HP_{avg} = \frac{22.1 \times 1 + 9.83 \times 3}{4} = 12.9 \text{ hp} \tag{16.65}$$

which suggests that a 15-hp motor might be adequate. But average power is a bad criterion for the following reason: Motor current is roughly proportional to load, but motor copper losses increase in proportion to current squared and hence roughly proportional to output power squared. Thus, a motor chosen on the basis of average power might overheat, and lifetime and efficiency would suffer.

**RMS-horsepower choice.** The loss considerations suggest that the rms horsepower is a better choice:[15]

$$HP_{rms} = \sqrt{\frac{(22.1)^2 \times 1 + (9.83)^2 \times 3}{4}} = 14.0 \text{ hp} \tag{16.66}$$

This result shows that the 15 hp are adequate. We may confirm this choice with a more careful analysis of motor losses.

**Motor losses.** The three motor losses are mechanical losses, iron losses, and copper losses.

- Mechanical losses are small and constant as long as the motor is running. Mechanical losses may be determined from the no-load speed of the motor, but should be at most 100 W for a motor of the size required for this load.

- Iron losses are also constant as long as the motor is operating. The iron losses are proportional to motor weight for a given maximum flux. We assume 1.5 watts/pound of weight in this analysis.

- Copper losses are proportional to current squared but only the in-phase component of the current increases with the load; by Faraday's law, the out-of-phase current is roughly constant.

**Loss analysis.** We estimate the losses of the 15-hp motor for the fluctuating load in Fig. 16.24. The allowed losses in the motor may be determined from the nameplate efficiency:

$$Loss = P_{NP}\left(\frac{1}{\eta} - 1\right) = 15 \times 746\left(\frac{1}{0.885} - 1\right) = 1454 \text{ W} \tag{16.67}$$

Of these, we assume 100 W of mechanical loss and 410 W of iron loss based on the weight, and, hence, we have 944 W of copper loss. Assuming that copper losses are proportional to current squared, the constant of proportionality is

---

[15] For a more general definition of rms housepower, see *Electrical Machines*, 5th Ed., by A. E. Fitzgerald, Charles Kingsley, Jr., and Stephen D. Umans, New York: McGraw Hill, pp. 377.

$$944 = K_{Cu} (38.4)^2 \quad \Rightarrow \quad K_{Cu} = 0.640 \tag{16.68}$$

To divide the current between the out-of-phase component, which is roughly constant, and the in-phase component, which is proportional to power, we must determine the power factor at the nameplate:

$$PF = \frac{15 \times 746/0.885}{\sqrt{3} \times 230 \times 38.4} = 0.8265 \; (\theta = 34.3°) \tag{16.69}$$

Thus, the in-phase current is 31.7 A and the out-of-phase component is 21.6 A. Consequently, a model of the motor loss as a function of output power is

$$\text{Loss (hp)} = 100 + 410 + 0.640\left[ (21.6)^2 + \left(31.7 \times \frac{\text{hp}}{15}\right)^2 \right] \text{W} \tag{16.70}$$

Using Eq. (16.70), we find that the loss during the high-torque period is 2205 W and during the low-torque period 1085 W, for a weighted average of 1365 W. This is less than the allowed loss of 1454 watts and indicates that the 15-hp motor is adequate. Other factors such as reliability, cost, lifetime, weight, and size should be considered in the final decision.

**Summary.** We analyzed a motor with a fluctuating load and considered several criteria for choosing a motor. The peak power gives a safe choice, but is an overdesign. Average power is not a valid approach, but rms power has more validity. A careful analysis of the motor losses is better yet, but many assumptions must be made in the absence of detailed test data.

### Check Your Understanding

1. For the per-phase equivalent circuit shown in Fig. 16.11, identify what element(s) account for the specified physical effects. If nothing on the circuit is a suitable answer, indicate "none."
   (a) Developed mechanical power.
   (b) Leakage flux in the stator.
   (c) Rotor-copper loss.
   (d) Mechanical loss.
   (e) Stored energy in the air-gap flux.
   (f) Iron loss.
   (g) Stator-copper loss.
   (h) Input three-phase voltage.

2. To operate with small slip, an induction motor should have rotor resistance that is large or small, or does not matter. Which?

3. For high starting torque, an induction motor should have rotor resistance that is large, small, or does not matter. Which?

4. As the load-torque requirements vary, the induction motor has approximately constant speed, constant torque, constant power, or constant rotor losses. Give one or more answers.

**5.** Choosing a motor to meet average power requirement often leads to an overdesign. True or false?

***Answers.*** **(1)** **(a)** $R_R(1-s)/s$, **(b)** $X_S$, **(c)** $R'_R$, **(d)** none, **(e)** $X_{ag}$, **(f)** $R_i$, **(g)** $R_S$, **(h)** none directly, although $V$ is the input voltage divided by $\sqrt{3}$; **(2)** small; **(3)** large; **(4)** constant speed; **(5)** false.

## 16.3 SINGLE-PHASE INDUCTION MOTORS

**Introduction.** The three-phase induction motor is rugged, reliable, long-lived, self-starting, smooth-running, and relatively inexpensive. But three-phase power is not available everywhere, so if possible we need single-phase motors with the same characteristics. In fact, single-phase induction motors have excellent characteristics and outnumber the three-phase variety. Most of the small electric motors used in home, farm, or office are single-phase induction motors of one type or another.

In this section, we show first that the single-phase induction motor runs if started. We look then into the ways that single-phase motors are started, and finally we survey various types of single-phase induction motors.

**Forward and reverse slip.** As we showed in Sec. 15.2, Eq. (15.33), a single-phase flux can be resolved into two equal counter-rotating flux waves. If the rotor is stationary, it will have a slip of unity relative to both waves and experience equal but opposite torques from each. Hence, no starting torque is produced.

**forward slip, reverse slip**

**Forward and reverse slip.** Let us assume that the rotor is rotating in the forward direction with an angular velocity $\omega_m$. The *forward slip* is

$$s_f = \frac{\omega_s - \omega_m}{\omega_s} = 1 - \frac{\omega_m}{\omega_s} \tag{16.71}$$

where $s_f$ is the slip relative to the forward flux wave. The synchronous speed of the reverse flux wave is $-\omega_s$, and hence the *reverse slip* of the rotor is

$$s_r = \frac{-\omega_s - \omega_m}{-\omega_s} = 1 + \frac{\omega_m}{\omega_s} = 2 - s_f \tag{16.72}$$

where $s_r$ is the slip relative to the reverse flux wave. However, because both slips can be expressed in terms of the forward slip, we drop the subscripts and use $s$ for the forward slip and $2 - s$ for the reverse slip.

**Torque characteristic.** We may estimate the torque characteristic of the single-phase induction motor from our results for the three-phase motor. Equation (15.33) shows that an oscillating flux can be divided into two counterrotating fluxes of half strength. Therefore, if $T_{3\phi}$ is the torque characteristic of the corresponding three-phase motor, then the torque as a single-phase motor, $T_{1\phi}$, for the same maximum flux would be

$$T_{1\phi}(s) = (\tfrac{1}{2})^2 \, [T_{3\phi}(s) - T_{3\phi}(2 - s)] \tag{16.73}$$

where the $(\tfrac{1}{2})^2$ comes from the equal division of the flux, because torque is propor-

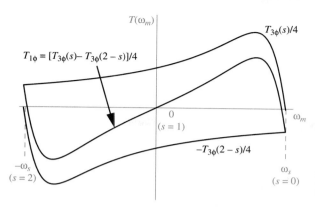

**Figure 16.25** The single-phase run characteristic can be derived from the three-phase characteristic. These curves assume that the motor is excited at constant current.

tional to the square of the flux, and the two terms represent coupling to forward and reverse fluxes, respectively. The torque characteristic of the single-phase motor is therefore as shown in Fig. 16.25. We note that the motor has no starting torque, but, once started, produces a torque in the direction in which it is rotating. Thus, it will run if started.

---

**EXAMPLE 16.10** **Single-phase motor slips**

Find the forward and reverse slip of a 60-Hz, four-pole, single-phase motor running at 1725 rpm.

**SOLUTION:**
The synchronous speed is 1800 rpm. From Eqs. (16.71) and (16.72), we find the slip to be $(1800 - 1725)/1800 = 0.0417$ relative to the forward flux and $2 - 0.0417 = 1.9583$ relative to the reverse flux.

**WHAT IF?** What if you want the electrical frequencies in the rotor?[16]

---

**Constant-current supply.** The argument supporting the use of Eq. (15.33) in explaining single-phase torque depends on having rotating fluxes that are not influenced by the currents in the rotor. This requires exciting the motor from a constant-current source. The characteristic shown in Fig. 16.25 is therefore unrealistic for normal ac sources, which supply constant voltage.

**Constant-voltage supply.** In practice, a single-phase induction motor is driven by a constant-voltage supply. By Faraday's law, the applied voltage determines the flux in the stator winding, but in this case, the flux is composed of two counterrotating fluxes, which are not necessarily equal due to the contribution of rotor flux.

---

[16] The rotor frequencies would be $s \times 60 = 2.5$ Hz and $(2 - s) \times 60 = 117.5$ Hz.

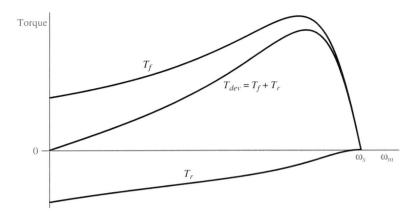

**Figure 16.26** Run-torque characteristic of a single-phase induction motor for a constant-voltage supply.

An analysis of the single-phase motor driven by a constant-voltage supply is beyond the scope of this text. Figure 16.26 shows the torque characteristic of a representative single-phase motor calculated for a constant-voltage supply. We show coupling to forward and reverse waves separately. Clearly, the reverse wave has a slight effect in the small-slip region. We conclude that the single-phase motor runs well; our problem is to start it.

**Starting methods for single-phase motors.** In addition to the main, or run, winding, the single-phase induction motor requires an auxiliary, or starting, winding. The starter winding is physically separated by $90°/(P/2)$ in space from the main winding and thus the stator has a two-phase geometry. In effect, the single-phase motor is started as a two-phase motor. The motor can be started in either direction by reversing the polarity of the auxiliary winding. The auxiliary winding may or may not be designed for continuous operation. We distinguish between several types of single-phase induction motors by how the phase shift is created between the currents in the main and auxiliary windings, and by whether the auxiliary windings are used continuously or only for starting.

**Split-phase motors.** The split-phase motor, whose circuit is shown in Fig. 16.27(a), has an auxiliary winding that would burn out if used continuously. Normally, the starting winding is disconnected with a centrifugal switch that opens at about 75% of the rated speed. Occasionally, the auxiliary winding is switched with a relay that is activated by the current in the main winding. Figure 16.27(b) shows the current in the main winding and the region where the relay would engage the auxiliary winding. Such arrangements are used in compressor motors, in which the motor is enclosed in a refrigerant system.

The phase shift between the main and auxiliary windings in a split-phase motor is created by their differing ratios of resistance to inductance. The auxiliary winding uses a small wire and hence has a higher resistance than the main winding. Thus, the auxiliary current is smaller and more in phase with the line voltage, as shown in Fig. 16.28. This method yields a relatively small phase shift between main and auxiliary currents, and hence gives low starting torque. Split-phase motors serve applications requiring low starting torque, such as fans and bench grinders. Typical power ratings are 1/20 to 1/3 hp.

To understand the characteristics and applications of the various types of single-phase induction motors

starting or auxiliary winding

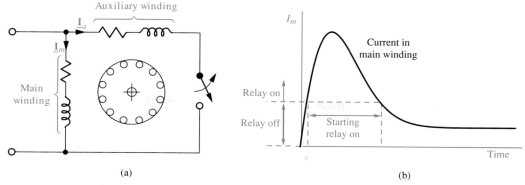

(a)                                         (b)

**Figure 16.27**   (a) For the split-phase motor, the auxiliary, or starting, winding is disconnected after the motor starts; (b) a current-sensing relay can be used to connect and disconnect the auxiliary winding.

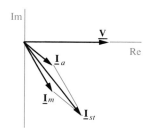

**Figure 16.28**   The starting current for the split-phase motor. The small phase difference yields low starting torque.

---

**EXAMPLE 16.11** | **Split-phase motor**

Find the phase shift in the starting current of a 115-V, single-phase induction motor if the main and auxiliary winding have impedances of $\mathbf{Z}_m = 3.3 + j4.0\ \Omega$ and $\mathbf{Z}_a = 6.0 + j3.8\ \Omega$, respectively.

**SOLUTION:**
The currents are

$$\mathbf{I}_m = \frac{115 \angle 0°}{3.3 + j4.0} = 22.2 \angle -50.5°\ \text{A},$$

and                                                           (16.74)

$$\mathbf{I}_a = \frac{115 \angle 0°}{6.0 + j3.8} = 16.2 \angle -32.5°\ \text{A}$$

The phase shift is $50.5 - 32.5 = 18.1°.$[17]

---

**WHAT IF?**        What if you want the starting current?[18]

---

[17] To three-place accuracy, based on the exact angles.

[18] 37.9 A.

**Capacitor-start/induction-run motors.** Figure 16.29(a) shows the circuit of the capacitor-start motor. A capacitor in series with the auxiliary winding produces a leading current. Ideally, the auxiliary current would lead the main current by 90° of phase for maximum starting torque, as shown in Fig. 16.29(b). The capacitor would be of the electrolytic type, designed for short-time operation, and the auxiliary winding would be disconnected after the motor is started. Such motors have good starting torque and are used for large appliances, some power tools, and large fans. Typical power ratings are 1/4 to 10 hp.

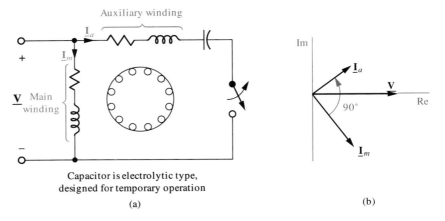

**Figure 16.29** (a) A capacitor may be used to increase the phase shift between the currents in the main and auxiliary windings; (b) a phasor diagram showing the 90° shift due to the capacitor.

| EXAMPLE 16.12 | Phase-shift capacitor |

What capacitor, placed in series with the auxiliary winding in Example 16.11, gives a 90° phase shift between the $\mathbf{I}_m$ and $\mathbf{I}_a$ at starting?

**SOLUTION:**
We require

$$\mathbf{I}_a = \frac{115 \angle 0°}{6.0 + j(3.8 + X_C)} = (\text{magnitude}) \angle -50.5 + 90°, \qquad (16.75)$$

therefore

$$\frac{3.8 + X_C}{6.0} = \tan(-39.5°) \Rightarrow X_C = -3.8 + 6.0 \times \tan(-39.5°) = -8.75 \ \Omega \qquad (16.76)$$

This reactance requires 303 μF at 60 Hz.

| **WHAT IF?** | What if you use 300 μF and want the starting current?[19] |

### Capacitor-start/capacitor-run motors.
The capacitor-start/capacitor-run motor shown in Fig. 16.30 has two capacitors. One capacitor is rated for short-time operation, for starting the motor; the other is rated for long-term operation, for improving the run characteristics of the motor. By giving a rotating wave that is more pure, the run capacitor improves the torque and efficiency characteristics of the motor and reduces vibration. Capacitor-start/capacitor-run motors are available in sizes from 1/4 to 10 hp and are used for conveyors, air compressors, and other heavy intermittent loads.

### Permanent-split-capacitor (PSC) motors.
In the PSC motor, shown in Fig. 16.31, the auxiliary winding is designed for continuous operation. This motor has a continuous-rated capacitor for start and run, and no switch. The auxiliary winding gives some help in starting torque and some help in run characteristics. The main virtues of the PSC motor are high efficiency and smoother operation. Power ratings of 1/6 to 3/4 hp are typical of PSC motors, which are often used for fans and direct-drive blowers.

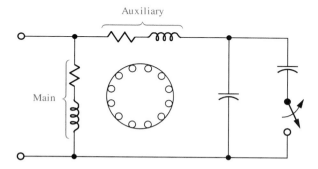

**Figure 16.30** Improved run characteristics result if the auxiliary winding is used continuously.

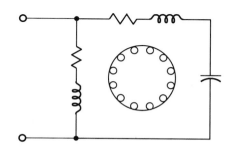

**Figure 16.31** The PSC motor has no switch.

### Shaded-pole motors.
Figure 16.32 shows two types of shaded-pole motor. This motor is characterized by having salient poles, partly encircled by conducting rings. As flux increases, current flows in the "shading ring" to delay flux buildup within the shaded portion of the pole. Later, as flux decreases, the current induced in the ring delays the flux decrease in the shaded portion of the pole. Hence, the flux maximum moves $1 \rightarrow 2 \rightarrow 3 \rightarrow 4 \rightarrow 1$, and so on. The motors shown in Fig. 16.32 turn in one direction only, but shaded-pole motors can be made reversible if both sides of the pole are shaded and the shading coils are brought out for external switching. As shown, the motors are fixed-speed, but multipole motors can be made to run at different speeds by exciting poles in various patterns. Shaded-pole motors are widely used in small fans, pumps, and small household appliances.

### Check Your Understanding

1. The single-phase induction motor runs in either direction, depending on which way it is started. True or false?

---

[19] 26.5 A.

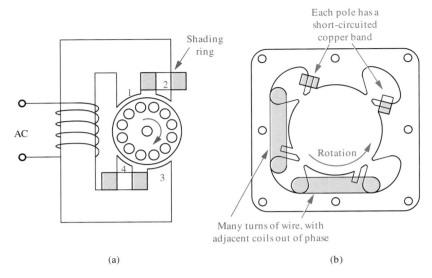

Shading
ring

AC

Rotation

Many turns of wire, with
adjacent coils out of phase

(a)

(b)

**Figure 16.32**  (a) A simple two-pole, shaded-pole motor; (b) the magnetic structure for a larger, four-pole, shaded-pole motor. Shading rings and coils are shown on half of the poles.

2. In a single-phase induction motor, the slip of the rotor relative to one rotating wave of stator flux is 6%. What is its slip relative to the other wave of stator flux?

3. A 60-Hz, single-phase induction motor turns 1740 rpm.
   **(a)** How many poles does the motor have?
   **(b)** What is (are) the frequency (frequencies) of the stator current(s)?
   **(c)** What is (are) the frequency (frequencies) of the rotor current(s)?

4. The unloaded ideal (no mechanical loss) single-phase induction motor will runs slower than synchronous speed. True or false?

5. Why does a capacitor-start, single-phase induction motor have greater starting torque than a split-phase motor?

6. A permanent split-capacitor (PSC) motor has less vibration at 120 Hz than a capacitor-start/induction-run motor. True or false?

7. Why does the standard shaded-pole motor turn only one way?

*Answers:*  (1) True;  (2) 194%;  (3) (a) four poles, (b) 60 Hz, (c) 2 Hz and 118 Hz;  (4) true, because of the reverse torque;  (5) the current in the start winding is more out of phase with the current in the main winding;  (6) true, because the rotating flux has a smaller counterrotating flux; (7) because the mechanism to make the flux rotate is built into the iron of the poles.

## CHAPTER SUMMARY

We began by investigating the induction principle used to produce torque in an induction motor. The three-phase induction motor was examined thoroughly, both at an intuitive level from basic principles and quantitatively through a per-phase equivalent circuit. The various types of single-phase induction motors were described.

**Objective 1: To understand the induction principle that produces torque in induction motors.** The rotor of an induction motor has imbedded conductors that are shorted to allow the free flow of current. Voltage is induced by the motion of the physical rotor relative to the rotating stator flux. The resulting current produces rotor torque that depends on the slip speed between the physical rotor and the rotating flux.

**Objective 2: To understand the physical origin of all elements in the equivalent circuit of an induction motor, and be able to use the circuit to predict motor performance.** A per-phase equivalent circuit for the induction motor was developed by considering the various energy processes in the motor. The energy converted to mechanical form was represented by a resistance that depends on the slip. The equivalent circuit permits calculation of output torque and input current and power factor, all as functions of motor speed. Starting current and torque can also be predicted with the equivalent circuit.

**Objective 3: To understand the characteristics and applications of the various types of single-phase induction motors.** The run principle of the single-phase induction motor was described. The various means for starting such motors were described. Applications of the different types of motors were indicated.

The electronic control of three-phase induction motors is described in Chapter 18. There we discuss the characteristics of three-phase induction motors as ac voltage and frequency are changed.

## PROBLEMS

## Section 16.1: Three-phase Induction-motor Characteristic

16.1. What relative values of dc current in coils $a$, $b$ and $c$ in Fig 15.11 give a horizontal flux, as required for the mental experiment?

16.2. A three-phase, 60-Hz induction motor has a nameplate speed of 1740 rpm. Find the following:
  (a) Slip.
  (b) Electrical frequency of the stator currents.
  (c) Electrical frequency of the rotor currents.
  (d) Mechanical rotational speed of the stator fields.
  (e) Mechanical rotational speed of the rotor fields.
  (f) Ratio of the developed power to the rotor-copper losses.

16.3. In a three-phase, 60-Hz induction motor turning 1720 rpm, the following losses are known: stator copper loss = 50 W; rotor copper loss = 65 W; iron loss = 80 W; and mechanical losses = 5 W. Find the following:
  (a) Number of poles.
  (b) Slip.

  (c) Air-gap power.
  (d) Output power.
  (e) Input power.
  (f) Efficiency.
  (g) Output torque.
  (h) Apparent power if the power factor is 0.85.

16.4. A three-phase, 60-Hz induction motor has the speed–torque characteristic shown in Fig. P16.4. The load characteristic is also shown. Find the following:
  (a) Number of motor poles.
  (b) Operating speed.
  (c) Slip at maximum torque.
  (d) Motor starting torque
  (e) Air-gap power at a slip of 1.0.
  (f) Output power at the operating speed (hp).
  (g) Approximate rotor-copper losses at the operating speed, neglecting mechanical losses.

16.5. A three-phase, 60-Hz induction motor has the following specifications: 5 hp, 1740 rpm, 230/460

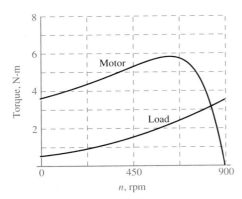

**Figure P16.4**

V, 12.8/6.4 A, efficiency 87.5%, and service factor 1.15.

(a) Find the slip of the motor at nameplate speed.
(b) Find the power factor under nameplate conditions.
(c) What is the air-gap power under nameplate conditions, assuming that 95% of the losses are electrical and 5% mechanical?
(d) If the motor were excited by 220 V, would the current be less than, equal to, or greater than 12.8 A with the same ouput power?

16.6. A four-pole, 60-Hz, three-phase induction motor operates from 460 V, draws 2.85 A at 0.76 *PF* (lagging). Of the input electrical power, 95% crosses into the rotor; of that power, 96% is converted to mechanical form; and of that, 99% is

output power. Find the following:
(a) Motor efficiency.
(b) Motor speed in rpm.
(c) Output power.
(d) Output torque.

16.7. A three-phase, 60-Hz induction motor has the following nameplate information: 2 hp, 1725 rpm; 230/460 V, 5.7/2.85 A, 87% efficiency; service factor 1.15. If the machine is operating under nameplate conditions, determine the stator-and rotor-copper losses, assuming the mechanical losses are negligible but iron losses are 60 W.

16.8. The nameplate information on a three-phase, 60-Hz induction motor is 15 hp, 1755 rpm, 230/460 V, 36.0/18.0 A, 88.5% eff; service factor 1.15. Assume that at nameplate speed, the mechanical losses are 0.5% of the output power.
(a) Find the number of poles.
(b) What is the slip at nameplate conditions?
(c) What is the power factor at rared output power?
(d) What is the output torque at nameplate output power?
(e) Find the sum of the stator-iron and-copper losses at rated ouput power.

16.9. A three-phase, 60-Hz induction motor has the following nameplate information: 2 hp, 3450 rpm; 230/460 V, 5.2/2.6 A, SF 1.15. At nameplate conditions, the stator-copper, stator-iron, rotor-copper, and mechanical losses divide in the ratios 4:2:3:1. Find the efficiency of the motor.

## Section 16.2: Equivalent Circuits for Three-Phase Induction Motors

16.10 Figure P16.10 shows the per-phase equivalent circuit for a three-phase induction motor. The slip is represented by *s*. At a slip of 4%, the current in the stator is 9.928 A and the current in the rotor part of the circuits is 7.063. Iron losses are ignored.
(a) Find the developed power.

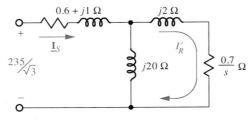

**Figure P16.10**

(b) Find the rotor-copper loss.
(c) Find the stator-copper loss.
(d) What is the power factor?

16.11 A three-phase, four-pole, 60-Hz induction motor is represented at one speed by the per-phase circuit shown in Fig. P16.11. The 8-$\Omega$ resistor represents the power being converted to mechanical form in the motor.
(a) What is the motor speed in rpm?
(b) Find the developed mechanical torque. The current in the rotor part of the circuit is 16.0 A.
(c) Estimate the starting torque? (Ignore 100 ∥ $j$16 $\Omega$.)

16.12 A three-phase, 230-V, 60–Hz induction motor has the following nameplate information: 10 hp, 90% efficiency, 0.82 power factor (lagging), 1740 rpm.

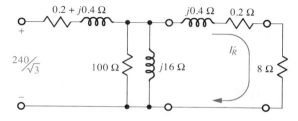

**Figure P16.11**

(a) Determine the apparent power rating of the machine.
(b) Find the reactive power required by the motor at nameplate operation.
(c) What is the output torque at nameplate operation?
(d) Find the total stator losses at nameplate operation, assuming 10 W of mechanical loss.

16.13. The per-phase equivalent circuit of a two-pole, three-phase, 60-Hz induction motor is shown as a function of slip in Fig. P16.13. Ignore mechanical losses.
(a) For an ouput power of 1 hp, find the speed of the two-pole motor. *Hint:* Use a Thèvenin equivalent circuit.
(b) For an output power of 1 hp, determine the input current and the efficiency of the motor.
(c) Estimate the starting torque for this motor.

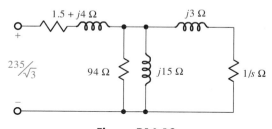

**Figure P16.13**

16.14. A 60-Hz, three-phase induction motor runs at 3599.5 rpm at no load and at 3500 rpm with 5 hp out. Assume operation in the small-slip region.
(a) Find the slip at no load and at 5 hp out.
(b) Find the mechanical losses, assumed independent of speed. Assume operation in the small-slip region.
(c) Find the air-gap power at 3500 rpm.

16.15. The per-phase equivalent circuit for a 60-Hz, three-phase, four-pole induction motor is shown in Fig. P16.15. At a slip of 4%, the input current is 49.75 A and the power factor is 0.9391.
(a) What is the input power to the motor at this slip?
(b) Find the air-gap power at this slip.
(c) What is the developed torque for the motor at this slip?
(d) *Estimate* the input current for starting the motor. (Ignore $j10 \parallel 44\ \Omega$.)
(e) *Estimate* the starting torque for the motor.

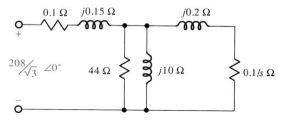

**Figure P16.15**

16.16. The equivalent per-phase circuit shown in Fig. P16.16 represents a 60-Hz, three-phase induction motor with six poles.
(a) Estimate the starting current. (Ignore $j20 \parallel 60\ \Omega$.)
(b) Estimate the slip for 25-hp output power, ignoring mechanical losses.

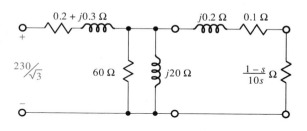

$$V_T = 130.4 \text{ V}$$
$$R_{eq} + jX_{eq} = 0.195 + j0.296\ \Omega, \text{ seen by rotor}$$

**Figure P16.16**

16.17. A 60-Hz, three-phase induction motor has the following nameplate information: 100 hp, 1780 rpm, 230/460 V, 244.0/122.0 A, 91.7% efficiency, service factor 1.15, and 732 lbs. Assume that mechanical losses are 100 W and that iron losses are 1.8 W/lb.
(a) Find the number of poles and the slip at nameplate operation.
(b) Find the three electrical loss components.

(c) Estimate the motor speed if the motor is operated at 115 hp continuously.

16.18. The per-phase equivalent circuit of a three-phase induction motor is shown in Fig. P16.18. The rotor current at a slip of 5% is 10 A rms.
   (a) Find the developed power of the rotor at this slip.
   (b) Estimate the efficiency of the motor at this slip.

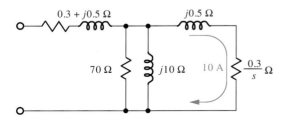

**Figure P16.18**

16.19. A 6-pole, 60-Hz, three-phase induction motor has the per-phase equivalent circuit shown in Fig. P16.19.
   (a) Determine the developed power at 1140 rpm.
   (b) At what speed does the motor produce 4 hp? assume 10 W mechanical loss and the small-slip region.

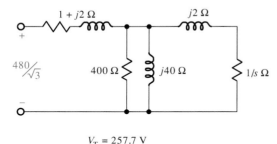

$V_T = 257.7$ V

$\underline{Z}_{eq} = 0.914 + j1.918$ Ω

**Figure P16.19**

16.20. A three-phase, 60-Hz induction motor has the following nameplate information: 25 hp, 1750 rpm, 230/460 V, 64.0/32.0 A, 91.0% eff; and 1.15 service factor. Assume negligible mechanical losses but a 500-W iron loss.
   (a) Find the reactive power requirement of the motor at nameplate conditions.
   (b) Find the stator-copper loss of the motor at nameplate conditions.

(c) Estimate the output torque at a speed of 1760 rpm.

16.21. An industrial-duty 60-Hz, three-phase induction motor has the following nameplate information: 20 hp, 3515 rpm, 230/460 V, 50.0/25.0 A, efficiency = 86.5%, and 320 lb. The mechanical losses are 100 W. Assume iron losses are 1.5 W/lb of weight. At nameplate conditions, find the following:
   (a) Air-gap power.
   (b) Stator losses.
   (c) Power factor.
   (d) Developed torque.
   (e) No-load speed.
   (f) The per-phase stator resistance when the motor is connected for 460-V operation.

16.22. The nameplate specifications of a 60-Hz, three-phase induction motor are as follows: 15 hp, 284-T frame, 1170 rpm, 67.3 lb-ft torque, 94.2 lb-ft locked-rotor torque, 135 lb-ft breakdown torque, 42 A, 230 V, 232 A locked-rotor current, 89.5% efficiency, and 1.15 service factor. (1 ft-lb = 1.356 N-m.) Assuming no mechanical losses but 300-W iron loss, find the following:
   (a) The power factor under nameplate conditions.
   (b) The rotor-copper loss under nameplate conditions.
   (c) The per-phase stator resistance.
   (d) The speed at which the motor output torque is 60% of the nameplate torque.
   (e) The air-gap power for $s = 1$.

16.23. Figure P16.23 shows the per-phase equivalent circuit for a six-pole, 60-Hz, three-phase induction motor. The stator circuit has been converted to a Thèvenin equivalent circuit.
   (a) Find the speed (rpm) for an output power of 10 hp. Assume the small-slip region.
   (b) The nameplate speed is 1135 rpm. Find the nameplate output power, assuming 1% of the developed power is mechanical loss.

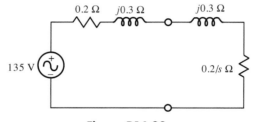

**Figure P16.23**

**(c)** From the previous information, estimate the no-load speed, assuming constant mechanical loss.

**16.24.** A three-phase, 60-Hz induction motor has the following nameplate information: 5 hp, 1740 rpm, 230/460 V, 12.8/6.4 A, efficiency 87.5%, service factor 1.15, blocked-rotor current 93 A at 230 V, blocked-rotor torque 180% of rated torque, and weight 95 lb.

**(a)** Find the power factor under nameplate conditions.

**(b)** Find the air-gap power under blocked-rotor conditions.

**(c)** What happens to the air-gap power under blocked-rotor conditions?

**(d)** Assuming that the iron losses are 1.5 W/lb of weight, find the stator per-phase resistance when connected for 230-V operation. Ignore mechanical losses.

**16.25.** A three-phase, 60-Hz induction motor has the following nameplate information: 2 hp, 3500 rpm, 230/460 V, 6.0/30. A, 80.0% eff, and 50 lb. Tests at 230 V shown that the motor has a no-load speed and input current of 3599.2 rpm and 3.2 A respectively.

**(a)** Find the mechanical loss, assumed independent of speed.

**(b)** Find the rotor loss at nameplate operation.

**(c)** Find the stator loss at nameplate operation, assuming 2-W/lb iron loss.

**(d)** Find the power factor at nameplate operation.

**(e)** Estimate the power factor at no load.

**16.26.** A three-phase, 10-hp motor has the following specifications: 60-Hz, 1750 rpm, 230/460 V, 88.5% eff; 26.2/13.1 A, and service factor 1.35. Assume that the mechanical losses are 0.5% of the output power at nameplate conditions and are constant throughout the small-slip region. Assume iron losses of 250 W.

**(a)** What is the output torque at nameplate conditions?

**(b)** Give the power factor at nameplate conditions.

**(c)** Find the per-phase stator resistance of the motor for 230-V excitation.

**(d)** *Estimate* the per-phase rotor resistance referred to the stator for 230-V excitation.

**16.27.** The (simplified) per-phase equivalent circuit in Fig. P16.27 is for a 460-V, four-pole, three-phase, 60-Hz induction motor. The motor has 200 W of iron and the mechanical loss, and the total losses

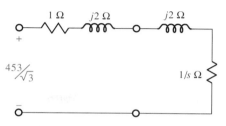

**Figure P16.27**

must be less than 900 W to avoid overheating.

**(a)** What is the approximate nameplate power rating for this motor?

**(b)** Estimate the slip at rated load.

**16.28** Figure P16.28 shows the per-phase equivalent circuit for a 50-Hz, three-phase induction motor. Estimate the speed for 4.5 hp out, ignoring mechanical losses.

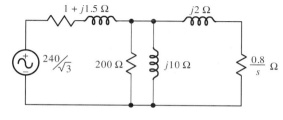

**Figure P16.28**

**16.29.** A three-phase, 60-Hz induction motor has the following nameplate information: 7.5 hp, 1755 rpm, 230/460 V, 19.4/9.7 A, 88.5% eff; and service factor 1.15. Neglect mechanical losses but assume 200 W of iron loss.

**(a)** Find the power factor at nameplate operation.

**(b)** Find the output torque at nameplate operation.

**(c)** Find the slip speed in radians/second at nameplate operation.

**(d)** Find the rotor losses at nameplate operation.

**(e)** Find the stator losses at nameplate operation.

**(f)** A load requiring $T_L(n) = 10 + 12.8\,(n/1800)^2$ N-m is connected to the motor. Find the speed at which the motor operates.

**16.30.** A three-phase, 60-Hz induction motor has the following nameplate information: 1/4 hp, 1725 rpm, 230/440 V, 1.1/0.55 A, 66.8% eff; and 1.35 service factor. Consider mechanical losses to be negligible.

**(a)** Find the output torque at nameplate operation.

**(b)** Find the power factor at nameplate operation.

(c) If the load torque requirement is $T_L = 0.004\omega_m$ N-m, find the speed in rpm at which the motor/load will operate.

(d) Under the conditions in part (c), estimate the rotor-copper losses.

16.31. A 60-Hz, three-phase induction motor has the following nameplate information: 40 hp, 1775 rpm, 230/460 V, 91.7% eff; 94.8/47.4 A, $1269.97 wholesale, and 548 lb. Neglect mechanical losses but assume 1 W/lb of iron loss.

(a) Find the slip speed in radians/second at nameplate conditions.

(b) Find the apparent power in kVA used by the motor at nameplate conditions.

(c) Find the power factor of the motor at nameplate conditions.

(d) Find the rotor-copper losses at nameplate conditions.

(e) Find the stator losses at nameplate conditions.

16.32 A junior engineer was given the task of evaluating the motor in the previous problem through a series of measurements, so as to producce a per-phase equivalent circuit. The engineer measures the mechanical losses as 10 watts and presented to the boss the equivalence circuit shown in Fig. P16.32.

(a) Does the $j13\ \Omega$ look reasonable? Explain why or why not.

(b) Does the $143\ \Omega$ look reasonable? Explain why or why not.

(c) Does the $0.28\ \Omega$ look reasonable? Explain why or why not.

(d) Does the $0.5/s\ \Omega$ look reasonable? Explain why or why not.

N.B.: These questions should be answered without a detailed analysis of the equivalent circuit. Your "reasons" should include some simple calculations.

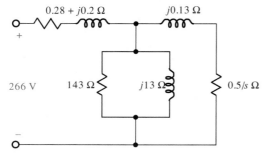

**Figure P16.32**

16.33. A 60-Hz, three-phase induction motor has the following nameplate specificationa: 20.5 A at 230 V; runs 1725 rpm with an efficiency of 88.0%. The no-load speed and current are 1799.2 rpm and 11.1 A, respectively. We ignore iron loss. A simplified per-phase equivalent circuit for the motor is shown in Fig. P16.33. From the given information, estimate as many of the equivalent circuit resistors and reactances as you can.

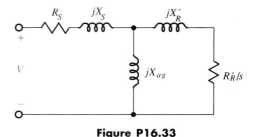

**Figure P16.33**

16.34. A three-phase, 60-Hz induction motor has the following nameplate information: 30 hp, 1750 rpm, 39.0 A, 460 V 87.5% eff; and 1.15 SF. A simplified per-phase equivalent circuit for the motor is shown in Fig. P16.34.

(a) From the given information, estimate the three impendance values in the circuit. Ignore iron and mechanical losses.

(b) The motor is connected to a load that requires a torque given by the equation

$$T_L(n) = 10 + 12\left(\frac{n}{1800}\right) + 30\left(\frac{n}{1800}\right)^2 \text{ N-m}$$

Assuming operation in the small-slip region, find the operating speed of the system. Do not use the equivalent circuit from part (a), but rather work directly from the nameplate information.

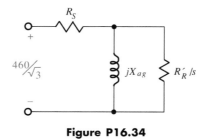

**Figure P16.34**

16.35 Design a motor-drive system for a load with the following characteristics: The motor is OFF for 2 seconds and ON for 1 second, and then the pattern repeats. While ON, the power required is 1.5 hp. The current required to start is 400% the rated current, but lasts only for 0.1 second. Neglect mechanical losses and assume 2 watts/pound of weight for the iron losses. Pick a suitable motor drive from Table 16.2 and confirm that your choice meets the specifications for the job through an analysis of the losses.

16.36. A high-slip, 30-hp, three-phase motor is used on an unbalanced pumping jack. The nameplate information on the motor is 460 V, 36 A, 1115 rpm, 86.4% eff; service factor = 1.0. Ignore mechanical losses. The equivalent circuit for the motor is shown in Fig. P16.36. The load is unbalanced, with a torque requirement of 250 N-m on the upstroke and a load requirement of −100 N-m on the down stroke, meaning that the motor acts as an induction generator and returns energy to the electrical power system. The gearing is such that the shaft turns 100 revolutions on the up-stroke and 100 revolutions on the downstroke.
(a) Find the total energy used by the motor on one up–down cycle.
(b) Is the motor overloaded in this application? Explain.

16.37. A load with the time-varying torque shown in Fig. P16.37 turns about 1750 rpm. We need to specify a motor-drive this load, to satisfy two criteria: (1) the load torque never exceeds 175% of the

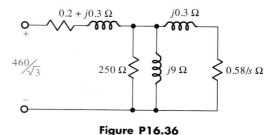

**Figure P16.36**

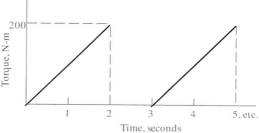

**Figure P16.37**

nameplate torque (avoid breakover); and (2) the rms horsepower required by the load does not exceed the nameplate rating of the motor (avoid overheating). To simplify, consider the speed to be exactly 1750 rpm. Determine the rating of a three-phase insduction motor to meet these criteria, using the motor information in Table 16.2.

## Section 16.3: Single-Phase Induction Motors

16.38. A single-phase, 120-V induction motor takes a current of 6 A. The electrical loss is 5% of the input power and the mechanical loss is 1% of the output power. If the total losses are 30 W, find the power factor of the motor.

16.39. A 115-V, 60-Hz, single-phase induction motor produces 2 hp at 3500 rpm with an input current of 18.8 A. Assume losses at this power to be 20% of the output power, divided between mechanical and electrical losses in the ratio 1:20. Find the power factor and the efficiency.

16.40. A 60-Hz, single-phase induction motor has the following nameplate information: 115/230 V, 8.2/4.1 A. 1725 rpm and 3/4 hp. Assume a power factor of 0.78 lagging.
(a) Determine the efficiency of the motor at nameplate operation.
(b) What is the output torque at nameplate operation.

(c) What are the electrical frequencies in the rotor at nameplate operation?
(d) Explain how the motor can be connected for either 115- or 230-V operation.
(e) Would you expect the motor to have better performance when connected for 115- or 230-V operation? Explain.

16.41. A single-phase, 60-Hz induction motor has the following specifications: 3/4 hp, 1725 rpm, 115/230 V, 11.6/5.8 A, ball bearings, and reversible.
(a) Assuming a power factor of 0.77, determine the efficiency of the motor.
(b) Find the output torque under nameplate conditions.
(c) Explain how to reverse the motor.
(d) If the motor were excited at 113 V, would the current be less than, the same as, or greater than 11.6 A for the same output power?

A high-efficiency, single-phase, 60-Hz induction

motors has the following nameplate information: 1/2 hp, 1725 rpm, 115 V, and 5.5 A. This is capacitor-start/capacitor-run motor.

(a) How many poles does this motor have?

(b) Assuming an efficiency of 75%, determine the power factor.

(c) What electrical frequencies exist in the rotor?

(d) What is the output torque?

(e) Draw the motor circuit that exists during starting.

16.43. A 60-Hz, 120-V, single-phase induction motor has a linear region described by the equation $P_{dev} = a + bs$. The motor runs at 1798 rpm at no load and 1740 rpm with 1-hp output power. Find the output power at 1785 rpm, assuming the same mechanical losses at all speeds in the problem.

16.44. A capacitor-start/induction-run, 60-Hz, single-phase induction motor has the following nameplate information: 2 hp, 1725 rpm, 60 Hz, 230 V, 10.3 A, and efficiency = 84.0%. Find the following:

(a) The number of poles.

(b) The slip at nameplate load.

(c) The power factor at nameplate load.

(d) The rated torque at nameplate load.

(e) The yearly operating cost based on 6 cents/kW-hour, 40 h/week, 50 weeks/year.

16.45. The circuit diagram for a 120-V, 60-Hz, single-phase capacitor-start/induction-run motor is shown in Fig. P16.45. The circuit applies only with the rotor at rest. After the motor comes to full speed, the current in the main winding is one-third of its value at the instant of starting. The auxiliary winding is connected only during starting. Find the ratio of the maximum starting current to the run current.

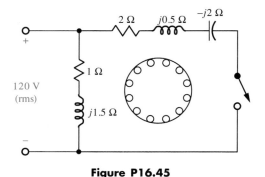

**Figure P16.45**

16.46 A single-phase, 60-Hz capacitor-start/induction-run

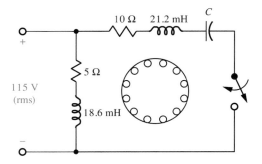

**Figure P16.46**

motor has the equivalent circuit (for starting) shown in Fig. P16.46.

(a) Find $C$ for a $90°$ phase shift between starting currents in run and auxiliary windings at starting.

(b) Determine the starting current for this value of $C$.

(c) Assuming the nameplate run current is 3.9 A, the speed is 1740 rpm, and the power is 1/4 hp, estimate the power factor and output torque of the motor under nameplate conditions. Ignore iron and mechanical losses.

16.47. A motor catalog lists a 60-Hz, high efficiency (capacitor-start/capacitor-run) single phase motor with the following nameplate information: 1 hp, 1725 rpm, 115/230 V, and 9.2/4.6 A. The catalog also claims that this motor saves 100 W compared to the normal capacitor-start/induction-run motor, which has the following nameplate information: 1 hp, 1725 rpm, 115/230 V, and 14.8/7.4 A. Assume that electrical losses are $K(I_{in})^2$, where $K$ is the same for both motors. Also assume that mechanical losses are 2% of the output power for both motors. Determine the power factors of the two motors.

16.48. A 1/4 hp, 120-V, 60-Hz, single-phase induction motor runs at 3599 rpm no-load speed and 3450 rpm at rated output power. *Hint:* Assume $P_{out} = a + bs$.

(a) Find the two electrical frequencies in the rotor at 1/4 hp out.

(b) Estimate the slip for 1/8 hp out.

(c) Find the mechanical power required to drive the motor at 3600 rpm.

16.49. A capacitor-start/induction-run, 115-V, 60-Hz single-phase induction motor has stator field parameters as shown in Fig. P16.49.

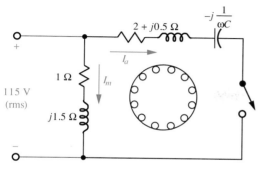

**Figure P16.49**

(a) What value of capacitor is required to produce a 90° phase shift between main and auxiliary currents for starting?

(b) Find the starting current with the value of capacitance determined in part (a).

16.50. Figure P16.50 shows a shaded-pole induction motor. The conducting bands "shade" a portion of the poles to create rotating flux.

(a) Estimate the flux in the iron.

(b) Estimate the input current to the motor if its output power is 25 W. Ignore iron losses.

(c) Mark the direction that the motor will turn.

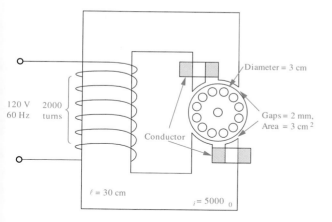

**Figure P16.50**

16.51. A 1/4-hp, 120-V, capacitor-start/induction-run motor has the current, PF, and speed characteristics given in Table P16.51.

(a) Find the efficiency at 60% and 100% of nameplate power.

(b) Is this motor designed to have maximum efficiency at nameplate conditions? Yes or no?

(c) Estimate the stator losses at no load. (*N.B.:*

Assume no mechanical losses. But there are copper losses at no-load because the rotor is in equilibrium between forward and reverse components of the rotating fields and losses due to each torque appears as rotor-copper loss. Consider the reverse-torque to be constant over the operating range of the motor.)

**TABLE P16.51**

| Power, hp | rpm | PF | Current |
|---|---|---|---|
| 0 | 1787 | 0.246 | 6.25 |
| 0.05 | 1777 | 0.292 | 6.21 |
| 0.10 | 1767 | 0.341 | 6.24 |
| 0.15 | 1756 | 0.392 | 6.28 |
| 0.20 | 1745 | 0.433 | 6.34 |
| 0.25 | 1731 | 0.476 | 6.41 |
| 0.30 | 1716 | 0.520 | 6.55 |
| 0.35 | 1702 | 0.561 | 6.78 |
| 0.40 | 1686 | 0.594 | 7.11 |
| 0.45 | 1669 | 0.625 | 7.55 |
| 0.50 | 1650 | 0.652 | 8.07 |

16.52. A single-phase induction motor has the following nameplate information: 1/3 hp, 60 Hz, 3450 rpm, 115/230 V, 9.8/4.9 A, and power factor 0.72, lagging. The equivalent circuit, connected for 230-V operation, is shown in Fig. P16.52. The resistance values are valid for starting, but change as the rotor moves to account for power transformed into mechanical work.

(a) Find the starting current for the motor.

(b) Find the stator-copper losses at nameplate conditions.

(c) If the no-load speed were 3585 rpm, estimate the speed for 0.25-hp output power.

16.53. The equivalent circuit for a single-phase motor is shown in Fig. P16.53. Under nameplate conditions, the currents in the two windings are equal in magnitude and 90° out of phase.

(a) What type of motor is it? Your choices are (1) capacitor-start/induction-run, (2) split-phase, (3) capacitor-start/capacitor-run, (4) permanent-split-capacitor, and (5) shaded-pole.

(b) The rotating field in this motor depends on one phase, two phases or three phases? Which?

(c) The input run current to the motor is 10 A.

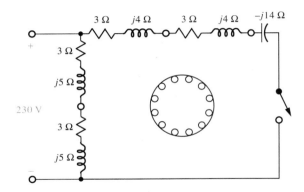

**Figure P16.52**

What is the magnitude of the currents in the windings?

**(d)** The run current in the winding without the capacitor lags input voltage by 45°. Find the value of the capacitor.

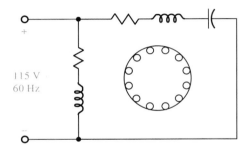

**Figure P16.53**

**16.54.** A single-phase motor drives a machine that has a duty cycle requiring 2 N-m for 15 s and 4 N-m for 5 s, and then repeats with a 20-s cycle time. The speed should be in the range 1650−1750 rpm, so a 60-Hz, 4-pole motor is indicated. A section out of a motor catalog is given in Table P16.54. Assume that all motors have an efficiency of 80%

## General Problems

**16.57.** A motor catalog lists the following motor: 5 hp, 230/460 V, 12.8/6.4 A, 1740 rpm, 60 Hz, 85.5% eff; 1.15 service factor, 60 lb. Assume operation at nameplate conditions and negligible mechanical losses. Assume further that the electrical losses divide between rotor and stator in the ratio 1:3.
**(a)** What type of motor is this: induction or synchronous? Explain how you know.
**(b)** In this a three-phase or single-phase motor?

when operating near their nameplate conditions and total losses are proportional to current squared and that current is proportional to torque. Select the best motor for the job.

| TABLE P16.54 | | | | |
| --- | --- | --- | --- | --- |
| hp | rpm | Amps | SF | Cost, $ |
| 1/4 | 1725 | 5.6 | 1.35 | 83.16 |
| 1/3 | 1725 | 8.0 | 1.0 | 85.14 |
| 1/2 | 1725 | 10.0 | 1.0 | 101.97 |
| 3/4 | 1725 | 10.8 | 1.25 | 141.57 |
| 1 | 1725 | 15.0 | 1.0 | 156.42 |

**16.55.** A 60-Hz, single-phase, capacitor-start/induction-run induction motor has the following nameplate information: 3 hp, 3450 rpm, 115/230 V, 30.0/15.0 A, service factor 1.15, $347.34, and 63.0 pounds. Measurements show the motor losses to be 600 W.
**(a)** Find the slip at nameplate conditions.
**(b)** Find the number of poles.
**(c)** What is the efficiency of the motor at nameplate conditions?
**(d)** What is the in-phase component of the current at nameplate conditions for 230-V operation?
**(e)** What is the out-of-phase component of the current at nameplate conditions for 230-V operation?

**16.56.** By accident, the run windings for the motor described in the previous problem are connected in series for 230-V operation, but the auxiliary windings are connected in parallel. The motor has 230 V applied. Explain the following:
**(a)** Will this affect the starting torque?
**(b)** Will this affect the starting current?
**(c)** Will this affect the run torque?
**(d)** Will this affect the run current?
**(e)** Will this affect the direction of rotation?

Explain how you know.
**(c)** What is the power factor of the motor?
**(d)** Find the rotor-and stator-copper losses and the iron losses.
**(e)** Find the per-phase rotor resistance, assuming 230-V operation.

**16.58.** Observe the comparison in Table P16.58 between similar 60-Hz, single-phase and three-phase induction motors:

**TABLE P16.58**

| Phases | hp | rpm | Volts | Amps | lb | Cost, $ |
|--------|----|-----|-------|------|-----|---------|
| 3 | 1 | 1750 | 230 | 3.5 | 32 | 120.06 |
| 1 | 1 | 1740 | 230 | 7.2 | 40.7 | 174.75 |

Indicate for the following statements: true, false, or uncertain, and explain.

(a) The single-phase motor is heavier because of the starting capacitor.

(b) The single-phase motor runs slower because it has a counter-rotating flux that opposes the principal rotation.

(c) The single-phase has higher current because it has a worse efficiency.

(d) Both motors have four poles.

16.59. Here are some short-answer questions:

(a) Two input power wires of an operating three-phase induction motor are exchanged suddenly. The slip at that instant would be about $-1$, 0, $+1$, or $+2$?

(b) Assuming voltages are OK, a single-phase induction motor can be operated from two wires of a three-phase system, but a three-phase induction motor cannot be operated off the two wires of a single-phase power system. True or false?

(c) A two-phase induction motor would have a torque/speed characteristic similar to that of a three-phase induction motor except it would have no starting torque. True or false?

(d) If a 60-Hz, single-phase induction motor were run at 50 Hz, the motor speed for the same torque would approximately 5/6 of the 60-Hz speed. True or false?

(e) If a three-phase induction motor were operating and one of the input wires became disconnected, the motor would stop immediately. True or false?

## Answers to Odd-Numbered Problems

16.1. $I_a = I$, $I_b = I_c = -I/2$.

16.3. (a) 4; (b) 4.44%; (c) 1460 W; (d) 1390 W; (e) 1590 W; (f) 87.4%; (g) 7.73 N-m; (h) 1870 VA.

16.5. (a) 3.33%; (b) 0.836; (c) 3890; (d) greater than.

16.7. Rotor = 64.9 W and stator = 98.1 W.

16.9. 87.2%.

16.11. (a) 1800 rpm; (b) 33.4 N-m; (c) 76.4 N-m.

16.13. (a) 3518 rpm; (b) 7.86 A, 77.8%; (c) 2.65 N-m.

16.15. (a) 16,800 W; (b) 15,100 W; (c) 80.1 N-m; (d) 298 A; (e) 141 N-m.

16.17. (a) 1.11%; (b) rotor = 839 W, iron = 1320 W, stator = 4500 W; (c) 1777 rpm.

16.19. (a) 8370 W; (b) 1182 rpm.

16.21. (a) 15,400 W; (b) 1390 W; (c) 0.866; (d) 40.8 W; (e) 3599.4 rpm; (f) 0.741 $\Omega$.

16.23. (a) 1166 rpm; (b) 12,200 W; (c) 1199.35 rpm.

16.25. (a) 12.4 W; (b) 43.0 W; (c) 218 W; (d) 0.780; (e) 0.341, lagging.

16.27. (a) 7660 W, about 10 hp; (b) 4.37%.

16.29. (a) 0.818; (b) 30.4 N-m; (c) 4.71 rad/s; (d) 143 W; (e) 384 W; (f) 1767 rpm.

16.31. (a) 2.62 rad/s; (b) 37.8 kVA; (c) 0.862; (d) 420 W; (e) 1730 W.

16.33. $R'_R \approx 0.4\ \Omega$, $X_{ag} \approx 11\ \Omega$, $R_s \approx 0.37\ \Omega$; reactances are small and not easily estimated except by careful measurement.

16.35. RMS hp suggests 1 hp; everage losses estimate to about 220 W, well below the allowed 290 W.

16.37. 30 hp, mainly on the maximum torque requirement.

16.39. 0.828, 83.3%.

16.41. (a) 54.5 %; (b) 3.10 N-m; (c) reverse the auxiliary winding connections; (d) greater than 11.6 A; approxiomately 11.8 A.

16.43. 167 W.

16.45. 3.60.

16.47. $PF_1 = 0.779$, $PF_2 = 0.543$.

16.49. (a) 1450 µF; (b) 79.8 A.

16.51. (a) $\eta_{60\%} = 37.9\%$, $\eta_{100\%} = 50.9\%$; (b) no; (c) 88 W.

16.53. (a) PSC; (b) two phases; (c) 7.07 A; (d) 115 µF.

16.55. (a) 4.17%; (b) 2; (c) 78.9%; (d) 12.3 A; (e) 8.53 A, lagging.

16.57. (a) induction motor: (b) three phase, because its power factor would exceed unity if it were a single-phase motor; (c) 0.856; (d) rotor = 129 W, stator = 388 W, iron = 118 W; (e) 0.789 $\Omega$.

16.59. (a) $+2$, because the synchronous speed reverses sign; (b) true: two wires give single-phase power; (c) false: it would have the same characteristics; (d) true: the synchronous speed is 5/6 of 60-hz synchronous speed; (e) false: it becomes a single-phase motor, which will run if started.

# Direct-Current Motors

1. To understand the physical basis for the equivalent circuit of a dc motor
2. To understand the speed–torque characteristic of the shunt-connected dc motor
3. To understand the speed-torque characteristic of the series-connected dc motor
4. To understand how to develop system models for separately excited dc motors from nameplate and load characteristics

We still need lots of dc motors for portable operation such as in automobiles, for control applications, and for household tools and appliances that, ironically, run on ac power. In this chapter, we consider operating principles and external characteristics of several types of dc motors.

**alternator**

**Importance.** The dc machine can be used either as a motor or a generator. However, because semiconductor rectifiers can generate dc voltage from ac with electronic power supplies, dc generators are unneeded except for remote operations. Even in the automobile, the dc generator has been replaced by the *alternator*, a synchronous generator plus diodes for rectification. On the other hand, generator operation must still be considered because motors operate as generators in braking and reversing.

Portable devices operating from battery power require dc motors, such as auto starters, window lifts, and portable tape players. Equally important, the dc machine is readily controlled in speed and torque and hence is useful for control systems. Examples are robots, elevators, machine tools, rolling mills, and large power shovels.

In this chapter, we examine the fundamental principles of dc motors and explore the wide range of characteristics that can be achieved through various motor configurations. DC generators are mentioned briefly, primarily because of the role of the back-generated voltage in the operation of dc motors. The universal motor, a type of dc motor that runs on ac power, is also discussed.

### Stator Magnetic Structure

**Salient-pole structures.** The stator magnetic structure for a dc machine is shown in Fig. 17.1(a). The dc machine uses salient poles,[1] which are extended in width to leave as little interpole space as practical. The field coils are wrapped around these poles. The rotor is cylindrical, with slots for wires, as shown in Fig. 17.1(b). The flux-density distribution approximates a square wave, as shown in Fig. 17.2 for the four-pole structure in Fig. 17.1(a).

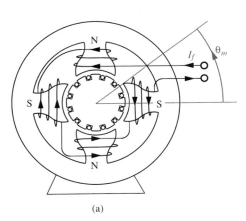
(a)

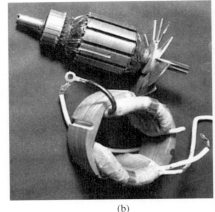
(b)

**Figure 17.1** (a) Salient-pole magnetic structure with $P = 4$ poles; (b) a small dc motor with two poles.

**Analysis.** The maximum flux density can be determined from Ampère's circuital law around a path passing through two adjacent poles.

---

[1] In this context, "pole" refers to the mechanical protrusion as well as the magnetic pole associated with it.

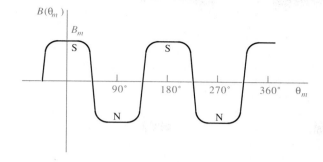

**Figure 17.2** Flux density for four-pole, dc magnetic structure. Flux is positive in the radially outward direction. This is also the form of the voltage generated in a single wire of a rotating armature.

$$\oint \vec{H} \cdot \vec{dl} = ni \quad \Rightarrow \quad B_m = \frac{\mu_0 2nI_f}{2g} \qquad (17.1)$$

where $B_m$ is the maximum flux density, $nI_f$ is the mmf per pole, and $g$ is the width of the air gap. The factor 2 in the denominator arises because the air gap is traversed twice by the path of integration, and the factor 2 appears in the numerator because $n$ is the turns on one pole and the path of integration passes through two poles. The mmf loss in the iron has been neglected.

---

**EXAMPLE 17.1** | **Field mmf**

A small dc motor has a rotor OD of $3.80 \pm 0.01$ cm and a stator ID of $3.90 \pm 0.01$ cm. Find the mmf/pole for a nominal flux density of 0.8 tesla.

**SOLUTION:**

By using the nominal diameters, the value of $2g$ in Eq. (17.1) is $3.90 - 3.80 = 0.10$ cm. From Eq. (17.1), the required mmf is

$$0.8 = \frac{4\pi \times 10^{-7} \times 2nI_f}{0.10 \times 10^{-2}} \quad \Rightarrow \quad nI_f = 318 \text{ A-t} \qquad (17.2)$$

**WHAT IF?** What if 318 ampere-turns are used, and the *maximum* possible flux density is desired?[2]

---

**Alnico**

**Permanent magnet fields for dc machines.** Figure 17.3 shows an automotive air-conditioner/heater-blower motor, which uses field of permanent magnets made from molded ceramic ferrite. Larger structures might use *Alnico*[3] permanent magnets.

---
[2] 1.0 tesla.

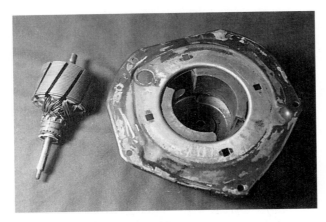

**Figure 17.3** Automotive fan motor. Permanent magnets on the stator produce the magnetic field. This stator has four poles

## Rotor Construction

**Rotor currents and flux.** The dc machine requires a brush-commutator system, indicated in Fig. 17.4, to produce currents out of the paper on the right side and into the paper on the left. The right-hand rule shows that the rotor currents produce a downward flux, a north pole at the bottom and a south pole at the top. These poles are attracted to their opposites on the stator and a counterclockwise torque is produced on the rotor from these currents.

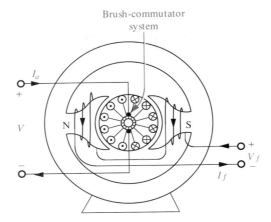

**Figure 17.4** A two-pole dc machine with two salient stator poles and a brush-commutator system.

**commutator, brushes**

**Brush–commutator system.** Figure 17.5 shows a brush and the commutator from a dc machine. The commutator has a cylindrical surface of wedge-shaped segments connected to the rotor conductors. The commutator is part of the rotor and participates in its rotation. The brushes are stationary and rub against the commutator as the rotor rotates. Figure 17.6 shows a schematic view of how the currents reverse due to commutation. The radial lines represent the active lengths of the rotor conductors,

---

[3] *Alnico* is a tradename of Alcoa for aluminum–nickel–cobalt, from which many permanent magnets are fashioned.

**Figure 17.5** An automobile generator.

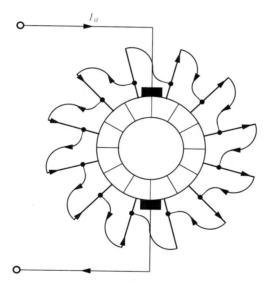

**Figure 17.6** Schematic diagram of the armature conductors. The heavy lines represent the active lengths of the armature conductors. The currents are in opposite directions on opposite sides.

and the current returns and internal connections are shown. The currents reverse on opposite sides of the rotor, as indicated in Fig. 17.6.

The brush–commutator system provides, therefore, two related functions:

- Electrical connection is made with the moving rotor.
- Switching of the rotor currents is accomplished mechanically in a way that automatically synchronizes switching with rotor motion.

Due to the brush–commutator system, the *spatial pattern* of the rotor currents is always the same, independent of the physical position of the rotor.

Many of the problems with dc machines arise due to commutation. Not only must the brush–commutator system carry large currents across a sliding contact, but the switching of currents in the individual coils causes an inductive effect that limits performance. These problems have been solved in measure, with the result that we have available dc machines with excellent characteristics, although they require occasional maintenance.

In dc motors, both stator and rotor magnetic poles remain fixed in space, and the mechanical rotor rotates relative to the rotor magnetic poles. The rotor conductors carry "ac" currents[4] under the control of the brush–commutator system.

## Circuit Model

**Equivalent Circuits**

**separately excited**

**Field circuit.** The field circuit is modeled in Fig. 17.7 as a series connection of resistance and inductance, with a field-voltage supply, $V_f$. The motor is *separately excited* because the field circuit is independent of the armature circuit. In steady-state operation, the field current follows from Ohm's law:

$$I_f = \frac{V_f}{R_f} \tag{17.3}$$

where $I_f$ is the field current and $R_f$ the resistance of the field windings. Neglecting magnetic saturation and residual magnetism, we may relate the flux to the field current through the reluctance of the magnetic structure, $\Re$,

$$\Phi = \frac{2nI_f}{\Re} \tag{17.4}$$

where $\Phi$ is the flux and $n$ is the equivalent number of turns/pole. Normally, magnetic saturation and residual magnetism are significant, however, and the relationship between field current and flux is nonlinear.

The number of poles runs from 2 or 4 for a small motor to as large as 30 for a large motor. As we will see, the number of poles has no effect on the speed of the motor.

**Armature circuit.** The armature circuit is located on the rotor. The circuit model for the rotor consists of a resistance and inductance in series with an emf, $E$. Figure 17.7 shows the armature resistance and inductance outside the brush–commutator system, which introduces the emf, $E$, into the armature circuit. The armature resistance, $R_a$, and inductance, $L_a$, belong physically between the brushes but customarily are shown outside for artistic reasons. In either event, it does not matter for a series connection.

**Mechanical output.** We indicate the mechanical output with symbols indicating rotation and developed torque. As a consequence of its rotation in a magnetic field, the rotor also has iron losses; however, these customarily are not represented in the electrical equivalent circuit but are combined with the mechanical losses because they depend on mechanical speed and not on the electrical variables in the armature.

---

[4] Actually, chopped dc currents.

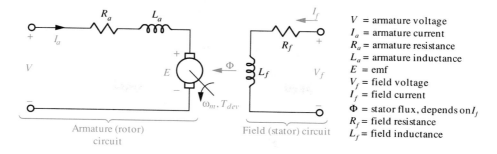

$V$ = armature voltage
$I_a$ = armature current
$R_a$ = armature resistance
$L_a$ = armature inductance
$E$ = emf
$V_f$ = field voltage
$I_f$ = field current
$\Phi$ = stator flux, depends on $I_f$
$R_f$ = field resistance
$L_f$ = field inductance

Armature (rotor) circuit

Field (stator) circuit

**Figure 17.7** Circuit model for a separately excited dc machine.

**back emf**

### Electromotive force.

When the rotor is rotated in the flux produced by the field, an ac voltage is produced in each rotor conductor. These voltages are rectified and summed by the brush–commutator system to produce a dc emf.[5] By Faraday's law, this emf is proportional to flux and rotation speed, and hence may be expressed by the relationship

$$E = K_E \Phi \omega_m \tag{17.5}$$

where $K_E$ is a constant that depends on rotor size, the number of rotor turns, and details of how these turns are interconnected.

### Developed torque.

If an armature current flows through the brush–commutator system, this current passes through the rotor conductors and a torque is developed. By Ampère's force law, this developed torque is proportional to flux and armature current and hence may be expressed as

$$T_{dev} = K_T \Phi I_a \tag{17.6}$$

where $K_T$ is a constant that also depends on rotor size, the number of rotor turns, and details of how these turns are interconnected. We soon demonstrate that conservation of energy requires that the constants in Eqs. (17.5) and (17.6) be the same.

## Power Flow in DC Machines

### Conservation of energy.

In steady state, KVL applied to the armature circuit yields

$$V = R_a I_a + E \quad \Rightarrow \quad I_a = \frac{V - E}{R_a} \tag{17.7}$$

where $V$ is the armature voltage, $I_a$ is the armature current, $R_a$ is the armature resistance, and $E$ is the armature emf. We may convert Eq. (17.7) into a power equation by multiplying by the armature current:

---

[5] In a motor called the *back emf*.

$$\underbrace{VI_a}_{P_{in}} = \underbrace{R_a I_a^2}_{\substack{\text{armature} \\ \text{Cu loss}}} + \underbrace{EI_a}_{\substack{\text{developed} \\ \text{power}}} \qquad (17.8)$$

**Conservation of Energy**

Equation (17.8) shows that the input power divides between armature-copper losses and $EI_a$, which represents power leaving the electrical circuit as mechanical power. Thus, conservation of energy requires the developed power to be

$$P_{dev} = \omega_m T_{dev} = EI_a \qquad (17.9)$$

The output power, $P$, is less than the developed power by the rotational losses, $P_{rot}$:

$$P = P_{dev} - P_{rot} \qquad (17.10)$$

**The machine constant.** If we substitute Eqs. (17.5) and (17.6) for $E$ and $T_{dev}$, respectively, Eq. (17.9) takes the form

$$K_T \Phi I_a \omega_m = K_E \Phi \omega_m I_a \qquad (17.11)$$

and thus $K_E = K_T = K$, the machine constant,[6] as asserted earlier.

**Motor action.** Combining Eq. (17.7) with Eq. (17.9), we may express the developed power as

$$P_{dev} = EI_a = \frac{E(V - E)}{R_a} \qquad (17.12)$$

When the armature voltage exceeds the emf, the armature current is positive relative to the reference direction shown in Fig. 17.7, electrical power is delivered to the armature, and the machine acts as a motor. In this case, the developed torque has the same direction as the direction of rotation, and mechanical power is delivered to the mechanical load.

**Generator action.** When the emf exceeds the armature voltage due to external mechanical drive, the current becomes negative relative to the reference direction in Fig. 17.7 and flows out of the + polarity mark on the armature. The machine then acts as a generator, and the developed torque is opposite to the direction of rotation. In many applications, the machine alternatively acts as a motor or generator, depending on changes in the mechanical load or armature voltage.

**Causality.** Figure 17.8 shows the causal factors governing dc machine behavior. Let us consider an at-rest dc machine with no mechanical load. If we apply voltage to the armature circuit, the resulting current will produce torque, which accelerates the rotor. As the rotor speed increases, so does the back emf, $E$, and the current decreases. The no-load equilibrium is reached when $E \approx V$ and a small armature current flows to supply rotational losses.

---

[6] The product of this machine constant and the magnetic flux, $K\Phi$, is also called "the machine constant." Context will make it clear which is meant.

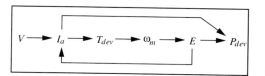

**Figure 17.8**  Causality in a dc motor.

**Effect of load.**  Continuing the previous discussion, we now apply a mechanical load. This slows down the rotor and the back emf is reduced proportionally. The lower emf causes an increase in current and torque until a new equilibrium is reached. Thus, we expect the motor to slow down with increasing mechanical load.

---

**EXAMPLE 17.2**  **Maximum power**

What is the maximum power that can be developed in an armature if armature voltage is constant?

**SOLUTION:**

For fixed $V$ and $R_a$, Eq. (17.12) describes a parabola with a maximum at $E = V/2$. Thus, the maximum power that can be developed is

$$P_{max} = \frac{V}{2} \times \frac{V - V/2}{R_a} = \frac{V^2}{4R_a} \qquad (17.13)$$

**WHAT IF?**  What if the voltage source in not ideal but has an output impedance, $R_{eq}$?[7]

---

**magnetization curve**

**Magnetization curve.**  Equation (17.5) allows the relationship between stator flux and field current to be represented as a *magnetization curve* of emf versus field current for a constant speed, as shown in Fig. 17.9. From the magnetization curve, we can determine the machine constant and the emf at other speeds, because the emf is strictly proportional to rotational speed by Eq. (17.5). Furthermore, we can also derive torque information because Eq. (17.9) gives

$$T_{dev} = \frac{E}{\omega_m} \times I_a \qquad (17.14)$$

where $E/\omega_m$ depends on field current and can be determined from the magnetization curve.

---

[7] $P_{max} = V^2/4(R_{eq} + R_a)$.

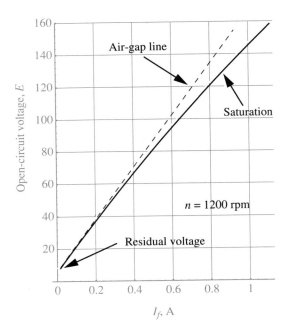

**Figure 17.9** The magnetization curve gives emf versus field current at fixed speed.[8]

---

EXAMPLE 17.3 **Torque calculation**

Find the developed torque of the motor whose magnetization curve is given in Fig. 17.9 if $I_f = 1.1$ A and $I_a = 5$ A.

**SOLUTION:**
At $n = 1200$ rpm and $I_f = 1.1$ A, $E = 159$ V. Hence, from Eq. (17.14),

$$T_{dev} = \frac{159 \times 5}{1200 \times 2\pi/60} = 6.31 \text{ N-m} \qquad (17.15)$$

---

**Residual magnetism.**   At zero field current, Fig. 17.9 indicates a small voltage. This effect from residual (permanent) magnetism in the stator magnetic structure plays an important role in the buildup of voltage if the machine is operated as a generator.

**air-gap line**   **Air-gap line.**   Figure 17.9 shows the effect of saturation in the iron of the magnetic structure. The linear approximation, *air-gap line*, is important in the following sections because, to derive approximate motor characteristics with the various means of field excitation, we often assume that the motor is operating with the stator flux proportional to field current. The results of such an analysis suggest the general features of the motor characteristics, but any resulting calculations are approximate.

---

[8] To aid in working examples and problems based on this magnetization curve, we confess that Fig. 17.9 was generated by the following parabola: $E(I_f) = 160 I_f - 21 I_f^2 + 8$. In pratice, it has to be measured.

**EXAMPLE 17.4** | **Output power calculation**

A 120-V dc motor has an armature resistance of 0.70 Ω. At no-load, it requires 1.1 A armature current and runs at 1000 rpm. Find the output power and torque at 952 rpm output speed. Assume constant flux.

**SOLUTION:**

From the no-load condition, we can calculate the machine constant and the rotational losses. The input power at no load is 120 V × 1.1 A = 132 W, and the armature loss is $0.70(1.1)^2 = 0.85$ W; hence, the rotational losses at 1000 rpm are 131.2 W. The emf at this speed can be calculated from Eq. (17.7) as $120 - 0.70(1.1) = 119.2$ V. Hence, the product of the machine constant and the stator flux is $K\Phi = 119.2/1000$.[9]

At 952 rpm, the emf is reduced to $E' = K\Phi \times 952 = 119.2 \times 952/1000 = 113.5$ V. This reduced voltage implies an input current of $I'_a = (120 - 113.5)/0.70 = 9.28$ A; and hence the developed power is $P_{dev} = EI'_a = 113.5 \times 9.28 = 1052.9$ W. Mechanical losses at 952 rpm are approximately the same as at 1000 rpm, and therefore the output power is $1052.9 - 131.2 = 921.7$ W (1.23 hp). The output torque is

$$T_{out} = \frac{P_{out}}{\omega_m} = \frac{921.7}{952(2\pi/60)} = 9.25 \text{ N-m} \tag{17.16}$$

**WHAT IF?**

What if the no-load current were 1.4 A and the rotational losses were proportional to speed? Find the output torque.[10]

### Check Your Understanding

1. On a dc machine, the magnitude of the rotor-stator power angle is about 90°. True or false?

2. DC motors are still used because they (a) can be portable, (b) have a good power factor, (c) can be controlled for speed, (d) can be controlled for torque, and (e) have low maintenance. Which? (May be more than one.)

3. DC motor torque is proportional to (a) armature current, (b) field current, (c) speed, or (d) developed power. Which? (May be more than one.)

4. DC motor emf is proportional to (a) armature current, (b) field current, (c) speed, or (d) developed power. Which? (May be more than one.)

5. To increase the speed of a separately excited dc motor, we would increase the (a) input voltage, (b) field current, (c) output torque, or (d) number of poles. Which?

6. The armature circuit of a separately excited dc motor is shown in Fig. 17.10. Determine the input and developed power of the motor.

---

[9] In this expression, the units for $K$ include the conversion between rpm and rad/s. Because we employ scaling principles, such conversion factors cancel.
[10] 9.31 N-m.

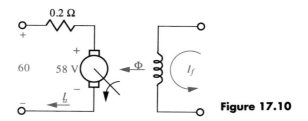

**Figure 17.10**

**Answers.** (1) True; (2) (a), (c), and (d); (3) (a) and (b); (4) (b) and (c); (5) (a); (6) 600 and 580 W, respectively.

## 17.2 CHARACTERISTICS OF DC MOTORS

**OBJECTIVE 2**

To understand the speed-torque characteristic of the shunt-connected dc motor

### Shunt-Connected Field

**Circuit.** Figure 17.11 shows a *shunt-connected*[11] motor. Here the field circuit is connected in parallel, or shunt, with the armature circuit. Normally, the field has a large resistance, so the field current is small compared with the armature current. The shunt-connected motor is similar to the separately excited motor, except that here the field current must be controlled by a field *rheostat*, $R_F$.[12]

shunt-connected,
shunt-excited,
parallel-excited,
rheostat

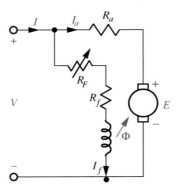

**Figure 17.11** Circuit model for a shunt-connected motor.

**Analysis.** We now derive the torque as a function of speed with fixed input voltage and fixed field current. The nonlinear behavior of the magnetic structure is not a factor because the field current is constant. We begin with KVL in the armature circuit, Eq. (17.7), eliminate $I_a$ through Eq. (17.6) and eliminate $E$ through Eq. (17.5).[13] The results are

$$V = R_a I_a + E = R_a \frac{T_{dev}}{K\Phi} + K\Phi\omega_m \tag{17.17}$$

---

[11] Also called *shunt-excited* and *parallel-excited*.

[12] A *rheostat* is variable resistor used to control a current.

[13] Recall that $K_T = K_E = K$.

Solving for developed torque, we obtain

$$T_{dev} = \frac{K\Phi}{R_a}[V - K\Phi\omega_m] \qquad (17.18)$$

If we assume the rotational-loss torque is constant or varies linearly with speed, the output torque will have the form of a straight line:

$$T_{out}(\omega_m) = C_1 - C_2\omega_m \qquad (17.19)$$

where $C_1$ and $C_2$ are constants.

---

**EXAMPLE 17.5**  **No-load speed**

Consider the machine whose characteristic is shown in Fig. 17.9. Assume the line voltage to be 120 V, the armature resistance to be 0.5 $\Omega$, and the total field resistance to be 120 $\Omega$, such that the field current is 1.0 A. The rotational losses at 1200 rpm are 25 W, assumed constant. Find the speed for no load.

**SOLUTION:**
With no external load, the power into the armature must supply armature resistive loss and rotational losses. For the moment, we ignore the electrical loss; hence, the input power to the armature is 25 W, and the required current is 25 W/120 V = 0.208 A. From KVL, we calculate the emf to be $120 - 0.208 \times (0.5\ \Omega) = 119.9$ V. From Fig. 17.9, we have, for a field current of 1.0 A, a generated voltage of 147 V at 1200 rpm. Hence, we scale the speed proportional to the generated voltage and estimate the no-load speed as

$$n_{NL} = \frac{119.9}{147} \times 1200 = 978.7 \text{ rpm} \qquad (17.20)$$

**WHAT IF?**  What if we assume rotational losses are proportional to speed? Find the corresponding no-load speed.[14]

---

**Finding the speed generally.**  Because back emf, $E$, and speed are strictly proportional, we may determine speed from developed power with Eq.(17.12), which is quadratic in $E$:

$$E^2 - VE + R_aP_{dev} = 0 \qquad (17.21)$$

Equation (17.21) gives two real and positive roots; the larger value of $E$ is the realistic solution. From the resulting $E$, the speed can be found, and from the speed and power, the torque can be calculated.

---

[14] 978.9 rpm.

EXAMPLE 17.6 **For 1 hp out**

Find the speed and torque for an output power of 1 hp for the motor in the previous example.

**SOLUTION:**
The developed power in the armature must now be $746 + 25 = 771$ W. From Eq. (17.21):

$$E^2 - 120E + 0.5 \times 771 = 0 \Rightarrow E = 3.30 \text{ and } 116.7 \text{ V} \tag{17.22}$$

Thus, for 1 hp out, the speed must drop to

$$n = \frac{116.7}{147} \times 1200 = 952.6 \text{ rpm} \tag{17.23}$$

The output torque for 1 hp and 952.6 rpm is

$$T_{out} = \frac{746}{952.6 \times 2\pi/60} = 7.48 \text{ N-m} \tag{17.24}$$

**WHAT IF?**   What if we assume rotational losses are proportional to speed? What then would be the speed at 1 hp output power?[15]

**Torque–speed characteristic.**   Equation (17.19) shows that the torque–speed characteristic for the shunt-connected dc motor is a straight line. Thus, the full-torque characteristic may be derived from two points. The speed is approximately constant because $E \approx V$ and $n \propto E$. The motor torque is limited by the ability of the armature to dissipate the armature-copper loss without damage, or perhaps by the ability of the brush–commutator system to handle the required current.

EXAMPLE 17.7 **Torque characteristic**

Find $T_M(n)$ for the motor used in the previous two examples.

**SOLUTION:**
From Eq. (17.19) and the results of the previous two examples:

$$
\begin{aligned}
0 &= C_1 - C_2 \times 978.7 \\
7.48 &= C_1 - C_2 \times 952.6
\end{aligned}
\tag{17.25}
$$

Thus, $C_1 = 280$ N-m and $C_2 = 0.286$ N-m/rpm, and the torque characteristic is shown in Fig. 17.12.

---

[15] 952.8 rpm.

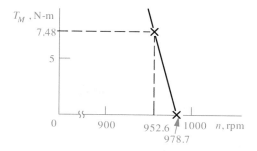

**Figure 17.12** Torque–speed characteristic. The shunt-connected motor maintains nearly constant speed.

**Rotational losses.**  The rotational losses of a dc motor consists principally of iron losses, with a small component of mechanical loss.  The iron losses occur in the rotor, which rotates in a stationary magnetic flux.  The ac frequency is proportional to motor speed and hence rotational power losses are approximately proportional to speed and hence the loss torque is approximately constant.

**Speed control.**  We note in Fig. 17.12 that for the dc motor, the speed is nearly constant over a wide range of torques.  We can control the speed of the dc motor by varying the armature voltage while keeping the field current constant, or by varying the field current while keeping the armature voltage constant. Both these methods are effective, but the control of the armature voltage offers broader range and more desirable dynamic properties. The armature voltage may be varied by several methods, such as the electronic means discussed in Chapter 18.

**Efficiency.**  In calculating the efficiency of the dc motor, the losses of the field circuit and rheostat much be charged against the motor.

---

| **EXAMPLE 17.8** | **Efficiency calculation** |
| --- | --- |

Find the efficiency of the motor in the previous three examples at 1 hp output power.

**SOLUTION:**
The armature current is

$$I_a = \frac{V - E}{R_a} = \frac{120 - 116.7}{0.5} = 6.61 \text{ A} \tag{17.26}$$

Thus, the input current to the motor is

$$I = I_a + I_f = 6.61 + 1.00 = 7.61 \text{ A} \tag{17.27}$$

and the motor efficiency is

$$\eta = \frac{P_{out}}{P_{in}} = \frac{746}{120 \times 7.61} = 81.7\% \tag{17.28}$$

---

| **WHAT IF?** | What if you wish to know the fraction of motor losses caused by the field circuit?[16] |
| --- | --- |

**Permanent-magnet (PM) DC motors.** Large numbers of dc machines are manufactured with fields provided by permanent magnets. Applications include fan and window-lift motors on automobiles, small appliances such as electric toothbrushes, tape recorders, and hair dryers, instruments like tachometers and novelties devices such as toy trains. Some large machines, up to 200 hp, are designed with permanent-magnetic fields to meet special requirements for size, weight, or efficiency. Machines with permanent-magnet fields have characteristics similar to separately and shunt-excited machines, except that field flux cannot be varied.

---

| **EXAMPLE 17.9** | **PM dc motor** |

A permanent-magnet dc motor has the following nameplate information: 50 hp, 200 V, 200 A, 1200 rpm, and armature resistance of 0.05 $\Omega$. Determine the speed and output power if the voltage is lowered to 150 V and the current is 200 A. Assume that rotational losses are proportional to speed.

**SOLUTION:**
First, we analyze the nameplate information to determine the machine constant and rotational losses. At the nameplate voltage and current, the emf is

$$E = V - I_a R_a = 200 - 200(0.05) = 190 \text{ V} \qquad (17.29)$$

and the machine constant in volts/rpm is

$$K\Phi = \frac{190 \text{ V}}{1200 \text{ rpm}} = 0.158 \text{ V/rpm} \qquad (17.30)$$

Thus, the developed power and rotational losses are

$$P_{dev} = 190 \times 200 = 38,000 \text{ W} \Rightarrow P_m = 38,000 - 50 \times 746 \qquad (17.31)$$
$$= 700 \text{ W}$$

With the input voltage at 150 V, and the armature current unchanged, the new emf is

$$E' = 150 - 200(0.05) = 140 \text{ V} \qquad (17.32)$$

We may determine the new speed by scaling:

$$n' = n \times \frac{E'}{E} = 1200 \times \frac{140}{190} = 884 \text{ rpm} \qquad (17.33)$$

This same result could be obtained from the machine constant in Eq. (17.30). The new developed power is

$$P'_{dev} = E' \times I_a = 28,000 \text{ W} \qquad (17.34)$$

We have assumed rotational losses proportional to speed, so the new losses are 516 W. Hence, the new output power is 27,500 W (36.8 hp). This is the rated output power of the machine at 150 V.

| **WHAT IF?** | What if the input voltage is 160 V? Find the new rated output power.[17] |

---

[16] 71.9%.

[17] 39.5 hp.

**Characteristics of shunt-connected and permanent-magnet-field dc motors.** The characteristics of the shunt-connected and permanent-magnet dc motors are as follows:

- For fixed field current and input voltage, the speed is nearly constant. This is true because the emf is approximately equal to the input voltage.

- For fixed field current, the speed is approximately proportional to armature voltage. Because the emf is proportional to the product of the rotational speed and the stator magnetic flux, for fixed armature voltage, the speed is inversely affected by field current. To increase motor speed, we must decrease field current.

- Reversing the input voltage to the shunt-connected motor does not reverse the direction of rotation because both stator flux and armature current reverse. To reverse the motor directions, we must reverse the polarity of either field or armature. The permanent-magnet motor reverses when input voltage is reversed.

**OBJECTIVE 3**

**To understand the speed-torque characteristic of the series-connected dc motor**

## Series-Connected Field

**Circuit.** Figure 17.13 shows a series-connected dc motor, where the armature and field carry the same current.

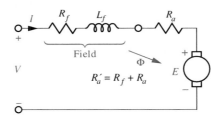

**Figure 17.13** Circuit model for series-connected motor.

**Speed–torque characteristic.** We now derive the torque–speed characteristic of the series-connected motor. We ignore magnetic saturation by assuming that the stator flux is proportional to field current; thus, we combine Eqs. (17.4) and Eq. (17.6):

$$T_{dev} = K\Phi I = \frac{K2n}{\Re}I^2 = K'I^2 \tag{17.35}$$

where $I$ is the current, $n$ is the number for turns/pole in the field, $\Re$ is the reluctance of the magnetic structure, and $K'$ replaces all the other constants. We let $R'_a = R_f + R_a$ represent the combined field and armature resistance; hence, KVL in the armature circuit becomes

$$V = R'_a I + K\Phi\omega_m = (R'_a + K'\omega_m)I \tag{17.36}$$

To obtain the torque–speed characteristic, we solve Eq. (17.36) for the current and substitute into Eq. (17.35)

$$T_{dev} = K'\left[\frac{V}{R'_a + K'\omega_m}\right]^2 \tag{17.37}$$

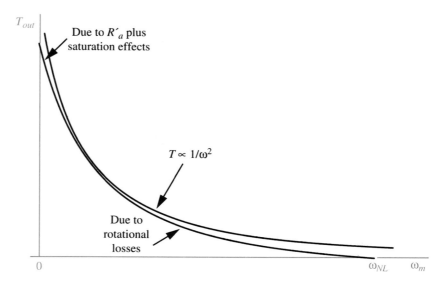

**Figure 17.14** Output torque–speed characteristic for a series-excited motor.

The torque–speed characteristic in Eq. (17.37), modified to include rotational losses and magnetic saturation, is shown in Fig. 17.14.

---

**EXAMPLE 17.10** **3 hp output**

A 50-V series-connected motor has $R'_a = 0.05\ \Omega$ and an output power of 1 hp at 500 rpm. Find the speed and motor current for an output power of 3 hp, ignoring rotational losses.

**SOLUTION:**

An approximate solution is easy. If we assume we are in that part of the characteristic where the effects of resistance and rotational losses are negligible, the torque is inversely proportional to the square of the speed. In this region, the power, $P = \omega_m T$, is inversely proportional to speed; hence,

$$P = \omega_m T \approx \frac{C}{n} \tag{17.38}$$

where $C$ is a constant and $n$ is the motor speed in rpm. From the given information, we know that $C = 500$ when power is expressed in hp; hence, for 3 hp, the speed, $n'$, must be

$$3 = \frac{C}{n'} \quad \Rightarrow \quad n' = \frac{500 \times 1}{3} = 167\ \text{rpm} \tag{17.39}$$

The current, $I'$, can be determined from conservation of energy, Eq. (17.8),

$$50 I' = 0.05(I')^2 + 3 \times 746 \tag{17.40}$$

The quadratic has two solutions, and we pick the smaller root as the realistic current, $I' = 47.0$ A. Although the speed was derived from an approximate analysis, the current was derived from conservation of energy and thus is exact.

We begin a more accurate analysis by calculating the current, $I$, for 1 hp out.

$$50I = 0.05I^2 + 746 \qquad (17.41)$$

Hence, $I = 15.1$ A. Because the torque for 1 hp is

$$T = \frac{746}{500(2\pi/60)} = 14.2 \text{ N-m} \qquad (17.42)$$

Equation. (17.35) gives $K'$ as

$$K' = \frac{T}{I^2} = \frac{14.2}{(15.1)^2} = 0.0621 \text{ N-m/A}^2 \qquad (17.43)$$

This value is used in Eq. (17.37), which we convert to a power equation by multiplying by $\omega_m$:

$$P = \omega_m T = K' \left[ \frac{V}{R'_a + K'\omega_m} \right]^2 \times \omega_m \qquad (17.44)$$

With the known values of power in watts ($3 \times 746$), input voltage (50 V), total resistance (0.05 $\Omega$), and $K'$ (0.0621), Eq. (17.44) is quadratic in $\omega_m$. The two roots are $\omega_m = 0.0397$ and 16.3 rad/s. In this case, the larger root, 156 rpm, is the realistic answer. The current for 3 hp was calculated earlier to be 47.0 A.

**WHAT IF?**     What if we want the speed for 2 hp?[18]

**Features of the series-connected motor.**     Reversing the polarity of the input voltage does not reverse the direction of rotation because both field and armature currents are reversed. To reverse the motor, we must reverse field or armature polarity separately.

The sloping torque–speed characteristic of the series-connected motor offers benefits for many applications. The motor gives good torque for starting without excessive current. For this reason, series-connected motors are used as starter motors for automobiles.

## Universal (AC/DC) Motors

**Principle of operation.**     The series-connected dc motor operates on alternating current. With the field in series with the armature, as shown in Fig. 17.15(a), the flux is proportional to the current, and a time-average torque is produced by ac current, as shown in Fig. 17.15(b). Thus, we may time average Eq. (17.35):

---

[18] 242 rpm.

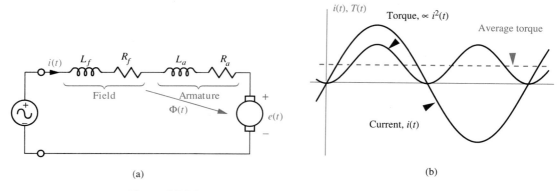

 placed near Check Your Understanding

**Figure 17.15** (a) Circuit model for a universal motor; (b) the ac current produces a time-average torque.

$$\langle T(t) \rangle = K' \langle i^2(t) \rangle = K' I^2_{\text{rms}} \tag{17.45}$$

where the angle brackets indicate time averaging. The speed–torque characteristic of the universal motor is similar to that for the series-connected dc motor in Fig. 17.14.

**Applications.** Although the machine operates on ac or dc, most universal motors are designed to operate only on ac. When you see an ac motor with a brush–commutator system, you recognize a universal motor. When an application requires speeds higher than 3600 rpm, a universal motor is required. Also important is the ease with which the speed of a universal motor can be controlled with a "dimmer" circuit.[19] For these reasons, universal motors are used for tools such as drills and routers and for household appliances such as mixers, blenders, and vacuum cleaners.

The torque–speed characteristic of the series motor serves many applications. For example, in a hand drill, we want a high speed for a small drill bit, but with the heavier load of a large bit, we would like a slower speed. The overall characteristic of the universal motor is to slow down and increase torque as the mechanical load increases and to allow stall at a moderate torque. The motor is, therefore, tolerant of a wide variety of load conditions. Finally, the universal motor gives more horsepower per pound than other ac motors because of its high speed, and thus universal motors are used for hand-held tools such as drills, sanders, and saws of various types.

### Check Your Understanding

1. A shunt-connected dc motor will reverse if the polarity of the input voltage is reversed. True or false?

2. A shunt-connected dc motor runs at 800 rpm. The field current is increased by 10% but the armature voltage remains constant. What is the new speed approximately?

3. A shunt-connected dc motor draws 10 A at 24 V. The motor torque drops to half its former value. What is the new input power?

---

[19] Discussed in Sec. 18.1.

4. A series-connected dc motor with constant input voltage will run with essentially constant (a) speed, (b) current, (c) power, (d) torque, or (e) none of these. Which?

5. A series-connected dc motor will reverse if the polarity of the input voltage is reversed. True or false?

6. Name the motor most likely to be used in an electric chain saw.

7. The starter motor in an automobile would be (a) shunt-connected, (b) series-connected, or (c) have a permanent magnet field. Which?

**Answers.** (1) False; (2) 727 rpm; (3) 120 W; (4) e; (5) false; (6) universal motor; (7) series-connected dc motor.

## 17.3 DYNAMIC RESPONSE OF DC MOTORS

**System component.** DC motors are frequently used in control systems. In this section, we analyze the performance of a dc motor as a system component, whether driven by a current source or a voltage source, using the methods and notation developed in Chapter 12. We treat only the separately excited motor with constant field current; hence, the armature circuit is analyzed for constant field flux. Figure 17.16 shows the armature circuit in the time domain with all time variables explicit.

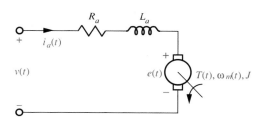

**Figure 17.16** Armature circuit of a dc motor. The voltage, current, developed torque, and mechanical speed are functions of time.

**Analysis of motor nameplate.** The system model involves motor parameters that can be deduced from the nameplate information plus the armature inductance and total moment of the rotating system. We begin by analyzing the nameplate of a specific motor that we use in the numerical examples: 1 hp, 180 V, 4.9 A, 1.78 $\Omega$ armature resistance, 30-mH armature inductance, and 1750 rpm (183.3 rad/s). The armature moment of inertia is $5.9 \times 10^{-4}$ kg-m$^2$; we assume a total moment of twice this value, $J_T = 1.18 \times 10^{-3}$ kg-m$^2$.

**Machine constant.** The machine constant can be determined from the nameplate, $NP$, conditions

$$K\Phi = \frac{E_{NP}}{\omega_{mNP}} = \frac{V_{NP} - R_a I_{NP}}{\omega_{mNP}} \tag{17.46}$$

$$= \frac{180 - 1.78 \times 4.9}{183.3} = 0.935 \quad \text{V}/(\text{rad}/\text{s})$$

**Rotational losses.** The rotational power losses are approximately proportional to speed, which means the loss torque is approximately constant. We may determine this loss torque from the nameplate conditions:

$$P_{rot} = V_{NP}I_{NP} - R_a I^2{}_{NP} - P_{NP} \tag{17.47}$$

$$= 180 \times 4.9 - 1.78 \times (4.9)^2 - 746 = 93.3 \text{ W}$$

and thus the loss torque is

$$T_{loss} = \frac{P_{rot}}{\omega_{mNP}} = \frac{93.3}{183.3} = 0.509 \text{ N-m} \tag{17.48}$$

**Load model.** The dynamics of the system depend also on the load characteristics. We assume a load with a moment of inertia equal to that of the motor armature and a torque requirement proportional to speed. We assume further that the load requires nameplate power at nameplate speed. Thus,

$$T_L(\omega_m) = K_L \omega_m \tag{17.49}$$

where the torque constant, $K_L$, can be determined from the nameplate conditions:

$$K_L = \frac{T_{NP}}{\omega_{mNP}} = \frac{P_{NP}}{(\omega_{mNP})^2} = \frac{746}{(183.3)^2} = 2.22 \times 10^{-2} \tag{17.50}$$

## Current-driven Motor Dynamics

**OBJECTIVE 4**

To understand
how to develop
system models for
separately excited
dc motors from
nameplate
and load
characteristics

**System model.** The system model for the current-driven dc motor result from combining motor equations with Newton's law. The developed torque is

$$T_{dev}(t) = K\Phi i_a(t) \quad \Rightarrow \quad \underline{T}_{dev}(\underline{s}) = K\Phi \underline{I}_a(\underline{s}) \tag{17.51}$$

The first equation is a time-domain equation; the second is the frequency-domain version. The transform of Eq. (6.48) is

$$\underline{s}J_T\underline{\Omega}_m(\underline{s}) + K_L\underline{\Omega}_m(\underline{s}) = \underline{T}_{dev}(\underline{s}) - T_{loss} \tag{17.52}$$

where $\underline{\Omega}_m(\underline{s})$ is the transform of the speed, and $J_T$ is the moment of the rotating system. Equations (17.51) and (17.52) may be combined:

$$(\underline{s}J_T + K_L)\underline{\Omega}_m(\underline{s}) = K\Phi \underline{I}_a(\underline{s}) - T_{loss} \quad \Rightarrow \quad \underline{\Omega}_m(\underline{s}) = \frac{K\Phi \underline{I}_a(\underline{s}) - T_{loss}}{\underline{s}J_T + K_L} \tag{17.53}$$

Equation (17.53) may be represented by the system diagram of Fig. 17.17. The input from mechanical losses is present if the motor is turning but would go away if the motor were at rest.

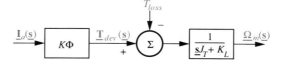

**Figure 17.17** System diagram for armature rotational response. The input variable is the transform of armature current.

**Time constant.** Equation (17.53) and Fig. 17.17 show the current-driven motor to be a simple first-order system. The natural frequency, $\underline{s}_n$, comes from the pole of the system function:

$$\underline{s}_n J_T + K_L = 0 \quad \Rightarrow \quad \underline{s}_n = -\frac{K_L}{J_T} \quad \text{and} \quad \tau = \frac{J_T}{K_L} \tag{17.54}$$

where $\tau$ is the time constant.

---

## EXAMPLE 17.11 Startup transient

Calculate the motor response from rest if nameplate current were suddenly applied to the motor just described.

### SOLUTION:

Because this is a first-order system, we need only initial and final values plus the time constant. The initial speed is zero, and the final speed is the nameplate speed because the load requires nameplate torque at nameplate speed. The time constant from Eq. (17.54) is

$$\tau = \frac{1.18 \times 10^{-3}}{2.22 \times 10^{-2}} = 53.2 \text{ ms} \tag{17.55}$$

Thus, the start-up transient is

$$\omega_m = \omega_m(\infty) + [\omega_m(0) - \omega_m(\infty)]e^{-t/53.2 \text{ ms}} = 183.3(1 - e^{-18.8t}) \text{ rad /s} \tag{17.56}$$

which is shown in Fig. 17.18.

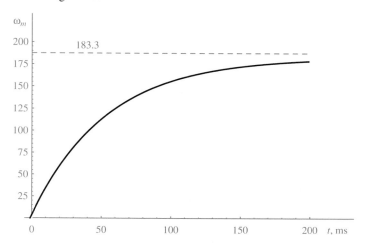

**Figure 17.18** Start-up transient response of motor speed to nameplate current.

### WHAT IF?

What if the speed were expressed in rpm?[20]

---

**Summary.** With a current-driven motor, the armature circuit is open-circuited and hence the energy stored in the inductance of the armature is not a factor in motor dynamics.

## Voltage-Driven Motor Dynamics

**System function.** We now consider a voltage-driven motor, in which stored electrical and mechanical energies interact. Kirchhoff's voltage law in the armature circuit of Fig. 17.16 is

$$v(t) = L_a \frac{di_a}{dt} + R_a i_a + e(t) \quad \Rightarrow \quad \underline{I}_a(\underline{s}) = \frac{\underline{V}(\underline{s}) - \underline{E}(\underline{s})}{\underline{s}L_a + R_a} \tag{17.57}$$

where $e(t)$ is the emf and $v(t)$ the armature voltage. The frequency-domain version of KVL is solved for the armature current, which drives the motor response as shown in Fig. 17.17. Equation (17.57) may be modeled with a summer and a block representing the armature impedance, as shown in Fig. 17.19. Because the emf is proportional to motor speed, Eq. (17.5), we have

$$e(t) = K\Phi\omega_m(t) \quad \Rightarrow \quad \underline{E}(\underline{s}) = K\Phi\underline{\Omega}_m(\underline{s}) \tag{17.58}$$

We may thus complete the system diagram of the voltage-driven motor with a feedback loop,[21] as shown in Fig. 17.19.

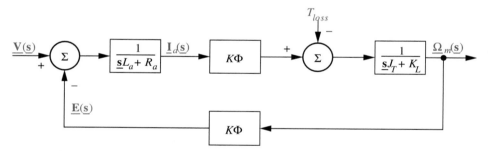

**Figure 17.19** System diagram for a dc motor that is voltage-driven. The motor contains an inherent feedback loop.

**Dynamic response.** The system now is second-order. We may determine the natural frequencies of the system from the loop gain, which is

$$\underline{L}(\underline{s}) = -\frac{(K\Phi)^2}{(\underline{s}L_a + R_a)(\underline{s}J_T + K_L)} \tag{17.59}$$

As shown on pages 639, the natural frequencies of the system come from

---

[20] $1750(1 - e^{-18.8t})$ rpm.

[21] This feedback loop is inherent to the motor and is not something we have added to the motor for control purposes.

$$1 - \mathbf{L}(\underline{s}) = 0 \quad \Rightarrow \quad (\underline{s}L_a + R_a)(\underline{s}J_T + K_L) + (K\Phi)^2 = 0 \tag{17.60}$$

The nature of the response depends on the parameters of the motor and load.

---

**EXAMPLE 17.12** **System response**

Determine the nature of the response of the motor/load system in Example 17.11 to the sudden application of nameplate voltage.

**SOLUTION:**
Equation 17.60 is

$$(0.03\,\underline{s} + 1.78)(1.18 \times 10^{-3}\,\underline{s} + 2.22 \times 10^{-2}) + (0.935)^2 = 0 \tag{17.61}$$

which has the solutions $\underline{s}_n = -39.1 \pm j156$ s$^{-1}$. Thus, the response is underdamped.

---

**Dynamic response.** We now know that the response is underdamped and can work out the total solution. The form of the answer is

$$\omega_m(t) = \omega_m(\infty) + Ae^{-\sigma t}\cos(\omega t + \theta) \tag{17.62}$$

where $\underline{s}_n = \sigma \pm j\omega$ are the natural frequencies of the underdamped system. The initial condition is zero speed, and the initial derivative of the speed must also be zero because the current, which generates the torque, is zero at $t = 0^+$.

$$\omega_m(0) = 0 = \omega_m(\infty) + A\cos\theta \tag{17.63}$$

and

$$\frac{d\omega_m(t)}{dt}\bigg|_{t=0} = 0 = A(-\sigma\cos\theta - \omega\sin\theta) \tag{17.64}$$

which are readily solved for the amplitude and phase of the start-up transient.

---

**EXAMPLE 17.13** **Transient response**

Determine the response of the voltage-driven motor if nameplate voltage is applied suddenly to the at-rest motor/load system.[22]

**SOLUTION:**
The final value is nameplate speed, 183.3 rad/s. From Eq. (17.64), the phase is

---

[22] Applying nameplate voltage to an at-rest system is not generally recommended, as it causes excessive currents and can damage the motor. We use nameplate voltage for convenience because we know the final speed to be nameplate speed. The nature of the response is independent of the magnitude of the input change.

$$\tan \theta = -\frac{\sigma}{\omega} = -\frac{39.1}{156} \quad \Rightarrow \quad \theta = -14.1° \tag{17.65}$$

and from Eq. (17.63), the amplitude is

$$A = -\frac{183.3}{\cos 14.1°} = -188.9 \text{ V} \tag{17.66}$$

The transient response is

$$\omega_m(t) = 183.3 - 188.9e^{-39.1t} \cos (156t - 14.1°) \text{ V} \tag{17.67}$$

which is shown in Fig. 17.20. The motor overshoots and oscillates around its final speed before settling down to steady state.

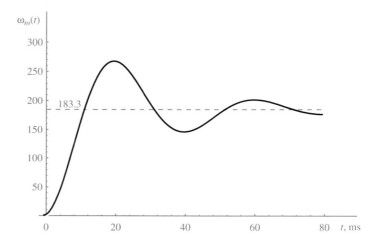

**Figure 17.20**   Transient response of the dc motor to rated voltage.

### Check Your Understanding

1. If the load required a constant torque, the current-driven motor would reach steady-state immediately. True or false?
2. If the load required a constant torque, the voltage-driven motor would reach steady-state faster. True or false?
3. Changing the motor field current would have no effect on the dynamic response of the motor. True or false?

*Answers.*  (1) False; (2) true; (3) false.

# CHAPTER SUMMARY

The dc motor is important for portable and control applications. In the dc motor, the motor flux is stationary in space and the rotor rotates physically with respect to its flux by means of a synchronizing switch, the commutator. The characteristics of the motor can be changed markedly by connecting the field in series or parallel with the armature. The voltage-driven armature exhibits a second-order behavior in control applications.

**Objective 1: To understand the physical basis for the equivalent circuit of a dc motor.** The field of the dc motor is on the stator and thus the magnetic flux of the machine is stationary in space. The rotor is the armature, and currents are brought through a brush—commutator switch that synchronizes flux direction with rotation.

**Objective 2: To understand the speed—torque characteristic of the shunt-connected dc motor.** The shunt-connected and permanent-magnet-field dc motors maintain fairly constant speed as output torque varies widely. If the field is separately connected, the speed can be controlled by the armature voltage, or the torque can be controlled by the armature current.

**Objective 3: To understand the speed—torque characteristic of the series-connected dc motor.** With the field in series with the armature, the dc motor speed depends on output torque. The series-connected motor is called a universal motor when operated with ac input power. Series-connected motors find applications in automotive starters, hand-held tools, and household appliances.

**Objective 4: To understand how to develop system models for separately excited dc motors from nameplate and load characteristics.** System models for the separately excited dc motor are derived from the analysis of the nameplate information, supplemented by knowledge of the rotating moment of inertia and the load-torque characteristics. We examine the dynamic responses of current-driven and voltage-driven armatures.

Electronic drive of dc motors is described in Chapter 18. We show that unfiltered rectifiers can drive dc motors, but motor characteristics differ from motors driven by pure dc sources.

## PROBLEMS

## Section 17.1:  Principles of DC Machines

17.1. A dc motor is shown in Fig. P17.1. The stator coil has 200 turns per pole and carries 7 A dc in the direction shown. The rotor is turning counterclockwise, as shown, and the rotor currents come out on the right and go in on the left, as shown. The width of the air gap is 1.5 mm on each side and the iron has $\mu_i = \infty$.

(a) Determine the direction of the stator flux and mark the poles N and S accordingly on the stator poles.

(b) Find the flux density in the air gap due to the field current. Assume a linear magnetic structure.

(c) What is the direction of the magnetically generated torque on the rotor?

(d) Is the machine acting as a generator or a motor?

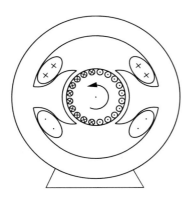

**Figure P17.1**

**17.2.** The magnetic structure for a dc motor is shown in Fig. P17.2. Each field pole has 1000 turns, the rotor radius and length are 10 cm, and the gap between rotor and stator is 2 mm wide. The rotor is turning at 5000 rad/s in the direction shown. The pole faces cover 75% of the rotor circumference. The rotor current is 10 A, and there are 18 rotor conductors, as shown. The air-gap flux density is 1.6 T. Assume a linear magnetic structure.

(a) What is the field current?

(b) Estimate the developed torque.

(c) Is the machine acting as a motor or generator? How much power is being converted between electrical and mechanical form?

(d) Estimate the armature voltage.

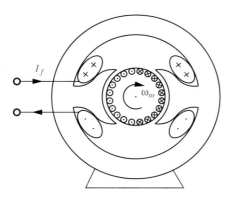

**Figure P17.2**

**17.3** A dc motor is separately excited, that is, has independent control over armature and field. The ratings are $P$ watts, $n$ rpm, $I_a$ amperes,

$V$ volts on the armature, $T$ newton-meters, and $I_f$ amperes of field current. Assuming a linear magnetic structure and ignoring losses, fill in Table P17.3.

**TABLE P17.3**

| Field Current | Voltage | Current | Speed | Torque | Power |
|---|---|---|---|---|---|
| $I_f$ | $V$ | $I_a$ | $n$ | $T$ | $P$ |
| $I_f$ | $V$ | | | $\frac{1}{2}T$ | |
| $\frac{1}{2}I_f$ | $V$ | $I_a$ | | | |
| $2I_f$ | $\frac{1}{2}V$ | $\frac{1}{2}I_a$ | | | |
| $I_f$ | $2V$ | | | | $P$ |

**17.4.** For the motor model in Fig. 17.7, the input voltage and current are 24 V and 10 A, respectively, the armature resistance is 0.10 $\Omega$, the field voltage is 24 V, the field current is 1.0 A, the rotational losses are 10 W, and the motor speed is 1200 rpm. Find the following:

(a) The input power, including that required for the field current.

(b) The emf.

(c) Developed power.

(d) The output power.

(e) The output torque.

(f) The efficiency.

(g) What is the machine constant in volts/(radian per second)?

**17.5.** An 80-V, 25-A dc motor is separately excited from a constant voltage, and thus has constant field current. The armature resistance is 0.100 $\Omega$. The motor is used to hoist an elevator weighing 500 lb (Fig. P17.5). Neglect rotational losses throughout this problem.

(a) What is the lifting rate in feet per second with the motor drawing nameplate current?

(b) The motor voltage is then reversed in polarity to lower the load. The voltage is adjusted to lower at the same rate as in part (a), again with nameplate current. What is the required voltage?

(c) What percentage of the energy used to raise the load is then returned to the electrical supply in lowering the load? Neglect rotational loss and the effects of acceleration and deceleration.

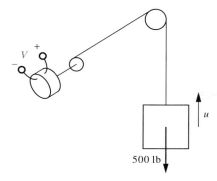

**Figure P17.5**

**17.6.** A separately excited dc motor has the following nameplate information: 180 V, 9.5-A armature

## Section 17.2: Characteristics of DC Motors

**17.8.** A separately excited dc motor runs 1000 rpm for a line voltage of 120 V dc, a field current of 2 A, and an output power of 2 hp. Give the effect on motor speed (speed up or slowdown, and whether the change is large or small) of the following changes, made one at a time and then restored before the next change is made. Assume negligible armature resistance and field flux proportional to field current.
  **(a)** The voltage changes to 60 V.
  **(b)** The output power doubles.
  **(c)** The output torque doubles.
  **(d)** The field current doubles.

**17.9.** The circuit model for a shunt-excited dc motor is shown in Fig. P17.9. The machine constant is 0.2 V/(rad/s). Find the speed in rpm for a developed power of 500 W.

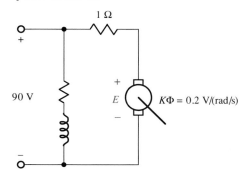

**Figure P17.9**

current, 1150 rpm, 1.03-$\Omega$ armature resistance, and 2 hp. Determine the no-load speed of the motor for the same field current, assuming the rotational losses are proportional to the motor speed.

**17.7.** An 80-V dc motor has a constant field flux (separately excited) and a nameplate speed of 1150 rpm with 710-W output power. The nameplate armature current is 10 A and the no-load current is 0.5 A. Assume constant rotational loss.
  **(a)** Estimate the rotational loss.
  **(b)** Determine the armature resistance.
  **(c)** What is the no-load speed in rpm?
  **(d)** Find the machine constant in V/(rad/s).
  **(e)** Find the efficiency at nameplate load, including field-circuit losses of 30 W.

**17.10.** A dc motor has the following nameplate information: 5 hp, 180 V, 25 A, 1200 rpm, and 0.25 $\Omega$ armature resistance. Assume rotational losses are proportional to speed. The motor is separately excited at nameplate field and must drive a load having a requirement $T_L(n) = 15 + (n/1200)^2$ N-m, where $n$ is the speed in rpm. Find the speed at which the system operates and the input current under this load.

**17.11.** A 1.5-hp shunt-excited dc motor has the following nameplate information: 180 V, 2500 rpm, 7.5 A, $R_a = 0.563$ $\Omega$, $L_a = 12$ mH, $I_f = 0.56$ A, and $R_f = 282$ $\Omega$. Assume rotational losses are constant. Consider the field current constant throughout the entire problem.
  **(a)** Find the total losses of the motor at nameplate operation. These are losses in the physical motor and do not include losses associated with external circuitry.
  **(b)** Find the rotational losses at nameplate operation.
  **(c)** Find the required current for a developed power of 1.2 hp with $V = 180$ V.
  **(d)** Find the output power if the developed power is 1.2 hp with $V = 180$ V.
  **(e)** Find the required input voltage for a no-load speed of 2800 rpm.

**17.12.** For the motor in Problem P17.8, the armature resistance is 0.8 $\Omega$ and the rotational loss is 30 W, assumed constant.
  **(a)** Find the armature current for 2 hp out.

**(b)** Find the no-load speed.

17.13. A shunt-connected dc motor operates from 24 V and has an armature resistance of 0.30 Ω. The rotational losses are 5% of the output power. The armature current is 10 A and the speed is 1200 rpm.
   **(a)** Find the input power. Ignore field losses.
   **(b)** Find the output power in horsepower.
   **(c)** Find the machine constant $K\Phi$.
   **(d)** Approximate the no-load speed in rpm.

17.14. The nameplate information on a dc motor is the following: armature 2 hp, 180 V, 9.5 A, 1150/1380 rpm (with reduced field), 1.03 Ω, 28 mH; field 120 V, 0.76 A for 1150 rpm. The motor is externally excited for operation at nameplate conditions, that is, with 0.76 A field current.
   **(a)** Estimate the field current at 1380-rpm operation with nameplate conditions (hp and armature voltage).
   **(b)** Find the efficiency at nameplate conditions, including the field loss.
   **(c)** Determine the rotational losses at nameplate conditions.
   **(d)** Find the no-load speed assuming constant loss torque.
   **(e)** Find the no-load armature current, assuming constant loss torque.
   **(f)** Find the speed at which the motor output is 1 hp, assuming constant loss torque.

17.15. A shunt-excited dc motor has an armature resistance of 0.5 Ω, a field resistance of 100 Ω, and an applied voltage of 90 V. The magnetization curve is shown in Fig. P17.15. Neglect rotational losses.
   **(a)** Find the no-load speed of the motor.
   **(b)** What input current is required for 10 N-m of developed torque?
   **(c)** Determine the efficiency of the motor with 2 hp out, including field losses.

17.16. A shunt-connected, 1-hp, 180-V dc motor puts out nameplate power at 1800 rpm but runs at 1850 rpm at no load. The rotational loss is a constant 50 W and field resistance is 810 Ω.
   **(a)** Draw a circuit of the motor.
   **(b)** What is the field current?
   **(c)** Determine the armature resistance.
   **(d)** Find the input current to the armature at nameplate load.
   **(e)** Find the efficiency, including field losses.
   **(f)** Find the torque out at nameplate load.

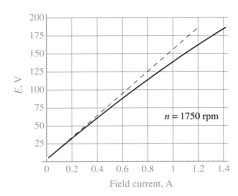

**Figure P17.15**

   **(g)** What is the machine constant in N-m/ampere?

17.17. A dc motor has the following nameplate information: 1.5 hp, 1750 rpm, 180 V in the armature, 7.3 A in the armature, 1.05-Ω armature resistance, 180 V for the field, and 0.55 A for the field. The motor is shunt-connected. Assume constant rotational losses in this problem.
   **(a)** Find the rotational losses at 1750 rpm.
   **(b)** Find the developed torque at 1750 rpm.
   **(c)** Determine the no-load speed.

17.18. A 180-V, shunt-excited dc motor runs 1150 rpm at nameplate load with 2 hp out and 1190 rpm at no load. Estimate the armature resistance. State assumptions.

17.19. For the motor with the magnetization curve shown in Fig. P17.19, find the voltage required for 5 hp out at 1000 rpm in shunt-connected operation with $I_f = 1.5$ A. The rotational losses at 1000 rpm are 100 W, and $R_a = 0.8$ Ω.

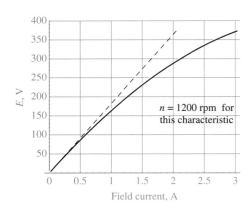

**Figure P17.19**

**17.20** For the motor with the magnetization curve shown in Fig. P17.19, determine the developed torque at the following currents:
  **(a)** $I_f = 2$ A, $I_a = 15$ A.
  **(b)** $I_f = 2$ A, $I_a = 10$ A.
  **(c)** $I_f = 1$ A, $I_a = 10$ A.

**17.21.** A 5-hp, shunt-connected, 180-V dc motor has 0.25-$\Omega$ armature resistance and 50-W rotational loss at the nameplate speed of 600 rpm. The field current is 0.5 A.
  **(a)** What is the developed torque at the nameplate output power of 5 hp?
  **(b)** What is the efficiency at 5 hp out, including field losses?
  **(c)** What is the no-load speed? Assume the same rotational losses.

**17.22.** A dc motor has the following nameplate information: armature 180 V, 7.3 A, 1.5 hp, 1750 rpm, and resistance 1.05 $\Omega$; field 100 V, and 0.5 A.
  **(a)** Draw the circuit for parallel excitation, including the field rheostat.
  **(b)** What value of the field rheostat resistance gives the nameplate field current.
  **(c)** Determine the rotational losses at nameplate speed.
  **(d)** Determine the efficiency at nameplate conditions.
  **(e)** The motor has a load described by $T_L(n) = 2 + 0.002n + 10^{-6}n^2$ N-m. Find the operating speed assuming rotational losses are proportional to speed.

**17.23.** A dc motor has the following nameplate information: armature 50 hp, 50 V, 80 A, 0.18 $\Omega$, 8.2 mH, and $1200 - 1350$ rpm; field 200 V, 10 A (for 1200 rpm), and 15-H inductance. Assume rotational losses proportional to speed.
  **(a)** Draw a circuit of the motor, connected for parallel excitation. Determine the range of the field rheostat for field speed control, assuming a linear magnetic field.
  **(b)** Find the efficiency at nameplate conditions, 1200 rpm.
  **(c)** Find the formula for the rotational losses as a function of speed in rpm.
  **(d)** Find the current to the armature for 20 hp out at 300 rpm with a 10-A field current. The voltage is reduced for this operation.
  **(e)** Would the motor operate successfully for long

periods of time under the conditions of part (d)? Explain.
  **(f)** If the machine's speed is up to 1350 rpm by reduction of the field current, what is the maximum output power possible at this speed?

**17.24.** Consider a dc motor with the following nameplate information: armature 2500 rpm, 1.5 hp, 180 V, 7.5 A, 0.563 $\Omega$ and 12 mH; field 0.56 A (2500 rpm), 0.43 A (2750 rpm), 282 $\Omega$, and 85 H. Assume the motor is separately excited at the nameplate field current (2500 rpm) and has a true 180 V (dc) on the armature throughout the problem.
  **(a)** Determine the rotational loss at nameplate conditions.
  **(b)** Find the motor current for 1 hp out, assuming constant rotational loss.
  **(c)** Find the motor speed in rpm for the condition in part (b).
  **(d)** Suppose you wanted the motor to be running 2000 rpm at 1 hp out, and you add a resistor in the armature circuit to slow down the motor. What value of resistance should you use?

**17.25.** A dc motor has the following nameplate armature information: 500 V, 40 hp, 66.2 A, and 1750 rpm. Field nameplate information is 240 V and 3.0 A. The motor is to be shunt-connected. Assume that armature-copper losses are equal to rotational losses under nameplate condition.
  **(a)** Draw a circuit diagram for the motor and put in a field rheostat resistance for nameplate condition.
  **(b)** Determine the total efficiency of the motor under nameplate conditions.
  **(c)** Find the no-load speed, assuming rotational losses are proportional to the speed.
  **(d)** Determine the output torque if the output power is 20 hp, assuming rotational losses are proportional to the speed.

**17.26.** A dc motor has the following nameplate: armature 1 hp, 1150/1380 rpm (with reduced field), 5.0 A, 180 V, 2.43 $\Omega$ and 0.049 H; field: base-speed field current $= 0.54$ A; top-speed field current $= 0.33$ A, 200 V, 282 $\Omega$, and 86 H.
  **(a)** If the field were really operated from 200 V dc, what range (max. and min.) of series resistance would have to be added to give the stated range of field current?
  **(b)** Find the rotational losses of the armature.
  **(c)** Find the no-load speed of the motor.

**(d)** Assuming that rotational power losses are proportional to speed, find the output torque as a function of speed in rpm.

**(e)** The field current is adjusted for 0.54 A and the armature voltage is 180 V. Find the input current if the motor drives a load with the torque requirement $T_L(n) = 2 + n/240$ N-m.

**17.27.** We have two motors. Motor A: three-phase induction motor, 60 Hz, 1 hp, 230/460 V, 3.4/1.7 A, 1735 rpm, 13-lb-ft locked rotor torque, 18-lb-ft breakdown (maximum) torque, 25/12.5-A locked rotor current, 0.968-lb-ft$^2$ rotor moment, 82% efficient, and service factor 1.15. A no-load test was performed on the motor and the speed of the motor was observed to be 1799.1 rpm, the input current to be 2.8 A, and the input power 95 W. Assume that mechanical losses are constant. Motor B: dc motor, 1 hp, 1750 rpm, 180 V, 4.9 A, 1.78-Ω armature resistance, 30-mH armature inductance, 0.14-lb-ft$^2$ rotor moment, 200-V field voltage, and 0.78-A field current. Motor A and motor B, both turning in the same direction, have their shafts connected together, so that they must turn at the same speed. Both are operated at nameplate voltage, and the dc motor is operated with nameplate field. Assume rotational losses in the dc motor are proportional to speed.

**(a)** Find the resulting speed.

**(b)** Find the power going down the shaft and the direction it goes, that is, which motor is the source and which the load.

**17.28.** A shunt-connected dc motor has an armature resistance of 0.2 Ω, a line voltage of 300 V, and a field resistance of 100 Ω. The magnetization curve is shown in Fig. P17.19. Ignore rotational losses.

**(a)** At what speed would the motor run with no load?

**(b)** A load is applied and the speed drops 5%. Find the input current and output power in horsepower.

**(c)** With the same torque requirement as in part (b), the input voltage is dropped to 250 V. Find the new speed.

**17.29.** A 12.6 V permanent-magnet-field dc motor has negligible rotational losses. The stall ($n = 0$ rpm) current is 30 A. Find the maximum output power (watts) this motor can produce when supplied with nameplate voltage.

**17.30.** A dc motor with a permanent-magnet field structure has the characteristics shown in Table P17.30:

### TABLE P17.30

| Condition | Armature $V$ | Armature $I$ (A) | Speed (rpm) |
|---|---|---|---|
| No load | 12.6 | 0.37 | 1210 |
| Full load | 12.6 | 5.85 | 627 |

**(a)** Find the armature resistance and the rotational losses at no load. Assume rotational losses are proportional to speed.

**(b)** Find the full-load power.

**17.31.** A 12.6-V, permanent-magnet-field dc motor is used to power a window lift in an automobile. The motor requires 10.2 A and runs at 1180 rpm when lifting the window, but requires only 7.6 A and turns at 1220 rpm when lowering the window (with reversed voltage, current, and direction of rotation). Assume friction and rotational losses are proportional to speed and hence can be represented by a constant loss torque.

**(a)** Determine the armature resistance.

**(b)** Determine the torque required to lift the window, excluding the effects of friction.

**17.32.** A 90-V, permanent-magnet-field dc motor has an armature resistance of 1.0 Ω and draws 10 A at 5000 rpm. Rotational loss at this speed is 100 W and is proportional to the speed.

**(a)** Find the output power at 5000 rpm.

**(b)** Find the no-load speed if the input voltage is decreased to 85 V.

**(c)** Find the speed at which the output power of the motor is maximum with 90-V input.

**17.33.** A 12.6-V window-lift motor on an automobile has a permanent magnet field and runs 800 rpm raising the window with a current of 8.1 A. The stall current (motor is stopped, with the window fully up) is 22 A. The torque required to lower the window is 80% of that required to lift the window because the weight of the window is aiding the descent. Find the current drawn in lowering the window and the corresponding speed. Ignore rotational losses in the armature.

**17.34.** A permanent-magnet-field, window-lift motor for an automobile runs at 2000 rpm and draws 10 A from a 12.6-V battery source. The stall current of the motor is 25 A.

**(a)** Find the developed power at 2000 rpm.

**(b)** What resistance must be placed in series with

the motor to give 1000 rpm if the power required by the load, including rotational losses, is 61% that for 2000 rpm?

**17.35.** An engineer purchased a dc motor with a permanent-magnet field. The nameplate gives 90 V and 9.2 A but does not give the rated power. The engineer applied 90 V to the unloaded motor and measured the input current (0.5 A) and speed (1843 rpm). The engineer then loaded the motor mechanically until the current reached 9.2 A and measured the speed (1750 rpm). The engineer assumed that rotational losses were constant, and determined from these data the output power at nameplate load. What was the result?

**17.36.** Assume a series-wound dc motor to have negligible rotational losses. The nameplate voltage is 24 V, the nameplate current 20 A, and the efficiency and speed at nameplate load are 78% and 3000 rpm, respectively.
(a) Find the combined armature and field resistance.
(b) Find the speed for an output power of 1/4 hp.
(c) Find the stall torque of the motor, assuming a 50% decrease in the magnetic flux (from the ideal value) due to magnetic saturation.

**17.37.** The circuit of Fig. P17.37 shows a series-excited motor. Ignore rotational losses.
(a) Find the current for 1 hp out.
(b) If the load torque is decreased by a factor of 2, what is the new current, assuming no magnetic saturation?

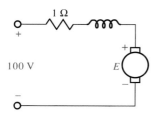

**Figure P17.37**

**17.38.** A series motor operates on 12.6 V and has a combined field and armature resistance of 0.4 Ω. At 2000 rpm, the input current is 6.8 A. Ignore rotational losses.
(a) Find the output torque at 2000 rpm.
(b) Find the speed at which the motor produces twice the torque found in part (a).

(c) Find the input current for an output power of 30 watts.

**17.39.** A series-connected dc motor runs at 1200 rpm with an input voltage of 180 V and an output power of 1 hp. Ignore all losses in this problem. Fill in Table P17.39.

**TABLE P17.39**

| Voltage (V) | Power (hp) | Speed (rpm) |
|:-----------:|:----------:|:-----------:|
| 180 | 1 | 1200 |
| 120 | $\frac{1}{2}$ | |
| 120 | | 1800 |
| | 1 | 800 |

**17.40.** An 80-V series-excited dc motor has an armature resistance of 1 Ω and a field resistance of 1 Ω. The motor turns 10,000 rpm with a load of 3/4 hp. Ignore rotational losses.
(a) Find the motor current for 3/4 hp out.
(b) Give an equation for the emf of the motor as a function of speed in rpm and current.
(c) At what speed is the power out of the motor a maximum?

**17.41.** An 80-V, series-excited dc motor draws 8 A at an output torque of 6 N-m. Find the torque at a speed of 1200 rpm. Ignore losses and magnetic nonlinearities.

**17.42.** A series-connected dc motor has a rotational power loss that is proportional to speed. Assume the armature resistance is negligible. A test of the output torque vs. speed produces the data shown in Table P17.42.

**TABLE P17.42**

| Speed (rpm) | Output Torque (N-m) |
|:-----------:|:-------------------:|
| 8000 | No load |
| 6000 | 0.86 |
| 4000 | 3.3 |
| 3000 | 6.7 |
| 2000 | 8.2 |
| 1000 | 10.4 |
| 0 | 11.6 |

(a) Find the loss torque of the motor.
(b) Estimate the maximum power out of the motor.

**17.43.** A 24-V, series-excited dc motor has a combined

armature and field resistance of 1.2 $\Omega$. The stall torque of the motor is 10 N-m, and the no-load speed is 10,000 rpm. Find the rotational losses at the no-load speed, assuming no magnetic saturation.

17.44. A 60-V, series-excited dc motor has a speed–torque characteristic as shown in Fig. P17.44. The motor has a loss torque of 3 N-m, which is constant over the range of speeds shown, except at rest and at extremely low speeds. At speeds below about 80 rad/s, the current is so high in the motor that magnetic saturation is a strong factor in establishing the torque.
(a) Estimate the factor $K'$ based upon the information supplied.
(b) Estimate the stall current, the current that would result if the motor were stopped with the nameplate voltage applied.
(c) Estimate the maximum power out of this motor and the speed at which it occurs.

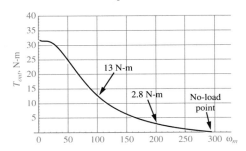

**Figure P17.44**

17.45. A series-connected dc motor has a combined field and armature resistance of 0.5 $\Omega$, an input voltage of 24 V dc, and runs at 5000 rpm with 1/4-hp output power. Ignore rotational losses in this problem.
(a) Find the output torque.
(b) Find the input current.
(c) At twice the input current for part (b), what is the speed? Assume that magnetic flux is proportional to current.

17.46. A dc series-connected motor drives a load whose input torque requirement is proportional to speed. The combined armature and field resistance is 3 $\Omega$. With an input voltage of 100 V dc, the motor input power is 50 W and the output speed of the load is 100 rpm. Derive the equation for the voltage required for other speeds. Assume that the flux of the field is proportional to the current. Ignore rotational losses.

17.47. Does the output power of a series-excited dc

motor increase, decrease, or remain the same as load torque increases? Explain.

17.48. A 12-V, series-connected dc motor has rotational losses that are proportional to speed. At no-load, the motor runs at 10,000 rpm and draws 0.83 A. Find the current and speed for an output power of 50 W. Assume no armature or field resistance.

17.49. A 90-V, series-connected dc motor has a no-load speed of 20,000 rpm. Its nameplate output power of 1.5 hp occurs at a speed of 10,000 rpm. Assume rotational loss is proportional to speed, but assume electrical losses are negligible. Find the no-load current.

17.50. A 24-V, series-excited dc motor has a current-vs.-speed curve given by Fig. P17.50. Find the range of torques developed in the normal operating region. Assume that magnetic saturation reduces the *starting* torque by 20%.

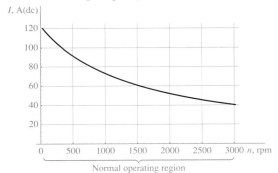

**Figure P17.50**

17.51. A hand-held drill powered by a universal motor runs at 1200 rpm with no load. With a 3/8-in. drill bit in operation, the drill slows down to 900 rpm. Ignore electrical loss and also the effects of inductance. Mechanical loss is assumed to be proportional to speed. Determine at the slower speed the following ratio: the output power to the bit divided by the rotational loss at the lower speed.

17.52. A 24-V, series-connected dc motor has a combined armature and field resistance of 2 $\Omega$. The motor runs at 5000 rpm with a developed power of 22 W. Find the maximum power that the motor can develop and the associated speed. Assume that flux is proportional to current.

17.53. A 250-V dc motor is equipped for speed control with both a field rheostat in the shunt field (0 to 150 $\Omega$) and a series armature rheostat (0 to 5 $\Omega$).

The resistance of the shunt field is 100 $\Omega$ and the armature resistance is 0.5 $\Omega$. Figure P17.53 shows the motor circuit. The rotational losses are 300 W at 5000 rpm and are proportional to speed. Assume the field is proportional to field current.

(a) With both rheostats set to zero, the motor draws a total input current of 18.5 A at 5000 rpm. What is the output power?

(b) Find the minimum no-load speed and the combination of field and armature rheostat resistances for minimum speed.

(c) Find the maximum no-load speed and the combination of field and armature rheostat resistances for maximum speed.

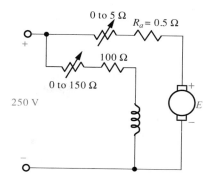

**Figure P17.53**

## Section 17.3: Dynamics of DC Motors

17.54. A dc permanent magnet motor has 0.8-$\Omega$ armature resistance and negligible inductance. The machine constant is $K\Phi = 0.12$ V/rpm. The motor is operated at 24 V with a load, inducing rotational losses of $T_L = 0.4 + 0.1\omega_m$, and the total moment of the system is 0.01 kg-m$^2$.

(a) Find the steady-state operating speed in radians/second with 24 V applied to the armature.

(b) With the motor running at the speed calculated in part (a), if the 24 V were suddenly removed and the armature circuit open-circuited, how long would it be before the motor/load would come to rest?

(c) With the motor running at the speed calculated in part (a), if the 24 V were suddenly removed and the armature circuit short-circuited, how long would it be before the motor/load would come to rest?

17.55. A dc motor has the following nameplate information: 3500 rpm, 15 hp, 54 A, 230 V, 0.153-$\Omega$ armature resistance, 1.1-mH armature inductance, and 0.068-kg-m$^2$ moment of inertia. The field is separately excited at the nameplate field current. The nameplate voltage is suddenly applied to the armature. Show that the armature-current-response transfer function is second-order and determine the natural frequencies. The motor is unloaded and rotational losses are proportional to speed.

17.56. A separately excited dc motor has the following nameplate information about the armature: 180 V, 1.05 $\Omega$, 22 mH, 1750 rpm, 1.5 hp, and 7.3 A. The field is excited at the nameplate value. The load-torque requirement is $T_L = \omega_m/20$ N-m and the total moment of the system is 0.01 kg-m$^2$. Assume that rotational losses are proportional to speed.

(a) If the armature is suddenly excited at the nameplate current, find the time constant of the response and the speed as a function of time.

(b) If the armature is suddenly excited at the nameplate voltage, find the natural frequencies of the response and the speed as a function of time.

17.57. A small permanent-magnet dc motor has an armature inductance of 5 mH and negligible resistance. Assume the load torque is proportional to speed. The motor has negligible inertia and runs at 1000 rpm with an input voltage of 12 V and a current of 3 A.

(a) Make a system diagram describing the operation of the motor in the frequency domain. Use numerical values in the boxes where possible.

(b) Using feedback theory, determine the transfer function of the motor, $\mathbf{M}(\mathbf{s}) = \underline{\Omega}_m(\mathbf{s})/\mathbf{V}(\mathbf{s})$.

(c) If the motor is at standstill and 12 volts is suddenly applied, calculate the speed as a function of time, $n(t)$ rpm.

17.58. A dc motor has the following nameplate information: armature 2 hp, 1150/1380 maximum rpm, 9.5 A, 180 V, 1.03 $\Omega$, 28 mH, and $J = 0.32 \times 4.21 \times 10^{-2}$ kg-m$^2$; field 189 $\Omega$, 0.76 A for nameplate speed, 0.43 A for max. speed, and 85 H. Throughout the entire problem, consider that the armature current is kept constant at the nameplate value of 9.5 A dc. The field is excited by a full-wave rectifier, as shown in Fig. P17.58.

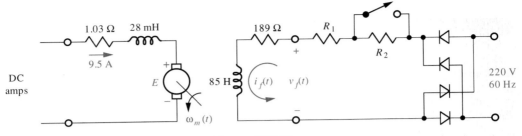

**Figure P17.58**

(a) The field circuit has two rheostat resistors and a switch to adjust the field current between the nameplate value (0.76 A dc) and the value for maximum speed (0.43 A dc). Find the value of $R_1$ and $R_2$. Assume ideal diodes.

(b) The load is of the form $\tau_L = K_L \omega_m$ and is such that at nameplate speed (1150 rpm), the motor produces nameplate power (2 hp). Further, the rotational losses are assumed to vary as the speed, $P_{rot} = D_R \omega_m$. Find $K_L$ and $D_R$.

(c) Assume that the switch is closed for a long time and then suddenly opened. Using the time-domain equations describing the system operation, derive a system diagram in the frequency domain with $\mathbf{V}_f(\mathbf{s})$ the input and $\Omega_m(\mathbf{s})$ the output. Let $I_a$ ($= 9.5$ A dc) represent the constant armature current. Find the motor system function $\mathbf{M}_f(\mathbf{s})$ under these conditions. Use symbols ($K\Phi$, $J$, $K_L n$, $\mathcal{R}$, etc.) on this part. The definition of the motor system function is $\Omega_m(\mathbf{s})/\mathbf{V}_f(\mathbf{s}) = \mathbf{M}(s)$.
*Note:* Although the field current changes are a result of a resistance change via a switch opening, the system diagram works out better if the field voltage is considered as the input variable. We can work out the initial and final speeds from the motor characteristics; after all we do not know the

field turns or reluctance. All we need from the system function are the natural frequencies.

(d) Find the response of the system $\omega_m(t)$ caused by the switch opening.

17.59. A dc motor has the following nameplate information: 15 hp, 230 V, 54 A, 3500 rpm, 0.153-$\Omega$ armature resistance, 1.1-mH armature inductance, and 0.068-kg-m² armature moment. The motor is driving a load requiring a torque proportional to speed and that requires nameplate power at nameplate speed. The load moment is nine times that of the armature; thus, the total moment is 0.68 kg-m². The system can be represented by the feedback system shown in Fig. 17.19.

(a) Find the load torque constant.

(b) Analyze the motor for the $K\Phi$ and $T_{loss}$ constants.

(c) Find the loop gain using numerical values.

(d) Determine the motor system function, $\mathbf{M}(\mathbf{s}) = \Omega_m(\mathbf{s})/\mathbf{V}(\mathbf{s})$ using feedback theory. Ignore the loss-torque effect.

(e) Find the natural frequencies of the system, and describe the response to a sudden change in armature voltage (underdamped?, overdamped?, etc.).

## Answers to Odd-Numbered Problems

17.1. (a) N on the right, flux from right to left; (b) 1.17 T; (c) CW; (d) generator.

17.3.

| Field Current | Voltage | Current | Speed | Torque | Power |
|---|---|---|---|---|---|
| $I_f$ | $V$ | $I_a$ | $n$ | $T$ | $P$ |
| $I_f$ | $V$ | $\frac{1}{2}I_a$ | $n$ | $\frac{1}{2}T$ | $\frac{1}{2}P$ |
| $\frac{1}{2}I_f$ | $V$ | $I_a$ | $2n$ | $\frac{1}{2}T$ | $P$ |
| $2I_f$ | $\frac{1}{2}V$ | $\frac{1}{2}I_a$ | $\frac{1}{4}n$ | $T$ | $\frac{1}{4}P$ |
| $I_f$ | $2V$ | $\frac{1}{2}I_a$ | $2n$ | $\frac{1}{2}T$ | $P$ |

**17.5.** (a) 2.86 ft/s; (b) –75.0 V; (c) 93.8%.

**17.7.** (a) 40 W (39.9 exact); (b) 0.500 Ω (0.501 exact); (c) 1227 rpm (1223 exact); (d) 0.623 V/(rad/s); (e) 85.5%.

**17.9.** 4013 rpm.

**17.11.** (a) 319 W; (b) 199 W; (c) 5.05 A; (d) 694 W; (e) 198 V.

**17.13.** (a) 240 W; (b) 200 W; (c) 0.167 V/(rad/s); (d) 1371 rpm (1364 exact).

**17.15.** (a) 1250 rpm; (b) 14.5 A; (c) 85.6%.

**17.17.** (a) 139 W; (b) 6.86 N-m; (c) 1820 rpm.

**17.19.** 211 V.

**17.21.** (a) 60.2 N-m; (b) 93.5%; (c) 618 rpm.

**17.23.** (a) $R_{F\max} = 47.4$ Ω and $R_{F\min} = 30$ Ω

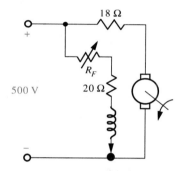

(b) 82.9 %; (c) 1550 $(n/1200)$ W; (d) 144 V for 126 A; (e) losses are 5250 W compared with the allowed 4700 W, so it is overloaded; (f) 46,000 W (61.7 hp).

**17.25.** (a)

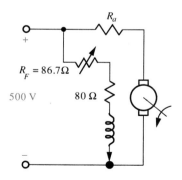

(b) 86.2%; (c) 1836 rpm; (d) 79.4 N-m.

**17.27.** (a) 1813 rpm; (b) 158 W, the dc motor is the motor and the ac motor is the load (generator).

**17.29.** 94.5 W.

**17.31.** (a) 0.205 Ω; (b) 0.105 N-m.

**17.33.** 6.48 A and 893 rpm.

**17.35.** 743 W (739 exact).

**17.37.** (a) 8.12 A; (b) 5.74 A.

**17.39.** 120 V for 0.296 hp at 1800 rpm; 120 V for 1/2 hp at 1067 rpm; 147 V for 1 hp at 800 rpm.

**17.41.** 4.32 N-m.

**17.43.** 20.1 W.

**17.45.** (a) 0.0391 N-m; (b) 9.75 A; (c) 1863 rpm.

**17.47.** $P$ varies as $\sqrt{\text{torque}} \times \text{constant} - T \times$ a small constant. Thus, the power at first increases, but eventually levels out and decreases.

**17.49.** 8.39 A with 74.6 W.

**17.51.** 0.778.

**17.53.** (a) 3570 W (4.79 hp); (b) 5042 rpm for maximum armature resistance and minimum field resistance; (c) 12,833 rpm for minimum armature resistance and maximum field resistance.

**17.55.** The natural frequencies are $\underline{s}_n = -69.5 \pm j7.52$ s$^{-1}$.

**17.57.** (a)

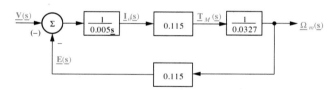

(b) $\underline{M}(\underline{s}) = 702/(\underline{s} + 80.2)$; (c) $n(t) = 1000\,(1 - e^{-80.2t})$ rpm.

**17.59.** (a) 0.0833; (b) 0.605 V/(rad/s) and 2.14 N-m;

(c) $\underline{L}(\underline{s}) = -\dfrac{(0.605)^2}{(0.0011\underline{s} + 0.153)(0.68\underline{s} + 0.0833)}$

(d)

$$\underline{M}(\underline{s}) = \dfrac{0.605}{1 + \dfrac{(0.605)^2}{(0.0011\underline{s} + 0.153)(0.68\underline{s} + 0.0833)}}$$

(e) $\underline{s} = -3.79, -90.9$ s$^{-1}$, overdamped.

# Power Electronic Systems

1. To become aware of the variety and limitations of semiconductor switches
2. To understand in full the operation of the common light-dimmer circuit
3. To understand the operation of a controlled single-phase, full-wave rectifier driving a dc motor
4. To understand the methods and complexities of ac motor controllers

"Power" and "electronics" do not seem to go together, but increasingly electronic techniques are used to control large power equipment such as motors and transmission systems. The recent appearance of semiconductor devices capable of switching large amounts of power has made possible these new techniques. We consider these switches and some basic applications in dc and ac motors controllers.

**power electronics**

**Introduction.** *Power electronics* applies electronic techniques to the control of electric power. The field is not new because vacuum tubes have long been used for this purpose. But recently, power electronics has grown rapidly as solid-state devices have been developed to control electric power, specifically, power transistors, silicon-controlled rectifiers (SCRs), and gate-turnoff thyristors (GTOs).

**HVDC**

Ordinary electronics deals with the control of electric power in small quantities, normally for its information content. Power is voltage times current; hence, ordinary electronic devices, such as transistors and diodes, must handle small voltages, or small currents, or both. Power electronic devices must handle large voltages and large currents. How large depends on the context. The variable-speed hand-held drill requires voltages around 200 V (peak) and currents of a few amperes. By contrast 4500-V, 2500-A SCRs can be operated in tandem to handle conversion of 200 MW of ac power to dc power for a high-voltage, direct-current (HVDC) transmission line. The principles are the same for both applications.

This chapter introduces basic concepts of power electronics. We begin by discussing semiconductor switches. We then analyze a simple power controller such as might be used in a light dimmer or hand-held, variable-speed drill. After giving some general principles of motor controllers, we discuss the electronic control of both dc motors and ac motors. Our purpose is to illustrate the principles of power electronic systems through the analysis of representative applications.

## Semiconductor Switches

<table>
<tr><td>OBJECTIVE 1</td></tr>
<tr><td>To understand how to become aware of the variety and limitations of semiconductor switches</td></tr>
</table>

**Introduction** As discussed on page 345, a switch is a device that has two stable states, ON and OFF. When ON, the switch has an impedance much smaller than its load, and when OFF, it has an impedance much larger than its load. Semiconductor switches have recently been developed to handle large amounts of power. In this section, we describe principles of operation, terminal characteristics, and limitations of four-level diodes, thyristors, gate-turnoff thyristors, and power transistors.

**Four-level diode.** Figure 18.1(a) shows the circuit symbol and Fig. 18.1(b) shows the structure of the *pnpn* diode, which consists of four alternating layers of *p*- and *n*-type semiconductor, forming three *pn* junctions. Two of the *pn* junctions face the same direction, and the middle one faces the opposite direction. Thus, you might anticipate that the device will operate as three diodes in series, with the middle one turned around. Hence, no current ought to flow in either direction, because at least one of the diodes will always be reverse-biased.

**Characteristics of pnpn diodes.** The characteristic displayed in Fig. 18.1(c) reveals that no current flows for negative voltages, where two *pn* junctions are reverse-biased; nor does current flow for positive voltages, where the middle *pn* junction is reverse-biased, until a threshold voltage, $V_{th}$, is reached. After this threshold voltage is exceeded, the four-level diode begins to conduct freely: It "fires," acting as if the middle *pn* junction has disappeared. The threshold phenomenon occurs because the doping levels in the four layers differ greatly. The outside *p* and *n* materials are doped heavily; hence, they have many carrier holes and electrons, respectively, available to diffuse into the middle *n* and *p* regions, which are lightly doped. Once the breakdown occurs in the

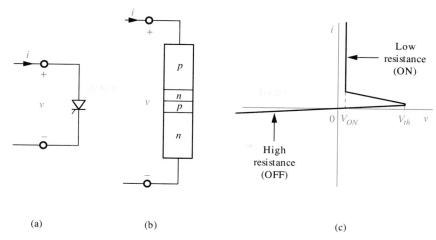

(a)　　　　　　　　(b)　　　　　　　　　　　(c)

**Figure 18.1** Four-level diode: (a) symbol, (b) structure, and (c) voltage–current characteristic.

middle junction at $V_{th}$, the holes from above and the electrons from below flood into the depletion region of the middle junction, where the internal battery–capacitor effect, described on page 330, reinforces their movement across the junction. Thus, this middle depletion region effectively disappears due to the carriers from the forward-biased junctions, and we are left with two forward-biased junctions in series. The small voltage for the *pnpn* diode in the ON state results from the contributions from each ON junction. The turn-ON voltage is typically less than 0.7 V because the excess carriers from each junction help each other.

**Voltage-actuated switch.** Thus, the *pnpn* has two states. It is OFF for negative voltage, and remains OFF for positive voltage until the threshold voltage is reached, after which it turns ON. It remains ON until the current is reduced to a small value, after which it turns OFF again. The value of the threshold voltage, $V_{th}$, can be controlled over a modest range by the semiconductor designer. Typical *pnpn* diodes have threshold voltages from 6 to 32 V. Thus, this device, like the *pn*-junction diode, is a voltage-controlled switch, except that the four-level diode requires much more than 0.7 V to turn ON.

**gate**

**Thyristor (SCR).** Figure 18.2(a) shows the circuit symbol and Fig. 18.2(b) shows the structure of the thyristor, or silicon-controlled rectifier (SCR). The thyristor has a *pnpn* structure with an external *gate* to turn ON the device. With no gate current, the SCR characteristic is that of a four-level diode, as shown. The important difference, however, is that the breakdown threshold occurs at a much higher voltage, indeed, high enough that the SCR should never conduct because the input voltage exceeds its threshold. On the contrary, the forward-biased SCR should fire only when a pulse of current is delivered to the gate. This is shown by the $i_G > 0$ characteristic in Fig. 18.2(c); in effect, the threshold is reduced to a very small value when the gate conducts. Physically, the gate injects holes into the lightly doped *p* region and floods the depletion region with carriers, thus initiating breakdown.

**SCR limitations.** From the instant when voltage is applied to the gate, there is a small delay before the SCR turns ON, but this is not a problem at power frequencies.

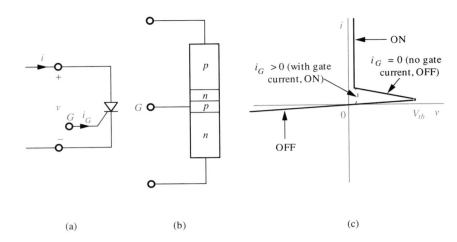

(a)    (b)    (c)

**Figure 18.2** Silicon-controlled rectifier (SCR): (a) symbol, (b) structure, and (c) voltage–current characteristic.

More problematic is the rate of rise of SCR current, which can cause device failure due to localized heating in the junction. If not limited by load inductance, an external inductor must be added in series to limit the $di/dt$ of the SCR.

Also critical is the rate of voltage rise of the SCR in its OFF state. In certain applications, a rapid voltage increase can initiate conduction, independent of the gate signal, and cause device malfunction. The *RC snubber* circuit[1] shown in Fig. 18.3 limits the $dv/dt$ across the SCR. With the SCR OFF, the small (10- to 100-$\Omega$) resistor in series with $C$ and the inductance in the load circuit limit the $dv/dt$ across the SCR, and the capacitor blocks dc current. When the SCR fires, the energy stored in the capacitor is dissipated in $R$ and the SCR.

To turn OFF, the SCR must be reverse-biased for a sufficient period of time for carriers to recombine and reestablish the blocking junction. This time can vary from 20 to 200 µs, depending on SCR size and type.

**Line and forced commutation.** *Commutation* refers to the switching of a conducting SCR from the ON state to the OFF state. As we have seen, an SCR may be commutated by reducing its current below the value required to sustain conduction. Normally, this is accomplished by reverse biasing the device for a period of time.

When in an ac cycle, the voltage across an SCR changes from forward bias to reverse bias, the SCR ceases to pass current and is *line commutated*. When an auxiliary circuit is used to commutate the SCR independent of the line voltage, the SCR has a *forced commutation*.

**Summary.** In the previous section, we discussed the use of SCRs as power switches. We gave the conditions for turning SCRs ON and OFF. The need for auxiliary circuits to force the commutation of the SCR is a serious liability, and for this and other reasons alternative electronic switches have been developed.

**snubber**

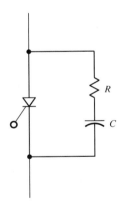

**Figure 18.3** The *RC* snubber circuit limits the rate of voltage rise of the SCR in its OFF state.

**commutation,
line commutation,
forced commutation**

---

[1] A *snubber* circuit protects a switch circuit from excessive voltage, current, energy, or power.

**Gate-turnoff thyristors (GTOs).** Figure 18.4(a) shows the circuit symbol for a GTO, which is like an SCR symbol except for a mark on the gate, and Fig. 18.4(b) shows GTO construction. The forward-biased GTO is turned ON by a pulse of positive current to its gate, but unlike the SCR, it is turned OFF by a pulse of negative gate current. The negative current removes carriers from the cathode region, and the inner *pn* junction blocks the forward current.

The switching characteristics of the GTO are excellent, and this device is appearing in a variety of power controllers. Development in GTOs and power field-effect transistors is very active, and the circuit designer has an increasing number of semiconductor devices to consider in power controllers.

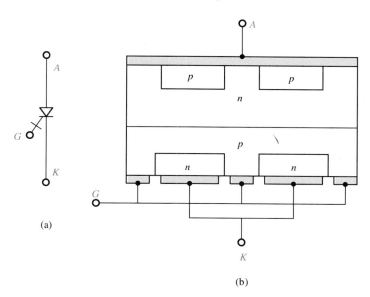

(a)

(b)

**Figure 18.4**   (a) Circuit symbol for a gate-turnoff thyristor (GTO); (b) construction of a GTO. The anode (A) and cathode (K) are the power terminals and *G* is the gate terminal.

**Power bipolar-junction transistors.**   Recent advances in bipolar power transistors (BJTs) have allowed their use in power electronic circuits. Although SCRs are still dominant in applicati  s requiring high voltage and high power, transistors are replacing SCRs in ac motor controllers for voltages below 460 V and power levels below 400 hp. The main advantage of transistor switches is that turn-ON and turn-OFF are controlled by the base current, and no forced-commutation circuit is required. Transistors also offer fast switching times, which is important in many ac motor controller circuits. The disadvantages of transistors are that they require medium-power base drive circuits and that they have higher switching and operating losses than SCRs. In this section, we consider transistor switches with resistive and inductive loads.

**rise time**

**Transistor switch with a resistive load.**   Figure 18.5(a) shows a BJT switching a resistive load, and Fig. 18.5(b) shows voltage and current during turn-ON. Base current is applied at $t = 0$. After a delay time, $t_d$, the collector current begins to rise and the collector–emitter voltage begins to drop. The *rise time*, $t_r$, is defined as the time required for the collector current to rise from 10 to 90% of its final value, $I_{Cp}$.

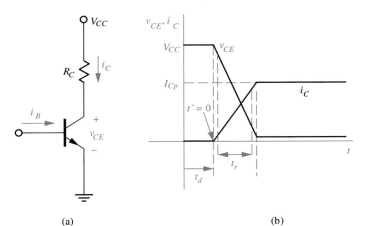

**Figure 18.5** (a) Transistor switch with a resistive load; (b) transistor voltage and load during switching.

**Switching losses.** When the transistor is OFF, it has no collector current and hence no power dissipation. After switching, the transistor is saturated and has a low collector–emitter voltage and hence low dissipation. During switching, however, the transistor has appreciable voltage and current; hence, the power level can become high. We calculate the power during switching and the total energy dissipated by the transistor during switching. We assume linear voltage and current transitions and assume an origin ($t'$) at the instant the current begins to rise. The voltage and current are, therefore,

$$i_C(t') = 0.8t' \times \frac{I_{Cp}}{t_r} \quad \text{and} \quad v_{CE}(t') = V_{CC}\left(1 - \frac{0.8t'}{t_r}\right) \tag{18.1}$$

where $t_r/0.8$ is the total time of transition and we have set the saturation voltage to zero. The expressions in Eq. (18.1) are valid only during the time $0 < t' < t_r/0.8$. The power into the transistor is the product of voltage and current:

$$p_C(t') = V_{CC}I_{Cp}\frac{0.8t'}{t_r}\left(1 - \frac{0.8t'}{t_r}\right) \tag{18.2}$$

which has a maximum value of $V_{CC}I_{Cp}/4$ at $t' = 0.625t_r$. For a 300-V, 100-A device, the peak power into the transistor during switching is 7500 W. The energy given to the transistor in switching, $W$, is the integral of the power.

$$W = \int_0^{t_r/0.8} v_{CE}(t')i_C(t')\,dt$$

$$= V_{CC}I_{Cp}\int_0^{t_r/0.8} \frac{0.8t'}{t_r}\left(1 - \frac{0.8t'}{t_r}\right)dt' = \frac{V_{CC}I_{Cp}t_r}{4.8} \tag{18.3}$$

which gives an energy of 12.5 mJ for each switching transition, assuming a 2-μs rise time. This appears small, but if the transistor is switching at a 2-kHz rate, this requires dissipation of 50 W from switching alone. During saturation, the collector–emitter voltage drop is about 1.2 V at high current levels, so the collector dissipation is 120 W while the transistor is ON. In the switching mode, the transistor would be ON approximately half of the time, so the average power would be 60 W due to the ON voltage. Therefore, the switching power is an important contribution to the total transistor dissipation.

---

**EXAMPLE 18.1**

## Resistive switching losses

A BJT with a rise time of 3 μs is used to switch 100 V to a 10-Ω resistor at a 5-kHz rate. Find the switching losses.

**SOLUTION:**

The peak current is $I_{Cp} = 100$ V$/10$ Ω $= 10$ A. Thus, Eq. (18.3) gives

$$W = \frac{100 \times 10 \times 3 \times 10^{-6}}{4.8} = 0.625 \text{ mJ/transition} \qquad (18.4)$$

Because there are $10^4$ transitions/second, the average switching power is 6.25 W.

**WHAT IF?**

What if the transistor saturation voltage is 1.0 V and the maximum allowable power is 8 W. What is the minimum load resistance?[2]

---

**Transistor switching losses with inductive loads.** Figure 18.6(a) shows a BJT with an inductive load. The free-wheeling diode is required to protect the transistor from large inductive voltages. Figure 18.6(b) compares the switching trajectory in the $v_{CE}$–$i_C$ plane for the resistive and inductive loads. To understand the trajectory for an inductive load, we must investigate the role of the transistor in controlling the current through the inductive load, and also investigate the importance of the time-average voltage in controlling the current through the inductive load.

**Inductive loads.** For the resistive load, the transistor turns the current on and off, and thereby controls the average voltage and power to the load. For an inductive load, by contrast, the transistor is turned ON and OFF to control the average voltage across the load, and this average voltage determines the average current through the load, as shown in the following paragraph. The current through the load does not cease because the inductance keeps it more or less constant, provided the transistor switching period is much smaller than the time constant of the $RL$ load.

**The Frequency Domain**

**Average voltages.** We now consider why the average current through an $RL$ load is controlled by the time-average voltage across the load. This is true for all periodic voltages and currents because the time-average voltage across the inductance must be

---

[2] 20.8 Ω.

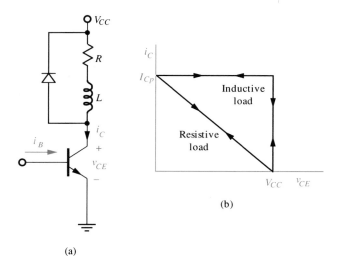

(b)

(a)

**Figure 18.6** (a) Transistor switch with an inductive load; (b) switching trajectories for resistive and inductive loads.

zero. To see that this is true, consider the current through the *RL* load as a discrete spectrum of sinusoidal harmonics, plus a dc component. The voltage across the inductance consists, therefore, of sinusoidal components, and the time average of a sinusoid is zero. Therefore, the time-average voltage across the inductance is zero. It follows also that the time-average voltage across the *RL* load is equal to the dc component of the current times the resistance of the load, because the time average of the resistor voltage due to the harmonics of the current must also be zero. Thus, the transistor controls the current in the *RL* load by controlling the time-average voltage across the load.

**Returning to the transistor.** The transistor in Fig. 18.6(a) switches ON and OFF, but the current through the inductor continues more or less constant. Therefore, while the transistor is OFF and any time the transistor is not carrying the full-load current, some current passes through the free-wheeling diode, and the collector voltage of the transistor is equal to the supply voltage, assuming an ideal diode. It follows that the switching trajectory for an inductive load is that shown in Fig. 18.6(b), with constant voltage at $V_{CC}$ while the collector current is moving from zero to $I_{Cp}$ and back during the switching cycle.

An analysis of the power and energy shows that the peak power into the transistor is four times that with a resistive load, and the energy per cycle is three times that required for switching a resistive load. The strain on the transistor is greatly increased, and snubber circuits are required to reduce the power requirement on the transistor.

---

**EXAMPLE 18.2** | **Switching losses**

A BJT switches 100 V to an inductive load with $R = 5\ \Omega$ and $L = 20$ mH. The transistor is ON for 0.1 ms and OFF for 0.2 ms. Find the average current and switching loss in the transistor if $t_r = 3\ \mu$s and $V_{ON} = 1$ V.

**SOLUTION:**

The $RL$ time constant is 4 ms, much longer than the switching cycle, so the current is essentially constant. The voltage across the $RL$ load is as shown in Fig. 18.7. The average voltage is 67.0 V, so the time-average current is $I_{dc} = 67.0 \text{ V}/5\,\Omega = 13.4$ A. As stated, the switch loss/transition is three times that given by Eq. (18.3):

$$W = \frac{V_{cc}I_{cp}t_r}{1.6} = \frac{100 \times 13.4 \times 3 \times 10^{-6}}{1.6} = 2.51 \text{ mJ/transition} \qquad (18.5)$$

Hence, the switching losses are $2 \times 2.51 \times 10^{-3}/0.3 \times 10^{-3} = 16.8$ W.

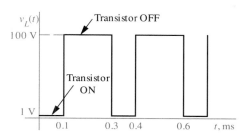

**Figure 18.7** The transistor is ON one-third of the time.

**WHAT IF?**

What if you want total transistor dissipation?[3]

---

**Summary.** The section introduced SCRs, GTOs, and power transistors as semiconductor switches. We considered how to turn these devices ON and OFF and discussed their limitations. In the next section, we analyze a light-dimmer circuit to show a common application of power electronic techniques.

## Common Application of Power Electronics

**Power electronic circuit.** In this section, we examine the operation of the circuit shown in Fig. 18.8. The ac source represents a standard 120-V, 60-Hz supply. The circuit in the box is a power controller, the resistor with the arrow represents a variable resistor, and $R_L$ represents the load receiving the power. The circuit uses a four-level diode and an SCR as semiconductor switches.

**Common applications for this circuit.** Circuits of this type are used in light dimmers. In this application, the variable resistor is adjusted by a rotary mechanism, and an on–off switch is normally built into the same mechanism. The load is an incandescent light. Variable-speed drills are controlled by this or similar circuits. In that application the variable resistor is adjusted by the squeeze trigger on the drill handle and the load is a universal motor, discussed in Sec.17.2.

**Four-layer diode function.** To explain the operation of the circuit in Fig. 18.8, we start with the simpler circuit shown in Fig. 18.9 to see how the SCR-gate current

---

[3] 21.2 W.

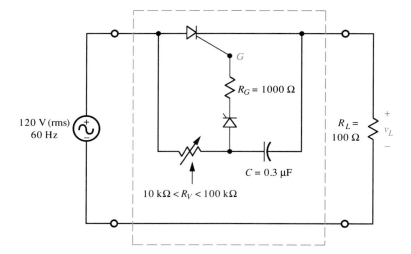

Figure 18.8 A power controller circuit.

pulses are formed. We begin with a discharged capacitor. Closing the switch at $t = 0$ allows current to flow and the capacitor voltage increases. The *pnpn* diode remains OFF and no current flows through $R_G$ until the voltage across the capacitor reaches the threshold voltage, $V_{th}$. Thus, until the *pnpn* diode fires, we have a simple $RC$ transient. The time constant is $R_VC$, the initial value of the voltage across the capacitor is 0 V, and the final value would be $V_p$ if the transient reached completion. Using techniques from Chapter 3, we determine the voltage across the capacitor to be

$$v_C(t) = V_p(1 - e^{-t/R_VC}) \tag{18.6}$$

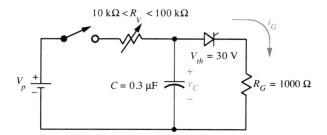

Figure 18.9 The four-level diode fires when $v_C = 30$ V.

The capacitor voltage increases according to Eq. (18.6) until the threshold voltage of the *pnpn* diode is reached. At this point, the *pnpn* diode turns ON and allows current to flow through $R_G$. Current from the dc source is limited by the large value of $R_V$, but the current from the capacitor discharge can be quite large. The time at which the discharge occurs, $t_\alpha$, is

$$V_{th} = V_p(1 - e^{-t_\alpha/R_VC}) \quad \Rightarrow \quad t_\alpha = -R_VC \times \ln\left(1 - \frac{V_{th}}{V_p}\right) \tag{18.7}$$

**EXAMPLE 18.3**

## Firing time

Let $V_{th} = 30$ V, $V_p = 120\sqrt{2}$ V, $C = 0.3$ μF, and $10$ kΩ $< R_V < 100$ kΩ. Find the minimum firing time.

**SOLUTION:**

Using Eq. (18.7), we calculate

$$t_\alpha = -10^4 \times 0.3 \times 10^{-6} \ln\left(1 - \frac{30}{120\sqrt{2}}\right) = 0.584 \text{ ms} \qquad (18.8)$$

**WHAT IF?**

What if $R_G = 1000$ Ω and $V_{ON} = 0.5$ V? What is the current in $R$ as a function of time?[4]

**Pulse cycle.** After discharge, the *pnpn* diode turns OFF, there being insufficient current flowing to keep it ON, and the cycle begins again. Hence, the capacitor voltage and the current through the small resistor are as shown in Fig. 18.10, where there is a 5-ms cycle time.

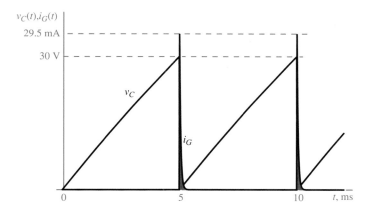

**Figure 18.10** Capacitor-voltage and gate-current waveforms.

**With an AC source.** We now consider what would happen if the dc source were replaced by an ac source, as shown in Fig. 18.11(a). We draw the input voltage as a sine function and show the capacitor voltage, $v_C$, as it would be if the *pnpn* diode did not conduct. If the capacitor were initially uncharged and if the four-level diode never fired, there would be a start-up transient, and then the voltage of the capacitor would lag the input voltage with a phase shift between 0° and 90°, depending on the value of $R_V C$. However, the four-level diode fires at the time labeled $t_\alpha$, when the capacitor voltage reaches the threshold voltage, Fig. 18.11(b).

[4] $i_G(t) = 29.5\, e^{-(t - t_\alpha)/300\,\mu s}$ mA.

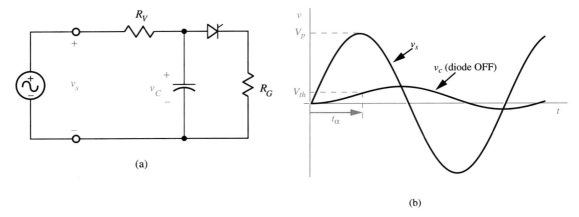

**Figure 18.11** Circuit response with a sinusoidal source.

**The Time Domain**

**Analysis.** The calculation of $t_\alpha$ combines transient and ac steady-state techniques but is basically a time-domain analysis. The steady-state voltage found by ac circuit techniques is

$$v_C(t) = \frac{V_p}{\sqrt{1 + (\omega R_V C)^2}} \sin(\omega t - \phi) \qquad (18.9)$$

where $V_p$ is the peak ac voltage, $\phi = \tan^{-1}(\omega R_V C)$, and $t = 0$ when the input voltage is zero. The transient portion of the capacitor voltage is $Ae^{-t/R_V C}$, where $A$ is a constant to be determined from the initial conditions. The capacitor is initially uncharged, so

$$0 = \frac{V_p}{\sqrt{1 + (\omega R_V C)^2}} \sin(0 - \phi) + Ae^{-0/R_V C} \Rightarrow \qquad (18.10)$$

$$A = \frac{V_p \sin \phi}{\sqrt{1 + (\omega R_V C)^2}}$$

**Firing time.** The firing time, $t_\alpha$, for the *pnpn* diode occurs when the capacitor voltage equals the threshold voltage of the *pnpn* diode:

$$V_{th} = \frac{V_p}{\sqrt{1 + (\omega R_V C)^2}} [\sin(\omega t_\alpha - \phi) + e^{-t_\alpha/R_V C} \sin \phi] \qquad (18.11)$$

**delay angle, firing angle**

The *delay angle*, $\alpha = \omega t_\alpha$, describes the position in the cycle when the *pnpn* diode fires. For the values of $R_V$ and $C$ that we show, the delay angle lies between 30° and 180°. Hence, we can control the firing time, or *firing angle*, with $R_V$ as we did with the dc source. When the four-level diode fires, the capacitor discharges through the gate resistor with a short time constant, as before. After the capacitor discharges, the four-level diode turns OFF, there being insufficient current passing through $R_V$ to keep it conducting. The capacitor voltage again begins building up and may fire the four-level diode again before the input voltage goes negative, but once the input becomes negative, the four-level diode does not fire again until the source voltage again goes positive.

**Summary.**   We can create a pulse of current with the four-level diode. The timing of this pulse of current is controlled by the $R_V C$ time constant and can be varied over a range of delay angles.

**Back to the original circuit.**   We now can investigate the operation of the circuit in Fig. 18.8, repeated in Fig. 18.12. Figure 18.12 shows the SCR gate circuit to be the "load" to which the four-level diode delivers its current pulses. The load of the SCR, $R_L$, has presumably a low impedance level and does not affect greatly the charging of the capacitor. Hence, when the input voltage goes positive, the capacitor begins charging through $R_V$ and the load. When the capacitor voltage builds up to the threshold voltage, the four-level diode fires and the current pulse passes through the gate, turning ON the SCR.

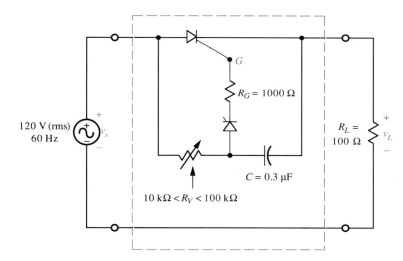

**Figure 18.12**   Power controller circuit (identical to Fig. 18.8).

**Load voltage.**   The voltage to the load is thus that shown in Fig. 18.13. By adjusting the delay angle with $R_V$, we can control the conduction angle of the SCR and hence the power to the load. The resistor in series with the four-level diode limits the gate current to an acceptable value. With the SCR gate for a load, repeated firing of the four-level diode does not matter. Once the SCR is turned ON, it remains ON until the input voltage goes negative to turn it OFF by line commutation.

---

**EXAMPLE 18.4**   **Gate current**

What resistance, $R_G$, should be put in series with the SCR gate to limit the peak gate current at 10 mA if the circuit is that used in the previous examples?

The voltage driving the transient is $V_{th} - V_{ON} = 29.5 \text{ V}$. Thus,

$$10 \text{ mA} = \frac{29.5}{R_G} \quad \Rightarrow \quad R_G = 2950 \ \Omega \tag{18.12}$$

**WHAT IF?**

What if you want the new discharge time constant?[5]

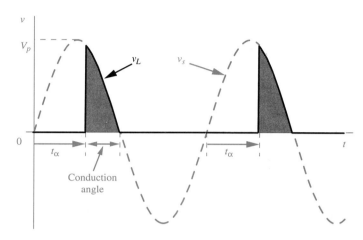

**Figure 18.13**  Load voltage for the circuit in Fig. 18.12.

**diac, triac**

### Diacs and triacs.

Figure 18.14 shows a nonrectifying power controller. The device replacing the four-level diode is called a *diac*. It is like two parallel four-level diodes facing in opposite directions and fires in either direction. Similarly, the device replacing the SCR is called a *triac*, and it functions like two parallel SCRs facing opposite directions. This circuit operates like the circuit in Fig. 18.12, except that it does not rectify. Hence, the load voltage is as shown in Fig. 18.15. This is the preferred circuit for light dimmers and universal-motor tools, which do not require dc voltage.

### Check Your Understanding

1. Turning ON an SCR requires (a) forward bias, (b) a pulse of current to the gate, or (c) both. Which?

2. Turning OFF an SCR requires (a) reverse biasing the SCR, (b) keeping the SCR reverse biased for a prescribed period of time, and/or (c) removing the gate signal. Which? May be more than one.

3. To operate successfully, the SCR must be protected from (a) high $dv/dt$ in the OFF condition, (b) high $di/dt$ in the ON condition, and/or (c) excessive reverse voltage in the OFF condition. Which? May be more than one.

---

[5] 885 μs.

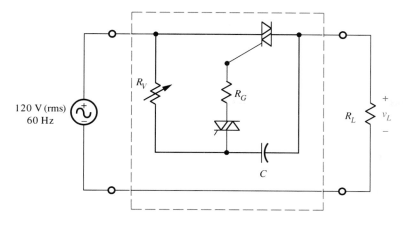

**Figure 18.14** Diacs and triacs fire in both directions.

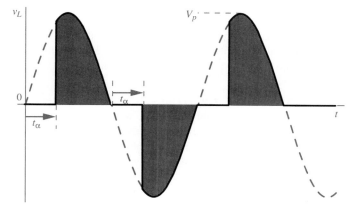

**Figure 18.15** Load voltage for the triac circuit of Fig. 18.14.

4. Does the SCR in the light-dimmer circuit of Fig. 18.12 turn OFF by line or forced commutation?

5. The power dissipation limits of a power transistor affect the rate at which it can be cycled as a switch. True or false?

6. If the *pnpn* diode in Fig. 18.9 fired at 20 V, what would be the resistor value required for it to fire in 3 ms?

*Answers.* (**1**) (c); (**2**) (b) and (c); (**3**) (a), (b), and (c); (**4**) line commutation; (**5**) true; (**6**) 79.7 kΩ.

## 18.2 DC MOTOR CONTROLLERS

### Introduction to Motor Controllers

**Power electronic converters.** A power electronic converter controls the power exchange between an electrical supply and a load, as shown in Fig. 18.16. The information that controls the power electronics may be a simple manual control, as in the previous section, or may be produced by a control system. The electrical supply may be ac or dc. The load may be a passive load, such as a bank of lights or an induction furnace,

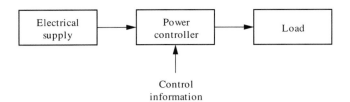

**Figure 18.16** General power controller.

or may be an electromechanical system, such as a dc or ac motor. The load may even be another electrical supply. Normally, the power flows from the electrical supply to the load, but for certain loads may flow in both directions. We introduce briefly the various types of systems:

**chopper**

- **DC–DC Converters.** A converter that takes fixed-voltage dc voltage and produces variable-voltage dc is normally called a *chopper*. We could, for example, control a dc motor armature circuit and hence control motor speed with a dc–dc converter.

- **AC–DC Converters.** An ac–dc converter is a controlled rectifier. In such a converter, the rectifier diodes are replaced by SCRs or similar switches, and the dc voltage is controlled by the switches. We will deal with single-phase converters of this type.

**inverter**

- **DC–AC and AC–DC–AC Converters.** A dc–ac converter is called an *inverter*. Combined with an ac–dc converter, we can develop an ac–dc–ac converter to make a variable-frequency ac source. For example, if we wished to control the speed of an induction motor, one approach would be to rectify the available 60-Hz ac to dc power and then invert the dc to ac at a controlled frequency to drive the motor. Such systems can also link together unsynchronized ac power systems for exchange of ac power between different power grids, sometime over a high-voltage dc, HVDC, transmission line. On a smaller scale, an ac–dc–ac converter can make a noninterruptable power supply if the dc portion maintains a battery bank to supply temporary dc power in case of a power failure.

- **AC–AC Controllers.** In addition to the ac–dc–ac converters described before, there exist ac–ac converters that perform direct conversion from fixed-frequency, fixed-voltage ac power to variable-frequency, variable-voltage ac power.

**Quadrants of operation.** Our principal concern is motor controllers. Figure 18.17 shows the four quadrants of motor operation. Because power is the product of torque and speed, the mechanical power out of the motor is positive in the first and third quadrants, which correspond to forward and reverse driving of the motor, respectively. In the fourth quadrant, the motor rotates in the forward direction, but the torque is supplied in the reverse direction, tending to slow down the motor. In this forward-braking region, the power output of the motor is negative, and the motor acts as a source of electric power. This power may be delivered back to the electrical supply or may be dissipated in the motor or the converter. Similarly, in the second quadrant, the motor is braked from reverse rotation. Operation in the second and fourth quadrants is sometimes called

**plugging, regenerative braking**

$$\begin{array}{c|c}
\text{(2)} & \text{(1)} \\
\text{Reverse} & \text{Forward} \\
\text{braking} & \text{drive} \\
\hline
\text{(3)} & \text{(4)} \\
\text{Reverse} & \text{Forward} \\
\text{drive} & \text{braking}
\end{array}$$

T (top axis label), $\omega_m$ (right axis label)

**Figure 18.17**  The four quadrants of motor operation.

*plugging*, or *regenerative braking*. As we will see, motor controllers are classified according to the quadrants in which they operate.

## DC Motor Model

**Equivalent Circuits**

**Time-average torque and power.**  We begin with ac–dc power electronic controllers for dc motors. We reexamine the model of a dc motor for the effect of periodic time-varying armature voltage and current.  Figure 18.18(a) shows the armature circuit of a separately excited dc motor. The armature emf is

$$E = K\Phi\omega_m \tag{18.13}$$

where $K\Phi$ is the machine constant, assumed constant. Although the voltage is periodic, the emf is constant because of the inertia of the armature and mechanical load. The armature current is also periodic, but the time-average torque is

$$T_{dev} = \langle K\Phi i_a(t)\rangle = K\Phi\langle i_a(t)\rangle = K\Phi I_a \tag{18.14}$$

where $<\ >$ means time average and $I_a$ is the dc component of the armature current. Because the emf is constant, the developed power also depends on the dc component of the armature current:

$$P_{dev} = \langle E i_a(t)\rangle = E\langle i_a(t)\rangle = E I_a \tag{18.15}$$

**Input voltage.**  Although the armature voltage, $v_a(t)$, is periodic, the dc component of the armature voltage is simply related to the emf and the dc current. Kirchhoff's voltage law in the armature circuit is

$$v_a(t) = R i_a(t) + v_L(t) + E \tag{18.16}$$

where $v_L(t)$ is the voltage across the inductor. As explained earlier on page 889, the time-average voltage across the inductance must be zero for steady-state operation, so the time average of Eq. (18.16) is

$$V_a = R I_a + E \tag{18.17}$$

where $V_a = \langle v_a(t)\rangle$ is the time-average voltage applied to the armature circuit.

**Quadrants of operation.**  Because torque is proportional to current and emf is proportional to speed, the four quadrants of operation in Fig. 18.17 correspond to identical quadrants in the $E$–$I_a$ plane shown in Fig. 18.18(b). For example, in the first quadrant, the emf and dc current are positive, which corresponds to positive torque and speed, hence to forward drive. The input voltage to the armature circuit is not identical

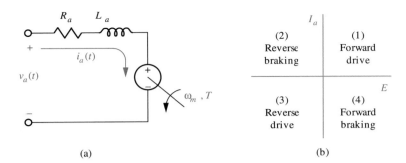

(a)                                                             (b)

**Figure 18.18** DC motor model.

to the emf, but in steady state, the emf follows the input voltage closely. Thus, we may assume that motor operation in the first quadrant corresponds to positive input voltage and current, and so on.

**Notation for switches.** In the remainder of this chapter, we symbolize a semiconductor switch as a "switch-in-a-box," as shown in Fig. 18.19. Because the SCR, GTO, and BJT switches allow current flow in one direction only and require forward bias in that direction to conduct, we have shown the allowed current direction by the orientation of the open end of the switch in a box, as shown. By this symbol we imply the existence of circuits to switch the device ON and OFF for forced commutation, including necessary protective circuits.

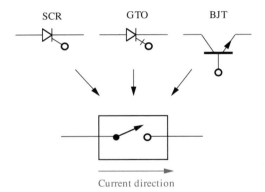

**Figure 18.19** The "switch in a box" represents a semiconductor switch. The allowed current direction is shown. All switches require forward bias in this direction to conduct.

## Single-Phase Uncontrolled Rectifier Analysis

**Introduction.** In this section, we analyze a single-phase rectifier that drives a dc motor from an ac source. A full treatment of this subject would analyze both single- and three-phase rectifiers and deal with dc motors with and without free-wheeling diodes. Due to limitation of space, we consider only two circuits: uncontrolled and controlled full-wave, single-phase rectifiers driving a dc motor with a free-wheeling diode.

**Problem description.** Figure 18.20 shows the circuit we now analyze. The full-wave rectifier uses a center-tapped transformer, but a bridge rectifier also works. The free-wheeling diode prevents the armature voltage from going negative, as can happen due to the inductance in the armature. We assume a separately excited motor with con-

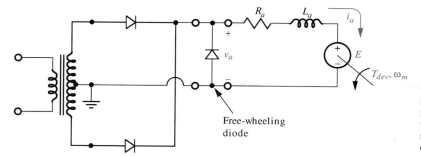

**Figure 18.20** Uncontrolled full-wave rectifier driving a dc motor with free-wheeling diode. The transformer could be replaced with a bridge circuit with four diodes.

stant nameplate field flux. The goal of our analysis is to determine the conditions required to drive the motor at nameplate conditions and to examine the performance of the rectifier–motor at other load conditions.

**Motor nameplate conditions.** Throughout this section we illustrate with the motor analyzed at the beginning of Sec. 17.3. The nameplate information is 1 hp, 180 V, 4.9 A, 1.78-$\Omega$ armature resistance, 30-mH armature inductance, 1750 rpm (183.3 rad/s), and 2050 rpm maximum. The nameplate emf and torque are $E_{NP} = 180 - 4.9\,\text{A} \times 1.78\,\Omega = 171.3\,\text{V}$, and $T_{NP} = 746\,\text{W}/183.3\,\text{rad/s} = 4.07\,\text{N-m}$, respectively. The brochure describing this motor states the motor should operate with full-wave controlled rectifiers with 230 nominal ac voltage input. However, we are at this stage of the analysis using uncontrolled rectifiers and leaving the ac voltage unspecified.

**Continuous current assumption.** The analysis of the circuit in Fig. 18.20 depends on whether the current in the armature is continuous or discontinuous. We assume the current to be continuous, that is, to flow throughout the entire ac cycle. These conditions follow:

- If the current is continuous, then one of the diodes is always ON.
- The diode that is ON must be the diode that is connected to the most positive input voltage. Thus, the armature voltage is always positive.
- The free-wheeling diode never conducts because the armature voltage is always positive.

These conditions lead to a relatively simple analysis. We therefore assume continuous current and nameplate conditions and check afterward to confirm the assumption of continuous current.

**The Frequency Domain**

**Armature voltage.** Because the diode connected to the positive end of the transformer is ON, the armature voltage is simply a full-wave rectified sinusoid, as shown in Fig. 18.21. Our analysis of the circuit is based on the Fourier series of the armature voltage:

$$v_a(t) = v_{FW}(t) = V_p \left[ \frac{2}{\pi} + \frac{4}{3\pi} \cos(2\omega t) - \frac{4}{15\pi} \cos(4\omega t) + \cdots \right] \qquad (18.18)$$

where $\omega$ is the radian frequency of the ac voltage, $120\pi$ for 60 Hz, and $V_p$ is the peak voltage from the centertap to the ends of the transformer. The voltage consists of a dc component plus the even harmonics.

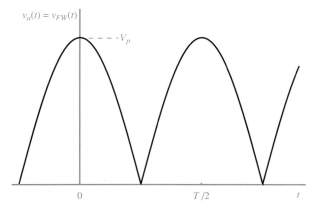

**Figure 18.21** With continuous current, the armature voltage is a full-wave rectified sinusoid. The Fourier series is given in Eq. (18.18).

**DC current.** At dc, the armature inductance is a short circuit, and the armature dc voltage and current are

$$V_a = \frac{2}{\pi}V_p \quad \text{and} \quad I_a = \frac{(2/\pi)V_p - E}{R_a} \tag{18.19}$$

---

### EXAMPLE 18.5  Required ac voltage

Find the required ac voltage into the full-wave rectifier for nameplate operation of the motor, assuming continuous current.

**SOLUTION:**

For nameplate operation, the input dc current is 4.9 A and the back emf is 171.3 A. With the resistance of the armature at 1.78 $\Omega$, Eq. (18.19) shows the dc voltage to be 180 V, which is, of course, the nameplate input voltage. Therefore,

$$\frac{2}{\pi}V_p = 180 \quad \Rightarrow \quad V_p = 282.7 \text{ V, or } 199.9 \text{ V(rms)} \tag{18.20}$$

The transformer turns ratio must be chosen to have approximately 400 V rms on the full secondary, or 200 V rms to the centertap.

---

**Second-harmonic current.** We must consider the fluctuations in the current to confirm that the current remains positive. At the second and higher harmonics, the emf, which is a dc source, is treated as a short circuit. The second-harmonic current magnitude is the second-harmonic voltage divided by the magnitude of the circuit impedance at the second-harmonic frequency:

$$I_2 = \frac{(4/3\pi)V_p}{|R_a + j2\omega L_a|} = \frac{4V_p}{3\pi\sqrt{R_a^2 + 4\omega^2 L_a^2}} \tag{18.21}$$

and similarly for the higher harmonics. The approximate condition for continuous current is that the second-harmonic peak current is smaller than the dc current; otherwise, the fluctuations of the current try to go negative. This requires

$$I_2 < I_a \quad \Rightarrow \quad \frac{(2/\pi)V_p - E}{R_a} < \frac{4V_p}{3\pi\sqrt{R_a^2 + 4\omega^2 L_a^2}} \tag{18.22}$$

Equation (18.22) places a limitation on the emf:

$$E < \frac{2}{\pi}V_p\left(1 - \frac{2}{3\sqrt{1 + 4\tan^2\phi}}\right) \tag{18.23}$$

where $\tan\phi = \omega L_a/R_a$ is the angle of the armature impedance at the fundamental frequency. Equation (18.23) gives the approximate condition for continuous current in the motor.

---

**EXAMPLE 18.6**  **Is the previous example valid?**

Confirm, if possible, that the motor in the Example 18.5 has continuous current.

**SOLUTION:**
The angle of the armature impedance at the fundamental is

$$\tan\phi = \frac{\omega L_a}{R_a} = \frac{120\pi \times 0.030}{1.78} = 6.354 \Rightarrow \phi = 81.1° \tag{18.24}$$

and thus Eq. (18.23) yields

$$E < 180\left[1 - \frac{2}{3\sqrt{1 + 4(6.354)^2}}\right] = 170.6 \tag{18.25}$$

which is less than the value of 171.3 at nameplate conditions. Thus, the current is not continuous at nameplate operation by this criterion.

**WHAT IF?**  What if the fourth harmonic is considered?[6]

---

**Conclusion.**  We conclude that this mode of operation is acceptable, but the analysis is not robust. The copper losses in the armature are increased by approximately 50% due to the second-harmonic current. This motor is designed for this type of operation and tolerates the extra losses. If the load demanded less than the nameplate torque, the motor current would become discontinuous. This would not hurt the motor; it would merely hurt our simple analysis. However, if the load were too small, the motor speed would increase dangerously.

---

[6] The harmonics are out of phase: $I_2 - I_4 = 5.29 - 0.53 = 4.76$ A, so the current is barely continuous.

## Controlled Rectifier Operation: Constant Speed Analysis

**Introduction.** We move on to the analysis of a controlled rectifier rather than analyzing the uncontrolled rectifier circuit for discontinuous current, because the latter is in fact a special case of the analysis we now undertake.

**Effect of gating.** Figure 18.22 shows a controlled full-wave rectifier circuit driving a dc motor. We replaced the diodes by controlled switches SW1 and SW2. The ac voltage is applied at $t = 0$, and we analyze circuit behavior for $t > 0$. Figure 18.23

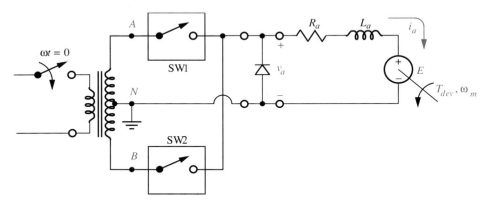

**Figure 18.22** A switched full-wave rectifier with a dc motor for a load.

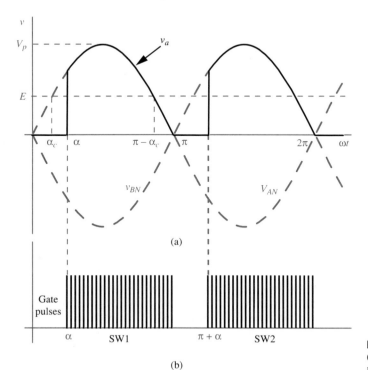

**Figure 18.23** (a) Applied voltage and (b) gating signals as a function of electrical angle, $\omega t$. The critical angle is $\alpha_c$.

shows the ac voltages and the gating signals with the time axis expressed in electrical angle. The gating signals consist of sequences of pulses beginning at $\omega t = \alpha$ for SW1 and $\omega t = \pi + \alpha$ for SW2 and repeated with the ac period. This type of gating signal is required because a switch may not conduct when first gated because it may be reverse-biased due to the emf.

**critical delay angle** **Critical delay angle.** If SW1 were gated before the critical delay angle, $\alpha_c$, it would come ON at $\alpha_c$ when the input voltage first exceeds the emf, $E$. This *critical delay angle* is

$$\alpha_c = \sin^{-1} \frac{E}{V_p} \tag{18.26}$$

where $V_p$ is the peak amplitude of the ac voltage. Similarly if $\alpha$ exceeds $\pi - \alpha_c$, neither switch will come ON and the rectifier supplies no current. We analyze for $\alpha_c < \alpha < \pi - \alpha_c$, because this is the region of normal operation. Figure 18.23(a) shows the input ac gated ON at $\omega t = \alpha$ and remaining connected to the armature until $\omega t = \pi$, when the free-wheeling diode prevents the armature voltage from going negative. The voltage marked $v_a$ would be the armature voltage if the current flows continuously.

**Three cases.** With fixed speed (fixed emf), we find three regimes of operation. When the firing angle is large, current flows through the armature for a short period of time and the free-wheeling diode never conducts. We call this Case A. Then there is a range of firing angles for which the motor current flows for a longer period of time, but not continuously, and the free-wheeling diode conducts for part of the cycle, Case B. Finally, there is a range of firing angles that causes the current to flow continuously, Case C. Each of these cases must be analyzed separately because different equations apply in each.

**Circuit operation for Case A.** Figure 18.24 shows the waveform applied to the load for $\alpha = 115°$, which is Case A. The input voltage is $230\sqrt{2}$ and the motor speed is $n = 1750$ rpm. Firing the switch begins a buildup of current in the load because the input ac voltage exceeds the back emf. The armature current builds up gradually due to the inductance, and thus the current remains positive after the source voltage falls below the emf. When the load current goes to zero and tries to reverse, the switch turns OFF by line commutation. During the periods when the instantaneous armature current is zero, the motor is not connected to the ac voltage and the load voltage is equal to the emf.

**Armature-current analysis.** The analysis of the circuit response involves a transient solution with a steady-state condition consisting of a sinusoidal and a dc response. Once SW1 is fired, the circuit is that shown in Fig. 18.25. The DE for the circuit is

$$L_a \frac{di_a}{dt} + R_a i_a = V_p \sin(\omega t) - E \tag{18.27}$$

and its solution consists of a transient and a steady-state response:

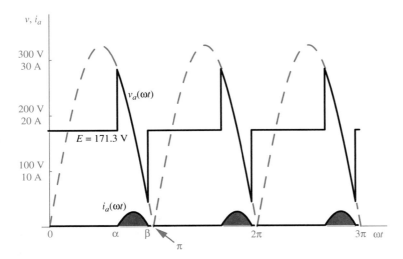

**Figure 18.24** Armature current and voltage for $\alpha = 115°$. This is Case A, where the free-wheeling diode never conducts. The plot is made for $V_p = 230\sqrt{2}$ and $n = 1750$ rpm.

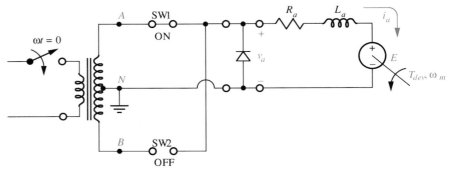

**Figure 18.25** Circuit after SW1 is fired, for the transient analysis.

$$i_a(t) = Ae^{-t/\tau} + \frac{V_p}{Z} \sin(\omega t - \phi) - \frac{E}{R_a} \tag{18.28}$$

where $A$ is an unknown constant to be determined from the initial condition, $\tau = L_a/R_a$ is the time constant of the transient, $Z = \sqrt{R_a^2 + (\omega L_a)^2}$ is the magnitude of the impedance at the input frequency, $\omega$, of the resistor and inductor in series, and $\phi = \tan^{-1}(\omega L_a/R_a)$ is the phase shift from the inductor. The sinusoidal portion of the current is determined from routine ac analysis, using the sine function for the ac source. The dc portion of the forced response involves only the emf and the resistor because the inductor and the ac source are short circuits at dc.

In Case A, $\alpha > \alpha_c$ such that SW1 fires at $\omega t = \alpha$. Because of the inductor, the initial current must be zero, so the initial condition at $\omega t = \alpha$ is

$$i_a(\alpha) = Ae^{-\alpha/\tan\phi} + \frac{V_p}{Z} \sin(\alpha - \phi) - \frac{E}{R_a} = 0 \tag{18.29}$$

where in the exponential we have replaced $t/\tau$ by $\alpha/\omega\tau$, and then replaced $\omega\tau$ by $\omega L_a / R_a = \tan \phi$. Solving for $A$, we find

$$A = \left[ \frac{E}{R} - \frac{V_p}{Z} \sin(\alpha - \phi) \right] e^{\alpha/\tan\phi} \tag{18.30}$$

and so the current is

$$i_a(\omega t) = \frac{V_p}{Z} [\sin(\omega t - \phi) - e^{(\alpha - \omega t)/\tan\phi} \sin(\alpha - \phi)]$$

$$- \frac{E}{R} [1 - e^{(\alpha - \omega t)/\tan\phi}] \tag{18.31}$$

**extinction angle**

Equation (18.31) is valid as long as $i_a > 0$. When the current tries to reverse, the switch turns OFF through line commutation, and the current ceases. The *extinction angle*, $\beta$, is defined as the angle where $i_a(t)$ crosses zero going negative, so $\beta$ satisfies Eq. (18.32).

$$i_a(\beta) = 0 = \frac{V_p}{Z} [\sin(\beta - \phi) - e^{(\alpha - \beta)/\tan\phi} \sin(\alpha - \phi)]$$

$$- \frac{E}{R_a} [1 - e^{(\alpha - \beta)/\tan\phi}] \tag{18.32}$$

Figure 18.24 shows $\beta$. For a specific circuit and value of $\alpha$, Eq. (18.32) may be solved for $\beta$ with numerical techniques; be sure to seek the first zero crossing after $\omega t = \alpha$.

---

**EXAMPLE 18.7** | **Find the extinction angle, $\beta$**

Find the extinction angle, $\beta$, for $\alpha = 115°$.

**SOLUTION:**
Equation (18.32) is nonlinear and may be solved by a "solve" routine on a calculator or computer. Another approach is to use Eq. (18.31) and seek the first zero crossing. For $\alpha = 115°$ and the system parameters given on page 901, we calculate the currents in Table 18.1.

| TABLE 18.1 Value of armature current for $\alpha = 115°$ | |
|---|---|
| $\omega t$ (deg) | $i_a(\omega t)$ |
| 160 | 2.675 |
| 170 | 1.273 |
| 180 | −0.939 |

*We interpolate between the last two values to find the zero crossing, which is the extinction angle.

The angle for which $i_a(\omega t) = 0$ may be estimated by linear interpolation to be 175.8°. Thus, the extinction angle is approximately $\beta = 175.8°$.

**WHAT IF?**   What if you want more accuracy?[7]

**Armature voltage for Case A.**   While the switch is ON and current flows, the armature voltage is equal to the input sinusoidal voltage, and the armature voltage is $E$ for the remainder of the cycle.[8] The time-average load voltage, averaged over one-half the period, is, therefore,

$$V_a = \frac{1}{\pi} \int\limits_{\alpha}^{\alpha + \pi} v_a(\omega t)\, d(\omega t) = \frac{1}{\pi} \int\limits_{\alpha}^{\beta} V_p \sin(\omega t)\, d(\omega t) + \frac{1}{\pi} \int\limits_{\beta}^{\alpha + \pi} E\, d(\omega t) \qquad (18.33)$$

$$= \frac{V_p}{\pi}(\cos\alpha - \cos\beta) + E\left(1 - \frac{\gamma}{\pi}\right)$$

**conduction angle**      where $\gamma = \beta - \alpha$ is the *conduction angle* in radians.

---

**EXAMPLE 18.8**   **Find voltage, current, and power**

Find the time-average armature voltage, current, and power for $V_p = 230\sqrt{2}$, $n = 1750$ rpm, and the motor parameters on page 901.

**SOLUTION:**

For $\alpha = 115°$ and $\beta = 176.2°$, the average load voltage is from Eq. (18.33)

$$V_a = \frac{230\sqrt{2}}{\pi}(\cos 115° - \cos 176.2°) + 171.3\left(1 - \frac{176.2° - 115°}{180°}\right) = 172.6 \text{ V} \qquad (18.34)$$

As we showed in Eq. (18.17), the dc current can be determined from the dc load voltage, the emf, and the resistance:

$$I_a = \frac{V_a - E}{R_a} = \frac{172.6 - 171.3}{1.78} = 0.744 \text{ A} \qquad (18.35)$$

The total power given to the emf is given by Eq. (18.15):

$$P_{dev} = EI_a = 171.3 \times 0.744 = 127.5 \text{ W} \qquad (18.36)$$

and the total power to the armature circuit is slightly higher because of loss in the armature resistance. The developed power minus the rotational losses gives an output power of 34.2 W for this condition.

---

[7] $i_a(175°) = 0.2868$ A and $i_a(176°) = 0.0432$ A; therefore, $\beta = 176.2°$.
[8] In Case A, the free-wheeling diode never conducts.

**Limits for Case A.** The maximum delay angle for Case A occurs when the input voltage falls below the emf, $\alpha = \pi - \alpha_c = 148.2°$. For larger values of $\alpha$, the switches are reverse-biased and never conduct. The minimum delay angle for Case A occurs when $\beta = \pi$, which requires

$$i_a(\pi) = 0 = \frac{V_p}{Z}[\sin(\pi - \phi) - e^{(\alpha - \pi)/\tan\theta}\sin(\alpha - \phi)]$$

$$- \frac{E}{R_a}[1 - e^{(\alpha - \pi)/\tan\phi}]$$

(18.37)

Equation (18.37) can be solved for $\alpha$ by numerical means. For our case, the solution is $\alpha = 109.4°$. The corresponding armature currents for Case A, $109.4° < \alpha < 148.2°$ are $1.12\ A > I_a > 0\ A$.

**Condition for Case B.** For $\alpha < 109.4°$, the extinction angle $\beta$ exceeds 180° and the armature voltage tries to go negative. For this case, the free-wheeling diode conducts for part of the cycle. Figure 18.26 shows the voltage and current for $\alpha = 75.2°$, which is the value of $\alpha$ that drives the motor at nameplate voltage.

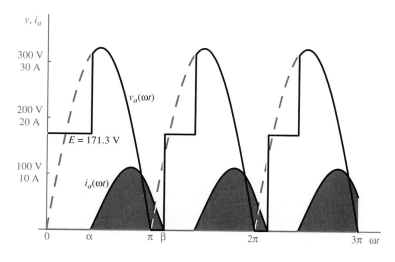

**Figure 18.26** Armature current and voltage for $\alpha = 75.2°$. This is Case B, where the free-wheeling diode conducts for part of the cycle.

**Role of the free-wheeling diode.** The current to the load is increased by the free-wheeling diode across the load. When SW1 is ON and SW2 OFF, the diode is in parallel with the source and is reverse-biased while the source voltage is positive. When the source voltage goes negative, the diode turns ON, and SW1 turns OFF by line commutation. The armature current is free-wheeling through the diode.

**Analysis for Case B.** The current for the period $\alpha < \omega t < \pi$ is given by Eq. (18.31) if we assume zero current when SW1 is fired. When $\omega t = \pi$, SW1 turns OFF, and the current is

$$I_a(\pi) = \frac{V_p}{Z}[\sin(\pi - \phi) - e^{(\alpha - \pi)/\tan\phi}\sin(\alpha - \phi)] - \frac{E}{R_a}[1 - e^{(\alpha - \pi)/\tan\phi}]$$

(18.38)

When $\omega t = \pi$, the free-wheeling diode conducts, SW1 is OFF by line-commutation and the current begins to decay in a simple dc transient such as we studied in Chapter 3. The initial value is $i_a(\pi)$, and the final value is $-E/R_a$; hence, the current for $\pi < \omega t < \beta$ is

$$I_a(\omega t') = -\frac{E}{R_a} + \left[i_a(\pi) + \frac{E}{R_a}\right]e^{-t'/\tau} \qquad (18.39)$$

where $t' = 0$ at $\omega t = \pi$. Extinction occurs when

$$\beta = \pi + (\omega\tau)\ln\left[1 + \frac{i_a(\pi)R_a}{E}\right] \qquad (18.40)$$

At extinction, the free-wheeling diode turns OFF, and the load current remains at zero until a switch is again gated ON in the next cycle. For the present case, we require that $\pi < \beta < \alpha + \pi$, which is true for $109.4° > \alpha > 36.5°$.

**Armature voltage for Case B.** The armature voltage is equal to the source voltage while the switch is ON, is zero while the diode is ON, and is equal to $E$ while both switch and diode are OFF, as shown in Fig. 18.26. The average load voltage is

$$V_a = \frac{1}{\pi}\int_\alpha^\pi V_p \sin(\omega t)\, d(\omega t) + \frac{1}{\pi}\int_\beta^{\alpha+\pi} E\, d(\omega t) \qquad (18.41)$$

$$= \frac{V_p}{\pi}(1 + \cos\alpha) + E\left(1 - \frac{\gamma}{\pi}\right)$$

which yields nameplate conditions of 180.0 V for $E = 171.3$ V, $\alpha = 75.2°$, and the circuit parameters given on page 901. Equation (18.17) gives the average load current as 4.90 A. The full range of currents for Case B is $1.12 < I_a < 8.68$ A. Thus, Case B covers the remainder of the operating region of the motor. However, for the sake of completeness, we discuss Case C, in which the armature current flows continuously.

**Analysis for Case C.** For $\alpha < 36.5°$, the current becomes continuous and a transient period passes before the current reaches steady state. Figure 18.27 shows the first three half cycles for $\alpha = \alpha_c = 31.8°$. The diode never conducts, and the average voltage in steady state is

$$V_a = \frac{1}{\pi}\int_\alpha^\pi V_p \sin(\omega t)\, d(\omega t) = \frac{V_p}{\pi}(1 + \cos\alpha) \qquad (18.42)$$

which is the same as Eq. (18.41) for a conduction angle of 180°. For this firing angle, Eq. (18.42) yields $V_a = 191.6$ V and the armature current is 11.4 A. As the firing angle continues to increase, the applied waveform approaches that of a conventional full-wave rectifier, and the dc current to the armature approaches that given by Eq. (18.19).

**Summary.** The controlled full-wave rectifier delivers dc voltage and current to the dc motor armature. The current may be continuous or discontinuous. A free-wheeling

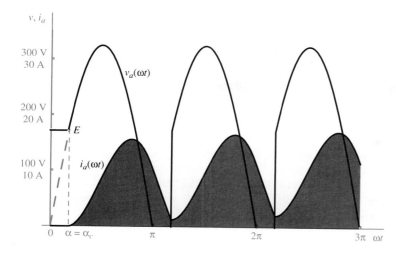

**Figure 18.27** For $\beta > \alpha + \pi$, the current becomes continuous and builds up to a steady state. This is Case C. We show the first three cycles for $\alpha = \alpha_c = 31.8°$.

diode across the load prevents the armature voltage from going negative and thus increases the armature current and reduces harmonics. Figure 18.28 shows the delay and extinction angles plotted against armature current for Cases A and B. These curves were calculated by first assuming the delay angle, $\alpha$, then calculating the extinction angle, $\beta$, then the armature voltage, and from that the current. The analysis must distinguish three cases, depending on whether the free-wheeling diode conducts and whether the current is continuous or discontinuous. As we shall see in what follows, there are even other states that can come into play.

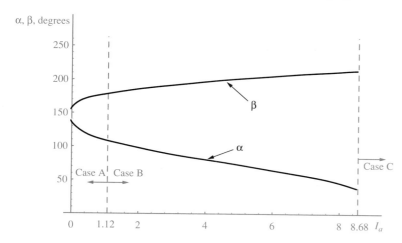

**Figure 18.28** Delay and extinction angle as a function of the resulting current. This assumes a fixed motor speed of 1750 rpm. The independent variable is the delay angle, $\alpha$, and the extinction angle, $\beta$, and armature current are calculated. For Cases A and C, the free-wheeling diode never conducts.

## Motor Performance with Constant Firing Angle

**Nameplate conditions.** As asserted earlier, nameplate conditions occur with $\alpha = 75.2°$ provided the load requires nameplate torque at nameplate speed. In this section, we analyze the motor with constant firing angle and determine the output torque as a function of motor speed. The procedure is to assume a speed, determine the back emf from the speed, and then find the extinction angle, $\beta$, from either Eq. (18.32) or (18.40), depending on whether Case A or B proves to be consistent.[9] From the firing and extinction angles, we can determine the dc armature voltage from either Eq. (18.33) or (18.41), and then the armature current and developed torque. After subtracting the loss torque determined in Eq. (17.48), we have the output torque.

**Case B conditions.** We now determine the limits for which Case B conditions exist. The minimum speed is that for which the conduction angle, $\gamma$, is 180°, which requires that $\beta = \alpha + 180° = 255.2°$. Thus, we can substitute this angle into Eq. (18.40) and solve for the emf, $E$. The result is $E = 112.6$ V, and the corresponding speed and armature current are 1151 rpm and 9.98 A, respectively.

The maximum speed for which Case B conditions exist is that at which the extinction angle is 180°. Thus, we can substitute $\alpha = 75.2°$ and $\beta = 180°$ into Eq. (18.32) and solve for the emf. The result is $E = 215.9$ V, which corresponds to a speed of 2206 rpm and current of 2.60 A.

**Case A conditions.** Case A begins where Case B leaves off and continues until the critical angle equals the delay angle. This occurs when

$$E = V_p \sin \alpha = 230\sqrt{2} \sin 75.2° = 314.5 \text{ V} \qquad (18.43)$$

which corresponds to 3213 rpm, $\beta = 119.4°$, and $I_a = 0.03$ A. Because the motor losses require more current than this, we conclude that this condition is not reached in practice. Indeed, this high speed could damage the motor and should be prevented from occurring in practice.

**Torque vs. speed for $\alpha = 75.2°$.** The results of the calculations described before are shown in Fig. 18.29 alongside the torque characteristic for fixed nameplate voltage of 180 V. We have marked the limits imposed by armature current and speed constraints. Clearly, active control of the system is required to prevent exceeding motor limitations as load requirements change.

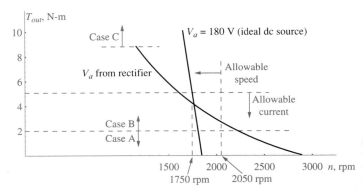

**Figure 18.29** Torque characteristic with fixed delay angle and fixed armature voltage. The armature speed and current limits are shown.

---

[9] Case C exceeds the motor limits and will not be considered.

## Harmonics in the ac line.

When a motor is driven by an controlled rectifier, the current that flows in the ac power system is nonsinusoidal, containing in general all the even harmonics of 60 Hz. The harmonics constitute noise for other users of the ac power circuit and can disturb sensitive electronic circuits. The issue of power quality is growing in importance to power companies as more power-electronic equipment comes into use.

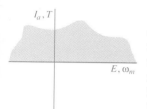

**Figure 18.30** The controlled rectifier in Fig. 18.22 operates in the first and second quadrants.

## Operation in the second quadrant.

Without the free-wheeling diode, the circuit can put out negative armature voltage for $\alpha > 90°$ and small or negative emf. As $\alpha$ is advanced more and more, the switches are gated ON and continue conducting when the input voltage is negative, making the load voltage negative. However, the load current must be kept positive in the indicated direction because the switches in the controlled rectifier in Fig. 18.22 permit only positive load current. This can occur when $V_a > E$. If $E$ is positive, $V_a$ has to be more positive. This can also occur if $E$ is negative and $V_a$ is less negative. This circuit controls motor torque, therefore, in the first and second quadrants, as shown in Fig. 18.30. The controller is incapable of drive in the reverse direction, but could operate as a brake if the motor direction were reversed by the mechanical system.

## Inverter operation.

In the circumstance where the emf is negative, but the current is positive, the emf acts as a generator and delivers power to the ac source. The system thus can function as an inverter, converting dc power to ac power. The same may be accomplished in the four-quadrant converter described in what follows, in which the current may reverse.

## Four-quadrant controller.

Figure 18.31(a) shows a controlled rectifier that operates in all four quadrants without a free-wheeling diode, as shown in Fig. 18.31(b). The original switches, SW1 and SW2, are gated for positive load current, and SW3 and SW4 are gated for negative load current. We can envision the rectifier operating with continuous positive current for small $\alpha$ and going into discontinuous positive current as $\alpha$ is increased. Somewhere near $\alpha = 90°$, the current reverses and the motor slows and reverses. Further increases of $\alpha$ drive the motor in the reverse direction. At some point, the current may become continuous in the negative direction.

The circuit in Fig. 18.31 is completely symmetrical and may be analyzed by the methods given before; indeed, the various formulas may be adapted for this type of operation. However, the control of the switches is complicated by the possibility of reversal of the load current, for the direction of the current flows determines which switches to turn ON.

## Check Your Understanding

1. A free-wheeling diode increases or decreases the armature current to a dc motor. Which?

2. If a dc motor draws continuous current from a source at a given speed, it will draw continuous current for higher speeds, everything else being held the same. True or false?

3. The peak of the current in Fig. 18.26 corresponds roughly to what condition between input voltage and emf?

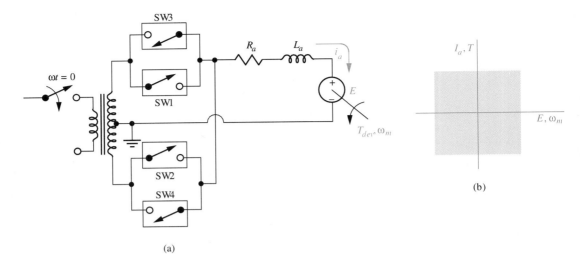

(a)

(b)

**Figure 18.31** A controlled rectifier capable of operation in all four quadrants.

**4.** For an uncontrolled rectifier drive of a dc motor, the value of $\alpha$ is always the critical value. True or false?

**5.** For a controlled single-phase rectifier, the extinction angle cannot be greater than the firing angle by more than 180°. True or false?

*Answers.* **(1)** Increases for Cases B and C; **(2)** false; **(3)** the current maximum occurs roughly when the input voltage and emf are equal because the armature impedance is largely inductive; **(4)** true, if the current is discontinuous; **(5)** true.

## 18.3 AC MOTOR CONTROLLERS

Many types of ac motor controllers are currently in use, and this is an active field of research and development, with continual innovations in response to improvements in semiconductor devices and control techniques. Controllers are tailored to specific types of motors, such as induction motors and synchronous motors. We limit our discussion to the control of induction motors, and examine the more common types of power controllers.

**Speed control of induction motors.** Of the various means for controlling the speed of a three-phase induction motor, we consider the two most common: variation of the magnitude of the applied voltage and the variation of frequency of the applied voltage.

Figure 18.32 shows the effect of lowering the voltage applied to an induction motor. The principal effect is to lower the torque, but with certain loads, this leads to a measure of speed control.

Figure 18.33 shows the torque characteristics of a three-phase induction motor as the frequency of the applied voltage is varied but the voltage amplitude is kept constant. Magnetic saturation has been ignored. At low frequencies, the impedance of the motor is low, current is increased, and torque is high. However, high currents cause magnetic

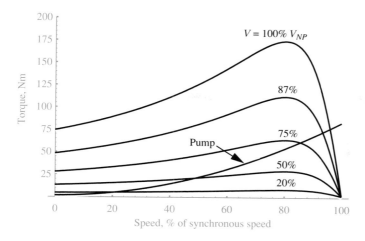

**Figure 18.32** Torque characteristics of a three-phase induction motor at various percentages of rated voltage. The torque scales with the square of the applied voltage. As the voltage is decreased, the intersection with the load requirement moves to lower speeds. The torque requirement of a pump is shown as a representative load.

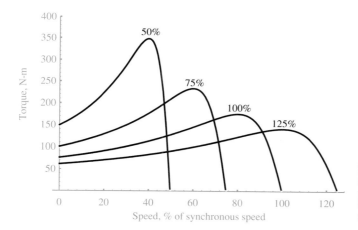

**Figure 18.33** Torque characteristics of a three-phase induction motor at various percentages of rated frequency. The applied voltage is kept constant. Magnetic saturation is ignored.

saturation and increased losses. For this reason, motor controllers vary applied voltage in proportion to frequency to keep the current roughly constant, which is known as constant volts/hertz drive.

**Voltage control of induction motors.** Figure 18.34 shows a fixed-frequency, variable-voltage controller for a three-phase induction motor. Such a controller is useful for loads whose torque requirements increase strongly with speed, such as fans and pumps. The controller consists of six back-to-back switches that switch the three-phase ac waveform. The output of the converter is an ac waveform that can be varied in amplitude, plus harmonics. The model for the induction motor is that of Fig. 16.14, except that for simplicity, we have treated the Thevénin voltage as the per-phase voltage and ignored mechanical losses.

**Equivalent Circuits**

**Torque characteristic.** Considering only the fundamental in the voltage applied to the induction motor, Eq. (16.37) gives the developed torque as

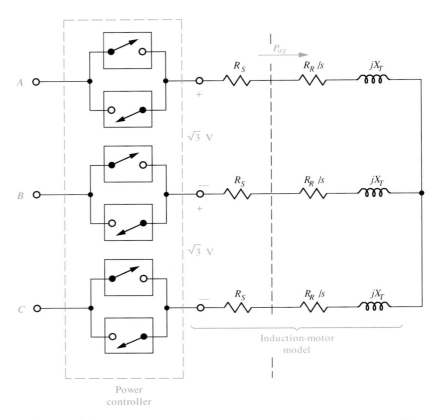

**Figure 18.34** Circuit model of a fixed-frequency, variable-voltage motor controller with a model of a three-phase induction motor. The slip, $s$, represents the motor speed and the air-gap power, $P_{ag}$, is proportional to the motor torque.

$$T_{dev} = \frac{3V^2}{\omega_s} \times \frac{R'_R/s}{[R_S + R'_R/s]^2 + X_T^2} \tag{18.44}$$

where $V$ is the per-phase voltage, $R_S$ is the stator per-phase resistance, $R'_R$ is the rotor per-phase resistance as seen from the stator, and $X_T$ is the total reactance per phase. Torque is proportional to the voltage squared, and thus the motor-load speed can be controlled if the load torque varies strongly with speed.

---

**EXAMPLE 18.9** **Induction motor with a pump as load**

Consider a six-pole, 230-V, 60-Hz, three-phase induction motor with $R_S = 0.2\ \Omega$, $R'_R = 0.2\ \Omega$, and $X_T = 1.0\ \Omega$. The load torque varies as the square of speed and operates with a slip of 4% at rated voltage. Calculate the system speed as the ac voltage amplitude is varied. Figure 18.32 shows the output torque of the motor and the load torque requirements.

**SOLUTION:**

The developed torque at 4% slip is from Eq. (18.44):

$$T_{dev}(s = 4\%) = \frac{3(230/\sqrt{3})^2}{40\pi} \times \frac{0.2/0.04}{[0.2 + (0.2/0.04)]^2 + 1^2} = 75.1 \text{ N-m} \qquad (18.45)$$

and because speed is proportional to $1 - s$, the load torque is generally

$$T_L(s) = 75.1 \times \left(\frac{1 - s}{0.96}\right)^2 \qquad (18.46)$$

Combining Eqs. (18.44) and (18.46), we have for the system,

$$75.1\left(\frac{1 - s}{0.96}\right)^2 = \frac{3V^2}{40\pi} \times \frac{0.2/s}{[0.2 + (0.2/s)]^2 + 1^2} \qquad (18.47)$$

which may be solved for slip or voltage if either is assumed. Figure 18.35 shows speed versus voltage from Eq. (18.47), and also the speed characteristics of a high-slip motor ($R'_R = 1.0\,\Omega$). We include the latter to demonstrate its improved speed-control characteristics, albeit at lower efficiency.

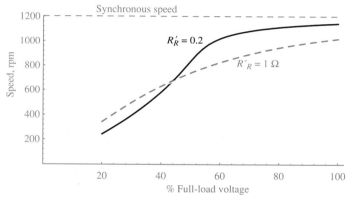

**Figure 18.35** Speed vs. applied voltage for a normal and a high-slip induction motor. The larger rotor resistance of the high-slip rotor improves controllability but increases losses.

**Discussion of fixed-frequency voltage control.**   This method is limited to smaller loads with favorable speed–torque characteristics. The efficiency is low, and harmonics are generated in the power system. The controller operates in the first and second quadrants, although the latter does not occur with typical loads.

## DC-Link Variable-Frequency Controllers

**Basic configuration.**   Figure 18.36 represents a dc-link variable-frequency motor controller. The input ac power is converted to dc, filtered, and then converted to variable-frequency three-phase ac by an inverter. The switches are numbered in the order that they are turned ON, with the complementary switch turned OFF simultaneously;

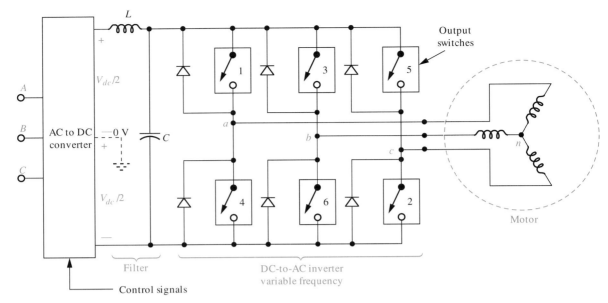

**Figure 18.36** DC-link motor controller.

that is, when switch 1 is ON, switch 4 is OFF, and so on. We examine several means by which the switches may convert the dc to three-phase ac power to drive an induction motor. The bypass diodes are required for reactive power flow and to limit the voltage to that of the dc supply. The filter we show supplies the inverter with dc voltage that is largely independent of load current. When the capacitor is omitted, the dc voltage may vary, but the inductor tends to keep the current constant, which offers some advantages. The ac-to-dc converter output may be fixed or variable voltage (or current), depending on the type of inverter scheme and filter used. We show the neutral as a dashed ground because no actual ground is required.

**Square-wave inverter.** In the square-wave inverter, each phase is connected alternatively to the positive and negative power-supply outputs to give a square-wave approximation to an ac waveform at a frequency of $\omega_e$ determined by the gating of the switches. The voltage in each output line is phase shifted by 120° to synthesize a three-phase source. Voltage waveforms for the square-wave inverter are shown in Fig. 18.37(a). The first three waveforms are voltage of phases $a$, $b$, and $c$ relative to the neutral on the center tap of the power supply. The bottom waveform gives the voltage of motor terminal $a$ relative to the ungrounded neutral on the motor. The circuit in Fig. 18.37(b) shows the configuration when $a$ and $c$ are connected to the positive dc voltage and $b$ is connected to the negative dc voltage. The two phases in parallel give half the impedance of an individual phase and thus get one-third the total dc voltage, whereas the unpaired phase gets two-thirds the dc voltage. Thus, for the first 30°, $v_{an} = \frac{1}{3}V_{dc}$ and for the next 30°, $v_{an} = \frac{2}{3}V_{dc}$, and so on. In this manner, the stair-step voltage for each motor phase is produced. The fundamental component in each waveform is about $0.637 \times V_{dc}$.

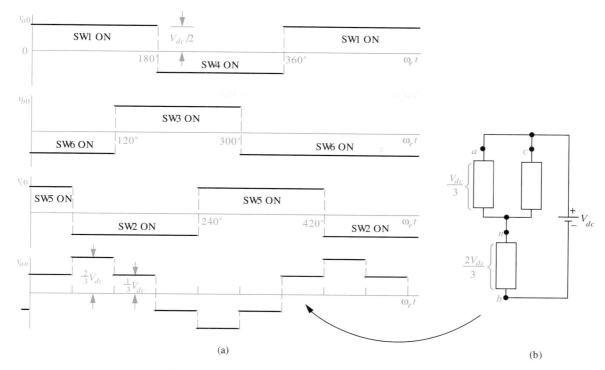

(a) (b)

**Figure 18.37** (a) The synthesis of the line-to-neutral voltage from a square-wave inverter. The stair-step waveform results from the changing neutral voltage on the motor. (b) Circuit configuration when $a$ and $c$ are connected to the positive and $b$ is connected to the negative dc voltage.

**Need for constant voltage/frequency.** At frequencies below the rated frequency of the motor, the applied voltage must be reduced. Otherwise, the current to the motor becomes excessive, as implied by Fig. 18.33, and causes magnetic saturation. This follows from Faraday's law:

$$\underline{\mathbf{V}} = j\omega_e n\underline{\mathbf{\Phi}} \tag{18.48}$$

where $\omega_e$ is the electrical frequency; clearly, the voltage must decrease as the frequency is reduced if the peak flux is to be kept constant. Thus, the square-wave inverter requires decreasing dc voltage as motor speed is reduced below rated speed. For this reason, Fig. 18.36 shows control signals to the ac–dc converter.

**The Frequency Domain**

**Harmonics.** The square-wave inverter has two types of problems with harmonics. At the input, the controlled rectifier that produces the variable dc voltage creates harmonics that constitute noise in the power system. These can be filtered, but the added complexity degrades the efficiency and power factor, which are already somewhat poor for a controlled rectifier.

The output waveforms also have problems with harmonics. The stair-step-output waveforms in Fig. 18.37(a) contain only odd harmonics. The third, ninth, and so on, cause no problems because they are in phase and thus self-cancel at the input to the motor. But the other harmonics, principally the fifth and seventh, cause currents that increase losses in the motor and produce no torque. Although these harmonics are filtered somewhat by the inductance of the motor, the combination of these problems has caused designers to look for alternatives. The pulse-width modulation (PWM) system discussed in what follows conquers these problem with a more complicated switching sequence.

**pulse-width modulation (PWM)**

### Pulse-width modulation (PWM).

Figure 18.38(b) shows 180 electrical degrees of a waveform that has been generated through pulse-width modulation. The basic idea in PWM is to chop pieces out of the wave to control the fundamental in the output, while in the same operation shifting the harmonics to high frequencies that are easily filtered by the inductance of the motor.

### Sine/triangle modulation.

Figure 18.38(a) shows one means for controlling the switches to create a PWM waveform. The triangle wave is a carrier, and its frequency is much higher than the electrical frequency applied to the motor. The sinusoidal waveform, of which only one-half of the period is shown, is the modulating waveform that controls the amplitude and frequency of the fundamental applied to the motor. Specifically, the electrical frequency of the ac applied to the motor is equal to that of the mod-

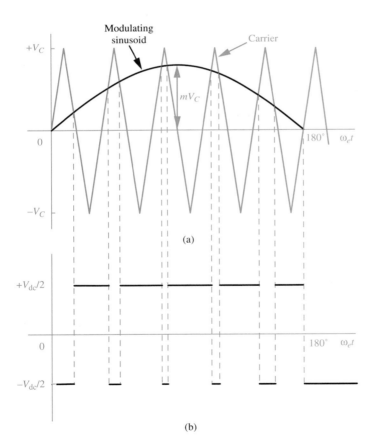

**Figure 18.38** (a) The switching sequence is generated by comparing a triangular wave with a sinusoidal wave. The modulation index is $m$. (b) The resulting waveform has a sinusoidal component proportional to $m$ at the frequency of the sinusoid in part (a).

ulating sinusoid, and the amplitude of the ac is proportional to the modulation index, $m$, defined in Fig. 18.38(a).

The relationship between the carrier, modulating sinusoid, and switched waveform is evident: Whenever the modulating sinusoid exceeds the carrier, the switches connect the motor to the positive dc voltage, and whenever the modulating sinusoid falls below the carrier, the switches connect the motor to the negative dc voltage. Note that if $m$ were small, the output would have roughly equal amounts of positive and negative voltage for this half-cycle and thus produce a small component of the fundamental. But as $m$ increases, the positive voltage dominates. The opposite would be true for the second half of the cycle. In this way, the modulating sinusoid controls the amplitude and frequency of the output.

**The Frequency Domain**

**Harmonics in PWM.** With PWM, the harmonics are shifted to frequencies comparable to the carrier frequency and thus are much higher than the harmonics of the square-wave inverter. The higher harmonics are filtered by the inductance of the motor, and the resulting current is sinusoidal with a small ripple.

We showed the modulated waveform for only one phase of the three-phase inverter. For the other two phases, the modulating sinusoids are phase shifted by 120° and 240° in the usual fashion. In this way, the inverter produces three-phase voltage of controlled frequency and amplitude.

**Hysteresis-current control.** Figure 18.39 illustrates yet another method for deriving the PWM switching sequence. The output current in each output phase is compared with a reference signal of the desired amplitude and frequency. When the output current falls below the reference signal by a prescribed error, the output is connected to the positive dc bus, and when the output current rises above the reference signal by the specified error, the output is connected to the negative dc bus. Thus, the current bounces between the two error bounds, following the reference signal. This method controls current, and thus torque, directly and is not greatly affected by the variation of the motor impedance with drive frequency.

**Benefits of PWM drive.** Pulse-width modulation controls motor voltage or current, depending on the modulation scheme, by connecting the motor to the positive or negative buses of a fixed-voltage dc supply. Such a supply has good efficiency and power

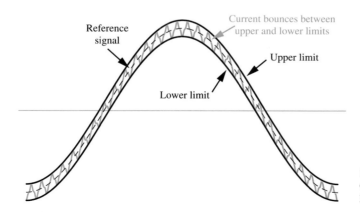

Reference signal

Current bounces between upper and lower limits

Upper limit

Lower limit

**Figure 18.39** Hysteresis-current control keeps the current within a prescribed range of a reference waveform.

factor and does not generate excessive harmonics in the power system. The PWM systems shift the harmonics to high frequencies that are filtered by the inductance of the motor.

### Check Your Understanding

1. The speed of an induction motor can be controlled by varying the drive voltage or frequency, but not both. True or false?

2. Figure 18.38 shows a sine/triangle modulation scheme. Sketch the voltage waveform if the modulation index, $m$, equals 1.5.

3. The speed of a synchronous motor cannot be controlled by a power electronics system because the slip is always zero. True or false?

*Answers.* (**1**) False; (**2**) almost a square wave; (**3**) false; the rotor position, and hence its speed, can be controlled precisely.

## CHAPTER SUMMARY

This introduction to power electronics began with a presentation of the properties and limitations of various semiconductor switches. We then showed how such switches are used in the simple ac power controller used in the common dimmer-switch circuit.

We analyze in detail a controlled rectifier circuit with a dc motor for a load. The various modes of operation lead to analytical complexities, but the behavior of the system is straightforward. We end by describing several motor controllers for ac induction motors, without detailed analysis.

**Objective 1: To understand the variety and limitations of semiconductor switches.** The solid-state revolution has produced a variety of semiconductor switches that can handle large amounts of power. We focus primarily on the switching losses and protection needs of such switches.

**Objective 2: To understand in full the operation of the common light-dimmer circuit.** This circuit in its simplest form uses one four-level diode as a voltage-controlled switch to control the firing of an SCR that in turn controls power to a low-impedance load. The thorough analysis introduces the time-domain analysis of such nonlinear circuits.

**Objective 3: To understand the operation of a controlled single-phase, full-wave rectifier driving a dc motor.** The unfiltered full-wave rectifier is analyzed with a dc motor armature as a load. We show that the motor characteristics are changed markedly in this application, and that lightly loaded motors can overspeed.

**Objective 4: To understand the methods and complexities of ac motor controllers.** The characteristics of the three-phase induction motor are examined when ac drive voltage and frequency are varied. The need for constant-volts/hertz drive is shown. Several types of variable-voltage and variable-frequency drives are described qualitatively.

Chapter 18 utilizes the time-domain viewpoint almost exclusively, a result of the nonlinear behavior of the switching devices. Many sections of this book are used in

Chapter 18. The time-domain analysis of nonlinear circuits is based on Chapters 3, 4, and 5. The electronic devices and principles are related to material in Chapter 7. The existence and effects of the harmonics are based on the frequency-domain viewpoint presented in Chapter 9. And, of course, knowledge of the motor characteristics comes from Chapters 15, 16, and 17. The material of this chapter, through challenging, makes a suitable summation of this book. Our survey of electrical engineering is finished.

## PROBLEMS

## Section 18.1: Introduction to Power Electronics

18.1. A snubber circuit, shown in Fig. P18.1, is placed in parallel with an SCR to limit the rate of voltage rise across the OFF device. If $120\sqrt{2}$ V were suddenly applied to the SCR and snubber circuit with the load shown, what would be the required value of $R$ to keep the $dv/dt$ of the SCR below $100$ V/$\mu$s? Treat the capacitor as a short circuit for the worst-case transient.

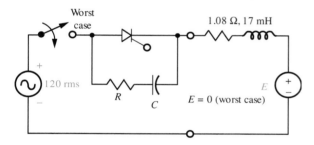

**Figure P18.1**

18.2. Verify the result of the integration in Eq. (18.3).

18.3. (a) Calculate the energy lost in the transistor for the inductive switching trajectory shown in Fig. 18.6(b). The voltage and current for the turn-ON switching operation is shown in Fig. P18.4(b). In both transitions, the collector voltage is at the power-supply voltage while the current makes its transition in $t_r/0.8$.

(b) What is the power in the transistor if it is switching with a frequency, $f_{sw}$?

18.4. A transistor switching an inductive load, Fig. P18.4(a) has the waveform shown in Fig. P18.4(b) for current and voltage. The switching cycle is short compared to the time constant; hence, the current in the inductor is essentially constant at $I_{Cp}$.

(a) Explain briefly why the diode is in the circuit.

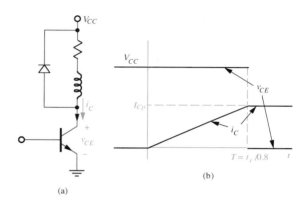

**Figure P18.4**

(b) Find the energy dissipated in the transistor in an OFF → ON transition.

(c) If the same energy is used in the ON → OFF transition and the transistor is driven ON → OFF → ON at a rate $f_r$, find the time-average power dissipated by the transistor.

18.5. On page 888, we work out the switching losses for a transistor switching a resistive load. The model used is linear, that is, the current increases linearly and the voltage across the transistor decreases linearly. Let us assume an *exponential* model and rework the problem for comparison. Let

$$i_C(t) = I_{Cp}(1 - e^{-2.2t/t_r}) \text{ and } v_{CE}(t) = V_{CC}e^{-2.2t/t_r}$$

In these expressions, $t$ is counted from the time the current starts to increase (same as $t'$ in the book.)

(a) Show that the rise time satisfies the definition on page 887.

(b) Calculate the energy delivered to the transistor during the switching.

18.6. The SCR in Fig. P18.6 has infinite resistance when OFF and a voltage of 0.3 V when ON. A pulse of

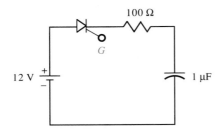

**Figure P18.6**

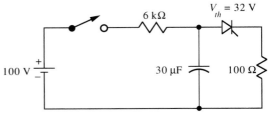

**Figure P18.8**

current occurs at the gate at $t = 0$. Find the following:
**(a)** The current in the circuit before the gate pulse.
**(b)** The maximum current that can flow in the circuit.
**(c)** The time constant of the current.

**18.7.** Commercial airplanes carry flashlights that have a light-emitting diode (LED) that flashes occasionally to show that the batteries are still good (and also presumably to allow one to find the flashlights in the dark). A circuit that accomplishes this flashing is shown in Fig. P18.7. Assume that the *pnpn* diode fires at 2.2 V and has 0.7 V when ON. The LED requires at least 10 mA of current at 0.7 V to glow. Find $R_1$ and $R_2$ so that the LED glows for at least 4 ms every 10 s.

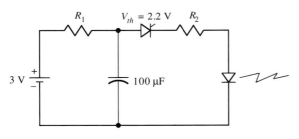

**Figure P18.7**

**18.8.** For the circuit shown in Fig. P18.8, the capacitor is initially uncharged and the switch is closed at $t = 0$. The *pnpn* diode has a threshold voltage of 32 V and has an ON voltage of 0.3 V. Find the maximum current in the 100-$\Omega$ resistor and the time when the maximum current occurs.

**18.9.** If the gate of the SCR in Fig. 18.12 is limited to 10 mA of current, what value of resistance should be placed in series with the *pnpn* diode to limit the

gate current to this value. Assume that the *pnpn* diode fires at 30 V and that the equivalent resistance of the gate is 15 $\Omega$.

**18.10.** For the circuit in Fig. 18.9 and $V_p = 120\sqrt{2}$ V, determine the exact minimum and maximum delay time if the *pnpn* diode has a threshold voltage of 26 V.

**18.11.** The circuit shown in Fig. P18.11(b) contains *pnpn* diode, whose characteristics are shown in Fig. P18.11(a), and an ideal SCR. The switch closes at $t = 0$.
**(a)** At what time does the SCR conduct?
**(b)** What is the maximum current in the 5-k$\Omega$ resistor?
**(c)** What is the maximum current in the 300-$\Omega$ resistor?

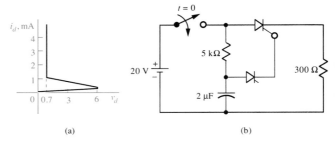

**Figure P18.11**

**18.12.** For the circuit shown in Fig. P18.12, the switch is closed at $t = 0$. Before the switch is closed, the capacitor is uncharged. The four-level diode turns ON at 10 V, has a voltage of 0.5 V when ON, and turns OFF when the current through it falls below 10 mA. Sketch the voltage across the 10-$\Omega$ resistor as a function of time for $t > 0$.

**18.13.** For the circuit in Fig. 18.12, what would be the maximum $R_V C$ time constant for the *pnpn* diode to reach 30 V and fire the *pnpn* diode? *Hint*: The

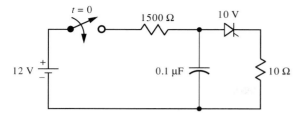

**Figure P18.12**

exact solution is difficult due to the nonlinear character of the equations. A good numerical approach would be to ignore the exponential term in Eq. (18.11) for a first approximation and then include it for subsequent approximations.

18.14. The circuit in Fig. 18.14 represents a dimmer switch, and the load represents a 150-watt light bulb. The voltage is turned ON and the circuit is adjusted to cause the bulb to glow slightly. Circle the change (brighter, dimmer, or no change) for the following changes:
   (a) The amplitude of the input voltage is increased.
   (b) The phase of the input voltage is increased.

## Section 18.2: DC Motor Controllers

18.17. Consider a separately excited 180-V dc motor with armature resistance of 1.05 $\Omega$ and inductance of 22 mH. Nameplate ratings are 1750 rpm (2050 rpm max.), 1.5 hp, and 7.3-A armature current. The motor is driven by an uncontrolled 60-Hz full-wave rectifier with $V_p = 230\sqrt{2}$ V. The emf of the motor is 201.9V. The current is discontinuous and flows for 91.6% of the time. What is the extinction angle $\beta$ in radians?

18.18. Consider a separately excited 180-V dc motor with an armature resistance of 1.05 $\Omega$ and an inductance of 22 mH. Nameplate ratings are 1750 rpm (2050 rpm max.), 1.5 hp, and 7.3-A armature current. The dc motor is driven by an uncontrolled 60-Hz full-wave rectifier.
   (a) Find the required input voltage to the rectifier for nameplate operation, assuming that the current to the motor flows continuously.
   (b) Find the required emf of the motor for continuous current, considering only the second-harmonic current.
   (c) Is the current for this emf below its nameplate value?

(c) The frequency of the input voltage is increased.
(d) The resistance, $R_V$, is increased.
(e) The capacitance, $C$, is increased.

18.15. For $V_p = 120\sqrt{2}$, $f = 60$ Hz, $V_{th} = 30$ V, $R_V = 30$ k$\Omega$, and $C = 0.3$ $\mu$F, determine the firing time, $t_\alpha$, from Eq. (18.11). This requires a graphical or numerical solution unless you have a calculator that solves nonlinear equations.

18.16. Normally, the firing time in SCR operation, $t_\alpha$, shown in Fig. 18.13, is described in terms of a "conduction angle," where $\gamma = 180° - 360° \times t_\alpha/T$, where $T$ is the period of the frequency, usually 1/60 s. Clearly, $\gamma$ is the amount of phase angle during which the SCR fires each cycle.
   (a) For a conduction angle of 90°, $V = 120$ V (rms), and $R_L = 100$ $\Omega$, what is the dc current and the total power in the load? Note that the total power is a measure of the total heating effect on the load and is more than the dc power.
   (b) Repeat part (a) for a conduction angle of 120°. Part (a) can be solved without evaluating any integrals, but part (b) requires two integrations.

18.19. Consider a separately excited 180-V dc motor with an armature resistance of 1.05 $\Omega$ and an inductance of 22 mH. Nameplate ratings are 1750 rpm (2050 rpm max.), 1.5 hp, and 7.3-A armature current. The motor is supplied by an uncontrolled single-phase, 60-Hz full-wave rectifier.
   (a) Determine the minimum input voltage (rms) such that the armature current flows continuously at 90% of nameplate speed. Consider only the second harmonic.
   (b) Find the current under these conditions.

18.20. A series-excited dc motor has the following nameplate information: 24 V, 5 A, 0.8-$\Omega$ armature plus field resistance, 0.05 H-armature plus field inductance, and 800 rpm. The motor is driven by a full-wave rectifier connected to the 120-V, 60-Hz power with a center-tapped transformer.
   (a) Find the turns ratio of the transformer, $n_s/n_p$ so that the motor is driven at nameplate conditions, assuming that current is continuous.
   (b) Confirm that current is continuous.

(c) At what speed does the current in the motor current become discontinuous?

18.21. Consider a separately excited 180-V dc motor with armature resistance of 1.05 $\Omega$ and inductance of 22 mH. Nameplate ratings are 1750 rpm (2050 rpm max.), 1.5 hp, and 7.3-A armature current. This motor is driven by a controlled rectifier. The ac source is 230 V rms.
(a) If the firing pulses begin at $\alpha = 0°$, estimate the no-load speed of the motor? Ignore losses. *Hint*: The motor accelerates to a speed where very little current flows, that is, the critical delay angle is approximately 90°.
(b) With no load, what range of $\alpha$ has no effect on the speed?
(c) With $\alpha = 90°$ and $E = 180$ V, the extinction angle, $\beta$, is 101.8°.
(1) What is the conduction angle, $\gamma$, in radians?
(2) What is the dc armature voltage?
(3) Find the developed torque in the motor.

18.22. Consider a separately excited 180-V dc motor with armature resistance of 1.05 $\Omega$ and inductance of 22 mH. Nameplate ratings are 1750 rpm (2050 rpm max.), 1.5 hp, and 7.3-A armature current. The dc motor is driven by a single-phase controlled rectifier with $V_p = 120\sqrt{2}$ V, and 60 Hz.
(a) If the firing pulses begin at $\alpha = 0°$, what is the no-load speed of the motor? Ignore losses.
(b) With $E = 150$ V, what range of $\alpha$ has no effect on the speed?
(c) With the firing pulses beginning at $\alpha = 0°$, what range of emfs gives continuous conduction?

(d) With the firing pulses beginning at $\alpha = 0°$ and $E = 150$ V, the extinction angle, $\beta$, is 145.2°.
(1) What is the conduction angle, $\gamma$, in radians?
(2) What is the dc load voltage?
(3) Find the armature current?

18.23. Consider a separately excited 180-V dc motor with an armature resistance of 1.05 $\Omega$ and inductance of 22 mH. Nameplate ratings are 1750 rpm (2050 rpm max.), 1.5 hp, and 7.3-A armature current. This motor is driven by a single-phase, controlled rectifier drive. The input voltage is 220 V rms, 60 Hz, for each half of the transformer supplying the rectifier. Consider that the motor is running at nameplate speed.
(a) Determine the critical $\alpha$ for the circuit, $\alpha_c$, in degrees and radians.
(b) Assuming the firing pulses begin at $\alpha = \alpha_c$, write the equation for the current in the period of time $\alpha_c < \omega t < 180°$. Assume zero current at $\omega t = \alpha_c$ and solve for all constants in the equation.
(c) Calculate $i_a(180°)$ to see if we have Case A.
(d) If not Case A, is it Case B?

18.24. A full-wave gated SCR rectifier provides adjustable dc power to an *RL* load, as shown in Fig. P18.24(a). The resistance is 10 $\Omega$ and the inductance is unknown. For a circuit delay angle the voltage applied to the *RL* load is that shown in Fig. P18.24(b). No free-wheeling diodes are used, so the voltage can go negative due to the inductance.
(a) What is the delay angle?

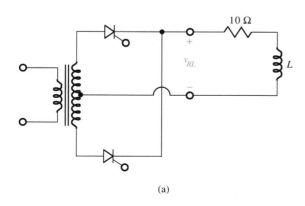

(a)

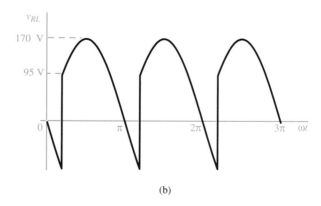

(b)

**Figure P18.24**

**(b)** Is the current continuous or discontinuous? Explain.

**(c)** Find the minimum value of inductance to give the voltage shown and 60-Hz operation.

**(d)** Determine the dc current in the *RL* load.

**18.25.** The circuit in Fig. P18.25 shows a single-phase, full-wave uncontrolled rectifier battery charger. The load is a dc battery with an emf that varies from 11.8 V (discharged) to 12.6 V (charged), and an equivalent resistance of 0.03 Ω. The peak value of the transformer secondary voltage is 13.3 V, such that no current flows into the battery when fully charged because the diodes require 0.7 V to turn ON.

**(a)** For a discharged battery, 11.8 V, what is the critical delay angle, $\alpha_c$, of the diodes?

**(b)** What is the peak current in the discharged battery?

**(c)** What is the average current in the discharged battery?

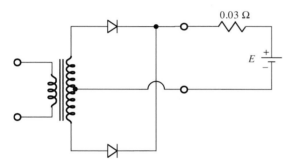

**Figure P18.25**

**18.26.** The circuit in Fig. P18.26 shows a single-phase, full-wave controlled rectifier. The top switch is

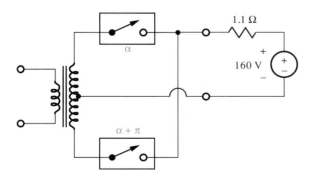

**Figure P18.26**

gated at $\alpha$ and the bottom at $\alpha + \pi$. The load is a dc motor with an emf of 160 V, an armature resistance of 1.1 Ω, and negligible armature inductance. The secondary voltage of the transformer is 120 V rms. With negligible inductance, the current cannot go negative, so no free-wheeling diode is required.

**(a)** What values of $\alpha$ actually affect motor voltage and current?

**(b)** For $\alpha = 90°$, what is the peak instantaneous current in the motor?

**(c)** For $\alpha = 90°$, what is the average current in the motor?

**18.27.** A dc motor has the following nameplate information: 230 V dc, 1750 rpm, 20 hp, 74.0 A dc, 0.180-Ω armature resistance, and 2.93-mH armature inductance. The field current is separately excited for nameplate operation. For the motor turning at nameplate speed, with 230 V rms driving it via a controlled full-wave rectifier, with a prescribed delay angle, the current is as shown in the shaded area in Fig. P18.27. The current begins at a phase angle of 70°, reaches a maximum value of 33 A, and ceases at an angle of 182°. There is a free-wheeling diode.

**(a)** What is $\alpha$?

**(b)** What is $\beta$?

**(c)** Sketch the voltage applied to the motor. (The full-wave rectified sinusoid is given for reference.)

**(d)** What is the developed power in the motor?

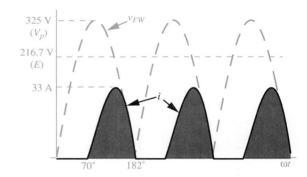

**Figure P18.27**

**18.28.** A dc motor is driven by an ungated full-wave rectifier circuit. The motor nameplate information is 1 hp, 1150 rpm, 180 V, 5.0 A, 2.43-Ω armature resistance, and 49-mH armature inductance. The field current is that required for nameplate operation.

**(a)** Find the rms voltage to the rectifier input such that the motor draws continuous current at nameplate conditions.

**(b)** Determine approximately the speed of the motor if allowed to run at no load.

**(c)** Estimate the dc current into the motor if allowed to run at no load.

**18.29.** A model train locomotive has a permanent-magnet dc motor. For full speed of 1 ft/s, the motor requires 6 V dc, and 2 A dc. The motor armature has 2 Ω in series with 10 mH. The motor is to be driven by a full-wave rectifier using pn-junction diodes (assume ideal), connected to a 120-V, 60-Hz power source via a transformer whose secondary is center-tapped for the rectifier. A variable resistor (rheostat) is connected in series with the motor for speed control.

**(a)** Draw the circuit of the rectifier, rheostat, and motor model.

**(b)** Find the turns ratio of the transformer (total primary turns/total secondary turns) to drive the train at full speed with the rheostat set to zero resistance. Assume that current flows continuously.

**(c)** Confirm that the current flows continuously.

**(d)** Find the resistance of the rheostat to give a train speed of 0.5 ft/s if the current required is 1.6 A.

**18.30.** A dc motor has the following nameplate information: armature: 1.5 hp, 2500 rpm (2750 max. with reduced field), 180 V, 7.5 A, 0.563 Ω, and 12 mH; field: 0.56 A (0.43 A for max. speed), 282 Ω, and 86 H. A full-wave rectifier is installed to give the required 180-V input, as you can

confirm from the circuit diagram in Fig. P18.30 using the usual equations for the dc from a full-wave rectifier. However, the engineer who designed the power supply (transformer plus the full-wave rectifier) found that, with the motor running with nameplate speed and torque, the voltage at the output is not 180 volts at nameplate operation, but is higher.

**(a)** Explain why the voltage is high. Support your explanation with numerical calculations.

**(b)** The engineer then found that adding an external inductor in series with the motor armature, as shown in Fig. P18.31, reduces the voltage. Calculate the minimum inductance to give the required 180 V at nameplate operation.

**18.31.** A permanent-magnet-field dc motor is driven by a 60-Hz, uncontrolled, full-wave single-phase rectifier with a free-wheeling diode. The no-load speed and current of the motor are 1925 rpm and 0.8 A, respectively. The current becomes continuous at 930 rpm, and the full-load speed and output power are 900 rpm and 2 hp, respectively. Assume rotational losses are proportional to the mechanical speed. The armature resistance is 1 ohm.

**(a)** Find the emf at full load.

**(b)** Estimate the armature inductance.

**18.32.** An engineer is operating a dc motor with an electronic box, but does not know what is in the box. The engineer knows the frequency, 60 Hz, and the armature resistance of the motor, 1.05 Ω. To learn what the electronics was doing, she looked at the output voltage of the box with an oscilloscope. What she saw is shown in Fig. P18.32: The voltage was sinusoidal for part

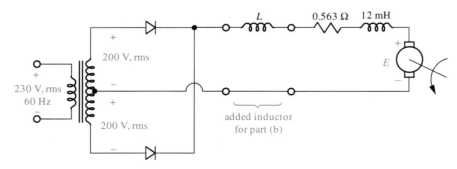

**Figure P18.30**

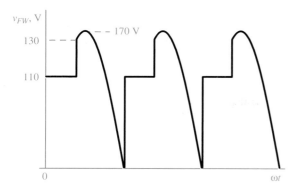

**Figure P18.32**

of the cycle, was zero for about 0.5 ms, jumped to 110 V and was constant for a while, then jumped to 130 V, and becomes sinusoidal again. From this, the engineer learned a lot about the system:
(a) Continuous or discontinuous current?
(b) EMF of the motor?
(c) Delay angle of the drive?
(d) Extinction angle?
(e) Time-average motor current?
(f) Developed power?

18.33. A dc motor has the following nameplate information: 1.5 hp, 2500 (2850 max.) rpm, 180 V, 7.5 A, 0.563-$\Omega$ armature resistance, and 12-mH armature inductance. The motor is separately excited at rated field current for operation at nameplate conditions. The motor armature is connected to a 460-V secondary of a transformer, center-tapped for 230 V(rms), 60 Hz each half, and diodes are used to rectify the ac for the armature circuit, as shown in Fig. P18.33. Find the motor speed at which the current becomes continuous. Is the motor operating within its allowed limits?

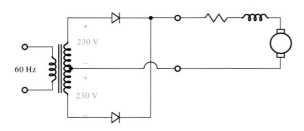

**Figure P18.33**

18.34. A 230-V, 60-Hz single-phase rectifier-type motor controller drives a dc motor. The motor nameplate information is 180 V, 8.5 A, 1150 rpm, 1.03-$\Omega$ armature resistance, 28-mH armature inductance, 2-hp output power. The motor is separately excited for nameplate conditions. A free-wheeling diode is used to reduce harmonics and increase armature current. The motor is turning 1150 rpm. The delay angle is set to 40°, and the first pulse of current is observed as shown in Fig. P18.34. From this information, determine the time-average torque developed by the motor.

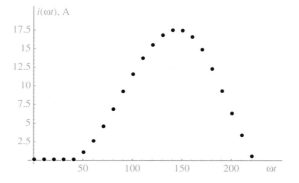

**Figure P18.34**

18.35. A dc motor has the following specifications: armature: 1 hp, 1150/1380 max. rpm (with reduced field), 5.0 A, 180 V, 2.43 $\Omega$, and 0.049 H; field: base-speed current = 0.54 A; top-speed current = 0.33 A, 200 V, 282 $\Omega$, and 86 H. This motor is to be used in an application where it is to run at 1000 rpm with an output torque of 3.5 N-m, driven by an ac source and a full wave rectifier.
(a) Because 230-V, 60-Hz, single-phase power is available, a transformer must be used to convert the voltage for the application. Determine the transformer voltage required to drive the motor at this speed and load. Assume the nameplate current of 0.54 A for the motor field. Assume rotational power losses proportional to speed.
(b) Draw the entire circuit, including the field circuit and the ON/OFF switch. You are supposed to excite the field from the same rectifier, adding a rheostat if required.

18.36. A dc motor with a free-wheeling diode has the following nameplate information: 5 hp, 1750 rpm,

220 V, 20 A, 0.5-Ω armature resistance, and 2.5-mH armature inductance. The motor is driven by a 60-Hz, single-phase controlled full-wave rectifier with a voltage of 460 V rms, center-tapped for the rectifier ($V_p = 230\sqrt{2}$). For an emf ($E$) of 210 V (nameplate speed), the conduction angles are calculated from Eq. (18.32), as follows:

| $\alpha$ | 30° | 40° | 50° | 60° | 80° | 100° | 120° | 140° |
|---|---|---|---|---|---|---|---|---|
| $\gamma°$ | 148.8 | 138.8 | 128.5 | 117.6 | 93.8 | 66.8 | 36.0 | 0.000 |

(a) Confirm one of the data points except the last by direct calculation.
(b) What portion of the calculated data is relevant to system performance?
(c) Estimate the value of $\alpha$ to drive the motor at nameplate conditions.

18.37. A dc motor with a free-wheeling diode is driven by a gated full-wave, single-phase bridge rectifier. The armature voltage is shown in Fig. P18.37, along with critical voltages and angles in electrical degrees. The dc motor nameplate information is as follows: 2500 rpm, 3 hp, 180 V, 14.5 A, 0.313-Ω armature resistance, and 7-mH armature inductance. Assume ideal diodes. Find the following:
(a) The rms voltage of the ac system.
(b) The delay angle, $\alpha$.
(c) The critical delay angle, $\alpha_c$.
(d) The extinction angle, $\beta$.
(e) The motor speed.
(f) The developed power.

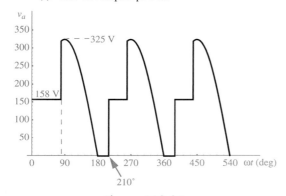

**Figure P18.37**

18.38. A 240-V, 60-Hz, gated, full-wave single-phase rectifier drives a dc motor with an armature

resistance and inductance of 3 Ω and 30 mH, respectively. At a speed of 1350 rpm, the critical delay angle is 20°. A free-wheeling diode is used.
(a) Determine the delay angle required such that the operation is borderline between continuous and discontinuous conduction. This requires a trial-and-error solution.
(b) For the delay angle determined in part (a), find the developed power in the motor in hp.

18.39. A dc motor has the following nameplate information: 1 hp, 1150 rpm (1380 with reduced field), 180 V, 5.0 A, 2.43 Ω, 0.049 H, and 0.076 kg-m² moment (armature only, no load). The field is 200 V, 0.54 A for 1150 rpm and 0.33 A for 1380 rpm. The machine is operated with separately excited field, with nameplate field voltage (200 V) and nameplate current (0.54 A). The armature is connected to a 230-V(rms), 60-Hz, single-phase source via a full-wave rectifier (assume ideal diodes). A series resistor is connected between the power source and motor to limit the voltage to the motor to 180 V under nameplate conditions.
(a) Find the emf under nameplate conditions.
(b) Find the rotational losses under nameplate conditions.
(c) Find the value of the series resistor to ensure nameplate conditions from the rectifier.
(d) Confirm that the current is continuous at nameplate conditions.
(e) Determine the overall efficiency at nameplate conditions, including field losses and losses in the series resistor. Consider only the dc power out of the rectifier, that is, neglect any power in the higher harmonics.
(f) Find the maximum value of the series resistor to give continuous current at $n = 1150$ rpm.

18.40. An electromagnet has a resistance of 120 Ω and an inductance of 0.5 H. The magnet is activated by a 60-Hz, 240-V, single-phase ac power source. Two schemes are considered. One uses ac current only to activate the magnet, and the other uses a full-wave rectifier to convert the ac to dc. In both cases, the lifting power of the magnet is proportional to the square of the rms value of the current.
(a) Draw the circuit diagram for the rectifier scheme, showing the ON/OFF switch and a free-wheeling diode if required. Use a bridge rectifier circuit.

**(b)** Determine the rms current in the magnet with the rectifier. If you assume a continuous current, show that this assumption is justified.

**(c)** Determine the rms current with the ac source connected directly. Compare the performance of the two schemes.

18.41. An electromagnet is designed to work in a junkyard lifting junk cars, as shown in Fig. P18.41(a). The geometry is cylindrical, as shown in Fig. P18.41(b), and the coil has 500 turns and a 500-$\Omega$ resistance. The OD of the inner pole is 24 cm, and the ID and OD of the outer pole are 30 cm and 38 cm, respectively, as shown. Due to the irregular nature of the loads, assume a nominal air gap of 1 cm. Two methods for exciting the electromagnet are being considered: a 240-V, 60-Hz ac source, and a dc source produced by full-wave rectifying the 240-V source with a bridge rectifier. Determine the current due to each and make your recommendation as to the best approach. Assume lifting power is proportional to the square of the rms current. *Hint*: In the reluctance calculation, consider the two air gaps in series and use the average area.

## Section 18.3: AC Motor Controllers

18.42. Determine the speed vs. percent full-load voltage curve for the motor described in Example 18.9 if the full-load slip were 11% and the rotor resistance were 0.5 $\Omega$. The stator resistance and the total reactance are unchanged. Hint: Assume values of $s$ and then calculate the voltage required.

18.43. Figure P18.43 shows an approximate per-phase circuit for a three-phase, two-pole, 60-Hz induction motor at nameplate frequency. At a slip of 3%, the developed torque is 8.18 N-m for nameplate voltage.

**(a)** Find the torque at 80% of nameplate voltage if the slip is constant.

**(b)** Find the torque at 80% of nameplate voltage and 80% of nameplate frequency if the slip is changed to 5%.

18.44. A six-pole, 60-Hz, three-phase induction motor has the simplified per-phase equivalent circuit

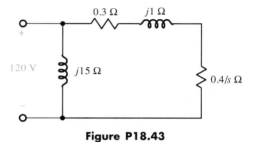

**Figure P18.43**

shown in Fig. P18.44. The motor load requires a torque given by the equation:
$T_{dev} = 1.4 \times 10^{-5}\omega^3$ N-m. Find the per-phase voltage required to drive the motor at 1155 rpm.

18.45. The equivalent circuit in Fig. P18.45 is a simplified model for a 230-V, four-pole, 60-Hz induction motor that is operated from a variable-

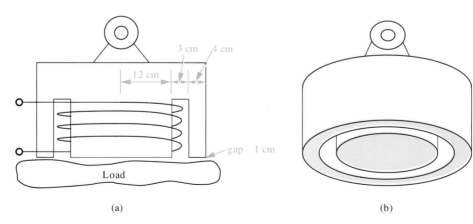

(a)

(b)

**Figure P18.41**

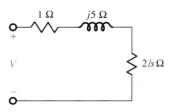

**Figure P18.44**

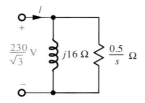

**Figure P18.45**

frequency, variable-voltage power electronic drive. At 60 Hz and nameplate voltage, the motor operates with a 5% slip with a certain power to the load. By keeping the input-current magnitude constant and the developed power at 60% of the previous power, the driver frequency is reduced to 45 Hz. Find the new speed and voltage.

18.46. The simplified per-phase equivalent circuit in Fig. P18.46 describes a 230-V, 60-Hz, four-pole, three-phase induction motor in the small-slip region. The motor generates the required torque in a certain application at a slip of 5% when operated at 60 Hz. The motor is driven by an ac controller that can vary the frequency to control speed and the voltage to control the motor current. What voltage should be applied to the machine if operated at 30 Hz if the torque and input-current magnitude are to remain the same as for the nameplate conditions? Ignore mechanical losses.

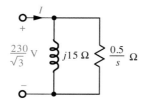

**Figure P18.46**

18.47. An induction motor runs with a 4% slip at nameplate frequency and voltage. The frequency

is reduced to 80% of nameplate frequency and the motor voltage is also reduced to 75% of nameplate voltage. Determine the slip at the reduced speed if the developed torque is the same in both cases. Assume that the motor operates in the small-slip region in both cases.

18.48. The speed of an ac induction motor is controlled by varying the applied voltage and frequency of the ac input voltage. The motor runs at 1164 rpm at full voltage and 60 Hz. Estimate the speed at 60% of nameplate voltage and 70% of nameplate frequency. Assume small-slip operation and constant load torque.

18.49. The load for a three-phase induction motor requires constant power. The motor is driven by a power electronic circuit to control speed. The motor operates with a slip of 3% at nameplate voltage and frequency. Estimate the slip at 80% of nameplate frequency and 80% of nameplate voltage. Ignore mechanical losses. Assume the motor is operating in the small-slip region.

18.50. The circuit of Fig. P18.50 is a simplified per-phase equivalent circuit for a three-phase induction motor. At the nameplate frequency of 60 Hz and the nameplate voltage of 230-V rms line voltage, the motor draws the nameplate current of 22.1 A, has the nameplate slip of 4%, and develops the nameplate torque of 18.7 N-m. If we allow the frequency and slip to vary, but not the voltage, what is the maximum torque the motor can produce without exceeding the nameplate current of 22.1 A?

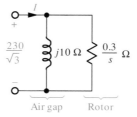

**Figure P18.50**

18.51. A 60-Hz, four-pole, three-phase induction motor is represented by the per-phase circuit shown in Fig. P18.51 at nameplate voltage and frequency. The developed torque is 10.3 N-m at the nameplate slip of 5%, which you may check if you wish. The motor is driven by a variable

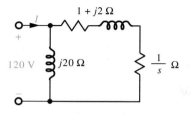

**Figure P18.51**

frequency, constant-volts/hertz power electronic drive.

**(a)** Find the drive frequency to produce 3 N-m of developed torque at 875 rpm. Assume operation in the small-slip region.

**(b)** Find the motor input current at the new frequency and compare (find the ratio) with the nameplate current.

18.52. A two-pole, 60-Hz, three-phase induction motor has the simplified equivalent circuit shown in Fig. P18.52 at 60 Hz. The motor is driven by a constant-volts/hertz variable frequency drive and drives a load with a torque requirement $T_L = 3 + \omega_m/100$ N-m. Neglect motor mechanical losses.

**(a)** Find the mechanical speed of the system as a function of the electrical drive frequency. Use the small-slip approximation.

**(b)** Considering the small-slip approximation valid for $s \le 0.15$, find the lowest electrical frequency at which the expression in part (a) is valid.

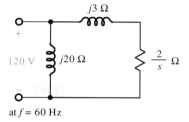

at $f = 60$ Hz

**Figure P18.52**

18.53. A synchronous motor is to be controlled by a power electronic drive, as shown in Fig. P18.53. The "phase" input corresponds to the $\omega_e t$-axis in Fig. 18.37(a). In effect, the "phase" input consists of triggering signals to the six electronic switches in Fig. 18.36.

**(a)** If the motor is to turn at 356 rpm, how often is a single diode turned ON and OFF?

**(b)** If the switches are held in a single state, the rotor takes certain fixed positions. In effect, the motor becomes a stepper motor with certain output angles. What is the smallest increment of angle that can be commanded by this system?

18.54. To speed up an induction motor by 20% and keep the output torque roughly constant, one should (choose one answer): (a) increase the voltage, (b) increase the frequency, (c) increase the voltage and frequency.

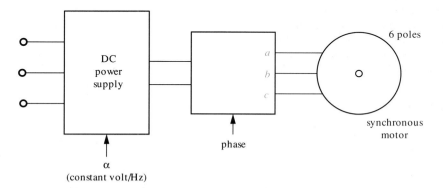

**Figure P18.53**

# Answers to Odd-Numbered Problems

**18.1.** Less that 10 kΩ.

**18.3.** (a) $V_{CC}I_{Cp} \int_{0}^{t_r/0.8} \dfrac{0.8t'}{t_r} \, dt' = \dfrac{V_{CC}I_{Cp}t_r}{1.6}$;

(b) $\dfrac{V_{CC}I_{Cp}}{1.6} \times 2f_{SW}$.

**18.5.** (a) $0.999t_r$; (b) $V_{CC}I_{Cp}t_r/4.4$.

**18.7.** $R_1 = 39$ kΩ; $20 \, \Omega < R_2 < 100 \, \Omega$.

**18.9.** 2915 Ω.

**18.11.** (a) 3.57 ms; (b) 4 mA; (c) 64.3 mA.

**18.13.** About 26 ms.

**18.15.** About 3.3 ms.

**18.17.** 203°.

**18.19.** (a) 254 V peak; (b) 6.49 A.

**18.21.** (a) 3303 rpm (should be avoided); (b) $0° < \alpha < 90°$; (c) (1) $11.8° = 0.206$ rad, (2) 189 V, (3) 8.39 N-m.

**18.23.** (a) 33.6°; (b) $i_a(\omega t) = 37.2[\sin(120\pi t - 82.8°) - e^{(0.587 - 120\pi t)/7.90}\sin(33.6° - 82.8°)] - 164[1 - e^{(0.587 - 120\pi t)/7.90}]$; (c) $i_a(180°) = 12.0$ A; (d) $\beta = 212°$ so Case B.

**18.25.** (a) 70.0°; (b) 26.7 A; (c) 3.82 A.

**18.27.** (a) 70.0°; (b) 182°; (c)

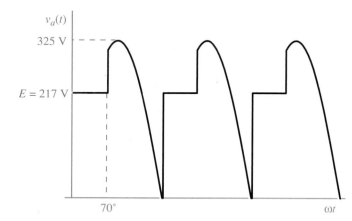

(d) 4970 W.

**18.29.** (a)

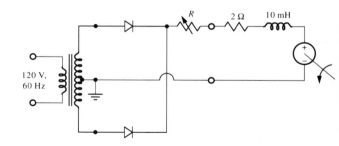

(b) 12.7; (c) $E < 4.97$ V; (d) 2.13 Ω.

**18.31.** (a) 46.5 V; (b) 4.83 mH.

**18.33.** 2823 rpm, 15.2 A is too much.

**18.35.** (a) 170 V, rms; (b)

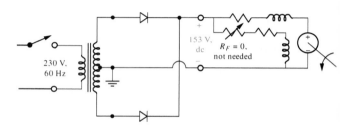

**18.37.** (a) 230 V, rms; (b) 80°; (c) 29.1°; (d) 210°; (e) 2251 rpm; (f) 3740 W.

**18.39.** (a) 168 V; (b) 93.3 W; (c) 5.41 Ω; (d) $168 < 178$ V, so OK; (e) 65.2%; (f) 8.52 Ω.

**18.41.** $I_{dc} = 0.432$ A, $I_{ac} = 0.426$ A, so a rectifier is better.

**18.43.** (a) 5.23 N-m; (b) 10.5 N-m.

**18.45.** 44.2 Hz, 174 V.

**18.47.** 5.69%.

**18.49.** 4.77%.

**18.51.** (a) 30.0 Hz (exact = 29.95); (b) 0.720.

**18.53.** (a) 56.2 ms; (b) 20°.

# Index

## Physical Constants

1. Velocity of light in vacuum, $c = 2.998 \times 10^8$ meters/second
2. Charge on the electron $e = -1.602 \times 10^{-19}$ coulombs
3. Mass of the electron, $m_e = 9.110 \times 10^{-31}$ kilogram
4. Electron charge/mass ratio, $|e| / m_e = 1.759 \times 10^{+11}$ coulomb/kilogram
5. Mass of the proton, $m_p = 1.673 \times 10^{-27}$ kilogram
6. Permeability of vacuum, $\mu_0 = 4\pi \times 10^{-7}$ henry/meter
7. Permittivity of vacuum, $\varepsilon_0 = 8.854 \times 10^{-12}$ farad/meter
8. Boltzmann's constant, $k = 1.381 \times 10^{-23}$ joules/Kelvin
9. Voltage equivalent of temperature, $kT/|e| = 25.9$ millivolts at 300 Kelvin
10. Typical mass density of magnetic steel, $\rho = 7.65$ grams/cubic centimeter

## Conversion Factors

1. Horsepower to watts: 1 hp = 746 W
2. Torque from English to mks units: 1 lb-ft = 1,356 N-m
3. Moments of inertia from English to mks units: 1 lb-ft$^2$ = $4.214 \times 10^{-2}$ kg-m$^2$
4. Angular velocity from rpm to radians/second: 1 rpm = $2\pi/60$ rad/s

## Three Fourier Series

1. Square wave (see Fig 9.5):

$$v(t) = V_s\left[\frac{1}{2} + \frac{2}{\pi}\cos(\omega_1 t) - \frac{2}{3\pi}\cos(3\omega_1 t) + \frac{2}{5\pi}\cos(5\omega_1 t) - \cdots\right]$$

2. Half-wave rectified sinusoid (see Fig. 9.6):

$$v(t) = V_p\left[\frac{1}{\pi} + \frac{1}{2}\cos(\omega_1 t) + \frac{2}{3\pi}\cos(2\omega_1 t) - \frac{2}{15\pi}\cos(4\omega_1 t) + \cdots\right]$$

3. Full-wave rectified sinusoid (see Fig. 7.10)

$$(t) = V_p\left[\frac{2}{\pi} + \frac{4}{3\pi}\cos(2\omega_1 t) - \frac{4}{15\pi}\cos(4\omega_1 t) + \frac{4}{35\pi}\cos(6\omega_1 t) - \cdots\right].$$